UTOPIAN THOUGHT
IN THE WESTERN WORLD

Expulsion from Paradise, ca. 1445
Giovanni di Paolo
Metropolitan Museum of Art, New York
(Robert Lehman Collection, 1975)

UTOPIAN THOUGHT
IN THE
WESTERN WORLD

Frank E. Manuel
and
Fritzie P. Manuel

THE BELKNAP PRESS
OF HARVARD UNIVERSITY PRESS
Cambridge, Massachusetts

Library of Congress Cataloging in Publication Data

Manuel, Frank Edward.
   Utopian thought in the Western world.

   Bibliography: p.
   Includes index.
      1. Utopias—History.   I. Manuel, Fritzie Prigohzy,
joint author.   II. Title.
HX806.M33   335'.02   79-12382
ISBN 0-674-93185-8 (cloth)
ISBN 0-674-93186-6 (paper)

Preface

OUR BOOK is constructed of seven major utopian constellations and a few minor ones, arranged in chronological order, preceded by two exordia, one methodological and the other mythological, the whole crowned with a prophetic peroration. An essay form that selects examples and suggests general lines of development but does not pretend to exhaustiveness was deliberately chosen. There has been no attempt to string out long lists of titles, which are easily available in a growing number of bibliographies. Unlike Erasmus, who claims to have composed *The Praise of Folly* in a week, we have been preoccupied with the utopian thought of the West for more than a quarter of a century. It is time to call a halt.

We have included pictures, as Giambattista Vico did in his *New Science,* and with the same end in view: "to give the reader an idea of the work before beginning and to allow him to recall its content the more readily, with the help of his imagination, after having finished." Happily, an underlying conception of our study was prefigured in two fragments of a predella painted around 1445 by Giovanni di Paolo of Siena. In one, Adam and Eve are being pushed out of the Garden of Eden, while God the Father points to a map of the barren world to which they are banished. Four rivers flow out of the earthly paradise, symbolizing to latter-day commentators the ancient and medieval wellsprings of the idea of utopia, with its yearning for a return to the blessed state from which mankind has been exiled. Even while utopian man hopes to re-create paradise on earth, he consoles himself with the vision of a paradise in heaven—the subject of a second fragment of the same predella. There the saintly ones, clad in graceful fifteenth-century costumes, are engaged in gentle converse with one another in a tranquil garden. The gnostic Simon Magus likened paradise to the womb—an analogy recognized in the map of the island sketched for the Louvain 1516 edition of *Utopia.* We have always been aware of the creators of the Western utopian tradition as persons. Without prejudice to the rest, a few have been singled out as illustrations from among the thousands who have renewed the myth of paradise in a secular translation: Thomas More, Jan Amos Comenius, Jean-Jacques Rousseau, Restif de la Bretonne, Charles Fourier, Karl Marx, William Morris.

Earlier versions of parts of the text appeared in issues of *Daedalus* on "Utopia and Utopian Thought" (Spring 1956), "Myth, Symbol, and Culture" (Winter 1972), "In Praise of Books" (Winter 1976), and "Rousseau for Our Time" (Summer 1978). We owe much to the Editor of *Daedalus,* Stephen R. Graubard, who over the years has been a steadfast friend and forthright critic. *The Prophets of Paris* (Harvard University Press, 1962) has been drawn upon freely, and so have "The Philosophes in Doubt," a lecture published by the William Andrews Clark Memorial Library (1978), and "Reconsideration: Thomas More," *The New Republic* (June 24, 1978).

In addition to the credits in the notes, further acknowledgment is made for quotations from the following: *The Yale Edition of the Complete Works of St. Thomas More* (Yale University Press, 1963–1976); *The Yale Edition of the Selected Works of St. Thomas More* (Yale University Press, 1961–1976); Filarete, *Treatise on Architecture*, translated and edited by John R. Spencer (Yale University Press, 1965); John Donne, *Satires, Epigrams, and Verse Letters*, edited by W. Milgate (by permission of Oxford University Press, 1967); Johann Valentine Andreae, *Christianopolis*, translated by F. E. Held (Oxford University Press, 1916); *Ancient Near Eastern Texts Relating to the Old Testament*, edited by James B. Pritchard (Copyright © 1955 by Princeton University Press; reprinted by permission of the publisher); Ernst Herzfeld, *Zoroaster and His World* (Princeton University Press, 1947); A. L. Morton, *The English Utopia* (Lawrence & Wishart, Publishers, London, 1952); J. M. Edmonds, *The Fragments of Attic Comedy* (E. J. Brill, Leiden, 1957); *Hesiod*, translated by Richmond Lattimore (University of Michigan Press; Copyright © by the University of Michigan, 1959); S. N. Kramer, *Sumerian Mythology*, revised edition (Harper & Row, 1961); J. W. Montgomery, *Cross and Crucible: Johann Valentin Andreae (1586–1654), Phoenix of the Theologians* (Martinus Nijhoff, The Hague, 1973).

A Research Fellowship at the Australian National University in the summer of 1974 and a year at the Institute for Advanced Study in Princeton (1976–77) provided a chance to work uninterruptedly on the book and to profit from the comments of learned colleagues. We are especially grateful to the President and the Trustees of Brandeis University for their encouragement and for furnishing us with the skilled assistance of Mrs. Linda M. Schell in the final preparation of the manuscript.

For errors of fact and the vagaries of our interpretations, we have no one to blame but ourselves—or rather, each other. One of the joys of collaboration is the almost limitless opportunity it affords for mutual recrimination.

F. E. M.
F. P. M.

Contents

UTOPIAN THOUGHT
IN THE WESTERN WORLD

Map of the Island

Utopia, first edition, Louvain 1516
Pierpont Morgan Library, New York

INTRODUCTION

The Utopian Propensity

ANTHROPOLOGISTS tell us that blessed isles and paradises are part of the dream-world of savages everywhere. The dogged wanderings of the Guarani tribe in search of a "Land-without-Evil" have been tracked over the length and breadth of Brazil, and the contemporary cargo-cults of Asia and Africa have been investigated for their marvelous syncretism of Christian and native para-dises. Neither pictorial nor discursive philosophico-religious utopias are exclu-sive to the Western world. Taoism, Theravada Buddhism, and medieval Mus-lim philosophy are impregnated with utopian elements. There are treatises on ideal states and stories about imaginary havens of delight among the Chinese, the Japanese, the Hindus, and the Arabs, but the profusion of Western utopias has not been equaled in any other culture. Perhaps the Chinese have been too worldly and practical, the Hindus too transcendental to recognize a tension be-tween the Two Kingdoms and to resolve it in that myth of a heaven on earth which lies at the heart of utopian fantasy.

In the Beginning Was the Word

For some time before the publication in 1516 of the *De Optimo Reipublicae Statu deque Nova Insula Utopia Libellus Vere Aureus,* Thomas More and his friend Erasmus had been referring to it simply as the "Nusquama," from a good Latin adverb meaning "nowhere." But then the spirit of neologism pos-sessed the future saint. He combined the Greek *ou,* used to express a general negative and transliterated into the Latin *u,* with the Greek *topos,* place or re-gion, to build Utopia. In the playful printed matter prefixed to the body of the book the poet laureate of the island, in a brief self-congratulatory poem written in the Utopian tongue, claimed that his country deserved to be called "Euto-pia" with an *eu,* which in Greek connoted a broad spectrum of positive attrib-utes from good through ideal, prosperous, and perfect. Guillaume Budé, the great French humanist and a well-wisher of More's, added to the confusion by remarking in his complimentary Latin letter to the author that he had heard the place called "Udepotia," or "Neverland," from the Greek for "never." Fi-nally, Germain de Brie, otherwise known as Brixius, author of the sarcastic *Antimorus,* heaped scorn on both the Greek of More's title and the many new words crowded into his Latin text. Through the centuries utopias have pre-served the complexity of the original nomenclature.

In the sixteenth and seventeenth centuries, descriptive works that imitated the *Utopia* were called utopias, with a minuscule, and they adhered more or less to traditional literary devices that More himself had received from Lucian of Samosata, who in turn had inherited them from Hellenistic novels, many of them no longer extant. The invention of printing made readily available trans-lations of tales of this character from one European language into another, and

they came to constitute an ever-expanding corpus, in which stock formulas
and concepts can be traced historically and their modifications charted. The
principal elements are a shipwreck or chance landing on the shores of what
turns out to be an ideal commonwealth, a return to Europe, and a report on
what has been remarked. If arranged in chronological order these works, considered "proper utopias" by bibliographers, form a sequence in which the imitation of predecessors is patent.

How to classify the Morean utopia as a form of rhetoric and a way to
knowledge was taken up as early as 1595 in Sir Philip Sidney's *Defence of Poesie*. There he coupled utopia with poetry and ranked them both above philosophy and history as more persuasive in leading men to virtue than a weighty
philosophical argument: "But even in the most excellent determination of
goodnesse, what *Philosophers counsaile* can so readely direct a Prince, as the
feined *Cirus* in *Xenophon,* or a vertuous man in all fortunes as Aeneas in Virgill,
or a whole Common-wealt, as the Way of Sir Thomas Moores Eutopia?"
Courtier of Elizabeth and loyal member of the Church of England, Sidney discreetly avoided what might have been interpreted as unqualified commitment
to the political ideal of a Papist executed for treason; but his praise of the genre
was unaffected. "I say the Way, because where Sir Thomas Moore erred, it
was the fault of the man and not of the Poet: for that Way of patterning a
Common-wealth, was most absolute though hee perchaunce hath not so absolutely performed it."[1] Sidney's pithy definition of poetry, "a speaking *Picture,*
with this end to teach and delight," was applied equally to utopia.[2] The term
utopia speedily made its way into other European languages. By the early seventeenth century it was not uncommon for great writers—Cervantes, Shakespeare—to interpolate a utopian episode or allude to utopian conceits by name.
Francis Bacon made a point of mocking utopias and labeling the *New Atlantis* a
fable, but contemporary compendia-makers forced him into the utopian company of More and Campanella.

Before the sixteenth century was out, the adjectival form "utopian" was
born, and when it was not a merely derogatory epithet, connoting a wild fancy
or a chimerical notion, it could refer to an ideal psychological condition or to
an idealizing capacity. The use of the word by John Donne, a descendant of
More's, may be its subtlest early extension to imply a general emotional attitude. In a verse letter to Sir Henry Wotton, who had spent many years in the
courts of Venice and Florence, the poet wrote:

> I thinke if men, which in these places live
> Durst looke for themselves, and themselves retrive,
> They would like strangers greet themselves, seeing then
> Utopian youth, growne old Italian.[3]

By the seventeenth century utopia was no longer restricted to a speaking
picture, a dramatic narrative portrayal of a way of life that is so essentially
good and fulfills so many profound longings that it wins immediate, almost
instinctive, approbation. It could embrace as well the underlying principles of
an optimum society expounded and argued either by the author directly or by
several interlocutors. Utopia also came to denote general programs and platforms for ideal societies, codes, and constitutions that dispensed with the fictional apparatus altogether. When the discursive, argumentative utopia as-

sumed a place alongside the speaking picture, the line between a utopian system and political and social theory often became shadowy. In *A Voice in Rhama* (1647) Peter Chamberlen, an English royal physician and a Fifth Monarchy man—not so improbable a combination as might be imagined—wrote of his hope that the world would return to its "first simplicity" or to a "Christian utopia." John Milton, in his *Apology for Smectymnuus* (1642), and his friend Samuel Hartlib, who had been appointed an official "Projector" by Parliament, both used utopia in the sense of a model for an ideal commonwealth. In the Pansophic utopia of Campanella, Andreae, Comenius, and Leibniz, the boundaries of an ideal Christian republic were enlarged to encompass the whole world. While religious commentaries on what heavenly paradise would be like kept up a constant flow of images as they had for two thousand years, the conception of a millennium as a real society on earth covering a fixed period of time gave rise to speculations about what events would occur in that blessed epoch, what government would be instituted, and what social relationships would prevail. Whenever the vaguely oracular mode of prophecy was set aside in the seventeenth century, the millenarian utopia could respond to concrete, matter-of-fact questions. Fifth Monarchy men of England even committed themselves to a specific tariff policy for their millennium.

Toward the end of the eighteenth century, in a growingly de-Christianized Europe, even while the old isolated island and valley utopias and a newer type of awakened-dreamer utopia continued to be regurgitated, there came into greater prominence the branch of utopian thought that spurned any fictional backdrop, broke with the limitations of specific place, and addressed itself directly to the reformation of the entire species. The Frenchmen Morelly, Dom Deschamps, Restif de la Bretonne, and Condorcet wrote what in effect were constitutions for a new secular, global society, and conceived of themselves as universal lawgivers, as would the utopian socialists of the post-Revolutionary era. By the early nineteenth century innovative utopian thought had all but lost its enclosed space. The novels portraying encapsulated and protected pictorial utopias, while they have continued to be sold in millions of copies into our own time, were often in content residual and derivative, dependent upon revolutionary utopian theory that others had propounded. A utopian genius like Charles Fourier might still initiate his project with the description of a single phalanstery, and on occasion one detects the rudiments of a story among his papers, but his phalanstery was conceived as a cell in an international movement that he hoped would soon spread throughout the globe, with similar communities joined in a vast federation.

In these rationalist, systematic utopias whose province was the whole world, the means of reaching utopia was transformed from an adventure story or a rite de passage to Elysium into a question of political action: How do you change a present misery into a future happiness in this world? The method of reaching utopia and the speed of travel, usually peripheral in the novelistic form, were now central, and the prickly issues of revolution, evolution, the uses of violence, the mechanics of the propagation of a new faith, determinism and free will, the imperatives of blind historical destiny, and the requirements of human freedom became intrinsic to utopian thought. In the early utopia the mode of access did not alter the nature of the perfect society. In the discursive universal utopia, though the idea was rarely spelled out, the way of attaining the ideal city affected the nature of the city itself. The vision of perfection was henceforward either disfigured or enhanced by the path to utopia. When utopia became attached to global philosophies of history, practitioners of that form of knowledge were turned into unwitting utopians or anti-utopians as they prognosticated the ineluctable end toward which mankind was moving.

Utopia thus became laden with meanings as it moved through time: a literary genre, a constitution for a perfectly restructured polity, a state of mind, the religious or scientific foundations of a universal republic. Many French eighteenth-century works called by their authors *rêves, codes, robinsonades, voyages imaginaires* were patently utopias in the conventional sense. Utopia could always be used either positively or pejoratively. In philosophe circles, Grimm and Meister's literary newsletter applied the disdainful epithet *espèce d'utopie* to the flood of stories that, with constantly changing content, imitated Morean devices. In the positivist tradition of the nineteenth century Littré's French dictionary defined *utopie* as *chimère*, noted its early appearance in Rabelais's *Pantagruel,* and seized the opportunity to deliver a brief homily on the deceptions of utopian promises. Over the years a utopian vocabulary entered the French language—*utopie, utopique, utopiste, utopiens*—though not all terms were welcomed into the Academy. In English a utopian became a person who inhabits a utopia or one who would like to be in a utopia or has a utopian cast of temperament. Some men were utopographers, a seventeenth-century word for the writers or inventors of utopias. The researcher into the utopian propensity of mankind, though he is one of a long line going back to Aristotle, has no particular name, and must rest content with the plain appellation historian, though his subject has been dubbed utopology by a recent innovator.

Two further neologisms have proved to be of use to us in designating different aspects of the subject, and we have accepted them without slighting the time-sanctioned coverall of utopia. The term uchronia, no time, was invented in the late nineteenth century by the French philosopher Charles Renouvier to characterize a fictitious history of the past written on the supposition that a critical turning point had had a different outcome. There has been a sizable literature of such exercises since the end of the eighteenth century, none of it noteworthy. We took the label uchronia, rashly altered its spelling to euchronia, good time, and applied it to a major departure in Western utopia and utopian thought that occurred when good place, good state of consciousness, and good constitution were all translated to a good future time. The Germans have coined a word for the speaking-picture euchronia, the *Zukunftsroman.* The other neologism, eupsychia, was introduced by the psychologist Abraham Maslow to signify an ideal state of consciousness; though the idea had already been incorporated into utopia in the sixteenth century, we have had occasion to borrow its new name.

This abbreviated overview of historical semantics with its limited terminological armature may help to guide us through a broad and loose-jointed universe of utopian discourse.

The Shadowy Boundaries of Utopia

The descriptive and the discursive rhetorical modes in utopia are never, or rarely ever, found in a simon-pure state, since the living portrait of a utopia rests on a set of implicit psychological, philosophical, or theological assumptions about the nature of man, and the discursive exposition of utopian principles frequently has recourse to illustrations from ordinary events, proposes hypothetical situations, and analogizes from other realms of being. In the course of time, "proper" utopias, discussions of utopian thought, and portrayals of utopian states of consciousness have so interpenetrated that the perimeters of the concept of utopia have to be left hazy. From the time of its first discovery, the island of King Utopus has been shrouded in ambiguity, and no latter-day scholars should presume to dispel the fog, polluting utopia's natural environment with an excess of clarity and definition. Thomas More himself could not get straight the exact length of the bridge that spanned the River Anydrus at Amaurotum in Utopia. Was it five hundred paces or three hundred? he asked his friend Peter Giles. No greater precision than he was able to muster should be expected of historians of utopian thought. A fluid identity will have to suffice, for our primary purpose is to dwell on the multifarious changes of utopian experience through the centuries, and, as Nietzsche taught, only that which has no history can be defined.

The bypassing of a rigid definition may distress some philosophical intelligences who demand that at the opening of an inquiry its terms be spelled out in contractual language; but as the whole of this work is intended to endow the idea of utopia with historical meaning, those looking for a dictionary label or a pat phrase had better try elsewhere. Utopia acquires plural meanings in the course of our study, in which we presuppose the existence of a utopian propensity in man as William James in his famous lectures assumed a "religious propensity" while pointedly refusing to define religion. We aim to communicate the diversity of experiences in which this propensity has manifested itself in Western society. Experience is here a mental act that takes the form of speech. The utopian propensity is no more equally distributed among men in all times and places than the religious propensity, though it is doubtful whether anyone is totally devoid of it. There may even be a utopian vocation.

Any strict compartmentalization of future utopia and nostalgia for an idealized bygone human condition is invalidated by their constant interplay in Western thought. In the fiction of the original Morean utopia, the ideal already exists somewhere on a faraway island and has been seen by human eyes. The discourse bears with it the implied argument that the model reported on should be imitated. Similarly, the widespread Christian belief that the Garden of Eden, or earthly paradise, continued to exist in a particular place, even after the expulsion of Adam and Eve, fed the hope that a paradisaical state was possible this side of heaven and provided a model for it. The discovery of a utopia in the past was often an essential rhetorical way of justifying a radical future innovation in the centuries when tradition rather than innovation was the guiding principle of life. Unearthing an ancient or primeval ideal society allayed the anxiety of the utopian, reluctant to introduce unprecedented novelty. One of the strengths of Plato's discursive dialogues, when read as utopias, derived from the assertion that the ideal city had in fact once existed as ancient Athens. From Plato's evocation of an Athens of the distant past in the *Critias* through the English longing for the age before the imposition of the Norman yoke and the primitivism of the eighteenth century, the nostalgic mode has been an auxiliary of utopia.

Since the end of the eighteenth century the predictive utopia has become a major form of imaginative thought and has preempted certain scientific techniques of forecasting. The distinction between utopia and prophecy (with or without scientistic apparatus) is often difficult to sustain. The long-term prediction—applied to centuries rather than a few decades—that is cut loose from present-day moorings, mostly statistical, ends up as an expression of utopian desire or, what amounts to the same, radical counter-desire. Any doomsday prophecy opens wide the potentialities of paradise or hell. Futurology, which is normally mere extrapolation, can become utopia in disguise, especially if the prophecy offers a choice of alternatives at many crossroads on the long journey. The bimorphic predictions of J. D. Bernal in *The World, the Flesh and the Devil* (1929) in effect spell out the possibilities of two different utopias. While prophecy can be nightmarish rather than comforting, the contemporary utopia has a way of becoming more and more intertwined with a philosophical history that binds past, present, and future together as though fated. From the eighteenth century onward, many utopias, especially the euchronias, have harbored an element of determinism. The state they depict appears virtually ordained either by God or by history; there is a carry-over of millenarian certainty, and if disciples, religious or secular, discover that a specific timetable has not been realized, they manage to revise it ingeniously and preserve the credibility of the whole unfulfilled prophecy. The Sabbath of the apocalypse, the days of the Messiah, and the millennium were inspired by divine revelations, but it would be difficult to detach them from utopian longing. Even when the prediction is based on the soundest and most carefully assembled scientific evidence it can hardly escape the leaven of desire.

Though the nightly dreamer rarely utters a negative, derision of the great utopian dream has paralleled utopian thought from its very inception. The histories of utopia and dystopia are a landscape in chiaroscuro. The anti-utopia was not the twentieth-century invention of Aldous Huxley and Yevgeny Zamiatin: *The Parliament of Women* by Aristophanes was contemporaneous with Plato's *Republic,* though any connection between them is today doubted; More's *Utopia* provoked mocking parodies; and in many a deadpan utopia a mischievous little imp raises its head to debunk. Such intrusions and the satirical utopia, or what has been variously called the dystopia, anti-utopia, devolutionary utopia, or counter-utopia, cannot be entirely excluded from consideration, but our focus is on the utopian yea rather than the dystopian nay. If in the background of every utopia there is an anti-utopia, the existing world seen through the critical eyes of the utopia-composer, one might say conversely that in the background of many a dystopia there is a secret utopia.

Utopias, like postage stamps, have attracted avid collectors. Resort to modern bibliographies allows one to assemble a fairly complete list of speaking-picture utopias in action and books with discursive utopian matter written up to the twentieth century, when the subject explodes in all directions and one does not know what parts of futurology, science fiction, or predictive science to encompass. The eighteenth century probably produced as many utopian texts as the sixteenth and seventeenth put together, and the nineteenth quintupled that number. But quantifying utopias is not a very fruitful exercise. While a few prototypes enjoy great longevity, scores of utopias are fugitive. Since we are writing a true history, not drawing up a catalogue, any student of bibliographies will realize how many books that are undoubtedly utopian in title and spirit receive no mention. In describing the triumphs and defeats of the utopian imagination it is not incumbent upon us to name and evaluate every participant in the battle. When a writer has imprinted his personality upon a movement of ideas he is singled out, but many utopians deserve the oblivion into which they have fallen. We shall deal principally with exemplars, not with an army roll call, and scores of unsung utopians will remain unsung. This critical inquiry into utopian thought necessarily betrays a predilection for those utopias in which the will to achieve social transformation predominates over the vaporous fantasies that are meant merely to amuse or titillate. Eighteenth-century utopias that were intended to divert an increasing number of literate ladies, in which the adventures of heroes and heroines all but drown out the didactic element, are worthy of study, especially in an inquiry into the history of women and of male conceptions about their literary tastes, but they are not a major concern of serious utopian thought.

Our latitudinarian and ecumenical conception of utopia draws its documentation from "extraordinary voyages," moon-travelers' reports, fanciful descriptions of lost worlds in a state of nature, optimum constitutions, advice to princes on the most perfect government, novels built around life in a "proper" utopian society, millenarian prophecies, architectural plans for ideal cities. It includes men like Owen, Saint-Simon, and Fourier, who would surely have spurned the epithet utopian thrust upon them by Karl Marx; and Marx himself, who tried so hard to differentiate his vision from theirs; and finally a group of modern philosophical psychologists and biologists who would be ambivalent about the term, as well as a number of contemporary philosophers of history and practicing scientists who have ventured to speculate about the future of man. More and Patrizi, Bacon and Campanella, Andreae and Morelly, Fénelon and Condorcet, Restif de la Bretonne and Edward Bellamy, H. G. Wells and Theodor Hertzka, Wilhelm Reich and Norman Brown, Erich Fromm and Herbert Marcuse, Julian Huxley and Pierre Teilhard de Chardin all have a place on the roster of utopians—some, to be sure, against their will.

But if the land of utopia were thrown open to every fantasy of an individual ideal situation the realm would be boundless. The personal daydream with its idiosyncratic fixations has to be excluded. The ideal condition should have some measure of generality, if not universality, or it becomes merely a narcissistic yearning. There are utopias so private that they border on schizophrenia. *The Description of a New World, called the Blazing World* (1666) by Margaret Cavendish, Duchess of Newcastle, has much in common with the delusions of Dr. Schreber analyzed by Sigmund Freud in a famous paper.[4] Uncounted utopian worlds of this stripe, many of them highly systematized, are being conjured up every day, in and out of hospitals, though few of them are ever set in print. (The title of Giulio Clemente Scotti's *Lucii Cornelii Europaei Monarchia Solipsorum ad Leonem Allatium* [1645] suggests a solipsistic utopia, but the work turns out to be a utopian parody of the Jesuit order.) We have preferred to steer clear of solipsistic manifestations and continently restrict ourselves to those utopias that have won a measure of public acceptance and become at least folie à deux, the author and the printer. When, however, a solipsistic utopia is projected into a social utopia, it falls within the permissible sphere, especially if the creator of the psychic *monde idéal* happens to be Jean-Jacques Rousseau. It would require a bit of stretching to incorporate Diogenes the Cynic's concept of autarchy into utopia, though a fragment on an ideal primitive condition is imputed to him, and his notion of shamelessness has found a counterpart in Reformation and present-day eupsychias.

Nor should every political and economic prognostication be considered utopian. In mid-eighteenth-century England, a Tory gentleman outlined the future history of European wars in the twentieth century under the reign of a George VI.[5] He predicted Russia's penetration deep into Europe, the occupation of Scandinavia, and the defeat of France by England. Nothing in the life of the British Isles is portrayed as remarkably different from what it was under George III, except that the empire is administered from a Versailles-like capital called Stanley. The changes envisaged are not radical enough—they do not strike at the roots of existence—to be included in the utopian orbit. They are nothing but minor, false prophecy. A perennial question arises as to how to distinguish a program of reform or a five-year plan from a utopia. The reply that the difference lies in the extent of the proposed transformation begs the question, because one man's trivial revision is another man's upheaval. Utopia should probably exclude mere futurist projections of existing series, short-term predictions still fettered to the present. Final judgment in these instances has to be subjective, though perhaps some historical testimony or contemporary consensus can be invoked.

The facile extrapolations of a scientistic futurology that looks only to tomorrow, or to the year 2000, and engages in immediate problem-solving are of a different order from the leap into a new state of being in which contemporary values in at least one area—the critical one for the utopian—are totally transformed or turned upside down. In the *Utopia* of Thomas More, who was anguished over greed and corruption in the Christian polity, such a transvaluation was symbolized in the conversion of gold specie into chamber pots and jewels into children's baubles, and was embodied in conceptions of work, pleasure, and property. And in the seventeenth century, when the new science, which had earlier been obliged to apologize for its existence, was glorified as the foundation stone of a world Christian society in Pansophic visions from Bacon through Leibniz, a real world in which science had either been feared or despised was metamorphosed by utopia. Condorcet's flights of imagination in his commentary on the *New Atlantis* and the recent projections of those who expect a self-alteration of species man in an extraterrestrial environment may have been regarded by these scientist-utopians as reasonable predictions. Many of their foretellings have in fact come true, and the developments they envisaged could be read as possible, if daring, extensions of contemporary knowledge. But their revolutionary character has produced the pattern for a human condition that is totally new by any standard.

We have deliberately separated utopian theory and invention from attempts to put them into practice. Studying the actual experience of those who sought to implement utopias would bring us too dangerously close to reality. There have been thinkers who, having given birth to an idea, proceeded to act it out, men who founded movements and organized schools, who formed conspiracies and hatched cabals, who led bands of followers to strange places. Some, like Thomas Müntzer and Tommaso Campanella and Gracchus Babeuf, paid dearly for their ventures; others, like Fourier, Owen, Comte, and Marx, ended up in constant bickering with their disciples. The fortunate ones, like Henri Saint-Simon, initiated their followers into the system and then had the good judgment to die. But usually there has been a functional division of labor between writers of utopias and the activist utopians who have established utopian communities or launched revolutions for the sake of seeing the glory of utopia with their own eyes. When we analyze popular millenarian or revolutionary movements, it is the content of the dreams, manifest or hidden, not the strategies for their realization, that primarily engages us. Were a new science to be founded—and we have no such pretension—it would be valid to distinguish between theoretical utopistics and applied utopistics. Utopian practice, if indeed it is not a contradiction in terms, has sometimes affected later theorists; but on the whole the ardor of a utopian innovator in the moment of creation is overwhelming and is not dampened by his knowledge of previous defeats.

Popular hope literature has not been excluded from this study on principle, or without awareness that a police or other judicial record, or a hospital casebook, or a prize essay contest in a provincial French academy, might reveal an unnoticed utopian thinker operating in his own world whose dreams could be more representative of large segments of the population than a formally printed utopia. The lines had to be drawn somewhere, and the task of capturing the utopian consciousness of great masses of people has been left to others, some of whom have already begun their explorations. A distinction has to be made between a collective utopia that exists in a passive state among a large segment of the population and a utopia expressly written for the purpose of instructing men and persuading them to some action. Doubtless the unwritten popular utopia of a country is constantly undergoing change, but access to the transformations would involve the development of new strategies that will have to await other historians. The complete speaking-picture or finished discursive utopia is usually the product of deliberate educative intent, and it is explicit and organized in its presentation. This may be both a virtue and a limitation.

The problem of the relations between the book utopia and other more popular manifestations of similar ideas has not been wholly resolved. There are times when both have been swept up by a wave and carried away in the sea of a common utopia. The utopia of the people has been mediated by members of the literate classes in Attic comedy, in Midrashic literature, in trial records of the Inquisition and interrogations of millenarians, in police spy reports, in court trials following riots and uprisings. The mutual interpenetration of popular utopian elements and literary documents appears obvious. If a group or a class is isolated, it will evolve a utopia unique to itself; its archaeological reconstruction is another matter. But there is reason to be leery of the eighteenth-century *Bibliothèque bleue,* written for, but not by, "the people," as a mirror of the utopian *espérance* of the masses. Folktale and folksong may yield a more authentic picture, though the decipherment of their universal images demands skills beyond those of the professional historian and their message may be ahistorical.

This history is not in search of the utopian ideas most widely diffused in the population of the West at particular moments, one living head being counted as the repository of one utopian idea. Kant's reading of Rousseau's primitivist utopia is not equivalent to everyman's. Since for most ages the popular utopia is largely inaccessible, or the materials still remain to be assembled, the present work tends to dwell on the utopian thought of the literate classes in Western society. Through time they have changed in character and in numbers and so has the representativeness of their utopias. But the study of utopian thought in books composed by philosophers and litterateurs does not limit the significance of the enterprise to upper-class culture. Often the utopias of the "educated classes" have had a way of seeping into popular action programs and general social movements, so that in considering today's upper-class utopia we may be witnessing a preview of tomorrow's mass demands. (This is not always so; many major utopian conceptions remain literary.) Though the utopia is inspired by one man's experience of his society, he may well become the voice of whole silent segments of the population. He creates consciousness, as the chapbooks say. Virtually every one of the major slogans that expressed the hopes of French and English working-class movements of the first half of the nineteenth century was plucked from the gardens of the printed works of utopian writers.

The Critical Study of Utopia

Like the utopias themselves, the analytic and historical study of utopia has had precedents going all the way back to the Greeks. That proposals for "ideal states" demanded objective critical examination was first argued by Aristotle in Book II of the *Politics,* where he entered the lists against forms "designed by theorists" and took on seriatim Plato, Phaleas of Chalcedon, and Hippodamus of Miletus.[6] If we forgo for the present a laborious tracing of Aristotle's successors and restrict ourselves to relatively modern times, the earliest known academic treatment of utopian thought is probably a stillborn Latin dissertation published in 1704 by the hapless Henricus ab Ahlefeld, whose fame has been obscured by cataloguers' attributing his work to Georg Pasch, the professor who approved the thesis.[7] But it was not until Louis Reybaud's *Etudes sur les réformateurs ou socialistes modernes* (1840) that the *utopies sociales,* which he branded subversive, really received detailed consideration as a type. Simultaneously, on the other side of the Rhine, Robert von Mohl drew up a list of some twenty-five utopias from Plato down, baptized them *Staatsromane,* and bravely proposed to incorporate them into political science.[8] Utopia became a subject of contention in world revolutionary movements when Marx in the *Communist Manifesto* and Engels in the *Anti-Dühring* conceived of their doctrine dialectically as at once an outgrowth of earlier utopian thought and its contradiction, and condemned utopias as outdated and historically superseded fantasies, though anyone ploughing through the *Marx-Engels Gesamtausgabe* is immediately aware of a constant preoccupation with utopians of the past.

Although utopianism attracted a few champions in the 1920s and 1930s, to many observers it was a corpse. The nails were hammered into the coffin with resounding blows struck by Marxists at one end and Fascist theorists at the other. The latter group, adapting the language of Georges Sorel, grandiloquently proclaimed the superiority of their own creative myths as "dynamic realities," spontaneous utterances of authentic desires, over the utopias, which they dismissed as hollow rationalist constructs. For a whole galaxy of other lished oppositions between utopia and ideology, utopianism and millenarianism, the utopia and the pastoral.

Our way falls somewhere between the stools. Acknowledging that the utopian propensity is pervasive, we would avoid both the microscopic analysis of individual units in succession and the evocative summation of the whole experience under one or two rubrics. Our aim has been to settle on a middle level: to try to identify historical constellations of utopias with reasonably well marked time-space perimeters and common elements that are striking enough to permit framing generalizations, while still respecting the concreteness of the individual experience. The origin of the utopian propensity is, in an absolute sense, not knowable; its application and incorporation in given utopian configurations or constellations are. These become the main subject of our inquiry. Commentary upon them, with psychological knowledge of persons and historical analysis of circumstances, constitutes the body of this narrative. Historical analysis involves recognition of the persistence of symbolic and residual utopian forms, as well as consciousness of the "hot" motivation generated by immediate socioeconomic, political, or philosophico-religious dissatisfaction and anguish.

Looking for anticipations, forerunners, prefigurations of utopian ideas is a legitimate historical enterprise. Though utopians who are contemporaries appear to resemble one another more than they do their predecessors or descendants, until recent times a utopian was almost invariably aware of the existence of some of his major antecedents; he had read their writings or at least heard about them. Even a cursory review of utopian thought through the centuries reveals interesting relationships, returns, resumptions, and repetitions, as starry-eyed grandchildren reproduce the fantasies of grandfathers who have been denied by their sons. The sequence is not orderly and the filiations cannot always be firmly established; but one soon recognizes that in the utopian lineage dominant ancestors lord it over the generations that follow. More or Patrizi of Cherso or Campanella is inconceivable without Plato. The German Pansophists were the first to publish Campanella, who likened himself to Plato and More, and Comenius announced himself the successor of Andreae. Condorcet's evocation of a world dominated by scientists was a revival of Bacon's plan. Owen, Saint-Simon, and Fourier prepared the way for Marx. Saint-Simon had devoured his Condorcet and Fourier his Restif. The utopian novelists of the nineteenth century, whether Cabet, Chernyshevskii, Bellamy, Morris, or Hertzka, were either illustrations of or reactions to earlier utopians of the century. Since utopian themes are often handed down from one generation to another, with modifications and variations of recognizable thought patterns and pictorial details, and utopia-writers either invoke the authority of their predecessors or engage in explicit or implicit debate with them, there is an evident continuity that can be established and described. This justifies a history of utopia. Some old utopian themes drop by the wayside and new ones are introduced, but few utopias written since 1450 represent a creation ex nihilo. Most utopias are born of utopias, however pretentious the claims to complete novelty may be.

The historical longevity of certain mythic themes in utopia that evoke associations remote and deeply rooted in Western consciousness can help us to understand the fascination utopias have exerted over the minds of men. Anyone

born into a culture is likely to imbibe a set of utopian fantasies even as he inter-
nalizes certain prohibitions at an early age. We do not know whether these
utopian elements are part of a collective unconscious. The problem of conformities in the symbols of utopia is not unlike that of dream symbols. They may
be ahistorical and acultural, though always found in a specific context, social
and psychological. But even as we probe in this study for the continuities in
Western utopian thought, we are acutely aware of the temporal and geographic
fractures and demarcations that separate one utopian constellation from
another.

Particularly rich utopian moments have been attached to political revolutions and the dictatorships that follow in their wake, such as the English Civil
War or the Age of the French Revolution—periods, incidentally, in which de
facto restrictions on printing disappear for a while and allow a host of new
conceptions to surface. At such times all things seem possible, and the utopian
appears no madder than other men. Religious schisms and intellectual revolutions like the emergence of the new science in the seventeenth century, or the
dramatic introduction of new modes of production in the nineteenth, or the
exploration of new space in the Americas, in the South Seas, or beyond the
bounds of this sphere, have all sparked novel utopian ideas and led to the formation of startling new utopian constellations.

Despite the thesis in Victor Dupont's grand compendium on utopia and utopian thought in English literature—that there is a special affinity between the
English national temperament and utopia—the utopian propensity is common
to the Western world.[16] The Italian architectural utopias of the Renaissance
and the French social utopias of the eighteenth and nineteenth centuries were
among the heights of utopian expression, and the Pansophic vision of the seventeenth century had a deep Germanic and Lutheran coloration. In a particular epoch the spirit of utopia may have been more active in one national culture
than in others or a utopian form may have flourished in only one land; but
utopia in general has not been geographically exclusive. The relative unity of
Western culture has guaranteed the rapid diffusion of utopian ideas irrespective of the countries in which they originated. We consider Russian and
American utopian thought before the late nineteenth century an overflow of
European types—Prince M. M. Shcherbatov's *Journey to the Land of the Ophirs*
(1796) and New England millenarian sermons are derivative. A long tradition
identifies the colonies and the United States with utopia, but, curiously, those
who were actually fashioning that utopia were dreaming about it in European
terms. The writings of the Puritans with all their millenarian imagery and the
later utopian proclamations of the victorious colonial insurgents are extensions
of European idea systems. The seven books of Cotton Mather's *Magnalia
Christi Americana: or, the Ecclesiastical History of New-England, from its first planting in the year 1620, unto the year of our Lord, 1698,* constitute a mammoth, self-
adulatory utopia whose spiritual roots are in England, where it was first
published in 1702. The Winthrops and the Mathers were putting utopia into
practice, building a Christian utopia and a New Jerusalem in their commonwealth with imported thoughts and symbols, even as in the nineteenth century
New England Transcendentalists would experiment with Fourierist ideas in
Brook Farm. The absence of a sustained utopian tradition in Spain is peculiar,
though free-floating utopian affect may have somehow attached itself to the

figure of Don Quixote. The manuscript of an Enlightenment utopia, *Descripción de la Sinapia, península en la terra austral,*[17] has recently been published, but it hardly modifies the generalization that Spain was relatively untouched by the utopian main current until the penetration of Marxist and anarchist thought. Danes, Swiss, Poles, Czechs, and members of other European nations have written utopias, though the overwhelming number of Western utopias—whatever their national origin—were first printed in Latin, English, French, Italian, or German.

Not all utopias can without straining be squeezed within the chronological benchmarks and attached to the ideational clusters that we shall outline, but one can seek out those constellations of utopias and utopian thought in each epoch that have embodied significant innovations and new content. Although virtually all utopias deal with major aspects of living, such as work, government, love and sexuality, knowledge, religion, beauty, the tone and quality of life, dying, each of these subjects has at one or another time preempted a central position in utopian consciousness and has inspired new forms. Works that spew forth worn-out themes, even when numerically weighty, have been neglected or underplayed here in favor of new departures. Nobody can really copy straight even when that is the intention, and hence there are minor intrusions of novelty in the most hackneyed utopian thought; these offshoots, however, are to be distinguished from authentic innovations, when the rather repetitive series is broken by a genius who establishes a new style. Though in most utopian thinkers the past is present, there are rare moments of disjuncture too acute to allow for the utopian past as a prime catalytic agent in a new creation. We have usually hurried over the pabulum of an age, the chewed cud of previous epochs, and looked for fresh invention.

The underlying pattern of this book involves identifying the major historical constellations of utopian thought in the Western world. Our task has been to explore the main lines of transmission, without enslavement to a chain of influences, and at the same time to mark and highlight innovations, fractures, and discontinuities, the formation of new clusters, without accepting every self-proclaimed discoverer in utopia at his word.

Mapping the Constellations

The fixing of a point of departure confronted us with our first problem. One possibility entailed going all the way back to the paradisaical fantasies of the Near East in the third millennium before Christ, another to Plato's presentation of both the *mythos* and the *logos* of an ideal city. But the unique character of utopia in the West was in our judgment best brought out by initiating the history in medias res, so to speak, with its baptism in the Age of the Renaissance. Utopia is a hybrid plant, born of the crossing of a paradisaical, otherworldly belief of Judeo-Christian religion with the Hellenic myth of an ideal city on earth. The naming took place in an enclave of sixteenth-century scholars excited about the prospect of a Hellenized Christianity. While we may loosely refer to ancient and medieval works with some utopian content as utopias, the Western utopia is for us a creation of the world of the Renaissance and the Reformation. Since that period, the history of utopia has been reasonably continuous. Works and parts of works that entered utopian consciousness from the ancient Judeo-Christian, Hellenic, and medieval worlds have been considered not in themselves but as the vital prehistory or underthought of modern utopia, that strange absorption in a heaven on earth, the desire for both worlds. In this context we have read the ancient works, in the first instance, not as they might be reconstituted in their native habitat by present-day scholars, but as they appeared to Renaissance Europeans who laid the foundations of the Christian utopia. After tracing the Judeo-Christian and Hellenic strands in the underthought of utopia, we advance directly to our first historical constellation, marking the principal figures in the age of birth and naming.

The period of the latter part of the fifteenth and the early sixteenth centuries recommended itself as a starting point because of the confluence of diverse intellectual and social forces whose relation to the creation of modern utopia was provocative, if not causal: the translation of Plato's *Republic* in the fifteenth century, to the accompaniment of a tumultuous debate on Italian soil among Byzantine émigrés over the admissibility of Plato's communist politics into Christian society; the printing within a century or so of a large part of the Greek and Latin corpus, which made available to the learned a thousand years of experience with the ancient rationalist problem of what an ideal condition in this world would be like; the overflow into print and into organized social movements of a stream of paradisaical, apocalyptic, and millenarian visions that had had a continuous existence since the Christian era and some roots going further back to the early cultures of the Near East; the discoveries of lands to the West, throwing open the windows of the utopian imagination to novel social and religious arrangements, as Alexander's push eastward had given rise to Hellenistic exotic novels.

A Renaissance utopian did not have to seek out esoterica buried in the Greek and Latin corpus. If he had access to Aristotle's *Politics*, Plato's *Republic* and *Laws*, and Cicero's *Offices*, what Aristotle called the study of the form of political association that was "the ideal for those who can count upon the material conditions of their life being, as nearly as possible, just what they would themselves wish" could be nourished with the fundamental texts inherited from antiquity that were necessary for a discursive utopia.[18] The speaking-picture utopia had a storehouse of images in Homer, Hesiod, and Ovid, in Xenophon's historical romance, the *Cyropaedia,* in excerpts from Hellenistic novels incorporated as geography in Diodorus Siculus' *Library of History,* and in Plutarch's lives of Solon and Lycurgus. Aristophanes and Lucian provided materials in a lighter vein, but when they were read in a humorless, literal fashion the ideal cities and government projects they mocked could inspire earnest utopian disquisitions. Reports from explorers to the New World fitted in neatly with classical sources and medieval accounts like Sir John Mandeville's of exotic peoples living in a state of happiness. Paradisaical, apocalyptic, and millenarian fantasies had been kept alive throughout the Middle Ages in scores of heretical and some orthodox movements of reformation. The publication of the works of Joachim of Fiore spread more widely ideas about a third *status* on earth, the reign of the Holy Ghost, an age of peace and love. And medieval fabliaux preserved the delights of a cokaygne utopia, sustained by a collective gastronomic unconscious whose manifest images had surfaced in Attic comedy, the Midrash, and the Church Fathers.

The two ancient beliefs that molded and nurtured utopia—the Judeo-Christian faith in a paradise created with the world and destined to endure beyond it, and the Hellenic myth of an ideal, beautiful city built by men for men without the assistance and often in defiance of the gods—were deeply embedded in the consciousness of Europeans. The utopia born in the Renaissance was of course designed for a society whose cities, jewels in a rural landscape, were assuming new dimensions to which both the Eastern paradise and the community of the small Greek city-state in pursuit of perfection were profoundly alien. There were also inherent contradictions between the two myths, which the Christian utopia of the sixteenth and seventeenth centuries attempted to gloss over. Moreover, neither the paradisaical nor the Hellenic myth was a monolith; the legacies transmitted were rich and varied, full of contrarieties. But though the powerful arguments of the Greek philosophers and the authority of the philo-sophical poets were in many respects profoundly different from the prophetic spirit of Judaic and Christian enthusiasm, there were times when they fortified each other. The Greek golden age and biblical paradise were recognized to have striking similarities, readily explained by the Church Fathers and Renais-sance commentators as the classical poets' piracy from Moses. On rare occa-sions the Greco-Roman and the Judeo-Christian worlds shared a utopianized historical reign, like that of Cyrus, though the divergent perceptions of Xeno-phon and Isaiah are illustrative of the different tempers of their two societies, briefly joined in common celebration. But even when the Hellenic and the Judeo-Christian elements were uncongenial to each other, they coexisted in utopia, a synthesis often on the verge of falling apart.

The conception of a heaven on earth that underlies Western utopian thought presupposes an idea of perfection in another sphere and at the same time a mea-sure of confidence in human capacity to fashion on earth what is recognized as a transient mortal state into a simulacrum of the transcendental. Judeo-Chris-tianity and Hellenic culture provided Europe with two distinct versions of an otherworldly state which could be conjoined. But the relation of the utopian to the heavenly always remains problematic. Utopia may be conceived as a pro-logue or a foretaste of the absolute perfection still to be experienced; it then resembles the Days of the Messiah or the Reign of Christ on earth of tradi-tional Judaism and Christianity, with the vital addition of human volition as an ingredient in the attainment of that wished-for state. Or the utopia, though originally implanted in a belief in the reality of a transcendental state, can break away from its source and attempt to survive wholly on its own creative self-as-surance. Whether the persistence of the heavenly vision in a secularized world, if only in some disguised shape, is a necessary condition for the duration of utopia is one of the unresolved questions of Western culture. At that moment in time when utopia first came into existence faith in a Christian heavenly paradise was still unshaken and the assertion of human talent to invent, dis-cover, and devise was as if reborn.

The utopian constellations of the period from the mid-fifteenth to the early eighteenth century, still united by their total commitment to Christianity, have a common driving purpose: the radical transformation of the nature and domain of the Christian world. The main line of this utopia runs roughly from Thomas More and Thomas Müntzer to the death of Leibniz. In Italy one has to reach back to Alberti and Filarete and Francesco di Giorgio Martini in the fif-teenth century for the Renaissance rediscovery of the symbolic radial form of

the ideal city, thereby spoiling the perfect symmetry of a simultaneous beginning everywhere in Europe but gaining the advantage of initiating the modern
utopian world with the printed recovery of the corpus of classical antiquity.

The utopia that was born and bred in the Christian society of Europe has
been divided into two separate constellations, one covering the period of its
birth, the other its seventeenth-century flowering and final demise. The chronological beginning of the first constellation could conceivably have been
pushed back to the Middle Ages. The rule of the Benedictines and subsequent
regulations for the government of monastic institutions doubtless left prototypes for an ideal Christian existence on earth, and the passion for ordering the
minutiae of every aspect of existence made its imprint upon later utopias,
which often are reminiscent of monastic establishments. Ramón Lull's *Blanquerna,* a didactic romance written in Catalan between 1283 and 1285, and
Pierre Dubois's *De recuperatione Terre Sancte* (ca. 1305–1307) might be considered embryonic Christian utopias, but they appear to have left no significant
traces in Western utopian literature before the seventeenth century. The philosophical writings of Lull then joined the main current of utopian thought and
and were assimilated by the Pansophists. Campanella and Leibniz were aware
of Lull's ideas when three centuries after his death they again tried to interest
princes and popes in projects for Christian unity and militant propagation of
the faith among the heathen in order to establish one heavenly community on
earth, but both Lull and Dubois have to be regarded as precursors rather than
initiators of a new mode.

Similarly, the second constellation of the Christian utopia could have been
prolonged to include residual manifestations in the eighteenth and nineteenth
centuries, examples of a surviving Christian utopian force in a de-Christianized Europe: the ideas behind the communal organization imposed upon the
Paraguayan Indians by the Jesuits, the various forms of the Herrnhut communities founded by Count Ludwig von Zinzendorf, the intermittent recrudescence of millenarian conceptions among groups like the Shakers, the Catholic traditionalist political theory of Joseph de Maistre and Louis-Gabriel-
Ambroise de Bonald, the mystical visions of Pierre-Simon Ballanche, and
even the Christian anarchism of Tolstoy. But in our judgment the principal
utopian concerns in the eighteenth and nineteenth centuries were secular,
and Christian utopia was a feeble remnant. It is primarily in the sixteenth
and seventeenth centuries, when nascent secular utopian and Christian otherworldly strains of thought interpenetrate, that the tension of the Christian utopia is at its highest. It does not matter that major utopias, such as More's little
book, Campanella's *City of the Sun,* and Vairasse's *History of the Sevarambians,*
portray pre-Christian or non-Christian societies; all are confronting the problems of Christianity in a world that is approaching the crisis of secularism.
Utopian thought is a fair barometer of this spiritual contest.

Under the rubric of the Birth of Utopia we have treated three different geographic and temporal units. The Christian humanist utopia of More has been
read in the spirit of northern humanism common to Erasmus and Rabelais,
though here can also be discovered conceptions of work and honest pleasures
and equality that have an enduring resonance and a complicated *fortuna* as
More goes through scores of translations. The Italian Renaissance utopia of the
città felice (from the title of Patrizi of Cherso's book), embodied both in words

and in architectural drawings, is one of the rare moments when the idea of beauty permeates utopia and creates an aristocratic Christian fantasy that is conscious of two levels of social existence, symbolized perhaps by the two-layered city of Leonardo's sketches. As a celebration of radial form, the architectural utopia responds to a variety of military, symbolic, and hygienic needs that live together in close disharmony. Finally, in the Germanic world of the early sixteenth century the utopia of the common man, the *Gemeinermann*, rises out of the mystical and political sermons and the legend of Thomas Müntzer and the radical Anabaptists.

Christian utopian thought in the seventeenth century, which saw its apogee and decline, while forming one overall cluster, has been examined in its varied geographic manifestations. The protracted upheavals of the English Civil War allowed for a massive discharge of utopian fantasy. A few of the radical utopians acknowledged a distant relationship to Müntzer and the Anabaptists and referred to them with favor; for the most part, however, their thought, steeped in bibliolatry, has a distinctive national character, and its magnificent vituperative style was not for export. By contrast, the Pansophic dream of a universal Christian Republic that would be nourished by the new science is European in its contours (there were influential Comenians in England and in the American colonies), though if a principal locus were to be established it would be the Central European world, devastated by war. Pansophia is anything but a populist utopia; its propagators are learned men associated with universities and courts, most of their all-too-voluminous tracts and treatises are in Latin, and the scholars engaged in the enterprise look to ruling princes, rich burghers, the Pope, the Emperor, the Czar as the divine instruments for its implementation. The Pansophists of the Germanic world, Italy, and England are closely linked with one another and are the bearers of the last great Christian hope for a unified religious society of all men everywhere. A third utopia of the seventeenth century is relatively minor, as parochially French as the creations of the English Civil War are English. Both Huguenot and Catholic utopians of the latter part of the century, Vairasse as well as Fénelon, repudiated the luxury-ridden society of Versailles forged by the triumphant monarchy of Louis XIV and moved off to Sevarambia or La Bétique. Since they recounted daring exploits and wrote in French (readily translated into other vernacular tongues), they appealed to a far broader audience than the scholarly Pansophists.

The utopian constellations of the Enlightenment and of the French Revolutionary era lose the focus of the earlier centuries as their authors are pulled in different directions. Old hopes of the Christian utopia have been forsaken and there is not yet full commitment to the euchronian constellations that dominate the next epoch. The *patres majores* among the French philosophes, with their troubled ambivalence toward utopia, and even Rousseau's enigmatic *moi commun* and *monde idéal,* are transitional. The philosophes have to be left in utopian limbo, which is just where they belong. They were not emancipated enough from the classical doctrine of the cyclical vicissitudes of states and empires to be convinced of an endlessly dynamic future. There is no article on utopia in the *Encyclopédie,* and old utopians are treated with contempt. Nonetheless, the eighteenth century proliferated utopias of every type—Morean, Robinsonian, physiocratic, communistic, sexual. On the eve of the Revolution, disquisitions on sexuality, ideal architectural forms, property, and equality cropped up all over the place in a utopian format, signaling alternative paths for a return to nature, or, faute de mieux, to a quasi-natural state in the midst of civilization. A babel of utopias trumpeted in the Revolution. Its many tongues were the education of party chiefs, but however radically the visions may have differed from one another, in toto the eighteenth-century utopia was still framed in terms of an agrarian society.

Unfortunately, chronological models are rarely neat, and Turgot, Condorcet, and Mercier, the initiators in different styles of the new euchronia, in which good place gives way to good time, had the bad grace to be Enlightenment stalwarts, bred in its Parisian womb. In this instance nothing avails but to call the dialectical principle to the rescue: In the bosom of a utopia of agrarian calm felicity a utopia of endless, dynamic change in science and technology was born. This switch to euchronia was heralded with the awakened sleeper of Sébastien Mercier's *L'An 2440* and with the utopian projections in the Tenth Epoch of Condorcet's *Esquisse*. The vision of a future society of *progrès indéfini* predominates through the emergence of Marx on the utopian landscape. Paradoxically, un-Christian euchronia represented a resurgence of a strong millenarian, paradisaical, and apocalyptic current in secular form. The free rational choices of the Morean Utopian lawgiver or the Renaissance architect were abandoned to history: Utopia became less Hellenic and more Judeo-Christian. Older rhythms of thought from millenarianism and Joachimism were secularized, and translations of Judeo-Christian apocalyptic rhetoric into new terms became the stuff of the transformation.

Both in fertility of invention and penetrating insight into the human condition, the French thinkers from Saint-Simon through Fourier, Comte, and their schools were a luminous constellation of modern utopian thought: Work and love were brilliantly analyzed and their felicitous union was established as a prerequisite for an ideal society. Robert Owen and German originals like Wilhelm Weitling were lesser lights of the same species. Marx brought the triumph of euchronia to a European climax by incorporating French, German, and English elements into a unique synthesis, condensed in that banderole of the *Gotha Program Critique*, "From each according to his abilities, to each according to his needs." After Marx, there was a falling-off in utopian invention. The utopians of the earlier part of the nineteenth century were reacted against, assimilated, cribbed, echoed, regurgitated, and watered down in a variety of new forms, discursive and novelistic. The anarchist utopia is the most virulent of the utopian forces competitive to the Marxist; and the "Utopia Victoriana," typified by the works of Chernyshevskii, Morris, Bellamy, and Hertzka, is its most genteel dilution. Lenin treasured his executed brother's copy of Chernyshevskii's *What Is to Be Done?* but clearly Lenin's field of specialization was applied utopistics.

At a time when utopian formulas still enjoyed a great vogue, two intruders broke into heaven on earth: Darwin and Freud. Popular Darwinism and the new utopia of science and science fiction that flowed from it at once opened vast new vistas and closed others. The new utopia to counteract a Darwinian cosmic pessimism was epitomized by the noösphere of Teilhard de Chardin and the scientific utopia of Bernal, with its marvels of biological engineering and the projection of humanity into outer space as an ultimate destiny. Freud, the trenchant critic of "lullabies of heaven," was followed by an outcropping of Freudo-Marxists, who tried to soften the Freudian sermon on the eternity of aggression. Their works culminated in Marcuse's utopian "Ende der Utopie," with its exaltation of a new utopian value that he called sexual-aesthetic.[19] The diffuse manner in which the utopian imagination has responded to the dystopian forces of Darwin and Freud represents a weakening and an attenuation of earlier ideas and imagery, and suggested the phrase "twilight of utopia" as descriptive of the most recent period.

The Pluralism of the Commentary

Utopias can be considered from a number of points of view: geographical, historical, psychological, sociological; as a form of belles-lettres; as philosophico-moral treatises; as a new mythology. Just as there have been monist theories that pretend to explicate all myths, so those who have psychologized, sociologized, or historicized utopias or treated them as a literary genre or a philosophical principle have had a tendency to constrict their significance within the limits of a single discipline. The partial validity of all of these interpretations ought to be accepted—a reading would have to be far-out indeed not to contain at least a grain of meaning and truth. But we have tried to avoid the parochialism of exclusive disciplinary discourse by studying the same utopian constellation on many different levels.

An easy, though restricted, access to utopia is through its historical geography. The historian of "proper utopias" twirls a globe dotted with ideal societies on distant islands with specific geographic locations, in isolated valleys, remote mountain fastnesses, underground galleries, caverns in the bowels of the earth, inaccessible jungle clearings. Fortunate peoples inhabit floating platforms in space, the moon, the sun, Mars, Venus; they populate an infinity of worlds.

Much of Western utopia can be related to the acquisition of the known visible world by the peoples of the peninsula of Europe. This development cuts across the individual historical constellations. Imaginary societies are situated along the general path of actual conquests, discoveries, and explorations. In the wake of Alexander's drive to the heart of Asia, Euhemerus, a Hellenistic Greek, found a good order of society on Panchaïa, an island in the Indian Ocean. The trader Iambulus, probably a Syrian metic, abandoned to the sea by his Ethiopian captors as a sacrificial offering, told how his boat had drifted to Islands of the Sun somewhere near the east coast of Africa. Other Greek writers claimed acquaintance with the happy Hyperboreans and the men of Ultima Thule on the edge of the European continent. The Romans rarely stretched themselves far beyond the boundaries of the Greek romances; in their imperial triumph many Romans were too complacent and too self-satisfied to dream of ideal polities; for them, Rome itself was utopia. But after the fall of Rome and throughout the Middle Ages new lands were constantly being incorporated into the utopian *mappamundi* from the seas to the west of Europe and Africa. Saint Brendan's Fortunate Isle, the most famous of them, was a Christianized gift of Celtic fantasy. Often the creation of medieval utopias was incidental to a search for the eastern site of the terrestrial Garden of Eden or to a quest for the Holy Grail, in whose presence the knights would be overcome by feelings of ineffable joy. Eldad ha-Dani, a Jewish traveler of the late ninth century, came upon a perfect society on the other side of the River Sambatyon, where the ten lost tribes of Israel had migrated. And in the fourteenth century Sir John Mandeville was carried by his reveries to the mysterious East, to the Isle of Bragmans, where there was "neither thunder ne levening, hail ne snow, ne other tempests of ill weathers; ne hunger, ne pestilence, ne war, ne other tribulations."[20]

Within a few decades after Europeans had broken through their continental shell in the fifteenth century and sailed off in ships to possess the world, Utopia itself was "discovered" by Raphael Hythloday, a Portuguese mariner who had purportedly participated in Amerigo Vespucci's expeditions and returned to recount his adventures to Thomas More. For two hundred years thereafter the imaginary encounters of literary voyagers with stranger peoples kept close pace with the real adventures of their seafaring counterparts in America and Asia. Sometimes the utopias prophetically preceded rather than followed historical landings of Europeans in new places: Toward the latter part of the seventeenth century, at a time when the South Sea islands and Australia were still unexplored, the utopians outstripped the sailors, and the Huguenots Gabriel de Foigny and Denis Vairasse situated kingdoms in the Mers Australes. For some, there was no longer enough wonderment attached to the coastline of the Americas. Happiness was where they were not, beyond the horizon. During the course of the next century ideal societies multiplied in a balmy region of the Pacific—in Tahiti and on the island of Nouvelle-Cythère—*rêves exotiques* bred by the real voyages of Captain James Cook and Louis Antoine de Bougainville in the same area. After 1800 the wilderness of the American West, opened to travelers, yielded up utopian worlds in hidden valleys and on the broad plains and plateaus. New territories were progressively annexed to utopia until the whole face of the earth was covered and men had to seek elsewhere.

The astronomical and mechanical studies of the seventeenth century had already encouraged the utopian imagination to soar into outer space, giving a strong impetus to explorations that had been begun rather gingerly by the Greeks and the Romans. The Neoplatonists Plutarch and Plotinus, through an ingenious and daring exegesis of Homer, had translated Elysium from the ends of the earth to the moon, and Lucian's mockery of the whole Greek corpus of utopian expeditions had kept the moon site prominent all through the Middle Ages. But extraterrestrial utopian societies really began to crowd one another only after 1600, when moon travel dependent upon breaking through the gravitational pull and attaining a state of weightlessness for most of the journey became a theoretical scientific possibility. Johannes Kepler's *Somnium, seu Opus Posthumum de Astronomia Lunari* (1634) placed a human on the moon to observe the earth, and John Wilkins' *Discovery of the New World in the Moon* (1638), a popular-science treatise on the mechanics of lunar voyages, though not a utopia, discussed the feasibility of living on the moon. The utopian excursions of Francis Godwin, Cyrano de Bergerac, and a host of others were not long delayed once the idea became a commonplace. The universe beyond the earth was peopled in man's fantasy for centuries before the giant step on the moon in 1969; and a proliferation of works of science fiction and predictive science in the twentieth century prefigured the event.

Since the fabrication of utopian societies and the expeditions to new lands ran parallel, it is not surprising that their two geographies, the imaginary and the real, were sometimes confused. Like the voyages of the Argonauts and of Sinbad the Sailor, utopian adventures never completely severed their ties to the phenomenal world. At times the utopia-writer lent such verisimilitude to the description of his fantasy land that fictional names, such as those of the East Indian islands in the Huguenot François Misson's *Voyage et avantures de François Leguat* (1708), found their way into serious geography books and remained there for centuries. The novel by the trader Iambulus, preserved in the histories of Diodorus Siculus, was reprinted in Giovanni Battista Ramusio's mid-sixteenth-century collection of voyages (though he hedged a bit about its authenticity, suggesting that it was part truth, part fable),[21] and it survived as an inspiration of Tommaso Campanella's *Città del Sole* (1602). A great utopia like Thomas More's exerted a more profound and subtle influence. It penetrated the consciousness of literate men and colored their whole view of reality. More's perception of things stamped the European mind so indelibly that the schema of Book II of the *Utopia* was adopted in scores of genuine, as well as imaginary, travel accounts, and became an accepted framework for circumstantial reporting on newly discovered lands.

Not content with inventing a fabulous universal geography, the Western imagination has waved a magic wand over many of the great historical societies, so that idealized depictions of Egypt, Sparta, Athens, Scythia, Persia, Rome, Israel have in a way become part of the utopian corpus. Plutarch's Lycurgan Sparta and Xenophon's Persia, long after the historical passing of these states, assumed separate existences as utopian polities worthy of imitation by all mankind. Egocentric eulogists have composed self-adulatory utopias, painting their own societies in colors so dazzling that those not possessed can hardly recognize even the outlines of actuality. The sixteenth- and seventeenth-century myth of Venice as the ideal commonwealth would boggle the minds of twentieth-century men were we not inured to the apotheosis of societies whose ugliness and depravity we have beheld with our own eyes. There is hardly a polity so vicious that it cannot be transformed into a paragon of virtue by the power of the imagination interweaving utopian and historical modes.

Every utopia, rooted as it is in time and place, is bound to reproduce the stage scenery of its particular world as well as its preoccupation with contemporary social problems. Here analogies to the dream and the psychotic fantasy may be telling. Observers of paranoid behavior report that though the disease remains relatively constant, the mysterious, all-seeing forces that watch and persecute their patients change with time and technology. They may be spirits, telephones, radios, or television sets in successive periods. Utopias are not an illness; but to a large degree they avail themselves of the existing equipment of a society, perhaps its most advanced models, prettified and rearranged. Often a utopian foresees the later evolution and consequences of technological development already present in an embryonic state; he may have antennae sensitive to the future. His gadgets, however, rarely go beyond the mechanical potentialities of his age. Try as he may to invent something wholly new, he cannot make a world out of nothing.

If utopias are classified by the style of their furniture, sociological and historical, and the style is related to a contemporary social reality, the utopia can be studied as a reflection of the specific crises that it presumes to resolve. That utopia is tied to existing social conflicts and that the utopian often aligns himself with one side or the other has been profusely illustrated. In Hesiod one senses the state of decline after the heroic epoch of Hellas, in Plato the temper of growing luxuriousness in Athenian life and the impending demise of the polis. The utopias of Alberti, Filarete, and Patrizi communicate the spirit of a new Renaissance aristocracy of wealth as distinct from a rough, feudal nobility, and the elegant patricians of their ideal cities keep themselves aloof from both the swashbuckling condottieri and the plebeians on the lower levels of society. Thomas More, it is said, is reacting against the enclosure movement, but whether in the name of the new burghers of London or of nostalgic medieval agrarianism or the spiritual ideals of a Christian humanism remains debatable. The great seventeenth-century utopias strive to mend the political and religious schisms in the Christian world and to reconstitute a universal order on the basis of Christian virtues bolstered by the new science. Many eighteenth-century utopias with their ever-normal granaries and orderly physiocratic policies directed by a wise paternal legislator and a meritocracy in the spiritual and temporal realms point the way to ending the endemic hunger of the ancien régime and ridding society of its vestigial feudal institutions. Saint-Simon and Fourier had the perspicacity to respond to the economic and psychic dislocations of the new industrial society long before its griefs had become plainly visible. Marx sought to master the same forces at a maturer stage of capitalism and Hertzka at an even later stage, when the problems of industrialism were complicated by imperialist expansion. Present-day utopians are trying to cope with the anxieties and potentialities of what has been called postindustrial society. But since most epochs in the West have been turbulent, the proposition that the utopias they have produced are related to economic and social upheavals becomes truistic. To announce in tones of dramatic revelation that a utopia mirrors the misery of the working classes or the squeeze of the lesser nobility between the peasants and the royal power is to say something, but not enough. To identify elements in utopias of the seventeenth and eighteenth centuries as manifestations of *Frühkapitalismus,* a current fashion, is to mistake a rubric for a statement of content.

Identifying the sources of a utopia in historical reality can of course be done with more or with less sensitivity. Granted that the utopia-maker reflects the historical moment, in the rare instances where he has genius he reveals the inner depths, the essence, of that moment rather than mere externals. He has the capacity to achieve a measure of distance from the day-to-day controversies of the marketplace and to view the life of his society in the light of its manifold possibilities. Even though he may not be so insightful as a sublime poet, the utopian can capture the anguish of an epoch in a striking metaphor. In dissecting the urgent requirements of his times, he may also lay bare age-old, if not eternal, needs of man. Limiting an interpretation to the immediate environment of the utopian, tying him down too closely and mechanically to the precise circumstances and incidents that could have triggered his writing, fails to recognize that he may have something ahistorical to say about love, aggression, the nature of work, the fulfillment of personality. The truly great utopian is a Janus-like creature, time-bound and free of time, place-bound and free of place. His duality should be respected and appreciated.

Certain historical generations are peculiarly susceptible to utopian thinking and it is not uncommon to find the same young men possessed by a succession of utopias and stumbling from one utopian movement into another. English seekers of the Civil War, though primarily embarked on an individual quest for a way to God, became involved, as they wandered from sect to sect, with the social utopias related to each new doctrine. Rootless young Frenchmen of the generation of 1798, when they reached maturity under the Restoration, made the rounds from Saint-Simonism to Fourierism to Comtism (not always in that order). The spiritual migrations of the 1930s and the 1960s tell similar stories in the United States. Such concentrations represent far larger numbers than the interplay of an exclusive band of northern Christian humanists, or the Renaissance architects of the ideal city, or the Pansophists of the seventeenth century. And yet in their own small way the young Rhineland academics touched by the Rosicrucian hope of reforming the world underwent psychic experiences that were not dissimilar to those of the French Romantic utopians. A historical sociology of utopian movements or, better, affinity groups would have to go back to the Pythagoreans, the Essenes, the radical sectaries of the Middle Ages and the Reformation, if it were not to get bogged down in the parochial though rich nineteenth-century American experience with utopian communities. We have been preoccupied chiefly with the thought behind these movements, but some consideration of their character and organization throws light on the ideational substance.

Utopias have been powerful dynamic forces in the political arena, though not necessarily when first published. If their astute empirical diagnosis strikes a chord that has resonances among some classes of their society, they become famous; failing, they are forgotten, or may wait in some utopian limbo to be revived at a future date. The *fortuna* of the original document is an inseparable part of its meaning, and should be examined along with the changed content that new generations have constantly poured into the old utopia. A work can hardly escape fundamental transformation as its audience changes: More's Christian-humanist *declamatio* becomes a revolutionary manifesto; Marx's notebooks in which a young man is trying out his ideas are read as dogma a century later; Comenius' massive systematic manuscript, *General Consultation on an Improvement of All Things Human,* aimed at effectuating a radical universal reform, ends up as a mere historical curiosity, a scholar's felicitous discovery three hundred years after the author's death and of interest only to a limited number of specialists. Of late, statistical records of the past compiled by government officials with one specific intent, when placed in another context have begun to speak a very different language to researchers. Similarly, utopian ideas assume new meanings as they are moved about from series to series. A commentator focusing on utopian sexual fantasies will not pluck the same meaning from an account of a Ranter assemblage during the English Civil War as did a contemporary presbyter. The observer of utopia over a period of hundreds of years is constrained to consider each event as having roots in the past and sending out tentacles to the future and to coevals scattered over a broad area. No important utopian event is encapsulated or autonomous, because future history has embraced it. A critical history, while it can never escape its own historicity, may succeed in combining a measure of distance with its empathy and antipathy.

The changing size of the reading public is part of the commentary that illuminates utopias. Thomas More's Latin *libellus* was originally accessible to a far smaller public than Edward Bellamy's *Looking Backward,* but it was large compared to Winstanley's Digger *Platform* or a Ranter sermon that made its way into the hostile report of Thomas Edwards' *Gangraena.* Marx's definition of the higher stage of communism in the *Critique of the Gotha Program* has surely been read by a far greater number of persons in contemporary China, where it is said to be discussed at peasant study sessions, than it was in the 1890s when it was published. And if we would pursue fragments of utopias that penetrate the rhetoric of popular movements, we enter a world of diffusion where solids have become gaseous and impossible to isolate. Confronted with a shifting readership and the utopian's mobile or ambivalent original purpose, the critical historian who reviews the whole process ought not to take too rigid a stance, for the same text tells many different things about utopian thought at widely dispersed times, and even among different classes of contemporaries.

The Utopian and His Creation

As a mental event, a utopia takes the form of a written document and is usually composed by one man. On rare occasions a group of men may concert together to formulate a utopian program; for that moment, at least, they give the appearance of being of one mind and they share a common utopian experience. The utopian may, as politician, reformer, revolutionary, prophet, use bits and pieces of his own utopian structure. Others may cannibalize his utopia and incorporate it into their manifestoes for action, inscribe its slogans on their banners. But every subsequent usage of utopian rhetoric after the initial creation involves a tearing apart and perhaps even a total destruction of the original. A history of utopian thought may deal with the preliminaries in the life of the individual utopian, the dynamic internal psychic forces that climaxed in the recording of the utopian experience, and the communication, popularization, vulgarization, stereotyping, or rigidifying of the utopian event in the course of time. But in the process the mental event itself should not be diluted to the point where it is hardly distinguishable from the waters that flowed in and those that poured out; it remains a unique creation.

At a time when individual psychological analysis flourishes, one is tempted to turn to the person of the utopian for the illumination of his fantasy. Though a poet has related the utopian mode to youth and the attraction of ideal world systems may be most powerful in adolescence, there are many middle-aged utopian fantasts, and the utopian propensity is not restricted to any one stage of the life cycle. More wrote his utopia in his late thirties, Restif and Saint-Simon composed theirs when they were about forty. One version of Rousseau's utopia was a deathbed revelation and Diderot's *Supplément au voyage de Bougainville* was the daydream of an aging man. Since the illusory world serves some purpose in the psychic economy of its author, interpreters have undertaken to ferret out and relate the utopian's hidden drives to major elements of his imaginary society. The effort should not be scorned. For many, such as More, Comenius, Bacon, Jean-Jacques, Fourier, Marx, the data are richly available and the quest is rewarding; for others, the psychological perceptions that can be mustered are severely limited, since we may know nothing but the author's name, perhaps a nom de plume at that, or only a family name as with Morelly, whose *Code de la nature* was a signficant utopian landmark and played a major part in the intellectual world of Babeuf. But paucity of materials does not discourage the convinced believer in the paramountcy of his psychological techniques. He can reconstruct a personality on the basis of psychological disclosures in the fantasy and then triumphantly interpret the fantasy in terms of its creator. An ideal visionary type, the perfect utopian, would probably both hate his father and come from a disinherited class. A bit of schizophrenia, a dose of megalomania, obsessiveness, and compulsiveness fit neatly into the stereotype. But the utopian personality that is more than an item in a catalogue must also be gifted and stirred by a creative passion. The great utopias—and they are not numerous—are marked but not necessarily marred by the scars of their authors. Sometimes the wounds lie well concealed, as was More's hair-shirted and lacerated body beneath the inky cloak of the Holbein portrait.

There is a sense in which the mental act of creating a utopian world, or the principles for one, is psychologically a regressive phenomenon for an individual. In this respect the utopian is kindred to the religious, scientific, and artistic creators who flee to the desert, suffer psychic crises, become disoriented by the contradictions between accepted reality and the new insights of which they have a glimmer. In the first instance the utopian is overwhelmed by the evil complexities of existence. The great utopians have all borne witness to their anger at the world, their disgust with society, their acute suffering as their sensibilities are assailed from all sides. They withdraw from this world into a far simpler form of existence which they fantasy. The escape from everyday conflicts and disappointments has a childlike quality. And their way back from utopia, their return to the real world they had abandoned, is often characterized by devotion to a fixed idea with which they become obsessed. They clutch frantically at this overvalued idea that at once explains all evil and offers the universal remedy, and they build an impregnable fortification around it. The one idea becomes a fetish that they worship and defend with marvelous ingenuity. To outsiders they are monomaniacs. These reflections naturally apply only to the select number of authentic utopians who endure the travail of new birth, not to the hundreds of utopian imitators who crowd bibliographies as poetasters do histories of literature.

Utopians are almost always tragic or tragicomic figures who die unfulfilled; the future does not begin to conform to their fantasy. Then appear the disciples or curious readers who have not been shaken in their innermost being with anything like the intensity of the original utopian visionary, and they adapt, prune, distort, refine, render banal, make matter-of-fact the utopia, so that it reenters the world as a force for good or evil. Compromises with existence are effected; the ironclad formula is relaxed. To measure the pure utopian theory by the achievements of "applied utopistics" is fatuous, as is any attempt to make fathers responsible for the sins and barbarities of their putative sons. By definition, the utopian creation born of a yearning for return to a simple haven or of a descent into the lower depths of the unconscious cannot be put into practice.

One of the most prickly tasks for the commentator on utopia is to assess the commitment of a utopian author to his own work. Appraisals range from the mere jeu d'esprit through rhetorical *declamatio* as a didactic device, from the utopia as wish rather than anticipation to zealous conviction of the need for or expectation of the total implementation of the utopian principles on the morrow or at most the day after. When the utopian is torn by doubts, on the manifest or covert level, an evaluation becomes acutely problematic. Restif de la Bretonne, a type familiar enough to modern psychologists, wrote both expansively permissive and obsessively repressive utopias. Some utopians wear a mask of harlequin, as Fourier did on occasion, to attract attention with absurdities and scandalous utterances. Many who conceived of their utopias as popular forms of a Platonic idea would have been content with far less than complete realization in this world. Others, possessed by the spirit of religious ritualism, would not allow for the changing of an iota in their system lest the magical efficacy of the whole be impaired. Both proper and discursive utopias are literary texts in which ambivalence and ambiguity are very often inseparable from the thought itself. Obviously, once they have left their author's hands they lead lives of their own, and the most ironic or hyperbolic positions can subsequently be read as if they were biblical commandments, mathematical demonstrations, or the triumphs of academic discourse in which points are proved and disproved. This applies not only to Thomas More's work, where divergent contemporary commentaries are at last making the Christian humanist tone evident, but to many other utopias that to this day are interpreted in a doltishly straight-faced manner because the doubt of the author has been ignored. Searching for the utopian intent, almost always elusive, comes to occupy a significant part of this historical commentary.

Paradoxically, the great utopians have been great realists. They have an extraordinary comprehension of the time and place in which they are writing and deliver themselves of penetrating reflections on socioeconomic, scientific, or emotional conditions of their moment in history. They have discovered truths that other men have only vaguely sensed or have refused to recognize. The utopian often emerges as a man with a deeper understanding of the drift of his society than the hardheaded problem-solvers with their noses to the grindstone of the present, blind to potentiality. Perhaps the utopians stand out because of the tenacity with which they hold to their ideas. They have a penchant for focusing the full glare of their insight on a particular aspect of the world and leaving much unnoticed. But if they are fixated on one face of reality, this face they understand as other men have not. Their knowledge serves them as a springboard for a jump into a future which could be either a total negation of the present or so sharply lateral that others would at first glance consider it chimerical, fantastic, improbable—in a word, utopian. There is an almost inevitable inclination in a utilitarian society to value most those utopian visionaries whose "dreams came true," not the best criterion for judgment. The short-term prognosticator can be a bore. He is merely a meteorologist, useful in planning an outing or a military invasion.

Without taking leave of reality, utopians have performed symbolic acts to dramatize their break with the present. They have located their ideal societies at a distance in space—this was the normal device of the Morean utopia that required the rite of passage of an ocean voyage. King Utopus cut the isthmus that had once attached his newly conquered kingdom to the mainland as one would snip an umbilical cord. In the twentieth century Bernal required a light-year of flight to establish the necessary pathos of distance for one of his artificial planets. Men have fallen into holes in the earth to get to the ideal center of things; they have crossed impassable mountain ranges to descend into pleasant valleys; they have broken the time barrier of the present through machines or through sleep; they have distinguished between evil prehistory and utopian history. The critical negation may be incorporated in a separate book and composed after the utopia proper. We now know that More's Book I postdated the composition of Book II; the whole is a study in contrasts. In other Morean utopias the negative and the positive are intermingled in the same account, as the strangers, or the utopians (who are sometimes all-knowing), play a counterpoint between Europe and the newly discovered island, or the present and the future. The movement back and forth between heaven and hell is precipitous, so that the reader is constantly made aware of the antithesis.

The utopians whose repudiation of the present is in the Greek tradition tend to seek a more rationalist and analytical way to expose what to Aristotle were the defects in existing forms. In the Judeo-Christian corpus the revulsion against the pervasiveness of religious sin is more emotive. But the logical argumentative character of the classical search for perfect forms may only disguise the force of the underlying negative affect. The medical metaphor of Plato, diagnosing his contemporary city as suffering from an inflammation, and the summary condemnation in his Seventh Epistle of "all the states which now exist" as "badly governed" dramatize the feeling that preceded or accompanied the analysis.[22]

It would be deceptive to stress the utopia as negation of present reality to the neglect of curiosity, inventiveness, the exploratory drive that has led man on the most daring adventures. The two strains have had changing relative potencies at different epochs. There are times when the utopia of calm felicity dominates Western culture and the imagery of a return to the protective womb of paradise seems to suffuse the emotional atmosphere; then a Promethean element breaks through and utopian existence becomes the dramatic torch race of which Bacon wrote in *Wisdom of the Ancients*. Utopians are often intrepid, bold explorers whom many of their contemporaries consider wild because they neither repeat existing rhetoric with variations nor pursue familiar directions. If a utopia is merely or primarily reflective of existing reality it is trivial. On the other hand, when the imaginary world is cut off from all relationship with reality, it becomes a vaporous fairy tale, formless and pointless, like many *voyages imaginaires* and *songes* and *romans cabalistiques* of the eighteenth century and much of contemporary science fiction, where the utopian elements are so feeble they are only sedatives, pastimes, narcotics. The great utopia startles and yet is recognized as conceivable. It is not a sleepy or bizarre vision but one that satisfies a hunger or stimulates the mind and the body to the recognition of a new potentiality.

PART I

The Ancient and Medieval Wellsprings

The Heavenly Paradise, ca. 1445
Giovanni di Paolo
Metropolitan Museum of Art, New York
(Rogers Fund, 1906)

I

Paradise and the Millennium

OF THE TWO ELEMENTS which flowed together in the underthought of Western utopia, the Judeo-Christian and the Hellenic, the first has had the more continuous existence. A natural history of the paradises of the Judaic and Christian religions assembles some of the intellectual and emotional materials that accumulated in European society and constituted an ever-growing storehouse in the culture. Paradise in its Judeo-Christian forms has to be accepted as the deepest archaeological layer of Western utopia, active in the unconscious of large segments of the population, even when they did not read the books in which the varieties of this experience assumed literary shape—testimony to the enduring power of religious belief to keep alive the strange longing for a state of man that once has been and will be again. The paradisaical myth is virtually universal in mankind, but in Western culture it has been assimilated by each succeeding generation in specific new guises. By the time Western utopia was born in the fifteenth and early sixteenth centuries the belief in paradise was present on all levels of psychic existence. Its name need not be uttered by the utopian creator; its fragrance was in the air he breathed, sustaining his existence. Perhaps Purgatory and Hell were more constant preoccupations of European Christians at the historic moment when utopia first saw the light, but the solace of paradise was still a part of the ritual of dying and being buried among Christians and Jews.

Though utopia proper remains a creation of the world of the Renaissance and the Reformation, the visions of the two paradises (Eden and the World to Come), of the Days of the Messiah, and of the millennium have so tenacious a hold on Western consciousness that they are a constant presence—in multiple variations—in all subsequent utopian thought. The history of paradise is a prolegomenon and perennial accompaniment to utopia without which the powerful religious emotion that infuses this experience can never be captured. Images of paradise and the millennium constitute a treasury on which utopian thinkers draw, though they are not always conscious of their borrowing. The psychological roots of the paradise myth and of millenarian hope, never to be divorced from the apocalypse—with its dual prophecies of terror and salvation—are so profound that their existence may sometimes be taken for granted or overlooked. The very language used in the descriptions of successive paradises, the foretelling of a thousand-year reign of Christ on earth, and the prophecies of Joachim of Fiore have remained alive in the discourse of all European societies. Millenarian speech has been adopted by scores of secular revolutionary movements. Joachim of Fiore's conceptions reappeared, often by name, among Christian utopians from Müntzer in the sixteenth through Campanella in the seventeenth and Lessing in the eighteenth centuries. When translated into secular terminology the "three states" of Joachimism became,

33

in the nineteenth century, the dominant philosophy of history ending in a utopia.

Since the time of Christ the Jewish and Christian religions have wrestled with parallel great expectations in their conceptions of the Days of the Messiah and the millennium, in the fantastic new worlds of the Kabbala and Joachim's Third Age, in popular versions of both the terrestrial and celestial paradises. Through a thousand avenues of intellectual influence the different conceptions of Jewish and Christian belief have interpenetrated. A later Christian utopian did not have to have direct access to the documents of Judaic thought to experience its weight.

The idea of a millennium or of the Days of the Messiah came closest to utopia before the emergence of utopia itself. And certain Christian institutions such as monasticism are embodiments of the best possible life on earth for a Christian who has taken vows. The existence of such imaginary states and of real forms of human organization is a long-living memory in utopian consciousness.

The Paradise Cult

A revealing way to examine the psychic life of Judeo-Christian civilization would be to study it as a paradise cult, isolating fantasies about another world as they found expression in sacred texts, in their commentaries, and in their secular adaptation. It would not be a mere thin-spun web of dreams: Grand enterprises of Western man, among them the Crusades against Islam, millenarian revolts during the Reformation, the overseas explorations of the sixteenth century, and the settlement of the American continent, drew sustenance from the body of this myth. The emotive forces behind the quest for the Holy Grail, the need to conquer Jerusalem—the umbilicus of the world that held the sepulture of Adam from whose mouth grew the tree of the Cross on which Jesus was crucified—and the search for the earthly paradise imparted to mass movements an intensity that cannot be explained in the language of politics and economics alone. In visions of paradise terrestrial and celestial, men of the West have been disclosing their innermost desires, whether they have thrust them backward into the past, projected them forward into the future on earth, or raised them beyond the bounds of this sphere. As in dreams, men have displaced themselves in time and space and compressed their manifold wishes into an all-embracing metaphor—the "garden eastward in Eden" of Genesis, the "World to Come" of the rabbis, the "city of the living God" of the Epistle to the Hebrews, the "ineffabile allegrezza" of Dante's *Paradiso*.

Academic documentation of the paradisaical state over the centuries is now almost complete—a bold assertion. But anyone who today embarks upon this perilous three-thousand-year journey will of necessity have to change his mentors along the route. Unlike that more fortunate Florentine seeker after paradise, he will find no solitary Vergil, Matelda, or Beatrice waiting for him at appointed stations. Instead, for every portion of the way he will have to choose from among a clamorous throng of guides all of whom pretend to a preeminent knowledge of the terrain. At some crossroads the guides are friendly competitors, like those professors of literature who treat of the golden age and an earthly paradise in the Renaissance poets and have a way of tossing garlands to one another, though not without a concealed thorn here and there. At other points where new discoveries have been made—the scrolls in the Qumran caves—rival scholars heave great boulders from the desert and engage in such bitter learned disputation that the traveler is bewildered and must find a path through the wasteland of apocalyptic literature on the Messianic age virtually without assistance.

In the beginning paradise was a myth with all the ambiguities of a myth; in time it became a religious belief in Israel and eventually a theological doctrine in Judaism and in Christianity. Like all orthodoxies it was then subject to imaginative deviations that strayed far from the dogma of the ecclesiastical establishments. Toward the end of the Middle Ages paradise ceased to be speculative alone and became enmeshed with action programs, often of a violent revolutionary character. As simple religious faith in the existence of paradise waned, the unconscious material of the original myth was preserved in a literary genre, the utopia, and in a political form, the movement. Today even among those who no longer believe in paradise in an elementary sense residues remain—last vestiges about to become extinct or seeds waiting for the moment to germinate.

A Garden Eastward in Eden

The canonical version of paradise, an account of the Garden of Eden in Chapter II of Genesis, has been recognized, at least since the eighteenth century, as a composite of separate texts one or more of which was written around the ninth or possibly the eighth century before Christ by priests of Israel. Contemporary criticism, no longer content with attempts to isolate and date the discrete versions of Genesis—the Jahvist, the Elohist, the priestly, and the other creations of the learned imagination—conceives of each of them as itself an embodiment of traditions going back much further in the religion of Israel, so that the date of final redaction loses some of its significance. While there was a time in the late nineteenth and early twentieth centuries when it was fashionable to view all elements of the biblical Garden of Eden as derivative from fragments of epic literature in the cultures of the Tigris-Euphrates valley of the third and second millennia before Christ, the weight of biblical studies today is rather on the uniqueness and complexity of the myth in Genesis, and there is a tendency to underplay "origins" suggested by the reading of cuneiform texts. The Near Eastern myths nonetheless remain an integral part of the history of the paradisaical state, even if they no longer explain away the novelty of the biblical invention. Both are related to the oldest cultural stratum of Mesopotamia. Recent discoveries of a rich library in Ebla, Syria, may in the future revolutionize our knowledge of Sumerian culture, the creation of a strange non-Semitic, non-Indo-European people who dominated southern Babylonia from the beginning of the fourth to the end of the third millennium B.C. For the time being, we must rely on known texts. Sumerian cuneiform writing spread throughout the Near East, and with it a mythology that penetrated the spiritual life of the Akkadians, the Canaanites, the Hebrews, and the Greeks.

The memory of a lost paradisaical age is evoked in a Sumerian epic poem whose hero, Enmerkar, ruled in the city of Erech sometime during the fourth millennium B.C. In a distant past—the "no" in the text means "not yet"—the world was free of savage and noxious creatures and the supremacy of man was unchallenged. The cohesion of the peoples, their security and union in religious worship, are recollected with yearning.

> In those days there was no snake, there was no scorpion, there was no *hyena,*
> There was no lion, there was no *wild dog,* no wolf,
> There was no fear, no terror,
> Man had no rival.
>
> In those days the land Shubur (East), the place of plenty, of righteous decrees,
> *Harmony-tongued* Sumer (South), the great land of the "decrees of princeship,"
> Uri (North), the land having all that is *needful,*
> The land Martu (West), resting in security,
> The whole universe, the people *in unison,*
> To Enlil in one tongue *gave praise.*[1]

The tablet of a Sumerian poem inscribed sometime before 1500 B.C., first published by S. H. Langdon in 1915, tells of the purity and peace of the mythic land of Dilmun, provided with water by Enki, and of the health and agelessness of its inhabitants. The place is described in a series of negatives that simultaneously conjure up before the mind's eye the spectacle of the evils of this world. "In Dilmun the raven utters no cries,/ The *ittidû*-bird utters not the cry of the *ittidû*-bird,/ The lion kills not,/ The wolf snatches not the lamb,/ Unknown is the kid-devouring *wild dog* . . . The dove *droops* not the head,/ The sick-eyed says not 'I am sick-eyed,'/ The sick-headed [says] not 'I am sick-headed,'/ Its old woman [says] not 'I am an old woman,'/ Its old man [says] not 'I am an old man.' "[2]

In the Akkadian Epic of Gilgamesh, for which versions exist from the second millennium, Utnapishtim, survivor of the deluge, was made immortal and was settled with his wife "far away at the mouth of the rivers." "Then Enlil went up into the ship./ He took my hand and caused me to go aboard./ He caused my wife to go aboard and to kneel down at my side./ Standing between us, he touched our foreheads and blessed us./ 'Hitherto Utnapishtim has been but a man;/ but now Utnapishtim and his wife shall be like unto us gods./ In the distance, at the mouth of the rivers Utnapishtim shall dwell.' " After conquering the scorpion-people who guard the gate, Gilgamesh himself penetrates a beautiful garden whose trees, shrubs, and vines are all of precious stones— the carnelian and lapis lazuli bearing fruit lush to behold—and there Siduri dwells. Rare stones and minerals—gold, bdellium, and onyx—reappear in Genesis and are even more common in an "Eden the garden of God" in Ezekiel—the sardius, topaz, carbuncle, diamond, beryl, onyx, jasper, sapphire, emerald—and in apocalyptic and Midrashic paradises.[3] Are these merely signs of wealth and prosperity, or do the gems recall the first glistening objects upon which the nursing infant is riveted, its mother's eyes?

While reasonable similarities can be found, there now is grave doubt whether the Sumerian epic of Dilmun and Sumerian tablets relating to the Fall of man are tales of paradise in the sense of Genesis. The first is considered to be a myth of the divine couple Enki-Ninhursag; the second, a story of the disobedience of man who failed to perform the work he owed the gods. If the land of Dilmun is the home of gods, not men, it has the same relation to paradise as Olympus has to Elysium. Of the gardens appearing in the Gilgamesh epic, many are abodes of the gods, not terrestrial paradises for man; and the paradisaical land where Utnapishtim was borne to immortality is more like Hesiod's Isles of the Blessed and Homer's Elysium than a Garden of Eden. There may be, it is allowed, a number of paradisaical images in the "cedar mountain, abode of the gods, throne-seat of Irnini," and in the garden of Siduri; and the Babylonian story of creation, the *Enûma Elish* (When Above), is probably mirrored in biblical cosmogony. But the identification of proper Hebrew names in Genesis with Sumerian words is an open question, and so is the origin of the Fall in the Babylonian-Assyrian Adapa myth, where a man squanders his chances to gain immortality. After a long period during which the higher criticism found virtually everything in the biblical paradise in texts of the Sumerian, Babylonian, and Assyrian world, the newest scholarship finds very little—though this may change again. But whatever the sources of the lines in Genesis, one stands in awe before the vast sea of commentary and hundreds of imaginative elaborations which over a period of almost three thousand years have surrounded this handful of verses in Judeo-Christian culture, as each generation reads into them its own ever-renewed fantasy of a garden in the beginning of things.

In the Hellenistic and Roman periods, tales of primitive peoples living in a paradisaical condition in the wilderness beyond the borders of civility were the products of a restless, discontented urban imagination. Soon enough this sophisticated primitivism incorporated the imagery of the myth of the golden age and the Judaic and Christian Garden of Eden. When new lands were discovered and explored, their primitive inhabitants were perceived in the light of the Greek and Hebrew myths, which psychically predetermined what Europeans saw. Primitivism has an almost uninterrupted history from its inception through episodes of the Alexander legend and travel reports from the Hyperboreans, islands beyond the gates of Hercules, tribes on the Roman marches, and, in the Middle Ages, from the mysterious East. The search for the realm of Prester John, which captured the imagination of the late medieval world, is at once Christian paradisaical and primitivist. This stream of thought finally becomes dominant, during the period from the sixteenth through the eighteenth centuries, in the myth of the noble savage with its syncretism of paradisaical longings and the exaltation of the virtues of uncivilized man. Missionaries were quick to see the Indians as living in either a golden age or a terrestrial paradise, a perception dependent for the strength of its impact upon revolutionary transformations in Jewish and Christian conceptions of paradise. By the time Europeans set forth in ships to cross the Atlantic and the Pacific and trekked over the vast continental expanses of America, always in quest of an earthly paradise, that dream had for many centuries been suffused with religious feelings of great potency—a historical continuum that is sometimes ignored by those who blithely write of the *rêve exotique* of the seventeenth and eighteenth centuries as an independent creation of that period.

The Shaping of Belief in the Talmud and the Midrash

The word paradise was not used by the Jews in the canonical writings of the Bible. The spread of conceptions of an ideal future state in another world as a reward for the righteous is usually postponed by scholars until after the Babylonian captivity, Persian influences being the supposed stimulus to the introduction of these beliefs. As anyone who has immersed himself in academic literature on paradise knows, whenever novelty intrudes there is an initial temptation to trace it back to the "East." The original Persian *pairidaēza* seems to denote a surrounding (*pairi* = Greek *peri*) wall made of a sticky mass (*daēza*) like clay or dough—an etymology to which, as Freudians of sorts, we are naturally partial, since it is more womblike than the blander "royal park." In Persian mythology the oxhorn tree with a surrounding wall and vegetation rises from the worldwide sea of Vouru Kaša and is similar to the world mountain, a frequent Eastern location for the paradisaical garden.[4]

The idea of an otherworldly paradise also has a parallel in the Zoroastrian doctrine of aeons, known in the West through crude summaries in Herodotus and Plutarch. The final *apatiyārakīh* has been translated as "state-of-no-more-being-contested," and the Song to the Sōšyant (Savior) about resurrection and eternal life has been reconstructed to read: "Astvatrta will set forth/ from the water Kansaviya/ the champion of AhuraMazdāh/ and his other companions, that they make humanity *frašam,*/ not-aging, not-dying,/ not-decaying, not-rotting,/ ever-living, ever-flourishing./ When the dead will rise up,/ the reviver, the imperishable will come,/ he will make humanity *frašam,* please God!" *Frašam* implies a condition beyond "the last day of history, when the world has finished its ninth round, when time stops and eternity begins."[5]

While the Hebrew word *pardes* (garden), of Persian origin, appears in a number of places in the postexilic books of the Old Testament, the first use of the Greek *paradeisos* (the "royal park" of Celaenae in Xenophon's *Anabasis*) to translate *Gan Eden* (Garden of Eden) is in the Septuagint begun in the third century before Christ. In Greek and Latin Christianity this was the term employed for both the Garden of Eden and a future otherworld, and it was diffused into all European languages. The rabbinic texts of the Talmud never adopted the word paradise; they held to the phrases Garden of Eden, this world, the Days of the Messiah, and the World to Come to define the major divisions of time. As Jerusalem came to occupy a central role in the life of the Jews, this model of urban perfection, related to an idealization of the reigns of David and Solomon and symbolically represented by the Temple, became another equivalent of the paradisaical state and the source of the idea of a heavenly Jerusalem.

At one time the messianic age of the Old Testament prophets referred solely to a future tribal or ethnic triumph of Israel over its neighboring enemies and was devoid of miraculous or unnaturalistic epiphanies; only after the return from Babylon did universalist overtones keep insinuating themselves until the Days of the Messiah became a kind of wonder-laden prolegomenon to a final judgment and an otherworldly paradise. Those curious about the origins of so radical a conception as the idea of a Messiah can turn to hypotheses about the recrudescence in an abstract form of a primitive ritual of the death and resurrection of a king-god whose being sustains his people. There is also a suggestive study of the dying Messiah as an archetype by a member of the Jungian school.[6] And if these explanations fail to satisfy, one can always turn to the East.

The nature of the Days of the Messiah and of the events that would precede and follow them enjoyed no general consensus in the sixty-three tractates of the oral law of the Talmud, whose interpretations of Scripture ranged over a period of almost a thousand years until their final codification in two different versions, the Babylonian and the Jerusalem, in the fifth and sixth centuries A.D. The eleventh chapter of the tractate *Sanhedrin* in the Babylonian Talmud is devoted to the determination of who has a part in the World to Come. After an opening manifesto in its Mishnah—a division of the Talmud that incorporates the opinions of an early generation of rabbis known as the Tannaim and was already fixed by about A.D. 200—that "all Israel" has such a portion, the rabbis withdrew substantially from this open-ended promise. Certain grave sinners were denied entry: "he who maintains that the resurrection is not a Biblical doctrine, the Torah was not divinely revealed, and an Epikoros" (an adherent of the Epicurean philosophy and by extension one who led a dissolute life).[7] Ordinarily there was in the Talmud an underlying contrast between *Olam Haze,* this world, and *Olam Haba,* the World to Come, but that amphibious period on earth known as the Days of the Messiah continually intervenes to complicate matters temporally; nor is there any agreement about the substantive relationship between the World to Come and the Eden of Adam and Eve in the beginning of things, though there are doctrines of prefiguration to account for the resemblance of the two states. At intervals in the history of the Jews there has been a powerful resurgence of belief in the reign of the Messiah in this world, usually accompanied by a conviction that the epoch was imminent or had in effect already dawned. Faith in the advent of the Messiah was probably most intense in Judaea in the second century before Christ during the persecutions by the Seleucids, in the age of Bar Kochba's uprising against the Romans, and during the mid-seventeenth-century movement of Shabbethai Zevi, which gripped Jewish communities throughout the world; but in some form, trust in a messianic age at an unknown future time is one of the constants of postexilic Judaic religion.

Some Talmudic schools issued stringent admonitions against those who presumed to compute the precise time of the coming of the Messiah, condemning them as propagators of disbelief. In the tractate *Sanhedrin* Rabbi Samuel ben Naḥmani is reported to have said in the name of Rabbi Jonathan: "Blasted be the bones of those who calculate the end. For they would say, since the predetermined time has arrived, and yet he has not come, he will never come."[8] But such imprecations did not prevent other rabbis from making rough estimates of the three periods into which human existence on earth was destined to be apportioned: "The world is to exist six thousand years. In the first two thousand there was desolation; two thousand years the Torah flourished; and the next two thousand years is the Messianic era; but through our many iniquities all these years have been lost."[9] Judah the Protector, in a flight of fancy, reckoned the duration of the messianic age at 365,000 years. Rabbi Joḥanan held that the son of David "will come only in a generation that is either altogether righteous or altogether wicked."[10]

As for the nature of the other world, Talmudic opinion is equally inconclusive. Disputations about the resurrection of the dead, intimately related to paradisaical conceptions of the World to Come, rocked Judaic sects in the last centuries before the Christian era, the Sadducees and the Samaritans denying the validity of any such doctrine. Corrupted texts led to the perpetuation of many frivolous problems related to the resurrection, like the saucy question

"Queen Cleopatra" is reputed to have posed for Rabbi Meir as to whether the dead arise naked or in their garments.[11] The birth of Christianity made the whole problem of the coming of the Messiah and an otherworldly paradise an extraordinarily sensitive one in Judaic thought, as the rabbis found it imperative to demonstrate that the resurrection of the dead was first foretold in the Torah and was not in any way related to Christian revelations. The proper manner of distinguishing a true from a false Messiah became critical for traditional Judaism, and a vast body of law grew up to make the identification at the appropriate moment.

There are many examples of loose Talmudic usage of the terms World to Come and Days of the Messiah, both of which were occasionally embraced by an even vaguer one, the Future to Come (le-atid lavo). In some texts the World to Come quite clearly refers to the plenitude of the paradise-like Days of the Messiah on earth, not to an otherworldly state. A baraitha (an opinion reported without the name of its authority) in tractate Baba Bathra tells of the diversified crops that will then be allotted to every man: "[In] this world [should] a man possess a cornfield he does not possess an orchard; [should he possess] an orchard he does not possess a cornfield, [but] in the world to come there will be no single individual who will not possess [land] in mountain, lowland, and valley."[12] Patently this is not the other world. Similar promises dating from the period of the Tannaim in tractate Kethuboth remind one of the winy paradise of Attic comedy: "In this world there is the trouble of harvesting and treading [of the grapes], but in the world to come a man will bring one grape on a wagon or a ship, put it in a corner of his house and use its contents as [if it had been] a large wine cask . . . There will be no grape that will not contain thirty kegs of wine."[13] In the compilation known as the Pesikta Rabbati, Rabbi Judah makes a valiant attempt to distinguish among the three stages of time by remarking upon the growing complexity of the harp that will be used in each one—there were seven strings in the harp of the Temple, there would be eight in the Days of the Messiah, and ten in the World to Come.[14] Obviously quantity is to be transmuted into quality. In other Talmudic passages the Days of the Messiah recall in a measure the ease of Hesiod's golden age when the earth yielded fruit spontaneously. "There will be a time when wheat will rise as high as a palm-tree and will grow on the top of the mountains . . . the Holy One, blessed be He, will bring a wind from his treasure houses which He will cause to blow upon it. This will loosen its fine flour and a man will walk out into the field and take a mere handful and, out of it, will [have sufficient provision for] his own and his household's maintenance."[15]

From the period of the Talmud on, there was always a conservative body of opinion that strove to minimize the distinction between this world and the messianic age. Samuel, in Babylon of the third century A.D., maintained: "This world differs from the Messianic era only in respect of the servitude of the Diaspora."[16] Under the Sassanian dynasty there was a concerted attempt to bank the fires of messianism. For many, even the World to Come after the resurrection would mean a continuation of the benign activities of this world. Often there is a deliberate decision to stand silent on the otherworldly paradise. Rabbi Ḥiyya ben Abba said in Rabbi Joḥanan's name: "All the prophets prophesied [all the good things] only in respect of the Messianic era; but as for the world to come, 'the eye hath not seen, O Lord, beside thee, what he hath prepared for *him that waiteth for him.'*"[17] Even the patriarchs Abraham, Isaac, and Jacob, though as a rule well informed on the future of things, were, according to some rabbis, kept in the dark about the next world. And that nineteenth-century grandson of two rabbis, Karl Marx, remained in the same laconic tradition when it came to being circumstantial about his world to come.

Compared with the Talmud, whose reserve about the World to Come may be a reaction against the profuseness of Christian prophecy, unincorporated Midrashim ascribed to individual rabbis, which represent a more popular layer of thought and are often of a later date, are rich in pictorial detail. As in the Hellenic world there are class preferences in the representation of heaven. The otherworldly paradises of the common man's imagination allow for rather grand oral pleasures—the eating of Leviathan, for example, which God created with this ulterior purpose in mind. In the popular Midrashic paradise there will be much feasting, drinking, joyousness, and each fruit will have a savor different from the next; the problem of sameness in heaven is resolved by providing 15,000 tastes and as many perfumes. David will sing and say prayers, the angels will dance before the faithful. In the *Seder Gan Eden,* a Midrash in which Mohammedan influences may be at play, "sixty angels stand on the head of each and every just man and urge him to eat honey with joy because he occupied himself with the Torah and to drink wine preserved in the grape from the six days of creation."[18] There are grand canopies to cover the heads of the elect and magnificent buildings for their habitation. Thomas Aquinas was later troubled about the age of a man at the time of resurrection. In the Midrash there are four transformations a day—childhood, youth, adulthood, and old age—as the whole of the epigenetic cycle, with joys appropriate to each state, is recapitulated. All men in heaven are as beautiful as Joseph and Rabbi Joḥanan were said to have been.

Of the few virtuous men who while yet in this world were vouchsafed a visit to paradise—such as Simon ben Yoḥai and Joshua ben Levi—all brought back the report of a play of blinding light from gems and precious metals. The tradition penetrated deep into Ethiopia, where the pious hermit Gorgorios under the guidance of the archangel Michael was shown the heavenly temple, a vision still preserved by the Jewish Falasha in the twentieth century: "There was in it a white sea pearl which shone brightly. Its light was brighter than the light of the sky. It was made of a shiny pearl and of pure gold, and the crown on its top was made of a green pearl like an emerald, adorned with three white pieces of silver that shone with so brilliant a light that no eye could look at it."[19] In paradise, as in the beginning, there shall be light.

In addition to oral, visual, auditory, and olfactory satisfactions—touch is excluded—the inhabitants of Judaic paradise are engaged in a major pursuit not featured in other heavens, the constant study of the Torah. This holds for both the Days of the Messiah and the *Olam Haba* in the Talmud, the Midrash, and the medieval Hebrew philosophical tradition. In the two future worlds, absolute freedom from material necessity permits a greater concentration on the Torah, in marked contrast with the relentless harassment by satanic forces and Gentile persecution to which Israel is subject in this world. In a number of popular Midrashic paradises God himself is director of studies; He finally unravels mysteries and explains the reasons for commandments whose meaning is now obscure, such as the dietary laws. In the various heavenly mansions each subdirector of studies is especially suited to guide the particular inmates. According to the *Midrash Konen* (Of the Correct Order), which has the most complete account, the Garden of Eden of the World to Come is divided into various classes of the just, and each occupies a separate structure.[20] Gathered in groups of families and tribes, they allocate their time between learning and praising God. The divine effulgence is enjoyed by each according to his deeds and his devotion to the study of the Torah in this world, a hierarchy of merit that has its parallel in the paradises of Augustine and Dante.

Finally, there can be discerned in the Talmud and the Midrash the beginnings of a mystical tradition on paradise that is different from both the sober and reticent rabbinic one and the earthy sensate one of the people. Its esoteric speculations and secret doctrines culminate in the Kabbala; but that contemplative paradise of which certain just men have a glimmer in this world partakes of the mystery of all Gnostic doctrine and can only be communicated to adepts. The Kabbalist conception of alternative world orders far superior to the one in which we languish did not reach its full-blown development until the thirteenth century.

Symbolic Interpretations

In the first century of the Christian era the Garden of Eden was subject to a form of interpretation that came to be sanctioned by both Judaism and Christianity. In Hellenic culture it had long been accepted that myth had a *hypnoia,* an underthought, and that the literal sense was not the most profound one. Similarly, the oral law in Judaism was based upon the conviction that the commonsensical reading of the Scriptures yielded only one of a number of possible meanings. There were set rules for uncovering ancillary ideas and the secret, as contrasted with the overt, significance of each word and letter in the Bible.

Philo Judaeus of Alexandria, where at least half a million Jews lived in the first century, adopted the methodological tools of the rabbis in his commentary on Genesis, but he wrote in Greek and the spirit that animated him was often as Platonic as it was Hebraic. The precise relationship between some Midrashic interpretations of Scripture and the reading that Philo first designated as "allegorical" and passed on to the Church Fathers is much in dispute. When rabbis said that the four rivers of the Garden of Eden represented the four world kingdoms which were to be, did they use an allegorical method in Philo's restricted philosophical sense? Whichever way one resolves this learned debate with its delicious evasive compromises—such as calling Midrashic readings "foresteps of allegory"—Philo's pivotal position in the history of allegorizing in Judeo-Christian thought has been firmly established.

While Philo did not depart from the Jewish tradition that accepted the biblical narrative as true in a literal sense, he left no doubt about his preference for an interpretation of the Garden of Eden in the spirit of Platonic philosophy: The fruits of the garden were the virtues of the soul and the working of the garden the observance of the divine commandments. Many Church Fathers, though with different purpose, followed in his path: Origen, Irenaeus, and Cyprian made Eden an allegorical prefiguration of the church. "Of Paradise," Philo wrote in *Questions and Answers on Genesis,* "so far as the literal meaning is concerned, there is no need to give an explicit interpretation. For it is a dense

place full of all kinds of trees."[21] Since it was on earth it ought to be somewhere, but Philo was unconvinced by the location generally assigned to the
Garden of Eden in the Armenian mountains. "In that place there is no Paradise, nor are there two sources of the river. Unless perhaps Paradise is in some
distant place far from our inhabited world, and has a river flowing under the
earth."[22] Clearly he was more comfortable with the Garden as an allegory for
wisdom or knowledge of the divine and the human and of their causes. "God
sows and plants earthly excellence for the race of mortals as a copy and a reproduction of the heavenly . . . By the rivers his purpose is to indicate the particular virtues. These are four in number, prudence, self-mastery, courage, justice. The largest river of which the four are effluxes is generic virtue which we
have called goodness."[23]

Once the Garden of Eden was opened to symbolic interpretation, the
method could induce the most untoward associations. To see the Garden as a
typology for the future paradise in heaven was an easily acceptable extension
of the meaning of Genesis; but soon Gnostics of the first century, flirting with
Judaic and Christian tradition, resorted to extravagant fantasy. Simon Magus,
the most notorious of the Gnostic heretics who perverted the doctrine of
Christ and "foolishly and knavishly paraphrased the law of Moses," claimed
that the Garden of Eden was not a real place but an allegory for the womb.
Saint Hippolytus (A.D. 170–236), author of *The Refutation of all Heresies,* the
hostile source for Simon Magus' opinions, left an argument so congested with
analogies between Genesis and the physiological state of a fetus in utero that it
is often impossible to ascertain where the views of the heretic end and those of
the bishop begin. While we despair of an accurate translation of his tract, it is of
more than passing interest that a first-century Gnostic established a connection
between the Garden of Eden and a womb. "Moses, says Simon, has given alle-
gorically to the womb the name Paradise, if we ought to rely on his statement.
If God forms man in his mother's womb—that is, in Paradise—as I have said,
then let the womb be Paradise and the after-birth Eden, 'a river flowing forth
from Eden, for the purpose of irrigating Paradise.' This river is the navel. This,
he says, is divided into four branches; for on either side of the navel are placed
two arteries, which serve as conduits for breath, and two veins, which serve as
channels for blood."[24] Simon Magus' insight will be applauded by disciples of
the Jungian school of psychoanalysis. To Carl Jung paradise was the positive
aspect of the archetypal mother, and he related it to the Kingdom of God and
the Heavenly Jerusalem, symbols of a longing for redemption.[25] Understandably, Jung has more to say about paradise and the millennium than Freud, who
on clinical grounds was reluctant to stress universal symbols in the dreams of
his patients. One looks in vain for paradise in Freud's collected works.

Symbolic interpretations of the Garden of Eden have been many and varied.
Ancient Hermetic writings saw it as the head rather than the womb. Church
Fathers said that it meant *serenitas mentis;* the *Zohar* that it connoted woman.
Protestant commentators from the sixteenth through the eighteenth centuries
were especially skillful in evading the literal meaning of the words of Genesis
and discovering in them a hidden, abstract philosophical significance consonant with their own moral principles. By the seventeenth century, it was not
uncommon to identify the historical origin of man's sense of guilt with
Adam's discovery of his sexual nature in Eden, and, on the basis of superficial

phonetic resemblances, the garden where Adonis and Venus cavorted was equated with the Garden of Eden. Adriaan Beverland in his *Peccatum originale* (1679) read every word in Genesis as a sexual "hieroglyph." The apple was *amoris symbolum; donare* was equivalent to *coire;* and *ramus, flos,* and *arbor* to *membrum virile.*[26] Some present-day scholars have continued this tradition, seeing in the etymology of Eve's name and in the story of the Fall symbolic renderings of the birth of sexual awareness. Most attempts at symbolic interpretation—and their authors included men of the stature of Immanuel Kant, whose *Conjectures on the Beginnings of Human History* (published in the *Berlinische Monatsschrift* of January 1786) transformed the narrative of Genesis into a hypothetical account of the birth of reason and free will—have had brief lives and leave one with the feeling of *suum cuique.* One major body of speculation on Genesis, however, the Kabbala of the thirteenth century, made a deep and lasting impress on Western thought, both Judaic and Christian.

Jewish Apocalyptic

By the beginning of the Christian era the Greek and the Judaic clusters of ideas on paradise were generally accessible in writing or through oral tradition to literate persons of the eastern Mediterranean, and elements from improbable sources were constantly cropping up in alien contexts. There are parallel visions in Jewish and Christian apocalyptic, as there are in patristic writings and Talmudic accounts of the messianic age and paradise. By now it is well established that personal relationships existed between Jewish and Christian seminarians in the same cities of Syria during the early Christian centuries, and the adaptation of Talmudic and Philonic exegesis on the Garden of Eden and paradise in the works of Church Fathers can be amply documented.

That strange corpus categorized during the last hundred years as "Jewish apocalyptic" was composed from about the second century B.C. to A.D. 150 by visionaries who in their writings assumed the identities of personages from an earlier epoch to lend credibility to their prophecies. It is a body of conceptions of an earthly paradise that was to accompany the messianic age, not always distinguishable from an otherworldly paradise. In the seventeenth century Uriel da Costa, a tragic rebel who was expelled from the Amsterdam synagogue, was the first to point out that the one complete canonical work of Jewish apocalyptic, the Book of Daniel, had not been written during the reign of Nebuchadnezzar, King of Babylon, as the text itself pretends, but had been produced later under the Seleucid hegemony by the Pharisees to buttress their belief in a Messiah and in the resurrection of the dead. Apocalyptic passages in other books of the Old Testament, as well as those not included in the canon, like the Book of the Secrets of Enoch, the Book of Jubilees, Sibylline Oracles, Testament of the Twelve Patriarchs, II Baruch, and IV Ezra, have been the subject of passionate scholarly inquiry for more than a century since Friedrich Lücke pioneered *Apokalyptikforschung* in the early 1830s. The texts as they have survived—sometimes only in Slavonic, Syriac, or Greek translation—are now thought to be composites of manuscripts from different periods and their identification and dating is a major enterprise. The discovery of the Dead Sea scrolls in 1947 has excited renewed interest in the subject, vastly enriched the literature of Hebrew apocalyptic, and lent another dimension to our understanding of the spiritual world into which Christianity was born. In a new interpretation of apocalypticism, origins have been pushed back to the sixth century before Christ, and the mythic material of Jewish apocalyptic has been related to a recrudescence of "old Canaanite" mythic lore—without, to be sure, eliminating from its later development Persian, Mesopotamian, and Greek borrowings.

We cannot dispel the mysteries that still enshroud the relations between Jewish and Christian apocalyptic or judge between the "oriental" and Canaanite origins of the grotesque animal symbols of the apocalypses. Whether the predictions of the visionaries represent a sharp break with ancient Jewish belief or are an outgrowth of Old Testament prophecy, and whether or not the apocalypses were normative during the early Christian era when Talmudic Judaism was taking form, are questions that have not been resolved. We stand in that period at a parting of the ways in the history of paradise. One branch moves in the direction of a legalistic, matter-of-fact, and philosophic statement that will finally rigidify into dogma in the synagogue and the church; the other will lead a more turbulent existence as it wanders through dark and mysterious caverns. Apocalyptic and mystical paradises with their marvelous predictions of heaven on earth and their poetic raptures about life in the other world were always suspect to the authorities, but they were never uprooted.

The bare elements of Jewish apocalyptic are clear enough. The paradisaical reign of a messianic king is foretold after the destruction of the enemies of Israel and probably of all evil in great and dreadful clashes. Vials of wrath are poured upon the unrighteous. In manuscripts from Qumran the final contest has a mildly Zoroastrian cast: "When the children of Perversity are shut up then Wickedness shall retire before Righteousness as darkness retires before the light."[27] The imagery of conflict in other works of Jewish apocalyptic, as in the most terrifying apocalypse of all literature, the Revelation of Saint John, is crowded with monsters, fornicators, prostitutes, Whores of Babylon, crawling things of uncleanness: The innocence of the Garden of Eden has been polluted for the visionaries, and vengeance is theirs. Howls of rage precede the rebirth of the kingdom of virtue. The evocation of an imminent messianic era is far more vivid and dramatic, more tinged with the miraculous, more sibylline and cryptic, than the rather grave, sparse utterances of the Talmud. In the tractate *Sanhedrin,* 'Ulla, dismayed at the prospect of slaughter and devastation that would herald the appearance of the Messiah, cries out: "Let him come, but let me not see him."[28] Apocalyptic shows no such abhorrence of destructive fantasies; it revels in them.

The messianic age that follows the holocaust is an amalgam of paradisaical fantasies reminiscent of both the golden age nostalgia in Hesiod and Ovid and the "messianic" prophecies of the Old Testament. Peace will prevail, an earthly Sabbath that prefigures the eternal Sabbath of the World to Come. The enemies of Israel having been driven from the holy places, there will be friendship among the kings of the earth. For men there will be inner serenity and freedom from care, no unwilling engagement with practical things, and no forced labor. "The reapers shall not grow weary. Nor those that build be toilworn. For the works shall of themselves speedily advance."[29] Sin, corruption, punishment, and tribulation will be banished as demons are either eliminated or subjugated. (Apocalyptic literature develops a complicated demonology and an equally intricate angelology.) There will be no more blind, poor, or hungry, no sadness or illness—birth itself will be painless—no mourning and no sighing, no tempests. In the latter half of the first century, II Baruch told of what would come to pass in the end of the days: "And disease shall withdraw, And anxiety and anguish and lamentation pass from amongst men, and gladness proceed through the whole earth . . . And judgments, and revilings, and contentions, and revenges, And blood, and passions, and envy, and hatred, And whatsoever are like these shall go into condemnation when they are removed."[30] These euphoric prophecies from the tongues of men in extreme anguish have been models for the apocalypse ever since.

In apocalyptic literature there is no one Messiah type, but a spectrum from the savior of the Jews to the miracle-worker to the son of God. In Jewish apocalyptic he is a king of the House of David, or a priest, or a priest-king, or, in the Qumran texts, the Rightful Teacher. Fission takes place and he can become more than one: There are Messiahs ben Joseph, ben Ephraim, ben Menashe, Messiahs called Moses and Aaron. The Hebrew Book of Enoch has two messianic ages in succession, each preceded by a cataclysmic struggle. In the middle of the second century A.D., Phoenicia and Palestine were still literally swarming with Messiahs each proclaiming the advent of the new age in his own person, often with words of fire and brimstone. Origen in his *Contra Celsum* has quoted Celsus' pastiche of a messianic sermon, a distillation of apocalyptic modes: "I am God; I am the son of God; or, I am the divine spirit; I have come because the world is perishing, and you shall see me returning again with heavenly power. Blessed is he who now does me homage. On all the rest I will send down eternal fire, both on cities and on countries. And those who know not the punishments which await them shall repent and grieve in vain; while those who are faithful to me I will preserve eternally."[31] The juxtaposition of aggression against enemies and the outpouring of love for true followers and believers, with promises of ineffable joy in victory, is a pattern of rhetoric for which Jewish apocalyptic provided a prototype much used through the centuries, often against the Jews themselves.

Early Christian Millenarianism

The Danielic prophecy of what would succeed the destruction of the Fourth Monarchy, the Apocalypse of John (probably written during the persecutions of Nero and Domitian), and a variety of Sibylline Oracles of Judaic origin all fed the Christian millenarian spirit of the early centuries after Christ. In a strict sense, millenarianism, or chiliasm, was originally limited to a prophetic conviction, derived from a commentary on the fourth verse of the twentieth chapter of the Apocalypse of John, to the effect that Christ would reign for a thousand years on earth. The pivotal events of the transition to the days of the millennium were depicted in well-worn images of catastrophe: During a time of troubles empires crumble, there are titanic struggles of opposing armies, vast areas of the world are devastated, nature is upheaved, rivers flow with blood. On the morrow, good triumphs over evil, God over Satan, Christ over Antichrist. As existential experience the millennium of early Christianity is the counterpart of the Days of the Messiah in much of Jewish apocalyptic. The bout of violence reaches a grand climax, and then and only then is there peace —primitive priapic scenes are the inescapable analogy.

However similar the spectacles of devastation, the angelology and demonology, the animal symbolism, and the homilies on the reign of justice on earth, the belief in Jesus separates Christian from Jewish apocalyptic. For Christians the Messiah has already come and expectations concentrate on a second coming; for Jews the messianic age, whatever its attributes, is a part of the future. The Qumran texts enormously improve our knowledge of the perfect order of the Essene communities in which these ideas grew and they enrich our comprehension of the background of Christianity, illuminating the flow of religious ideas throughout the Near East; but in the Qumran literature the Messiah has not yet become a heavenly savior. After the birth of Christ the barrier between those who believed that the Messiah had appeared and those who still awaited him was insurmountable. The paradisaical fantasies of Judaism and Christianity drifted apart but, as we shall see, not so radically as might be expected; both matured into orthodoxies and acquired heterodoxies.

Sabbatical millenarianism in the early Christian church developed a specific form of eschatology. A literal exegesis of the Psalmist's wonderment that a thousand years are as one day in the eyes of the Lord facilitated the reading of Genesis as at once an account of creation as it had actually happened and a prefiguration of the seven-thousand-year history of the world. The early Church Fathers Papias, Irenaeus, Justin, Tertullian, and Lactantius were all millenarians of this sort. Irenaeus, a second-century bishop of Lyons, was one of the first to divide world history into seven millennia, the last of which would be the reign of Christ on earth. Church Fathers of the second century committed to the doctrine of the millennium were adroit in adapting images and rhetorical devices from the Talmud, Jewish apocalyptic, and popular fantasies. In his diatribe *Against the Heresies* Irenaeus prophesied in language that recalls the speaking victuals of Hades in Attic comedy: "The days will come in which vines shall grow, each having ten thousand branches and in each branch ten thousand twigs, and in each twig ten thousand shoots, and in each one of the shoots ten thousand clusters, and on every one of the clusters ten thousand grapes, and every grape when pressed will give five and twenty metretes of wine. And when any one of the saints shall lay hold of a cluster, another shall cry out 'I am a better cluster, take me; bless the Lord through me.' In like manner [the Lord declared] that a grain of wheat would produce ten thousand ears, and that every ear should have ten thousand grains, and every grain would yield ten pounds of clear, pure, fine flour."[32] In the *Divine Institutes* Lactantius, after foreseeing that the enemies of Christ would be condemned to perpetual slavery, rhapsodized over the millennium in turns of phrase borrowed from the pagan poets: "The earth will open its fruitfulness, and bring forth most abundant fruit of its own accord; the rocky mountains shall drip with honey; streams of wine shall run down, and rivers flow with milk."[33]

The particular form of the correspondence between the history of the world and the seven days of Creation depended upon whether a millennium was conceived literally as a thousand calendar years or was a conventional term signifying an indefinite period of time, and upon whether the reign of Christ was interpreted materially or symbolically. Sabbatical millenarianism raised ominous questions. Was the seventh millennium to be an earthly kingdom like the poets' golden age under Saturn, as Lactantius held, or did the Last Judgment end the world at the close of the sixth? Justin's seventh millennium was still of this world, though it was characterized by a complete cessation of sexual activity. Would there be a new creation on the eighth day?

Saint Augustine put the quietus on millenarianism as an official church doctrine, and the growth of ecclesiastical power in the Roman Empire coincided with the decline of this belief. For Augustine the dominion of Christ, the last of the epochs, had already begun; and the eternal Sabbath that was to follow the end of the sixth period was not of this earth. Christian millenarianism, however, was never extirpated and its recrudescence as heresy was continual, if sporadic, among Manichaeans, Messalians, Paulicians, Bogomilians, Patarians, and Albigensians, until its spectacular outburst in the age of the Reformation.

Western Monasticism and Utopia

That the monastic orders should be considered even peripherally in a study of utopias in the West may appear paradoxical: *Monos* is Greek for "alone," which seems to contradict the basic principle of a social utopia. But the memory of the Western monastic order cannot be considered irrelevant to the organized utopia of the city of man in a Christian society. At least two of the most noted early utopia-makers, Thomas More and Tommaso Campanella, were deeply involved with the ideal of the monastic life. More longed for it but considered himself incapable of fulfilling its vows; Campanella was made a novice of the Dominican order in his early youth and spent the rest of his life in rebellion against the requirements of obedience. But when toward the end he had to defend the feasibility of certain utopian institutions in his *City of the Sun,* he drew upon the experience of monastic life to bolster his apology. Some of the same impulses toward original monasticism in the West—the desire to separate oneself from the world as it was and to build an order of perfection in this life—underlay the search of the utopian as they had that of the monk. Both monasticism and one type of utopianism are man-created orders, attempts to escape the unbearable disorder of the world by building in the imagination de novo—in some faraway place or future time.

Communal societies, in particular the Essenes, had been known in Judaea and were described by Philo in the first century A.D. Though Saint Anthony is called the first Christian anchorite, the father of monks of the communal life was Pachomius (286–346), whose rule has come down to us in the Latin form transmitted by Saint Jerome; this expression of Egyptian Christianity, which in many ways was a full-fledged monastic order with an abbot and work rules, did not long survive its founder. The introduction of communal monasticism into the West was relatively slow; though the originality of the Rule of Saint Benedict of Nursia, written in 535–545, has rightly been questioned, his became the basic frame for the ideal monastic order for at least six hundred years.

The constitution of the monastery was simplicity itself. A monarchical abbot elected for life by his monks ruled with the advice of the brethren. The general council of all participated in grave decisions, and a smaller council of elders was consulted in minor matters. The monastery, though in the world, seemed totally cut off from it, and lived in a state of autarchy. It was self-sufficient, isolated by sea or forest or rivers or mountains, and containing within itself all that was necessary for a Christian life. There was provision for the intervention of the bishop in case an abbot should egregiously violate the letter and spirit of the rule, but in general this community of men committed for their lifetime was conceived of as autonomous and perfect in its order, like a Morean utopia. Admittedly, in utopia the practice of the religious life is not the core of existence, and work for sustenance is not the primary mission of the monastery; but governments in both have to deal with all human activities and all men are regulated. Having taken vows or made commitments, monks and utopians are ideally free because of their inner acceptance of the rules.

Modern scholarship has rejected the tradition of the unbroken continuity of the Benedictine rule from Monte Cassino to the great abbeys of the eleventh century, but despite institutional fractures the rule gradually spread throughout the West and became the dominant model, though inevitable variations were introduced through time in different localities. With the foundation of the Abbey of Inden (815) near Aachen by Benedict of Aniane, a uniform Benedictine code was established for all monasteries in the Carolingian Empire by Louis the Pious and probably inspired the famous *Klosterplan* for St. Gall. With the foundation of the Cluniac monasteries, a modified Benedictine rule did in fact become a system with more than a thousand houses spread throughout Europe. The abbot of Cluny governed all the monasteries, but his relations with local heads of monasteries followed a feudal pattern. The problem of the interrelations of individual utopian entities to one another and to a central authority will, as with the monasteries, mirror changing contemporary forms of organization. In More each of the cities on the island of Utopia will be directly under the King; by the time Fourier appears with his phalanxes, a more complex system is evolved with national capitals (Nevers for France) and an international center in Constantinople—to spite Paris. The Cluniac model of centralized administration lived on in Campanella's federation of cities of the sun under a reformed papacy. Utopian revolutionary movements well into the twentieth century wrestled with the problem of achieving unity without stifling diversity. Cells, national parties, the International were the structures into which communist parties fell in the twentieth century in much the same way as the great international monastic orders, like the eleventh-century Cluniacs and sixteenth-century Jesuits, blundered into their different patterns of organization.

The monastery as a paradigm for Christian living in this world in a state of community endured in utopian foundations. The House of Salomon in Bacon's *New Atlantis,* the product of one of the least saintly of utopia-makers, is in effect a monastic establishment. Drawings of Fourier's great house in the phalanstery make it resemble an abbey; and even the Saint-Simonians in their adolescent heyday repaired to Montmartre, toyed with celibacy, and for a time lived a monastic life in which former bourgeois donned workers' clothes and tilled the soil—to the amazement of Parisians who came to witness the spectacle on holidays. The breakdown of the simple system of equality outlined in the Benedictine rule in the great abbeys of later centuries and the introduction of separate classes of manual drudges (oblates, bearded monks, *conversi*) to support the intellectual labors of the monastic elect have not been unknown in communist practice. The Cistercians were innovators when they developed the concept of a federated union of equal, independent houses. They also abolished infant oblation and formally integrated a lay brotherhood into the order. The fellow travelers of the revolutionary communist cells of the 1930s were not unlike the *fratres sed non monachi* introduced by the Cistercians. The ideal forms of Western monastic life are almost as varied as the utopian, and it is peculiarly fitting that in the sixteenth century these parallel ideals should have been joined in Rabelais's dream of an Abbey of Thélème.

Monasticism suffered the same fate as utopianism: Both became dynamic, encompassing ever-wider spaces and functions, until they embraced the whole world. Both surrendered their protected isolation on an island, in a forest, on a high place. Neither, of course, was at any time hermetically sealed. From the very beginning, the Benedictine rule was relaxed to give charity to those who were in the vicinity of the monastery; Thomas More's Utopians received the visitors who touched their island with monastic hospitality. The Utopians assembled a few client states that acted as a buffer against the world, and Utopian emissaries were secretly despatched to spy upon other peoples. In the early monasteries and the early utopias there is a pervasive feeling that the outside world presents a danger of contamination. For the sake of continuity, the monastery must constantly draw children, novices, even lay converts from the outside. Utopia lives on its own progeny. Both nevertheless represent the displacement of the organic family by another fundamental unit of existence.

In the monastery and in the closed utopia there is also recognition of an internal threat, the vice of *luxuria*. Hence they are committed to simplicity and restricted to the necessary. The monastery's way of abstracting itself from the world was to accept a regular order of liturgical prayer, meditation or reading, and the exercise of manual skill for six hours a day or more. This was also the workday of More's Utopians. A thousand years before Saint Thomas More, Saint Benedict had freed labor from Aristotle's denigration and the biblical curse. Saint Benedict's monastic inmates worked in the garden, and at Monte Cassino the *coloni* performed the more arduous labors in the field. Slaves were not unknown in More's Utopia. The rule of equality in either ideal should not be interpreted with the absolutism of a Babeuf.

The Benedictine rule of obedience to an abbot is the unique characteristic of monastic life. The abbot is the father present in person, a surrogate for a higher power. Well through the end of the eighteenth century the monarchical or patriarchal form of governance will be preferred in utopia. But what stands out in both the monastic rule and the later utopia is their changeless character. Ideally neither the monastery nor the Morean utopia has a history once it has been founded. Innovations are prohibited. Saint Bernard even discouraged the introduction of a better mill. Time regulates the day and events of the year, but historical time that brings novelties does not exist.

There is in the Benedictine code great reliance upon external orders and rules. Doubtless needs of the common life are provided for by the meditations of Christian love, but the monastery, like the early utopias, does not spurn legal regulations to insure tranquillity. The monastery is not a house of perfection and the rule supplies guidance when the inmates fail. Similarly the early utopia has to incorporate punishments for violation of the order of the optimum republic.

The analogy, to be sure, is limited. The monastery tends to encourage avoidance of converse when it does not prohibit speech altogether. The nourishment of early Christian writings and the advice of elders are considered sufficient for moral guidance, and practical concerns are covered by the rule. Prayer holds the first place among the duties of a Benedictine; it does not occupy the same role in the life of the Utopian, who takes time out from his daily tasks for religious contemplation. The early Benedictine rule encouraged *lectio,* but it was *lectio divina.* The delight of More's Utopians in pagan literature approximates earlier monastic copying of manuscripts and the preservation of culture; in the beginning, a monastery recognized only the Scriptures and Church Fathers.

For all the differences between monasticism and early utopianism, the European monastery was the first institution to wrestle with the quintessential Christian utopian problem, the creation of a society that was both a simulacrum on earth of a divine order and a preparation for the beatitude of a future time.

The Paradise of Medieval Orthodoxy

Unlike many rabbis of the Talmud, the Church Fathers unhesitatingly poured forth detailed expositions of how men would feel in the otherworldly paradise. While Talmudic depictions, such as they are, tend to be preoccupied with admission requirements, external arrangements, and the doings of the blessed, the Church Fathers dwell on the psychic state of the inner man. Saint Augustine, perhaps the greatest psychologist of religious life, has presented a subtle projection of his own deep needs and desires in a portrayal of paradise in the final chapter of the *City of God.* There is no equivalent in Judaism until the *Zohar.*

The felicity of the otherworldly paradise will be total, Augustine tells us; no conceivable good will be lacking. Conversely, it will not be tainted by any evil. Since heaven is freedom from labor, there will be nothing to prevent man from consecrating all his efforts to the praise of God. "Nam quid aliud agatur?"[34] God has promised Himself as the reward, and loving Him is an activity that can go on without end, without alloy, without weariness. The whole human being will now be free to dwell on God since those bodily organs that on earth are devoted to the necessities of life will no longer be absorbed with such functions. Men do not now understand the true nature and purposes of many parts of the body, surely not the meaning of their rhythms and proportions and harmonies. These will first be discovered to them in paradise and will then become available for laudation. If Augustine has moments of doubt about his capacity to define the power of movement that bodies will possess in heaven, he knows that their appearance both at rest and in motion will be beautiful. But these delights of the physical body are as nothing compared to the harmony that will prevail between body and spirit. Everything will be fitting. Neither body nor spirit will do contradictory things and the conflict raging in the breast of every man in this world will subside. In heavenly paradise there are no inner spiritual wars, and no one will suffer opposition either from himself or from others. Had Augustine but foretold the end of alienation, the portrait of psychic wholeness would have stood complete for all time. Or perhaps only in Augustine's heaven can alienation from God the Father, the original terror of the religious man and the source of worldly feelings of alienation, be wiped away with transports of mutual love.

There will still be free will, though not freedom to sin; an intellectual remembrance of the bygone ills of the soul, without a sensible experience of their pain, even as a doctor knows the diseases of his patients. Paradise means the reign of eternal peace, the great Sabbath without evening. "There we shall rest and we shall see; we shall see and we shall love; we shall love and we shall praise. Behold what shall be in the end without end! For what is our end but to arrive at that Kingdom which has no end?"[35]

Commentators have signaled the communal nature of being in Augustine's heavenly state, *socialis,* whereas this world is *privatus.* His homilies use words like *familia, societas, consortium,* and *patria communis* to convey the prevailing spirit.[36] The *Enarrationes in Psalmos* keeps dilating upon the community of heavenly joys: "Commune spectaculum habebimus Deum; communem possessionem habebimus Deum; communem pacem habebimus Deum."[37] The painful privatization of man that a late Roman understood so well comes to an end as creatures are joined in everlasting harmony.

Despite the union of all men in the love of God, Augustine's heaven will not be an egalitarian society: A hierarchy of merit obtains, though Augustine cannot foresee precisely how the different degrees of honor and glory will be awarded. Whatever the system of distribution, it will have the unique quality, inconceivable in this world, of arousing no envy. And why should it? Do angels envy archangels? The finger does not seek to be the eye when both members are consonant parts of the body. The gift of contentment, to desire nothing other than one has, is the supreme virtue of the heavenly condition.

There are of course less attractive aspects to paradise in some of the earlier Church Fathers, when the triumph of Christianity was still far from assured and its enticements had to compete with the cruel and debased pleasures of the Roman arena. Abrasive Tertullian had reserved the blessedness of direct reception into paradise immediately after death for martyrs only: "The sole key to unlock Paradise is your own life's blood."[38] Ordinary Christians would have to remain in safekeeping in a Hades until the day of the Lord. Other passages in Tertullian bear out Nietzsche's contention that much of the Christian otherworldly paradise is the invention of a slave man's *ressentiment* and a fantasy of vengeance against his masters. The *De Spectaculis* comes to a climax in a vivid apostrophe: "What a city, the New Jerusalem! How vast the spectacle that day, and how wide! What sight shall wake my wonder, why my laughter, my joy and exultation? As I see all those kings, those great kings, welcomed (we are told) in heaven, along with Jove, along with those who told of their ascent, groaning in the depths of darkness. And the magistrates who persecuted the name of Jesus liquefying in fiercer flames than they kindled in their rage against the Christians! . . . Such sights, such exultation—what praetor, consul, quaestor, priest, will ever give you of his bounty? And yet, all this, in some sort, is ours pictured through faith in the imagination of the spirit . . . I believe things of greater joy than circus theatre or amphitheatre or any stadium."[39]

From among the Schoolmen, perhaps the opinion of Saint Thomas Aquinas will suffice to show that orthodox institutional Christianity after Augustine lived for hundreds of years with a fairly constant official view of the other-worldly paradise. With the same skill that he used to refute Gentile heresies Aquinas dismissed those who held to a millenarian reign of Christ on earth. Firmly fixed in the central tradition of the church, he knew that there was to be one Last Judgment, without intermediary paradisaical ages. But what would existence be like after the universal raising of the bodies, the good and the evil, and their summons before Christ?

In the Thomist drama there is an initial movement of souls to their desig-nated areas in heaven and hell immediately upon the separation of the soul from the body. But the Last Judgment, conducted by Christ and his assessors, is an event of a different order. The evil bodies are condemned to eternal suf-fering because their souls are set forever against God, while the good souls re-join their bodies for a life everlasting—resurrected at their best age, the age of the young Christ. We are assured in the *Summa contra Gentiles* that bodies will retain all their physical characteristics male and female, as well as the organs for ingestion, even though they will be of no practical utility since neither genera-tion nor corruption will take place and there will be no purpose in copulation or eating. Bodies will be totally submissive to souls and not have refractory wills of their own, and souls will be interested only in the contemplation of God.[40] Aquinas was repelled by what he considered the sensate paradises of the Mohammedans and the Jews, with their pleasures of venery and eating. Though the resurrected are not ghosts or spirits, their joys are wholly spiritual. More than five hundred years later, a mad French genius, Auguste Comte, in painting the future of humanity translated the Thomist heaven into nine-teenth-century biological language. In the earthly paradise of his Religion of Humanity, the ape of Catholicism, he foresaw a new man nourished solely on odors (a compromise with the total spiritualization of Aquinas) and procre-ation through female parthenogenesis without the intervention of a male seed. Sexuality remained for centuries the forbidden fruit of maternal paradises, ce-lestial and earthly.

The major philosopher of medieval Judaism, Moses Maimonides, was as in-imical to any miraculous Days of the Messiah as Aquinas was to millenarian doctrines; that was to be expected from a stalwart of the Judaic establishment, Aquinas' opposite number. For Maimonides the Days of the Messiah, because of long traditional sanction, was a necessary state before the World to Come; but like some Talmudic rabbis he did the next best thing to eliminating it en-tirely when he reduced it to a natural part of this world's time, distinguished from the rest primarily by the termination of Israel's exile and subjection.[41] Maimonides interpreted the prophecy of Isaiah in a naturalistic manner as a promise of the reign of a Judaean King-Messiah, and the lying together of the lion and the lamb became an allegory for a future age when the Gentiles, li-kened to wild beasts, would stop their vexation of Israel. "Think not," he wrote in *Hilkhot Melakhim* (The Laws of Kings), "that in the Days of the Mes-siah any terrestrial custom will be nullified, or that there will be any novelty in creation; but the world will pursue an ordinary course . . . The [great] desire of the Sages and the prophets was not for the Days of the Messiah, not that they might rule over the whole world . . . or eat and drink and make merry, but that they might be accounted worthy of life in the World to Come."[42]

Other Worlds in the Kabbala

If Maimonides epitomized conservative medieval Judaism, there was that other world of the Kabbala, rich with an inheritance of Gnostic and Midrashic traditions and fertile with inventions on all aspects of creation—a world that lay open to those who risked entry into the mystical garden. The doctrines of the Kabbala were given their magnificent canonical form in the *Zohar* (The Book of Splendor), whose basic text is believed to have been written by Moses de Leon in pseudo-Aramaic sometime after 1275 and which represents an ingathering of Kabbalist traditions that had been accumulating in Germany, Provence, and Catalonia. What most Christians came to know of the Kabbala in the Renaissance and in the seventeenth century were the allegorical interpretations in the *Zohar,* and from this canon stemmed the great Jewish efflorescence of Kabbalist thought in the sixteenth century that is associated with the name of Isaac Luria of Safed. The commentary on Genesis with which the *Zohar* opens identifies Adam and Eve as the Father and Mother; the Garden as the Shekinah (Divine Radiance and Female Principle) on earth; Eden as the supernal Mother; and the man as the Central Column. "The Shekinah was to be his plantation, his spouse who was never to depart from him and was to be his proper delight. Thus God at that time planted Israel as a holy shoot, as it is written, 'the branch of my planting, the work of my hands, in which I glory.'" The medieval Kabbalist lived in the presence of paradisaical images of this character, whose full meaning was revealed only to initiates. An entire section of the *Zohar,* called the "Rav Mithivtha," is a visionary journey through future paradise and a discourse by one of the heads of the celestial academy on the destinies of the soul in the other world. The décor is traditional: glistening columns, rivers of floating pearls, fragrant reservoirs. There is more attention paid to the fortunes of just women than in Talmudic paradise, and though males and females are segregated during the day, the souls of spouses are allowed to embrace at midnight.[43]

The Kabbalistic allegorist in this world had access to a vision of the *Merkaba,* the throne-chariot of God, and could in anticipation absorb something of the odor of those secrets and mysteries of the upper world that strictly speaking belonged to the messianic age and were preserved on high for the time to come. Ritual action here below on celestial and cosmic reality forged mystery relationships that were subversive of traditional rabbinic performance. In Kabbala each ritual served a function in the eternal order; it was not an individually limited act but had cosmic consequences, and without it a void would have been created in the universe. A pious human deed effected a change leading to the final redemption of Israel and the coming of the paradisaical world.

A part of the existing text of the *Zohar* known as the "Raya Mehemna" (Faithful Shepherd) is a very late thirteenth-century interpolation written in imitation of the rest of the work; it is of inferior literary quality with none of the glorious imagery that distinguishes the original composition. While the anonymous author still honors the traditional centrality of the law, he is seriously troubled by the nettlesome problem of the role assigned to the 613 commandments in the Days of the Messiah, when human nature will have changed. Are not all prohibitions and precepts made supererogatory by a spiritual revolution in mankind? Instead of living under the rule of the tree of good and evil, man will be restored to the Edenic rule of the tree of life, and the divine will be suffused through all things. The Torah will continue to be the guide, but its commandments will assume a new and more profound meaning. There are contemporary scholars who discern here the influence of the Spiritual Franciscans who preached the eternal gospel of Joachim of Fiore. The ambivalence of the Kabbalist author, the tension between his commitment to the law of the Torah and the need to envisage a spiritual transformation in the Days of the Messiah, has a manifest parallel in the Joachimite prophecy of the third *status* and the new man of the Reign of the Holy Ghost.

In the Middle Ages Judaism and Christianity thus continued to harbor within them deviations that promised a heaven on earth to a regenerated man, a baffling creation of the religious imagination forthrightly rejected by the authorities. More astonishing, both of these doctrines so interpreted written Testaments and Torahs revered as eternal and absolute that they were transcended.

An even more heterodox Kabbalist tradition was excluded from the *Zohar* and embodied in an anonymous work, probably of Catalonian origin and with roots in the school of Gerona, that was known by the year 1280 as the *Sefer ha-Temunah* (The Book of the Image). It had its partisans and practitioners, along with the *Zohar,* and in periods of messianic possession like the mid-seventeenth century it enjoyed great prestige. A late-thirteenth-century commentary on the *Sefer ha-Temunah* has made a good deal of its esoteric symbolism comprehensible, though the present-day master interpreter of this text confesses that even to him the language is not always pellucid. The parallelism between the conceptions of the Catalonian Kabbalists and those of the followers of Joachim of Fiore, who died in 1202, is striking, though there is no convincing proof of any direct relationship or mutual influence between them; nor can it be demonstrated that Joachim was of Jewish descent, an accusation made during his lifetime. The two are coupled in this study because they represent contemporaneous complex doctrines of other worlds that were in flagrant contradiction to their respective religious establishments and yet were allowed to survive. In a way the *Sefer ha-Temunah* is the more far-out.

Traditions about a plurality of worlds that would succeed one another in the course of cosmic revolutions have ancient origins—Hindu, Magian, and Greek. The idea that divinity was not restricted to one creation but would continue to fulfill itself in a whole series of creations assumed a radical form in the *Sefer ha-Temunah,* where the doctrine of aeons, or Schemiṭṭas, broke through the confines of traditional biblical chronology with its five- to six-thousand-year timespan and posited a long succession of worlds. The Schemiṭṭas are cosmic cycles with beginnings, middles, and ends, and human existence is qualitatively different in each of them—this is no Stoic doctrine of eternal recurrence. Our world is in the second Schemiṭṭa under the sign of *Gevura* (Power) or *Din* (Law) and by all odds is the worst of all possible aeons. Both the preceding one that was dominated by *Hesed* (Benevolence) and the next one under *Rachamim* (Compassion) are far superior in nature, and so will be all future worlds until the coming of the aeon of *Sabbath.* While we now live under the force of law, we can look back to a paradisaical aeon in which there were only pure souls luminous as clear water; there were then no diaspora, no transmigration of souls as punishment, no lost souls, no serpent, no evil desire, no uncleanness.

In the past Schemitta, worship was not regulated but was a spontaneous effusion. Abraham, symbol of benevolence in our world, was a remnant of what all creatures once were like. This world is always a struggle with desires and our Torah is full of prohibitions that raise a barrier against them. The Torah of that former world had only commandments "to do," no "thou shalt nots." The coming aeon of Compassion will witness a return to wholeness in all things. Even the moon will not wane. There will be no families, only one great family, no death until the end of the Schemitta and then death with a kiss. The symbols of light and water are pervasive: Men will lead bright and translucent lives, like the angels. They will eat manna, not grain; their sabbaths will be long; absolute equality will prevail among them.

That the Torah was one and immutable was an article of Jewish faith defended with fierce tenacity against the pretensions of the Christians and the Mohammedans to new revelations. Along came the dauntless author of the *Sefer ha-Temunah* to posit a Torah with a new phase for each Schemitta, depending upon the character of its controlling force. Instead of one revelation, that of Mount Sinai, there are at least three: the first a Torah Kaduma, a heavenly Torah that was the paradigm, so to speak, which God looked into when he created the world; the second, the written Sinaitic Torah; and the third, a Torah that is amenable to constant transformation. When this fluid conception of the Torah is combined with a doctrine of Schemittas, a different view of past, present, and future emerges that is quite alien to dominant rabbinic thought as enshrined in the Code of Maimonides. The idea that a whole new letter might be added to a future Torah is only hinted at, but the revolutionary possibility that the known and revered Torah might be entirely revamped dismayed the orthodox. The only path to conciliation lay in the belief that each of the new Torahs was but a finite and partial revelation of the Torah Kaduma according to which the world had once been fashioned.

The complex numerology of the cycles and their duration until the fifty-thousand-year jubilee need not detain us, nor the intricate changes in the Hebrew alphabet of successive aeons. For our purposes, the most compelling aspect of this work is the combination of a paradisaical retrospect and a paradisaical prospect on a cosmic scale. Unlike similar formulas in Jewish apocalyptic, each aeon fulfills its course in a slow, natural way, and the awful, catastrophic crises of epochs of transition to the Days of the Messiah are conspicuously absent, as they are in Joachimite thought. Tenderness and softness fill the spiritual atmosphere, and there is a palpable unease with the rigor of the law.

The Joachimite Reign of the Holy Ghost

Toward the end of the twelfth century the Abbot Joachim, a Calabrian monk who had known the mighty at the Norman court of Sicily, a former Cistercian who had fled to the wild mountains of San Giovanni in Fiore to found a more stringent rule, was illuminated with a vision of the true meaning of cryptic passages in the Old and New Testaments, and was inspired to write of a new historical order in which the Church of Christ would be superseded by the Reign of the Holy Ghost on earth. To this day Joachim has remained under a cloud in the Catholic Church, though during his lifetime he was honored by popes and was never declared a heretic. There are rival schools of thought on virtually every aspect of his life and teachings. Some have discovered in him the hidden inspiration of the whole of Dante's *Divine Comedy,* the clue to the enigmatic Veltro; others have transformed him into a great historical villain responsible for what they call the secularized gnosis of all modern revolutionary movements.

Joachim was heir to the exegetical, topological, allegorical, and numerological traditions on paradise, the Days of the Messiah, and the millennium that had been accumulating in the West for centuries. These he fashioned into a symbolism uniquely his own. There are three states (*status*) in progression, corresponding in their essential natures to the three persons of the Trinity; each state is in turn divisible into seven periods (*aetates*), which are named after characters from sacred history. The *Concordance of the Old and the New Testament,* one of his few authenticated works, is the mystical key to the system. Every saintly father in the first dispensation has an opposite number in the second; the saints of the third state, which is just dawning, are precursors for the *Dux* of the new age, and Joachim regards himself as a John the Baptist. Life in the world is no longer a relentless Augustinian struggle between two cities only one of which can be victorious, but a stadial ascent toward goodness and absolute love. The Reign of the Son that was born of the Reign of the Father is to give way to a new perfection in the Reign of the Holy Ghost on earth.

To depict the persons of the Trinity not only as theological but also as historical realities was a hazardous innovation when it entailed an order of excellence among them, flagrantly diminishing the position of Christ and downgrading the Gospel to a prologue of an earthly state of perfection. Whether Joachim envisioned the total and absolute supersession of the clerical and sacramental church or only its spiritualization, with perhaps a shift of monasticism from a peripheral to a central position, remains moot. With doctrines of renewal and progression there is always a problem as to whether renovation can take place within the establishment or whether the order has to be completely refashioned. In all forms of messianism and millenarianism a cleavage exists between those who require a new birth, with the imagery of a return to the womb and an expulsion from it (as in the eighth-century Midrash known as the *Pirke de Rabbi Eliezar*) and those who would minimize the differences of the new and see it as a mere restoration of the old or a fulfillment of what the ancients had always intended. Joachim at no time defaulted in his personal obedience to papal authority, and he may not have been aware of the profundity of the chasm between his views and the institutions of the church.

The reign of love on this earth, love from the heart, can dispense with the law of both Testaments. Judgment Day is indefinitely postponed and its awesome sting is removed by the transitional third stage of the Holy Ghost. The great expectation for which Joachim prepares the faithful is not an apocalyptic end of the world and a transcendent resolution in heaven, but a more immediate event, the appearance within a generation of the Holy Ghost on earth. As with the Greek Orthodox tradition of a benign apocalyptic emperor whose reign precedes the Second Coming of Christ, so the third state of Joachim eases the passage to the Last Judgment, rendering the break between this world and the next far less frightful than it is in Augustinian Christianity.

Joachim's numerological symbolism is an intrinsic part of his work; everywhere he finds meaning in the numbers twelve and seven and forty-two, and they serve to give arithmetic solidity to the equation of parallel periods and generations among the three states. The crucial date of the new era was 1,260 years after Christ, proved with an exegetical virtuosity that ranges from Daniel and Revelation through the book of Judith, who waited in her widowhood three years and six months or forty-two months, which contain 1,260 days—ergo the reign of the New Testament will last 1,260 years. But though the Joachimite predictions and the secret numbers of the heterodox Kabbalist writings are comparable, there are also important differences between them: The Kabbalists dealt with cosmic processes, while Joachimism, however interpreted, remained absorbed with changes that occurred on earth alone.

Joachim's cumbersome arithmetical apparatus is less significant than the attributes with which he clothed his three states. To their radically different characters he devoted the zeal that other mystics poured into their definitions of God. The *Concordance* tells us that in the first state we were under the law, in the second we were under grace, and in the third we shall be under still richer grace. The first was knowledge, the second was the power of wisdom, the third will be the fullness of knowledge. The first was spent in the submission of slaves, the second in the obedience of sons, the third in freedom. The first in suffering, the second in action, the third in contemplation. The first in fear, the second in faith, the third in love. The first in starlight, the second in dawn, the third in broad daylight. Joachim's was a rich symbolic vocabulary that had resonances for centuries after his death. The ardent longing for a new man breaks through, the man who has seen the vision of Jacob's Ladder and the heavens thrown open, when the Holy Ghost descended on earth to teach him the fullness of knowledge and to strengthen his will. "Life should be changed because the state of the world will be changed."[44] The active life immersed in dross must be replaced by the pure contemplation of spiritual man, who will also be wise, peaceful, and lovable, a man stripped of the vice of envious emulation. "We shall not be what we have been, but we shall begin to be other."[45]

From the thirteenth century on, followers of Joachim were fired by his progressionist history to preach of the new man of the Third Kingdom and of the eternal gospel. The record of the reverberations of Joachimite prophecy in the later Middle Ages has been assembled in Marjorie Reeves's voluminous study.[46] That Joachim was a hidden force in heterodox medieval thought is proved beyond question by the inventory of his manuscripts—authentic, probable, possible, and false—that have survived in European libraries. Many a thinker on the borderline of Catholic orthodoxy discovered in him a predecessor, and either adopted his writings or ascribed his own to him, so that in time there emerged within the church an amorphous body of Joachimite thought, an uncondemned heresy or one that was formally denounced only in its most extravagant pretensions. The name of Joachim became a magnet that drew to it hopes of a most diverse character ranging from the aspirations of the two new monastic orders, the Dominican and the Franciscan, whose existence seemed to confirm his prophecy, through the Arthurian romances and the quest for the Holy Grail, to fanatical anti-ecclesiastical exponents of a new age beyond the church. The Joachimite tradition had an active, unbroken existence well into the seventeenth century, even though the content of life in the kingdom-to-be underwent a series of transformations and the savior changed with the soil in which the prophecy was acclaimed: The *Dux* was successively an angelic pope in Italy, a reborn Charlemagne in France, a Third Frederick in Germany, even a universal Spanish monarch who in an act of self-denial would hand over his power to the pope—the fixed idea of Tommaso Campanella, who during his interrogation by the Inquisition insisted that he was merely reviving the prophecies of Joachim.

In addition to the monastic rule, the constantly recreated literary images of the two paradises (at the beginning in Eden and in the next world), and Joachimism, medieval Christianity bequeathed two universalist visions that approach utopias in form and content. These two works of the late thirteenth and early fourteenth centuries, though not widely known, are prefigurations of the speaking-picture utopias to come. *Blanquerna* (first published in Valencia, 1521), by the Catalan scholar and philosopher Ramón Lull, recounted the life of a fictional saintly Pope, his upbringing, reluctant acceptance of the Holy Office, resignation, and final choice of a hermit's existence. In the course of the narrative Lull depicts the institution of an ideal apostolic state. Twelve papal emissaries dispatched throughout the world report on abuses of the Christian life and attend to its reformation. They aim at unifying the customs and languages of all the peoples of the earth in order to end misunderstandings and assure a lasting peace. Elaborate plans for the conversion of the Saracens, the Jews, and the inhabitants of India are set in motion. Pope Blanquerna also orders representatives of all the communes of Italy, ravaged by endemic warfare, to assemble annually in a secure and neutral place where they will constitute a chapter and settle their disputes and differences. The sanction for failure to abide by the decisions of the chapter is the typical "puniment de moneda." There is an echo of *Blanquerna* in Pierre Dubois's proposals in *De Recuperatione Terre Sancte* for the convocation of an extraordinary assembly of prelates and Christian princes presided over by the Pope to preserve universal peace. The detailed outline for the government and educational establishments of the Holy Land after its capture from the Turks is in its own way a realistic utopian project for an ideal society on earth.

Of lasting significance in the history of utopian thought was the attempt of the medieval church to keep alive and to nurture the longing of mankind for eternal peace. Though the idea had its roots in the Greco-Roman and Judaic worlds, the movement for a Peace of God and a Truce of God which spread through Christendom after the great fear of the year 1000 left an enduring imprint on Christian life. In one of their aspects the works of Lull and Dubois reflected the dream of universalizing sporadic local efforts for peace in feudal Europe. In Guillaume Postel's *De Orbis Terrae Concordia Libri Quatuor* (1544), Eméric Crucé's *Le Nouveau Cynée* (1623), and the Abbé de Saint-Pierre's *Projet pour rendre la paix perpétuelle* (1713), the tradition of utopian projects for peace among warring nations was reaffirmed, culminating in Immanuel Kant's philosophical essay *Eternal Peace* (1795), a secular version of the Christian hope. The utopian chain then continued unbroken into the slaughterhouse of the twentieth century.

Columbus at the Parting of the Rivers

For many centuries the Church Fathers debated the question of whether an earthly paradise still existed. Although there was some sympathy for Philo's allegorical interpretation of the second chapter in Genesis, the weight of opinion favored a literal reading of the text and excluded any skepticism about the reality of a garden from which the four rivers of Pison, Gihon, Hiddekel (Tigris), and Euphrates flowed and which still harbored a few blessed ones. But if it was an actual place and not a symbol for wisdom or virtue, where was it? The Tigris and the Euphrates were easily identified; the other two rivers were not, and relating them to the Ganges and the Nile only complicated the problem of discovering a common origin. The Bible said that the Garden of Eden was to the east, a direction that shifted with the stance of the commentator and the geographical world view of his time. Medieval maps bear witness to the widespread conviction that there was an actual place called terrestrial paradise. Usually Jerusalem was in the center of a circular *mappamundi* and paradise was above it, at the edge of the water in which the island of the earth floated. Well into the seventeenth century Christian scholars devoted themselves to composing treatises on the situation of Eden. Bishop Huet's in 1698 was perhaps the most famous of modern times.[47] Since then, new locations have been regularly proposed, including a recent one beneath the polar ice cap.

In their descriptions of the Garden of Eden, medieval poets introduced new elements from patristic commentaries, and in the thirteenth century, romances about the search for the Holy Grail became related to the quest for an earthly paradise. The tradition that the crucifix came of a tree that had once stood in the Garden cemented the connection between a crusade for the recovery of the True Cross and a longing for the terrestrial paradise. According to Lars-Ivar Ringbom's bold hypothesis, motifs and architectural forms from the Zoroastrian sacred city of Šiz (excavated in 1937) continued to influence European pictorializations of paradise throughout the Middle Ages.[48] Khosar II, the Sassanid king, had invaded Jerusalem in A.D. 614 and carried off the Cross to his own capital; in revenge, the Emperor Heraclius sacked Šiz ten years later and retrieved it. During this movement back and forth numerous decorative details from the royal palace at Šiz were supposedly transmitted to Europe, where they reappeared in Paleo-Christian churches, in hermits' visions of paradise, and in the romance of the Holy Grail by Albrecht von Scharffenberg.

The belief was common in the medieval world that things physically contiguous were similar to each other. If the Nile was one of the rivers flowing out of paradise, the nearness of Ethiopia to its source made inhabitants of the region seem rather paradisaical to the Christian imagination. Penetration of the Garden of Eden itself was prohibited by the archangel with the flaming sword, but one might come upon almost blessed peoples in the areas adjacent to it. The legend of the Christian Ethiopian Emperor Prester John was related to paradise because his lands bordered the Nile; he also answered the need for an ally on the eastern flank of Islam and fitted in with Joachimite belief in the coming of an Emperor Redeemer. In 1460, the last year of his life, Henry the Navigator still hoped to pay him a visit, and Vasco da Gama carried letters addressed to him. Pierre d'Ailly's *Imago Mundi,* which Christopher Columbus studied with great care, gathered up all the tales of Prester John. The paradisaical myth was like a web growing ever more intricate as the centuries passed and fibers that were once quite distinct became entwined with one another.

Columbus' letter on his third voyage in 1498, when he reached the mouth of the Orinoco River and its four tributaries and then hastily withdrew in fear, exemplifies the continued force of the myth of paradise in the Western imagi-

nation well into the Renaissance. It also affords at least an inkling of the unconscious psychic meaning that paradise has had for some men. The facts of Columbus' overt behavior are plain enough. According to his reckoning of
elevation as he approached the Orinoco (he had been taking measurements by
the North Star), he seemed to be mounting; and the turbulence of the currents
at the mouth of the river indicated that the waters were running downhill from
some high place. The idea that the Garden of Eden was at the highest point on
earth was supported by the knowledge that it had survived the flood, which in
turn was proved by the fact that the living Enoch and Elijah had been wafted
there. The four rivers into which the Orinoco branched, like those of Eden,
were sweet; the natives were nude, handsome, and gentle, to be expected of
those living in the neighborhood of paradise. As the Book of Genesis and Ezekiel reported, there were gold and precious stones in the vicinity. And, on the
basis of Columbus' calculation of his geographic position, the mountain garden was located toward the east. The arguments from authority, the descriptions in Genesis, the astronomical measurements, the evidence of his eyes, and
the taste on his lips all coincided and led him to surmise that he was at the foot
of the Holy Mountain. There was only one difficulty: This great elevation
around the equinoctial line ran counter to the view he had accepted before he
embarked on his voyages that the world was a perfect sphere. Now that he had
discovered the mountain of paradise, he would have to reject d'Ailly and Aristotle and conceive of a new shape for the earth. In a burst of fantasy, he concluded that it was for the most part indeed round like a *pelota muy redonda;* but
on one side it had a stalk that protruded and pointed upward toward the
heavens. (He used the word *pezón,* which can be both the stalk of a fruit and a
teat.) The earth was thus more like a pear than a sphere (*en la forma de una pera*),
rather like a woman's breast with a nipple on it (*una teta de mujer*).

One can hardly avoid reflecting that it was in the proximity of the terrestrial
paradise that this image of the nipple on the breast thrust itself into Columbus'
revised theory of the earth's shape. References to the mountain of paradise as
the *pezón de la pera* and the *teta de mujer* both appear twice, in two different
places in the same letter; it was no casual analogy. Columbus was manifestly in
a state of disarray. He was close by the terrestrial paradise, but he knew, as he
wrote to the Spanish sovereigns, that no one might enter it except with the will
of God. Frightened by the forbidden paradise and the ultimate secret it held, he
fled back to Hispaniola.

We have the letter Columbus wrote to Ferdinand and Isabella only in a copy
by Bartolomé de las Casas, but its contents jibe with the published testimony
of Peter Martyr on the history of the voyages.[49] Columbus' report is replete
with references to traditions on paradise in d'Ailly, the Book of Ezra, Isidore
of Seville, Bede, Ambrose, and Scotus. And a mere perusal of Columbus' annotations on his copy of d'Ailly's *Imago Mundi* shows at a glance how frequently he had underlined and commented on references to Joachim of Fiore
and his prophecies of a new paradisaical age.[50] Columbus always insisted that
his "execution of the affair of the Indies" was a fulfillment of prophecies in
Isaiah and not a matter of mere reason, mathematics, and maps. Whether the
great voyages of discovery represent a need for rebirth, as a contemporary psy-
choanalyst has conjectured, we do not know;[51] but Columbus' strange conduct
suggests that the paradise fantasy not only has power to draw men to the place

related to memories of the earliest moments of happiness, but also can be inhibitory.

We are prepared to accept the idea that mother-yearning has underlain a great many of the quests for paradise, that Western images of paradise have enfolded recollections of existence in the womb or the early months of life, and that some paradisaical images describing a future rebirth recapitulate the actual experience of birth. But granted that the myth of paradise as a maternal symbol has meaning, this association of ideas should not lead to simplistic reductionism. Paradise is more than a longing to reestablish the blissful union of mother and child. It is a complex state that has had a history—mythic, dogmatic, mystical, activist. The manifold uses of paradise have surely not been exhausted here. We have avoided discussing its two most magnificent embodiments in Western culture, the poems of Dante and of Milton; nor have we dared undertake a study of the paradise of the painters and an inquiry into their iconography.

The Living Myth of Paradise

The biological and anthropological discoveries of the nineteenth and twentieth centuries helped to subvert the Edenic myth—the further back one went the more bestial man appeared, and the idea of a heavenly paradise could no longer have a prototype on earth in the beginning of things. The earthly euchronias of the nineteenth century were thus born into a barren spiritual landscape, and their creaky character as ersatz religions is apparent. They point up how difficult is the search for a terrestrial paradise when man is bereft of belief both in a Garden of Eden that might serve as a restorative model and a future otherworldly heaven.

But written and oral tradition on the paradisaical state is far from extinct. There is still a paradise in the collective conscious of the West, a rich repository with myriad interconnections available to those who write fantasies or organize movements. The emotional potency of these images derives from aspects of the myth that reanimate deep-rooted psychic experiences and may kindle a hope for rebirth, for another change. The myth, religious or secular, serves a purpose in the psychic economy, for it makes possible the continuance of living in the unease of civilization. This fantasy, as Freud thought of all religion, is perhaps unworthy of adults; but it has its consolatory role, like the narcotics whose perennial utility Freud seems to have recognized, without becoming quite so incensed about them as he was about religious narcosis. To bathe in the waters of paradise or utopia for a precious while has made existence bearable for man under the most ghastly conditions. There is even a mild gratification in reading and writing about paradise.

The paradise fantasy is still alive, whether in the form of Baudelaire's "paradis artificiels," or in revolutionary utopias, or in the survival of old-fashioned Christian millenarian religions, or in the cargo-cults of primitive peoples. But the unique contemporary predicament of Western civilization, with its frantic demand for paradise *now*, can be understood only against the shadowy background of those two other paradises "in the beginning" and "in the world to come" whose images grow ever dimmer. The question remains: Can paradise be anything but ephemeral when two of the three paradises—the past and the future—that composed a traditional triune will have vanished and paradise has to be compressed into the fleeting present? Of the thousands of paradisaical settlements that have been founded in Europe and America since the seventeenth century, only the religious ones, which recognized the other segments of time, have exhibited any signs of longevity—which augurs ill for the life span of the current spate of communes in young America. For those without faith, there is probably only a chemical paradise as the alternative to the reality principle. And who knows which is the bitterer?

At intervals one is seized with a desire to be free of the childish fantasy of paradise once and for all, to be rid of those Messiahs, pseudo-Messiahs, half-Messiahs, prophets and charismatic leaders, the sons of God, the ben Josephs, the ben Davids, the ben Menashes, the ben Ephraims, the world-historical personalities, who promise a heavenly kingdom on earth after an apocalyptic combat with the incarnation of evil and who in the end turn out to be as horrible in the flesh as the monsters they have slain. But if paradise was born of that mystical union between mother and child, is it not man's fate to oscillate forever between a longing for the return of that state and disillusion when it finally arrives? The flux and reflux of belief in paradise then becomes a part of the order itself, and do what we may—destroy its orthodox religious foundations, abolish Eden and the world to come—paradise will reappear in a new place, still drawing its children to Joachim's Reign of the Holy Ghost on earth, to the third state of Auguste Comte, to Marx's Higher Stage of Communism, to Teilhard's Noösphere, and even, caricature of caricatures, to Consciousness III.

2

The Golden Age of Kronos

THE GREEKS were richly endowed with the gift of utopian fantasy, in marked contrast with the practical Romans, who, except for occasional glosses on the works of their Hellenic predecessors, were singularly devoid of interest in such unrealistic manifestations of the human spirit. Extraordinarily varied in content and remarkably enduring in time, the Greek utopia had no unified canon; it did not even have a proper name, dispersed as it was among many types and branches of literature over a period of a thousand years. And yet some half a dozen different shapes can be readily recognized as utopian in character.

There is a Greek utopia in which mythic, otherworldly elements not dissimilar to the paradise cult of Judeo-Christianity intrude. But the Greeks also wrestled with the concrete organizational problems of an earthly city in a high state of civilization, and ideal urban forms of life became a central preoccupation of their philosophy and political theory. Modern Western utopia has constantly been torn by the polarity of the paradisaical religious fantasy and the rationalist ideal of a city of men created by the Greeks.

The Greeks early invented—though invention does not preclude remote antecedents of their ideas—the myth of a golden age, a perfect human condition sometime in the distant past, along with the ancillary myth of the Elysian fields where heroes lived happily on into the present, and a whole congeries of civilization myths honoring Prometheus the firebringer and other innovating benefactors of mankind. From Homer and Hesiod through the tragedians of the classical age, Greek literature gave expression to these legends in forms of great beauty that have long since been deeply embedded in Western consciousness, a parallel to the paradise cult and an integral part of the mythic substratum of modern utopian thought.

Beginning about the middle of the fifth century before Christ, the Old Comedy reflected a rather different type of utopia—the sensuous fantasies of the ordinary people of the city of Athens, their desires for gross gratification, as well as their hopes for community, equality, and lasting peace. Though the comic poets ridiculed the impracticality and extravagance of these daydreams, they were not without a measure of sympathy for the popular yearnings. Aristophanes is the brisk, if ambiguous, spirit of this Athenian utopia.

With Plato, Greek genius gave birth to the grand philosophical utopia of antiquity, a plan for a just and harmonious urban society based on a hierarchy of virtues and instinctual repression, which continued to attract and often to enthrall later generations. Aristotle wrote the first sober critique of the ideal societies of his predecessors, accompanied by a rather low-keyed utopia of his own. The schools of Greek philosophy that came after Plato and Aristotle—Stoics, Cynics, and Epicureans—also spawned utopias, though little now remains of them beyond the title and list of contents of a primitivist utopia ascribed to Diogenes and isolated fragments of a *Politeia* by Zeno. Many of the

later philosophers were oriented so completely in the direction of highly individualistic, even solipsistic, solutions to the choice of a way of life that they
hardly qualify as social utopians, though their dominant tendency to privatize
the human ideal is in itself significant.

Greek pastoral, or bucolic, poetry, which came to fruition in the Alexandrian Age and is associated particularly with the names of Theocritus, Mos-
chus, and Bion, inspired a nostalgic utopia in which erotic themes, set against
the backdrop of a natural landscape, were interwoven with an idealization of
the countryman's life. Though the subject matter of the idylls was varied and
sometimes even struck an elegiac note, the poems that were admired and imitated by later ages celebrated rustic tranquillity and the herdsman's simple
joys. The appeal of the pastoral utopia to sophisticated and decadent societies
need not be labored: It echoed in Vergil's *Eclogues* and among Renaissance followers of Theocritus, and found a reductio ad absurdum in the shepherd-shep-
herdess playacting of eighteenth-century French courtiers.

Following the death of Alexander the Great there was an outcropping of
rather prosy depictions of life on fortunate isles at the ends of the earth, fiction
usually cast as authentic geography or travel accounts. Though only a handful
of these Hellenistic novels have survived even in excerpts, they established a
literary genre and set a dreary narrative pattern for thousands of later utopias in
the West. Lucian's parodies of the novels enjoyed lasting popularity and kept
the memory of the tales alive even when the texts had disappeared.

While the great lawgivers of city-states, Solon and Lycurgus and Pythagoras, anchored the good society in philosophical views of human nature and
were among the first to translate their ideals into functioning political structures, the fact that their models were put into practice, that they were historical
realities, did not dull their utopian aura for later generations. Eventually the
laws of Solon and Lycurgus assumed a quasi-mythic character, and became an
essential ingredient of the European utopian tradition through the age of the
French Revolution. Men opted either for the Athenian or for the Spartan
model.

The Greek philosophical utopia was concretely embodied in the architectural design of ideal city plans from the classical through the Hellenistic
periods, of which only scattered cursory notices survive, and in experiments
projected or actual of which little can be said with certainty. Such were the
communities of the Pythagoreans in Magna Graecia, the Ouranopolis (City of
Heaven) that the philologist Alexarchus, brother of King Cassander (d. 297
B.C.), is said to have founded in Macedon, calling himself its Sun and bestowing upon it a language and laws,[1] and a Platonopolis that Plotinus (A.D.
205–269/70) tried to persuade the Emperor Gallienus to build on the site of a
ruined Pythagorean settlement in Campania. Among the architectural treatises
of the ancients, the work of the Augustan Vitruvius was preserved intact and
became the canonical text for Renaissance Europe.

Popular uprisings to effect cancellation of debts, agrarian reform, and a redistribution of power in the city-state have been related to utopian thought in
the classical world. The third-century revolutions in Sparta culminating in the
accession of Cleomenes III (235 B.C.) have been utopianized and so have the
power plays of his successor Nabis. Perhaps the plans of Tiberius Gracchus in
second-century Rome should also be included in the utopian corpus, if only

because of their later reverberations in the French communist utopia of Gracchus Babeuf. The Stoic philosopher Blossius, tutor of the Gracchi, was certainly involved in their conspiracy in some way, and his flight to Pergamum, where he joined Aristonicus, bastard son of Eumenes II, in an appeal to the slaves and non-Greeks and the proclamation of a Heliopolis, lends support to the idea that Stoic concepts of universality and equality inspired the creation of a utopia in action—though it seems farfetched to connect Aristonicus' City of the Sun to Iambulus' utopian novel about the Islands of the Sun, as some literary commentators have.[2]

The principal utopian fixation of Rome was Rome itself, a model of a universal society under law, most pompously presented by Cicero in the *Laws* and in the *Republic*. Roman emperors—Augustus, Nero—and their poets used Greek golden-age imagery to lend glamor to their reigns. The famous Messianic Eclogue of Vergil and passages in Ovid were the key texts for transmission of the Greek myth of the golden age to the Middle Ages and later times, since Latin was more current in the schools than Greek.

Utopian thinkers of the Renaissance, no matter how imbued they were with a sense of their original genius, breathed the intoxicating air of the Greek utopias. In the century after 1450, virtually the whole of the extant Greek corpus was published. Homer and Hesiod, Plato and Aristotle, Aristophanes, Lucian, and Plutarch appeared in the original, in Latin translations, and in the vernacular languages. Classical universal histories that confounded Hellenistic utopias with actual societies and Latin compendia that incorporated summaries of Hellenistic utopian novels became available to humanists and their patrons. Some of the Greek utopias were also known through paraphrases in the Church Fathers. After the recovery and diffusion of this Greek literature, Europeans had access to more varied examples of Greek utopian thought than most Greeks had ever had. The utopias in print gave Europeans a common pool of fantasies, imagery, and plans. Without this Greek legacy the utopia of the Renaissance is hardly conceivable.

Among the varieties of thought transmitted from the Greco-Roman world to modern utopia, two types can be distinguished, even though the boundary between them is sometimes vague. One is more purely mythic and relates to the *aurea aetas* in its multiplicity of poetic, dramatic, and novelistic forms; it is a substratum that is diffuse and rather protean, even when it can be illustrated by specific texts. The other is more stable and is centered on the institutions of an ideal city as reported or conceptualized by the philosophical and literary minds of antiquity. Of the two, the legend of the golden age takes historical precedence.

Hesiod's Golden Race

Sometime around 700 B.C., a Greek merchant sailor from Kyme, a commercial center on the mainland of Asia Minor, returned to the countryside of southern Boeotia from which his ancestors had fled in the wake of the Dorian invasion. There he bought land on the slopes of Mount Helikon, cleared the fields of rocks, and built a farm. After he died, his two sons fell to wrangling over their inheritance. One, who was the poet Hesiod, took the occasion to write an expostulation to a disappointing brother as an introduction to his great moralizing epic of Greek rural life, *Works and Days*. Sadness over the loss of fraternal love was intermingled with a more universal feeling of man's bleak isolation in an age of social disarray.

Twilight had descended upon the age of the heroes and the tone of life was melancholy. Agglomerations of wealth had been dispersed and there was a pervasive atmosphere of decline. Hunger had become a familiar in the house of the Boeotian farmer. The barons who ruled his destiny were venal and rapacious—they had taken bribes from brother Perses. Hesiod saw little hope for the future, for he was of the men of the iron age. Bickering and strife, suffering and travail, were their daily lot, and the gloom was relieved only by rare intervals of good fortune. When in the course of their steady degeneration the present race of men were born grayheads, the poet-seer prophesied, Zeus would put an end to them, a fate they deserved, for they were incapable of justice and righteousness and controlled, lawful behavior. Hesiod cried out in despair:

> And I wish that I were not any part
> of the fifth generation
> of men, but had died before it came,
> or been born afterward.
> For here now is the age of iron. Never by daytime
> will there be an end to hard work and pain,
> nor in the night
> to weariness, when the gods will send anxieties
> to trouble us.
> Yet here also there shall be some good things
> mixed with the evils.
> But Zeus will destroy this generation of mortals
> also,
> in the time when children, as they are born,
> grow gray on the temples,
> when the father no longer agrees with the children,
> nor children with their father,
> when guest is no longer at one with host,
> nor companion to companion,
> when your brother is no longer your friend,
> as he was in the old days.[3]

The bitter lament concluded a long mythic sequence on the five races of men, in which is embedded the most famous passage in Western culture on the golden age. Hesiod's disheartened strophes on the age of iron were preceded by a nostalgic evocation of a primeval epoch of ease and innocence, when a fortunate golden race peopled the earth. Through a curious though not uncommon historical dialectic, the dark world of Hesiod gave birth to its opposite, the canonical Greek version of the golden age of Kronos, a myth that in time was amalgamated with the companion myth of the Blessed Isles and with a rich inheritance of Near Eastern visions of paradise. Eventually the three myths, syncretized in a thousand different shapes, became powerful subterranean currents in utopian thought. From this early mythopoeic experience there is neither escape nor recovery; it remains an inexhaustible source of great strength and tragic weakness for European man.

In the opening verses of Hesiod's description of the golden race, many elements of the utopia of calm felicity, a dream of happiness that will endure until the end of the eighteenth century, are already present. The abode of the golden race has no name, but it is a serene and tranquil place where food grows without cultivation and the curse of hard labor has not yet fallen upon mankind. The earth gives forth fruit of itself, *automate,* a fantasy that will often be renewed in the utopian imagination and contrasts dramatically with the unremitting toil of the iron men. The golden ones, in a state of eupsychia, spend their days merrymaking and feasting. The life they lead is free from violence and grief—a pastoral idyll. Evils of old age are outside their ken, and so are the terrors of dying: In their golden well-being they glide into death as if they were falling asleep. Great utopias always provide for good dying as well as for good living.

> In the beginning, the immortals
>   who have their homes on Olympos
> created the golden generation of mortal people.
> These lived in Kronos' time, when he
>   was the king in heaven.
> They lived as if they were gods,
>   their hearts free from all sorrow,
> by themselves, and without hard work or pain;
>   no miserable
> old age came their way; their hands, their feet,
>   did not alter.
> They took their pleasure in festivals,
>   and lived without troubles.
> When they died, it was as if they fell asleep.
>   All goods
> were theirs. The fruitful grainland
>   yielded its harvest to them
> of its own accord; this was great and abundant,
>   while they at their pleasure
> quietly looked after their works,
>   in the midst of good things
> [prosperous in flocks, on friendly terms
>   with the blessed immortals].[4]

Perhaps only one adornment of later utopias is conspicuously absent: While the golden race is beloved of the gods, there are no women. The "golden generation of mortal people" antedated the events narrated in the myth of Pandora, even though in the present arrangement of Hesiod's poem the misogynous tale of the gods' vengeful creation of woman as the origin of evil is placed before the myth of the races. The men of the golden race were sons of Mother Earth and were conceived without the intervention of the male, either divine or human—a sharp contrast to the creation of Adam, which is accomplished by the Lord, a paternal figure, acting alone.

After the golden ones there was an abrupt decline, and the race of silver men who succeeded were born abject and vicious. Maturing late, they remained children hanging on to their mothers' skirts until a hundred, and in the brief span of adult life allotted to them were incapable of refraining from savage insolence toward one another. The bronze race, even more bestial, were possessed by psychic evils. They were bloodthirsty creatures who reveled in war, and aggression became endemic among them. The race of heroes, which Hesiod interpolated at this point, has no metallic equivalent. Toward this generation immediately preceding his own iron men he betrayed a measure of ambivalence. The heroes of Thebes and Troy could not be ignored, though their inclusion interrupts the general pattern; but there is no unreserved admiration for the Greek intruders who launched a thousand ships against the land of his father's birth. The Homeric warriors were not practiced in the virtues of diligence and industriousness that Hesiod extolled. Nonetheless, their life span over, they were allowed to dwell in the Islands of the Blessed in circumstances approximating those of the golden age, while the bronze race were despatched to Hades.

This literal-minded recapitulation of Hesiod's myth of the five races assumes that Hesiod existed as a historical personage and was not a mere name for a collectivity of Boeotian bards; and it passes over a multitude of scholarly interpretations to which the seemingly innocent lines have given birth over the past century. Some recent readings are so subtle and sophisticated that the farmer-poet of Askra might have had difficulty in comprehending their arguments. But the rationalist commentators who have raised a host of queries in the spirit of the higher criticism should not be dismissed without at least a hearing. If Hesiod intended to present the decline of the races as inevitable, they ask, how could the myth serve to encourage either his brother or the rest of mankind to return to the ways of work and justice? Does the interjection of the race of heroes between the bronze and the iron races, on the face of it rather clumsy, have a more recondite meaning? Is he telling of a one-way, linear descent from golden excellence to iron degeneracy, or does he hold forth the promise, or at least the remote possibility, of a renewal of the metallic cycle from the beginning? Does he allow for a countermovement as the genealogy of the races is reversed and they swing pendulum-like from iron to heroes to bronze to silver to gold in a variant of the theme of eternal recurrence? If the underlying four-metal division of the races was transmitted from the Orient, from Indian or Zoroastrian mythology or both—as many scholars believe—was Hesiod's originality limited to the invention of the race of heroes? Do the metals have hidden symbolic significance, gold being identified with royalty or divine brilliance, or was the myth a poetic, real history of the progressive introduction of new forms of metallurgy, a model for our archaeological nomenclature?

The conclusions of present-day interpreters are nothing if not ingenious. The opening myths of *Works and Days* are looked upon as two related accounts of the origin of evil in the world that recall in passing a time before the existence of sickness, suffering, and death. There is a moral behind the myth of Prometheus and Pandora: Men must accept the harsh decree of Zeus that henceforward the sustenance of life will be hidden from them and they must work to survive. The myth of the five races was a lesson to Hesiod's hapless brother Perses as well as to the mighty princes of the earth that they must pursue *Dike* (Justice) and shun *Hubris* (Insolence) or suffer the dismal fate of the evil races. Alternatively, for critics who stress the final destiny of the races, the myth serves as an explanatory system of the world natural and supernatural. The first two races become daimones, the bronze men are the people of the dead in Hades, and the heroes have been wafted away to the Blessed Isles. Alongside the immortal gods, the superseded races continue to exist in another form, and the myth establishes the extramundane structure of the universe, a total hierarchy of being.

Skeptical of the traditional acceptance of the chronology of the races, some mythographers deny any vital links among these self-contained entities. The sequence is not temporal but is an order of merit, and the serialization of the myth is disregarded as a latter-day innovation. This is an attractive hypothesis, though the heroes, who are in fourth place, are manifestly superior to the bronze race who are in third, thus upsetting the descending ladder of excellence. One commentator interprets the myth as a constant dialectic between Dike and Hubris, rather than a simple decline from race to race. He posits a major break after the first two races, who represent higher types of reality, embodiments of justice—gold the positive image and silver the negative. The third and fourth races can only be defined in terms of violence, the opposite of justice. While the first two become daimones and are worshipped by the pious, the third and fourth, inferior beings, are not comprehended in the ranks of the divine. The iron race is the most complex of all, for it has two stages of existence: in one, Justice still rules, moral laws are obeyed, men go through a natural life cycle, and good is mixed with evil; in the other Hubris alone will triumph, a state of absolute evil symbolized by the birth of grayheads and neglect of the laws of filial piety, hospitality, and respect for oaths. Hesiod thus conceived of himself as living in a transitional moment of the iron age, when Dike and Hubris still coexisted and men had a choice between good and evil. The moral admonition to brother Perses is now understandable. A world ruled by Hubris alone inspires terror, though there is a prospect that after the reign of Hubris is over, Justice may return. It is the poet's anguished complaint that he was not born either in an earlier generation or later under a new reign of Justice.

Provocative as these interpretations are, the encrustations of recent scholiasts have rendered the myth virtually unrecognizable, like barnacle-covered statues raised from the bottom of the sea. Prior to the projections of modern scholarship, most of Western culture was content to read Hesiod at the surface level, without probing for secret complexities. Whatever Hesiod's desire may have been—and he was not rigorously rationalistic and philosophical, but probably used older mythic materials in a free and poetic way—in the three thousand years following his death, his golden race, or the golden age into which it was soon transformed, was cherished as a shining ideal of human existence, and the remaining races or ages were lumped together as times of sorrow. Of the entire myth, often only the golden-age utopia was remembered and the anti-utopia of the other periods forgotten. A didactic epistle in verse addressed to a wayward brother, exhorting him to lead a continent, blameless life by tilling the soil and forswearing contentiousness, seems an unlikely place to find the Greek counterpart of the Garden of Eden. But *Works and Days* remained the locus classicus of the idea, and its phrases reappeared countless times in utopias well into the eighteenth century. Lifted from its context, Hesiod's myth of the golden race lived on, adapted, altered, telescoped, amplified, and historicized.

The Metamorphoses of a Myth

In antiquity, the metamorphoses of Hesiod's myth of the golden race vied in number with those of the gods. As the myth was passed along through the

Greek and Roman literary worlds, the conditions of life for the golden race were constantly modified to accord with current philosophical and religious preconceptions. Eventually the myth of the golden race, with all the ambiguities of a myth in Greek culture, was reduced to a matter-of-fact description of an actual historical epoch. In the intermediate stages along the way, the mythic and historical components were inextricably intermingled. At some point difficult to establish, but surely by Hellenistic times, Hesiod's five races were completely supplanted by four ages (the race of heroes was dropped) and the golden race became a golden age. When this occurred, the temporal and historical character of the myth was firmly established.

In the second century before Christ, the original Oriental myth of four metallic ages from which Hesiod's idea may have derived sprang another offshoot, the redaction of the myth in a mixed Hebrew and Aramaic form in the Book of Daniel. When adopted into the biblical canon, Nebuchadnezzar's vision of the colossus composed of four metals and feet of clay gave rise among interpreters to the doctrine of the Four Kingdoms, the most tenacious frame for universal history until the eighteenth century.

Greek lyric poets of the sixth and fifth centuries before Christ evoked a bygone age of innocence and virtue without calling it golden, but Hesiod's imprint on their writing is unmistakable. Theognis of Megara bewailed the passing of the pious men among whom had once dwelt Hope and Good Faith and Moderation and Justice, in a vein reminiscent of Hesiod, though his vision may have been much narrower. He may only have been deploring the usurpation of power, once exercised by his own social class, the good nobles, by the evil, vulgar upstarts greedy for money and without any sense of fidelity to the old ways. The Agrigentine poet Empedocles, in a fragment appropriately preserved in a treatise on vegetarianism written by the Neoplatonist Porphyry eight hundred years later, added "abstinence from blood" to the attributes of an age anterior to and even more perfect than the reign of Kronos. In Empedocles' mystic cycle of Love and Strife, the primal age corresponds to a time when Strife is yet unborn. Kupris, who in this fragment is Aphrodite and the cosmic force of Love, reigns a solitary goddess at the beginning of things. She is honored with animal offerings, not in the flesh, not in life-destroying ritual sacrifice, but merely through images. "They had no god Ares nor Kudoimos nor king Zeus nor Kronos nor Poseidon, but Kupris as queen. Her did they propitiate with holy images, with paintings of living creatures, with perfumes of varied fragrance and with sacrifice of pure myrrh and sweet-scented frankincense, casting to the ground libations of golden honey. Their altar was not steeped in the pure blood of bulls, but rather was this the greatest abomination among men, to tear out the life from the goodly limbs and eat them."[5] Empedocles' text on the alternation of the ages of Love and Strife has recently given rise to as many variant interpretations as Hesiod's apparently diachronous order of the races, though for most of Western culture Empedocles was simply the poet of the contrariety of Love and Strife in a temporal sequence.

In the *Dialogues,* Plato used the myth of the races in a variety of ways. The third book of the *Republic* incorporated a transformed version of Hesiod's myth into the noble lie, a technique for imposing hierarchic order upon the ideal city. "While all of you in the city are brothers, we will say in our tale, yet God in fashioning those of you who are fitted to rule mingled gold in their generation, for which reason they are the most precious—but in the helpers silver, and iron and brass in the farmers and other craftsmen."[6] In the third book of the *Laws,* his last work, he used the first part of the same myth for an entirely different purpose. He told of periodic geological catastrophes after which civilization had to start its cycle of existence over again with only a remnant of mankind, and in a limited sense each new beginning became a golden age. By this time the myth of Hesiod had been wedded to an origins-of-civilization myth. Through the mouth of the "Athenian," Plato reconstructed the life of the few survivors of the human race preserved somewhere on the mountaintops on the morrow of one of the great periodic deluges. The first generations after the flood, bereft of all arts and sciences, lived in a primitive state of innocence. Though simpleminded, they had exalted natures; and Plato appreciated their unspoiled way of life. Civilized mankind could not recapture their guilelessness; but Plato linked the ideal state of the past with the future good society when he tried to inculcate their moral virtues into his urbanized citizenry, whom he would strip of useless and corrupting luxury. Men of the first age were kindly disposed and friendly toward one another because they had the necessaries, but not the superfluities, of life. "Now a community which has no communion with either poverty or wealth," he argued, "is generally the one in which the noblest characters will be formed; for in it there is no place for the growth of insolence and injustice, of rivalries and jealousies."[7]

Many later utopias would seek to reproduce the continence and benevolent spirit of Plato's early ages of mankind. More than two thousand years after Plato, a young French engineer, Nicolas Boulanger, member of the philosophical circle of the Baron d'Holbach, revived much of the Platonic phraseology in his *L'Antiquité dévoilée* (published posthumously in 1766), an impassioned re-creation of the human condition after upheavals in the physical structure of the earth. His purpose was to relate the naturally moral postdiluvians to the rational good men who were being fashioned in European society by the Enlightenment. The Platonic lawgiver aimed to institute at one fell swoop what the most sanguine of the eighteenth-century philosophes hoped to achieve only gradually. What for Plato was still a myth became scientific truth for the engineer-philosophe, who could prove that the deluge had in fact occurred by pointing to seashells on the mountains, and who derived the image of tender and gentle postdiluvian man from mythology and Plato's text. Nothing in Plato ever died; in new guises his images were reborn in the utopian fantasies of later generations.

The vision of man in a primitive state of nature in Rousseau's *Discourse on the Origin of Inequality,* its most noteworthy modern envelopment, makes only peripheral reference to Plato's fable of early mankind, though Rousseau knew the *Dialogues.* From his notes we gather that he was inspired rather by the work of a later writer, Dicaearchus of Messana, a pupil of Aristotle who spent most of his life in Sparta. His *Bios Hellados* (Life in Greece), the first universal history of culture ever written, is preserved in a summary by Porphyry in that same treatise to which we owe the fragment from Empedocles on the primitive reign of love, and came to Rousseau circuitously through excerpts in Saint Jerome. Dicaearchus completely demythicized the golden age and reduced it to plain historical reality. Virtually all the physical and moral qualities that grace Rousseau's state-of-nature man have an antecedent in this Hellenistic portrait of the first generation, an age extolled as the best life ever enjoyed by men, when they were truly like unto the gods. They ate little—no heavy foods—and therefore did not sicken from being loaded down with foul matter. The arts had not yet been invented, and men thrived, without care or toil, on the spontaneous fruits of nature. Similarly, Rousseau's natural man was superior to societal man in "physique" and in "morale," he never suffered from disease, and he needed no doctors, the bane of civilized existence. Both in Dicaearchus and in Rousseau the acorn sufficed the peaceful primitives. There was no conflict or emulation among them because there was nothing of value about which to contend. To the later multiplication of desires Dicaearchus, a true forerunner of Rousseau, imputed all the evils that had beset mankind.[8]

By the time Aratus of Soli wrote his astronomical poem, the *Phaenomena*, for the Macedonian court in the third century before Christ, the temper of the golden age had been subtly changed. No longer depicted as primitive, it was a philosophical epoch in which the first men practiced the rationalist moral virtues esteemed by the author. When Aratus reached the Maiden in his versified description of the constellations, he was minded to celebrate her ancient beneficent reign: "But another tale is current among men, how of old she dwelt on earth and met men face to face, nor ever disdained in olden time the tribes of men nor women, but mingling with them took her seat, immortal though she was. Her men called Justice; but she assembling the elders, it might be in the market-place or in the wide-wayed streets, uttered her voice, ever urging on them judgements kinder to the people. Not yet in that age had men knowledge of hateful strife, or carping contention, or din of battle, but a simple life they lived. Far from them was the cruel sea and not yet from afar did ships bring their livelihood, but the oxen and the plough and Justice herself, queen of the peoples, giver of things just, abundantly supplied their every need."[9] Life had lost something of its easygoing character as men ploughed the fields with oxen, but the air of the pastoral idyll was preserved: Existence remained simple, nature was generous, and the pernicious influences of foreign trade had not yet corrupted men by stimulating a taste for luxury. The poem of Aratus was popular in the Roman world; it was translated by Cicero and adapted by Hyginus, who added nothing to the original.

The Romans, who had virtually no utopias of their own invention, dreamed of the happiness of the reign of Saturn, whom they identified with Kronos, and in the Saturnalia enjoyed, if only for a brief moment and in a debauched form, a revival of the golden age. In the great philosophical poem of Lucretius, *De rerum natura*, the idea of the golden has, strangely enough, a negative connotation and characterizes the epoch of the fall after the founding of cities, the invention of property, and the discovery of gold. If his history of mankind in Book V has a benign early period it is the age of *amicitia*, after the emergence of men from brutish isolation. "Then it was that humanity first began to mellow . . . Then neighbours began to form mutual alliances, wishing neither to do nor to suffer violence among themselves."[10] In Roman literature generally the epithet golden is used in a positive sense and is applied to a historical period rather than to a mythic race. Vergil, however, in the imagery of his Fourth, or Messianic, Eclogue returned to Hesiod's conception of a golden race. He combined it with the Age of the Maiden, Justice, conjured up by Aratus, and foretold the renewal of a reign of peace to be inaugurated by the birth of a son—to precisely whom is still a matter of scholarly debate. "Now the Virgin [Justice] returns, the reign of Saturn returns; now a new generation descends from heaven on high. Only do thou, pure Lucina, smile on the birth of the child, under whom the iron brood shall first cease, and a golden race spring up throughout the world." At the birth of the babe, flowers will bloom spontaneously. Unprodded, goats will wend their way homeward with udders full of milk. Savage lions, serpents, and poisonous plants will be no more. After the child grows up and the world is once again torn by a great war, crime will disappear, seafaring and conflict will be eliminated, the earth will produce abundant food and drink without cultivation. Transported by his own rhetoric, Vergil scales giddy heights that surpass the golden-age rhapsodies of the Greek poets: "The ram in the meadows shall change his fleece, now to sweetly blushing purple, now to a saffron yellow; of its own will shall scarlet clothe the grazing lambs."[11]

Far better known than the Greek poets, Vergil and especially Ovid were pivotal figures in preserving and handing down the myth of a golden age. The Fourth Eclogue was later read as heralding Christianity, and largely accounts for the reverence in which Vergil was held in the Middle Ages. Beginning with the Renaissance, Ovid's *Metamorphoses* was one of the most popular schoolbooks in Western Europe; and his portrayal of the golden age in Book I, which filled out Hesiod's spare text, was the definitive form in which the myth was infused into utopian thought. Ovid, who was a friend of Hyginus, did not disguise his close kinship with Hesiod, for all his rich embellishments of the *aurea aetas;* but the atmosphere had become heavily scented with the primitivist nostalgia of an oversophisticated society. "Golden was that first age, which, with no one to compel, without a law, of its own will, kept faith and did the right. There was no fear of punishment, no threatening words were to be read on brazen tablets; no suppliant throng gazed fearfully upon its judge's face; but without judges lived secure. Not yet had the pine-tree, felled on its native mountains, descended thence into the watery plain to visit other lands; men knew no shores except their own. Not yet were cities begirt with steep moats; there were no trumpets of straight, no horns of curving brass, no swords or helmets. There was no need at all of armed men, for nations, secure from war's alarms, passed the years in gentle ease. The earth herself, without compulsion, untouched by hoe or plowshare, of herself gave all things needful. And men, content with food which came with no one's seeking, gathered the arbute fruit, strawberries from the mountain-sides, cornel-cherries, berries hanging thick upon the prickly bramble, and acorns fallen from the spreading tree of Jove. Then spring was everlasting, and gentle zephyrs with warm breath played with the flowers that sprang unplanted. Anon the earth, untilled, brought forth her stores of grain, and the fields, though unfallowed, grew white with the heavy, bearded wheat. Streams of milk and streams of sweet nectar flowed, and yellow honey was distilled from the verdant oak."[12] As one moves from Ovid through time, the literary rendering of a golden age becomes ever more laden with ornaments until in the epics of the Italian Renaissance the exuberance of detail is oppressive and suffocating. The reign of natural righteousness without legal sanctions, with which Ovid began, was in itself utopia for the law-ridden society of Rome and its heirs. The elimination of any need for the external compulsions and restraints of law remained a dominant theme in utopian thought down through Marx's *Critique of the Gotha Program,* albeit his concept was animated by a romantic idea of *Gemeinschaft* which no Roman would have countenanced.

In the dramas of the human imagination, events can readily be shoved about to form a different sequence and their props moved along with them. Though there are those who would sharpen the distinction between the vision of a glorified past in Hesiod and a complete utopia that looks to the future, many Western thinkers have joined the notion of a primitive golden age with a promise that the happy epoch now vanished will be reborn. Secular versions of this union of ideas were widespread in the eighteenth and nineteenth centuries: A typical history of mankind began with an age of blissful innocence, followed by an interim of misery, and concluded with a progressive attainment of a state of terrestrial happiness. While Hesiod's epic reflected an age of social disintegration and looked backward, the fortunate human condition of the age of Kronos could be made part of a utopian vision if translated into the future, as in Vergil's Messianic Eclogue. Utopian fantasy, like the dreamworld of our nightly existence, is not very insistent on precise chronology. Early in the nineteenth century Henri Saint-Simon stood Hesiod's mythic conception on its head and proclaimed: "The imagination of the poets placed the Golden Age in the cradle of mankind, in the ignorance and brutality of early times. It is rather the Iron Age that should be relegated there. The Golden Age of the human species is not behind us, it is before us."[13]

The Translation of Elysium

Another mythic element in utopia, Elysium, which first appears in Homer's *Odyssey*, is said to be a survival from Minoan religion. It is a death-free, comfortable retreat for selected heroes in a place that is neither Olympus nor Hades. "But for thyself, Menelaus, fostered of Zeus," the royal hero was assured by Proteus, "it is not ordained that thou shouldst die and meet thy fate in horse-pasturing Argos but to the Elysian plain and the bounds of the Earth will the immortals convey thee, where dwells fair-haired Rhadamanthus, and where life is easiest for men. No snow is there, nor heavy storms nor rain, but ever does Ocean send up blasts of the shrill-blowing West Wind that they may give cooling to men; for thou hast Helen to wife, and art in their eyes the husband of the daughter of Zeus."[14]

In Hesiod's version of the same myth, when Kronos, king in heaven during the golden age, was overthrown by his son Zeus, he was banished to the Islands of the Blessed to rule over the heroes. Conditions in the Islands were about the same as those that prevailed for the golden race:

> And there they have their dwelling place,
>   and hearts free of sorrow
> in the islands of the blessed
>   by the deep-swirling stream of the ocean,
> prospering heroes, on whom in every year
>   three times over
> the fruitful grainland bestows its sweet yield.
>   These live
> far from the immortals, and Kronos is
>   king among them.[15]

The stream of the ocean is common to both versions of the Elysian myth, though only in Hesiod is the haven explicitly an island. The human fetus too is an island, and in their island utopias men have often expressed a longing for the protective fluid that once surrounded them. The maternal symbols of most Elysian, golden-age, and paradisaical utopias are compelling and the point need not be labored. The enclosed gardens, islands, valleys have reappeared with constancy through the ages. There is free feeding, security, peace, plenitude, and no rivalry. The vagueness of Homer's language in locating Elysium at "the bounds of the earth" gave the exegetes an opportunity for play, and they shifted its site about until they landed it on the moon, another female. And though Hesiod stressed the distance of the Islands of the Blessed from the immortal gods, inevitably there was a blurring of the line between the blissful existence of the heroes under King Kronos and the carefree ways of the gods on Mount Olympus, the grandest creation of Greek utopian fantasy.

In Greek and Roman mythology there were many permutations of Elysium and the Isles of the Blessed. They assumed kindred shapes as the garden of the Hesperides, the Isle of Ogygia where Calypso offered Odysseus immortality, and Leuke, the white island, to which Thetis carried the body of Achilles. The related idea of Elysium-like places that were the abodes of mortals was born early. Homer himself left a description of good King Alcinous' orchard, where "the fruit perishes not nor fails in winter or in summer, but lasts throughout the year; and ever does the west wind, as it blows, quicken to life some fruits, and ripen others . . ."[16] Servius, the commentator on the *Aeneid,* identified Elysium with the Fortunate Isles. Belief in an earthly garden paradise for mortal men thus had Greco-Roman as well as Judeo-Christian origins.

By the time of Pindar, a Theban of the fifth century before Christ who became the philosophical poet of Orphism, the character of the population in Elysium had radically changed. In Homer, the next world had been located in two distinct regions, the dark underground Hades across the River Styx to which most men repaired as shades and the exclusive Elysium reserved for the immortal heroes in a rather unidentifiable faraway place at "the bounds of the earth." Under Orphic influence this aristocratic division was modified by a doctrine of punishments meted out for breaches of the laws of the gods and by a belief in the transmigration of souls through successive existences and purifications until the final release of a select group to the Islands of the Blessed. Pindar's Second Olympian Ode and a few threnodic fragments that are ascribed to him expressed the Orphic faith of Theron, tyrant of Acragas. The Orphic cult had taken root in Sicily, and in this ode, at least, Pindar accepted its mystic eschatology. The ode has a consolatory opening on the vicissitudes of life addressed to Theron, and it closes with a baffling attack on Pindar's literary rivals; but its magnificent central passages are devoted to a prophecy of the fortunes of the soul in afterlife that has elevated the poem to a religious revelation. Immediately after death on earth, good and evil spirits would be judged in a nether Hades, Pindar foretold, and their fates determined. The righteous would lead a life of ease and the wicked suffer pains that no one dared look upon. After purgation some good souls would be sent back to earth to experience again the cycle of life and death. Only a small group who had survived this process of reincarnation three times and remained innocent of wrongdoing both on earth and in Hades might then proceed along the highway of Zeus to the Islands of the Blessed. The cooling ocean breezes of this abode of the pure recall Homer and Hesiod, but the environment has been newly enriched. Radiant trees and flowers of gold blaze all about and the blessed ones entwine their arms and crown their heads with chaplets. According to a threnody that has been related to the ode, the immortal souls are more sportive than in the passive Homeric Elysium: "Some there delight themselves with feats of horsemanship and the athlete's practisings. Some with draught-play, others with the music of lyres."[17] In the ode itself the governance of the place has been entrusted by Kronos to Rhadamanthus, its ruler in the Homeric version as well, and Pindar gives a partial list of the goodly company assembled there—Peleus and Cadmus and Achilles.

Though secular portions of the ode celebrated Theron's victory in the chariot race in 476 B.C. and praised wealth and hard-won achievement—frequent Pindaric themes—salvation in Elysium depended not upon earthly good fortune or success in contests, but upon freedom from wrongdoing demonstrated in repeated trials in this world and in Hades. Whereas in Homer Elysium had been the predestined lot of a few humans who were transported there as relatives of the gods, in Pindar the Islands of the Blessed became the reward for a life of struggle and of overcoming sin. It coexisted with a Hades where the wicked were tormented. Achievement of felicity had become a more active goal; translation to the Islands of the Blessed was not a birthright but required a life of strenuous effort, a moral equivalent of the athlete's training. The Church Fathers would have to go only one step further than Pindar, when they allowed the saints in Christian heaven, who had endured in virtue, to gaze out of the celestial windows and rejoice in the spectacle of the torture of the damned. In their emphasis on orthodoxy and chastisement some modern "utopian" societies have closer affinities to Christian heaven than to the calm Elysium of Homer.

While in the *Phaedrus* Plato accepted into his own myth of the soul an Orphic doctrine, not unlike Pindar's, of three incarnations and a final release of the soul for the philosopher without guile or the philosophical lover, he was bitterly scornful of other Orphic renderings of the afterlife in Elysium. In the second book of the *Republic,* speaking through the mouth of Adeimantus, he denounced as contemptible the materialist rewards that some Orphic poets in the name of the gods dangled before those who lived in justice and piety, and he mocked Musaeus and his son Eumolpus for their song of alcoholic gratification in the next world that awaited righteous initiates into the mysteries: "They conduct them to the house of Hades in their tale and they arrange a symposium of the saints; where, reclined on couches and crowned with wreaths, they entertain the time henceforth with wine, as if the fairest meed of virtue were an everlasting drunk."[18] This utopia of vulgar delights was repugnant to Plato the censor, who would expel the poets from the city—even Homer and Hesiod—for prating about physical pleasures as a recompense for upright conduct.

In later Greek writings the Elysian Fields were often transposed to other planets or to the celestial sphere. Doubt over their whereabouts beset the Neoplatonists, in part because Plato had shifted the final haven of the soul from one to another of his eschatological myths. Plutarch and the third-century disciple of Plotinus, Porphyry, interpreted the Homeric text on Elysium to mean that the poet had situated the fields of the blessed on the moon. In his *De facie in orbe lunae* (*Face One Sees on the Moon*), Plutarch supported his conclusion with evidence from an ancient parchment found at Carthage, which maintained that Persephone, who receives the souls of the dead, is not the queen of the underworld but of the moon. Contrary to the myth, she spends all her time with her husband, who is the atmosphere of the moon, though periodically she approaches Demeter the earth-mother and their shadows are intermingled in space. Homer's "bounds of the earth" is therefore the moon, because it is the place to which the earth's shadow extends, and the space between the earth and the moon is an atmospheric purgatory through which souls still sullied must pass. Once having found peace on the moon, the spirit is separated from the psyche and returns to its origin, the sun, while the psyche retains its exterior corporeal form and continues for some time to live an attenuated dreamlike existence—much like that which Homer recounted of the shades in Hades. In his *Eclogues* the fifth-century compiler Stobaeus quoted a fragment of Porphyry to prove incontrovertibly that Homer's Elysium flourished on the moon. Porphyry starts with an etymological argument—that Elysium derived from *heliosis,* meaning that side of the moon exposed to the sun and enjoying brilliant illumination. The hypothesis is then reinforced by an astronomic explication of the enigmatic Homeric words "bounds of the earth": "Night say the mathematicians [he meant the Pythagoreans] is nothing but the shadow of the earth which often falls on the moon. The moon is thus really the extreme limit of the earth, since its shadow cannot hit anything beyond the moon."[19]

The newly established lunar site of Homer's Elysium became a favorite destination of extramundane voyagers in search of a perfect society. From Lucian through Cyrano de Bergerac and Godwin, more or less serious lunar utopias proliferated for centuries—though the marked preference voiced by American astronauts for the plains of Texas over the face of the moon may presage the definitive extirpation of this fantasy from our consciousness. The physical presence of man in a place where he had once situated his utopia will invariably desacralize it and make him look elsewhere. The moon has suffered the fate of Tahiti.

The Old Comedy and the Land of Cokaygne

The common man's gustatory utopia, which was caricatured in the Old Comedy of Athens, is the vulgar, sometimes obscene, counterpart of the genteel and poetic imaginary worlds of the golden age and Elysium and Pindar's Orphic Hades.

Among the 238 manuscripts brought by Giovanni Aurispa from Constantinople in 1423—a major act of intellectual transmission from East to West—was a long-winded symposium in some thirty books called the *Deipnosophistai,* variously translated as *Banquet of the Learned* and *The Gastronomers.* The work entered the collection of the great humanist and Platonic scholar Cardinal Bessarion, and through the gift of his library to the Venetian Senate ultimately reached the Marciana. Its author, Athenaeus, who flourished about A.D. 200, was a Graeculus born in Naucratis, Egypt. If Plato's is the utopia of the soul, these long, turgid discourses are a repository of fantasies of the appetites. The characters of the *Deipnosophists,* attending a symposium at the house of a rich landowner in Alexandria, instead of discussing lofty philosophical ideas in the Socratic manner, while away their time quoting from the whole corpus of Greek literature as far back as the eighth or ninth century before Christ on gastronomy, sexual behavior, medicine, law, and music, and reporting on customs associated with sensate pleasure throughout the world. The result is an anthology of sorts, a pedantic display of learning, which has acquired historical importance because many of the literary citations have survived nowhere else. When the editio princeps appeared in 1514, it put at the disposal of Renaissance humanists a miscellany of factual information on the social life of the ancient Greek world.

Though in dull imitation of Plato occasional dramatic incidents break up the dialogue, a large portion of the work is a monstrous lexicon of experiences in eating. There is not a hint of the intense religious rivalry among Christians, pagans, and Jews in the Alexandria of the period, nor are any controversial political subjects broached. The book echoes the tone of life among the upper classes in Egypt under Roman imperial domination. It is a sybarite's vision, a utopia of contemplative concupiscence for the surfeited, an extension into the imagination of a lust for gorging among Alexandrians who could eat no more.

For the scholar, the excerpts from Greek comedy in the sixth book of the *Deipnosophists* reflect popular Athenian daydreams of a luxurious existence in the latter half of the fifth century before Christ, an entirely different world. But while the gastronomic utopia was treated by the poets of the Old Comedy in a light and bantering spirit, Athenaeus collected and preserved these extravaganzas of gluttony with humorless, encyclopedic obsessiveness. The spirit of popular utopian fantasies in ancient times is difficult to capture because their expression is ordinarily mediated through sophisticated writers; but Attic comedy comes as close to the original source as we may hope for. Not only is it worthy of consideration in its own right, but many of these fragments were quoted and requoted in later ages. In addition to their testimony, eleven complete works of the towering genius of the Old Comedy, Aristophanes, have survived relatively unscathed, profusely explicated by Byzantine scholiasts. The Renaissance revival of utopia drew sustenance from this well-dunged soil.

One of the recurrent ploys of the Old Comedy was to render grotesque the contemporary ambitious projects of universal reform, another to jibe at the common man's notions of a gastronomic Elysium or his nostalgia for the age of Kronos. The two were not unrelated, for the grandiose schemes of Athenian demagogues always featured abundance of food and drink. Nothing is respected in the Old Comedy, neither the age of Kronos, nor Elysium, nor the prospect of a future utopia that would revive the golden age, nor the new ideal constitution-making and city planning that accompanied the Athenian founding of colonies. But if utopia was mocked in Attic comedy, the writers were nevertheless close enough to their audience not to dismiss their vulgar aspirations with philosophical contempt. The comic poets ridiculed the grossness of popular utopian desires, they did not brush them aside with lofty disdain. They even betrayed a certain sympathy for them. Many of the comic heroes are outsized, like the giants of old—true ancestors of Gargantua and Pantagruel.

In the *Metalles* (*The Miners*) of the poet Pherecrates, who flourished about 438 B.C., a character that may be Persephone paints a sensuous utopia in the nether world. The gluttony of the dead is an occasion for black humor, as Persephone's comrade salivates at the prospect of groats "be-snowed with cream," juicy legs of lamb, roast thrushes fricasseed and dressed, all "craving ingurgitation" by ghostly lips.

> O'er each head
> The finest pippins swung, of no tree bred;
> If any thirsted, drink was drawn for him
> Through pipes by slender lasses ripe and trim
> Arrayed in silks, bumpers of wine to wit,
> Crimson and sweet, for all that wished for it.

Sexual desires are but lightly alluded to. Emphasis is upon the consumption of enormous quantities of food and drink and their spontaneous replenishment. "And when one took of these things, bite or sup,/ Straightway the loss was more than twice made up."[20] This Elysium-in-Hades reproduces the same gastronomic utopia that Crates and Teleclseides located in the golden age or in a demagogue's imagination. In the *Beluae* (*The Animals*) by Crates a politician promises a regime in which men will not need slaves, as the animated victuals and cooking utensils respond to voice command: "Rise loaf! It's time the beef was done; saucepan, deliver it!" Not to be outshone, a rival demagogue offers in competition a bathtub utopia: ". . . *my* people nice hot baths will get . . . all they'll do,/ Will be to say 'On with the water, you!'/ And to each bather soap will come unsought,/ His sponge uncalled-for, and his shoes unbrought."[21] Cratinus in *The Wealth-Gods* and Teleclseides in *The Amphictyons* evoked an age of Kronos in which choice food and drink were spontaneously generated and prepared for ingestion:

> Since black loaves and white at men's lips used to fight
>   each asking the hungry to take it
> If they liked their bread fine; and as for the wine,
>   it filled ev'ry brook; and the fishes
> Came perfectly willing and did their own grilling
>   and served themselves up on the dishes.[22]

Almost identical fantasies remained alive well into modern times—for example, in J. A. Etzler's nineteenth-century utopia of automated machines, *The Paradise within the Reach of All Men,* which scandalized Thoreau. Greek imagination simply skipped the early machine age and went directly to automation.

For the poets of the Old Comedy, the golden age was neither a venerated sacred myth nor a true history, but a subject of merriment. Subsequently, through a process of adaptation, plays that were initially satires on the golden age and Orphic Hades became an integral part of the Western world's utopia, just as Lucian's works, written in mockery of classical utopias, served as a rich source for the local color and equipment of scores of modern ideal societies from Thomas More on. The free consumption of wine that an Athenian artisan hankered after, when set in another frame, could assume a mystical, or Christological, significance. The daydream of a life in which every extravagant appetite is instantaneously appeased—aptly named the Cokaygne utopia after its reappearance in the fabliau of the Land of Cokaygne ("little cake") in early fourteenth-century France and England (the German equivalent is *Schlaraffenland,* Lubberland)—has had an extraordinary vitality. Even the promise of green pastures in paradise paled before the robust reality of the medieval ballad-maker's Cokaygne west of Spain. In paradise there was only water to quench man's thirst; but in Cokaygne, where all things were held in common, water was reserved for washing, while great rivers ran with oil, milk, honey, and wine, and roast geese flew about advertising themselves "Gees al hote, al hot." Many of the same conceits, down to minute details, not only have been shared by Attic comedy, English mummers' plays, and popular fables, but are repeated in Judaic and Christian descriptions of paradise, in legends of the Holy Grail, in the paintings of Breughel, and in nineteenth-century European and American ballads like the *Big Rock Candy Mountains:*

> The little streams of alcohol
> Come a-trickling down the rocks
>
> . . .
>
> There's a lake of stew and of whisky too
>
> . . .
>
> I'm bound to stay where they sleep all day,
> Where they hung the Turk that invented work.[23]

Whether the images of the land of Cokaygne, *Schlaraffenland,* and the Old Comedy were diffused in a literary form and through oral transmission or whether they are part of a collective gastronomic unconscious remains a tantalizing question that might agreeably exercise the academic mind.

The marked preponderance of oral over sexual pleasures is characteristic of Greek as well as Jewish popular fancies of utopia, which may either throw light upon their infantile character or bear witness that bread and wine have always been the heaven of the poor and the hungry. Of the three great religions, only Islam's Koran graces the couches of the elect in the future Gardens of Delight with damsels "restrained in glance, wide-eyed, as if they were eggs [or pearls], well-guarded."[24] The women depicted in the earthly paradises of the Renaissance epics, still deeply Christian in spirit, are, like Lilith, dangerous creatures. In the West, paradise and sexual love did not often coexist before the eighteenth century.

The Uses of the Hellenistic Novel

In the Hellenistic novels the myth of the golden age was incorporated into adventure stories and imaginary voyages that catered to a contemporary taste for the bizarre and the exotic. The fragments of these novels that survived in the Church Fathers, in Greek and Roman universal histories, and in Latin compendia of knowledge set the narrative pattern for the later utopian novel and for much of its concrete pictorial detail. But of far deeper significance, the vision of static, changeless happiness in these early novels possessed the vast majority of modern utopias from the Renaissance to the French Revolution.

The Hellenistic age was a period of lively utopian creation, and there are evident resemblances between this epoch and the Renaissance, which witnessed a similar flowering of the utopian imagination. In one, the independent Greek city-states were being gobbled up by the massive imperial structures of Alexander's successors; in the other, the loose, disintegrating framework of feudal society was yielding to new, centralized, dynastic states. In both there occurred dramatic expansions of the known world to encompass distant lands and peoples. The conquests of Alexander, which pushed the intellectual and artistic horizons of Greece eastward, had their counterpart in the great European explorations of the late fifteenth and early sixteenth centuries, with their far-reaching moral and socioeconomic consequences. Geographical discovery helped to make utopia plausible in both epochs. As strange lands were penetrated, the windows of credibility were opened wide. Authentic narratives about new nations and kingdoms with hitherto unheard-of customs were in themselves so marvelous that they lent verisimilitude to the imaginary utopia, however wild it might be. The boundary line between real and unreal, possible and impossible, faded. The present-day proliferation of utopias, stereotyped though they are, and of science fiction has been partly stimulated by the exploration of new dimensions in outer space.

Alexander's conquests prepared the believing ears of city-dwellers on the shores of the Hellenic Mediterranean for accounts of India to the east, of the land of the Hyperboreans to the north, of Ultima Thule itself. Greek reasoning about the ideal city-state had reached its zenith in the works of Plato and Aristotle on the eve of the destruction of the independent Greek polis. After the organization of the new Ptolemaic and Seleucid empires, men stopped debating with the tools of logic about the nature of an ideal city; abandoning the rigors of the Socratic dialogue, they surrendered themselves to the imagery of the golden age and spun reveries. The utopias became myths again, sleepy fantasy-wishes, passive daydreams, airy descriptions of faraway places with no discursive rationalist system to hem them in. The Blessed Isles, the Fortunate Isles, the Elysian Fields, the race of golden men were transplanted into a strange and lush environment. Travelers' tales of happiness in the lands they visited replaced dialectical controversy about the type of polity in which man might attain the highest perfection. Determination of the institutions of civil government, vital to Plato and Aristotle, lost meaning for the utopia-makers living under the new imperial regimes. The Hellenistic utopia was escapist, uncommitted, and gelatinous.

An element of the Stoic and Epicurean privatized morality penetrated the Hellenistic utopia, a longing for a psychic state of calm felicity. Even when the governmental forms described in the novels preserved vaguely Platonic outlines, the temper of life was an admixture of Stoicism and Epicureanism that valued peace and quiet over athletic exertion of body and spirit. The bonds of a tight political community that Plato had forged at the expense of the family were loosened, giving way to a diffuse, much diluted feeling of universal brotherhood. Hellenistic authors were more concerned with evoking utopian moods than with the institutional framework of society. In their fables they idealized the Indians of the East two thousand years before the Indians of the West were glorified by Europeans in the myth of the noble savage—both suggestive of self-denigration. Primitivist tendencies had emerged before in the Greek world, but with the triumph of Alexandrian exoticism the Scyths and the northern tribes, the Indians and the Ethiopians, and even anthropoid creatures who had undergone weird physical alterations, were exalted as somehow closer to nature or to the first, golden age of the world.

The Hellenistic utopia broke the mythic confines of Greek religion and established ties with the Garden of Eden and the paradisaical themes of the civilization of the Tigris-Euphrates that lie behind Genesis. Tales of wonder from ancient Greek and Oriental seafaring traditions and golden-age images, even direct quotations out of Homer and Hesiod, were mixed with adaptations of Indian myths. Pliny in the sixth book of his *Natural History* makes mention of a Hellenistic novel about the Attacoreans by one Amometus, which is related to the Indian myth of the land of the Uttara Kurus, north of the Himalayas, where it was neither hot nor cold, where sickness was unknown and pleasure uninterrupted, where everything a man might desire—fruit, garments, beautiful women—grew on trees, though the women were fated to die each nightfall.[25]

Of what was undoubtedly a large body of Hellenistic novel utopias, only brief excerpts from a few authors have survived. The tales of Theopompus of Chios, Hecataeus of Abdera, Iambulus, Euhemerus, and Antonius Diogenes can serve to illustrate the genre.[26] Like the writers of utopias during the Renaissance and the Enlightenment, some of the Hellenistic fabulists appear to have been homebodies who never ventured to far-distant lands; but they may have been inspired by the oral testimony of returned voyagers. As Thomas More later had access to the letters of Amerigo Vespucci, so Euhemerus may have heard the reports of seamen with Alexander's expedition to India. Except for Theopompus, whom exile forced to travel, little or nothing is known about the persons or social condition of the Hellenistic novelists. Some of them were probably hangers-on at the courts of the Ptolemies or the Seleucids. From the fact that Iambulus' name is said to be Syrian or Phoenician it has been surmised that he was a metic, not a proper Greek. Perhaps the intense yearning for another world that these utopias betray is the mark of a member of a disadvantaged class in the hierarchic society of the Greek occupiers of Egypt and Syria, an alienated "native," solacing himself with a reverie. Then again, this may simply be exotic literature for the market.

Theopompus is less a cipher than the others. He was born in Chios in 377/376 B.C. and early became one of the wandering Greeks of the time of troubles. His family, banished because of its Spartan sympathies, was ultimately restored by Alexander for its opposition to the pro-Persian oligarchy of the island. On the death of Alexander, Theopompus, whose passionate temperament and vituperative judgments won him a host of enemies, had to flee to Egypt, and Ptolemy, even though well-disposed toward writers and artists, considered doing away with him. Having resolved to devote himself to historical research, Theopompus moved throughout the eastern Mediterranean gathering materials for what was to be a continuation of Thucydides down to the year 394 B.C., though written, he bragged, in a style superior to his predecessor's. The result was the *Hellenika*. When his interests switched to contemporary history, he composed the fifty-eight books of a *Philippika*. Of these ambitious undertakings only disjointed pieces have been collected, a hodgepodge of history and myth. Generally Theopompus' reputation among ancient historians was not good, though at the present time his stock is rising. Our concern with him derives solely from a brief digression in his long historical panegyric on Philip of Macedon, for which the classicist Erwin Rohde included him among the Greek utopians—though not without raising a minor learned controversy in the leisurely world of late nineteenth-century German scholarship over the intent of the fragment.

After recounting various prophecies and dreams in the eighth book of the

Philippika and boasting that he knew more about India than either Herodotus or Ktesias, Theopompus launched into a description of the Meropians and other fictitious peoples. The story begins with King Midas of Phrygia, who outwitted Silenus by getting him drunk and manacling him in the depths of a well full of wine. Upon awakening from his stupor, the demigod was forced to reveal his secret wisdom as the price of release. In his response Silenus delivered himself of a lament on the wretchedness of mankind in the rest of the world, in contrast to the happiness of a vast continent situated at the end of the earth, beyond the ocean seas in which the islands of Europe, Asia, and Africa were afloat. There men and beasts grew to enormous size and lived twice as long as ordinary creatures. The two largest cities were Eusebes (Pious) and Machimos (Bellicose). In Eusebes the inhabitants were always at peace and the soil offered its products spontaneously, without being worked. The Eusebians were free from disease and died as cheerfully as they lived. The gods often visited them in tribute to their renowned piety. Men of Machimos, not quite so peace-loving, died hurling rocks at one another. Their land was rich in precious metals, but gold was valued less than was iron among the Greeks. Apparently they had once crossed over to the islands of the known world; when, however, they encountered the Hyperboreans, reputed the happiest of men, they turned back at the sight of so much misery. The huge continent was also peopled by the Meropians, perhaps named for Merope, daughter of Helios. (Through the centuries personifications of the sun constantly reappear in utopian stories and experiments.) Meropians had many great cities, but the most remarkable spot was the pitlike Anostos (Place of No Return), located at the extreme boundary of their land, and surrounded by the River of Mourning and the River of Desire. Those who ate of the fruit trees along the River of Mourning cried themselves to death, and those who ate of the fruit trees along the River of Desire grew progressively younger until they faded away into nothingness. Apart from these fancies about different ways of dying, a recurrent utopian theme in Western society, Theopompus offers nothing very convincing about the bliss of the Meropians. The survival of the fable is due in large measure to its inclusion in the third-century compilation of sundries on human life and history, the *Varia Historia,* written in Greek by Claudius Aelian, a Roman of freedman stock.[27] (There are also brief references to the Meropians in Tertullian's *De Pallio* and *Adversus Hermogenem.*)[28] If Clement of Alexandria is to be credited, Theopompus himself, something of a Machimonian, had strong convictions about the way to die. If life were secure, he wrote, it would be reasonable to wish for its prolongation; but since it was threatened by so many imminent perils, it was better by far to court death in battle.

The Hyperboreans rivaled the Meropians as exemplars of people actually living in a golden-age condition. The quest for a source of all wisdom was rather frequent in the cosmopolitan world of the Hellenistic period. Even Pyrrhonism could, like all extreme skepticism, conceal longings for a perfect good and a supreme wisdom to be discovered in far-off places—now in India, now in Egypt, now among the Jews. Hecataeus of Abdera, mentioned by Josephus as a contemporary of Alexander's who lived at the court of the first Ptolemy, is said to have been a follower of Pyrrhon. Though there are many passages in the poets praising the virtues of the Hyperboreans, who lived beyond the North Wind, Hecataeus was the first, or so at least it is recorded in the scholia to Apollonius Rhodius, to undertake writing a whole book about them. Only brief summaries of the work are extant, in the universal history of Diodorus Siculus, written in Greek in the first century before the Christian era, and in Claudius Aelian's *De natura animalium,* another of his miscellanies.

In the second of the forty books of his history, Diodorus, without discriminating between mythical and contemporary peoples, treats of the Hyperboreans, Indians, Scythians, and Amazons. Of the last, however, whose historicity he is inclined to accept, he grants that what he has to say is "so marvellous that it will resemble a tale from mythology."[29] The Hyperboreans live in the regions beyond the Celtic territory on an island as large as Sicily, enjoy great abundance, and are devoted to Apollo. Since there are two harvests a year and a favorable climate, they have leisure to play the lyre and sing the praises of the god—the equivalent to the eternal harp playing and golden horn blowing of Judeo-Christian heaven. There is on the island a magnificent precinct dedicated to Apollo, in the midst of which a spherical temple stands. The Hyperboreans are well-disposed toward the Greeks, especially the Athenians and the Delians, and there is a tradition among them that in olden times Greeks had landed on the island, leaving rich offerings. Modern scholars have proposed that the tale of the Hyperboreans indicates an early acquaintance of the Greeks with the inhabitants of Britain, and that the sacred precinct of Apollo is none other than Stonehenge.[30] Astronomic and religious elements are interwoven in Diodorus Siculus' version. "They say also that the moon, as viewed from this island, appears to be but a little distance from the earth and to have upon it prominences, like those of the earth, which are visible to the eye. The account is also given that the god visits the island every nineteen years, the period in which the return of the stars to the same place in the heavens is accomplished; and for this reason the nineteen year period is called by the Greeks the 'year of Meton.' At the time of this appearance of the god he both plays on the cithara and dances continuously the night through from the vernal equinox until the rising of the Pleiades, expressing in this manner his delight in his successes."[31]

Aelian's *De natura animalium,* also drawing upon Hecataeus, further elaborates upon the grandeur of the Hyperborean religious ceremonial. "This god has as priests the sons of Boreas and Chione, three in number, brothers by birth, and six cubits in height. So when at the customary time they perform the established ritual of the aforesaid god, there swoop down from what are called the Rhipaean mountains Swans in clouds, past numbering, and after they have circled round the temple as though they were purifying it by their flight, they descend into the precinct of the temple, an area of immense size and of surpassing beauty. Now whenever the singers sing their hymns to the god and the harpers accompany the chorus with their harmonious music, thereupon the Swans also with one accord join in the chant and never once do they sing a discordant note or out of tune, but as though they had been given the key by the conductor they chant in unison with the natives who are skilled in the sacred melodies. Then when the hymn is finished the aforesaid winged choristers, so to call them, after their customary service in honour of the god and after singing and celebrating his praises all through the day, depart."[32]

The Hyperboreans have an existence independent of Hecataeus of Abdera, for they are usually included in the works of Roman geographers and in universal compendia by such authors as Pliny the Elder. From these Latin compilations the Hyperboreans made their way into medieval travel literature and the writings of the Renaissance polyhistors; and once in print the utopianized Hyperboreans, in any number of versions, were available to seventeenth- and eighteenth-century authors. Some isolated details of their works can be traced all the way back to Greek and Roman sources; others are later accretions; and the minor innovation that each new treatment introduced is often revelatory of the sensibility of the historical moment in which it was invented.

Pomponius Mela of Tingentera (near Gilbraltar), for example, included the Hyperboreans in the third book of *De chorographia,* a survey of universal geography written in the first century A.D. either under Gaius or early in the reign of Claudius. His Hyperboreans live on the spontaneous products of a land of woods and groves and are spared the back-breaking labor of agriculture. Arboriculture is generally the utopian symbol of freedom from the curse of toil on the land—Fourier, for example, showed a predilection for fruit-picking over hoeing. Though the Hyperboreans have themselves remained just and honest, they have come to experience the wickedness of neighboring peoples to whom they once blindly entrusted maidens with first fruits destined for delivery to Delos. Pomponius Mela's Hyperboreans live longer than other peoples, but they too must finally die, and the problem of how to terminate a paradisaical existence is resolved in a rather original manner that was imitated by a number of seventeenth- and eighteenth-century utopians. Excessively long life can become a curse, one of the cruelest mockeries of man's utopian passion for longevity, as it does in Swift's depiction of the loathsome *struldbrugs,* who are immortal. Some seventeenth-century utopias, such as Gabriel de Foigny's *La Terre australe connue,* after wrestling with death in utopia, invent pleasant forms of suicide, as had the Meropians. Pomponius Mela describes the Hyperboreans' search for death in the fullness of time. "And when sufficiency of living rather than boredom has come upon them, laughingly they wreath their heads with garlands and throw themselves headlong into the sea from a certain rock. This is their strange funeral rite."[33] In passing, Pomponius Mela, like so many utopians, had a flash of self-revelation: We Romans feel *taedium;* the fortunate Hyperboreans die when they reach *satietas,* sufficiency of living.

Pliny the Elder's *Natural History* added nothing to the utopia of the Hyperboreans beyond a circumstantial description of their way of life during the six-month day (a chronological deceleration others had previously noted): "They sow in the morning periods, reap at midday, pluck the fruit from the trees at sunset, and retire into caves for the night."[34] Similar pictures of the Hyperboreans appeared in Solinus in the third century and in Martianus Capella in the fifth. Thenceforth the Hyperboreans became fixtures in Western utopian fantasy, especially after Diodorus Siculus, Pliny the Elder, and Pomponius Mela were printed.

Iambulus is known to us primarily through Lucian, who satirized him in *A True Story,* and Diodorus Siculus, who summarized his adventure to the Islands of the Sun, as he did the tale of the Hyperboreans in Hecataeus of Abdera and Euhemerus' novel about Panchaïa. The significance of Iambulus for the utopian imagination was enhanced by his inclusion in Giovanni Battista Ramusio's mid-sixteenth-century collection of voyages, in which the great Renaissance compiler of travel literature translated the fragment from Diodorus

Siculus into Italian and devoted a rather extended and sophisticated discussion to the authenticity of Iambulus as history. Without delivering a clear-cut verdict, Ramusio suggested that the story was part truth, part fable. In a French translation of the work of the Moorish traveler Leo Africanus published in Lyons in 1556, Iambulus' story and Ranusio's commentary were appended among records of other voyages, thus implying that Iambulus' account could be credited.[35]

According to the narrative, Iambulus was a learned young man who, upon inheriting his father's business, traveled as far as the southwest corner of Arabia in pursuit of trade. There he and a companion were seized by brigands, who made shepherds of them. Subsequently captured by the Ethiopians, they were put into a boat with six months' provisions and cast out to sea as an expiatory offering that was made every six hundred years; Iambulus and his comrade were threatened with death if they should turn back. By sailing directly south, after a four-month voyage they came upon a group of seven islands similar in size and equidistant from one another. Since they were located near the equator, night and day were of the same duration. The surrounding waters were sweet, the climate mild; hot and cold springs abounded; fruits were plentiful and ripened throughout the year as in Homer's land of the Phaeacians, cited by Iambulus for comparison. To his paraphrase of Iambulus on the fertility of the islands and the lushness of all growing things, Diodorus appends a tacit stricture against contemporary gluttons. The islanders "do not indulge in the enjoyment of this abundance without restraint, but they practise simplicity and take for their food only what suffices for their needs. Meat and whatever else is roasted or boiled in water are prepared by them, but of all the other dishes ingeniously concocted by professional cooks, such as sauces and the various kinds of seasonings, they have no notion whatsoever."[36]

Whether because of their abstemiousness or not, the inhabitants, who are devoted to all branches of learning including astrology (as Iambulus himself was reputed to be), are of great physical beauty, with hairless bodies that are vigorous and supple and bones as sinewy as muscles. They are rarely afflicted with disease, but after reaching the stipulated age of 150 they take their own lives by lying down upon a special plant with the property of lulling them to sleep and imperceptibly killing them. Their social organization is simple. They live in kinship groups of about four hundred, led by the eldest, practice division of labor, do not marry, and suckle and rear children in common, mothers often failing to recognize their own offspring. Among the more dubious blessings of the islanders are their double tongues, which enable them not only to imitate various forms of human and animal speech but also to converse with two persons at one and the same time.

Euhemerus is a name to which a body of ideas and doctrines have been attached through the centuries, and it is now virtually impossible to discover the true Euhemerus in the welter of stray references to what is usually called *The Sacred Description* in classical literature and in the Church Fathers. He is as unknowable as the origin of the gods whose divinity he is said to have debunked. Nothing by Euhemerus himself has been preserved and most of the purported quotations from his novel were first written down hundreds of years after his death. Majority opinion among scholars now makes him out to have been a native of Messene, though whether the Peloponnesian Messene or the Sicilian

Messina is undetermined. Other testimony that he was from Agrigentum or Chios or Cos has been rejected. His dates are equally uncertain. According to Diodorus Siculus, the prologue to the *Sacred Description* claimed that Euhemerus' voyage to the island of Panchaïa somewhere in the Indian Ocean was undertaken at the behest of Cassander, King of Macedon, who is linked to utopian exploits also through his eccentric brother Alexarchus. The poet Callimachus has Euhemerus writing in an Alexandrian temple beyond the city limits after his return from his travels.[37] One authority dates Euhemerus' voyage to the last years of the fourth century and the composition of the account to about 270 B.C., when he was an old man.

The work is expressive of the general political and moral disarray following the death of Alexander. Like other Hellenistic novels it is escape literature with standard exotic motifs. The drafting of an atheist manifesto may not have been its author's original purpose; but once the work was read in this spirit, its religious iconoclasm was accepted as the central theme. There is far more evidence about the uses to which the novel was put in later centuries—and it had a long history—than about Euhemerus' intention in writing it, more about its influence than the thing itself.

The *Sacred Description* is known primarily from substantial excerpts in Diodorus Siculus and references in Lactantius' *Divine Institutes,* the latter based on a Latin translation said to have been made by the poet Ennius.[38] In the late classical world Euhemerus was brought on stage by two opposing parties: The defenders of paganism like Callimachus, Eratosthenes, Polybius, and Plutarch attacked him as an atheist, while the Church Fathers, beginning with Clement of Alexandria, quoted him to prove conclusively through the testimony of a pagan himself that the gods of Olympus were mere political fabrications. The pagan and Christian polemists who created Euhemerus' reputation were far less absorbed in the social order of Panchaïa, which interests us, than Euhemerus' supposed discovery of a stele on which the deeds of King Zeus and his forebears, all of them men, not gods, were commemorated. The finding of King Zeus's grave was final demonstration of the human and historical birth of the gods.

The Epicurean philosophy of Lucretius meshed well with the apparently antireligious implications of the *Sacred Description.* The historical interpretation of the origin of the gods in the pagan pantheon, in contrast with the divine revelation of the true religion, was welcome to both the Greek and the Latin Fathers of the Church, and Euhemerus was quoted with great regularity in ecclesiastical apologetics. With the Renaissance revival of interest in patristic literature, the Church Fathers' interpretation of the doctrine of Euhemerus was widely adopted in secular studies of ancient history, and by the seventeenth century a "euhemeristic" reading of pagan mythology had virtually supplanted the allegorical readings that the Stoics had introduced. Isaac Newton, in his less-well-known role of mythographer, for example, still cited "Euhemerus the Coan" with approval. On the rare occasions when Renaissance writers referred to the social order on the island rather than the stele of King Zeus, as Alberti did in his *De re aedificatoria* (*Ten Books on Architecture*), the Panchaïans were treated as a historical people.

The finding of the stele is only one incident in the total description of the island, and the work belongs to the general category of Hellenistic novels that

were written as geography or travel literature and that seem to have had a utopian slant. While Euhemerus may conceivably have participated in voyages to
Arabia and India led by Alexander's admirals, much of the narrative is imaginary and the attempts to locate Panchaïa precisely are failures. The portrayal of
the island is in the accepted utopian vein: It is rich in flowers and fruit trees and
springs of fresh water. According to the historical traditions Euhemerus is
supposed to have gathered, Zeus, a King in Crete, had once headed an expedition of his countrymen all the way to Panchaïa, where in their new homeland
they constituted themselves a priesthood, the first of three castes, to whom
were assigned the artisans. The second caste consisted of farmers, the third of
soldiers, to whom were attached the shepherds. Together they fashioned a
perfect functional society. In addition to the indigenous Panchaïans, the settlers on the island included immigrant Scythians, Cretans, Indians, and Ocean-
ites, an admixture that perhaps reflects the universalism furthered by Alexander's imperial ambitions. The castes were more or less equal in prestige
except for the priests, who had a loftier status than the rest, exercised final authority in community affairs, and enjoyed the trappings of luxury and refinement in their style of life. The pattern, it has been pointed out, is not a revolutionary departure from the general plan of an ideal society put forth by
Hippodamus of Miletus, which Aristotle had criticized along with Plato's *Republic*. Houses and gardens were privately held by the Panchaïans, but all products and revenues were turned over to the priests, who allotted a just share to
every man—reserving for themselves twice as much as for the others. Though
a general spirit of equality predominated, there were incentives to stimulate
production, and a wise exploitation of the natural riches of the soil and the
mines of precious metals had led to prosperity.

Historians and geographers had described similar, tightly knit, caste societies in India and Egypt, with no crossing of social barriers, each caste exclusively dedicated to a single occupation. Megasthenes listed seven hereditary
castes in his description of India, and Herodotus recorded the existence of
cowherds, swineherds, tradesmen, boatmen, and interpreters, in addition to
the privileged soldiers and priests, in Egypt.[39] Perhaps the major difference between the social pattern of the empires with which the Greeks were coming
into closer contact during Alexander's conquest and the ideal cities that had
been proposed before in the Hellenic world was the intrusion of a separate,
independent sacerdotal class of great importance. A caste of this dimension
was rather alien to Greek life. The seclusion of the priestly order of Panchaïa in
a sacred precinct called Panara, the riches of the temple, and the profuse display
of ornaments connected with religious worship were Oriental rather than
Greek. Euhemerus' utopia represents the syncretism of Greek and Asiatic elements that Alexander himself had dreamed of—an Oriental environment and
Greek principles.

The significance of the gold stele in the sacred temple, written in King
Zeus's own hand and enumerating his exploits, was far from atheistic. The
King in Panchaïa was made a god because of his benefactions to mankind. This
did not resemble the creation of a remote Pharaonic image of a king-god, but
was similar to the Hellenistic deification of kings in whom the divine quality of
reason was worshiped. Euhemerus had no "euhemeristic" or atheistic motives
in writing the work; he may even have been furthering the policy of the Helle-

nistic monarchs by showing that the great gods of the Greco-Roman cult themselves had their origins in the gratitude of mankind for the services that King Zeus as a man had rendered his subjects and that the lesser deities were meritorious subalterns upon whom Zeus the conqueror had lavished honors. There are passages in Euhemerus that seem to point to an original worship of natural forces among the inhabitants of Panchaïa prior to the divinization of King Zeus, and this may make Euhemerus a prototype of those worshipers of nature who so often people utopias ancient and modern.

This is far from the spirit in which Euhemerus has been read through the ages. Divinization of kings in the later euhemeristic interpretations usually implied trickery and deceit, when it did not involve the reduction of "sacred history" to court scandal, as in the speech of the cook in Athenaeus' *Banquet of the Learned:* "You evidently do not know, gentlemen of the banquet, that even Cadmus, the grandfather of Dionysus, was a cook. They all fell silent at this and he went on: Euhemerus of Cos, in the third book of his *Sacred Register,* tells a story on the authority of the Sidonians that Cadmus was the king's cook, and that, taking Harmonia, a flute-player who also belonged to the king, he eloped with her."[40]

Of *The Marvels beyond Thule* by Antonius Diogenes there remains only a long summary which the ninth-century Patriarch of Constantinople, Photius, included in his compilation *The Library.*[41] The manuscript text was in Cardinal Bessarion's famous collection and was given to the Republic of Venice in 1469. It was first published in 1601 in an Augsburg edition by David Hoeschel; a Latin translation by André Schott followed five years later. Though utopian elements in the Antonius Diogenes piece are slight, the romance is the prototype of a literary genre with pretensions to being more than picaresque novels. The confluence of plots enfolding subplots, the amorous episodes, the description of fortunate peoples in distant lands, and the simplistic morality—evildoers are ultimately punished, virtuous ones delivered from harm—reappear in many seventeenth- and eighteenth-century "extraordinary voyages." Antonius is believed to have been a Greek living under Roman rule, either the freedman of a Roman or a recent Roman citizen who assumed his patron's name. The latest possible date for the novel is about A.D. 300, since it is mentioned by Porphyry in his biography of Pythagoras. Rohde pushes Antonius back to the second half of the second century, before Lucian.

In the opening scene, set in Tyre, the aged hero Dinias is conversing with his fellow countryman Kymbas, come to fetch him back to the community of the Arcadians. Since he is too old to travel any more, he refuses to accompany Kymbas. Instead, he regales him with an account of his life since leaving his homeland, and enjoins Kymbas' companion, who is literate, to inscribe his deeds on tablets of wood—in duplicate. In some respects we may consider ourselves fortunate to possess no more than Photius' précis of the long-drawn-out recital of misfortunes. Dinias and his son Demochares had left home on a quest for knowledge. Traveling over the Black Sea and the Caspian and passing the Rhipaean mountains, they moved on to the Eastern ocean and the lands of the rising sun. After many taxing adventures they finally reached the island of Thule. There Dinias fell in love with Derkyllis, a young noblewoman of Tyre who had herself got to Thule by a circuitous route. She had been forced to flee her home because she and her brother, Mantineas, through the machinations of the wicked Egyptian priest Paapis, had involuntarily put their parents into a deathlike sleep. Her path had led to Rhodes, Crete, and Italian Cimmeria, where she descended to Hades and was shown about under the guidance of a former servant. Up from Hades, she visited the grave of the Siren in the company of Keryllus and Astraeus, from whom she learned a good deal about Pythagoras. They then repaired to a city in Iberia whose inhabitants saw only by night, pressed on to the wild Celts, and returned to Spain among a people whose women did the fighting. In Sicily Derkyllis was seized by a tyrant. She rediscovered her brother, long separated from her, and heard his stories of strange lands, animals, and plants. In a renewed encounter with Paapis, Derkyllis and her brother succeeded in stealing his magic. An oracle consulted about the thralldom of the young Tyrians advised Derkyllis to go to Thule, where after much suffering she would be able to expiate her unwitting parricide. Derkyllis and her brother arrived with the evil Paapis in hot pursuit. By spitting at them, he made them die every day and allowed them to revive only at night. Paapis finally met his end at the hands of a Thule man enamored of Derkyllis. From the priest's magic books the brother and sister learned how to break his spells, and forthwith returned to Tyre to awaken their parents from the trance—but not before they imparted their harrowing tales to Dinias, who incorporates them into his narrative.

With the departure of Derkyllis and Mantineas, Dinias and his son resumed their journey northward. They came to a region under the arctic circle, where days and nights of a month's or even a year's duration were not exceptional. At last the two wanderers touched upon the moon, whose inhabitants enjoyed the immediate fulfillment of their personal prayers. When this lunar power was bestowed on Dinias, he had himself transported straightway to Tyre, where he was reunited with Derkyllis and eventually sought out by the Arcadian emissaries. His autobiography completed, Dinias conveyed one copy to Derkyllis, with the request that at his death it be entombed with him. And, Antonius recounts, the story came to light through the accidental unearthing of the tablets during Alexander's conquest of Syria.

The Hellenistic novels have more to do with the literary form and exotic spirit of many baroque utopias than with their thought content. The hero-narrator of the Hellenistic utopian novel tends to be a rather rigid figure who hardly utters a word on his own and betrays no emotional response to hair-raising events. This blasé protagonist gets lost or is shipwrecked, observes, sometimes falls in love, returns to the Greek world, and writes his memoirs. The substance of the ancient novels is generally quite meager, and one would hardly wish to overplay their influence. But Meropians, Hyperboreans, Arcadians, Solarians, and men of Ultima Thule became stereotypes in European utopia, bearers of pagan golden-age imagery into the Christian world.

Once Greco-Roman culture was assimilated by the church, elements from the similar though distinct Greek myth of the golden age and its variants commonly fused with visions of paradise. But on balance the Hellenic stream was tributary to the main paradisaical cult. The Church Fathers were always quick to assert that histories of the golden age in Greek poets from Hesiod on were either literary plagiarism of the true story of the Garden of Eden, or at best prefigurations. When during the classical revival of the Renaissance the imagery of the golden age threatened to establish itself as a separate entity, poets and philosophers sharply reaffirmed the religious and historical primacy of the Christian over the pagan myth, which was denigrated as mere imitation.[42] As the myth of paradise assumed a secular form in Thomas More's *Utopia* and hundreds of works were composed after his model from the sixteenth through the eighteenth centuries, pictorial details from the classical corpus of golden ages, cities of the sun, imaginary Hellenic societies, and ideal Greek philosopher-states were allowed to intrude. The underlying psychic force, however, remained profoundly Judeo-Christian. The most incongruous devices and fragments from Greek and Roman literature could be incorporated into paradise, without impairing its religious character. In the monastic visions of the Middle Ages and in the romances that flowered in the thirteenth century, Celtic and Norse myths were also admitted, as Islamic motifs had been during the Crusades, but only when they could be rendered harmonious with Judeo-Christian paradise.

3
The Great Transmission

AMONG THE HETEROGENEOUS group of ancient Greek writers who presided at the birth of modern utopia in the fifteenth and early sixteenth centuries, four are preeminent—Aristophanes, Plato, Plutarch, and Lucian. Their legacies were contradictory both in form and content, which may in some measure account for the ambiguity of spirit that often marks the utopias of the Renaissance. While the modern utopia had remote mythic origins, it also drew upon specific literary sources, some of them two thousand years old, that in the half century after the invention of printing charmed the humanist scholars as if they had been scintillating novelties.

Ancient Lawgivers

Western Europe inherited idealized images of historical ancient societies that played powerful roles in shaping fantasies of utopia—the cities of Sparta and Athens, the kingdom of Persia, and the Pythagorean settlements in Magna Graecia. There was some knowledge of the ascetic communities of the Essenes, described in Greek texts by Philo of Alexandria, but their Judaic religious character excluded them from the secular corpus. One of the oldest and most widespread Hellenic traditions imputes the promulgation of a new order of society to *nomothetai,* lawgivers, who founded or regenerated their cities. Solon, the "archon and reconciler" of early sixth-century Athens, was a historical figure who justified his intentions in verse of iambic tetrameter, fragments of which have come down to us. His constitutional reforms were analyzed by Aristotle and his biography was written by Plutarch. The dates of Lycurgus of Sparta, if he is not a mythic personage, have been set anywhere from the twelfth to the sixth century B.C., with some recent authorities preferring the late ninth. Though he is mentioned by Herodotus, the details of his achievements were delivered to the literate world by Aristotle in his *Lacedemonian Constitution* and by Plutarch in his *Parallel Lives,* which made of Lycurgan Sparta an early Greek utopia. A similar function was performed for Persia by the Athenian Xenophon (ca. 430 to ca. 354 B.C.), whose *Cyropaedia,* an idealized biography of the wise and tolerant Cyrus the Elder, founder of the Achaemenid Persian Empire in the second half of the sixth century, provided seventeenth- and eighteenth-century utopians with a third model to imitate. A fourth renowned lawgiver was Pythagoras, who lived in the late sixth and early fifth centuries and founded a religious and political order in Croton that for a while dominated the whole of the surrounding region. By Aristotle's time his communal regulations had already become legendary. In the fourth century, when Greek colonial expansion and the founding of new cities were at their height, disciples in Plato's Academy were trained as constitutional advisers and despatched throughout the Hellenic world to help institute ideal societies. These constitution-framers were venturing to do again what had already been accomplished by the revered ancients. Thus from mythic times onward there was a succession of lawgivers for ideal societies, reaching its zenith in Plato and continuing after him.

The establishment of the Pythagorean communities in southern Italy was perhaps the most famous utopian experiment of the ancient world, and it was not lost on Plato. The chronology of their rise and fall is reasonably well documented. The order was founded in Croton about 530 B.C.; as the doctrine spread, a countermovement gained strength culminating in the burning of the house of Milon; fifty years later there was a final exodus back to Greece. Whenever Pythagorean adepts, who had been initiated into an esoteric philosophy and a strict rule leading to an ideal way of life, came to power in some part of Magna Graecia, they tried to fashion the state in conformity with their mystic, aristocratic model. The reported Pythagorean admixture of political and religious elements became a utopian precedent for the German Rosicrucians of the early seventeenth century, and the manner of the Pythagorean infiltration of the civil order of southern Italy suggests comparison with the activities of Freemasonic societies in eighteenth-century Europe.[1]

But the history of the Pythagorean communal movement, of the misadventures of Plato and his disciples in trying to realize the ideal city, and of a number of similar experiences in the Hellenistic world, while they were passed on to posterity, did not exert an influence remotely comparable to that of the myths bequeathed by Athens and Sparta to future generations up to the end of the eighteenth century. At the time of Herodotus, Lycurgus was already the object of cult worship at Sparta. His new order had been approved by the oracle at Delphi, if not entirely ordained by it. Solon's law was secular; it had been dictated by his own conscience. Yet with time the polities instituted by both Solon and Lycurgus acquired a vaguely religious aura; inhabitants of both cities believed that obedience to their great lawgivers would insure prosperity, that departure from their commandments was a certain portent of communal defeat and suffering.

For Western Europeans the two polar constitutional ideals of Athens and Sparta came to represent contradictory ways of life, different psychologies, opposing views of the optimum society. Their confrontation in the Peloponnesian War has often been presented as an ideological battle, and speeches in Thucydides helped to fix the stereotypes of the Athenian and the Spartan between which later utopians felt called upon to make a choice. In modern times, the opening passages of Rousseau's *Discourse on the Arts and Sciences* are a rather shrill, melodramatic rehearsal of the ancient quarrel. In broad terms, many Christian utopias from the Renaissance through the French Revolution were either ascetic and communistic in the image of Lycurgus' Sparta or loosely democratic and tolerant of sensate pleasure in the image of Solon's Athens. There was an occasional attempt at a syncretism of elements from both; but for centuries every modern European utopian with a foot in antiquity tended to select as his model one of the two lawgivers.

Though the images of Athens and Sparta remained rather fluid, partaking of a mythic quality, after the recovery of the classical corpus a number of specific documents depicting their polities became primary sources of utopian inspiration. Beyond the restricted circle of great humanist scholars, the Athens idealized is the Athens of Plutarch's Solon and of the Periclean funeral oration of Thucydides; Sparta, that of Plutarch's life of Lycurgus. These texts formed the core of many utopias of later ages, modified only in peripheral details when writers were cognizant of other accounts of the perfect cities. Plutarch's *Parallels,* or *Parallel Lives,* was first published in Latin in Rome, 1470, through a cooperative enterprise that involved a galaxy of Italian humanists, and the sixteenth century produced authoritative Greek and Latin texts, along with a flood of translations into the major European languages. Jacques Amyot's French and Sir Thomas North's English translations became popular classics in their own right. There were only a few lawgivers in Plutarch's roster of antique heroes and they are easily recognizable as prototypes of More's King Utopus, Campanella's Sol, Vairasse's Sevarias, and a host of other fictional fathers of utopian commonwealths.

Utopians have occasionally been introspective thinkers highly self-conscious about their historical role. Solon is the first who left a moral apology for the provisions of his ideal constitution, a philosophical self-image enshrined in his poetry. From the fragments of this first Athenian poet, often writing after his hopes had been shattered and the tyrant Pisistratus had arisen, a utopia of sorts emerges. It had been Solon's dream to submit the society of Athens to *eunomia,* lawfulness, order, and *arpos,* that which is fitting, without recourse to tyranny. In all things he extolled the middle way. The people were not to be left too free, nor were they to be oppressed. He had emancipated the earth itself from the ignominy of servitude by abolishing the enslavement of farmer-citizens for debt. Athenians who had been sold into bondage abroad had been redeemed and those who once trembled before the changing moods of their masters had been liberated. In the conflict of classes, the shield of Solon's might had been opposed to both hostile parties, and neither had been allowed to win a decisive victory.

> For to the common people I gave so much power as is sufficient,
> Neither robbing them of dignity, nor giving them too much;
> And those who had power, and were marvellously rich,
> Even for these I contrived that they suffered no harm.
> I stood with a mighty shield in front of both classes,
> And suffered neither of them to prevail unjustly.[2]

The poor were granted sufficiency, the rich only that which rightfully belonged to them. In the name of conscience Solon had summoned the rich to set bounds to their arrogance and intemperance and desires for goods. He rebuked them for avarice and high-handedness and urged them to use moderation in the enjoyment of their wealth. Living in the midst of civil strife that threatened to destroy the city, he conceived of himself as the great conciliator. The early nineteenth-century French utopian, Henri Saint-Simon, assuming a similar role, addressed Solonic appeals to the men of property and the propertyless—it was his mission to avert revolutionary disaster.

Solon himself, especially in his youth, was committed to the intimate pleasures of love and song and wine and wrote poems in their praise, cherishing them as much as great possessions; a man could also be content with children and horses and good hunting dogs and friendship. But his vision of the good society was not privatized, and he promulgated a law, again reported by Plutarch, that disfranchised those who stood neutral in a sedition. His political ideal was a rather loose, mixed democracy that approved pleasure under restraint and sanctioned class distinction as long as the mighty kept their power in check and the masses were safeguarded from rabble-rousing demagogues.

Solon knew that there were men dissatisfied with his halfway measures in dealing with the rich, but he refused to divide the goods of the rich among the poor and to push the society into total equality. He would not equalize the men of fortune, the "good ones," with the poor, "the bad ones," in the possession of land. While he had alienated many from both parties, he had won the greater glory. What he had been able to do for the common people they had only dreamed of before. And the great and powerful would sing his praises if they but realized how a demagogue would have acted in his place. Fighting on all sides like a dog surrounded by wolves, he firmly opposed the usurpation of tyrannical power. Though some called him mad, he took the solid stance of a boundary stone between both parties. But Solon's warnings against greed and factionalism went unheeded. After he embarked on his travels abroad, dissension broke out among the people, whom he compared to a calm sea whipped into turbulence by unscrupulous leaders, and ended only with the ascendancy to power of the tyrant Pisistratus.

If utopianism were restricted to confidence in the possibility of a life of perfect felicity, then it could hardly embrace Solon's credo. In the famous anecdote of his confrontation with King Croesus, reported by Plutarch, Solon philosophized about the vicissitudes of fortune and the folly of judging happy a life that had not yet reached its end. "O king of Lydia, as the Deity has given us Greeks all other blessings in moderation, so our moderation gives us a kind of wisdom which is timid, in all likelihood, and fit for common people, not one which is kingly and splendid. This wisdom, such as it is, observing that human life is ever subject to all sorts of vicissitudes, forbids us to be puffed up by the good things we have, or to admire a man's felicity while there is still time for it to change. For the future which is advancing upon every one is varied and uncertain, but when the Deity bestows prosperity on a man up to the end, that man we consider happy; to pronounce anyone happy, however, while he is still living and running the risks of life, is like proclaiming an athlete victorious and crowning him while he is still contending for the prize; the verdict is insecure and without authority." Plutarch observes drily that after this sermon Solon departed from the royal presence, "leaving Croesus vexed, but none the wiser for it."[3]

Ever since Aristotle's discussion in the *Politics,* there have been academic disputes about the precise character of the historical Solonic reform; but Solon left behind the image of a benign democratic lawgiver who rose above the interests of faction to bestow an "admirably tempered" constitution upon Athens, a model for later times. Pericles' funeral oration, that masterpiece of Athenian smugness, far exceeded the moderate self-appreciation of Solon's utopia.

Athenian society as described by Thucydides and Plutarch had less attraction for some utopians than Sparta, whose authoritarian nature was more in tune with their regulatory passion. Fundamentally, Plato's *Laws* and Plutarch's Spartan fantasy reinforced each other. If on his travels Lycurgus was influenced by Cretan practice, as his ancient biographers report, then it is of no significance whether Plato in the *Laws* was inspired directly by Crete or drew upon Spartan institutions that still bore the imprint of Lycurgus.

What we know about the laws of Lycurgus derives mainly from Herodotus, Plato, Xenophon, Aristotle, and above all Plutarch. Virtually nothing about the subject enjoys a general consensus, neither the historicity of Lycurgus, his dates, his actual reforms as distinguished from earlier and later Spartan customs imputed to him, nor the purpose and meaning of the innovations with which he is credited. The most modern, sophisticated, textual hypercritics of the sources differ widely among themselves. The account in Plutarch is the most circumstantial, but contemporary reading of this text departs from the rather loose, commonsensical one that prevailed in Western Europe—before our time.

Plutarch's description of Lycurgus' Spartan constitution drew not only from Plato and Aristotle but from direct observation, albeit when he visited Sparta the ancient institutions had long since become corrupted. Whether or not Lycurgus the lawgiver of Sparta was a historical figure, the institutions identified with his name became influential in designs for a hard, ascetic utopia. There is scarcely a detail of the constitution of Sparta and the way of life Plutarch described that failed to be picked up and incorporated into some seventeenth- or eighteenth-century utopia. While historical Athens left the memory of a rather easygoing society devoted to the arts but contaminated with moral faults, Sparta in its period of obedience to the laws of Lycurgus was the archetype of the most upright commonwealth. The civic virtues of the Spartans and their sense of duty were praised, and their military success made their constitution worth emulating.

Sparta became the example of perfect social cohesion, of patriotic devotion, to be admired by the young of all nations. "No man was allowed to live as he pleased; but in their city, as in a military encampment, they always had a prescribed regimen and employment in public service, considering that they belonged entirely to their country and not to themselves . . ."[4] If later more enlightened generations were repelled by the inhumanity of the Spartan treatment of the Helots, they merely passed over it in silence, keeping the remainder of the utopia intact. When Christian Europe made extramarital sexual relations, even with their husbands' consent, a heinous crime for women, the adulators of Lycurgan Sparta simply denied the charge that such practices had ever existed among its citizens. The Spartan encouragement of amorous relationships among men could be eliminated or overlooked. The strict educational system, the common tables, the suppression of individual caprice, the egalitarianism, the continence, the abstinence, the obedience became much-exalted attributes of the ideal society. The anecdotes in Plutarch's Lycurgus about the fortitude and courage and bravery and self-effacement of the Spartans were cited to inculcate similar virtues in the young. Schoolchildren were brought up on the tale of the unflinching boy who was disemboweled by a stolen fox that he concealed on his person, but who would not reveal his theft.

Sparta was a warrior state that spent its whole existence either fighting or preparing for battle. From birth to death the agents of the state—the kings, elders, and appointed platoon leaders—supervised every act of life. Among themselves all Spartans were equal. The division of the land into lots of the same size, which Lycurgus had enforced, set the pattern for future utopian plans of agrarian communism. Marriage was totally subordinate to eugenic purpose, the procreation of strong progeny fit for battle. Women as well as men were toughened because of a prevalent belief that their state of health at the time of conception would determine the strength of the child. This emphasis upon the physical training of women as well as men was in sharp contrast to the softness and luxury in which upper-class women lolled in advanced societies that produced utopias.

Marital customs that even Plutarch regarded as rather bizarre were observed: An older man might persuade a younger to inseminate his wife, and women might be granted to eugenically sound men who desired them. Some of the sexual regulations, such as the dressing of women in men's clothing and the shearing of their hair on the wedding night, the brevity of the early heterosexual encounters followed by the return of the young husbands to the sleeping quarters of their fellows, may today be interpreted in homosexual terms, but Plutarch praised them both on eugenic grounds and as a means of keeping the flame of passion alive. As late as the end of the eighteenth century, the prolific French utopian Restif de la Bretonne devised all manner of social mechanics to prevent young married couples from having easy access to each other, in order to stimulate desire. Childless men, barren women, were held in disrespect by the Spartans, and bachelors were subjected to a humiliating ritual that involved walking about in wintertime scantily clad and singing satirical songs about themselves because they did not allow their vital energy to function. Spartan marriage remained outlandish to Europeans, even after their travel and exploration literature had acquainted them with strange practices.

Infants were subjected to the test of a wine bath, Plutarch relates, in order to ferret out those weaklings who should be exterminated in accordance with the Spartan criteria. Present-day commentators stress the ritualistic character of this baptism, of which the ancients do not seem to have been aware. Children were taken away from their parents at an early age and reared along with their peers under the strict supervision of state authorities. The paideia was unintellectual, consecrated to the development of the body, the suppression of the ego, the promotion of military skills, and above all the flowering of the virtues of courage and self-control. Discipline for endurance, initiated at birth, was meant to produce hardy warriors, and the killing of the weak was looked upon as a necessity. Punishments were severe and to a reader unilluminated by the newer sciences either outrageously cruel or downright peculiar: Not many would interpret a supervisor's biting the thumb of a pupil who replied stupidly to a moral question as a propitiatory act to protect the young Spartan's power. And teaching boys to steal was regarded by innocent Christian readers as a great blotch on the Spartan escutcheon. Not until classical scholarship met up with anthropology was the scourging of Spartan boys interpreted as a fertility rite and the encouragement of their thefts as a way of nourishing an impulse to arrogate to themselves the military and sexual powers of the elders, whom they were dispossessing of food.

The boys and men seem to have spent most of the time in one another's company exercising, learning the art of war, eating, and sleeping together. Plutarch describes them as jocular, given to bons mots and intolerant of long speeches. He readily acknowledged that there was intense love among members of the same sex. Respect for a higher age class was one of the bases of the whole structure. Since Lycurgus had divided the land equally, all Spartans contributed to the common table, but only that which was necessary. Luxuries were banned and a few tonsorial and sartorial embellishments were allowed only on the eve of war. There was competition among the Spartans in sport and in military skill, and those young men who were deficient were mocked at ceremonial games by half-naked maidens, participants in the formal processions. Each Spartan rejoiced in victory, not for himself but for the state, and there was no envy. Priests did not play a great role in the portrait of this society of warriors, though war and gymnastics had a solemn religious character.

Vices such as adultery without the husband's consent were unknown among Plutarch's Spartans. Drunkenness was discouraged in the young by showing them intoxicated Helots, and gluttony was impossible because food was available only in sparse quantities and at the common table. While arts pandering to luxury were forbidden, martial music and heroic poetry were fostered. With such superb moral and physical training the Spartans advanced in battle without quivering and were never defeated. At the same time they were generous to the vanquished and refrained from hacking them to pieces—a stratagem that encouraged their enemies to surrender.

This society of total dedication to physical and moral training did not allow for any work on the part of the citizenry. For this purpose they had serfs and slaves, whom they treated with great severity lest they revolt. To terrorize their Helots, young Spartans were encouraged on occasion to go into the fields and slaughter some of them. Spartans did not engage in trade. Migration and travel were prohibited, and foreigners were not admitted among them lest they introduce alien corruption.

According to Herodotus, the changes introduced by Lycurgus had brought about a total reversal of Spartan fortunes. From a period of depression and constant defeat at the hands of the Tegeans, the Spartans suddenly emerged victorious and had remained so ever since. Thucydides too imputed Sparta's power in the latter part of the sixth century to the Lycurgan reform three or four centuries earlier. Both historians created the image of a city-state whose very nature was changed by a revolutionary reform that brought triumph instead of defeat on the field of battle and established a durable, constant order. Later utopians constantly adverted to the intimate connection between the Lycurgan reform and subsequent military victory. Crediting the fathers of Greek history, a European utopian who wished to depict a state that had endured and achieved success in war chose Sparta, the perfect model of a "well-ordered government."

Aristophanes and Lucian Christianized

The Renaissance humanists received the writings of Plato, Aristophanes, and Lucian as if they had been composed by contemporaries, and felt a peculiar closeness toward these classical authors. More and Erasmus lived with them as intimately as with each other. But the humanists were acutely aware of their own individuality; they adopted diverse conceptions from their favorite ancients without being dominated or overwhelmed by any one of them. More's *Utopia* is neither Platonic nor Lucianic; it is both. Aristophanes and Lucian had made fun of Socrates and were never moved by his high seriousness. Thomas More could jest about the *Republic* and at the same time live devoutly by its ideal. If Rabelais is added to the humanist brethren, the jocular so far outstrips the grave that allegiance to Aristophanes submerges any admiration for Plato.

But even in the midst of the Rabelaisian ribaldry a solemn processional tone obtrudes as in the magnificent utopian fantasy of the Abbey of Thélème. The utopia of the northern Renaissance, born of both the philosophical and the satiric Greek traditions, used and commingled the literary artifices of both, which endowed it with a special complexity.

A rather substantial corpus of works by Aristophanes and Lucian was transmitted relatively intact to the expanding European intellectual world of the fifteenth century. The fact that they had written nearly six hundred years apart and represented different literary genres did not prevent their assimilation to each other for purposes of quotation and imitation. They were ordinarily coupled and alluded to in the same breath. When the northern humanists undertook their mission to reform mankind there were no guides more ingenious than these ancient masters of the art of castigation, the great debunkers of pomposities, of arrogant official philosophers, of warrior-heroes who devastated the world, of soothsayers and false prophets who deceived and robbed the credulous, of greedy plutocrats and cruel tyrants. The humanists subtly appreciated the immunity that their ancient friends had gained by putting on the comic or satiric mask. For More, Erasmus, and Rabelais were not open rebels against their society, they were its admonishers. True, Aristophanes and Lucian did not hold up before mankind a lofty or a transcendental goal; some scholars today even doubt any moralizing intent on Aristophanes' part. But the Renaissance humanists had Jesus Christ and the evangelical spirit as their ultimate source of illumination; they needed no other. Their own profound religious commitment was never for a moment in question, and the absence of an ideal in the writings of the pagan satirists did not trouble them. Moreover, if a reformed Christianity needed counsel from an ancient philosophy in creating a model of conduct in this world, there was always Plato, or Aristotle freed from the glosses of the Schoolmen. The basic rhetorical devices of utopia were learned from Aristophanes and Lucian.

The Greeks obliquely attacked flagrant evils, such as the devastations of war, the blind lust for possession among the wealthy, the devious ways of slander, the pretensions of philosophers and system-makers, the hollow promises of demagogues, all of which were normally accepted as inevitable in the course of human affairs, by daringly experimenting with the opposite condition. The real world was turned topsy-turvy in the area on which the writer concentrated his fire. At other times they exaggerated a proposed reform or utopian scheme to monstrous proportions and unfolded its comically catastrophic results. Or they mixed the themes, both highlighting the absurdities and iniquities of this world and poking fun at panaceas and quack remedies.

What if there really were peace on earth, Aristophanes muses. He brings about a glorious epoch of tranquillity through a grotesque invention: An old man flies up to the heavens on a beetle fed by dung en route, and contrives to return to earth with the Goddess of Peace. Or a canny woman forces peace by denying the warriors access to the instrumentalities of sexual pleasure. Or two Athenians fleeing the turbulent politics of their native city build an ideal Cloudcuckooborough for the birds. Or a popular longing for common ownership or sexual freedom is appeased when a group of women, disguised and falsely bearded, seize the assembly and pass communist laws, leaving young men victims to the importunities of amorous old crones and the state paralyzed by sensible citizens who withhold their private goods from the common treasury. Through all this tomfoolery, Renaissance humanists recognized in Aristophanes a profound and serious moralist. Once the plays were printed in 1498, there was a constant stream of translations.

Aristophanes is related to the history of utopian thought through many different lines, not all in harmony with one another. When he exploited the farcical potentialities of utopias of total gratification in which no one had to work, he became a source of dystopian argument and imagery. But his jesting at an Athenian's dream of idleness did not preclude a more sympathetic treatment of the ordinary man's privations. In his last comedy, the *Ploutos,* the hardships of the virtuous poor were portrayed in a play that was one of his most popular in both the ancient and the medieval worlds. Its exposure of greed and covetous wealth fitted in with a canonical Christian denunciation of avarice, and it was more acceptable than the plays that were tainted with obscenities. Any reading of More's *Utopia* should keep in mind the *Ploutos.* It was received as a utopian fairy tale, a plain man's fantasy of the way out of his wretchedness. The change could not be effected by the state; it required an act of the gods to set straight the unjust economic order that they had established. The once purblind God of Wealth, his sight regained, no longer favored the rich rascals but shed his bounty on the deserving poor. In Aristophanes, peace, decent plenty, a chance for pleasure after work added up to a little man's commonsensical utopia. Paradoxically, he resorted to utopian extravaganzas in order to plead for the decent conditions of life that would promote domestic virtues (with occasional breaches of monogamy), home cooking, and neighborliness.

Insofar as Aristophanes' comic heroes have healthy appetites for food and sex, he belongs to the tradition that extolled robust, sensate pleasure as the most reasonable goal of the individual man. He exposed the frauds—the religious, political, philosophical pundits who could only make empty promises. The greatest banes of existence were war and poverty, which reduced men to frugal diets and sexual abstinence, and obliged them to bustle around frantically instead of taking their ease and enjoying themselves. Perhaps Aristophanes was not a moralizing pacifist, but a pacifist in the name of the lower pleasures.

Sometimes Aristophanes sounds like a staunch believer in the "good old ways." When utopian schemes exalted communism or condoned unnatural behavior, he ridiculed them to death. He was skeptical of any institutional arrangements to bring about a better world, and contented himself with negative injunctions: Stop wars, silence demagogues, banish crooked priests and pretentious philosophers. His utopia was individualist and sensate, and grandiose schemes were for the *Birds.* Aristophanes has been made out to be the conservative voice of the oligarchic faction, a rural democrat, a Panhellenist, a spokesman for the Athenian peasantry in conflict with the interests of the new urban population. More plausible is the idea that he had a utopia of his own that has been called "petty bourgeois," anachronistic as the term is when applied to fifth-century Athens.[5] To try to discover a unified political theory in Aristophanes seems fruitless. Later ages, however, admired him for his moral strictures, and this helps to account for his survival: His comedies were re-

garded as morality plays. Even if his aim was laughter and his attacks on society were in the tradition of the Old Comedy, it was the consensus of the
learned that his comedy served a high moral purpose.

In the end the opposition is not between Plato the utopian and Aristophanes
the anti-utopian, but between rival guides to the good city. While Plato regarded war as the ultimate test of the ideal city-state, Aristophanes was bored
with battle from the very beginning. All the writers of the Old Comedy were
Athenian citizens, but they were commoners, and the heroic ideal that Plato
the aristocrat embodied was alien to them. They neither despised the body nor
did they seek to suppress its natural instincts, and they preserved the materials
for a sensate utopia to which Western fantasy would return time and again
when it grew weary of Platonizing. On the eve of the Reformation, the northern humanists were not so completely immersed in Plato that they failed to
appreciate the moral worth of the sallies in Aristophanes' utopia of materialis-
tic, utilitarian common sense, which recognized the existence of the passions
and provided for their satisfaction but eschewed impractical and outlandish
plans. Peaceful work and honest allowable pleasures were never derided by
Aristophanes—a position not too far from Thomas More's in 1516, despite
their very different concepts of decorum. But if most humanists regarded
Aristophanes as a moralistic mirror of vices, for Rabelais at least he became
much more—the source book for an exuberant utopia of peace and abundance
that had a destiny of its own in European culture.

Lucian had a somewhat different fortune. He would have rejoiced at being
joined with Aristophanes—a "wise and truthful man," he said, "whose writings are distrusted without reason."[6] Though certain vulgarities had to be
overlooked, many passages out of Lucian had been used by the Church Fathers
as witness against the false pagan prophets. If Saint Gregory Nazianzen and
Saint John Chrysostom could quote him, why should northern humanists feel
inhibited? Among the small library of books Raphael Hythloday leaves with
More's Utopians, the works of Plato rank first; Aristophanes leads the list of
poets, which includes Homer, Euripides, and Sophocles; the Utopians are very
fond of Plutarch, but "captivated by the wit and pleasantry of Lucian."[7]

When Giovanni Aurispa and Francesco Filelfo brought manuscripts of Lucian's works from Constantinople in the first quarter of the fifteenth century,
the whole group of Italian humanists, Battista Guarino, Rinuccio Aretino,
Poggio Bracciolini, Giovanni Pontano, and Coluccio Salutati, set about translating them. They were joined by the Germans Rudolf Agricola and Willibald
Pirckheimer and even Philipp Melanchthon himself. More and Erasmus both
had a special predilection for Lucian. His transmission became a communal enterprise of European humanist scholarship, with each writer preparing a few
dialogues. Before 1500, at least twenty-one distinct editions of thirteen different dialogues had been published in Latin. The so-called translations are often,
more accurately, adaptations. In the Dialogues of the Dead, endings are changed
to suit current political exigencies. Melanchthon's rendering of Lucian's Slander is related to false accusations against the Lutheran reformers. More trans-
lates the Tyrannicide and then in characteristic fashion writes against it—he has
a double satisfaction. Ulrich von Hutten learned Greek in Bologna by reading
Lucian and Aristophanes, and much of the early pamphleteering of the Reformation imitated Lucian's style and literary devices.

Virtually all the major utopian themes of the novelistic Greek utopias are parodied in the *True Story* of Lucian. This second-century rhetorician and satirist had served as an administrator for the Romans in Egypt, and in the spirit of the new overlords of the Mediterranean world showed little sympathy for the utopian imagination, though he was well acquainted with its expressions from the mythic tales of the golden age through Plato and Iambulus. In his *True Story*, which was translated into Latin and published in the same volume as the first book of Diodorus Siculus' history in a 1476 edition, he indiscriminately tossed all the great philosophical and military heroes of antiquity into an island community and recounted with malicious delight the ensuing involvements — except for Plato, isolated in a republic he had constructed for himself in accordance with a constitution and laws of his own devising.

Though Lucian's aim was to satirize, his influence was not unequivocally anti-utopian, and many a light conceit from the *True Story* and the *Saturnalia* found its way into serious utopian literature. His picture of the Island of the Blessed, which he described with deliberate and studied exaggeration, piecing together a montage out of elements from the whole body of Greek utopian literature, was sometimes read as a straight-faced account. In his own way, Lucian conveniently synthesized the popular and the literary Greek utopian traditions for later generations. Seventeenth- and eighteenth-century utopia-makers in search of stage sets simply lifted them out of his writings. If Plato dominated the rational argument and formal structures of utopian thought in early modern times, it was Lucian, favorite of More and Erasmus, who supplied many of the colorful details and some of the extravagant imagery.

The inhabitants of Lucian's community of heroes and philosophers in the *True Story* knew no death and whiled away the time in pleasure and laughter. The climate was mild and constant, the fruit ever ripe. "There are great trees of the clearest glass around the table, and instead of fruit they bear cups of all shapes and sizes. When anyone comes to table he picks one or two of the cups and puts them at his place. These fill with wine at once."[8]

There was outdoor swimming in perfume and indoor swimming in great glass buildings heated with cinnamon wood, where warm dew instead of water filled the troughs. The world was suffused with the soft, gray twilight of predawn, which spared the blessed ones both darkness and the glare of day. The stillness was broken by a chorus of boys and girls directed by the great poets and alternating with a choir of singing swans, swallows, and nightingales, while the murmuring of the woods responded to the gentle zephyr. Lovemaking took place openly in the sight of all, with both men and women, who "think no shame of it at all."[9] There were no Stoics in the company — apparently, Lucian tells us, they were still climbing up the steep hill of virtue.

The friends of More who read the *Utopia* were thus prepared for this type of exercise. Lucian's mocking exaggeration and the fantasy play were part of their habitual literary practice, even in personal correspondence. But this does not mean that More's *Utopia* was merely a Lucianic performance, as one recent critic proposes, a parody of a utopia in the sense that Lucian's *True Story* was a parody of the ideal city plans and golden-age myths and fantasy places in Hellenistic novels. The majesty of Plato's presence pervades the Kingdom of Utopia. And while Lucian deliberately caricatured events so that they became unmistakable flights of fancy into the realm of the impossible and the absurd,

More employed another kind of artistry. He embraced the paradoxical in the spirit of Aristophanes and Lucian, but he incorporated into his work so many realistic details that he gave it the semblance of a genuine "true story," in a matter-of-fact, not a Lucianic, meaning.

The Baptism of Plato's Republic

The initial reception of Plato's *Republic* in fifteenth-century Europe was turbulent. It could not be assimilated casually like the works of Aristophanes and Lucian, whose obscenities were dismissed, overlooked, or expurgated as extrinsic—the privilege of jesters—while what was considered their moral teaching was appreciated and imitated. Plato, whose dialogues pretended to impart true doctrine about virtuous conduct, was encroaching upon a domain where the Church allowed for neither alternatives nor flippancy. Plato was ushered into the Latin intellectual world of the fifteenth century to the accompaniment of vitriolic attacks and counterattacks from newly arrived Greek émigrés fighting among themselves about the worth of his philosophy. Theirs was rough, partisan scholarship. When the humanist Niccolo Perotti joined the fray he demanded that Georgios Trapezuntios, one of the more contentious Byzantines, be suspended upside down and spat upon by passersby. Plato did not quietly assume his place in the calm of a Socratic dialogue or of an elegant conversation at a Medici court. From the moment of his reentry into the learned world of Europe he had to struggle for his existence.

When manuscript translations of the *Republic* into Latin began to be diffused in fifteenth-century Italy, the manifest contradiction between the ideal society of Plato and the *Ethics* and *Politics* of Aristotle, which had been an accepted part of Christian culture for more than two hundred years and had been newly translated by the Florentine humanist Leonardo Bruni in 1414 and 1437, became the focus of spirited controversy. The original motive for Pier Decembrio's translation of the *Republic* in 1437 was, he confessed, a desire to compare on his own the text of Aristotle's attack on Plato in the *Politics* with what Plato himself had written about the community of women and property in the fifth book, though Decembrio had access to the Latin version prepared three decades earlier by his father, Umberto Decembrio, and the Greek scholar Manuel Chrysoloras. After the Council of Trent (1545–1563), with its formal incorporation of Aristotle and the Scholastics as orthodoxy, there were times when an acknowledged adherence to Plato in any area of thought could be dangerous: Witness the condemnation of the *Nova Philosophia* of Francesco Patrizi, Bishop of Cherso, and its inclusion on the Index of Prohibited Books. But for more than a century after his reintroduction Plato had competed with Aristotle for the spiritual allegiance of Christian Europe, in politics as well as in metaphysics.

It is generally recognized today that emphasis on the blackout of the Platonic tradition during the Middle Ages was at one time much exaggerated. There are various kinds of latter-day Platonism, many types of *Platonici*, different aspects of Plato himself—metaphysical, theological, political, erotic, poetic—and they experienced independent fortunes. Some medieval thinkers distinguished between the cosmological Plato, author of the *Timaeus*, a *tractatus de naturali iusticia*, and the moral-political Plato, whose *Republic*, known only at second hand, was called a *tractatus de positiva* (or *populari*) *iusticia*. And there was simply no great interest in the politics of Plato until the fifteenth century. When a large number of translations, paraphrases, attacks, and apologies began to appear about mid-century, the moral and political Plato suddenly gained widespread notoriety. In addition to the Latin translations of Chrysoloras, Decembrio father and son, and Cassarino, there were esoteric works like Elia del Medigo's rendering into Latin of a Hebrew version of Averroes' Arabic paraphrase of the *Republic*. The polemics of the Greek émigré scholars Georgios Gemistos and Georgios Trapezuntios, and Bessarion's masterful reply to Plato's detractors were probably the most famous writings in a prolonged debate that involved some twenty tractates, many of which have never been printed.

The plain reason for the difference between the medieval and the Renaissance Platos was that knowledge of his writings, once limited to secondary sources (except for the *Timaeus* and parts of the *Phaedo*) was now augmented by the dialogues themselves either in Greek or in Latin. After the publication of Marsilio Ficino's translation of the Platonic corpus in 1484—a fateful year for European culture—doctrines that had once been discussed on the basis of mere hearsay or critical accounts like that of Aristotle or excerpts preserved in the Church Fathers became available in their totality, along with commentaries and summaries. And Ficino's Latin version was soon supplemented by sporadic translations into French, English, and other popular languages. In whatever tongue the Platonic dialogues on politics and morals appeared, they had the attraction of novelty and the piquancy of dangerous heterodoxy.

Even on casual acquaintance, Plato's vision of the ideal city was embarrassing to humanists who adored the spiritual beauties of his other writings. Leonardo Bruni refused to translate the *Republic* because, he said, "there are many things in these books that, to our ways, are loathsome," and for the honor of Plato it was better to leave them alone.[10] There were parts of the *Republic* that ran flatly counter to ordinary Christian moral practice, that could not readily be theologized, metaphysicized, or sublimated into expressions of divine love or mystical experience. In fact, the political Plato became a handicap to defenders of the theological or cosmological Plato. How could they accept the metaphysical ideas of a man who forthrightly espoused the community of women, infanticide, the free exercise of naked youth of both sexes, and who was suspected of condoning pederasty? The exquisite aesthetic pleasures Plato afforded the humanists, the mystical elevation of the soul experienced by those who read him in the language of Neoplatonism and Egyptian hermeticism, were marred by accusations that Plato was a threat to the Christian faith. The cosmology, the metaphysics, the moral attributes of the philosopher-king, the extolling of virtue and justice, the praise of unity and self-sacrifice, the expulsion of mendacious poets and pagan mythology were all admirable. Even communal property could be countenanced by a society that esteemed the monastic life. The doctrine of love could be sublimated, poeticized, made religious. If the Song of Songs could be allegorized, why not Platonic love? But in Plato's descriptions of educational and sexual institutions, the matter-of-fact detail resisted idealization. Other apologetic techniques had to be brought into play.

The aged Byzantine scholar Georgios Gemistos had come as an adviser to the Greek churchmen attending the Council of Florence, and had stayed to in-

sinuate more dangerous doctrines than even the heterodox theological opinions for which he was attacked by Latin ecclesiastics. Because of his learning he
was warmly received at the court of Cosimo de' Medici, and his Greek lectures
were generally acclaimed, though skeptics have questioned whether they were
much comprehended by an audience for whom Greek was still an enigma. He
was hailed as a reincarnation of Plato himself and, as if to advertise the affinity,
he added to his name the epithet Pletho, a synonym for Gemistos, or "full." In
the twentieth century this has led to alliterative flights of fancy in German
scholarship—there is a dissertation appropriately entitled *Zu Plethon und
Platon.*

Gemistos was a Platonist of the Proclus and Plotinus order, and there is a
story that he had studied with Jewish Kabbalists in Constantinople. His enthusiasm for the Platonic philosophy seemed at times to outstrip his allegiance to
Christian belief, and enemies spread word of his deathbed prophecy that a new
religion was about to supersede both Christ and Mohammed. In his tract on
the distinctions between the philosophies of Plato and Aristotle, written in
Greek and heavily weighted on Plato's side, he was not above a mean slur,
identifying Christian Aristotelians with the Muslim Averroes. While the main
thrust of his attack on Aristotle was metaphysical, he also went after the Aristotelian moral doctrine of the golden mean and, in a rather sophisticated analysis of Plato's hierarchy of virtues, condemned Aristotle for a theory of happiness that recognized no absolute spiritual perfection as the ideal.

Among the acrimonious retorts to which Gemistos' manuscript gave rise—
it was not published until 1532, some eighty years after his death—Georgios
Trapezuntios' defense of Aristotle in 1455, *Comparationes phylosophorum Aristo-
telis et Platonis,* which in turn elicited Bessarion's Platonic counteroffensive,
created the greatest stir in that close circle of scholars living in Italy. Written in
Latin, Trapezuntios' apologia (though it, too, was published posthumously)
reached a larger number of readers than Gemistos' Greek treatise. It used heavy
ad hominem arguments against Plato's person and derided the hollowness of
his rhetoric. Trapezuntios found the Trinity in Aristotle, while he contested
Plato's supposed belief in the immortality of the soul. From the *Phaedrus* he
drew inferences about the indecency of Plato's love life and then leveled a barrage against the most vulnerable sections of the *Republic,* which dealt with the
role of women and their "prostitution." The *Laws* showed Plato corrupting
the youth in drunken debauches, rousing their lusts with exercises in the nude
in which both sexes participated. Trapezuntios denounced Plato for glorifying
sins of the flesh and encouraging gluttony. And he mocked him for trying to
preserve his wretched little state with inadequate means: Restricting offspring
to two would have led to catastrophic depopulation in the event of plague.
Trapezuntios' tract in large measure determined the subjects around which
discussion of the moral and political works of Plato would revolve for many
years.

Bessarion's *In Calumniatorem Platonis libri quatuor* (Four Books against the
Calumniator of Plato), a response to Trapezuntios, contained by far the most
significant summary and defense of Plato's political ideas in the Latin world of
the fifteenth century. Originally composed in Greek, it was translated into
Latin and printed in 1469, one of the first books from a Roman press, and there
were two subsequent editions before the masterful critical publication of both

versions by Ludwig Mohler in Paderborn, 1927. Bessarion's was a pivotal role in the transmission of Plato, for he was the first to discuss the whole of Plato in all its multifarious aspects, in a printed work. Bessarion, a Byzantine monk and titular patriarch of Constantinople who favored unification and was made a cardinal in the Latin Church, exerted influence not only through his writings but also through the private academy he established in Rome, where Latins and Greeks, erudite laymen and theologians, foregathered for discussion; through his magnificent collection of manuscripts; and through his patronage of men like Lorenzo Valla, Michael Apostolios, and Francesco Filelfo whom he had known in Constantinople. Many of the ideas of the *In Calumniatorem* had been voiced in Bessarion's academy and the language retained the flavor of oral delivery.

The fourth book was devoted entirely to Plato's social, political, and sexual principles, and was more defensive than the other three. Based on traditional biographies of Plato as well as on his writings, it was the ultimate vindication of his person and his social thought. Its central topics were the doctrine of love, marital arrangements, education of the young, the general attitude toward pleasure and desire. Bessarion reminded his readers that Plato was not Christian but pagan, and therefore should not be judged by Christian standards. Keeping Christ out of utopia was to be one of the standard ways in which adventurous later writers secured for themselves a measure of latitude.

Bessarion's Plato was chaste and ascetic, ate little—mainly olives, bread, and water—and hardly slept. It was an error, Bessarion insisted, to accept the opinions of various participants in the dialogues as Plato's own. Socrates alone was his true mouthpiece and he had sharply distinguished the divine love that he apotheosized from the earthly love that was barely tolerated. He had even expelled the poets from the ideal republic for teaching immoral ideas. In the *Laws* he permitted intercourse only for the sake of progeny, and he condemned all unnatural sexual relations.

In explaining eugenic breeding and the pooling of women and children, Bessarion accepted the premises of Plato and demonstrated the consistency of his reasoning. Seeing in the meum-tuum a source of radical evil was by no means out of harmony with the dicta of many of the Church Fathers. Granted the assumption that private ownership was the root of all conflict and divisiveness in the state, it had to be eradicated completely; it would have been a betrayal of principle to eliminate individual property while retaining privacy of wives and children. Moreover, Plato had reconsidered the extreme position of the *Republic;* in the *Laws* he had permitted family life for purposes of procreation and had mitigated the rigorous austerity of total communism. But even in the *Republic,* the sexual arrangements were regulatory mechanisms serving rational social ends, not opportunities for lust. Though Plato's community of women was shocking and repugnant to the Christian conscience, many ancient peoples had practiced it—Bessarion had combed the literature—and thus it was not bizarre for earlier ages. Bessarion was not, of course, an advocate of this community; he merely found some explanation for it in terms of reason, local custom, and historical reality.

Plato had exercised foresight in devising a plan for a totally new society, Bessarion argued, for the ancient city-state was in fact breaking down. Aristotle's way, the middle way of the *Politics,* did not save it from destruction. What

Aristotle hoped to achieve through love and respect within the family, Plato had entrusted to the educative institutions of the state. Platonic education in general was deserving of high praise. Pernicious books, idolatrous conceptions, anthropomorphism, debauch were condemned, and there was strict supervision of the young, with punishment for violations of the prescribed rules of conduct and study.

Ficino's life of Plato, which introduced the Latin translation of his works, included an "Apology of Plato's Morals" with sections on his *continentia, gravitas, pietas,* and *magnanimitas.* In the commentaries that prefaced his rendering of the *Republic* and the *Laws,* Ficino advanced the same kind of arguments that Bessarion had employed against Trapezuntios. The practice of community was not outlandishly rare: It had been tried in Prague (he may have had in mind the Taborites or Hussites). He also recalled a passage in Diodorus Siculus about a communal island off the African coast—a reference to Iambulus' Hellenistic novel. Many philosophers believed that the Garamantes practiced community, as did the philosophical Brahmins, Gymnosophists, Essenes, Pythagoreans, and a number of saints of the Republica Christiana. Ficino had to admit that the rules governing sexual intercourse had something disturbing about them. But he noted as an extenuation that Socrates had made the proposals only with great trepidation and after invoking the protection of the goddess Adrastia. Furthermore, the community of women was not to be an isolated institution, but an integral part of the total equality of men and women guardians in war and in peace, and was to be strictly regulated and controlled by the magistrates. Men and women who pursued an identical course of studies were comrades-in-arms. If there were breaches of the sexual ordinances, the resultant offspring would not be killed but would be taken away and brought up in obscurity, which did not violate Christian canons. In defense of Plato's community of all things among the guardians, Ficino deplored the madness and universal discord engendered by the obsession with private property and individual ownership in his own society—a pious moral reflection that a member of Lorenzo de' Medici's grand entourage could make without upsetting the social order.

Ficino continued to exercise a subtle influence for centuries through his translation and the commentaries that accompanied it. Well up to the end of the eighteenth century anyone who read Plato in Latin absorbed the Renaissance problems and Ficino's particular brand of Platonism along with the text. The place of Ficino and other fifteenth-century apologists of Plato in the resurrection of the myth of an ideal city has usually been neglected because of the more obvious role they played in the diffusion of Neoplatonic sensibility in European literature and art. But their part in removing the stigma attached to Plato's morals and politics helped his assimilation by orthodox Christians and even by a future martyr-saint. When the English scholars who had studied in Italy brought Plato home with them, he was an idealized figure, cleansed of calumnies. The Socrates-Christ of Erasmus and Thomas More was in the offing.

Italians of the fifteenth and sixteenth centuries who apologized for Plato or were inspired by him were not engaged in putting his ideal society into practice or even recommending it; the utopia in action is a later, Reformation fantasy. Neither Bessarion nor Doni nor Patrizi entertained the notion that in

Plato's political dialogues there was a program to be implemented. They were absorbed with humanist discourse about ideal Platonic love, metaphysical forms, the Platonic paradigm of the perfect society. Utopia was the subject of intellectual disquisition: There was much worth contemplating there. To become a political program utopia had to await the millenarian zealousness of the Protestant world.

The opposition between Plato and Aristotle, which was played up in the Italian literature of the fifteenth century, should not obscure the fact that they communicated a common moral tone to the first centuries of the modern utopian tradition in the West. If one takes an overview of the whole of utopian thought, the distinction between Plato's and Aristotle's rival visions of the best commonwealth fades. The dramatic cleavage in the history comes with the materialist utopia-makers of the eighteenth century, who abandoned the glorification of spirituality. Though Aristotle's repudiation of his master's ideal society is unequivocal, even scornful, both considered utilitarian man seeking sensate pleasure as somewhat less than human. Supreme virtue or spiritual excellence, albeit differently conceived by the two philosophers, was the unquestioned goal of individual life.

Aristotle diverged sharply from Plato, however, on how much the ideal commonwealth should concede to animal elements in man. Plato would allow almost nothing, and would dole out pleasures to his guardians in driblets. While the sexual act was not quite covered with the obloquy with which Christianity invested it, fornication was considered unseemly or unnecessary in a man of virtue who had reached a certain age; and something more than minimal consumption of food was permitted only because it sustained the state's military power.

Advancing arguments that would be repeated by anti-utopians throughout succeeding ages, Aristotle balked at the rigid tripartite class division of Plato's Republic, at the degree to which specialization had been driven, at the imposition of one function upon a man for the whole of his life, at the exaggerated emphasis on unity as the end of the state. He was sensitive to the varying needs and capacities of men at different stages of the life cycle, an idea that would long be absent from utopian fantasy until it was recaptured by Restif de la Bretonne and Charles Fourier. Aristotle drew his military guardians only from the young; in the fullness of manhood they advanced to the magistracy; and in old age they became keepers of the sacred precincts. Plato's rulers and military auxiliaries were categorized for life. Aristotle was impressed with the intensity of the passion for equality—it was the motive drive behind all revolutions in the city—and under ideal circumstances he would give every freeman a chance to exercise some form of authority.

For Aristotle the total communism that Plato decreed for the guardians and his abolition of the family made paternal and filial love watery since it was spread over a whole age-group, and excluded warm personal friendships, which could not be cemented with generous gifts once private ownership had been outlawed. Though both Plato and Aristotle eschewed the extremes of great riches and wretched poverty as destroying any feeling of community in the city, Aristotle rejected pure communism as too restrictive and inflexible to sustain the good life. He viewed externals such as status, honors, property as real, not factitious, goods, as inducements, not impediments, on the path to virtue. He seemed to doubt the worth of the very myth of an ideal city, though his *Ethics* and *Politics* were guides to optimal moral behavior and he praised the contemplative life. The golden mean of Aristotle was set up against the transcendental ideal of Plato.

If Christians of the late Renaissance could not quite comprehend what was meant by *arete,* which became somewhat confused with Roman and Christian virtues, they nevertheless respected the two philosophers as ancient witnesses that the way of mere physical enjoyment was brutish, and in writing about society they often combined elements from both heathen sages. A lofty spiritual atmosphere in the Platonic mode could enshroud Aristotelian political forms, especially those of the household, and commonsensical theories of human nature. To hardheaded realists free from utopian fantasy, Aristotle appeared to balance individual needs with those of the commonwealth and to make the best disposition of both. They took him at his word when he criticized ideal forms of government designed by woolly-headed theorists as running counter to his own rather more pluralist views on political associations. But for those in search of the absolute, only Plato left a model elaborated in detail that could be imitated, and in the history of utopian thought his influence is paramount. In the Hellenic world the debate on the ideal community had gone far beyond the consideration of mere governmental mechanics to pose the major question of the feeling tone of human relations, which would become a perennial problem, sometimes hard to grasp and put into words, in all significant utopian thought. The desirable degree of fusion, or symphysis, of individuals and the community was central to the differences between Plato and Aristotle. In modern sociology, analysis of the contrasting temper of life in a *Gemeinschaft* (community) and a *Gesellschaft* (society) has acquired a new vocabulary, but the topic made its appearance early in utopian discussions and is absent only from mechanical and stereotyped utopias.

The translation and publication of Plato's moral and political dialogues made of him a rich source book not only for the fundamental utopian themes but also for pictorial decorative elements. Since utopia-makers were reasonably literate—until the twentieth century—there is a presumption that they knew Plato in the original, in translation, or at least through excerpts or commentaries. Utopian fantasies are as book-ridden as philosophical arguments, dependent upon an eternal dialogue with forerunners. We cannot hold with those who brush aside the literary tradition, who ascribe every artifact in the later world of utopia solely to a contemporary event or situation and constantly assure us that the deviations from Plato are more significant than the conformities. No utopian who read ever laid the ghost of Plato.

Whether the *Republic* and the *Laws* are in fact utopias or integral parts of the whole of Platonic philosophy is not our question; in the sixteenth and seventeenth centuries utopians recognized Plato as their eminent predecessor and forerunner whenever they took the trouble to write historical introductions to their own works. If Thomas More is the father of the utopian tradition, Plato still looms in the background, and up to the end of the eighteenth century his impress is ineradicable. Even when the stage scenery of utopia was drastically refurbished, the serious part of the program remained largely determined by Plato. It was he who really formulated the questions that were asked centuries later by shipwrecked travelers as they encountered the inhabitants of uncharted continents in remote parts of the globe. Above all, in Plato later utopians found the first serious attempt to distinguish between need and desire, which lies at the heart of the utopian problem of modern man.

Pulling the *Republic* out of the Greek intellectual world of the fifth century B.C. is perhaps as grave a transgression as lifting Thomas More or Francis Bacon or Tommaso Campanella out of his Christian matrix; but since we are looking not for the recovery of the historical Plato but for Platonic elements that endured in the modern utopian imagination, much of the virtuosity of contemporary scholarship in establishing his original and true meaning will have to be foregone. Many of the subtleties of his thought were lost in the course of transmission.

Plato bequeathed to Western utopia the idea of a city of perfect justice ruled by an aristocracy that was educated to abide by a set of absolute values; the techniques, primarily eugenic, for maintaining the stability of a rigid, hierarchical class structure insofar as possible, given the changing nature of all things; the definition of authentic human needs in contradistinction to mere desires, and mechanisms for the perfect meshing of authentic needs and unique natural talents; and a faith in community to the point where the individual would cease to conceive of himself as an independent entity. Paradoxically, Plato also sowed the seeds of universal communist and egalitarian conceptions, though he himself had limited such proposals to relationships within the small ruling class of his Republic.

For centuries utopias based upon strict sumptuary controls were sustained by the thesis in Book II of the *Republic* that the growth of luxury and excess corrupts the good society and must lead to wars of aggression and ultimately to degeneration. Some utopias surpassed Plato's in austerity, others were more lenient; but Professor Arthur Lovejoy was correct in his estimate that the preponderant influence of Plato was in the direction of what he called "hard primitivism," the belief that men's authentic needs were few and simple. This idea dominated the main current of utopian thought until the end of the eighteenth century; by comparison the cokaygne utopia had few exponents in the literary world up to the nineteenth century. Plato had presented contemporary Athens as a city far along in history that had developed its arts, crafts, and desires to so exaggerated a degree that it had become putrescent with riches. It was now "suffering from an inflammation," a malady that utopian writers of later ages recognized in their own societies by the same symptoms.

Plato's conception of human need involved the exercise of athletic capacities of both body and soul among the guardians of the Republic. Certain civilized oral satisfactions above a bare minimum were permissible, and the ideal city was to be embellished with grand public buildings that elevated the soul in quest of forms of perfect beauty. But life in the Platonic Republic was never facile; it was an arduous struggle with the unruly elements of concupiscence in man's soul, with the dark forces in his anarchic nature that made him dream of fornicating his mother. Unless there was a constant battle with the vicious desires that many men often had, and nearly all men had sometimes, the Athenians of Plato's Republic would become like the Atlanteans of old and go down to ignominious defeat as they had. The ease of the golden age is brusquely rejected in the *Republic*. Life in Plato's utopia demands eternal vigilance. The souls of the guardians—and they are the only class in which he was vitally interested—had to be supervised at every moment in life. Animalian desire was to be suppressed whenever it represented the least danger to the polity. There was one supreme, overriding need in the city to which all others were subordinate, its unity.

Aside from raising the basic problems that must confront a philosopher-king, perhaps the most significant heritage Plato left to utopian thought was the conviction that an ideal society was in some measure feasible. Until the Republic became a reality, a just and philosophical man could not wholly fulfill himself. In time this idea was extended to mean that *no* man could realize his potentialities outside a utopian society. At the same time the Republic is also a paradigm in the heavens, and the failure of attempts to bring it down to earth is an integral part of the Platonic tradition that More inherited. The memory of Plato's tragic voyages to Syracuse in the hope of converting into a philosopher-king the tyrant Dionysius, a foppish, unstable intellectual, has haunted the history of utopianism.

From Paradise to Utopia

When plain belief in religious paradise became attenuated, utopia came into being. The natural history of paradise might serve as an introduction to the history of the self-conscious, deliberately fabricated utopias of modern times, for in most of them vestiges of paradise can be discovered, like the structures of superseded forms in biological evolution. One need only be reminded that *Utopia* itself was written by a Christian martyr who achieved sainthood. Pansophia, which underlies the serious utopias of the seventeenth century—those of Bacon, Campanella, Andreae, Comenius, and Leibniz—is still profoundly Christian and in the direct paradisaical, often mystical, tradition. There is hardly a problem related to Eden, the messianic age, or the otherworldly paradise that is not rehearsed in secular utopian literature.

But there is also a distinction between religious paradise and modern utopia that establishes a caesura and bestows a unique character upon the utopias that are born in the fifteenth and early sixteenth centuries. The paradises of Judeo-Christian religion were brought into being by a transcendent God, and the time and nature of His Creation were dependent upon His will alone. Utopia is man-made paradise on earth, a usurpation of His omnipotence. It is a Promethean act of defiance of the existing order of the world, and though the order that is substituted usually partakes of the soft, maternal attributes of a religious paradise its founder is a bold human hero. King Utopus was a conqueror who cut the umbilical cord, a strip of land that once joined the island of Utopia to the mainland; Bacon's New Atlantis was the invention of the wise Solamona; the ruler of Campanella's City of the Sun—and solar imagery is universally masculine—was an all-knowing, all-loving, and all-powerful man; Vairasse's Sevarambians were defeated by King Sevarias who then became their monarch and lawgiver. Virtually all of the utopia-writers identified themselves with their activist heroes—More daydreamed that he was King Utopus, and Vairasse's Sevarias was an anagram of his own name. In Hesiod's myth, Prometheus hid the fire he stole in the hollow of a fennel stick, a marvelous advertisement of male sexual potency; and utopian authors—Bacon and Campanella and Marx—were great admirers of the Prometheus figure. The Messiahs of Judaism and Christianity, too, may have been prototypes for the utopian rulers; but the religious saviors were always direct emissaries of God, carrying out His will, while in the utopias, even when the fiction of a vague, otherworldly power is preserved, it is remote and the stress is on the initiative and autonomy of the earthly leader.

Utopia burst upon European consciousness in three radically different shapes. One received a name that established itself in European culture, Thomas More's *Utopia*. The other two, which can be related to More with only tenuous threads, had independent existences. The Italian type never acquired a separate designation that was widely recognized. Terms like *città felice, città perfetta,* and *mondo nuovo* were used rather loosely. The German or Central European utopian mode broke the bounds of a literary creation and was quickly identified with a popular religious movement and a renewal of belief in the millennium. Its enemies denounced it as an *Aufruhr* or mocked it as a *Schlaraffenland,* its supporters used words like *communia* to describe its content and *Gemeinermann* to identify its new elect; but perhaps *Christliche Verbündniss* was the contemporary term which best characterized its nature— it was Thomas Müntzer's own.

More's *Utopia* caught the imagination of the Western world and it is reasonable to preserve the generic name for the birth of utopia as a European phenomenon, even though the other two types had separate origins in social and geographic soils very different from those of Tudor England. *Utopia* was rendered into German in 1524 and into Italian in 1548 but it never served as a guide for the major German or Italian ventures into utopia.

Of the three utopias born in the century following the invention of printing, one was chiefly embodied in plans for a city of stone, another was a speaking picture of life in a remote island republic, and the third was enveloped in a radical theology of resounding religious manifestoes and sermons. Such sharp disparities among the three types should at the very outset lay to rest the fiction of a uniform utopian spirit even among contemporaries. The two Thomases who stand at the fountainhead of utopian thought died on the executioner's block within eight years of each other. The apocalyptic utopia of Thomas Müntzer, who was beheaded first, has been more closely reflected in political action programs, while the utopia of Thomas More, nominal progenitor of the tribe, has spawned a greater number of literary descendants. Oddly enough, the apocalyptic utopia sometimes incorporated matter from the Morean one to flesh out its vision of the Sabbatical future. In comparison with the other forms, the rationalist constructs of the Italian architectural utopia have surfaced only sporadically.

While the little book written in Latin by an English ambassador became the prototype of a novel way of depicting an optimum society on earth and had an enduring influence in the Western world, the Italian *città felice* was more parochial; it was so bound up with sensate needs and Platonic and Vitruvian ideals of beauty that its significance tended to be limited to the artistic flowering of the Renaissance Italian city-state and was not readily universalized. The radical revolutionary utopia of the Germanic world left behind the memory of a group of symbolic historical figures who with time became legendary. Bound up with the recrudescence of Christian millenarianism, this utopia of the common man was close to the Protestant sectarians who would hasten the coming reign of Christ on earth through direct action. It became the source of a long, not yet extinct, tradition, the utopian with a sword ushering in the rule of community and equality.

The Christian utopia of the Western world was thus born with three heads, though only More bestowed a lasting name upon his. The Judeo-Christian paradisaical element was strongest in the Germanic utopian movements of artisans and peasants led by preachers, the Hellenic urban ideal was predominant among the Italian philosophical architects, while More, whose imprint was the deepest, wrestled with the two traditions and achieved only a precarious balance between them. The utopias which were scholarly and humanist in England were aristocratic and aesthetic in Italy, violent and populist in Germany. But all of them were profoundly Christian.

PART II

The Birth of Utopia

Sir Thomas More, 1527

Hans Holbein the Younger
Frick Collection, New York

4

The Passion of Thomas More

IN A LETTER of July 23, 1519, to the German humanist Ulrich von Hutten, Erasmus has left a winning description of the affectionate friend who called him his darling. "In company his rare affability and sweetness of manner lift the saddest spirits and relieve the pain of the grimmest circumstance. As a boy he was already so delighted with jokes that one would think he was born for them alone, but he never jested to the point of buffoonery, nor had he ever any taste for biting sarcasm. As a youth he wrote farces and acted in them. When something was said wittily, even though it was at his expense, he enjoyed it, so heartily did he appreciate bright and original sallies. When he was a young man he played with epigrams and was especially charmed by Lucian. It was in fact More who urged me to write the *Moriae Encomium,* which was like setting a camel a-dancing."[1] Erasmus understood something of More's passionate nature. Because he could not put by his desire for a wife, Erasmus confided, More chose to be "a chaste husband rather than a licentious priest."[2] But Erasmus also knew of the darker, ascetic side of More, of his early attraction to the monastic life of the Carthusians, from which he turned to enter the law courts in order to please his father. In the Tower, More later watched three Carthusian brothers going off to Tyburn to be hanged, drawn, and quartered; he was finally joined to them in death.

More's own letters in his twenties tell of his suffering periods of black despair. To John Colet, his spiritual counselor, he described his utter contempt for the world's passions and ambitions, and his fear of falling into grim despondency, "almost the very gates of hell."[3] "Wherever you betake yourself, on one side nothing but feigned love and the honeyed poisons of smooth flatterers resound; on the other, fierce hatreds, quarrels, the din of the forum murmur against you. Wherever you turn your eyes, what else will you see but confectioners, fishmongers, butchers, cooks, poulterers, fishermen, fowlers, who supply the materials for gluttony, for the world, and the world's lord, the devil."[4] More lived with this despair bordering on a weariness with existence both before and after the *Utopia.* Man was born into a vale of tears and life was a search for salvation, communion with God, liberation of the soul from the prison of the body. Though active in the law courts and in the King's service—he was a master of requests, an ambassador, an under-treasurer of the Exchequer, a lord chancellor of England—from his early youth More longed for a Christian *vita contemplativa* and emancipation from the business of the marketplace, sometimes from life itself.

When More was only six his mother, to whom he was deeply attached, died, and his father, Sir John More, a lawyer of humble origin who had made his way in the City, brought home three wives in succession. Thomas More lost his own first wife, Jane, then married Dame Alice, who was devoted to her stepchildren, and composed an epitaph for Jane voicing the hope for a ménage à trois in heaven that fate and religion had excluded on earth.[5] Jesting about death and dying, making death a familiar, was one way of exorcizing its terrors.

The final decision and will of this worldly humanist and skillful lawyer to embrace his death as a supreme sacrifice of self to his God remains the enigma of Thomas More. The legalities of his refusal to acknowledge the King as supreme head of the English church, his insistence on remaining mute over Henry's divorce from Queen Catherine in order to marry Anne Boleyn pale before the universal meaning of his act of conscience, for which he had been preparing himself throughout his life. The lines between the temporal and the spiritual powers were always a matter of dispute in medieval England, where contests were resolved by murder or execution. As royal power expanded, the king was loath to have a great number of his subjects outside his jurisdiction when royal justice was involved. The balance of forces between king and ecclesiastics shifted from reign to reign. With the wealth of the church increasing, the exclusion of its lands from royal interference became a grievous affront to Tudor hegemony. While More as a lawyer defended positions that were not always consistent with one another, whenever there was a serious conflict between the secular and the sacred, he fought for the inviolability of the sacred jurisdiction. In the third part of the *Tres Thomae,* published in Douai in 1588, the theologian of Louvain, Thomas Stapleton, placed More by the side of Thomas à Becket. The broad political context of Thomas More's death is all too easy to outline. It is the person of Thomas More that continues to confound us half a millennium after his birth.

Apart from his martyr's end on the executioner's block for what his outraged sovereign called treason—a charge supported by trumped-up evidence that More was implicated in the revelations of the Nun of Canterbury foretelling Henry VIII's doom—More's fame rests upon a pithy little work he wrote when he was thirty-eight. The freshness of *Utopia,* its rich substance and piquant style, have not been abraded by more than four centuries of imitation and misapplication, the muck of scholarly analysis, and even the ministrations of Roland Barthes's semiology. More the author of a witty book and More the saint (as of the year 1935) have traveled their separate ways through history. It is perhaps time they met again, not to be reconciled but to be confronted anew in all their tragic contradiction.

A Victor over Plato

More was born in 1478 in a provincial country on the periphery of continental Europe, where a small group of scholars for a number of decades had been engaged in bringing back into the corpus of learning the moral writings of the ancient Greek philosophers, whose teachings came to be appreciated as a great rhetorical presentation of how good men should behave. Lorenzo Valla and others before him had debated the rival claims of Stoics, Epicureans, Plato, and Aristotle as guides to conduct in this world. For all their delight in the pagans, however, few if any English scholars would have considered the wisdom of an ancient sect or combination of sects to be as powerfully illuminating as the supreme light of Revelation, whose dictates as interpreted by the Church were unquestioned. Greco-Roman learning gave spiritual pleasure and had a unique force of persuasion, since it was close to ordinary human desires and passions, and by example and through experience taught men how to act. Humanists were concerned not with harmonizing the moral principles of the ancients with the Gospel, but with applying both to life and behavior; the idea of conciliation is a latter-day view of their convictions. The pre-Christian teachings of Plato were in their essence a truth. The beliefs of More's Utopians were another version of the truth, perhaps purified of details that had provoked criticism of Plato's political ideas when they were communicated to Italian scholars by Byzantine émigrés in the fifteenth century. But the ultimate message was in the Gospel.

More was of the second generation of Englishmen who were enthralled by Hellenic culture. Older scholars had themselves traveled to Italy and had learned the Greek language in which the moral lessons from antiquity had been communicated. More never managed to receive the word directly from the Italian humanists, but there were living English intermediaries whose books were appearing in print and with whom he enjoyed oral converse. Thomas Linacre, a fellow of All Souls, had left Oxford in 1487 and returned five years later. Grocyn resigned his readership at Magdalen College in 1488 to spend three years in the south of Europe. John Colet, though no great scholar of the Greek language, was the master who defined most sharply the role of Platonic philosophy for Englishmen brought up in the Christian tradition. And then there was Erasmus, who came to England in 1499, the favored brother-in-arms in the scholars' crusade for the regeneration of Christianity.

Though Plato was the central figure in the fifteenth-century renascence of Greek literature, he was flanked by those less decorous writers, Aristophanes and Lucian, who in their own boisterous and ribald way had become vehicles of moral truth. When the northern humanists proposed to regenerate mankind within the framework of the existing political and religious order, they could hardly find cleverer models to imitate than these master critics. More's Hellenic studies also embraced ancient writers of utopian novels, known to him through fragments preserved in Diodorus Siculus, and Greek biographies as recorded by Plutarch. Scholars have traced parallels between *Utopia* and the tales of Iambulus and Euhemerus, and have suggested that King Utopus was inspired by the revolutionary Spartan monarch Agis IV.[6] The devices, traditions, and mannerisms of different genres of Greek literature were artfully commingled in *Utopia,* to achieve an effect of density without loss of elegance and grace—a dramatically new creation.

The Platonic legacy in the *Utopia* is indelibly marked on the face of the first edition (1516), whose front matter is full of teasing remarks about the relations of the island of Utopia to Plato's Republic. On the second unsigned leaf a quatrain in the Utopian vernacular, a language whimsically invented by More, boasts that good King Utopus has built a "philosophical city" without the aid of abstract philosophy,[7] a mild jest at Plato's expense, a kind of kidding on the square, for More grounded the virtues of his optimum republic in moral, not metaphysical, principles. The verse also highlights the island nature of Utopia, though it had originally been a "non-island." On the map drawn opposite, the umbilical cord that once joined Utopia to the mainland has been cut. On the next page Anemolius, the island's poet laureate, announces in the name of Utopia: "I am a rival of Plato's Republic, perhaps even a victor over it."[8] With appropriate fanfare More has entered the lists in a tourney of ingenuity with Plato as he might a literary contest with one of his fellow humanists. More's friend Peter Giles, in a letter to Councillor of the Emperor Jerome Busleyden that serves as a deliberately obfuscatory preface, outrightly claims for *Utopia* superiority over the *Republic*.[9] The excuse for all this immodest bragging is that Plato argued abstractly, whereas More painted a picture, exhibiting the inhabitants of Utopia, their laws and resources, so skillfully that in reading the little book one felt as if one were actually living there.

The idea behind this bumptious self-praise, a private joke in the circle of humanists, derived from Plato himself and they all knew it—the distinction between discursive philosophical argument about an ideal city and the circumstantial description of a utopian society, telling a story, a significant dichotomy in utopian thought that can be found in the dialogues of Plato traditionally presented as sequels to the *Republic*. In the opening of the *Timaeus* Socrates expressed a need for a pendant to the *Republic,* a complementary work depicting the ideal state in movement. "I may compare my feeling to something of this kind: suppose, for instance, that on seeing beautiful creatures, whether works of art or actually alive but in repose, a man should be moved with desire to behold them in motion and vigorously engaged in some such exercise as seemed suitable to their physique; well, that is the very feeling I have regarding the State we have described."[10] Socrates wanted to see the Republic at work. In recognizing the need for both discursive and pictorial elements, Plato established a pattern for later utopias. Since none of the characters of the *Republic* reappear in either the *Timaeus* or the *Critias* doubt has been cast on an integral relationship among the three, but a connection was surely assumed in the Renaissance.

Socrates feigned a constitutional inability to present a dynamic portrait of the ideal republic on the pretext that it lay outside the range of his experience; but his interlocutors Timaeus, Critias, and Hermocrates were fitted for the task by nature and nurture, since they had participated in public affairs. Cajoled, Critias accepted the challenge and undertook to relate the story of the conflict between the lost island of Atlantis and ancient Athens, the ideal city, as its tradition had been handed down from Solon, who had it from the priests of Saïs in Egypt. "And the city with its citizens which you described to us yesterday," Critias says to Socrates, recalling the Republic, "as it were in a fable, we will now transport hither into the realm of fact; for we will assume that the city is that ancient city of ours, and declare that the citizens you conceived are in truth those actual progenitors of ours, of whom the priest told."[11] In this passage, at least, Plato meant to treat the ideal city as though it were historical reality, its likeness having existed in Athens in the period before Atlantis was submerged in one of the countless cycles of annihilation and regeneration through which the world passes.

It had been agreed that Critias would be preceded by Timaeus, their best astronomer, who would speak about the origin and nature of the universe and the beginnings of mankind. The cosmological discourse delivered by Timaeus was virtually incorporated into Christian theology in the Middle Ages; but Critias did not fulfill his part of the bargain, at least not in the extant texts. The truncated dialogue, a fragment that bears his name, never reached the climax of action and covered only a more or less surface description of Athens and Atlantis, the two great antagonists of the ancient world—on the one hand the wicked Atlanteans, driven by a desire for conquest, and on the other the just, ancient Athenians, who vanquished them because of the virtues of their perfect, or nigh perfect, state. But even in the fragment, the institutional forms that supported the combatants in the titanic battle reveal something of their contrasting natures: One is utopian, the other dystopian. Athens is a prosperous city-state with an agricultural hinterland, Atlantis a far-flung empire with colonies spread over the western Mediterranean. Athens is governed by a military aristocracy, Atlantis is ruled by an alliance of ten hereditary kings, brother monarchs, one of whom is the chief. Atlantis is literally sunk in luxury, while the Athenian military aristocracy, which has no resources beyond its own agricultural lands, pursues a middle course between extravagance and meanness. The military guardians of ancient Athens, who are explicitly identified with the guardians of Socrates' Republic, live in a state of communism. From the *Critias* it is manifest that a city such as Athens of old would have the fortitude to trounce the most magnificent imperial hosts.

The unfinished state of Plato's *Critias,* its failure to present the ideal city as had been promised to Socrates, created an opportunity for More nearly two thousand years later to conceive of his own book as a completion and fulfillment of the Platonic dialogue. Deliberately picking up the thread where the sage of the antique world had left off, he would show the active ideal republic. More could be breezy about his superiority over Plato, for his veneration of the *Republic* as a model was not in question. By the time it was brought to England, the bitter fifteenth-century Italian controversy over Plato's moral acceptability had petered out. In London More had read the *Republic* in Greek under the guidance of the English humanists, and throughout his life, in personal domestic arrangements as well as in critical moments of existence and on the very eve of death, he turned to Saint Socrates for guidance. In the Platonic tradition, More's *Utopia* marvelously interwove rational argument, moving scenes, and history, creating an artistic balance not often achieved by latter-day utopians.

Two thousand years had passed from Plato to More and it would be preposterous to imagine that the spirit of the Athenian aristocrat, still embittered over the judicial murder of his master by a democratic assembly, could have entered the mind of an English ambassador engaged in economic negotiations, a Christian humanist, a practicing lawyer, and a sheriff chosen by the burghers of London. Yet without the *Republic,* More's *Utopia* is incomprehensible. More's relationship to Plato was that of a pious, yet independent, son, seeking his own way without flaunting his rebellion. In a long passage in the first book of the *Utopia* Raphael Hythloday lays down the principle of absolute community of property and passionately defends it in Plato's name, while More interjects stereotyped arguments from Aristotle and Aquinas against it. There is no reason to accept the voice of the mariner as the true More and More's rejoinder as a mere literary or protective artifice. The dialogue is a dramatic exchange that expressed More's ambivalence toward Father Plato. In the end Thomas More is his own man, and his genius is never suffocated by his reverence for the ancients. The Greek philosopher, moreover, had been introduced to a young man already deeply immersed in the revelations of both the Old and the New Testaments, and Greek was the key to the ultimate truth of the word of Christ as well as the precepts of Plato.

The Manifest Content

Everything in More's *Utopia* should be read on many different levels; if it is pinned down too tightly on one, the whole vision has a way of evaporating. But this is not to say that the book is in essence an airy jeu d'esprit. For More's intention was to teach as well as please, to persuade not by the windy exposition of an abstract argument, for which he seems to have had little capacity or taste, but by telling a fable that relied on the blandishments of style and wit to engage the readers in his eminently serious purposes. On first approach, everything on the island of Utopia is to be taken at face value. Digging for the underthought, however tantalizing, should not lead to neglecting the manifest content, because it gave weight to More's reflections on contemporary society and pointed the way to its spiritual reform.

Utopia purports to be the record of a long conversation in the garden of Peter Giles's house in Antwerp written by Thomas More, Henry VIII's ambassador, who some time after the occasion carefully noted down everything he had heard. It is in large part a monologue by a wild-eyed, learned Portuguese mariner, Raphael Hythloday, who knew many of the courts of European lords secular and ecclesiastic, was a member of Amerigo Vespucci's expedition to America, and became the leader of a party of even more intrepid explorers who had left Vespucci and ventured as far as the domain of King Utopus. Ambassador More, having been introduced to Hythloday by Giles on the way out of church, acts as a curious interlocutor who occasionally provokes and contradicts the hero but for the most part does not argue with him, since he recognizes that he has encountered a man possessed by a vision who is not amenable to rational objection. In drafting the final account of the dialogue, however, More hazards a few sparse afterthoughts of his own that take issue with Hythloday.

Book I, which was written after Book II, is given over to a story within a story—Hythloday's version of a conversation about the sorry state of the realm of England that took place at the table of the venerable Cardinal Morton (in whose household More himself had served as a young man). Book II does not feature conversations, but describes all aspects of utopian life—social, moral, political, religious, intellectual—setting a pattern for authentic travel literature for centuries to come. The whole world of the Utopians is seen only through the eyes of the fierce Hythloday, who is so carried away by his depiction of their calm felicity that in the telling he becomes as mild and gentle as they are. In contrast to the full-blooded, intemperate characters of the first book, those of the second, somewhat pallid to be sure, are "gentle, merye, quycke, and fyne wytted, delytynge in quyetnes, and, when nede requyreth, able to abyde and suffre muche bodelye laboure. Elles they be not greatelye desyerous and fonde of yt: but in the exercyse and studdye of the mynde they be never werye," to quote Robinson's earthy Tudor translation.[12]

More's delight in dramatic opposition might have been called romantic in the early nineteenth century. In the opening of his history of Richard III, he juxtaposed the villainous Richard with Edward IV, so heartily beloved by his subjects: "Whiche favour and affeccion yet after his decease, by the crueltie, mischiefe, and trouble of the tempestious worlde that followed, highelye towarde hym more increased."[13] The same kind of contrariety is established between Books I and II of *Utopia,* where the worlds of England and Utopia confront each other. Neither society is in accord with the moral and religious truth of Christ, the Utopians because they never heard of the Gospel until the coming of Hythloday and his companions, the English because in many spheres of life they have abandoned His guiding rules. The good way, which is implicit throughout, has always been available to man in some form even before the propagation of the Gospel. Greek philosophers had taught a truth, based on their knowledge of things, which corresponded to the Christian; the Jews through their prophets had preached a similar truth; and the Utopians had independently arrived at moral and political truths not unlike those of the Gentile philosophers, truths they had actually put into practice and had preserved unchanged for more than a thousand years since the founding of their kingdom. While the Utopians were not Christian and therefore could not know the absolute truth—nor could any man on earth, though he might strive to approach it through the exercise of the will—their excellence resided in their moral action, a preference for practice over mere philosophy More had inherited from his master Colet. When compared with the modes and institutions of contemporary English society, Utopian life was indubitably nearer to Christian truth. The greater the shame of Europeans, who had the advantage of Christian teaching.

But the kingdom of Utopia was not a second paradise. In other works More would hold to a firm belief in the literal meaning of Genesis and attack exclusively allegorical readings of the Bible that cast doubt on the continued existence of terrestrial paradise. The original paradise had survived somewhere on earth. This was More's conviction throughout his life, as it was that of most European Christians in the sixteenth century. "[Any man may] teache us certayne convenient vertues understanden bi the four flouds of paradise, and tell us that paradise is grace, out of whych all the floodes of all vertues flowe and water the earth . . . But mary if he would . . . teache us such a spiritual sense, to make us believe that those wordes were to be none otherwise understanden besyde, but that ther wer no such floodes flowing foorthe of paradise, nor such paradise at all, I wold wene verely that he were a very heretike."[14] More's son John prepared a translation of a supposed report from the Kingdom of Prester John in Ethiopia, where according to widespread opinion the original paradise was located.[15] The Utopians, who had attained to moral and political truths of a high order through their own collective efforts, were nevertheless not living in a paradisaical state. Even though they had stripped their society of most vanities, they had to work and there was still crime within the state and war against outside enemies. The Kingdom of Heaven was not of this world, while Utopia was a society that provided for the natural desires and authentic needs of man on earth. Following a practical as well as a philosophical interpretation of their pleasure principle, the Utopians had arrived at the optimum state of a commonwealth in this world. But it was not to be compared with paradise. At best, Utopian society could fit its members for the heavenly afterlife.

Not only does *Utopia* depict an earthly society, however virtuous its inhabitants; it is an urban society, conceived by the son of a London lawyer and the grandson of a London baker. The Arcadian mode, much imitated in the Renaissance, was alien to the first utopia. Though he had passed a brief period in Oxford, More was very much a city man, educated in London, practicing law in the courts or listening to public lectures and sermons, often indistinguishable from one another. More's teacher Colet had established his school of humanist education at St. Paul's in the heart of London. The English humanists were less interested in creating a new social hierarchy than in infusing the old one with a civic spirit, in Hellenizing Christian England, and Hellenism without cities would have been a contradiction in terms. The island kingdom of Utopia, composed of many cities spaced throughout its territory, resembles the realm of England or the Holy Land more than it does a self-contained Greek polis or a contemporary Italian city-state; but though the dimensions of the ideal have changed, the model of the individual cities on the island, which are all alike, may still be ancient Athens as depicted in the *Critias*. *Utopia* is pointedly antifeudal—there are no great baronial estates or manors; nor does it glorify a return to nature. The society is composed of families who have all tilled the soil at one time or another, but who come back from their rural stint to dwell in the cities. The fundamental institutions of Utopia are urban.

In the Utopian cities, it is taken for granted that the *optimates* in goodness and learning will be chosen for public office, thus establishing a nonhereditary aristocracy that enjoys virtually no privileges beyond esteem. There is equality among citizen heads of large family units, within which order and degree depend upon age and sex. The Utopian order is patriarchal, and women and the young meekly accept their subordinate position. Society is not immobile, though stability is implied in the simple observation that sons tend to follow in their father's footsteps, as did most people in Tudor England including More himself. The calm meritocracy of More's fancy would soon be violated by Anabaptist enthusiasts and rebellious German peasants bearing arms, whose rival utopia would in his eyes be the devil's handiwork.

Great warrior nobles and their retainers are barbaric enemies in Utopia. The cities will manage to defend themselves with mercenaries and through the bribery and subversion of foreign courts. For the most part the heroic virtues are superfluous. The monarch depends upon civilian councillors in Utopia as in contemporary England, where ambassadors were lawyers and great clerics, not soldiers. The high valuation of learning in Utopia was not revolutionary; it was an extension of what was already taking place in the royal service of many European monarchies.[16] More was the educator of the new merchant classes who were related by birth and marriage to scholars and lawyers. Colet and More were both members of the Mercers Company by patrimony. More also knew of the evil world of the warrior nobility.

Two of More's major innovations in the *Utopia* are markedly un-Platonic, the complete equality of property for all free inhabitants and the intricate hierarchy of pleasures. Plato would not have countenanced the abolition of class distinctions and he surely would have contemned More's constant preoccupation with the appeasement of natural desires among ordinary people. More's Christian humanist way of reasoning here diverges from the *Republic*.

In the *Utopia* the root of all evil in society is the lust for possessions, a passion that leads men to behave like beasts toward one another. From Hythloday's graphic characterization of the enclosure movement in Book I—"Your sheep, which are usually so tame and so cheaply fed, begin now, according to report, to be so greedy and wild that they devour human beings themselves and devastate and depopulate fields, houses, and towns"[17]—to the concluding reflection that existing society is nothing but a conspiracy of the rich to defraud the poor,[18] there is an underlying Christian thesis: The pride that accompanies the accumulation of useless and superfluous wealth must be curbed. If a commonwealth, Hythloday muses, would only prohibit the amassing of wealth, distribute property and produce equally, enforce a rule of labor for all, there would be no opportunity for the sin of pride to raise its monstrous head. It is not only inequality of possessions in itself that is repugnant to Hythloday, but the moral consequences of monopoly on the one hand and abject poverty on the other. Vast possessions mean idleness among the powerful and sloth among their retainers. Unemployed soldiers and farmers chased off the land by enclosures are driven into crime, and the multiplication of executions is a futile attempt to deter criminals whom despair has goaded into iniquity. Extirpate the profound causes, Hythloday admonishes, banish hunger and idleness, educate the young in the morality of simple pleasures, and all men will enjoy lives of calm felicity. Moralist censure of wealth and cupidity was a part of common Christian and Hellenic teaching. Lucian's *Menippus,* which More had translated, described the miserable fate of the rich and powerful after death, detailing a new ordinance that required their bodies to be tormented in Hades, while their souls entered donkeys on earth and were driven by the poor for 250,000 years.[19]

With provision in Utopia for the care of the sick and security in old age, the gnawing anxieties that any poor, propertyless man suffers in the course of a lifetime will be eliminated. It would be anachronistic to regard More as the discoverer of an active passion for equality among all men. Equality is a mechanism for the eradication of the gravest Christian sin, the arrogance that led to the Fall. In Utopia there are decent honors for elected magistrates, priests, and scholars, but no accumulation and hoarding of wealth that permit the poor to starve while the granaries of the rich are bulging.

More's *Utopia* is inconceivable without a belief in the immortality of the soul and in rewards and punishments in the next world. Were these doctrines not the common element in virtually all religions on the island of Utopia, the benign conduct of the inhabitants would not generally be guaranteed by equality of property alone. Both considerations, the religious and the mundane, were interwoven to create the favorable psychic climate of Utopia. By far the majority of Utopians worship a divine, omnipotent, eternal being, diffused throughout the universe in power, not mass, whom they call father. The other Utopians also believe in a supreme being but he is regarded by different persons as having different forms, though among all the Utopians his name is Mithras. Those few who do not accept the elementary doctrines of religion are not actively persecuted, but they become second-class citizens: The magistracy is closed to them. More has no name for such persons; later French translations supplied the lack: in seventeenth-century renderings they are called *libertins,* in the early nineteenth *matérialistes*—examples of the manner in which *Utopia* could be constantly refurbished to keep up with the times, moving ever further from the original.

The Utopians are pre-Christians; the absolute truth of Christ had not been revealed to them before the arrival of Hythloday and his companions. But many of the Utopians are quick to grasp the Christian message, which has already been prefigured in their own beliefs. Their views about social behavior are at one with the teachings of Christ, Plato, Epicurus, and the Stoics, and they are spontaneously drawn to the Greek pagan books and to the New Testament brought by Hythloday, all of which mirror the Utopian moral outlook. Their contempt for gold parallels Christ's driving the money changers from the Temple, their family order is Biblical in character, their joy is seemly in the manner of Biblical lessons and Platonic dialogues. Precedent for their common ownership of goods could be found among the Church Fathers and in the Biblical conception of the Jubilee, as well as in Plato and Pythagoras.

Some of the Utopians have been baptized, but as there is no priest to administer the other sacraments, they remain imperfect Christians, which permits More to let them engage in markedly un-Christian practices without arousing scandal. Against the advice of the Europeans, a zealot among the newly baptized proclaims that those who do not admit Christ will suffer eternal hellfire. But his threats only seal his own doom, for King Utopus had ordained from the beginning "that it should be lawful for every man to follow the religion of his choice, that each might strive to bring others over to his own, provided that he quietly and modestly supported his own by reasons nor bitterly demolished all others if his persuasions were not successful nor used any violence and refrained from abuse. If a person contends too vehemently in expressing his views, he is punished with exile or enslavement."[20] Utopia was tolerant and the sacral did not extend over a large part of existence. When, however, the *Utopia* is stripped of its religious dress, as it is in some accounts, we may have a utopia, but it is not More's.

There are lawbreakers in Utopia—adulterers and disturbers of the public peace. These malefactors are punished severely, though under ordinary circumstances they are not put to death. Instead, criminals are laden with golden chains as symbols of their shame and are set to hard labor; there would be no point in depriving society of their work by executing them. The criminals about whom More is particularly concerned are not thieves or murderers, types virtually eliminated from Utopia, but the adulterers and religious zealots. Apparently sexual coveting would continue to threaten Utopian calm even after property was equally distributed—a prospect Freud would later remark upon—and the sin of pride, though no longer nourished by possessions, would take the form of an excessive proselytizing fervor that could become criminal.

The tranquil life of Utopia might be upheaved by war, forced on its inhabitants by other peoples less virtuous than they were. Guillaume Postel and great seventeenth-century utopians would have visions of universal peace, as Pierre Dubois had had in the early fourteenth. More himself, strolling along the Thames with his son-in-law Roper, told him of his ardent longing for "perfect uniformitie of religion" and his wish that "where the most part of Christian Princes be now at mortall warre, they were all at one universalle peace."[21] But even as in *Utopia* he contented himself with less than the ideal in religion, so he presented his peaceful kingdom as a single state in a potentially hostile world. Long passages on the military and colonial policy of the Utopians today seem incongruous; some commentators even make a proto-imperialist out of More, since the Utopians justify the occupation of underutilized neighboring lands in language that could be adapted to nineteenth-century expansionism. But to have painted a society without war in the early sixteenth century would have deprived the book of the verisimilitude More was aiming for.

War-making does not, however, play the crucial role in Utopia that it did in Plato's Republic or in More's contemporary Europe. Triumph in battle is no longer the ultimate test of the good society. War, like crime, is inevitable because there is still evil in the world, but the peculiar manner in which Utopians wage war has been rightly seen as the ultimate caricature of aristocratic military heroics and thus of war itself. The comical aspect of Utopian war may well have been inspired by the battles between moon-people and sun-people in Lucian's *True Story*. While the Utopians have a militia and they train themselves for war, they prefer to use mercenaries, or they buy off potential enemies with their superfluous gold and silver and employ sophisticated propaganda techniques to undermine a hostile government rather than face open confrontation in the field. They have allies and they requite injuries inflicted upon them, especially upon their merchants, but the allies are rather like satellite states who welcome Utopians as administrators. When war is thrust upon the Utopians, they are invariably victorious. They make every effort to minimize the number of casualties on both sides and their priests play an active role in restraining slaughter in the first flush of triumph. Most of the slaves in Utopia are war booty, men whose lives have been spared after their defeat in conflicts they unjustly provoked. It is unimaginable that the Utopians should declare a war that is not righteous. While More could not depict eternal and universal peace, he could make the costly European wars among Christian brothers appear stupid and futile.

The tolerance of slavery by a Christian humanist has been related to the discoveries of the New World. More's retention of the institution in Utopia for its criminals, certain categories of the conquered, and foreigners who put themselves voluntarily into Utopian servitude has obvious analogies with practices in the world of the revered ancients. But the slaves are not significant in the Utopian economy, which for the most part maintains itself through the free labor of its own citizens. More's rehabilitation of the idea of physical labor was a milestone in the history of utopian thought, and was incorporated into all socialist systems, from Saint-Simon's dictum that "all men shall work" through Mao. Christianity had begun to liberate Western man from the Greco-Roman disdain for physical work, so that society founded upon equal labor had become at least conceivable in Utopia. The elitist spirit of the pure Platonic tradition was far better preserved by the humanist Italian bishops writing utopias for leisurely aristocratic patrons. Though in a sense More's ideal is still an aristocratic one, the behavior of all free citizens in Utopia has been ennobled. There are no feudal lords who live by the sword and there is no riffraff. All men are imbued with the values of a philosophical spirit that respects learning and leads to the practice of virtue.

In the end, the meaning of pleasure in Utopia is perhaps the best key for opening the door to this kingdom. The Utopians believe that the chief part of men's felicity rests in pleasure—not wild and vulgar concupiscence, but honest, moderate enjoyments leading to contentment. Morean *voluptas,* or pleasure, includes "every movement and state of body or mind in which, under the guidance of nature, man delights to dwell."[22] More Christianized the idea of pleasure by extending it far beyond classical *voluptas* and identifying it with joyfulness and sweetness.

Having established the doctrine of pleasure as the highest good, More proceeded to set perimeters around it, lest it be associated with popular, "Epicurean" conceptions. Though the Utopians are constantly engaged in free discussion on the nature of pleasure, these are no sybarites talking about sensuality when they are not actively given over to its pursuit. Despite divergences among them, there is general consensus about the rank of the pleasures, those of the mind having clear superiority over those of the body and those of the body being sharply divisible into true, honest pleasures and spurious, adulterated ones. Above all, the pursuit of pleasure is subject to two limitations: No pleasure is permitted if it brings pain in its wake or is harmful to others, and no lower pleasure is chosen in preference to a higher one. More fired a salvo against the dismal morality that conceived of value and pleasure only by their contrast with the pain and deprivation of others, an evil propensity of mankind that he formulated concisely.

Many were the pleasures to be enjoyed without rancor or gloating over the discomfiture of others. Eating, drinking, defecating, copulating, even scratching are tolerated as pleasures, more or less on an equal plane, as long as there is no overindulgence; their purpose is either to restore the body or to eliminate excess matter that would otherwise generate pain. But these are not pure pleasures since they are always preceded by a measure of discomfort. Excessive preoccupation with these pleasures would violate More's fundamental rules of the pleasure principle and be a sign of grossness, for while nature was generous to man in affording him delightful alleviations of hunger and thirst, these pleasures were not to be prized in themselves. The satisfactions of beautiful sounds and sights were recognized by the Utopians to be of a higher, more spiritual order, and the pleasures of learning were among the worthiest of all, though More recognized that the greatest part of pleasures of the mind "arise from the practice of the virtues and the consciousness of a good life."[23]

There is some inkling of the spiritual pleasures More had in mind for his Utopians: good conversation and the study of classical literature, with a preference for Greek over Latin. There were profound reasons for the Utopians' intense interest in the Greek books that Hythloday brought with him. Here were the true origins of humanist values, the very sources of the culture More respected and cherished both in philosophy and in religion. As befitted an admirer of Pico della Mirandola, he included Plato himself in the first rank, but Aristotle was not denied. As a literary artist, More made his obeisance to Aristophanes and Lucian. As a Christian, he gloried in the language that gave him access to the Greek text of the New Testament and the Greek Fathers of the Church, who were closer to the apostolic tradition than were Jerome and his Latin Bible. Erasmus and More were seeking the fountainhead of their faith in primitive Christianity, and Greek was the medium. Toward the whole Scholastic tradition of medieval Christendom there is more than a little coldness at this stage of More's life. The fascination of the Utopians with the works of ancient Greek literature brought by Hythloday surpassed their interest in the inventions of Western technology, though they could be competent in practical arts when they served a lofty purpose such as producing printed copies of his books. Disinterested inquiries into nature that could be related to the glorification of God were respected, but there did not prevail among the Utopians anything like the later dedication of the priest-scientists in Bacon's *New Atlantis*.

One of the rare criticisms that Hythloday, More's philosophical hero, ventures to make about Utopian customs and opinions has to do with their exaggerated emphasis upon pleasure as the highest end. This passage may offer a clue to the spirit of the entire work, for it establishes a certain separation between More and the Utopians. Hythloday expounds the doctrine of the hierarchy of pleasures and then, as if catching himself, confesses his uneasiness that the Utopians may be somewhat too absorbed with the way of pleasure—a gentle reprimand, a word of caution, a protective caveat, who knows?[24] For More the Christian humanist the highest good must still be concentration upon God and the imitation of Christ, as John Colet taught even after his return from Italy. Colet had never accepted the equivalence of the two theologies, the ancient Greek and the Christian. Throughout, Utopian pleasure is encompassed within a traditional humanist frame, for the Utopians are intellectually preoccupied with the philosophical problems of pleasure, which at once puts them in a different category from heedless joy-seekers. If the general position maintained is Epicurean, it is the doctrine, not of the Epicurus who was the monster of Judaic and Christian belief, but of the Epicurus whom Erasmus had rehabilitated and likened to Christ as a teacher. The humanist, Christianized Epicurus of Lorenzo Valla and Erasmus who stood for continent, minimal gratification, not maximal indulgence, was the one More accepted.[25]

In a few areas related to work and pleasure, the egalitarianism of the Utopian society was slightly modified or amended. Those who had extraordinary natural endowments for learning were recognized early and were freed from manual labor to devote themselves wholly to study. Some could thus become benefactors to society and would have statues erected in their honor. A few Utopians who were allowed to become priests also remained outside the regular rational functioning of the Utopian pleasure principle. An exemption from the normal balance of work and pleasure was permitted, moreover, to a small group who for some reason had an unquenchable desire to labor for the community—building public works, toiling in the fields, and performing other good deeds far beyond usual expectations. Those who denied themselves their just allotment of pleasure might, out of a religious need to serve others, even remain celibate, and they were revered for their selflessness and love of God. The rest of the ascetics, not moved by a religious purpose, were tolerated though considered rather eccentric.

More was keenly aware that the amount and duration of indulgence in the pleasures of consumption would in the end depend upon the results of the collective labor of the Utopians, and here he made a vital regulatory decision. Then, as now, the key economic utopian questions revolved around the amount of labor required to fill the needs of the society, and a definition of the character and extent of those needs. More concluded that men should work just enough to provide an ample supply of basic necessities, plus a substantial surplus for defense purposes and as insurance against drought—but not one whit more. If the Utopians perform their appointed tasks cheerfully, the vast majority of them nevertheless do not like work for its own sake and would not protract it in order to purchase additional sensate pleasures, surely not for the sake of the host of false pleasures to which non-Utopians are passionately addicted. Utopians cannot understand the absorption of other nations in gaming, that most repetitive, dull pastime. The bestial hunt is outlawed on the ground that it inures men to cruelty, though other sports and exercises are cultivated for the good of the body.

Plato had already dealt with the fundamental distinctions between mere desire and authentic need in the good society. Present-day utopian thought is again raising the question of authentic need and artificially stimulated need—this time in the social context of a popular superfluity that More could hardly have conceived of. More rejected with particular vehemence the non-Utopian vanity of personal adornment, a false need, and some of his most effective dramatic scenes depict the bewilderment of a foreign ambassador bedecked with gold chains and jewels, who becomes an object of ridicule to the Utopians since they fetter their prisoners with chains of gold, and pearls are worthless playthings for their children. Gold chamberpots are the ultimate symbols of the transvaluation of European values in Utopia. The mockery of personal adornment perhaps owes something to More's familiarity with travel literature and especially Vespucci's account of his voyages, printed in 1507, which described the savages of the New World as despising gold and precious stones.[26]

The honest pleasures of the Utopians (with a few obvious exceptions) are enjoyed in public, and there is no lurking in dark corners in pursuit of secret vices. While there is a chance for quiet contemplation in the dim temples erected for religious communion, there is not much privacy in Utopia. It is not a recognized need. Travel is restricted because it is a disruption of the body politic and is a pointless activity inasmuch as the fifty-four Utopian cities are virtually identical. "The person who knows one of the cities will know them all," wrote More in words that call to mind a less admirable observer of the human condition.[27] Occasionally the agreeable routine of work, honest pleasures, religious worship, and holidays on the first and last of the month is interrupted by a great undertaking, such as the transplanting of an entire forest nearer to the city. The object, however, is not simply to achieve an impressive feat of engineering, but to diminish labor by making wood more accessible to consumers. Whatever time the community can spare from work is devoted to learning and discussions both of a scientific and a moral humanist character. Work is curtailed in the name of the higher, not the lower, pleasures.

The Original Spirit and Intent

At the time of its publication in 1516, *Utopia* was More's most ambitious literary venture, and though a man of eminence in the realm, he behaved very much like a young author uncertain of the reception of his first book. Other saints have experienced the seductions of vanity and its pains. Up to that time he had been known as the translator of a few pieces from Lucian, the author of a refutation of his dialogue on tyrannicide, a composer and translator of epigrams, a translator of a brief life of Pico della Mirandola, a lecturer on Saint Augustine's *City of God* in a London church. He was respected as a poetaster, lawyer, scholar, and sometime public servant for Henry VIII, but mostly as a private man, hospitable and charming and the educator of his family.

When More sent Erasmus his "Nowhere" he added the punning remark that it was "nowhere well written."[28] But he took great care with its publication, saw to it that Erasmus commanded for the addenda an appropriate letter of praise from a reluctant Jerome Busleyden, and at the same time coyly intimated that he had never meant to have the slight thing printed but that it had been ravished without his knowledge by Peter Giles. With humanist mannerism he protested too much; the self-denigration was laid on with a trowel. To his Italian friend Antonio Buonvisi he wrote that his *Utopia* deserved to be hidden away forever on its own island;[29] to William Warham, Archbishop of Canterbury, he sent a copy calling it a none too witty little book written in undue haste.[30] But when Cuthbert Tunstal praised it More wrote excitedly to Erasmus: "You have no idea how thrilled I am; I feel so expanded and I hold my head high."[31] To Tunstal himself he gushed: "I cannot express my delight that your judgment is so favorable."[32] More cushioned himself against the possible shock of a negative reception by telling Erasmus that after all a utopia for two would suffice: "To my way of thinking, we two are a crowd, and I think I could be happy with you in any forsaken spot."[33] If *Utopia* was a humanist exercise, More in 1516 was far from indifferent to the plaudits of his equals and to worldly fame.

The spirit and intent of the *Utopia* at the time of its composition are to some extent discoverable, despite the studied ambiguity of the work. We know something of the man, though not all his innermost secrets, and we are quite well informed about how the book was received and interpreted among that small band of mutual admirers for whom it was written in Latin—the northern humanists Busleyden, Erasmus, Peter Giles, Ulrich von Hutten, Jean Desmarais, Jean Le Sauvage, Guillaume Budé, Tunstal, Warham. They were not at all confounded by the work. Erasmus had been in on the game from its inception. It was he who had suggested that his friend try his hand at "Nusquama nostra." In the *Moriae Encomium* he had defied the monks to go and inhabit the skies of the Abraxsceni, and Utopia is called Abraxa before its renaming by the King. Erasmus could say with some authority that More's design was to show the things that "occasion mischief in commonwealths; having the English constitution especially in view, which he so thoroughly knows and understands."[34] Busleyden, interpreting *Utopia* as a Platonic paradigm, praised More for delineating for rational beings an ideal commonwealth and perfect model of conduct. Carried away by his enthusiasm, he advised contemporary states wishing to survive the vicissitudes that had destroyed Athens, Sparta, Rome to follow the Utopian pattern and "not depart from it, as they say, by a hair's breadth."[35] Guillaume Budé, the leading French humanist, wrote with elaborate flourishes: "In Utopia the assertion could be made that Aratus and the ancient poets were dangerously close to being mistaken when they stationed justice in the Zodiac after her flight from the earth. If we are to believe Hythlodaeus, she must have remained behind on the island of Utopia and not yet have made her way to the sky.

"I personally, however, have made investigation and discerned for certain that Utopia lies outside the limits of the known world. Undoubtedly, it is one of the Fortunate Isles, perhaps close to the Elysian Fields . . . content with its own institutions and possessions, blessed in its innocence, and leading a kind of heavenly life which is below the level of heaven but above the rabble of this known world." In this letter from Paris on July 31, 1517, he concluded that "our age and succeeding ages will hold his account as a nursery of correct and useful institutions from which every man may introduce and adapt transplanted customs to his own city."[36]

In none of this extravagant praise is there any suggestion that More's friends thought he had written an action program to which he or they could subscribe. They commented upon the style of the book, in private not always favorably; they rejoiced in its conceits; and in acknowledging his presentation copies they exchanged fantasy for fantasy. More returned their lavish compliments and reported his dream of glory to his friend Erasmus—a fetching picture of himself as King Utopus, welcoming his friend to the island domain: "I can see myself now marching along, crowned with a diadem of wheat, very striking in my Franciscan frock, carrying a handful of wheat as my sacred scepter, thronged by a distinguished retinue of Amaurotians, and, with this huge entourage, giving audience to foreign ambassadors and sovereigns; wretched creatures they are, in comparison with us, as they stupidly pride themselves on appearing in childish garb and feminine finery, laced with that despicable gold, and ludicrous in their purple and jewels and other empty baubles. Yet, I would not want either you or our friend, Tunstal, to judge me by other men, whose character shifts with fortune. Even if heaven has decreed to waft me from my lowly estate to this soaring pinnacle which, I think, defies comparison with that of kings, still you will never find me forgetful of that old friendship I had with you when I was but a private citizen. And if you do not mind making the short trip to visit me in Utopia, I shall definitely see to it that all mortals governed by my kindly rule will show you the honor due to those who, they know, are very dear to the heart of their king."[37] More's beguiling fantasy vanished as he awakened, he told Erasmus, but he took comfort in the thought that his ephemeral Utopia had endured about as long as real kingdoms in this world.

While in *Utopia* the allegro mood is dominant, even at this euphoric moment in More's life a melancholy undertone can be detected. Hythloday, having returned from the island of Utopia, has despaired of reform in Europe. The chances that any prince will follow the excellent Utopian model are virtually nil. Slaughter, treachery, abject fawning were the way of a world in which the devil and his minions were constantly at work. Utopia is a lecture sermon in an imaginative literary format borrowed from the ancients, and its author, like Colet delivering his sermons, was under no illusion that in this world all his precepts would be followed by men of sin assailed by the lusts of the flesh. There is something about the *Utopia* that suggests a book written "on the eve of"—a premonition of disaster, a sense of imminent catastrophe that gives urgency to the wish for salvation. And on sober appraisal there is not too much hope. More came out of the dream of Utopia to the reality of Henry VIII's England and pre-Reformation Europe. *Utopia* closes on a rueful note: "But I readily admit that there are very many features in the Utopian commonwealth which it is easier for me to wish for in our countries than to have any hope of seeing realized."[38] In his commentary on More, Father Edward Surtz felicitously juxtaposed this sentiment with a quotation from a letter by Erasmus, who had a few years earlier written to Antony of Bergen, the Abbot of Saint Bertin at Saint Omer: "As for us, we can wish for the best, but wish only."[39]

The idea that More hoped some of his proposals might conceivably be translated into action should not be rejected out of hand. Perhaps European princes would become more peaceful, the enclosure movement and the disinheritance of hard-working farmers might be stopped. At one time More toyed with the idea of dedicating *Utopia* to Cardinal Wolsey, who preceded him as chancellor of England, and the book may have been instrumental in effecting a few statutory changes in Tudor land policy. But it is farfetched to suppose that More was espousing economic communism for England, or remotely expected it. Was he an advocate of community of women because in his youth he had written a rhetorical exercise in its defense, or composed an epitaph about living with his two wives in heaven? Utopian viewing of prospective spouses in the nude, perhaps less related to sensuality than concern about venereal disease, was nonetheless so far beyond the pale of Christian conduct that More can hardly be suspected of having seriously proposed it. The precise measure of his earnestness with respect to specific Utopian institutions must continue to be elusive; he may not even have determined it himself. A reforming zeal could be combined with skepticism about the prospects for change, and the wildest of utopian plans could be dramatically thrown on the table to attract attention to the ills that needed remedy. More used the dialogue form in nearly all his works: It puts a certain distance between him and the reader, perplexes and tantalizes him, hints that the interlocutor is the author's alter ego considering the merits of a contrary point of view. But however fluid More's position, this seasoned lawyer, who served as a London judge and was engaged in diplomatic and commercial negotiations under Henry VIII and Wolsey, was no starry-eyed prophet or reformer, no innocent when it came to assessing the violence, caprices, and blind egotism of those at the apex of power.

Though More leaves doubts about the degree of his commitment to any particular Utopian institution, the underlying spirit of the Utopian laws enjoyed his approval in 1516. The More of the *Utopia* was for his period a humanist of good and free will both in personal and in public life, and his predilection was distinctly reflected in the book. In 1516 he would give men a large measure of doing what they would, as long as they caused no pain to themselves or to others. If taken in a commonsensical way, this principle is a startling novelty in Western thought. The Utopians are individual householders —an eighteenth-century French translation even calls them *bourgeois*—and they keep their own separate homes and gardens for a ten-year period. They may eat privately if they wish, though a common kitchen provides better food with less expenditure of labor. Goods are distributed in sufficient quantity to meet the requirements of each household, and no one wants more than enough —one of the more dubious Morean postulates. The Utopians enjoy great latitude in choosing the artisan work they perform, as long as they put in a normal six-hour day and have had some agricultural experience. In this relatively static society men can even get permission to move out of town, if their object is not to shirk labor by going to a new city.

This hardly seems a society driven by "want," as some scholars have held, or one in which there are excessively burdensome regulations. In the sixteenth century the Utopian workday would have appeared rather easy and the options numerous. There was an amplitude of choice, despite the ban on taverns, travel, and "lurking holes." Training is by example in the community, not through the harsh dictates of Plato's athletic masters or his vigilant old men in the secret, nocturnal council of the *Laws*. There is mutual respect among all men in private and in public relationships. The family is a spiritual institution and ecclesiastical functions like the confession are transferred from priests to fathers. Utopia is a benign patriarchal society in which age confers minor privileges on elders, who in turn encourage the growth of virtue among the young. At moments More seems to be reproducing the climate of his own household in Chelsea that so enchanted Erasmus, a "school and gymnasium of the Christian religion," where idleness and gaming were banished, intellectual pursuits encouraged, and the paternal authority unquestioningly accepted.

Utopia was free in its atmosphere, free of the chains of folly and greed, cheerful in the temper of its daily activities. It was not a rigorously regulated and repressive society whose constraints were dictated by fear. The preordained arrangements were limited to those necessary to permit everyone to do what he liked. This is the feeling conveyed to later generations. Utopia was a society of do's, not do not's. Excessive proselytizing zeal was repugnant to the Utopians because they believed that men should be allowed to go their own way as long as they intended no harm; the thunderous noise of converting missionaries only created public disturbance. Perhaps the Utopians were low on the transcendental, esteemed commodiousness too much, but they lived in peace and tolerance. More set the tone for the utopia of calm felicity that dominated much of Western consciousness up to the end of the eighteenth century: a quiet, stable existence free from anxiety, marked by honest allowable pleasures.

More's *Utopia* embarked on its long and checkered career first as a novel form of rhetoric, a way of teaching through entertainment. Its mood was one of mockery and earnestness combined, the precise measure of the parts depending upon the perception of the reader as much as upon the intent of the author. Others were writing in the same vein. Rabelais later opened *Gargantua* with an admonition to the reader to look for the marrow in the bone, though in the next breath he sowed confusion by poking fun at those who always searched for recondite meanings in literature. Invoking the spirit of Aristophanes and Lucian, Erasmus in his *Moriae Encomium* (1509) had tried to achieve the perfect balance between play and moral precept. If northern humanism was dedicated to both the "sweet and the useful," as a poem in praise of *Utopia* put it, a book had to be tested by this double standard. More's *Utopia* should be read in conjunction with Erasmus' *Moriae Encomium* and Rabelais's *Gargantua* and *Pantagruel,* despite the different dates of composition and varying styles. The resemblances lie not in specific descriptions and arguments, but in the temper of the works. Rabelais knew More's book well. Gargantua addresses letters to his father from Utopia, and it has even been conjectured that the English scholar Thaumaste, who engages Panurge in the famous pantomime debate, is Sir Thomas himself. Among a number of utopian excursions in Rabelais's writings, the most significant are the administration of the Abbey of

Thélème in *Gargantua* and the digression in *Pantagruel* in which Panurge tells of a wonderful city of happy debtors. Panurge's glorification of the city illustrates that favorite humanist device, the paradox. A man's falling into debt is generally assumed to be a calamity. On the contrary, it would be a delightful world if everybody were in debt, if everyone owed something to everyone else. How they would love, cherish, protect, and speak well of one another to safeguard their loans! The conceit is played out to the limit of its possibilities and a delirious logic proves incontrovertibly that if all men were debtors, society would be ideal. The regimen of the Abbey of Thélème flagrantly violates all monastic rules—there are no fixed hours, no vigils; but instead of begetting chaos, the reversal creates a magnificent sanctuary with a perfect order as the inhabitants, women as well as men, all spontaneously want to do the same things at the same time. More's *Utopia* deals with gold in the same paradoxical manner. The prize for whose possession men have struggled and slaughtered one another is deemed worthless, fit only for prisoners' chains or chamber pots. That which is most valued in the world is most debased in Utopia, and this upside-down scale is the cornerstone of a happy kingdom. Paradox is built into the very structure of the *Utopia,* and More has recourse to it again in his condemnation of the enclosure movement. The lamb, most guileless of creatures, symbol of Christian goodness, provider of sustenance and clothing, has become a monster that devours men. Its triumph, the extension of pasturage, has driven Christian farmers off the land and turned them into thieves who are hunted down and hanged or into starving beggars.

The motto of the Abbey of Thélème is: "Do what you will." The phrase has been related to a letter of Erasmus on freedom of the will, which in turn recalls the way of life in Utopia where, except for restrictions in a handful of laws, everybody does as he wishes. The handsome aristocrats in the Abbey of Thélème disport themselves in much the same fashion as do the small elite in Utopia freed from manual labor because of their special talents. They are engaged in a *philologia perennis,* the very activity that so gratified More and Erasmus when they were at leisure. True, there is far less drinking and random copulating in More's *Utopia* than in the society of Pantagruel, but the Abbey of Thélème, which represents an ideal existence in Rabelais, is anything but a spectacle of Roman debauchery. Gluttons and lechers are both excluded from its library, richly stocked with books in many languages.

More's vision of the good society in the *Utopia* did not require a conception of a perfect man. Christian humanism was not as absolutist as a religious millenarianism. More did not anticipate the reign of the Holy Ghost on earth and his Utopian is not a "new man" in the Abbot Joachim's or Thomas Müntzer's sense. He is a modified "old man," not wholly good by nature but capable of both good and evil—the Christian Platonic dualism persists—and the best in him is elicited by appropriate institutional arrangements. His pride, the most deadly vice, his satisfaction in his own elevation and another man's belittlement, is stifled by the prevailing rule of equality. For the rest, More has the Utopians once again reverse the expected order of things with a novel exegesis of the Biblical injunction about loving one's neighbor. "When nature bids you to be good to others, she does not command you conversely to be cruel and merciless to yourself."[40]

Before the schism of the Reformation, Christian humanists were beset by

doubts, conflicting beliefs, opposing loyalties. And they were candid enough
to express their misgivings and their ambivalences, to deliver themselves of
paradoxes, to say something and then partially retract it, to examine the potentialities of an idea without totally embracing it, to call attention to a present
evil by proposing an outrageous remedy like the *Utopia* and then withdrawing
from its advocacy. All this, of course, was possible only before the great upheaval. When Luther's breach became final and the whole politico-religious atmosphere was saturated with mistrust, intolerance, and hatred, More's view of
the world was radically altered, and so was the meaning of his *Utopia*.

After the Lutheran Heresy

After staring at the Holbein painting of More dated 1527, asking whether this
is the head of a martyr or of the author of *Utopia,* one recalls the plain chronological fact that the book had been written some twelve years before, in 1515,
and may have incorporated notes that went as far back as a conversation with
Erasmus in 1509. The neck around which More wears the gold chain that was
the mark of shame in Utopia is closer to the chopping block, indeed only eight
years away. An X ray of the picture has revealed a face that Holbein reworked
in many areas and that resembles even less a humanist scholar mildly amused
by the foibles of the world than does the austere and haunted visage of the
final, official portrait (now hanging in the Frick Collection in New York). It is
difficult to recognize the author of the elegant *Utopia* in this picture of a man of
fifty about to become lord chancellor of England, who had recently written
violent polemics in defense of the King's theology against the "insane calumnies of Luther" [41] and who would continue to denounce in book after book the
"heretyques of oure tyme that go busylye aboute to heape uppe to the skye
theyr foule, fylthye dunghyll of all olde and newe false, stynckyng heresyes,
gathered uppe together againste the trewe catholike faithe of Christ." [42]

Shortly after the *Utopia* was published, the schism in the Church had become open, and the whole intellectual world was turned upside down, but in
ways very different from the reforms of King Utopus. By 1520, fanciful innovations ceased to be laughing matters. The playful days were over; one did not
toy with utopias while Christendom was being torn asunder. The purported
demands for community of property by Thomas Müntzer and other Protestant leaders of the Peasant Wars of 1525, who were said to quote *Utopia* in a
German translation, revolted and alarmed Thomas More. The marriage of
nuns and priests and wild tales of Hussite sexual license disgusted him. Once
the "pestylent errours" and "pernyciouse heresyes" [43] had infested the Continent, More regretted much that he and his friend Erasmus had written. He
considered himself responsible for the consequences of his earlier works, as he
did in 1529 for the burning of a neighbor's grain through a fire that accidentally broke out on his property. He did not rewrite his past; but since he was
now wrongly interpreted he would not again publish in such a manner or encourage the diffusion of ideas that might lead men into error and bloody revolt. Erasmus (More means himself, too) had not been at fault, because he had
been trying to cure current evils and did not have in mind future ones. But
More advised greater caution in expression, and made it abundantly clear that
now he would not compound the evil he had unwittingly promoted by allow-

ing Erasmus' *Praise of Folly* or his own *Utopia* to appear in English: "I wolde not onely my derlynges bokes but myne owne also, helpe to burne them both wyth myne owne handes, rather than folke sholde (though thorow theyr own faute) take any harme of them."[44] The glee with which he had once hailed books like Ulrich von Hutten's *Letters of Obscure Men* that mystified and perplexed the boors was gone. There was a tinge of remorse that he had devoted so much of his time to levities that were misunderstood, and in 1533, when he composed a lengthy epitaph for himself during a period of illness, he dismissed his lighter writings with the terse remark: "He engaged to some extent in literary matters."[45] More always recognized degrees of evil, as his Utopians appreciated degrees of pleasure, and the evils he had deplored in 1516 occupied a less significant place in his order of vices fifteen years later. It was the heretical books, "growen so faste and sprongen uppe so thykke,"[46] that had killed more souls than the famine of lean years had killed bodies, and he attacked them with the vigor he had employed in the *Utopia* to denounce social and economic injustices.

More turned to writing a long succession of theological diatribes in English against the heretical enemies of the Catholic Church. The Latin literary writings of the period before 1520 belong to the European humanist tradition. The attack on Luther in Latin and the later English works are a defense of Catholicism in England against all those who would rend the seamless garment of Christ. After More's death his writings were collected either by men who sought to present before the world the brother-in-battle of Erasmus, the mocker of monks and theologians, the reviver of the evangelical spirit of Christ, or by coreligionists who saw only the enemy of Luther, Tyndale, and Frith and the martyr for the Roman faith. There was a tendency in his family and among English Catholics to ignore the writings of 1510–1520, while Continental humanists featured them and suppressed the attacks on Luther. William Roper managed to narrate his father-in-law's life without even a mention of the *Utopia*. In the same spirit, the Louvain 1565 edition of the *Opera Latina* expunged a section of the first book of the *Utopia* on the idleness of the monks and omitted many of the earlier writings, such as the correspondence with Erasmus and Martin Dorp and the letters on Biblical exegesis.

The hundreds of pages of invective More wrote in earthy English accessible to everyman are full of polemical devices that are more often Scholastic than classical in their inspiration. The vehemence of the attacks on Tyndale and Luther is worlds away from the graceful style and manner of *Utopia*. The heretics were within the city, Christendom was threatened, and the King and he were defenders of the faith—soon only he alone. He spewed forth his venom in a letter to Erasmus in 1533: "I find that breed of men [heretics] absolutely loathsome, so much so that, unless they regain their senses, I want to be as hateful to them as anyone can possibly be; for my increasing experience with those men frightens me with the thought of what the world will suffer at their hands."[47] More returned them polemical blow for blow. To keep his readers from nodding he was not above resorting to the scatological turns of phrase in which Luther excelled, or making oblique references to the hot sexual passion aroused by fair devils. The images he used were those of ordinary speech, the examples came from his wide experience in the law courts. With blunt coarseness he described Luther as a *cacadaemon* and invented a string of variations on the verb *cacare*.[48] Tyndale was denounced as "a bolde beste and a shameless whoremaster" and his writing as a "poysened stynkynge tayle of some stynkynge serpent."[49] John Foxe made of Thomas More the polemist a creature of the bishops, a man whose "finenesse of wit and scoffing termes" they found useful. Quoting Edward Hall's *Chronicle,* he offered a characterization of More's famous wit very different from that of Erasmus' eulogy. "For as by nature he was endued with a great wit, so the same againe was so mingled . . . with taunting and mocking, that it seemed to them that best knew him, that he thought nothing to be well spoken, except he had ministred some mocke in the communication."[50]

The Hair Shirt and the Quip

If sentiments voiced in *Utopia* are taken as humanist ideals that More could at least wish for and are compared with reflections in the *Apology* or the *Dialogue of Comfort* (1534), his very late works, it is difficult to hold to the thesis of his marvelous consistency that some modern expositors have propounded. But why should the moral utterances of a man of thirty-eight displaying his ingenuity in friendly rivalry with fellow humanists match the solemn reflections of that same man approaching death twenty years later, after catastrophic revolutions in Christendom and in the constitution of the kingdom he had served? The seasons change and so does the man. While in *Utopia* economic equality is the fundamental law, in the *Dialogue of Comfort* More's venerable spokesman Anthonye advances the threadbare arguments that if all property were divided equally nobody would be much better off than a beggar, and if a society was to function one man had to give work to many. Obviously, this does not square with the passionate defense of equality in all things made by Hythloday, or with the description of its salutary moral consequences. In attempts to reconcile the two attitudes toward property, *Utopia* has been called a Christian apostolic view, while the *Dialogue of Comfort* is supposed merely to mirror worldly reality. But one cannot help feeling that the German peasant uprisings and Anabaptist scandals had profoundly modified More's attitudes toward established laws and customs. In the *Dialogue of Comfort* he returned to traditional Christian concepts of charity. The former position that the problem of poverty was, ideally at least, amenable to a social institutional solution was abandoned.

While honest, allowable pleasures are the norm of Utopian life, the *Dialogue of Comfort,* through the mouth of Anthonye, merely allows a man "to take now & than some honest worldly myrth." More writes: "I dare not be so sore as utterly to forbyd yt, syth good men & well lernid have in some case alowid it, specyally for the diversitie of divers mens myndes."[51] Thus, what has been the general spirit in *Utopia* is in the *Dialogue* a rare and stinted concession. Man cannot reach heaven in a featherbed. Tribulation is not an evil, but a way to God—that is the burden of the *Dialogue.* The Utopians, in accordance with their rule of pleasure, had tried to eliminate pain entirely; they had even sanctioned euthanasia.

That life was a prison, an antechamber to death, was a Platonic and Christian image constantly renewed in More's writings, from the early Latin epigrams Erasmus appended to the Basel edition of *Utopia* through the last *Dialogue of*

Comfort More left for all Christian readers in adversity. But what was a sentiment among other Christian feelings couched in the late medieval language of piety—and we are fully aware of the convention—was often so intense that it broke the bounds of a layman's religion. Toward the end remembrance of death possessed More completely. Since the world was a prison, what mattered it whether one slept in a palatial chamber or in a tiny cubicle? Worldly affairs should be indifferent to men awaiting Judgment Day as they trembled for the salvation of their souls, and More fervently prayed in the Tower that he might "abstayn from vayne confabulations" and "estew light folysh myrth and gladnesse."[52] When he was writing the *Utopia,* he may sincerely have believed that distributive justice in the world was of pressing consequence to a Christian. Not by any stretch of the imagination can this be said of his later writing, surely not of the *Dialogue of Comfort.* In those years More could not even wish for, let alone hope for, the world of Utopia because the Turks were possessing Europe: the real Turks in Hungary, the Lutheran heretic Turk in Germany, and in England the monster Turk who was his King. More feared for his soul, for the souls of all European Christians, and he lived in trepidation that he would not stand up to the torture that he conceived of as a possibility— a ghastly dread from which he tried to shake himself free by relating long-winded jesting anecdotes about voluntary decapitation in the *Dialogue of Comfort.*

More himself told of his rage against the heretics. As an official he personally conducted raids on the German merchants in the Steelyard in London to search out copies of the Bible in the vernacular;[53] and he is accused of ordering a boy heretic to be whipped in his garden, and not with peacock feathers (the instrument for chastisement of his own children). Foxe's *Book of Martyrs* has left a circumstantial record, perhaps more true than false, of the cruel burning of Protestants under his chancellorship, which made More's name anathema to Englishmen for centuries. His epitaph gloried in his achievements as castigator of heretics, thieves, and murderers, who were regularly executed during his incumbency. Yet Hythloday had known no heretics in Utopia and had pitied the English thieves. The official word-portrait of More as a gentle humanist that Erasmus composed in 1519 for Ulrich von Hutten may hold for that date, but not for the bitter partisan who excoriated his opponents as idolaters more offensive to God than those who exalted "Beel, and Baal, and Belzabub, and all the devyls in hell."[54] If son-in-law Roper never heard him utter a word in anger, as he maintained in his biography, English heretics who suffered his taunts before their martyrdom might have borne witness to another side of his nature.

While changes in More's social and religious outlook readily find an explanation in the revolution of objective realities, his emotional tone invites a deeper inquiry. Only a psychology that is undaunted by polarities and ambivalences and contrarieties and paradoxes can presume to make sense of Thomas More without decapitating him psychically as the executioner did physically. For all his beguiling humor, More was always obsessed with death. This was a constant of his psychic existence. Among his youthful English poems was the couplet: "The head that lay easily and full soft,/ Instede of pylows lyeth after on the blocke."[55] At the time of Henry VIII's greatest favor toward him, More observed to Roper that the King would unhesitatingly part with his learned chancellor's head to "winne him a castle in Fraunce."[56] On another occasion he told Roper that if only Christendom could be united again he would gladly have himself thrown into the Thames in a sack,[57] a vision of self-immolation inspired by the passion of Christ; he would die that the world might be saved. And in his English works death was a recurrent theme: "We dye all the tyme we lyve"; "What cause shoulde make us to dye willingly"; "Of lothnes to die and gladnes to dye"; "The lackes that cause one loth to Dye"; "Dye we must, lyve we never so longe"; "Death determineth the wretchedness of this lyfe"; "Death a nygh neighbour"; "Death the dreadful messenger of God."[58] The common Christian need to reflect on death had more than a formal character in his writings. To a Latinist, More's very name echoed the sound of death, *mors,* intermingled with folly, *moria,* preceded by a doubting Thomas. According to Nicholas Harpsfield, one of his early biographers, More composed punning Latin verses on the "folly" and "death" in his name: "You are foolish if you entertain any long hope of remaining here on earth. Even a fool can advise you, More, on this score. Stop being foolish and contemplate staying in heaven; even a fool can advise you, More, on this score."[59] Among the English verses young More composed for hangings of fine painted cloth in his father's house the fifth verse accompanied an image of death. "Though I be foule, ugly, lene and mysshape,/ Yet there is none in all this worlde wyde,/ That may my power withstande or escape."[60] The lad's doggerel revealed no extraordinary poetic talent in the making, but was the first of scores of similar reflections. More's Latin epigrams, translations from the *Greek Anthology* as well as his own original poems, abound in traditional commentaries on the futility of life, the omnipresence of death, the fear of death, the progress toward death. But though the themes are treated in the manner of the age, their prominence has its own significance.[61]

A Treatise on Ecclesiastes 7, "Remember the last things, and thou shalt never sin," apparently written in 1522, only seven years after *Utopia,* is a memento mori many of whose thoughts reappeared in the *De Tristitia Christi* written in the Tower. "If you consider this well, thou mayest look upon death, not as a stranger, but as a nigh neighbor. For as the flame is next the smoke, so is death next an incurable sickness; and such is all our life . . .

"Which measuring of time and diminishing of life, with approaching towards death, is nothing else but from our beginning to our ending, one continual dying: so that wake we, sleep we, eat we, drink we, mourn we, sing we, in what wise soever live we, all the same while die we. So that we never ought to look towards death as a thing far off, considering that although he make no haste towards us, yet we never cease ourselves to make haste towards him." Anecdotes and examples from men carted to the gallows all bear the same moral: Even a young man is on the way to execution, though he may have a little longer time than others to traverse the road. The analogies to life as a prison and men as the waiting victims occur over and over again. "We be very sure that we be already condemned to death, some one, some other, none of us can tell what death we be doomed to, but surely can we all tell that die we shall." The "dainty body" is juxtaposed with the "stinking carrion."[62]

In More's last year in the Tower, contemplation of death bore him to new heights of religious feeling. The debate with himself on death and martyrdom in the *De Tristitia Christi* gave expression to thoughts that he had harbored many years, and that now possessed his whole being. With moving candor he struggled with his fear and weakness. "To expose one's self to death for Christ's sake when the case clearly demands it or when God gives a secret prompting to do so, this, I do not deny, is a deed of preeminent virtue. But otherwise I do not think it very safe to do so, and among those who willingly suffered for Christ we find outstanding figures who were very much afraid, who were deeply distressed, who even withdrew from death more than once before they finally faced it bravely." [63] In the end he transcended his fear of death and identified himself with Christ in magnificent passages where his own triumph shines through. "How is it that now, by a sudden reversal, you [Christ] leap up and spring forth like a giant running his race and come forward eagerly to meet those who seek to inflict that passion upon you?" He preached to himself and all mankind to follow Christ's example. "Hither, hither let all hasten who are faint of heart. Here let them take firm hold of an unwavering hope when they feel themselves struck by a horror of death." [64] But More lost nothing of his psychological acumen in prison. In *De Tristitia Christi* he analyzed the raving madness and perversity of Judas. "The ingrate desires the death of the very victim he has unjustly injured. So too, the person whose conscience is full of guilty sores is so sensitive that he views even the face of his victim as a reproach and shrinks from it with dread." [65] Henry VIII was not named, but his role in the passion of Thomas was barely disguised.

The salvation of man's soul through penitential exercises to crush the lusts of the flesh was one Christian way, and More had worn a hair shirt till the blood flowed onto his clothes. Thomas Stapleton, the Louvain theologian, has reported on the preservation of More's instrument of self-punishment as a relic by his family. "Throughout his whole life on certain days and at certain times he wore a hair-shirt and took the discipline . . . More than twenty years ago Margaret, the wife of Dr. Clements, showed me the holy man's hair-shirt when I was at Bergen near Antwerp . . . The hair-shirt was knotty, like a net, much rougher, I should think, than are commonly hair-shirts of religious. His discipline, through some negligence, had been lost." [66] Penance had a broad meaning for More, related to the need to inflict pain upon himself as a religious duty. It was a punitive revenging of his sins upon himself, a payment for sin through sacrifice, for he owed some immense debt beyond redemption. As Anthonye told his beloved Vyncente in the *Dialogue of Comfort,* adapting from Jean Gerson, "the lesse affliccion that he felith in his sowle, the more payne in recompence let hym put uppon his body, & pourge the spirite by the affliccion of the flesh." [67]

More's gloomy inner recesses and his urbane, attractive facade were always present together, though at different periods in life either the penitential or the jocular side of his nature was more in evidence in books, in the family circle, in public behavior. The hair shirt, the self-flagellation with knotted ropes, the vigils, and the fasts were there, even when his dark view of man's journey on earth was covered over with a cheerful demeanor and a jesting way of speech that served to hide his inner torment. For many years anxiety was drowned in constant activity in the law courts, taking care of the king's business, following the royal household from manor to manor, robbing himself of a few hours of sleep to study and write. As time passed and cataclysms broke over Christendom, with ugly manifestations in England from which More could not extricate himself, his penitential passion became stronger and the uses of this world ever staler to him. But even in the last dialogue written in prison, even on the scaffold, the joking mask was not completely dropped. Only in the manuscript notes of his prison psalter has the balance been upset, as he writes in the margin over and over again: *demones, demones, demones.*[68]

Reviewing his whole life, the beginning that prefigures the end and the end that clarifies the beginning, one might say that More's deep melancholy bespoke aggression turned inward, while his wit, which, *pace* Erasmus, could be bitter and scratchy, was a sign of aggression turned outward, a protective device against the mortal danger of a violence directed entirely against the self. The ferocious sarcasm of his polemics against the heretics was an outlet for the angry passion that was consuming him. More's final willing of death was a surrender to the cup of temptation that had been close to his lips throughout his adult years; and he celebrated the event in character, with a quip to the executioner.

Of the many brilliant attempts to define laughter, wit, and humor in man's psychic economy, the distinction between wit and humor that has been essayed by Jean-Paul Richter and by Sigmund Freud may give us a window into the troubled breast of Thomas More. There is a wit that can be barbed and cruel, that vents its aggressive energy against a person or thing, and there is a humor that is a triumph, a transcendent exercise that liberates its possessor by separating him from his interests and anxieties, diminishing them through distance, making them childish, unreal, a fitting subject of merriment.[69] Both wit and humor were Thomas More's guardian angels, intervening at the gravest and most critical junctures in his life.

"Humour is not resigned; it is rebellious. It signifies the triumph not only of the ego, but also of the pleasure principle, which is strong enough to assert itself here in the face of the adverse real circumstances." The penitential More would doubtless have been taken aback by such an analysis of his behavior on the scaffold, yet in many ways he was an outstanding illustration of what Freud was contending. The elements of humor in *Utopia's* denial of reality and the liberating humor of More's last moments on earth are brought together. "By its repudiation of the possibility of suffering it [humor] takes its place in the great series of methods devised by the mind of man for evading the compulsion to suffer—a series which begins with neurosis and culminates in delusions, and includes intoxication, self-induced states of abstraction and ecstasy."[70] To this list Freud might have added utopia-making as a mental exercise.

More's wit and satire were meant to correct, chastise, wound. His aggression ran the gamut from tame to carnivorous. In the *Utopia,* when he was animated by a desire to reform institutions, not turn his back on them as worldly matters unworthy of his concern, he ridiculed diplomatic pomp by decking out an ambassador in the gold that Utopians used for chamber pots; and he derided the English judicial system with savage attacks delivered through the mouth of the wild prophet Hythloday. He poked fun at the clergy, writing his friend Peter Giles that a theologian had already asked to be named Bishop of Utopia. (Later the tale sprang up that a credulous canon of St. Paul's and rector of Merton College had asked for the appointment.) The wit could assume a teasing character. More loved to confound literalists, many of whose present-day heirs have turned his jokes into history and political theory. At other times satiric jibes were weapons of theological warfare intended to degrade and demean enemies. In his burning tirades against the heretics More could not resist interrupting the flow of apocalyptic language with malevolent jests about the persons of his adversaries. When he was harpooning Tyndale with every lethal rhetorical device at his command he heaped scorn upon his antagonist's clumsy style. "Though I can not make hym by no meane to wryte trewe mater, I wolde have hym yet at the leste wyse wryte trew englyshe."[71]

In the final period of his contest with Henry VIII the witticisms assumed the nature of a reckless play with instruments of violence that could ricochet against More himself. As his opposition to the King hardened and it became clearer that he could maintain the purity of his Christian conscience only at the price of open defiance, he challenged and demeaned the royal will. Declining the bishops' invitation that he accompany them to the coronation of Anne Boleyn, he warned them about the impending loss of their virtue through the seemingly innocuous act of their attendance, and entertained them by telling a witty tale with a concealed dart—all meant to be reported. "[It] putteth me in Remembrance of an Emperour that had ordained a lawe that whosoever committed a certaine crime, except it were a virgen, should suffer the paines of death, such was the reverence he bare to virginitie. Now so it happened that the first committer of the offence was indeede a virginne; whereof the Emperour hearing, was in no smale perplexitie, being greatlie desierous to have the lawe put in execution, and by example of Iustice to terrifie others. Whereupon when his Councell sate long, solemnlie debating the matter, sodenlie there arose one amongst them, and saide, 'Why make you so much adoe, my lordes, about so smale a matter? Let her first be defloured, then after may she be devoured' . . . Now, my lordes," said More, "it lieth not in my powre but that they may devoure me; but, by godes holie grace, I will provide yey shall never defloure me."[72] The lecherous King who had deflowered so many others would not have him. This punning, rhyming wit was a fiery instrument that seared its victims.

But it was humor rather than aggressive wit that in the final days came to More's aid and helped him face death, jests that placed him outside the reach of his own circumstances and made him invulnerable. With gallows humor he was able to annihilate reality. Imprisoned in the Tower, he told a visitor, or spy, that he had changed his mind. When a document approving the royal marriage was hastily brought for his signature, he claimed that he had been misunderstood; he had changed his mind merely about shaving his beard before the execution.[73] In his very last moments he found solace in deflating the dreadful solemnity of a public execution, though it was his own. As he ascended the stairs to the scaffold, he appealed to an officer: "Help me up with your hand, for as for my comming doone, let me shift as I may, for by then I ame sure I shall take no great harme."[74] It is easy to discover in later utopians of stature ambiguities and aggressive violence akin to Thomas More's. There are martyrs among them. But none to our knowledge achieved his transcendent humor.

The quips and puns More directed at himself and others now give delight as a mild release of our own desire to hurt, but the physical penitential reality of More's personal existence is so strange and brutal one begins to suspect that self-destructive drives are in operation beneath the affable exterior. Preoccupation with death may be dismissed as a common experience of sixteenth-century man, or of everyman. The terrors of purgatory and hell loomed large in More's time. But if all men were absorbed with death, its pangs were not equally intense, and the unconscious mechanisms More used to combat the death wish were not always available to others. The gifts of wit and humor are not universal.

Five hundred years after More's birth we are still perplexed by him. Even a secularist who is mocking of the doctrine of papal supremacy for which More died can admire the courage of his stance in the face of absolute royal power, bedecked with the laws of the realm, demanding positive, overt, verbal obedience. More engages our sympathies. But when we remember that he meted out similar punishments to "his heretics," we have to draw back, in the realization that religious zeal has been among the most barbarous of human vices. One man's martyr is another man's persecutor. As John Foxe moralized: "Thus Bishop Fisher and Sir Tho. More, which a little before had put John Frith to death for heresie against the Pope, were themselves executed and beheaded for treason against the King."[75]

There is a hidden violence in More and a controlled rage that is the more startling when it breaks through the calm surface in controversy and acts of authority. The source of his deep melancholy—the violence turned inward— has been looked for in the traditional places, in the early loss of a mother, in the dominance of a father who brought home three successive stepmothers, in the death of a beloved wife; but nothing quite accounts for the polarity of More's jocular and penitential nature. He who wanted to become a monk was forced by his father to be a lawyer, and in the end he rose to a spiritual order higher than the protected monastic servant of God. He became a martyr. But then the historic anomaly intrudes: He had written a little book that has appeared in over 150 editions and has sparked movements of men he would have considered diabolical in a literal sense. That More who was haunted by the fear of death and the fear of wishing death wrote a book about an order of worldly contentment in which death appears only casually as euthanasia may be one of the triumphs of the utopian imagination. *Utopia*, toppling the existing world order in fantasy, an innocent act of destruction, may have been for More, as it was for many who came after him, a saving act of sublimation.

The Later Fortune of Utopia

if one turns from the person of More to the *Utopia* after More's death, the significance of things seems once again radically transformed. Tracing the later history of *Utopia*, its *fortuna,* the readings of successive ages, is an endeavor that involves the uses to which *Utopia* was put in other men's works and reveals the dynamic power of the book as a font of revolutionary slogans and vivid images of human suffering and hope, often transplanted to a wholly alien context. When in the nineteenth and twentieth centuries the *Utopia* began to be treated as a document reflective of the socioeconomic or intellectual state of sixteenth-century Europe, an expository tradition was initiated to which belong some of the more dismal and outlandish theses about the book.

Should it have been given to Thomas More in the afterlife to contemplate the long and convoluted stream of scholarly interpretations of his writings, he must indeed be enjoying a jolly spectacle, since the anguish that underlay his jocularity during his lifetime has in paradise doubtless been assuaged, if not entirely wiped away. A man who was rarely more gratified than when his readers or his auditors in the family circle guessed his meaning wrongly or took seriously a flash of humor or a joke solemnly delivered would derive no small pleasure—if such mild forms of aggression are allowable in heaven— from the bewildered efforts of the expositors of *Utopia* in later times. He must have been entertained by William Morris turning him into a prophet of socialism, John Stuart Mill of utilitarianism, Karl Kautsky of communism, Gerhard Ritter and Hermann Oncken of British imperialism, Russell Ames of bourgeois democracy. The Catholic writers who in celebrating his elevation to sainthood found it appropriate to dismiss his *Utopia* as a mere jeu d'esprit may have annoyed him as much as R. W. Chambers' attempt to see him only looking backward to corporate life in the Middle Ages. Having passed through the fire of a trial by Benedictine scholars and achieved sainthood, he is in no need of such rewriting of his history. The ingeniousness and subtlety of Father Surtz, with his evocation of parallels in other men's learning and his artful demonstration of the total consistency of More's ideas in all seasons, must appear somewhat strained to a man as self-revealed as More was. The present interpretation may find no greater favor with Saint Thomas, unless psychological analysis has made further progress in heaven than it has among academic historians on earth.

By the time the reductionist readings of More began to proliferate, Europeans had become involved with various versions of a dynamic, revolutionary utopia, and the utopia of changeless, calm felicity to which More and his followers were committed was assessed for its part in a dynamic historical process: More was appreciated as either furthering the revolutionary utopia of Western man in one or another of its definitions, or striving to stay its advance in the name of a medieval corporate Christian ideal. He was a chapter in the history of democracy, communism, individualist utilitarianism. Squeezing *Utopia* under such rubrics is like reducing *Hamlet* to a play about the Danish succession.

When More described the varieties of religious worship in Utopia nobody at the time could have imagined that he was advocating religious liberty in John Stuart Mill's sense. And nothing could be more anachronistic than Mill's contention that More's Utopian doctrine of pleasure was an early version of the principle of utility, unless it is the position assumed in Robert Southey's colloquy, in which More laments "the decay of the feudal system";[76] or Karl Kautsky's attempt to adopt More as a member in good standing of the Social Democratic party of the early twentieth century; or Father Surtz's presentation of More as an enlightened, perhaps slightly heterodox, member of the present-day Jesuit order, a man who would be called to account from time to time by the director general, but who would nevertheless be treated with respect as a sort of Renaissance Teilhard de Chardin; or Russell Ames's identification of More as a precursor of Diderot, Jefferson, and Sun Yat Sen, and his description of *Utopia* as "a product of capitalism's attack on feudalism, a part of middle-class and humanist criticism of a decaying social order."[77]

Literary readings have been almost as lopsided. Taking off from C. S.

Lewis' theme of the playful jest Dorsch has endeavored to show that the whole of the *Utopia* is pure Lucianic satire, an updated *True Story*, whose real aim is to make fun of all ideal societies. In concentrating almost exclusively on the mocking names in Greek—Hythloday the babbler, Anydrus the dry river, Amaurote the dim city—Dorsch makes the jocular completely submerge the grave. If any Morean dialogue was deadly earnest in its purpose it was the diatribe against Luther in 1523; yet its protagonist in the original version of the work was a Spaniard called Baravellus, a name that sounds quite as absurd as Hythloday. A recent study reaches into the newer criticism for its recondite analysis and turns the whole of the *Utopia* into an existentialist contest between More and Hythloday over the limits of "consciousness-in-conscience" and the duty of man in society. There is even available a French structuralist rendering of *Utopia*.

Hexter and Prévost, Donner and the Delcourts and Süssmuth have restored More the Christian humanist to his time and place, and in many respects they have together contributed to a certain consensus about *Utopia*, though the problems of consistency, of the extent of More's advocacy of the Utopian society, and of the balance of his personality remain at issue. More's ambiguity is contagious and a commentator has no sooner uttered a definitive judgment on meaning than he feels a need to retract part of it. Great philosophical dialogues have invariably led to sharply conflicting interpretations—witness the works of Hume and Diderot. One who uses the dialogue form too adroitly is likely to suffer a strange fortune for his pains: *Le Neveu de Rameau* becomes a hippy manifesto, *Utopia* a communist one.

If there is an important break between the More of the *Utopia* and the later More, an even wider chasm separates the *Utopia* from its historical, as differentiated from its scholarly, destiny.

Once More had been recognized as a founder of a race of Utopians who traced their ancestry back to him, *Utopia* became an inspirational text to which men of action turned for sustenance and support. It became a dialogue of comfort for men subversive of their social order. Particularly in the English-speaking world, felicitous turns of speech in the free, Robinson translation of 1551, with its vibrant Tudor phraseology, were used to reinforce age-old, amorphous, revolutionary feelings and to quicken awareness of the dichotomous conflict between rich and poor, oppressors and oppressed. Passages toward the end of the second book, passionate outcries against injustice, had a universal resonance. The order of society was unjust, a condition due primarily to the usurpations of the rich, who through the mechanism of the laws palmed off their rule as justice. The moral indignation that later excited men who read Rousseau or Marx was captured here in pithy formulas, which seeped down into popular culture.

"Consequently, when I consider and turn over in my mind the state of all commonwealths flourishing anywhere today, so help me God, I can see nothing else than a kind of conspiracy of the rich, who are aiming at their own interests under the name and title of the commonwealth. They invent and devise all ways and means by which, first, they may keep without fear of loss all that they have amassed by evil practices and, secondly, they may then purchase as cheaply as possible and abuse the toil and labor of all the poor. These devices become law as soon as the rich have once decreed their observance in the name of the public—that is, of the poor also!"[78] Pamphlets of the English Revolution like the anonymous *Tyranipocrit Discovered* (1649) faithfully echoed the *Utopia* when they denounced the rich thieves "who make a combination and call it a law, to hang a poor man if he do steal, when they have wrongfully taken from him all his maintenance." In the course of British history, Hythloday's outburst at Cardinal Morton's table, where he epitomized enclosures as sheep devouring men, was paraphrased in a hundred different settings by agrarian rebels, and the image was carried over into the industrial revolution, translated into the spectacle of machines devouring the men who made them. It would be supererogatory to trace in detail the history of such apostrophes, which carry along with them a utopian hope for the opposite of the condition they describe; they saturate the modern revolutionary atmosphere, the air of all revolutions.

No one in later generations cared whether or not Hythloday quoted Plato inaccurately when he announced that this "sage" foresaw the one and only road to the general welfare as "the maintenance of equality in all respects."[79] In despite of themselves, Plato and More were together enlisted in the ranks of the economic egalitarians who would abolish private property and money and institute communism in all things for all men. Phrases and formulas from *Utopia* were assimilated with the language of Rousseau and Owen and Marx. Rousseau himself cited passages from *Utopia* to demonstrate the moral degradation of a civilization of gross inequality that based one man's pleasure on another's pain, and Marx quoted More on the inhuman devastations of the enclosure movement as symbolic of ruthless capitalism from its very inception.

The simple affirmation that money is the root of all evil became the foundation stone of countless utopian fantasies, many of them still very much alive. One is not obliged either to quote Sallust as More's source or consider More the inventor of the idea to perceive that Hythloday's words in themselves were powerful historical catalysts. Abolish money and all the ills of mankind would be resolved. "Who does not know that fraud, theft, rapine, quarrels, disorders, brawls, seditions, murders, treasons, poisonings, which are avenged rather than restrained by daily executions, die out with the destruction of money? Who does not know that fear, anxiety, worries, toils, and sleepless nights will also perish at the same time as money?"[80] When revolutionaries read Hythloday's resounding attack on the evils of filthy lucre, they may not have followed his Christian argument that pride was the sin which had wedded mankind to money; nor did many bother to ponder More's closing reflection that he had refrained from answering the prophet Hythloday because he knew that he would brook no opposition anyway. In the history of utopian thought the dramatic phrases that packed a punch, encapsulations of massive and amorphous protests, demands, hopes, were remembered by themselves and reiterated. More's demurrer—"I cannot agree with all that he said"[81]—was forgotten.

More's is not the only work of utopian thought whose enduring significance as a historical force has resided in its pungent rhetoric, rather than in the fine nuances of thought that twentieth-century scholarship has laboriously discovered wherever they exist in the text and even where they do not. Jean-Jacques is an eighteenth-century parallel. And anyone who has observed students thumbing Herbert Marcuse's ponderous Hegelian dialectic and coming away with a slogan will recognize the same phenomenon in our own time. More's role in the history of utopian thought derives from a surface, simplistic, and fast reading of the text, and is not much illuminated by scholarly expositions, however admirable, that point out recondite precedents in the Church Fathers, among contemporary humanists, or in classical literature. The *Utopia* served as a revolutionary document in the same sense that the *Discourse on Inequality* did —against the manifest will of its author. What survived was the passion of Hythloday, not the caution of his ambassadorial interlocutor, Thomas More.

But the uses of More's *Utopia* have by no means been restricted to fostering an egalitarian revolutionary spirit, first among English radicals, then French revolutionaries, finally Marxists. Over the centuries it has been adapted to diverse purposes in the Old World and New—and not all of them would have gratified Thomas More. As early as 1520, the German author of a vitriolic attack on the papal extortion of monies from Germany advertised his connection with More's work by using the nom de plume "Philalethes civis Utopiensis."[82] A few decades later a Mexican judge, Vasco de Quiroga, introduced a Utopian constitution into a network of Indian hospital-villages in Santa Fe, with common ownership of property, alternation of rural and urban employment, the six-hour workday, and distribution of goods according to need.[83] A French lawyer, René Choppin, cited the Lex Utopiensium in 1574 in a treatise, *De privilegiis rusticorum libri tres,* to support a proposal that every Frenchman should at some time engage in agriculture and that rural life should not be abandoned for the sake of the city—though Choppin's principal concern was productivity, not the condition of the peasantry, and he would have been quite out of sympathy with More's curtailment of the working day.[84]

Translations of *Utopia* into many languages including the Japanese and the Chinese—a steady progression for more than four centuries—have tended to update the little book as each generation and society have refashioned the island kingdom to serve their own needs. In retrospect, one of the most outlandish reincarnations is a 1780 rendering into French by M. T. Rousseau, dedicated to Count Vergennes, Minister of Foreign Affairs, which extols his regime as a fulfillment of the laws of More's Utopia and a final realization of its humanity. Lest his patron be offended by too close a comparison with the English martyr, Rousseau concluded his eulogy with a comforting prediction: "The happy lot you will enjoy till the end of your days will be the only respect in which posterity will find you different from that great man."[85]

The deft combination of moods of More's *Utopia* has never been reproduced. In this sense it has had no progeny, only epigoni. When utopia became entirely serious, an important shift occurred in European consciousness. Among all the elements that have entered into Western utopia, millenarianism played no part in Erasmus, More, and Rabelais. When millenarianism was married to utopia in the Anabaptist uprisings, More was profoundly shocked and dismayed. For him the heavenly city was separate from an earthly optimum republic. One might speculate about it, dream about it, measure the shortcomings of contemporary society against it; but true bliss belonged only to the other world, which could not be brought down to the terrestrial sphere.

There is something as fundamentally paradoxical about the utopian tradition that derived from Thomas More as there is about the man himself. The *Utopia* was the offspring of a nostalgia for what in the early sixteenth century was conceived to be the spirit of ancient Greece and for what evangelicals believed to be the moral truths of apostolic Christianity; yet the later utopian passion for happiness in this world was a potent force in wiping out both of these traditions. The temper of the original Christian humanist utopia in More, Erasmus, and Rabelais was gay, playful, tolerant, skeptical, amusing in varying degrees; by the seventeenth century the utopian tradition that stemmed from it became grave, absolutist, self-righteous, assured of its truth, apocalyptic, vehement. That More's *Utopia* was read in the spirit of the deadly earnest reformers and revolutionaries is perhaps the dialectical destiny of many great works. Posterity often turned Utopia into its opposite; no place became some place very specific, and the utopian who was going there knew precisely where it was, how to get there, and what he would find when he landed. The *Utopia* itself is a sport in the history of utopian thought, since the main current from the Reformation forward moves in a different direction. The utopias of absolute faith recognize no compromise, virtually no distinctions among greater and lesser evils. The utopia of Christian humanism could still ridicule itself as well as the miserable real world in which the colloquy took place. In later utopias there are no jokes worth telling, no absurd scenes to narrate.

5

A *Città Felice* for Architects and Philosophers

THE COUNCIL OF TRENT had already been sitting for three years when a couple of footloose literary scamps, Ortensio Landi and Antonio Francesco Doni, given to excoriating the vices of the age in a flamboyant style and to inventing wild fantasies, collaborated on the publication in Venice, 1548, of Thomas More's *Utopia* under the title *La Republica nuovamente ritrovata del governo dell'isola Eutopia* (The Newly Discovered Republic of the Government of the Isle of Eutopia).

The Reception of More in Italy

Landi was acquainted with the family of Antonio Buonvisi, a patrician from Lucca who had been close to More during a stay in London and to whom More had addressed a moving, affectionate letter in the last days of his life. It was probably through the Buonvisi that Landi came to know the *Utopia,* and seized with its charm he prepared a translation for Italian readers. Though it does not bear his name on the title page, he acknowledged his connection with it obliquely by signing his other works "Philalethes ex Utopia," "Polyto-piensis civis," or "Messer Anonymo di Utopia." This restless doctor and soldier of fortune fancied the idea of hailing from Noplace. His critical writings, the *Quattro libri de dubbi* (Four Books of Doubts), 1552, and the *Commentario delle piu notabili, et mostruose cose d'Italia* (Commentary on the Most Notable and Monstrous Affairs of Italy), 1548, are violent diatribes against the brutishness of Italian society and the "Sardanapali" and "Epicuri" who ruled its states from Sicily to Venice; there are passages that recall Raphael Hythloday's bitter invective against oppressors of the poor in early sixteenth-century England. In the *Commentario,* Landi reversed the Morean fable and played the role of a citizen of Utopia bearing witness to the depravities of contemporary Italy.[1]

Landi's collaborator Doni, a defrocked monk and bankrupt printer, compiler of writings ancient and modern, was the editor of the Landi translation, and it was he who signed the letter of dedication to Gieronimo Fava praising More's republic for its excellent customs, forthright government, and real human beings. Actually the book was a bowdlerized paraphrase rather than a translation. Four years later, in 1552, Doni tried his own hand at utopia-making in a dialogue entitled "Mondo Savio," included in his extravaganza *I Mondi celesti, terrestri, et infernali, de gli accademici pellegrini,* a conversation between a sage and a madman who had been conducted into a perfect, star-shaped city, the setting for a reformed society. Its laws and manners—among them the promiscuous resorting to women, who are quartered in a separate district, and the abolition of marriage—turned out to be more offensive to devout ears than those of More's *Utopia.* On the whole the piece is pretty dull fare, neither funny nor subtle. *I Mondi* went through many editions in Italian and in French translation, though later versions were thoroughly expurgated by order of the church censors. Doni's *I Marmi* and some of his other works were tainted with heresy, but his satirical style and his mask of buffoonery gave him a measure of protection.[2] While on any particular subject one can never be certain whether or not Doni is jesting, his general moralizing intention is not in doubt.

In 1561 More's *Utopia* became more widely known in Italy when Francesco Sansovino included in his compendium of comparative politics, *Del governo dei regni et delle republiche cosi antiche come moderne libri XVIII* (Eighteen Books on the Government of Kingdoms and Republics Ancient and Modern), long passages from the Landi translation under the rubric "Del governo della republica d'Utopia," by "Tomaso Moro cittadino di Londra, & huomo santissimo di vita." A bizarre commingling of the real and the imaginary such as Sansovino produced is not uncommon in the history of utopian literature. Other orthodox Catholic writers were harder put to assimilate More, and his reception was sometimes ambivalent. Though written by a martyr, his work if taken literally was streaked with religious and moral doctrines anathema to the church militant of the Counter-Reformation. As an individual More was widely admired for his heroic defense of the faith, was depicted in dramas and essays as a gentle Christian saint, and was eulogized by the formidable Cardinal Bellarmine. Ellis Heywood (the son of More's friend John Heywood), who found refuge in Italy, where he changed his name to Eliseo Heivodo, composed the dialogue *Il Moro* (Florence, 1556) dealing with the nature of true happiness, one of the first books to attempt an evocation of the character of More.[3] And Traiano Boccalini in his *Ragguagli di Parnaso* (1612), a potpourri that included a pseudo-utopian excursion and was republished more than twenty-five times in the course of the seventeenth century, called More a "santissimo literato." But his person aside, there were specific proposals in the text of *Utopia* that had to be either explained away or overlooked if his golden *libellus* was to be unequivocally approved in Counter-Reformation Italy.

Most apologists interpreted *Utopia* as a mere literary contrivance to castigate contemporary society for its corruption, or suggested that the book had been written at Cardinal John Morton's behest to offer a model of life in a terrestrial paradise and was not to be taken literally as a prescription for Christian behavior in the present world. Ignored were King Utopus' banishment of religious zealots, the disquisition on pleasure, the premarital review of prospective spouses, and the boldness of advocating common ownership of property. A number of judicious alterations made by Sansovino in the excerpts from *Utopia* that he published facilitated More's integration into post-Trentine society. Landi's *voluttà*, a proper translation of the original, was replaced by *volontà*, which made utter nonsense of many sentences in More's discussion of *voluptas* in Utopia. More's martyrdom, a measure of allegorizing, and a bit of word-twisting all contributed to the work's survival in Italy without getting on the Index. (It did not fare so well in Spain, where in 1583 the Archbishop of Toledo prohibited it.)[4] In 1620 the Latin text was republished intact with a Milan imprint. Not until 1625 was a serious attack leveled against More, in one of the *Dialoghi* of Lodovico Zuccolo entitled "L'Aromatario, overo della Republica d'Utopia," a trivial piece in which virtually no aspect of *Utopia* escaped criticism. The whole idea was condemned as impossible from the outset because men by nature resembled savage beasts rather than More's pure-hearted citizens. Zuccolo's attempt at demolition was really intended to clear the way for his own jejune and boring utopian exercises, "Il Belluzzi, overo della città felice" and "Il Porto, overo della Republica d'Evandria," idealizations of the republic of San Marino.[5]

In the second half of the sixteenth century a brief flurry of earnest utopian dialogues had followed the diffusion of More's ideas by Landi and Doni. Francesco Patrizi's *La Città felice* (1553), a brief youthful essay by a great philosophical intelligence, was far more profoundly Platonic and Aristotelian than it was Morean, but it was in some sense a response to Landi's translation. The solemnity of Patrizi was completely alien in spirit to Thomas More's playfulness; and this holds for virtually the whole of the philosophical utopian experience of the Italian Renaissance—it is More stripped of ambiguities. Roman *gravitas* presides over Italian utopia, with the obvious exception of Doni's and Boccalini's mad capers. In Patrizi's sketch there were already intimations of a commitment to heterodox Platonic doctrines which, when voiced in the *Nova de Universis Philosophia* of his mature years, brought him to the notice of the Inquisition, notwithstanding his elevation to the bishopric of Cherso.[6] Portions of Uberto Foglietta's dialogues about the vices of the old Genoese nobility, accompanied by proper reformist proposals, in *Della republica di Genova libri II* (Rome, 1559), are occasionally included in anthologies of Italian utopias, though perhaps without much justification. In a zealous endeavor to gather all the strands of sixteenth-century Italian utopian thought, one scholar has even drawn in the paradoxical *Encomium Neronis* by the Milanese genius and libertine Girolamo Cardano. In this work, which followed his son's condemnation for murder by the Senate of Milan, Cardano advocated a powerful monarchy, with Nero, the archenemy of the senators, portrayed as the protector of poor wretches from the exactions of aristocrats and the merciless verdicts of their justice.[7] The shocking conceit of turning Nero into a hero recalls the inversions of *Utopia,* and the denunciations of aristocratic justice echo the indignation of Hythloday, but that is as far as the similarity goes. Ludovico Agostini's dialogue about an imaginary republic, probably written in the late 1580s and closer to More in form if not in spirit, remained in manuscript in Pesaro until the twentieth century.[8] Its author was a doctor of laws and a devout court poet, moved by the mystical spirit of the Counter-Reformation, which found an echo in his Christian ideal republic. In Agostini's original manuscript the imaginary republic, located in his native city of Pesaro, was a digression buried away in a traditional commentary on Genesis at the point where the Mosaic polity was conceived.

There were many humanist treatises in the sixteenth century, unrelated to More's *Utopia,* that skirted the idea of an optimum commonwealth—long, windy tomes with flowery dedications to princes on what were the ends of government, which of the three fundamental types discussed by Aristotle was the best, and how to administer a state of many orders. The work of the Spaniard Antonio de Guevara, *Libro llamado Relox de los principes* (1529), which included a utopian episode on an imaginary visit of Alexander the Great to the gentle, peace-loving Garamantes, was the most widely known of these manuals and achieved fame in England in Sir Thomas North's translation under the title *Dial of Princes* (1557); but virtually every Renaissance potentate could boast a scholar in his realm who exercised his wit on the same subject. Often the treatises focused on Aristotle's critique of Plato's *Republic,* and the Italian authors, officials in city-states, understandably tended to side with the preserver of private property against the idea of communism, which they discussed as though Plato would have applied it to the whole society. Works of this character, like *La Republica regia del Signor Fabio Albergati,* dedicated to the Duke of Urbino and posthumously published in Bologna in 1627, were reactions to Machiavelli's denial of the religious virtues. Given the corruptibility of human nature but at the same time man's sociability and his access to religious morality, how should the prince best govern his kingdom? Albergati's answers were eclectic and essentially mere rationalizations of existing political arrangements. The "republica perfetta" was lost in a mass of erudite citations and noble platitudes to the effect that true greatness was to be judged not by the size of a polity and its riches, but by the *felicità* of its inhabitants.

Another form of political disquisition, perhaps more relevant to the history of utopian thought, is one in which the contemporary government of an Italian city-state is presented as the optimum commonwealth through a historical and analytic study of its institutions. Florence had once enjoyed this kind of idealization in the work of Leonardo Bruni. By the sixteenth century it had been supplanted by Venice as the prototype of the ideal republic. In the Renaissance any conception of a lasting optimum republic inevitably ran up against a deeprooted conviction of the natural mutability of all things and of the historical vicissitudes and revolutions of states and empires, as well as the traditional Christian belief in original sin. But in the sixteenth century a number of Venetian apologists began demonstrating that there was one exception to this law of the circular destiny of nations, and that was Venice, which for a period of eleven hundred years had been free of internal strife and had warded off all foreign enemies. Cardinal Gasparo Contarini, a native son and the most noted formulator of the myth of Venice, wrote a description of its institutions that was a self-congratulatory utopia, the *De Magistratibus et Republica Venetorum Libri Quinque* (1543). Sixteenth-century Venice with its decadent oligarchs, its lust for gain and dominion, its refined pleasures of art and philosophy, by a strange alchemy was transformed into a realization of the Platonic republic. The Della Rovere, the Sfondrati, and the Valieri, living in an opulent Elysium above a world of slaves and servants and merchant adventurers, by their mere existence affirmed the happiness of the *città felice.* The myth of Venice was distinguished from the run of Italian philosophical utopias in its impact upon the history of thought well beyond the borders of Italy. It penetrated English political theory in the seventeenth century and bolstered revolutionary doctrines that favored mixed government. The myopic view of the Venetian oligarchy as a fortunate balance of monarchical, aristocratic, and democratic elements is an illustrious example of man's capacity to utopianize any reality.

The Ideal City of the Renaissance Architects

Of far greater interest in the history of utopian thought than these politico-philosophical inquiries is a genre in which the Italians of the Renaissance were marvelous innovators, rather than more or less imitative derivers from Thomas More or Greek thinkers. As a corpus, the ideal cities graphically depicted in Italian architectural treatises from the mid-fifteenth to the mid-sixteenth century represent one of the grand moments of independent utopian creativity. The Italian architects flourished before More's *Utopia* was published, but there is nothing in *Utopia* to suggest that More, despite his interest in humanists like Pico della Mirandola, was aware of the Italian artists and their visions even when they anticipated him by half a century. While More turned outward for inspiration, to the newly discovered continents and to the primitives depicted in the early voyage literature, the Italians in the utopian mode were still totally embedded in the literary and artistic traditions of the ancients and impressed with the image of their own communes. The gusty winds of the Atlantic that blow through More's *Utopia* and enliven it with the excitement of a new world become possible, at least on an imaginary island, are absent from the Italian works, which have a bookish smell.

Unlike the cities in Utopia, which were havens of good sense and practicality, rather provincial and rather parochial, the ideal cities of the Italian architects were bedecked with mystical significations. Though both were related to the recovery of classical texts, the genius of place took over and the same epoch gave birth to distinctive utopian types in England and in Italy. In the period before More's *Utopia* was translated, the primary Italian Renaissance utopia was figurative and devoted to the cult of sensate beauty. There are few other epochs in Western history when the architectural embodiment of the ideal occupied so prominent a place in utopia. The geometric plans of Boullée and Ledoux at the end of the eighteenth century, the Gothic revival of William Morris, and perhaps the structures of the contemporary architectural seers Le Corbusier, Wright, and Soleri are examples of the same preoccupation. Both the Renaissance ideal of the city and the stark forms of the late-eighteenth-century architects may have been born of nostalgia for the strength, simplicity, and harmony of what was conceived to be antiquity. The manifestations of the utopian aesthetic were of course radically different in the later epochs.

The contrast between the cities in *Utopia* and the ideal cities of the Italian architects is visible at once on the facades of their stone structures. "The buildings, which are far from mean," More wrote, describing the houses of the capital city early in the second book of the *Utopia,* "are set together in a long row, continuous through the block and faced by a corresponding one. The house fronts of the respective blocks are divided by an avenue twenty feet broad. On the rear of the houses, through the whole length of the block, lies a broad garden enclosed on all sides by the backs of the blocks."[9] There is hardly a word about the decoration of the row houses or of the great hall in which the members of a synography take their meals together. By contrast, in the Italian Renaissance utopias the pursuit of beauty in the city was the essence of the good life. The Italians shared Plato's recognition of the potency of art in molding the souls of the young, without heeding his strictures against the poets and against the luxury of the Atlantean monuments. Utopians of other ages have valued beautiful forms, but have usually relegated them to the role of mere adornment; they have been secondary attributes. Only in the patrician fantasies of the Italian Renaissance did beauty become identified with the very meaning of existence.

Unlike the narcissistic aesthetes of the fin de siècle, who worshiped beauty in the hookah dreams of their private cabinets, the Renaissance utopians dedicated themselves to the life of beauty in community. Not all men, however, had equal access to beauty, and the Italian utopia was by definition aristocratic, its finest fruits reserved for those few whose souls, through the contemplation of noble forms, could rise to heights of divine exaltation. In this respect it was in an authentic tradition of Plato. The city became a setting for a life of thought and refined pleasure; within it were fashioned harmonious, perfect beings who chose to express themselves in quasi-mystical, Neoplatonic language. In this community whose end was the flowering of an aristocracy, the material and grosser occupations of men were mentioned but kept under cover, hidden away in corners, submerged in sewers. The Italian Renaissance utopians, dreaming of a beauty they called ancient and abiding by the rules of their goddess *Misura,* took the proportions of the human body as their model and enshrined what they conceived to be the classical tradition of the human in moral behavior and the conduct of life.

Of all the utopian goals of Western man, this aesthetic humanist way, aristocratic to the bone, appears the most remote from present-day prospects, despite the efforts and rich ideological vocabulary of twentieth-century architect-planners of genius, with their mystique of the physical environment and the power of its influence on men. Even the grandest structures of Renaissance architecture patterned after the humanist ideal have become difficult to appreciate in a modern city. Who can still recognize Bernini's sketch of a human form—the head, arms, body, and legs—in the church and colonnades of St. Peter's and the houses of the Borgo in Rome, as the automobiles whir through the piazza?[10]

The traditions of Hippodamus of Miletus and Vitruvius were revived by Renaissance artists in a rich treasury of plans for the founding of ideal cities— Leone Battista Alberti in *De re aedificatoria* (published in 1485), Antonio Averlino, known as Filarete, in the *Sforzinda* (composed between 1461 and 1464), Francesco di Giorgio Martini in the *Trattato di architettura* (begun about 1481), Leonardo da Vinci in his sketches, and a host of lesser figures, whose writings often remained in manuscript until the twentieth century. The draughtsmen may not have been sanguine about the prospects of seeing a utopia rise on the chaotic foundations of a medieval commune during their lifetime; it was far more likely that the ideal would be realized in stage scenery for a courtly play with architecture as a backdrop. Nevertheless there were from time to time actual attempts, though usually abortive, to implement ideal plans under the patronage of pope or podesta: Nicholas V in Borgo Leonino (1450), Pius II in Pienza (where a complex by Bernardo Rossellino, 1460–1464, still stands), Ludovico Sforza (Il Moro) in Vigevano. And the dukes of Tuscany toyed with the notion of transforming Portoferraio into Cosmopoli, a city of *érudits* in which only Latin would be spoken. Alberti's relationship to the grand design of the mid-fifteenth-century papacy to establish a seat of power and magnificence in Rome has been studied in meticulous detail.[11] While these plans appear to transcend the bounds of an ideal city-state, the unit of most architects, they represent an amalgam of Hellenic and Judeo-Christian elements in utopia: the eternal city of God embodied in stone.

Among the authors of architectural codices in the fifteenth century, Alberti, Filarete, and Francesco di Giorgio exercised a lasting influence upon city plans well into the seventeenth century. They are all exemplars of the universal man of the Renaissance to whom no art or knowledge was alien. Only Alberti, born in Genoa in 1404, was the scion of a noble family, who had been exiled from their home in Florence; he returned to become one of the most illustrious of Florentines. The other two were of the people, Filarete the son of a stone carver of Siena, Francesco di Giorgio Martini of peasant origin.

Alberti, the most philosophical of the three, was probably more a moralist than a professional architect, and his utopian ideas, set forth in his famous architectural work, are also dispersed in writings like *Della famiglia* and *De Iciarchia*.[12] The publication of his *De re aedificatoria,* completed around 1450 when he was at the court of Pope Nicholas V, gave it an audience that neither Filarete nor Francesco di Giorgio enjoyed since their treatises remained in manuscript. Alberti's work was translated from Latin into Italian in Venice, 1546; a steady stream of editions in all European languages has made it the most significant treatise in the history of architecture.

Filarete was a great sculptor and worker in bronze as well as an architect. In his *Sforzinda* he laid down abstract principles and then made an effort, albeit a feeble one, to tell a story, and a story within a story, to dramatize for his patron the actual building operations of the ideal city, replete with startling incidents such as the chance discovery of an ancient work on architecture that, mirabile dictu, conformed in every particular to Filarete's own ideas about the beautiful city.[13] He led an adventurous life, courting danger in war and caught up in the intrigues of Renaissance courts and city-state popular governments. Sometime between 1445 and 1449 he was accused of attempting to steal the head of John the Baptist from San Silvestro in Rome and was tortured before his final release. The charge against him is not wholly implausible; such heads were often peripatetic, and in 1411 Pope John XXIII himself had been prepared to sell the Florentines the reliquary of their patron saint.

Francesco di Giorgio Martini was as famous a builder of fortifications and a painter as he was a city planner and a diplomat. Much in demand as an engineer, he also wrote one of the most orderly and well-reasoned architectural treatises of the Renaissance, embellished in the margins with varied and imaginative drawings of ideal cities.[14] Francesco di Giorgio had begun his career as an engineer in the Sienese water works before he moved into the service of Federigo da Montefeltro in Urbino, where he participated in the building of the ducal palace and the reconstruction of the church. Federigo called him "mio dilettissimo archietecto."[15] During the wars between Urbino and Florence he served both as a military engineer and an ambassador. Even after he assumed the post of official engineer of Siena, he was loaned out to other cities. The Aragonese hired him in Naples and he was largely responsible for the destruction of the French garrison there in 1495. He could work in many artistic media and is sometimes called the Sienese Leonardo. A letter of thanks for his advice on plans for the Milan cathedral reads: "If we have not presented him with worthy rewards, in such manner as the greatness of his genius required, let him bear it with equable spirit because the Immaculate Virgin will bring him better remuneration."[16]

No starry-eyed dreamer, Francesco di Giorgio wrote theoretical works that were closely bound up with his practice—he did not indulge in architectural conceptualization abstracted from detailed rules and methods of actual construction. The treatises were inspired by an ambition to outstrip Vitruvius, but he was driven also by the need to solve urgent technical problems of fortification for his patrons. Alberti and Filarete restricted themselves largely to civil architecture; Francesco operated with equal facility in both the military and the civil fields. As a follower of Vitruvius, he established the predominance of the antique wherever he went, but he never accepted the theory without verifying it by studying its precise application in the Roman monuments that had survived. Architectural historians consider his work to be more concrete, though less organic, than Alberti's. An attempt has been made to distinguish between the guiding spirit of Filarete, who in the *Sforzinda* appears primarily as the servitor of a court establishment, however ambitious his projections, and the prevalent tone in the writing of Francesco di Giorgio, whose flights of utopian fancy are considered to be a denial of *principi e potenti* and the incarnation of the values of an authentic artisan class jealous of its liberty and conscious of its newfound social dignity. The contrast is much exaggerated. Though glorying in his own gifts, Francesco looked to princely protectors for the implementation of his ideas—to those who aimed to live honorably and free from worldly cares. And he designed public buildings that could be converted into fortresses for all eventualities, in particular for resisting the "volubilità e furie de popoli." [17]

It may seem to be stretching the idea of utopia beyond tolerable limits to include these illustrated treatises on architecture and city planning, since they were usually meant to serve pragmatic ends, to acquaint patrons, the dilettante-tyrants of the Italian city-states or the rulers of republics, with the architect's virtuosity and workmanlike principles. The admission of Alberti and his successors into the realm of utopia perhaps requires some justification. Alberti, who was providing doctrinal support for Pope Nicholas' restructuring of Rome, aware that architecture spoke with religious significations, was no mere planner of comfortable urban organisms to serve passing human needs. He was a philosopher who invested objects with moral and religious meaning without abandoning interest in their practical utility. The ideal city of Alberti was the only place where a man would be able to fulfill himself by exercising his *virtù*. To provide that city with the most perfect structure was an integral part of the ideal because men were constantly subject to its influence. Need for cover and the utility of a protective wall were elementary, but Alberti had a broader vision. He planned a city whose inhabitants would be able to accommodate to one another in creating a good life.

The architect's role was no mean one: The ultimate success of the enterprise, the longevity of the city, might depend more upon his skills than upon the power of the government and the fortunes of the military captains. The architect who could discover the inner reason of the soul would have the key to binding the citizens together into a harmonious whole, whatever their condition. Since building would in some respect involve all the inhabitants, through this common work they would find themselves united. Francesco di Giorgio wrote that a walled agglomeration of houses could be called a city only when its inhabitants had formed a union enabling them to pass their brief life span more commodiously. [18] Filarete planned not only to construct beautiful, useful, and enduring structures, but to reinstitute a perfection that once had been. The architectural treatises are utopian in that their authors have discovered the means for creating the bond of sympathy among the inhabitants that could make the city *felice*. The citizens would gain in dignity and honor if they lived among the architect's perfect designs. Alberti makes frequent reference to Plato's Republic as a model and to reports of other excellently governed peoples such as the Panchaïans of Euhemerus. The line between the real and the imaginary was not sharply drawn.

The ideal of Alberti was a harmony of *commoditas* and *voluptas,* of function and of beauty. Plato would not have given too deep thought to the commoditas. But despite commitment to commoditas, abstract and ideal considerations continually obtrude in Alberti, like the Pythagorean theory of numbers, a vision of the cosmos. The image of the city is again infused with a hieratic quality. The city mirrored the soul of the just man or at least it should in its underlying divisions, so that true harmony of unequal parts would prevail. This transcendental quality is all but absent from More's commonsensical republic, though it was not foreign to his own innermost religious being. Unlike Plato in his obsession with absolute unity, Alberti was interested in variety, multiplicity, complexity. His defense of curving streets is revealing: "I ask you to consider how much more pleasant the view will be if at every step you see new forms of buildings." [19] Instead of Platonic constancy, the eye has begun to seek continual novelty and refreshment as part of the ideal. For Alberti "the city" has two meanings: a grouping of edifices in a certain pattern and a meeting of men. Plato described the architecture of the Atlanteans and of the ancient Athenians their contemporaries, but the buildings and layout of the city were hardly on a level of importance with molding the character of the citizens.

Whatever their political leanings, Alberti, Filarete, and Francesco have in common the rediscovery of the radial city plan, a form that has deep roots, sacred and profane, in the human imagination, and the development of the conception of *misura* handed down from Vitruvius. They all accepted the existing class stratification of the Italian commune which, with a little cosmetic effort, could be seen as a replica of the Platonic hierarchy in the perfect republic. And they had the same concern with military defense and political survival, manifested not only in the fortifications of the city but in the strategic location of the princely palace or seigneury of the republic, both of which were in constant danger of attack from enemies within and without the state. They had a commitment to an aristocratic ideal of life to which both mob violence and arbitrary rule were repugnant. It was their abiding passion to create a city that would be unvarying in social structure, a city whose beauty would serve to enhance its durability since the inhabitants would be moved by aesthetic considerations to preserve it without modification. Theirs was the apotheosis of the static utopia: Perfection having been embodied in stone, there was nothing further to do but to hold it intact.

Plato's ideal—and that of most utopias up to the mid-eighteenth century—was immutable institutions, the changeless society, though he knew it could never be attained. Alberti and his followers planned structures fitting for such a society. In a sense, what Plato tried to achieve with eugenically selected persons and with laws, Alberti hoped to accomplish with stone. The Renaissance city plan, centralized and harmonious, with different types of buildings for the residences of the various classes and for their occupations, was a framework which through its very nature would ensure stability. Since that which was to last had to be beautiful, it was the mission of the architect-creator to fashion forms worthy of duration. There were to be no changes or the least change possible. The city could not long survive without obedience to rightful authority, which for Alberti in theory was natural authority, such as a father exercised over a son, a captain over sailors, a doctor over his patient. All these forms of authority restricted liberty in the name of a higher good. No more than Plato would Alberti open the floodgates to innovation: If laws were to be respected they could be altered only very rarely. In the opening pages of Book III of *De Iciarchia,* written about 1469, he counseled: "As they say, it is better to preserve an ancient order, even if it is not without faults, than break it with new rules."[20] Alberti saw no virtue in the multiplication of laws: The wicked could not be restrained by them and the good did not require them.

The Renaissance ideal city was planned to endure, not forever—for the predominant conception of cyclical vicissitudes in history militated against any such pretension—but at least as long as the great monuments of the ancients, some of which had been immune to the ravages of time for many centuries. At first glance the very idea of utopia is precluded by acceptance of the mutability of all things. In the face of eventual decline, what worth could a "stable" utopia have? The answer may serve to distinguish sharply the Renaissance utopia from what came to be the Christian millenarian and Pansophic visions of the seventeenth century, as well as the secular, dynamic, progressionist utopias that possessed Western thought from the end of the eighteenth century onward. For Renaissance theorists the cycle could not be broken, but once the apex had been reached, degeneration could be slowed. The good institutions of Jean Bodin, the craft of Machiavelli's prince, and the skill of the Italian Renaissance utopian were all directed toward that same end.

Sforzinda

The Italian utopias, both philosophical and architectural, tend to be discursive, and few of them bother with sophisticated literary inventions after the manner of either the Hellenistic novel or More's *Utopia.* Filarete's *Sforzinda* of the 1460s, which has an elaborate fictional envelopment, is a rare exception, and its early date makes it worthy of special notice. The opening scene is a table conversation in which the architect is fighting off detractors, much as Raphael Hythloday later did at Cardinal Morton's court in the first book of *Utopia.* Filarete's defense of the Florentine style of architecture against the Lombard is interrupted with long digressions on the discovery of an ancient city plan drafted by one Onitoan Nolivera (an obvious anagram for Antonio Averlino), on hunting parties, and on the practical problems of construction. The *Sforzinda* was probably designed for reading aloud to Filarete's patron, Francesco Sforza of Milan, while he dined, which may account for the introduction of the divertissements. The conceit of inserting in an architectural treatise the detailed description of an entire city built by the mythical King Zogalia and his architect in the "antique style," with excursions on the functioning of its schools, law courts, brothels, and prisons, is a major innovation. Filarete thus bestowed the sanction of antiquity on his own new creation, an artful way of reconciling an ideal city with a cyclical view of the world.

Filarete's tale of the discovery of an ancient work on architecture, though a literary artifice, was not fabricated out of whole cloth, for Renaissance models of the ideal city were deliberately drawn from antiquity, and the predominant conceptions of the architect-planners rested on Greek and Roman authorities —selected, emended, reinterpreted, and inevitably distorted. Plato's communism for the guardians of the Republic was lightly dropped from city plans drafted for absolutist Renaissance princes, while the rigidity of the rest of his class structure was maintained. The Italian podesta who replaced the philosopher-king was in most respects a radical departure from his Platonic prototype, but a vague connection was somehow suggested. The Renaissance architect-utopian did not appeal to his patron in the name of Plato's idea of justice, but instead raised the seductive image of the Alexandrian and Roman goddess of fame to persuade the ruler to undertake vast building projects, "beautiful, with no expense spared," the most brilliant jewel in the crown of his achievements.[21] Filarete, for one, was not above coupling the appeal to glory with utilitarian economic and social considerations: A gigantic building program involving thousands of workers (102,000 masters and workmen, not counting overseers and additional laborers to assist in laying the foundation) would contribute to the well-being of the citizenry and help subdue their unruly passions.[22] Plato had also proposed the construction of grand public buildings for the Republic, though not so lavish as to lead to the excess of luxury into which the Atlantean monarchs had fallen, to their ultimate disaster; Plato, however, would never have measured his ideal plan by the realization of such lowly objectives as the maintenance of full employment among the men of brass, whose existence hardly touched him. Yet it would be misleading to stress exclusively the utilitarian or political purposes of the colossal program. As he contemplates the great architect's sensuous joy in building, Filarete is carried away. "Building is nothing more than a voluptuous pleasure, like that of a man in love. Anyone who has experienced it knows that there is so much pleasure and desire in building that however much a man does, he wants to do more."[23]

Occasionally a utopia will express the Renaissance temper in a minor detail, as in *Sforzinda* when Filarete describes the incredible speed with which the new city is to be constructed. In the fourth book of his treatise he explains how an army of workers laying 30,000,000 bricks could raise city walls in ten days. In eight days all the radial streets are built and the canals are dug. Medieval cathedrals were constructed over centuries; private palaces in Sforzinda are built in twenty days. Once the heavy labor is completed the greatest artists of Italy are to be summoned to decorate the new city. The schedule truly bespeaks the tempo of a new age, despite the obeisance to antique models.

In Filarete's treatise, popular religious superstitions and a belief in auguries and signs still played a role in determining the auspicious moment to begin the construction of the radial city. *Sforzinda* is graced with symbols, omens, and moral homilies drawn from both pagan and Christian tradition. Vases filled with grain, water, wine, milk, oil, and honey are to be embedded in the foundation of the first building, along with marble and bronze records of the names and deeds of the prime movers in the construction of the city and of other worthy men. When questioned by his patron as to the reason for their incorporation into the building, the architect replies: ". . . as every man knows, things that have a beginning must have an end. When the time comes, they will find these things, and know our names and remember us because of them, just as we remember when we find something noble in a ruin or in an excavation. We are happy and pleased to find a thing that represents antiquity and [gives] the name of him who had it done." On the cover of the vase of grain are depicted the three fates, of whom one spins, one receives the thread, and one breaks it. On the vase are inscribed only two words, Life and Death, for there is nothing else in the world except living and dying. "A city endures for the term conceded to it," the architect explains. The vase of water is included because water "is an element that in itself is clean, pure, and clear and very useful to everyone. If it is not dirtied by other matter, it is always clear and lucid. In the same way the inhabitants of the city should be clear and clean and useful to others. As water becomes turbid and spoiled by filthy matter or by things not suited to it, so men of the territory are spoiled and become turbid through bad practices."[24] On the dome of the cathedral over the apse where the high altar was placed were mosaic figures of Christ and the Madonna in Judgment, seated amid rays of gold on a blue field.[25]

The City of Symbolic Forms

In the earliest Greek studies of the polity, plans for the physical structure of the city were intimately related to political theory, which was almost always concerned with a quest for the ideal. In ancient Greece, the shape of the city was a subject of political and moral speculation because it was believed to be as pervasive in its effect on the conduct of the citizenry as the allowable music and poetry. Both visual and auditory impressions penetrated to the core of the soul. Sometimes the basic form of the city had an astrological significance, but the supreme goal to which everything else was subordinated was unity, and the radial pattern seemed most conducive to this end.

In fifteenth-century Italy the bond between political thought and the city plan was reaffirmed through the heavy reliance of Renaissance writers on examples in the texts of the ancient theorists, and the architects of the ideal city, though no great philosophers in their own right, were men of the court steeped in its dominant intellectual fashions. In the manner of the Greek and Roman philosophers, they too believed that a harmonious physical environment was a benign mold that would render perverse mankind more tractable, its parts more consonant one with another. In Alberti's conception of the perfect city, beauty was a supreme value in its own right, but it also had an educative function in fashioning the moral character of individual citizens. The artist, particularly the architect, could enshrine the ideal in a *disegno* (model) for reality to approximate. An architect-planner was the highpriest of the ideal, no mere artisan-builder, and the creation of his model was endowed with Platonic overtones: It was a *paradigma*. Under the influence of this new Renaissance aesthetic, the architect-philosophers turned their backs on the formless, haphazard pile of the medieval city, grown in depth with the accumulation of refuse and in breadth with the expansion of trade, to embrace a city-state ideal *all'antica*, in which one of the fundamental geometric shapes embedded in man's consciousness was given supreme expression—the mystic circle. That the radial form is among the oldest patterns for the organization of human agglomerations seems borne out by reports of recently excavated neolithic sites in the Kiev region of Russia and in aerial views of other ancient centers.

In reviving the radial city of antiquity the Renaissance architects attached to it, consciously or unconsciously, magical and religious attributes and symbols that had once played a part in the founding of cities throughout the ancient world. To humanists of the Renaissance, susceptible to Kabbalistic and Neo-platonic rhetoric, circularity had hermetic significance. If man was to concern himself with making a perfect earthly abode, the circle was the form most appropriate to his lofty, godlike nature. The ideal city as a mirror of the celestial sphere is an obvious analogy, and the frequent resort to twelve radii in the city, recalling the twelve signs of the zodiac and the twelve apostles, has astronomic and astrologic as well as religious implications. The idea of necessary correspondence between the shapes of the lower and the upper worlds was fostered by Christian thinkers from antiquity well into the eighteenth century, one of its last great proponents being none other than Isaac Newton.

Literary sources for the model of the radial city inherited from antiquity were abundant. Aristotle's *Politics* included a critical discussion of the ideal plan of Hippodamus, a city composed of three classes, artisans, farmers, and soldiers, with its land area divided into three types, sacred, public, and private. Aristotle's attack is in the same spirit as his criticism of Plato's community system, the voice of sobriety in the face of an absolutist ideal that is dismissed as unclear and impractical. And Aristotle was not above an ad hominem argument, mocking Hippodamus as a fellow who wore his hair long and expensively adorned and tried to win attention by eccentricity in clothes and manners.[26] But for the Renaissance architects, Hippodamus evoked another image—he was the master architect, founder of circular cities. About 445 B.C. he was supposed to have built Piraeus, then to have journeyed to Sicily or southern Italy, where he was entrusted with the construction of Thurioi, a city that men of the Renaissance found described in Diodorus Siculus' *Library of History*. The radial city must have been talked about in the time of Aristophanes in connection with the colonial movement of the fifth century B.C. and the establishment of new settlements—witness the passage in the *Birds* that ridicules a city to be built in the clouds, with streets laid out in star shape. One can reach far back to Indian and Persian culture and discover parallels or remote origins for the circular city with a temple in the center. Some of these early Asiatic experiences with urban plans were recorded by Alexander's historiographers, by Diodorus, and by Strabo, and their reports were there for the Renaissance architects to read. The architecture in Plato's *Republic* is related to the conceptions of Hippodamus: It is clearly monocentric, with all public buildings concentrated in one area. In the *Laws,* the identity of all the dwellings is explicit, the purpose of structural uniformity being to make everything in the city appear part of one great house. In the *Timaeus* and the *Critias* the lost city of Atlantis is circular. Echoes of the Platonic city reverberated through the ancient world, and many details of Plato's plans in both his utopia and his anti-utopia are reflected in the writings of the Renaissance architects.

But of all the sources, the treatise of Vitruvius, *De architectura,* was by far the richest inspiration to Renaissance planners, because of the abstract principles it enunciated and the circumstantial descriptions of ancient cities it included. Vitruvius, an imperial official involved in the rebuilding of Rome, is said to have written his work before 27 B.C., and it was one of the early classical texts to be recovered. There are extant manuscripts dated to the Carolingian period, and the memory of Vitruvius seems never to have entirely faded. The *De architectura* was one of the first books on architecture to be printed (the editio princeps is Rome, ca. 1486), but it was also available to architects in many fourteenth- and fifteenth-century manuscripts.

In a eulogistic dedication to Augustus, Vitruvius set the pattern for the ideal relationship between princely patron and architect. He voiced the proud conviction that Augustus and he were together building a "memorial to future ages," and the Renaissance architects later wrote of themselves in similar vein.[27] They too were building, though perhaps on a smaller scale, eternal Romes. Vitruvius' preference for the radial form seems to have been dictated chiefly by hygienic concerns. His aim was to protect the many arteries of a city from the prevailing winds by allowing the streets to radiate from a single center. Appended to his texts was a radial, octagonal city plan, so conceived as to prevent gusts of air from swirling through the streets and breeding illness.[28] This matter-of-fact Roman does not seem to have been aware of the transcendental aspects of his plan; practical and unmystical, his object was to eliminate drafts, not reflect the divine. His description of the city of Halicarnassus, with a form "like the curvature of a theatre," built on the mainland over against Cos by Mausolus, King of Caria (377–353 B.C.), provided a concrete historical example for the Renaissance theorists.[29]

For fifteen hundred years after Vitruvius the radial city had not played a great role in practice. The Romans did not generally follow his plan in establishing new cities, preferring the grid pattern of their camps for provincial towns like Nîmes, Arles, Turin, and Padua. In the Middle Ages, images of the circular city were perhaps best preserved in visions of the heavenly Jerusalem and in manuscript illuminations depicting its earthly counterpart. Illustrations of Saint Augustine's two cities, a heavenly city of angels and an earthly city in strife, sometimes gave the earthly city a circular shape. To please Frances Yates, the influence of the magical city of Adocentyn that Hermes founded in Egypt should be mentioned. Its description in *Picatrix*, a twelfth-century Arabic work well known in the Renaissance, does not firmly establish its circularity, but the central castle with four gates leading in four different directions, the adjacent Temple of the Sun, the guardian spirits posted around the circumference of the city, as well as the presence within of a philosopher-ruler, are elements that reappear in many later utopias. Despite medieval antecedents, however, the radial circular or starlike city plan came as a great revival in Italy of the fifteenth century, if not a complete innovation.

In Filarete's *Sforzinda* the basic shape of the city is a star, in the center of which are grouped communal structures from which eight streets radiate to the gates and eight canals lined with columns radiate to the towers of the outer circle. At the intersections of the inner circle with the streets there are eight major squares on which churches are erected and eight smaller squares without them. Nearly a century later, when Doni adopted the stellar form for his utopian *mondo savio*, he carried it to numerically obsessive extremes: a hundred doors to the cathedral in the center of the circle leading to a hundred avenues divided into streets, each devoted to a separate trade or occupation, a hundred priests in charge of the hundred avenues, and one *capo della terre* who was the oldest of the priests. Doni, of course, emphasized the sacerdotal or mystical meaning of the radial city far less than its utility: You could not get lost in it, for wherever you were you had only to return to the center and start all over again. (Many European countries built their railroad systems on this pattern.)

Francesco di Giorgio included in his treatises all manner of diagrams of circular hill cities that had in common a castle or church at the summit. In perusing these fantasy plans, one is struck by the analogy to the mountain of paradise in Eastern and Western religions.

As the authority of Vitruvius was a determinant in the Renaissance preference for the radial city, so was it again Vitruvius whom the architect-planners invoked in propounding the doctrine that bodily proportions should be the measure of all manmade structures. Treating Vitruvius as a sacred text on ideal forms, the Renaissance theorists quoted him as a preacher might the Gospel, and applied his theories at every point, to parts of individual buildings and to the city as a whole. In Book I Vitruvius had written:

"Proportion implies a graceful semblance; the suitable display of details in their context. This is attained when the details of the work are of a height suitable to their breadth, of a breadth suitable to their length; in a word, when everything has a symmetrical correspondence.

"Symmetry also is the appropriate harmony arising out of the details of the work itself; the correspondence of each given detail among the separate details to the form of the design as a whole. As in the human body, from cubit, foot, palm, inch and other small parts comes the symmetric quality of eurythmy; so is it in the completed building."[30]

The last sentence became crucial for the Renaissance concept of *misura*, the architectural law of the ideal city and the ultimate humanist commandment. The late Erwin Panofsky has traced it back to the Stoics and from them through their followers Vitruvius, Cicero, Lucian, and Galen. It was enshrined by Alberti as the primary law of nature and the universal principle of aesthetics. Filarete, who derived from him, wrote in the second folio of his treatise that man was "fatto colla misura," and to imitate his form was both natural and true, for the human figure was geometrically perfect and had an ideal harmony of parts. "As everyone knows, man was created by God; the body, the soul, the intellect, the mind, and everything was produced in perfection by Him. The body [was] organized and measured and all its members proportioned according to their qualities and measure."[31] This ideal system of relationships was to govern the basic form of all great structures like cathedrals and the design of the city itself. In the *Sforzinda,* Filarete provided a historical justification for the idea of misura that rooted the concept in the earliest acts of civilization-building. Man's first care after his eviction from Paradise was bread; next was architecture. "The first need and necessity of man, after food, was habitation; thus he endeavored to construct a place where he could dwell. From this, then, public and private buildings were derived . . . Since man is made with the measure stated above, he decided to take the measures, members, proportions, and qualities from himself and to adapt them to this method of building."[32] The central aesthetic problem was to discover the exact proportions of the parts that would achieve perfect harmony and balance. The proportions could be gleaned from diverse places: the writings of the ancients, numerological theory (often with mystical implications), and observation. But whatever the source, this canon dominated the aesthetic conceptions not only of Alberti, Filarete, and Francesco di Giorgio, but of Lorenzo Ghiberti, Luca Pacioli, Leonardo da Vinci, Pomponius Gauricus, and Albrecht Dürer.

Like Filarete, Francesco di Giorgio extended to the city, "un organismo unico e complesso," the precept of Vitruvius that the proportions of a work of art should follow those of the body: All the parts of the city were to correspond and be proportionate to the human body. A manuscript of Francesco's treatise in the Biblioteca Reale of Turin depicts anthropomorphically a fortified city including within its circumference a human figure with arms outstretched and legs akimbo. In the middle is a circular piazza dominated by a "tempio"; the head is the citadel; towers at four points correspond to the extremities of the limbs.[33] In the margin of a manuscript, now in the Biblioteca Laurenziana in Florence, that describes many octagonal radial cities, Francesco di Giorgio again draws human bodies enclosed in circles to illustrate the correspondence between man and city.[34] Leonardo may well have seen this codex. Book III of Francesco di Giorgio's treatise, which also covers the "economia generale" and the "perimetri della città," follows the Vitruvian precept to the letter by establishing analogies between the parts of the three orders of columns and the human body. An Ionic column encases a female nude, the head fitting into the capital, the rest of the body below the shoulders being the shaft of the column. The city was a human body; each structure within it was human; each column of whatever order had human proportions.

But the city of man also had necessary correspondences with the heavens. The ideal city of the Renaissance was by no means a totally secular conception, and even when its originators were immersed in technical particulars and exigencies of warfare, there was a sacral meaning to their art. While Italian Renaissance planners were anything but indifferent to the mundane problems of military security, comfort, and hygiene, they do not seem to have fixed on the radial city only for reasons of defense and sanitation. Feelings that were more metaphysical, hermetic, and religious were constantly brought into play. Doubtless practical considerations and ideal images were interwoven. It may be that only those willing to delve into the history of the human unconscious can fathom the full meaning, the profound transformation in the psyche of Europeans, that this predilection for the radial, circular city bespeaks. And it long remained a utopian fantasy of urban perfection. Perhaps its most noteworthy embodiments were the plans of L'Enfant for the city of Washington, when America was still a utopia. In pursuit of symbolic forms architect-engineers sometimes even sacrificed military advantages. In the context of an eighteenth-century utopian city plan the circular form might represent pure Cartesian reason secularized; in the Renaissance the same form reflected divine Platonic reason.

Platonic ideas of the perfect were translated into mathematical terms. The zodiac with its division of the heavens into twelve constellations was an astronomic form that could be reproduced in a radial city of hexagonal shape. Sacred numerical relationships were implicit in its axes and gates, the height and breadth of its walls. Though a discrete, perfect, and complete unit, the ideal city was not isolated or independent from the general schema of the universe. It stood midway between the cosmic order of nature and, at the other end of the scale, corporeal man. Related to both realities, the city reflected them in its very structure, which incorporated divine and human proportions. These two analogues of the city, the human body and the heavens, did not seem incongruent to an intellectual society that could assimilate on different levels multiple interpretations of the same scriptural text.

Diverse elements flowed together and coalesced in the ideal city of the Renaissance philosophical architects. The preference for the symbolic form of the radial city, with its roots in prehistory, was strengthened by the prestige of a revived Greek antiquity and the canon of Vitruvius. Christian significations were attached to the city, sanctified by the central position of the church and the symbolic number of its gates. Military objectives were served by the bastions at the end of each avenue, points in the star-shaped octagon or hexagon of the ideal form. Designating quarters for different occupations satisfied civil, hygienic, and aesthetic requirements. In serving a multiplicity of purposes simultaneously the architect gave expression to the fullness of his own and his patron's needs, religious, military, aesthetic, hygienic, and economic. There is no evidence that the architects established a hierarchy among these needs, and attempts of latter-day Marxist architectural historians to demonstrate the primacy of economic considerations over all others have not been convincing.

After the completion of the city of Sforzinda, a visiting nobleman, who has been identified as Lodovico Gonzaga, Marchese of Mantua, had an aesthetic experience as moving as a religious rebirth. "My lord," he said to the prince, "I seem to see again the noble buildings that were once in Rome and those that we read were in Egypt. It seems to me that I have been reborn on seeing (*rinascere a vedere*) those noble buildings. They seem very beautiful to me."[35] The architect had so thoroughly convinced his patron of the superiority of the ancient over the modern (which in his lexicon meant the Gothic, a corruption of the natural, antique way) that the prince vowed never again to heed praise for any other forms[36]—though it would require an extraordinary flight of imagination to recognize in Filarete's drawings anything that even remotely resembles what we know of Roman architecture.

In the architectural utopias of the Renaissance, existing social relations were ennobled by being placed in a more beautiful and more perfect setting. A conception of life that Italian humanists, beginning with Leonardo Bruni, had expressed in words was now to be concretely realized in cities planned by architectural geniuses. The ideal city of Alberti reflected the natural order and then transcended it in an image of a Platonic republic adapted and transformed. The worldly order was meant to endure, to legitimize a social structure whose class divisions would be perpetuated in stone, but the hope for eternity imparted to the buildings an otherworldly dimension. There was acute awareness of the mutability of things and the tendency to corruption in all natural works; yet, paradoxically, the philosophical architect was preoccupied with planning the individual edifice and the organic complex of the whole city so that, insofar as humanly possible, they might be immune to change. The architect and the prince together composed the Platonic philosopher-king who would create the ideal city. In Filarete's *Sforzinda* the prince was recognized as the seminal element, the architect as the mother who carried the child, nourished it, and brought it to life. This duumvirate had a number of ancient models to imitate: Plato and Dionysius, Dinocrates and Alexander, Aristotle and Alexander, but especially Vitruvius and Augustus.[37]

Inspired by such relationships, the authors of the architectural treatises aimed to instruct their patrons and other architects in the art of building. In no sense was it their initial purpose to construct an ideal society de novo. The Renaissance architects were not rebels but respected members of the dominant establishments of the city-states in which they worked, whether republican, aristocratic, or tyrannical. Though their individual inclinations may have manifested themselves, they were not men bent on unseating the political powers for whom they drafted plans. Their intention was to provide housing for the inhabitants of the city without upsetting the existing order, to clothe its institutions in grand vestments that would help prolong its life. A more orderly, beautiful city would strengthen internal allegiances and prove invulnerable to foreign enemies, so that it would survive until kingdom come, or at least as long as had the ancient Roman buildings.

The Beleaguered City

The Italian Renaissance utopias, architectural and philosophical, were almost uniformly aristocratic. While the ideal city was ruled by a single prince, the general tone of life was usually set by a noble elite and the architectural plan was fashioned to serve them. There was a great divide between the gentlemen and the commoners. In the Renaissance utopian fantasies attempts were made to resolve the tensions in the physical and spiritual relationships between potentially hostile classes, and a surface appearance of harmonious calm prevailed. But if the Platonic aura surrounding most of the Italian utopias of the fifteenth and sixteenth centuries is lifted, one sees embattled cities into which problems of security internal and external obtrude to dim the luster of the ideal vision. The foreign wars and class conflicts endemic in the real world were inevitably reflected in the optimum commonwealths. The radial city of the Renaissance architects was enveloped in an atmosphere of suspicion. In these beleaguered ideal cities planning was directed toward the retention of power by the aristocratic elite as well as the enhancement of beauty and utility. For all their absorption with numerological mysteries and correspondences with configurations in the heavens and the proportions of the human body, the great architects were also skillful military engineers.

With rare exceptions like Doni and Agostini, the Renaissance utopia was courtly and answered to aristocratic needs. But Plato's sovereign disregard of the men of brass and of their living arrangements and conduct had given way in the Renaissance to a realization that the commoners were a potential political and sanitary menace, which made it unutopian to disregard them. The architect-planners were keenly aware that in the city all the inhabitants were subject to a common fate, particularly when a pestilence raged. The Black Death and recurrent plagues were grim reminders that even an aristocratic utopia could not neglect the plebeians and survive. (Leonardo submitted to Ludovico Sforza his grand design for the reorganization of Milan after the plague of 1484/5 had taken 50,000 lives.) The architects of the ideal city were under some constraint to deal with the choice of salubrious sites, with drainage, with communal hygiene, with a rational and orderly communications system, and with housing for the lower classes as well as the *nobili*.

Both the architectural and the philosophical treatises usually begin with a circumstantial description of the best possible location for their city. (Even shrewd, realistic observers like Claudio Tolomei, Ludovico Guicciardini, Giovanni Botero discussed ideal locations for cities.) As in classical visions of the Islands of the Blessed, a mild climate is an important element in the happiness of Patrizi's città felice. Extreme heat and cold are to be avoided and, to take account of the changing seasons, he summons the aid of an architectural planner who knows the ways of the winds. Freely circulating air is a requirement, and if the site of the città felice is wisely chosen, its inhabitants will be spared the savage ministrations of doctors, surgeons, barbers. Part of Patrizi's city is built on a "colle rilevato," for climatic reasons as well as purposes of fortification and to assure a pleasant view.

Alberti had been aware of contradictory opinions among philosophical architects about the optimum site for the city. Some chose a harsh climate and an inaccessible natural environment for greater security from enemy forces; others favored fertile lands where produce was plentiful and easily available. For Filarete, for example, a healthy and salubrious valley plain surrounded by mountains was the optimum site. On balance, Alberti appeared to favor the pleasant atmosphere and the rich soil, though he sided with Plato in giving precedence to the internal structure of the society, letting the inhabitants accommodate themselves to the necessities of the place. He did, of course, presuppose a propitious environment that would facilitate the founding of an optimum city, for neither he nor Plato envisaged the good society as one whose members would have to expend their energies in fighting for sustenance. Alberti's summary of Plato's remarks in the *Republic* interpreted them as favoring an ideally situated city endowed with all conceivable natural advantages.[38]

In working out the building patterns of their ideal cities, the utopian architects took as their point of departure the social arrangements that had been inherited from past ages. Medieval groupings of artisans in guilds had been preserved, and workers' quarters and shops were generally isolated from noble habitations. In the opening of the fourth book of his *De Re Aedificatoria* Alberti divided the city into different social orders after the manner of the "wise Founders of ancient Republicks,"[39] Theseus, Solon, Romulus, the Panchaïans of Euhemerus, Hippodamus, the Indians as described by Diodorus Siculus— all eminent utopian forebears. Alberti would first identify the men of reason and entrust them with the care of the city and the power to moderate in all disputes. The next in place were those who created wealth either by husbandry or commerce. "All the other Orders of Men ought in Reason to obey and be subservient to these as chief."[40] The architecture was to reflect the social order. "Now if any Thing is to be gather'd from all this to our Purpose, it is certainly that of the different Kinds of Building, one Sort belongs to the Publick, another to the principal Citizens, and another to the Commonality."[41]

In the end the major distinction was between the principal citizens and the common sort, and the housing plans were drawn up accordingly. Everywhere a reasonable distance had to separate the noble from the ignoble, the mature from the infantile. The houses of the prince and the magistrates would be situated far from the noisy populace so that the *nobili* might repose in peace just outside the city. The second chapter of Book V of Alberti's treatise on architecture provides further for the removal of the master's apartments away from children and maids, among whom there was incessant chatter. Also out of sight would be "the Dirtiness of the Servants."[42] Nunneries and monasteries were located midway from the center of the city to the outskirts—not too remote lest they be overrun by robbers, not too near lest their inmates be distracted from their religious purposes. Filarete's *Sforzinda* had also made model houses for "each class of person," using Doric proportions for gentlemen, Corinthian for merchants, and Ionic for artisans, the sizes running from 200 by 100 *braccia* for the first to 30 by 50 for the last, not a very dramatic range. And Francesco di Giorgio designed four types of houses for the four lower orders of the city's inhabitants, peasants (*villani*), artisans (*artefici*), intellectuals (*studenti*), and merchants (*mercanti*), as well as residences for the *nobili*.[43]

For all its rational orderliness, the ideal city remained a threatened utopia. Since criminal passions could not be entirely extirpated, and cupidity and resentment nourished malevolent designs among domestic and foreign enemies, the planners exercised their ingenuity in devising means to discourage or suppress rebellion against authority and to protect the city from external attack. Military installations were vital fixtures of the Renaissance utopia. A shrewd architect and engineer like Francesco di Giorgio prudently placed the arsenal near the central palaces where it would be available for defense, limited the number of doors to the seigneury so that the mobs might not invade from all sides, and constructed special listening devices for the prince that were an adaptation of the ear of Dionysius.

Taking cognizance of the differing needs of various types of government, Alberti understood that the palace of a free republic would be unlike that of a recent usurper, who would have to rely on more elaborate security measures. Crenelated walls betrayed a fearful tyrant prepared to do evil. But despite Alberti's abhorrence of tyranny and his preference for a mild paternal authority, the possibility of foreign war or of an uprising of seditious inhabitants in his own ideal city was clearly present in his mind. Arsenals and granaries were strategically located; buildings were thickly walled and fortified, bastions within the city. The senate chamber had many porticoes and anterooms so that retainers could protect the aristocrats from sudden mass incursions.

Filarete planned Sforzinda for a podesta; the unity of the city and the fusion of the sentiments of the inhabitants depended upon his person. In the dedication ceremony of the newly built city this cohesiveness was to be symbolized by a vase of honey to indicate that the city should resemble a beehive. The negative associations that such an analogy would now evoke would not have occurred to a Renaissance philosophical architect constructing an orderly, productive society.

The animals that produce honey are industrious, severe, and just. They desire and have a lord and ruler over themselves and they follow all his commands. Everyone has his task and everyone obeys. When their ruler becomes so old that he can no longer fly, through justice and clemency they carry him. Thus should the men of the city be. They should be industrious, do their duties, and do what their superiors command them. They should love and obey their lord and when he needs them, either because of war or some other necessity, they should aid him like their own father. The lord should be just and severe when it is needful and at times clement and merciful.[44]

Whenever the prince made his appearance on the building site he was greeted with tumultuous cries of "Viva, viva, il nostro Signiore!"[45]

Schools for the sons and daughters of the poor and other charitable institutions draw *Sforzinda* closer to the populist utopia, but Filarete was far from espousing egalitarian conceptions. Though God created man in perfection, there were differences, often attributable to celestial constellations and planetary influences. "As is seen, [some] have more intellect than others."[46] Filarete's description of the prison expresses the prevalent merciless attitude toward any common lawbreakers who were a threat to the city. His punishments were, in the temper of the age, cruel. The idea of utility had penetrated *Sforzinda* to the extent that the death penalty was abolished as wasteful of productive capacity; instead, in the ideal prison of the ideal city as described in King Zogalia's golden book those who deserved to be hanged, beheaded, burned, or quartered, each according to his merits, served in a different area called either Hard Labor, Torment, Hunger, or No Peace, wearing the symbol of the death he deserved embroidered on his clothing.[47]

It was Leonardo da Vinci who proposed the most radical architectural solution to the problem of plebeians in an aristocratic utopia. He advised the decentralization of crowded agglomerations like Milan into about ten separate communes, and in a famous sketch he designed a two-level city, the lower level for the commoners, the upper for the nobles, who would be free to move about without being molested by carriages and wagons and provisions, which were confined to the roads of the lower city. Public toilets would be set on landings between the flights of stairs joining the levels.[48] There would literally be two layers of existence: the nobles on the elevated platform in the sun, and the common people down below with the canals, sewers, and carts. If a whole segment of a radial hexagonal city were given over to the refuse and smells and noise of the artisans, its perfect balance could not be maintained. But if the city were so constructed that carriers and workmen were relegated to the world underneath and the upper level was one vast area for free movement on foot by the patricians, then the beauty of the superior parts would not be spoiled. The hierarchy of values in the aristocratic utopia would receive concrete embodiment in the city plan. Leonardo's text accompanying the sketch in Manuscript B, now in the Institut de France, is a stark statement of the aristocratic character of the Italian Renaissance utopia.[49]

The most forthright philosophical apology for the aristocratic utopia was written by Patrizi. There was a necessary division between those who could afford to devote themselves with their whole souls to civil and contemplative virtue and those who could not. Citizenship in the *città felice* was therefore limited to three classes who enjoyed leisure: the soldiers, the magistrates, and the priests. It was denied to the classes whose lives were spent in low occupations and burdensome labor: the peasants, the artisans, and the merchants. Patrizi's bifurcation of the city was absolute; there were two kinds of human beings with two different destinies—one servile and poor, the other noble and happy. The term citizen was reserved for those who enjoyed the honors and dignities of the republic and participated in its rule.[50] There were slaves in Patrizi's *Città felice* as there were in Plato's *Republic* and More's *Utopia;* but since they might not accept their servitude as philosophically as he did, he counseled precautionary measures: Slaves with blood ties were not to be allowed to live together lest they conspire and revolt. The slaves and the common people had inferior souls and the only reason for their existence was the role they played in facilitating the noble's way to the river of happiness by leveling the ground before him.

To label the utopian ruling classes aristocratic is, to be sure, insufficiently descriptive. Were the aristocrats to be warrior-guardians, priests, nobles, high bourgeois, patricians, moneyed men, scientist-priests, engineers, artists, inspired prophets, bureaucrats? In Plato's city they had been warrior-guardians; in Alberti's Florence they were rich, educated merchants for whom Plato would have had nothing but contempt; in Castiglione's Urbino they were learned and witty courtiers, humanists, for whom More would have had great personal sympathy but who would not have found a place in his egalitarian utopia of workers. The character of Alberti's ideal ruling class was spelled out in *De Iciarchia*. The tone of life would be very different under his businesslike aristocrats, who organized commerce and were patrons of literature, from that under the rather ascetic warrior-guardians of Plato or, to make a historical leap, under Burke's Whig landed gentry. What separated Alberti's elite from commoners were the same qualities that differentiated men from brutes—reason and the knowledge of useful arts, to which could be added prosperity of fortune. A small number of men outstanding for one or another of these gifts would be entrusted with the chief offices of the city. The verbal ideal was still Platonic, the reign of reason and justice; but implementation had changed the very nature of the ideal by finding in the rationalist, upper-class merchant-patricians and their friends the embodiment of reason.

In the same tradition, Francesco di Giorgio in the opening of his architectural treatise would have men of reason rule because this attribute elevated them above the other levels of the hierarchy. Patrizi's nobles were perhaps more contemplative than Alberti's, and Agostini's more pious and ascetic. But none of them mirrored the rough old feudal nobility. The centuries-long class war that convulsed the communes had been definitively settled in favor of the new patricians, at least in utopia.

Among the aristocrats themselves equality prevailed. The free and easy manner of the conversationalists in Castiglione's *The Courtier* (1528) is fitting aristocratic behavior. Castiglione's "speaking picture" is a pendant to the argument about the nature of an aristocratic utopia set forth in Patrizi's *Città felice*. Perhaps Castiglione's courtiers are engaged in somewhat livelier exchanges than the Bishop of Cherso's nobles; surely they are not grave enough to inhabit Agostini's imaginary republic, in which the somber spirit of the Counter-Reformation has taken over. But if there is an Italian Renaissance aristocratic utopia in action, it emerges from Castiglione's report of the learned witty society of Urbino, with its admixture of nobles and scholars occupied in pleasant converse about the parts and accomplishments of a perfect courtier, an aesthetic utopian ideal concentrated on itself.

The maintenance of carefully measured equality in the distribution of powers and dignities among aristocrats eliminated noble feuds. Patrizi would give every noble citizen access to the magistracy in turn and thus all would participate in the honors of the city. *Invidia* would be banished. But Patrizi counsels that only the *savi* and the *prudenti* should rule, leaving some doubt as to whether all citizens automatically would take turns at the helm or only the wise and prudent. His other attempts to eradicate aggressive hostility among the powerful families are equally feeble and simplistic, if set against the background of the private wars of the Renaissance city, immortalized by Shakespeare. Patrizi divides the city into clans so that there may be no formless irresponsible hordes. Starting from the banality that there will be no internecine wars when people love one another, and that to love they must know one another, he proposes a series of public festivals for all the inhabitants at least once a month, reviving the ancient practices of mythical King Italo.[51] The fruits of a piece of public land would be reserved exclusively for these celebrations. With peace thus ensured, the aristocrats of the città felice would go their happy way unperturbed. Plato would never have countenanced such fraternization.

The hostility to mercenaries is as sharp in Patrizi as it was in Plato and Machiavelli, but the future bishop, knowing the frailties of human nature in a world somewhat less ideal than Plato's, is prepared to combine mechanisms of appeal to private interest with the call to communal loyalty in defense of the state. Each man's property is so divided that only a part of it lies within the city itself; the rest is on the outskirts, so that the citizens are moved to unite quickly in war before an enemy reaches the walls. In his later years, when the Turks were menacing the Venetian empire and the Spaniards became a pressing danger to the whole of Italy, Bishop Patrizi turned from writing about the città felice to treatises on military affairs.

In Agostini's imaginary republic of the 1580s, while the rule of the nobility is still recognized, a leveling influence penetrates the aristocratic citadel. Men of all classes must work set hours, and the privileged nobility and those engaged in the contemplative sciences enjoy only half an hour a day more rest than do other citizens of the città nuova. Laziness is prohibited, the infistoliti oziosi (inveterate idlers) are denounced, and everyone has to busy himself, according to his capacity, with manual labor, commerce, or the pursuit of knowledge, on which an especially high value has been placed. Agostini is imbued with a monastic reverence for work and a suspicion of idleness. The supreme need of the free citizen of antiquity, leisure for contemplation, is conspicuously absent, and much like a Lutheran, Agostini gives worth to all callings and rejects the traditional distinction between noble arts and vile occupations. The regulation of commerce and of the labor of artisans and peasants was left to representatives after the manner of medieval communal regulations —each università of artisans or merchants had its confraternity and procurator to defend it against the depredations and encroachments of the powerful. Essentially Agostini preserved the existing system of corporations, perhaps emphasizing the importance of the protector saint of each trade. It should be remembered that the divine Plato in the Republic wasted no time on the details of organization for the men of brass engaged in commerce and agriculture and mechanics.

The work ethic of the post-Trentine European world was not restricted to Calvinists. In fact, the rule of work was respected among Italian utopians as far back as Alberti and Filarete. Filarete, for example, saw to it that each artisan group had its guild statutes and separate quarter, as in a medieval city. Both in More and in Alberti, good Catholics, all men work; idleness not only is a great moral evil for Alberti, but in the creation of any object—and he does not limit this to the fine arts—there is something of the divine. The ideal of work and the appreciation of creative effort penetrated Alberti's conception of the aristocratic utopia, even if it did not alter the average Italian aristocrat's attitude toward labor. The Renaissance artist, to exalt the products of his own labor, ended up bestowing new respect on the work of all artisans. In Doni, work is light and there are days of rest, devoted for the most part to religious worship. There is no strife or litigation, hence no need for lawyers, because there is nothing to fight about, neither food, nor clothing, nor women. Government is sacerdotal, but the priests do not bear a very heavy burden in regulating the polity. The city is built on a specialized division of labor, though it is less a psychological division into human types as in Plato than a medieval functionalism.

The exclusive role of the nobility in political affairs was still safeguarded in Agostini's imaginary republic. Since Christ sanctioned civil law, armed rebellion was forbidden on religious as well as secular grounds; an erring authority was to be admonished through the mouth of the bishop. The nobility were conceived of as loving elder brothers in Christ, and Agostini chided the Venetian and Genoese aristocrats for their aloofness. Though trenchant criticism of the existing order was a frequent concomitant of utopias, attacks against social conditions in Italy rarely had the bite of Thomas More's invective. They can occasionally be found—in Alberti's depiction of the contemporary family, in Marco Girolamo Vida's denunciation of the vice-ridden city, in Uberto Foglietta's diatribes against the ancient Genoese nobility—but the violence of Agostini's castigation of the "inhuman rich" is exceptional. His sermons against the speculators and engrossers were not published in his lifetime and this may account for their free-flowing acerbity, or they may simply represent a resurgence of the medieval social doctrine of the just price expressed with religious passion. "Contrary to human piety and Christian charity," he wrote, "they traffic in the blood of the poor without any deep feeling of pity." Christ had never been absent from the Italian utopia, but this minor poet, author of the fervent *Cries to God*, no longer turned away from ordinary men with the cold indifference of Francesco Patrizi, Bishop of Cherso. Agostini even allowed himself a seditious utterance that ran sharply contrary to his own prevailing social doctrine, which countenanced no civil disobedience: "If the poor classes, whose ranks are more numerous than the others, were also more courageous and united, they could not do better in similar cases than turn on the inhuman rich and make of them what the Licaonians made of the monstrous serpents who advanced on them."[52]

Commoditas without Luxuria

In the aristocratic utopias of the Italian Renaissance, happiness or felicity was a state of harmony in which material needs were so satisfied that free play was allowed the spiritual forces of man's nature. This implied neither a surfeit that suffocated the spirit with material luxuries, nor so meager an appeasement that the spirit remained tormented with fleshly hunger because of the inadequacy of the body's restoration. Confronted by the polarities of luxury and minimal necessity, the Italian utopians usually assumed a position midway between sumptuary extremes; and often their regimen approximated the liberal temper of Aristotle's *Politics* more closely than the austerity laid down for Plato's guardians. An ideal of *commoditas* was defined that was far more generous than mere necessity and yet did not lapse into *luxuria*.

In *Della famiglia*, Alberti's treatise on rules of conduct for a perfect aristocratic family, he struck a golden mean between niggardliness and reckless profligacy of expenditure. The patrician family was obligated to save, use up less than it earned, for there was no point to eating beyond what was necessary; but the ideal of parsimony was balanced by an injunction that the family household should live in beauty and splendor. Thrift was not encouraged for its own sake or in pursuit of an ascetic goal. Alberti's family was advised to be continent for reasons quite different from those of Weber's Protestant ethic—the family needed a surplus in order to dispense Christian charity freely, to embellish the household, and to support artists. This was a unique ideal, neither Platonic nor Protestant. Alberti would combine the Aristotelian virtue of liberality toward friends with the Christian virtue of beneficence and the Renaissance ideal of magnificence, all made possible through the practice of household economy.

Alberti wrote at least two utopias that are readily connected, one ˚for the gentleman's family, the other for the city. The family utopia was a block in the total utopian edifice. The perfection of the household should correspond to the perfection of the city, which corresponded to the perfection of the divine cosmic order. The two mundane orders reflected the celestial one insofar as it was feasible; they could not be absolutely perfect. The more excellent the order of the city in its stone structure, the greater would be the tendency of the family to incorporate its virtues; the greater the number of aristocratic families that were disciplined to the ideal order of Alberti, the more excellent the city might be. The ultimate model was in the heavens.

The *Della famiglia* took the form of a dialogue in which a number of Albertis were gathered in the house of the dying Lorenzo, natural father of Leone Battista. Lorenzo gave his final counsel on the ideal measures for raising a gentleman's family. There was stress on the inculcation of a love of God and of learning, physical exercises were recommended, and the acquisition of an honorable art or trade as a hostage to fortune was prescribed. The distinction between animal love and conjugal affection was explored. The psychic ideals were tranquillity and honor. Commerce was not disapproved as long as the occupation, free from evil passions, could be exercised with sobriety and honesty. In the treatment of family economics, both the stingy and the prodigal were deprecated. The Albertis had suffered the humiliations of exile and there was a nostalgia for the good old days when the family devoted to *virtù* found its rewards and recognition in the city. But Alberti did not succumb to a totally privatized family utopia despite strong arguments presented on its behalf. The city, even when at fault, was preserved as the human ideal.

Patrizi's sumptuary idea of a century later was still an abundance of food and clothing and other necessities of life. Necessities were not restricted to a bare minimum, since even Plato in the *Laws* had emphasized that mere subsistence was insufficient for the good life. After Patrizi, however, there was a break in the continuum of Italian utopias, and by the time Agostini was writing in the closing decades of the sixteenth century, the voice of the Counter-Reformation was making itself heard and the ideal of moderate abundance was transformed into meticulously controlled communal feeding. In Agostini's imaginary republic, at public houses staffed by expert chefs, each head of a household could purchase no more than his family allotment, a rule that might be suspended only on holidays and with episcopal permission. To make up for this festive gorging, twice a week all adults had to observe a partial fast and content themselves with one meal a day. When Finito, the weak character in

Agostini's stilted dialogue, pleads for more feasts and time for play in the ideal society, he is disdainfully rebuffed by Infinito.

Even Agostini's aristocrats are rigidly confined in their enjoyment to "everything that is allowable and honest" (*ogni cosa lecita e onesta*), an almost literal translation of More's "honest pleasures."[53] The pleasures turn out to be limited to conversation and physical exercise and to exclude pomp and ceremony and masquerades, as well as dancing, a pastime that Agostini feared might lead to violations of the Decalogue's prohibition against coveting. Stringent rules governed personal adornment, and garments of many colors were the sole prerogative of the magistrates. Sleep was curtailed to seven hours a night, and no one was allowed to lie abed during the day. At the appointed mealtimes, music was freely provided in the vicinity of the palaces, but when this entertainment was over everybody returned to work; no eating between meals was permitted and there were no taverns to frequent. Harsh punishments from Deuteronomy or the *Laws* were meted out for violations. Again, when Finito, speaking for poor, feeble, human nature, complains that Infinito is bent on tearing up all pleasures by the roots, he is brushed aside by the superhuman Infinito, who sternly observes that he is not depriving anyone of temperate pleasures, only of those conducive to vice.

In the *Republic* Plato allowed the lower classes to go more or less their own concupiscent way, and limited austerity to the aristocratic guardians. Agostini, in the new ascetic egalitarian spirit of the Counter-Reformation, imposed prohibitions upon all men. No matter how rich a noble might be, the plan of his house required approval by the architect of the city, and nothing that overstepped the bounds of uniformity was sanctioned. No one escaped Agostini's revivalist censures; he was particularly vehement against those clergy "who live scandalous lives with excessive display and gluttony, sensuality, and covetousness."[54] The earlier utopian ideal of happiness in Alberti and Patrizi had been spiritual without being quite so ascetic and monastic, since *commoditas*— comfort, convenience—was conceived as an aid rather than an impediment to spirituality.

Commoditas was a general moral and philosophical ideal. In its pursuit, many Renaissance utopias, especially those in architectural treatises, had shown an interest in new technology, and had introduced hygienic measures to prevent the ravages of pestilence. Waterworks, harbor construction, canals, and drainage systems were all part of Filarete's *Sforzinda*. Francesco di Giorgio designed lavatories and stables, and they figured prominently in what remains of Leonardo's sketch of the two-level city. Francesco di Giorgio's treatise is divided into sections on general principles, the essential features of a commodious city constructed for a social animal, the ornaments of cities and fortresses, the temple to God, the fortifications for dominion, and the technology necessary for construction. The lodestar of this architectural dreamer remains commodiousness, as he moves from the perfect stable through the perfect chimney to the perfect lavatory.

Even Doni, whose egalitarian laws do not quite fit into the general pattern, nevertheless recognizes the principle of commodiousness without luxury, though in a different way. His espousal of community of property in the satire "Mondo Savio," in which the dialogue of Savio and Pazzo reflects Doni's ambivalence about the utopian world, is idiosyncratic, like his sexual arrangements. There is absolute equality among citizens and private ownership is excluded. All people dress alike, banishing jealousy, though the simple garments are colored differently for the various age groups. Common kitchens are open to all the hungry, and when one hostelry has finished distributing its allotted victuals, people repair to another. Much of this is patently under Morean influence, but a novel element is introduced: There is an almost Platonic emphasis upon the specialization of a wide variety of tasks, while at least half the inhabitants of More's Utopia engage in simple agriculture. The underlying assumption in Doni's fantasy is that for every thing and every person there is an optimum use, and an ideal world is the consequence of utilizing each object and each human being in a perfect way. In this freak satire of Renaissance Italy, we are jauntily on the way to "each according to his abilities." In virtually all communist utopias from More to the nineteenth century, repression of desires makes egalitarian commonality possible. Excess or surplus is associated with vices that are likely to disrupt the calm of the polity. Hence there is no money in Doni's city, and anyone who requires goods applies directly to the specialized artisan-producer, from whom he freely receives what he needs. But production is regulated by the standard of elementary need, and no accumulation that could breed *luxuria* is permitted. The inhabitants of Doni's *mondo nuovo* make the same crucial decision that underlies the ordinances of More's King Utopus. They prefer to work less, quitting two hours before dark, rather than to consume more. There is a little of everything, but not too much of anything. Commoditas without luxuria.

The appeasement of sexual needs was not usually considered an aspect of commoditas. Nevertheless, sexual regulations, a province normally reserved for ecclesiastical authorities and therefore discreetly avoided by most Italian Renaissance writers, were brazenly incorporated into the utopias of two writers, Filarete and Doni. At their hands, need and *commodità* received a realistic extension neglected by other Italian utopians. Filarete provided for a House of Virtue and a House of Vice in the very center of Sforzinda, places for Venus and Bacchus, for baths, taprooms, and such like appurtenances, as well as "games and other swindles, as is the custom, though an unfortunate custom."[55] Courtesans, brought to the House of Vice by their neighbors for violating decent behavior, were nevertheless respected. Luxuria was appropriately condemned in the symbolic decorations of Sforzinda, but necessary vices were tolerated—though this is no wildly licentious society and there are punishments for "things that cannot be permitted,"[56] even in the House of Vice. Portraits of Nero, Elagabalus, Sardanapalus, and unidentified contemporaries accused of monstrous crimes were displayed to discourage unnatural proclivities among the frequenters of these establishments.

The sexual regulations spelled out in early editions of Doni's work would have been totally unacceptable to any other Renaissance utopian, since they designated a section of the radial city for all women, who would be "used" in common. The rationale for this arrangement is, one suspects, mostly tongue-in-cheek. Consider how many evils would be avoided by this community of women, Doni's Savio tries to convince the reluctant Pazzo. The absence of identifiable progeny eliminates from the city much weeping and wailing over lost relatives because death is no longer an individual tragedy. There is a spirited attack on the evils of marriage and the rapes, tumults, blood feuds, and assassinations that follow in its wake. Community of women would put an end to the "uproar of the wedding, the stealthy smuggling of bridegrooms, the procuring, the lawsuits over refusals, the embezzlement of dowries, and the pitfalls of the deceptions perpetrated by rascals."[57] The argument that lovers would be anguished is countered with a sly twist of rhetoric out of Plato. Since love is the deprivation of the thing loved, when the city will have a plethora of love objects freely available, amorous suffering will be banished from the city. But Doni's and Filarete's utopian sexual institutions are sports in the Renaissance.

The Dilemma of Christian Aristocracy in Utopia

The Italian Renaissance utopia is full of contradictions unresolved. The beautiful shapes expressive of ideal philosophical relationships were not always in perfect harmony with the utilitarian functioning of the ideal city. Commitment to both a rigid class division in the social order and to the radial form of city plan involved contrarieties that could hardly be reconciled even in utopian fantasy. When religious or mythic needs, the exigencies of the power structure, and the demands of the new hygiene collided, they led to clumsy compromises. Finally, the whole notion of a terrestrial ideal city that retained its Christian character was problematical and required apology in Renaissance and Counter-Reformation Italy.

The Christian dilemma was the central one. Admittedly, the very absorption with a perfect city on earth implies at least a measure of alienation from the City of God as it had been conceived by Saint Augustine. There is something autonomous, Epicurean, and neglectful of God about a worldly utopia. Are not those who assume the possibility of great happiness in this world guilty of the sin of pride? The antagonism between Christianity and utopia may be smoothed over, but it is not dissolved even when the cathedral is raised on a lofty mount in the center of a radial city, as in Francesco di Giorgio's famous drawings, or when felicity is defined primarily in spiritual and moral rather than sensate terms, as in the writings of Patrizi, whose città felice preserves the meaning of blessed city. Saint Augustine taught that men of the City of God during their sojourn in the earthly city were in constant struggle with the evil ones among whom they lived intermingled in faulty human societies until the final resolution of Judgment Day. If this world is a mere antechamber to the beatitude of the next, then plans for a supreme good on earth are presumptuous.

Yet perhaps the break is less sharp than might be imagined between the late medieval Christian outlook embodied in the self-image of Italian city-states and the ideal earthly vision of the Renaissance. By the thirteenth century the Italian commune had already begun to conceive of itself as a thing of beauty in which religious and aesthetic elements were fused. There was thus a preparation for the utopia of the Renaissance. There is matter-of-fact evidence of this new consciousness in the statutes of the period. When the commune of Brescia, for example, prohibited the destruction of buildings whose owners had been condemned for heinous crimes—an ancient act of vengeance related to the uprooting of sin—the justification for the new ordinance was "*Quod civi-*

tates facte sunt ad similitudinem paradisi" (For cities are made to the likeness of paradise).[58] The analogy of any great city with Jerusalem assumed concrete shape when processions at Easter transformed the commune, with the aid of decorations, into a Jerusalem prepared for the entry of Christ. A city square could be turned into a simulacrum of the Holy Land, complete with a River Jordan and other sacred places. The cathedral, which in isolation had once stood for the City of God, became an integral part of a city that in its totality, not only in its church, corresponded to a sacred reality. Though a traditional reading of Saint Augustine would restrict the City of God to heaven and to godly representatives on earth, some passages in his writings allowed for betterment in the society of the earthly city. The rise of the medieval city has usually been considered in economic and social terms, but there were also religious conceptions that bathed it in a paradisaical light and served as a transition to the Renaissance idea of a perfect city. There is thus a continuity between the medieval ideas of *ordo* and *aequalitas* preached by the great Schoolmen and the institutions of the *città felice.*

Despite the insinuation of aesthetic ideals from pagan antiquity, the Italian city-utopias remained deeply Christian. Agostini, a mystic who made a pilgrimage to the Holy Land, is an example of the penetration of the religious spirit of the Counter-Reformation into utopia. He dwelt on *misericordia* as the virtue that bridged the gap among classes. In adopting for his imaginary republic the regulations of the markets of Venice as the best in the world, he added a gloss on the compulsory daily celebration of the mass: "Since the most important part of a Christian (or civilized man) is religion, I do not intend to open the businesses of my city until the whole people . . . has heard and seen the sacred mystery of the Altar, and the priest has exhorted them in a brief sermon to carry out the doctrine of the Gospel that has been read, and they have been dismissed with his blessing."[59] For all of Doni's shocking community of women and property, the center of his radial city was dominated by a church four to six times higher than the majestic Duomo of Florence. Apart from their stress on Christian virtues and ceremonials, the utopia-makers of the Renaissance remained Christian dualists, for whom evil was ineradicable even in the optimum republic. In their writings there is no echo of Joachim of Fiore's eternal gospel, the heterodox belief in absolute love under the millennial rule of the Holy Ghost on earth as the third stage of mankind. Patrizi taught in *La Città felice* that man, who like all other creatures desired his own good, had to rest content with the *humano bene,* a finite good, for more he could not attain in this world. There was a limit to *beatitudine* (general happiness), which consisted in the rule of the body by the soul, or the subservience of the body to the soul.

The Two Modes

There is a marked distinction between the fortunes of the architectural treatises and of the Italian philosophical utopias, the works of Doni, Patrizi, Agostini, at the time of their composition and subsequently. The two modes were not, of course, quite so unrelated to each other in content as bald titles might suggest, since the plans of the architects were unfolded in narrative form and their arguments often involved them in expounding social and even metaphysical concepts. But each of the types reached its high point in a different period, and for the most part neither was cognizant of the other's existence. The most important illustrated treatises were written in the second half of the fifteenth and the early sixteenth centuries, while the strictly philosophical utopias began to appear only around the time of the Council of Trent and were compressed into the latter half of the sixteenth century, with some spillage over into the early seventeenth.

The manuscripts of the architectural utopias, highly prized, were deposited in the libraries of the ducal patrons to whom they were dedicated, and successive generations of architects had access to the writings and sketches of their predecessors. Occasionally it is known precisely when one of the manuscripts was read by a stranger and when a fresh copy was made. The architectural ideal cities with their magnificent illustrations thus had a fertile existence, while the later, purely philosophical discourses of Patrizi and Agostini, though noticed by contemporaries, left no offspring. Long omitted from histories of utopian thought, the Italian philosophical utopias of the latter part of the sixteenth century did not enter the main current, and remained an underground rivulet that surfaced only with the explorations of twentieth-century Italian scholars avid for literary curiosities. The period of Fascism witnessed a minor revival of interest in this group of thinkers, as if the Aesopian language of utopia might be used against the regime. And in the first years after 1945 a few academic studies on sixteenth-century Italian utopias accompanied the search for a way out of the tragic postwar condition: This was really grasping at straws.

Despite the different shapes it assumed, the varying fortunes of its two principal modes, and the broad time span it covered—from the middle of the fifteenth to the early seventeenth century—the utopian experience of the Italian Renaissance, both philosophical and architectural, can in most respects be viewed as a whole. The towering Italian philosopher-utopians Bruno and Campanella have been intentionally excluded because their universalist visions, though in part they harked back to medieval and early Renaissance hermeticism, really belong to another sphere, to seventeenth-century Pansophia, a utopia of Christian unity that was rooted in a new scientific world view and transcended the limits of the predominantly aristocratic, rather mystical, and aesthetic utopia of the earlier period.

In Renaissance visions of the ideal society it is possible to identify discrete Platonic and Aristotelian elements, and there is no dearth of citations from both philosophers—though the mere use of a quotation does not stamp a work as belonging definitively in one camp or the other. In narrative Italian utopias the imitation of Plato is more obvious because there was a completed model to follow, while Aristotle was critical and discursive; but the personal virtues of the good citizen were still set forth in the language of Aristotle's *Ethics* and *Politics,* and Roman Stoic values as transmitted by Cicero and Seneca always remained active ingredients. Yet the Italian Renaissance utopias are not mere syncretisms of classical themes. For all their superficial archaisms, they represent a distinctive ideal world of their own. A Platonic atmosphere, vague and mystical language about the spirit enshroud the writings with a mist so opaque that it often obscures the marked differences between the Renaissance ideal city and Plato's Republic. But even when men of the Renaissance thought that they were copying, imitating, rediscovering, they were in fact creating anew, especially in two respects: The Italian utopias reflected a very different class structure from that of the polis, and the relationship of an ideal city in this world to a future heavenly Jerusalem, though sometimes not explicit, was never wholly lost from sight. The utopias were Platonic, but their Plato had been thoroughly Christianized.

The outburst of ideality among the Renaissance philosophical architects was brief; the actual structures they built outlasted the passion for city planning. By the second half of the sixteenth century, while the Vitruvian formula became canonical in the designs of private palaces, individual churches, and government buildings, the philosophical concept of the ideal whole withered away. Palladio symbolized this transformation when he initiated his treatise *Quattro libri dell'architettura* (1570) with a consideration of individual houses, explaining that these structures were to be grouped in *borghi* and the borghi would constitute the *città*. Filarete had operated in an inverse order: Beginning with the site and radial form of the whole city, he then fitted different types of public and domestic edifices into their appropriate places within the general pattern. Francesco di Giorgio, builder of palaces and citadels, never lost sight of the organic whole of the city. The *grandi* of the latter part of the sixteenth century may no longer have wielded political power, but they retained the economic capacity to display their own opulence at the expense of the city's unity. In the plans he drew for schools, factories, churches, and other public buildings, Bartolomeo Ammannati was probably trying to recover the fifteenth-century conception of a total city; but the model of the city as a tangible architectural expression of the continuity between the nature of the cosmos and a civil society governed by natural laws was by that time lost. While parts of the architectural plans of the utopians had been realized, their vision in its entirety remained imaginary, the ideal expression of a cultural moment in high Renaissance Italy.

6

Heaven on Earth for the Common Man

THOMAS MÜNTZER'S utopia was born of a consciousness of brutal social conflict in the German towns in which he served. Thomas More had wished for the reordering, spiritualization, and stabilization of society. Müntzer cried for an upheaval, a massive destruction succeeded by the reign of Christ. More's utopia was an escape to a blessed isle; he was creating not the perfect, but the optimum, human republic, for true beatitude resided only in heaven. Müntzer would resort to the sword to usher in the Kingdom of Heaven on Earth. More read the Bible as real history made present and was leery of interpreting the text as philosophical allegory rather than direct moral precept. For Müntzer Scripture was to be read freely and translated into contemporary events, the revelation of the reader directing his understanding. While More dreamed of uprooting the source of violence in human relationships, Müntzer reveled in turmoil. His paradise would be brought about through the organization of a mighty host marching against the princes of evil. In a seventeenth-century woodcut by Romeyn de Hooghe, Müntzer is portrayed with a Bible under his arm and his sword unsheathed.

Brothers of the Free Spirit, Taborites, Anabaptists

Toward the end of the Middle Ages paradise ceased to be merely the dream of a future life and became a catalyst for brazen and adventurous deeds on earth. Religious enthusiasts, no longer content with passively waiting for the blessedness of the next world, demanded the consummation of the times, the immediate founding of the glorious kingdom. The main geographic areas of prophetic contagion were Central Europe and the Rhineland, but the movement spread throughout the Continent in a web of secret channels, many of them still unexplored. Influences from the heart of Russia are turning up in Bohemia and Moravia and the doctrines of sectarians in the Lowlands have been tracked to England.

In the centuries before the Lutheran Reformation, millenarian belief and movements of social revolt interpenetrated. During popular uprisings of artisans and peasants, which joined religious hostility toward dignitaries of the church to the endemic antagonism of the poor against rich lords and burghers, men turned to the Bible for a model of society to replace the odious one they were rejecting. The rationalist urban utopias of the Greek philosophers were beyond their ken. Perhaps echoes from the ancient cokaygne utopia lingered on in popular folklore; but they were ephemeral compared with the paradisaical images that could be drawn from the Bible and its prophecies. In fourteenth-century England John Ball and the Lollards found in the Gospels a sanction for social and political protest: Scripture presented them with a sacred picture of what the world ought to be. The Hussites of Bohemia dreamed of a patriarchal order whose rulers would imitate the Fathers of the Old Testament. Flemish weavers went further back, to the Garden of Eden, and had fantasies of the nudity and simplicity of the first man, the naked truth. A quest for the truth spiritual and the nakedness of the body have accompanied visions of rebirth down to our own day, though the former is not a necessary condition for the latter. Müntzer too, would admonish believers to come before God empty and naked.[1]

Affinities have been remarked among the visions and activities of the leaders of the *pauperes* during the Crusades, the delusions of the *pastoureaux,* the legend of Kaiser Frederick's future reign after awakening from a long sleep, the paradisaical beliefs of the Brothers of the Free Spirit, and the apocalypse of the Taborites, a wild offshoot of the Hussites. A prophet is the charismatic leader. Antichrist and his cohorts are identified with the rich, the powerful, the Jews, the ordinary clergy. A day of reckoning with much bloodshed is foretold, to be followed by an earthly reign of the good emperor or the mystic leader or Christ himself. The language common to the sects is an admixture of the prophecies in Daniel, Revelation, and the Sibylline Oracles. The millennium is suffused with peace and love, though the punishing and destructive fervor that marks the last days before the good reign is inaugurated spills over. In a manuscript by the "revolutionary of the Upper Rhine," a violent millenarian recently identified as Conrad Stürtzel, a jurist at the court of the Emperor Maximilian who wrote his "hundred articles and twenty statutes" about 1498, the rebirth of a rigorous punitive religion is related to a prediction of the universal hegemony of the Holy Roman Empire under the Black Forest Kaiser and his Knights, a medieval fantasy mixed in with a promise of equality, appeals to the common man and the common people, and an obsessive revulsion against court officials that prefigures both More's Hythloday and Müntzer.[2]

Some idea of the earthly paradise instituted by the Brothers of the Free Spirit was extracted from John of Brünn during his interrogation about 1330. Initiates went through two stages: first an ascetic one, during which they surrendered all their property and became mendicants; then one of absolute liberty in which, their old natures having been killed, they were enjoined to heed all the promptings of their new, emancipated natures on pain of falling away from freedom and dropping from the eternal into the mere temporal. Those who were in true liberty could not be commanded by anyone, or excommunicated, or forbidden anything. Neither the pope nor an archbishop had authority over them, for they were free and did not come under the jurisdiction of any man; therefore they obeyed neither the statutes nor mandates of the Church. "I am of the Free Spirit," the new believer proclaimed, "and all that I desire I satisfy and gratify. Should I seek a woman in the still of the night I satisfy my craving without any feelings of bad conscience or sin; for the spirit is free, and I am also a natural man. Therefore I must freely fulfill my nature in deeds."[3] If union with God was achieved, man could do no evil.

The Taborites were part of God's army to be led out of cities, villages, and castles, before the imminent destruction of the rest of the world. They chose five cities to be spared in the general conflagration, and multitudes gathered in these havens to establish communal societies. Laurence of Brezova's Hussite chronicle reports on a wild Adamite wing of the Taborites: "In the second advent of Christ before the Day of Judgment, all kings and princes and prelates will cease to be. Those elect still living will be brought back to the state of innocence of Adam in Paradise, like Enoch and Elijah, and they will know neither hunger nor thirst, nor other spiritual or physical pain. And in holy marriage and with immaculate marriage-bed they will carnally generate sons and grandchildren here on earth and on the mountains, without pain or grief, and without original sin."[4] Under the leadership of one they called Moses the Adamites wandered shamelessly about like the first man and woman in the Garden, dancing naked and lying with each other. In the history of utopias there is an alternative to the more prevalent rule of strict sexual regulation in a fantasy of promiscuity, but the phenomenon is comparatively rare in Western culture.

Melodramatic stories about millenarians of the Reformation period who acted out their dreams of freedom from repression have been told often. The restoration of primitive Christianity, the reinstitution of patriarchal polygamy, and the overnight establishment of community lend themselves to easy ridicule. The Anabaptists were an international sect whose territory stretched into Alsace, the Netherlands, Switzerland, Bohemia. They believed neither in the Church alone nor in the letter of the Bible, but taught that God still revealed himself to those with open hearts, prepared through suffering to receive His illumination. In hearings that followed the quelling of peasant revolts in Germany it became clear that these poor and uncomprehending people, who had declared their emancipation from the old Church hierarchy, blindly obeyed their sectarian pastors and did whatever they bade them. Prophetic seizures, the advance of peasant rebels against the bullets of the enemy armed with nothing but faith in the prophet, the executions and plundering, famished men, women, and children eating grass like beasts while awaiting the millennium bore witness to the deception and madness of paradisaical fantasies. The spectacle of John of Leyden, the Anabaptist butcher who proclaimed himself King of Justice and King of the New Jerusalem in Münster, gorging while his subjects starved in community, was difficult for later egalitarians to live down. When David Hume in his elegant treatise on morals wished to dismiss the idea of communism with a phrase he raised the specter of the Anabaptists

The Wandering Pastor

Thomas Müntzer can be considered as a theologian of the early Reformation, or the leader of bands of artisans and peasants destroying monasteries and castles, or the wretched and inept military tactician of a benighted horde who fell easy prey to the troops of German nobles. He was also the creator of a vision of life on earth. The content of his utopia has to be gleaned from a few manifestoes, articles of union among the sworn elect, a small collection of letters to friends and enemies, replies to Luther's attacks, a published sermon, a printed confession that purported to be the record of his interrogation by his captors after the massacre of Frankenhausen. The brief passages uttered or written down under a wide variety of circumstances hardly constitute a speaking-picture utopia of an alternative or future state of society, nor can they by any stretch of the imagination be regarded as a discussion of the principles that should underlie the conditions of life in an ideal city. Müntzer was acquainted with Plato's *Republic*—the record shows that he owned a copy—but his one passing reference to it is derogatory. What, then, is Müntzer the prophet doing among the utopian elect? His acceptance among the elect of God is not open to question, because it derives from his own inner conviction that he heard the voice of God after passing through the awesome trials, pains, and tribulations of the set stages that preceded mystical illumination.

Müntzer has become the prototype of those who preached the modern religious utopia of the millennium, a form that has exerted a powerful influence far beyond the sectarian confines of its origins. If utopian thought in Western society were limited to purely secular works, one of its vigorous currents that runs from the early Jewish and Christian apocalypses through Leibniz would have to be blotted out. Among the multiplicity of shapes assumed by the Christian utopia through the centuries, one rested on belief in a divine promise communicated directly to men with prophetic gifts and not requiring the intervention of the Word of God written in the Old and New Testaments. The two grandest moments of this spiritual utopia occurred in the early Reformation and during the English Civil War.

Millenarianism has never ceased to produce its steady stream of prophets, the exact time for initiating the millennium being constantly pushed forward as a prophecy was not fulfilled and illusions went underground to reemerge on the morrow. Millenarians addicted to exegesis of the word and practitioners of the art of *gematria*—a technique for interpreting Scripture by giving numerical value to letters and words—had a way of impaling themselves on specific dates. The Anabaptist Hans Huth, Müntzer's friend, proclaimed May 15, 1527, the day of final judgment, then had to postpone it to 1529. Others contented themselves with merely announcing the imminence of the Kingdom of Heaven on Earth. Thomas Müntzer belongs to the tradition that eschewed dates, conveying in vivid language the feeling that the moment had in fact already arrived. Millenarians can be divided between those who passively awaited the intrusion of the Lord into history and those who held to the conviction that it was the duty of man to participate in God's work with direct action, preaching, converting, witnessing truth, and on occasion brandishing the sword against the minions of Antichrist, the enemies in the divine battle. Müntzer, a leader of the activists, became the symbolic hero of revolutionaries, religious and secular.

The early sixteenth-century uprisings in South Germany have a local, medieval aspect. Yet Thomas Müntzer was far more than a provincial visionary. Amid a host of stereotyped millenarians, he is emerging as a unique figure. His yearning for spirituality, his intense feeling for the misery of the human condition, the universality of the message that excluded neither Jew nor Turk nor a man of any status in society if he endured the psychic trials of illumination raise him above the crowd of preachers of what has come to be called the Radical Reformation. At the same time, his polarization of existence into salvation and damnation, and the sharp Joshua-like cut between those for his gospel and those against it, established him in modern millenarian and apocalyptic thought as a figure who would alternately be despised and exalted to the heavens. He probably belongs more to the prologue of a revolutionary utopia than to the drama itself. He set a precedent. The concentration on violence, the rejection of alternative paths, the heightening of the intensity of the struggle imprinted a pattern. The anguished process of reaching utopia and the absolutism of surrender to the band of the elect are in themselves the very definition of the spiritual utopia of the reign of Christ on earth.

Thomas Müntzer was no ignorant peasant possessed by a vision. Of all the activist millenarians, this preacher was the most learned in Scripture, in the Church Fathers, in the writings of medieval prophets. He even had more than a passing acquaintance with contemporary humanist literature. Born in Stolberg about 1488 or 1489,[5] he attended the universities of Leipzig and Frankfort and acquired a knowledge of both Hebrew and Greek. Citations in his works and manuscript lists of books now preserved in Dresden include Platonic dialogues, Eusebius' world history, Apuleius' *Golden Ass,* tracts by Erasmus. Leaving the academy, Müntzer became a preacher who wandered restlessly through Central Germany, roaming as far south as Basel and as far east as Prague. During a period when he served as father confessor in a nunnery, he earnestly sought a way to God through a study of the mystical theologians Heinrich Seuse and Johann Tauler, whose writings had recounted the assaults of doubt and despair that could overwhelm a true Christian before the birth of God in his soul. The freedom of Tauler's imaginative and allegorical interpretation of the Bible was adopted by Müntzer in his social-apocalyptic reading of the text. But though he used the same mystical terminology, he was not a *Schwärmer,* a ranting enthusiast.

An early supporter of Luther, Müntzer was militantly antipapist from the outset, and on Luther's recommendation was appointed to the post of "supply pastor" in Zwickau, an important trading and cloth-manufacturing city close to a silver-mining area, and an intellectual center. Georg Agricola, the pioneer mineralogist, taught there at the time. And Zwickau, where Müntzer soon gained notoriety as a popular preacher who scandalized the rich, was on the road to Prague, heart of the Radical Reformation. Ties had been established between members of the Zwickau clergy and Bohemian millenarians like the Nicolaites, named after Nicholas Wlasonic, a farmer who was frequented by angels. Among the chiliastic preachers of Zwickau, monkery was caricatured in language as vitriolic as anything Voltaire later concocted. There was a tradition of heresy in the locality; in 1462 Waldensians had been executed there. Zwickau was torn by deep-rooted antagonism between the old corporations of weavers and the new, prosperous mining interests. Partisanship over status in the community and partisanship in religious beliefs reinforced each other. The weavers, suffering from a prolonged economic depression, sided with the religious innovators, while the rich newcomers who controlled the exploitation of the mines and could afford masses remained faithful to the Catholic Church. Nikolaus Storch, a Zwickau weaver who had revived the old Taborite doctrines, was reported to be a proponent of polygamy, adult baptism, seizure of the property of the rich, the overthrow of civil authority and the priesthood. A dissident Beghard tradition had survived among the poor weavers and dyers, who worshiped in little conventicles at night in their own manner and were a fertile breeding ground for rebellion.

Müntzer was about thirty when he was caught up in a whirlpool of heresy and social discontent. At the beginning of his career he had been rather like the humanist, book-learned Lutherans whom he now began to despise and revile. As late as 1520, with a bequest from his mother, he had ordered some seventy-five learned volumes from a bookseller, a substantial library for those times. He did not belong by birth to the class of peasants and artisans with whom he identified himself after receiving his mission. His revolt against the erudite professors and resentment toward his respectable burgher father, with whom he quarreled over a legacy, are a denial of his origins and a search for the chosen people, the elect of God, among others, not his own kind. His complaint that his father treated him like the son of a whore may help us understand his rage against the powerful in the world, but we know too little about the boy and the youth to begin to account for his mighty anger and his commitment to the wretched of the earth.

Under attack for his harsh sermons against the Franciscans in Zwickau, Müntzer had appealed to Luther for support, still considering himself one of his followers. But he soon moved in the direction of Storch and the millenarians and away from the more stolid Lutheran reformers. He preached that the external, audible word of the priests was theirs alone, not God's, and therefore should not be sacrosanct to men. An uprising against the bishop led to charges that Müntzer was fanaticizing his congregation and he was expelled from the city. He sought refuge in Prague among the Hussites, Taborites, and Anabaptists, and preached to them through an interpreter. The Almighty still communicated with men through the Holy Spirit, he assured them, and adherence to the literal word of the Bible, sacred to Luther, could become another kind of servitude to the flesh. In his denunciation of Lutherans, issued in Latin, Czech, and German, he ridiculed the belief that God no longer spoke with people, as if He had suddenly been struck dumb. The Holy Spirit could reveal itself in any age of the world and was not confined to the apostolic. God again talked through *him,* Müntzer boasted. ("And before he turned around he was lying with a few thousand men in the muck," was Luther's mockery of his pretension to direct illumination on the morrow of the defeat at Frankenhausen, in a triumphant announcement of God's awful judgment on the false prophet.)[6] God's will was absolutely free, and a free God could move the spirit of a man even though he might be ignorant and poor. The German radical missionaries and preachers of this new gospel had occasional illusions about converting dukes, electors, or city councillors; but whatever their class origins and education, during their most militant and influential periods they were bound to the common people, to ordinary peasants and artisans.

When Prague in its turn proved inhospitable, Müntzer roamed through Thuringia and Saxony until he was summoned to Allstedt, a small town near the Mansfeld copper mines, where he settled and married a former nun. There he formed a *Verbündniss* among artisans and miners, a union that was intended ultimately to embrace all of Christendom, called upon princes and lords to leave their palaces and live as Christians, and threatened with death those who would not heed his gospel. When Duke George of Saxony and Count Ernst von Mansfeld forbade their subjects to attend his services, he challenged them and their priests to show where he contradicted Scripture, and wrote defiantly to the Count on September 22, 1523, "And you should know that in such mighty and righteous matters I am not afraid of the whole world. But you want to be feared more than God himself, as I can show from your actions and orders . . . I'll deal with you a hundred thousand times worse than Luther did with the Pope." He signed himself "Thomas Müntzer, A Destroyer of the Unbelievers."[7]

Luther recognized the danger in Müntzer's social gospel and his megalomaniac claims, was suspicious of his evasive replies when he summoned him for questioning, and finally visited upon him the full fury of his chastisement. In a letter addressed toward the end of July 1524 to Frederick the Wise, Elector of Saxony, and Duke John of Saxony, Luther bragged of an encounter with the prophet some years back, in which he had been worsted. "He was punched in the nose once or twice in my presence at the cloister in Wittenberg."[8] That Luther was constantly fighting Müntzer in letters, sermons, and table talk refutes those who have assiduously tried to expunge him from the historical record of the Reformation as a trivial preacher of no great account. There are more than a hundred attacks in the collected works that have now been carefully assembled, one even in Luther's last sermon on February 15, 1546, when Müntzer had been dead for more than twenty years.[9]

Theologian with a Sword

Müntzer saw a universal upheaval of the existing order as part of God's design and read the inchoate demands of the peasants as heralding the imminent establishment of the Kingdom of Heaven on Earth. But he did not rest with prophetic evocations of a new and glorious reign of justice. In the history of modern utopian thought he stands out as a formidable exponent of man's obligation to join actively with the will of God and not shrink from performing deeds of violence to carry out His purposes. Acts, not words alone, would clear the path to salvation. When in the summer of 1525, not long after Müntzer's execution, Luther decided to marry the former nun Katharina von Bora, he crudely caricatured Müntzer's doctrine by announcing that he too would celebrate the Gospel not only in the Word but in the Act. In Allstedt Müntzer had proceeded to acts. In a new liturgy he had stripped off every last vestige of pagan ceremonial and had concentrated on the inner communion between God and man. Thousands flocked to hear him. But at Mallerbach at the very gates of his city stood a Catholic chapel in which men, like heathens, adored a statue and left waxen votive offerings to it. The devil was being worshiped there under the name of Mary. Müntzer exhorted his congregation to end this brazen idolatry, and then he watched in triumphant righteousness as the chapel was put to the torch.

Müntzer's doctrine of inner illumination opened wide the possibilities for a new social interpretation of the Gospel. Evangelical texts on spiritual hunger were rendered into language that spoke of plain physical needs. And Müntzer took the prophecy of Daniel in Chapter 7, verse 27, that the power of the heavens would be given to "the people of the saints of the most High" to mean the common people. Though he esteemed the Abbot Joachim of Fiore, his own imminent Kingdom of God belonged not to a sacred monastic brotherhood but to ordinary folk, flesh-and-blood peasants who rebelled against their masters. In a letter of May 13, 1525, to the men of Erfurt, just before the fateful encounter at Frankenhausen, Müntzer declared: "According to the seventh chapter of Daniel and Revelation 18 and 19, authority should be vested in the common people. Virtually all judgments in the Bible bear witness that the creatures must be free, otherwise the pure word of God will be undone."[10] Müntzer established an important conjunction in world history, the union of a particular body, the common people in action, and a religious teaching based on a new interpretation of Scripture. The wrath of Moses and the prophets was alive again, vented against local princelets who were identified with ancient sinners of Judea and Israel.

In the Italian città felice the patricians were the natural rulers of the perfect society; in More's *Utopia,* the pillars of the kingdom were the learned heads of households. Müntzer's choice fell upon the common people, who were capable of suffering in their quest for God and of martyrdom in the fulfillment of His will. Worldly authority held no terrors for that brotherhood of Christians who had fought their way to God and become a new elect. Because they had been purified and exalted, these soldiers enlisted in the army of the righteous could strike out against evil with abandon. Müntzer's ally Andreas Karlstadt was troubled by his friend's insistence on the organization of the peasants into a brotherhood to bring about the Kingdom of God. There was an implied derogation of His omnipotence in this newfound need for the assembling of a *Christliche Vereinigung,* a Christian Union. Could God not inaugurate the reign of the just by Himself? Karlstadt had warned Müntzer that in this world men lived in the land of the dead and as long as they were subject to the demands of the flesh the justice of Christ could not triumph. Müntzer denied the limitation. He preached a heavenly life on earth that could be attained by bestowing the power of the sword on the whole community and by cultivating internal perfection and the understanding (*Verstand*) of the poor. In Müntzer, the millenarian doctrine of the earthly paradise assumed something of a class character, a revolutionary moment in the history of the idea. The conception that before the inauguration of the reign of Christ the elect should form a *Bund* that would unite them in war and peace was given great prominence by Müntzer's Allstedt *Verbündniss.* A covenant as a solemn commitment to action among the elect carried the idea forward. In the course of time, like so many sectarian forms of the Reformation, it was secularized in the secret society that would lead the revolution to a worldly utopia.

In Müntzer's Kingdom of Heaven there was no room for pedantic theologians, surely not for Luther, whom he scorned as Doctor Liar (*Doctor Luegner*). There is a strong anti-intellectual undercurrent in Müntzer's preaching, as there would be among the Diggers and Ranters of the English Civil War and in nineteenth-century American populist revivalism, though he was perhaps moved less by simplistic obscurantism than by a desire to raise the self-esteem of the ignorant, virtuous poor and to castigate the learned who used their gifts only for corrupt ends. In sermon after sermon Müntzer read into the text of Jeremiah attacks on wealthy merchants and the book-learned and an appreciation of the faith of ordinary peasants. But his discovery in the Gospel of a new order of righteousness did not encase a Christian in the letter of the law and hold him captive. Everyman had the same power to find his way to God through the inner word as through the biblical text itself, a theological position that had forced a chasm between Müntzer and the orthodox Lutherans. The doctrine of the "inner word" has always appeared a threat to the ecclesiastical establishment of any scriptural religion. "Well, perhaps you inquire how the

Word gets into the heart?" Müntzer asked rhetorically. "Answer: It gets down from God above when you are in a high state of wonderment . . . And this wonderment, whether it be the word of God or not, begins when one is a child of six or seven, as is alluded to in Numbers 19 . . . And any man who has not become aware and receptive through the living witness of God, Romans 8, really has nothing to say even if he stuffed himself with a hundred thousand Bibles."[11]

True Christian belief was a rarity in Christendom, Müntzer taught. Light-hearted belief was no belief at all. The Bible was not necessary to acquire true belief; it could be attained by those who had never heard of Scripture or of other books. The Bible merely bore witness as to how belief had been achieved by men in other times, but it did not itself create belief. The potency for the common man of a doctrine of direct infusion of the Holy Spirit, in contrast to Luther's "Bibel Babel Bubel," will be witnessed time and again in the history of the revolutionary utopia. The confrontation of the Luther type with a Müntzer type will often be repeated. Winstanley the Digger will incarnate the Müntzer image and will be defeated by the Puritan bibliolaters. And when the millenarian revolutionary utopia is secularized, Marx with his book will ultimately be victorious over the anarchist spiritualizers who talk on about their inner feelings of right.

The common man, the common people, were the bearers of divine justice in the world, for they understood the meaning of the Kingdom of Heaven better than did the scholars. In Müntzer's "social" interpretation of Old Testament prophets the peasants were exalted over the great ones of the earth. The bestial drinkers and gluttons who had never known suffering, what could they understand of the Kingdom of Heaven? Despite an occasional lapse into despair over the stupidity and ignorance of the people, Müntzer raised them above their polluted rulers. The absolutism of his position, however, did not prevent him from writing with a certain humility to Frederick the Wise, calling upon him to lead the crusade against the godless. There was always that remote hope that a mighty prince would suddenly see the light, a fantasy that has a way of possessing many utopians in times of crisis.

The Scriptures held within them the truth of the new order, Müntzer conceded, but—and this is a peculiar feature of his dispensation—its meaning and practice were not equally accessible to all Christian laymen. The common man was superior in his understanding of Scripture to the upper classes, whose luxurious situation blinded them to a full comprehension of the Word. Though Christian brotherhood and union were the basis of the new order, only honest laborers could grasp its meaning—such was the new election, the reverse of the later Calvinist order with its preference for the socially powerful in the congregation, marked with the sign of grace by their prosperity. The poor were the true elect and their understanding of Scripture had to be hearkened to because they alone had been visited by the Fear of God (*Gottesfurcht*). Devotion to the reign of God on earth required prior emancipation from pride and self-seeking; and only those who were already encumbered with nothing were capable of that freedom. "For the stone, torn from the mountain without hands, has become mighty. The poor laymen and peasants see it more sharply than you do," Müntzer thundered at Duke Johann of Saxony and his son Johann Friedrich at Allstedt on July 13, 1524, in the sermon on Daniel explicating

Nebuchadnezzar's ominous dream.[12] This famous *Fürstenpredigt* was published in Allstedt and earned its printer an expulsion from Thuringia. In his sermon to the princes Müntzer exhorted, admonished, and threatened. His wrath against those who held power was inflamed by the recognition that though such authority carried with it the Christian duty to lead the common people to a spiritual regeneration, the mighty ones refused to fulfill their office and instead hindered others in the propagation of true belief. Müntzer foretold the gruesome punishment of the princes in language adopted from the Old Testament prophets and turned into common everyday speech.

Documentary evidence of concrete demands made by Müntzer and his followers is flimsy. A curious proposal emerging in his last interrogation—that a prince be limited to eight horses and a count to four—seems to have been aimed at easing the burden of feeding the animals when nobles and their retinues appeared at assemblies. In the records that remain, Müntzer delivered no forthright tirades against private property in and of itself. He denounced only the vast holdings of the lords and championed the peasants in their struggle to retain their own parcels of land and in their fight against expropriation of the commons. Far from spurning material things, he demanded the satisfaction of ordinary needs and decried the harsh yoke of the rich on the neck of the peasantry as an impediment to the realization of their spiritual worth. The Word of God could be choked by the sorrows of this world to which the mass of the people were condemned. The necessity of appeasing ordinary needs as a requirement for spiritual preparation would persist in seventeenth-century Moravian and Puritan doctrines. In correspondence with peasant communities Müntzer devoted his attention to concrete objectives without forgetting the ultimate goal of the reign of God and of perfect righteousness on earth. He was not altogether lost in apocalyptic visions: He took thought for the daily problems, the grievances, of peasants and artisans, guiding their negotiations for ridding the communal lands of the lord's animals and for dividing confiscated Church property among the poverty-stricken, intervening in individual peasant quarrels and disputes among neighboring villages. Luther had inveighed against plundering by the peasants during their uprisings and called for bloodshed in reprisal. Müntzer defended their cause in a tart, plainspoken retort to the "soft-living flesh" in Wittenberg. "And so they let God's commandment be spread among the poor and they proclaim, God has commanded, Thou shalt not steal. But it does not work. Since they cause any man who lives, the poor ploughman, handworker, everyone, to shove and scrape. Micah chapter 3, so as soon as he does the least thing wrong, so he must hang. Whereupon doctor liar says, Amen. The lords are themselves to blame that the poor man is their enemy. They do not want to do away with the cause of the uproar, how can it ever be good in the long run?"[13]

Müntzer the defender of the poor used an earthy German speech that is far from the humanist Latinity of Thomas More and the Italians; he was competitive in robust language with Doctor Luegner himself. Men ought to behave like brothers, he wrote to the people of Allstedt on August 15, 1524, and not offer the pitiable spectacle of Christians sacrificing one another on the butcher's block.[14] His words of incitement pierced the minds of his hearers, as he raised for them the images of Joshua and Gideon and those who had been ordered by God to drive the Philistines from the land. Any definition of

Müntzer depends in part upon a feeling for the tone of his sermons, more authentic than the impressions that can be gleaned from the debatable histories penned by his enemies. Though he hailed the destructiveness of the peasants in the uprisings of 1524–1525—some forty monasteries were sacked in the Harz and in Thuringia within a two-week period—in language crowded with imagery from the Prophets, especially Isaiah and Micah, his was not simply traditional Old Testament preaching. By the end of April 1525 he was moving toward the final confrontation when he wrote to the people of Allstedt: "All the German, French, and Italian lands are wakeful; the Master wants to play games . . . If you were only three who with faith seek His name and glory, you need not fear 100,000 . . . Go to it! Go to it! Go to it! Pay no attention to the howling of the godless. They will entreat you so gently, they will whimper, they will implore you like children. Show no pity, as God has commanded through Moses." He told the men of Allstedt to rouse the people in towns and villages, especially the miners. "Do not let your sword grow cold. Strike the anvil with the hammer—*pinkepanke*." [15] In Müntzer's sermons there is a harsh wit and irony. A deadly, megalomaniac earnestness takes over as he challenges the whole world. Through Müntzer's adaptation of the words of the Hebrew prophets, general and abstract terms in the original text were rendered concrete: The "people" became "poor ploughmen and artisans." Though his sermons and letters are spotted with biblical quotations—Amos on righteousness, and divine vengeance in Jeremiah and Judges and Kings— he honors only the spirit of Scripture, not its letter. The medieval prophets who foretold the reign of the Holy Ghost had neither developed an emotive attachment to the poor of this earth nor used their ordinary speech. Müntzer's definition of the new man who would emerge after an apocalyptic holocaust is not entirely without precedent, but his coarse language lends the conception fresh vigor.

Müntzer was clearly aware of the writings of Joachim of Fiore at the end of the twelfth century and of the German mystics of the thirteenth and fourteenth; but Luther exaggerated the Joachimite origins of Müntzer's thought in order to compromise him. His doctrine of the inner word was a dangerous denial of the literal meaning of the Bible, a heresy that Luther traced to Joachim with his rather free interpretation of texts in accordance with the harmony he established between the Old and New Testaments. Müntzer, though he wrote to Hans Zeiss on December 2, 1523, "For me the witness of the Abbot Joachim is great," [16] was careful to counter the allegations of the "bookmen" and Luther that he had copied all his doctrines straight from Joachim and was merely repeating ideas from the Eternal Evangile imputed to him. Müntzer had intended to prepare a complete commentary on Scriptures after the manner of Joachim, but one that would highlight his differences from the medieval prophet. Müntzer was no imitator.

The glaring distinctions between the theological and social outlooks of Joachim and of Müntzer make Luther's accusation groundless. Progression in the development of consciousness, which Joachim traces through three ages, is not really an evolution of human understanding, but represents three discrete stages in the revelation and unveiling of truth by God. In Joachim's vision, numerological predestination is absolute and human effort and will have nothing to do with the chronology of illumination. Man is passive. Not until Spengler does an important thinker again enclose himself in such an iron arithmetical mold. At a given moment in time a new spiritual development takes place, the reign of the Holy Ghost on earth, but no man need do anything to bring about the transformation. Modern secular stadial theories, even when they are determinist, admit of human involvement in the transformation of consciousness far more frequently than chapbook presentations of their ideas allow for. In this respect Müntzer is in the modern, not the medieval Joachimite, temper. The conflict between Müntzer's elect, "the poor laymen and peasants," and the priests is not a mystical vision for which hidden clues can be discovered in Scripture. After the Medes and the Persians, the Greeks and the Romans, the existing Holy Roman Empire—the Fifth Monarchy—is "also of iron." "The Fifth Monarchy is this one, that we have before our eyes," he charged in the *Fürstenpredigt*.[17] The heathen and Jews would turn to the church only when they witnessed the triumph of the true faith in actual Christian conduct; their conversion depended upon their conviction of the superiority of Christian practice in this world. For Joachim the reign of the Holy Ghost will be the last kingdom on earth, after which there will be another Judgment and a Heavenly Kingdom. Müntzer does not make any sharp chronological break between the victory of Christ and a movement to heaven.

Man is now in the status of the brute creatures through his absorption in the flesh. It is the mission of reformed Christianity to return him to God: Christ having become man shows him the way to become a divinized man inseparable from God. Only if man is in a state of fear of God, a state of consciousness about his moral being, can he receive grace and be illuminated. In a commentary on Luke, the *Ausgedrückte Entblössung des falschen Glaubens der ungetrewen welt* (Mühlhausen, 1524), Müntzer's anthropology assumed a startling form. "For believers, what in nature was considered impossible actually takes place . . . We fleshly earthly men become gods through Christ's becoming human and thus we are pupils of God with Him, taught by Him Himself and made divine by Him. Nay far more. We become altogether transformed so that the earthly life changes over into heaven."[18]

In Müntzer's radical Christian utopia entry into the Kingdom of Heaven on Earth and into heaven itself had about the same requirements. The compromises of the Morean humanist republic are not recognized here nor are the frailties of the humans who inhabit it. The revolution of the elect, both in their own souls and in action, is itself the ideal condition, consummated by uniting in battle. The Morean utopia could live with the ambiguities of wishing for more than one could hope after. For the world and for himself Müntzer wanted freedom from the doubt that assailed him. Its complete eradication from the bosom of every man was the very heart of his gospel. The powerful preacher opened before his believers the portals of a paradise of the heart that transported his listeners into a state of eupsychia. At least for the moment the torments of ambiguity were silenced as he wielded the hammer that became his symbol, mowed down the enemy, wrote hymns to existence in a state of godliness, and preached the merciless destruction of the unbelievers. To be in a condition of revolutionary enthusiasm was the utopia. A historical course to the end of the days had been fixed. The elect pursued this way in word and deed. Time and again their suffering would be renewed, as God, to temper the steel of his chosen ones, appeared to stop their advance. But He had never abandoned the elect to their enemies and He never would. In due time vengeance would be their reward and their triumph was assured.

Müntzer's promise of a heaven on earth, which he tied to the peasants' clamor for land, involved a complete transformation of religious consciousness, the positive recognition by the ordinary man of his own unique spiritual worth. There is much that is theologically innovative in Müntzer, who devised a vigorous, highly personal religious vocabulary to describe the states a man might experience as he fought his way through doubt to attain Fear of God. His five states of the soul before the descent of the Holy Spirit into a man's heart began with an early unfleshing and climaxed in a state of deep disbelief and outward despair. The coming on of faith (*Ankunft*), the first movement of the Holy Spirit in a man, could occur at any time and in any place. The next stage was contemplation, active wonderment at the total sphere of existence and all its creatures. But in its turn the contemplation was interrupted by great agitation of the spirit. In his tribulation and doubt, man was brought to the brink of an abyss. Surmounting the waves of spiritual conflict, through his struggle he finally won a way to God.

Those who would reduce Müntzer to just another peasant leader are deaf to the power of his rhetoric as he draws a map of Christian experience. In drafts of an epistle to the brethren in Stolberg, sent on July 18, 1523, he was more graphic than in the final text. "Before it comes to that, that man is certain of his salvation, there come so many outpourings of the waters and frightful roarings that the desire for life departs from a man; for the billows of this wild sea swallow up many a man who may think that he has already won through. Therefore a man should not flee this billow but smash into it masterfully, as the skillful boatsmen do. For the Lord will give no one His holy witness before he has struggled his way through with his wonderment. Therefore, the hearts of men are rarely burdened with the true spirit of Christ."[19] The psychic struggle to reach God is depicted in images with a long history among those who have articulated their religious anguish and ultimate triumph. The passive receptivity that is central in the self-revelations of many Christian mystics is underplayed by Müntzer, whose victory comes after a hard-fought, aggressive contest. As he wrote to his friend Christoph Meinhard in Eisleben on May 30, 1524, elucidating the Eighteenth Psalm, "When a man in the wild sea of movement becomes aware of his origin, when he is in the midst of the maelstrom, then he must do as a fish does. He turns about, swims against the current back through the water, in order that he may come back to the place of his first origin."[20] The theological sources of so many of the terms associated with modern revolutions—like *Bewegung* (movement), *Entfremdung* (alienation)— along with the rhetoric of salvation and emancipation are patent. Müntzer's doctrine of the heart made empty through suffering and the Cross, so that it might then, and only then, be filled by the Holy Spirit, was in flagrant contradiction to Luther's contention that he had received God's gift through reading and hearing Scripture.

Müntzer refused to be judged by Christian theologians alone. His was a universal religion that soared beyond belief in the Testaments, for it admitted of the possibility that heathens and Turks could be penetrated by the Holy Spirit. Only those who had had the actual religious experience were capable of judging others of the universal elect, a body of men independent of the written word or any particular ritual. To address learned theological unbelievers was like throwing pearls before swine. Only those who had gone through *Anfechtung,* the state of tribulation and despair, and the breakthrough of belief were in a state to hear and participate in what Müntzer preached. The believing *Volk* of the elect were themselves the justifiers, no others. Müntzer's universalism, scandalous in the sixteenth century, later became an integral part of the Pansophic utopia.

The times were about to be fulfilled, Judgment Day was at hand, and Müntzer was a Daniel come to life to guide those who were willing to renounce the corruptions of this world and let the fear of God suffuse their whole being in preparation for the imminent apocalyptic event. Orthodox Lutherans denied the right to take up arms against authority, even to hasten the accomplishment of God's work. Luther's acceptance of the external dominion of the German princes alongside the Christian liberty of the inner man was for Müntzer a satanic doctrine that involved acquiescence in the wicked order of this life and a deflection to mere creatures of part of the fear of God that should have been concentrated on Him alone. For Luther a worldly order could never be related to the Gospel, which referred to spiritual, not earthly, things. Christian law demanded subordination to authority, irrespective of whether it was just or not, and he preached the lawfulness of serfdom. Müntzer rejected Luther's two orders, one according to the natural law, the other the Christian rule. For Müntzer there could be no separate, imperfect, wicked worldly order that might somehow serve as the environment for a spiritual gospel; there was but one order of perfection. His *Ausgedrückte Entblössung* denounced the luxurious regimen of princes as a descent to the state of animality. Men could not honor at the same time these *Kreaturen* and God, because they represented two opposite realms of being. The princes were not lords but external, fleshly objects without meaning for the spiritual elevation of man. It was not the princes, but the elect who were to be obeyed, for they would lead those who believed to a higher state of being.

Müntzer and his followers had declared that princes were worthless and contemptible. When Luther was confronted with this disdain for authority he rose to the attack. He tore the mask from the pretensions of the peasants and their leader: They were not opposed to all rule, merely the princes' rule, while all the time they coveted lordship for themselves. Deflation of the revolutionary utopia by attacking its egalitarianism as disguised ambition has had a continuous history ever since Aristophanes, and has not been altogether groundless. Luther charged Müntzer with wanting to be a new Turkish Kaiser, trying to make the sword an arbiter in theological disputes, and declaring war on the secular rulers of society with the fiendish intent of putting himself in their place. He could not abide the arrogance of this apostle to the peasants. Who had appointed him to the task of cleansing and Christianizing the temporal order? In a letter to Nikolaus von Amsdorf on April 11, 1525, Luther bitterly mocked the grasping of the lowly preacher for worldly power: "Munzer Mulhusii rex et imperator est, non solum doctor."[21] Theological differences between them were ignored as he focused on Müntzer's designs for personal aggrandizement. (Philosophical leaders of the French Revolution and Marx and Lenin would be the objects of similar denunciations.) The "doctor" wished to be "imperator" and was using the peasants to destroy all vestiges of order, while driving them to their doom. Luther's Müntzer was the Arch-devil (*Erzteufel*). As long as this devil spoke with tongues, Luther had been in favor of allowing him a hearing so that the diabolical origins of his own words would betray him. When the monster turned to deeds, he had to be annihilated.

There is truth in the accusation that Müntzer bestowed upon the elect the right to slaughter unbelievers. It would be divine justice in the same sense that the massacre of the Canaanites and Ammonites was ordered by God. In Müntzer's writings there are hints of a doctrine that goes even beyond neces-sary violence, a belief that slaughter must be accepted and condoned, and opens the gates to that tragic coupling of utopia with creative violence whose force as a revolutionary idea is not yet spent. Müntzer's social-religious teach-ing mirrors in the large his own mystical experience as he ascended through the stages before he incorporated Christ in himself and became like unto Christ. He had to be emptied of all easily accepted ideas, undergo the tortures of total alienation from God, face the abyss, become like a field that had been devastated and lay barren. Nothing of the old self could survive and the de-struction of concupiscent, whoring, gluttonous man had to be total and abso-lute. In the same precise sense and not merely by analogy to the individual ex-perience, the old order of society had to be completely torn down and pulverized before the new could be raised. The Old Testament was a reposi-tory of scenes describing the extermination of the enemies of Israel that could readily be translated into Müntzer's German, a vehicle he manipulated with a touch of genius. His cruel and merciless tirades against the fleshly lords could vie with Luther's ranting against the peasants. They were fired by the same biblical texts.

Müntzer had no gift for depicting the great Sabbath that was to succeed the outpouring of the vials of wrath in the apocalypse. After the godless were de-stroyed, the pious elect would establish a "peaceable kingdom" and reign on earth. What the reign would be like remains veiled. But it is precisely this mist-iness about what happens on the morrow of victory that has given birth to one of the most powerful utopias of the Western world. A word about things being held in common, or as if in common, about brothers in Christ, and about the satisfaction of need, has been enough to send men into battle. If all men were possessed by the Holy Spirit, from being earthlings they would be-come new heavenly creatures. This is turned into as overwhelming a utopia as the story that piles up pictorial details about an ideal government and its economy.

For all the egalitarian formulas that are attributed to Müntzer, his is a Chris-tianity of the elect, as exclusive as the patrician aristocracy of the Renaissance utopians. The elect in the first instance have to choose themselves by fighting through to God. Once the individual victory has been won, they may preach to others as Müntzer did, showing them the path of thorns that must be tra-versed, challenging them to undertake the journey, mocking false leaders like Luther and his ilk, who promised an easy way to faith and belief. Müntzer doubtless caricatured Luther's doctrine, but Müntzer's elect were granted no such easy crutch as the biblical word that Luther extended to his followers. Belief in the word was not enough. The Bible might be used to tell ordinary people tales of the sufferings endured by God's true servants in the past, but if a man was to become one of the elect he himself had to undergo the same bitter experience. There was no short way to faith and the men of Wittenberg who attracted adherents by allowing them to continue easy living along with faith were deceptive guides.

Müntzer's ministry has been identified with weavers and miners and peasants in the towns where he preached. But turning him into a revolutionary utopian of one social class alone on the ground that he incited with his sermons only the wretched of the earth ignores his goal of winning all Christian men, including burghers, municipal authorities, and nobles, to his doctrine of Christ through pain. There is nevertheless one critical point at which Müntzer has left a legend of a class character for posterity, the inference in his sermons that the demarcation between the elect of Christ and the agents of Antichrist is likely to be drawn along lines that distinguish the rich and the powerful from the poor and miserable. The common man had the better chance of becoming one of the elect because, Müntzer thought most of the time though not always, the poor had fewer objects of fleshly desire to weigh them down on their course. Those who wallowed in luxury and lay on the backs of ordinary men whom they treated like beasts of burden were doubly culpable. They were so sunk in whoredom that they could not respond to the voice of the preacher, let alone exert their wills in traversing the stages of the Christian pilgrimage. But they bore the additional stigma of being public authorities who usurped God's glory by bedecking themselves with titles and who, by oppressing the common man, reduced him to so low a state of animality that he too was often incapable of moving toward God.

The tone of the ideal reign that was soon to be inaugurated was rigidly ascetic. Sexual intercourse for pleasure was condemned as whoring. Müntzer's doctrine of marriage, on which Luther's *Table Talk* reports, held that a man was to have sexual converse with his wife only if he were certain through divine revelation that he would create a holy child; otherwise it was a whore's marriage.[22] The conception is harmonious with Müntzer's ideal of the spiritualization and sanctification of life under the new order. There would be no whores' sons, only divine children. In depicting the morrow after victory, Müntzer granted his adherents the right to take from their oppressors only what was necessary (*nothaft*). No popular cokaygne utopia with a plethora of sensate things was conjured up to kindle their enthusiasm for the struggle. Peasants who went into battle under his standard may have had daydreams of a *Schlaraffenland,* as Melanchthon charged, but there is no evidence that Müntzer implanted them. The passion of Christ on the Cross was still the heart of his doctrine.

When a decade later the Anabaptists took possession of the city of Münster, the scandal of their licentious behavior redounded to Müntzer's ignominy in Western culture. Lutherans tried to eradicate him from the history of the Reformation. Müntzer's ideas lived on in the underground of popular utopian movements, but they never surfaced in a form that remotely recalled his original purposes, confused as they may sometimes appear.

The Debacle at Frankenhausen

The apostle of violence became its victim when his straggly and outnumbered troops, wielding pikes and sticks against the cavalry and cannon of their overlords, were routed at Frankenhausen and Müntzer their leader, who had escaped and was found hiding in a cellar, was dragged off to the castle of Count Ernst von Mansfeld, the noble to whom Müntzer had written with scornful braggadocio a year and a half before. There in the presence of the Count, Duke George, a torturer, and a scribe, Müntzer was submitted to inter-rogation. What was published shortly afterward was not a precise, nearly ver-batim, record such as a trained team of Venetian inquisitors might produce later in the century, but a bald summary that in brief compass surveyed Müntzer's activities in the centers where he had preached and formed unions. The captors were trying to pile up a record of agitation that would make of his work a series of plots. Müntzer divulged the names of his associates, but no extraordinary revelations were extracted from him. His role in most of the riots and tumults he had instigated was well known. Müntzer stuck to his claim that killing the three prisoners on the eve of battle was divine justice. He did not elaborate any refined theology in the course of the examination. His apology was couched in biblical language interpreted according to the gospel of Müntzer. In Christendom all should become equal, and those princes and lords who refused to accept this belief should be driven forth and struck dead. A few laconic sentences in this spirit were said to have been his justification of the uprising. Whether or not Müntzer actually spoke the words of the pub-lished confession or whether the scribe put into his mouth sentiments with which his name was ordinarily associated remains moot; but nothing out of harmony with the principle of the Allstedt Christian Union was added.

The report of the interrogation of May 16, 1525, flatly stated the purposes of the Allstedt Union: "This was their belief and what they wanted to put into practice: *Omnia sunt communia.* Each and every one should be given what he needs when he needs it. If any Prince, Count, or Lord did not want to do this, and had been warned, he should have his head chopped off or be hanged."[23] These sentences have been subject to a wide diversity of interpretations, and given the circumstances under which they were presumably spoken as well as the discrepancies between manuscript and published versions, any reconstruc-tion of what Müntzer really said or meant on this occasion must remain du-bious. To see a protocommunist pronouncement in a few slogans about equal-ity, the high-flown Latin formula of *Omnia sunt communia,* and the threat of killing noble rejectors of the new rule is to build intellectual castles that tower above Ernst von Mansfeld's stronghold where Müntzer was taunted and tor-tured by Catholic lords for his abuse of the Christian sacraments. The formal organization of a *Bund* and the military action may raise the captive Müntzer's rhetoric to a higher level of utopian consciousness, and the image of him as a communist may be enhanced by phrases culled from his sermons on the immi-nent apocalypse, the regeneration of mankind, willful action in the name of Christ, the humble elect, and above all divine vengeance against the wicked who had usurped power over the common man—though all of it hardly adds up to a communist manifesto.

The interrogators made of Müntzer a man whose whole life was a rebellion against authority. They discovered a *Verbündniss* against the bishop when he was a young man in Ascherleben and Halle. His "confession" became a chron-icle of radical evil that mounted to a climax in the insurrection of Frankenhau-sen and the great slaughter. Müntzer was said to have harbored plans for do-minion over territory covering a ten-mile circle around Mühlhausen and over land belonging to Philip of Hesse, a purpose in contradiction with his Christian spirituality but not his character. John of Leyden was in the wings.

Duke George, preoccupied with the murders and the uprising, did not absorb himself with theological niceties. On the other hand, Luther and Melanchthon expressed disappointment at the captors' failure to explore more thoroughly the question whether Müntzer's claim to divine revelation had been his own invention or whether it had in fact been inspired by the devil. Upon receiving a report from Johann Rühel, Luther wrote back: "Such a confession is nothing but a piece of devilish, hardened, obduracy."[24] The prisoner himself, a contumacious heretic both to the Catholic lords and to the Lutheran Protestants, seems at the end to have been resigned to his fate. The last letter written to his Mühlhausen friends from the castle at Heldrungen on May 17 can be read either as an authentic recantation of his course of violence or a forced reversal in writing to protect some of his followers and his family. It has even been interpreted with theological overtones: The terrible defeat is a divine warning and he is enduring the torments of a Christ to expiate the sins of those who at Frankenhausen had sought their own gain and had not entered the struggle with the wicked princes solely in order to join in God's design. The request that his wife and child be provided for, that she be given his books and goods, strikes a gentle note rarely heard in his sermons and polemics. He pleaded with his followers: "Treat each other with friendship and do not embitter the lords any more as many have done through self-interest . . . Above all flee from spilling blood, about which I wish to warn you in good faith. For I know that most of you in Mühlhausen were not partisans of the tumult and self-seeking."[25] In his final farewell he wanted to lift the burden from his soul with the repeated admonition that "no more innocent blood should be spilled." That Müntzer was ever the prime instigator in the disorganized peasant uprisings that were sweeping through Germany is dubious. And they continued after he was executed. Eventually the Müntzer legends became more powerful than the events in which he had participated.

The sixth and eighth summary points of the interrogation, which preceded the beheading by eleven days, answered one of the prepared questions that had been asked of all the captives. "If matters had gone their way what would they have done?" On point eight the version published by Wolfgang Stöckel in Leipzig had an important variant from the accepted manuscript. The famous *Omnia sunt communia* reads *Omnia simul communia,* "Everything should be as if it were held in common."[26] Müntzer evidently had some notion of a *communio rerum,* as one contemporary report has it, and he made a distinction between *Gemein-nutz* (common use) and *Eigen-nutz* (private use). But this does not equate his views with a Platonic holding of all things in common. Müntzer still thought primarily in terms of the peasant "commons" that were being expropriated by the lords, and he was far more concerned with the souls of the victorious elect and their hard-won religious belief than with material goods and their equitable distribution. The peasants and artisans who flocked to his sermons in Allstedt and joined ranks under his captaincy at Frankenhausen may well have heard only his tirades against their lords' amassing of fleshly things. Perhaps Müntzer misled his poor listeners, as Luther charged, and was himself carried away by the force of his preaching. But in the texts that remain there is an obsession with the Holy Spirit and the individual soul of every man that makes it difficult to relate Müntzer to a postapocalyptic world of material riches.

For the Lutheran reformers, Müntzer represented a corrupter of Scripture, a propagator of subversive doctrines respecting temporal authority, a preacher of dangerous ideas about the methods of individual spiritual illumination, a promoter of extravagant expectations that could not be fulfilled. With his death, the aura of magical invulnerability that had once clung to him would be dissipated. In a letter of May 19, 1525, to his Bamberg friend, Joachim Camerarius, announcing the defeat of the peasants and the execution of Müntzer, Melanchthon exulted not only in the quelling of a seditious rebellion but in the defeat of a heresy and the exposure of a false prophet. "I am happy that the leader of the uprising has been captured. Not so much because there is any hope that in the future things will be calmer, but because it has become manifest that the spirit they boasted about had no authority. Dear God, of what kind of kingdom did they have such sweet dreams? With what fabricated prophecies did he lead the stupid mass of the people to take up arms? How many promises that in the near future the order of the state would change on command of the heavenly oracles?"[27] After his execution, Müntzer became the symbol of the defeated peasant uprising, and other radical preachers hastened to dissociate themselves from him by parading the letters they had written against the doctrine of violence and in opposition to the Christian Union of the peasants. Even Müntzer's friend Karlstadt maneuvered to exculpate himself from the accusation that he had acquiesced in Müntzer's "uproar." But though theologians in all camps were eager to bury his memory, Müntzer in death was still a foe to be reckoned with. Echoes of his theology resounded in many directions, and his spiritual presence was long felt among the Anabaptists of Germany. By 1531 so many people in Mühlhausen had come to visit the spot where his severed head had been exposed that Luther feared popular adulation would make a saint of him.

The Müntzer Legends

During his lifetime Müntzer was buffeted about in the social and religious storms of the early Reformation; almost five hundred years after his death, partisans are still wrangling over his remains. He has been likened to a saint, a red poppy that bloomed on the stony field of Christendom, or treated as a murderous incendiary and archfanatic, a leader of seditious, destructive peasants. Some have dismissed him as a crackpot preacher with a reactionary, theocratic vision; others have revered him as a social revolutionary martyr who died for the cause of emancipating the working classes.

Müntzer's role in the Peasant War is difficult to assess, because those who triumphed and survived to write about him were his enemies and they had a variety of differently shaped axes to grind. Some contemporary Catholic writers like Johannes Cochläus saw him as a natural outgrowth of the Lutheran heresy and explained the Lutherans' magnification of his part as an attempt to remove the stigma of rebellion from themselves. Luther and Melanchthon inflated him into the demonic leader of the Peasant War and launched a propaganda campaign to discredit a doctrine that offered a rival vision of great potency. A late-eighteenth-century German pastor, Georg Theodor Strobel, attributed to Müntzer's inflammatory teachings the shedding of the blood of thousands and the devastation of castles and churches in Thuringia. He completed his life and works of Müntzer in 1794 at the height of the Terror in France, with the hope that Germany might be spared the repetition of uprisings like Müntzer's *Aufrahr* of 1525.[28]

By now it is virtually impossible to divest Müntzer of his legends—in the plural, for they are many and contradictory. The factual information in the possession of detractors and adulators alike is scanty. His nine tiny pamphlets (including his liturgical music) published in 1523 and 1524 hardly constitute a treasury of utopian thought. A few of his sermons and a collection of his letters were edited with critical care in 1968. An extensive biography by Walter Elliger, a lifelong Müntzer scholar, has assembled the factual record, turning it into a monument commemorating a revolutionary hero.[29] In *Die Histori Thome Muntzers des Anfengers der döringischen Uffrur*, attributed to Melanchthon, his teachings had been crudely caricatured: "He taught . . . that all goods should be held in common as is written in the Acts of the Apostles and that they should throw in all goods together. In this way he encouraged the people not to work any more. If anyone needed food or clothing he went to any rich man and demanded it as a Christian right. For Christ wanted people to divide with the needy. If the rich man did not give willingly, it was taken from him by force."[30] This *History of Müntzer* accused the warrior-preacher not of initiating the peasant rebellion but of providing an evangelical justification for it. No such iniquitous religious apology had backed previous peasant uprisings. Whatever the content of Müntzer's social doctrine—and the evidence is still the subject of heated argument between historians of East and West Germany—a stock set of beliefs has clung to his name. According to the *History of Müntzer*, he believed that no one must be raised above another, that all must be free and hold things in common, and that "to each was allotted according to his need" (a manifest prefiguration, it might be said, of Marx's higher stage of communism in the *Critique of the Gotha Program*). In addition there was an isolated report that in 1521 Müntzer had upheld other precepts: to love one's enemies, not to seek revenge, not to swear, and to institute the community of things. Stray phrases are the basic substance of the communist legend of Thomas Müntzer.

There was a rationalist core in Müntzer's sermons, rare among the Reformation enthusiasts, that led some late-eighteenth- and early-nineteenth-century Germans to latch on to him as a predecessor of the Age of Reason. The historian Wilhelm Zimmermann, on whom Friedrich Engels largely relied in *The Peasant War in Germany*, singled out Müntzer as a respectworthy precursor of one wing of Enlightenment thought and of the French Revolution.[31] In the wake of Zimmermann, Marx and Engels continued the rehabilitation of Müntzer and transformed Luther's Archdevil into the first self-conscious revolutionary hero of modern times, who transcended his own moment to proclaim the ultimate goal of the communist revolution. Engels differentiated the intermittent jacqueries of the Middle Ages from the German peasants' revolt of 1525 and proclaimed this war the first act of the European bourgeois revolution. In Engels' history, Müntzer's movement reflected the emergence of "embryonic proletarian elements in the city," especially those lower on the social scale who were, in origin, peasants driven from their lands and excluded from the rigid medieval corporate structures of the German urban artisans. In landless peasants Engels discovered the beginnings of the present-day proletariat, "red flag in hand and the community of property on their lips."[32] Müntzer was doomed to defeat from the outset, but Marx and Engels had a kind word for selected foretellers of the communist future even when they failed to appraise accurately the "objective conditions" of their historical epoch. Karl Kautsky, in his bloated *Vorläufer des neueren Sozialismus* (Forerunners of Modern Socialism), rejected this appreciation of Müntzer and labeled him an epigone of the medieval communistic sects who was completely lacking in originality, a mere propagator of ideas that had long been held by the Brothers of the Free Spirit.[33] The differences between Engels and Kautsky stem from opposing views of the origins of modern socialism: Kautsky apparently found them in the medieval corporations of artisans, Engels among the footloose disinherited of the Reformation period who had broken with the medieval world.

In the history of modern utopia, Müntzer has remained frozen in the mold into which Engels cast him, the revolutionary before his time. Isolated radicals of the English Civil War had already attached themselves to his legend and they could be fitted into the chain of the history of communist thought. In East Germany and Soviet Russia Müntzer's story is still being elaborated within this framework, though with far greater subtlety. Müntzer has become the harbinger of a world communist revolution operating through the German peasantry, who, in opposing the German nobility, were effectively furthering the bourgeois revolution that was a necessary condition of the proletarian revolution. Müntzer's earliest extant manuscript, a fragment of a liturgical poem, was presented by the Saxon government to Joseph Stalin on his seventieth birthday. This apotheosis of Müntzer in the communist world has survived de-Stalinization, though it has become more difficult to assess him as the factual material about the Radical Reformation in Central Europe accumulates and the data have to be squeezed into the preestablished disharmony of objective conditions and subjective intent.

There was a time when Marxist historians could bypass Müntzer's theology as vapid nonsense and go directly to the historical forces that Müntzer is presumed to have unleashed. Of late it has become fashionable and necessary to show that the theology itself secreted revolutionary power. The more sophisticated Marxist transformers of Müntzer have discovered in his proclamations and sermons a protocommunist anthropology. The revolutionary is made to emerge out of his theology as a figure of colossal dimensions rivaling Luther himself. Müntzer's demand that each and every man must experience for himself the spiritual victory over all obstacles as he struggles his way to God can be so translated that it becomes, mutatis mutandis, a prefiguration of the spiritual conflict a true communist of the twentieth century must undergo before he overcomes all doubts and is prepared for membership in the Communist *Vereinigung*. Müntzer's eschatology can be interpreted to resemble a secular philosophy of history and his prophetic sense of mission, even if it has its pathological moments, can be placed in harmony with the dedication of any leader of a political movement.

Some West German and English historians of theology have rejected this communist interpretation but have been as zealous as the Marxists in reclaiming Müntzer from obscurity. While eschewing any depiction of him as a forerunner of Marx, they value him for the pure theology in his teachings. They have been unable to discover in Müntzer's authenticated writings any promise of rich material rewards for the artisans and peasants. The spiritual freedom of being possessed by God is for these theologians a conception that harks back to earlier mystical ideas rather than looks forward to a sensate heaven on earth under communism.

The most recent histories of the Radical Reformation seek to amalgamate the theological Müntzer and the social revolutionary into an integrated whole, instead of allowing them to proceed their respective ways without hope of a convergence. But in the end the contradiction between the two Müntzers has only been raised to a higher plane. Granted that there are social roots to theological conceptions and that social doctrines can germinate in theological soil, the argument now turns on where the weight of historical judgment should rest, on the side of the spirit or on the side of matter. Refinements of this controversy have become the staple of a scholarly industry surrounding Müntzer and the Radical Reformation. The *Müntzerbild* is not yet complete. The final impression of the rough, psychically torn leader who was lost in the turmoil of the Reformation has not been struck.

With the suppression of the radical elements of the German Reformation, the legend of Müntzer went underground. The hundred and twenty years between the Peasant War in Germany and the English Civil War were marked by intermittent peasant uprisings in different parts of Europe. Some took on the traditional aspect of flash outbursts in the countryside provoked by famine; others, as in Catalonia, were demands for the restoration of ancient liberties; and there were occasional attempts, like Campanella's Calabrian revolt, to seize power in an isolated province. But with the exception of the Calabrian revolt, none of these passing explosions can be associated with a utopian vision of a radical and popular restructuring of life. The politico-religious climate of the latter part of the sixteenth century in Western Europe, the world of the Counter-Reformation, was hardly propitious for the blossoming of new worldly utopias. The Italian philosophical writings of the sixteenth century were, after all, not among the most original expressions of utopian thought. The Catholic Church militant was consolidating its forces, as were the dynastic states of France and England. Protestant theologians in the Lutheran, Calvinist, and Anglican areas were preoccupied with settling the intricate problems involved in formulating new religious dogmas.

Utopian fantasy of the period was impoverished, compared with the outburst in the century from 1450 to 1550 and with its revival in new forms around 1600. Nostalgic pastorals abound; there are a number of imitations of More's *Utopia;* architectural invention of a privatized character flourishes. But the utopian imagination of the West was dormant before the magnificent awakening in the first decades of the seventeenth century with the works of Bacon, Campanella, and Andreae. The Escorial, begun in 1563, was perhaps the symbolic structure of this anti–utopian age, Teresa de Jesús and John of the Cross its mystical expression, the Society of Jesus, founded in 1540, its ideal social organization.

PART III

Flowering and Death
of the Christian Utopia

Jan Amos Comenius, 1658–1660

Juriaen Ovens
Rijksmuseum, Amsterdam

7

Pansophia: A Dream of Science

EUROPE IN THE seventeenth century was a traditional Christian society in turmoil. Internal social and political crises were aggravated by a chronic state of fratricidal war among the dynasts in which religious loyalties played a significant, though not always a determining, role. In all states—Catholic, Lutheran, Calvinist, or Anglican—intellectual and spiritual institutions were by their very nature conservative and ecclesiastical authorities were jealous of their prerogatives. Doubtless there were men in religious establishments who were prepared to accept something of the new science that was beginning to raise its head as long as the scientists, an inchoate assemblage without a formal collective name until the nineteenth century, introduced their wares slowly, without fanfare, in driblets, practically unnoticed. When Harvey presented his theory on the circulation of the blood reasonably, within a traditional Aristotelian framework, nobody was perturbed. And even the greatest innovators like Isaac Newton at times maintained rather modestly that they had merely rediscovered what ancient philosophers (under the mask of mythmakers) had once taught. But scientific activity in many shapes, alchemical, Paracelsian, academic, mathematical, experimental, was becoming too conspicuous to be simply assimilated or accommodated by the old spiritual order without creating a ripple.

The Christian Utopia

The practice of science as a virtuous activity in Christian, aristocratic, seventeenth-century Europe could not be taken for granted. It had to overcome the inveterate prejudices of various segments of the population, not only the wariness of members of the ecclesiastical establishments. One group of the religious looked upon the absorption with secondary causes as a deflection from contemplation of the divine Primary Cause and hence suspect, if not heretical, especially when propositions like the Copernican hypothesis, touted as absolute truths, contradicted the literal sense of the Bible. Aristocrats who had an Aristotelian contempt for manual labor and a certain fastidiousness in personal habit were offended by the very idea of a man of quality dirtying his bare hands with offal and black coals and animal carcasses. The mass of the people, not free from the image of the scholar–magus as a sorcerer or one possessed by the devil, were frightened by tales of clandestine experiments said to bestow dark powers upon the natural philosopher. And some literary wits, envious of the honors that began to accrue to men who were engaged with rulers and triangles and circles rather than lofty poesy, soon found an easy mark for ridicule in the portrait of the obsessed scientist.

The sheer accumulation and increasing weight of the new science made a showdown with its detractors inevitable. When an encounter finally takes place in which rival corps such as scientists and ecclesiastics do not seek to annihilate each other completely—with the possible exception of Giordano Bruno we recognize no pretenders to the total destruction of the existing spiritual order, and even his purposes are too wild, changeable, and ambivalent to be readily categorized—men try to invent myths or metaphors that delimit jurisdictions, prevent frictions and encroachments, and ensure mutual forbearance, if not interdependence. They also concoct utopias of harmony and conciliation.

Baldly stated, two major conceptions about the possible relations of science and religion in European society were evolved during the seventeenth century. One can be subsumed under the broadly used metaphor of the two books, the Book of Nature and the Book of Scripture, both viewed as equivalent sources of Christian knowledge, both leading to truth but remaining separate, with distinct languages, modes of expression, institutional arrangements, and areas of specialization. The other myth, far more utopian in character, was Pansophia, a new Christian synthesis of organic truth that would replace the relatively stable body of beliefs Europe had supposedly entertained around the year 1500, prior to the great religious schisms and the serious attacks on the inherited conceptual framework of Ptolemy, Aristotle, and Galen—to use an abbreviation for the science that had become acceptable to the churches of Europe. Among many theorists who participated in its elaboration, Pansophia entailed a virtual amalgamation of the two spiritual corps, the scientists and the ministers of religion, into a single body, putting an end to the conflict before it assumed disastrous proportions.

Two such conceptions or metaphors immediately raise as many questions as they answer, because they are antagonistic to each other and betray palpable internal difficulties. An intellectual metaphor adopted by an age is often a passionate attempt to forge at least the appearance of a solution to an almost insoluble problem. Since the relation of science and religion was critical at a vital turning point in European culture, the verbal and imaginative structures it created, or borrowed from previous ages and adapted, are worthy of examination in their own right. Understanding what transpired in the course of the century involves a bookish study of rational arguments, warranties from sacred texts, and emotive longings expressed in utopian philosophical dialogues and private letters. In addition to the metaphor of the two books and Pansophia, there was of course a third attitude, that of the mathematician Pascal turned Jansenist, the outright denial of any intrinsic worth to the works of science; but analysis of his thought and its implications is beyond the bounds of our subject.

The kind of people who did most of the writing on the relations of science and religion can be roughly divided into three types. First, those who were the trumpeters of the new science, men who were not themselves *virtuosi* or *investiganti,* but who either heralded the new creators or drafted ambitious programs for them. By definition they were apologists and defenders, who tried to work out a favorable relationship with religion for the new philosophy. Bacon in England, Campanella in Italy, and Andreae in Germany are exemplary figures of this character, writing at about the same time; Comenius repeated the attempt in the next generation. Then there were the major scientists themselves, Kepler, Galileo, and Newton, who in moments of crisis when they were under attack, or because an attack from some quarter was imminent, or for a variety of personal reasons, expressed their own religious ideas, or wrote about the relations of the two books and the autonomy of science. Finally, the philosophers—Descartes and Spinoza, Locke and Leibniz—on a more abstract level than the trumpeters or the scientists sought to draw out the implications of what was going on. This tripartite division among the protagonists is not meant to lock any individual into a single role, for some seventeenth-century men of genius appeared in all three parts at one time or another in their lives and works.

Antagonists of science ensconced in positions of spiritual power are an integral part of the story, but they do not yield so rich a harvest of thought as those involved in some affirmative way with the new philosophy. The outlook of the traditionalists emerges in debate with the defenders of science. And not all the churchmen were devils; some were fools, some showed their teeth, and a few were wise men with a philosophical predilection for spiritual accommodation with the new forces. The last group found the metaphor of the two books particularly useful, as did many working scientists. In the end the separation of science and religion into two distinct domains became the predominant rhetorical solution of the problem, and remained so from the foundation of the Royal Society of London down to the present.

The Chain of Pansophist Philosophers

The second alternative, Pansophia, had a very different fortune. It was a utopian fantasy that never bore fruit, a lost cause, a seventeenth-century hope of a reconstituted Christian commonwealth in Europe that would be the harbinger of a universal millennium on earth, a millennium unpolluted by the violence and wild enthusiasm of the Anabaptists, a millennium based on calm and orderly science as a way to God. This utopia of a perfected Christian society assumed widely diversified shapes in a broad spectrum of writers. Under the Pansophic canopy one could include the works of the Italians Bruno and Campanella, the Englishmen Francis Bacon and John Wilkins, the Rhinelanders Alsted, Besold, and Andreae, the Moravian Comenius, and the expatriate Comenians in London, Hartlib and Dury. That supreme embodiment of European culture, Gottfried Wilhelm Leibniz, though he publicly rejected the Pansophic synthesis of Comenius, attempted to create a vision of a universal Christian republic in the same spirit. He stands apart as the most ambitious projector of a union of science and religion, and is at the same time the symbol of its tragic failure. Comenius, the major link in the chain, borrowed the term Pansophia for the movement from a now forgotten book by Peter Laurenberg published in Rostock in 1633, *Pansophia, sive Paedia Philosophica.*[1] As individuals these thinkers have been studied often enough before, and the last two decades have vastly expanded our knowledge of their persons and their ideas; a grasp of the total configuration of their enterprise may add something new. Though they were dispersed throughout Europe, they learned from one another and sparked one another's imaginations; the core of their grand illusion was the same.

Pansophia had distant origins in the writings of the thirteenth-century illuminated doctor from Majorca, Ramón Lull, whose *Ars magna generalis* foreshadowed many later attempts to fix the elements of universal knowledge and to use this new science as an instrument for the propagation of the Christian faith among infidel Mohammedans and Jews. With the sixteenth-century publication of his numerous writings, Lull was posthumously recognized as an eminent forerunner in quest of a logic that would unify the sciences, a methodical science of sciences, and an encyclopedia that would illustrate the unity of basic ideas in the diverse branches of knowledge. The writings of Lull, who was also the author of the historical romance *Blanquerna,* were suspect in the Church of the Counter-Reformation and in the standard instruction manuals for Roman Inquisitors Lullism was included in the long array of heresies ancient and modern that could lead to the stake.

The Christian-scientific utopians who followed in Lull's footsteps were unanimous in their rejection of dogmatic allegiance to scholastic Aristotelian philosophy, though there were different degrees of vehemence in their denial. In its stead, in the ideal Christian polity—whether patterned after the City of the Sun, Christianopolis, New Atlantis, the Christian Brotherhood of Comenius, or Leibniz' Grand Designs—men would be joined in knowledge *in rebus,* knowledge that was concrete, sensate, based on objects in the real world. All things and their relationships would be perceived with a new clarity. This would be true illumination. War was declared on purely verbal definitions that confused and obfuscated. Few diatribes have reached the peak of vituperation with which Bruno and Bacon denounced the empty definitions in the accepted Aristotelian tradition that still dominated the universities of Europe. In an early manuscript Bacon was mild-mannered, but deadly, on the whole of Greek philosophy:

Your learning we have said, is derived from the Greeks. But what sort of people were they? I mean to go in for no abuse. I shall neither repeat nor imitate what others have said. I am content simply to remark that that nation was always precipitate mentally, and professorial by habit—two characteristics inimical to wisdom and truth . . . What could be more childlike than a philosophy prompt to chatter and argue and incapable of begetting works, a philosophy inept in dispute and empty of results.[2]

In the latter half of the century, Comenius and Leibniz began to find a place in their all-embracing universal synthesis even for Aristotle, but he was dethroned as the sole arbiter of knowledge.

Among the Christian utopians of the seventeenth century, primary emphasis was placed upon the senses, above all sight, as a fundamental source of true understanding. Campanella prescribed that everything known about nature and the cosmos should be depicted in images on the circular walls of the City of the Sun for all men to see. Symbolic representation and mathematical signs were sound means for teaching and memorizing and for universal communication, and there was a certain derogation of words, surely of wit and literary conceits and flourishes. A predilection for plain speaking associated with this outlook was later reflected in the style laid down for the Transactions of the Royal Society, whose very motto is telling—*Nullius in verba.* John Wilkins' *Essay towards a Real Character and a Philosophical Language* (1668), a language of rational signs akin to ideograms, had numerous predecessors in the seventeenth century and many later admirers, not the least of them Gottfried Wilhelm Leibniz.

In the early decades of the seventeenth century the utopian program-makers of science maintained close ties through personal contact or through intermediaries, and the web of their interconnections can be reconstructed. Bruno was in England in the 1580s and remains a perplexing source that erupts in unexpected places—in the writings of the Rhineland polymath and millenarian J. H. Alsted, for example, who after Bruno's martyrdom printed some of his manuscripts and was the teacher of Johann Valentin Andreae at the University of Herborn in Nassau. It was Andreae's friends who contrived to smuggle Campanella's manuscripts out of prison and to publish them in Frankfort. In turn Andreae was the mentor of Comenius, to whom a youthful Leibniz paid his debt in verse, though by the 1670s the mention of Comenius' name had become taboo because he himself had announced his connection with a motley group of millenarians by publishing their forecasts. His absorption with the visionary prophets beclouded the Enlightenment perception of Pansophia, throwing it out of history. Earlier in the seventeenth century Bacon kept channels with the Continent open through the agency of his little favorite, the exiled Catholic convert Sir Toby Matthew, who wrote a preface to the Italian translation of Bacon's moral essays in 1618 and informed him about the work of Galileo. This is the Tobias Matthew whom Bruno praised in his dialogue on the infinite universe and contrasted favorably with academic pedants. John Wilkins, the English clergyman who was Cromwell's brother-in-law, in his apology for science freely borrowed arguments from Campanella's defense of Galileo; Samuel Hartlib wrote to Robert Boyle about Andreae's projects for the universal fraternity of "Invisibles" (the Rosicrucian mystification hovered somewhere on the borders of Pansophia); and Comenius cited both Bacon and Campanella with approval.

What is less evident than the multiple personal interrelationships is the ardent devotion to a common cause in the men from Moravia, Württemberg, London, Leipzig, Elbing, Nola, and Calabria whom we have identified as the chief bearers of the seventeenth-century Pansophic utopia. To discern similarities among these highly individualistic geniuses, whose voracious appetite for knowledge and whose philosophical stature appear larger than life-sized, is not to pare them down and fit them into a single system. Nevertheless, identical elements and shared ideals persist and form the basis of a collective utopia, one of the most imaginative creations of the Western mind.

In one sense, these men were extending the mode of thought that had been revived by Thomas More in the previous century, and his name was called to witness by Protestants and Catholics alike. But in spirit their new Respublica Christiana was radically different from his Christian humanist "Optimum Republic"; for by 1600 the idea of utopia had broken through the ramparts of his tight little island and fused with the new intellectual and scientific atmosphere of the age. Though utopia as a literary genre continued to follow the bare outline of More's fable, and some Pansophists still used the fictional device in an amended form, in the early seventeenth century the word "utopia" came more and more to connote visions of an ideal state of man in this world, without restriction to the tale of a returned traveler reporting on a distant society to astonished Europeans. Utopia was also applied to reformist projects of ambitious dimensions—designs or "ideas," as Samuel Hartlib's group called them. The overtones of the term fluctuated from mockery to admiration. If there were occasional parodies of utopia, such as Hall's *A World Different yet the Same* (ca. 1605), John Milton could write of utopia with glowing warmth as "that grave and noble invention which the greatest and sublimest wits in sundry ages, Plato in Critias, and our two famous countrymen, the one in his Utopia, the other in his new Atlantis chose, I may not say as a feild, but as a mighty Continent wherein to display the largenesse of their spirits by teaching this our world better and exacter things, then were yet known . . ."[3]

The enduring influence of Plato's *Republic* and More's *Utopia* in the Respublica Christiana is easily isolated; more amorphous and elusive are the traces of Joachimite prophecy in seventeenth-century social and political movements. The writings of Joachim of Fiore were first printed in Venice in the early 1500s and his sibylline phrases reverberated for centuries thereafter. Seventeenth-century Christian millenarianism derived from many sources, but much of the foretelling of a reign of light on earth under an order of brotherly love and community has a Joachimite resonance, though few may have read his works in the original. In his abortive utopian rebellion in Calabria in 1599 Tommaso Campanella deliberately adopted Joachim's style and said so to his Inquisitors. And in addition to Joachimism, paradisaical fantasies, never lacking in Protestant societies possessed by bibliolatry, constantly nourished the Pansophic dream. Nor was the Renaissance hermetic tradition, with its promise of plainly magical benefits to all mankind if they partook of its wisdom, alien to Pansophia, though the magical residue is far from the center of the seventeenth-century intellectual movement. Philosophical alchemy translated into a Christian myth was more readily assimilated in the Lutheran Pansophic orbit.

A growing realization that novelty was feasible in the physical world, both in geography and in experimental science, buttressed the Pansophic faith. The frontispiece of Bacon's *Great Instauration,* a sailing ship accompanied by a citation from the prophecy of Daniel, dramatized the dual aspect of discovery. If there were new lands and new inventions, there could be new societies molded by man's accumulated knowledge. The building of a New Atlantis, a Christianopolis, a New Jerusalem, a City of the Sun was eminently practicable. Explorations overseas strengthened the prospect of a Christian society comprising the whole of mankind, with pagans, Jews, and Muslims converted, even as it was assured by the revelations of the two Testaments. The Christian Commonwealth would be supported by a vast encyclopedia of knowledge of the concrete world and an expanding body of experimental science. Often the science of the literary Pansophists was no more than a dream of science expressed in nonmathematical terms; they clung to an older meaning of mathesis. The dreams of science are to be distinguished from the momentous scientific achievements of the age, which assumed a specific mathematical form; the most fervent Pansophist visionaries performed no significant experiments.

More had concluded Book II of the *Utopia* with a wistful reflection: He had little hope of seeing its society imitated. The seventeenth-century Pansophic utopians were imbued with a completely different spirit. Virtually all of them were men of action who believed that their plans could and would be crowned with success within a foreseeable, not a distant, future. They were engaged in a finite enterprise of plausible dimensions. As a young man in the first flush of adolescent universalism Bacon had intended to put his great reform of science and education into execution all at once, by fiat, and he wrote a letter to his uncle Burghley seeking an immediate governmental decision to assist him. The *Parasceve* of his middle age still expected the whole scientific system to be completed within a brief period of time. Utopia, having left the realm of fiction, became a manifesto. The religious schisms and their divisive political concomitants, the fanaticism of the Reformation and the obscurantism of the Counter-Reformation, were threatening Europe with wars of annihilation. Drafting comprehensive designs for the survival of Christendom was of the utmost urgency, and their inventors dedicated themselves to this sacred purpose, a few of them prepared to sacrifice their lives for its realization.

In the seventeenth-century Pansophic movement one senses that the learned had become keenly aware of the fragmentation of the Christian world— Erasmus may have foreseen the dangers before the definitive breakup—and felt a desperate longing to restore a measure of communication among Europeans. During the bloody polemics of the sixteenth century the reformers and counter-reformers spent themselves in violent tirades. By the seventeenth, a group of men had come forth who yearned to heal the wounds, to restore some communion among Christians, perhaps to embark on a new mission of conversion to the Indians, the Chinese, the Muslims. The Christian utopia of the Pansophists was very much alive. It bordered on a mystical vision while incorporating the new science. It sought avenues for the expression of Christian love and found them in projects for a universal language, plans for writing encyclopedias, schemes for Offices of Address, academies that would become international clearinghouses. Refugees and exiles necessarily played an important role, their very presence in a foreign country testifying to the survival of European man.

These seventeenth-century Pansophists made the last major effort to establish a unity of European culture upon a religious foundation free from sectarian malice. Their aspirations were authentically Christian in two respects: the extension of scientific research into all the possible powers of nature as a way of knowing and loving God; and the use of the new discoveries for the benefit of mankind as an act of Christian charity, of obedience to the commandment to love one's neighbor. In the preface to the *Great Instauration*, Bacon addressed a "general admonition to all" that the true end of knowledge should be charity, not power. Admittedly, Christ's role in Pansophia was often rather shadowy, though all of the Pansophic utopians, with the possible exception of Bruno, still incorporated Him into their systems as a mediator. Among the Lutheran Pansophists, Christ internalized as the Book of Conscience became a third way of understanding God's works, open alongside the Book of Scripture and the Book of Nature.

To advocate rebuilding the Christian polity with scientific underpinnings went far beyond a mere plea for toleration of the new philosophy; it implied the total reordering of European society. Most of the scientific and philosophical geniuses of the age who were working experimentalists and synthesizers kept such revolutionary pretensions at arm's length and preferred to ensconce themselves behind the metaphor of the two books, adhering to the principle of the autonomy of science and its separation from both the religious and the political powers in society. While they did not consistently abide by the tenets of their own rhetoric in either their public actions or their private religious lives, Pansophia and its related Rosicrucian and hermetic beliefs were often suspect in respectable circles and remained underground. Many seventeenth-century thinkers (including the young Descartes) flirted with Pansophic ideas at some point in their lives, but only a few were won over to them. Galileo and Kepler were too preoccupied with survival as practicing men of science faced with hostile political forces to entertain such extravagant notions, and the mature Descartes and Newton would have associated many of the proponents of Pansophia with religious enthusiasm, which repelled them on both Christian and scientific grounds. With the exception of Leibniz, none of the stars of seventeenth-century science and philosophy bothered to reflect in utopian language about an ideal society in this world. Kepler's *Somnium* told virtually nothing about the lunar inhabitants. Newton drafted a project for incorporating into the Royal Society a few paid fellows in various branches of natural philosophy; but beyond party loyalty to the Whigs he did not trouble himself too much about the order of this world. When he fantasized about an ideal state he was more likely to dwell upon the paradise of the world to come. Descartes mocked a universal language as a romance.[4] The Pansophists hoped to relate science with society and religion in a way that the major practicing scientists sedulously avoided.

The history of Pansophic utopian thought has a shape that transcends the mere chronological sequence of its preeminent figures. Bruno, Bacon, Campanella, Andreae, Comenius, and Leibniz are the great planets in the Pansophic system; in turn each is surrounded by satellites that play subsidiary roles as supporters or transmitters—men such as Wilkins, Hartlib, Dury, Alsted, Besold, who sometimes divert attention from the luminaries. Cultural movements like the Rosicrucian Brotherhood were related to Christian Pansophia, as were earlier attempts at a unification of the churches, projects for the creation of a universal language, secular schemes for the pacification of Europe, plans for the worldwide propagation of Christianity. In recent decades leading Pansophists have been studied in such detail as to give rise to separate fields of learning. Biographies have settled many factual questions, but the meaning of the vast corpus of enigmatic writings remains as controversial as ever and the innermost secrets of their authors continue to elude us. They have not yet been frozen into postures like the Enlightenment philosophes, and we do not presume to unravel all their mysteries or resolve their ambiguities. Often their inner conflicts and intellectual contradictions must be left in the raw.

In his old age Andreae wrote an autobiography, a condensed official vita that hardly ranks with the confessions of Saint Augustine and Jean-Jacques Rousseau; but like many such documents it tells more than the author intended to convey. In seventeenth-century Germany the autobiographical mode was undeveloped, though among utopian thinkers it was not altogether unknown. Comenius left a brief sketch of his stay in England, Leibniz told the mere beginning of his story in a fragment, Bruno was forced to narrate his biography in answer to interrogations by Inquisitors, Campanella kept sending his life history to prospective defenders like Gaspar Schopp, a convert to Catholicism who, he hoped, might help get him out of the dungeon. Much of Bacon's life is recorded, since he was born, lived, and died in the shadow of the gossipy English royal court, yet the complex motives of the man can only be guessed. A glimpse into his chambers is perhaps afforded by a diary he kept for a short period. The correspondence of Leibniz was vast (thousands of letters are to be found in Hanover, many still unpublished), but one should not expect to come upon indiscretions there, any more than in Bacon's letters, which his mother called "involuted." Comenius was more forthright, and his letters to the prophet Drabík, whom he had known since childhood, are marked by psychic tensions that are on the surface.

The Pansophists were polymaths whose utopian writings comprise only a part of their literary output. Since these men were philosophers and theologians, aspects of their theology, epistemology, and metaphysics are bound up with their utopias. Only recently has exploration begun into the intricacies of the philosophy of Bruno and Bacon, Campanella and Andreae, Comenius and Leibniz. With the exception of Bacon, critical editions of their total works are still incomplete or not yet in prospect; many of their manuscripts remain unpublished; even Bacon's *Works* could be illuminated by a new editor. A focus upon their utopias is a distortion of sorts, but it is the element that knits them together and allows for their incorporation into this history.

Science and the Social Order

The seventeenth-century utopian philosophers shared a presupposition that the reorganization of knowledge was fundamental to the reform of society. Their utopias bear the closest resemblance to one another when they concentrate upon this goal. Conjoined with the reorganization of knowledge was the revamping of the educational system, the best means for the communication of the new knowledge to rising generations in order to produce an ideal state in the world. Politics, economics, and the rules governing human relations are subordinate to the organization of knowledge. The political order flows naturally from the state of knowledge, not the other way around. If the utopians addressed themselves to princes in the first instance, it was to obtain their support in initiating the religio-scientific revolution; the secular powers were needed to launch the great transformation, but the substance of the new philosophy had to be developed by men like the Pansophists, men of learning.

A central problem of the Pansophist utopia was delimiting the body of knowledge. Knowledge would not be restricted to what was coming to be called natural philosophy, and surely not to experimental philosophy. The role of mathematics in the new schemes was a subject of constant debate; its prestige could vary, from Bacon's suspicious attitude through Leibniz' ecumenical embracing of both the mathematical and the experimental methods. Though Andreae knew mathematics (he had some of the same masters as Kepler in Tübingen) and Leibniz was a mathematical genius, neither of them conceived of mathematics as the ultimate key to knowledge. Bruno was mocking of the pretensions of mathematics; Comenius was doubtful of its centrality in universal science, and in his criticism of Descartes highlighted the shortcomings of the mechanical philosophy—after all, it had not squared the circle nor had it solved the problem of perpetual motion. And experimental, we might now say experiential, knowledge of the divinely created light of the inner man was still of a higher order than knowledge of matter. The practical reformers and projectors in England such as Samuel Hartlib, who considered themselves a part of the Pansophic movement, attracted to their circle the founder of political arithmetic, William Petty; but their activities were on the periphery of Pansophia. In bringing Pansophia down to earth, the English projectors somewhat reduced its dimensions.

Knowledge of God held the foremost place in the Pansophist hierarchy, from Bruno and Bacon through Leibniz, and there is nothing to confirm a supposition that this was merely a politic position maintained out of fear of religious persecution. The Pansophists provided new meanings to the concept of knowledge of God and proposed new ways of attaining it. They wrestled with the relations of this knowledge of God to other kinds of knowledge—the physical world, historical and theological traditions, ancient books of revelation, modern prophecies, the movement of the soul, consciousness and conscience. Knowledge of a good social order and of a world order were bound up with the knowledge of God. Mere contemplation of the divine or individual mystical experience was dismissed as insufficient. Individual enlightenment, the discovery of the divine spark in oneself, or in one's charges if one were a teacher, was an approved aspect of existence, but there was unanimity on the importance of works and the dissemination of knowledge or at least its fruits among all mankind. As knowledge of the external world that did not eventuate in works was always in danger of degenerating into verbalism, so knowledge of self that was not translated into action for the "general good" was suspect.

Campanella, Andreae, Comenius, and Leibniz, one following upon the other, were responsible for extending the scope of works into areas that had previously been secondary. Action was concentrated mostly in two politico-religious spheres: achieving unity among the churches at a sacrifice of the niceties of theological disputation, and extending geographic boundaries beyond Europe so that good works might encompass the whole world. (In the end, a measure of European intellectual unity was achieved not through the pacification of the churches, but by virtually throwing the party of religion out of the republic of letters, or pushing them into a corner where at most they could succeed in having a book burned by the public hangman after its condemnation by the Sorbonne.) Geographic universalism enveloped the thought of all these utopian projectors, though the earlier ones tended to think in terms of discovering new instrumentalities of conversion to their own sectarian position. Campanella's conceptions of religious unity, at least after his imprisonment, meant the propagation of the Catholic faith, cleansed of its vices. Bruno may have dreamed of creating a universal religion, but it was a religion of *Giordanisti* or a purified Catholicism. Andreae became almost as parochial as Campanella, surely after the brief Rosicrucian caper of his youth, when he settled down as a member of the Lutheran establishment. Though he expressed admiration for the rigorous social order of the Genevan Calvinists, whom he had visited as a young man, there seems to have been little that would have broadened his conception of a Christian society beyond the Lutheran church. With a certain reluctance Andreae and his circle accepted Comenius, the Moravian Brethren of the Unity, and a few of his Polish friends into their Christian society; but though they may have talked about "mankind" when they preached the coming regeneration, they stuck close to their German and Lutheran origins.

The utopian mantle inherited by Comenius was a coat of many colors. He directed his energies chiefly to the unity of the Protestant world, but he left the door open for the inclusion of Catholics and drew the line only at the papacy, the Whore of Babylon. He became enthusiastic about conversions among the Indians and anticipated Leibniz in hailing the Jesuit triumphs in China. The common danger from the Turkish penetration of Hapsburg lands led Comenius in his final years to mitigate his animosity toward the Catholic power that had destroyed his fatherland and driven him into exile. A generation later, Leibniz could espouse more openly the cause of the Jesuits in the dispute with the Dominicans over the "Chinese rites" and support their claim of having legitimately converted the mandarins. Leibniz was the proponent of a grand design for the unification of Catholics and Protestants and pulled in his horns only in the face of failure. He was prepared to learn from civilized pagans as well as to teach them. The "noble savage" was only an incidental figure in his Christian utopia, but the civilized Greek Orthodox religion and even the Chinese religion were made integral parts of a new universalism that was to have a religious foundation.

None of the early Pansophists was completely free of millenarianism, though it assumed varying forms and intensity. Campanella, never emancipated from the mystic significance of numbers, had been assured that the year 1600 would usher in a great renovation, and he was simply carrying out the role of an active millenarian when he raised the banner of utopian revolt in Calabria in 1599. Though the record remains obscure, there may have been a moment when an impending alchemical revolution or an awakening among pious Lutherans seemed to Andreae to herald the coming of Christ. Even if there was fleeting friendship with some millenarian naometricians who circulated the Rosicrucian fable, their influence was not of long duration. *Christianopolis* is the symbol of a Christian society; it does not presage a reign of Christ on earth and its Lutheran orthodoxy is not in question. Comenius, who was the propagator of the revelations of three notorious seventeenth-century prophets, has to be located in the millenarian tradition in order to be understood at all. The belief in the imminence of the reign of Christ on earth was no fugitive aberration; he held to this faith in the midst of all his Pansophic studies. The final version of his Pansophia, the voluminous *De Rerum Humanarum Emendatione Consultatio Catholica,* was explicitly grounded on a traditional millenarian view of world history: The sabbatical millennium was now at hand after the passage of almost 6,000 years since the beginning of things. Underlying this conviction was Comenius' deep sense of the wholeness and fitness and harmony of God's creation. God had made man so that he might ultimately comprehend His work; this purpose was inherent in the very act of fashioning a rational being with a spark of divine light in his soul. When man had come to the fullness of knowledge as embodied in Comenius' *Janua rerum,* there would be a fulfillment of the times. Bacon and Campanella before him had quoted and interpreted Scripture to sustain their conviction that the discovery of unknown lands and the full understanding of God's creation, parallel developments, were signs that the millennium was about to dawn.

While Bacon avoided dwelling on precise political or astrological omens, Campanella and Comenius had no such inhibitions. For Campanella, the scientific perfection of astronomy made it possible to read the universal timetable with greater accuracy. He vacillated on acceptance of the Copernican hypothesis, but he was no enemy of Galilean science. Leibniz, coming after the execu-

tion of Drabík and the posthumous disgrace of Comenius, avoided the numerical millenarian fixations of his predecessors, and though a passionate
advocate of the accumulation of knowledge, he eschewed circumstantial
chronologies of the future. Since both the acquisition of knowledge and the
religio-political triumph of true faith throughout the world were consequences
of the exertion of will for the general good, he could not devise a mechanical
schedule for the great reformation. Bold and utopian as were his plans for the
conversion of Russia and China to the new religion of the love of God, man,
and scientific knowledge, he never went so far as to establish dates for the
completion of his projects. Bacon and Descartes had thought of the whole scientific enterprise as capable of being concluded within a limited time period.
Leibniz left his utopia of science and the coming of true ecumenical religion
open-ended. An imp of self-mockery pushed him to express occasional doubts
about the entire venture, and philosophico-historical reflections on the cyclical
vicissitudes of things intruded to break up oversanguine hopes for a favorable
development. But even though the next step in human history was not determined it was his religious duty to endeavor to move mankind in the direction
of the good, to bring into actuality all that was potential in the fortunate conjuncture of physical science and geographic discovery. Leibniz was philosophically and perhaps psychically confident a good deal of the time that all of
creation formed a universal harmony, but he was also in accord with the contention of Jacobus Thomasius that modern prophecies were impostures.

In Thomas More's *Utopia,* while the favorite form of learning was the study
of ancient moral literature and philosophy (with a bias toward the Greek), the
Utopians also respected inquiries into nature as long as they were a part of the
glorification of God. For the rest of the sixteenth century, science was hardly
ever mentioned either in the discussions of ideal cities or in the speaking-picture utopias. It may happen, in the Italian architectural utopias of the fifteenth
and sixteenth centuries, as in Francesco di Giorgio's plans, that a separate section of the ideal city is reserved for *studenti,* but the nature of their studies is not
further detailed. Abruptly, in the speaking-picture utopias of the first two decades of the seventeenth century, the scientist was differentiated from other
men of learning and began to play the dominant role in the imaginary society.

The three outstanding Pansophic utopias, Campanella's *City of the Sun,*
Bacon's *New Atlantis,* and Andreae's *Christianopolis,* are important mirror
projections because, unlike most of the genre, they were long-lived in European culture. The role of the scientist and the institutions of science in these
three works set important form-giving patterns for many later scientific establishments, a rare example of utopian penetration into the real world of scientific practice. The fact that Bacon's slight work was written in English by a
man who had become lord chancellor helps to account for its enormous later
impact. Those who might be reluctant to wrestle with his *Great Instauration*
could easily assimilate the short text that he called a fable. In seventeenth- and
eighteenth-century academies and royal societies throughout Europe it became
customary to incorporate Baconian rhetoric into the founding charter. Of the
scores of works in print and manuscript that Campanella left behind, the
Città del sole was the only one widely read, with the possible addition of the
Discourse Touching the Spanish Monarchy, before his revival by nineteenth-century scholars. Andreae's plans penetrated into the Puritan world mostly

through the agency of Comenius, who considered himself the direct heir and instrument of Andreae. The Comenian attempt to alter the ultimate purposes and organization of science by promulgating a set of religious standards for its operation and a voluminous outline of his plans have begun to be studied only in recent years. Leibniz' grand designs, known exclusively to kings and princes during his lifetime, have turned out to be among the most imaginative discursive attempts to justify the reconstitution of the Christian Republic.

The undefined and often covert character of Pansophic allegiance does not make it less pervasive as a utopian intellectual orientation in seventeenth-century Europe. Its immediate concrete results may have been restricted to limited educational reforms, trivial when judged in the light of the grandiose visions of its principal protagonists. Pansophia was the swansong of Christian Europe—the Enlightenment virtually obliterated the memory of its existence. But in a secularized form its universalism, its faith in the power of scientific knowledge to modify human conduct, its conviction that human affairs could be emended were carried over into Enlightenment thought, even though the major philosophes were repelled by its systematizing pretensions and inflated theosophical language. Only the philosophy of Bacon—in their own rendering—was respected.

The six heroic enthusiasts forming the constellation of Pansophia should perhaps be presented as parallel lives. There were two Dominican friars of humble birth, Bruno and Campanella, from the Kingdom of Naples dominated by the Spaniards. Both were tried as heretics by the Inquisition, one burned at the stake, the other sequestered for three decades in jails of the secular arm. Two others were Protestant pastors, Andreae a Lutheran and Comenius a bishop of the Moravian Brethren of the Unity. Caught up in the depredations of the Thirty Years' War, they suffered in the flesh and in the spirit. And finally there were the courtiers Bacon and Leibniz, who spent their lives in the shadow of kings and princes. The friars were lone men with heterodox views on the sexual passions; the pastors married and sired many children; of the courtiers, Bacon married, but his amorous inclinations were reputed to be homosexual, and Leibniz remained a bachelor, his loves unknown. All six were polymaths who produced large numbers of books and left behind many manuscripts.

Their appearance depends upon the context in which they are set. A utopian universe of discourse requires that one ask them utopian questions, that one view them not solely as scientists, though all have found a place in the recent *Dictionary of Scientific Biography*, nor religious thinkers, though the relations of man and God were among their major preoccupations. The seventeenth-century Pansophists were revolutionaries in the bosom of Christianity, and with one possible exception, Bruno, they emerged as renovators and reformers within the Christian fold. In the Catholic world they announced the failure of Christian humanism and of the Counter-Reformation; in the Lutheran and Moravian lands they implied the inadequacy of the Lutheran reform as it had come to be practiced. Their quest broke sectarian bounds and pretended to a new universalism. They could be defined by negation. The dogmatic theological struggles had been recognized as a prodigious waste of human effort; Aristotelian doctrines in many spheres of knowledge were false and could no longer serve as a philosophical underpinning of religion. But the Pansophists were not secularists. All of existence was to be divinized and the sacral was not to be shunted off into a corner. The new science could not be isolated from religion as the Royal Society of London hoped. Men could not live with divided allegiances to priests and scientists.

Minor Utopian Modes

While the Pansophic vision was the most universal and innovative of Christian utopias in the seventeenth century, it did not occupy the whole field. Two other constellations, more restricted to national societies, made their appearance: the many popular utopias that sprouted in the ferment of the English Commonwealth period, and the significant Morean speaking-picture utopias of Vairasse and Fénelon that gave voice to a religious and social protest among Huguenots and dissident Catholics against the hegemony of Louis XIV. Of the English utopias, Levellers and Diggers in time became a part of the international utopia of radical egalitarianism, the Fifth Monarchy men a variant of Christian millenarianism. Only the Ranters remained virtually unnoticed until their revival by twentieth-century scholarship. The French pastoral idyll of Fénelon became a prototype of the nostalgic agrarian utopia that extended its influence to Rousseau and nineteenth-century romanticism.

By the early seventeenth century the Morean speaking picture had become an accepted literary form in all European countries, and the greatest writers of the age introduced utopian digressions or conceits into their works—minor asides often ironic in their intent. Shakespeare's *Tempest* has the honest old counselor Gonzalo fantasy a perfect society of primeval innocence, to the accompaniment of jibes from his shipwrecked companions.

> I' the commonwealth I would by contraries
> Execute all things: for no kind of traffic
> Would I admit; no name of magistrate:
> Letters should not be known; riches, poverty,
> And use of service, none; contract, succession,
> Bourn, bound of land, tilth, vineyard, none;
> No use of metal, corn, or wine, or oil;
> No occupation: all men idle, all;
> And women too, but innocent and pure;
> No sovereignty;—
>
> . . .
>
> All things in common nature should produce,
> Without sweat or endeavour: treason, felony,
> Sword, pike, knife, gun, or need of any engine,
> Would I not have; but nature should bring forth,
> Of its own kind, all foison, all abundance,
> To feed my innocent people.
>
> . . .
>
> I would with such perfection govern, sir,
> To excel the golden age.

Cervantes awards Sancho Panza the island of Barataria to govern and there he establishes an ideal order. Lesser writers also played with utopian devices. In his brief utopian digression, a poetical commonwealth of his own, in the

Anatomy of Melancholy, which he revised in successive editions from 1621 to 1640, Robert Burton bore witness that contemporaries were beginning to discern common elements in the works of Campanella, Bacon. and Andreae and to identify them with Plato and More. Burton's own utopia was pretty stereotyped, nothing more than his society stripped of its flagrant vices.

Moon voyages became popular in the 1630s, their underlying inspiration Galileo's telescope and the curiosity it piqued about the planet; but the way of reaching the new world on the moon was more important than the substance of an ideal society. Kepler's *Somnium* of a man on the moon viewing the earth was in the service of the Copernican hypothesis. Francis Godwin's *Man in the Moone: A Discourse of a Voyage thither by Domingo Gonzales* (1638) treats primarily of the mechanics of flight with the aid of a crew of birds. Cyrano de Bergerac's *Histoire comique,* with voyages to the moon and the sun (1657, 1662), is Lucianic; John Wilkins' *The Discovery of the New World in the Moon* (1638), scientific. But none of the adventures have the high seriousness and unified moral purpose of the Christian Pansophic utopia. The extraterrestrial site of a society revived an ancient theme, but its intent was usually satiric rather than utopian and it did not bear significant fruit until the twentieth century.

The sun came to play a central symbolic role in seventeenth-century utopian culture, and the sunburst achieved a new prominence in Christian iconography. Campanella's *City of the Sun* (1602) introduced Sole himself as ruler. Garcilaso de la Vega, the learned half-breed who wrote a tragic history of his mother's people (*The Royal Commentaries of the Incas,* 1609), bestowed deep meaning on the Peruvian belief that the Inca, who had established a perfect communal order of society, was the son of the Sun. And the King of Vairasse's Sevarambians (1675) identified himself as the Viceroy of the Sun. In the theological wrangle of the Catholic world with the new science, the sun was contesting the central position of earth. Into the works of the most orthodox Catholic writers, like the theologian Bérulle, an analogy between Christ and the sun insinuated itself (with a marginal reference to Copernicus). In the second discourse of his *Grandeurs de Jésus* (1623), Bérulle wrote: "For Jesus is the sun immobile in its grandeur and yet moving all things." When in European consciousness the sun rises as the dominant psychic force of life on earth, the terrestrial paradise emerges with a new brilliance. The nature of light, as well as movement, becomes a key problem of science, and knowledge as illumination of worldly things governs utopia.

The French are not conspicuous in our genealogy of Pansophists. There were, to be sure, French men of science who touched at the periphery of the movement. Father Marin Mersenne, active in the first half of the seventeenth century, appreciated the Pansophic ideals of Comenius, and received Campanella in Paris after his liberation, though with a measure of skepticism. Cyrano de Bergerac's utopian voyages to the moon and the sun, slight things in themselves, drew inspiration from Campanella and probably Francis Godwin. But Descartes, despite his mild, youthful flirtation with the literature of the Rosicrucians and with ideas of a universal science, mocked Pansophist projects and voiced contempt for the aged Campanella, who tried in vain to track him down in Holland. The French seem to have contributed primarily political schemes to the idea of Europe, and the excessive concentration upon political mechanics in memoranda like the Duke de Sully's Grand Design and in Eméric Cruce's *Le Nouveau Cynée* shows that their conceptions tended to be essentially plans for achieving a European peace through a balance of power, not an integrated Christian world order.

The relative insignificance of France in this enterprise may be explained in part by the simple reality that the consolidated French monarchy was providing a new framework for the reestablishment of hierarchy, whereas in revolutionary England, pulverized Italy and Germany, and chaotic Central Europe, which had no such centripetal force, the visionaries looked outward to a revival of the concept of universal monarchy. In the deliberations of the private "academy" of that strange French entrepreneur Théophraste Renaudot which served as brain trust and propaganda mechanism for Richelieu, there might be occasional mention of Bacon and Campanella, even of the Rosicrucians; but amid scores of practical projects of a scientific and philanthropic nature, many of which were copied verbatim by Hartlib, there is not a single grand conception. Even the Christian agrarian utopia of Fénelon was addressed primarily to the French monarchy; it was perhaps universalist and mystical in spirit, but its chief concern was the realm of France and it turned its back on the new science.

Scholars have begun to see Pansophia as a major European intellectual movement, a body of thought with a reasonable measure of internal cohesion that occupies the space between the philosophies of the late Renaissance and the Enlightenment. It was characterized, particularly in Protestant lands, by the need to present a unified system of thought comparable to the formally approved synthesis of Aristotelianism and Thomist theology that had emerged at the Council of Trent. Inevitably, those Catholics who exhibited Pansophic symptoms were accused of heresy, even though they were as critical of the intellectual and moral abuses of the northern religions as they were of their own.

Ancient doctrines left their mark on Pansophist thought. There was an assumption that the levels of creation from the highest to the lowest showed correspondences in their formal structures. The Pansophists held the conviction that Adam had possessed total knowledge but lost it at the time of the Fall, and that mankind had the capacity to reacquire through time and effort much of what had been forgotten. They recognized the power of evil in every newborn child, which had to be suppressed by vigilant nurture of his divine spark rather than through the administration of punishments, though these were not totally abolished. A cleansing of error and the institution of similar categories of thought among all peoples, through a uniform system of ideas and a correct universal language, were ways of ending meaningless theological disputes. The Pansophists preached the rehabilitation of nature, not in a romantic mode but as a source of truth, because every object in God's world contained within it a multiplicity of potential forces that should be brought by degrees into actuality. In manuscripts discovered in the 1930s Comenius wrote of a *mundus possibilis,* in its own way a philosophical designation of a utopian world.

Pansophism, Rosicrucianism, philosophical alchemy, and other hermetic and pseudo-kabbalist ideas, which are intertwined too closely to be kept distinct from one another, are full of exhortations to adepts to purify themselves and abandon the lusts of the world as necessary prerequisites for entrance into the higher stages of knowledge. Unlike European Neoplatonic and mystical movements, these theosophical utopias exalted things of the physical world, comprehended by sight and mathematical reason, as aids rather than impediments to spiritual elevation. But one should beware of pushing Pansophia into the late Enlightenment and the nineteenth century. Venery and the senses of taste and smell had not yet been divinized. They might serve as subjects of allegorical discourse, but Western culture had a way to go before the grosser senses were appreciated in themselves.

8

Bruno, the Magus of Nola

THE DOMINICAN friar Giordano Bruno of Nola lived no more than forty-eight days into the seventeenth century before he was burned alive at the stake, after having been handed over to the secular authorities by the Inquisition. Giordano was the name bestowed upon him when he entered the Dominican order. He had been baptized Filippo, and he oscillated between Filippo and Giordano with changes in fortune; in Geneva he was known as Philippe Brun. His father, to whom he makes respectful reference, served in the armies of the King of Spain as a retainer; his mother, Fraulissa, is a dim figure. Bruno identified himself less with his natural family or his monastic brethren than with the place of his birth. In his philosophical dialogues he appears as "the Nolan," and his friends addressed him that way. The practice was common enough, but for Bruno the exile and wanderer, the ancient, pre-Etruscan city of Nola, east of Naples, was the strongest tie to the earth. Nola lay in the shadow of both Mount Cicada and Mount Vesuvius, and in one of his poems Bruno wrote of the Cicada nearby and the distant Vesuvius as his parents. (His family owned a small plot of land outside the city gates.) The mountains addressed him familiarly, and taught him an early lesson in the relativity of sense perception, a lesson he carried over into the moral world. When he climbed Cicada its beauty and fertility overwhelmed him by contrast with bare Vesuvius; but he was assured that "Brother Vesuvius" was no less fertile and beautiful. From Mount Vesuvius, "Brother Cicada" looked dark and drear against the sky.[1]

A Daedalus of the Intellect

Bruno's formal philosophical training began in the monastery of San Domenico in Naples, which he entered as a novice of seventeen in 1565 and where he became a doctor of theology ten years later. Here he learned the language of disputation in the works of Aristotle and Aquinas. The first became the incarnation of all that was counterfeit in the world of man and nature. But Bruno never abandoned Aquinas, any more than did Campanella. These Dominican subversives conceived of themselves as rescuers of the true Aquinas from the grasping hands of those in the orthodox Catholic world who would transform him into a mere creature of the wicked pagan corrupter of Christianity. Bruno was as hostile to Aristotle's rules of poetry as he was to his physics and cosmology. He found for Plato and the spontaneity of heroic frenzy, making light of the middle way.

In various languages the Christian utopians of the seventeenth century praised expressiveness, creativity, and inventiveness; they rejected mere imitation and learning by rote. From Bruno onward they encouraged the development of the inner light in everyman. On one level that could mean growing in Christ and awareness of one's own particular spiritual essence; on another,

Bruno's, it involved esteeming novelty in poetry and in a philosophical-scientific comprehension of the universe. Before Leibniz, most of the Pansophists, who appeared rather indifferent to mathematics, harbored a sense that the mathematization of the world would reduce its many-sidedness. Bruno craved total knowledge, and its compression into the mathematical, the direction science would take after Galileo, would not have contented him; his major insights were poetic and philosophical, hardly scientific in a modern sense. Numbers interested Bruno not as keys to the universe, but as instruments of playful rhythms.[2] The subtitle of the *Ash Wednesday Supper* announces that it is composed of five dialogues, with four interlocutors, three reflections, around two subjects. Divinity was not yet restricted to number, weight, and size as the architectural frame of creation.

Bruno's experience as a Dominican novice was not unique. In monasteries throughout Catholic Europe, youths took their vows and were caught forever, no matter how unfit they may have been psychically and physiologically for the chosen vocation. If they were learned, there were books available in the rich monastic libraries that raised theological and philosophical doubts. The works of Erasmus, Ficino, Patrizi, and other writers likely to upset a simple orthodoxy had somehow found their way even into the establishments of southern Italy. As prohibited books, they were read in the secrecy of the privy. Luther's illumination during the evacuation of his bowels was only an instance of the heresies that flourished in these chambers. But the moderns were not the sole avenue through which evil thoughts infiltrated the minds of novices. Polemics of the Church Fathers quoted heretics in order to refute them, and despite the triumph of the Fathers, the apostates and pagan philosophers lay in ambush, concealed in permissible books, to corrupt later generations.

Bruno's rebelliousness early found an outlet in words and deeds. He was quarrelsome and was accused of sowing doubt in the monastic community in which he lived. To the consternation of his fellows, he removed images of the saints from his cell. Almost from the start he was in trouble with the authorities. But Bruno was not merely an intractable little Dominican awaiting ordination. In 1571 he was called to Rome to instruct the Holy Father himself in mnemotechny, an art that made Bruno famous and later won him entrance into the courts of kings and nobles throughout Europe; the secret art of memory recognized no boundaries of religious geography. And it was Bruno's virtuosity in this now neglected skill that was his undoing: When he was only twenty-three it had brought him to the notice of a pope, and twenty years later, through the intervention of a Venetian noble fascinated by the stories of Bruno's mnemonic power and eager to learn its magic, he fell into the hands of the Inquisition.

Sometime in 1576, already doctor of theology, Bruno fled Naples a jump ahead of the prosecutors who had instituted two proceedings against him with the Holy Office. Like other Italian clerics who forsook their homeland, he took off for the north, passing through Siena, Lucca, Noli in Liguria, Milan. During brief respites from his travels, he taught astronomy to nobles and grammar to little children. He crossed the Alps. His Dominican habit was doffed and donned again whenever it was expedient. He made a rash foray into the city of heretics, Calvinist Geneva, where he registered at the University and straightway published a theological attack on one of the main figures of the Consistory, the eminent professor of theology Antoine de la Faye of Chateaudun. Arrested and tried, he first repented, then took refuge in France, where he moved from Lyons through Avignon and Montpellier until he found a place at the University of Toulouse. There he delivered commentaries on Aristotle's *De anima*. From Toulouse he made his way to Paris, rising in the social scale, lecturing to the University on the divine attributes, and training Henry III in the *ars memoriae*.

Bruno never tarried long in any one place, and in the spring of 1583 he was off to London with royal letters of introduction from the King to his Ambassador at the Court of Queen Elizabeth, Michel de Castelnau. Bruno's arrival was preceded on March 28 by a secret warning from Sir Henry Cobham, English Ambassador at Paris, to Secretary of State Walsingham to the effect that "Dr. Jiordano Bruno Nolano, a professor in philosophy, intendeth to pass into England, whose religion I cannot commend."[3]

In England Bruno found an audience. At Oxford disputatious scholars challenged his arguments against Aristotle in debates that turned into public tumults. In London he enjoyed the society of Italianate Englishmen before whom he could display his wit and learning in symposia that he later adapted or refashioned in the form of dialogues, superb artistic creations in which characters are delineated with a few master strokes, ignoramuses are exposed, and Bruno's moral and physical system of the world is proclaimed in oracular statements. The Italian dialogues, published in London, bore Paris and Venice imprints. His earlier publications had concentrated on mnemotechny; now he won the plaudits of the English literary artists and noble poets, whose praises he returned generously in his writings. But though the Nolan was for a time appreciated and admired, he left no recognizable imprint on English thought of the period. There is a slim possibility that he met Francis Bacon in London; Bruno's name and wild notions are mentioned in the writings of the Lord Chancellor, who treats him disparagingly,[4] though some of the well-known Baconian aphorisms run parallel to Bruno's and the two men shared a common hostility to the prevailing sanctification of Aristotelian philosophy. Moderns, too, could make discoveries. Truth in science was the consequence of accumulation. "We are older and we have more years than our predecessors," Bruno wrote in *The Ash Wednesday Supper*.[5]

Bruno at first attracted friends and protectors, men fascinated by his person and his ideas. His fiery advocacy entranced booksellers and scholars, fellow monks and monarchs. For a while he had access to the circle of Sir Philip Sidney and Fulke Greville, the poet who was Queen Elizabeth's equerry; he became a fast friend of the famous Italian translator Florio; and he was housed in the French Embassy in London. *The Ash Wednesday Supper* is supposed to reenact a philosophical dialogue that actually took place. Bruno set up straw opponents in the persons of two pedantic doctors of philosophy, whom "the Nolan" caricatured with a few deft strokes and whom he worsted in an argument on the system of the universe, to the applause of entranced members of the English nobility. Queen Elizabeth was one of the few monarchs whom Bruno praised without stint in his writings—admiration for a notorious heretic that did not escape the investigators of the Inquisition. But a breach with friends was never long delayed. Soon enough Bruno was embroiled with the English poets, and he left in a huff to resume his wanderings on the Continent.

Back in Paris with Michel de Castelnau, Bruno published a book on Aristotle's physics and probably worked on his cosmological poems, later printed in Frankfort. In Paris he made an attempt at reconciliation with the Catholic Church, but adamantly refused to take up the monk's cowl again, and nothing came of his overtures to the papal nuncio. The itinerant scholar continued on his way in an abortive effort to capture the academic world of Central Europe. From Wittenberg, where he delivered himself of a panegyric on Luther, he headed east to Prague, thence north to Helmstedt. After this temporary haven in Brunswick he set off again. Furies pursued him as he dashed from Frankfort to Zurich and back.

Throughout Bruno's adult life the same compulsive behavior pattern was repeated: He showed up in a university town, registered as a master of arts, quickly searched out some eminent authority on Aristotle, found scores of errors in the pedant's readings and in Aristotle himself, then proceeded to engage in violent disputations from which, in his own eyes at least, he emerged a glorious victor. The authorities became involved in his quarrels and he had to move on. The calm of each European university center was disrupted in its turn—Padua, Toulouse, Geneva, Paris, Oxford, Wittenberg. He appeared and vanished like a comet. In each new place he adopted, or at least appeared sympathetic to, the dominant local religion, multiplying his apostasies with abandon.

Time and again this man of rage sought his own destruction. He was secretive, aggressive, possessed with the idea that people were plotting against him —and often they were. There is tragic plausibility to the self-image he painted in the dedication of his dialogue on the infinite universe: "If . . . I worked a plough, pastured a flock, cultivated an orchard, and tailored a garment, no one would look at me, few would observe me, by very few would I be reprehended, and I could easily be pleasing to everybody. But since I am a delineator of the field of nature, solicitous concerning the pasture of the soul, enamored of the cultivation of the mind, and a Daedalus as regards the habits of the intellect, behold one who, having cast his glance upon me, threatens me, another who, having attained me, bites me, and another who, having apprehended me, devours me. It is not one person, it is not a few, it is many, it is almost all."[6]

Of the more than fifty works or treatises Bruno composed, thirty-eight were printed and survive. One group centers around the *Ars magna* of Ramón Lull and affirms the underlying filiation of the great utopian visionaries of the seventeenth century with the Majorcan philosopher, who had died around 1315. Bruno's relations to Lull and the *Ars Magna* were kept alive in the seventeenth century by inclusion of Bruno's essays in Lazarus Zetzner's compendious editions of Lull's texts and their interpretation in 1609 and 1651. The Italian dialogues, which had been published in London, must have been much rarer. Echoes of Bruno's speculative philosophy of nature and holistic conceptions of knowledge reverberated through the seventeenth century; the moral dialogues tended to be forgotten. During Bruno's trial in Venice, the Inquisitors focused their attention upon the *Spaccio;* when later Leibniz referred to it in a letter he seemed to be so little aware of its contents that he raised a question as to why it had not been entitled *Specchio* (mirror).

Bruno usually made his living from his mnemotechnic treatises and his expositions of ancient and modern philosophical systems. The "magical works," written from 1589 to 1591, that earned him his underground notoriety are the hardest to evaluate. The degree to which he thought he could control the secret and hidden forces of nature through magical devices remains open to question. Like Kepler composing works on astrology for money, Bruno may simply have been faking. Or he may indeed have been convinced of the efficacy of his techniques. Mocking skepticism and credulous superstition have been housed in the same person before, and the existence of contradictions in Bruno is easy to accept. The earnestness of his rhetorical pretensions to magical powers when he was carried away by his own enthusiasm is more believable than the actual practice of magic. The recourse to hermetic or Kabbalistic formulae for practical purposes is difficult to credit in the author of the irreverent and scoffing comedy Il Candelaio (1582). What he read of astronomers ancient and modern was emended by his own fertile imagination—it is doubtful whether he did much or any astronomic observation or computation. He was quick to demolish predecessors in the study of natural phenomena, trampling upon them with rhetorical savagery whether or not he understood their arguments. His philosophical syncretism derived its elements from other writers, though none had spelled out the religious and moral implications of their speculative flights with Bruno's pathos. Though he left behind a spate of books on the art of memory, manuscripts on cosmology, even a salacious comedy, of all his ideas it was the infinity of worlds that became synonomous with his name. Belief in this heretical doctrine was one of the few purely philosophical charges leveled against him in the final list of his abominations.

In 1591, the roving Nolan managed to complete and publish the three Latin cosmological poems, De minimo, De monade, De immenso. And in that same year he took the fatal step of accepting an invitation from the scion of the patrician Mocenigo family to come to Venice, where he was to be paid to teach his art of memory and other esoteric knowledge. Evidence on the relations between Bruno and Giovanni (or Zuane) Mocenigo is contradictory. One can listen to either voice, the magus or the inquisitive noble disciple. Bruno wanted to return to Frankfort, ostensibly to see his latest work through the press. Mocenigo, afraid that Bruno's secret knowledge would then become common property, accused his master before the Holy Office. Bruno was arrested on the night of May 23, 1592, and thrown into prison. Three days later the official interrogation began, and what was asked and answered during these sessions was recorded with meticulous detail. Bruno's confession of faith before the Inquisition can be juxtaposed with depositions by others reporting what he said on different occasions in casual conversation. Admissions of guilt cannot be accepted on their face; the proud man was fencing for his life with skilled adversaries, and yet he would not retract everything. As in all such accusations, printed opinions were torn out of context, verbal remarks that may have been made in earnest or in jest were repeated undiscriminatingly.

The summary of each day's proceedings was attested to and signed, but the words hide as much as they reveal. Bruno swung between outbursts of arrogance and abject humility before the visible authority of a Church with which he had never completely broken—life outside it was virtually unimaginable. Bruno the philosopher might seek to demonstrate that his novel views could be tolerated within the ecclesiastical framework, he could try to dredge up support for his position from Fathers of the Church, but he could not affront the Church or conceive of existence without a religious sanction, if only as a necessary restraint on the behavior of the ignorant masses whom he despised. The breach of his monastic vows was beyond dispute, but the nature of his heresy remained open to question. Had he actually been converted to another religion in England or Geneva or some German principality? Was his crime perhaps even graver? Was he a heresiarch, the founder of a new clandestine religious sect in the bosom of a Church that had already been pillaged by Luther and Calvin and a host of others?

Bruno's interrogation at Venice reads like a stage play. With an extraordinary economy, in the course of a few sessions all aspects of his disordered life, his beliefs, and his published works were passed in review. The posturings of the baroque theatre were faithfully reproduced in the records of the diligent secretaries of the Holy Office: "He waved his hands wildly"; "He fell on his knees and extended his arms."[7] The prisoner was evasive with his persecutors. He prevaricated, feigned loss of memory, justified himself, admitted error, retracted patently heretical remarks, begged forgiveness, became irate, and then for a moment forgot his predicament as he allowed satirical boutades to drop, entrapped by his own brilliance.

The Venetian Inquisition had been curious about Bruno's sex life, and on May 29, 1592, Mocenigo provided the facts. They sound as if Bruno had been bragging.[8] He had told Mocenigo that he liked women a lot, though the number of his conquests had not yet equaled Solomon's, and that the Church committed a great sin in making a sin out of what nature had made such good use of. He considered the love of women a very great virtue. (Nothing is known about the actual sexual behavior of these great friars Bruno and Campanella, but from time to time they talked the language of sexual revolution.) The Inquisitor picked up Mocenigo's remarks and in the tonelessness of formal procedure asked Bruno's opinion about the sin of the flesh outside of the sacrament of marriage. Bruno replied with meticulous care, raising a few distinctions. He had indeed spoken of the matter, maintaining that in general the sin of the flesh was of a lesser order, but the sin of adultery was greater than the other, except of course if the other was the sin "against nature." As for simple fornication, he considered it so light a transgression it was almost venial. This he had sometimes said, he admitted to his Inquisitor, and he now recognized that he had delivered himself of error for he remembered the stricture of St. Paul that fornicators shall not possess the Kingdom of Heaven.[9]

Since sexual intercourse was "natural" and its practice universal and varied, in and out of wedlock, there was an element of cynical disdain in Bruno's ready acceptance of ecclesiastical prohibitions. A monk among monks who were interrogating him, he made a sardonic point of his repugnance to "unnatural" sexual relations. This wanderer over the highways of Europe, this priest who had listened to confessions in rural Italy and had lived in and around royal courts, was not prepared to be a martyr for the right to preach sexual liberty. He knew that in reality men and women did enjoy this freedom out of wedlock. He could jest about his own amorous conquests. When his Inquisitors taxed him with error, he piously intoned, with a mea culpa, the Pauline injunction that he had violated. The long exursions on women that break into the introductions of his most famous dialogues and even into the text of his astronomical speculations, sometimes without apparent reason, resemble excerpts from the common Renaissance literary and poetic debate on the nature of women.[10] Bruno could argue on either side with equal vigor. He could denounce women as the vilest of God's creatures in the thematic tradition that conceived of them as possessed in their wombs of an insatiable animal, and in the next breath he could exalt English women or the French Ambassador's wife and daughter as noble paragons of virtue and beauty. His eulogy of Queen Elizabeth was later read by the inquisitorial commission as another charge in the heavy docket of his crimes. What love and sexuality meant to Bruno beyond a conventional literary subject is hard to establish. Perhaps he considered sex an appetite to be indulged as a natural pleasure if kept within bounds; but the heroic philosopher had to guard against the frenzy of woman-love lest it distract him from his pursuit of the divine frenzy of the love of God.

When Bruno said to the Venetian Inquisitor that he was born in 1548, adding "so my people tell me," one imagines a supercilious tone. He was a man capable of outright defiance, of covering over his fear with wit, of blinding himself to the palpable dangers with which he was confronted—of all three in rapid succession. The record contains a number of feeble attempts at humor during the course of the inquiry, but no echo of laughter is noted in the solemn document. On one side of the bar, occasional forced levity; on the other, the flat questions of a set procedure. Bruno was accustomed to more disorderly confrontations in which he established the mood of the encounter.

Witnesses from distant places suddenly turned up in Venice—among them a bookseller who had known Bruno in Frankfort. Independent documents corroborate some of their testimony. Guillaume Cottin, Librarian of the Abbey of Saint Victor in Paris where Bruno used to study, kept a private diary in which Bruno's heterodox views were noted down, and though the Inquisitors had no access to this record, its contents bear out the accounts of the official informants. For the librarian Bruno defined the whole of Christianity as fostering *le bien-vivre*, an affirmation rather innocent in itself, yet ambiguous enough to suggest worldly "happiness" and "well-being." The nobleman Mocenigo, his principal betrayer, swore that during their many intimate conversations Bruno had blasphemed and denied basic tenets of the Catholic faith: Christ was a rogue, He and His disciples simulated miracles through magic, the world was infinite and eternal. Under the guise of an inventor of a new philosophy, Bruno had planned to become the head of a religious sect. Mocenigo's report may have faithfully reproduced some of Bruno's loose talk. The idea was widespread among reformers and millenarians and messianists in the seventeenth century that the world moved through cycles of corruption and regeneration; the depths of evil having been plumbed, the great renewal had to be close at hand. Mocenigo related to the Venetian inquisitors Bruno's heterodox ideas of religious tolerance and reform as he had picked them up in their discussions: "The Church today does not proceed as the Apostles used to proceed, for they converted men by their preaching and the example of a good life, but today whoever wishes not to be a Catholic must endure punishment and pain, for force is used and not love; . . . the Catholic religion pleases him better than any other, but this too has need of much reformation; . . . this is not good, but soon the world would see a general reform of itself, for it was impossible that such corruptions should go on . . ."[11]

Expulsion of the Triumphant Beast

It is doubtful that there was a coherent moral, philosophical, or scientific system in the political writings, treatises, and dialogues of this outrageous half-genius, half-charlatan, though of late scholars have bestowed upon inchoate thoughts, intuitions, and emotive utterances a structure that ignores their fluid character. The Inquisitors who closely interrogated Bruno in Venice about the fantasy of his conversations of the gods, *Spaccio della bestia trionfante* (*The Expulsion of the Triumphant Beast*), published in Italian in 1584 by a London press during his sojourn in England, believed that in Aesopian language it foretold the collapse of the Church and the foundation of a new religion. Through the device of a rehabilitated Jovian pantheon, in imagery that eludes interpretation in detail, he had created an allegory of the transformation of mankind under the reign of pure love free from concupiscence, of the exercise of a benign authority tolerant of human differences, of devotion to true knowledge devoid of Aristotelian pedantry, and of a reformed morality cleansed of vice and hypocrisy and false conceptions of the cosmos. Before his Inquisitors he steadfastly maintained that he was merely propounding philosophy and never meant to assail the Christian faith or the Church. But this stock defense could hardly be sustained in the face of his trenchant criticism of the ecclesiastical hierarchy and the Egyptian hermetic forms in which his utopian vision was enveloped.

Though at the Venetian trial Bruno paraded a sort of double-truth doctrine and represented his most heterodox conceptions as nothing more than a manner of speaking philosophically without religious implications, just as Catholic authorities might accept Aristotelianism without being pagans, in none of his writings is any such detachment of a part of existence from the whole countenanced. He was at once a theologian, a metaphysician, a moralist, and a political epigrammatist. Knowledge leading to the regeneration of mankind could not be compartmentalized or restricted to the mathematical, the astronomical, and the physical. Bruno hoped to penetrate the mysteries of harmonious proportions, of magic, of the right ordering of human conduct in worship and in government, of heroic frenzy. He was not a "scientific" thinker in the narrow sense; he recognized no neutral moral area of mathematical science isolated from human behavior and the service of mankind. He excoriated the vices of the upper classes, epitomized in the unnatural mothers who fondled their pets and abandoned their children and in the effeminate fops who wasted their lives in self-adornment and play. He pleaded for charity toward the poor and scorned the avaricious rich. But lest one make a populist hero of him, it should be remembered that he despised ordinary people as superstitious. There was something of the Adamite about him as he preached the emancipation of the flesh, albeit in cautious phrases. Eternal damnation was denied and ethics was reduced to the golden rule. Machiavellian wiles were denounced; in their stead, the image of the Roman Republic imposing restraints on the "beast" was held up before his contemporaries as the shining political ideal.

For the exposition of his conceptions Bruno had adopted the form of Lucian's dialogues. (It is odd that Lucian, who satirized utopia, should have so attracted the great utopians from More on.) But Bruno was no Hellenistic trifler, and his tone was passionately earnest. There may be more than a bit of the

South Italian fantast, of the hierophant, about him. His powerful style was a mallet with which he beat down the enemies of virtue and truth with a prodigious energy—a Hercules was cleansing the Augean stables of the world to prepare for a new revelation. It seems difficult to question either the sincerity of Bruno's reckless zeal to reform the whole world, or the tragically simple confidence that his doctrines were reconcilable with those of Thomas Aquinas and that the Pope could serve as an agent in the great work. Utopian thinkers in all ages have propelled themselves with a naive trust that they would gain influence over the most powerful men in the world and use them as instruments of a general reformation. Pope, emperor, king, financier, each in his turn served the utopians, until in the nineteenth century a new deus ex machina, the people, made its appearance and radically altered the utopian's mission. For Bruno, Campanella, and Bacon, the masses were still the heart of darkness. In the *Spaccio,* it was Jove himself who first had to consent to the expulsion of the triumphant beast before the renovation could be set into motion; mankind was a passive benefactor. Reform would have to come from on high.

Bruno's religious utopia, draped in parables and allegories, exerted only a feeble influence on Western thought because of the rarity of his books in the seventeenth century. One has to begin with him, however, in any history of the Pansophic vision, which combined a reinterpretation of religion with the new science. In his very extravagance he embodied the daring of those who would in one fell swoop substitute a science of things for what had become mummified abstractions. The science of things would serve as the foundation of a religion that would bind men together. "Natura est deus in rebus," he wrote. His was a pantheism that presaged Spinoza, if it did not influence him directly, a spiritualization of matter rather than its condemnation. He taught a new reverence for plain things, because they were infused with divinity. Resurrecting an ancient philosophical theme, he praised the very contrarieties of forces in the world as productive of the highest good.

In *The Expulsion of the Triumphant Beast* Sophia herself expounds the new theology:

God as a whole (though not totally but in some more, in some less, excellently) is in all things . . . Thus one should think of Sol as being in a crocus, a daffodil, a sunflower, in the cock, in the lion; and thus one should conceive of each of the gods through each of the species grouped under the divers genuses of the *ens*. For as the divinity descends in a certain manner inasmuch as it communicates itself to nature, so there is an ascent made to the divinity through nature. Thus through the light which shines in natural things one mounts up to the life which presides over them . . .

Those wise men, then, in order to obtain certain benefits and gifts from the gods, by means of a profound magic, made use of certain natural things in which the divinity was latent, and through which the divinity was able and willing to communicate itself for certain effects.[12]

In retrospect, Bruno's pantheism looms as the most radical justification of scientific inquiry presented to the seventeenth century: The infinite universe was not merely a creation of God, but the living divinity itself. God was immanent in the physical universe, and the least of material things secreted a divine inner being that gave it form. No distant Creator had abandoned His creation after the planets had been appropriately distributed and set a-spinning.

But the infiniteness of the universe was not identical with the infiniteness of God, for He was infinite in all His parts, while the universe was divisible into finite segments. The discovery of divinity in all things great and small was congruent with ancient hermetic writings, with Renaissance Platonizing, and with literary and artistic adoration of the sun; it surely could not be harmonized with any of the four major Christian theologies—Catholic, Calvinist, Anglican, and Lutheran. The worship of saints and relics for themselves was for Bruno as abominable as the worship of crocodiles and other beasts for themselves, a perversion of religion since it failed to discern the particular attribute of divinity in them that was to be adored. In the allegory of the triumphant beast the many-headed monster had to be expelled from the city that men might freely pursue, in diverse ways, the life of truth, a new order that a repentant Jove, foreseeing the end of his reign after the fulfillment of the cycle of the great year, had determined to institute. Since all things, like all men, bore contrarieties within them, the same planets that now exuded vices could by order of Jove emit virtues, which made a renovation of the physical and the moral world possible. *The Expulsion of the Triumphant Beast* predicted an imminent reformation. There would soon be a return to the pristine virtues of hermetic religion; vice, symbolized by the behavior of the old Jove of the pagan pantheon and his licentious companions, would be banished, perhaps not forever, but at least for another cycle of the great year. Jove performed a symbolic act: He ordered his firstborn, Minerva, to hand him the box kept under a pillow on his bed that held nine smaller boxes containing the medicated eye salve prescribed to purge the human mind both of its false knowledge and its evil dispositions. Though the council of the gods over which Jove presided was convened in pagan heaven, the moral values of Christian Europe were in question—a common type of subterfuge for the discussion of contemporary religion. But the golden age of pagan myth that looked backward was mocked by Bruno, since only in the harmony of civil society, not primitive animalian existence, was the identification of human with divine reason becoming manifest. An ideal world, a composite of elements from three past civilizations, the Egyptian Hermetic religion, Hellenic reason, and Roman law, with Christian and Judaic forms conspicuously underplayed, would be inaugurated after the expulsion of the triumphant beast. The Inquisitors were not far wrong in their conviction that the beast was intended to symbolize the Church.

The Inquisitors had hit upon the most obviously heretical of Bruno's allegorical dialogues. They did not have to single out the many passages from Renaissance hermetic literature that are either paraphrased or directly transcribed to recognize in this dialogue a transparent attack on all versions of Christianity. When the gods in council debate the treatment to be meted out to various mythological figures in the heavens, Momus turns on Chiron the Centaur and delivers a scandalous parody of belief in Christ and the Trinity: "Now what do we wish to do with this man inserted into a beast or this beast encumbered with a man, in which one person is made of two natures and two substances concur in *una ipostatica unione?* Here two things come into union to make a third entity; of this there is no doubt whatsoever. But the difficulty in this lies particularly in deciding whether such a third entity produces something better than the one and the other, or better than one of the two parts, or truly something baser."[13] Having got hold of an allegory to exploit, Bruno never lets go, toying with the analogy of the Centaur to one pant and one sleeve in all manner of combinations. At another point he satirizes a Kabbalistic tragedy to mock the Crucifixion.

Bruno was the Pansophist most alienated from any Christian establishment. Contempt for the practices of all existing positive religions, Judaism, Protestant sects, Catholicism, was joined with a derision of Christian theology for its blind involvement with the Aristotelian philosophy that had stifled thought. After his rejection of the inanities of Aristotle, Bruno tended to revert to the sibylline concepts of the pre-Socratics as correct reflections of the real physical universe. To the Church in which he was born he became a heresiarch. But Calvinists could take no comfort from his acerb portrayal of the Protestant temper. His trial before the Genevan Consistory for defaming one of its elders and his humble confession of guilt and repentance in order to escape imprisonment had left their mark. Proof of Protestant truth hinged upon whether it gave birth to fruits—to academies, universities, temples, hospitals, colleges, and institutes of arts and sciences. The promulgators of the new catechism were sharply examined: Would these establishments multiply or decay under Protestant tutelage after the old monastic foundations had been expropriated? Bruno was apprehensive lest the Protestants, in belittling good works, should suppress enthusiasm for all creative effort in the new science while at the same time neglecting the preservation of the old culture. During a period when he found hospitality at the University of Wittenberg the Lutherans enjoyed his approbation; but no sect could hold his allegiance for long. Some passages of the *Spaccio* have a marked anti-Protestant flavor:

Whilst no one works for them, and they work for no one (for they do no other work except to speak evil of works), yet they live on the works of others who worked for others beside them, and who for others instituted temples, chapels, inns, hospitals, colleges, and universities; wherefore they are open robbers and occupiers of the hereditary goods of others; who, if not perfect nor as good as they ought to be, yet will not be (as these men are) perverse and pernicious to the world; but rather necessary to the commonwealth, skilled in the speculative sciences, careful of morality, solicitous for increasing zeal and care for helping one another and maintaining society (for which all laws are ordained) by proposing certain rewards to well-doers and threatening criminals with certain punishments.[14]

Bruno was always more forceful in denunciation than in utopian portrayal. He included pedantic scholars and grammarians, indifferent to the public good, among the chief sowers of evil. His principal enemies were not abstract or distant powers but rivals in close proximity, the stupid professors who dominated establishments of learning. That the state of science and scholarship was the key measure of the quality of the world at any given moment was not open to doubt. Bruno never drew too far away from his personal situation; and his utopian vision preserved its academic character, narrowly construed. He would in passing take sideswipes at justification by faith alone and at the Calvinist denigrators of "good works," but his eye was primarily on activities in the seats of learning. No group among whom he sojourned was spared his corrosive humor. The Germans, who treated him rather well, were ridiculed for their traditional gluttony and drunkenness. The Calvinists and Lutherans were accused of slighting good works, when philanthropy should be a prime attribute of the human condition. The warlike French and the Turks were denounced along with the Jews. Moses and the great pair of horns branching from his forehead, the pontiffs with their two-horned mitres, the Grand Turk allowing his horn to rise in pyramidal form out of his turban—all this bestial symbolism was of a piece with that of the monks of Castello in Genoa, who called upon the faithful to kiss the tail of the blessed she-ass that carried Jesus to Jerusalem: "Adore it, kiss it, offer alms."[15]

Bruno's conception of a general reform involved a purification of institutions, not their total transformation. The Thomas More who had persecuted and martyred Protestants was not remembered with favor in the north of Europe, and in the Catholic world many passages of the *Utopia* sounded heretical. Bruno had heard of utopian projects, as an informant of the Inquisition reported, but he was not preoccupied with them. "Jordanus told me that he knew nothing of the city built by the Duke of Florence where one was supposed to speak Latin [the foundation of the story was doubtless a project to establish a city of Latin scholars in Portoferraio], but he did hear it said that the Duke wanted to erect a City of the Sun, where the sun would shine every day in the year, which a number of cities are famous for, among others Rome and Rhodes."[16] When Saint Victor's librarian, Cottin, mentioned a plan for a city that would be called Paradisus, Bruno evinced no interest. In a few years the Inquisitors of Naples would have occasion to hear more about a City of the Sun from another South Italian, who had fomented a revolt in Calabria in 1599. Whether Tommaso Campanella's implication in the Calabrian incident, which led to a characteristic jurisdictional wrangle between the Naples Holy Office and the Spanish Governor over possession of the victim, hastened the consummation of Bruno's fate is unknown. But reports of what happened to Bruno can hardly have been lost on Campanella, and even a generation later, on Galileo.

Bruno's reform was of a universal, psychic character, and the mechanics of enclosed utopias in the Morean manner did not much concern him. His utopia implied a changed state of the soul of man; it was a eupsychia. While he might lavish extravagant praise in the style of the age on aristocratic and royal patrons and their capacities for governance, political institutions and optimum republics did not claim his attention. In the *Spaccio* there are digressions on the power of Roman law to strike down men of iniquity, but the idealization of Rome is vague and at most the repetition of a banal stereotype. Bruno castigated the enemies of the good state of the soul, gave precedence to religious and intellectual regeneration as the key to the great renewal, but did not commit himself to a specific social or political order. He never wrote a *City of the Sun* or a *New Atlantis*. While he favored peace, he did not dream of an eternal Sabbath. His was not the ideal of calm felicity that dominated the Christian utopia from More through Leibniz. Bruno exalted energy and zeal. (Absence of zeal was a vice.) A world without heroic frenzy would be impoverished, but the frenzy was to be channeled into love and passionate inquiry instead of war. The utopia of calm felicity, as good a description as any for the Christian utopias in the Morean canon, was not his model.

Bruno approached closest to preaching social reform in the allegorical *Spaccio,* with its nonascetic, unmartial, utilitarian utopia, its respect for the Roman communal virtues of law and order. But this moralizing work, which condemned vices in church and state, denounced hypocrisy, and extolled virtues that were the contraries of the vices it deplored, hardly has the makings of a new gospel. Moralizing allegorical literature abounded in the sixteenth century. Ortensio Landi, Italian translator of More's *Utopia,* had written diatribes against the vicious Sardanapali who ruled Italy; but neither he nor his friend Doni labored under any delusion that the portraits of ideal societies they drew had the possibility of realization. Bruno's utopian vision found expression primarily in critical negation of existing social and religious behavior and a call to spiritual regeneration. A truly reformed religion would put an end to war and persecution and outlaw theological quibbling, banning punishment for those who held rival opinions about the universe. Aristotle the ass and his asinine followers would surrender their hold on the human mind as men turned to the study of God in things once again. But Bruno's view of the world and humankind excluded any facile optimism. Man's acquisition of learning meant an exacerbation of anguish, since with increased knowledge came the understanding that absolute truth was forever inaccessible. In the London dialogues, the promotion of knowledge of the physical universe to which Bruno was dedicated with a heroic frenzy was not expressed in neat metaphors of accumulation, such as those to which Joseph Glanvill and other apologists of the Royal Society resorted later in the seventeenth century. The immediate goal was divine illumination.

Bruno's shifting doctrinal positions had settled into one affirmation: The right to philosophical speculation even within the province of the Church was not to be denied. The speculative reasoning he stood for was remote from experimental philosophy; his natural philosophy was infused with elements considered in the Renaissance as benign natural magic, power exerted by men because of the sympathy among components of the human body, the physical world, and the planets. The Jewish Kabbala had systematized such conceptions and the ideas had penetrated Christian thought. Numerous natural philosophies of this character, fed by Platonic and hermetic writings, were floating around the Continent. Bruno's reason was not reason in Bayle's, Voltaire's, Diderot's, or Kant's sense; it was an untrammeled individual force that could become a heroic frenzy alien to the most daring men of the Enlightenment. An illustrious figure of eighteenth-century Italian *illuminismo,* Cesare Beccaria, once quipped that he wanted to save humanity without being martyred by it. Giordano Bruno, author of a dialogue on the *Heroic Frenzies,* could die for a heroic truth with which he was seized, impervious to the mob, the ancient authorities of the Church, the arguments of its keenest theologians. It was he and he alone whose substance was divine, who could live and die without auxiliary. A divinized intellect proclaiming its truth in heroic frenzy was in the end an absolute, individual act.

Bruno saw himself as a servant of truth, though a disbeliever in the exclusiveness of any discovered manifestations of truth. The relativity of sense perception that he expounded in *De l'infinito universo e mondi*—"Those who speak prudently will not say: this smells good, that tastes good, this sounds good, that looks beautiful, but will add: for me, at a certain time"—was extended to customs and manners.[17] Bruno demonstrated the existence of infinite worlds, of the variety of moral truths, and of a multiplicity of paths to truths that somehow had received their most perfect expression in the allegories of ancient Egyptian wisdom. The *Hermetica*, a collection of texts now dated to the second and third centuries after Christ, had been resurrected by Renaissance philosophers as authentic documents of early Egyptian religion and had been extolled as the pristine theological truth about God and His relation to the universe. Paraphrases and elaborations of these mystical writings were incorporated into Bruno's works, along with heady draughts of what Renaissance Christian philosophers believed to be the Kabbala. According to some contemporary scholars, Bruno actually intended to found and propagate a new religion that drew its inspiration from an amalgam of what he thought were pre-Christian doctrines, merged with his own highly idiosyncratic reading of Copernicus' treatise on the revolutions of the heavens. For orthodox Catholics, these syncretistic views quickly reduced themselves to a pagan sun-worship, which left far behind the trinitarian theology and Aristotelian philosophy that had been redefined by the Council of Trent.

Doubt remains whether Bruno in fact hoped to resurrect a true and pure primitive religion of the ancient Egyptians before its corruption by myths of the Greco-Roman pantheon. Greco-Roman "histories of avarice, lusts, thefts, hatreds, contempts, and shames" had been deplored in one of the obscure hermetic writings, the *Koré Kosmou* (translated and published by Patrizi in his *Nova de Universis Philosophia* in Ferrara, 1591). Was the complicated dialogue of the gods in the *Expulsion of the Triumphant Beast* simply an artistic medium that Bruno used to convey general hopes for moral reformation without committing himself to a historical sequence of religious degeneration that placed Christianity in the same box of corruption with the Hellenic mythology it superseded? To have Isis upbraid the glorious Greek gods and justify beast worship could have been a deliberate attempt to shock his readers. In the third dialogue of the *Expulsion* Bruno expounded the true meaning of ancient Egyptian animal-worship, so manifestly superior to the idol-worship of the Greeks and the Romans and, by implication, of a higher degree of spirituality than Christian saint-worship.

Thus crocodiles, cocks, onions and turnips were never worshipped for themselves, but the gods and the divinity in crocodiles, cocks and other things, which divinity was, is and will be found in diverse subjects insofar as they are mortal at certain times and places, successively and all at once, that is to say, the divinity according as it is near and familiar to these things, not the divinity as it is most high, absolute in itself, and without relation to the things produced. You see, then, how one simple divinity which is in all things, one fecund nature, mother and preserver of the universe, shines forth in diverse subjects, and takes diverse names, according as it communicates itself diversely. You see how one must ascend to this One by the participation in diverse gifts; for it would be in vain to attempt to catch water in a net, or fish in a plate.[18]

If Bruno's veneration for the hermetic writings as the foundation of a new religion is read literally, the reign of justice could be brought about by magic. Knowledge of the planetary virtues, of the minerals, and of the attributes of each planet in the physical universe would enable a religious magus versed in ancient lore and modern astronomy to manipulate metallic and planetary influences into benign conjunctures and avoid noxious configurations, with the ultimate aim of inaugurating the reign of virtue. But despite its hermetic language, the whole allegory can just as plausibly be read as a sensible moral homily directed to the individual and exhorting him to purify his own psychic state, rather than as a complex interplay of the planets, the metallic forces associated with them, and the passions of men. Perhaps there were moments when Bruno experimented with number combinations and, like an activist Kabbalist (as distinguished from a passive, contemplative one), imagined that he could affect the effluvia of the spheres and through them exert cosmic power for good on the world. When he visited Kabbalist centers like Prague, he may well have been touched by doctrines that would have meshed with the hermetic studies in which he was immersed. But there is no convincing evidence that he actually engaged in magical rites. It is conceivable that in periods of exaltation and enthusiasm he laid claim to occult powers to mystify his listeners, though the report of these claims comes from informants of the Holy Office and they were not beyond pushing a point. Bruno's written dialogues are witty, sarcastic, and artistically so sensitive to form that it is difficult to cast him in the role of a full-time solemn hierophant.

That Bruno speculated about an entirely new religion beyond the bounds of Christianity is possible. But while he consulted esoteric works and put whole parts of the hermetic writings into the mouths of interlocutors in his dialogues, any contention that he truly hoped to revive a pristine Egyptian religion is far-fetched. The poets of the Elizabethan court circle in which he cut a figure indulged in all kinds of literary play and contrivances. Sir Philip Sidney had felicitously called a utopia a speaking-picture. Bruno's dialogue dedicated to him resembles that kind of fare rather more than it does the manifesto of a priest of the Egyptian religion. His were poetic conceits, not the prophecies of a seer. He capered and cavorted preposterously, and though there was a serious undertone in his writing, it was a longing for a golden age of peace, not a summons to the adoration of Isis and Osiris.

Other Italian moralists in the latter part of the sixteenth century, such as Landi, denounced the social evils besetting the land in violent and graphic language. But though he signed himself "Philalethes ex Utopia" and More's Utopians were not Christians, Landi never abandoned the common faith of his nation. In like manner, Bruno's *Spaccio* describes the inauguration of a lawful society in which tyrants were restrained, the poor and the weak protected, the arts and learning encouraged. When the work was subjected to close scrutiny by a commission of theologians acting at the behest of the Inquisition, they had no difficulty in spotting outrageous references to central Catholic dogmas camouflaged in allegorical images. This does not prove, however, that Bruno was prepared to leave the social community of Christians. Patrizi of Cherso was able to amalgamate his hermeticism with Christian forms, and there is no reason to divest Bruno's reform of its essentially religious character, though Christ's person is certainly thrust into the background and on more than one occasion trinitarian doctrine is ridiculed.

The Impenitent Heretic

When the Venetian trial concluded Bruno fell to his knees, begging for condign punishment in order that his fate might serve as a warning to others.[19] Whether he was suddenly overwhelmed by the enormity of his blasphemies or this was a mere artifice, playacting to save his life, is not determinable. Nothing in what is known of the man points compellingly in either direction. The strongest have been broken in the presence of formidable power. Bruno had no one to sustain him, no sect of *Giordanisti*. He was out of reach of the stray students and amanuenses he may once have attracted with his ideas. Since the accused showed remorse and repented of his errors, the Venetian trial might have had a less tragic denouement, if political expediency had not impelled the Venetian Senate to comply with the request of Pope Clement VIII and agree to Bruno's extradition to Rome.

The records of Bruno's second trial have been lost or destroyed. All that remains is a summary published in 1942 by the head of the Vatican archives, Angelo Mercati.[20] One approaches with misgivings information gleaned from adversary proceedings in the trial of a man for his opinions. The Inquisitors set the terms of the accusation and selected from the testimony what was of most concern to them, not to the victim. Bruno, as cognizant as any ancient or modern of the relativity of an observation and the changing perception of an object not only among different persons but in the same man at different times, was called upon to deliver himself of laconic yea or nay answers to reports others had made of his opinions of the Church, Christ, sexual relations, the nature of the universe, human corruption.

Why the Holy Office turned Bruno over to the secular authorities to be burned at the stake is not at issue. His fate was overdetermined: Witnesses' accounts of his oral blasphemies, his published works, his own final refusal to withdraw from the seven heretical positions with which he had been charged by a Roman commission that included the most eminent theologians in the Church all pushed him to a gruesome finale. The strenuous efforts of the ecclesiastical authorities to obtain a confession were part of normal procedure, though Bruno may have enjoyed their special concern. It is not clear that he would have escaped execution even had he recanted. The theologians were fighting for his soul, and perhaps a last-minute confession could have mitigated the brutality of the punishment.

Some recent commentators have tried to separate out the purely religious accusations from interrogatories aimed at eliciting his philosophical and cosmological views. Though Bruno might have occasionally resorted to some such distinction, it is highly dubious whether the inner man recognized divisions of this kind. His philosophical utterances were no less dangerous to the core of orthodox belief than denying Christ's divinity, or considering the Scriptures a series of accounts not far removed in character from Greco-Roman mythology, or explicitly propounding a doctrine of universal salvation in the end of the days that abolished eternal hellfire and gave even the fallen angels hope. If there was an infinity of worlds, as Bruno maintained, for whom in particular had Christ died on this earth? If the universe was eternal, what would become of God the Creator? Acceptance of the Copernican cosmology was a religious act that bore serious consequences in its contradiction of the biblical texts.

In defending himself earlier at the Venetian trial, Bruno had tried to ingratiate himself with his interrogators. He had put the evidence into context, making light of it as considered opinion, even trying to ridicule it out of existence. Or he had attempted to show that his views were in fact allowable in the Church and that eminent authorities had subscribed to similar opinions. Finally, when pushed to the wall, he had simply confessed that his reported statements had not been in conformity with appropriate Catholic belief. In April 1599, after seven years during which he was abandoned to the horrors of isolation in the jails of the Roman Inquisition, he again confessed his guilt, continuing in this vein through August 24. Then a baffling reversal occurred. He became obstinate in his errors and refused to retract. What did Bruno die for? At any time in the protracted proceedings, which lasted nearly eight years in Venice and Rome, could he have got away unscathed? The man was, after all, a lover of the flesh. When he had fallen into the hands of the Calvinist elders in Geneva, he had bent the knee and asked forgiveness; and at the conclusion of the hearing before the Venetian Inquisition he had again dropped to his knees and formally pleaded for punishment. What brought about the subsequent reversal? Did he, like More, will his own death? What happened to Bruno during the long years he was in the prisons of the Roman Inquisition? Was he put to the torture, as one terse record may imply? Had he come to the definitive conclusion that his fate was sealed and that they were only wrestling with him for the possession of his soul, his soul which would not surrender to these defamers of true divinity? Did he imagine that to the end he could sustain his distinction between philosophy and theology, insisting upon liberty of thought while the Church demanded unquestioning belief in what the Fathers had for centuries held about the constitution of the world? Even by their own criteria as Bruno understood them, the churchmen were wrong in denying him the right to opinions that other churchmen had held with impunity. The theologians were not accurately interpreting the words of Augustine, Aquinas, Nicholas of Cusa, when they found Bruno in contradiction with some of their opinions about the world. The theologians of the Holy Office had locked the Church within the narrowly interpreted, finite universe of Aristotle's physics, had accepted his false doctrine about the movement of the four elements. And they were lying about the true relations of divinity and creation, for they restricted divinity to a tiny world of a few planets moving around the earth, when the plenitude of God's infinite power required the existence of infinite worlds peopled with numberless inhabitants. Bruno stood before his accusers as a defender of divine omnipotence and a plurality of forms, while they would constrict mankind into a dogmatic position that belittled divinity. If he had in fact made a psychic identification with divinity, their worldly fires could not touch him.

Perhaps *De gl' heroici furori* (*The Heroic Frenzies*), 1585, is a key to his vision and a prefiguration of his ultimate fate. "His love," Bruno writes of the enthusiast,

is completely heroic and divine . . . even though because of it he speaks of himself as afflicted by such cruel tortures; for every lover who is separated from the beloved (to which, joined by his desire, he would also be joined in act) finds himself in anguish and pain, crucifies himself and torments himself. He is so tormented, not only because he loves and is conscious that his love is most worthily and nobly employed, but because his love is deprived of that fruition which it would attain if it had arrived at the end toward which it tends. He does not suffer because of that desire which enlivens him, but because of the difficulty of the labor which martyrs him. Thus others consider him as being in an unhappy condition because of the fate which seems to have condemned him to these torments; as for himself, despite these torments, he will not fail to render thanks to it, because it has brought an intelligible form before his mind. For in that intelligible form, although he is enclosed within the prison of the flesh during this earthly life, bound by his sinews and confined by his very bones, he has been permitted to contemplate an image of the divinity more exalted than would have been possible had some other species and similitude of it been offered him . . .

A heroic mind will prefer falling or missing the mark nobly in a lofty enterprise, whereby he manifests the dignity of his mind, to obtaining perfection in things less noble, if not base . . . Certainly a worthy and heroic death is preferable to an unworthy and vile triumph . . . Fear not noble destruction, burst boldly through the clouds, and die content, if heaven destines us to so illustrious a death.[21]

Time and again Bruno resurrects the Platonic image of the cave, and exalts the heroic frenzy of those who escaped the condition of the stupid, base multitude. Those capable of divine contemplation could only be few in number. As he wrote at the end of the third dialogue, the heroic enthusiast, having grasped the nature of divine beauty and goodness, takes flight on the wings of the intellect and of the intellectual will, rising to divinity and abandoning his baser form. "From a more vile creature I become a God."[22]

The final tragic resolution of his conflict with the Church could be reduced to a series of accidents. But there may also have been deep-rooted psychic drives that converged and in a unity of contrarieties forced him to perform the act of will that is called martyrdom, the sacrifice of self. But martyrdom for what? The query goes to the heart of Bruno's conception of himself as a person with a divine mission and his idea of that mission in Christian Europe as the papacy was celebrating the sixteen-hundredth year under the star of Christ. The Bruno who believed himself called by the living God who was everywhere to smite the purveyors of falsehoods about God's universe and about the duties of men was devoured by the heroic frenzy to which he sang hymns of praise. The man who was fleshly, satirical, vengeful was at moments so possessed that life itself could be surrendered, as he was dissolved in the ocean of divinity. When scholarly virtuosi contract his transcendent purpose to a revival of the hermetic religion primarily on the evidence of quotations from esoteric texts inserted into his writings, they are forcing him into a tighter straitjacket than ever the Church would have thrust upon him. Bruno was the founder of an invisible ecclesia without known adherents. One of the Inquisition's informants accused him of planning to establish a new religion of *Giordanisti;* when he was burned, the whole abominable sect died with him, for he was its only member.

Other more secular considerations may have come into play. The intellectual life was a combat in which Bruno had been the doughtiest of warriors, managing to survive until the last engagement, an uneven battle of wits with the interrogators of the Holy Office. Within a decade of his execution a Spaniard created the figure of the knight errant Don Quixote, who combed the world in search of rivals to defeat in honor of his Dulcinea. Bruno the disputatious monk had roamed from one university center to another issuing challenges against all comers, anyone who would dare enter into public debate with him, shame and ridicule the price of defeat. In the heat of the fray, he laid on the blows in a frenzy—in a printed leaflet one rival was accused of making a hundred errors in a single lecture. Bruno's Dulcinea was Sophia, the goddess who announces the new moral law for mankind in *The Expulsion of the Tri-*

umphant Beast. Don Quixote is often worsted, but he rises again and fantasy transforms humiliation into victory. Though most of Bruno's scholastic combats left behind no record except his own proclamations of triumph, other sources disclose his submission in a few instances, even his ignominious abandonment of the field of battle. But though Bruno, when faced with overwhelming power, sometimes collapsed and confessed his errors to escape punishment, he never forgot his shame. Had the Genevans not made him suffer dishonor—the word is his—he might have accepted their religion, he later told one of the Inquisition's informants.[23] In the dialogue of *The Ash Wednesday Supper,* he did not fail to record the slights to which "the Nolan" had been subjected by the English aristocrats who were among his auditors. While his attacks on others were merciless, he himself was a thin-skinned, sensitive Don Quixote, and any derogation of his person was an affront to Sophia, whose devoted worshiper he was. Whatever the military rank of his father might have been (he was, it seems, an ordinary retainer), he was a noble warrior in the fantasy of the son, who inherited an aristocratic sense of honor. It may be that in the last months of his life the concept of soldierly honor which he had often violated—fawning before benefactors, genuflecting in the presence of Calvinist elders and Catholic Inquisitors, repenting of his ways—took hold of him. Ultimately, he refused to admit to the formal charges punctiliously drawn up by the commission of theologians and to suffer who knows what degradation at their hands, even though he had already confessed in principle. Men more skeptical and even cynical than Bruno have been known to embrace death at critical moments, rather than besmirch once again the already tarnished escutcheon of their honor, which becomes the definition of their manhood.

Bruno did not accept martyrdom for the sake of hermetic theology whose imagery he had borrowed to give voice to his un-Christian pantheism. The details of his cosmology were not expounded with religious fervor, though he held them to be true. The particulars of his false doctrine that made light of sexual violations when he knew they were sins were not central propositions of faith for him. He could have explained away as levity, as he had before, his utterances on the venial sin of fornication. Particular views could have been interpreted in a variety of ways. But the last proceedings somehow touched a secret core of his being. The final rejection of the accusations may be more related to the soldier's sense of honor than to either his religious or his philosophical opinions. He was, after all, the son of a man of arms—he had identified his father to the Inquisitors with these words—and the enemy was dishonoring him.

For Holy Year 1600 more than three million persons were crowded into Rome. There were parades of pilgrims, processions of flagellants. The city was in turmoil, as robberies and murders multiplied. The number 1600, composed of a nine and a seven, had magical meaning; perhaps it signified that the end was near. Prophets prophesied. In the meantime, the penitents who expected to amass the necessary absolutions from sin before it was too late were fleeced by the noble Romans. One of the minor attractions for February 17 was announced in fly sheets. The Nolan, a most stubborn heretic, was being burned in the Piazza Santa Fiore. A witness was a German converted to the Catholic faith, a scholar who never missed a major theological contest, Gaspar Schopp. He hovered over the final days of Bruno, vulture-like, picking up his last words and spreading them about. To him we owe the report of Bruno's defiance of his judges in Santa Maria sopra Minerva: "I daresay you are more afraid to hand down the sentence against me than I am to receive it." And after the burning, Schopp dispatched a gloating account to the rector of the University of Altdorf: "Thus he perished wretchedly by roasting, and he can go tell in those fantastic worlds he dreamed up how in this world impious blasphemers are dealt with in Rome."[24] Schopp would reappear in Campanella's cells a decade later and dish out promises to work for his deliverance, while plagiarizing the manuscripts he could get hold of.

The Inquisition was a law-abiding institution. Its punishments were graded and assigned with care. The secular arm could be advised to behead the victim, have him choked before he was burned, or tear his tongue out and roast him alive. Bruno's martyrdom was not a Christian one. While the Church supplied him with a whole retinue of monks who prayed for his soul as he was marched to the stake, he himself had issued a counterjudgment upon his judges. His last recorded words were not those of a *homo religiosus*. Proud as Satan, he tacitly threatened his judges with the condemnation of posterity, while he stood in a Roman heroic posture, unflinching, unafraid. Lest Bruno be turned into a religious hierophant for whom worship of the omnipresent divinity in all things was the sole passion of existence, one must also listen to the paeans of praise to glory that break through in his dialogues. The glory is worldly fame, a Roman reward for virtue that was never accommodated with the otherworldliness of Christianity and increased the psychic tension of many a Christian hero. The *De monade* entrusted his fame to "secla futura." Whether or not he toyed with the idea of a hermetic religion, in the hour of need he found support for his moral stance neither in Christ nor in Hermes, but in the heroic tradition of the noble Roman, which he had assimilated. Cicero, Vergil, and Horace have dominated the conduct of utopian visionaries from Bruno through Condorcet; they taught them how to behave in extremis. When Bruno called upon the Pope as the only one capable of judging him, he was evoking a Pauline image of appeal to the Emperor on the part of a Christian who was a Roman citizen.

There is no easy solution to the enigma of Giordano Bruno, a strange genius drunk with a cosmic spirit. He was Theophilo, a lover of God, a footloose wanderer, a man possessed of more than a measure of paranoia and a violent, combative nature subject to uncontrollable outbursts, a wit, a sarcastic speaker who scratched and clawed his adversaries, a sycophant when need be, a lover of the society of the great, a confessed hater of the mob, a respecter of no positive religion, a playful literary artist, a hard-necked and obstinate man, a believer in the uniqueness of his destiny, an admirer of honor—the aristocratic virtue that infuses a whole person in body and spirit with an extreme susceptibility to derogation and insult—a fantast who juggled planets and worlds with speculative ease, a master of dialectic, a critical doubter, a naive believer in transmigration of souls and in the effluvia of different planets, a man with a prodigious memory, and finally by his own account a great lover of women. He sanctified all worldly things and made profane what the four Christian religions held sacred. A knower of ancient mythologies, he treated Christianity as a myth, sometimes as a great deception. He was imbued with a sense of the contrarieties in all persons and things, sometimes even in himself. He talked of his command of magical powers, and yet one is not entirely free from the suspicion that he was putting on his interlocutors. Like many prophets of new cults, which proliferated clandestinely in the bosom of Christianity in the seventeenth century, he was ambivalent toward the Catholic hierarchy, Aquinas the Doctor of the Church, and Christ Himself, whom he sometimes considered a magus and sometimes a mere pitiable wretch. Bruno was a man who loved dramatic invention, who saw personal incidents in the heightened form of a stage play in which he was featured in the principal role. In poems and casual utterances he prophesied that he would be a tragic hero. At moments he had no understanding of the reality of the power into whose clutches he had fallen. At other times he displayed consummate skill as he dueled with the most formidable men of the canon law that the Church could assemble, headed by Cardinal Bellarmine.

Once Bruno was betrayed into the hands of the Inquisition and destroyed as an "impenitent heretic," he was virtually forgotten—though it may be that Campanella and Galileo at moments remembered his fate all too well. He did not really come alive again until deists like John Toland discovered in him a soul mate. In that Protestant world of the eighteenth century Bruno became the symbol of the new science martyred by religious superstition, though neither his method of attaining knowledge of the physical universe nor his use of mathematics had any relation to the experimental philosophy that came to dominate Western science. When the anticlericals raised a monument to the martyr for science on the Campo dei Fiori in Rome, it was the Pope, in the role of champion of modern science, who denied him all claim to positive achievement. Many of Bruno's manuscripts, now at the Vatican, were published for the first time in the mid-twentieth century, when he rose phoenixlike from the ashes in the city where he had been burned.

9

Bacon, Trumpeter of New Atlantis

FRANCIS BACON was born January 22, 1561, in an ancient mansion on the Thames, York House, and he died on April 9, 1626. Giandomenico (later Tommaso) Campanella, about seven years his junior, son of an illiterate shoemaker in Stilo, Calabria, a center of Greco-Byzantine culture, was born on September 5, 1568, and died in a monastery on the rue Saint-Honoré in Paris on May 21, 1639. The two could hardly have been more different in character, native culture, religious training, and personal fortune. Yet so mighty are the contemporary winds bearing ideas that these men were driven to compose utopias intimately related in spirit. Both were of the late Renaissance, post-Trentine heralds of the new philosophy, whose concise utopias of science, little more than pamphlets in size, came to enjoy a wide circulation and after their death exerted extraordinary influence upon men of action of the most diverse persuasions. The direct impact of Bacon's College of the Six Days' Works on the founders of the Royal Society of London and on the sponsors of many eighteenth-century European academies is attested in the formal histories of the learned societies and in their charters.[1] Campanella, after notoriety in the seventeenth century and oblivion in the eighteenth, has had an even more bizarre fate in modern times: He has become a hero of the Russian Revolution.[2]

The Watchful Eye

Though Bacon's *The Great Instauration,* his major philosophical work, did not appear until 1620, after at least twelve revisions, the first decade of the century was for him a period of prodigious invention during which he composed nine different works, only two of which were printed in his lifetime: *Of the Proficience and the Advancement of Learning* and *The Wisdome of the Ancients.* The *New Atlantis,* probably written in a first draft about 1614, was published posthumously in 1626.[3] The private life of this corrupt and self-revealed man was in some respects a constant denial of his spiritual vocation; but his ideas and felicitous phraseology crop up everywhere, and his all-encompassing program for the new science in a Christian commonwealth initiated an independent intellectual stream that swiftly flowed through Europe and merged with Campanella's. Bacon's whole scientific scheme was incorporated into the first Continental encyclopedias of the seventeenth century—Alsted's, for example; Campanella's theological manuscripts quote the epigraph of *The Great Instauration,* "Multi pertransibunt & augebitur scientia," with a Baconian interpretation.[4]

Francis Bacon was the last and the littlest of the creations of Nicholas Bacon, Lord Keeper of the Seal for Queen Elizabeth. At the time of his son's birth, the middle-aged father was at the height of his powers, a huge hulk of a man, yet subtle, lively, reputed for his wit and capacity to summarize arguments with clarity and to formulate the most complicated statutes or council decisions in a

simple, straightforward manner. He was a newly risen man in the Tudor bureaucracy, whose father had been an official—one source says the sheep reeve
of the Abbey of Bury St. Edmonds. Like other members of his class who participated in the dissolution of the monastic properties under Thomas Cromwell, Nicholas ended up acquiring a goodly share of them for himself. The
new men not only seized the lands of the church, they began to invade the
strongholds of learning, the universities where clerks were once trained, and
throughout the rest of the century there was a rising tide of gentry and nobles
matriculating at Oxford and Cambridge. One of the early recruits to the new
learning, Nicholas spent a few years at Bennet College in Oxford before entering upon a legal career at Gray's Inn.

Along with two friends, Nicholas is said to have devised a scheme for employing the revenues of the dissolved monasteries to found a college in London
where young men of good family would perfect their knowledge of civil law,
Latin, and French, in order to serve the Crown in its foreign embassies. Nothing came of the notion, but his son outstripped him in the building of airy
colleges, and in the next century the idea came to fruition in a host of societies
and academies. Francis Bacon's original scientific projects were thus indirectly
related to training for royal service and the formation of a body of secular
clerks. The Bacons, father and son, led the transition from one ruling spiritual
class to another. The elder participated in the liquidation of the monastic
houses which had for centuries preserved the old learning, the son drew plans
for the glorification of the new. Though Nicholas Bacon might ape the nobility in manners and literary sensibility, he was concerned with practical things
—when he built a manor he had water piped into every room. This positive
valuation of mechanical objects was given philosophical justification by
Francis Bacon: Of all the achievements of the past, only the discoveries of artisans had preserved real knowledge about how nature worked; inherited book
learning was false.

Every one of Nicholas' male children was persuaded to follow in his footsteps and become a lawyer and parliamentarian. When the sons of his first marriage had finished their training, he presented them lands in the counties and
contracted advantageous marriages for them. They cut significant figures in
their localities, well-rooted in the soil and independent of the royal caprice—
which Sir Nicholas was not. From his second marriage he had two sons, about
two or three years apart. In some ways their birth initiated a new life for him.
He built an estate at Gorhamsbury, though he was well settled at York House
on the Thames over the Whitehall Bridge, close by the palace and the great
houses, and the Queen was a frequent guest at his sumptuous entertainments.
Both of his sons were rather sickly: The elder, Anthony, was frail-bod-
ied, almost carried away by a fever when he was two, and by the age of thirty
was "impotent in both his legs"; the younger, Francis, frequently took to his
bed. His ailments have not been diagnosed, but Anthony observed that Francis
worsened when in bad temper after a political defeat. There was talk of gout,
of crippling back pain, of a tendency to faint. In fits of extreme depression, he
retreated into isolation and denied admission even to urgent messengers. Enemies cited his ill health to support their claim that he lacked the stamina to
sustain the cares of high office.

Francis' mother, Anne, born in 1528, was the daughter of the scholarly Sir

Anthony Cooke, who had educated all his five daughters in the humanist learning of Greece and Rome and in the French and Italian tongues. He was in the midst of the great religious controversies when the parochial Anglican version of Protestantism was being shaped, and was open to Zwinglian and Ochinian influences. His daughters, too, were deeply immersed in the current disputations and Anne translated into English Ochino's sermons and Jewel's Latin apology for the English Church, for decades the standard justification of Anglicanism. While Nicholas Bacon was a man of the law and directed public policy for Queen Elizabeth, his wife was absorbed with the intricacies of Calvinist theology, preoccupied with predestination, election, sin, duty, vocation, credit in this world, and damnation in the next. She was suspicious of servants, fearful of spies in high and low places, full of physical dread at the contamination of papist effluvia that threatened her sons whenever they dealt with Catholics. By the time she died in 1610 she was quite "frantic," according to a Court journalist.

When her sons were over thirty, Anne Bacon still treated them as minors. Her letters, written in an almost undecipherable scrawl, afford an inkling into their upbringing. There are outbursts of verbal violence, curses, followed by effusive concern, admonitions against what might injure their health, presents of delicacies they liked to eat and home-brewed beer to strengthen them. She held important legal strings on their property, and they always addressed her respectfully, though they tried to avoid her. After the death of Sir Nicholas in 1579 there do not seem to have been intimate relations between the two families he had fathered. Anne's sisters all married men of parts, and Francis turned to them, especially his uncle, Lord Treasurer Burghley, more often than to his half brothers. Frequently he was rebuffed.

Anne Bacon poured her frenzied passion onto her first born. In young Anthony she would live as the learned male her father Anthony had wished for. When the brothers roomed together, she wrote mostly to Anthony, and the distance from Francis, his father's favorite, was marked. Francis feared her, never crossed her, and later revealed his deep hurt, perhaps inadvertently. In an essay on parents and children, he censured those, especially mothers, who showed preference for one child over another. And in his last will, he asked to be buried by her side. Whenever he met failure in the active life, he turned to the learning with which his mother was identified.

Accusations of homosexuality against Francis Bacon are founded upon more than a phrase in John Aubrey, who had heard anecdotes about him from Thomas Hobbes, one of his secretaries. His love for Sir Toby Matthew, the Italianate English convert to Catholicism, whose mannerisms were the butt of literary ridicule, was notorious. Bacon came into his own as adviser to King James and his favorite, Villiers. Denunciations of pederasty, a classical form of sexual self-revelation, flowed from Bacon's pen as readily as they did from James's.

Apart from Toby Matthew, the only strong affective relationship that Bacon revealed was to his brother. They were educated together, for long periods shared a home, and in the last ten years of Anthony's life were bound in a firm political alliance in the entourage of Lord Essex. "The brothers," as they were referred to in contemporary correspondence, behaved as twins sometimes do. They mothered each other. At one point Bacon wished his brother's ills on himself, as a desperate parent might. Both were engaged in ferreting out secrets—Anthony, operating as a spy, unraveled the diplomatic secrets of Europe, Francis the secrets of nature.

That Bacon sought to repeat his father's career in homage to his revered ancestor has been noticed before. At every stage of the course he compared himself with his dead father. The law and the office were his heritage. There is more than one instance of implied rebuke that Sir Nicholas had left him no inheritance, that he failed him in dying without completing arrangements for a grant of land and in abandoning him to the bounty of the family; provision had been made for all the sons except him. The father had been a formidable figure. Identification with him was complete, but was also crippling. The son could never be as great as the founder of his estate and everyone knew it. He was physically small, weak, chronically ailing. Nicholas Bacon had always stood on his own feet. There are reports of his delivering open and frontal insults to men of power, Burghley and Archbishop Parker. Nicholas was jovial, Francis sarcastic. Time and again Francis Bacon had to summon the shades of his father to his aid, call upon men to pay their debts to his ancestor. In the end, as soon as he reached the heights and surpassed Sir Nicholas, he fell precipitously downward, like those characters in Shakespeare and Marlowe when they have reached the apogee. It was not this they wanted. Bacon had betrayed "sophia" in lusting after office. All his life he wished to pursue philosophy and somehow was deflected from his course. His last years were a pitiful display, an attempt to recover King James's favor and to devote himself to the conquest of nature at the same time. The disgrace was hard to bear. He had shamed his father in his father's office and robes. Bacon was obsessed with parricide. He found the laws too lenient: The crime should have been equated with treason, not plain murder. To kill the father was to kill God, or the divine king. But in that dream of his eighteenth year—remembered and described in the *Sylva Sylvarum* when he was sixty-five—in which his father's house was plastered with black mortar, was he not wishing his father dead and his mother a widow?[5] And when, upon returning to England from France, he found him dead, was he not seeing his criminal wish fulfilled? He explained the dream and the event as perhaps telepathy among those with close sympathies.

As a child Francis Bacon was brought to Court by his father, and amused the Virgin Queen he later served in the most bewildering episode of her reign. Except for occasional journeys abroad on official business, he did not stray far from the center of power at the Court to which he was bound. He died as he was born, a courtier, his whole existence dependent upon the will and whim first of a masterful woman, Queen Elizabeth, and then of a weak king, James I. It was a circumscribed world of castles and great houses, where one learned to watch hawkeyed and interpret with analytic subtlety the slightest alteration in the mood of a fellow protagonist in the political drama. Francis Bacon did not write Shakespeare's plays of courtly passion and intrigue; he performed in them every moment of his life. His whole career was interwoven with public affairs foreign and domestic, crises of war, of royal prerogative, of parliamentary privilege, of the ecclesiastical establishment. In the midst of the stately exits and entrances, the private Bacon is lost to view. Loves and hates burned beneath the minister's frozen mask. The religious and scientific visions that had seized him early in his youth were suppressed or set aside as he sought palpable power and gold in the governance of the realm. From time to time throughout his life the grand philosophical designs of his early years again laid hold upon him, but he surrendered to them completely only after his downfall, when it was already too late. His death from a chill caught during an amateurish experiment with a frozen chicken was close at hand.

Francis Bacon wrote aphoristically and not always consistently about the ancients and the moderns. He himself was proof of the natural order of things, that the youngest generations were the wisest. The moderns, the latest of mankind chronologically, were superior to the ancients—"For rightly is truth called the daughter of time, not of authority," a phrase that Bruno had used and Bacon may have heard in the 1590s.[6] The philosophical babblers Plato and Aristotle were not, however, the real wise men of Greece. The true wisdom of the ancients, Bacon taught, lay in the works of the pre-Socratic atomists, who studied nature itself and like Thales did not disdain material goods and commerce with things. The great mythmakers had instructed mankind in parables about scientific accumulation through time. If one denied Father Aristotle, one could seek refuge among the mythic sages of Egypt, as Bruno had, or the Greek ancients, as Bacon did.

Psychically, Bacon was one of the uneasy ones, placed at the end of the line in his own house, and the age in which he lived became a projection of his image of himself. This was the age "of not having enough." Men had once complained to the gods about Prometheus because he had not given them more and they were right, Bacon wrote in *De Sapientia Veterum* (The Wisdome of the Ancients), 1609: "having inough, is to be accounted one of the greatest causes of having too little."[7] There is no recorded moment in Bacon's life when, except for temporary relaxation before a new bout, he would rest content. He was voracious for more honors, more knowledge, more power. And when he reached the apogee and became lord chancellor, there was nothing to do but reverse the process. His fall seems a self-inflicted punishment.

Bacon was not profusely honored for his philosophy during his lifetime. He may have died with the conviction that he had inaugurated a new epoch in human thought, a creative century after a long period of darkness, but few of his English contemporaries shared this belief. He treasured the rare compliments he garnered from his foreign correspondents. Bacon was admired more for his style, his conceits, than for his philosophy, which, as James I said, was beyond understanding. Devout Protestants had denounced Plato and Aristotle as impious pagans; but an attack on their doctrines in the name of a new philosophy of things was not readily comprehensible or acceptable, and James set the tone of the popular response when he made fun of *The Great Instauration*. In 1609 Bacon tried to communicate the virtues of the new philosophy in the guise of an explication of ancient myths, but men took *The Wisdome of the Ancients* to be a mere exercise in wit that gave meaning to the parables, a book to be set alongside the other learned explications of ancient fables that had multiplied during the Renaissance, from many of which Bacon had derived symbols and other details. He was read for entertainment, and little of his thought crept into men's minds during his lifetime. The elegance and the imagery were too successful, the disguise of the mask was too effective.

In *The Wisdome of the Ancients* Bacon set forth ideals of moral conduct that he was himself incapable of achieving. The voluptuary Epimetheus, who esteems only what is most sweet in the present and who inevitably brings forth miseries, could be a caricature of Bacon. But he is not uncritically in favor of the Promethean martyr type who denies himself lawful pleasures and is full of anxieties and fears, the hero whose liver is gnawed by the eagle. His real idol is Hercules with his fortitude and constancy of mind, foreseeing without trepidation, enjoying without loathing, suffering without impatience; this is the god that delicate, neurasthenic Francis Bacon would have wished to resemble. Puny Francis Bacon who dreamed of Hercules wanted the fame and the delights of fortune that came easily. The denial of an office threw him into a depression; for decades, from his late adolescence through his marriage at forty-five, he could not extricate himself from debts and endless lawsuits. He was both profligate and apprehensive.

Theoretically, Bacon resolved to keep the Kingdom of Man and the Kingdom of God apart. But analogies between the two worlds penetrated his thoughts and slipped from his pen, and he had to take them back after they were on the page. Hercules coming across the sea in a cup to rescue Prometheus bears a similarity to the Divine Word coming in the flesh as in a fragile vessel to redeem man from the slavery of Hell. "But," he quickly adds, "I have interdicted my penne all liberty in this kinde, lest I should use strange fire at the altar of the Lord."[8] The nature of his religious life remains as obscure as that of most eminent Elizabethans; he committed sexual sins for which all contemporary Christian sects would have burned him if they obeyed their laws, but in many of his writings the intensity of his religious feeling breaks through.

Bacon does not make much sense if one is looking for an integrated character, a balanced man. One should apply to him his own psychological insights into behavior. For him most men are torn by contrarieties, and this is what he looks for in unraveling their secrets. They do what at least one part of them would not. All the personages he analyzes in the Court and in literary exercises are self-deceived; they are aliens to themselves. Late in life he tried a self-analysis and concluded that he had spent himself in "busyness," his word for activity in public affairs, whereas he was fittest for philosophical studies. Parliament men thought him haughty, as had everyone since his youth; yet he wrote to Burghley with extraordinary insight that he was really bashful.

Sometimes Bacon tried to reconcile the opposites. Studies were not useless for the man of action, and he could profit from the researches of the analytic mind. As if conscious of his own weakness, Bacon was always trying to ally himself with great power, with Elizabeth, Essex, Buckingham, James I. Toward the end he sought a union with practical men of science who, he hoped, would appreciate his message and rush to his side to perfect the grandiose design for the ingathering of all knowledge about the world of nature. At one time he may have thought of his brother Anthony as a partner, creating a perfect unity, bound by love.

In reality, Francis always ended up as a third person, a supernumerary. He was the go-between, first between Elizabeth and Essex, then a more cautious aide in the relationship between James and Buckingham, aware now that he must go through the channel of the favorite to reach the King, avoiding direct access or keeping the favorite informed of every move he made in the royal direction. On the philosophical plane Bacon saw himself as the intermediary between the men of the world and the discoverers, between the King and a mythic scientific establishment for the new philosophy; he would be the trumpeter of science to all mankind. The historical model for this ideal relationship was Alexander and Aristotle.

Like a Iago, Bacon was always reading other men's minds, manipulating them through his knowledge, his study of their countenances and their words. In the triplexes in which he was involved, it is hard to be sure where his true love lay; he did not himself know. To have power over nature, his mother, Elizabeth, or the effeminate monarch who succeeded her, he had to proceed by indirection. All approaches had to be devious. And when he announced that he was being plainspoken—fear Bacon singing a song of forthrightness. Incautious men of power like Essex and Raleigh ended on the executioner's block. In both cases Bacon participated in the legal ceremonial as the prosecutor of these willful, uncontrolled, hot males. At one time he attempted to guide Essex's behavior with keen and subtle advice, trying to exercise power through him, but the man was unteachable. When Bacon became certain that Essex was too wild, he abandoned him to his fate and then rewrote the history of their relationship. The image of the stage is recurrent in this Elizabethan world of play-actors in high places. Grand actions were divided into theatrical scenes, each of which had to be meticulously planned. Bacon was the playwright, and, depending upon whether or not his advice was accepted, the history would have a tragic or a comic ending.

There was a cruel streak in this man—witness the description of the naked, whipped boy in the apothegms, the "vexing" and torturing of nature. The personality was classically anal. There was a constant preoccupation with bowel movements, congestion, order in the administration of physic. He even allowed his absorption with defecating to affect his style, occasionally indulging himself in a naughty pun. In omitting from the Latin version of his *Advancement of Learning* passages that might give offence to Catholics, he acted as his own *index expurgatorius,* he said, and would not "pen up in the matter" what he hoped to diffuse widely abroad. Bacon's learned Calvinist mother was the original source of his terrors. She laid down the law to her errant sons. There were divine vocations and there were estates; one should be content to fulfill what was ordained. Earls were earls, but Bacon should not model himself after a carousing, gambling fellow like Essex. Sinful companions were to be avoided, for sin was an easily communicable disease of the soul. One should live within one's income, shun idleness. If Francis was refused a charge, he should accept the divine chastisement. Francis and his brother cavorted with their servants. She scolded them for making bed and coach companions out of them. There should be no trust in persons, surely not in servants who by the definition of their status were close to evil.

Rebellion against his father, never openly expressed, manifested itself in violent antagonism to the whole philosophical and educational tradition in which Francis had been brought up. He wiped clean the slate on which are inscribed the names of the ancient and modern contrivers of philosophico-scientific systems. Not one of them passed muster: "In ancient times there were philosophical doctrines in plenty; doctrines of Pythagoras, Philolaus, Xenophanes, Heraclitus, Empedocles, Parmenides, Anaxagoras, Leucippus, Democritus, Plato, Aristotle, Zeno, and others. All these invented systems of the universe, each according to his own fancy, like so many arguments of plays . . . Nor in our age, though by reason of the institutions of schools and colleges wits are more restrained, has the practice entirely ceased; for Patricius, Telesius, Brunus, Severinus the Dane, Gilbert the Englishman, and Campanella have come upon the stage with fresh stories, neither honoured by approbation nor elegant in argument."[9] Aristotle, Plato, the Scholastics, the Paracelsians, the alchemists—the whole of his training was dismissed as useless.[10] These philosophers dealt in phrases, vapors, airy constructions; he wanted to ferret out the real secrets of nature. Nature had to be "vexed" in order to be shaken in her innermost depths; otherwise, she did not respond. The reputed Greek fathers of learning had multiplied verbal syllogisms that he knew all too well. He wanted to fathom nature's hidden powers, to capture them for himself.

The violence of Bacon's attack against philosophical authority is equaled only by Campanella's. To strike out against the political order would mean facing his father and to cast doubt on religion was an assault against his mother. The Baconian rebellion assumed two more innocuous forms, transgression in personal conduct and hostility against "the philosophers." In Elizabethan England, outside the university philosophical opinions were a matter of indifference. Bacon's was a cautious rebellion; society was attacked where no one seemed to care. In Campanella's Calabria, Aristotle could not be torn apart with such impunity; there was a watchful Inquisition. In England there were permissible and impermissible positions about Church organization and the doctrines relating to it. As for philosophy, it was not a subject of paramount concern. The university curriculum long remained impervious to the verbal attacks of Bacon and the Baconians. As long as nothing was said against the divine right of kings, who would be troubled by a revolt against a long-dead Greek philosopher, especially one who enjoyed particular favor among the accursed papal enemies of England? The university was still an establishment for the training of clerics, and nobody bothered much about what these poor fellows did or did not believe.

The part that was allotted Bacon in the historical drama by most of his contemporaries in high places was an ugly one. He was a trimmer, a false friend who prosecuted Lord Essex, his patron. He was an officer of the Crown, the administrator of justice who confessed to the taking of bribes. Then, from the mid-seventeenth century for the next 150 years, he was transformed into a grand symbolic figure, the prophet of reason and the new science, only to be denigrated as a mere rhetorician of science and forgotten again during the positivistic nineteenth century. In recent years he has emerged as far less free from the magical and the occult than men of the Enlightenment had imagined.

The Scientist as Priest

After his impeachment for taking bribes, disgraced but still living in comfort, Bacon published a *History of the Winds* and a *History of Life and Death*. He had read the great moralists to learn how to endure old age and to die well. A certain calm came over him—unlike Campanella, who never knew a moment's rest from his furies. The two treatises gave promise of a great natural and experimental history to come that would be a model of the world as it truly was, with sections on matters political, physical, and psychological and "tables of discovery" in all subjects. Bacon sensed that time was running out: *The History of Life and Death,* planned as the conclusion of the series, was advanced out of sequence. The collecting of materials for the natural history should have been, Bacon wrote, a work for a king or pope, or some college or order. Shortly after his death, his secretary William Rawley published the *Sylva Sylvarum: or a Natural History, in Ten Centuries* (1626 [1627]), little more than an outline of experiments in diverse fields, despite its grandiose title. In a somewhat apologetic foreword to the reader, Rawley recounted: "I have heard his lordship speak complainingly, that his lordship (who thinketh he deserveth to be an architect in this building), should be forced to be a workman and a labourer, and to dig the clay and burn the brick; and more than that, (according to the hard condition of the Israelites at the latter end) to gather the straw and stubble over all the fields, to burn the bricks withal."[11]

The *New Atlantis* had been designed for publication after the *Sylva Sylvarum,* and it was in fact printed in the same year. Its final composition has been dated 1624 by Bacon's editor James Spedding, though drafts may go back a decade earlier. Bacon had imposed six-month deadlines on himself for a whole series of projects, and had abandoned the unfinished *New Atlantis* in favor of the "Natural History." Perhaps the observations on life and death seemed more immediately fruit-bearing than an ideal frame of laws of the best state or mold of a commonwealth. That project seems to have been left to another secretary, Thomas Hobbes, who completed it half a century later with a picture of society that from our vantage point bears little resemblance to that of Bensalem. Spedding called Bacon's *New Atlantis* "an image of himself made perfect," and in many respects it remains the best example of a utopia as a projection of a man's overt, and sometimes even hidden, tastes and desires, the contradictions ironed out. "The account of the manners and customs of the people of Bensalem is an account of his own taste in humanity; for a man's ideal, though not necessarily a description of what he is, is almost always an indication of what he would be."[12] In his discussion of the College of the Six Days' Works, Bacon credits the historical Solomon with authorship of a "Natural History" of all plants and all things having life and motion, and suggests that Bensalem's ancient king, Solamona, "finding himself to symbolize, in many things, with that king of the Hebrews (which lived many years before him) honoured him with the title of this foundation."[13]

The truncated *New Atlantis* was called a utopia within decades after Bacon's death and was spoken of in the same breath as Thomas More's *Utopia.* Writing utopias was beginning to be a professional hazard of English lord chancellors. And yet few who read Bacon's sophisticated dissection of the complexities of conduct of Elizabeth, Essex, and himself in their triangular relationship would have imagined that he was capable of delineating an optimum society. What is Francis Bacon doing among the utopian prophets? His works contain slighting references to utopias and ideal societies.[14] Bacon was still generally committed to the common Renaissance theory of vicissitudes in describing the philosophic history of states and empires, and at first glance the idea of a static reign of total happiness on earth is foreign to him. He was a great "projector," as they would say later in the century, overflowing with designs for reform of the higher educational system, the method of accumulating knowledge about nature, the penal laws of England; but there are few passages in which he pretends that these changes would result in a stable, moral society. Declension was inevitable, and at least in one passage in *Of the Advancement of Learning,* he does not doubt that in morals "this age of the world is somewhat upon the descent of the wheel."[15] For the past, at least, Bacon accepted the historical tradition of a whole series of destructions or declinations after great periods of flowering in the arts and sciences. (In *The Wisdome of the Ancients* he tried to rediscover the knowledge of the ancients during the one previous noteworthy period of man's achievement.)

But belief in vicissitudes and great destructions in the past could be combined with a present-day utopia about whose duration a man might be ambivalent. Or a philosopher might vacillate between the notion that the new order would be definitive and an awareness that the eternal turning of the wheel could not be stopped, at least not until final Judgment Day. Campanella was possessed by similar doubts. The alternatives were not always future utopia or future declension; mankind might have both. And there was a third alternative for a Christian, the millennium before Judgment Day. Bacon did not see the improvement of man's earthly condition and a belief in a heavenly paradise as mutually exclusive. Prolongation of life on earth was no sin: The most beloved of the disciples, John, reached ninety-three, and the most saintly hermits were long-lived. Campanella taught that a paradise on earth would only make men believe more fervently in an eternal paradise. There was no necessary contradiction between heavenly paradise and earthly utopia for a growing number of seventeenth-century thinkers.

Bacon's own view of his purposes in undertaking the grand work of a new instauration was complex. When as a young man he wrote his uncle Burghley soliciting financial support for his project for the reorganization of knowledge, he listed a number of possible motives for engaging in an enterprise so alien to his station. A drive to utopia was not one of them. "I have taken all knowledge to be my province . . . I hope I should bring in industrious observations, grounded conclusions, and profitable inventions and discoveries; the best state of that province. This, whether it be curiosity, or vain glory, or nature, or (if one take it favourably) *philanthropia,* is so fixed in my mind as it cannot be removed."[16] Charity toward his fellowmen was a necessary religious accompaniment of the achievement of great power over all things in nature because he was aware that power without a Christian sanction could be destructive of the truth of religion and of humaneness. Even if men turned to his system of knowledge, without the moral dictates of religion they would not achieve the Christian life. Unlike More's Utopia, which knew only a primitive monotheism before the arrival of the European sailors, Bacon's Bensalem had received the Christian revelation through a miraculous intervention. But though Salomon's House had been in full operation for many centuries, there were still poor people in the city. The *New Atlantis* makes no pretense to being a social utopia for all men, even though one populist touch—new cloths are plentiful —has been inserted by a man hardly reputed to love the masses, whom he, along with Bruno and Campanella, considered the heart of dark superstition.

Bacon described in detail only the ordering of the college for the acquisition of knowledge; he dropped or failed to complete his original plan to give laws and a constitution to his model commonwealth. The House of Inventions appears to be distinct from the government of the island, whose character is left vague. One has to imagine the nature of the general society of Bensalem from the few incidents that are described, and the inferences do not add up to a well-organized picture. In the long history of utopias that concentrate upon revolutionary scientific and technological transformation, the social relations of the inhabitants tend to remain shadowy. Theft is not unknown on New Atlantis: One of the strangers is in fact robbed and intercedes for the culprit. It can be surmised that there are needy citizens, since Bacon describes the alleviation of poverty. The family structure is patriarchal and there is great respect for age; one episode depicts the ceremonial honoring of a man who has contributed thirty living progeny to the state—this from the childless Francis Bacon over sixty. We learn virtually nothing about the motivation of the mass of the people or why they accept the hegemony of their king, who never appears on the scene. The atmosphere is cold and formal, and the conduct of life is grave. This was the ideal existence conceived by the shy son of a chilly and domineering mother. There is solemnity, a certain pity on the part of the hieratic scientist who walks among the people. Renaissance paintings of ideal cities sometimes convey this temper: The architecture is balanced and symmetrical, the human beings are in lifeless poses. Everyone on New Atlantis is thoughtful enough of the physical needs of the shipwrecked sailors and their questions are answered, but passion has been banished from utopia. The inquiries are methodical and orderly and they produce results because proper procedures are followed. Works of the imagination, which received a place in Bacon's systematic division of knowledge, are not mentioned in the *New Atlantis,* and works of memory are not prominent.

Plato's Republic had spirited guardians to mediate between the pure contemplative reason of the philosopher-rulers and the mass of the working people. Bacon has only administrative officials who scrupulously carry out orders. They are polite, considerate, and uninventive. The ideal administrators know their place and there are no intrigues among them. The mature Bacon had no affection for parliaments and there are none in Bensalem. At least three times the strangers attempt to reward officials of Bensalem paid by the state for their services; the gratuities are repeatedly rejected with the rhetorical query: "Twice paid?" They seem content with the official estimate of their worth. This is an odd personal touch from a Lord Chancellor who was impeached for taking bribes and openly confessed his guilt. Courtesy in Bensalem is elaborate and there is much bowing and saluting. Even the common people who line the streets to receive the strangers greet them in a formal manner. There are no tumults and nothing like a mass of Elizabethan groundlings. No one raises his voice in Bensalem. The whole city is a court in which everyone is respected in accordance with his rank. Above all, there is no expression of emotion. Life is a dignified procession. By contrast, the foreign sailors, uncouth Europeans, have to be restrained by admonitions from their leaders, and though they behave well enough it is out of self-interest, lest they be ejected before they have recuperated sufficiently to continue their journey.

That Bacon's preferred form of government was a monarchical absolutism hardly remains in doubt, and when R. H.—possibly Robert Hooke—in 1660 wrote a continuation to the *New Atlantis* supplying the political part, all power spiritual and temporal was vested in a king-bishop. What takes place beneath the surface of New Atlantis is not difficult to discern. Bacon is king, and the lords and potentates he served in real life, who acted out of caprice and were driven by violent passions, play no role in society. More's daydream that he was King Utopus could not have been recorded by a man like Francis Bacon, who rarely jested, and, when he did, was contriving to insinuate a politic idea into his august listener. Yet who is the head of New Atlantis but a man who was Bacon's idealized self-image, the ruler of a hierarchy of scientists, the master of universal knowledge?

In his introduction to the *New Atlantis* Rawley says that it is a model or description of a college for the interpreting of Nature, or, alternatively, a College of the Six Days' Works before God rested on the seventh. Though Bacon uses a number of standard Morean and Lucianic devices, such as the chance discovery of an isolated island by a group of sailors, and though he provides a history of the island, the emphasis is very different from More's. Whereas More had concentrated upon the social system, the order of the family, and religion, the heart of Bacon's truncated sketch is one institution, Salomon's House, the center of scientific discovery and invention. Though called a "fable," the *New Atlantis* is closer to an action program. In contrast with the dubiety of More toward the realization of his optimum republic, Bacon expected a large measure of practical fulfillment, and forthwith. According to Rawley, he was prepared to withdraw a little, to recognize that the model was "more vast, and high, than can possibly be imitated in all things." But this did not make of it utopian nonsense: "Notwithstanding, most things therein are within men's power to effect."[17] Bacon, as was his wont in dealing with intricate psychological situations at Elizabeth's or James's Court, was rooted in the realm of what he conceived to be the possible.

Since he broke off the fable of *New Atlantis* and never supplied those sections that concern the best state or "mould of a Commonwealth," the unique role of science may have received undue emphasis; but the succinct characterization of this part as "the very eye of the kingdom" makes it hard to overestimate the central role of science even had the society been completely delineated. While Bacon wrote longer works that have had their changing fortunes, this fragment durably imprinted a new popular image of the scientist on literate Western society. The Dr. Faustus who sold his soul to the devil was not entirely ousted—the legend still terrifies mankind—but Bacon succeeded in creating a scientist-priest cleansed of demonic attributes, a fit leader of a Christian society. Bacon's scientist was accompanied on his travels by an attendant bearing a pastoral staff. The only Christian priest explicitly identified as such in the *New Atlantis* was the Conservator of Health of the city, a government official hardly on a par with the thirty-six Elders constituting the core of the personnel of Salomon's House; but the Elder blesses the people in his passage as if he were a priest.

After the reader of the *New Atlantis* has been given a sketchy view of the accommodations in the Strangers' House (where the sick sailors have been fed a few pills), has heard a lesson on the advantages of a balanced budget, has witnessed the magnificent ceremonial honoring the patriarch who had thirty living progeny, the main event takes place: the dramatic confrontation between the European chosen to represent his fellows and one of the touring Elders of Salomon's House.

This Elder had not visited the city in a dozen years and there is a pathos of distance between him and the people. Francis Bacon, grandson of a sheep reeve, son of a powerful builder of Queen Elizabeth's empire, adored grand displays in which he could picture himself the central actor. The Elder's passage through Bensalem was an opportunity to lay on the pomp with a trowel. Some elements would seem to be derived from Bacon's sexual fantasies: Fifty young men in white satin coats to the mid-leg and stockings of white silk accompany the Elder. A touch of Christ's entry into Jerusalem is there. This scientist-priest is no wild magus or shaman. Although the carriage in which he is borne is luxurious, his own garments are austere black and white, fitting for either academic or sacerdotal robes. A Calvinist scholar surrounded by the trappings of James I's Court appears to be the combination.

The day being come he made his entry. He was a man of middle stature and age, comely of person, and had an aspect as if he pitied men. He was clothed in a robe of fine black cloth, with wide sleeves, and a cape: his undergarment was of excellent white linen down to the foot, girt with a girdle of the same; and a sindon or tippet of the same about his neck. He had gloves that were curious, and set with stone; and shoes of peach-coloured velvet. His neck was bare to the shoulders. His hat was like a helmet, or Spanish montero; and his locks curled below it decently; they were of colour brown. His beard was cut round and of the same colour with his hair, somewhat lighter. He was carried in a rich chariot, without wheels, litter-wise, with two horses at either end, richly trapped in blue velvet embroidered; and two footmen on each side in the like attire. The chariot was all of cedar, gilt, and adorned with crystal; save that the fore-end had panels of sapphires, set in borders of gold, and the hinder-end the like of emeralds of the Peru colour. There was also a sun of gold, radiant upon the top, in the midst; and on the top before, a small cherub of gold, with wings displayed.[18]

In the chariot the Elder sits on plush cushions. "He held up his bare hand, as he went, as blessing the people, but in silence." If he is not a Christian priest he behaves like one and is endowed with sacerdotal functions. The mood of the society is not ascetic, but neither is it sybaritic; the grandest feast of Bensalem never lasts above an hour and a half. When the Elder receives the representative of the strangers in private conference, he is seated on a low, though richly adorned, throne. He wears the same black and white cloak, and every visitor kisses the hem of his tippet and receives a blessing.

The Elder's discourse carefully followed Bacon's rules of rhetoric: The *partitio* was precise. The relation of the true state of Salomon's House was presented under four headings, which he first named and then proceeded to elaborate with details in careful order, like a lawyer presenting a brief: the end of the foundation, the preparations and instruments for its works, the employments and functions of the fellows, and the ordinances and rites that were observed.

First, the purpose of the foundation, perhaps the most frequently quoted succinct goal of science set forth in literature: "The end of our foundation is the knowledge of causes, and secret motion of things; and the enlarging of the human Empire, to the effecting of all things possible."[19] If modern science has a banderole these words have been inscribed upon it, though their meaning has been radically modified with the secularization of Western society. Bacon had voiced similar sentiments when he was speaking in his own name, though in his longer writings there are commentaries on the meaning of this sibylline utterance and numerous caveats against too simplistic or too broad a reading of the dictum. As might be expected, the limitations on science, which Bacon set forth in other works, have often been forgotten.

The second part of the discourse is devoted to the preparations and to the instruments of Salomon's House.[20] The Elders and their assistants and voluntary aides work in caves of various depths. Some caves start at the top of hills and descend three miles beneath the ground, the purpose being to create chambers protected from the beams of the sun and the heavens and from the air. In these caves new conditions are created for coagulations, indurations, refrigerations, and the conservation of bodies. The scientists can also produce imitations of natural wines and develop new artificial metals, which are stored for years. The cave experiments are not limited to organic and inorganic materials. There are human volunteers, hermits, who choose to live there; the scientists test cures of various diseases upon them, and devise methods for the prolongation of life. They experiment with earths and cements, producing porcelains finer than the Chinese (great rarities in Elizabethan England) and a variety of composts that make the earth fruitful. The range of their constructions above the level of the earth equals those of the caverns. Set on high mountains, towers half a mile in height allow for a view of at least three miles. Bensalem thus has three regions, high, middle, and low, and at each level the same experiments are performed. Within the towers the fellows of Salomon's House can, with the aid of volunteer hermits, observe winds, rain, snow, hail, even fiery meteors.

Some of the same experiments are performed in the watery environments of lakes, both salt and fresh, and on the rocky shores of the sea where the action of its vapors is studied. Torrential streams and cataracts allow the Atlanteans to investigate machines in motion. Artificial fountains and wells make possible observation of the effects of various tinctures; and one of them, the Water of Paradise, is especially prized for the prolongation of life. In great, spacious houses the scientists can generate bodies in the air and make them descend in an artificial rain, imitating one of the plagues visited upon Pharaoh. The orchards and gardens, which yield many new types of fruit through grafting and inoculation, allow for a great variety of beverages, the synthetic fruits surpassing the natural ones in taste and smell. The Atlanteans have mastered the techniques of either accelerating or slowing down the season of growth.

It would be possible to trace back many, though not all, of the Atlantean concoctions to the popular cokaygne utopias, which have had a continuous existence for a few thousand years, and to supplement them with paradisaical images of the varied tastes and smells and sights with which the just are rewarded in Midrashic and medieval Islamic and Christian accounts of heaven. By 1600, golden-age and paradisaical descriptions had become burdensomely lush. The collective gastronomic unconscious, however, does not require the mechanism of literary transmission. And though Baconian science may draw from these fantasies, the purpose of the activities in Salomon's House is not the pursuit of pleasure—the experiments center around a medical utopia dedicated to the cure of disease and the prolongation of life. "For although we Christians ever aspire and pant after the land of promise," Bacon wrote in *The History of Life and Death,* "yet meanwhile it will be a mark of God's favour if in our pilgrimage through the wilderness of this world, these our shoes and garments (I mean our frail bodies) are as little worn out as possible."[21] Since the sickly Francis and his brother Anthony were dosed with all manner of compounds, as his tutor's account book shows, there may be a personal element in the disproportionate space devoted to natural health foods, drugs, and a large variety of medicines. The general availability of these items at low cost in dispensatories or shops of medicine in Bensalem might attract an ordinary reader of the *New Atlantis* to the whole venture.

Passages in the *New Atlantis* dealing with the dissection of birds and beasts are directly related to the question of what could be wrought on the human body: how men might continue to live with parts removed. Biological engineering, even human engineering, later became a fixture of utopian fantasy. It would be a number of centuries before belief in the stability of the species would be shaken, which makes Bacon's "commixtures of animals and copulations of divers kinds, and them not barren," among the most daring activities in Salomon's House.[22] Bacon's harmonizing with Scripture the new machines and the study of bodies under different conditions was not unorthodox: Man was merely bringing into actuality what was potentially there. But in creating new animals that Adam himself had not named Bacon approached a religious abyss.

There are instruments in the College of the Six Days' Works that deal with heat and cold and that produce various forms of light. Without naming them, Bacon describes telescopes and microscopes enlarging the empire of sight. The same extension of manipulation takes place with music and the imitation and transformation of the sounds of beasts. The Atlanteans also are able to convey sounds in trunks and pipes in strange lines and over great distances. As he moved along in his discourse, the Elder alternated between accounts of the creation of new smells and tastes and those of war machines, many of them long a part of the fantasy world of Western man. Magnifying the potency of instruments of war was an old utopian notion that reached a high point with the "vril-power" of Bulwer-Lytton's post-Darwinian utopia. More esoteric were Bacon's machines for "some degree of flying in the air"[23] and ships for going under water. The Elder also talked of "some perpetual motions," which would remain a standby of utopian science for many years.

The sparse description of the mathematical house as a place "where are represented all instruments, as well of geometry as astronomy, exquisitely made," a total of thirteen words, is as good an indication as any of the chemical and biological and medicinal emphasis in the Baconian inquiries.[24] The dichotomy between mathematical and experimental science, which Thomas Kuhn has stressed, is quite explicit in Bacon's slighting of mathematical knowledge. The image of the scientist evoked by the few pages of the *New Atlantis* is far removed from the stargazer or mathematical theorist as the central figure, despite the fact that he is not entirely excluded.

In making a division of labor among the fellows—described under the third heading—Bacon set up a model of a highly centralized scientific organization. The thirty-six Elders of Salomon's House (a number that bears overtones of the Judaic belief in the thirty-six just men who sustain the world) constitute a unified community of scientists working in a set direction as a collegiate body. The manner of the controls is not described, but in this exemplary institution of science, individual *investiganti* and *virtuosi* are not running off on their own; nor is there room for the lone genius later immortalized by the picture of the young Newton. In his imagination Bacon made the leap into the system of highly coordinated scientific inquiry that would not be a reality for centuries.

A rather substantial number, a full third of the body of Elders, are always on their travels, gathering information on experiments in other countries of the world, which in part accounts for the superiority of the science of Bensalem over anything known in Europe. The Atlanteans not only inherited intact the Natural History of Solomon, but are apprised of all recent innovations that have been made elsewhere through the reports of their secret agents. The table of organization of the home-based scientists provides for three Depredators to ransack the contents of books, three Mystery-men to collect mechanical experiments, three Pioneers who try out new experiments, three Compilers who draw observations from the work of the previous nine. In another group are three Benefactors who examine the researches of their fellows to extract from them things for the use and benefit of men. When the whole body meets, three who listen to the reports are deputed to direct the undertaking of new experiments of a higher light, more penetrating into nature. These Elders are called Lamps, and they are joined by Inoculators who execute the experiments that have been approved. Finally, there are three Interpreters of Nature who distill from all the experiments general observations and axioms.

Since the Elders have a great body of servants and attendants as well as novices and apprentices to second them, enabling the total work to proceed without interruption in case of death, the activity of Solomon's House appears to be a limitless process. The highly unified scientific enterprise goes on indefinitely, it would seem, though in some of his writings Bacon voices the belief that the whole undertaking, when completed, will yield principles that can be contained within the covers of a book no larger than Pliny.

For most of the narrative it is unclear how appointments are made, though collegiate co-option is implied. What is more explicit is the relation of Solomon's House to the state and the inhabitants of the island. The body of thirty-six is completely independent. They have regular consultations about which of the inventions and experiments should be published (by "published" Bacon means made known to everyone) and which should not, and they are bound by oath not to reveal those that are to be kept secret. The guiding principle governing their decisions, though not set forth, appears to be *caritas,* which Christianizes all their activities. The Elders also must decide when to impart secret inventions to the state alone: "Some of those we do reveal sometimes to the State, and some not."[25] Those inventions approved for general public consumption are announced during circuits of the principal cities. In the course of these journeys, the Elders perform good works in preventive medicine and in mitigating the effect of such disasters as they can predict. The absolute neutrality of scientific discovery is further restricted in Bacon's other writings. He is especially censorious of endeavors that run contrary to Christian charity and that might threaten the mental and spiritual equilibrium of the scientist. Among the few rites at Solomon's House, spelled out in the scanty fourth part, there is a prayer of thanks to God for his marvelous works and an imploring of his aid that the discoveries be put to good and holy use.

The *New Atlantis* went through eight editions in the first half of the seventeenth century in England, was translated throughout the Continent, and became a model of moral intent for the new scientific academies founded in the seventeenth and eighteenth centuries. Literally scores of colleges of science, mostly short-lived, were established during the thirty-five years following Bacon's death, and though none followed his tightly knit plan his name was regularly invoked as a patron saint.

What stands out in the Baconian structure is the total coordination of the efforts of the scientists, who followed a common collegiate direction. This was utopian, and was not realized in the actual experience of science for centuries. In reality, the separation of science from the state has rarely been carried out, though violent confrontations have been avoided. But pervading the *New Atlantis* is the notion that science has to be governed by higher values and that not all its works are spontaneously in harmony with *caritas*. Of the Baconian testament the part that looked toward implementing the utility of the discoveries received most widespread recognition in an outpouring of popular works. By the time the Comenian conception of the scientific undertaking, influenced by Bacon, came to England it had merged with two other utopian strains, one from Campanella and the other from Andreae, both of which stressed even further the sacerdotal character of the scientific enterprise.

The *New Atlantis* is hardly a popular utopia of social regeneration; its purpose lies elsewhere. For all its absorption with inventions, New Atlantis is socially static. The monarchy and the class divisions, the exaltation of the richly robed inhabitants of Salomon's House, constitute an order for perpetuity. Foreigners are excluded to eliminate the threat of subversive ideas from abroad. There is no suggestion that the steady flow of discoveries from Salomon's House has basically altered over the centuries or would affect the fixed arrangements of the society. The *New Atlantis* is the vision of a *raffiné* Elizabethan courtier-official aping the old aristocracy, a man who would have his servants shod in Spanish leather, not out of solicitude for them but because he could not endure the smell of any other boots. The priest-scientist elite in Bensalem can be likened to the nobles free to lead lives of contemplation in Patrizi's *Città felice* and to the priest-rulers of Campanella's *City of the Sun*. Ordinary persons are treated with varying degrees of contempt or condescension.

Bacon was more keenly aware of the religious than the social implications of his vast scientific program (only cursorily outlined and illustrated in the *New Atlantis*). Charity toward fellowmen was a necessary Christian accompaniment of the exercise of power over all things in nature because power without moral direction could be destructive of the truths of religion and of humanity. When the eighteenth-century philosophes abstracted the Baconian method and plan from this profoundly religious context, they were doing violence to the spirit of his work. His major books—and though its influence was enormous Bacon would not himself have reckoned the *New Atlantis* among them—are dotted with cautions that the scientists must not try to overreach themselves, to ascend the ladder of knowledge without any restraints. The limitations to scientific aspiration are three: "The first, that we do not so place our felicity in knowledge, as we forget our mortality: the second, that we make application of our knowledge to give ourselves repose and contentment, and not distaste or repining: the third, that we do not presume by the contemplation of nature to attain to the mysteries of God."[26] In discussing the second limitation, Bacon warns of the danger that science may become sullied with human emotions, giving rise to anxieties in its practitioners, or delusions of grandeur, or inordinate desires—perhaps an admonition against Paracelsian and Faustian pretensions. There are other cautions in this vein in his writings. The man was preaching to himself as well as to others.

Bacon established a point beyond which scientists should not seek to fathom the unknowable will of the Calvinist God whom he had inherited from his

mother theologically and who was embodied in that great, ponderous Keeper of
the Seal who was his father. He was aware that there had indeed been instances
of erudite men losing their faith because they presumed to believe that secular
learning would lead them to a perfect understanding of the divine: "Divers
great learned men have been heretical, whilst they have sought to fly up to the
secrets of the Deity by the waxen wings of the senses."[27] Nevertheless, the
scientist had a religious duty to inquire into God's creation as a Gloria, to vex
and contort nature and force it to yield up in works all the potentialities inherent in creation. If God made the winds, Bacon reasoned, and man's science,
through an understanding of winds, invented sails, then man was merely
bringing to realization what had always been present, though hidden, in that
initial creation. The New Atlantis was a society of scientist-priests who were
Christian and submitted their works to the teachings of the Gospel, expunging
from the world-utopia both pagan philosophy and pagan moral principles.
This was the ideal of the new union of science and Christianity.

Bacon can be turned into a representative of the rising bourgeoisie, with its
lust for power symbolized in his college of experimental science for practical
ends, only by ignoring the moral and religious frame of his works, which led
Comenius and his followers to incorporate them into Pansophia. When Rosicrucians and other mystics like John Heydon plagiarized parts of the *New Atlantis* in their religious utopias, they were not doing as much violence to
Bacon's spirit as some twentieth-century commentators, who have transformed him into an industrial engineer interested in the multiplication of big-
ger and better gadgets. If Bacon's medical works emphasize the cure of disease,
it is not with a view to prolonging sensate pleasures but to ease the passage of
man through this vale of tears into the next world.

But to right the balance in the presentation of Bacon's utopia, lest the religious Judeo-Christian element be overplayed, it is wise to introduce a quotation from one of his earliest manuscripts that exudes a very different spirit, one
that borders on hubris. In the *Masculine Birth of Time* (ca. 1602) he addressed his
imaginary disciple:

"My dear, dear boy, what I purpose is to unite you with *things themselves* in a
chaste, holy, and legal wedlock; and from this association you will secure an
increase beyond all the hopes and prayers of ordinary marriages, to wit, a
blessed race of Heroes or Supermen who will overcome the immeasurable
helplessness and poverty of the human race, which cause it more destruction
than all giants, monsters, or tyrants, and will make you peaceful, happy, prosperous, and secure."[28]

The contrarieties of Bacon's personality are clearly mirrored in the ambivalences of his world view.

10

Campanella's City of the Sun

THE ANIMUS of Francis Bacon against Aristotle was equaled by that of his contemporary a thousand miles away, the monk Tommaso Campanella, who virtually at the same moment was venting his fury against the dominance of the pagan Greek in Christian philosophy. Aristotle was stifling these young geniuses. Wherever they turned, into whatever field of knowledge they ventured —the physical world, logic, metaphysics, poetics—he stood impregnable, his dicta mumbled through the mouths of hundreds of unthinking schoolmasters throughout Christian Europe. By the end of the sixteenth century the orthodoxy of Aristotle was all that the official theological establishments of the Christian churches had in common. Aristotle had been attacked earlier in the century by the northern humanists, and vain Scholastic logic-choppers had been satirized with wild glee in the writings of Rabelais. But Aristotle had lived on in the textbooks of schools and seminaries as if his reputation had never been impugned. Now the dam suddenly burst, and he became the symbolic target of young rebels. In the post-Trentine Catholic world, to criticize Aristotle for whatever reason was an advertisement of heresy. Amid the bewildering, subtle, theological controversies of the Reformation and the Counter-Reformation, heterodoxy could disguise itself in a thousand masks, and it soon became evident to the Catholic authorities that antagonism to Aristotle warranted their immediate suspicion. When in his first printed work the son of a Calabrian shoemaker declared himself an open enemy of Aristotle's system, which he derided as overornamented raving, his fate was sealed.

Prometheus in a Naples Dungeon

Campanella attended local schools in the ancient town of Stilo, Calabria, where his phenomenal intellectual gifts were early recognized. The possibility of a career in the law was dependent upon higher studies in Naples, and a relative there was prepared to accept him into his household. Instead of pursuing a secular calling, which his father favored, Campanella became fascinated by a traveling Dominican preacher, and in 1582, at the age of fourteen, he entered the monastery of Placanica. After a year's novitiate he became a Dominican monk, adopted the name Tommaso, and throughout his life remained loyal, by performing marvelous feats of exegesis, to the doctrines of Saint Thomas Aquinas. The young Campanella had been beguiled by eloquence, the miracles of the saints, and the iron power of the syllogism.

The brilliant neophyte quickly aroused hostility among his fellow monks, of whom he was contemptuous, and he was advised to escape to Germany or to Constantinople, but he stayed on. At San Giorgio Morgeto he studied Aristotelian logic, physic, and metaphysics in accordance with the accepted rule, while devouring in secret the whole corpus of ancient science and philosophy

—Democritus, Plato, the Stoics, Galen—and retaining in his memory whatever he read. His first colossal project, the "De Investigatione Rerum," began to take shape, and he conducted a constant dialectical war with his professors and the authors he was reading. Once he had embarked on a course of eternal negation, the prelude to new creation, his own destructive prowess flung him into the depths of despair. He has told of his suffering through the long night, as the weakness of Aristotelian arguments on the immortality of the soul was gradually revealed to him.[1]

At Nicastro, where he was sent after a reorganization of studies in the Dominican order, his battles with Aristotle and with the professors who were his advocates grew increasingly acerb. For Campanella, as for Bruno, Bacon, and a whole line of later Pansophists, Aristotle was the monster whom a new Saint George had to slay, a negative identity, a satanic philosopher. Campanella was outraged at the thought that Christianity had enslaved itself to an Antichrist who affirmed the eternity of the world. It was this same Aristotle, Campanella later complained to the cardinals and the Holy Father from his Naples prison, who had rendered him odious to his brethren and caused him to be persecuted by the priests of his own church.[2]

With a warning that he would come to a bad end, in 1588 Campanella was despatched to a theological house of studies at Cosenza. There he knew the rapture of a great illumination when the monks, who used to pass forbidden books among themselves, gave him the works of Bernardino Telesio of Cosenza, a South Italian master. Though Campanella composed an elegy on Telesio's death, he never succeeded in meeting his heroic spiritual mentor, who drew his truths from the *natura delle cose* and not from the assertions of mere men. The teachers of Scholastic philosophy were troubled by Campanella's infatuation with Telesio, and he was sent off to a retreat.

Campanella left the monasteries of Calabria without the consent of his superiors and joined the occult group of investigators in the circle of Giambattista della Porta in Naples. The *Philosophia Sensibus Demonstrata*, published in 1591 when Campanella was only twenty-three, was a manifesto in Telesio's spirit and provoked the first of Campanella's many trials for demonic practices and heresy—with charges of sodomy thrown in. The ponderous tome of more than five hundred pages grandiloquently announced itself as a work in which the errors of Aristotle and the Peripatetics, including their recent apologist Jacobus Antonius Marta, were exposed, and the thought of Telesio and of Plato and other ancient writers confirmed. The young hero appeared in battle array to defeat Aristotle by his own words. But what of that other Thomas from the south of Italy, the heavenly doctor from Aquino whose work had been incorporated as dogma in the decisions of the Council of Trent? Had he not leaned on Aristotle? With a loyalty to Aquinas that neither he nor his even more rash contemporary, Giordano Bruno, ever abandoned, Campanella turned the great Schoolman's seeming dependence upon Aristotle into a mere dialectical exercise that had really aimed at uncovering his pagan falsehoods. And for further support Campanella amassed direct citations from Saint Augustine against the heathen philosopher who had dominated the Christian world. Campanella drew the line sharply between friends and enemies. The book was dedicated to a noble, Mario del Tufo, who had sheltered him in Naples, and was prefaced by an account of Campanella's quarrels with his Dominican teachers. Campanella was proud of his vocation and of his birthplace, and he identified himself on the title page as "a Calabrian of Stylo and of the order of preachers."

Campanella remained orthodox in his affirmations of dogma: the virginity of Mary, the Fall of man and his redemption through the Son of God, the creation of the world ex nihilo, the truth of Scriptures, the authority of the Church. The nature of man was conceived in terms of a Platonic triad—body, mind, spirit. But the Aristotelian doctrine of matter and form was outrightly rejected and the truth of the senses validated. Bold declarations about the separation of science and religion accompanied Campanella's professions of faith. Physical science, knowledge of the physical world, was not a matter of faith and the Holy Church had no concern with it.[3] Campanella presented himself as the restorer of a pristine truth about the world that had been forgotten. Telesio had reduced the natural world to a dyadic metaphor after the manner of the pre-Socratics—the polarity of heat and cold. Campanella adopted a more ancient symbolic dualism—father-sun and mother-earth. A radical reliance on the senses as the source of truth about the natural world and an uncompromising denial of Aristotle could hardly be tolerated by the Church hierarchy, especially when accompanied by violent polemics against teachers and colleagues.

Though Campanella denounced astrology in his first book, there were tales that he engaged in occult practices. Ugly stories were spread about his relations with della Porta and with a young Jew who had taught him the Kabbala. Among the lower social classes all science was tinged with an imputation of diabolism and witchcraft. But Campanella was moving out of his class into the circles of the rich and the powerful, who nurtured the new ideas out of curiosity. Wealthy dilettantes played the Maecenas to the young genius endowed with a terrifying, captivating energy, and they supplied him with books. For years Campanella avoided his native town, so that his father and brother did not recognize him when he returned. His father could neither read nor write and thought of his son's fortunate connections in terms of money—perhaps he might help marry off his wretched sisters.

In 1592 Campanella was arrested on the denunciation of a monk who was his adversary and he was imprisoned in the jail of the papal nuncio. His Naples appearance before a tribunal of Dominican friars drew enough attention to be commented on by the ambassador from Tuscany, who extolled him as one of the "più rari ingegni" in Italy.[4] Campanella succeeded in refuting the accusation of his envious monastic brother that he had a "familiar spirit"; but the plaguing questions of his fellow monks continued. Where had this son of a poor shoemaker who had attended only monastery schools, never a university, acquired all this knowledge? The suspicion that he had a demon could not be downed. With the insolence of youth, Campanella answered his judges that he burned more oil in his lamps than they consumed wine.[5] Monastic cannibalism and superstition pursued him throughout his life. But there were some monks who dared to join the prodigy despite the prevailing animosity. Others felt an adoration tinged with fear. Later he even acquired apostles: There was a Fra Dionysio who thought him a Messiah. The sentence imposed at the end of Campanella's first trial was unusually mild. He was ordered to return to Calabria and to recite penitential prayers and the office of the dead three times on the Sabbath. The accusation had been reduced to his approval of the doctrines of Telesio and his failure to follow Saint Thomas.

The sojourn in Naples had been a period of explosive creativity. He dashed off in all directions writing books almost as fast as he had once devoured them: In addition to the *Philosophia Sensibus Demonstrata,* he composed a treatise on dreams (*De Insomniis*) and *De Sphera Aristarchi,* a comparison of the Pythagorean with the Copernican doctrine. More and more he turned to the early philosophers with whom the South Italian world of Magna Graecia was identified, and established a filiation with them. The man who sprang out of nothing found himself a spiritual ancestry. Like Pythagoras he would lead a sect to save the world. His heroes all hailed from the regions south of Naples—Joachim of Fiore, Thomas Aquinas, Telesio of Cosenza, Pythagoras, Empedocles. But there was also another South Italian prophet whose name was soon unmentionable: Giordano Bruno of Nola, burned in Rome while Campanella was being tried again, this time on more serious charges, in Naples.[6]

Instead of returning to Calabria after his first trial, Campanella defied his superiors and set off for Rome, Florence (where he hoped to arrange a professorship at Pisa or Siena), then Padua. En route, at Bologna, a group of "false friars" robbed him of all his manuscripts. At Padua he met Galileo and other scholars.[7] After successfully defending himself against a charge of immorality, he enjoyed a rare year of peace, which gave him an opportunity to recompose some of the philosophical works that had been torn away from him. In early 1594, his manuscripts were seized and he was arraigned before the Holy Office in Padua for discussing matters of faith with a Jew, writing *De Tribus Impostoribus,* accepting Democritus, and criticizing the order and doctrine of the Church. At the trial, he was absolved of being a Democritan and of writing the notorious atheistic tract, but the case was referred to Rome for further consideration. There he was tortured and in 1596 sentenced to abjure publicly his heretical doctrines. A year later he was jailed again on a charge of heresy, but released on condition that his Dominican superiors confine him to a monastery, and in August of 1598 he was returned to Calabria.

In the provincial exile to which he was banished Campanella followed his vocation rather lackadaisically. There are reports that from time to time he involved himself in local affairs. He tried to make peace between the bishop and the king's fiscal; he drew up plans for a church. Monks caught him standing in the choir abstracted, not praying. In the *Quod Reminiscentur* he later confessed that the temple of God was hateful to him. Instead of singing God's praises, he considered prayer a chore, like ploughing and digging. Arrogant, he thought himself more worthy than his brothers and he disdained his superiors. He managed to absent himself from his monastery, roaming the countryside, curing the sick, leading the peasants to believe that he was gifted with thaumaturgical powers.[8]

As early as 1593 Campanella had become the prophet of a plan for a universal organization of society under a new papacy, set forth in his treatises *De Monarchia Christianorum* and *De Regimine Ecclesiae,* and two years later in the *Discorsi ai principi d'Italia* and *Dialogo politico contro Luterani, Calvinisti ed altri eretici.* Campanella was possessed by a vision of the reordering of humanity, a total reformation of the Church, and a return of mankind to a state of innocence. The time of troubles was upon the world, witness the incursions of the Turks in Calabria, the internecine conflicts within the Church, the religious schisms, the wars of Christian kings, and the strange configurations in the heavens—all signs of a coming great transformation.

Campanella never focused exclusively on one enemy. Aristotle might remain the chief antagonist; but this passionate son of the Bay of Squillace encompassed the whole political and moral world, and the ruthless local barons and officials of the Spanish monarchy made him a violent opponent of both the political and the ecclesiastical establishments. Orthodoxy is indivisible, and the young monk who alienated his superiors with his dialectical skills became the foe of Spanish hegemony over his native province, where ancient liberties had been wiped out and the venerable traditions of independent cities had been trampled upon. But the poetic tirades of Campanella are not overflowing with sympathy for the sufferings of the peasantry. In one of his later poems he lashed out against the people, who remained for him, as for a long line of utopian reformers in modern times, the *bestia*. Hatred of the Spanish overlord was not balanced by intense love of the people. There was another alternative, the reign of a philosopher-king or of a pope who would become both the temporal and spiritual ruler of the world.

The approach of the year 1600 spawned millenarian visions, prophecies, and Kabbalist numerological demonstrations of great changes to come. Few potentates turned a deaf ear when glorious futures were predicted for them. The combination of a nine and a seven in the millenarian count was irresistible. An astronomer like Kepler out of necessity played the astrologer, and the writers of almanacs who foretold wars, natural disasters, plagues, assassinations of kings and princes, famines, and devastations could not be far wrong as long as they remained shrewdly general in their prognostications. The passing of the year 1600 did not end the passion for futurology. When the religious wars drove troops of barbarians through the heartland of central Europe, the prophets became more precise as the wretched of the earth demanded concrete consolations. Monarchs who had been persuaded to follow a course that proved disastrous then simply executed the false prophets. But no one could stop seers from interpreting portents and other men from believing them.

Before the fateful year 1600 Calabria had been torn by factions of petty barons and small-time condottieri. Conflicts raged between Spanish officials and local bishops, who excommunicated them and then had to flee for their lives. The people eked out a wretched existence from a hard soil; prey to superstitions, they lived in a world of devils and witches. Campanella, the monk with secret powers, was both feared and admired. As a Dominican preacher he moved crowds with his eloquence. When he talked of signs and omens, earthquakes and floods, they knew he spoke truth because they had witnessed such prodigies of nature. In South Italy an undercurrent of heterodox doctrine and belief flowed on beneath the surface of approved institutional teaching. The Waldensians who settled in Calabria may have spread their heresy. The learned son of a shoemaker and brother of a shoe peddler, related to a nun who was clairvoyant, could be a new savior. He later compared himself to the prophet Amos, but he also dared to think that he was destined for an even greater part in the divine plan.

In 1599 Campanella was implicated in a conspiracy to oust the Spaniards and establish a republic in Calabria. In this plot to liberate his native province disparate elements converged—libertine monks, freedom-seeking zealots who detested the foreigners, declassed nobles hardly differentiated from bandits. But Campanella the utopian visionary never conceived of the affair as a mere local episode. Everything he touched was set in a universalist frame. After the

Spanish yoke had been cast off, the reign of a pure religion in a Republic of the Sun would be inaugurated, a faith bolstered by arguments from astrology, history, sacred prophecies—a babel of foretellings.[9]

A summary of Campanella's beliefs at this period, detailed by fellow monks turned informers, was bursting with heresies, enough for burning. The hodgepodge of sacrilegious and blasphemous utterances need not be credited, but this is what his judges heard from terror-struck witnesses:

There is no God. There is only nature which we call God. The name of God is an empty name. All the sacraments of the Church are nothing but the rules of dominion, or reasons of power for states, and there is nothing else in the sacraments. The sacraments were not established by God, but invented by men as signs of social cohesion. The most awesome sacrament of the Eucharist is a triviality and is not truly the Body and Blood of Our Lord. Demons do not exist, nor does Hell or Paradise. Nobody has ever seen devils. These things were invented and recounted to instill fear in men and make them fervent believers. The words "Every time that you do this, do it in memory of me" do not have the meaning that the Church credits, but mean only "When you eat, remember me." The crucifix is not to be adored. Mary Magdalen and Martha were sister-lovers of Christ in the wicked sense. The most Holy Virgin was not a virgin. The act of making love is permissible. Miracles are not true but are considered so from way back by common opinion. The miracles were recounted by the apostles who were friends of Christ and thus are not to be believed. Campanella himself can perform miracles. Moses did not part the Red Sea miraculously; the phenomenon of division was caused naturally by the ebbing of the tide. The Trinity is not true, but fake and monstrous because it is presented with three heads. The dimming of the sun at the moment of Christ's death was not miraculous and universal, but natural and local. Christ did not rise again, but was pilfered from the grave. The Pope is Antichrist. The authority of the Pope is usurped and tyrannical. Singing in church is silly and something of an insult to God. The initials J. N. R. J. on the Cross do not signify Jesus of Nazareth King of the Jews, but a Hebrew word vulgar and abusive. The abstention from meat on certain days is not a moral rule; one ought to eat it deliberately. Sin is nothing except when it is linked to punishment and is known as such by men. Misdeeds secretly committed are not sins. Brother Tommaso Campanella declared himself chosen by God to preach the new law and eliminate abuses in the Holy Church of God, especially those of prelates. Brother Tommaso Campanella wants to strive with the Roman Pontiff in matters of faith and persuade him to yield by virtue of the miracles he has made. Brother Tommaso Campanella considers himself invulnerable. No weapon can hurt him.[10]

At the Naples trial after his arrest on September 6, Campanella was charged with both heresy and insurrection, and under torture he confessed. (The record meticulously included shrieks of rage in Calabrian dialect and the earthy curses of the people among whom he was born.) To escape the death penalty, he feigned madness,[11] or so it is conjectured, a posture he maintained through thirty-six hours of further interrogation on the rack. The trial closed in 1602 with a sentence of life imprisonment pronounced by the Holy Office. It is hard to understand why they did not do away with him. Perhaps the two rival jurisdictions of the Holy Office and the Viceroy of Spain, who were both concerned with Campanella's crimes, negated each other. It is perplexing that what may have been stage insanity was accepted as real, since such behavior was not rare, and manuals and compendia carefully drawn up to guide Inquisitors specifically warned them to be wary of simulated madness.[12] Campanella carried it off, sometimes keeping up the lunatic antics back in his cell so that his keepers and other prisoners thought him crazy. Yet when the prosecuting attorney of the Viceroy placed informers in cells adjacent to Campanella's, he seemed to converse rationally with one of them. They talked in Latin, and if the reports are correct they cast doubt on sustained madness, though there may have been sporadic outbursts. Campanella himself is hardly a reliable witness on his behavior, as he kept altering the story of his persecutions.

During Campanella's twenty-seven years in the jails of Naples, from 1599 to 1626, barbaric treatment alternated with ordinary detention. For long periods he was chained in a dank dungeon and almost starved to death. In a manuscript introduction to the *Atheismus Triumphatus* he told of being dragged through fifty jails and formally tortured seven times.[13] But with time and reports that his madness had lifted, he acquired books, received letters, was allowed visitors. The physical suffering had made him cunning; it did not rid him of his messianic fantasies. Successive Spanish governors of the prisons—he ended up in secular custody—conversed with him for their own diversion. In repeated pleas for his liberation, Campanella rehearsed the history of his life, touching up the self-portrait to suit the occasion. He was set free in Naples on May 23, 1626, through the intervention of Pope Urban VIII, only to be reimprisoned in Rome. On January 11, 1629, he was released once again, but his life was jeopardized by rumors of his complicity in a plot purportedly engineered by his disciple Pignatelli, and he was forced to take refuge in a monastery at Frascati. Finally, in 1634, on the advice and with the complicity of the Pope, he escaped from Italy and with the help of the French ambassador clandestinely made his way to France.[14]

During his incarceration after the Calabrian fiasco, Campanella finished the Italian version of the *City of the Sun* (1602). For thirty-seven years thereafter he continued to labor for the realization of a utopia on a world scale through the most outlandish political mechanisms. Though Bruno was rarely mentioned by Campanella in his writings, his destiny was an uncanny replica of his predecessor's.

Campanella drew from the same hermetic sources as Bruno had, though the Christian nature of his utopia is less debatable. If Bacon considered himself the trumpeter of the new science, Campanella in a word-play on his name thought he was heralding its triumph from the "campanile" and his books published in the 1630s bore the symbol of the bell on the title page. His life is testimony to the power of a fixed idea to maintain itself and the human being it possessed, transcending physical and spiritual agonies. He fascinated his followers and his persecutors alike. But toward the end of his days, though he was received by the King of France and by Richelieu, Descartes and other French men of learning treated him like a crackpot, a miserable old relic of another age and another world.[15]

Convert or Dissembler

After his capture by the Spaniards during the Calabrian conspiracy, the imprisoned Campanella at first remained defiant. Finally, the content and tone of his works began to alter, and the rebel of 1599 appeared to become a docile defender of Catholic orthodoxy and papal supremacy. Was the change a deception to end persecution? Was it the overt doctrine preached while his covert belief remained the same, a duplicity practiced for almost four decades? Or was it monkish Machiavellianism, a ruse to draw men to his system by indirection? Or is there greater moral consistency between his first stance and his last, which shows a growth and maturation of ideas rather than a volte-face? For more than a century these questions have absorbed scholars intrigued by a philosophy that becomes increasingly difficult to penetrate with the publication of additional manuscripts from an original hoard of over a hundred. As with so many figures of the Italian past, the alignment of contemporary clericals and anticlericals makes the controversy vituperative.

The lives and works of men cannot escape the vicissitudes of fortune over the course of time. But few authors have been read from such a bewildering variety of perspectives as Campanella.[16] Seventeenth-century English writers referred to him as a "second Machiavelli," and as recent a historian as Friedrich Meinecke allowed him a chapter in the history of the idea of *Staatsraison*. Campanella has made no great splash in the history of philosophy, and Hegel devoted a scant eight pages to him, less than to Bruno. But in the seventeenth century a whole group of Rhenish Lutheran professors and ministers were attracted to his works and he became a major source for the Pansophic doctrines of the Germanic world. Today literate Europeans and Americans associate his name with his speaking-picture utopia, *The City of the Sun*.

Not many scholars outside Italy have ploughed through his politico-philosophical and theological treatises or read his poetical works. Yet his name has found its way into the most unlikely places. On an obelisk in Red Square in Moscow it is inscribed among the fathers of the Russian Revolution. Giovanni Di Napoli, whose book is one of the more recent of the general synthesizing works on Campanella, candidly proclaimed his intention to return to the Catholic Church what belonged to it:[17] Campanella was perhaps an innovator, but he was no heretic. Luigi Amabile, a nineteenth-century professor of pathological anatomy, had combed the archives of the Church and of every major country in Europe in search of Campanella, and his five large volumes of texts and biographical commentary discourage any latecomer from going over the same territory to pick up gleanings after the great thresher has moved through. Amabile was the first to examine the archives of the Holy Office when they became temporarily available in the 1880s, and his conclusions were unequivocal: Campanella played a major role in the Calabrian conspiracy against the Spanish monarchy, and his ideas were heretical. He was an anticlerical, a patriot, a freedom fighter, and a herald of the new science. His madness was faked with the hope of escaping the Inquisitors and carrying on the battle for his heterodox principles. Anything he wrote or said after torture was a deliberate attempt to circumvent and outwit his persecutors. Amabile created a Campanella who, once apprehended, acted out a "continuous simulation" for the sake of his native province and the whole world.[18] The City of the Sun was the kind of society Campanella wished to see implanted everywhere.

Neither Amabile, Di Napoli, nor their partisans conceived of the ambivalence of the prophet to his mission, what might be called the "Jonah complex."[19] The academic rationalists of the 1880s had to take forthright and definitive positions, to draw the lines sharply. Campanella either did or did not feign madness; the *City of the Sun* was a passing fancy or it was an action program to be realized in the near future; his ultimate vision was a naturalistic manifesto or a reborn universal papal theocracy. That the grand utopian obsessives have moments of anguish and doubt; that commitment to a principle could be accompanied by great fluidity in its mechanisms of achievement; that the hysteric who puts on an act is a sufferer; that under torture, lines are blurred between the hero, the traitor, and the dissimulator—such propositions were unacceptable to the bookmen. What did Campanella believe in: a deist-like primordial wisdom; the truth of Hermes Trismegistus as revealed in the Renaissance; Jesus Christ? Or was he, Tommaso Campanella the system giver, the new angelic doctor for the Church, like that other doctor of Aquino whose name he inherited when he became a Dominican monk? If the rigid academic division between clericals and anticlericals obfuscates more than it illuminates, Campanella's self-image revealed in his poetry and his letters is easier to grasp. Megalomania triumphed over self-abasement. He was Prometheus bound to the rock in the Caucasus; he was the Campanella (campanile) calling men to drink their mother's milk; he was Columbus whom everyone mocked when he said he had discovered a new world; he was the new Messiah, like the Galilean whose life was a prefiguration of his. At thirty-two had come his great trial.

Some scholars have posited a break in Campanella's life around 1606, when he began to despair of liberation. To the subsequent period belong his apparent reconversion to orthodox Catholicism (under the direction of his confessor Berillo)[20] and his abandonment of the notorious ideas that had become attached to his name. Since many of his works originally composed during the 1590s were stolen, lost, or confiscated by the Holy Office, he had to reconstruct them during his quarter-century of imprisonment. That despite his amazing memory these writings were altered during their redrafting is a plausible conclusion, but a question persists to what degree they were deliberately modified by his new circumstances and what portions were composed with the primary purpose of ingratiating himself with the Spaniards and the papacy, in order to secure a release that would permit him to carry on his mission. The evidence is ambiguous. Remnants of a youthful vision became entangled with politic argument. Campanella could assume almost any position and defend it with consummate dialectical skill and citations from respectworthy Church authority—witness the convoluted arguments with which he espoused community of women (of service, but not of the bed) and his demonstrations that the most venerated Fathers of the Church had attacked property and advocated community.

After the turn of the century, Campanella was not engaged in intellectual speculation, he was arguing for his life. Half of his years were spent in verbal self-defense in which he tailored his reasoning to his listener—an inquisitor, a pope, an emperor, a Spanish viceroy, a foreign visitor who might conceivably intervene in his behalf. With time his boldness, or foolhardiness, was softened. Ideas that he had once proclaimed with bravado were modified, their sharp edges smoothed. He could even fawn and beg. Surely he modified his views about the imminence of the great transformation. In 1599 he was still in the activist millenarian tradition: The end was near and he was hastening the Coming. But in the course of his incarceration he acquired a new appreciation of the power that held him in its toils and lacerated his flesh. The talk of an immediate "mutation" in the nature of things that had captivated his followers during the Calabrian conspiracy—one Giovanni Battista Vitale testified before the Inquisition that Campanella read the signs for the year 1600 to mean the coming of a "new law" and the return of every man to his "libertà naturale"— gave way to visions of the resurrection and the reign of Christ far less precisely dated. The theological manuscripts of the second decade of the seventeenth century forcefully repudiated the libertinism of the Beghard heretics and those who pretended to be free from the restrictions of the laws of God. Campanella preached obedience to Church rules.

Throughout the early interrogations that followed upon the Calabrian plot Campanella had contended that his plan for a republic was contingent upon other political events. Prophecy had taught him that a great religio-political upheaval was about to transpire, perhaps the triumph of Antichrist just before the victory of Christ. There were portents that the Turks, who had been making successful incursions along the coast of Calabria, would land in force. In that event the faithful, following the example of the ancient Venetians or the Christians during the Saracen invasion of Spain, would flee inland to a mountain stronghold. Campanella's Republic of the Sun was to be the government of Christian refugees if the Spaniards were defeated and the Turks triumphed, and from their fortress the citizens were to launch the reconquest. He had only devised a means of succor if the dire prophecies for the year 1600 were fulfilled. Happily they had not come to pass, but he was innocent for he had made no predictions himself; he had simply been misled by Daniel, Joachim, Saint Brigida, and others.[21]

As for the charge that he meant to join with the Turks against the Spanish king, even Maurizio di Rinauldi, the local freebooter, in his final confession before he was executed for participation in the uprising, had not claimed that Campanella was privy to negotiations with the fleet of Cicala the Turkish commander. If his accusers would read his works written in the 1590s, Campanella pleaded in his apology, they would realize that he had always favored the Spaniards as the saviors of Christendom from the infidels and seen in their universal monarchy the preliminary to the spiritual lordship of the papacy over the whole world.[22]

Fra Dionysio and Fra Pietro were the dearly beloved; the monks who had informed against him were wretches and bearers of false witness. Maurizio and Contestabile were bandits. He had met with them only in order to effect a peace among warring local factions, and at one time they had threatened his life. Admittedly, he had favored a republic, but since it was only a provisional plan in case the Spaniards were defeated, he did not merit the death penalty. Besides, he was a monk and should not be tried by the civil authority. His interrogators hoped to gain favor with the king by convicting him, his accusers were liars who led scandalous lives.

In prison the grapevine kept members of the group apprised of how each had borne up under torture, who had informed, who had retracted. Campanella composed love sonnets for those who remained silent and he vilified the squealers. Then he himself was broken and confessed to the plan for a republic, though he soon reversed himself and explained it away. There were moments of shame at his incapacity to endure, along with self-justifications that varied as the years dragged on. Witnesses died, papers were destroyed or misplaced, and the heaps of testimony lay neglected until the nineteenth century. On July 6,

1638, he wrote to Ferdinand II de' Medici, "The future age will judge us because the present always crucifies its benefactors; but then they will resurrect us on the third day or the third century."[23]

The City of the Sun

For some scholars the first Italian manuscript version of the *Città del Sole,* a dialogue between a Knight Hospitaler of Jerusalem and a Genoese sea captain just returned from Taprobane (an ancient name for Ceylon or Sumatra), remains the most authentic expression of Campanella's thought. The Latin editions of Frankfort (1623) and Paris (1637), published in his lifetime, and the posthumous text of Utrecht (1643), as well as a variety of manuscripts, present alternatives significant for students of Campanella's deviations, but the core remains unchanged.[24] The work is surely the most succinct of his writings and has become the mark of his identity in Western culture, setting a utopian pattern for scores of imitators. The Calabrian revolt had been described by the informants of the Inquisition in Naples as Campanella's attempt to create a state in which philosophers like himself would rule. Though he had at one point tried to relate his action to the millenarianism of Joachim of Fiore and other prophets, later there emerged a quasi-rational pattern in the universalization of an uprising that would move in stages from the possession of Calabria to the Kingdom of Naples to the Mediterranean and to the world. The City of the Sun was a model in petto for the whole earth.

Through the report of the Genoese mariner, a feeble reincarnation of More's Hythloday, Campanella presented a city under a single ruler called Sole, or the Metafisico, who incorporated in himself all power, all knowledge, and all love. Under him were three aides, Pon, Sin, and Mor, or Potestà, Sapienza, and Amore, representing each of the three jurisdictions into which the city was divided. Thus Sapienza had supervision over all the sciences and of the doctors and teachers of liberal and mechanical arts. Under his direction were as many officials as there were *scienze,* though it is not quite clear from their titles precisely what areas of knowledge they covered. There was an Astrologo, a Cosmografo, a Geometra, a Loico, a Rettorico, a Grammatico, a Medico, a Fisico, a Politico, and a Morale. The categories seem quite traditional, with few innovations. What is new is the role that scientific knowledge played in the administration of society. Science occupied a third of the directing personnel of the state. Through these supervisors, vital information on eugenics was transmitted to the important branch of government that regulated sexual intercourse. Moreover, Sapienza did not allow knowledge to proliferate at random; it had to be incorporated in a single book, read to all the people as in the Pythagorean utopia of scientist-rulers. The precedent came naturally to a son of Stilo, a citizen of Magna Graecia, highly conscious of his pre-Christian and pre-Roman culture.

Not only the attempt to popularize scientific knowledge but the manner of doing so was imaginative. Scientific knowledge was translated into pictures painted on both sides of all seven concentric walls of the circular city and on a globe beneath the cupola of the central temple, where the sphere with its constellations was drawn in the traditional manner. This conception is related to Campanella's emphasis on the visual and on concrete illustration as the superior means for communication, in contrast with Scholastic and Aristotelian abstract verbalization. The world seen in pictures was believed to be more real than the world described in words—this was a major Campanellan notion that more than three hundred years after the composition of *The City of the Sun* had curious repercussions in Soviet Russia. Gorki had read the utopia in Italy, talked about it to Lunacharsky and Lenin, and the brief passage about the depiction of science on walls became an inspiration for official dicta on realistic socialist art. One need not pretend that this was the sole basis for the freezing of artistic expression in the Soviet Union; but the patronage of Campanella was openly acknowledged.

In *The City of the Sun* the illustrations on the seven rings of walls were a way of presenting both the unity and the proper division of knowledge. Captions identifying each picture were limited to a few words of explanation. The city itself became a total book of knowledge displayed in a set order, not unlike the cycles of frescoes in a Christian church—the facts of science have replaced the events of sacred history. On the outside wall of the Solarian church located on a hill in the center of the city the stars were depicted and labeled. From the roof of the temple there hung seven golden lamps, named after the seven planets, which burned eternally. (Some recent commentators have conceived of them as protective hermetic astrological devices, though the 1643 edition noted a parallel with the biblical description of the Temple.) The concentric city walls displayed mathematical figures, more numerous than the inventions of Euclid and Archimedes, together with their important propositions; a map of the whole world with a table of all its provinces, their rites, customs, and laws, and the Solarian alphabet superimposed over their languages; a collection of metals; all manner of wines and liquors and carafes containing medicines that cured "almost" all illnesses; various kinds of herbs and trees, their virtues and the correspondence of their natures with the stars and metals and parts of the human body, information of use in the practice of medicine. (The Paracelsian doctrine was incorporated as a science in a manner that Bacon would not have approved but that was not alien to the medical chemistry of the Rhineland Christian utopians who accepted Campanella.) Then followed sea creatures, animals, and reptiles, as well as perfected animals of which Europeans had no knowledge. The inside of the sixth ring featured the mechanical arts and their inventors, while outside were portraits of lawgivers and religious leaders along with Alexander, Caesar, and other heroes, "whom they do not make much of." Christ and the twelve apostles were depicted in a special location, where they were honored as *supra homines*. When the Genoese admiral—his status changes in different manuscripts and texts—asked the Solarians how they knew about the historic figures of Europe, they answered in words almost identical with those of Bacon's Elder on Bensalem: They had clandestine ambassadors in all countries who reported on these matters. As a consequence of the pictorial display, children while playing learned all the sciences before they were ten years old.

The possibility that Bacon saw the Frankfort (1623) edition of the *Civitas Solis* cannot be excluded, since it is not definitively known when Bacon last put his hand to the *New Atlantis*. Andreae and his friends probably were aware of Campanella's work well before the publication of the *Christianopolis* (1619)[25] and *The City of the Sun*, since Wense at one time wished to call their Christian fraternity a "civitas solis," the name Campanella used in his Latin version. The whole issue of priority is trivial, because the three prototypes of a seventeenth-century speaking-picture utopia differ radically from one another in most of their exterior institutional arrangements. What the utopias of Bacon, Campanella, and Andreae do have in common is the prominence of physical science and men of science as the moving spirit of future society, a major conceptual landmark in Western culture.[26]

The scandal of the Campanellan utopia was not its worship of science but its abolition of the family and of private property. Three decades after its composition Campanella was still defending his conceit as an ideal philosophical republic according to the law of nature. Affects in *The City of the Sun* are transferred from possessions to the *patria*. The Solarians have so much love for their country that it even surpasses that of the legendary Romans. Half a century earlier, in a more playful Italian utopia, Doni had extolled the advantages of freedom from personal ties and affections in a communal order. But while Doni was half joking, Campanella was in deadly earnest. In an aside, he surmised that Christian priests and monks, if emancipated from parental relationships and desires for advancement in the dignities of office, would become more holy and charitable. Apart from the powerful love of country, friendship was the bond that held together Solarian society, a sentiment that found ample opportunity for expression in war, in sickness, and in the pursuit of scientific knowledge. Where people constantly helped one another, "amor proprio" disappeared. Campanella was more circumstantial than More in communicating this new kind of feeling as the foundation of society.[27] In answer to the contention of the Knight Hospitaler that nobody wanted to work and everybody expected his neighbor to do so instead—an argument that runs through the whole history of anti-utopian thought—the mariner responded that love of country supplied the necessary motivation.

The fundamental organizational principle of the Solarians was monarchical, and their Metafisico was kept informed of everything that transpired. When the four chiefs who united in themselves spiritual and temporal power conferred, the Metafisico delivered the final decision. The officials were singled out in early childhood as embodying the virtues of liberality, magnanimity, chastity, gratitude, and pity. Below Sole the rest of the order was hierarchical: He had three subordinates, each of whom had three, each of whom in turn had three, to make a total of forty, a number that had a tradition behind it only slightly less venerable than Bacon's thirty-six Elders. All except the top four were elected; these major heads remained in office until someone who knew more than they did appeared, whereupon they voluntarily vacated their posts. Each person was rated by the head of his department, and punishments could include exile, death, an eye for an eye, prohibition of the common table, or deprivation of the right to speak to women. The prisoner in the fortified castles of Naples allowed for no jails in the City of the Sun.

The educational system was the key to the longevity of the ideal city. Elders taught the children to read while they were playing about the walls, and began to take cognizance of their special inclinations by visiting the shops of artisans with them. Bacon was rather vague about the training that prepared novices for Salomon's House; Campanella and the Continental educators of Pansophia emphasized as crucial the identification of the special calling of each individual at the earliest possible moment. There was a presumption among the Lutherans and Moravians who derived from Campanella that in each child a divine spark corresponded to one minute aspect of the divinity that was in all creatures and things. Education meant developing to the utmost that particular knowledge of which every human being was capable. In the City of the Sun the moral inclinations were watched vigilantly to ward off devilish wiles that might assail the child, who, though born with a capacity for sin, could be deterred from evil through supervision. All the Solarians acquired both a general education and an area of special competence. They attributed the development of their keen intelligences to the excellence of their pedagogic methods: Solarian children learned more in a year than Europeans in ten or fifteen.

From the age of seven on, Solarians spent four hours a day on natural sciences (*scienze naturale*), an activity that was alternated with physical exercise. Then they turned to mathematics, medicine, and other sciences. There was great competition among the young in their disputations because both in the acquisition of the sciences and in mechanical knowledge a *capo* (head) who excelled was always recognized—for all Campanella's talk about universal love he did not eliminate *concorrenza* (rivalry). The same held for those who worked in the fields, where anyone outstanding was honored as the nobler person. One of the principal elements in the Solarian system of equality involved a recasting of the very concept of *nobilità*. We, said the Genoese admiral, consider workers ignoble and call the idlers (*oziosi*) noble, an order reversed in the City of the Sun, where work had been rehabilitated. In the Italian Catholic Renaissance tradition that runs from Alberti through Bruno and Campanella, including Agostini and Doni, work does not need the elaboration of a Protestant ethic as its justification. Labor was cleansed of its stigma and everyone worked. In a rare direct reference to contemporary conditions, Campanella contrasted the Solarians' respect for labor with life in Naples, where only 50,000 of 300,000 persons were employed and the rest of the inhabitants were given over either to impoverished idleness or to luxury. En passant, Campanella improved on More and reduced the length of the working day to four hours. The Solarians were in the habit of contrasting their fortunate egalitarian condition with the miserable spectacle of other societies, where extremes of poverty and wealth corrupted everybody, where the poor were vicious, cunning, crooked, sly, bearers of false witness, while the rich were insolent, arrogant, ignorant, treacherous, pretentious about what they were not. Solarian *communità* made everyone at once rich and poor, rich because they had everything they needed, poor because they were not given to accumulation of goods. No human being was left useless. In old age the Solarians counseled the young; even a man who had only one limb could be of service in spying things out for the republic. The hardest labor generally earned the greatest honors, though mechanical arts were not deemed quite so worthy as speculative arts, whose outstanding practitioners became priests.

The Metafisico, or Sole, was the epitome of knowledge of every kind, history, mechanics, mathematics, physics, and astrology—"tutte le scienze." The only allowable limitation on this omniscience lay in the area of languages: Sole could have recourse to an interpreter. Above all, Sole had to be a metaphysician and a theologian who understood the hierarchical gradations of being and the correspondences among celestial, terrestrial, and marine things. He also had to be deeply learned in prophecies and astrology. The director of the City of the Sun was thus more than an Elder of the type that inhabited Bacon's House of Salomon. The markedly theocratic figure of Sole could not be under thirty-five, and he held office as long as he was unrivaled in knowledge. The Hospitaler in the dialogue interrupted at one point to voice his doubt that anybody could be so erudite and to observe that someone preoccupied with the sciences would not understand how to govern. The Genoese had already raised this objection with the Solarians, who in reply had contrasted the superb capacities of their Sole, a philosopher-king endowed with all three virtues of power, love, and knowledge, with the European monarchs among whom the notion prevailed that men, though ignorant, were born to rule because of noble birth or their capacity to be elected by powerful factions. No matter how dismal Sole might be at governing, one who knew so much would surely not be very cruel or wicked or tyrannical.

Through the mouth of the Solarians Campanella was again afforded a chance to attack his bête noire, Aristotle, and the belief of Europeans that one became learned by knowing the rhetoric and logic of Aristotle or some other author. Cultivating a servile memory made of a man a passive creature; he ceased to observe things, giving heed only to books, and his soul was degraded by these dead objects. Ignorant of how God ruled the universe, he understood neither the ways of God nor the ways of nature. Sole could not have managed to know so much if he were not gifted with general ingenuity, a quality that also made him skilled and alert in governance. Anybody who devoted himself exclusively to one science acquired from a book became inert and heavy. Sole's quick wit made all forms of knowledge come easily to him. Campanella drew the portrait of a ruler that was a mirror image of himself with his own temperament and in accordance with his own esteem of himself as a man of universal learning.

In Campanella's eulogies of the City of the Sun, the adjective *commune* constantly recurred. The Solarians were brought up in communal dormitories and both speculative and mechanical arts were taught to men and women in common. The women tended to perform lighter work, such as household chores and gardening, while the men took care of heavy labor. Music was wholly a feminine province and so was cooking; children served at the table. Men and women ate separately to the accompaniment of readings and music. Doctors directed the diet of the young, the aged, and the sick.[28] But despite the stress on equality and community, the officials got better victuals than others and offered a portion of their good food to those who had triumphed in scientific discussion or military exercises. The aged were supervisors, discipline was strict, and corporal punishment was not banned. Cleanliness was enforced, and the Solarians changed their white garments four times a year, when the sun entered Cancer, Capricorn, Aries, and Libra.

In the course of the educational process Solarian brotherhood was fostered within a peer group born under the same constellation. Its members were believed to be related in temperament; they dressed alike and were joined by a special bond. Names were not given by parents but by the Metafisico, who bestowed appellations upon individuals first in accordance with their character and then, as they grew up, in harmony with their performance in the arts and sciences and in war. Honored names awarded in recognition of military victories were highly prized.

When the Genoese reporter was asked about the jealousy of those not chosen to be procreators, or Solarians frustrated in some other ambition, he answered that there were no ill-disposed people among them and that everything was governed by the public, not the private, weal. Solarians did not need to resort to Plato's deception whereby the guardians were made to believe that lots, hence blind fortune, determined mating partners, since all spontaneously and voluntarily heeded the wisdom of the eugenicists. The sexual controls Plato restricted to an elite were extended to the whole society. Solarians lacked nothing of the necessities of life, by which Campanella meant simple food and clothes, and for the rest they were content to obey their officials with religious punctiliousness. Women needed no cosmetics or other artifical embellishments. Love (as distinct from sexual converse) was not prohibited and Solarians were allowed to talk about their affections and to write verse to their beloveds.

Following Plato, both men and women were trained in the art of war. The *Città del Sole* was virtually a unisex society, and in the Platonic tradition, men and women performed many of the same functions. There was only a slight difference in battle dress, women wearing their *sopraveste* below the knee, men above. They were fearless in battle because they believed in the immortality of the soul. Warlike exercises were constant to prevent the Solarians from turning into cowards, and preparation for battle became a unifying force in society. Though women did not venture far from the city they assisted the men. Children on horseback were thrust into the midst of the battle so that, like *lupicini,* they might become accustomed to the taste of blood. The existence of four other kingdoms on the island whose inhabitants were envious of the Solarians kept them on the alert. Sometimes they liberated a city that was being tyrannized, allowing the enemy a brief opportunity to submit voluntarily before they let loose their troops. Ordinarily Potestà made the military decisions, but in matters of great moment he turned for advice to Amore, Sapienza and Sole, and everyone twenty and over, including women, joined in a grand deliberative assembly. Desertion in the face of the enemy was severely punished, even as extraordinary bravery in helping a comrade was rewarded with a Roman triumph. When the enemy was defeated the Solarians immediately destroyed his walls and killed his chiefs, the whole procedure taking place in a single day. Then a firm peace was promptly established. Campanella had read his Machiavelli.

Many details of the *Città del Sole* were lifted straight out of More's *Utopia,* and Campanella was proud of his model. Gold was despised in both societies. The Solarian children laughed when they saw foreign merchants part with their goods for a few coins, just as Utopian children were hilarious at the sight of ambassadors wearing gold chains. The Solarians protected themselves from being infected with the evil customs of slaves and foreigners. They either sold slaves captured in war or assigned them to work outside the city limits. Foreigners were fed for three days, taken on a tour of the city under Solarian guard, and, should they wish to become citizens, were tested for a month in the surrounding area and a month in the city. If approved, they were received with great ceremony. Though convinced that the whole world would ultimately come around to their way of living, Solarians maintained contact with China, Siam, Cochinchina, and Calcutta, in order to adopt any better techniques practiced among them and to forestall surprise moves on their part.

The City of the Sun had been established under optimal astrological auspices, which the Genoese sailor enumerated for the Knight Hospitaler. Their Brahmin heritage had first led the founders who hailed from India to reject meat, but when they came to realize that even consuming grass meant killing living things, they were persuaded that the ignoble had been created to feed the more noble. The Solarians were temperate and did not suffer from diseases, which they imputed to the exercises that purged their humors. Solarian society was lively, full of movement, busy, joyous—"giocando, disputando, leggendo, insegnando, caminando, e sempre con gaudio."[29] "There were no sitting games," wrote the Dominican fettered in the dungeon of the Inquisition.

In the concluding interchange of the *Città del Sole* the Knight Hospitaler, entranced by the tale of the Solarians and eager to learn more, sought to detain the sea captain with entreaties of "Wait! Wait!"; but he hurried off, shouting back "Non posso! Non posso!" The impetuousness of the sea captain, who is Campanella, was contained through long years of solitude, disgrace, and torture. He had steeled himself to endure, a personal triumph to which he made a pointed reference in the text. The citizens of the City of the Sun believed in the absolute freedom of the will of each individual, and as an example of this power they told of a philosopher who had been horribly tortured by his enemies for forty years without their drawing out of him a single word of what they were intent upon. Not even the stars could force a man to act against his will, because at most they exerted a weak influence from afar.

Campanella's utopia of science in a communal order was neither known nor appreciated in the land of his birth for many decades and found its first admirers only among the Protestant Pansophists north of the Alps, who sometimes put it to strange uses. In the later years of his imprisonment, Campanella reread his earlier works and interpreted them in the light of his new expectations. *The City of the Sun* was no longer the action program for an ideal state written a few years after the Calabrian conspiracy had been crushed; in an apology of the work written in 1620 and published in 1637,[30] it was transformed into a prophecy, or an imaginary republic after the manner of More. Campanella astutely protected his original fantasy by translating its fulfillment to an indefinite future time. For the purpose of subsequent refutation, he reviewed the whole body of ancient and modern attacks on utopia, playing the devil's advocate. Since an optimum republic free from crime had never existed and never would, why bother about it? Even if it were possible to institute the order of the City of the Sun in one place, it could never be extended to a whole kingdom. Where would one find a city uncorrupted by commerce with other peoples or by subject nations? More had isolated his Utopia; but Campanella, citizen of a land torn by endemic internal civil strife and foreign war among its rival principalities, could hardly ignore the possibility of uprisings against the austerity of his Solarian rulers. Was this rigid society not beyond the endurance of the mass of mankind? If Plato had foreseen the downfall of his Republic through a mere eugenic error, the misplacement of a base, brass man among the golden guardians, how could Campanella's city survive attacks of foul air, war, hunger, the plague, wild beasts, or an excess of population? What of the warnings of the apostle about those who claimed to be free of sin? Or Aristotle's arguments against Plato's community of women and of property? Might not the suppression of one vice generate a host of others? If the communistic order of the City of the Sun were the optimum one, why had it been rejected by all nations and the common opinion of mankind? The enclosed character of the city, its very defense against alien forces, would lead to sterility. It was more natural for man to study the works of God by moving throughout the world, by investigating new things in action. Sequestered behind their walls, would not the Solarians become desiccated, like those bookmen who rejected the truths of Galileo and the discoveries of Columbus because they contradicted what was written in texts? How prevent the vice of verbal obscurantism against which Campanella had inveighed throughout his life?

Campanella refused to concede that his republic was not possible: Witness the community of the early Church and the rule of the monastic orders, a state of community destined to be revived after Antichrist was destroyed. The regimen of the Solarians was judged excessively stringent only by those who lived outside it. Mockers of Plato's Republic were the Lucians of this world, over whom Campanella preferred a thousandfold the Fathers of the Church who spoke Plato's praises. The City of the Sun was not contumacious; it was the fulfillment of a Christian prayer that God's will be done on earth as it is in heaven. Buttressed by patristic citations community held its own. Owners of property were not free to dispose of it as they pleased; they were only custodians like bishops. Saint Chrysostom in Chapter 6 of his homily on Luke had been forthright: *mendacii verba sunt meum et tuum* (mine and thine are lying words). Property was not in accord with natural law, not a right, but an institution introduced by man's iniquity. At most it could be said that natural law neither affirmed nor denied the division of property. Saint Thomas had distinguished between natural and positive law; and property accumulation was not allowable when it exceeded natural needs. In his defense of the community of property Campanella combed theological disputations that had gone on among Christians for more than a thousand years. The textual exegesis was impeccable. Community emerged as the nobler, more virtuous, and more Christian form of social order.

Campanella answered less convincingly the objections to community of women. Aristotle had contended that if all men of a generation considered themselves brothers and their elders fathers, love would be so diffuse as to be no love at all, like a drop of honey diluted in a vast quantity of water. The individual would not be bound to the city with stronger ties if familial ones were eliminated. A particular love is concentrated, tragically sometimes, on one person or on very few, but utopian love without a family will be spread thin and will lose in intensity what it may achieve in extension. The practical difficulties of extending love to embrace a whole generation were conceded by Campanella. Would not a father and son recognize each other by their physical similarities? Would there not be disputes about uncertain paternity? Was it not natural to want to recognize one's own progeny in whom one was perpetuated? What about incest, jealousies, and other disorders resulting from the community of women? Did not the biblical "erunt duo in carne una" preclude such community beyond a one-to-one relationship? For Campanella all these considerations were outweighed by the manifest benefits of community. In any event, he had never espoused the community of women, only of women's service, and far from encouraging promiscuity he had provided that sexual intercourse be carefully regulated by the authorities to bring about the improvement of the race.

When the aged Campanella in the freedom of Paris reviewed the *Quaestiones* against his perfect society of the City of the Sun, he concluded with satisfaction that nothing in the little book he had composed thirty-five years earlier when incarcerated in a dungeon required emendation.

The New Papacy

Campanella's politics remained the same throughout his life and in all his writings. That was the firm position of the seventy-year-old refugee in 1637, when one of his principal works, the *Philosophiae Realis Libri Quatuor,* was republished in Paris with the royal privilege and dedicated to the Chancellor of France. In addition to reproducing the texts of the *De Politicis* and the *Civitas Solis* prepared for the Frankfort press by Tobias Adami in 1623, Campanella listed his numerous treatises on the organization of society in manuscript and in print, from the 1590s on.[31] He included the *De Monarchia Hispanica;* a panegyric to the princes of Italy; two books of the *Monarchia Messiae;* the tractate *De Juribus Regis Catholici in Novum Orbem; De Regimine Ecclesiae* (1593); and *De Monarchia Christianorum* (1593). The master dialectician with a seemingly bottomless bag of quotations from Scripture, the Fathers, and Aquinas could gloss over apparent inconsistencies with ease and conciliate every detail of his description of the pre-Christian republic of the Solarians with his doctrines of a universal papal theocracy and politic advice to the Spanish monarchy about stratagems for achieving world hegemony as a prelude to turning over the empire to the rule of the pope.

There is no reason to doubt that from his mid-twenties onward Campanella had in mind a plan, at least in embryonic form, for an ideal world political order under a single spiritual head. And this allows Catholic apologists to claim him back as a loyal son of the Church. But he did, after all, compose individual works for specific purposes at different periods in his long, tragic life, and the doctrinal stresses changed radically from one writing to another as he became involved in the espousal of different aspects of his total system. When he was carried away with a portrayal of Solarian life in an imaginary society without the revelation of Christ, a strong suspicion arises that he appreciated this natural state in its own right. Any reader of his advice to the Spanish monarchy on how to divide its enemies, spread confusion among them, convert the Indians of the New World into slaves or faithful clients, could detach this counsel from the grand design and adapt it to another power, as Campanella's English translator observed in 1654. The advocacy of papal supremacy could become so ardent in Campanella's plea for a universal theocracy as the ideal form for a paradisaical age on earth that the communal nature of the society was pushed far into the background.

The historical modes of Campanella's political doctrines were bound up with his changing religious philosophy and sentiments, especially his attitude toward the legitimacy of direct, overt action to bring about a renovation of the existing spiritual power in society. The beliefs of the Calabrian rebel of 1599 were not of the same emotional character and tenor as those of the imprisoned poet of 1606, who had resigned himself to God and accepted the establishment of the Church as the sole agent of its own reform. In Calabria he had tried to force the hand of God, so to speak; the victim of the Inquisition was persuaded to assume a more passive attitude toward the Church. Yet he continued to permit his militant schemes to be republished, and it is difficult to envisage Campanella as a quietist in any period. Whenever he was given an opportunity, he burst forth with new projects that were expressions of his own titanic will and imagination and did not denote mere acceptance of a providential design. A fleeting admission of his proud contumely in the face of the Church, followed by confessions and repentance, did not transform this man imbued with a sense of his election into an abject servant. The drive of his divine mission was too compelling for him ever to abandon the arena of combat. The mystic moments of religious illumination were succeeded by the feverish writing of works of political agitation, an outpouring that never ceased. He may himself have fallen into states of contemplation; but the contemplative life does not appear to occupy a prominent place in *The City of the Sun*. It is not necessary to posit a complete fracture between Campanella up to 1606 and the Campanella of his last thirty years; the leading ideas were fashioned early and remained with him. But their nature and meaning were altered even when origins can be traced to his youth. The wild monk from Calabria was not the same person who sat in secret conclave with Urban VIII.

Foreign ambassadors have reported that Campanella and the Pope, closeted in Rome in 1628, conducted elaborate rites to ward off the evil effects of an eclipse of the moon that threatened the Pope's life. One should not be fazed by the inconsistency of Campanella's preparing for Urban VIII a bull against astrological practices not of Ficinian vintage. That Campanella prepared complicated astrological rituals and described them in his *Astrologia,* published in Rome in 1629 (probably without his consent), does not affect the principles of his political system. Full-fledged astrological practices were a rather late addition to his repertory. They were absent from the first editions of *The City of the Sun,* where an *astrologo* was among the officials but could not be differentiated from an astronomer and where recourse to astrological signs during mating only faintly suggests the elaborate paraphernalia of astrological prophylaxis invented by Campanella later in life. In the edition of 1637 seven magical lights corresponding to the planets were introduced to protect the Solarian city, and on his deathbed Campanella employed other astrological techniques as preventive measures against the eclipse of the sun due on June 1, 1637.

Enlistment of the aid of planetary angels could be harmonized with traditional Christian beliefs. Even Aquinas, the canonical enemy of astrology, allowed a measure of determinism through astral influences on the body. Campanella was not in flagrant violation of the Council of Trent when he took into account astral effects on body and spirit, though not on the soul, and was prepared to adopt countermeasures against unfavorable astrological predictions. The movement of the sun was of especial predictive value in foretelling the rise and fall of empires and the coming of the great renovation, though it was not the sole portent. Campanella should not be reduced to a magician or converted into an exponent of a hermetic religion, though he quoted from hermetic writings and practiced astrological magic, any more than Bruno should be distorted into an Egyptian hierophant because he avowed belief in the correspondences between astral and terrestrial bodies (but to our knowledge did not practice astrology). The papacy itself provided Campanella with the opportunity for his exercises, while Bruno was cut off too soon. From time to time both Judaism and Christianity have tolerated new magical rites or preserved ancient ones in a new guise without sacrificing whatever essential quality they may possess.

If Campanella's utopia of science incorporated elements that would now be considered magical, the powers he came to believe he possessed were not supernatural; they were the result of astrological inquiries indistinguishable in character from other investigations into the forces of nature. Campanella would draw on any source that dealt with real things, such as the power of light, the emanations of the planets, or any force that struck the senses. Only the philosophical abstractions of Aristotle about form and matter were vapid. The rituals of astrology were not unlike the medical nostrums the monks of his order had exchanged with one another. Echoes of hermeticism, of the works of Hermes Trismegistus, and pictorial details of the medieval Arabic astrological work known in Latin as *Picatrix,* with its mystical city of Adocentyn, have been recognized in *The City of the Sun,*[32] but they hardly constitute its core. The political heart of the Campanellan system was not profoundly modified by a few astrological antics, though their existence should not be forgotten.

As Campanella came to maturity, the two most urgent global tasks confronting the Christian world were the conversion of pagans and heathens, whose numbers were suddenly revealed by the new geographical explorations to be five times those of Christians, and the reconstitution of the Christian Republic by subordinating the secular powers of kings to the papacy, healing the great schism in the body of the Church, and restoring Christian unity. Both of these transformations had to proceed simultaneously because they were dependent upon each other. Moreover their success was contingent upon a new understanding of Christian theology, purged of pagan Aristotelian pollution and rooted in a sound, scientific philosophy of nature—which meant his own, Telesio's, and the fundamental theories of Galileo when he learned of them (despite vacillation on the Copernican hypothesis).

As an activist, Campanella devoted a great part of his later years to the formulation of plans for the conversion of Mohammedans, Jews, and infidels to Christianity and of Protestant schismatics to Catholicism. His schemes were so ingenious and detailed that both in his own day and in modern times they have often been classified as the plots of a Machiavellian. Campanella was convinced that he and he alone, because of his prodigious learning, knew how to convert. This much-tried prisoner of the Inquisition became one of the spiritual founders of the Congregation for the Propagation of the Faith. Propaganda was a sacred mission whose art he had perfected, a cornerstone of his whole visionary structure, the necessary prelude to the reign of Christ through a pope preeminent in both the temporal and the spiritual rule of the world.

Only a rational foundation of religion could serve as a means for the conversion of Protestants, Jews, and pagans. For purposes of polemic, in *Atheismus Triumphatus* (1631) Campanella placed himself in the enemies' doctrinal strongholds to disprove their contentions. His rationalist arguments have led some interpreters to regard his position as bordering on deism, when in fact he was manipulating rhetorical devices, demonstrating with arguments of reason and citations from the sacred texts of the unconverted themselves how heathens and heretics could be led to Catholic truth.[33] The reason of the new science was enlisted to combat the false reason of the disbelievers. Telesio's philosophy of nature was integrated with Christian theology as a substitute for

Aristotelian deductive reasoning. But Campanella's exaltation of the sensate, of the concrete, and of experience does not warrant identifying him with plain materialism or sensism. "The Telesian Philosophy is the most excellent of all; seeing it comes the nearest to the Holy Fathers, and makes it appear to the World, that the [pagan] Philosophers knew nothing; and that Aristotle, who would have the Soul to be Mortal, and the World to be Immortal, and denyes Providence also, (on which Christianity is grounded) talks very absurdly, notwithstanding all his so specious Reasons; seeing that the same are refuted by stronger Reasons, fetcht in like manner from Nature," he wrote in the *Discourse Touching the Spanish Monarchy*.[34]

Campanella's religion of reason was not above all positive faiths. The one universal religion remained Catholic, a reformed Catholicism, armed with invincible, scientific, polemical weaponry, the instrumentalities of reason, and expounding the truth about God's world. As long as the Catholic religion was fettered to the false pagan philosophy of Aristotle, the Church had no sound, rational instruments with which to propagate the faith among heretics, heathens, and Jews. If the Church became pure and truthful as a consequence of a radical spiritual reformation, it would draw the heretics to itself by the example of its very existence. As he wrote to Pope Paul V in 1606: "Universal reform is the only remedy. No reform is possible if the Roman clergy does not reform itself . . . Force is appropriate to make animals behave; but with men, right conduct is instilled through imitation of those who are better." Campanella urged an end of civil law, for canon law alone would suffice. Christ was the Supreme Reason, Wisdom, the Word of God the Father. The vicar of the Supreme Reason and of Supreme Wisdom was pastor of all reasonable men, hence of the whole human world. "He who is not subject to reason is not subject to the Pope. And the Pope *omnia potest*."[35]

Campanella may have moved from an early commitment to primordial reason as a source of truth to an identification of reason with Christ and His reign on earth. Some commentators have exaggerated a youthful involvement with hermeticism, with or without Christ, and others have insisted on an unblemished orthodoxy that was constant throughout his life, but neither extreme position need be maintained in a modern perception of this mercurial thinker. For the mature Campanella, truth was already present in natural wisdom but was only fulfilled in the revelations of Christ and was entrusted to the Roman Church, whose mission it was to spread His doctrine throughout the world. Seventeenth-century utopian polymaths like Campanella could readily conciliate and assimilate Adamic truth, the hermetic tradition, a measure of judicial astrology, and the truth of Christ and the Church.

While men of all religions potentially recognized Christ in their reason, the faith had to be preached militantly among Christians, Jews, Mussulmen, and pagans in order to be made manifest. Campanella would fit his methods to his subjects, converting the Indians by teaching them history "in brief form," not in such "prolix, tedious forms as our modern writers use nowadays." In his propaganda to the Hebrews, who had thus far rejected Christ the Messiah, the superior truth of Catholicism would be demonstrated not only through its spiritual nature but through its capacity to bring about temporal perfection here on earth as a foretaste of Christ's eternal reign in heaven. When the Hebrews saw proof that the golden age was imminent, their obstinacy against

Christ would vanish and they would be among the first to sing His glories. The paradise of this world—and the conception filled one entire section of the voluminous *Theologicorum* (written from 1613 to 1624 and only now in course of publication)—would at once show up the deceptions of the Machiavellians and the error of the Hebrews in denying Christ's reign on earth. After unbelievers were addressed by Campanella in terms of their respective false doctrines, they were summoned to a great ecumenical assembly, at which, under the presidency of the pope, they would make a spiritual leap into the true faith.

Campanella's digression, "Of the Terrestrial Paradise," in the *De Homine*, the fourth book of his theological manuscripts, lapsed into the contemporary learned debate about the actual location of an earthly paradise and rejected all the current geographic candidates (including America, which he dismissed as savage and uncultivated), along with the proposals that it might be on Venus or the moon. The most salubrious climates—those superior in sky and sun— did not necessarily produce the best or happiest men, else his native Calabria would have carried off the laurels in Italy, as Italy would have in the rest of the world. His own opinion about the precise site of the celestial paradise was equally inconclusive. The existence of paradise was never in doubt, but its meaning led him to an original turn of thought in a modification of the Philonic allegorical tradition. "Finally, I believe that the whole world is a paradise for men who use to a virtuous purpose the marvelous works of God, recognizing and admiring in them the Creator. And after having lived and worked virtuously in this paradise and died, they will be translated to the paradise that is beyond the sky and above the stars. The specific place of paradise God alone knows."[36]

The fundamental idea of the *Quod Reminiscentur,* the most complete statement of the plan for converting unbelievers, like all Campanella's major conceptions had already been adumbrated in the 1590s. In Chapter 10 of the *De Regimine Ecclesiae* (written at the end of 1593), Campanella had included "Proemii da farsi agli eretici e scismatici ed agli Giudei e Machomettani per convincirli"; and in 1595 he had composed a *Dialogo politico contro Luterani, Calvinisti ed altri eretici.* He reverted to the idea again in a letter of 1606, where he proposed writing a book to proselytize the Gentiles of both the East and West Indies.[37] He kept referring to his work in progress, dwelling on specific aspects intermittently until 1616, when the definitive quadripartite text of the *Quod Reminiscentur* was finished.[38] From 1621 through 1628 there were protracted attempts to obtain an imprimatur from his superiors, during the course of which the permission to publish was granted, withdrawn, and the text revised to comply with censorship, then again approved and disapproved. Only in the twentieth century has it finally been printed.

The *De Monarchia Hispanica Discursus* (the Latin text appeared posthumously in Amsterdam, 1640) in which Campanella appointed Spain the divine agent for the institution of a universal monarchy that would then be handed over to the papacy for governance in a paradisaical age, was first published in German in Tübingen, 1620, by one of the key figures of the Rhenish circle around Andreae, Christoph Besold.[39] His conversion to Catholicism has made him anathema to the Lutherans, among whom he was once greatly admired. The same ideas reappeared in another form in Campanella's *Monarchia Messiae* (a first version of which can be traced back to 1593) in a Iesi, 1633, edition printed "superiorum permissu." Though the techniques Campanella recommended to the Spaniards for attaining world power varied from one work to another, the underlying argument was rather consistent. The devil had invented a fishhook, he wrote in the *Quod Reminiscentur*,[40] and baited it with the Kingdom of Naples. While the two gigantic fish, France and Spain, avid for food, were fighting over the bait, in the rear the Turk was capturing in great nets all the nations blinded by their greed. The Kingdom of Naples was the source of the evil. Rescue it from the sea, turn it over to the pope, convert the Spaniards and the French to his supremacy in temporal as well as in spiritual affairs, and Christendom would be prepared for the paradisaical age. In his plans for conquering the enemies of Spain, Campanella tried to out-Machiavelli Machiavelli for an anti-Machiavellian purpose: He advised the Spaniards to subdue the Low Countries not by facing their rebellious subjects frontally in battle but by first sowing dissension among them. The ultimate goal, however, was not the glory of Spain, but the predominance of a Christian spiritual force.

One of Campanella's most paradoxical schemes, set forth in Chapter XX of the *Monarchia Hispanica,* involved exploiting the natural sciences to further the cause of the Spanish monarch. Campanella counseled the King to foster them in his own domain as a means of enhancing world renown, for *fama* was a help to conquest. Sciences should also be sponsored among the English nobles with the different aim of deflecting the aristocracy from warlike enterprise to higher things. And if insinuated among the terrible Turks the sciences might help to bring them down by sowing controversies and divisions among them. It was Campanella's experience that intellectual disputations rendered an empire easy prey to a warrior nation. Yet the same sciences in transalpine Europe were expected to promote world monarchical government and turn the "wits" from heretical theological debates that undermined the papacy to benign discussions of natural philosophy. Campanella would shut off the teaching of the Hebrew and Greek tongues because they had become vehicles of heresy, and in their stead would emphasize the learning of Arabic, so that Western scholars, forsaking internecine quarrels, would spend their energies in converting the Turks, using Arabic as the primary means of communication.[41]

In the English-speaking world the *Monarchia Hispanica* gained notoriety as a Machiavellian document when it was translated under the title *A Discourse Touching the Spanish Monarchy* (London, 1654) and was cited as evidence of papist conspiracies during the Commonwealth and the Restoration. When the translation was reprinted in 1660, William Prynne wrote an admonitory preface in which the whole history of the English Civil War was presented as the doing of Campanella.[42] This second Machiavelli had counseled the Spanish King to create a division between the English King and Parliament in order to alter the government from kingdom to commonwealth, embroil the English in a civil war, and divert them from interfering with the Spaniards, who were bringing Indian treasure into Spain, while Holland would be reduced in a conflict with England and other seafaring countries. The intention was to make the King of Spain master of England and the Low Countries, and straightway the sole monarch of Europe and the greatest part of the New World. By 1670 Campanella's arguments on the advantages to the Spanish monarchy in stimulating British science were used by Henry Stubbs in his famous attack on the Royal Society.[43]

The English interpreted Campanella's prophecies of Spanish victory as part of a plot to destroy them, but he had his eye on the next step, the papal hegemony that would follow unification of the world under Spain. The first of the *Discorsi della libertà e della felice suggezione allo Stato ecclesiastico* (Iesi, 1633)— which formed the second part of the *Monarchia Messiae*—ended with a series of propositions utopianizing papal rule.[44] Campanella, who had been sequestered and tortured in papal prisons (though in his declining years he owed his freedom to the pope), declared in print that in no empire, whether governed by a prince, by an aristocracy, or by a democracy, did so true a liberty prevail as in Rome under the pope; that this republic contained within itself popular, aristocratic, and monarchic elements, with all their convenience, utility, and freedoms, including freedom from famine, plague, and strife, without the inconvenience and servility found elsewhere. This government of virtuosi from every part of the world, where neither the virtuosi nor the magistrates were hereditary, shaped a republic so sublime and wonderful that philosophers could never have imagined anything better or even equal to it. To conceive of it as coming from anyone but God was impossible. When the "monarchy of the Messiah" was established world history would have completed its movement from ignorant tyranny to dominion through love. Of course, even this worldly government of Rome was not absolute perfection. "If you are looking for a Republic without ministerial abuse, you will have to go to Heaven and fashion it after the manner of Plato and Thomas More, or," Campanella added with his customary modesty, "like the City of the Sun."[45]

Campanella's argument for the supremacy of the papacy over all temporal princes was a recapitulation of the historic apologies for this position, climaxed with a Campanellan summation. Dominion naturally required a unity incorporating within itself supreme power, wisdom, and love; election was superior to succession, religion was the soul of the republic, the amalgamation of governance with the priesthood was the original condition of society; unity was the best safeguard for the laws, for security against heresies, for firmness in the face of rebellion. All this was confirmed by the history of the nations. When Campanella's vision of the circular nature of things was adapted to his prophecy of the ultimate reign of one Christian monarch, the whole of world history became a single grand movement, the return to the perfection of the original paradise from which man had been expelled. The felicity of the golden age would prevail. Since this had been the natural order of things in the beginning it would be so again under the reign of the Messiah. With unity scientific knowledge would be augmented, life would be prolonged, and easy communication among the regions of the sacerdotal empire would diffuse useful information throughout the world. It was the devil who had first introduced a multiplicity of princes and brought about the present wretched state of mankind.

Campanella's dogmatic assertions were interlarded with cogent examples from the past of the union of the sacerdotal and temporal powers, and with copious citations from Scripture and the Fathers. Upholders of the imperial power like Dante were denied. Nature, prophecy, the interest of the princes and their vassals, all pointed to one ruler over a united Christendom. Neither the two-swords doctrine nor the conciliar theory was tolerated. The emperor was not another sun, only a moon dependent upon the sun. Campanella traced the movement of world history as it was embodied in universal monarchy "beginning from the East, and so coming at length to the West, having passed through the hands of the Assyrians, Medes, Persians, Greeks, and Romans." (Two centuries later Hegel's World Spirit would pursue the same solar course with different protagonists.) The whole bore witness to a providential design. Traditional prophecies from Daniel, slightly amended, showed that in universal history the power of man appeared only outwardly. There was always "the concurrence and co-operation of the finger of God, though not so visibly seen." On occasion God carried out a great stroke of business, as when He came forth directly upon the stage and raised Arbaces against Sardanapalus. God had selected both the agent and the event. Campanella latched on to Augustine to prove that the Romans too had once been chosen by God for hegemony. And now Spain was divinely enjoined to overthrow the Turks and assume universal dominion.

Campanella continued to predict the coming end of individual monarchies, with proofs from prophecy, astrology, and numerology. The year 1600 had passed and it was composed of seven and nine, numbers fatal to all monarchies. "I say, that the end of Monarchies is now come, and that we are now come to that Age, wherein all things are to be in subjection to the Saints, and to the Church; which is to be, after the end of the four Monarchies, and the death of Antichrist, who shall continue for the space of three Weeks and a half . . ."[46] All empires were naturally subject to the vicissitudes, a cycle of rise and decline. "For, Humane Things do, as it were Naturally encrease sometimes, and sometimes again decrease; after the example of the Moon, to which they are all subject. And therefore it is a most High, and weighty undertaking if not such a one as is above the Power of Man, to endeavour to Fixe them, & keep them in one Certain, standing Condition; that so they fall not from the pitch they had arrived at, nor grow worse, and fall to decay."[47] But if Campanella were released from prison, he assured the Spanish King, and became his advisor, he could arrest the cycle. Conservation would be his aim, and eternal stability would be achieved with the aid of his genius. It was not true that only ancient philosophers such as Aristotle could serve as guides to the conduct of policy. "This Age of ours hath also Its Solons, Lycurgusses, and Josephs, which are sent by God himself: but they are kept under, and are not admitted to the Presence of Princes: And that Common Saying, namely, that there are no Solons, or Aristotles born now adaies, is most false. For indeed there are such born even in these our daies; and such as are better than they too: but they lye hid, and concealed; whiles that Gentiles are had in admiration; but Christians are envied."[48]

In the course of his long life Campanella proposed diverse men and kingdoms as instruments for the regeneration of mankind. To inaugurate a republic under the protection of the Turks (an accusation leveled against him in the trial of 1599) was no more excluded than the later rallying of the Christian princes against the threat of Islam. From dominion over Calabria to dominion over the Kingdom of Naples, the Mediterranean, and finally the whole world, was a natural progression of stages in the institution of a new order, and Campanella long dreamed that a *pax hispanica,* successor to the *pax romana,* by uniting the world under one law would serve, like the rule of the ancient Romans, as a prologue to the reign of Christ. Such a proposal was not unprecedented in the Christian world, but to preach to the Spanish monarchy that it would then have to subordinate itself to papal rule was a kind of lunacy.

Finally, despite years of enthusiasm and persistence, Campanella abandoned the choice of the Spanish monarchy as the agent of renovation once he found a refuge in France. Absurd as it may sound, the dying Campanella, disillusioned with the Spaniards, hailed the government of Richelieu as the incarnation of the City of the Sun in the new edition of his book in 1637.[49] The eclogue he wrote on the birth of the Dauphin, the future Sun King Louis XIV, attests to Campanella's flexibility:

> The Cock will sing. Peter will spontaneously reform himself; Peter will sing; the Cock will fly over the whole world, but will submit it to Peter and be guided by his reins. Work will become a pleasure amicably divided among many, for all will recognise one Father and God . . . All kings and peoples will unite in a city which they will call "Heliaca," which will be built by this noble hero. A temple will be built in the midst of it, modelled on the heavens; it will be ruled by the high priest and the senates of the monarchs, and the sceptres of kings will be placed at the feet of Christ.[50]

Whatever grand monarch became the standard-bearer of world reform, Campanella saw the man of learning as under a special obligation to spiritualize humanity. He constantly argued that every great power, ancient and modern, was dependent for its success upon co-opting men of science.[51] It was in the genius of his native province to spawn philosophical sects that could spearhead a general reformation. Campanella keenly appreciated the role of his predecessors, the ancient Pythagoreans in Magna Graecia, and thought of himself as the chosen instrument of God for a similar task. When he failed, he became Prometheus chained to the rock in the Caucasus, as he wrote in the poems he composed in prison. But the drama of Prometheus had many alternative denouements, and in one, the omnipotent Zeus was ultimately reconciled to him. Perhaps this was a prefiguration of what Campanella had hoped from the papacy. Even when he repudiated the idea of absolute perfection in this world in his theological manuscripts, he never doubted that all things were "capable of a beatitude, proportionate to their capacity," and that relative felicity for all the people was the end for which society was created. The epilogue of the *Metaphysica* concluded in his prophetic vein: "The nations of the world are agreed that the souls of men have reached the uttermost limits of discord, of disease, and of corruptions. They also believe that the age of corruption is about to end and that the world has to be renewed. All things are on the verge of a return to their beginnings. Centuries of a better order are to follow, and in a changed time that is absorbed in eternity, when death will be transformed into life, a blessed God will be exalted for having transformed all things into all things."[52]

By 1637 Campanella saw *The City of the Sun* as serving a double purpose. It could teach the Gentiles that they should live righteously if they did not wish to be forsaken by God, and, at the same time, through this perfect model the Christians could be persuaded that the Christian life was in accord with nature. Catholic interpreters, accepting at face value the old man's view of a work he had written in a dungeon thirty-five years before, hold that the naturalistic utopia was never conceived as a substitute for historical Christianity but only as a demonstration that a utopia according to the law of nature was very close to Christianity. The utopia of the City of the Sun then becomes a mere premise of the higher ideal, the papal state predicted in the *Monarchia Messiae,* which was itself an amplification of the lost *Monarchia Christianorum* of 1593. The consistency of the Campanellan doctrine is thus preserved intact, perhaps too tightly to bear psychological credence. While the position of the anticlerical Italian scholars that *The City of the Sun* is evidence of Campanella's unadulterated secular naturalism is hard to sustain in the light of writings of the 1590s and scores of manuscripts, letters, and printed documents subsequent to its composition, it is equally implausible to make of this protean genius, subjected to lifelong persecution by his Church, a simple stalwart of the faith. And yet the portrait of Campanella as a Machiavellian secularist also lacks the stamp of authenticity. Reason of state, Machiavellianism, was diabolical, anti-Christian, the very force that had kept Campanella incarcerated. Machiavelli had reduced religion to a historical-political invention, an instrument of potentates, the degenerate condition from which Campanella hoped to rescue it.

The parochial debates of clericals and anticlericals about the orthodoxy of Campanella vanish into thin air if he is placed in the Pansophic chain of Western society. He then appears as a Christian of the seventeenth century moved by a vision in the universalist spirit of Bruno, Andreae, Comenius, and Leibniz, a utopian world in which science and religion strove to achieve a new synthesis for the spiritual renovation of all mankind. In this catena Campanella leads directly to Andreae and the Germans who rescued many of his works.

I I

Andreae, Pastor
of Christianopolis

JOHANN VALENTIN ANDREAE, a Lutheran pastor, son of a pastor who dabbled in chemistry and alchemy and grandson of the theologian responsible for the *Concordienformel* that settled the official Lutheran position on the Eucharist, was the author of more than a hundred published Latin and German works of piety, belles lettres, polemics, and autobiographical confessions of his wanderings in the wilderness of error and doubt. In 1619 he published in Strasbourg a utopia, the *Reipublicae Christianopolitanae Descriptio,* after he had dramatically broken with the Rosicrucians of Tübingen and their plans for a secret brotherhood that was to serve as a nucleus for the "reform of the whole of mankind," a phrase that was the actual title of one of the more ambiguous pamphlets attributed to them. Despite Andreae's return to respectability, which opened the way to prominent posts in the Lutheran religious establishment of the Rhineland, the *Christianopolis* preserves something of the spirit of the movement that he had ostentatiously disavowed. On the model of Luther's seal, Grandfather Jakob had established the family crest as a Saint Andrew's cross and four roses —a rosy cross.

Andreae and the Invisibles

Andreae was born August 17, 1586, in Herrenberg, the heart of Lutheran orthodoxy, where his father Johannes (1554–1601) was Superintendent. His son has described him in the standard terms befitting a gentle pastor—temperate, exceedingly kind, sociable, musical, a man of generous disposition—though his liberality was undiscriminating and he appears to have been an easy mark for alchemist impostors. About his mother, Johann Valentin waxed more eloquent: She was an *optima, dulcissima, beatissima mater,* interested in pharmacology and occupied with preparing remedies for the ailing poor. When this "chemical wedding" was broken by the premature death of her husband—Johann Valentin was then fifteen—she became court apothecary to Duke Friedrich. She taught Andreae chemistry and the pharmaceutical arts and in her old age lived in his house. Alchemy, pharmacology, chemistry were forms of knowledge well within the bounds of Lutheran orthodoxy.

Herrenberg is situated ten miles northwest of Tübingen, and from his earliest years Johann Valentin and his four brothers were bound up with the life of its university. He was a sickly child and for ten years he was tutored at home by two young medical students. Late in life Andreae still remembered the excitement that ushered in the year 1600, that fateful number pregnant with portents of joy or disaster, according to one's persuasion. After his father's death in 1601, the family moved to Tübingen, where his grandfather Jakob (1528–1590) had been chancellor of the university and his mother was given the *ius civitatis* of this great center of Lutheran theology that was discreetly open to new ideas. The mathematician-astronomer Michael Maestlin, who had once taught Kepler, became Andreae's professor and so did Christoph Besold, a complex, troubled polymath who poured forth books on theology, history, jurisprudence, translated Campanella, and ended in the bosom of the Catholic Church. He was godfather to Andreae's children and his intimacy with the Andreae circle cannot be glossed over. Besold was deeply immersed in hermetic writings.

The enigma of the Rosicrucians in the early seventeenth century continues to intrigue historians. Report of the existence of a far-flung network of adepts, who promised a universal reordering of the world through a theosophy, spread across Europe from England to Poland—even Descartes was once accused of membership. A motley group of mystics, alchemists, and Christian reformers, men like Michael Maier and Robert Fludd, considered themselves part of the clandestine Fraternity and defended the principles set forth in its canonical text, the *Fama Fraternitatis,* published in Cassel in 1614. In the seventeenth century more scholarly young men were at one time touched by the Rosicrucian faith than were willing to confess to it when they had grown old and staid.[1]

Many of the data on the early seventeenth-century Rosicrucians are still in dispute. There doubtless existed in Germany clandestine fraternities committed to doctrines soaked in the Kabbala and in the literature of philosophical and experimental alchemy. Among the Rosicrucians, some pretended to the discovery of a medical panacea and to psychic powers that rendered them capable of divining other people's thoughts even at a distance. Membership was kept secret lest the initiates be accused of sorcery by the ignorant. The term "Invisibles" that was sometimes applied to them referred either to their secrecy or to their supposed capacity to make themselves invisible. Modern Rosicrucians who are true believers have pretended in their official histories that Bacon, Comenius, Descartes, Spinoza, Newton, and Leibniz were all either members of the Fraternity or at the least fellow travelers. Twentieth-century historians of the movement have discussed and rejected these claims; Andreae alone is still identified with the Fraternity in some manner. Descartes's famous three dreams on the night of November 10, 1619, while he was on military service in Germany, may have been affected by his reading of Rosicrucian literature, as a curiosity if nothing more, though his early biographer, Adrien Baillet, has quoted Descartes's staunch denial that he ever joined a Rosicrucian Fraternity.[2]

Andreae's connections with Campanella from whom he derived and with Comenius who was his direct disciple are amply documented. The utopia of these thinkers, both in its heretical Rosicrucian envelopment and its later orthodox Lutheran and Moravian form, can be related to esoteric movements that had survived from past ages. Even when heralds of the new science repudiated philosophical alchemy, judicial astrology, millenarianism, Kabbalist numerology, hermeticism, Gnostic theosophy, or Neoplatonic mysticism, the ancient beliefs were intermingled with the most commonsensical scientific and political insights. The two worlds often lived together in the same persons. Only in modern times have the rationalist aspects of the Pansophic utopians been isolated in compendia of thought, which have pared away the living flesh and spirit to expose mere dry bones.

Present-day scholarly debates over questions of priority in utopian discovery among partisans of Bacon, Campanella, and Andreae are anachronistic. Theirs was an intellectual commonalty. Oral converse and the exchange of manuscripts were important, and ideas were freely transmitted and borrowed. The sequence of printed books is not a determinant of precedence in invention. When some of Campanella's philosophical works, including the *City of the Sun* itself, were printed for the first time in Frankfort, 1623, in Latin, they were prefaced with a moving introduction about the sufferings of the author written by Tobias Adami, who had carried the manuscripts north and had earlier published a précis of Campanella's philosophical doctrines. The major figures sometimes copied from one another verbatim, as Comenius certainly did from Andreae, but plagiarism is not the word for their incorporation of one another's ideas or phraseology. The bitter quarrels among practicing physical scientists that streak the seventeenth century with cries of "thief" are not repeated here. The Christian utopian brethren were contributors to a common treasury and in their dreams of Christian science there were no sharp disputes about priority.

Bruno, Andreae, and the tradition of Paracelsus all extol the creativity of the inner man; his soul forms matter even as God created the world. The violence of their antagonism against school philosophy, logic-chopping, the precepts of Galen and Aristotle is motivated in part at least by the desire to clear away the inherited bookish debris so that the divine spark of knowledge in every man may be free to glow. In the Germanic world, Pansophia was the scientific equivalent to the theological revolt of Luther a century before; both centered upon the powers of man the willful maker rather than upon external authority vested in institutions.

Johann Valentin Andreae is a fine example of utopian youth, grown old, administrative. The remorse of the aging, pious superintendent of Lutheran clergy over his youthful sins is a less fertile field of inquiry than the plans and writings of the young academic theologian whose name was associated with the Rosicrucian mystification. Since the beginnings and multifarious activities of what Andreae in his maturity denounced as an idle and dangerous fantasy remain cloudy, the part he played in its invention and propagation is problematic. In the light of recent studies, one may feel some doubt that he was the prime originator of the legend of Christian Rosencreutz, without swinging fully in the opposite direction to read the life and works of Andreae, the tormented, limping Swabian, as those of an orthodox Lutheran who never for a moment swerved from the beaten path.[3]

The scandal of Andreae's participation in the secret society of the Rosicrucians, if it ever existed in an organized form, was heightened by the eminence of his ancestry. Since his grandfather had fixed Lutheran Christological dogma into a mold, his father had been a dutiful Lutheran superintendent in Herrenberg, and his brothers were pastors without fault, how had Andreae, destined for a prominent place in the Lutheran establishment of the Rhineland, become entangled with the heretical fabrication of a new book of revelations, an alien confession, and a clandestine religious society of adepts who pretended to remold the whole world?

The name of Christian Rosencreutz, the legendary German prophet of the new dispensation, first appeared in two small works published anonymously in 1614 and 1615, the *Fama Fraternitatis* and the *Confessio Roseae Crucis*. It was also featured on the cover of a German work, *Chymische Hochzeit Christiani Rosenkreuz. Anno 1459* (Strasbourg, 1616), whose authorship Andreae openly acknowledged, though he later denigrated it as a youthful folly that had been grossly misinterpreted.[4] The problem of Andreae's relationship to the Rosicrucians initially has to do with his part in the composition of the *Fama* and the *Confessio.* Many apocalyptic, Kabbalistic, hermetic, and Freemasonic works are pseudonymous. Since antiquity bestowed great authority, prophetic utterances acquired prestige through the simple device of predated authorship. Once some of the prognostications of a seer had been borne out, a reasonable presumption was established that foretellings not yet fulfilled would also come to pass. The Rosicrucian Fraternity followed the customary practice. The works themselves told of the discovery in 1604 of the coffin of one Christian Rosencreutz, which when opened revealed his testament. He was said to be a knight who in the fifteenth century had traveled east, to the land of Damcar, and had brought back esoteric wisdom learned from Arabian philosophers. This secret lore was now to be imparted to a select few who were known only to one another and who would use it to concoct an elixir, transmute metals, and bring about the reformation of the whole world through their hidden powers. The rosy cross became the emblem of the new order, whose promise of imminent transformation made existing ecclesiastical arrangements supererogatory. The idea of a secret brotherhood that through its covert influence would remake the world has numerous antecedents, and Rosicrucianism could be linked with any of them—the Pythagoreans, the thirty-six just men who would save the world in early Talmudic Judaism and later folklore, the Twelve Apostles, the Christian monastic orders. The alchemical coloration of the Rosicrucian wisdom is easily associated with the sixteenth- and seventeenth-century efflorescence of alchemy and the growth of the new philosophy. The formal confession of Rosicrucian faith was often merely an adaptation of existing creeds, and its numerology is quite banal. What is novel is the universality of the message and the fervor of commitment in a small group of believers sworn to effect an immediate moral revolution.

Along with the *Fama* and the *Confessio* another work, *Allgemeine und general Reformation, der gantzen weiten Welt* (Cassel, 1614), has sometimes been labeled Rosicrucian, but as far back as the late eighteenth century it was recognized to be a translation of a fantasy in Traiano Boccalini's *De' Ragguagli di Parnaso* (Venice, 1612) entitled "Generale Riforma dell'Universo dai sette Savii della Grecia e da altri Letterati, pubblicata di ordine di Apollo." Far from being a serious program, as its German title implies, it has patent elements of a satire on projects of universal renovation. The scene is a meeting of wise men called under the Emperor Justinian at the Delphic palace to draft a general plan of reform because the times are evil and the number of suicides increasing. The solutions presented are deliberately extravagant: Thales recommends inserting a window into each man's breast so that his heart will be open to all. Cato proposes another flood destroying all women and all men over twelve, leaving to future mankind the task of procreation without the female sex. The sixteenth-century philosopher Giacomo Mazzoni, having had the patient, the Present Age, brought into the assembly and undressed, finds it totally corrupt. After further horseplay a manifesto of the Sages is finally read to the multitude fixing the prices of sprats, cabbages, and pumpkins as a panacea. Conceivably,

Boccalini's jest mocked the popular reform proposals of previous ages as an introduction to the unveiling of a true reformation. The idea of a council of gods discussing the evils of the world had already appeared in Bruno's *Expulsion of the Triumphant Beast*—the fantasy that his Venetian Inquisitors laid hold upon as the repository of his manifold heresies. It was the opinion of the Lutheran alchemist Michael Maier in 1618 that the binding together of the *Allgemeine Reformation* and the *Fama* in 1614 was simply a bookseller's device.

Once the story of Christian Rosencreutz got about, learned men and charlatans throughout northern Europe convinced themselves that they were members of the secret brotherhood. As the myth ballooned, the orthodox of all religions began to suspect the beliefs of any members of the faith who appeared to be straying, and accused them of being heretical Rosicrucians. Public denials were not enough, not even when it was recognized that those suspect had not taken Rosicrucian vows at any time in their lives. For who knew when Rosicrucian-like hopes might have invaded their dreams? Andreae denied his sometime adherence to the Rosicrucian Brotherhood with increasing vehemence as the years advanced. In the *Menippus* (1617) the chapter entitled "Fraternitas" still conceded an early attraction to the Brotherhood: "When I became disgusted with the whole spirit of the age, I really wanted to go over to them, but not for lucre."[5] The Rosicrucians had become identified with the prospect of an imminent discovery of the philosopher's stone, which would allow them to transmute metals and provide them with enough gold to improve the conditions of life for great masses of people. Andreae's divorcement from the plan was coupled with more than a hint of their drawing power; he had been at least a fellow traveler of the Fraternity, if not one of its guiding spirits. By 1618 his doubts, whatever they were, were turning into pronounced hostility. He assured the public that he had been skeptical from the beginning about the Brotherhood's ability to bring men closer to Christ or to stop the impaired world of men from creaking, and he had been suspicious of the high-flown Rosicrucian rhetoric that resembled the speech of magic-makers and charlatans. As practical alchemy and mystical notions became more prominent in Rosicrucian circles he revised the memory of his previous attitudes toward the Fraternity. Andreae's new Fraternitas Christi was founded in sharp opposition to what he called the Rosicrucian laughing-stock. The *Peregrini in Patria Errores. Utopiae* (Strasbourg, 1618) and the *Civis Christianus, sive Peregrini Quondam Errantis Restitutiones* (Strasbourg, 1619) continued in the same spirit.

It is impossible to establish the intellectual boundaries of Rosicrucianism. The extent and tenacity of adherence varied, and as the Brotherhood became notorious throughout Europe, its doctrines acquired local geographic idiosyncrasies that bore little relationship to the credo of that nucleus of Rhineland academicians who in the second decade of the seventeenth century proposed to cure all the ills of Christian society. When Andreae returned to a more orthodox brotherhood in Christ, he saw Rosicrucianism as bearing the mark of the devil, as a satanic attempt to undermine the fellowship of Christians and usurp its place, as a heresy from whose clutches he had narrowly escaped. The fear grew upon him that Rosicrucians were diluting the Gospel and shifting the focus of the Lutheran religion away from the marriage of Christ and the Church to a new Messiah. The millenarian character of the Rosicrucian manifestoes was forthrightly denounced in the *Invitationis ad Fraternitatem Christi*

Pars Altera (1618).[6] Dissociating himself from the evil doctrines of his youth turned into an obsessive preoccupation for Andreae. Ideologues who for a variety of politic and psychic reasons seek to wipe out a piece of their past tend to fall prey to such repetition neuroses. The *Turris Babel* (Strasbourg, 1619) had as its subtitle *sive Judiciorum de Fraternitate Rosaceae Crucis Chaos,* and Andreae there let loose the full barrage of his satiric eloquence. In *Turbo* (1616), Truth announced in orthodox Lutheran rhetoric that human error was "hopeless," without possibility of emendation, and that anyone who believed he could transform mankind for the better was only a greater fool than his fellows. Instead of unifying mankind Rosicrucianism would breed utter confusion. By the time Andreae wrote the *Theophilus* (1649) he was praying that all Rosicrucian writings would be consigned to the flames.[7]

Continuing the apology, Andreae's most recent Lutheran biographer has denied that his hero had anything to do with the composition of either the *Fama* or the *Confessio,* and has singled out a certain Simon Studion, author of a 2000-page "Naometria" (1604), still in manuscript, as the probable perpetrator of the mystification of Christian Rosencreutz. If this be so, in the course of time the verbose Studion surely acquired new skills in conceptual compression. Scores of works all over Europe, many of them never printed, heralded a great reformation around 1600. In order to exonerate Andreae completely from Rosicrucian complicity and preserve his unblemished image as an impeccable Lutheran, the origin of Studion's chiliastic doctrines has been pushed back to 1593, when Andreae was less than seven.

Whoever the author or authors of the *Fama* and the *Confessio* may have been, these writings emerged from the Lutheran academic world of the Rhineland, where alongside a certain relaxation of Lutheran standards of behavior and a settled organization of the church and its dogmas, there were currents of intense spiritual unease. Youths born to formal evangelical orthodoxy faced the challenge of the reformed church of Calvin, of Counter-Reformation Catholic faith, of mystics, of the new science; and many of them went through spiritual crises: They felt themselves lost in the world, strangers in a society whose religious doctrines were ignored in the practices of everyday life. Andreae has faithfully recorded their anguish, their sickness unto death, in passages of his *Turbo.* "O God, bring back blind chaos! Woe! Woe! Woe! To die! To die! I can no longer endure the light of the sun, nor men, nor night, nor myself. Where, where am I? I drag around Turbo, wretched Turbo."[8] The confused were wanderers. Some went on pilgrimage to the Holy Land and passed through the dens of iniquity in Rome and Naples, bastions of the Inquisition. Or they landed in stern Calvinist Geneva. The mystics they read were foreign Catholics and German writers of the pre-Reformation period. In an attempt to find the way of light the young Lutherans endangered their immortal souls.

These men seeking a new life often ventured upon strange pathways. The university provided them with a rich classical background and they expressed themselves in novel modes of speech—elliptical, symbolic, imagistic. They looked for hidden Christian meanings in pagan myths, and they invented allegories that gave utterance to their own religious bewilderment and often served to cover their adventures beyond the pale of orthodoxy. Absorption in philosophical alchemy coexisted with a fervid desire to know their inner conscience, to discover all the secrets of nature, to prepare for the millennium, to synthesize ancient, Christian, and modern learning. University life made it possible to communicate their esoteric ideas to a few trusted colleagues without risking publication. A desire to reform the Reformation was a threat to an establishment that only recently had resolved its major theological questions and separated itself with a wall of dogma not only from the Whore of Babylon in Rome, but from Calvin's Geneva.

Wanderings of a Limping Swabian

Andreae was a prototype of the seeker. In 1607 a group of theological students in Tübingen were condemned for association with prostitutes. Andreae's involvement in the affair has given rise to different interpretations. One has it that the Ducal Chancellor, Matthias Enzlin, used the incident as a pretext to punish the scion of an important bourgeois family in an assertion of ducal absolutism. The event is clouded over with Andreae's account of a dream that was a prognostic of his fate. Whatever the specific facts of his misadventure, he fled Tübingen, first taking refuge with friends of his father and grandfather in Strasbourg. There he met Lazarus Zetzner, a printer of Paracelsus and of alchemical literature for the whole of Europe, who was to be Andreae's publisher for twenty years. Andreae's peregrinations continued through Heidelberg, Frankfort, Mainz, and on more than one occasion he approached the fires of Romanism, especially at the Jesuit college in Dillingen. Back in Tübingen, still denied the clericate, he became a tutor of young noblemen, learned mechanical arts and music, and wrote a treatise on the education of youth, disguised as fiction. In 1610 there was another period of travel, obscured by allegations that it followed upon a second ouster from Tübingen, this time because of involvement with occult studies and societies. Now Andreae moved toward French-speaking Switzerland (either before or after journeys to France, Italy, and Spain). The order of Geneva, city of the Calvinists, was a great utopian revelation, or so the aging Lutheran official recollected it in his autobiography.

Christianopolis later embodied the spirit of the strictly supervised life of Calvin's Geneva, rather than the comparative looseness of the Rhineland university towns occasionally interrupted by the punitive forays of Lutheran directors. A twentieth-century youth of the West would be repelled by the idealized portrait of Geneva that Andreae sketched from memory, but the values of a seventeenth-century Christian utopia were rooted in concepts of obedience to civic authority, whose spiritual meaning is now difficult to grasp. Political freedom conjoined with absolute authoritative religious guidance of moral behavior could be attractive to a young man accustomed to Lutheran acceptance of the autocratic will of the ruling princelet and his chancellor. Freedom was conceived as the fulfillment of God's command, but in the more activist spirit of his generation, Andreae was not content with mere verbal obeisance to belief in the general good; he required the union of wisdom and charity, manifested in the cultivation of arts and sciences as visible acts of Christian love.

Upon his return from the second period of wanderings, Andreae studied theology in earnest in the Tübingen seminary that had once harbored Kepler and was to shelter Schelling and Hegel. In the university towns men could be close friends without having identical views on the extent to which a Lutheran might involve himself in astrology, alchemy, Paracelsian doctrines of the macro-microcosmic correspondence, the chiliastic mysticism of naometrianism, the writings of Jacob Boehme, and sundry other theosophies and millenarianisms without falling into the mire of outright heresy. Esoterica attracted many in various degrees for shorter or longer periods. Early enthusiasms and later repudiations were frequent, and a passing phase should not be regarded as stamping a man for life. The concept of knowledge (*scientia*) was fluid, the canons of experimental science and demonstration hardly fixed. One might betray an inclination toward one aspect of a theosophical position without having swallowed it whole (though professorial and theological enemies might be prepared to make much of even the mildest flirtation). In his oration at his friend Tobias Hess's funeral, Andreae was careful to allude to Hess's early addiction to chiliasm—he once called him "Utopiensis Princeps" —and then to assure the assembly that he had died an orthodox Lutheran. In the *Mythologia Christiana* (1619) Andreae employed an earthy Luther-like image in justification of his friend, who in this conceit has had his brain examined in an autopsy by Vesalius: "Curiositatis excremata bene evacuarat."[9]

In the Tübingen seminary the group that was once committed to the reformation of the whole world soon returned to orthodoxy and forgot Rosencreutz. As might be expected, Lutheran writers are eager to underplay the role of Christoph Besold (1577–1638) in their circle, but however one plots the constellation of relations among the twenty-five men who, along with Andreae, founded the orthodox *Societas Christiana* in 1618, the future heretic who defected to Catholicism appears to occupy a prominent place.[10] Through Besold, Andreae got to know Wilhelm Wense, who traveled in Italy from 1614 to 1616 and visited Campanella in prison; and through Wense Andreae became acquainted with Tobias Adami, who had earlier penetrated the dungeon where Campanella lay buried and by 1613 had begun to spread the Italian Dominican's ideas in the Rhineland. Andreae quoted from Campanella's manuscripts as early as 1619 and published German translations of Campanella's Italian sonnets, among them the "Delle radici de' gran mali del mondo."

Campanella's works were a bizarre intrusion from the very bowels of evil, the dungeons of the Inquisition. Papers had been smuggled north into the heart of the Lutheran theological establishment in the seminary of Tübingen. The ideas of the young Lutheran reformers were inchoate—they had just returned from their travels (Adami had gone as far as Jerusalem) and their early writings bear witness to a troubled theology and the difficulties they encountered in assimilating what the "new philosophy" represented. The issue of Campanella's influence on the German group is one of those "appearance problems" in which the history of ideas sometimes becomes enmeshed. Andreae's mentality was fashioned in a Lutheran theological world and Campanella's, despite his many heterodoxies, in a Thomist one. Campanellan formulas were contagious—tyranny, sophistry, and hypocrisy as the age's trinity of evil —and the writings of this victim of Catholic persecution could at one point be read sympathetically in Germany. But Andreae's myth of the progress of the soul in search of Christ is remote from Campanella's project for a universal papal theocracy. These men did not share the same political or religious outlook, and the gap between them widened as each embraced his respective orthodoxy. Before Leibniz tried to effect a great conciliation between Catholicism and Protestantism, the idea of accepting Rome was repugnant to an orthodox Lutheran. When Andreae, in imitation of Luther, reflected on Rome, he echoed Luther's verdict: "Orbis quondam, nunc scelerum caput."[11] Andreae's *Verae Unionis in Christo Jesu Specimen* (1628) had voiced a "consensus Christiani, pro unius Religionis sincera professione"; but Andreae could only conceive of the single religion as the unique and true Evangelical Religion, distinguished by the name of the incomparable hero Luther, and he would have no truck with Calvinism, Anabaptism, Weigelianism, Rosicrucianism, and pseudochemical impostures, not to speak of papism. Tobias Adami finally broke with Campanella because of his virulent attacks on Luther, and Andreae ended up denouncing Campanella for demeaning himself by a belief in fate and the stars.[12] Thirty years earlier, Andreae's sentiments were more favorable.

But though Andreae and Campanella grew in different intellectual soils, they were contemporaries, and time stamped similitudes upon them. If any influence was exerted, its direction was manifestly from Campanella to Andreae. Both visions were essentially independent variations on the Pansophic utopia, and searching the two for like images and phrases is a pedant's task. Campanella would have remained unknown for decades in northern Europe, if some of his ideas had not penetrated the German Lutheran world through the conduit of Adami, Wense, and Andreae, who were the intermediaries to Comenius. Books published in Frankfort were readily distributed throughout the northern Protestant lands, and Adami's preparation of Campanella's manuscripts for the press was a major act of intellectual transmission. Andreae's conceptions were not immaculately conceived, but a spongy brain such as his makes it difficult to establish the paternity of many of his ideas. This much is certain: No upstanding Lutheran could live in the Campanellan City of the Sun, but he would find a haven in Christianopolis. The southern vagrants moved in an astronomical and astrological world—the planets danced in Bruno's imaginative constructs. The northerners awaited marvels from the alchemical laboratory, which Luther had sanctioned. The alchemical concoctions required cellars, while in Campanella's city teaching took place in the open air and the temple was crowned by an observatory.

Andreae used a variety of literary devices to enhance his apostolic message. One was derived from the Epistle to the Hebrews, chapter 11, verses 13–16, where Paul wrote of those who confessed themselves "strangers and pilgrims on the earth," who now "desire a better country, that is, a heavenly." It led to a description of a pilgrim's progress in the land of the wicked and the discovery of the city of God. The image of Cosmoxenus is said to reflect the writings of Sebastian Münster, or if one looks for deeper origins in Andreae's early life, a painting in the Herrenberg Stiftskirche by Jerg Ratgeb depicting the apostolic company as it goes forth into the world.[13] Another way to propagate the faith involved the translation of the language of alchemy, the experience of the various stages of the traditional chemical processes, into religious terms. Alchemy became a rich storehouse of Christian symbols in Andreae's *Chemical Wedding*. This symbolization of alchemy was an approved practice going back to Luther himself. The search for Christ could be rendered in a variety of images that saturated the spiritual atmosphere. Dreams reflected bookish fantasies and associations from the alchemical laboratory; in turn literary renderings of emotional religious experiences assumed a dreamlike quality. Later generations lost the alchemical keys to these symbolic forms and they became merely bizarre. Finally, the whole of pagan mythology and all the astrological signs were Christianized. All these were new ways of propagating the faith, the creation of Christian myths that would appeal to the hearts of men, fables to teach the unknowing. The myth of the *Christianopolis* was Andreae's ultimate achievement, the myth of Christian Rosencreutz was one with which he wrangled until he recognized its dangers, but along the way he brought forth other syncretic images, many of which were far too recondite to penetrate the general culture of Christian Europe. The sciences became Christian experiences, not mere studies of objective nature. Christian doctrines, rites, articles of faith were read into the practices of the sciences, which were then used as emotional demonstrations of Christianity, a means to strengthen Christian belief through the operation of the senses in the laboratory. In the *Herculis Christiani Luctae XXIV* (Strasbourg, 1615), the pagan hero was completely Christianized and his labors became Christian trials.[14]

The wanderer in a strange country, a myth that could take the form of a dialogue, a homily, poetry, permitted Andreae to adapt Lucianic and Erasmian wit to expose the folly of false rhetoricians, inflated mathematicians, lucre-lusting—as contrasted with Christian—alchemists, and, once he was aware of their threat to Christian faith, the Rosicrucians. The pilgrim of the *Peregrini in Patria Errores* (1618) was directed in *Civis Christianus* (1619) to the discovery of Christ. In a rather late work, the *Opuscula Aliquot de Restitutione Reipub. Christianae in Germania* (Nuremberg, 1633), Andreae voiced his fears that in his own Evangelical Church the state, unless it was reformed in a Christian spirit, might replace the papacy in a new confusion of the gospel.

In a letter to Duke Augustus of June 27, 1642, Andreae recounted the truncated life of the Societas Christiana, whose promise had been shattered by the outbreak of the Thirty Years' War. The original roster of membership included a number of impeccably proper Lutherans, and Andreae later contended that the Society had been unalterably opposed to the "unworthy fantasy" of the fictitious Rosicrucian Fraternity. After a quarter of a century, the earlier fascination of at least a portion of the respectable scholars was soft-pedaled. Some members of the Society may have once shared with the Rosicrucian Fraternity a passion for the renovation of the Christian world, but the openness, common sense, and straightforwardness of the Society contrasted sharply with the Fraternity's affinity for naometria, practical alchemy, and a variety of occult sciences. The idea of the Society stayed with Andreae, and in 1626 he tried again to form a *Unio Christiana,* but with little success. In a letter of September 16, 1629, to Comenius, who offered to enlist in the Union, Andreae focused on the crucial distinction between the vain, pretentious, worldly aims of the Rosicrucian Fraternity and those of the new Society, in which Christ was restored to His proper place in the order of the universe.[15] By that time Andreae had been overwhelmed by despair and had resigned himself to the role of a David forbidden to build the temple of the Lord, a task left to a future Solomon. Comenius responded to the challenge, and his writings heralded a new Solomon who would erect the Temple of Pansophia, with the support of a new Plato, himself.

Christianopolis and the Societas Christiana may have been the ideal solution for the tender Lutheran conscience of Andreae. If he could show that all the ideas necessary for a general reformation were already in the Gospel, there was no need for a new confession of faith. Since Christ Himself was teacher, Christian Rosencreutz and his Arabic "science" learned in distant Damcar and his rediscovered tomb became a supererogatory mystification. Wilhelm Wense was credited by Andreae in a funerary homage with originating the idea of the Christian Society.

He labored to bring together in a kind of society a certain number of men eager and able to work for the betterment of the age, who, dispersed throughout Germany, would communicate with each other, and, in the bonds of friendship, analyze corrupt conditions both in literature and in the Christian life and discuss remedies for the same. For at a time when a certain deceitful (*fictitia*) fraternity had imposed upon inquisitive minds far and wide, he believed that the opportunity had arisen to reply (as I mentioned in my *Christianopolis,* p. 15), "If these reforms seem proper, why do we not try them ourselves? Let us not wait for them to do it . . ."

Following Wense's advice, Andreae composed, he tells us, the two *Invitationes ad Fraternitatem Christi,* and two small pamphlets, the "Christianae Societatis Imago" and the "Christiani Amoris Dextera Porrecta." Campanella's title was preserved, its meaning transformed.

The society was called the "Civitas Solis," and the two of us had as our goal to unite—under a kind of rule and a head (we had settled upon Augustus of Lüneburg, that phoenix of princes and living ideal for such a plan)—a certain number of Germans who were orthodox in Lutheran faith, conspicuous in erudition, and trustworthy in character (but without discrimination as to family or fortune), in order that they might apply themselves earnestly to the cultivation of truer piety, the correction of dissolute moral life, and the restoration of a literary culture that had fallen into decay . . . But the storm of the German calamity fell upon us and made trial of all these—in my opinion not at all unpraiseworthy—endeavors, thus frustrating and overturning my whole "Christianopolis."[16]

Some scholars have bifurcated the life of Andreae into the young esoteric thinker of the pre-1634 period and the rather narrow, orthodox Lutheran preacher and administrator of later years. Similar attempts have been made to saw in two the life of Campanella, of Marx, and of hundreds of other thinkers. The texts show a reasonable moral consistency in Andreae throughout the years, though the alchemical symbolism became less pervasive as he got older and grew more verbose and prosy. His *Rei Christianae et Literariae Subsidia* (Tübingen, 1642) is a dull, 600-page compendium, in which sections on universal knowledge in science, art, and learning rub elbows with chronology, Christian apologetics, a harmony of the Gospels. At one point he lists four men in each of fifteen spheres of human activity where moderns have been innovators, ranging from theology through law, medicine, history, mathematics, astronomy, philosophy, rhetoric, criticism (classical scholarship), poetry, encyclopedism, geography, cosmography, art, music, printing. More than a third of the men named were engaged, at least part-time, in what would today be called science; but a good number of them were alchemists and iatrochemists.

Not only had the Thirty Years' War dashed the hopes of Andreae's Societas Christiana. He experienced its ravages in the flesh in the loss of his possessions and in the sufferings of the flock whose shepherd he was. At Calw, where he had served for nearly two decades as Spezialsuperintendent (Chief Pastor), his library and paintings were burned, his manuscripts destroyed. After the disaster and the years of reconstruction, in 1639 he was appointed court preacher and consistorial councillor to Duke Eberhard III at Stuttgart. Andreae bewailed his lot like Jonah—"I have been tossed out of my ship, Calw, and swallowed by the leviathan, the Court"[17]—but with time he overcame his "nausea rerum" and proceeded to reorganize and reform Lutheran institutions in his jurisdiction. When ill health demanded that he be freed of some of his responsibilities, he was made Abbot and Generalsuperintendent of Bebenhausen, a Cistercian cloister that had become a Lutheran school. Finally in 1654, the year of his death, he was awarded a sinecure as Abbot of Adelberg, a burned abbey, and allowed to retire to Stuttgart, his *refrigerium,* a place of refreshment and consolation. But the memory of a Rosicrucian past haunted him all his life. In his Autobiography he had again reaffirmed his orthodoxy with passionate invective. "Therefore, both privately and in the public light of the Christian church, and against the lovers of darkness, we solemnly declare that we do not have, have not had, nor will have anything in common with the mire of Papism, the grandiloquence of Calvinism, the blasphemies of Photinianism, the hypocrisy of the Schwenkfelders, the craze of the Weigelians, the dregs of Anabaptism, the reveries of the Enthusiasts, the predictive calculations of the curious, the slipperiness of syncretism, the abomination of libertinism—or, in short, with any vanities and illusions of impostors."[18] He managed to incorporate both Arndt's pietism and Hafenreffer's theological orthodoxy; but the proportions of the sacred formula were not constant throughout his life. The ardor of youth and the frigidity of age gravely affected the balance.

Christianopolis

Of his hundred-odd writings the *Christianopolis* was the one work through which Andreae entered general histories of utopian thought. In this portrait of an ideal Christian society science and orthodox Lutheran religion are completely integrated; while knowledge of Christ is the highest good, physical science becomes a major human preoccupation that has been sanctified. As early as Robert Burton's *Anatomy of Melancholy, Christianopolis* was classified with More's *Utopia,* Bacon's *New Atlantis,* and Campanella's *City of the Sun* as a utopia. In his funeral oration for Wilhelm Wense, Andreae had called the *Christianopolis* the literary pendant to the Societas Christiana. It became one of the recognized progenitors of the Comenian Pansophia and a foundation of Leibniz' universal projects. Since it was composed in Latin and was not translated into German until the eighteenth century, its direct influence was generally restricted to the learned world; but there it was often imitated, extending its imagery over a broader field as the ideas appeared secondhand in the vernacular.[19]

Andreae's utopian masterpiece is written in his satiric, imagistic, Erasmian, often cryptic style, more apt for the description of spiritual experience than for arguing the fine points of theology. The *Christianopolis* departs in significant ways from its utopian contemporaries. It is fervently Christocentric, and the observer who is the protagonist is not a wooden robot; he is psychically transformed by the experience of the holy city. *Christianopolis* is the history of an adept in an ideal Lutheran community, and the alterations of his inner being, his exaltation through the sight of the meticulously ordered Christian city, is the heart of the work. By contrast, nothing much happens to Bacon's sailors shipwrecked on New Atlantis; though they feel amazement and gratitude for the kind treatment they receive, they do not undergo a spiritual conversion. As for the Genoese captain who has seen the glories of Campanella's City of the Sun, he is nothing but a figurehead, in haste to sail away once his tale has been recounted.

The hero of *Christianopolis* is Cosmoxenus Christianus, a stranger, a pilgrim who suffers from the corrupt uses of the world; the allegory is not disguised. Raphael Hythlodaeus, the hero of More's *Utopia,* is presented as a member of Vespucci's expedition functioning on a realistic level, and More's artifice throughout is to preserve verisimilitude. Andreae's pilgrim embarks on the ship named Fantasy; after it is wrecked, he is washed ashore on Caphar Salama (named for the place where Judas Maccabaeus conquered Nicanor's forces), an island whose inhabitants live in community under a spiritual rule. Caphar Salama is described in fifty chapters covering all aspects of the society under as many headings. The guardians of Christianopolis first submit the outsider to a moral examination, which he passes. Immersion in the sea, represented as a baptism, has prepared him for a new life. In stages he is shown the city. First there is a review of the material order, the things that concern the historians of mechanical utopias—agriculture, artisans' work, public projects. Then Cosmoxenus ascends to the innermost shrine of the city, where the institutions of justice, religion, and education are located. On entering the holier region he is confronted by twelve articles inscribed in gold. They are Christological, orthodox in their formulas on the ministry of the word, free forgiveness of sin, general resurrection of the flesh. Part of the credo testifies: "We believe in an eternal life by which we shall obtain perfect light, ability, quiet knowledge, plenty and joy; by which also the malice of Satan, the impurity of the world, the corruption of men shall be checked, by which it shall be well with the good, and evil with the evildoers, and the visible glory of the Holy Trinity shall be ours forever."[20] To Andreae, Satan was as palpable as he had been for Luther, and men had to give him combat through word and deed. In few other utopias are explicit creedal utterances so prominently featured. More's Utopians require only a belief in God, the immortality of the soul, and rewards and punishments in the next world; religion is reasonably tolerant of deviations. Bacon's Atlanteans have become Christian through a miraculous epiphany, but not much is made of the whole matter beyond observance of certain Christian restraints on behavior. Christianopolis not only has a detailed creed, but some articles are believed *toto corde,* "with all our heart"—a pietistic intensity has suffused religious belief.

Andreae's man has been restored to the dignity forfeited by Adam's transgression, and through the Holy Spirit he has entered upon a new relationship with nature. Article VIII reads: "erudimur supra naturam, armamur contra naturam, conciliamur cum naturam."[21] In the interrogation to which Cosmoxenus submitted before entering Christianopolis, one of the failings to which he confessed was that "by . . . inexcusable folly" he had neglected the countenance of nature.[22] In another passage, Andreae reflected: "For what a narrow thing is human knowledge if it walks about as a stranger in the most whole-some creations and does not know what advantage this or that thing bears to man, yet meanwhile wanders about in the unpleasant crackle of abstractions and rules, none the less boasting of this as a science of the highest order!"[23]

The mood of Christianopolitan society conforms to the Morean rule about "honest allowable pleasures," not quite monastic in its austerity, but hardly indulging in superfluities. "Oh," says the narrator, "only those persons are rich who have all of which they have real need, who admit nothing merely because it is possible to have it in abundance!"[24] The evils of disorder, hunger, misery, and war prevalent in the outside world are lamented as impediments to spiritual fulfillment. The ideal secular institutions of Christianopolis, the educational system that fosters excellence and the utopian mechanics proper governing production and consumption, are not ends in themselves, but merely a preparation for the spiritual feast, the theosophical stretching of the soul. They are preliminaries that insure against the loss of spiritually creative members of the community through want and neglect. In a specially appointed place in Christianopolis where the qualified inhabitants convene for lectures on metaphysical science, the chosen ones acquire a mystic vision of God in the Christian Neoplatonic tradition. Rapture makes them oblivious of all earthly concerns—"they find themselves again."[25] Though this is not an enduring or continuing state, they return to earthly matters ennobled by the experience. Differences are recognized in the capacity of various men for such an exalted spiritual achievement. The highest stage of theosophy, a science reserved for a select group capable of receiving God's direct illumination, begins where the knowledge of nature ends. It is secret and is communicated through the vision of the Cross. Andreae has drawn on the rich German mystical tradition, into which images from the new science have been infused, as a way of finding union with God. More's Christian humanist utopia allowed for an elite, but they were far closer to all other men than the awesome scientist-priests of Bacon and Campanella or the spiritual directors of Christianopolis.

In a passage leveled against excessive emphasis upon sterile logic, Andreae defined the intellectual temper of the island in language at once theological and scientific: "They incite their talented men to recognize what reason has been entrusted to them and to test their own judgment of things lest they find it necessary to seek everything outside of themselves and to bring in theories from without. For man has within him a great treasure of judging if he prefers to dig it up instead of burying it with mounds and weight of precepts."[26] The inhabitants of Christianopolis turn to modern mathematics and geometry for sharpening their wits, rather than to Aristotelian logic. Both the Baconian empirical science and mathematics were integrated into the Christian science; but such knowledge was not autonomous or sufficient unto itself.

Surely that supreme Architect did not make this mighty mechanism haphazard, but He completed it most wisely by measures, numbers and proportions and He added to it the element of time, distinguished by a wonderful harmony. His mysteries has He placed especially in His workshops and typical buildings, that with the key of David we may reveal the length, breadth, and depth of divinity, find and note down the Messiah present in all things, who unites all in a wonderful harmony and conducts all wisely and powerfully, and that we may take our delight in adoring the name of Jesus.[27]

The secret brotherhood, the elect alone, learn of the mystic numbers and proportions of things. Despite the generally communal spirit of the society, the esoteric character of the highest knowledge in Christianopolis excludes the "rabble," and even the most illuminated must accept the existence of bounds to their knowledge of God and His ways, an idea of human limitations Andreae shared with Francis Bacon. Millenarian prophecy is rejected.

In this *cabala* it is advisable to be rather circumspect, since we have considerable difficulty in present matters, grope in events of the past, and since God has reserved the future for Himself, revealing it to a very limited number of individuals and then only at the greatest intervals. Let us then love the secrets of God which are made plain to us and let us not, with the rabble, throw away that which is above us nor consider divine things on an equal basis with human; since God is good in all things, but in His own, even admirable.[28]

In Christianopolis there is a negative attitude toward the traditional Aristotelian classics of philosophy and even a certain ambivalence about the printing press because it has propagated so much irreligion and absurdity, but there is no such denigration of the chemical laboratory. Here true nature, God's world, is revealed without falsification. Only direct exploration of nature yields truth; everything the ancients wrote about nature is prima facie suspect since they were heathens. "Whatever has been dug out and extracted from the bowels of nature by the industry of the ancients, is here subjected to close examination, that we may know whether nature has been truly and faithfully opened to us."[29] While Luther in his table talk may have denigrated astronomy in general (and perhaps Copernicus in particular), he had not been opposed to alchemical inquiries. The new astronomy could run up against the literal, precise Lutheran interpretation of scriptural text, but alchemical chemistry and mathematics were not exposed to such risks since their content was by no stretch of the most punctilious scholar's imagination covered in the Bible. It has even been surmised that the Lutheran dogma of the real presence in the Eucharist could lead to a veneration of the world of nature in all its chemical complexity. The pharmacy in Christianopolis is a veritable microcosm of the whole of nature. "Whatsoever the elements offer, whatever art improves, whatever all creatures furnish, it is all brought to this place, not only for the cause of health, but also with a view toward the advancement of education in general." Pharmacology and chemistry have become the exemplar sciences, whose teachings can by analogy be extended to public affairs. "For how can the division of human matters be accomplished more easily than where one observes the most skillful classification, together with the greatest variety!"[30]

The *laboratorium* in the center of the city is described with meticulous detail. "Here the powers of metals, minerals, vegetables, and also animals are investigated, refined, increased, and combined for the use of the human race and the improvement of health. Here sky is married to earth, and the divine mysteries impressed upon the earth are discovered; here one learns to master fire, make use of air, measure water, and analyze earth. Here the ape of nature has wherewith it may play, while it emulates her principles, and through the traces of the great machine forms something minute and most elegant."[31]

The evils of the world, the brevity of life, the weariness and plagues of existence are taken for granted; but men need not be broken by them. Andreae propounds no progressionist doctrine of science in the Condorcet manner, nor does he foresee a great prolongation of human life, the Baconian goal. The traditional allotted span would be sufficient, if it were not misspent in debauchery and avoidable suffering. Both Bacon and Andreae lay emphasis on the chemical and biological sciences as the clue to whatever transformations are to occur on earth. Galilean mathematical science, though respected, had not yet been conceived as applicable to human behavior. In Christianopolis the anatomy of animals is studied in order to be able to assist the struggles of nature, and Andreae is distressed that men outside the utopian island do not understand the internal operations of their own bodies.

Most sections of the *Christianopolis* are devoted to an account of the basic, everyday requirements of a society in which material necessities are readily provided for in a communal order. Houses are not privately owned, and cooked food is obtained from a central storehouse, though consumed at home to avoid the tumult of public mess halls. Work is freed from the biblical curse and is reconceptualized as an expression of man's divinity, an act of creation imitative of God the Creator. Necessity is no longer the whip that forces men to labor: They do not have to be driven to work like pack animals to their tasks. Having been trained in accurate knowledge of the science that underlies their work, they find delight in manipulating the innermost parts of nature. Science, work, and techniques have been interrelated. If a person in Christianopolis does not investigate the minutest elements of the world, filling in gaps in knowledge by devising more precise instruments, he is considered worthless. The worker-scientist-artisans, the predominant class, labor "in order that the human soul may have some means by which it and the highest prerogative of the mind may unfold themselves through different sorts of machinery, or by which, rather, the little spark of divinity remaining in us, may shine brightly in any material offered." [32]

The combination of the artisan and the scientist in one person was the natural consequence of a realization that the artisans were the repositories of scientific knowledge, of the Baconian test of science as knowledge that results in practical works, and of the new spiritual valuation of manual labor. There is mockery of the "carnal-minded" [33] who avoid science because, with aristocratic affectation, they shrink from touching earth, water, coal, and other material objects required in scientific experiments, while they boast of their possession of horses, dogs, and harlots. The whole state of Christianopolis can be considered one great workshop of educated artisans skilled in different sorts of crafts, who work short hours. Since there is no slavery or forced labor their work is not irksome to the human body. There is a great variety of products to be freely exchanged, since pecuniary gain is not a motive of production. Everything is clean and neatly arranged as befits a proper appreciation of the gifts of God. A minister, a judge, and a director of learning, combining in their persons religion, justice, and science, take care of public administration, and a state economist has supervision over the division of work tasks and produce. "For though no one in the whole island ever goes hungry, yet by the grace of God or the generosity of nature, there is always abundance, since gluttony and drunkenness are entirely unknown." [34]

But concentration on the utopian earthly order was not an end in itself. In a subtle, paradoxical sense the perfect order of this world achieved in Christianopolis becomes a means to freedom from earthliness. The director of learning had a way of at once valuing and transcending the knowledge of material things. "For he insisted that a close examination of the earth would bring about a proper appreciation of the heavens, and when the value of the heavens had been found, there would be a contempt of the earth."[35]

Andreae does not rely on the mere mechanics of a social utopia to bring about the general reformation of mankind. They are a part of the propitious setting for a Christian renewal; but only after men have undergone an inner transformation can they realize a terrestrial Christianopolis that will be both a simulacrum and a foretaste of the heavenly city. Universal brotherhood, godliness in men's hearts, must precede the establishment of Christianopolis. There is no authoritarian legislator as in More's *Utopia;* his function is replaced by the experience of religious and scientific conversion. The pursuit of science is recognized as the occupation most worthy of man and most acceptable to God because of its religious character.

Spiritual regeneration in Christianopolis takes place within the limitations of fallen man. The origin of life, like death, is putrid. Ultimate blessedness is not of this world; it is only of the resurrected body purified and refined in heaven. In this world science raises fallen man and restores him to a state that approximates the prelapsarian condition—an apology for science that would be reborn with Wilkins and Glanvill in the Royal Society and would survive as a secularized image as late as Saint-Simon. While Plato's spirited guardians exercised their bodies and listened to prescribed music, and More's Utopians at leisure were humanist scholars who learned moral truths from ancient literature, by the seventeenth century scientific activity became the principal preoccupation of the elite in *The City of the Sun,* the *New Atlantis,* and *Christianopolis.* At a time when Italian cardinals still refused to look into Galileo's glass, Andreae's community was equipped with "the very valuable telescope recently invented,"[36] with models of the heavens, tools, instruments for astronomical study and observation of the "spots on the stars." Galileo and Kepler were known, as were Bruno's "short cuts in memorizing."[37] There is no battle of the two cultures, and Andreae takes the stand that a man ignorant of science and mathematics is only half-educated. In *Christianopolis* a marked contempt for contemporary scholars ignorant of science obtrudes and echoes Kepler's *Nova Astronomia:* "If like strangers in a foreign land they shall bring to humanity no assistance or counsel or judgment or device, then I think they deserve to be contemned and classed with the tenders of sheep, cattle, and hogs."[38] But though science plays an important role in this and other utopias, most of the inhabitants are still primarily engaged in agricultural pursuits affected neither by the new science nor by technological innovation. In Christianopolis "the agriculture of the patriarchs is reproduced, the results being the more satisfactory the closer the work is to God and the more attentive to natural simplicity."[39] What Andreae imagined the agriculture of Abraham and Isaac to have been is not disclosed.

The educational reforms of Comenius are presaged in Andreae's ideal city, even as the pictures of scientific matter writ large on the walls of Campanella's City of the Sun were repeated in Comenius' *Orbis Sensualium Pictus.* The goals of education were first to teach the worship of God, then to instill the virtue of chastity, finally to develop intellectual prowess. As in the City of the Sun,

competitiveness and striving were encouraged; the pupils had to exert themselves to learn. Schools were airy, sunny, and decorated with pictures. Teachers were directed to acquire a sense of the individual psychological character of
the children in their charge, and praise or disgrace were the instrumentalities
that replaced the scourge, now restricted to exceptional cases. As corporal punishment of children was virtually banished among advanced utopian thinkers
from Andreae and Comenius through Rousseau and Fourier, shaming was
substituted—the replacement of physical by psychic pain as a desperate last resort. Teachers in contemporary schools, who were the dregs of society, were
attacked by Andreae for raining blows upon their pupils instead of displaying
generosity and kindness. Andreae may have been drawing on personal experience when he wrote that those who had suffered indignities at the hands of
schoolmasters bore witness with bodies enfeebled for the rest of their lives.
The training of girls did not exclude learning, though much of their effort was
devoted to domestic art and science; girls as well as boys studied Hebrew,
Greek, and Latin. Andreae would not drop ancient languages from the curriculum, but he voiced the Lutheran argument against excessive emphasis upon
this branch of knowledge: God understands the vernacular well enough. The
summit of happiness was to be able, with one and the same effort, to preserve
the safety of the republic and secure the future life, and education was the key
to both. "The children which we bear here, we may find to our satisfaction
have been born for the heavens as much as for the earth."[40] An idea has been
introduced that will have great potency in secularized versions of utopia.
"Happy and very wise are those who anticipate here on earth the firstlings of a
life which they hope will be everlasting."[41]

Christian renovation was dependent upon the integration into a whole of the
benign efforts of men, which were now divided into autonomous parts. Upon
his penetration of the innermost shrine of Christianopolis, Cosmoxenus
learned that the truly religious man would not sever connections with things
human and adopt a theology directed only toward the divine. Nor would he
exercise power and rule without the check of Christianity. Nor would he imitate those learned men who, instead of seeking truth for the sake of God and
men, were motivated primarily by vanity and self-love. In the real world there
was discord because of the separation of divinity, sovereign rule, and knowledge into compartments; in the ideal city there was *concordia*. "Christianity . . . conciliates God with men and unites men together, so that they
piously believe, do good deeds, know the truth, and finally die happily to live
eternally."[42]

Dynastic wars made more vicious by religious differences had brought
about a world in disintegration. Andreae's brotherhood of the learned and the
Christian societies he founded were the instrumentalities he hoped to use to
propagate a belief in the new unity. Where Wallenstein's troops struck, men
were reduced to an animalian state without rule, godliness, or knowledge. The
Continental wars of the seventeenth century awakened men of virtually every
religion in Europe to the disaster of the major Christian schism, and the English Civil War soon revealed the fragmentation of religion into literally hundreds of rival sects. The Christian utopia of Andreae answered to an anguished
longing for a restored unity, without which there could be no renovation as
Christian energies spent themselves in bloody internecine strife. A gulf sepa-

rates More's utopia, composed on the eve of the Reformation, from the seven-teenth-century religious utopias, whose main purpose was to put the pieces together again into a new whole.

Theoria and Praxis

It is common to stress the Christology and theocentrism of Luther and to belit-tle his social and ethical concerns. The attacks on the peasants and his sum-mons to the princes, along with his bitter hostility to Müntzer and what he came to represent, support this interpretation. In the seventeenth century the pietist resurgence within Lutheranism hoped to obliterate the false dichotomy between social doctrines and the quest for personal salvation. Through his writings and ministry Andreae strove to bridge the chasm between inner reli-gious consciousness and overt social behavior, and to make utopian renovation an integral part of the Lutheran creed. Often he suffered the despair of failure as invading armies destroyed what he had built and left parishes desolate.

In his youth, Andreae had been greatly impressed by Calvinist Geneva, and the aging Lutheran could still write a panegyric to its social order, much as his dogmatic beliefs differed from its religious doctrines.

> While I was at Geneva, I noted something of great moment which I will remember with nostalgia till the end of my days. Not only does this city enjoy a truly free political constitution; it has besides, as its particular ornament and means of discipline, the guid-ance of social life. By virtue of the latter, all the mores of the citizens and even their slightest transgressions are examined each week, first by neighborhood supervisors, then by the aldermen, and finally by the senate itself, according to the gravity of the case or the obduracy and insolence of the offender . . . The resultant moral purity does so much honor to the Christian religion, is so consistent with it and so inseparable from it, that we should shed our bitterest tears that this discipline is unknown or completely neglected in our circles; all men of good will ought to labor for its restoration. Indeed, if religious differences had not made it impossible for me, the harmony of faith and morals at Geneva would have bound me there—and so from that time I have striven with all nty energy to provide the like for our churches.[43]

After his rehabilitation Andreae had turned his Lutheranism outward to the reconstruction of church order and to eradicating social evil in his province. He had once poured forth works of theory, especially in the productive decade following his marriage, on the theme of the Christian as pilgrim in this world. To the traditional metaphor of the two books, Andreae's pilgrim had added the Book of Life and the Book of Conscience. In his Autobiography, Andreae wrote with an epigrammatic scratch about the necessity of relating theory and practice, excoriating those who led corrupt lives while they preserved dog-matic purity: "theoria quidem limpidissima, praxis vero lutulentissima est, doctrina integerrima, vita corruptissima."[44] Christ said to Peregrinus, "Know that you cannot have my book without my Cross." Descartes and the great mathematical astronomers and physicists tried to divide the realm of the sacred from that of the profane. The Pansophist Lutherans bore witness to the reli-gious impossibility of separating the two worlds of power and knowledge. They would deny that this divorcement had ever been Luther's intent; and in any event, the renovation of Lutheran doctrine required the integration of the secular and spiritual kingdoms. Campanella's prescriptions of unity in the *Ci-*

vitas Solis, though written to further the advancement of a different religious creed, were adapted by the Lutheran Pansophists.

For all his concern with social practice, Andreae's Christian myth (his term) was not a blueprint for a future reality in the commonsensical meaning of the word. The *Christianopolis* was perhaps the purest version of the myth, once presented in another form in his *Turbo.* Though the Lutheran Andreae wove a social gospel into the fabric of his ideal city, unlike Campanella he could not conceive of this earthly world as turning into a paradise. Forever each person had to live through the Christian experience of doubt and despair, before his individual discovery of Christ. Andreae's Christian communist society was not a project for immediate implementation, nor was it a prefiguration of a millennial state; it was the image of an ideal that might move Christians to strive for the improvement of Christian daily life. Even in its ultimate perfection the Societas Christiana was to be under a secular head, a Lutheran Christian prince. Though the members of Andreae's group were committed to work for the betterment of the age by conjuring up prospects of a more pious city, there is no proposal in the writings of the mature Andreae for a leap into a perfect society. He had become suspicious of charismatic experience. Ever since More, utopias have been disavowed by their inventors when the powder of violent action has spread its acrid smell around them. Individual utopians can be set into a spectrum: At one end are the militant reformers red hot with the expectation of instant fulfillment of their schemes, at the other end the visionaries whose dreams, though they may affect human conduct to some degree, were never meant to be realized in this vale of tears. The mature Andreae intended his *Christianopolis* to remain a *paradigma.* In his younger days he may have been more sanguine.

Andreae's ideas are still alive among present-day Rosicrucians and theosophists and in some faint degree among Freemasons. To approach God through inquiries into the secrets of the macrocosm both spiritual and physical, to be undertaken by a Christian brotherhood, led to the idea of a universal republic of science. The brotherhood and the Christian city bore witness that man, in imitation of his Creator, was capable of mastering chaos, of celebrating spirit and its capacities. Andreae posed the problem for the German Enlightenment: How does man order and spiritualize his earthly existence? Those of his utterances that could be interpreted as evangelical optimism were later picked up by major thinkers of the eighteenth century—Thomasius, Lessing, and above all Herder, who translated and revived a number of Andreae's works at a time when he had been virtually forgotten in the German world. In seventeenth-century England, however, echoes of Andreae were more commonly heard —in Samuel Gott's *Nova Solyma,* for example. There are references to Andreae's thought in Hartlib's correspondence with Boyle in 1647, and the religio-scientific admixture of the *Christianopolis* was not alien to the first generations of the Royal Society.[45] It fortified the message of the *New Atlantis.*

12

Comenius and His Disciples

DESPITE HIS DERISION of other hierophants, it was the fate of Comenius to build a baroque system of the same order, with one major difference—it was open, and all men, according to their capacities, could acquire the knowledge he freely dispensed. He invented neologisms as clumsy as those he mocked, and compiled volumes that were keys to foreign languages, that instructed men in wisdom, in the art of teaching, in ecumenical religion, in the science of all things. But before his death he suffered the same contempt that he had once heaped on the Rosicrucians. However obstinate his denials, his own roots were in the works of mystagogues close to those who had first fabricated the arcana of Christian Rosencreutz. Comenius picked up where Andreae had left off, and through one project after another tried to realize the Rosicrucian ideal of universal renovation. Millenarian prophets replaced Rosicrucian alchemists as the active agents of reform. The vast storehouse of his writings was a mixed bag—a contemporary called them a farrago.[1] One finds in his works insights of genius, practical educational plans of immediate applicability that reveal a knowledge of children and men, but also much sheer nonsense and a great utopian's jungle profusion of plans whose density would not be equaled again until the nineteenth century.

The Moravian Exile

Born on March 28, 1592, in Comnia, Moravia, he was called Johann in memory of the Johann Hus who was burned in 1415 in Constance, his ashes strewn over the Rhine. It was the custom of the faithful who traced their origins to Hus to name the second child Johann. In the seventeenth century the Moravian Brethren were close to the Lutheran Evangelicals and Komenský (Comenius) was sent away to be educated in the Protestant universities of Herborn and Heidelberg. Upon his return to his native land he became a teacher, then administrator, and finally a bishop. He married, sired children, saw his family wiped out by the plague, remarried, fathered more children. In the Battle of the White Mountain in 1620 the Bohemian forces were defeated by the Catholic League, and the years of exile began. First the Brethren of the Unity, as they were called, found a refuge in Leszno in Poland; from Poland Comenius went on missions to England, Sweden, back to Poland, then to Hungary, then back to Leszno again. The Moravian refugees were supported by Protestant, mostly Lutheran, donations. When in 1656 Leszno was ravaged and burned, piles of Comenius' manuscripts were destroyed. His final haven was the home of the de Geer family in Amsterdam, where he spent the last fourteen years of his life, published a collection of his long-winded repetitive works, the *Opera Didactica Omnia,* and prepared the manuscript of his *De Rerum Humanarum Emendatione Consultatio Catholica* (General Consultation on an Improvement of All Things

Human), a utopian legacy of mammoth proportions. The full version of the *Consultatio,* completed in 1666, was not printed in its entirety until three hundred years later, after having been buried away in the library of an orphanage in Halle.[2]

What was published in Comenius' lifetime was only a small portion of his accumulated works, comprising 450 items, according to a recent Czech bibliography. The seven-part system of the *Consultatio* consists of a Panegersia (Universal Awakening), Panaugia (Universal Dawning), Pansophia (Universal Wisdom), Pampaedia (Universal Education), Panglottia (Universal Language), Panorthosia (Universal Reform), Pannuthesia (Universal Admonition), the first and last sections being largely hortatory.[3] Even though unacquainted with these manuscripts, learned contemporaries throughout Europe knew by word of mouth of his plan to inculcate universal wisdom in all men capable of receiving it, using a universal language as a mechanism and an encyclopedia as a repository, with the eventual goal of a reformation of all mankind in a Christian spirit. Translations of Comenius' didactic works into Arabic were made in Aleppo, and there are stories of renderings into Polish, Turkish, and "Mongolian." He became the educator of the American Indian when his textbooks were introduced into Harvard, where an Indian college had been established.[4]

Comenius had the utopian passion that Charles Fourier in the early nineteenth century labeled "unityism," and he lamented the "Scientiarum laceratio" that paralleled the tragic political and religious fragmentation of Europe.

Metaphysicians hum to themselves only, Natural Philosophers chaunt their own praises, Astronomers lead on their dances for themselves, Ethical Thinkers set up laws for themselves, Politicians lay foundations for themselves, Mathematicians triumph for themselves, and for themselves Theologians reign . . . We see that the branches of a tree cannot live unless they all alike suck their juices from a common trunk with common roots. And can we hope that the branches of Wisdom can be torn asunder with safety to their life, that is to truth? Can one be a Natural Philosopher who is not also a Metaphysician? or an Ethical Thinker who does not know something of Physical Science? or a Logician who has no knowledge of real matters? or a Theologian, a Jurisconsult, or a Physician, who is not first a Philosopher? or an Orator or Poet who is not all things at once?[5]

But Comenius was aware that, no matter how compelling the need, unity in any sphere of endeavor could not be established by fiat and had to recognize diversity. He was realistic about Christianity's minority position in the world, assigning it only a sixth of the known regions of the earth, while the Mohammedans had a fifth and the heathens nearly two-thirds, and he reached the conclusion that amid such a host of religions, unity, peace, and love among men could be attained only through liberty, consent, and harmony, not through coercion. "But the World will then onely be happy, when it shall once become Universal, that is as large as the very Universe itself; and mens minds like to Truth itself, noble and free, and not narrow, but large spirited and diffusive, like the infinite Creators, who would have all men to be saved, and that by persuasion, and not force, because impossible."[6]

In 1623 Comenius had written in Czech a guide to the perplexed for his sorely tried brethren, *The Labyrinth of the World and the Paradise of the Heart,* the double title representing the two phases of a Christian utopia. In a spirit of

ecumenism he included in the book episodes in which both More and Campanella figured, and symbolized his irenic conception of Christianity by a great
church with many different sectarian chapels on all sides. The *Labyrinth*
opened with a wanderer's description of the miseries and deceptions of the
marketplace in an allegorical city, the anti-utopia, followed by a portrayal of
the state of eupsychia he attained after the discovery of the divine spark of light
in his own soul, the true paradise of the heart. Scholars have praised the beauties of this pilgrim's progress in its original version; the subtleties have not
been communicated in translation. Comenius had labored for almost a decade
on this record of self-revelation and conversion, which became a book of consolation for Moravian expatriates.

As Comenius' stranger roamed through the city he encountered groups of
pretenders to truth and wisdom, each of whom he satirized—scholars, philosophers, Rosicrucians, doctors, jurists, rival religious disputants, sybarites, men
of power and fame. The thirteenth chapter, devoted to the secretive Rosicrucians, ridiculed their claim to the possession of an elixir, their promises of long
life, their preachings of universal brotherhood and happiness. The stranger
told how, of a sudden, thousands descended upon the Rosicrucians to purchase
their wisdom in packages labeled Portae sapientiae, Fortalitium scientiae,
Gymnasium universitatis, Bonum macro-micro-cosmicon, Harmonia utrius-
que cosmi, Christiano-cabalisticum, Antrum naturae, Arx primaterialis, Di-
vino-magicum, Tertrinum catholicum, Pyramis triumphalis, Hallelujah, and
other windy combinations. When the packages were opened, they turned out
to be empty. The buyers were then informed that only adepts of the secret
knowledge had access to the mysteries.

By the time he was fifty, Comenius was a major figure in the Protestant
world, the propagator of a complete system of knowledge that he called Pansophia and a new pedagogy to implement its precepts. England, the Netherlands, Sweden, East Prussia, Hungary were way stations from which he diffused his ideas. His reputation led to a story that he had been asked to accept
the presidency of Harvard College. Cotton Mather later recorded in Book IV
of the *Magnalia* his disappointment that the invitation to "illuminate this *Colledge* and *country*" had been refused: "The solicitations of the *Swedish* Ambassador, diverting him another way, that incomparable *Moravian* became not an
American." [7]

Comenius was torn between the demands of patrons interested in his practical didactic work and the adulation of true disciples, who saw all this activity as
a waste of his genius on tasks that any schoolteacher could accomplish, while
the great work for which he was ordained languished. When they snatched bits
of manuscript away and printed them he was both nettled and pleased. In Sweden, Chancellor Axel Oxenstierna paid him to develop his practical educational writings and produce textbooks, but was far less enthusiastic about the
universalist fancies of Pansophia. [8] Ecumenical affairs in Lithuania and Poland,
proselytizing ventures among skeptical potentates, the devastations of war, involvements with prophets whom he sheltered and whose visions he transcribed, interrupted work on his grand design for the reformation of the
world; but he always reverted to it. His life was consumed in money-raising in
behalf of his Moravian brethren, in stately appearances before Protestant
princes, to whom he became the symbol of persecution by Catholic powers.

To all who would listen he proffered his voluminous system of knowledge, human and divine, as the guiding light in the wilderness, the revelation that would save Christian civilization from destruction by the Turks and by the internecine, fractricidal wars of European sovereigns. What is perhaps most difficult to understand is that ambassadors attended his sermons even during the peace conferences of warring powers. Comenius at Breda is almost as anomalous a figure as Robert Owen at the Congress of Aix-la-Chapelle—and yet both were allowed to deliver their utopian messages.

In Holland in 1642 Comenius met with Descartes, who uttered polite words of praise for the monumental projects, but unless Comenius was completely blinded by his own enthusiasm he must have noticed from the outset that a chasm separated Pansophia, which sought to amalgamate all science and religion into an integrated whole, from Descartes's carefully circumscribed demarcation of the boundaries between rational philosophy and faith.[9] Comenius could never have accepted Descartes's absolute separation of philosophical mechanical studies from the study of divinity. Both took place in the mind and body of the same man. Nor was all knowledge dependent upon external sense impressions. The divinity in every man was itself creative because it partook, even if only in a minute degree, of the divine creative nature. In the last decades of his life, Comenius attacked Descartes as the major philosophical enemy because of his false conception of man, especially his isolation of the cognitive element in human nature. Comenius' man was an integral whole, Descartes would break him up into segments. What were dreams if not free creations of the autonomous inner man? Comenius asked. He was not aware, of course, of Descartes's three dreams on the night of November 10, 1619, which by his own interpretation, allegorical and analogical, had announced the discovery of the cogito. Perhaps the feeling for history and tradition that the later Pansophists preserved represents the major contrast with Descartes, the archdenigrator of the historical. For Leibniz, history would be one of the repositories of the infinitely varied forms of existence. Comenius assimilated the past in a similar spirit in his own turgid writings, as he indiscriminately heaped up citations from the scholarship of the previous two centuries, all pointing to the solution of Pansophia.

From an initial *Janua linguarum reserata*, a new method of teaching Latin, Comenius had jumped to the conception of a total Pansophia, a *Janua rerum reserata*. Like many utopian projectors, he was driven by the need to make his general plan known immediately, as soon as it was conceived. His most ambitious designs were presented in provocative outline form long before they had been thought through, and they were accompanied by pleas for economic or political help to complete the project. Maecenas or prince was needed to sustain the holy work. The learned of all nations were summoned to join in collaboration because the task was beyond the capacities of any one man. Comenius the prospectus-writer was not ashamed to confess his ignorance in many areas of knowledge. What he wanted for himself was control of the overall enterprise. A wish, a glint in the utopian eye, becomes an easy reality. If one can conceive of the idea why should it not be brought to pass?

With long dry intervals, Comenius was engaged on the *Consultatio* for thirty-three years. Pieces of his plan were written out, portions of manuscript were even printed. Collections of papers were lost, destroyed, rewritten. The imagination of a few men caught fire. The Hartlib circle in London—John Gauden, John Dury, Joachim Hübner, Theodore Haak, John Pell, Gabriel Plattes—wrote treatises in a Comenian spirit and persuaded Parliament to invite Comenius to England with the intention of having him found a Pansophic college in London, in Thomas More's Chelsea, perhaps. When wars and revolutions wiped out Comenius' prospects, the wanderer started over again, strengthened by an inner illumination, a conviction of inevitable success, reassured by millenarian and political prophecies. Though he promised the Swedish Chancellor Oxenstierna pedagogic guidance for schools, Comenius felt weighed down by the practical didactic tasks for which he was most famous and he spoke of them resentfully as a heavy yoke. He failed to fulfill his prosaic obligations as he got swept away by the grand design or by ecumenical religious negotiations that unfailingly ended in fiascoes. Collaborators never proved adequate, printing problems continually plagued him, and he was discontent with what came off the press. Ultimately a few hundred copies of a *Novissima Linguarum Methodus,* or *Analytical Didactic,* appeared in a Leszno edition of 1648, a mere foretaste of the banquet of Pansophia that was always in the offing.

In the *Consultatio* Comenius consciously cannibalized Renaissance and earlier seventeenth-century scholarship. He listed twenty-five of his predecessors from the world of learning whom he had fitted into the universal synthesis. Despite the reverence for Comenius aroused in recent years by the belated publication of the *Consultatio,* it remains what most of his writings are: outlines, sketches, projects that have a grand architectural symmetry and express the fantasy wishes of Christian Pansophia, but often consist of mere chapter and section headings. The contents tend to be skimpy—old Comenian slogans and catchwords repeated, suggestive neologisms—and like any skeletal framework they do not fulfill the expectations he aroused. Often they are dry bones that modern commentators have covered with alien flesh. Only on occasion does the passion of the religious seeker after a Christian Pansophia erupt in a moving prayer: "O Lord, give us the true Philosophy; give us pure Religion; give us a peaceful Polity! So that wisely, piously, serenely, we can live in the present age, then be borne aloft to You, and dwell with You in Your blessed eternity without end! . . . O Lord, have mercy on the age! Do not despise the works of Your hands!"[10]

In the end, Comenius remains the disseminator of earlier ideas in the Pansophic movement, a synthesizer and structure-builder rather than an inventor of new conceptions. By now it has become possible to divest him of his often obfuscatory private language and to appreciate the manner in which he wove together strands from Bruno, Bacon, Campanella, and Andreae into one grandiose system. For Comenius there was no contradiction between a belief in the imminent end of the world and the active launching of Pansophic projects for gathering knowledge of the real world in colleges and for the writing of encyclopedias of all things. Through exegesis of biblical texts validation could be found for the idea that the fullness of knowledge and the millennium would occur more or less simultaneously. Comenius made the conjuncture explicit. "There was born on my hands a tractate with the title 'Via Lucis' [The Way of Light], that is, a reasonable disquistion in what manner the intellectual light of souls, Wisdom, may now at last, at the approaching eventide of the world, be happily diffused through all minds and peoples. This for the better understanding of those words of prophecy in Zachariah 14.v.7: 'But it shall come to pass, that at evening time it shall be light.'"[11]

Teaching All to All

The origin of evil lay in the individual quest for pleasure and the failure to seek universal harmony. In the present corrupted world, from the earliest years of man's education, knowledge was an egotistic goal that served human pride. In the harmony of the All, wisdom would become a general duty. It was not enough that a man labored for the salvation of his own soul or individual illumination; knowledge had to bear fruit for others. Among many sects, the dangerous idea was ingrained from childhood that those in most need of light were outside the circle of the brethren and should be denied admission to the church. Pansophia conceived of mankind as a whole. It was at once a *politia,* a *philosophia,* and a *religio,* Comenius taught in the *Prodromus,* a unifying principle that brought all men within its orbit and excluded no one.

Comenius' chosen instrumentality for inculcating a spirit of voluntary obedience in all members of the Christian commonwealth was education made attractive, and for most people he remains primarily an educational utopian. The course of life in the ideal Christian republic was open to talent, and spiritual leadership fell to those who had a natural vocation for it. The others, according to the gospel laid down in the *Great Didactic,* were not taught beyond their needs and capacities. And even though the higher forms of education were accessible to women, as a rule they would be excluded from exalted studies. If there was a careful regulation of pleasure in his utopia, hardship and pain in training were not extolled as salutary. The learning process was to be gradual and easy, chastisement rare and never brutal—Comenius too recalled his boyhood schools as "slaughterhouses."[12] As in Andreae's *Christianopolis,* under the new system teachers would strive to uncover and understand the concealed, inborn characters of their charges, in order to be able to guide them effectively. The careful gradation of learning from concrete, immediate things to the complex and the abstract was an imitation of the divine chain of being. Wherever Comenius' system was instituted in some degree, there was a revolutionary departure from learning by mere rote. A measure of educational reform was perhaps the most enduring achievement of the seventeenth-century Pansophic utopians.

In the Pansophic utopia spiritual power in society was acknowledged as manifestly superior over its ancient temporal rival, and both were vested in the same bodies. The rulers were to be philosopher-kings, or an aristocracy of scientist-priests governing a virtual theocracy. It was taken for granted that spiritual power was to be founded upon scientific knowledge as the Pansophists understood it. Though Comenius once possessed a copy of Copernicus' famous work in manuscript, he never committed himself to the heliocentric hypothesis.[13] The great scientific geniuses of the seventeenth century would not have accepted either Comenius' philosophy of nature or his theosophy into their experimental world. Like many of his predecessors, he talked of the new science without mastering it.

Comenius aimed to raise the intellectual, moral, and religious level of mankind. His ideal was not mechanically egalitarian, since men were not equally endowed with capacities for development. The climax of the plan is a call for the full education of the whole of humanity challenged to the utmost limits of its potentialities, "not any one individual, nor a few, nor even many, but all men together and each singly, young and old, rich and poor, noble and lowly, men and women . . . in a word, everyone who happens to be born a human . . ."[14] The insistent rhetoric is repeated over and over again as the schoolmaster Comenius hammers away in the *Pampaedia*. Man was created all potentiality. Education had to fashion him so that he became as perfect a being as possible. His formation, however, was not to be limited to the development of skills and the acquisition of factual knowledge about the external world, significant as these might be. The main concern was always moral and religious perfectibility, else the accumulation of mere sensate knowledge would sow chaos. The prime mover in every man is a creative spark related to divinity. Conscience is an active force that defines a man, and its fostering is the prime duty of the teacher. If the educational ideal is realized, the world will become utopia, "full of order, light, and peace."[15] If not, individuals will degenerate and the world will be the nightmare Comenius experienced during his harrowing years as a victim of plundering armies in the Thirty Years' War. Man could disintegrate into nonman if the force of education were not exerted as a counterpoise.[16] "Bring light and he will straightway see."[17]

While there are outlines for government institutions, these are not the central focus of the Comenian utopia. Real power is in the hands of the teacher, who can kill or make alive. This awesome capacity should not, however, breed in him overweening pride, for the master remains a servant, not a lord, of the inborn nature of his charge.[18] It is not his role to transform the quintessential nature that is put before him, but to cultivate it. Access to inner man is through the senses, not reasoning, and surely not the reiteration of stock phrases. Everything that is to be learned should be placed insofar as possible before the senses, and if the objects themselves are not available the master ought to obtain copies or models.[19] Even abstract concepts could be reduced to images— an idea not original with Comenius, as the numerous Renaissance iconographic manuals will testify. The purpose of everything taught is to be made immediately evident to the student in terms of its practical value for daily life. In his zeal to relate all things taught to definite ends, Comenius would occasionally lapse into derogation of the term utopia itself and write negatively of Plato. "The pupil should understand that what he learns is not taken out of some Utopia or borrowed from Platonic Ideas, but is one of the facts which surround us, and that a fitting acquaintance with it will be of great service in life."[20] And yet he clearly cuts a utopian page from Campanella's *City of the Sun* when he advises the teacher to display on the school walls abstracts of all books used in class and to illustrate their contents with pictures.[21] Matter presented should be entertaining as well as practical.

On the other hand, as a popular educator Comenius was not writing an *Emile* for a single tutee or a *Telemachus* for a prince. He was providing for mass education and numbers in the classroom did not frighten him. He resorted to homely analogies: "As a baker," he writes in the *Great Didactic*, "makes a large quantity of bread by a single kneading of the dough and a single heating of the oven, as a brick-maker burns many bricks at one time, as a printer prints hundreds of thousands of books from the same set of type, so should a teacher be able to teach a very large number of pupils at once and without the slightest inconvenience."[22] In the *Pampaedia* Comenius faced up to the question whether nobles and commoners should be allowed to mingle in the ideal schools of his imagination.[23] For a moment he hedged, remembering the biblical example of David, who entrusted Solomon to Nathan to be privately reared. But pedagogic egalitarianism finally triumphed. Since it was not certain that in biblical times there were public schools of the type he proposed, the Israelite precedent was not binding, and he wondered whether the time was at hand when the Isaian prophecy would be realized and the calf and the young lion would lie down together.

If Comenius' universalism faltered for a moment at the crossing of class lines, he was not in doubt about the need to liberate barbarous peoples from the shackles of their barbarity through enlightenment. "No strange skill is called for. If man is but raised from barbarism, i.e., from brutalizing conditions, and transferred to where he has the opportunity to perceive different things with his senses, to study different things with his reason, and to learn from report or history of different things beyond his purview, then we shall soon see brutes made into men and Anacharses born even in Scythia."[24] Human nature was *one,* what one wanted all wanted, and to know one was to know all.[25] Pansophia preached the conversion of the heathens. They should not be forsaken in their benighted condition, for one sick limb easily affected another and the dangers to the whole human race were palpable.[26] Long before Leibniz concerned himself with the Chinese, Comenius hailed the success of the Jesuit missionaries at the court of Shun Chih. In appreciation of their widespread achievements in conversion, Comenius cannily decided not to attack frontally either the Jesuits or the papacy, but to cajole them into accepting Pansophic principles. "If we win them we win the whole world."[27]

The Comenian educational utopia embraced all humans at all stages. "The whole of his life is a school for everyman, from the cradle to the grave."[28] Except for the paradise of the elect in heaven, no previous utopia had broken down barriers of sex, age, class, ethnic status, to fling open the gates to knowledge. Comenius may have hesitated about the equality of intellectual endowments in nature, but he never retreated from his conviction that all persons could be developed to the uttermost limits of their capacities. He would make of the school, and by extension the world, a "little Paradise, full of delights."[29] As the world was drawing to an end—it was on the threshold of eternity—it was ordained that it return full circle to the lost paradise, even if imperfectly.[30] At the beginning of the fourth stage of the *Pansophia,* he quoted Campanella to support his theory that all things were founded in nature and no one could be a good artisan, or doctor, or theologian, or statesman, who was ignorant of its laws.[31] Youths would enter the theatre of the world and penetrate the secrets of nature so that they moved among the works of God and the works of man with open eyes.[32] In the *Panorthosia* Comenius evoked the academic utopia of a supreme college of light, uniting all colleges of learned men, for the eternal Father of Light Himself called them to join in the community of light.[33]

Though scholars have found in Comenius' *Labyrinth of the World and Paradise of the Heart* not only the general idea-system of Andreae but whole passages from the *Peregrini in Patria Errores,* the *Civis Christianus,* the *Reipublicae*

Christianopolitanae Descriptio, such transmission was not plagiarism in any present-day sense. After Andreae had freed himself from the mystification of the Rosicrucian escapade and founded a Societas Christiana of men of good will who were joined in brotherhood to propagate Christian love and the knowledge of all things, Comenius wrote to him asking to be enrolled in the brotherhood. Andreae, sounding weary of the world, passed his mantle on to Comenius, who in return attempted to comfort his spiritual master. A long excerpt from Andreae opened Comenius' *Opera Didactica Omnia* of 1657, and he proudly announced his divine appointment to carry on Andreae's mission.[34] But though Comenius' acknowledgment of discipleship was made often enough, at one point their relationship had undergone a severe trial. Andreae in his preface to the *Brunswikische Evangelische Kirchenharmonie* (1646) referred to some who in contempt of Luther were "sowing the infelicitous tares of Scholastic Pansophy," a remark that roused the ire of Comenius, the proud Czech and Pansophic philosopher.[35] He struck back in a letter of August 22, 1647, saying that he had never sown in Luther's or Calvin's field but derived his Reformation from Bohemia's son, Hus.[36] The quarrel was patched up and Comenius accepted an explanation that no insult had been intended. Andreae had by that time abandoned the arena of active combat in behalf of universal reformation, while Comenius was to die a believer in the mission formulated by his forerunners Bacon, Campanella, and Andreae, whom he called "Philosophiae restauratores gloriosos."[37]

Though Comenius praised Bacon's method of induction as useful for the discovery of the secrets of physical nature and recommended the study of "whatsoever comes to passe of its owne accord by those dispositions implanted in things,"[38] there were important parts of Pansophia not derived from nature. He set "art" in a place of primacy; by art he meant nothing aesthetic, but whatever was emcompassed by human industry, a sector of knowledge that included thoughts, words, and actions. Knowledge of art was the uniquely human province. "Things are knowne as they are, when they are knowne according as they were made,"[39] a dictum that might have sprung out of Vico's *New Science* (though Vico, to our knowledge, was unacquainted with the writings of Comenius). But things could be made only in accordance with a proper idea of them, and art, which is human, borrows the ideas of its works from nature, which in turn derives them from God, who "hath them onely from himselfe."[40] Comenius had spent some of his younger years as an artisan and conceived of human activity in artisan terms. The artisan first had an idea of his work and then he created it.

In his educational system Comenius would have the teacher and child repeat the relationship that obtained in any original discovery or invention. The pupil-teacher bond was akin to that of an apprentice and a master artisan, and a discovery somehow imitated God's way with nature. When Leibniz, fascinated with the art of invention, tried to persuade the great scientists to record down to the minutest detail how they had chanced upon a new discovery, he was attempting to gain insight into the divine act of creation through thinking by analogy with an artisan who invents a new technique. Reading these reflections one thinks primarily in utilitarian terms, as if Leibniz were only searching for some principle of creativity or for a mechanical way of accelerating the advancement of scientific knowledge. In the world of Pansophia to which

Leibniz and Comenius belonged separate compartments did not exist. To invent was to imitate on an infinitesimal scale the act of God in creating the world. "For seeing an Idea," wrote Comenius in an early Latin version of Pansophia, translated into English as *A Reformation of Schooles,* "is a certaine rule of things, God cannot bee thought to doe any thing without Idea's, that is, without a certaine rule, as who is of himselfe the rule of all rules: So likewise Nature when she effects most orderly workes, cannot worke without a rule; as neither can Art, which is natures Ape." [41] When his English disciple Samuel Hartlib talked of any of his utopian projects as an Idea he meant it in Comenius' sense, a formulation that in its simplicity would hardly be acceptable to an ancient or a modern Platonist, but one that was quite satisfactory to the utopian projectors of Christian Pansophia. Pansophia is the knowledge of all things, first as they are, but then, what is intrinsically more important, things as they should and might be if addressed by human art. The fulfillment of potentiality becomes the driving force of the utopia.

Pansophia has nothing of the primitivist fantasy in its baggage train. While recognizing that things, states, religions have been corrupted, in seeking to restore them Comenius envisions an ideal state that is not a primitivist paradise, but paradise altered through human art. Art imitates the secrets of nature, but is itself not primitive nature. The Comenian utopia, which was born in libraries and schools and princely courts, was urban. The artisan transforming a natural object was the utopian. In pursuit of his craft he studied nature, learned God's way, and labored to produce new forms for his brethren.

The universe had an order and in imitating that order society should move from the known to the unknown, from the simple to the complex, in slow and easy steps. At each stage in time in the ideal school system it is possible to communicate knowledge of the whole universe and of all things in it to all men. The mode and difficulty and vantage point may change year by year throughout the school curriculum and then through life. The formula that all things can be taught to all men was not understood in a literal sense; its fundamental principle survived, however, since it was taken for granted that the level of complexity would vary with age and different natural capacities.

Victim of the Prophets

Comenius has become a saintly figure in the Slavic world, communist and noncommunist. He can be secularized and transformed into a popular hero who suffered from the persecutions of the Catholic Counter-Reformation in Bohemia, an educator who believed in the educability of all men and women. Communist theorists have been fascinated by this fervent believer in the great potentialities of most human beings. To be sure, his millenarianism and belief in the fulfillment of instant prophecies have to be expunged from his thought to make him assimilable by the atheist world. Posterity has dealt unevenly with Comenius' reputation: The Enlightenment saw only the superstitious believer in false prophecies, the twentieth century looks upon his ardent faith in revelations as a mere foible. In reality the two apparently contradictory strains in Comenius' thought reinforced each other. The deep Christian millenarian roots of the utopia of expanding individual human capacities are annoying only to those who would translate the rich Christian utopian corpus of Western society into purely secular terms. The seventeenth-century Pansophists could not abide by the apparently easy solution of the metaphor of the two books any more than did the major scientists. Newton could not avoid the method of scientific demonstration in interpreting Scripture. Once it was conceived that there was divinity in everyman, all his actions and thought had to be interrelated. Teilhard de Chardin is the modern who comes closest to resurrecting this seventeenth-century holism.

Throughout his life, Mikuláš Drabík the false prophet was Comenius' nemesis. In the early 1660s Drabík's prophecies continued to arouse curiosity in Protestant Europe. Nobles like Pembroke-Montgomery, even natural philosophers like Boyle and Oldenburg, were attracted by the foretellings. Men of Port Royal and the young Louis XIV made inquiries. And Comenius continued to be one of the major agents of transmission of Drabík's visions, translating his Czech into Latin. While the elders of the Brethren of the Unity expressed doubts and misgivings, Comenius never wavered. Even when particular prophecies failed of fulfillment he remained Drabík's outstanding defender, suffering ridicule on his account in old age.

Comenius' ties to Drabík went back to childhood and the prophet maintained a strange hold over him, sometimes treating him as a subaltern. Stories of Drabík's debauches could not shake Comenius' faith in the revelations. At the same time Comenius never communicated to him his own studies on "the improvement of all things human" and candidly gave the prophet the reasons —Drabík could not keep quiet and would not understand them. But Drabík had the gift of tongues, and the very crudeness of his manuscripts vouched for their authenticity. The fact that their author himself did not understand them was no hindrance to Comenius' belief. When Drabík was interrogated by the sober pastors of the Brethren of the Unity about what God looked like and how His heart was joined to Drabík's heart, he pleaded ignorance of God's ways. When they denounced his reports of Christ's words rendered into clumsy Latin verse, Comenius took the blame upon himself, explaining the difficulty of translating from the Czech.

At a meeting of the Brethren of the Unity on July 10, 1663, the aged seer was again warned by the elders to think on his fate should he prove to be an impostor. Defiantly Drabík affirmed the truthfulness of his experience and swore a mighty oath, which Comenius had himself composed, to confute the doubters. The whole assembly was overwhelmed and the critics ceased to enjoy the support of the Brethren. Comenius could not believe that Drabík would endanger his soul by lying, nor could he give credence to the idea that an evil spirit spoke through him. Drabík was showered with gifts for distribution among the poor, a duty he did not always discharge. Comenius was cognizant of the weakness of his character. Though Comenius tried to dissuade him, Drabík continued to predict the impending doom of the Hapsburgs at the very time when the Turks were triumphing. Soon the charge would be made that he had summoned the Turks into Hungary, and he would be executed. On the basis of Drabík's prophecies the imminence of the thousand-year reign had been proclaimed first for 1656, then for 1671 or 1672. Comenius did not live to be disappointed a second time.

Andreae's most recent biographer has sought to highlight a contrast between Andreae's Christ-oriented theology, with its emphasis on the experience of conversion, and Comenius' more optimistic view that man is an entire small world in which the whole of science is already arranged Pansophically and has only to be brought into actuality through an educational process. He argues that Comenius, unlike Andreae, is not centered on the Cross and man's radical need for redemption. The *Labyrinth* of 1623 appears Christological enough, but there is a point to the contention. The unrelieved millenarianism of Comenius is alien to Andreae in his later years. Comenius resembled those classical utopians incapable of envisaging and living with a long *progressus*. Once the Pansophic prinicples were accepted or revealed through education, radical evil would disappear overnight. As Comenius endured one disaster after another—fire, plague, exile, disappointment in the fulfillment of the precise political prophecies to which he was addicted—he might falter, but the overall renovation would always be coming soon. As an active millenarian, he had a mission to hasten the day.

Comenius was a strange figure who combined rational ideas and mystical propensities that to most men were incompatible, though less so in the seventeenth century than they would be in ours. In 1657–1658, the same years when he issued a collection of his pragmatic educational writings, including the textbook that revolutionized elementary education in many lands, the *Orbis Sensualium Pictus,*[42] there appeared *Lux in Tenebris,* an extensive Latin translation of the politico-millenarian prophecies of Kotter, Poniatowska, and Drabík. Comenius combined his appreciation for the learning of Western European culture with an apocalyptic vision that follows one of the traditional patterns in the Revelation of John. In the *Generall Table of Europe representing the Present and Future State thereof . . . The Future Mutations, Revolutions, Government, and Religion of Christendom and of the World from the Prophecies of the three late German Prophets Kotterus, Christina, and Drabicius,* an English-language version of *Lux in Tenebris,* he predicted: "And then indeed to be the peaceful, illuminate, Religious State of the World, and of the Church under the whole Heavens; Universal illumination of the Gentiles; the Earth to be filled with the knowledge and Righteousness of the Lord; and the kingdoms of the World to become the Kingdom of the Lord, and of his Christ; Universal Liberty, without tyranny and slavery of Body and Soul; Universal Unanimity, without Wars, Quarrels, Dissension, Divisions, Schisms, sects, and Factions; In one word, Universal Righteousness, Peace, and Love, even till the time when Satan shall again break loose and trouble things: But Christ by the last and final fire, shall destroy the circled and ungodly with the World itself."[43]

Typical inventor of a utopian universal system, Comenius was a zealot who reacted violently against those who doubted him, a victim of the wars of Central Europe in the second quarter of the seventeenth century, a godly man, a practical educator with acute psychological insight, a dupe, and for men of the French Enlightenment a charlatan of the same order as the prophets who had deceived him. The reader of Pierre Bayle's *Historical and Critical Dictionary* was entertained with a portrait of Comenius as a fanatical millenarian and a crook whose pompous notions and fancy pedagogy had hood-winked trusting souls into parting with their money. Herder had a more favorable estimate, and when histories of education came to be written Comenius found a respectable place as an educator who was against excessive punishments and would make learning easier by introducing pictures of things into books.[44] In modern times his writings have often been separated into two parts, the theosophical sections cast aside as aberrations of the age, the secular plans preserved as the works of a universalist reformer, a believer in the right of every man and woman to self-actualization, a savior of little children who in schools that followed his method were liberated from the stupefying blows of brutal masters.

Hartlib and the Grand Projectors

Samuel Hartlib served as a bridge from Comenius to the more respectable utopians of the English Commonwealth, even if at first glance they appear to be concerned more with economic projects for the improvement of agriculture, relief of the poor, and organization of public employment offices and clearing houses for scientific information than with the final hopes of Pansophia. Though civil war intervened and the leaders of Parliament who had invited him to England in 1641 failed to carry out their promise to found a Pansophic college, Comenius' impress was deep on a group of Puritan "projectors" and on John Wilkins, Joseph Glanvill, and Robert Boyle. Whenever his special advocates in England, the expatriate Prussian Hartlib and the Scottish divine John Dury, turned their attention to specific reforms limited in scope, they always conceived them as parts of the great reform of mankind through Pansophia, partial fulfillments of the universal goal. Hartlib's various "offices of address for accommodations and communications," planned for the mobilization of England's scientific and economic resources, were explicitly committed to the implementation of the grand designs of Bacon and Comenius.

The English Civil War presented a golden opportunity for making the Pansophic dream a reality. Hartlib and Dury had been wholly converted to Pansophia and saw the possibility of capturing the entire realm for the doctrine. There were enough scholars in the two great universities to fill the gaps in Comenius' knowledge, and Hartlib and Dury themselves were practical men of affairs with the energy and skill to direct the enterprise. There has been a tendency to enclose Hartlib and his group within the confines of the island where they had settled. From the perspective of the founder of the international movement they were merely one outpost; the center was somewhere in the heart of Europe, despite the transfer of Comenius' household to Amsterdam. The English version of Pansophia yielded a rich intellectual harvest once the Civil War was over, even though, looked at from Comenian heights, the Hartlib dispensation was very much watered down. Except in the eyes of a few eccentrics, Comenius' susceptibility to prophecy robbed him of credibility as soon as the commonsensical spirit of the Restoration settled over England, but during the Civil War, Hartlib as the agent of Pansophia cut no mean figure in the Cromwellian world. Economic and social projects that were, so to speak, lateral to the existing organization of labor and intellectual life were in the hands of a circle of men who lived and functioned within the parliamentary order as it was constituted early in the Civil War. They were the sensible religious-philanthropic voice of the Pansophic utopia, practical and matter-of-fact, not aiming at the abrupt upheaval of existing institutional relationships. However bold their projects, their intention was to operate within the bounds of the establishment—Samuel Hartlib himself received a parliamentary appointment in 1649 as an official utopian of the Commonwealth with the title "Agent for the advancement of universal learning and the public good."[45]

The elder Hartlib was the son of a Polish trader of German origin who had been obliged to flee his native country when the Jesuits took control. Having settled in Elbing, Prussia, he chose for his third wife the daughter of a wealthy English merchant and thus fathered a half-English son, Samuel. The younger Hartlib took up residence in London about 1628, made frequent business visits to the Continent, and through his relatives enjoyed wide connections in English society. Lord mayors, members of Parliament, professors of both universities, nobles, rich merchants, doctors, economists, diplomats, and divines interested in the unification of the churches, "the best of archbishops," were among his acquaintances (though their number did not include Archbishop Laud, for whom ecumenical activities were mischievous).[46] Milton praised Hartlib and dedicated a treatise on education to him. He was seconded in most of his projects by another "outsider," John Dury, who had been reared in Holland and France and had been minister to the English company of merchants at Elbing. Dury was possessed by a passion to end religious strife, and traveled from court to court in behalf of his ideal. In one of his numerous memorials, he voiced the hope that King and Parliament would be moved to summon a general synod of Protestants for settling "weighty matters in the Church, which now trouble not only the consciences of most men, but disturb the tranquillity of publick States, and divide the Churches one from another, to the great hindrance of Christianity, and the dishonour of Religion."[47]

That Hartlib may well have furnished the English with "intelligence from foreign parts" does not taint the Pansophic loftiness of his purposes; anyone who conducted a wide foreign correspondence for scientific or religious ends was likely to get enmeshed in some political intrigue.[48] Henry Oldenburg (who became Dury's son-in-law) was the target of similar charges while secretary of the Royal Society under the Restoration. For his services, Hartlib received occasional emoluments from official government sources, which he forthwith expended on one of his favorite projects for the good of mankind. He was an easy touch for inventors, especially those who knew how to make a perpetual-motion machine.[49] No less a personage than Robert Boyle, congratulating him in May 1647 on an award of £300 by Parliament, praised him for his enthusiastic devotion to the new science and all its works: "You interest yourself so much in the *Invisible College,* and that whole society is so highly concerned in all the accidents of your life, that you can send me no intelligence of your own affairs that does not, at least relationally, assume the nature of Utopian."[50] John Evelyn's diary affords a glimpse of the Projector on November 27, 1655: "Thence to visite honest & learned Mr. Hartlib, a Publique Spirited, and ingenious person, who had propagated many Useful things & Arts: Told me of the *Castles* which they set for ornament on their stoves in *Germanie* (he himselfe being a Lithuanian as I remember) which are furnished with small ordinance of silver on the battlements . . . He told me of an Inke that would give a dozen copies . . . This Gent: was Master of innumerable Curiosities, & very communicative."[51]

Hartlib's contacts even extended to luminaries of the New World. In the forties he had met John Winthrop, Jr., later governor of Connecticut, during his sojourn in England, and in 1659 Winthrop wrote to him avid for news about the activities of his circle, discoveries in the celestial bodies, and perpetual motion. He sensed that Hartlib was at the center of exciting intellectual events. Winthrop sought especially to know whether "that learned mr. Comenius be yett living and where, and what remarkable from him etc. I mett him once; and saw a copy of a letter of his at Wedell with mr. Ristius Pastor there wherein he mentioned that he had found out the motum perpetuum . . . I am full of more quaeries but I pray excuse me thus farr, for we are heere as men dead to the world in this wildernesse."[52]

Pansophists like Dury appreciated the intimate connection between the expansion of commercial relations, the spread of an ecumenical Protestantism, and the dissemination of knowledge. Whenever Dury traveled he sought to convert reigning monarchs and merchants to his views. From his correspondence with Hartlib in 1636 it appears that chance encounters on voyages opened up the prospect of winning the Emperor of Russia to their side. Russia was seen as virgin territory for propagation of the faith. If the Emperor would only let them establish a school in some safe place it might become a "seed of learninge to convert that nation from superstition."[53] "Muscovia" was then conceived as an area through which they could penetrate as far as the East Indies. "Now where trade beginneth and commerce with forraine nations, there all other things may be advanced," Dury wrote his friend.[54] This was no commercial enterprise plain and simple; the propagation of true Protestant religious ideas with an ecumenical flavor, the spread of Pansophic knowledge, and the fostering of trade were all intertwined. Political or economic ends such as gaining the right to establish a colony or a settlement were always pursued with the other objectives in view.

Dury's letters to Hartlib are suffused with a millenarian passion. "Let us bee busy while wee have tyme," he exhorted his friend, "the dayes are evill, therefore the tyme might be the more redeemed."[55] Hartlib constantly urged Comenius' Pansophic and pedagogical aims upon Dury. A letter from Dury to Hartlib in 1639 illustrates the close interrelation of science and millenarian religion, cemented with shrewd practicality, in the minds of these activist disciples of Comenius. "Mr. Tassius was with mee before I went from Hamburg, wee did discourse: 1. of the general method of delivering sciences demonstratively whereof I have of late had some peculiar thought, never soe come in former time into my mind, which he said he liked, because they agreed with the mathematical way of scientifical knowledge: and 2. of my demonstrative analysis of scripture, whereof he never had conceived the principles in former time . . . I have shewen the letter for the procurement of meanes towards a learned correspondence and for the maintenance of Comenius and Pansophical studyes to M. R. [Rosenkrantz], who did declare himself very affectionate to the scope and seemed not unwilling to contribute his quota. Hereafter I will see how to come neerer home to him to try whether or noe, these appearances have reall grounds."[56]

Extravagant rumors about mysterious Christian kingdoms in the East were easily credited among the Pansophists, and science, visions of utopian states of well-being, methodized biblical exegesis, and direct prophetic revelations were harbored in the breasts of men prized by their English fellows for their down-to-earth common sense. A letter to Hartlib in May 1643 reports on a meeting with an Austrian baron named Bernard de Callen, "a very gallant and learned gentleman," who had spent more than 20,000 Reichsdollars on alchemical experiments. He had brought from the Netherlands a treatise called "Clangor Buccinae Propheticae de Novissimis Temporibus," judged to be the best book ever written about the reign of Christ on earth, that a French correspondent believed would be very welcome to Hartlib's friends the English millenarians. The Austrian baron had recounted a most wonderful tale. Two persons of quality, recently arrived from the Indies and lodged with a Dr. Haberfeld at The Hague, had disclosed the existence in the Indies of a godly society of Christians with their own king and social order, the "Societas Coronae Equestris Ordinis," who, unlike the Rosicrucian Brotherhood, did not indulge in "imaginary and shady" affectations. The two men, "skilled in almost all languages," were emissaries of this Christian Commonwealth sent to survey the condition of God's faithful who professed the Protestant religion and to offer succor to those in need. The Societas apparently abounded in great treasures of gold and other riches and was capable of despatching armies for the deliverance of the godly. Since the Austrian baron narrated all this in good earnest as a certainty, Hartlib was to write to his confidants in Holland and seek confirmation from Dr. Haberfeld himself.[57] The elements of which the story is composed are readily identifiable. Bacon's New Atlanteans regularly sent spies to Europe to discover what events were transpiring there. The notion of lands with a limitless supply of gold dates from the age of exploration and was fortified by the alchemical passion for transmuting other metals that possessed Europe. Finally, the legend of Prester John of Ethiopia kept alive the idea of a blessed Christian kingdom in the East. What is remarkable about the story is that it was not allowed to rest as myth; serious men of letters set about verifying the baron's confabulation and reported it true that there was such a kingdom comprised of seventeen or eighteen countries named for the "Golden Sunne." Alas, the clandestine messengers from the East, after traveling through Germany, concluded that Protestants there were as wicked as other Christians and hastily returned home before they were infected with European vices.[58]

Hartlib expected great things from the Parliament that opened on November 3, 1640, changes that would go far beyond mere constitutional reform in the relations of King and Parliament.[59] Here were godly men wielding a divine instrument: They had the power to reform education, raise material and spiritual standards throughout the realm, and then turn their attention overseas to create a union of Protestant churches. He forthwith began to publish projects for their guidance. Some were submitted to him by friends; others were lifted from the works of Comenius or the Frenchman Théophraste Renaudot. Many of Hartlib's fellow projectors preferred to remain anonymous, or regarded themselves merely as contributors to a common treasury of plans. When Hartlib signed his own name to another man's work or quoted from it at length, no one accused him of plagiarism; he made himself into a sort of collective, a stock company of designs, projects, even little utopian novels. Modern scholarship has begun to sort out the attributions of his published and unpublished papers; seventeenth-century writers did not much care.[60] Some of his projects in turn were picked up by economists, scientists, Levellers, Fifth Monarchists, and incorporated into their pamphlets. Hartlib himself never joined any of the sects, and his reputation for political impeccability, whoever was in power, was untarnished.

Hartlib's interest in popularizing the ideas and works of Comenius among Englishmen dates from about 1637, when he printed a treatise that was a succinct summary of most of the strains of Pansophia: *The Gate of Wisdom Opened; or the Seminary of all Christian Knowledge: being a New, Compendious, and Solid Method of Learning, more briefly, more truly, and better than hitherto, all Sciences and Arts, and whatever there is, manifest or occult, that it is given to the Genius of man to penetrate, his craft to imitate, or his tongue to speak: the author that Reverend and most distinguished man, Mr. John Amos Comenius (Conatuum Comenianorum Praeludia: Porta Sapientiae Reserata).* There followed a small duodecimo volume entitled *Comenius' Harbinger of Universal Knowledge and Treatise on Education (Comenii Pansophiae Prodromus et Didactica Dissertatio),* 1639.[61] A flimsy traditional utopia from the Hartlib mill, *A Description of the Famous Kingdome of Macaria; shewing its excellent government: wherein the inhabitants live in great prosperity, health, and happinesse; the King obeyed, the nobles honoured; and all good men respected; vice punished and virtue rewarded. An example to other nations* (1641), recently ascribed to Gabriel Plattes, was dedicated to Parliament.[62] In this pedestrian dialogue, the totality of Hartlib's ideas was presented in the fictional manner of Thomas More and Francis Bacon. More was daringly invoked by name; ordinarily, sectaries were cautious to avoid all mention of the papist, though his rhetoric echoes among them. The author composed in an optimistic vein, certain that the Long Parliament would not close its sessions before it had effectuated great reforms for the happiness of the world, and he offered his ideal state for their inspection. Between 1628 and 1635 Hartlib had been corresponding with friends about the founding of a colony in Virginia to be called Antilia, meant to be part of an Andreaean-like Societas Christiana, and projects for Antilias and Macarias occupied him for the rest of his life.

The setting for *Macaria* (from *makarios*, "happy") is conventional. A traveler from Macaria encounters a scholar in the City of London, and during a walk in the country the Londoner is made acquainted with the wonders of the distant land. As if it were proposing nothing very extravagant or extraordinary, *Macaria* redirected the economy of a modern state, relieving Parliament of its responsibility for economic and social policies, which were transferred to five occupational corps, one each for agriculture, fisheries, trade on land, commerce on the seas, colonies. Each authority would make its own departmental laws. The land authority would tax a twentieth of all inherited property and use the revenues for agricultural improvement and roads and bridges. Macaria was a well-cultivated garden state; if anyone should persistently neglect the tillage of his land, he would lose title to it. Fisheries were expanded. Domestic trade was regulated by keeping the number of apprentices stable, increasing or decreasing the years of training as circumstances required. Foreign commerce was grudgingly permitted only if it enriched the kingdom. Since colonies drained off excess population, emigrants were subsidized during the early years of a new settlement.

There is no consideration of lofty philosophical problems of happiness, the aesthetic or moral improvement of the species man, love relations and their antinomies, the city as a mirror of divine perfection. Macaria is a simple, regulated, puritanical society for the provision of work and the creation of wealth, a bread-and-butter utopia that does not trouble itself with ideal forms. Violators of the Macarian order are punished by the confiscation of their property. The physical health of the citizenry is cared for by colleges of doctors. Pastors have two functions that they exercise simultaneously, the *cura animarum* and the *cura corporum.* Thus the Baconian priest-scientist of the *New Atlantis* is rehabilitated in modified form. He is no longer a remote, awe-inspiring hieratic figure, but a country doctor-pastor. Hartlib himself was always interested in techniques for the betterment of husbandry, and the traveler from Macaria has conveniently come to England with a new book on agricultural production whose rules, if instituted by Parliament, would make it possible to sustain double the population of England at a higher level of prosperity. The Long Parliament was occupied with other matters, however.

What emerges in the *Macaria* is an embryonic, characteristically English utopia based upon advanced agricultural methods. There has been a marked shift from the concerns of the Pansophic soul to those of the body's nutrition. Agricultural reform, by doubling the population, will also make England impregnable to foreign invasion. The institution of the Macarian society everywhere does not have to await Judgment Day, for the whole reformation could be realized through education in the Comenian manner. Once people were trained —and the printing press made universal education feasible and inevitable— they would no longer submit to tyrants. The scholar, who has at first listened to the tale of the man from Macaria with a measure of skepticism, when finally converted expresses a rapture that would be repeated again and again by utopians: "I am imparadised in my minde, in thinking that England may bee made happy, with such expedition and facility." [63] Condorcet at the conclusion of the Tenth Epoch of the *Esquisse,* contemplating the future happiness of mankind, would reflect that the philosopher was already enjoying in the mind the transports of the Elysium that would be. Utopia becomes a state of feeling, and Samuel Hartlib's philanthropists already lived in bliss because they believed that utopia could and soon would be in England. So entranced was the scholar with the traveler's relation that he promised to meet him again in order to hear about Macaria's laws, customs, and manners, even if he were ill and had to be carried to their rendezvous in a sedan chair. The book closes with his assurance that the English, sensible of their own good, would soon model their land on Macaria, "though our neighbour Countreys are pleased to call the English a dull Nation." [64]

The underlying philosophical preconceptions of Pansophia were again expounded to Englishmen in 1642, when Hartlib translated two essays of Comenius and entitled them *A Reformation of Schooles.* They presented the goals of the religio-philosophico-didactic movement in language that avoided some of the more arcane and lofty theosophy and remained on the familiar ground of a golden age, albeit a spiritual one.

We therefore in this present age being so well stored with experiences, as no former ages could have the like, why should we not raise our thoughts unto some higher aime? For not onely by the benefit of Printing (which Art God seemes, not without some Mystery, to have reserved to these latter times) what soever was ingeniously invented by the Ancients (though long buried in obscurity) is now come to light: but also moderne men being stirred up by new occasions, have attempted new inventions: and Wisdome hath beene, and is daily miraculously multiplied with variety of experiments. According as God hath foretold of these latter times, *Dan.* 12.4. Whereunto may be added the erecting of Schooles every where more, then any Histories record of any former ages: whereby bookes are growne so common in all Languages and Nations, that even common countrey people, and women themselves are familiarly acquainted with them; whereas formerly the learned, and those that were rich, could hardly at any price obtaine them. And now at length the constant endeavour of some breakes forth to bring the Method of studies to such a perfection, that whatsoever is found worthy of knowledge, may with much lesse labour, then heretofore, be attained unto. Which if it shall succeed (as I hope) and that there be an easie way discovered of teaching all men all things, I see not what should hinder us from a thankfull acknowledgement, and hearty embracing of that Golden Age of light and knowledge, which hathe beene so long foretold, and expected.[65]

When Comenius arrived in England in 1642, the whole group of projectors planned for a total revamping of education in a Baconian and Comenian spirit, a restructuring of the two great universities, which were royalist strongholds and quite moribund, the building of a new urban university in London, the establishment of a national council on education, and the formation of a union of English and Continental scholars through a network of correspondence. Hartlib's portfolio began to bulge with grand projects for a universal society of committed Christian reformers (excluding papists, of course), for scientific institutes that would draw international scholars to work on philosophical language reform, for libraries to diffuse knowledge. This tireless projector is an early example of a utopian eager to harvest immediate fruits, a type that appears rather frequently in England, the lower-keyed utopian reformer, the Fabian. Many utopian socialists of the nineteenth century, like Robert Owen, were men of entrepreneurial vision who had to begin on a small scale, as if they were exercising their skills with projects of limited scope, while awaiting the opportunity for the grand reformation of the whole world. The philosophy of projection common to the Hartlib circle was articulated in *An Idea of Mathematics written by Mr. Joh. Pell to Samuel Hartlib, 1650* (bound together in London, 1651, with John Dury's *The Reformed-School: and the Reformed Librairie-Keeper*): "And this is the *Idéa,* which I have long framed to my self, according to my fashion, with whom this passeth for an undoubted truth, that the surest waie to com to all possible excellencie *in anie thing,* is to propose to our selvs the perfectest *Idéa's* that wee can imagine, then to seek the means tending thereto, as rationally as may bee, and to prosecute it with indefatigable diligence; yet, if the *Idéa* prove too high for us, to rest our selvs content with *approximation.*"[66]

Hartlib started a private agricultural college to initiate on a small scale what the public magistracy would later develop for the whole realm. He was constantly preoccupied with founding companies for "our private & Publique Good," designs that usually started with a society of subscribers as if they were plain business ventures; but the ultimate ideal was to encompass the nation. He was intent on working within the system, or in the interstices between existing institutions where no one's interests would be damaged. While his eye was on the "Idea," the design, and its national and even universal dimensions, he was willing to start with the small model, a private little body. He would implement utopia in easy stages. The Hartlib circle argued against those who doubted the practicality of their schemes and were naively surprised that others did not rush to join with them. They pleaded for social experimentation on a minimal basis, proving like merchant adventurers that any initial investment would be secure, refuting traditionalist objections against newness: "Which of all those (almost infinite) wayes or means, by which man hath been made Instrumental to the increase of his own well-being, was not in one age or other, as *new* as this *Invention* of mine doth seem to be in this?"[67]

In 1648 *Macaria* was seconded by a project entitled *A Further Discoverie of the Office of Publick Addresse for Accommodations,* which proposed registers of every conceivable form of productive enterprise on one side, and on the other a list of needy persons in search of employment.[68] The Platonist Henry More waxed eloquent over the scheme: "Whatever is like that fruit which comes of the spirit of Christ, Tender-heartedness, equity, and common love, which in my apprehension your Office of Address do plainly tend to, I do most affectionately wish may be promoted."[69] Supplementary statistics and inventories of equipment were to be gathered together in one central office, so that all economic activity in the realm, like the movements of the planets in the heavens (Hartlib's analogy), could be charted and, if need be, directed. Doubtless the men of the Hartlib circle contributed to the "historical atmospherics" of the grand flowering of English science in the latter part of the century; in the Commonwealth period it was the rhetoric of science that spilled over onto utopian social projections.[70] A central place to receive and give information about all commodities, an employment office, would eliminate disorder in the economy. The original idea for the Office of Public Address came from an actual commercial establishment founded in Paris, Théophraste Renaudot's *Bureau d'adresse.*[71] Hartlib's project won the support of William Petty, the great English statistician and economist and one of the founders of the Royal Society, who added plans of his own to the common enterprise.[72] The coordinated statistical utopia would become in the eighteenth century a physiocratic dream culminating in Quesnay's grand tableau.

With the Hartlib group was born the technocratic utopia, a controlled economy organized for universal well-being. The rather primitive agrarian mechanisms of Thomas More, which required no formal regulation and would produce no more than was necessary, had been left far behind. In Hartlib's utopia, the pursuit of science, Pansophia, was tied to technologies leading to improvement in the food supply, the increase of consumption, the maintenance of employment, and a full use of the productive forces of society for the benefit of all. The theoretical implications of this new machine geared to expanding production were not elucidated because immediate concern was still centered on the appeasement of hunger and the alleviation of poverty, but utopia was beginning to grapple with the complexities of a commercial manufacturing society. The England of the projectors was starting to outgrow its agrarian swaddling clothes.

Among Hartlib's schemes was another central institution, an Office for Communications, whose province was inward things touching the souls of men—religion, learning, and "ingenuities"—as the Office of Address for Accommodations was related to the conduct of outward things. The head of the Office for Communications would know and maintain correspondence with learned men everywhere. It was one of his functions, later taken over by the secretary of the Royal Society, to stimulate erudite men to the exercise of their scientific faculties by suggesting new subjects for research. The head of this scientific-technical bureau was to make periodic reports to Parliament on "the substance of all his discoveries" throughout the world, and his operations were to be reviewed annually by an oversight committee of professors of all sciences in both English universities as well as the heads and masters of colleges. In this way every year some stones would be added to Bacon's structure of organized scientific knowledge.[73] "In Matters of Humane Sciences, the End of his Nego-tiation should be, 1. To put in Practice the Lord *Verulams* Designations, *De Augmentis Scientiarum,* among the Learned. 2. To help to perfit Mr. *Comenius* Undertakings, chiefly in the Method of Teaching, Languages, Sciences, and of Ordering Schooles for all Ages and Qualities of Scholars . . . In the Matters of Ingenuity his End should be to offer the most profitable Inventions which he should gaine, unto the benefit of the State, that they might be Publikely made use of, as the State should think most expedient."[74]

Even the library system could become an agency of universal reformation. John Dury, himself appointed in 1650 Library-Keeper of the books, medals, and manuscripts of St. James's Palace, was the main impetus behind the library project. The Chief Library-Keepers were to conduct correspondence "for the beating out of matters not yet elaborated in Sciences,"[75] and would exchange books with foreign scholars. No gifts of books were to be refused, for there was something useful in all learning. Dury would use the library and its net-work of scholarly relationships to inculcate the truths of religion as the highest goal of science, "for there is nothing of knowledg in the minde of man, which may not bee conveniently referred to the virtues of God in Christ."[76] The sci-ences had to be subordinate to this purpose, for otherwise the increase of knowledge would only increase strife, pride, and confusion, whence the griefs of mankind would be multiplied and reproduced for generations to come.

In men such as Hartlib and Dury and Pell there was a patriotic reformer's zeal to bring honor and glory to the English nation by promoting schemes for the advancement of the arts and sciences. They proposed an inquiry into the method and art of discovery itself. "Yet such an Art may men invent, if they accustom themselvs, as I have long don, to consider, not onely the *usefulness* of men's works, and the *meaning* and *truth* of their writings, but also *how it came to pass* that they fell upon such thoughts, and that they proposed to themselvs such ends, or found out such means for them."[77] A study of the psychology and history of invention was often suggested by men in their circle, an interest sparked by a desire to duplicate the conditions that had produced results in the past. Chance was not wholly ruled out; but for Dury, as for Bacon before him, creativity was not entirely a mystery or an accident. Invention could be spurred and made intentional by institutional mechanics: foundations, univer-sities, endowments, eradication of false methods, implementation of the reason-producing apparatus, even inducing an optimum psychic state. Similar notions would be revived by Leibniz. For the puritanical projectors under Comenius' influence, it was no more presumptuous to nurture and discipline the inventive faculty of man than it was to regulate his passions. For everything there was a way of "methodising," and the projector was a taskmaster of the enterprise. The political-religious sectarians favored governmental and constitutional panaceas; by contrast, the projector-utopians cautiously eschewed politics and expected a radical renovation of mankind to eventuate from plans that could coexist with any political regime allowing for free inquiry and favoring pro-ductivity.

In John Dury's *The Reformed-School: and the Reformed Librairie-Keeper* (1651), the Pansophic projects were framed in an amended version of lapsarian theol-ogy. Man had sustained defects through the Fall, which deprived him of "nat-ural happiness," a condition that could be restored through the organization of knowledge, an educational system, and the diffusion of ideas. "The true End of all Humane Learning is to supply in our selves and others the defects, which proceed from our Ignorance of the nature and use of the Creatures, and the disorderliness of our naturall faculties in using them and reflecting upon them . . . Nothing is to be counted a Matter of true Learning amongst men, which is not directly serviceable unto Mankind towards the supply of some of these defects, which deprive us of some part of our naturall Happiness."[78] (John Wilkins, much admired by Comenius,[79] used the same lapsarian argument about compensating for the defects of the Fall in his books of popular science, *Mathematical Magic* and *The Discovery of the New World in the Moon*, both of which Isaac Newton knew at an early age.)

The Comenian doctrine of the need to actualize the divine spark in each man underlay the educational projects. There were two parts to education, one relating to the inward principle of morality to be instilled in the young; the other, to outward behavior, its supervision and regulation. Dury's educational theory was not punitive, intent as he was upon the consideration of every individual humor. But scratch the skin of the system, and the puritanical code of living ever under the vigilant eye of one's neighbor and one's God is written clear and distinct. "This then is the Master-peece of the whole Art of education, to watch over the Childrens behaviour in their actions of all sorts, so as their true inclinations may be discovered; that the inward causes of their vicious disposition and distempers being found out; the true and proper Remedies thereof may be applyed unto them."[80] Dury offered prizes to his students for the revelation of their fellows' falsehoods and deceits. Nothing was to be kept secret or private in utopia.

Hartlib's enthusiasm for knitting relationships among diverse peoples and taking advantage of their unique natural resources in different parts of the world for the benefit of mankind was boundless. No venture was too small to escape his notice, or too great to warrant at least a nibble at the vast undertaking. His genius for discerning the potentialities of the least significant of God's creatures was brilliantly illustrated in a work published in London in 1652 and reprinted in 1655 as *The reformed Virginian silk-worm*. As usual, he was picking other people's brains and advertising the results. A young Englishwoman had chanced upon a speedy and easy way of feeding silkworms on the mulberry leaves of Virginia. Once the Indians realized that the whole procedure required neither great art, skill, nor pains, they would set about making silk and would then have "silk-bottoms" to sell the English in exchange for goods they needed. British commerce would be benefited and the civilizing of the Indians achieved in one fell swoop. An exhilarating awareness that there were virtually limitless possibilities—though a cautionary "almost" was introduced—in the development of a polity's economic prosperity through new inventions and experiments in agriculture was voiced in Cressy Dymock's *An Essay for Advancement of Husbandry-Learning: or Propositions for the Erecting a Colledge of Husbandry. And In order thereunto, for the taking in of Pupills or Apprentices, And also Friends or Fellowes of the same Colledge or Society* (1651): "Our Native Countrey, hath in its bowels an (even almost) infinite, and inexhaustible treasure; much of which hath long laine hid, and is but new begun to be discovered. It may seem a *large boast* or meer *Hyperbole* to say, we enjoy not, know not, use not, the one tenth part of that plenty or wealth and happinesse, that our Earth can, and (*Ingenuity* and *Industry* well encouraged) will (by God's blessing) Yield."[81]

There was a growing body of doctrine among the projectors that it was sinful as well as uncharitable not to exploit God's bounty, whether the fruit-bearing capacity of trees, the potential fertility of the fens, or the hidden capacity for invention in an individual, through ingenuity and industry. Organization, science, experimental inquiry not only made up for human defects but demonstrated that this world was given to man to be a garden. The Puritan projectors were matter-of-fact Baconians with an activist entrepreneurial sense of the possibilities of nature. Charity—the banishment of poverty, disease, idleness—turned out to be both religious and profitable. The Calvinist ethic was not submerged, but the prospect of increasing the number of the elect leading orderly religious lives free from sloth was substantially extended. The legal and military battles about political and constitutional and religious forms that absorbed the major parties in the Civil War were bypassed in favor of work projects suitable for all classes in society. As the conflicts became bloody and the fanatics ruled the day, projectors like Hartlib retreated into private societies of "Invisibles"—in a dismal period of the Civil War John Evelyn's diary depicts in detail his fantasy about a scientific monastic refuge—a few of which later developed into one of the most luciferous and fructiferous of modern institutions, the Royal Society of London.

13

Topsy-Turvy
in the English Civil War

POLITICAL REVOLUTIONS and the dictatorships that follow in their wake proliferate utopias. The revolution gives the appearance of turning the world topsy-
turvy, imaginative energies are released, and all new things seem possible. The
dictator, whether called Protector or Emperor, towers as a divine lawgiver capable of molding society to his free will. Utopians, often people without political weight or authority, cling to the hope that men of great power will put
into practice and make real the "idea" that they, the superior creators, have
invented. To capture the ear of a potentate has been a constant utopian expectation from Plato, who journeyed to the tyrant Dionysius of Syracuse, through
the French system-makers of the early nineteenth century, Saint-Simon and
Fourier, who first addressed their appeals to Napoleon. Unfortunately, the
"Ear of Dionysius" has acquired nefarious connotations as an architectural device for spying on dissidents, and dictatorships have ordinarily been more cunning in surveillance and denunciation than ingenious in social innovation. The
revolutionary epochs, inclusive of the dictatorships that function as settlers of
the revolution, nonetheless leave behind a welter of novel conceptions about
the restructuring of society which, though forgotten on the morrow of the turmoil, are picked up again by later generations. The ideas go underground and
then resurface in a new setting.

Israel in the Garden of England

Utopians of the two decades of the English Civil War may not have spoken
with tongues as divine as some of them believed, but they had the lesser gift of
historical tongues. A few centuries after their temporary eclipse they sound
like bold and farseeing prophets. The popular utopias spawned during the English Civil War and Cromwell's rule as Protector, generally neglected in the
eighteenth and nineteenth centuries by official British historiography, were revived by Friedrich Engels in his equally official history of communist thought.
New heroes who composed utopias have since been discovered in the ranks of
the people. Radical thought in the Civil War has become the appanage of
Marxists, sometime Marxists, and somewhat Marxists, who have tenderly
nurtured each Leveller, Digger, and Ranter as they recovered them from
oblivion. As the Psalmist said: "The stone which the builders refused is become the head stone of the corner." Inevitably, in righting the balance, the
revisionists have made more of the utterances of the sectarians than they may
deserve in a history of thought that frankly favors the high and middle culture.
  Since this Civil War literature is not epitomized in any compact, polished
artistic creation of the order of Thomas More's *libellus,* anyone in search of the
utopia of ordinary folk has to resort to general impressions gleaned from the
incomparable collection of hundreds of pamphlets assembled by the indefati-

gable George Thomason,[1] each carefully dated as it appeared on the streets, an omnibus of popular thought and sensibility, alive with every facet of dissident desire, running the gamut from extended projections of a political solution to the internecine hostilities, to revelations during trances, to the verbose spewings of mountebanks, crackpots, fakirs, feeders on forlorn hopes. The old socialist and anticlerical practice of abstracting these popular utopians from their religious ambience is coming to an end among present-day historians of the English Civil War. Even those most appreciative of the English radicals as the authentic voice of the wretched of the earth who wanted more food, less burdensome toil, a chance to govern in place of the traditional classes, and a less stringent sexual law—all in the name of a God who was loving and had decreed sensate as well as spiritual communion—are aware of the religious heart of their utopias. By now it can be accepted as a commonplace that theological questions, however recondite, and disputes over ritual had social meaning and vice versa.

What should England be like once the legal and constitutional disputes that triggered the Civil War were settled against the royalist party and the prelates? In response, at least half a dozen different utopian patterns took shape. At some point during the course of the war, most partisans turned utopian, if only for a while: The losers looked backward and idealized the recent past of the nation whose control had been wrested from them; the winners concocted programs as though they would effect a total regeneration of society. The only militant nonutopians in England were the Clubmen, who organized locally to keep the ravaging armies away from their lands and would have been content to let the war pass them by. That those indifferent to the chief protagonists may have represented the overwhelming majority is an observation frequently made about revolutionary epochs.

Since the utopians in this period were not mere bookmen but were deeply involved in day-to-day partisan activity, they had their canny, politic side and often adopted compromise positions that were halfway marks on the road to the "happy commonwealth" or to the millennium. Their ad hoc political statements can be separated only with difficulty from the utopian visions that lie behind them, for the dividing line is blurred and wavering. The English utopias were not composed in the solitude of garrets or prisons (writing in the Tower does not count because it was a much trafficked center with a frequent replacement of inmates), nor were they salon exercises or literary games. As platforms of men in the political arena they usually took the form of polemical pamphlets hot off the press. Once the censorship authority of the Archbishop of Canterbury was abolished by the Long Parliament, the whole system of the Stationers Company monopoly broke down and unlicensed printing presses sprang up in shops all over London. Parliamentary attempts to restore a central authority were unavailing and for most of the period even a frenetic Ranter could find a clandestine printer and distributor. A number of printers, like Giles Calvert, specialized in this literature out of conviction and were vital agents in the dissemination of unorthodox ideas. Freedom of the press was not a reality—men were charged by Parliament and local justices for outrageous writings attributed to them—but the printing industry was out of control and allowed for a wild efflorescence of opinion. Tracts dashed off in a passion were quickly published and promptly answered. The air was thick with theological animadversions and apologies, and ideal social and political orders constructed one day were toppled the next.

From 1640 to 1660 the utopian situation, like the political one, was fluid. Virtually every sect carried its own utopia, and individuals moved easily from one circle into another, punctuating their advent and departure with an appropriate religious revelation. Men dropped in and out of groups, recanting previous errors, writing confessions and testimonials, when they were not deliberately prevaricating to get out of prison or to save their tongues from being burned through. Attempts have been made to differentiate the individual sects on a class basis. The Levellers John Lilburne and William Walwyn had strength among London artisans and small merchants; the Diggers were footloose farm laborers or tenants, though the most rational visionary among them was a former merchant; Fifth Monarchy Men are even harder to pin down because of the widespread diffusion of millenarian belief; and the Ranters were itinerant preachers or artisans (though again, their most imaginative writer, Abiezer Coppe, was an Oxford man) who defy close definition. As in all such periods of tohubohu, the edges of one sect merge with another; the nucleus can be identified, but not the constantly changing form of the whole cell. The groups we have isolated are far fewer in number than contemporary pamphleteers and memoirs writers spotted. In mid-seventeenth-century England there were experts in heresies and sects, veritable taxonomists of "sectarisme," who were able to list by name and record as many as 199 species.

It was incumbent upon each of the radical sects to distinguish itself from the teeming mass, and much energy was expended upon touting the superiority of one future society over its rivals. Enemies of the sects, on the other hand, were busy obfuscating the distinctions among them, so that they could smear them all with the same brush that was a composite of their iniquitous doctrines. Before the Levellers had had their moment of triumph, when Gerrard Winstanley had not yet ventured to dig up the commons and invite the homeless to live in community, when Fifth Monarchy Men were still acceptable to the staff of Cromwell, and when the Ranters had not yet stood trial, a London preacher, the Presbyterian Thomas Edwards, published a book on the sects, the *Gangraena* (1646), that immediately ran through three editions, each fatter than its predecessor, and provoked a spate of angry responses from the victims of his castigations. He gave his readers a synopsis of the "Errours and strange opinions scattered up and down, and vented in many Books, Manuscripts, Sermons, conferences."[2] Fellow Presbyterians were assured that "the very same opinions and errours are maintained and held over and over in severall books and manuscripts, so that to have given them the Reader as I found them, would have been to have brought the Reader into a Wildernesse, and to have presented to publick view a rude and undigested Chaos, with an heap of Tautologies."[3] Edwards was only the most noteworthy of the specialists who, in cataloguing a wide variety of abominable heresies, theological and social, succeeded in conveying the impression that they were all of one ilk. Ephraim Pagitt's *Heresiography* (1645), more restricted in its field of inquiry, treated of some twenty sorts of Anabaptists alone: Muncerians, Apostolikes, Separatists, Catharists, Silentes, Enthusiasts, Liberi, Adamites, Huttites, Augustinians, Beucheldians, Melchiorites, Georgians, Mennonites, Servetians, Libertines,

Denkians, Orantes, Pueris Similes, Monasterienses, Plungers. And even this list was not exhaustive, for "almost every one of them hath some peculiar toy or figment in their heads, upon which they are divided, and oft excommunicate one another."[4]

A modern classifier must inevitably be found wanting by the standards of the seventeenth century when he scoops out of the maelstrom only a handful of prominent and provocative categories. While it is to be hoped he is more perceptive than the nineteenth-century historians who saw nothing but a war between King and Parliament, he wanders uncertainly, a stranger in this sectarian jungle. We shall nonetheless single out a few of the sects by name in an effort to make of each of them something of a separate unit, though aware that complete cohesion never existed. The major utopian positions—other than those of Hobbes and Harrington, whose works entered the main current of European political thought—enjoyed in turn but a brief moment of fame, though faint echoes lingered on after their decline, even into the Restoration. In establishing a sequence, allowance has to be made for an inchoate period during which a particular popular utopia achieved an identity and for the spillage and seepage of thought from one to another; but a rough, overall succession can be discerned.

The Levellers were oratorical, critical, bitter, demagogic, no respecters of persons however exalted. Their moment of grandeur in 1647–49 followed the military victory of the Independents and their program continued to enjoy significant backing among London tradesmen and artisans—though their danger to Cromwell's hegemony has recently been somewhat overplayed, doubtless in reaction against the attempts of the traditional historians Green and Gardiner to discount them completely. The Diggers were born of rural protest. Their practice of digging up and planting commons was suppressed soon after they came into being in 1649, but they left behind the image of Gerrard Winstanley as an original English theoretician of "community," and in his *Law of Freedom in a Platform or True Magistracy Restored* (1652), a rare document, a complete, discursive utopia. The Fifth Monarchy Men, who had been pouring out pamphlets on what the millennium would be like since the early 1640s, and many of whose leaders had once served Cromwell as the forerunner of the Messiah, in the fifties went into active opposition against his settlement. Their attempted coups and subsequent prosecution gave them a measure of notoriety and a few quickly forgotten martyrs. The Ranters were feared as the wildest of the sectaries and though an amorphous group they lasted longer than most, until many of them recanted and sought refuge in the bosom of Quaker quietism, a polar oscillation not unknown to such movements.

Confronted by the multitude of English utopian projects, platforms, designs, visions, and a few traditional story utopias—a rich harvest in these two decades that is not matched anywhere in Europe until the first half of the nineteenth century in France—one searches for some underlying principles or preconceptions in the mass of texts. Diverse as these writings are, can common elements be discerned in the rhetorical devices and in the kind of evidence Englishmen deemed most persuasive in leading their countrymen along the path to utopia? Or are there only the distinctions that bestow upon each utopian species its relative cohesiveness? For relative it must be, since one can always probe more deeply and find within any of these groups differences in the ideal society that each leader saw in his mind's eye. Lilburne, Walwyn, and Richard Overton were all called Levellers, but each had dreams particular to himself. The Civil War spirit of dissidence and independence fostered individuality, and even within a single soul the turnings of light and darkness were frequent, bringing forth a new or altered utopia. The collective documents issued by a group, their manifestoes, pleas to Parliament, petitions, indicate some agreement about a political platform, but fail to reflect the inner conscience of individuals; and many of the utopians of the Civil War were men of far greater complexity than a formal tentative accord can disclose.

Whether or not Hobbes had grand designs worthy of the company of radical utopian masters remains problematic, and he will be left in limbo, summoned only to bear witness to the existence of certain utopian turns of thought that crossed party lines. His *Leviathan* (1651) and Harrington's *Oceana* (1656) are sui generis; they are rather detailed plans for a definitive establishment of government, the first a grandly conceived treatise on politics in the mathematical spirit of the new sciences, the second written in the fictional style of the old utopias. Hobbes's inclusion among the English prophets upon whom he heaped scorn may raise scholarly eyebrows, but in the present work we declare writers to be utopians by sovereign fiat. Harrington's *Oceana,* which still enjoyed the plaudits of liberal and radical Englishmen like Tawney and Brailsford earlier in this century, is a waterless Sinai for the present generation, despite its remarkable influence upon constitution-makers and reformers on both sides of the Atlantic for more than a century. But it is the very multiplicity of social projectors, rather than preeminent individuals, in this period that makes it stand out in the history of utopian thought. John Milton, himself no mean innovator with his audacious opinions on divorce and a free press, has left a vivid contemporary portrait of the intellectual fervor of the age:

"Behold now this vast City; a City of refuge, the mansion house of liberty, encompast and surrounded with his protection; the shop of warre hath not there more anvils and hammers waking, to fashion out the plates and instruments of armed Justice in defence of beleaguer'd Truth, then there be pens and heads there, sitting by their studious lamps, musing, searching, revolving new notions and idea's wherewith to present, as with their homage and their fealty the approaching Reformation: others as fast reading, trying all things, assenting to the force of reason and convincement."[5] Understandably, Sir Edward Dering was far less enthusiastic about what he saw in 1642: "The vulgar mind is now fond with imaginary hopes. What will the issue be, when hopes grow still on hopes?" Another royalist reported in a similar vein: "All sorts of people dreamed of an utopia and infinite liberty, especially in matters of religion."[6] But among the victors the very word utopia had begun to assume positive rather than pejorative overtones.

The English utopias are radical in the sense that they seek to strike at the roots of social, moral, and religious evil and to reorder the estates of England in a fundamental way. In this respect Hobbes's *Leviathan,* which would abolish the conception of King in Parliament as the fountainhead of law in favor of the absolute power of the sovereign, was no less radical than Winstanley's *The Law of Freedom in a Platform or True Magistracy Restored,* which would "set the land free to the oppressed Commoners."[7] At the same time almost all parties and political thinkers conceived of themselves as restorers of a pristine state that had originally been ordained by God, rather than as revolutionaries who were bringing an unprecedented man-made scheme into the world, an idea that the seventeenth-century English mentality could not yet countenance. There are exceptions among the Ranters, and occasionally Levellers and Diggers exhort men to forget the past and take a brazen fresh look at the present world; but most of the English utopians clung to the myth of a remote good age to be revived, however they differed about its name—pre-Norman, Apostolic, Mosaic, Edenic, Adamite.

The utopias of the Civil War have an unmistakably parochial flavor. They are in the first instance directed to Englishmen, and only secondarily to the rest of the world. A self-centered island utopia is still the limit of their immediate ambition, even when Fifth Monarchy Men chart a foreign policy leading to the destruction of all Catholic powers and climaxed by the defeat of the papal Antichrist. Men of every shade of opinion were prone to indulge in a bit of patriotic boastfulness. All addressed themselves to the English, a people designated by God to inaugurate the reformation of their realm; He was clearly less preoccupied with the fate of other countries. In their zeal to win converts, the utopians intimidated their readers with the veiled threat that if they failed to seize this propitious moment to demand fundamental changes, they might suffer the ignominy of seeing the mantle of divine election pass from England to some other nation.

Utopians differed about precisely who in England was to be included in the category of the chosen people, and only Winstanley and the Ranters were ready to embrace all Englishmen to full membership in the commonwealth. Even the Levellers excluded servants, beggars, and sometimes wage earners who had masters. Two classes in society enjoyed universal contempt as worthless, lawyers and university scholars. (The elimination of kings, aristocrats, and prelates was taken for granted.)

There may have been personal reasons for the abomination of lawyers among the sectarians—many had been engaged in ruinous, protracted suits— but there was virtual unanimity of antagonism to the profession, which stood for the preservation of the existing material order in the same way that prelates did for the spiritual. A typical roster of grievances can be found in John Rogers' *Sagrir: or Doomes-day drawing nigh, With Thunder and With Lightening to Lawyers, In an Alarum for New Laws, and the Peoples Liberties from the Norman and the Babylonian Yokes. Making Discoveries of the present ungodly Laws and Lawyers of the fourth Monarchy* . . . (London, 1653). The lawyers were Antichrists and a state army of locusts who perverted the plain honest law of England that had prevailed before the Norman Conquest. They were the defenders of usurpation, who in addition used their profession to delay the administration of simple justice for their own profit. Winstanley raged in *Fire in the Bush* (1650): "For he [the Law] is a mighty Beast with great teeth, and is a mighty devourer of men; he eats up all that comes within his power; for this Proverb is true, goe to Law, and none shall get but the Lawyer. The Law is the Fox, poore men are the geesse; he pulls of their feathers, and feeds upon them."[8]

University scholars who held to the traditional practice of commenting on Aristotle as the source of all knowledge had been under attack since Bacon; now Hobbes and Winstanley, Fifth Monarchy Men and visionaries of the inner light joined in a combined assault on these stalwarts of the church establishment. "The Universities have been to this nation," Hobbes wrote in *Behemoth*, "as the wooden horse was to the Trojans . . . From the Universities it was, that the philosophy of Aristotle was made an ingredient in religion, as serving for a salve to a great many absurd articles, concerning the nature of Christ's body, and the estate of angels and saints in heaven; which articles they thought fit to have believed, because they bring, some of them profit, and others reverence to the clergy, even to the meanest of them."[9] Winstanley belabored the universities as engrossers of knowledge who paralleled the monopolists in land and trade. Overton the Leveller excoriated the universities for producing clergymen gifted with black coats, fancy speech, and the external advantages of the arts and sciences. For those who received their knowledge directly from God through personal illumination, the pretensions of book learning were an impediment to religious exaltation.

Yet despite antipathy toward lawyers as oppressive quibblers and academics as false reasoners, the bulk of English utopian literature in this period is discursive and argumentative in accordance with Aristotelian reasoning and the principles laid down in the law courts. None of the utopians are good at drawing speaking pictures of the ideal society, even when they are motivated by a lofty purpose: Hartlib's (or Plattes's) *Macaria* is a bore and Harrington's *Oceana* dismal and arid. The utopians are more skillful at debating fundamental principles, carefully numbering their subjects and topics in accordance with the rules of rhetoric. The documents they draft breathe the spirit of the English judiciary. Ranters like Abiezer Coppe, who denounced the rich and the powerful in street sermons and incorporated his dreadful threats in tracts like a *Fiery, flying roll* (1649), were uniquely immune to this legalistic thinking. He proclaimed the day of the Lord with a gnashing of teeth and conveyed his ideas in dramatic parables that are among the most vivid depictions of an outcast's rage against the rich, the hypocritical do-gooders, the repressors of human desires for food, drink, sex, fraternal feeling—all written by an Oxford man in a personal style that is free of many contemporary stereotypes.

The legalism that possessed John Lilburne the Leveller locked him into untenable political positions, as he constantly played the amateur barrister in his own and in his party's defense. "I am an Englishman born, bred, and brought up," he declared to representatives of Parliament who had dared to arrest him, violating proper forms and procedures, "and England is a Nation Governed, Bounded, and Limitted by Laws and Liberties . . . therefore Sir, I now stand before you upon the bare, naked, and single account of an Englishman."[10] A hostile preacher was reviled as one of those "unnatural, un-English-like men."[11] Lilburne was insistent that everything in the future had to be ordered exactly in accordance with his platform down to the last jot and tittle or it was invalid. A world without an army of magistrates to enforce commands was inconceivable even to most Fifth Monarchy Men, and there are articles in Winstanley's utopia that would increase rather than decrease their number in the land. Utopians sometimes take the same attitude toward the minutiae of their imaginary structures that shamans do toward their ceremonials. A Judaic insistence upon punctiliousness in the observance of ritual reinforced the English legal tradition among seventeenth-century utopians, even when they denounced lawyers. In writing his little book Thomas More emancipated himself for a time from his own legal profession. The platform-drafters of the Civil War, though they were unanimously agreed that the English law as practiced by the "vultures" had to be simplified, could not free themselves of their veneration for legal procedures. In the end the mechanics of the law, a new constitution, a new law that was really the old law rediscovered and purified were the instruments that would bring about a state of contentment. Once again the Ranters stood apart in the absolutism of their anarchist preaching and their refusal to recognize the existence of crime, since all was from God.

The reasoning of the new science—which virtually all utopians accepted—was in harmony with the legalist spirit. Hobbes announced that he was writing his treatise in accordance with mathematical principles, and though his own excursions into mathematics were unfortunate (he had the temerity to lock horns with John Wallis of the Royal Society), the idea of scientific method as he conceived it pervades his work. We now know that Locke wrote his treatises of government before the publication of Newton's *Principia* and the beginning of his warm friendship with the scientist, and that by mid-century scientific reasoning influenced even popular theorists of society. The mechanical analogy between the state and a machine antedated the perfection of Newton's "world machine." Harrington in his *Oceana,* published in 1656 before the founding of the Royal Society, was already obsessed with the achievement of an ideal balance in society through the manipulation of intricate voting procedures that relied on mathematical proportionality.

Finally, the methods of biblical exegesis dominated every Protestant writer whatever his sectarian persuasion might be. Hobbes quotes Scripture no less frequently than a Fifth Monarchy Man. The Ranters who attacked the Bible as a worthless collection of fictions did so in a prose style bursting with metaphors from the King James version. In calling the Bible the work of the devil they betrayed their intimacy with both. Among most utopian sectaries each major proposition on a social and moral problem was backed up with the citation of a verse from the Old or the New Testament appropriately interpreted. Since the authors of the English utopias were either divines themselves, or had been brought up on a constant flow of Sabbath sermons and church lectures in which preachers displayed their exegetical virtuosity, this method of reasoning was second nature to them. But the role of the Bible in English utopian literature was not limited to that of a source book for divine words explicated and quoted as authority. Whatever historical examples could be mustered for a future utopia were drawn from the one Book that united them all. The utopians recognized their contemporary villains (who were many) and their heroes (who were few) as replicas of familiar biblical persons.

The Bible was the ultimate source for the primal utopia of God. The Old Testament as a guide to specific ideal laws was more significant than the New, for in matters of government the long historical experience of the Israelites before the advent of Christ offered many more examples of good and evil polities than accounts of Christ and the Apostles, who had lived in one brief period of time. The glorified portrait of historical Mosaic Israel covered most aspects of life in authoritative detail. The Mosaic commonwealth was revealed above all in the laws of the Pentateuch—perhaps less in the actual practice of the kings of Israel, who flagrantly violated that code in their sinful excursions. The utopians were reasonably united in the intent of making the commonwealth of

England into the perfect simulacre of the Kingdom of Heaven, as the land of Canaan had been when God issued commandments for its governance. During the course of the Whitehall Debates in the Council of Officers of the Army, in which rival populist utopians of different political stripes had a free-for-all, one of the more radical speakers, John Goodwin, evoked the image of ancient Israel as a model: "Canaan is the Kingdom of Heaven, as we all generally know. There was a necessity, that land being a type of perfect holiness and of the Kingdom of Heaven, that there should be laws and ordinances of that nature which should keep all things as pure and [as] free [from corruption as] to worship, as possibly might be. Otherwise the visage, the loveliness of the type, would have been defaced."[12]

When the utopians fought among themselves they ended up arguing about the correct meaning of the Word of God plainly incorporated in a biblical text or the appropriate lesson to be derived from an event in Old Testament history. They quarreled about how to achieve the Mosaic society in the Garden of England, and about the deviations or compromises that might be desirable. Utopians were at some pains to demonstrate that their schemes, whatever their other virtues, were consonant with the scriptural government instituted by Moses. But Winstanley and many Levellers gave the biblical utopia a rather unique interpretation: They would hold to its spirit, not its letter, a continuation of Müntzer in another language. Cromwell, though he may have accepted the proposition of a "type" in a general way, was far from certain that the Judaic model should be imitated down to the last particular, abrogating all current judicial practices. Many Puritans, however, wanted to follow it meticulously, including the harsh punishments of Deuteronomy. Fifth Monarchy Men eager to reintroduce every law in the Old Testament were drawing up compendia of these commands of God in preparation; nothing fazed them, not even death for Sabbath-breaking and adultery. Harrington used the Hebrews as one of the ancient exemplars of excellence, with their balance of class interests among royalty, priests, Levites, and ordinary Israelites. Moses, he demonstrated, had promulgated a mixed constitution not too unlike that of Venice — an analogy that is strained even by the standards of seventeenth-century political theory. On occasion there was an evocation of institutions that postdated the Babylonian Captivity, such as the Jewish assembly of the Sanhedrin. Though rabbinic commentaries in the Talmud were not often quoted directly, contemporary English and Dutch scholarship laboring on a reconstruction of ancient Jewish law had seeped down to reorganizers of the English commonwealth — their utopia had to be made to fit some Israelite frame, if possible.

An alternative model, the image of the law of England in the ages before it had been corrupted by William the Conqueror, appealed most to Levellers and to Winstanley, though on occasion the Levellers went even further back to invoke the law of nature, and Winstanley, to a state of innocence before man's fall into the pit of buying and selling. Alfred the Great's kingdom had both advantages and disadvantages when compared with that of the Israelites. Since it bequeathed no Deuteronomic code, all manner of notions about an Englishman's birthright could be read into that fortunate time. Yet the absence of legal guidelines sometimes left the legend too vaporous to have any cogency. Those who held to the Norman yoke thesis preached a return to pre-Conquest equality or to a state of nature, after the King and his Norman Cavaliers had been eliminated. Lilburne attacked his judges as Norman interlopers. Winstanley argued sophistically that either conquest was a legitimate basis of right and power or it was not; if the theory that it was could be sustained, then the Norman conquerors had finally been trounced by the ousting of the King and no longer had a claim to govern; if conquest was not a valid basis of right, then men of God had but to efface the evil of centuries by returning to the equality of the time of Creation.

With rare deviations the radical transformers of the realm clung to the models of Israel and ancient England, sometimes in combination. (Again, the Ranters imposed no such restriction upon themselves.) By contrast, those who were least utopian and most conservative of existing social relationships had recourse to the experience of the classical world because it was rich with examples weighted on the antidemocratic side of the scale. The dangers of unchecked popular rule could be most profusely illustrated by citations from the Greek and Roman historians and philosophers.

Since the Wars of the Roses, Englishmen seem to have refrained from mass slaughter of one another; they have suffered nothing comparable to the French and American civil wars. The uprisings and rebellions for kings or Chartist democracy were abortive and relatively bloodless. The mid-seventeenth-century Civil War has been singled out as an exception, but some historians, applying the yardstick of twentieth-century massacres, have come to belittle the upheaval and to call attention to the fact that many parts of the country were untouched. This contention is supported by the testimony of English eyewitnesses themselves. An anonymous pamphleteer styling himself J. Philolaus contrasted the good fortune of his countrymen with the lot of the Germans and the French, who had vainly endured the most dreadful carnage: "When I consider the strange dispensations of providence upon us of this Nation, I cannot but be swallowed up in admiration and deepest acknowledgement, how it hath been pleased to scourge us but with light afflictions . . . we among whom for almost a decad of years there hath been a continual effusion of blood, know neither Rapes, nor Desolations, nay are ignorant almost of the common calamities of war, while we have puld down those powers of the earth that stood between us and our Felecity . . ."[13]

Englishmen's hostility to one another may be said to have taken itself out in a combat of words. There is a magnificent English vituperative tradition that assumes a class form, with expressions of contempt, anger, and repugnance equaled only by an outward appearance of deference and paternalism. It is a verbally violent society. The capacity for mutual recrimination reached a high point in the pamphlet literature of the seventeenth century, with titles like Josiah Ricraft's *A Nosegay of Rank-smelling Flowers, Such as grow in Mr. John Goodwin's Garden. Gathered Upon occasion of his late lying Libell* . . . (1646). What is at first glance less evident, these violent declamations nurtured by the language of the English Bible, especially the Old Testament, were the foreword to a utopian vision of an England that would be an Eden under God. Images from the Apocalypse dominate many sectarian utopias: first a bloody holocaust, then a reformation of the realm that would ravish the hearts of men. Most of the verbal energies were spent in depicting present horrors and foretelling the vengeance of the Lord. By the time the utopia proper was reached, the vital spirits were exhausted, invention was drained, and the prospect was flat and dry. Of course, the same charge may be made against virtually all utopias: More's Book I with Hythloday's accusations is more entertaining than Book II; Rousseau's incisive critique of the social state more convincing than the daydream of the *monde idéal;* Fourier's devastating analysis of man's choked-up passions more dramatic than his prescriptions for happiness; Marx's condemnation of capitalism, even his cry of alienation, more compelling than the banalities he was able to produce about the future.

English pamphlets of this period can still be read because of the forceful prose style that prevailed in all ranks of literate society, but the pamphlets are untranslatable into other idioms; they are bound to passing events in a complex political and religious interplay and would hardly be comprehensible outside their English context. French revolutionary oratory and philosophe terminology have been easily universalized. The talking pamphlets of the Levellers and Diggers are so entwined with the immediate circumstances of Englishmen, fantasies about their birthright and the past history of their island, that foreigners cannot readily grasp their meaning. Strangely enough, the extremist Ranters spoke a less parochial language, joined as they were with Familist predecessors and the long modern utopian series that proclaims the death of God and sin, emancipation of the flesh, and the end of instinctual repression. Since the sectarian utopians were tied to a scriptural religion in English and rooted in a tradition of the English customary law that was unique in Western society, the English utopia of the Civil War was not for export.

The Agreement of the Levellers

The Levellers were thrust into the thick of the political and social battles, and they fought for their utopia until the very end, when they were overwhelmed and crushed by Cromwell. The term Leveller was one of denigration hurled at John Lilburne's friends and other Army Agitators who participated in the joint debates of officers and men at Putney in October 1647. Anti-Leveller pamphleteers classed Levellers with utopians. The anonymous Philolaus wrote in *A Serious Aviso to the Good People of this Nation, Concerning that Sort of Men, called Levellers* (1649): "I am verily of opinion that Fantastick Eutopian Common Wealths (which some witty men, some Philosophers, have drawn unto us) introduced among men, would prove far more loathsom and be more fruitful of bad consequences than any of those of the Basest allay yet known."[14] The label stuck despite attempts of the political leaders of the movement, Lilburne, Overton, and Walwyn, to get rid of it.

John Lilburne had left Cromwell's army, where he had risen to the rank of lieutenant colonel, because he could not in good conscience support a House of Lords that had authority over a commoner. Imprisoned in the Tower for sedition, he contrived to write and disseminate his ideas from there, holding the allegiance of a strong following in the London area that was organized by William Walwyn, a prosperous silk merchant. Whenever Lilburne was molested by the authorities, a spate of anonymous pamphlets appeared in his defense. He was one of the early heroes of the rebellion, having been whipped by the tyrant for his denunciations of prelacy. By Lilburne's side stood his wife, Elizabeth, perhaps the first significant modern revolutionary figure who was a woman. If Lilburne and his followers are lifted from their tumultuous religious environment and from the political conflicts among Presbyterians, Independents, Baptists, and other sectarians, their vision, radical in content though simple in proposition, loses its essential character. Lilburne saw his soul clothed with the glorious righteousness of Jesus Christ, and when he flouted the minions of Cromwell in the *Picture of the Councel of State* he declaimed like a saint armed by the Lord: "If every hair of that Officer or Souldier they have at their command, were a legion of men, I would fear them no more than so many straws, for the Lord Jehovah is my rock and defence, under the assured shelter of whose wings, I am safe and secure, and therefore will sing and be merry; and do hereby sound an eternal trumpet of defiance to all the men and divels in earth and hell . . ."[15]

Lilburne's utopia cannot be reduced to unicameralism or a utilitarian conception of possessive individualism. From the scores of platforms and pamphlets published during their active period by Lilburne, Walwyn, and Overton, the society they yearned to live in can be constructed, though the edges are rough and there are contradictions, compromise agreements with Army Grandees, and Aesopian formulations that obscure their real intentions. The framework of an optimum commonwealth emerged from *Englands Birth Right Justified* (October 1645), *The Humble Petition of the Officers and Souldiers* of March 21, 1647, which was provoked by Parliament's rejection of the Army's demands at the time of its disbandment, and the *Petition* of May 1647, ordered burned by the House of Commons. The constitutional objective of parliaments annually elected by free manhood suffrage—with exceptions of course —was the coverall for the Army's and the people's just rights and liberties.

For a time, Cromwell and the Army Grandees were constrained to join forces with Lilburne against the Presbyterians in Parliament; but profound differences underlay the uneasy alliance. Cromwell feared Lilburne's "hurly burlyes" in the Army, and once the Presbyterians were ousted and the Independents securely ensconced, the Levellers were dropped. In defeat, Lilburne and Walwyn charged that the quarrel of King, Parliament, and the great men of the City with the Army had degenerated into a dispute over "whose Slaves the poor shall be," the poor being those who depended on farms, trades, and small pay.[16] The tactics of Cromwell were far more sharply focused on the seizure and maintenance of power than those of the Leveller leaders. "I tel you Sir," he is reported to have shouted to the Council of State after Lilburne's arrest, "you have no other way to deale with these men, but to break them in pieces . . . if you do not breake them, they will break you."[17]

Walwyn, the cultivated merchant who was the intellectual and spiritual conscience of the group, articulated their doctrine of absolute religious toleration and freedom from any state intervention whatsoever in language that was surpassed in vigor only by Milton's. In defiance of Calvinist precepts, Walwyn stoutly held to the position that there was free justification by Christ alone and that grace came to anyone who repented of his sins. References to Lucian, Thucydides, and Plutarch were joined to a formidable array of biblical quotations in support of freedom of belief. There are passages in Walwyn's religious autobiography, *A Still and Soft Voice from the Scriptures* (1647) that echo the spirit of Erasmian humanism, with its emphasis on moral conduct rather than theological dogma, before the great schism in the Church. "I have no quarrell to any man," Walwyn wrote, "either for unbeleefe or misbeleefe, because I judge no man beleeveth any thing, but what he cannot choose but beleeve; it is misery enough to want the comfort of true beleeving, and I judge the most convincing argument that any man can hold forth unto another, to prove him-selfe a true sincere beleever, is to practice to *the uttermost* that which his faith binds him unto: more of the *deeds of Christians,* and fewer of the arguments would doe a great deale more good to the establishing of those that stagger." [18] Walwyn was partial to Montaigne's portrayal of the noble, happy cannibal and his natural goodness. An embryonic Rousseau amid the Puritan saints is a paradoxical apparition.

It is difficult to reconstitute the atmosphere of petty puritanical spying, squealing, gathering false witness, tale-bearing, plain hallucination, and myth-omania that prevailed among the sectarians. Walwyn was accused of being "an Atheist and denier of Scriptures, a loose and vitious man," one who patterned himself after the "arch-anabaptist Müntzer." [19] There was an attempt to frame him with a lewd woman who was supposed to elicit from him a blasphemous attack on the Bible. Egocentric paranoids, balanced men persecuted, ven-geance-seekers, were intermingled in a pit of venomous creatures who spat out invective that was sometimes inventive if painfully long-winded. Political uto-pias were born among these screeching, scratching preachers, all invoking the living God.

The best abstract statement of Leveller principles is *An Agreement of the Free People of England,* signed by Lilburne, Walwyn, Thomas Prince, and Overton, and dated May 1, 1649. It is stripped of Walwyn's religious passion and Lil-burne's narcissism, and cleansed of any suspicion of economic egalitarianism. These are no Babouvists on trial or Anabaptists under torture; they are simply prisoners in an English institution—the Tower—that has housed so many em-inent utopians it might be considered a veritable chrysalis of utopian thought, or at least their place of retirement. The Levellers' program, a futile attempt at a reconciliation with Cromwell that advertised its conservatism, was a skeletal outline that deliberately left to future parliaments the task of fleshing out the details. Broad executive power was bestowed on the annually elected parlia-ment, but the "Agreement" was sanctified as an everlasting, changeless law that disallowed the right of any future parliament to "level mens Estates, de-stroy Propriety, or make all things Common." The Government could raise money "only by an equal rate in the pound upon every real and personall estate in the Nation." [20] The Levellers would abolish all economic privileges and spe-cial allowances, though not existing property holdings. Strict limits were set on the power of the law to deprive men of their physical liberty. No one was to be imprisoned for debt.

The "Agreement" included a set of constitutional provisions and guarantees of English liberties that were manifestly utopian in their own day and re-mained so for centuries after Britain settled down to orderly monarchical gov-ernment and rotten boroughs: annual parliaments of four hundred members whose reelection was prohibited because, as the pamphleteers commented, running waters flowed sweet; exclusion from parliament of public officers civil or military; universal manhood suffrage (except for "servants" and those receiving alms, or the miscreants who had sided with the late King); freedom of religious conscience; abolition of religious disabilities to the holding of pub-lic office (except for papists); revocation of excise and customs; universal trial by jury. Elections to parliament were to be based on the old jurisdictions (though parliament could establish different subdivisions if it chose), and there was to be no imposition of parliamentary officers on local administrative bodies. Army levies were to be equally allocated among the counties, cities, towns, and boroughs, which would pay the troops and appoint the officers themselves (except for the generals); and there was to be no forced service in the military. "Punishments equall to offences" was to be the fundamental rule of law, with no deprivation of lives, limbs, liberties, or estates upon trivial or slight occasion.[21] In all, a charter of political and religious, but not economic, equality for a society very much like the existing one thoroughly purged of its more flagrant political abuses.

Richard Overton, in *An Appeale from the Degenerate Representative Body of the Commons of England Assembled at Westminster* (London, 1647), was more partial than his friends, perhaps, to the decentralization of authority in giving each county control over the impeachment of its own representatives. But in general the Leveller utopia could be interpreted as a loose federation of local bodies exerting more power than the annually elected parliament. According to his enemies, Walwyn even toyed with the prospect of a society without formal permanent magistrates, a sort of random judicial administration. There would be no need of standing officers, or a committee, or judges. If a dispute arose or a crime was committed, a cobbler from his bench, or butcher from his shop, or any other tradesman that was honest and just, heard the case, passed judgment, and then betook himself to his work again.[22]

The Levellers, though they sought to convert members of the Model Army to their opinions, had no vision of a body of militant Christian saints enforcing the will of God. The Army would be disbanded soon after acceptance of their political utopia of parliamentary representation, for then the wheels of state would turn easily. The Levellers suffered from the illusion that somehow the truths they held to be self-evident would be subscribed to by the "people" and accepted by authority in an act of self-abnegation. Manipulatory capacities for raising a crowd in London were combined with a goodly measure of naiveté, faith in the promises of temporary allies, belief in the easy penetration of ordinary minds by plainly salutary principles.

The tone of the Leveller utopia was communicated in a long-winded preamble to the *Agreement of the Free People of England,* which for all its differences seems to echo in the Declaration of Independence, framed by a more respectable group of dissident Englishmen more than a century later:

And being earnestly desirous to make a right use of that opportunity God hath given us to make this Nation Free and Happy, to reconcile our differences, and beget a perfect amitie and friendship once more amongst us, that we may stand clear in our consciences before Almighty God, as unbyassed by any corrupt Interest or particular advantages, and manifest to all the world that our indeavours have not proceeded from malice to the persons of any, or enmity against opinions; but in reference to the peace and prosperity of the Common-wealth, and for prevention of like distractions, and removall of all grievances; We the free People of *England,* to whom God hath given hearts, means and opportunity to effect the same, do with submission to his wisdom, in his name, and desiring the equity thereof may be to his praise and glory; Agree to ascertain our Government, to abolish all arbitrary Power, and to set bounds and limits both to our Supreme, and all Subordinate Authority, and remove all known Grievances.[23]

The Leveller utopia was philosophically overdetermined: The laws of nature, the laws of Christ, and the precepts of good government all pointed in the same direction, toward the goal of "communitive Happinesse."[24] The devils in this world were the greedy pursuit of interest and arbitrary power. The Levellers dedicated themselves to a variant of the principle of calm felicity that would not disrupt the existing social order—"the enjoyment of those contentments our several Conditions reach unto us."[25] Striving and struggling were primary sources of unhappiness among men, and the good commonwealth was a happy nation of men satisfied with their lot. Acceptance of one's social condition was a requisite element in contentment. Political and religious, not social or economic, equality was the foundation of the Leveller utopia.[26] But Lilburne refused to settle for a merely nominal political change, by which he meant a switch from monarchy to republic. The essential regeneration of England could be brought about only by purified parliamentarism.

The constant charge against the Levellers was that of "levelling," that they would level all men's estates and abolish all distinctions of order and all dignities. Not so, they reiterated with tiresome frequency. Levelling, the taking away of the proper right and title that every man had to his own, was most injurious unless—and the condition is writ clear and large in their program—"there did precede an universall assent thereunto from all and every one of the People."[27] Such an eventuality being manifestly impossible, the Levellers were not levellers. The community of primitive apostolic Christianity was rejected as a model for England; it had in any case been voluntary, not coercive. Lilburne kept protesting that the enemies of the Levellers were smearing them with a doctrine of secret belief they never entertained. Orders and dignities were necessary for the maintenance of magistracy and government. A charge of anarchy was refuted with the forthright assertion that between the extremes of tyranny and popular confusion, they would always choose tyranny as the lesser evil. They were accused of being royalists, Jesuits, tools of unnamed "others," but they spoke candidly and only on their own behalf. As for their religion, they rejected atheism and professed a belief in God. Lilburne saw himself as another in an illustrious line of the persecuted defenders of righteousness who had been denounced as heretics.[28] Overton defied

what all the men and divels in earth or hell can do against me in the discharge of my understanding and Conscience for the good of this Common-wealth; for I know my Redeemer liveth, and that after this life I shall be restored to life and Immortality, and receive according to the innocency and uprightnesse of my heart: Otherwise, I tell you plainly, I would not thus put my life and wel-being in jeopardie, and expose my self to those extremities and necessities that I do; I would creaturize, be this or that or any thing else, as were the times, eat, drink, and take my pleasure; turn Judas or any thing to flatter great men for promotion: but blessed be the God of Heaven and Earth, he hath given me a better heart, and better understanding.[29]

The manner of God's communication with man was simple: His will was written first in their hearts and then in Scriptures, a sequence that was important, but the Levellers denied being anti-Scripturists. At the same time they conceded that they were not strict in prescribing rules and ceremonials for His service. God's love in Christ was the core of their religion; and God was goodness itself, not the God of vengeance and punishment and eternal wrath. There was evil in the world and corruption and the actions of wicked egotistic interests, but those were not God's creation. The Levellers were fully aware of diabolical enticements and the strength of the argument that once in power men became tyrants. They had witnessed the defections of so many men who had succeeded to authority that they did not remove themselves from the human community, or play the game of the elect and the saints. Experience made them mistrust even their own hearts. The purpose of what they called their "Establishment," or plan of government, was to arrange the political order in such a manner that even if men in power succumbed to worldly temptation, they would not be able to do much injury to others. More than a century later their political utopia was resurrected in spirit by the formulators of a similar American instrument, though the Americans abandoned the simplicity of the Leveller attempt at a revival of ancient democracy and got themselves knotted up in the numerical gimmickry of Harrington's *Oceana*.

Commonwealth apologists like Marchamont Nedham in his *Case of the Commonwealth of England, Stated* derided the Levellers as impossible changelings whose desires were unknowable: "What these people aim at and how they would settle is as hard for me to determine as in what point of the compass the wind will sit next, since they are every jot as giddy and rapid in their motions."[30] They were "a certain sort of men of busy pates" that had "a mind to seem somebody," who took a few phrases touching the liberties of the people in the declarations of Parliament and the Army "to frame such comments and chimeras of liberty as might fit their own ends and fantasies; and in time disseminated such strange principles of pretended freedom among the common sort of soldiery and people that it became evident to all the world they sought not liberty but licentiousness."[31] Their ideal of a commonwealth founded on equality of political rights would inevitably lead, Nedham threatened, to equality of estates and agrarian laws. The Levellers were a prelude to the Diggers and aimed to renounce towns and cities and hold all things in common like the old Parthians, Scythian nomads, and other wild barbarians. The multitude, whom the Levellers aroused, were brutish, oscillating between extremes of cruelty and kindness, and could become a most pernicious tyrant.[32]

Among present-day English critical historians, a debate has been joined between those who believe the Levellers advocated only a modest extension of the franchise to holders of some property and to men who had served in the Army and those who assert that, whatever temporary agreements the leaders may have been forced into by circumstance, the *fons et origo* of the movement was a popular desire to return to every freeborn Englishman, irrespective of his social status, the right to choose his representatives. They argue over whether the "servants" excluded from the franchise in platform proposals referred only to body servants, or included apprentices and artisan dependents who worked for wages and lived in a master's house. No one doubts the exclusion of beggars. Depending on their alignment, the historians cite either limiting texts in programmatic statements or open-ended affirmations in pamphlets about everyman's birthright and the equality of rich and poor. The protagonists carry on the controversy as if Levellers had one secret inner voice, as if their leaders were not the volatile creatures we know them to have been, as if there had not been an ounce of rabble-rousing populism in pure Leveller blood, as if the seventeenth-century orators had drawn out the statistical implications of every promise and flourish delivered in the heat of debate. Anyone reading French Revolutionary speeches about the people, the rights of man, and the new liberty, equality, and fraternity would have a hard time to discover there the particular restrictions on the franchise imposed by successive French constitutions. The rhetoric of the Putney Debates was threatening to the Grandees, however minimal the extension of the voting base that a speaker actually favored. With men like Lilburne and Walwyn, the suffrage hinged upon the existence of a free and independent will and could not readily be granted to servants bound to masters who could control their votes, to papists whose allegiance to England was questionable, and to footloose beggars with votes to sell. Perhaps, as in Marxist theory, there was a lower and a higher stage of levelling.

Were there two political theories at war in the breast of the Leveller movement, one binding a political right to the holding of property and the other vesting it in the inalienable heritage of each Englishman? Were they thinking of a utopia of village democracies loosely held together? Were they London artisans and tradesmen who could be called out whenever their hero Lilburne was in danger, incarcerated in the Tower or on trial in the courts, though they understood little about legal procedures and the rights of Englishmen? "Levveller" probably came to be one of those generic labels on bottles whose contents could be mixed, watered, adulterated as the occasion required both by friend and enemy. Henry Denne, himself a sometime Leveller, bore witness to the variety of doctrines among the group: "We were an Heterogenial Body, consisting of parts very diverse one from another, setled upon principles inconsistent one with another."[33] There are Leveller utterances, Leveller tendencies, Leveller bogies, no coherent Leveller theory. Lilburne the apprentice who had been flogged through London, Walwyn who lived as a well-to-do merchant should, and Overton who could rip through an opponent with a pen dipped in bile were possessed by their own words. They were Proteus-like utopians who turned themselves into many shapes and forms, "according to severall occasions and times," as Edwards wrote of the sectaries.[34] But they had a sense of historical drama and they could make the most of a public confrontation.

Overton boomed in October 1646 in *An Arrow against All Tyrants and Tyrany, shot from the Prison of New-gate into the Prerogative Bowels of the Arbitrary House of Lords:* "For by naturall birth, all men are equally and alike borne to like propriety, liberty, and freedome, and as we are delivered of God by the hand of nature into this world, every one with a naturall, innate freedome and propriety (as it were writ in the table of every mans heart, never to be obliterated) even so are we to live, every one equally and alike to enjoy his Birth-right and priviledge; even all whereof God by nature hath made him free."[35] And an echo resounded two months later in Lilburne's *In the Charters of London* (December 1646): "The only and sole legislative law-making power is originally inherent in the people and derivatively in their commissions chosen by themselves by common consent and no other. In which the poorest that lives hath as true a right to give a vote, as well as the richest and greatest."[36] The programs they signed in common were graced with less high-flown speech and were less ominous for the preservation of existing power relations.

In the 1650s, the Leveller leaders faded into the English landscape. Lilburne ended up among the Quakers, the friends of inward light. He had despaired of direct action to bring about the true commonwealth. Walwyn became a practicing physician, wrote a book on doctoring, *Physick for Families* (posthumously published in 1681), and lived to a ripe old age. When Lilburne, only forty-three, died on August 29, 1657, his old Leveller friends and new Quaker brothers fought for the possession of his corpse.[37]

Gerrard Winstanley and the Diggers of George Hill

Gerrard Winstanley was a small clothing tradesman without formal education, an immigrant from Lancashire to London. When he went bankrupt at the beginning of the Civil War, he sought refuge among friends in Surrey, where in 1649, while pasturing his neighbor's cattle, he had a vision in which he was commanded to assemble a community, dig up and plant the commons, and live on their produce. For some years he had been one of those troubled souls whom contemporaries called Seekers, and had preached and written of his experience of God. *The True Levellers Standard Advanced,* published in 1649, described his trance and the voice that commanded: "Work together, Eate bread together, Declare this all abroad."[38] He came into conflict with local authorities over digging up the commons, was summoned before Fairfax and other Commonwealth leaders, and got enmeshed in lawsuits. The original declaration of the Diggers in 1649 was addressed to the powers of England and the powers of all the world; yet the parochial English ingredient was not absent. If there was to be a world revolution, "The State of Community opened, and Presented to the Sons of Men,"[39] it would after all begin on George Hill, near Walton, in the County of Surrey.

For a while Winstanley won the allegiance of a few hundred converts and attracted public notice in London; but by 1652 interest in his ventures petered out. He went back into business again, and while some say he found a resting place among the Quakers, others deny him this consolation. It was not his deeds, but his writings, that won him a niche in the history of communist utopian thought.

Winstanley's published works, a corpus of about a thousand pages, printed by the same Giles Calvert whose presses were open to Levellers, Ranters, and Fifth Monarchy Men, cover a brief four-year span from 1648 to 1652. They begin with *The Mysterie of God concerning the Whole Creation, Mankinde,* in which the personal mystical experience of the author and his idiosyncratic interpretation of the meaning of Genesis are interwoven, and end with *The Law of Freedom in a Platform or True Magistracy Restored,* a complete scheme in about ninety pages for the radical reconstruction of society around the principle of community. Ideas of community were already present in Winstanley's early religious writings, and his last work is still infused with a theosophical spirit, despite the dry formality of regulations and ordinances piled up in chapter after chapter. These years were marked by Cromwell's firm entrenchment, the demise of the political Levellers in London, and the spread of Ranter contagion in the countryside, and Winstanley was affected by the winds of changing doctrine and opinion.

The London Levellers' goal was too restrictive for Winstanley—he was a

"True Leveller"; yet he was equally repelled by the outpourings of Ranter preachers whose inner light led them to deny the usefulness of any order in society that repressed desires, and in his pamphlet *Englands Spirit Unfoulded* (written in 1650 but not published until the twentieth century) he cautioned lady Diggers to shun the blandishments of the "ranting crew," who would get them with child and then abandon them. It is difficult to distill a consistent doctrine out of Winstanley's works. The same man who had once denounced the death penalty with righteous indignation against the oppressors of the people, in 1652 included the ultimate sanction of capital punishment among his own rules of discipline for the restoration of a good society. Doubtless an exegete would be able to reconcile the passages that ring with the rhetoric of freedom and those that impose forced labor under a taskmaster and prescribe whipping, cutting off the head, shooting, and hanging by an executioner in utopia: After all, the earlier outcry against harsh punishments was directed against the unjust chastisement of innocent commoners, the later severity against violators of Winstanley's own Law of Freedom—a double standard whose logic any twentieth-century revolutionary would understand.

Despite the contradictions, there are persistent themes in Winstanley's thought: the Norman yoke theory; a history of the fall from innocence that introduces a war between the powers of light and darkness in every soul; a history of mankind that echoes a Joachimite tri-stadial theory; a denial of heaven and hell as particular places of reward and punishment and a rereading of the words heaven and hell as descriptions of an inner state of love and hate in everyman. The term Reason designates the spirit of God in each individual, a seed capable of germinating. (Winstanley uses the word Reason as Müntzer uses *Verstand*, in a mystical religious sense that has no secular Enlightenment connotations.) When Winstanley descended from the metaphysical to the world of the senses, he singled out the promiscuous buying and selling of everyman's share in the heritage of the Creation as the major source of evil, and looked forward to the restoration of sowing and reaping in common. "Man had Domination given to him, over the Beasts, Birds, and Fishes; but not one word was spoken in the beginning, That one branch of mankind should rule over another."[40] Winstanley was reluctant to advocate seizure of privately owned property by violence and hoped that after the rich landowners saw how happily the Diggers got along by tilling the village commons together, they would eagerly forsake all covetousness, sharing and working with their fellows. The commons may have meant to Winstanley and the original Diggers about a third of the land of England not yet enclosed by individual proprietors, which left a sizable portion of the country available for communal exploitation, without confiscating private property directly.

In *The Saints Paradise: or, The Fathers Teaching the only satisfaction to waiting soules. Wherein Many Experiences are Recorded, for the comfort of such as are under spirituall Burning. The inward Testimony is the Souls strength*, probably written in the summer of 1648, Winstanley had bared his inner life to the public with a confession of the deadness of his religious past and exultation over his recent experience of God: "I spoke of the name of God, and Lord, and Christ, but I knew not this Lord, God, and Christ; I prayed to a God, but I knew not where he was, nor what he was, and so walking by imagination, I worshipped that devill, and called him God; by reason whereof my comforts were often shaken to pieces, and at last it was shewed to me, That while I builded upon any words or writings of other men, or while I looked after a God without me, I did but build upon the sand, and as yet I knew not the Rock."[41] The climax of religious experience for Winstanley, as for scores of other Seekers, was the sudden discovery of God within himself, accompanied by a depreciation of all exterior sources of divine knowledge, no matter how eminent the preachers or hallowed the book. Once God was internalized, He would sit upon the throne within a man (a perfect image for Freud's censor), judging and condemning the unrighteousness of his flesh, filling his face with shame and his soul with horror, even if no one else saw or was acquainted with his evil actions or thoughts.

"King flesh is very covetous, self-loving and self-honouring; it likes them that say as it saith, but it would imprison, kill, and hang every one that differs from him [in the end, Winstanley himself fitted this description]; he is full of heart-burning, either of open envy, and bitter distemper, or else carries himself in a smooth, quiet way of hypocrisie, walking in a shew of truth, like an Angel of light, but when he gets an opportune power, he turns to be a tyrant, against the way of the spirit."[42]

The virtues and vices recognized by Winstanley were those catalogued by all the Puritan saints. Injustice, covetousness, rash anger, hardness of heart toward others, uncleanness of the flesh, adulterousness, promiscuous pleasure, seeking of revenge were evil. Justice, faith, meekness and tenderness of spirit, sincerity, truth, holiness, and chastity were good. To be under grace did not free a man to wallow in the flesh. Winstanley's was a puritanical utopia, with no suggestion of Taborite or Ranter or Adamite sensuousness and permissiveness. Winstanley himself had known temptation: "I can hardly hear a sin named, but I have been tempted to it,"[43] he admitted with a candor that may have held a trace of boastfulness, but now he was regenerated.

Once a man felt the spirit of righteousness within himself, he was forthwith brought into communion with the whole of creation. The original Prophets experienced the Lord, the others only walked by the legs of the Prophets. And it was not the writings of the Apostles, but the spirit that dwelt in them that was life-giving and peace-giving. Those ignorant in the learning of men could become "abundantly learned in the experimentall knowledge of Christ," which would create a mystical communion among all men: "And so we being many, are knit together into one body, and are to be made all of one heart, and one minde, by that one spirit that enlightens every man."[44] Individuals going through the same experience could only arrive at the same experimental knowledge, and having the same knowledge would make them one.

This knowledge of God was progressive, as Winstanley realized even as he penned his preface "To my beloved friends, whose souls hunger after sincere Milk" in *The Saints Paradise*: "I see more clearly into these secrets than before I writ them, which teaches me to rejoyce in silence, to see the Father so abundantly at work."[45] The world movement of God's spirit among mankind had commenced and was growing, pouring out upon sons and daughters, and though "it yet seem small, it shall speedily increase, and the Father will not despise that day of small things; proud flesh shall die, and raign King and governour in man no longer."[46] In the Bible, God spoke to the "capacity of men,"[47] the old Calvinist doctrine, by which Winstanley meant that before the illumination of the world now taking place God had used the Bible with its images to give men an inkling of His Being, for that was all they were yet capable of comprehending; but He was about to speak directly, without intermediary aids. Then preaching would cease, for this verbal way of conveying knowledge would no longer be necessary. Words were inadequate to express Winstanley's experimental knowledge of God, which "sticks lively in me";[48] but soon everyone would experience this knowledge through love. God would give a "feeling experience to the heart,"[49] and such teachings, unlike book learning, were infinite. Winstanley saw himself driven to speak of his own experience of God because the King of Righteousness had thus far manifested Himself only to a few persons scattered throughout the world. Before these revelations, the earth had been overspread with the black cloud of darkness, but when the Divine Light shone upon the elect, the world began to be transformed. To render the coming of this enlightenment, Winstanley's early writings borrowed from the mystical imagery of all ages—springs and fountains gushing, streams flowing, light shining through.

Denigrating the bookish tradition as contrasted with the actual experience of God was part of a widespread radical religious sensibility. John Saltmarsh, one of the most eminent preachers of the period, who described the experience of the inner light in a series of brief works in the mid-1640s, had compared the mystical experience of God with the experimental knowledge of the scientist. Winstanley's reflections on the poverty of received book knowledge recall the denunciation of Aristotle by the trumpeters and heralds of the new science, Bacon and Campanella. Such inherited knowledge was regarded by Winstanley as knowledge of the fleshly imagination. Experience mystical and experience scientific were both the sphere of the inner spiritual man. The mystical experience had the quality of direct illumination for Winstanley, independent of the niceties of theological argument, even as the understanding derived from scientific experiment was distinct from the storehouse of inherited notions and was even at variance with it. Winstanley's tirades on the university system should be translated into hostility against the learned culture that concentrated on the ancient world and the false theological controversialists, not against the spread of a knowledge of things that had a useful function. Above all, he was antagonistic toward the creation of any special class of scholars or law interpreters or divines or magistrates. Everyone had direct access to the word of God.

Winstanley harked back to earlier English and Continental mysticism. Netherlands cults that practiced community of property like the "Family of Love," founded by Henry Niclaes, or Nicholas, whose pamphlets had also been published by Giles Calvert, had crossed over to England. During the Civil War period translations of Jacob Boehme (1645) and Nicholas of Cusa (1648) responded to the growing need for works on mystical experience and the experimental truth of God's revelation. Winstanley came to believe in the Arminian doctrine of universal salvation, even including the damned in hell. The power of inner illumination could recover the original purity before the Fall, to which he gave a fresh doctrinal twist. It was a fall from community and from delight in the spirit to preoccupation with the fleshly objects of the Creation.

The Law of Freedom in a Platform or True Magistracy Restored, Winstanley's proper utopia and final work, is dated 1652 and includes a dedicatory "Epistle to Oliver Cromwell" of November 5, 1651. Like Jonah, Winstanley was impelled to speak to Cromwell for his conscience' sake, "lest it tell me another day, If thou hadst spoke plain, things might have been amended."[50] Cromwell is addressed with the same threatening urgency that later marked the appeals of Saint-Simon and Fourier to Napoleon. Winstanley was as passionate as More when he depicted the sufferings of the downtrodden; but now the spokesman was no longer a learned mariner in a dialogue but the people themselves bearing witness:

And is not this a slavery, say the People, That though there be land enough in *England*, to maintain ten times as many people as are in it, yet some must beg of their brethren, or work in hard drudgery for day wages for them, or starve, or steal, and so be hanged out of the way, as men not fit to live in the earth, before they must be suffered to plant the waste land for their livelihood, unless they will pay Rent to their brethren for it? wel, this is a burthen the Creation groans under; and the subjects (so called) have not their Birth-right Freedomes granted them from their brethren, who hold it from them by club law, but not by righteousness.[51]

With the exception of certain Ranters, whose pantheism recognized God in all things and human actions, rejected the difference between good and evil (except murder), and railed against the hypocrites who denounced fornication, theft, and lying and hanged or burned men for it while they committed the same acts with impunity, all sectaries and utopians held to the existence of ineradicable powers of good and evil at war in the breast of everyman. Even when they posited the existence of a relatively good life for man sometime in the past, it was with the consciousness that there were latent forces of evil. The Levellers, who perhaps took the most favorable view of human nature and saw in it possibilities of love and benevolence toward fellow creatures, were aware through self-analysis that they also had potentialities for lusting after power and seeking after other men's positions. That was why they wished to be judged by their policy and not their persons. And in whatever procedures they proposed for electing members of parliament and choosing magistrates, they hedged their laws with provisos that would inhibit long-term usurpations of authority.

The spirit of Winstanley's final utopian project is even more wary than that of the Levellers. His *Law of Freedom in a Platform* portrayed an ever-vigilant society, not an easygoing pastoral idyll. He elaborated a system of production under the control of magistrates who were themselves subject to an intricate network of supervision. Even in Winstanley's utopia men might be prone to idleness, to stealing from one another's private households, taking more meat from the common storehouse than was necessary for their families, raising a tumult and announcing the reestablishment of the wicked right of property, reviling and slandering neighbors, committing rape and adultery and other offenses that merited capital punishment. There is nothing loose about Winstanley's ideal society once he gets down to promulgating regulations and leaves off his mystical interpretation of Genesis. Overseers and taskmasters operate at every stage in the hierarchy, and the price exacted for transgression, while moderate by some seventeenth-century standards, was cruel. Public admonitions, whipping, hard labor under a taskmaster, and finally beheading or hanging were normal gradations of punishment. Overseers took care that men contributed sufficient labor under threat of entering this system of escalating penalties. Shopkeepers who distributed the common stocks were closely watched. The education of children was rigorous and the disobedient were thrashed.

Looked at from the vantage point of the mid-twentieth century, Winstanley's utopia is an austere gerontocracy. For a product of the Civil War period in which many of the important protagonists were quite young, Winstanley exhibited a strong distrust of youth on the ground of its inexperience, a suspicion that is in harmony with the generally punitive temper of his utopia. Men below the age of forty had to work and could not be elected to the magistracy except in rare cases. After forty they governed as magistrates or taskmasters. Whenever Lilburne the Leveller was in trouble with Cromwell's agents, it was the "young and apprentices" of London who came to the rescue as they demonstrated and issued petitions under that title. Winstanley's requirement that rulers be limited to men over forty would have found little favor with the youthful hotheads. The laws of the society were clear-cut, were read over and over again on the Sabbath, which was workless, and were known to all. The familial structure was the existing one, but fortified by the official magistracy of the father. Sobriety was enforced in a puritanical spirit, and there was no idle babbling. Love was mentioned but once: Marriage would take place by mutual consent.

Winstanley laid down the law of the imperative to work and justified it, not on the biblical grounds of the Fall, but in the name of health physical and psychic and the welfare of the commonwealth. Labor was emancipated from both the aristocratic curse of Aristotle and the theological notion of punishment for sin. If one ate, there was no freedom to idle. "And the reason why every young man shall be trained up to some work or other, is to prevent pride and contention; it is for the health of their bodies, it is a pleasure to the minde, to be free in labors one with another; and it provides plenty of food and all necessaries for the Commonwealth."[52]

The passages on knowledge are most revealing of the moral tone of Winstanley's society. Universities as constituted, with their emphasis on theology, were eliminated and there was no concern with literature. Direct inquiry into God's creation was the only approved knowledge; and those who wished could deliver public discourses on the Sabbath on natural history, astronomy, astrology, husbandry, and human behavior, with the proviso that they restrict themselves to what their own "trials" had actually discovered. The antitheologism of some of the sectaries opened the door to the study of science as a replacement. Men could know God only in His works, the rest was pretense. There was overt hostility to the existing university system among all sectaries —Levellers, Diggers, and Ranters. In Winstanley's structure antagonism to the verbal scholarship of "divinity" led to a prohibition against any man's devoting himself entirely to mere book learning. In *A Declaration from the Poore oppressed people of England* he jeered at the "Parrat-like speaking, from the Universities, and Colledges for Scholars."[53] Knowledge was a supplement to work and not a substitute for it (as it could be in More's *Utopia*). Winstanley would have no learned elite, nor any special class of perpetual administrators, though he suggested incidentally that supervisors should further the talents of young persons who showed ingenuity. But his was not a novelty-seeking utopia despite its acceptance of science. Insistence upon the dissemination of the new science (yet unnamed) in popular lectures was in the same egalitarian spirit as his provision for equal shares of produce. He would brook no separate intellectual class such as the clergy that would be divorced from the ordinary people. Knowledge had to be close to practice and there was an underlying repudiation of abstract knowledge that did not directly yield fruits.

The theological foundations of Winstanley's utopia had early been set in the allegorical interpretation of the story of the two trees in Genesis. The tree of knowledge was the source of evil in man because it represented "imaginary" knowledge—fears of hell and punishment, terrors, superstitions, false dicta about obedience to elder brothers and conquerors and conniving priests. The Fall was man's enslavement to this so-called knowledge of imaginary things. Under the Norman conquest, under a lying theology, men had been dominated by this knowledge. But there was also the tree of life, knowledge of real things, knowledge of nature that would help them achieve agricultural abundance. In contrasting the two trees in *Fire in the Bush*, Winstanley had presented a dichotomous view of the world in a rhetoric that seems timeless, going back to Empedocles and forward to Freud and present-day Freudo-Marxists. The ideal was the state of innocence antedating the Fall, before the Zoroastrian conflict of real with imaginary knowledge became the fate of mankind. "As soone as Imagination began to sit upon the throne (Mans heart), The seed of Life began to cast him out, and to take his Kingdome from him; So that this is the great battaile of God Almighty; Light fights against darknesse, universall Love fights against selfish power; Life against death; True knowledge against imaginary thoughts."[54]

In 1649, when his public career began, Winstanley had spoken in language reminiscent of Joachim's three stages, and the age of universal love appeared imminent. Three years later, in the practical utopia dedicated to Cromwell, the spirit was Manichean, as he elaborated a mechanism to curb the powers of evil in human nature. The mystical triumph of universal love receded into the background, and he lost himself in that labyrinth of political gadgetry common to English utopias of the period. After submitting oneself to Winstanley's reign of the aging taskmasters, so orderly, regulated, lacking in joy and spontaneous effusions of love and hate, one begins to long for a bit of Ranter unrationality with its stripping of the false faces of do-gooders.

The World of the Ranters

Winstanley's utopia of inner conscience still preserved a conception of wrongdoing, and, while committed to equality, erected barriers to the freewheeling of man's evil nature. During the Civil War there were individual preachers who boasted that they were emancipated from any sense of sin and who proclaimed that everything was "from nature"—a kind of popular pantheism that saw Godliness in each act of their fellow creatures, drinking, smoking, fornicating, making merry. The term Ranter was loosely applied to this attitude toward God and men. The Ranters were not a proper sect, nor did they adhere to any formal manner of worship. Some among them not only felt God within themselves and in all living things and "ejaculated with prayers" when moved by Him, but believed themselves to be gods. One gathers—from their enemies and their own dubious recantations when apprehended by the authorities—that they had assembled small, self-contained groups around leaders who engaged in promiscuous converse with "she-disciples."

The ideal of liberation from guilt and the utopia without repression had never died in the West. The tenets of certain Gnostic sects had survived through the Middle Ages to reappear among the Taborite millenarians and the members of the Family of Love. In the mid-seventeenth century there were Continental sects both Christian and Judaic who believed that the Messiah would come when men were all good or all evil, and since the prospect of the former seemed remote there was a tendency among them to accept freedom of the will, without the restraints that traditional Christians and Renaissance humanists had imposed upon themselves. Many of these ideas crossed the Channel to England.

When societies are cut adrift from their moorings, instinctive drives break loose from the repressive psychic forces implanted in individuals by their upbringing. Groups arise among the ordinary people to demand public sanction for instinctual gratification that the upper classes have long enjoyed. In scriptural religious societies the demand for gratification presupposes total emancipation from written prohibitions in the commandments of God the Father. One Father Laurence Clarkson, or Claxton, told about his Ranter beliefs after he had abandoned them in favor of Muggletonianism. "No man could be free'd from sin, till he had acted that so called sin, as no sin . . . till you can lie with all women as one woman, and not judge it sin, you can do nothing but sin . . . no man could attain perfection but this way."[55] Those who were moved by the Ranters wanted not only to sin, but to sin with the approval of the Father. Rarely is such rebelliousness authentic liberty; usually it is an inadequate way of flouting paternal authority, for the internalized censor cannot be overthrown as readily as a king can be beheaded or a prelate ousted.

The Ranters' proclamation of freedom from sin and guilt was still soaked in the old religious rhetoric. God gave free grace; He was in everyman. God was in everything and in every action, adultery, theft, drinking, singing. The Presbyterian minister Thomas Edwards, who had studiously gathered the record of sectarian utterances throughout the realm, repeats the words of one of their preachers that "though a believer should commit as great sins as *David*, murther adulterie, there was no need for him to repent, and that sin was no sin to him, but a failing."[56] The preaching of pleasure was usually accompanied by tirades of great violence against the hypocritical upper classes who enjoyed these delights themselves but denied them to everyman. Among many Ranters the espousal of the doctrine of pleasure and the rejection of hell and its punishments assumed the form of a universalization of feelings of love and a special solicitude for the cast-off drunkards, whores, wastrels, thieves, beggars. The death of sin was widely celebrated, though the death of God was heralded but rarely. Instinctual freedom among the Ranters was of course only partial: Murder was usually excluded, and sexual enjoyment, at least as defined in print, meant genital sexuality with women, without marital restrictions. Room was left for novelty in the sexual utopias of the next major European revolution, for de Sade and Restif. Among the Ranters, unmentionable vices remained unmentionable, though their enemies charged them with sleeping two women to a man, with bestiality, and with drunkenness, generally approved in the very midst of their preaching as helping to see Christ the better. Occasionally blasphemous remarks and acts were reported—mockery of the idea of God, of the Virgin's chastity, of the Bible, of the body and blood of Christ in caricatures of the Mass during which they ate meat and drank beer.[57]

Ranters like the former Oxford undergraduate Abiezer Coppe bristled with bitterness and sarcasm as they flailed the upper classes. Coppe's *Fiery, Flying Roll,* condemned by Parliament in 1650 and burned, demanded instant parity, equality, community, universal love, universal peace, and perfect freedom. He threatened those in possession of honor, nobility, gentility, property, superfluity: "The rust of your silver, I say, shall eat your flesh as it were fire . . . have all things common, or else the plague of God will rot and consume all that you have . . . Howl, howl, ye nobles, howl honourable, howl ye rich men for the miseries that are coming upon you."[58] Coppe idealized the wretched of the earth in tales that contrasted the niggardly, penny-pinching charity of the "well-favored harlot and holy scripturian whore" carried within him by everyman with the great love burning hot toward a beggar that impelled Coppe himself, on horseback, to cast all he had into the poor wretch's hands, doff his hat to him, bow seven times, and say: "Because I am a King, I have done this, but you need not tell anyone."[59] The good Samaritan, Saint Martin, and Saint Francis all contributed to Coppe's hagiographical self-image. The mystical experience of Abiezer Coppe is further confused by a little tract published in London, 1649, by Giles Calvert, *Some Sweet Sips, of some Spirituall Wine, sweetly and freely dropping from one cluster of Grapes, brought between two upon a Staffe from Spirituall Canaan (that Land of the Living; the Living Lord.) to late Egyptian, and now bewildered Israelites. And to Abiezer Coppe* [in Hebrew letters] *A late converted Jew:* "Only I must let you know, that I long to be utterly undone, and that the pride of my fleshly glory is stained: and that I, either am or would be nothing, and see the Lord all, in all, in me. I am, or would be nothing. But by the grace of God I am what I am in I am, that I am. So I am in the Spirit—The Kings and the Queenes and the Princely Progenies; and the Presbyters, the Pastors, Teachers, and the Independents, and the Anabaptists, and the Seekers, and the Family of Loves, and all in the Spirit; in a word God, Christ, the Saints."[60]

Coppe's intemperate language and reports of his scandalous conduct led to his arrest, and won him the unwelcome attentions of a parliamentary committee. In the manner of some of his utopian predecessors, he feigned madness before the investigators, muttering to himself and throwing nutshells around the room. In the course of his subsequent imprisonment he recanted, at least overtly, and ended his life in Surrey, practicing medicine under the alias "Dr. Higham."

Ranter pamphlets allow us to look into the more extravagant manifestations of the English popular utopia during the Civil War period. Against the vehement, puritanical condemnation of coveting one's neighbor's wife or handmaiden, freer sexuality as a preoccupation is understandable, though hardly innovative. There was one area, however, in which the Ranters left a rich record of human satisfaction. Though it has existed in other societies, it assumed a unique role in this age—the need to relieve one's wrath with mighty oaths and imprecations. Swearing was extolled both by Abiezer Coppe of the activist

Ranters and by Joseph Salmon of their quietist wing. A hostile reporter described Coppe in the pulpit belching forth curses and "other such like stuff" for a whole hour.[61] Coppe himself carefully discriminated between "swearing ignorantly, i'th dark" and "swearing i'th light, gloriously."[62] This may not be a major addition to utopian invention; but only when defilement of the first commandment still had critical significance could swearing have been raised to its proper place in a life free from inhibitions.

The Millennium of the Fifth Monarchy Men

Millenarian programs were announced early in the Revolution and they died late. Most of the authors of these tracts are ciphers except for their names and occupations.[63] Henry Archer's *The Personall Reign of Christ Upon Earth* (1642) is divided into four parts that comprise the requisite sections for a perfect utopian plan. "1. That there shall be such a Kingdome. 2. The Manner of it. 3. The Duration of it. 4. The Time when it is to begin."[64] For a good part of the Civil War, activist Fifth Monarchy Men supported Cromwell, and John Rogers tried to persuade him to institute a "Synedrin" of seventy virtuous men, while Colonel Okey favored thirteen. Cromwell, who was not unmoved by the millenarians as long as they refrained from obstructing his policies, ended up with a Council of State composed of himself and twelve others. Once the Fifth Monarchy Men broke with him, they had only to amend their earlier identification of the little horn in the prophecy of Daniel, substituting the Protector for Charles the First; the rest of the prophecy could remain intact. Except for an abortive uprising or two, English millenarianism was respectable and most men of the Commonwealth subscribed to the doctrine in some degree; but it was generally a tame millenarianism that offered only an innocent spiritual existence, a far cry from the lusty promise of the Taborites.

Though the English Fifth Monarchy Men had a less precise general program than the Levellers and the Diggers, their objectives were not so vague as their detractors claimed. On the face of it nothing could be simpler than the intention to remold the whole of society in accordance with the laws of the Bible after the apocalyptic destruction of every last remnant of the wicked Fourth Kingdom. But, as with all historical determinisms, secular as well as theological, an immediate practical problem arises: Does a Fifth Monarchy Man sit back and wait for the Coming or does he take up arms to destroy the Fourth? Debates between activist Fifth Monarchists and the Presbyterian Saints could revolve around the proper interpretation of chapter 7 in Daniel. The Fifth Monarchist Colonel Thomas Harrison, who was Cromwell's aide, leaned heavily upon verse 18, "The saints shall take the kingdom," while Edmund Ludlow, more cautious, preferred verse 22, "Judgment was given to the saints."[65] Neither, of course, hesitated to identify the "saints" as Fifth Monarchy Men.

John Tillinghast, a militant, announced that they had no right to *"sit still and do nothing"*;[66] and the anonymous *Witnes to the Saints* (1657) proclaimed, "A Sword is as really the appointment of Christ, as any other Ordinance in the Church . . . And a man may as well go into the harvest without his Sickle, as to this work without . . . his Sword."[67] One faction among the Fifth Monarchists actually attempted a few feeble uprisings, and rumor had it that in June

1659 they threatened to burn London. But they were never a serious danger to Cromwell. A plot engineered in 1657 by Thomas Venner, returned from New England, by no means enjoyed the support of all Fifth Monarchists and most of them held off from action even in the manifestly ordained year of 1666. The less ardent were prepared to remain in their chambers until they heard a clear and certain call, waiting in silence, still in weeping and supplication. They could not agree among themselves as to whether it was proper for a Fifth Monarchy Man to hold office under the abominable Fourth; perhaps their policy changed with the "objective situation."

Activist or quietist, Fifth Monarchy Men could not dodge concrete problems about the nature of the millennium, even if there was no consensus as to the manner of its coming. Would Christ appear and reign in person, would He come for a while and then withdraw, or would He postpone His epiphany until the millennium was over? One group of dissidents even doubted whether He would show at all. Tillinghast conceived of a two-act Fifth Monarchy—a Kingdom of the Stone, or evening kingdom, organized by Fifth Monarchy saints on their own and called by Tillinghast the "working kingdom," to be succeeded by the Kingdom of the Mountain, or morning kingdom of Christ, when the saints would bask in the glory that was their just reward.[68] The nature of the political system during the millennium was equally controversial, some opposing monarchy as anti-Christian while others were more circumspect in their pronouncements lest so definitive a judgment exclude Christ Himself. Fifth Monarchy saints shied away from popular electoral procedures because the prospect of ungodly participants in government was an abomination. There was a marked preference for a Jewish Sanhedrin type of collective leadership, seventy or seventy-two members, depending on how the ancient rabbinic system was read. Chance observations about the "fundamental rights of Englishmen" may have been attempts to broaden the political base of the saints, but such unbiblical references were not in the saintly mainstream. Choice by lot was suggested in some prospects because it provided for divine participation in the selective process.

In the millennial preaching there was no Ranter-like hostility to magistracy; the office plays too prominent a role in biblical accounts of the future to be slighted. Magistracy might even be extended, it was surmised, to assure virtue and terrify the evildoers—the swearers, drunkards, and whoremasters. The millennium is portrayed as a solemn epoch and no flippant jests would be allowable, though the leaders differed about the absolute sinfulness of laughter. Most millenarians ordered dress to be plain and considered long hair effeminate. Their enemies mocked them as subversives who would make the rulers of the earth sit "bare-breeched upon Hawthorn-Bushes."[69] But since many Fifth Monarchy Men came from the upper classes, there were those who in anticipation of the rich apparel of the saints during the millennium wore scarlet coats laden with gold and silver lace.

It is not possible to define a unified Fifth Monarchist class theory. In general these saints were opposed to the Cavaliers in the Civil War, since true nobility consisted of inward grace and piety. And the radical wing of the movement believed that there would be no class distinctions in the future society, a prophecy whose fulfillment Venner anticipated by refusing to uncover his head before Cromwell, thus joining the Levellers, Ranters, and Diggers in stressing the symbolism of the hat—perhaps the only doctrinal canopy that sheltered them all. And yet, the prophetess Anna Trapnel foretold that the saints would be earls and potentates, and John Spittlehouse referred to them collectively as "our new built Arrastocracy."[70]

Millenarian social policy usually avoided anything resembling True Leveller phraseology. Spittlehouse defended liberty and property,[71] and Peter Chamberlen, a royal physician, for all his grandiose projects to use confiscated church lands and contributions by the rich as capital to establish manufactories for the unemployed and to provide holdings for the poor, was contemptuous of "mechanick Church wardens" and the confused rabble.[72] Frederick Woodall denounced propagation of the idea of community of persons and things as more wicked than an act of adultery. Attitudes toward the Münster Anabaptists and Thomas Müntzer are a fair indication of the divergences among the millenarians on social questions. Henry Danvers accepted them, while condemning their atrocities; William Aspinwall, another Fifth Monarchist who had sojourned in New England, and John Canne rejected them; and John More and Spittlehouse acknowledged filiation with Müntzer and Storch.[73] But Fifth Monarchism was essentially an urban movement, not a peasant rebellion, and there was no apotheosis of the common laborer on the land.

Like the more prosperous Presbyterians and Independents, many Fifth Monarchists joined in the general contempt of the respectable for able-bodied beggars and the poor, who somehow deserved their fate. Morgan Llwyd preached a redistribution of land so that the rich might not have an excess, but even the radical Venner announced his respect for private property, though he was not averse to seizing wealth forfeited for treason that would provide a treasury for the furtherance of God's work under the direction of the Fifth Monarchy Men.[74] Despite oratorical predictions of much groaning and grieving among the "merchants of Babylon" and the promise that in the end of the days men would not toil that others might live in idleness, the millenarians guaranteed the ownership of those who took the necessary precaution of casting their lot with them. Venner, Aspinwall, Spittlehouse, Benjamin Stoneham, and Vavasor Powell all predicted that there would be no need for taxes, excise, customs in the days of the Messiah. Christopher Feake hedged: People would voluntarily give the godly magistrates whatever they required. In the millennium, according to Chamberlen, peace and safety, plenty and prosperity would overflow the land.

Most of the Fifth Monarchists were against the lords, the richest merchants, and the monopolists, and they formulated an economic policy fit for an island kingdom that lived on trade. As protectionists, they demanded high duties on foreign finished goods and tolls on exports of raw materials, while they advocated the free export of manufactured articles and import of raw materials— they wanted it both ways.[75] Venner's manifesto of 1661 got down to specifics and gave assurances that in the millennium there would be a strict ban on the export of unwrought leather and fuller's earth used in cleaning cloth.[76] This millennium had powerful attractions for master artisans and shopkeepers. But the Fifth Monarchy Men made converts in all ranks of society, and recent attempts to provide a pattern of their class distribution, based on a sample of 233 identifiable persons, is an academic exercise not to be contemned, but not to be overvalued.

Fifth Monarchy Men were militant crusaders in foreign affairs, smiters of the Amalek. To end the reign of Antichrist, England had to lend succor to those who fought the Pope, the Turks, the Hapsburgs, the French. If they approved the war against Dutch Protestants, they could justify their position by explaining that their purpose was to force the Dutch to join them in battle against the Whore of Babylon. Ideological movements have usually been adroit at rationalizing their support of pragmatic foreign policies.

Though it would be difficult to trace direct influence, the Fifth Monarchists reverted in their portrait of the millennium to the sober delineation of the Days of the Messiah in the works of Moses Maimonides, which at this time were being translated and excerpted by learned English and Dutch university professors. His conception eschewed any miraculous distinction between present life on earth and the messianic age, except for the liberation of Israel from oppression and the triumph of righteousness. There would be no fundamental change in human business. Such ideas were consonant with those of the English Fifth Monarchy Men, who merely substituted England for Israel and the millennium for the Days of the Messiah.

After the lively array of Pansophic projectors, Levellers, Diggers, Ranters, and Fifth Monarchy Men, it is painful to report that the utopia of the Civil War period exerting the deepest influence on later generations was James Harrington's *Oceana,* as arid a work as has sprung from the mind of utopian man.

Harrington and the Myth of Venice

James Harrington is one of a long line of utopians who were betrayers of their class. Scion of the ancient nobility, but a republican and an opponent of the mighty lords, he followed the scent of future historical development instead of heeding the pulsations of his blood, bringing down upon himself J. Lesley's royalist curse in a letter with a scribbled title, "A Slap on the Snout of the Republican Swine that rooteth up Monarchy" (1657).[77] In Lincolnshire, where he was raised, Harrington witnessed the new economic prosperity of the gentry and the corresponding decline of the great families. By the beginning of the seventeenth century the Harringtons themselves had passed their zenith, though the illustrious Sir John of Kelston (d. 1612) wrote poetry and invented the water closet. James Harrington traveled on the Continent, studying the governments of the countries he visited, and was indelibly impressed by what he saw as the stability of the Venetian Republic, which appeared to be immune to the vicissitudes suffered by other states, peoples, individuals. John Toland in his biography of Harrington describes this extraordinary adulation of Venice, which we now realize had already descended from the pinnacle of its power: "He prefer'd *Venice* to all other places in *Italy,* as he did its Government to all those of the whole World, it being in his Opinion immutable by any external or internal Causes . . ."[78] It may be that the Venetian Grand Council, which he had observed in action, inspired the intricate balloting contrivances Harrington proposed to his fellow Englishmen as a way of settling their internal strife.

A century later, when the Baron de Montesquieu, an aristocratic young Frenchman destined to occupy a far loftier place than Harrington's in the history of political theory, made a similar tour, he was repelled by the corruption of despotic Venice. In the interim the myth had been exploded. But in the se-

venteenth century Venice was still an admired political model, the modern incarnation of the principles of the two most successful polities of antiquity,
Sparta and Rome. According to an idealized history, Venice—founded in the
islands of the Adriatic by refugees from the barbarian invasions—by a stroke
of fortune had managed to preserve in its constitution the political wisdom of
the ancients and to survive without change, a principal utopian virtue. The
Venetian constitution was based upon Aristotelian conceptions of the nature
of man as a political animal: Since he had a passion for equality that had to be
appeased and an appetite for usurping and monopolizing power, it was necessary to balance these conflicting tendencies if the state was not to be torn apart
by constant turmoil. In the eyes of secular theorists, the *governo misto* of Venice
answered to this need. There were differences of opinion as to the ideal proportions of monarchy, aristocracy, and democracy in the constitutional con-
coction, but almost universal agreement on the principle of a mixed polity.
Naturally, the Venetian idea of the democratic ingredient has little resemblance to present-day conceptions.

This model of mixed government was extolled by Cardinal Gaspar Contarini at one end of the political and chronological spectrum and by English
Republicans of the seventeenth century at the other. Both clung to the vision
of the Most Serene Republic of Venice as the optimum political creation.
Founding his opinion on Contarini's description, the English translator of 1599
concluded that the Grand Council "seemeth to bee an assembly of Angels,
then of men."[79] In 1581 the Grand Council, comprised of all patricians—that
is, nobles whose names were inscribed in the *Libro d'oro* and who had arrived at
the age of twenty-five (and a few at twenty, chosen by lot)—reached the number of 1,843 (out of a total population of 134,890). This was considered the
democratic element. The signory was the monarchical element and the senate
the aristocratic. If utopias are obsessive in the meticulousness of their ordinances, the Venetian constitution qualifies in this respect at least. The intricacies of selecting senators, councillors, and the doge involved an admixture of
the lot and secret election. The manifest purpose was to avoid the formation of
set factions, to give many a chance to govern in a rotary system, and to encourage a choice of the most capable men. Though the doge was elected for life, his
powers were defined anew at each accession, being increased or decreased as
circumstances required.

While for some Venice was the equal of Sparta and Rome, others were carried even further by their enthusiasm to assert that it surpassed them: The
Roman Republic in particular was criticized for having yielded to excessive
"popularity" at the expense of aristocracy. To Machiavelli's dissenting voice
that Venice was too aristocratic and unheroic, that it was merely a government
of preservation, Contarini opposed a baleful account of the consequences of
Roman military victories. After the defeat of Carthage the same martial spirit
that had led the Romans to triumph had turned inward and erupted in bloody
internecine strife. Venice experienced no such disasters because it was not addicted to war.

The idealization of Venice in England, so much in evidence in Shakespeare's
plays, continued into the Commonwealth period, and at a time when political
forms were unsettled, some, like Harrington, hoped to make this model a reality in the realm of England. Both Venice and England were maritime powers.

If he were stripped of his pretensions to royal prerogative, the king of England could be likened to a doge. The ultimate doom of Venice as a consequence of the new geographic discoveries and invasions of Italy by European powers was not foreseen. It is paradoxical that Venice captured the imagination of theorists of the optimum commonwealth at a time when its position had already been undermined. Contemporary testimony on a great society is often fallible; the fate of Venice recalls that of Rome under the Antonines and Britain after Versailles, when both had colored the world map so deeply and extensively. That men of the Renaissance could have utopianized what to most of us now appears to have been a narrow oligarchy should not surprise a generation that has seen the idealization of brutal tyrannies as the final triumph of freedom.

There were of course iconoclasts who tried to shatter the idol of Venetian excellence, like Sir Robert Filmer in his *Observations upon Aristotles Politiques* (1652), where the "intricate Solemnities" and elaborate governmental machinery of Venice revered by some observers were taken to be merely evidence that the Venetians lived in perpetual jealousy and suspicion of one another under an oppressive aristocracy that taxed the people more heavily than had the Turks and extorted money from courtesans in return for tolerance.[80] But such debunking efforts largely fell on deaf ears and the reputation of the Venetian Republic remained untarnished for another century.

James Harrington's *Oceana* (1656), dedicated to Oliver Cromwell, was advertised as the system that would set the commonwealth into a peaceful and enduring mold. As a friend of Charles I, Harrington had once tried to mediate the disputes between King and Parliament. After the failure of his efforts and Charles's execution in 1649 Harrington discreetly withdrew from public affairs for a time. His later statement during interrogation in the Tower of London after the Restoration has it that the *Oceana* was a "commissioned" utopia, apparently one of the first that was made to order in fulfillment of a specific demand. "Some sober men came to me and told me, if any man in *England* could shew what a Commonwealth was, it was my self. Upon this persuasion I wrote . . ."[81]

Oceana combines the two aspects of Western utopias: the speaking picture of how the perfect commonwealth is achieved, and the argument—proofs historical, psychological, scriptural, economic—as to why the new society is best. The argument takes the form of a debate on the government in process of being instituted under a great legislator, the Lord Archon, in the course of which various personages who have made special studies of ancient or modern constitutions present their individual provisions and proclaim their virtues.

Harrington was one of the fathers of a constitutional system of meticulously weighted restraints and balances, the larger and the smaller planets in the system all exerting their force to create enduring stability. His whole scheme revolved around the redistribution of suffrage and units of government on a rational basis. It also depended upon a bicameral legislature: the House of Knights, or Senate, to propose and debate and the House of Deputies to resolve. The *Oceana* announced itself as a utopia of moderation, mixed government, in which there was a balance of monarchical, aristocratic, and popular elements, based on the realities of landownership and nurtured by prudent examples from all the durable governments of antiquity and modern times. To the present-day reader it appears to be more like a ball manufacturer's utopia. Secret balloting with round balls variously colored and marked is at the heart of the decision-making process. A report on setting up the voting mechanism for Oceana conveys the essential flavor of the work.

So the whole territory of *Oceana,* consisting of about ten thousand Parishes, came to be cast into one thousand hundreds, and into fifty Tribes. In every Tribe at the place appointed for the annual Rendezvous of the same, were then, or soon after, begun those Buildings which are now call'd *Pavilions;* each of them standing with one open side upon fair Columns, like the porch of som antient Temple, and looking into a Field, capable of the muster of som four thousand Men: Before each Pavilion stand three Pillars sustaining Urns for the Ballot, that on the right-hand equal in height to the brow of a Horsman, being call'd the *Horse Urn;* that on the left-hand, with Bridges on either side to bring it equal in height with the brow of a Footman, being call'd the *Foot Urn;* and the *Middle Urn,* with a Bridg on the side towards the Foot Urn, the other side, as left for the Horse, being without one: and here ended the whole work of the Surveyors . . .

The estimated charges for installing the complex system came to a mere £339,000.[82]

The immediate impact of a utopia can in a way be sensed by the dystopias it provokes. In March 1657, a year after the publication of *Oceana,* the weekly newspaper *Mercurius Politicus* ran a series of satirical "Letters from Utopia." The fifth letter is a takeoff that penetrated to the core of Harrington's plan: "The Agrarian-Wits of the five and fiftieth order, of the Commonwealth of Oceana, do humbly conceive, That no Government whatsoever is of any Weight but in their Balance, and that if you go to Venice to learn to Cog a Die with a Balloting Box you'll soon get money enough to purchase a better Island than Utopia, and there you may erect a commonwealth of your own. For (SIR) you are to know, its no great charge, when the accompt is cast up, as it is set down by the learned Author and founder of our most famous Oceana . . ."[83]

Harrington's principle of the necessary correspondence between the form of government and the distribution of landed property led him to the conviction that property should be so allocated among the many that no one man or group of men could acquire more than the rest of their countrymen combined. "If the whole People be Landlords, or hold the Lands so divided among them, that no one Man, or number of Men, within the compass of the *Few* or *Aristocracy,* overbalance them, the Empire (without the interposition of Force) is a Commonwealth."[84] In the Aristotelian manner Harrington recognized various forms of stable government—rule vested in the one, the few, or the many— but, whichever form was adopted, it was the prerequisite for stability that the ruler or rulers should control more than half the property of the realm. Through a historical process of the redistribution of land, the many were in fact achieving this control in England.

The balance of ownership was subject to change from unforeseen causes, but the law of Oceana was meant to counteract the tendency to disequilibrium—a situation in which actual power ceased to be in the hands of those who owned more than half the property—and prevent the resulting shambles of a civil war. The mechanisms Harrington advocated are available to the scrutiny of the curious. English political theorists have lately shown that the system he proposed for maintaining the balance lacks even mechanical consistency.

Whether the gentry are included among Harrington's aristocratic few or the people's many exercises a slew of academic interpreters. Nonetheless he provided England with an illusory formula that it lived by for centuries, that of a mixed government in which the nobility, though well versed in the military arts and possessed of ancient virtues, had an underbalance in the ownership of the total lands of the realm. The many (the people) held more than half of the property and thus ultimate political power; hence in accordance with Harrington's postulates they had no fear of noble or gentry presence in the leadership of their commonwealth.

Harrington told his inquisitors in 1661 that *Oceana* was directed against the usurper Cromwell, a remark that hardly jibes with his dedication to the Protector (though permission to publish the book was granted only after intercessions by Cromwell's daughter and assurances that it was nothing but a "political romance").[85] Surely the description of the Lord Archon's abdication could not have gratified Cromwell, with its tacit suggestion that he go and do likewise:

MY Lord ARCHON . . . saw no more necessity or reason why he should administer an Oath to the Senat and the People that they would observe his Institutions, than to a Man in perfect health and felicity of Constitution, that he would not kill himself. Nevertheless wheras Christianity, tho' it forbids violent hands, consists no less in selfdenial than any other Religion, he resolv'd that all unreasonable Desires should dy upon the spot; to which end that no manner of food might be left to Ambition, he enter'd into the Senat with a unanimous Applause, and having spoken of his Government as LYCURGUS did when he assembl'd the People, he abdicated the magistracy of ARCHON. The Senat, as struck with astonishment, continu'd silent; Men upon so sudden an Accident being altogether unprovided of what to say; till the ARCHON withdrawing, and being almost at the door, divers of the Knights flew from their Places, offering as it were to lay violent hands on him, while he escaping left the Senat with the tears in their Eyes, of Children that had lost their Father; and to rid himself of all farther importunity, retir'd to a Country House of his, being remote, and very privat, in so much that no man could tell for some time what was becom of him.[86]

In what was doubtless intended to be an affecting scene, it seems obvious that Harrington fancied himself the Lord Archon (even as More had dreamed he was King Utopus), who after instituting the perfect government insisted upon relinquishing power and status and returning to obscurity, while his bereaved countrymen tried vainly to detain him.

Dullness is apparently not an inhibitory factor in the extension of a book's influence, else Harrington's *Oceana* could not have prospered so mightily. As R. H. Tawney suggested in the delightful essay, "Harrington's Interpretation of His Age": "The reader . . . is unlikely to reproach him with lack of sobriety."[87] The favor that *Oceana* enjoyed among eighteenth-century Englishmen and Americans is baffling. Even skeptical David Hume, after cavalierly dismissing the whole utopian genre in his essay "Idea of a Perfect Commonwealth," had a good word for Harrington's invention. "The *Oceana* is the only valuable model of a commonwealth, that has yet been offered to the public."[88] Debates in the early assemblies of the American and the French revolutions testify to the esteem in which constitution-makers held this incredibly dreary work, at a time when revolutionaries in quest of models had a way of looking backward, just as Harrington himself had rummaged through the stockpile of what he thought were the constitutions of Greece and Rome, Israel and Venice, before fashioning his ideal structure. Like many utopians intent upon immediate realization of a dream, Harrington was not an artist concerned with the literary form of his work. He was committed to an idea, and could present it in a verbose book like *Oceana,* or boil it down to four pages and two lines, as he did on February 6, 1659, in a brief pamphlet with a long-winded title, *The Ways and Meanes Whereby an Equal & Lasting Commonwealth May be suddenly Introduced and Perfectly founded with the Free Consent and Actual Confirmation of the Whole People of England* (London, 1660).

All constitution-making is in a way utopian, since its substance is an imaginative plan whose eventual consequences cannot be clearly foreseen. Late-eighteenth- and nineteenth-century constitution-makers all follow Harrington's schema to some degree. They rarely have more to say, though they may say it with more eloquence and elegance, about the balance of interests, the mechanics for holding off a tyrannical monopoly of power in one person or class, the wisest methods of choosing and deciding. *Oceana,* born of a misconception of the Venetian constitution and a history of changing landownership patterns in England, much appreciated by those who saw here a world-shaking discovery of the relations between property ownership and political power, seems to have exerted its attractions on later moderate revolutionary governments, the American and the early French assemblies, which hoped to couple the rhetoric of popular government with the reality of elitist control. The American constitution-makers abhorred Plato's metaphysics and adored Harrington's arithmetic practicality. Today his work is cited as a document of social history: The importance he bestows upon the knights in his utopia is interpreted as proof of their actual rising influence in England at that time. Marxists see in Harrington an early formulation, of which there are so many, of some aspects of the theory of historical materialism, for he made the point that the constitutional framework of a commonwealth reflected economic and social power as it had spread or been concentrated in certain hands.

Harrington's scheme failed because the monarchical principle was chosen as the safest haven after the storms of the Civil War; but his republican ideas would continue to have a small following in England for hundreds of years. As a utopian he was not one of the wilder sort. He remained close to sea level and the immediate economic and social realities of English life. His was the gentry's utopia, as the Italian bishops and humanist architects had written aristocratic urban utopias. Some commentators have praised Harrington's scientific detachment in evolving the principles of *Oceana* even though he was in the midst of a civil war. He was rather original in his overall view of the evolving structure of English society after the end of the Middle Ages: His ideal state represented a constitutional consolidation of these changes, and in this respect is one of the early modern utopias with a solid historical base. But for all his worthiness he is much duller reading than an oratorical Leveller, a theological Digger, a boisterous Ranter, or even a Fifth Monarchy Man.

14

The Sun King and His Enemies

TODAY THE *History of the Sevarambians* by Denis Vairasse, a Huguenot exile, is virtually forgotten. Volume One first appeared in English in a London edition of 1675, and only later, 1677–1679, was the full text published in French with the approval of the royal censor. (Further editions in French followed, as well as German and Italian translations.) The *Journal des Sçavans* for 1676 announced it as straight travel literature about a newly discovered land in the Southern Seas, though the reviewer entertained a measure of doubt concerning its reliability as geography. Only a portion of the book is a standard utopia describing the laws, customs, and religion of the inhabitants of Sevarambia; around this core are woven tales of adventure and narratives of *crimes passionels* and their punishment that display the utopia "in motion," as Plato would have had it. Learned men—Leibniz and Pierre Bayle among them—were sufficiently intrigued to inquire around in the republic of letters about the person of the author. Rousseau praised the *Sevarambians* along with More's *Utopia,* and Vairasse's work was ordinarily classified with Bacon's *New Atlantis* and Campanella's *City of the Sun,* though it hardly achieved their fame. For the most part the style is uninspired, and only the practice of "communism" among the subjects of the absolute monarch Sevarias accounts for the modern publication of the book in Soviet Russia[1]—belated recognition for Vairasse, whose name, unlike Campanella's and Saint-Simon's, has not been chiseled on the granite obelisk in Moscow's Red Square among the worthy predecessors of revolutionary thought.

The Huguenot Condition

The Revocation of the Edict of Nantes in 1685 was the climax of a long period of increasing harassment of a twentieth of the population of France who were Protestant. Louis XIV had an ambition to become the Catholic king of a united people, perhaps of the whole world; but his policy was not exclusively dictated by royal whim—it was reinforced by an upsurge of popular resentment against a refractory minority. Petitions reached the King from the council of the clergy and royal intendants, from zealous bishops and from ordinary peasants and envious shopkeepers, all inveighing against the heretics and the privileges they enjoyed.

Some French Protestants endured with resignation the billetings of royal troops meant to impose crushing burdens; others emigrated clandestinely; a sizable number gave lip service to conversion and drew their six-franc fee, only to relapse and be converted again. Peasants in the Cévennes remained steadfast in their faith, were stirred by millenarian preachers, and in the eighteenth century were able to hold a large portion of the French army at bay. Huguenots in the eastern provinces of France close to Protestant countries stole across the border despite the vigilance of royal guards, who transported those they caught to the galleys or to hospitals indistinguishable from insane asylums and prisons. Refugees along the Atlantic coast and the English Channel, rescued by Dutch boats, established settlements in Holland and England, where they suffered the usual vicissitudes of political and religious émigrés. The more fortunate were integrated into the commercial life of Amsterdam and London while preserving their Huguenot identity. A few scholars found a place for themselves in the nascent English scientific establishment, where they were befriended and patronized by Isaac Newton. And then there were the stray intellectuals without special occupation or remarkable talent, who eked out an existence as best they could as language teachers or dancing masters, acting as tutors to the sons of the English nobility, serving as scribes or secretaries, attaching themselves to the powerful. Though Huguenots supported one another in exile, many lived on the margins of society and moved back and forth across the Channel between Holland and England as the political winds shifted. Those who failed utterly in the countries where they had sought a safe haven returned home, to lose themselves in the labyrinth of Paris.

One body of Huguenot exiles formed a tight community in Holland dominated by that formidable pastor of righteousness, Pierre Jurieu. But while these émigrés—Israel in the diaspora—preached from afar that it was the Christian duty of the Huguenots to abandom the idolaters and flee the accursed country of the Antichrist, there were other Huguenots who opted for accommodation, encouraged for a time by Louis XIV's Gallican and antipapal policy. They hoped for a reunion of the churches under a king who, after breaking his ties with Rome, would institute a state religion flexible enough to include the Protestants. To this new church they were prepared to make doctrinal concessions, and in their adulation of the great monarch who would undertake a separation from the papacy they surpassed the most extravagantly flattering courtiers of Versailles. Louis XIV was called the true representative of God on earth, and his military victories and triumphs of diplomacy all bore witness to his divine ordination. Huguenot accommodators were bolstered by coreligionists who were relatively indifferent in matters of religion or conceived of it in Hobbesian terms as primarily an agency of the state to maintain public order. It was far easier for them to accept a Sun King than papal doctrine or conversion to a Roman Catholicism that their preachers and devout ancestors had stigmatized as the work of Beelzebub and that was psychically repugnant to them, however little they cared about their own inherited form of revealed religion. While they still drew a line at liberty of private conscience, most men of this persuasion would have gone far in putting up with uniform external practice to present their king with the spectacle of a harmonious union of all his subjects. The spiritual dilemmas of the philosophical Huguenots were prickly rather than soul-searing, but they had trouble forging a personality for themselves once they were cut loose from the moorings of their fathers. By contrast, the orthodox Huguenots who had fled to Holland and founded churches of their own were in a solid position.

The Fantasy of a Huguenot Exile

Denis Vairasse d'Allais (ca. 1630–ca. 1700) had been trained in French law, but he could not find a substantial post in the courts of the countries where he sought refuge. He shuttled between Paris, Amsterdam, and London, managing to subsist as a hanger-on of English nobles like the Duke of Buckingham— in and out of favor—a teacher of languages, geography, and history, an author of French grammar books, perhaps a minor diplomatic agent occasionally engaged in espionage. His utopia was the dream of a typical Huguenot accommodator who admired the works of Louis XIV and would have embraced most of them if only his kind of people had been tolerated, if the French monarch had really been a Sun King and not a tool of the Jesuits.

Huguenots were early associated with utopia. Protestant unease in Catholic France found a voice back in 1616, when an original French utopia was published in Saumur, a paltry little thing entitled *L'Histoire du Royaume d'Antangil,* with a vaguely Protestant air about it—though we do not know the name of its author. Huguenots were numerous among the sailors and naval officers of France, and in the accounts of early French explorers the idea of a refuge for their coreligionists crops up from time to time. The Marquis de Duquesne, son of a Protestant admiral of France who was explicitly exempted from the Revocation of the Edict of Nantes, laid plans for a utopian colony on the Ile de Bourbon. The disabilities suffered by Huguenots on all social levels sent them roaming throughout the world, and the idea of establishing a more perfect society was a recurrent theme in travel and novelistic literature whenever explorers or voyagers in fantasy chanced upon a salubrious climate, abundant food and water, and noble savages, whose myth they diligently cultivated to allay the fears of their coreligionists worried about the prospect of anthropophagy. The Abbé Prévost, in his popular novel *Le Philosophe anglais ou Histoire de Monsieur Cleveland* (1731), introduced Huguenot utopian commonwealths into the adventure story of his oddly pedigreed hero, the illegitimate son of a former mistress of Charles I and a youthful, peccant Cromwell. On the island of St. Helena, where the shipwrecked Cleveland was cast up, he found a Huguenot colony living in a communal, theocratic utopia, albeit distressed by a paucity of males. A number of Huguenot settlements were founded in America, and their experiences, like those of the New England colonies of Dissenters and William Penn's venture with the Quakers, were touched with utopia. John Locke's constitution for the Carolinas is a utopia of sorts; and among his manuscript notes there are a few pages of detailed marital regulations for an establishment labeled "New Atlantis." (During a stay in England, Vairasse had made the acquaintance of Locke, and may have been influenced by his Carolina constitution in elaborating the framework of the Sevarambian state.) In New England Cotton Mather soon celebrated the Puritan ideal society in a sermon addressed to the General Assembly of the Massachusetts Province and entitled *Theopolis Americana* (1710). But most of the Huguenot plans did not come to fruition, no great ingathering of the exiles took place, and their yearnings were recorded principally in a few Morean utopias, of which Sevarambia was in its day the most famous.

The *History of the Sevarambians* reflects the search for utopia of one Huguenot wanderer in the seventeenth century, an uprooted intellectual no longer bound to the doctrines of his Calvinist ancestors, who became flotsam and jetsam in the turbulent philosophical waters of the age. The novel, an attempt to make sense of his existence by building an imaginary society in the unexplored southern continent of Australia, filled an urgent personal and collective need, and, like much eclectic émigré literature, it made provocative new combinations out of ideas alien to settled, French homebodies with restricted horizons. Who should be a utopian if not the expatriate longing for a promised land where he hopes to find a measure of tranquillity?

A Baroque Tale

Four separate stories are intertwined in the history of the Sevarambians: the early life of one Captain Siden, a European who happened upon them in the Austral lands and left behind the manuscript on which the book is based; the history of Sevaris the Parsee who led an expedition to these territories in the fifteenth century and became the conqueror and original lawgiver of the autochthonous population; an account of the traditions of the natives, benighted victims of conniving priests before their redemption by Sevaris; and finally the utopia itself, the society observed by the shipwrecked Europeans who under Captain Siden came among the Sevarambians in the seventeenth century. Compared with the utopias by More, Campanella, and Bacon, which were remarkably compact little books, the work of Denis Vairasse is long-winded, discursive, replete with digressions that are stories in themselves. It prefigures those lengthy utopian novels that were to become a major literary genre in the eighteenth century, de-Christianized rationalist utopias which increased in size and quantitative output until the French Revolution put a temporary quietus on them. One exemplar, the *History of the Sevarambians,* should appease the appetite of even the most voracious consumer of this type of fare, which on the eve of the Revolution was spread out in C. G. T. Garnier's 36-volume compendium of *Voyages imaginaires, songes, visions et romans cabalistiques* (Amsterdam, 1787–1789).

Commentary on pre-Conquest Peru had brought to Europeans an account of a magnificent Incan society of shared wealth under a benign sun god. Why not a high civilization in the Austral land mass that was just being charted? Vairasse mixed real and fictitious events in the Hellenistic and Morean manner in order to enhance credibility. He had verified the fact of a shipwreck off the Australian coast with Pieter Van Dam, advocate of the Dutch East India Company, and the story of the sinking of Captain Siden's "Dragon d'Or" is in complete accord with documents now in the Royal Archives at The Hague. Having landed somewhere in Australia, the survivors of the wreck, four hundred strong, organized a temporary society, and advanced under the military command of Captain Siden to explore the island, eventually making contact with the baffling Sevarambians. From an adventure story about a group of shipwrecked passengers struggling for existence, Vairasse now moved to a confrontation between the Europeans and another, hitherto unknown, civilized society, the same circumstance that had been faced straightaway by the sailors who landed on More's and Bacon's islands.

Forging their way to the capital of Sevarambia, the Europeans discovered cities and buildings of a uniform character (noted as a virtue), great tunnels, canals, and funiculars, whose technology was much admired, even as Vairasse himself had been impressed by the Canal du Midi. A mammoth utopia in the tradition of Filarete's *Sforzinda* (which Vairasse could not possibly have known), the *History of the Sevarambians* is distinguished by its emphasis on grandiose public works and on symmetry in all things. The capital, Sevarinde, whose buildings had all been constructed of stone from the same quarry, astonished the new arrivals with its regularity and beauty, two interchangeable excellences in this aesthetic. The first king had been both conqueror and founder, so that he could by fiat make the city plan conform to an ideal social structure. The living area of Sevarinde was surrounded by a thick wall, beyond which lay fields, gardens, and an aquatic basin. In the middle of the city rose the palace of Sevarias, and in its center stood the Temple of the Sun, a configuration that derived from Campanella and the architectural utopians of the Renaissance radial cities. The inhabitants were lodged in compounds known as *osmasies,* which were grouped around the central governmental nucleus.

As in all sun cults and most utopias of the centuries of European dynastic rule, the fortunate Sevarambians owed everything to a single male founder, an incomparable legislator who literally lifted them out of barbarism, and his laws, emanating from one focal point like the rays of the sun, preserved the society's existence. The original fifteenth-century Sevaris, before the "a" was added to his name as a mark of his new dominion, traced his ancestry back to the Parsees, who had inherited the religion of the sun from remotest antiquity. (Vairasse knew the explorer Chardin, whose report on Persia was one of the most famous contemporary accounts of that kingdom and of the Zoroastrian religion.) Sevaris had been born along the shores of the Persian Gulf, eldest son of a lord who was the grand priest of the sun. During the lifetime of his father the family, persecuted by the Mohammedan Tartars, lost its fortune, and Sevaris after many adventures reached the Austral lands in 1427 (by the Christian calendar) when he was thirty-three, the age at which Jesus had been crucified. The persecution of the Parsees by the Tartar Mohammedans should be read as an analogue to the sufferings of the Huguenots at the hands of the French Catholics.

The utopia is patently autobiographical, with its idealized images of Denis Vairasse in the persons of both Captain Siden and King Sevarias (simple anagrams for the author's names)—one the great voyager to undiscovered countries, the other the brave hero in battle and founder of a perfect society. Vairasse brought his linguistic skills into play when, faithful to the Morean model, he devised a new vocabulary for his Sevarambian subjects. And he took his vengeance for the years spent in the study and practice of the hated legal profession: Though his Captain Siden had also been a law student in his youth, there were no lawyers in Sevarambia.

The trials of Sevaris before reaching the Austral lands were in the banal picaresque tradition. After enslavements, liberations, and voyages to many Asiatic lands, his curiosity had been aroused by sailors who told of a people of sun worshipers in the Southern Seas, and he fitted out an expedition to visit them. His early deeds suggest a condensed account of the conquests of the Mexican and Peruvian civilizations in the sixteenth century; but instead of decimating the natives after the manner of the Spaniards, Sevaris bestowed a perfect society upon them. With the sun cult to render them tractable—and the force of his indomitable artillery—he was able to mold the savages, who were in the state of nature, according to the principles of right reason.

Sevaris the *politique* chose the occasion of a grand festival to prompt a notable of one of the indigenous tribes to propose the election of a single chief who would rule over all the nations. After Sevaris' prayer for guidance, peace, and justice, a strange voice of a woman or young man was heard from the dome of the Temple; the Sun, it announced, had decided to reserve the monarchy for himself alone and would brook only a lieutenant as their governor. Like Louis XIV, Sevaris thus derived his authority by "divine right." The voice introduced during the building of the Temple was an artifice such as Fontenelle would describe in his analysis of pagan priestly tricks in the *Histoire des oracles* (1686); but it was a limited and benign kind of deception, since most of the educated Sevarambians whom Captain Siden met two centuries later were aware that it was a mechanism to lend authority to government and thought none the less of Sevaris–Sevarias for his astuteness.

The Social and Political Order

After briefly considering an imitation of the European system that would have divided the population into seven classes ranging from tillers of the soil to seigneurs, Sevarias conceived of a better and more just model of government. Having concluded that all wars and dissensions were rooted in pride, avarice, and idleness, he decided that a hereditary nobility would only foster a pernicious desire to be superior to others. Seigneurs fancied themselves born to command, forgetting that "la nature nous a faits tous égaux,"[2] portentous words in the 1670s. Hence Sevarias' final determination that there should be no more than one fundamental distinction among the citizens, that separating the magistrates from private persons. Only inequalities of age would be marked by inequalities in dignities. Age as the basis for precedence and hierarchy, regarded as indispensable in some form, is common in egalitarian utopias before the French Revolution.

Writing in Restoration England, Vairasse betrays no sympathy for rebellions and insurrections and revolts against authority. Total subordination to the sovereign arbiter of all things is taken for granted since this submission of will is to the Sun himself and no one feels imposed upon. There is a sense of freedom in this voluntary obedience through custom to what the Sevarambians have come to appreciate as an order of reason and justice; the rational will of the Sun-God has been internalized. "They are early inur'd to a strict Observation of the Laws," the foreigners were told, "which therefore, by long habit, becomes natural to them: and their Submission to them is still the more free and voluntary, seeing the more they reason upon them, the more just and equitable they find them."[3]

Sevarias' code of laws was communist, extending to all ranks Plato's community of goods for the guardians by abolishing private property altogether and assigning everything to the state. Since excessive ease and pleasure constituted dangers to such a society, a benign variation of the Protestant ethic came to the rescue and dictated that the people be kept active in the performance of moderate and useful work, each day being divided into three parts, one for labor, one for rest, and one for pleasure. The organization of labor was easily solved, for Sevarambians, unlike More's Utopians, liked to work and no coercion was necessary. A "moderate, daily Exercise, of eight Hours only" procured all the necessities, conveniences, pleasures, and diversions for a man, "his Family, and all his Children, even tho' he should have never so many."[4] Since no one consumed any more than was necessary, there was no accumulation and no inheritance. The Sevarambians had nothing to leave to their children but a "good Example for their imitation."[5] The definition of needs is plainly Morean: "the Necessaries and Conveniences of Life, as likewise . . . all such Things as contribute to lawful Pleasures."[6] As in More, there are slaves for the mean chores of the household.

After More's *Utopia,* Vairasse's equal distribution of goods does not sound very revolutionary. There is, however, more specialization of labor in Sevarambia than in Utopia. Vairasse provided storehouses for each product, from which officials of every administrative unit took only enough for their own group. *Osmasies* for each particular industry, a communication network to facilitate distribution, and a statistical apparatus to control the balance of supply and demand assured the orderliness of the system. Needs were static, defined as a reasonable quantity of consumer goods without the superfluities of luxury, a formula that appears and reappears for centuries in utopian projections of a communal society and still has auditory plausibility if one refrains from probing too deeply. There was a set sumptuary quota. Once the norm was established the regulation of production was a simple mathematical operation, and the society remained stable forever. The granaries and storehouses, having laid in extra supplies for emergencies, could support the same level of consumption irrespective of good harvests or drought. Some variety was imparted to existence by the succession of the three basic human activities— work, sleep, free enjoyment—during the course of a single day and by the six monthly holidays. Beyond that, sameness without want was the lodestar of the state. Models were all about Vairasse—in Garcilaso's description of the ancient Incan empire, in Colbert's plans for a productive class society in which all men either worked or fought, in ancient communist states among the Pythagoreans and Spartans, in Plato and in Thomas More.

The economic communism and the prestige of the magistrates superficially recall the Platonic ideal state, but the purpose and tenor of the utopia are totally different. We are beginning to hear the cry of the poor and of those tormented in mind and body by excessive toil; Christian sentiment penetrates the Platonic quest for justice as harmony. The *History of the Sevarambians* already has the bite of modern egalitarian revolt, and anticipates in an embryonic way the Marxist slogan: "To each according to his needs." Sevarambians were not distressed by inequality in state dignities because these were reserved for true worth. We are also on the way to the Saint-Simonian hierarchy of merit in an administrative order, though a modern humanitarian rejection of poverty and a critique of undeserved advancement do not fit too well with the underlying Calvinist theory of human nature that suddenly pokes its head into Sevarambia.

Though the utopia is labeled "despotical" in nature by its author, the government is essentially an admixture of aristocratic and democratic elements. The despotic character consists in the absolute power of the monarch, who is the Sun himself, worshiped by all. Actual rule is left to a Viceroy selected for life by an aristocratic council that in turn has been elected democratically by five thousand *osmasies,* the productive units into which Sevarambia is divided. In the grand pyramidal structure, the head of a family and the head of an osmasie occupy in their small spheres the same position spiritual and temporal as the Viceroy of the Sun does in the large. All forms are replicas of one another; they vary only in size and in the number of their subordinate units. The globe, the kingdom, and the osmasie mirror one another in different dimensions. Vairasse's Sevarambia is an example of one kind of utopian fixation, the repetition of identical forms in different magnitudes.

A basic equality in the satisfaction of sumptuary needs is combined with a hierarchy of honors, salutations being punctiliously regulated by position. Distinctions between ordinary people and magistrates express themselves primarily in the color of their garments. The clothes are simple, but the Sun Kingdom is not quite so sartorially egalitarian as More's Utopia, for the higher magistrates wear cloth of gold and silver, the lower of silk, and the common people linen, cotton, and wool. Colors are changed every seven years as a Sevarambian moves through the life cycle, from the white of little children through yellow, green, blue, red, and black for the aged. Purple is reserved for the magistrates. A glance suffices to know anyone's status in society and his age group, so that each person can be accorded the proper degree of respect. In addition, women are awarded a purple stripe for each child they have raised to the age of seven. Garments and underclothes are renewed at regular intervals, and the Sevarambians bathe at least once every ten days, more often than the Sun King at Versailles. Married couples perform their ablutions together in the river. Simple furniture is provided for the living quarters, but the houses are not cluttered with utensils because meals are usually taken in common in the osmasies, though the evening repast can be eaten at home with family and friends, so that there is a private social life.

Officials are chosen for their virtue, and there are elaborate provisions for the suspension or removal of the Viceroy should he betray symptoms of unreason in his behavior. The only perquisite of office is the right to take a plurality of wives from among the unmarried virgins and widows, a mixed blessing since most pretty girls, cognizant of the law, tend to reject suitors who show signs of being overambitious and are likely to be designated for public office.

Life in Sevarambia appears to drift along in an almost Rousseauistic state of natural goodness, until one is brought up short by the intrusion of a Calvinist affirmation that Sevarambians believe man has a natural proclivity for vice. To counter this secular version of original sin, the Sevarambians have made the educational system the cornerstone of their utopia as it was of Plato's Republic. Suspicion of raw human nature obtrudes, but social institutions and the force of education transform the dross of mankind. The purpose of education in man, a battleground of good and evil, is to stifle the seed of vice at an early age insofar as possible and to cultivate virtue. To this end the neutral authority of a state is required to show neither love nor hatred in its inculcation of the principles of reason—a rather chilling prospect.

The Sevarambians are conditioned early to feel the strongest emotional ties to the state. After a few years of maternal care, the umbilical cord binding the child to the family is cut, and in an elaborate ceremonial the parents surrender their offspring, who are thus removed from the danger of being pampered. Vairasse makes allowances for demonstrations of parental tenderness up to the seventh year, and even thereafter the parents retain the love and respect of their progeny, but all authority over them is transferred. State education stifles any tendency toward egotistic and privatized action. Once again the Platonic pre-

scription for the guardians has been applied to the whole polity. Though segregated, boys and girls receive virtually the same upbringing, and almost all
the youth are given an identical basic education, which is pratical, not religious: reading, writing, dancing, military drill; then farming for both sexes.
Here Plato, Plutarch's Lycurgus, and perhaps even a breath of Comenius may
be detected. At fourteen the youth are trained on the job as artisans or they
become agricultural laborers or masons, the most common occupations in this
utopia devoted to agriculture and public works. Especially gifted persons,
those capable of scientific speculation about the nature of things—the origins
of plants and animals, the age of the earth, the beginnings of religion—are sent
to colleges for advanced studies; and in order to keep abreast of the inventions
of other continents, qualified Sevarambians are despatched throughout the
world on secret missions of investigation, a practice borrowed from Bacon's
New Atlantis. But the Sevarambians do not have complete confidence in their
emissaries and—presage of our contemporary communist societies—those
who go abroad have to leave at least three children behind as hostages.

Upon reaching puberty, boys and girls are paired off, after they have had a
chance to examine each other during formal promenades. Marriage partners
are freely chosen. Premarital breaches of the sexual code are not tolerated and
postmarital violations are punished with public whipping. Vairasse inter-
sperses his exposition of the severe laws governing sexual chastity with stories
of their violation, elaborate intrigues involving transvestism, clandestine meetings of the guilty lovers, and finally their exposure and chastisement, all described in such lurid detail that the pornographic intent of the author is obvious. New techniques were being devised to keep the reader of utopias from
nodding.

In general, the attitude toward sexual intercourse is eugenic. Barrenness is
deplored and regarded as a justification for taking another wife. Those women
who produce the greatest number of children for the state are the most venerated; yet there is a prejudice, on purported medical grounds, against any but
temperate sexual relations among married couples. In their youth, sexual pleasure is restricted to one night in three out of apprehension that children born of
parents who indulge themselves too frequently will be feeble, a common belief
that persisted in utopia over many centuries.

For a European writing after the devastations of the Thirty Years' War, the
problem of maintaining a stable population, one of the key utopian preoccupations in antiquity, had ceased to exist. Population meant strength, and there
was a pervasive fear among state dynasts of a population slump that would
render them weak and vulnerable to hostile forces. Thus, though Vairasse is
careful to balance consumption and production, there were no restrictions on
population increase among the Sevarambians since the opposite danger, a de-
populated countryside, appeared universally threatening. Among the Sevarambians the prevailing community of goods obviated the problem of individual support, and girls of sixteen and boys of nineteen were regarded as
marital candidates, though they were obliged to defer consummation of their
desires for a few years. At eighteen for females and twenty-one for males, marriage became obligatory, not a far cry from official Colbertian policy, which
granted tax exemptions for early wedlock. Polygamy for magistrates was another means of increasing the population and avoiding the survival of old

maids and widows. In the sixteenth and seventeenth centuries, Protestant hostility to monastic celibacy rendered the practice of polygamy in imitation of the patriarchs at least a subject for discussion, though there were not many proponents of its general acceptance. In Sevarambian society, any consideration of the pleasures of sexual intercourse was subordinate to state policy on procreation, and the Viceroy intervened to assure not only a numerous progeny but the practice of sound eugenics. If eugenic controls failed and weak children were born, the ancients, they knew, had exposed them to the elements; since the Christian Vairasse could not quite countenance such brutality, his Sevarambians exiled the deformed to a remote part of the country.

The Sevarambians had universal conscription and a national army, which reflected both the tradition of the Hebrews dear to the Huguenots and the reorganization on something like a permanent footing of the monarchical army of Louis XIV, under whom the military establishment ceased to be a horde gathered by noble chiefs for limited finite purposes. The war policy of the Sevarambians was akin to that of the Morean Utopians: slow expansion along the borderlands as it was required by population increase, but no territorial aggrandizement merely for the glory of the ruler. Defense was the primary purpose of the military, and the Sevarambians customarily preferred client states to vanquished ones, another direct borrowing from Thomas More.

The Tone of Life

Of the eight or ten commonly known utopias written before the French Revolution, the *History of the Sevarambians* was the most eclectic. Its underlying spirit was libertine in religion, Hobbesian in the despotic centralism of government, Calvinist in the appraisal of human nature, rather Lucretian in natural philosophy, Colbertian in economic organization. The communism and state education derived from the long utopian tradition itself. Vairasse departs from More in shrinking the importance of the family, in slightly increasing industrial specialization and technology, and in elevating the magistracy to a position of privilege. Unlike More's Utopian households, the osmasies are differentiated from one another by the tasks to which they are consecrated, and some are devoted to industry rather than agriculture. The passion for experimentation among the elite of Bacon's New Atlantis and religious spiritualism of Campanella's Solarians have given way to an orderly uniformity that is prosaic and unchanging, but nobody complains of boredom. Vairasse borrowed from contemporary travel literature local color and details such as costuming, for he lacked inventiveness: Johan Nieuhof's accounts of China (1660), Jean Chardin's stories from Persia, and Garcilaso de La Vega's reconstruction of Incan society contributed to the embellishment of Sevarambia. But it has none of the transcendence of the Pansophic utopia; it is all matter-of-fact. The moral tone Vairasse conveyed was one of just and sensible contentment. And this flat, two-dimensional utopian model endured, with minor alterations, for some two hundred years in France, one specimen hardly distinguishable from another. Cabet's *Voyage en Icarie* was its most popular nineteenth-century exemplar. Alas, the insipid platitudes of his constructs of a perfect society were persuasive enough to lure Frenchmen to their deaths in the Red River swamps of Louisiana.

The Sevarambians, virtuous largely because of their training, are kept so by a regime of repression that is reminiscent of the Calvinist communal order of mutual espionage, though there is none of that hostility to play of which the more dour Puritans have sometimes been accused. The Sevarambians are not a grave lot. Vairasse insists upon their gaiety and good humor, though profound respect for women and abhorrence of adultery are so deeply ingrained that any levity about sex immediately jeopardizes a man's reputation and chance of advancement through election by his fellows. Sevarambians are by nature rather vengeful, but education and the laws operate to modify this character defect. "In a word, if we take a nice view of the Happiness of this People, we shall find that it is as perfect as any thing in this World can be, and that all other Nations, compar'd with them, are in but a poor wretched Situation,"[7] Captain Siden concludes in his manuscript notes. The mood of the Sevarambians is livelier than that of Epicurus in the garden, but he remains one of the hidden gods; perhaps there is an uneasy union with the Stoic idea of service to the state, creating that syncretic Stoic-Epicurean ideal that dominated the philosophes of the next century. The benign disposition of the Sevarambians is the best proof that they have fashioned an ideal system. Since they are sober and temperate, well exercised, free from diseases (especially the venereal), they live to be 120. They never suffer from care or anxiety. Robust, very tall, and handsome, they are blessed with soft, smooth skins, agreeably pink and white, and sleek bodies. They may not have the delicate fine faces that are like waxwork and pass for beauty in Europe, but they are healthy and attractive, not overrefined. Repeatedly Vairasse returns to his definition of the golden mean in the conduct of life: to enjoy with moderation the lawful pleasures.

On occasion, though not often, Vairasse, who led a wretched existence as an exile, let himself go and contrasted the just and equitable Sevarambian world with the harsh inequities of European society. "For we have, among us," he bursts out, "Persons who abound in Substance and Riches, while others want all things; we have some who spend their Lives in Idleness and Luxury, and others who are forc'd daily to get their Bread by the sweat of their Brow; we have some of Rank and Quality, who are neither worthy nor capable of the high Posts they possess; and we have also others of extraordinary Merit, who, being destitute of the Goods of Fortune, are still oblig'd to drudge miserably on in the Dirt, and even perpetually condemn'd to a low, servile State of Action, which the Generosity of their Temper abhors."[8]

Vairasse's epigrams are not as pithy as More's, but they continue the tradition of social protest against gross inequalities in the human condition, which will rise in a crescendo among utopians, religious and secular, decade after decade until it culminates in Babeuf's *Manifesto of the Equals*. In Sevarambia all are rich, "even from their very Cradles." Merit alone determines preferment, and one Sevarambian may not reproach another with the meanness of his birth, or boast of his own lofty stature. All are both nobles and peasants. "No person has the mortification to see others live idle, while he is forc'd to work hard to support their Pride and Vanity."[9] We are approaching Rousseau's thunderous attack on the psychic sufferings of both the underdog and his master in the state of civilization, the ultimate embodiment of unnatural inequalities. Vairasse often does not know where to land. He favors basic equality, and yet his rather dim Calvinist view of human nature, damned in its penchant for vice and violence, drives him to establish an absolute father authority at the head of the state. He dares not tamper with that awesome figure, and exalts him to the position of Viceroy of the Sun, invests him with despotic power in matters spiritual and temporal, and houses him in Oriental splendor (decorations by the travelers to the East, Chardin, Melchisédech Thévenot, Jean-Baptiste Tavernier, and Nieuhof). But once the absolute monarch has been placed on his pinnacle, all the sons beneath him must be more or less equal.

Even before Montesquieu, Sevarias I knew that the wise legislator had to fathom the esprit of his people and manipulate their dominant, often contrasting, traits of character in order to direct them to the good. It was his observation that the Sevarambians were natually proud, which meant that they were more amenable to praise than to tangible riches. Hence his magistrates were instructed to be profuse in their commendations of good deeds in men and virtue in women. Sevarambians were extremely scrupulous in their conduct and wary lest their good names became besmirched and they lost public credit and a reputation for merit. (The care for one's public standing is painfully Protestant.) By the same token, calumny was severely punished by the laws because it robbed the victim of his dearest possession, his good name. As an alternative to truth-saying, Sevarambians might seek refuge in silence; by implication an element of policy was thus introduced into the categorical imperative against lying, a loophole that Immanuel Kant would not have countenanced, though the Sevarambians had fewer occasions to speak falsehood than did Europeans because they had no need to dissimulate for gain or profit or to please superiors. And there were no bad examples for the young to imitate in this puritanical society where oaths and curse words were unknown. Early training and good models along with judicious praise and harsh punishments for violations fashioned a tractable Huguenot utopian.

Religion and Cosmology

In the latter part of the seventeenth century a *libertin* was a skeptic in matters of orthodox religion, unconvinced by the proofs of revelation, not necessarily an atheist, though the condition could be suspect, especially in the usage of the devout. That God-intoxicated Jew of Amsterdam, Spinoza, was often put in this category along with his unphilosophical admirer Saint-Evremond and a variety of popularizers of Gassendi's Epicureanism. The definition of the libertin was sometimes expanded to include the sort of moral conduct that implied an inclination to sensate pleasure, though of the moderate and refined sort, restrained by a philosophical awareness that gross pleasures were self-defeating. In the closing decades of the century the two aspects of the libertin would become detached from each other and a spiritual libertin might be a virtual ascetic or a man as little addicted to pleasure as Epicurus himself. Then the religious content of the word gradually eroded as the anticlerical crusade progressed, and libertin came to be used more and more frequently as a description of conduct rather than of belief, with a marked emphasis upon sexual promiscuity or debauchery. This is the meaning of the term in the *Encyclopédie,* and by the time the Marquis de Sade employed it, it denoted one who excelled in sexual depravity.

Denis Vairasse was exclusively a *libertin d'esprit,* at least in his writings, for we know little about his personal life. One of the propositions illustrated by his good society of Sevarambians was that a state religion which was by no stretch of the imagination Christian, and might even be considered a parody of both Catholicism and Protestantism, could become the prop for a highly moral society, one that in fact was more virtuous than the European way of life—a parallel to Bayle's paradoxical affirmation that there were virtuous atheists whom God preferred to idolaters.

Vairasse's religious position was a combination of the doctrines of Hobbes and Spinoza. The de-Christianization of utopia had begun in earnest. Religion was necessary for civility—despite the evidence of a few travel reports, Vairasse could not conceive of an atheistical society—and its institutions served exclusively political purposes. Without abandoning belief in an invisible monotheistic God, Vairasse became another promulgator of the sun religion that experienced so dramatic a revival in sixteenth- and seventeenth-century Europe. The rebirth of the solar religions has been associated with the growth of centralized dynastic states and the Copernican heliocentric theory of the universe. Utopian sun cults were doubtless inspired by both of these developments, as well as the Renaissance revival of images from what was believed to be Egyptian hermeticism. Accounts of Mexican and Peruvian sunworship fortified the idea that this was the primordial natural religion of man, to which he would return when theological Christianity had disappeared.

The religious settlement of the Sevarambians is what a Protestant accommodator would have asked of Louis XIV. There was an official public religion, but in private men could entertain whatever doctrine about divinity they liked and there were even set times each year when in colleges they could openly debate their opinions, as long as everyone behaved in a decent and respectful manner. Both the headship of the cult and that of the civil government were vested in the Viceroy and High Priest of the Sun, the office one party of Huguenots would have wished Louis XIV to assume after he had broken with Rome and proclaimed himself the religious chief of a Gallican Church. External conformity to a state religion did not trouble Huguenot libertins as long as they were not required to submit to Rome, and outward practices were not of paramount significance to them if they were vouchsafed freedom of conscience. Exalting the power of the King as God's representative on earth, allowing him to establish the laws of the cult and of the polity, was one way to end the religious disputes that were tearing the state apart.

The Sevarambian clergy were like ancient Roman priests; their religious status was not important and they could simultaneously hold civil office. A union of spiritual and temporal power, along with official indifference about matters of private conscience, fostered public tranquillity, the ultimate goal of the state, a *politique* position that became the normal one for most of the philosophes in the next century. Religious passion was as subversive of good order as avarice and sexual passion. The Sevarambian way of avoiding schism and civil war was to lower the temperature of religious controversy, to cool religious ardor. Toleration was extended to admit Catholics into the Sevarambian state. There was an end to fanatical persecutions, which Vairasse perceptively diagnosed as mere covers for the exercise of cruelty or for pecuniary interest—the sufferings of the Huguenots had been branded upon his consciousness. Simulated piety, the hypocritical religious conduct of court nobles seeking to please a king's mistress, were the actuality of one segment of the French religious establishment.

The stamping out of sectarian malice brought spiritual peace. The state religion was philosophical, founded on human reason, with revelation playing only a minor role that wise Sevarambians knew was a political invention. Since his book was published with royal approbation, Vairasse gave lip service to the superiority of the "celestial enlightenment of the Gospels" over the Sevarambian creed; but his general position was akin to Montesquieu's later views on Stoicism. Had he not been a Christian, Vairasse would have been a Sevarambian sun cultist. The limits of intellectual tolerance were broader in France than in the southern part of Europe, and Vairasse's Sevarambian religion could include a belief in the infinity of worlds for which Bruno had been burned by the Inquisition. The syncretistic Sevarambian theology symbolized in a black curtain that hung in the Temple the invisible infinite God whom men with their weak understandings could only sense obscurely, while their religious worship was regularly addressed to a visible Sun. Since the invisible God could be perceived only with the eyes of the mind, He was the object of formal adoration only once every seven years.

In the Sevarambian trinity the three persons have an order of excellence: the first is the invisible God, the black cloth, worshiped in one's inner being and represented by the reason that unites all men; the second is the Sun, a globe, object of love and gratitude for palpable benefits conferred upon the whole earth; and the third is a female symbol, the image of a mother nurturing many children, which is related to a particular good, the country of one's birth and the immediate source of nourishment and education. In this imitation of the Christian trinity the most revolutionary substitution is motherhood as the symbol of the land of one's birth. While it may be premature to talk of a Sevarambian nationhood, the political base is not too far removed from that of Bossuet's Gallican religion.

Religion was still crucial in the Sevarambian utopia, for it was in this sphere that pain had been inflicted on the Huguenot libertin. Under the civil religion of the Sevarambians men like Vairasse could have lived in peace, free from Catholic persecution. The sharing of wealth and communal education were old utopian ideas already explored by Thomas More and Campanella; but the Sevarambian religious settlement had a unique character. The cosmology was rather Cartesian, with a touch of Neoplatonic imagery that Vairasse might have picked up in England. About one Christian doctrine he was cautious— the immortality of the soul. Most ordinary Sevarambians believed in it, with the Sun the ultimate source of birth and resurrection; but the great minds among them were divided, some holding that the soul perished, others that it was material and eternal. Through the device of a multiplicity of private beliefs that prevailed in Sevarambia, Vairasse could toy with outrageous ideas that sound like adaptations from Porphyry and Plutarch and were part of the libertin stock-in-trade.

Previous utopias had either Christianized their inhabitants in a miraculous manner as Bacon had in the *New Atlantis,* or left them nominal adepts of a pre-Christian natural religion as in More and Campanella, thus avoiding the difficulties of conciliating some of their moral doctrines with the Church. Vairasse was more audacious. The descendants of Giovanni the Venetian, tutor of the first Sevarias, were devotees of a Christian cult, the one exception to the universal sun religion, but it was a substantially altered Christianity, in which Christ was an angel and the Eucharist a symbolic act. Despite the fact that they were concentrated in one osmasie and allowed to celebrate their religion openly and absent themselves from solar festivals, the Christians had not prevailed over the public cult nor even disturbed it. The mass of Sevarambians trusted in reason too much to be persuaded to credit Christian miracles. Sevarambians were emancipated from superstition, and reports of apparitions in the clouds were explained scientifically; Sevarias nevertheless honored what he knew of Christianity as serving a moral purpose. He was hostile, on the other hand, to Mohammedanism and Greco-Roman idolatry, whose myths were banned outrightly, in flagrant violation of the principle of free conscience. Here again, as at many other points, a Calvinist antipathy to sensuousness asserts itself in the Huguenot utopia.

There is a strange interplay of the mechanical and the organic in Vairasse's conception of the world, an amalgam of Cartesian ideas and Stoic speculations about the periodic exhaustion of nature. The mathematical arrangement of things, which is the work of man, militates in the direction of repetitive sameness, but nature itself surveyed over centuries has an organic pattern of growth and decay. On a universal scale entire peoples die and even the globe itself is doomed to extinction. The arts and sciences serve to maintain a balance in the world, but there is an underlying natural movement toward regression and even toward evil. The order of society cannot overcome this cosmic law, for, as the wisest of the Sevarambians know, in the infinite universe worlds are constantly dying and being born, like individuals, preserving a fixed quantum of matter and of spirit in the whole. Cyclical processes are constantly at work in nature and only a few are subject to modification by human will. The Sevarambians have rediscovered the arts and sciences of antiquity and there is reason to believe in their further progression during this cycle of history, though not in infinite progress because the earth, like all planets, ultimately has to be destroyed.

When the wise legislator thwarts bad will, superstition, greed for power, sexual lust, deception, arrogance, he is maintaining the equilibrium of the state as long as possible, but without any illusion that it can last forever. In punishing outbursts of passion among the Sevarambians, the Viceroy of the Sun is acting as a regulatory force. The passions, like sin for a Calvinist, are lying in wait to wreak havoc, often assuming the most benign and pleasing masks. The raison d'être for the mathematically organized nightmare of Sevarambia was the brute lurking in the background. "Men by nature have a strong tendency toward vice, and if good laws, good examples, and a good education do not correct them, the evil seed they bear within them will grow large and strong and often will crush the seed of virtue that nature has planted in them. Then they abandon themselves to their unruly appetites, and, allowing their impetuous and ferocious passions to rule their reason, they are flung into every sort of evil."[10]

The Archbishop's Pastoral Idyll

François de Salignac de la Mothe Fénelon was born in the ancestral chateau of Fénelon in Périgord in 1651. A younger son, destined for the Church by the order of his natality, he turned out to have an authentic religious vocation.

Périgord had been flooded by waves of Christian mysticism in the seventeenth century, but his was no mere precious religious sensibility; between the ages of twelve and fourteen, he had been educated by the Jesuits of Cahors in their rationalist mold. At Saint-Sulpice he was trained in the spirit of a reborn Catholic devoutness in which the charity of works became the core of the Christian mission without impeding the development of a rich inner life of contemplation. His later encounter with Madame Guyon only brought to the surface a subtle spirituality which had been latent since his youth. An acute reasoner and a religious enthusiast lived in the same man. The compatibility between religious sensitivity and political astuteness, even guile, is no longer open to question; the combination has been frequently noticed in the most renowned religious leaders. Fénelon was a formidable adversary, and both his worshipful friends and his enemies have left witness to the beguiling charm of his person. Few men and even fewer women withstood the seduction of his words when delivered from the pulpit, addressed to royal charges in private, or written as personal letters to troubled souls in search of direction.

Fénelon would seek out the self-love of his penitents in the most secret recesses of their self-abuse. "There is a very subtle illusion in your suffering," he wrote to the Countess de Montberon,

because you appear to yourself to be completely absorbed with what is due to God and his glory alone but at bottom you are in suffering about yourself. You really want God to be glorified but you want it to be through your perfection and thereby you return to all the refinements of your self-love. This is only a subtle detour to reenter under a better pretext into yourself. The true image to make of all the imperfections which you seem to discern in yourself is neither to justify them nor to condemn them (for this judgment will revive all your doubts) but to abandon them to God, making your heart conform to His in all things about which you cannot see clearly, and remaining at peace because peace is of the order of God in whatever state one might be.[11]

As a young man Fénelon had been patronized by Bossuet, and when a bitter dispute later arose between this stalwart defender of Gallican institutional Catholicism and the dissident Fénelon, his former protector took more than one occasion to allude to that period of tutelage. Fénelon's advancement was rapid. He became spiritual director for a school of young female Catholic converts who had either escaped from Huguenot parents or been abandoned by them. Once he had dreamed of an ambitious scheme, of leading a movement for the propagation of the faith in the Near East. Devotion to Greek studies had aroused in him a longing for the white light of the eastern Mediterranean, and he hoped to head a mission to the Christian lands ravaged by the Turks. In his mind's eye he saw the infidels fall back as he reunited the Christians east and west in a new bond. But his ecclesiastical superiors thought otherwise and he was sent in the opposite direction, to the Huguenots of the western provinces of France to persuade the heretics to return to the fold.

Writing about the state of the missions to the Huguenots in February 1686, Fénelon zealously defended the goal of Louis XIV's religious policy but advocated a different method: He would woo the heretics with sweetness rather than severity.[12] While authority must be unflinching, he counseled, in order to restrain these unruly people, some means had to be found for making their lives in France agreeable and dissuading them from leaving the country. The object of punishment was not to wreak vengeance but to direct consciences.

Fénelon tirelessly argued with the Huguenots, demonstrating with chapter and verse the rightness of the Catholic cause, trying to forestall the application of cruel measures, though always quite aware of the power in reserve. The great psychologist of the Christian life was not content with mere acquiescence. Somewhere between the lip service that satified the formal religionists and the dark absolutism, almost blind to charity, of the Jansenists, stood this believer in discipline who was nevertheless moved by the sufferings of recalcitrants upon whom the rod was wielded. He called for "gentle preachers" to assist him, men who could make themselves loved. In order to obtain credit with potential converts, Jesuits were advised to intercede with the authorities for the mitigation of royal punishments, even if they knew they would fail in their pleas—a bit of Machiavellian craftiness from the lips of the saint. In the utopia that he later came to write he similarly tempered discipline with affection, firmness with love, allowing for benign deceptions in the cause of virtue. Rousseau's system in the *Emile* was a secular version of the same path to a utopian *paideia*. A religious psychologist genuinely preoccupied with how to touch the souls of men, Fénelon subtly depicted the religious disarray of the French Huguenots bombarded at the same time by letters from their coreligionists in Holland and by the preachings of the Jesuits; he understood their troubled consciences and their secret shame.

During his mission to the Huguenots, Fénelon formed a close friendship with M. de Beauvillier. When this fellow aristocrat became the official tutor of the Duke of Burgundy, Fénelon was appointed his preceptor and the task of forming the character of a future king of France was entrusted to him. He had already written a treatise on the education of aristocratic young ladies which was highly approved; and in his new capacity he continued to compose works for the guidance of his royal charge. According to the witness of the Duke de Saint-Simon, Fénelon exerted a profound influence upon the boy and transformed his unruly character overnight. With extraordinary insight he analyzed his pupil's fits of rage, alternately directed outward against those surrounding him and turned inward in episodes of blaming and self-denigration.

Fénelon never thought of himself as a writer, and unlike the salon intellectuals in the eighteenth century he spent no time worrying about his literary fortunes. During his life individual works were published either without his consent or by editors who often knew little about his intentions. Not until the ancien régime was drawing to a close did the Assembly of the Clergy of France recognize in him the last significant Catholic apologist and proceed to a gathering of his works. The edition of nine volumes that appeared from 1787 to 1792, when God's house was already going up in flames, still preserved an official cast—all of Fénelon's controversial writings on quietism and Jansenism had been carefully expunged. The Bourbon Restoration finally discovered him as the embodiment of the Christian ideal and the priests of Saint-Sulpice prepared a thirty-five volume edition of their most famous predecessor, illuminated by a fairly accurate reconstruction of the political and ecclesiastical controversies that had engaged him. But even they refrained from publishing the *Maximes des Saints,* which had once brought down upon him a papal condemnation. Since then, extensive collections of his letters have been printed and new light has been thrown on his relations with Mme. Guyon and Mme. de Maintenon. His spiritual correspondence has come to be appreciated as a magnificent example of religious sensibility, and the political significance of this saintly archbishop living in the world is now better understood.

There is no reason to doubt Fénelon's testimony that he wrote *The Adventures of Telemachus* to instruct his student the Duke of Burgundy while diverting him. The work was not intended for publication, but two years after its composition a copyist apparently arranged to have the manuscript printed without permission. In 1698, word of its contents reached the Court, and the sheets were seized. Official suppression only caused the pirated editions to multiply. Voltaire reports a remark by Louis XIV that Fénelon had the finest and most chimerical mind in the kingdom, and he was chimerical indeed if he expected the Sun King not to take umbrage at this educational exercise. By this time Fénelon was no longer in the good graces of the monarch, having become involved with the quietist Mme. Guyon and sharing, at least in some measure, her views on the nature of the true Christian spiritual life. A contest had developed between Bossuet and Fénelon and at a formal inquiry the propositions of one of his works were condemned. He was disgraced and exiled to Cambrai in August 1697. Fénelon publicly retracted every one of the doctrines declared false by the Church, but the forthrightness of his withdrawal failed to regain the royal favor. The appearance of *Telemachus* in 1699 only compounded Louis's displeasure.

Mystic Communion and Utopia

Mme. Guyon's "moyen court et très facile" for attaining mystical illumination and knowledge of God, which Fénelon espoused against the attacks of Bossuet, was a spiritual foundation for Fénelon's utopia. Since God is within us, if we only had communion with our divine natures in peaceful self-examination, we would be able to make a good world. (We have heard the same message from the mouth of an English Digger.) Such mystic ways were suspect to institutional religion, for they elevated the worth of a passive religious state that prepared the suppliant to receive the direct spirit of God above formal confession, good works, and the rituals of a Gallican Church. Fénelon was hardly circumspect in his opposition to the Archbishop of Paris, who was directly involved in the harassment of Mme. Guyon. Complex intrigues involving papal policy, Gallican rights, personal animosities, pitted Bossuet and Fénelon against each other in a battle of ecclesiastical titans over the authenticity of the inspiration of a prophetess; but the ultimate issue was the nature of Christian society in a world of dynastic states. Bossuet, fixated upon man's sinful, rebellious nature, which had to be held in check by secular and sacerdotal powers, reserved paradise for the next world.

Ecclesastical establishments and political absolutisms are inveterately hostile to the religious man who believes that the divine spark within him can be ignited without the intervention of the officers of church and state, that pure love alone can guide man to God. A pillar of the church establishment and the state like Bossuet astutely sensed the heretical potentialities of a doctrine that relied on the power of religious illumination, as English prelates had half a century before. Fénelon's Christian universalism ran counter to Bossuet's acceptance of the civil divisions of mankind into dynastic states as permanent and necessary and to his castigation of religious mystics who would deny the di-

vine origin of these states. For Bossuet church and state were laden with sufficiently heavy burdens even if they only maintained an elementary order of society; Fénelon would have had the state activated by love into creating the best
possible republic, a utopia on earth—though he carefully eschewed the term.

In Fénelon's *Adventures of Telemachus* the hero is an amalgam of the noblest
aspects of the young David of the Psalms, the young Telemachus of Homer,
and a noble, converted Canadian Indian, set against a background drawn
from Anacreon and Ovid. Theologically Fénelon's utopia is rooted in the quietist conception that the cultivation of a passive, trusting, childlike attitude
would bring about a union with the divine and the approbation of a good king,
since both the king and God would be readily accessible to the obedient people. Evil derived from wicked monarchs who betrayed their trust. Orderliness
and regulations in excess were not needed; societies under wise mentors led a
natural idyllic existence without great struggle. The Salentians and the men of
Boetica—the utopians Telemachus learned about on his travels—performed
their tasks effortlessly, as though engaged in salutary exercises. Fénelon
evoked the spirit of antique Greece and the hills of Judea, which turn out to be
kindred; those who administered Plato's laws and the laws of the Israelites
were transmuted into gentle fathers of their people.

For pious abbés like Fleury and the young Fénelon, the ancient world they
knew from literature was bathed in a supernatural light of pure simplicity. Antiquity was experienced as a pastoral idyll, whose inhabitants, godlike figures
no matter how humble their station, wore the same loose-flowing garments
whether they lived in Judea, Egypt, the isles of Greece, or early Rome. And
little distinction was preserved between one century and another—all of it was
the blessed ancient world. Exaltation of antiquity made educated men of the
French "classical age" capable of achieving prodigies of transformism. The
warrior tribes whose history was narrated in Deuteronomy and the Books of
Kings were perceived by the Abbé Fleury in his *Moeurs des Israélites* as a gentle
people and their laws as the benign regulations of an ideal republic, interchangeable with his friend Fénelon's shepherds of utopian Boetica and the citizens of Salentum, the second-best utopia in *Telemachus,* after Mentor's reforms had been instituted. Poussin's paintings of the Seven Sacraments (in the
National Gallery, Edinburgh) convey the same syncretic atmosphere—Christian ceremonies performed by men in Greco-Roman costume against an Arcadian backdrop. The whole formed a spiritual unity that could become a
longed-for ideal among Catholic priests reacting with distaste to the ruffle-be-
decked, high-heeled, mannered nobles of the French Court. Fénelon differed
from the contemporary Pansophist utopians of the seventeenth century because he was both ignorant of the achievements of science and suspicious of
cultivation of the arts as an indulgence in superfluities. He paid them even less
heed than did the humanist More, remaining steadfast in his preference for
agrarian simplicity and for an emotional communion with God that had no use
for the new science. The knowledge that guided the Pansophists to God was
alien to him. It is an exaggeration to find all the roots of secular enlightenment
in Fénelon: One vital ingredient, the new science of things, is conspicuously
absent. He was a throwback, a nostalgic evocator of a bucolic contentment that
had never existed.

There is something paradoxical about Fénelon's role. How does a Christian saint teach at the court of Louis XIV? What meaning do his words have as they echo in the royal bedchamber through the pious lips of Mme. de Maintenon? Her scores of secret tiny notebooks full of devout homilies exerted little effect on the military policy of the Sun King. In France, traditionalist Catholicism died in a revery; the Archbishop spent his last years an exile in Cambrai tending to his pastoral duties. But by the end of the eighteenth century the French monarchy had undergone so radical a change that the same *Adventures of Telemachus* which had so outraged Louis XIV was prepared in a special edition by the royal presses for the guidance of another Bourbon king, a king who never reigned, one who was to have been the seventeenth of his line.

The Demise of the Rural Aristocracy

Sometime between 1688 and 1695 official spokesmen for the aristocracy at the Court developed a full-blown political ideology of an antimercantilist character. Documentary support for the reaction against Colbert's policy was drawn from an investigating commission report of 1687 that had graphically depicted the poverty and hunger of the French countryside. An anonymous memorandum of February 23, 1688, to the King had dramatized the situation: "The poor frequently have no bread, not even the blackest; lately they have been compelled to live off roots or gleanings. Most of them no longer possess even household furnishings for [the tax collector] to seize. They sleep on straw in the clothes on their backs, frequently half-naked. Haggard, thin, and languishing, having neither provisions to live on nor anything in reserve, all are driven to beggary . . . Is this the flourishing state of the realm about which we hear so often?" A similar portrait of the French peasants appeared in the 1689 edition of La Bruyère's *Les Caractères,* published after a catastrophic depression of agricultural prices: "Dispersed over the country certain wild animals, males and females, are seen bent over the ground which they turn with an invincible persistency." In the anonymous memorandum extravagance bred by social emulation was denounced in terms become stale and familiar in present-day mobile, competitive societies: "You no longer plan your expenditures according to what you have, but according to what others do."[13] Paris and the army consumed the surplus of the countryside. Those who worked in luxury industries by definition led an unstable existence because they were dependent upon the whims of fashion. Constant economic turbulence was the essence of antiutopia for men inspired by an admixture of Epicurean and Stoic virtues Christianized.

In the courtly manifestoes of the last decade of the seventeenth century, an economic reality was integrated with a religious philosophy that had roots in French piety and a demand for the reconstitution of aristocratic power. Behind the writings of Boisguilbert, Fleury, and above all Fénelon lay the vision of an agrarian society, a placid landscape in which a benign monarch settled his people in fixed estates—highest among them an aristocracy of birth that no one envied because it was natural—and governed them in a Christian spirit that had banished the demons of power and the lust for territorial aggrandizement. The mercantilists had insisted that the source of strength and wealth of the kingdom was industry: It stimulated trade, attracted foreign money, which then circulated throughout the realm and ultimately found its way into the

King's coffers to support his grandeur. The agrarians' intellectual revolt discovered the mainstay of the good Christian polity in the cultivation of the land, and a whole moral view of the world was attached to their choice. Industry had awakened unnecessary desires and led to the spreading evil of luxury, which brought on softness and undermined character. A sound people enjoyed all the necessaries of life, were continent and hardy, and had nothing but contempt for gold and fripperies. They were satisfied with their lot in whatever station of life they happened to be born. Commerce was allowable only within narrow limits and as long as it did not excite superfluous needs and introduce vices.

An agrarian suspicion of commerce and industry is one of the oldest utopian themes in the West. The pastoral idyll, a literary portrait of the good peoples of antiquity living peacefully among their flocks and tilling the soil, sustained this conception. The misery of the French peasantry, blamed directly on Colbert's mercantilist policy, was proof positive of the catastrophic consequences of enticing the laborers of France away from the rich lands of their fathers. Aristocrats in and out of the Church could look back nostalgically to smiling prosperous fields, untroubled by drought and unravaged by war—a bookish dream if ever there was one. Economics, morality, aristocracy, and religion spoke with one voice. The opposition to Louis XIV's system might be reduced to a class conflict, the attempt of the aristocracy to regain a status usurped by the parvenu merchants; but the new ideology was a complex superstructure, crowned by one of the most widely read utopias of the age.

Utopian agrarian ideas had been around for a long time and could easily be rooted in the wisdom of antiquity. The Abbé Fleury, a noble cleric, had expounded them in his *Pensées politiques* written between 1670 and 1675; and he had discovered a speaking picture of them in the way of life of the ancient Israelites as recorded in the Bible. The end of the state was to render its people happy, contented, suffused with a feeling of calm felicity and piety. Happiness had none of the orgiastic and passionate connotations that came to be attached to it in some quarters by the end of the eighteenth century. Thomas More's allowable pleasures and his censorship of the unnecessary were accepted as the positive and negative images of the ideal way of life. There is in Fleury's thought a strong undercurrent of prejudice against any large urban agglomerations—the growing attack on the cities that culminated in Rousseau had already begun in earnest, and the agrarians proffered the same psychological reasons for their antagonism to city life, a complete reversal of the dominant classical view that had lived on from Greece into the Middle Ages and the Renaissance and had conceived of the city as the perfect embodiment of everything that was social and human in existence. The isolation of urban inhabitants from one another, their mutual fear, the great and visible disparities in wealth, the weakness of the social bond were depicted in stark and simple terms. "The multitude of inhabitants is so great," Abbé Fleury complained, "that most of them do not know each other, they have no ties, no friendships; often, even those living under the same roof become suspicious of one another and take continual precautions. This is no longer a society."[14] The utopias of the Renaissance had always been cities—More's island of Utopia was dotted with cities, Patrizi wrote a *Città felice,* Campanella's Sun Kingdom was a city, as the great visionary republics before them had been ever since Plato and Hippodamus. The phenomenal growth of London and Paris in the seventeenth century had turned the city into an anti-utopia. Towns to which farmers returned at night were acceptable in the agrarian utopia, but the provincial capitals, then perceived as monstrous urban agglomerations, were denounced as the ruin of whole regions. A single dense urban center was growing at the expense of a countryside whose settlements would become sparse to the point of extinction. The ideal was an evenly populated agricultural area rather intensively worked, neither the territorial extension of empire to no purpose nor the artificial concentration of persons in cities, with their deleterious physical and spiritual consequences.

Agrarians were generally also anti-Machiavellian and anti-Hobbesian. They were rationalists who believed that a sound, successful, powerful government could be moral. The idea that men were totally depraved was rejected. The same dismal view of human nature that Fleury fought in his refutation of Machiavelli, his friend Fénelon would repudiate in his virulent opposition to the somber Jansenists. A wise king could, through institutions, curb whatever evil propensities there were in man and encourage the good. This is what Mentor taught Idomeneus in the *Adventures of Telemachus*. And Fleury charged in *Réflexions sur les oeuvres de Machiavel*: "But you [Machiavelli] say that if the Prince is good he will not survive because men are bad. First, they are for the most part neither very bad nor very good . . . Moreover, you, who wish to govern, have the duty of making them better: this is the goal of true politics . . . "[15]

The Mirror of the Good Prince

Fénelon had ventured to address Louis XIV like the prophet Nathan before David in passionate memoranda that pointed a finger at him (it is doubtful whether Fénelon's letters were ever seen by the King): "They have vastly increased your revenues and your expenditures. They have elevated you to the heavens . . . and impoverished all of France so as to introduce and maintain an incurable and monstrous luxury at Court. They wanted to raise you on the ruins of all the classes in the State, as if you could become great by oppressing your subjects on whom your Grandeur is founded."[16] When Fénelon had largely given up on the vain, aged sinner, he concentrated on the young Duke of Burgundy, placing great confidence in the future king for whom he wrote *Telemachus* sometime between the last months of 1694 and the end of 1696, a storybook version of what Fleury and Fénelon had been saying in private communications to Louis XIV. His mirror for a prince was not an idle fantasy, but a practical utopia that he hoped to see implemented by a young monarch under the aegis of seasoned mentors.

Telemachus, a text heavy with anachronisms, incongruities, and an eclectic imagery, begins with the shipwreck of the hero, who under the guidance of the wise Mentor (really Minerva in disguise) has set off in search of Ulysses. He falls into the hands of the goddess Calypso, who would smother him with her love, the unrequited passion for father Odysseus now transferred to the son—a flattering prospect to growing princes ancient and modern. She cajoles him into recounting his adventures, which affords Fénelon an opportunity to pass in review an array of wicked monarchs of the ancient world who had successively held Telemachus in their clutches after his many other shipwrecks and captures by piratical enemies. One of the most iniquitous of kings is the Phoenician Pygmalion, who so ground down his people with extortionate levies and his interference with free commercial enterprise that their naturally industrious qualities were stifled. The tyrant lived in terror of his subjects, had to sleep in a different bed each night to thwart those who plotted to murder him, bolted his doors, operated a network of spies; he was dominated by his power-lusting capricious mistress, who constantly deceived him. Sesostris of Egypt, a good man by nature, inadvertently committed evil deeds because of his reliance on ministers who misled him. The inhabitants of the island of Cyprus had been reduced to luxury and softness by their devotion to the single passion inspired by their goddess Aphrodite.

In almost every section of *Telemachus* at least one of the evils of Louis XIV's reign is denounced—his mercantilist manipulation of commerce, his sexual inconstancy, his wasteful wars of conquest, his expensive building projects, his dependence upon ignoble ministers, his spendthrift practices that were ruining the naturally rich agricultural economy of the realm. Fénelon's pointed references to monarchs who embarked on military adventures and mulcted their peoples for their own glorification can hardly be construed as anything but direct slaps at the Sun King, however vigorous the denial of any intent of lèse majesté. Who could believe that the description of the kings in Pluto's hell was mere playful fantasy against an antique backdrop, or a purely educational device, dreamed up without reference to contemporary reality, simply to instill virtue into the young Duke of Burgundy? If in the *Telemachus* Fénelon was merely excoriating vice in the tradition of the "mirror of princes," an old literary genre common to both the Islamic and the Christian worlds, he was laying it on with a trowel. Such an attempt to inspire good conduct in the Duke was surely an affront to a grandfather who was still very much alive.

One did not require a detailed key to recognize the characters in the tale and assimilate them to court personages. Fénelon's profound disapproval of the ways of Versailles, which he was at no pains to conceal, cast a shadow of doubt upon the innocence of his motives in writing the *Telemachus*. In a letter of July 4, 1695, to the Countess de Gramont, he sketched a melancholy portrait that was an antecedent of Rousseau's condemnation of the hypocrisies of life in Paris: "Versailles does not, after all, make one younger. You have to put on a smiling face there, but the heart does not laugh. No matter how few desires and how little sense of pride are left, one always finds here something to make one age . . . A host of fugitive little worries await you each morning upon rising and do not leave you until night; they take turns in agitating you. The more popular one is, the more one is at the mercy of these devils. That is what one calls the fashionable world, the object of envy among fools." [17] The French Court was a hive of envious competitive creatures poised to injure one another, a spectacle of psychic evil chronicled by the Duke de Saint-Simon, great-uncle of the future utopian socialist.

Telemachus escapes from the amorous embraces of Calypso when Mentor literally pushes him into the sea, and the adventures are resumed. But suddenly amid the darkness of monstrous kings, shining lights appear in the form of two virtuous societies. It is the first, Boetica, described by Adoam, a Phoenician captain on whose ship the wanderers have found temporary refuge, that is the more ideal of the two, perhaps so perfect that it cannot exist among ordinary men. Salentum, though admirable, is less exalted; it belongs to the earthly sphere and is a goal attainable by good men in any age. Boetica is a paradise where shepherds dwell in family groups without fixed abodes, holding all things in common, living continent, peaceful lives amid their flocks. Nature is bountiful, their desires are few and easily satisfied, emulation and violence are unknown among them. The attributes of the land and the temper of the inhabitants are unadorned literary adaptations from the Greek and Latin corpus—the golden race in Hesiod, the golden age in Ovid, the Elysian fields of Homer, and the idylls of minor writers who derived from them. Arcadian images flood the nostalgic utopia. Metallic gold is evil when used as money to corrupt mankind, and the men of Boetica make axles out of it for their carts—a more genteel version of More's chamber pots. There are no artisans devoted to the manufacture of luxury products since the women weave the white wool of the sheep and everyone dresses alike. Conquerors of empires are held in contempt. Each father is king of his own group, but even he never punishes without consulting the whole family. The inhabitants of Boetica have learned wisdom by studying nature. The uselessness of arts and sciences, that ancient Greek and Latin theme, was revived by Fénelon. The tone is not so abrasive as in Rousseau's later tirade, but the ideas are already here.

When one speaks to them of peoples who know the art of making grand buildings, furniture of gold and silver, materials decorated with embroidery and precious stones, exquisite perfumes, delicious food, musical instruments that charm, they respond in these terms: These peoples must be very unfortunate if they have to spend so much labor and industry to corrupt themselves! This superfluity softens, enervates, confuses those who possess it. It tempts those who are deprived of it to want to acquire it through injustice and violence. Can one call good a superfluity which only serves to make men evil? Are the people of that country any healthier and more robust than we are? Do they live longer? Are they united among themselves? Do they lead a freer life, a more tranquil one, a gayer one?[18]

In its own day *Telemachus* was acclaimed by imitation. *Les Voyages de Cyrus* (1727) by Fénelon's friend and admirer Andrew Michael Ramsay, the Abbé Jean Terrasson's *Séthos* (1731), and a host of other stories distinctive only in their costuming all depict the aristocratic life of virtue in some idealized antique land. Amid these uninspired epigoni, it is a relief to come upon *Télémaque travesti,* a picaresque novel by the youthful Marivaux that borrowed a conceit from Cervantes. A young bourgeois and his uncle, by dint of having read too much of *Telemachus,* have gone batty and spend their days reliving the adventures of the ancient heroes. Under a jesting exterior, Marivaux demeaned Fénelon's stilted attempt to reproduce epic style and subject matter, and tried to portray instead the harsh existence of ordinary people. But the dissenting voice of *Télémaque travesti* was barely audible. The book was published in 1736, twenty years after its composition, and then only abroad. Though reprinted in truncated form in the last quarter of the eighteenth century, it did not come to light again in all its wicked glory until 1956, more than two hundred years after its first appearance.

The popularity of *Telemachus* in later periods bore no relationship at all to Fénelon's object in writing it. As scores of editions followed one another throughout the eighteenth and nineteenth centuries, the impact of the tale was far mightier than anything its author could have expected. The book served as a respectable primer to communicate elementary knowledge about the geography of the ancient world and about mythology; and its precepts of moral virtue were salutary by-products in a schoolbook. Young Americans in the early nineteenth century, like their European counterparts, learned virtue, French, mythology, and the ideals of a pastoral utopia all at once when they were fed Fénelon's *Telemachus*.[19] One never knows where the seed will sprout. In his memoirs the aged Jeremy Bentham recalled the reading of *Telemachus* as the crucial event in his life: "That romance may be regarded as the foundation-stone of my whole character; the starting-post from whence my career of life commenced. The first dawning of the principle of utility may, I think, be traced to it."[20]

But to his own and immediately succeeding generations the serious message of Fénelon's fable, when it was understood, was its implied attack upon the monarchy and social institutions of France, upon Louis XIV's policy of aggrandizement and Colbert's mercantilism. The eulogy of a continent life of work on the land was a foil for the decadence of Versailles, and a natural hierarchy of birth, extolled as the basis of social organization, a tacit rebuke to self-made bourgeois administrators. In *Telemachus* the Christian utopia found its last significant pictorial embodiment; sentimentalized French Catholicism of the Romantic era kept its memory alive and modern industrialism sharpened its nostalgic appeal, but by then its original meaning had been completely forgotten.

15

Leibniz: The Swan Song of the Christian Republic

ON NOVEMBER 14, 1716, Gottfried Wilhelm Leibniz pulled his nightcap over his head and died in the lone presence of his servant, without calling for the consolations of religion. With him was buried the fantasy of a Christian Panso-phia which had possessed a brilliant, if motley, array of European thinkers for more than a century. In later centuries encyclopedists, founders of universities and academies, originators of philosophical languages and new logics, apologists of science, supporters of ecumenical endeavors, reformers of the education of the young, visionaries of world peace, latter-day Christian mystics, and even proponents of a communist revolution might on occasion hark back to one or another Pansophist as a predecessor, perhaps choose a fragment of his writing as an inspirational text; but the dream as a whole was the expression of a unique moment in time and vanished with it, despite its political survival in an attenuated form in the mechanical schemes for perpetual peace of the Abbé de Saint-Pierre.

Though Leibniz never composed a "proper utopia" in the Morean manner, he read many contemporary story utopias, even the lighter ones like Cyrano's *Histoire Comique,* Vairasse's *Sevarambians,* Barclay's *Argenis,* and he devoted the major part of his life to one of the grandest of all utopias, the elaboration of a plan for establishing a Respublica Christiana throughout the world.[1] Born in Leipzig on July 1, 1646, two years before the end of the Thirty Years' War, Leibniz left poignant descriptions of its massacres and sackings. Europe was in a graver state of crisis than it had been since the Carolingian Empire. The political fragmentation was paralleled by spiritual anarchy, as theologians squabbled with one another over minor points of doctrine, and Holland and England became hives of skeptics and freethinkers. From the time of his youth, Leibniz had lamented the fratricidal conflict of Christians, which resembled the wars of frogs and rats: "They fight over precedence at the door of a chamber while the house is on fire," he wrote in 1703.[2] As a utopian of perpetual peace, Leibniz was part of a long chain that linked him to Lull, Dubois, Erasmus, Sully, and Cruce.

After leaving the University of Leipzig without his doctorate—he avoided the city for the rest of his life—Leibniz set forth upon his travels. In Nuremberg he met Johann-Christian von Boineburg, a diplomat with wide connections who had once flirted with the Rosicrucians, and he entered upon his career under the patronage of the older man. The first encounter with Boineburg, who also dabbled in alchemy, probably occurred in the spring of 1667, when Leibniz himself was serving as secretary of a Rosicrucian-like brotherhood. Ties with earlier Pansophists are documented: Leibniz wrote an encomium of Comenius in 1671, and studied his *Opera Didactica Omnia,* as well as the works of Andreae, Bruno, Campanella, and Bacon.[3] His judgment of these antecedents was not uniformly favorable.

This restless man was never content with the role of the closeted philosopher. Throughout his life he had an image of himself as the embodiment of *sapientia,* a reincarnation of the great lawgivers of antiquity, who could carry out God's mission only in partnership with *potestas,* for great rulers had the means to bring into actuality the projections of wisdom. The concert of two persons, the philosopher and the king, is a utopian tradition that has been revived intermittently in a variety of shapes, from the Renaissance architect and his podestà to Fourier and his millionaire who would institute the phalansterian system. Plato had conceived of the philosopher-king as one, but in practice the ideal monarch first had to be converted by a philosopher like himself. More and Campanella also had an alternative to the duumvirate, a single being endowed with both spiritual and temporal headship. Leibniz, not one to break with time-honored forms, always eager to see the changing world as an infinite series of small differences and transitions without abrupt leaps and discontinuities, infused the medieval dualism of pope and emperor with new content.

He called upon each of the great princes of Europe in turn to serve as God's primary agent in realizing his magnificent design. European culture had been threatened by the Turks at the gates of Vienna, and Leibniz later offered one of his few finished manuscripts, *The Monadology,* to the conqueror of the Turks, Prince Eugene of Savoy, in an act symbolic of their communion of purpose.[4] Inconstancy in Leibniz' admiration of one or another European ruler—and he switched his protectors often, as Campanella had before him—was of little consequence; princes were only emissaries of the Lord, first in the reconstitution of a Christian Europe, and ultimately in the Christianization of the whole world. His apparent fickleness can bewilder a critic: From a utopia that would resurrect the Holy Roman Empire with a dual headship for Christian Europe, the Pope and the Emperor, one functioning in the spiritual, the other in the temporal sphere, he moved to a hyperbolic eulogy of Louis XIV as the immortal prince of the age, to a rediscovery of his Teutonic heart and a denunciation of the Sun King, to a final apotheosis of Czar Peter of Russia. And yet these shifts, which depended upon who his patron or prospective patron might be at any given moment, do not make of him a mere opportunistic pamphleteer. Like many other utopians, while he was flexible in the choice of instrumentalities for the implementation of his grand design, he did not abandon the vital center of his system either in philosophy or politics.

In Leibniz, the philosopher, theologian, mathematician, diplomat, physicist, jurist, historian, and visionary are united. The man of universal knowledge was a man of the universal utopia, bombarding princes throughout Europe with schemes of political reorganization, with plans for the founding of universities, the advancement of science, the conversion of non-Christians, the unity of the churches. The projects were often chimerical, sometimes merely out of phase. Potentates listened to them with a measure of skepticism, even suspicion, and when he seemed to side with one European power against another, Leibniz was accused of treachery. His diplomatic memoranda should not be appraised primarily in the context of German nationalism, as they sometimes have been east of the Rhine. The independent German princelets spending themselves in internecine wars were creating confusion and anarchy, and they had to be welded together if Europe were to survive; but the "Teutscher" monad he was fashioning in his fantasy was only one element in the great hierarchy of Christian European society.

The inner depths of this most versatile thinker of Western society have not been fathomed. In the vast archive of his papers in Hanover intimate documents are rare. There are rumors of an illegitimate son, but only rumors. His self-portraits avoid reference to affective relations and dwell on his freedom from disturbing passions, an official version of a philosophical existence. He enjoyed the amenities of comfortable living, and was careful to amass an adequate number of pensions from his royal and aristocratic protectors. A few years before his death he chose to reveal formally the outward direction of his life. In a letter to Chancellor Golofkin of Russia dated January 16, 1712, he wrote a retrospective summary of what he conceived to be his manifest purpose in the world: "Since my youth my ultimate goal has been to labor for the glory of God through the advancement of the sciences, which best illuminate the divine power, wisdom, and goodness . . . I am always prepared to turn my thoughts toward this great goal, and I have only been looking for a prince who shared the same aim . . . In this respect I favor neither nation nor party . . . "[5]

Though in 1676 Leibniz toyed with the idea of becoming amphibious, passing half the time in Paris, the other half in Germany, he ended up spending most of his life in Herrenhausen. He was tied to his locality, and only in imagination was he the man of all monads and ages. As ducal librarian in Hanover, he was engaged for forty years in writing the history of a princely family, a rather tiny monad from which to view the world. To find the origin of the House of Brunswick, Leibniz once set out on a voyage of discovery through the archives and papers of the House of Este, and identified it twenty generations back in the person of one Azo. By an irony of fate, the wife of Azo was Cunégonde, a detail that Voltairean Frenchmen none too sympathetic to the heroic disorder of Leibniz' thought and papers cannot report upon without malicious delight. Leibniz used up three princes of the House of Brunswick. His service at the court began with Johann Friedrich (1665–1679), a Catholic prince in whose behalf he concocted a bold plan for the conquest of Egypt, the *Consilium Aegyptiacum,* that would divert France from designs on Germany to the extra-European world. Ernst August (1679–1698) was a Lutheran married to a Calvinist, and the Austrian alliance rather than the French became the pivot of his policy. Under Georg Ludwig (1698–1727), the achievement of the English succession was the main thrust of Leibniz' endeavors, but he was never comfortable with this prince. When he ascended the English throne as George I, Leibniz was abandoned to die in solitude in Hanover. He also had once expected to follow Princess Sophie-Charlotte to Berlin. After the crowns of Brandenburg and Prussia had been placed on her head, she was to establish him in an academy, from which he would extend philosophical tentacles to Vienna, St. Petersburg, and, who knows, farther east to China at the other end of the Eurasian continent. But his hopes crumbled when she died in 1704.

The complete collection of Leibniz' books, manuscripts, and letters, still in course of publication, is expected to extend to some seventy large volumes in quarto. But this prolific writer never finished a major work that encompassed the totality of his thought. He was constantly viewing all sides of every question, displaying his incredible erudition, repeating formulas and arguments over and over again. Like so many of the great visionaries, as soon as he had the flash of an idea he put it into writing. The original invention was what mattered; further insights would come later. And he left behind scores of intuitive manuscript prospectuses, unified by a single religious purpose, parts of a whole that he had in his mind's eye. Leibniz' Christian utopia has to be pieced together from youthful projects, from his voluminous correspondence with the princes of Europe, from occasional references to his ideals in the prefaces to his published works. Consistency in detail within a body of such diverse documents is not to be expected.

The Organization of Science

The advancement of arts and sciences was the heart of Leibniz' utopia, a religious duty that men in the perfected Christian republic had to fulfill for the glorification of God. The mechanics for the achievement of a state of harmony and love was the dissemination of a body of organized information about all things arranged in an encyclopedia and the acceptance of a common language, a universal "characteristic" or "character" that facilitated communication.

The fantasy of a universal character was typical of the Pansophic mentality of the seventeenth century and Leibniz acknowledged the accomplishments of his predecessors in this field, especially John Wilkins, one of the founders of the Royal Society. "This writing or language (if the characters were rendered pronounceable) might soon be accepted throughout the world because it could be learned in a few weeks and would provide a means of communication everywhere. This would be of great significance in the propagation of the faith and the education of distant peoples," Leibniz wrote in a letter intended for Duke Ernst August.[6] On this premise he proceeded to build an airy structure of a whole world in easy discourse from one end to the other leading to a facile conversion of all peoples to the true religion. Leibniz went further. The new writing would then become the basis of a sort of general verbal, conceptual algebra and one would reason as one calculated. Instead of arguing, people would say: "Let's count"; error would be immediately detected, putting a stop to futile controversies.[7] And even if it were not possible always to find definitive answers to questions, the most probable solutions could be determined. The Leibnizian version of the universal characteristic depended upon the formulation of precise definitions of all the major concepts in man's intellectual vocabulary, and Leibniz had in fact begun accumulating such definitions, of which he offered Duke Ernst August a few samples: Justice was the charity of the wise man or charity in conformity with wisdom. Charity was nothing else but general benevolence. Wisdom was the science of felicity, felicity was a state of lasting joy, joy was a feeling of perfection, and perfection was the highest degree of reality. "I mean to provide similar definitions of all the passions, virtues, vices, and human actions, insofar as they are necessary," he assured his patron.[8] Through this instrument the sight of the mind would be enlarged as vision was improved by spectacles. The unfinished letter closes with a confession of his need for further meditation and a plea for help in the classical utopian manner.

Leibniz was aware of the general tendency—he called it a conspiracy—to lump together all projects for the welfare of the human race along with fantasies such as More's *Utopia,* Campanella's *City of the Sun,* and Bacon's *New Atlantis.* Like so many of his fellow utopians, he was eager to distinguish himself from the proponents of such extravagant ideas and to differentiate sharply his own "practical" projects from theirs. He was no utopian; his was the authentic message of the providential design. In a draft memorandum he prepared in 1671 for the creation of a society in Germany dedicated to the advancement of the arts and sciences, the second article was devoted to the eminently pragmatic question of what sort of people would sponsor such an enterprise and what might be their motives.[9] He presumed that the benefactors would be men of high social status, men of fortune and prominence who needed nothing else in the world but a good conscience and immortal fame, men imbued with the conviction that they were subject to the judgment of God and posterity (a combination that at first glance may appear strange) and hoped for a favorable verdict. For their own health's sake they wished to experience contentment, tranquillity of spirit, an anticipatory taste of future blessedness and the pleasures of immortality—in a word, *coelum in terris.* With joy in their souls because of an expectation of eternal blessedness, having done everything in their power to deserve salvation, they could leave the rest to the grace of a good God. In some of its versions Leibniz' academic utopia is presented as a sort of independent capitalist venture, first supported by men of wealth eager to assure their fame and their salvation, and then carrying on with its own resources as shops for printing, for weaving and dyeing, for lens-grinding tools, in themselves profitable, became attached to the central academy. The utopia would then be a self-sustaining operation.

Leibniz constantly argued the necessity of a deliberate organization of the scientific enterprise in order to save Europe, a mission of science that could be mocked when it appeared in the diffuse writings of a Comenius, but had a different resonance in the memoranda of a man whose scientific genius was universally recognized. Though Leibnizian science was far closer to what the members of the Royal Society called science than to the natural-philosophy fantasies of the first half of the century, it was not wholly divorced from the more ambitious Pansophic projects. Coming at the end of the seventeenth century, Leibniz towered above the multitude of Pansophic utopians. He alone was capable at one and the same time of sustaining the ideal of Comenius and his forerunners and working out the laborious details for its achievement through philosophy, theology, a new logic, an *ars combinatoria,* diplomacy, and concrete scientific investigations. Leibniz had a monarchical image of science before him and he doubtless drew from earlier models, Bacon's New Atlantis, Campanella's House of Inventions, Andreae's Christianopolis, Comenius' grand design for a Pansophia. His own projects culminated a century later in the plan for scientific organization in Condorcet's *Fragment on the New Atlantis* and the Tenth Epoch of his *Esquisse* and in Saint-Simon's Napoleonic projects for the hegemony of science.

Leibniz was aghast at the contemporary waste of scientific effort. Individualistic science had for a long time been the rule. For most men the publication of their work in scientific journals had satisfied the need for the recognition of personal achievement and had fulfilled elementary requirements for the advancement of science as a whole. The rights of personal glory were preserved, the body of science profited from a degree of mutual aid and even gained through emulation. But there was a growing number of men in the seventeenth and eighteenth centuries who, like Leibniz, were not content with the haphazard accumulations of science either through chance or individual effort. And from Bacon at the beginning to Leibniz at the end of the seventeenth century a utopia of universally organized science was kept alive. Even the most individualistic figure in the galaxy of geniuses, Isaac Newton, outlined a proposal for the organization of science in its various branches and provided for a few stipends to be awarded by the Royal Society to men who produced at a regular rate, emoluments that were to be withdrawn as soon as their labors slackened. The grand projectors like Leibniz were far more venturesome, driven by a spirit that revealed a deeper insight into the prospective organizational needs of the new science. He likened contemporary *connaissances* to a storehouse or a *comptoir* that lacked order or inventory.[10] Nobody really knew the full contents of the scientific world and therefore existing knowledge could not be tapped when needed. A great number of worthwhile ideas and observations were recorded somewhere in books, but far more could be culled from the actual practices of each profession and guild if they were accessible. There was poverty in the midst of abundance and without constant usage much knowledge was lost. Leibniz was apprehensive lest the helter-skelter profusion of publications, "cette horrible masse de livres," would breed such an aversion for knowledge that mankind would sink into ignorance and barbarism.[11] Many scientific investigators gathered objects without any specific purpose in mind or for a mercenary end, for divertissement, out of mere vanity, without a thought for the general advancement of the sciences. In the age of genius, one of the most versatile minds of modern Europe concluded, perhaps prematurely, that the day of the isolated experimenter was virtually over. Only by pursuing common ends under unified direction was significant progress in science now possible. The supersession of possessive scientific individualism does not conform to the style of the rising bourgeoisie, even though in many other respects Leibniz fits in well with its ideal of plenitude and he had a decent regard for money.

The problem of supervising all of scientific creativity and at the same time preserving individual freedom of inquiry that plagued Turgot and Condorcet a century later did not trouble Leibniz. The idea of a coordinated Pansophic enterprise was in an embryonic stage and he was not disturbed about the crushing burden of political authority over science. For the elementary organization of teaching and research, even the establishment of primitive forms of cooperation between the men of action and the men of science was still a utopian goal. Obedience to authority was not regarded in a negative light. The monarchical principle was the best possible form in the universe, whether in the governance of God's world, or in the rule of states imitative of His order, or in the oversight of science, manufactures, and commerce.

A first move to end the chaos was to divide all knowledge into two parts, what Europeans already knew and what still remained to be discovered. What was known had to be assembled in proper order and indexed; materials in print and manuscript had to be subdivided into that portion which was properly labeled and that which was merely inserted in texts en passant and would be difficult to find. Where rare manuscripts were involved, their location had to be identified in what amounted to a world geography of scientific knowledge. Leibniz' respect for historical and philological learning was a far cry from Bacon's opinion that all past knowledge, Greek and medieval, had to be jettisoned. Leibniz had in mind an improved and far grander Photius, a Myriobiblon of solid information, and he called for universal repositories that were both alphabetical and systematic. He was not reluctant to use analogies to law books, though he believed that medical compendia containing empirical observations were far more urgently needed, and he vented his sarcasm on primitive aphorisms of medicine to which there were more exceptions than cases that followed the rules.

A perfect scientific order would afford aesthetic pleasure to man and be a Gloria to God. The ultimate achievement would be a unified system of scientific laws that would ravish men's minds with the beauty of its simplicity and inspire wonderment at the wisdom of God's creation, he wrote in a *Discours touchant la méthode de la certitude:*

The perfect scientific order is one in which the propositions are arranged in accordance with their simplest demonstrations, and in such a way that they are derived one from another, but this order is not known from the start, and is revealed gradually as the science perfects itself. One can even say that sciences become abridged as they are augmented, which is a very remarkable paradox, for the more truths one discovers the more one is in a position to recognize an orderly succession and to make even more universal propositions of which the others are only examples or corollaries, with the result that a large part of those discoveries which have preceded us will in time be reduced to two or three general theses. Moreover, the more a science is perfected, the less does it need big volumes, since once the elements are sufficently well established one can find everything with the help of *la science générale* or the art of invention . . . Besides, the beautiful harmony of truths that one perceives all at once, in an ordered system, satisfies the mind more than the most pleasant music and serves above all to arouse admiration for the Author of all beings, who is the fountain of truth, which is the principal use of the sciences.[12]

One of the most remarkable aspects of this scientific utopia is its deliberate rejection of elitist or esoteric science in favor of its democratization. Leibniz was far closer to the populism of the Moravians than to the secretive Baconian Salomon's House. All men, whatever their station and capacity, were respectworthy contributors to the common treasury of knowledge and to the utopian enterprise. There was no absolute superiority of theory over practice, and the artisan and scientist would become partners in invention. Whenever philosophy moved away from the practical world it became sterile. Leibniz expanded the chorus of those who chanted a Gloria to God to include any person who increased the *commodität* of living, helped feed the poor, kept people from crime, preserved order, ended hard times, plagues, and wars, and contributed to the happiness of mankind. When he wrote a memorandum to the Duke of Württemberg on the founding of a new university (1668–1669), he stressed the need for locating it in an urban area, lest scholars become immured in monkish cells and defeat the aim of free exchange between men of learning and ordinary citizens for their mutual edification and enlightenment.[13] Science had to enter the very life stream of the Christian polity.

The unwritten knowledge dispersed among the various arts and professions was more important than what had been recorded, and thus a major part of the world's information was simply unregistered. There was no vocation, however humble, which did not possess knowledge that now died with the professional practitioners. Manufactures, arts, finance, military affairs were dependent upon the perpetuation of such knowledge. Many savants still occupied themselves with vague abstract discussions when the field was wide open for solid subjects of inquiry advantageous to the public. Leibniz' conception of the learning to be derived from observation of existing work practices included activities that would rarely come to the minds of the learned: hunting, fishing, navigation, commerce, games of skill and chance. Even the play of children might interest the greatest mathematician.[14] Leibniz dreamed of a veritable *théâtre de la vie humaine* drawn from observation, far different from a *théâtre* compiled by a few *érudits* primarily interested in subjects for academic harangues and sermons.

Scientists had been grossly negligent in overlooking the corpus of artisan skills, while artisans were none too eager to impart their information to anyone but their apprentices. Leibniz hoped to bring ordinary workmen into the orbit of scientific civilization not only for their own benefit but to allow the higher culture to profit from their experience. Since, in the ideal world, academies were to be located in cities, the interchange between philosophers and workers would be easy and mutually profitable, realizing the necessary union of theory and practice that underlay his world outlook. He rejected the common prejudice that workers had to be driven to their tasks by necessity and want; once their basic needs were satisfied, other elements of their nature would blossom. His utopia of happy artisans was no mere abstraction. Leibniz conceived of practical ways of cajoling workers away from indulgence in drink and debauch to discussion of their crafts. He would have a reporter present during their ordinary conversations to record any new ideas about methods of production that might be generated in passing. Men singing contentedly at their work is an optimistic prospect that reappears intermittently in the history of utopian thought from Leibniz to Saint-Simon, a denial of both the Greek and the older Christian conception of labor as pain. Since most of Leibniz' projects remained in manuscript, Marx could not have read them, but he felt a spontaneous sympathy with the philosopher who proclaimed the union of theory and practice—stripped of his godliness of course.

In many of his memoranda Leibniz communicates his appreciation of the limitless creative capacities of men in all stations of life. Since their inventiveness often remained dormant, his utopia fostered and encouraged creativity through special institutions. Simultaneously, the mysterious hieratic aura surrounding elitist scientific discovery was to be dispelled by persuading scientists to set down in detail the particular circumstances of their inventions—not omitting an account of their psychological state at the instant of discovery—in order to learn how to maximize *ingenio*. Finding out the *Neigung*, inclination, of each individual student was one of the first and crucial obligations of the educational system, an idea that had been winning adherents in Central Europe ever since Comenius had begun to preach.

Propagation of the Faith through Science

While Leibniz was skeptical about egalitarian institutions and fixed forms of meritocracy because it would be impossible to find men who would agree in their judgment of merit, and while he left intact existing institutions for the organization of work and justice, he was always on the lookout for ways of giving these same institutions new functions. In all of his projects the pace of change was to be gradual; there was an infinity of stages in any series, and novelty emerged from the old forms only slowly. The unfolding of new shapes of things was naturally stimulated by a philosophical need for plenitude in God's universe and a psychological need for creation and discovery in every man. Yet, like so many utopians before and after him, Leibniz was possessed by the idea that there was a particular moment when, under the tutelage of a philosopher who represented theory and a great monarch who represented practice, the proliferation of novel forms could be forced, so to speak, to achieve an accelerated tempo. If the propitious moment was not grasped, temporary retrogression could stifle a civilization. The great projector should influence the potentates of the world to fashion a political and social environment that allowed for the maximal expression of each man's productive inclination. The attribute of inevitability in the process is muted, except that finally everything, including a temporary retrograde movement, if it occurs, serves a divine purpose. The progress of *connaissances solides et utiles*—the words Leibniz used to describe the new science—was a duty owed to ancestors, a sort of psychic debt that had to be repaid by the transmission of knowledge in augmented form to the next generation. Leibniz was convinced that his age was the perfect time to harvest all past experience, and unite it with the concrete new information that the art of printing, the compass, the telescope, and the microscope had put at the disposal of men. In the course of time new forms and combinations of matter would have emerged of their own accord by accident, but the science of chemistry now accelerated the process. Though no invention of an individual scientific genius made a permanent difference between knowledge and ignorance, because eventually in the course of time the same knowledge would have emerged through the tiny increments of anonymous artisans and inventors, organized science would hasten the tempo of fulfillment.

The academies Leibniz planned for German, Austrian, and Russian monarchs would not be limited to philosophy and experimental science, but would direct inquiries into botany and zoology, collecting records of new species in all parts of the world. Medicine was to study temperament, especially genius and natural propensities, and to seek ways of recognizing and utilizing them for the perfection of arts and sciences. The sense of urgency that inspired Bacon's *Great Instauration* was heightened in Leibniz, as he called for a scientific explosion in all fields; the moral and religious fate of Christian civilization depended upon it. Military science and other ways of perpetrating evil were evolving so rapidly that Leibniz could only hope the *sciences du réel et du salutaire* could keep pace with those of the harmful. In his overall prospect he was careful to divide the "good" and "bad" sciences in such a manner that the balance of universal harmony was not disturbed. The invention of cannon—an apparent evil—was a gift of Heaven, because its immediate consequence was the stemming of the Ottoman tide, and someday cannon might deliver Europeans completely from the Turks. Then Greece would be rescued from barbarism and allowed to enjoy the fruits of the sciences it had founded, while to Asia, mother of religion, were returned the benefits derived from the practice of the true faith.[15]

Carried away by an early adulation of Louis XIV, the young Leibniz had once been convinced that the will of this monarch alone could achieve more impressive results in science than all the knowledge that had thus far been accumulated. The time necessary for discovery would be abbreviated and a few years would suffice for what would otherwise require centuries. The inquiries Alexander had encouraged Aristotle to undertake would be dwarfed by comparison; in fact, the scientific memoirs presented at the French Academy and the operations of the Observatory already far outstripped the ancient duumvirate. If Louis XIV united the scientific efforts of men, it would be a monument, not only to his charity but to his glory, that was superior to his military conquests. He alone was in a position to inspire more discoveries than all the mathematicians and doctors taken together could make without him, for he could issue orders and publish regulations to put the sciences on a track of rapid increase. He was capable of amassing more knowledge necessary for piety and tranquillity, for the diminution of pain and the augmentation of man's power over nature, than all the nations of all previous ages combined. With such extravagant rhetoric Leibniz renewed the plea of Bacon to James I, of Campanella to the Spanish Monarchy and the Pope, of Andreae to the learned men of the Christian Society, of Hartlib and the Comenians to the English Parliament. In a fanciful fragment of 1675 Leibniz proposed to open a review of the present state and future potentialities of learning with an address to the French King that promised him nothing less than immortality. "Sire, I present to Your Majesty the account of a country where you will live forever. That is the Elysian Fields of the heroes, and one must pass through them to have relations with posterity." The apotheosis of Louis turned to hostility in the *Mars Christianissimus* (1684) once Leibniz was reintegrated into the Germanic world.[16]

In the tradition of Bacon, the application of theoretical findings had to keep pace with the findings themselves. Though Bacon and Leibniz may appear to belong to a utilitarian tradition, such a conclusion would be a reduction of their dream of science. Both science and its applications were first a Gloria to God. Pure science would reveal the wisdom of God; its utilization to create new measures of abundance and to alleviate pain would illustrate the goodness of God. Anyone who contributed his skills to a stage of this process, whether as inventor, artisan-manufacturer, or keeper of the public order, was participating in the Christian enterprise. There were no autonomous monads in the universal harmony of things. The love of God fixed a center for all human activities and saved them from dispersion. It helped those men who heeded the general good to rise above the claims of their individual lusts and to put their actions in accord with the will of God, to choose, from among an infinity of possibilities in the present, those types of activity most readily conducive to the fulfillment of God's plan for the world. If there seemed to be historical regressions, in the end of time these would turn out to have been necessary elements in the best of all possible worlds. Anyone discontent with the order of things simply did not love God as he should.[17] Despite occasional lapses, Leibniz exuded a general optimism in his *Theodicy,* which became the source for Voltaire's mockery in *Candide ou l'optimisme.* The modern utopia feeds on this spirit or general mood, even as its opposite, pessimism—a term popularized by Schopenhauer—is anti-utopian. Leibniz' numerous utopian projects are far less well known than the formula Pangloss repeats over and over again amid disaster and catastrophe.

The cohesive force of the love of God would hold the great work of science together. Leibniz did not foresee the fragmentation of science and technology as their various parts came to serve a multiplicity of alien gods. No scientific corps would carve out for itself an independent status or existence. Theoretically, the religious orders would themselves become scientific establishments, thus providing a perfect transition, without disruption, from the monastery to the scientific academy that would replace it. If it had been possible to follow a Leibnizian prescription, presumably the whole future revolutionary utopian movement of Europe would have lost its raison d'être as traditional spiritual institutions transformed themselves. Priests and monks would have become scientists. The grave destructive tendency of a spiritual corps divided into two hostile sectors of scientists and priests was uppermost in the consciousness of Pansophic utopians, a subject that would be revived in the nineteenth century when the bifurcation had become definitive.

In all projects for academies and scientific establishments Leibniz joined practice to theory, the mark of his system that unites him most intimately with his Pansophist forerunners. The aim of these institutions was not only to promote the arts and sciences, but to further the welfare of the country and its inhabitants in general by improving agriculture, manufactures, commerce, in short, all aspects of existence; also, to make discoveries that would increase wonderment at God's marvels, to propagate the Christian religion, and to institute sound government and customs among pagans, peoples civilized and uncivilized, even among savages. Learned societies would become the chief organs for the simultaneous propagation of the faith and the extension of civilization.[18]

Science would emerge as the primary instrument for spreading Christianity, *propagatio verae fidei per scientias,*[19] and the universal triumph of the true religion would multiply commercial relationships among all parts of the world. Individual academies would become links in an international network promoting peace among the peoples of the earth. The most dramatic proof that science was destined to be the conquering arm of the new Christian polity was the triumph of the Jesuit missionaries in converting so many of the mandarins of China, a success that Leibniz attributed to the admiration aroused by their introduction of European scientific inventions and discoveries.[20] Like Comenius, he saw a movement parallel to the Christian expansion in China on the other side of the globe, in the harboring of the Indian colleges by centers of learning —Harvard, and William and Mary. The scientific academies he proposed for Berlin, Dresden, St. Petersburg were conceived as a chain of outposts against barbarism and a defense of Christian civilization. Planted in the very midst of European society with all its crimes and foibles, the academies would constitute focal points free of antagonism. Through the radiation of their activities they were destined to alter the essential character of the whole world. Leibniz' academic projects of the 1670s did not seriously attract anyone at the time of their composition. Eventually, largely through the efforts of Leibniz and the two Jablonski brothers, Comenius' grandsons, they led to the founding of the Prussian Academy, whose internecine quarrels belied the sanguine hopes of Leibniz for the best of all possible academies. (He himself had become the first president of the earlier Royal Society of Sciences of Berlin in 1700.)

Though ordinary persons would participate, the responsibility for the utopia of science devolved especially upon the elect, a few men like Newton (Leibniz was writing before their final quarrel) who were, so to speak, of the privy council of God. Without false humility, Leibniz defined the role of men of intellect in the providential design: They were more important than the great captains and at least on a par with the worthiest of lawgivers in helping mankind achieve its ultimate goal. He referred to himself as "Solicitor General of the public good," to which he was devoted above all other considerations, "even glory and money."[21] Education for all according to their capacities, the promotion of arts and sciences, and a sound organization of society were the practical means of furthering the general good. As for distributive justice, Leibniz considered the equal apportionment of goods a vain dream. A communist arrangement would merely favor the laziness of the mass of the citizens. The right of property was absolute, but good citizens had to renounce a portion of their riches for the common welfare. There was a clear-cut division between the private sector, where individual activity was rewarded, and the public service of *le bien général*.

The Ecumenical Natural Religion

Leibniz set forth his religious credo in the *Confessio philosophi* of 1675. "It behooves anyone who loves God to be satisfied with the past and to try to make the future the best possible world. He, and only he, who is thus disposed can achieve the peace of mind that the austere philosophers pursue, the state of total resignation to the will of God that the mystics sought. He whose feelings are different, whatever the words may be that he has in his mouth—faith, charity, God, or neighbor—neither knows God as the supreme reason, nor does he love him."[22]

This natural religion of reason was unknown among primitive peoples, whose first dogmas and rites were nothing but dark superstitions. Leibniz was untouched by the nascent cult of the noble savage. A few ancient philosophers might have had an insight into true religion before Jesus turned it into law and it achieved the authority of a revelation. With Christianity, natural religion, once limited to isolated sages, became the religion of the nations. Mohammedanism did not violate natural religion, and with the conquests of Islam it won converts among some primitive peoples. Reason, which was the natural voice of God in all men, would have ultimately led them to natural religion, but revelation made it an overpoweringly persuasive force. Without revelation, the rapid victory of Christianity over large areas of the world would have been impossible. Strangely enough, natural religion did not render the theological dogmas of Christianity and Islam either superfluous or matters of indifference. The Leibnizian concept that every soul was inseparable from at least a minimal quantity of matter, that each monad was united to an organic body, was the basis for the doctrine of the resurrection of the body, which was part of the principle of immortality. A correct, deeply researched theological interpretation of extension and the essence of bodies would make it possible to conciliate Calvinist, Lutheran, and Catholic doctrines of the Eucharist, even to harmonize trinitarian Christianity with ancient Chinese religion. The Chinese concept of *Li,* the substance or universal entity of all things, could be assimilated with the Christian idea of substance.[23]

But Leibniz was no superficial latitudinarian; he required a digging into the dogmas of the various positive religions in order to unearth the golden nugget of truth buried away in each of them, excluding only the idolatry in primitive and pagan religions.[24] As long as there was rational civilization, a possibility of religious union existed. Primitives usually fall outside the bounds of Leibniz' chief concerns and their religions have little or nothing to contribute to the universal harmony, though his projects for the reorganization of Russia included training missionaries for the propagation of Christianity in the most barbarous regions of the empire. His irenicism was not based on compromise among hostile sects, but on the proof that Christian theology, with its Trinity, was actually present in the beliefs of all great religions. The rites and doctrines of the major non-Protestant religions were not to be condemned or combated, but were to be analyzed in order to show that they were harmonious with Protestant theology. He would never attempt to overthrow an existing religious institution, Catholic or Greek Orthodox, that was alien to his Lutheran faith, but rather would convince their priests of truths they could not controvert, and would encourage them to extend their future activities into fields of science and learning they had not cultivated before.

By 1703, Leibniz had become an outspoken enemy of prophets who could not demonstrate their internal illumination by external phenomena that all men could judge. As the experimental method in science gradually made its way, it would, he hoped, destroy religious enthusiasm because the inner conviction of the prophet was not backed either by universal reason or by the witness of the senses. Moses had been granted an external sign of his election in the burning bush; modern prophets had nothing but their own testimony to support their authority. Despite an early affinity with Comenian thought expressed in his youthful poem and the similarity of Leibniz' projects with those of Christian Pansophia—a universal language, the centrality of educational reform, the ordering of scientific research, the conversion of China—he tended to treat Comenius' memory with condescension. In a letter of 1672 to Magnus Hessenthaler, Professor of Politics and Rhetoric in Tübingen, Leibniz admitted that the works of Comenius were more profound than appeared at first sight, but he was put off by his chiliasm and his association with false prophets.[25] After Drabík's implication in the failure of the Polish enterprise and his subsequent beheading, guilt by association made references to Comenius indiscreet, and his name all but disappeared from Leibniz' letters. Leibniz was leery of any manifestation of zeal or fanaticism; religion infused with passion closed men's minds to the truths of rational theology. Only as long as rationalism prevailed was there an opportunity for religious union.

Utopianizing China and Russia

For Leibniz each historical moment was pregnant with an infinitude of possibilities. It was the duty of every man in his age to work toward the realization of that possibility most in conformity with the will and commandment of God, exerting his powers to the utmost upon present reality. Unlike the schemes of other utopians, Leibniz' projects were not a denial of the past and a repudiation of the present, but an attempt to ferret out in existing society those traditional elements that could be nurtured in order to foster the growth of an ideal future in harmony with Christian moral principles. He was less absorbed in the dialectic between the imagined future and the present than in the search for optimal projections among a host of contemporary potentialities. His ideal was circumscribed by the common religious and moral principles of Europe; the content of the utopia was determined by a political understanding of what could grow out of the present. Leibniz conceived of himself as midwife to a present that would give birth to the future. Karl Marx understood, despite vast differences in their conception of the dynamic tempo of the historical process, that they were brothers. Engels once presented Marx with a rug that had belonged to Leibniz. The revolutionary theorist was thrilled with the gift: Walking in Leibniz' footsteps, he too believed that the present was pregnant with the future.

Leibniz foresaw an end to the fragmentation of mankind in a series of stages —first the strengthening and unification of Germany, then of the Holy Roman Empire, then of Europe, finally of the whole world. To implement this progression he resorted to a baroque *Kabinettspolitik* that involved the interplay of transitory alliances and alignments. But in his mind's eye political manipulations were always integrated with a cosmopolitan vision. The public welfare (*le bien public*) was the supreme law; and by public he referred to all who acknowledged God and were thereby united in one *mundi civitas*.[26] Leibniz' universal ideal, however, was not a faceless cosmopolitanism. Individual cultures would preserve their national character as indestructible monads, while they were incorporated into a more complex order that would banish internecine strife among men.

Not all Leibniz' proposals for unification were innocent—there was at least one aberration. In 1671–1672, in conjunction with the memorandum (the *Consilium Aegyptiacum*) for the conquest of Egypt presented to Louis XIV, he devised a scheme that exploited, rather than respected, cultural differences. A new invincible army that could conquer the world was to be composed of recruits from a great diversity of nations, men unable to communicate with one another, deprived of wills of their own, "a splendid collection of half-beasts" (*pulchrum concilium semibestiarum*).[27] The Egyptian project has always been under suspicion as a mere political device for diverting the warlike energies of France away from the Dutch and the Germanic worlds and exhausting them in a conquest of the Mohammedans, and such objectives may well have played a part in the total strategy. But generally Leibniz' plans, even when calculated to give a patron an immediate advantage in the European balance, were tied to the grander prospect of ultimately establishing peace by civilizing and uniting the whole world. Egypt was a way station to the East, to China.

While the ideal of universal peace did not exclude war as an occasional instrumentality, more often the primary agency of conquest was directly intellectual: Through the union of minds and religious beliefs the world would be moved toward peace and harmony. The mechanisms concocted by Leibniz appear to be less extravagant than those of utopians like Fourier because they are composed of elements with which we are familiar—theological conciliations, the furtherance of scientific invention, diplomatic combinations, understanding through improved communication. But given the politico–social realities of the late seventeenth and early eighteenth centuries, they are no less radical as lateral departures from the possibilities of the world. This man who at a princely court could shrewdly diagnose a personal or political situation was capable of soaring into a realm of pure fantasy.

Though most of the political memoranda Leibniz prepared were intended for private individuals of lofty station, not for the multitude, and remained in manuscript, he actually published the *Novissima Sinica* (1697), a gift to the eighteenth century. The book, a miscellany of materials on China, has a preface by Leibniz that entreats Protestant potentates to submerge their differences and vie with the Jesuits for the spiritual possession of China as friendly rivals who share a common Christian culture. Interest in the Americas is minor if compared with his obsession with China, though at the height of his infatuation with Peter the Great he pressed for Russian expansion beyond the Pacific, overflowing the Americas. At each end of the Eurasian continent was a great civilization excelling in certain spheres of human activity, the Europeans in knowledge of things spiritual and in science, the Chinese in civil behavior and the peaceful organization of society. The two were destined to approach each other and to interpenetrate, civilizing the vast intermediary land mass. China as the instructor of Europe, even if intended as a paradox, was a shocking notion, not likely to be embraced in the late seventeenth century. "But it is desirable that they in turn teach us those things which are especially in our interest: the greatest use of practical philosophy and a more perfect manner of living, to say nothing now of their other arts. Certainly the condition of our affairs, slipping as we are into ever greater corruption, seems to me such that we need missionaries from the Chinese who might teach us the use and practice of natural religion, just as we have sent them teachers of revealed theology."[28] In the same spirit of reciprocity, he had not been at all fazed when during ecumenical discussions with Bossuet he was warned that under the projected circumstances of union the Protestants would be turning Catholic; after all, simultaneously the Catholics would become Protestants. In the projects of his last years, after he had met Peter the Great, Leibniz ceased conceiving of the Muscovite empire as a mere passive area for the spread of Western European culture, and nominated it the active agent in the movement eastward to China, fashioning a new bridge after the Jesuits had been repudiated by the papacy in the dispute over the "Chinese rites" and the Protestant powers had failed to hearken to his plea that they send missionaries to convert the mandarins.

There is not a word in the writings of either the Jesuits or Leibniz about the Chinese mentality or the Chinese race. There was one universal reason and one humanity. Infiltrating China served the religious purpose of strengthening world unity. When the Jesuits were prepared to compromise on the toleration of certain Chinese rites in order to win converts, Leibniz had come to their support. If only one could persuade the Emperor of China and the mandarins to accept the true religion, demonstrate to them that the earliest religious writings of their ancestors embodied ideas resembling those of the biblical patriarchs, which had somehow been diffused to China, the two great civilizations, Europe and anti-Europe, would find a common ground. Since Leibniz' irenic utopia would eventually have to embrace the Chinese religion, he engaged in extravagant philosophical and exegetical gymnastics to prove that there were no fundamentally irreconcilable antagonisms between the most ancient religious traditions of the two cultures. Once convinced on this score, the Chinese and the Europeans would join together in the enterprises of the new science, and along with all other peoples would make use of the new philosophical language of notations to express their thoughts. The cultural monads did not have to be identical, they merely had to understand the same language of logic and conceptual definitions recorded in an encyclopedia. When intellectual and spiritual harmony was achieved, the basis would be laid for the unification of the world.

Leibniz' need to return to origins and his plans for thorough theological studies of any alien civilization, the Chinese and later the Russian, did not grow out of antiquarianism, but were integral to his philosophy. Through the laborious investigation of remote historical beginnings, common elements concealed in the diversity of present forms could be revealed. This was no deistic position that viewed the multiplicity of rites and practices as mere corruptions of some pristine abstract truth. The traditions in their concreteness and specificity and historical detail bore witness to the community of ideas. Leibniz criticized the Jesuit missionaries in China for not penetrating far back enough in their study of Chinese traditions; and when in the last years of his life he shifted the focus of his utopian fantasy to Russia, he called upon the Greek Orthodox theologians and the Czar to institute widespread researches into the forgotten manuscripts buried away in monasteries throughout the empire.[29] Again his object was not the mere pursuit of esoteric learning. Both the Chinese and the Slavic religious heritages when brought into contact with the European would enrich and establish roots for the new universalism.

Leibniz would not in one fell swoop overwhelm those he aimed to convert with "mysteries heaped indiscriminately upon unprepared souls."[30] He had a strong conviction that there were transitional forms on the way to perfection, that nature did not make leaps.[31] Only toward the end of his life, with perhaps a feeling that he had thus far failed in all his enterprises, did the aging, rather solitary historiographer of the House of Hannover, whom Newton had managed to keep out of England, show signs of impatience and abandon his habitual prudence as he dashed off proposals for the total reorganization of Russian life, heedless of the conservative power of the Russian Orthodox Church and the abysmal ignorance of the peasantry. He began to urge what appears to be a swift, abrupt changeover into a new order. As a rule, his plans were intricately reasoned and involved many intermediary steps.

Europeans were baffled by the appearance of Czar Peter in their midst, a barbarian in personal conduct seeking guidance on how to westernize his people. For Leibniz, Peter's war against the Turks held the promise of liberating the Christians of the Ottoman Empire, though Protestant sympathies kept him from acclaiming with unmixed joy Russian victories against the Swedish monarch Gustavus Adolphus, who was the Protestant hero. Leibniz felt a close psychic kinship with the Slavic world. An autobiographical fragment begins by identifying his family name as Slavic in origin: "Leubniziorum sive Lubeniecziorum nomen slavonicum; familia in Polonia . . . "[32] He had heard stories of Peter's intelligence, activism, passion for learning new things, along with accounts of his cruelties. Leibniz was fascinated by the imperial monster who displayed to the German princelets his hands rough from work on the seventy-five ships he was building, while they vainly tried to get him to listen to Italian music.

Leibniz had a way of sending out political feelers in different directions at the same time. He was still applauding the Jesuit endeavors to convert the Chinese when he began to compose programmatic letters for Peter's eyes—more than a decade before he was formally designated a councillor of the Czar. Leibniz' commitment to any power as the instrument for the salvation of Europe was never without ambivalence. He knew that the divine mission had been entrusted into his hands, but the vessels available to him were not flawless. A perfect specimen of Europe's religious civilization, he was early aware of the barbarities of the Scythian whom he had chosen; God had recourse to strange vehicles for the fulfillment of His purposes in the world. Leibniz has sometimes been portrayed as the courtier-dilettante seeking out kings and emperors before whom he could display his ingenuity. The vain side of his character, his desire to consort with the powerful of the earth, to enjoy their intimacy, is not to be denied; but once he had fixed on a hero, the passion and persistence with which he attended him bear witness to a more binding servitude. When he was moved by the urgency of such a relationship he could write with a candor bordering on naiveté, as he did on September 2, 1709, to Urbich, the Russian minister in Vienna, seeking to become the Czar's "instrument en chef." "The honor I have of being among the oldest members of all royal societies . . . not to speak of the very important discoveries for which I am generally recognized, gives me hope that I may be entrusted with the direction of so great an enterprise; and I would prefer this to any other occupation."[33] Leibniz carried out his indoctrination of the Czar with a sense of his election as the great intermediary between Europe and China. There were three meetings, in Torgau in 1711, Carlsbad in 1712, Herrenhausen and Pyrmont in 1716. Leibniz felt that the day of Russian enlightenment had finally arrived. In January of 1716—the year of his death—he wrote: "It appears to be the will of God for science to circumambulate the globe and now at last to come also to the land of the Scythians."[34]

Leibniz had the *passio utopiensis,* but though immersed in grand enterprises, he did not lose the courtier's sense of humor about himself and a certain detachment about his prospects. At once a master unraveler of political intentions in Europe's complex diplomatic intrigues and the Lord's anointed, chosen to bring about the universal Christian republic, he could occasionally laugh at himself. His efforts were accompanied with a measure of self-deprecation and, as he grew older, some skepticism about bringing his projects to a successful issue. His utopian mood changed over the years. The Egyptian scheme of his youth was composed in deadly earnest; one is less certain about his ambitions for Czar Peter. By this time, in the Morean manner, he may have wished for more than he hoped after. In November 1712, after he had been invited to meet the Czar at Carlsbad where he was taking the cure, Leibniz wrote tongue-in-cheek to the Electress Sophie: "Your Electoral Highness will find extraordinary that I am to be in a way the Solon of Russia, although from afar. That is to say, the Czar has informed me through Count Golofkin, his Grand Chancellor, that I am to revise its ordinances, and draft regulations on law and the administration of justice. Since I hold that the briefest laws, like the ten commandments of God and the twelve tables of ancient Rome, are the best, and as that subject is one of the things about which I have been meditating longest, this will not give me much trouble; and moreover I won't have to be in any great hurry about it. For the Czar will be a lawgiver only when the war is finished."[35]

The plans for the reformation of Russia constitute Leibniz' last utopia, the final attempt to win the East for the Respublica Christiana. Projects were transplanted from a Western European context and tied to a wholesale reformation of Russian society under the aegis of the Czar. Suddenly the very primitive character of the Russian people took on the semblance of a virtue. The vast empire was a tabula rasa, on which the philosopher could draw his new order at will. With a momentary resurgence of childlike enthusiasm, this adroit old diplomat dreamed of a reorganization of the Russian educational system with the aid of the Orthodox Church, a restructuring of the bureaucracy, and the widespread establishment of arts and manufactures, to create a Russia independent of the West. In the Russian utopia, two of the prinicpal threads of Leibniz' futurist fantasy came together. Here was an empire that could be refashioned, with new laws, work rules, education, institutions of arts and sciences, everything he had once proposed for German states. Here, too, was a universalist project that envisaged Russia as a bridge to China, Czar Peter replacing the Louis XIV of Leibniz' early Egyptian *Consilium*. Even his ideal of religious catholicity would be served, for he tried to promote councils in which Russian Orthodox believers and Protestants might find a new meeting ground.

In Leibniz' proposal for the building of universities and schools throughout Russia, teachers would assume a new role. On the lower levels they would be the chief representatives of the state in the various localities, while professors would become veritable court councillors. The whole system, designed to relate theory to practice, formed a mammoth pyramidal structure culminating in a supreme college under a president, with all of its members imperial councillors of the Czar. There was no sharp division between intellectual and practical pursuits in the service of society. Schools for elementary education would discover the special talents of children, who would then be assigned to artisans or sent on to higher schools of education in accordance with their talents.

The Last Christian Utopian

In the last quarter of the twentieth century a historian of thought no longer has to force a major European philosopher like Leibniz into a Procrustean bed. When a man has labored for fifty years pondering the whole of God's work, the neat formulas that are sometimes used to epitomize his writings are sad impoverishments. The demonstration of a steady progression in his thought can become just as restrictive. A complex and sensitive man torn by contending forces, Leibniz had many lapses, and he even performed an occasional somersault under the impact of violent changes in the world of dynastic diplomacy, where he served throughout his life. But he had an abiding faith in the healing qualities of a Christian Pansophia that could save the order of European culture and through its propagation the whole world. The utopia was still essentially Europocentric, even though it looked east to include China and west to embrace the American colonies. It was scientific in its espousal of realia, real things, as the foundation of knowledge, but the controlling force was an overriding Christian spirituality. Leibniz, who strove to create a new logic and had a natural genius for mathematics, warned against the Cartesian contempt for historical experience. He sought an ecumenical Christianity, though his dogmatic position could not always free itself from its parochial Protestant shackles. His was the last great utopian vision that derived its meaning from the love of God and the exploration of His world in all its dimensions, geographical, historical, theological, and scientific. Perhaps Teilhard de Chardin is a twentieth-century incarnation of the same idea, though his vision divests the concrete historical reality of man's past of much of its significance.

The love of God as the driving force behind Leibniz' Christian utopia is no easier to communicate to a late-twentieth-century man than Newton's science conceived of as an expression of his duty to obey the commandments of God the Father. Leibniz turned his passion outward to the love of mankind in imitation of Christ. Newton, who lowered the Christ-figure in the divine Trinity, stressed personal obedience to an omnipotent Lord and Master; there is little emotional concern for mankind in Newton, even though he fulfilled the duties of Christian charity—he distributed Bibles to the poor—and performed the tasks of his calling with meticulous care. Leibniz' love of God required a more ample expression and became manifest in a life of action that entailed a social mission: guiding the whole of mankind in the direction of a progressive realization of God's will. The two loves, both Glorias of God, are not comparable. Newton saw himself in the Godhead, Leibniz became a grand projector.

When in seventeenth-century Europe old hierarchical structures in religious and state institutions and in economic relationships were falling apart, the utopia of Pansophia tried to reestablish a harmony by reintegrating the new science with traditional Christian culture. The attempt failed, though not without leaving some residue. The utopian quest was resumed in the next age, but under very different auspices. In a French version of eighteenth-century cosmopolitanism the universal vision became militantly anticlerical and even anti-Christian. Like Pansophia, the Enlightenment was naturistic and it was scientific. Its conception of nature, however, was sensuous and pleasure-seeking; and its science, popularized by the French philosophes, was used to fight the religious establishment and, for good and for evil, to secularize European culture beyond redemption.

PART IV

Eupsychias
of the Enlightenment

Jean-Jacques Rousseau

engraving after Cochin le fils for *Emile*

16

The Philosophes's Dilemma

IDLY THUMBING the pages of the *Encyclopédie* one is struck by the absence of an article on utopia as the entries move along in alphabetical sequence from *utilité* to Utrecht. A sampling of *Encyclopédie* articles on famous authors of utopias to see whether the subject is not treated in some fashion under their names turns up meager pickings. There is no piece at all on Thomas More; the expected eulogy of Francis Bacon is there, but makes no reference to his *New Atlantis;* and Campanella is denigrated for his philosophical fantasies: *The City of the Sun* is totally ignored. The grand philosophical designs of Leibniz for ecumenical peace and the conversion of the heathen are passed over lightly.

The rationalists of the Enlightenment either treated the seventeenth-century visionaries as hotheads whose imagination had outstripped their reason, leaving behind a mass of confusion—witness Pierre Bayle's sneering piece on Comenius in the *Historical and Critical Dictionary* and Diderot's biographies of Bruno and Campanella—or, in dealing with the geniuses of the previous age whom they deigned to accept into their canon, they reduced complex philosophical systems to plain statements of the matter-of-fact.

None of the *patres majores* of the French Enlightenment actually wrote a proper utopia, even though there are in their works utopian excursions whose intent, when probed, appears to be rather ambiguous. Utopian digressions in the writings of the stars among the philosophes, like the "History of the Troglodytes" in Montesquieu's *Persian Letters,* a sketch of El Dorado in Voltaire's *Candide,* an appreciation of the sinless, shameless Tahitian way of life in Diderot's *Supplément au voyage de Bougainville,* should not be construed as serious dedication to a utopian model. Diderot could go into raptures over the isle of Lampedusa, but he was skeptical about the adaptability of Tahitian sexual customs to Europe, as his concluding dialogue between "A" and "B" shows; Voltaire's piece was a parody of a utopia; and Montesquieu was merely being playful and, in the *Voyage to Paphos,* mildly pornographic.

On the rare occasions when Grimm, Meister, and their collaborators, who distributed a famous literary newsletter to European aristocrats, bothered to notice any of the hundreds of utopias written in the Morean manner, their reviews were uniformly derogatory. They dismissed the works with a disdainful *espèce d'utopie.* And most philosophical plans and projects for universal reformation received short shrift at their hands. A brief account of James Harrington's *Oceana,* buried away in the *Encyclopédie*'s geographical description of the County of Rutland where Harrington was born, allowed the Chevalier de Jaucourt, Diderot's man of all articles, to shrug off universal plans for imaginary republics: "Perfection and immortality in a republic are as chimerical as in a man."[1] All of this leads one to reflect upon what happened to the utopian mode in eighteenth-century thought. It was surely part of the world outlook of the age. But where was it hiding in the century of light and what shapes did it assume?

Reluctantly one dismisses the idea that a single dominant utopian prototype might be discovered, analogous to the Christian Pansophic vision of the seventeenth century. One would have to strain to find common features in the Archbishop of Cambrai's *Avantures de Télémaque* and the new civil constitution for France proposed by a libertine in the Marquis de Sade's *La Philosophie dans le boudoir,* to choose utopias from the beginning and the end of the period. There is no way out but to proceed by the rhetorical device of *partitio* so dear to Francis Bacon, favorite of the philosophes, and to abandon the prospect of summing up the phenomenological essence of all eighteenth-century utopias in one terse formula. The varieties of utopian experience are too great to be drawn together under a single head. And yet one can hardly rest content with the easy solution that each writer had his own utopia and that no pattern can be discerned in the vast literary agglomeration.

We have come to recognize about five rather different positions on utopia developed in the course of the century: that of the *patres majores,* of Rousseau the renegade from the philosophical cult, of the popular novels, of the theoretical communistic projects, and finally of the prophets of the future at the end of the century, Turgot and Condorcet, de Sade and Restif, Saint-Just and Babeuf, who belong in a separate category. The major philosophes are a transitional stage on the way to euchronia, and their doubts and misgivings can best be illustrated by their ambiguous attitude toward two of the most powerful conceptions of the new age—the idea of perfectibility and the myth of the noble savage.

Historical Vicissitudes

For most of the philosophes, convinced of recurrent decadence after each burst of flourishing civilization, an enduring optimum system was an improbable fantasy. And this was not in contradiction to Diderot's belief that men of his generation should labor to collect their factual knowledge into one grand encyclopedia, so that future generations might think well of them and trumpet their fame. The article "Encyclopédie," written by Diderot himself, contains the words that later became the title of Condorcet's *Esquisse,* "l'histoire des progrès de l'esprit humain"; but there is nothing approximating a commitment to the euchronia of *progrès indéfini.* There are self-congratulatory excursions on the manifold uses that an encyclopedia primarily directed toward the future might have in accelerating the accumulation of knowledge, but caveats are never absent. "Cyclical revolutions are ineluctable. They always have occurred and they always will. The length of the maximum interval between one revolution and another is fixed. This factor alone limits the extent of our labors. There is a point in the acquisition of knowledge beyond which it is not possible to pass." Nor will scientific knowledge ever cease to be more than the province of an elite. "The general mass of the human species is not capable of either following or understanding this march of the human mind. The highest level of education that it can reach has its limits."[2]

To the Encyclopedists morals and politics were not sufficiently rigorous branches of knowledge to allow for the drafting of ambitious models of perfect societies. Perhaps a philosophe might influence kings and empresses in the direction of the good, ending wars, secularizing the state, reforming the penal laws, bringing the benefits of prosperity to their subjects; but the idea of a lasting, stable, perfect society in the face of the mutability of things—a doctrine of vicissitudes inherited from the classical world and the Renaissance—aroused only doubt. Not until Turgot's *Sorboniques,* Mercier's dream of the year 2440, and Condorcet's *Esquisse* were hopes voiced for a future, qualitatively more perfect state of man that might endure as a consequence of inevitable progress. There could and should be an abolition of obvious abuses such as the contumely of aristocrats and the legal impediments to industriousness—about this there was a consensus. Fanatical religions should be extirpated, and men should feel freer and easier in their political and social relations. But the philosophes hardly imagined that the rivalries of empires and the depredations of war would end, or that all men would become as good and virtuous as they were.

The philosophes's position with respect to an ideal polity was akin to that of the early Stoics—to Zeno and Chrysippus. The virtuous man felt in his inner being what was good in any particular circumstance, and so he did not require an abstract system. If all men were virtuous or became philosophes, there would be no particular need for any sort of government. Short of this total transformation, which was deemed highly unlikely, human beings were apt to be variable, more or less good, their happiness in large measure contingent upon the personality of sovereigns who would also be good or evil, wise or stupid. But a utopia, a settled and lasting order, was beyond the philosophes's expectations. Such schemes smacked of the dogmatism, rigidity, and false paradisaical illusions of the cruel, deceptive religions that had held mankind in thrall. Posterity, with the progress of the arts and sciences, might improve on things in the course of this cycle of history; but there would forever be misfortunes in store for mankind, hence an alternation of better and worse periods of human history. The triumph of an evil man was always possible, and the onset of decadence—the consequence of exhaustion in nature or society—was fated at intervals. The Abbé Galiani, a favorite in the Holbach circle, had a conception of historical *ricorsi,* inherited from Vico, that precluded any enduring absolute good. Nicolas Boulanger, that strange engineer and explicator of myths, for whom Diderot entertained a deep affection, expounded a similar doctrine, rich with antediluvian illustrations.

Voltaire was not averse to playing with the idea of a highly civilized society composed of a small number of philosophical adepts living together in "some little corner of the earth."[3] After the condemnation of the Chevalier de la Barre for sacrilege in 1766, the septuagenarian philosophe, in one of his periodic depressions, kept recurring to this fantasy in letters to his friend Etienne Noël Damilaville: "This is my romance; it is my misfortune that the romance is not a true history."[4] He even went so far as to propose the founding of a society of philosophes on Frederick II's lands in Cleves. The King gave his consent to what he thought was a jest, stipulating that the philosophes would have to be reasonable, observe the rules of decency in their writings, and preserve the peace. Nothing came of the plan, which had acquired a code name and was embroidered with mystificatory paraphernalia that delighted Voltaire. For Frederick, it was an opportunity to deliver himself of sardonic reflections on the people and the philosophes who pretended to guide them to reason. "Rest assured," he wrote on September 13, 1766, to his fellow monarch at Ferney, "if *philosophes* founded a government, at the end of half a century the people would have fashioned new superstitions for themselves and would have fixed their worship on some object or other that struck their fancy; or they would make little idols; or they would revere the graves of their founders; or they would invoke the sun; or a similar absurdity would triumph over the pure and simple cult of the Supreme Being. Superstition is a weakness of the human mind; it is innate in the creature. It always has been and always will be."[5]

The Encyclopedists were willing to work for reform as philosophes, but as disabused philosophes, not starry-eyed zealots. They had diagnosed the contradictions inherent in static egalitarian systems such as those of the Anabaptists or frozen hierarchies after the manner of Plato's *Republic* (generally a bête-noire in their writings). In *An Enquiry concerning the Principles of Morals* their friend David Hume has a brief passage in which, with his customary acumen, the feasibility of community of property is exploded; and the article "Equality" in the *Encyclopédie*, after expressing adherence to the principle of natural equality, recoils with abhorrence from the prospect of a state of complete equality in civilized societies. The philosophes tried to influence sovereigns because they had the power to do good, but, in general, forms of government did not preoccupy them excessively, even though they occasionally expressed predilections based on their personal experiences. There is an argument in favor of republican government that rests on the rarity with which sovereigns of genius like Catherine the Great emerge in a hereditary line—Diderot forthrightly told her so in their private conversations in the palace as he slapped her thigh to emphasize the point. To raise these preferences into a system would have violated the spirit of the philosophes. They were anything but democrats, those adulators of Socrates whom a democracy had condemned to death. Mob rule or anarchy would be far worse for the philosophes than tyranny—this proposition holds for the whole line beginning with Montesquieu. The comparative tranquillity of absolute government regulated by laws was for many the best available form for their purposes, and that was hardly utopia.

The frenetic enthusiasm of the millenarian Anabaptists repelled the ironic philosophes, and they would have felt the same about the revolutionaries of the Terror had they lived long enough to witness their massacres. The Reformation had stifled the spirit of the early Thomas More, which still allowed for the cohabitation of wit and utopia. The supposedly perfect society of the Deuteronomic Israelites and their cruel laws were fresh in the memories of the philosophes. Most of them were too disorderly in their personal lives, despite regular protestations of virtue—inconsistencies of behavior were glossed over by their much-vaunted sincerity—to favor the closed system of a traditional utopia of static sameness. Utopias resembled Christian heaven too much for the taste of the philosophes. Life was mixed, an amalgam of pain and pleasure in tenuous balance, Voltaire had written in his attack on Pascal. The state of utopian happiness, of calm tranquillity unpunctuated by the intrusion of intense pleasures, was a bore, monotonous, like a Christian paradise crowded with saints.

Diderot the Incorrigible

More than any other figure of the Enlightenment Denis Diderot epitomized the dilemmas that the idea of an enduring optimum republic raised for the philosophes.

In an imaginary conversation with Grimm inserted in the *Salon* of 1767, Diderot posed once again the perennial question of the influence of luxury on the fine arts and then moved on to a "Satire against Luxury after the manner of Persius" that far transcended the bounds of the subject with which he had begun.[6] Diderot juggles the problems of an ideal society in his usual scintillating style. Through negating a succession of utopianized historical societies of Western culture, he finally comes back to his own safe and sound position, an eyrie with limited horizons. Only we do not quite believe him because we know he will not remain there. The dialogue with his alter ego goes far toward defining the doubts that he experienced—at that instant at least.

Diderot twitted his other self for his jaundiced view of the diverse historical societies of the human species. There was nothing for his disenchantment but to retrieve the golden age. Not at all, answered the other Diderot. The romantic eighteenth-century version of the pastoral was accepted as the description of the golden age and then knocked on the head. Diderot was no advocate of a life passed sighing at the feet of a shepherdess; he wanted a real world for man and that entailed work and suffering. On the face of it, this appeared to be a resignation to the awesome verdict of the Jehovah of Genesis, but Diderot was moved by reflections of another order. He was not heeding a divine commandment, merely acting as a secular physician. In a state of nature, derived from Hesiod's golden age, in which produce came forth *automate* and the branch arched itself to extend its fruit within human reach, man would become a *fainéant*. And, may the poets forgive him, *fainéant* spelled wicked. Whatever else would go on in Diderot's ideal society, all men had to work. While the condemnation of idleness was not stamped with the religious intensity of a Protestant ethic, it was supported by the observation that those men in society who did nothing became mean-spirited. Unrelieved leisure was dangerous. Leisure, the Aristotelian prerequisite for the philosophical free citizen, was rejected. A man had to achieve something to be able to live. Freud in the same spirit would later declare *leisten* ("to achieve"), a word sometimes wrongly translated as "to work," one of the two pillars of life (the other was *lieben*). As for the milk and honey of the golden age—with fine impartiality Diderot mixed a promise from the book of Joshua with the golden age of Greek and Latin poetry—he himself could never have endured it. Milk would aggravate his biliousness and honey was cloying.

Since he had refused the golden age, his interlocutor mockingly offered him savagery, an even earlier stage in the eighteenth-century image of anthropological history. Let him undress naked, follow the advice of Rousseau, and become a savage. Rousseau never made any such proposal in the *Discourse on Inequality*, but for the moment Diderot picked up the challenge in jesting support of the position imputed to him. Savagery would surely be a better condition than the present so-called happy state of society. Diderot cited Rousseau's dictum that in savagery there would be only natural inequalities among nature's children. The primeval forests did not resound with the plaints that numberless evils now forced men to pour forth in anguish.

When Diderot could not really be seduced by Rousseau's utopia of savagery, in desperation Diderot's double tried another tack. If he would not tolerate either the golden age or savagery, what about the Spartans' ideal and their much-extolled customs? Under such a rule men would not be choked with the gold, the sumptuous meals, the elaborate furniture of present-day society that wounded Diderot's sensibilities. (Diderot was not above insinuating that the philosophes were anything but indifferent to the luxuries of Baron d'Holbach's table.) Alas, the Spartan utopia too had to be bypassed. Diderot's tender feelings of humanity could not endure the spectacle of those armed monks, and his heart overflowed with compassion at the sight of the miserable Helots. The tyranny of an American colonial slave-master was less cruel.

Diderot was laughingly offered the age of early Rome, when great warriors tilled the soil and hung their helmets on the horns of their cattle. He could not belittle those noble Romans, but he quailed before the lurid vision of imperial Rome wallowing in luxury, with the whole universe under the heel of its tyranny. "That is not my home." The Diderots did not even bother to raise the revolting image of a Christian medieval century. Where then? What should be their spiritual haven? The bewilderment persisted. "I no longer know in which age, in which century, in which corner of the earth, to place you."[7]

A proposed solution was to love one's country and one's contemporaries, to accept the existing order for better or for worse. If it had defects, one had to rely upon its rulers to remedy them. But how could Diderot endure this order? How stay and watch a people that presumed to be civilized put up state offices for sale? In a tirade against venality, Diderot made of that fault the symbol of the whole of France, a world consecrated to the worship of gold that ruined moral character in all ranks of society from the highest to the lowest. The pursuit of luxury bought by gold became the dominant drive of existence and determined the moral nature of the whole.

Ah, but did not luxury permit the flowering of the arts? Bah! Who cared for the arts if gold destroyed love in the family and made of all men enemies? Perhaps there was a way out. If agriculture were accorded its true worth, then riches would be evenly distributed, not concentrated, leading to widespread prosperity. But this would require a new social outlook in which offices could not be bought but would be the reward of merit and virtue. To the hackneyed argument that the accumulation of wealth in a few hands was necessary for the preservation of luxury and the arts, Diderot responded with a new economic version of the circular theory of history. Destiny, which rules the world, decrees that all must pass. The happiest condition of man, of a state, has its limits. Everything bears within itself a secret seed of its destruction. Agriculture, beneficent agriculture, admits Diderot turned Physiocrat, fosters commerce, industry, and riches, and riches generate population increases. A great increase in population causes fortunes to be divided. Divided fortunes restrict the sciences and the arts to the useful. Everything that is not useful is disdained. Time is too precious to be employed in idle speculations. Is anyone concerned about the grand monuments that have never been built? Does happiness reside in them? "Virtue, virtue, wisdom, morals, the love of children for their parents, of parents for their children, the solicitude of a sovereign for his subjects, of his subjects for their sovereign, good laws, good education, general well-being—that, that, is what I hope for. Show me the country where these real advantages are enjoyed and I will go there, even if it be as remote as China."[8]

On second thought, however, Diderot could not wholeheartedly embrace the popular eighteenth-century idealization of China. Even that sublime society had its shortcomings. "Cunning, bad faith, no great virtue, no heroism, a mass of petty vices, children of the commercial spirit and the litigious life. Where then shall I go? Where will I find a state of constant happiness? Here, a luxury masking wretchedness, there, a luxury that, born of superfluity, produces only a passing felicity. Where, then, shall I be born or live? Where is the home that promises me and my posterity lasting happiness?"[9] The final resolution is even more paradoxical and fragile than his first tentative proposal. "Go where evils exacerbated to the extreme are about to yield to a better order of things. Wait until affairs are righted and then enjoy that moment . . . My posterity? You are a madman. You look too far ahead. What were you to your ancestors four centuries ago? Nothing. Regard with the same eye the creatures that are to come into being at a time equally distant from you. Be happy. Your descendants will become whatever it pleases destiny, which disposes of all. In the state, Heaven raises a master who reforms or destroys; in the cycle of races, a descendant who restores or overthrows. This is the immutable decree of nature. Submit to it."[10]

Two years later Diderot was in a different mood. A monk called Dom Deschamps who was a fellow guest at a dinner party had presented a treatise laying the foundations of a communist utopia. It was one of the most violent and original works Diderot had ever seen. All at once there was unveiled before him a social state that mankind reached by abandoning the state of savagery, passing through the civil state, and coming into a new society where one realized the vanity of everything one had most valued. The human species would remain miserable as long as there were kings, priests, magistrates, laws, a mine and a thine, words connoting vices and virtues. "Imagine how much this work, badly written though it is, must have pleased me," he wrote a friend, "Suddenly I found myself in the world for which I was born."[11]

Coming home from the encounter, Diderot had a utopian experience. He began to dream about the implications of the principles propounded by the corpulent Benedictine with the manner and tone of an ancient philosopher. There was not a line he would alter in the entire bookful of bold assertions. His friend d'Alembert, who knew about the book, hardly shared his enthusiasm, but Diderot readily explained this reluctance as professional deformation. Geometers like d'Alembert were always bad metaphysicians as they were bad gamblers. In the understanding of nature as in successful gambling one had to have presentiments of things to come that were not amenable to calculation. One had to feel them. Geometers made bad politicians, too, because they had no nose for discovering and tracking the scent of fugitive phenomena that could not be formulated in terms of x and y.

Sophie Volland got an even more circumstantial report of the meeting with Dom Deschamps. Diderot was then at the height of his powers, engaged in writing his most daring dialogue, *D'Alembert's Dream,* in which philosophical conceptions were put into the mouth of a dreaming man, a neat trick, if he had to say so himself. It may well be that the encounter with Dom Deschamps encouraged Diderot to record some of his own extravagant notions, such as the famous aperçus about the different animal species that had preceded the men of his time and those that would succeed them. Dom Deschamps and the fellow monk who accompanied him to dinner were a continual source of astonishment to Diderot. After the atheistic treatise had been read, he was informed that theirs was common doctrine in the cloister of their abbey. The pair of atheistic monks were big shots (*gros bonnets*) in their house, but they displayed wit, gaiety, and learning, and he wagered that they would perform their duties punctiliously. What most amused Diderot were the efforts of the apostle of materialism to find sanction for his theories in the eternal order of things. Apparently Dom Deschamps was convinced that his system conformed to what was most sacred and that it would not lead him into difficulties. Diderot thought a single line of it enough for burning.[12] Dom Deschamps was in quest of a convert, a philosophe who would sponsor his "true system" before the public. After a number of meetings full of good cheer, with Diderot doing most of the talking, the Benedictine disappeared from view.

A letter received by Diderot from the cultivated Scottish artist Allan Ramsay—Diderot said he painted badly but reasoned well—about Beccaria's little book on crimes and punishments is further confirmation of the ambivalence with which any bold plan of reconstruction like the revamping of the penal system was received. Ramsay classified Beccaria's work as a utopia and mocked the contract theory that underlay it, arguing that society was the rule of the strong, that reform was at best an effort on the part of those imbued with a feeling of benevolence to persuade the mighty to alleviate some of the more extreme punishments they inflicted in order to secure their necessary domination. Punishments were in fact to be measured not by the severity of the crime, but by the degree of security a state enjoyed, and this was extraordinarily varied in London, Paris, and Constantinople. Ramsay's letter, preserved only in Diderot's translation, was an attack against the espousal of revolutionary means to bring about a utopian condition. For the present generation a violent revolutionary transformation would be a strange madness. Whether this great misfortune would have compensation in the well-being of future generations was most uncertain. Speculative utopias like Beccaria's were akin to Plato's Republic. They demonstrated the intelligence, humanity, and goodness of their authors but could have no influence on contemporary affairs. Instead of such speculations Ramsay proposed "experimental knowledge" and study of existing governments, the interest of their leaders, their security.[13] Diderot apparently thought Ramsay's strictures merited serious consideration and prepared a French version, but refrained from sending it off to Beccaria because he believed him too sensitive.[14]

Scornfully dismissing the Abbé Morellet's plans for economic reform Diderot could use utopian terminology pejoratively, as did Ramsay, Grimm, and other philosophes: "Stick all your fine pages in a utopia."[15] But in 1774, in a notebook meant only for the eyes of Catherine II, he sketched a utopian plan of his own, a strategy for the institution of a peaceful revolution in human values. As Catherine's adviser on the creation of an ideal free society, Diderot revived once again the fantasy of Plato on his journey to Sicily. "If I had to mold a nation to liberty, what would I do?" he asked himself, and responded, "I would plant in its midst a colony of free men, very free, like the Swiss, for example, and I would meticulously preserve their liberties. The rest I would leave to time and to their example . . . Slowly this precious yeast would change the whole mass and its spirit would become the general spirit."[16] The idea that utopia would be generated by contagion from a single successful example had a long prehistory before it became the fixed tactic of Fourierism and Owenism. Diderot's notion of utopian imitation was restated in Fourier's work, but the organization of Diderot's "colony" was *toto caelo* different from the obsessive heaping up of detailed procedures and techniques that would characterize the phalanstery. If Diderot's free men in a colony were allowed simply to go their own way, freedom would emanate from them. Philosophes would teach by example, but Diderot was too close to a kind of loose anarchic utopia to counsel minute and stringent regulations. His was a fantasy of the secular preaching of philosophical virtue, without resort either to political power imposed by an enlightened despot or to revolutionary action and mob violence. If the philosophes recognized the underlying failure and hypocrisy of the Church in its attempt to convert through force, they would follow a different path. Under no circumstances would they imitate the bestial tactics of the Inquisition or compel conversions. Preaching the word without raising the sword, a commitment to nonviolence (in theory at least)—that was the way.

Despite the absence of an article on utopia in the *Encyclopédie* and Diderot's frequent mockery of utopianizing, there is a sense in which a utopian idea, bearing resemblance to the proposal he submitted to Catherine, lay behind the whole ambitious enterprise: the belief that a small band of men of good will, learned and moderately zealous, through the propagation of ideas on the sciences, arts, and trades could serve as a leaven to raise the general consciousness of their society. Their discussions were deliberate attempts to mold public opinion and—allowance made for interludes of doubt—they believed in the power of secular matters of fact to alter human behavior. There had been cells of fixated monomaniacs often enough before; the group around Diderot appeared to be relatively free of the crippling symptoms of obsession. Their neuroses were under control. They worked hard on their design and at the same time enjoyed themselves; they did not reach the level of intoxication where egos merge into an all-consuming general will. At the beginning the philosophes were less torn by misgivings than the Erasmian humanists of the sixteenth century. Nor were they possessed like the Rosicrucian mystificators, drunk with a Pansophic vision of the direct and immediate general reformation of mankind. They were surely not a closed conspiracy to seize power for themselves or a social class, their playful cabals notwithstanding. They were neither so pompous nor so acerb to one another as members of the Vienna psychoanalytic society clustered around Freud in the first decade of the twentieth century. And they were far more balanced than, say, the Bloomsbury circle in London.

For a precious while, contributing to the *Encyclopédie* and belonging to the Holbachian synagogue was itself a utopia. Its members were living in an Elysium of their imagination while working to win the plaudits of future generations. They were attacked as a sect by their enemies. In a way, they were inhabiting their island of Lampedusa in Paris and its environs. A certain ease, generosity, openness, a tolerance of inconsistency among themselves, saved them from the punitive spirit of a Protestant sect, and the fanatic revolutionary utopian spirit was still unborn—Babeuf and the future Jacobin leaders reached maturity as the old philosophes began to die off. Theirs was a fortunate moment: they experienced their utopia and could make fun of it, too. They were not without nails with which to scratch at one another and they recognized a certain pleasure in the occasional flick of a whip, but their weaponry should be distinguished from the fangs of future utopian activists. All men grow nails and most deliberately pare them. The claws of revolutionary utopian sectarians have come to represent something quite different.

It is strange that in the eighteenth century Morelly's *Code de la nature* was attributed to Diderot. He wrote nothing in the inflexible, static temper of this utopia. Diderot was forever dialoguing about ideal states, the better and the worse; his philosophical evolutionary biology would have excluded Morelly's type of fixity and control. Diderot was by temperament a noninterventionist. He could even voice misgivings about the difficulties created when an original seed like the son of Rameau's nephew was tampered with through education. Rousseau was the interventionist, the manipulator of Emile. Diderot would let things take their course. A refreshing anarchist streak made him leery of too much interference, at least on most occasions.

In the course of his life Diderot assembled a whole bag of instruments for the conversion of mankind to philosophy, many of them childishly naive. Since he loved the theatre, he proposed making the stage a pulpit from which the actor, raised to an exalted status, would proclaim great truths that inculcated virtue. The teachings of the actor-playwright, a new apostle, would be sweet and easy to imbibe. Actually, many of the authors of dreary eighteenth-century novelistic utopias were moved by similar notions. Since truth and virtue could not be instilled as dry philosophical principles, the *dolce* had to be injected to make more palatable the rationally *utile,* the true and the virtuous. A few philosophical principles could be stealthily introduced, while the narrative was padded with exciting adventure stories, much love interest, the suspense of shipwrecks and sudden confrontations with savage peoples.

When Diderot in the *Entretiens sur le fils naturel* elevated the actor to the new moral priesthood, he prefigured the Saint-Simonian gospel of the social role of the artist in educating mankind, a rival to the priest-scientist of Bacon's *New Atlantis*. His first visits to the theatre as a young man had encouraged Diderot to daydream of wresting virtue from the bigots, sourpusses, and all those dedicated to a cult of pain and self-denial. If only Christianity had been a religion of sensual rather than spiritual love, if a Magdalen had appealed to one side of Christ's nature and the buttocks of John the well-beloved to another, what a religion of joyous virtue would have been granted to mankind: The theatre would have become a temple of virtue. When Dorval, one of the protagonists of the dialogue, attended a play, he was grieved as he compared the potential usefulness of theatres with the feeble efforts devoted to the training of dramatic companies. He exclaimed: "If we ever go to Lampedusa to found, far from shore, amid the waves of the sea, a small, happy people, there we shall have our preachers, and we will be careful to choose them in accordance with the importance of their ministry. All peoples have their sabbaths and we shall also have ours. On those solemn days we will perform a fine tragedy to teach men to beware of the passions; a good comedy, to instruct them in their duties and inspire them to like them." [17]

Perhaps in his *Observations sur Garrick* Diderot struck the note that best expressed his middling position about the social order. In a well-arranged society individual rights and the good of the whole were orchestrated. The individual had to be subordinated, but the proper degree of subordination would be determined by the upright man himself. There is an analogy with the great actor who knows exactly how much of his individuality must be restrained for the benefit of the whole ensemble. In the theatre the actor with a cool head, in society the upright man—they alone are capable of measuring the necessary sacrifice. Diderot is the great exponent of spontaneity in behavior. He would have us believe that he follows his pen wherever it flows. No good society can be happy without the free self-expression of human beings like himself; on the other hand, no society can endure without harmony and controls. On the stage, the poised actor knows how to manipulate himself in the very midst of his passionate outbursts. In society, the wise man plays a similar role. [18]

But this sounds too pat. In a fragment labeled *Le Temple du bonheur* Diderot unveiled himself with less discretion. He had been in the company of the witty, skeptical Abbé Galiani on Holbach's estate. Galiani's exasperated announcement that if he had to spend another quarter of an hour in the country he would throw himself into the canal near the Château du Grand-Val led Diderot to conclude that one man's happiness was not another's. Treatises on happiness disgusted him—and this included utopias, too, because they were merely accounts of the particular happiness of those who wrote them. About his own view of happiness he was appropriately ambivalent. On the one hand, he recognized in himself a fervent intellectual commitment to convincing men that to be happy in this world they had to be virtuous, a word that in his lexicon involved a composite of attributes: benevolent, kind, gentle, full of empathy, sociable, causing no harm to one's neighbor. And one part of Diderot adhered to this conception of virtue as it was expounded by *moi,* the philosopher in the dialogue with Rameau's nephew. Diderot was aware that this was a social gospel; he had to engage himself in demonstrating his inner conviction to others, in teaching.

On the other hand, men simply would not accept his premise that to be happy they had to be virtuous. Instead, they were prey to their dominant passions or vices: They ran madly after women, they were possessed by avarice or ambition. If denied satisfaction, they sank into wretchedness; but if appeased, did not the consequences of their unbridled desires ultimately render them more unhappy than if they had reined them in? "Upon my word, *je n'en sais rien.* Every day I see men who would rather die than reform themselves." [19] Diderot realized that true virtue and true happiness could be attained only in a devilishly ideal condition—a state without a king, judge, priests, laws, mine and thine, movable or immovable property, or distinction between virtues and vices. There was no resolution of his dilemma. It made it impossible for him either to embrace or abandon a utopian vision. Like a swallow he flew back and forth between the utopia of Lampedusa and the counter-utopian present, from which there was no real escape because of the very nature of things.

By October 1773 Diderot was ready to accept the repose of the valetudinarian. Like Grimm, who had promised himself a long stay on earth and expected it to be brilliant, honored, dazzling, respected, exciting, he wanted to make a splash. "I have done it," he wrote his wife, "I am still doing it. Now the time for rest, tranquillity, silence, withdrawal, obscurity, being forgotten, has come . . . Nothing is more absurd than an agitated old age. The soul of an old man should sit in his body the way his body sits in his armchair. The soul, the body, and the armchair then make a good, well-integrated machine."[20] Could Diderot ever really endure repose? At sixty, he still had fantasies of going to China, Constantinople, Carthage, Italy. The eye was not yet full. But he returned home from Russia the sensible way.

The *Encyclopédie* article "Happiness" holds forth on the insipidness of an enduring state of pleasant tranquillity that is not interrupted by intoxicating transports of pure passion. Unfortunately the human condition cannot tolerate the perpetual infiltration of violent pleasures, and the most perfect happiness we can hope to achieve in this life is a state of tranquillity broken here and there by a few pleasures. A straightfaced medical piece, "Penis," is even more to the point: "Without an erection it is impossible to launch and to lodge the seed in the place that was destined by nature. If this erection were perpetual or constant it would be virtually impossible to safeguard it from injuries, not to speak of the loss of desire that would be a consequence of a constant erection."[21] The Christian utopia was an unaltered state, a contradiction of man's biological and moral nature.

Neither the aging Diderot, nor the old Voltaire, nor the withdrawn Rousseau wanted to upheave their society and establish a wholly new order. Perhaps Diderot kept up the militant pose longer in salon talk—he was ever the enfant terrible. He was really more at home at Baron d'Holbach's sumptuous table, denouncing priests. Life was intimacy for Diderot—family feelings, quarrels, gentle play; even with strangers he drove right to the heart of their personal existence. Utopias are distant, cold, general; nobody jokes, asks after one's health, talks about the colic. Nothing could have been less congenial to him. A dialogue with a *Diogenes redivivus,* yes; but not with the awesome head of Salomon's house on New Atlantis. There was something too solemn about most utopias; it was not his genre. The *Supplément au voyage de Bougainville* was a plea for the alleviation of repressive Western laws governing sexual relations (not their abolition) on the ground that there were some physical acts that entailed no moral consequences. (Though completed early in 1773, this charming dialogue was not available until years after his death.) Diderot was never of one mind; his reason and his fantasy moved in different directions. He did not write his dialogue between a Catholic chaplain and a Tahitian to depict an ideal society for Europeans, though his artistry led him to create the atmosphere of an exotic idyll that we may now read as a primitivist utopia. Everything is there: antique simplicity, philosophical reverie of otherness, the sheer delight of imagining what life could be like in Tahiti, indignation at the severity of sexual restraints in European marriage, whose bonds Diderot had broken, though perhaps not so often as he would have wished. And now that he saw age approaching, there was an element of plain sexual fantasy—Diderot-David yearning for young girls. But he was far too sensible to conceive of a Tahitian utopia on the Left Bank of Paris.

If the philosophes were suspicious of the *esprit de système* in abstract philosophy, a fortiori a rigidly framed social system could not enjoy their confidence.

There is no systematic theory of history, no dogmatic political doctrine, and no fixed utopia in Diderot; and his general attitude, despite occasional exceptions, was shared by most of his collaborators on the *Encyclopédie*. If the cornerstone of the seventeenth-century utopia was a Christian Pansophia, with its creation of a common European philosophical language and an ordered, hierarchized body of knowledge leading to God that would enjoy universal comprehension and consent—vide Alsted's completed and Comenius' abortive encyclopedic projects—Diderot satirically distorted this prospect of cohesion and uniformity. He favored an alphabetical arrangement for knowledge in the titanic enterprise to which he devoted his middle years. The Encyclopedists exulted in the achievements of the arts and sciences since the Renaissance, but no member of the Baron d'Holbach's *synagogue,* as their circle was called, believed in the feasibility of either an integrated corpus of all thought or a perfect society.

A chasm separates Rousseau from his quondam friends: He did have a utopia and a political absolute and a hypothetical history of the human species. History in the *Encyclopédie* is a minor form of knowledge, part of the art of memory, not a rational science. The major uses of history have been abuses —outstandingly, the faked "historical proofs" that supported the positive religions. Knowledge in politics, unlike the physical sciences, was always contingent and conjectural (the adjectives are Diderot's). We must await Condorcet, the very last of the philosophes, who moves into the revolutionary era, for a futurist utopia founded upon what he called *sciences sociales* in the Tenth Epoch of the *Esquisse* and in the *Fragment on the New Atlantis.*

Most of the philosophes had been co-opted by the political establishment, they and their ideas. When they dined with the great, they were no longer dangerous men, and by the end of the ancien régime the mighty of the earth came to use their philosophical vocabulary and rhetoric. Everyone, including Louis XVI in his decrees of the 1780s, adopted the language of "humanity." Voltaire was borne in triumph, his bust crowned on the stage of the *Théâtre français;* Diderot's home town erected a statue in his honor, much to the disgust of his brother, a priest; Rousseau died in the bosom of the nobility. Good Turgot had even had an opportunity to form a brief philosophical ministry, in the course of which he was, alas, forced to hang bread rioters. The American War of Independence made it fashionable to extol those philosophical transatlantic natural men either from across the sea or in the person of Benjamin Franklin when he was an American commissioner in Paris. In supporting the insurgents the Encyclopedists idealized them in some measure, ignorant as they were of the profound internal social conflicts within the newly independent states. As for the American Founding Fathers themselves, they were by no means utopians, as debates over the framing of the Constitution disclose. John Adams filled the margins of the French books he acquired in Paris with attacks on Rousseau's state of nature—he knew what Indians were really like—and he ridiculed Condorcet's idea of progress.

The Uses of the Noble Savage

Throughout the Enlightenment the utopia of the noble savage, one of the great myths of modern times inherited from the classical world, remained a prickly subject among the philosophes. The "naked philosophers" of America were fixtures of much eighteenth-century thought; but there was no greater consensus in their portrayal than there had been in European literature ever since the first discoveries. Savages, dummies adorned with feathers and beads for the ventriloquist philosophers of the rue Saint-Jacques, could deliver moral harangues on the major themes of Stoicism and Epicureanism, or they could be viewed as sexually degenerate and miserable victims of the monstrous superstitions of their own fanatical priests and kings, or they could be noble men of nature, or they were creatures reduced to a pitiable state by vicious conquerors from Europe. There were witnesses from afar to the practices of ferocious and anthropophagous tribes who, we are informed in the *Encyclopédie*'s authoritative article on savages, still inhabited most parts of the Americas. The New World was an amorphous ink blot onto which writers could project their terrors of the wild and of the unknown primitive, as well as their hopes for a less repressive, freer way of life—sometimes on the same page. Europeans have often faced the pre-Conquest natives with anguished, conflicting emotions, feelings that have been carried over into white attitudes toward blacks to this day. One idealizes and diabolizes in the same breath.

A dominant preconception of the age common to Jesuits and David Hume held that the primitives were incapable of abstract reasoning; they had only concrete images and immediate fears. But there were also currents of philobarbarism, admiration for the powerful imagination of the primitives, their stoic virtue, their indifference to luxury. What later became the heart of the nineteenth-century utopian ideal, the simultaneous development of all human capacities, rationalist and imaginative, was called into question. If there was a stadial evolution of the consciousness of mankind—and notions of this sort in embryo are in Vico, in Turgot, and in the English philosophers—the philosophes identified change from one stage of the cycle to another with loss as well as gain. Hence their profound ambivalence toward the primitive. They despised him and they longed for his idealized state, a war in the breast of man from which he is not likely to be emancipated as long as the myth of the noble savage has a breath of life.

Voltaire, who mocked the simple, primitive life, made a counter-utopia out of the American savage condition. If the Mexicans and the Indians were massacred by the conquistadores, it was all to the good—better for mankind to exterminate these bestial peoples addicted to bloody sacrifices. When Voltaire condemned the European seizure of the American continents, it was not out of sympathy with the Indians for the sufferings inflicted upon them, but out of bitterness over the waste of energies on the desolate places they inhabited. Such vital forces might have been spent to better advantage at home. About the only American settlement he admired without qualification was the Jesuits' establishment in Paraguay, because they had succeeded in taming the savages at minimal cost in lives and money. The lot of the inmates of what came to be the Paraguayan utopia was a subject of perennial controversy in the eighteenth century—either you could see them as living in bondage to Jesuit overlords who luxuriated at their expense and filled the coffers of the order with the surplus from their labor, or you could admire the Jesuits for abolishing barbarism and establishing a regime of law, order, communal living, and happiness. The Paraguayan community could become the exemplar of a successful utopia in practice, a positive image that recurred in socialist literature of the nineteenth century from Charles Fourier on. The Jesuit experiment purportedly demonstrated that "community" was possible, just as did the Herrnhut settlement of the Moravian Brethren.

For Voltaire, whatever happiness men could attain—and limitations were inherent in the nature of things—was a consequence of civilization. He had nothing but disdain for the attempt of another Jesuit, Lafitau, who had labored in North America, to identify the Iroquois with Homeric heroes. In evident ridicule of Rousseau, in the introduction to the *Essai sur les moeurs* Voltaire asked rhetorically: "Do you mean by savages two-footed animals walking on their hands in their distress, isolated, roaming the forests, *salvatici, selvaggi,* mating by chance, forgetting the women to whom they were united, recognizing neither their sons nor their fathers, living as beasts without either the resources or the instincts of beasts? Some have written that this is the true state of man and that we have done nothing but degenerate into wretches since we left it. I do not believe that this solitary existence ascribed to our ancestors is true to human nature."[22] Voltaire's riposte to Rousseau's *Discours* is well known: "Thanks for your letter against the human species."

But then, on other occasions, for polemical purposes Voltaire could judge the subhuman condition of the savages to be superior to that of the European wretches who labored for others like animals, they knew not why, watched religious ceremonies they could not conceivably understand, and went off to war to get killed for reasons beyond their comprehension. Since the American Indians were "free," they had some advantage over the European beasts of burden in human shape; but their way of life was far from utopian. When Voltaire ransacked the literary stockpile for an authentic portrait of native Americans, he chose the one sketched in the Abbé de Pauw's *Recherches philosophiques sur les Américains* (Berlin, 1768–69), where Rousseau's thesis on the state of nature was stood on its head. Before the coming of the Europeans the savages were impotent and enfeebled and, if anything, their state had since improved.

Perhaps the works of the professional scientist-explorers of the eighteenth century contain the most telling examples of the moral dilemmas presented by the existence of the savage. While the generalizers who never left Paris in their innocence tended to lump together all the savages north and south and did not draw lines between the sedentary village societies of Mexico and Peru and those of the Plains Indians or the Caribs, the scientists who undertook long voyages were usually better informed. Nonetheless, the great naturalist La Condamine in his circumstantial description of the Indians in *Relation abrégée d'un voyage fait dans l'intérieure de l'Amérique Méridionale* (Paris, 1745) had arrived at the same conclusion as Voltaire: man in the state of nature was a mere brute. Bougainville, who circumnavigated the globe and left a record of his experiences, was in many ways the best of the realistic philosophical voyagers in the new eighteenth-century style. He had all the requisites—science, courage, a keen eye—and he was close to d'Alembert, who had taught him mathematics. He was no admirer of Rousseau and travelers who made the facts conform to their imaginings. Bougainville landed in Paraguay just when the Jesuits were being expelled. From a distance he had participated in the general appreciation of this peaceful, laborious society, holding everything in common; here were happy savages knowing neither riches nor poverty. But he soon learned that the Jesuit practice had been a far cry from the theory. On-the-spot inquiries led him to a very different evaluation. The Indians had been so tyrannized and terrified by the Jesuit Fathers that for minor infractions of the rules adults allowed themselves to be whipped like schoolboys. The hours of work and rest were so meticulously regulated by the clock that their whole existence was rendered monotonous. They were so overwhelmed with tedium that they died without regret, never having lived. The philosopher's calm felicity had to be punctuated from time to time by intense pleasure if happiness was to be attained. The lackluster attitude of the Paraguayans was a warning that there were bounds to the uses of an orderly, planned existence. Such negative aspects of utopia had been pointed out before, by Raguet, for example, a little-known continuator and critic of Bacon's *New Atlantis;* and the reappearance of this dystopian psychological argument in the latter part of the eighteenth century is not astonishing. Bougainville also learned that the Jesuits, who wanted to control the innermost thoughts of their Indians, had organized a system of espionage and secret surveillance from which there was no escape. The evils of a totally regulated society were clearly perceived by this worldly eighteenth-century ship's captain. The Jesuits, the learned Bougainville observed, had ample precedent for their system both in their own order and in the writings of an ancient proponent of a meticulously supervised republic, Plato, in the *Laws,* where a nocturnal, punitive council of elders manipulated a similar information network.[23]

After Bougainville had visited Tahiti, he once again bore witness to the flaws in what, at first sight, appeared to be a paradisaical utopia. When he entered the harbor, beautiful naked maidens who clambered aboard his ship, driving his young seamen mad with excitement, made him forget for a moment his scientific mission; at the sight of the gentle landscape and the profusion of Venuses, he dredged up the description of Eden in Genesis and Ovid's golden age and Anacreon in rapid succession. But after a time, realistic observation stained the image of perfection and beatitude. There were two races in Tahitian society and the "great ones" exercised the power of life and death over the common people. (Meat and fish were reserved for the magnates.) The inhabitants were in a state of perpetual warfare with tribes on other islands, and they suffered from venereal diseases.[24] Manifestly, Diderot had expurgated Bougainville's original account in a radical manner when he extolled the ways of Tahitian society in his fanciful *Supplément au voyage de Bougainville.*

The ambivalence of the philosophes to the state-of-nature utopia is most forcefully illustrated, toward the close of the ancien régime, in the Abbé Raynal's voluminous *Histoire philosophique des deux Indes,* one of the most widely read works of the period if the book-counters are to be credited. He summarized the body of travel literature and used it as the basis for a slashing indictment of the Europeans as destroyers of whole peoples, a veritable chronicle of genocide. But Raynal was no worshiper of the state of nature. His appraisal of the primitive way of life was in many respects the normative one for the Encyclopedists, full of inconsistencies. Sometimes his views are painfully Emersonian, to take refuge in an anachronism. "Ranging from the most bestial state of nature to the highest state of civilization, things seem to balance each other out, more or less—the vices and the virtues, the physical goods and the evils. In the forests as well as in society, the happiness of one individual may be more or less great than that of another. But I suspect that nature has imposed limits on the possibilities open to agglomerations of human beings, beyond which there is about as much happiness to lose as to gain."[25]

Then, in a passage of Book IV of his *Histoire philosophique* Raynal advanced a perceptive hypothesis to account for the popularity of the image of the noble contented savage of the New World who led a hard, Spartan existence. This portrait, he conjectured, was put together by philosophers to console those Europeans who had to endure as tough a life as the Indians. The depiction of the savages leading a rugged existence, struggling for survival, yet happy, also served to salve the consciences of the rich and the aristocratic in the enjoyment of their ease amid poverty-stricken compatriots. The savages were, after all, healthy and satisfied with their lot even as European peasants were, or at least should be. By a curious dialectic—he did not use the term—the savage utopia of the travel literature was turned into a justification of the existing power relations of society. Jean-Jacques's return-to-nature utopia, to which the aristocrats lent so attentive an ear, was thus an apology for their domination; they had in their imaginations rendered their peasants felicitous by assimilating them to contented primitives. If only the aristocrats were as fortunate as their peasants! Raynal of course considered this reasoning specious, for he knew that poor Europeans had their life span cut short by their exertions. "Travail modéré" was healthful; excessive toil crushed.[26] And yet, Raynal reasons, the vision of the savage state, though it started as the apology of contemporary oppression, might for future generations become a great source of enlightenment. Men in advanced societies would learn that the evils they suffered were not originally present in nature, but derived from institutions created by men, from superstitions instilled by men, from deceptions propagated by men. This realization had not yet borne fruit, but the "ignorance of the savages has in a sense enlightened civilized peoples."[27] When enlightenment came, however, it would not be definitive or enduring. The faltering movement of progress toward a better future could only be compared to the effect of the wind on a weathervane.

As for the present, this was the time for demolition. The discoveries of the quasi utopia of the savages would constrain Europeans to revise their law codes, clearing a space once encumbered with the refuse of time, custom, and the sovereign authority of priests. It would become possible to delineate the form of the new structure only when the space had been rid of the debris of the old order.[28] Such outspokenness made Raynal the most daring of the original group of philosophes. The *parlement* of Paris on May 25, 1781, had condemned the *Histoire philosophique des deux Indes* as impious, blasphemous, seditious, encouraging peoples to challenge sovereign authority and destroy the fundamental principles of civil order, and in salon talk Grimm violently denounced Raynal, a former collaborator, as an incendiary. But who should then rise to his defense? The aging, unpredictable, meteoric Denis Diderot, who had, by the way, contributed many of the eloquent digressions in Raynal's work.

The old philosophes were sensitive about their dependence on nobles and rich bourgeois, and to assure themselves of their virtuousness they still uttered scandalous phrases from time to time. Dying Voltaire would not hear of that man Jesus from a special ecclesiastical emissary even at the risk of being denied decent Christian burial, which he wanted. But in general, the anticlerical fire-eaters were quite tame on political subjects. Diderot dolefully foresaw the likelihood of an end of what for him was the "revolution"—the cyclical turn that had brought forth a temporary flowering of arts and sciences in modern times, as it had in the Augustan Age. As the Revolution with a large R approached, salon boutades and slogans from dissertations originally written for learned societies were repeated in the streets with a completely new intonation by a different generation. The people and their publicists spelled out what the philosophes had vaguely implied, and everyone was confounded, not least the few surviving minor philosophes themselves, or writers like Restif who had earlier published utopias and now, with terror in their hearts, watched the people of Paris in action.

Embarkation for Nowhere

In the eighteenth century the utopian mode found its most common expression not among the sophisticated philosophes, but first and foremost in Rousseau and then among the writers of popular novels, who catered to a widespread taste for the exotic and incorporated pornographic elements in their tales. Ambiguous and complex utterances by the great writers were reduced in these novels—and moral treatises disguised as novels—to simple, unequivocal images. Despite their vulgarity and triviality, it was they, surely as much as the *patres majores,* who were responsible for the creation of a utopian ideal with which the ancien régime was contrasted, by which it was judged and found wanting.

If a historical survey of the eighteenth century were to assign space to a novelistic utopia in proportion to the estimated size of the audience it attracted among contemporaries, the largest segments would have to be devoted to Fénelon's *Avantures de Télémaque* and Schnabel's *Insel Felsenburg* (published originally 1731–1743 with the title *Wunderliche Fata Einiger Seefahrer*). Such a study would not be worth either writing or reading. Despite the efforts of that branch of the present-day French historical school that is fascinated by statistics, we do not, of course, know with any preciseness how many people read a particular best-seller in the eighteenth century—the growing role of the lending library and private borrowing are unmeasurable. It was rare for a utopian novel to be limited to a single edition, and we have some notions about numbers of copies published. Yet even if a meticulous reckoning were made of both authorized and pirated editions, major questions about the relative importance of utopian concepts would remain unresolved. Quantity, a fair index of trends in mass culture, can hardly be the sole criterion of historical judgment even when ample data are available.

Once the unity of the seventeenth-century Christian utopia of Pansophia was dead, in their attempt to fill the moral emptiness men conjured up a multiplicity of wild, even grotesque forms for the optimum republic. The utopian fantasy of Western society had lost an inner core, and in the eighteenth century utopias moved off in diverse directions. While the number of specimens increased enormously, there was no harmony among them, no recognizable focus. The formlessness of the body of popular utopian literature in this period, we can now remark with historical hindsight, is perhaps characteristic of a society approaching a breakdown. New voices are clamoring on all sides, and the utopia caters to a wide variety of tastes, many of them frivolous, bearing no relationship to the high moral purpose and earnestness of the utopias of the previous century. The dream of a reconstituted Christian world order based on science and knowledge had evaporated.

All manner of people toyed with the utopian genre, including the King of Poland, that elegant soldier of fortune the Prince de Ligne, and the great physiologist von Haller. The hero and heroine of Casanova's five-volume *Icosaméron* (1788) discover a pre-Adamite utopia among the Mégamicres, aborigines who inhabit the Protocosmus in the interior of the globe, amid flying horses, mechanical music, a form of electrical telegraphy. These fortunate people, to whom love is the substance of existence, can control lightning and are free from the scourges of flood, famine, war, and slavery. But paradoxically, the eighteenth century, which witnessed a great proliferation of what by any definition of the term would be called proper utopias, many of them gigantic and shapeless novels, did not produce a single major work in the traditional utopian form, no one document that would be for the Enlightenment what More's golden *libellus* was for the sixteenth century and the books of Andreae, Bacon, Campanella, and Comenius were for the seventeenth. There was no great English utopia; a magnificent dystopia, *Gulliver's Travels,* holds the place once occupied by More and Bacon. No German work of distinction has survived, though a four-volume compendium of utopian adventure stories, the incredibly jejune *Insel Felsenburg,* in its day sold more copies than the writings of all the philosophers of Germany combined. In the eighteenth century, utopian ideals are dispersed among a thousand works rather than encapsulated in a single masterpiece. There are new utopian motifs in the novels—the projection of an emotional state of inner harmony, a stress upon the needs of production and the centralized organization of work, an attempt to come to grips with the intricate problems of sexuality. But their artistic expression is, to say the least, undistinguished. Writers descended into the marketplace from the lofty pinnacle held by the seventeenth-century religious philosopher-utopians, who with the death of Leibniz had experienced the tragedy of total defeat. Only toward the end of the century, on one side of the Rhine in the works of the Germans Lessing, Kant, and Schiller, and on the other in those of the Frenchmen Turgot and Condorcet—all intimately related to Rousseau—were vistas leading to the grand euchronia of the nineteenth century opened wide.

Though there is no single, overarching utopia in the eighteenth century, there is a certain uniformity in the rejection of the existing order. But the denial assumes a wide variety of tones and forms, from the Naudelians of Lesconvel, whose island is merely a touched-up portrait of the centralized French monarchy, to the rigid and dogmatic egalitarian communism of property in Morelly's *Code of Nature* and Babeuf's *Manifesto of the Equals;* from the traditional patriarchal family society of most islands discovered on extraordinary voyages, to the rather personalized sexual fantasies of the Marquis de Sade and the peasant's son Restif de la Bretonne; from the Stoic republic of virtue of most of the rationalist philosophes, who were touched with skepticism of all utopia, to Rousseau's dream of a new man imbued with a love of his fellows so profound that the line between individual and general will would become blurred; from the sexually liberated women, indistinguishable from men, in Rustaing de Saint-Jory and Laclos, to the pious, submissive daughters of Fénelon's Christianized antiquity. We now cannot avoid looking at the age as a prolegomenon to the French Revolution: The psychic disarray to which the utopian fantasies bear witness bespeaks an emotional revolution prior to the political outburst. At one time or another everything in the existing order was called into question, the family, private property, sexual normality, the very definition of pain and pleasure, the Christian religion, aristocracy, reason, self-interest.

The utopias are fragmented. Men feel individual pains and they build whole societies around their obsessive manias. The panaceas are specific and particular: a new sexual code, a meritocracy, the abolition of private ownership, the end of differentiation between the sexes, a new emotional apparatus, a new synthetic religion, a vast organization of secular science that could be transmuted into moral progress. Sometimes the remedies are combined. But single or multiple, the utopian alternatives are as chaotic as the social reality. In a way, social evils appeared less critical than in the previous century—men had become accustomed to the breakdown of the Christian world order, and drifting in a sea of moral turbulence no longer seemed intolerable. With the exception of Rousseau and de Sade, the tone of the utopias is rather bland; the passion of Bacon and Leibniz, Bruno and Campanella, Andreae and Comenius is largely absent. Not until the Revolution itself would Condorcet and Babeuf revive the fervor of the previous century. As for Voltaire and Diderot, Montesquieu and Hume—they were not wholly discontent with their times and they all died in bed, respected citizens of the world.

In the eighteenth century the plain Morean fable renovated was still the dominant popular literary device, but variations both in the manner of getting to utopia and in its physical situation had multiplied and the underlying spirit had changed. The relative weight of the adventure story leading to utopia and the utopia proper that was contained in the tale had been altered in favor of the "action." If the novel is long enough and the shipwrecks frequent enough, the hero and heroine may even find time to do some utopia-hopping, to visit more than one ideal society in the course of a lifetime. The social content of More's utopia far outbalanced the tale of the traveler who discovered the new land; in many banal eighteenth-century works the shipwrecks and mishaps of the Europeans bulk so large in the narrative that the sections devoted to a description of the optimum society are all but submerged by picaresque details. Much of this literature was meant to amuse or to excite its audience—the author's eye was cocked on the growing assortment of female readers of all ages, who were presumed to have a limited tolerance for the sober portrayal of social institutions, however praiseworthy. The sugarcoating had become thicker than the remedial content of the utopian pill.

In many respects the adventure utopias with hackneyed plots of hair-raising captures and rescues are not distinguishable from the flood of escapist literature of an exotic cast that was inundating the Continent. With some effort, standard eighteenth-century moral values preached by the philosophes can be distilled from this organic mass, though other forms of eighteenth-century literature presented the same ideas more cogently. At some time in the course of his many harrowing experiences the hero comes upon a good natural society and here the utopia is inserted. This may occur as a mere episode, as in the Abbé Prévost's voluminous *Le Philosophe anglais, ou Histoire de Cleveland, fils naturel de Cromwell* (1728–1738), or it may absorb most of the compact tale. To a present-day reader, the monotony of these stories is unrelieved. They may be compared to those Hellenistic utopian novels of which we have a few fragments: In their inane activism they suggest the drying up of an inner life among readers who resorted to this vapid literature. The genre is far from dead at the present time in numerous versions purveyed by our own mass media. The element of thought that remains is so minuscule that one may be excused for neglecting to follow it doggedly century by century, though its pollution of the psychic atmosphere is hardly on the decline. When this claptrap first appeared it had a touch of novelty. By juxtaposing a portrayal of the terrible Inquisition that held Gaudentio di Lucca in its clutches with an account of an ideal civilized country in the heart of Africa, Simon Berington produced a popular thriller. Some writers like the Dane Ludvig Holberg went underground for their perfect societies. Charles Tiphaigne de la Roche and Nicolas Bricaire de La Dixmerie indulged in such extravagant biological transformism or excursions among spirits that their inclusion in a compendium of human utopias becomes moot. As elaborate conceits were stuffed into eighteenth-century utopias, many lost all artistic credibility and their present oblivion is well deserved.

Robinson and the Robinsonades

Daniel Defoe's *Robinson Crusoe,* which has survived, launched a new utopian form with a magnetic appeal both in the original and in scores of imitations that became known among contemporaries as *robinsonades*. Many elements are preserved from the classical Morean utopia and the ordinary adventure story, but something unique has been added—a man alone building civilization from the state of nature up, without the encumbrance of inherited institutions. This, some commentators believe, symbolically expressed the dynamism of the rising middle classes and their growing feelings of competence; it flattered the self-esteem of the new self-made man. It also demonstrated the good that could come directly from the state of nature, if the corruptions of society were avoided, though a close scholarly reading of *Robinson Crusoe* in recent years finds in Mr. Crusoe's reflections less admiration for the state of nature than long soliloquies about the terrors of a condition in which he stood naked, bereft of the conveniences of civility. And Crusoe was able to construct the new society only because he had brought with him accurate and full recollections of the techniques of civilization. Be that as it may, Robinson Crusoe fed the cult of the state-of-nature utopia, whatever Defoe's intentions may have been.

It is customary among literary people to distinguish the pragmatic, realistic robinsonade from the utopia. Actually, these lines need not be drawn too sharply. The robinsonade is wedded to the utopian mode and helps transform it from a mere hope or a wish with no great prospect of fulfillment into an assertive proclamation that man can do anything fresh if he has the will and the wit. Robinson may be a kind of aggressive bourgeois Prometheus. In French models where an initial robinsonade becomes a utopian society through procreation, the story recapitulates the world-historical process under ideal conditions, with tyrants and priests omitted. Of course, the robinsonade had limited utopian potentialities unless the stranded voyager was accompanied by a fe-

male castaway, or provided with a girl Friday, making it possible to raise a
new society conceived in love. The circumstances of a shipwreck allowed for
"misalliances" between members of widely separated social classes that would
not ordinarily be countenanced in European society, as well as unions without
the blessing of an ecclesiastical establishment. The original couple not only
brought forth a numerous progeny but established a utopia, for as the families
multiplied, natural laws had to be promulgated by the patriarch to assure the
preservation of the society that had been organized spontaneously by the light
of natural reason and that, with the increase of population and its removal
from the original state of nature, might otherwise be in danger of corruption.
Guillaume Grivel's utopia, *L'Isle inconnue* (1784–1787), originates in a robinsonade à deux demonstrating the thesis that monarchy had its source in a fa-
ther-legislator, not a conqueror. After 1764, the society of such natural utopias
often illustrated the principles of Rousseau's *Social Contract* in action. The robinsonade utopia spread throughout Europe and assumed myriad forms: There
were German, French, Italian, even female and Jesuit Robinsons.

Enlightened Despotisms Idealized

Another type of utopian novel rather common in France depicts a benign, enlightened monarchy in an antique setting—a touched-up portrait of the centralized French government, or at least the hopes of that government, the
warty "feudal remnants" of existing society having been excised. These utopias are usually agrarian-physiocratic in philosophy. If a prosperous bourgeois
or a royal intendant wrote a utopia it tended to fall into this category. Fénelon's *Telemachus* became a prototype and enjoyed extraordinary repute
throughout the eighteenth century, its profound Christian elements overlooked and its subtle attack on Louis XIV forgotten.

China too was metamorphosed into a benign enlightened despotism in
many eighteenth-century travel accounts and histories. Although the celestial
empire was never quite raised to the exalted status of the Spartan utopia, it had
its admirers from Montesquieu onward; everyone remembered that in *The
Spirit of the Laws* the Emperor of China was depicted as symbolically ploughing the fields each year to inspire his people with workmanlike virtues. The
idealization of the populous, prosperous, industrious Chinese society run by
philosophical mandarins was as close as many French philosophes ever came to
utopia; it represented an Oriental parallel to their own self-image.

Many enlightened-despotism utopias are absolutist in their monarchical centralization and committed to a more rationalized economic and social organization then even Colbert or any other royal minister would have dared impose
upon the French state. Others, far fewer in number, are chaste, more or less
communistic, agrarian republics that seem to descend from Vairasse's *History
of the Sevarambians*. The enlightened-despotism utopias preserve the furnishings of their contemporary society, but uproot every last vestige of seigneurial
privilege. The territory is divided into equal units arranged in a neat pyramid,
at the apex of which stands a king who enforces equal justice in the realm
through the agency of governors more powerful and effective than French intendants could ever hope to be, because customary law and local usage and
impediments to the free movement of produce have been abolished by a philosophical monarch. In Pierre de Lesconvel's *Idée d'un regne doux et heureux, ou*

Relation du voyage du Prince de Montberaud dans l'île de Naudely (1703), dedicated to the Duke de Berry, famine was eradicated through the establishment of an ever-normal granary. All occupations were controlled, as the bourgeois minister Colbert would have wanted them to be. The hereditary nobility was suppressed and in its place was installed a nobility of merit that spurred the whole body of the citizenry to feats of industry and virtue in the hope of attaining noble eminence. The clergy were men of God completely devoid of any pretensions to secular authority. There were no vagrants, no unproductive or lazy paupers. State taxes were readily collected, which allowed the king to maintain so formidable a military establishment that no other power or combination of powers had the temerity to attack Naudely. Peace, prosperity, and glory reigned—though not military glory.

More's *Utopia,* in a translation made by one M. T. Rousseau in the last decade before the Revolution, was so altered in spirit that King Utopus became a mirror image of an ideal enlightened despot. The solemn dedication to the Comte de Vergennes, Louis XVI's minister, hailing him as the inaugurator of a utopian regime, is not incongruous, though it startles one when the book is first opened. A partisan travel literature that idealized the Emperor of China and his workmanlike people and philosophical mandarins was harmonious with enlightened-despotism utopias that chose ancient Greece, Persia, or fictitious kingdoms for their locales. One is hard put to it in France to find highly organized utopias that in their outward form are not benevolent monarchies into which democratic elements are incorporated. All citizens were more or less equal beneath the king among the Frenchmen of the year 2440 in Mercier's dream. The royal apartments were more luxurious than those of other men, to lend dignity to the office, but even this distinction was not always accorded him in enlightened-despotism utopias. Without hereditary aristocracy, elaborate court ceremonial, or etiquette, the king behaved like a good bourgeois. Mercier's Louis XXXVI walked about Paris like Louis Philippe, minus an umbrella. In a very real sense, these political utopias were authentic renderings of the modest objectives of the major philosophes; there was nothing to dismay anyone except perhaps the ecclesiastical establishment. It is often said that 1789 was a bourgeois revolution; one group of utopias certainly prefigured the event.

But the influence of the popular utopian literature was insidious. Explorers, missionaries, curious travelers, and shipwrecked sailors discovered or believed they had discovered in the new countries where they landed the ideal republics with whose utopian imagery their imaginations were already crowded. Almost any travel book has a tendency to become tinged with utopia. By the eighteenth century a reader could be expected to regard skeptically a traveler returned with tales of monsters and natural prodigies after the manner of medieval voyagers to the East; but he could readily be convinced that somewhere among the gentle people living in a state of nature or in a simple state of civility there was an ideally happy society. The joys of the optimal order of society replaced the wonders of physical nature as subjects of enthusiasm for the writer of extraordinary voyages, real and fancied. The ancien régime doubtless went to its doom on a graph of rising prices and falling wages, as Ernest Labrousse would have us believe; but it may also have foundered in a sea of expectations nurtured by imaginary voyages and visions of happiness where such ugly economic realities left no traces at all.

17

The *Monde Idéal* of Jean-Jacques

IN 1779, a year after Rousseau's death, there appeared in rural Lichfield, England, a volume in French entitled *Premier dialogue;* in manuscript it had been called *Rousseau juge de Jean-Jacques.* This was the last work of a man in his midsixties, seriously ill with an aggravation of numerous maladies of the urinary tract. He was obsessed with preparing a justification before posterity and an apology before God whose judgment he was soon to face. Most of the work is a tiresome rehearsal of his accusations against the philosophes, who had maligned his character, betrayed his friendship, deliberately distorted the meaning and intent of his writings, created an image of him as an unnatural monster. The dialogue is a rhetorical tour de force in which the patronym Rousseau accuses Jean-Jacques in absentia of heinous moral crimes; in the end, after a presentation of the evidence in Jean-Jacques's defense, the Frenchman, a character who represents everyman, is moved to exonerate him. The discussion is a whirlpool in which a multiplicity of psychic currents crisscross and intermingle. Rousseau lashes himself in a verbal display of those masochistic drives of which he was conscious from earliest childhood and which marked his sexual nature—witness the account in the *Confessions* of the pleasure he derived from his first spanking by the female relative who brought him up and his later stories of relationships with women in which he consistently played a submissive role. If we look beneath the surface, the *Premier dialogue* continues on another level motifs that had been suggested in the early pages of the *Confessions.* The Rousseau of the *Premier dialogue* is in a sense also the father in the *Confessions,* who had held Jean-Jacques responsible for having robbed him of his wife in childbirth. Little Jean-Jacques and his father weep together over the lost beloved; but Jean-Jacques perceives that his father both feels bitterness toward him for the murder of his mother and loves and will kiss and embrace him as a replacement for her. From the searing anxiety caused by his father's "sighs" and "convulsive manner" Jean-Jacques never recovered, except in a fantasy world he created for himself and for the rest of mankind. The tormenting ambivalence between fear of submission, which would make a woman of him, and longing for submission, to which his sexuality was tied, was banished only when he dreamed of a state in which he was another man, an integrated, totally assertive self, absolutely free, dependent upon no one else.

The Conflict of Polar Forces

When one examines the different faces of Rousseau, one is tempted to throw up one's hands and dismiss him as an incorrigible changeling, a schizoid personality whose moods are too elusive to be captured. He moved in and out of the Catholic and Protestant religions, ending up with a religion of his own, the confession of the Savoy Vicar. He praised the natural feelings of the ordinary peasant in one breath and railed against the people in another, reviling them as a mob of underlings who slavishly followed the lead of their masters. He denounced all revolutions, tumults, and political plots only to be accused of undermining the foundations of civil society, and posthumously he did in fact become the supreme rhetorician of the French Revolution, if anyone can be assigned that role. He was the most dependent of creatures, clinging like a babe to the skirts of Mme. de Warens and then to his "gouvernante" and nursemaid-wife, Thérèse Levasseur, at the same time that he proclaimed his need for total independence. A masterful rationalist dialectician when he wanted to be, he heralded the dethronement of reason and exalted the passions. He wrote the most famous treatise in modern times on the education of a boy and a young man and left his own five children in an asylum—if he ever really sired them. At first he was a darling of the philosophes and then they were his enemies. A denigrator of social status and mere inherited titles, a self-styled republican, he was for many years a hanger-on of aristocrats and lived in houses on the grounds of their châteaux. This man who advertised his indifference to material things kept the most meticulous accounts of his expenses.

Everything about him was polar. He longed for the love and approval of men and despised them. He sought the warmth of others and when they extended their affections to him he recoiled in terror or struck out against them. During the last decades of his life he was convinced that a plot to destroy him had been engineered by the philosophes and with all the subtlety of his genius he saw every act of his erstwhile friends as a part of the grand conspiracy. His behavior fits into clinical stereotypes of the paranoid personality. While intimately conversing with David Hume, who had befriended him and made available a cottage in the English countryside as a refuge, he suffered the delusion that the eyes of the philosopher were seeking him out wherever he moved in the room. A suspicion that the stone lintel over a door had been loosened by Hume so that it would fall on him and kill him was suddenly dissipated by an onrush of love, in the course of which he jumped onto the lap of the bewildered philosopher and overwhelmed him with protestations of affection. That Rousseau the incisive analyst and eternal observer of his own conduct was aware of a strong feminine component in his nature—as the feminine was conceived in his society—is indicated by the violence with which effeminacy in men was denounced whenever the subject was even remotely approached. Throughout his life his ideal of man was the Spartan hero, the self-contained male, brave, bold, and unflinching. And yet this adulation of the Spartans as seen through Plutarch's eyes went along with the knowledge that homosexual love was part of the education of the Spartan youth, a detail to which the author of *Emile* never adverted in his writings.

In all of his works and in the very fabric of his style, Jean-Jacques left traces of the conflicts of polar forces in his personality and his passionate craving to be rid of them. "Man was born free, and everywhere he is in chains" is the opening thrust of the first chapter of the *Contrat social*. The greatest evil is dependence upon others, yet final liberation can be achieved only through the instrumentality of the general will, which has absorbed into itself all individual wills, has put an end to the clash of wills, and has eradicated every vestige of independence.

Living in a World of Fantasies

During his grand tour of the Continent, young James Boswell was received at Môtiers by Rousseau, then fifty years old, and they hit it off well. Boswell described him as a "genteel black man in the dress of an Armenian" and in his notes recorded their dialogue in abominable French.

Rousseau: Sir, you don't see before you the bear you have heard tell of. Sir, I have no liking for the world. I live here in a world of fantasies [chimères], and I cannot tolerate the world as it is.
Boswell: But when you come across fantastical [chimériques] men, are they not to your liking?
Rousseau: Why, Sir, they have not the same fantasies as myself.[1]

Yet this was true only in a very narrow sense. Rousseau holds men enthralled precisely because his fantasies were theirs in far greater measure than he acknowledged. The prophet who admonished his contemporaries from on high also revealed their hidden desires to them.

Though Rousseau never composed a proper speaking-picture utopia, in virtually all of his works he had a way of falling into the discursive utopian mode. He had read the ancient dialogues on ideal cities in Plato,[2] their criticism in Aristotle, and the portraits of good societies in Xenophon's *Cyropaedia* and Plutarch's "Lycurgus," and had soaked up Judeo-Christian paradisaical and Hellenic golden-age imagery. He knew More's *Utopia*, Vairasse's *History of the Sevarambians*, Fénelon's *Adventures of Telemachus*, much of the writing of Mably and Morelly. He fell heir to the Abbé de Saint-Pierre's papers on political projects for universal peace and evaluated them with perspicacity.[3] Though he avoided the term in defining his own role, utopia as a concept did not suffer from his sneer as it did among the philosophes even when they toyed with it. Utopias were *chimères*, but in his lexicon this was not a pejorative word. Throughout his writings, in the *Discours, La Nouvelle Héloïse*, the *Contrat social, Emile*, the *Rêveries, Rousseau juge de Jean-Jacques*, he delivered himself of fragments—not always harmonious with one another—about an ideal world.

"Suppose for a moment," Rousseau mused in the first of the *Lettres écrites de la Montagne* (1764), "that the profession of faith of the Vicar [of Savoy] were adopted in some corner of the Christian world, let us see what would be the good and the evil consequences."[4] The world governed by the Vicar's religion, expounded in Emile, would in effect become an ideal world identical with his other portrayals. Upon examination, the psyche of a true convert to the religion of the Savoy Vicar and man's psyche in the ideal world of the *Premier dialogue* turn out to be intrinsically the same. Rousseau, inconsistent and fickle in many of his political utterances, was the victim of one persistent psychic fantasy, a genius entrapped in his *idée fixe*. The state of nature of the *Discours sur l'inégalité* was a hypothesis, "a state that no longer exists and that perhaps has never existed,"[5] and Rousseau was explicit in asserting that mankind could not regress to it, enviable though it was. Perhaps in character the *Discours* falls somewhere between a heuristic device and a sketch of a utopian consciousness, and too tight a definition of its method would establish categories that were alien to its author. He can be read as vainly yearning to return to the womb of the first state, or wishing to restore in some future state the virtues and especially the pleasures that had been lost (the bereaved orphan's dream). Nostalgia for the past and futurism are often conflated in an imagination that does not live by, let alone experience, rigid chronological sequences. Since Rousseau's image of an ideal world was never wholly imparted to his readers in a finished work it is not free of ambiguity, but in the long history of utopian thought there is a haze that lends enchantment. "I offer my dreams as dreams, leaving it to the reader to discover whether they have something useful for waking people," was Rousseau's disingenuous disclaimer in the *Emile*.[6]

Richly endowed with a utopian propensity, Rousseau confronted some of the prickly questions that characterize the Western utopian way in both argumentative discourse and description. The degree of symphysis, or cohesion, that should exist among individuals in society is probably the most deep-rooted utopian problem in the rationalist tradition; in what kind of social unit will this ideal find appropriate expression? What is the place of the ideal world as an age in the eternal passage of time? Granted the crucial significance of sexuality in mankind, what is the optimal pattern of relationship between the two parts of the species? Since education is the key to any society, what is the perfect model for upbringing? What should be the relationship between need and desire? What happens to individuality in the communal utopia? Is there an ideal religious spirit that should be infused into the feeling tone of society? What part of man's nature should by preference be perfected, his moral or his intellectual faculties?

In his rustic utopia Rousseau turned his back on the city, the jewel of Western civilization. "Cities are the abyss of the human species."[7] The myth of the ideal city inherited from Plato had been preserved in the urban architectural utopias of the Italian Renaissance, in the essentially urban agglomerations of More's island, in Bacon's Bensalem, in Campanella's seven-walled City of the Sun. But Jean-Jacques's constitution for Corsica knows no cities and conforms to the wild, natural world of the island. He searches out a little village at the foot of the Alps in which to enact the drama of Julie's death and resurrection in utopia. The event is unthinkable in an urban environment. Emile can be reared only in the countryside; in the truncated sequel to *Emile,* as soon as the hero lands in Paris he is almost, though not quite, destroyed. In the wake of Fénelon, Rousseau reversed the urban Christian utopia that had dominated European consciousness for more than three centuries. The citizen of Geneva repudiated his citizenship. The Rousseauan longing for a pastoral idyll is not yet dead. Twentieth-century revivals of utopian practice have fled the city gates and sought a haven in the bosom of nature. In the end the agrarian and pastoral nostalgia of Jean-Jacques and his followers is of interest principally for the history of small, escapist ventures. There is another face of Rousseau, however, that has retained its vitality: Rousseau the fabricator of a eupsychia, an optimum state of consciousness, in a society whose material structures tend to fade into the background. To appreciate Rousseau's eupsychia the usual mechanics of utopias have to be filtered out. The institutional arrangements for achieving and perpetuating the eupsychia are subsidiary exercises that have bedeviled political scientists for two centuries. Those who dwell upon Rousseau's rationalist arguments can, by trimming a few rough edges, produce a reasonably consistent political philosophy, but only at the sacrifice of its essence.

"I" and the Communal "I"

Rousseau's eupsychian legacy is the fantasy of a perfectly autonomous, fulfilled "I" for everyman, the wholeness of a communal "I" that is an organic unity, and the integration of the entire, individual "I" with the communal "I" with hardly a ripple on either surface. The amalgamation was achieved in rhetoric and philosophical argument not only in Rousseau but in those who came after him, Hegel and Marx. One may be unmoved by the logic of any of their presentations and nevertheless remain profoundly convinced of the continuing emotional potency of the utopian goals they posed. Rousseau's magical speech articulated these fantasies in enduring form. They have seeped into the atmosphere in which we live and breathe. Rousseau's utopian "I" has been embraced by a branch of psychology and has been spread about in multiple versions; the communal "I" is a political dogma taught over half the globe; and their fusion is part of a world revolutionary credo.

The eloquent diagnostic pronouncements of Jean-Jacques, grand doctor of the soul, if not his rhetorical remedies, can still intoxicate. The first book of More's *Utopia* depicts the state of anti-utopia, sixteenth-century England; and the eighteenth century developed a magnificent vocabulary for portraying the anti-utopia of contemporary civilization, to which the utopia offered an alternative. Others had preceded Rousseau in analyzing the *mal moral;* but once he spoke, the minor prophets who succeeded him could not free themselves from his spell. His words reverberate in documents as diverse as the writings of Kant and the youthful correspondence of Babeuf, not to speak of Dom Deschamps, Restif de la Bretonne, the Marquis de Sade, Mercier, William Godwin, and Marx. After two hundred years the Rousseauan anti-utopia has lost nothing of its intensity and pungent irony.

The utopian yea that accompanies Rousseau's nay is first and foremost the communication of a state of feeling. He delineates the healthy psychological attributes of man in a hypothetical state of nature and, as a prelude to unveiling his psychic utopia, bears testimony to the anguish of the present "difforme contraste" of passion that thinks it is reasoning and of understanding gone mad.[8] In the world of today, Rousseau declaims, human feelings, words, and actions are in flagrant contradiction with one another. Action was once in measured balance with primitive desire; now action and desire are in complete imbalance; in a future ideal condition—if it is ever achieved—action will mirror only real desire. Without benefit of Vico, Rousseau knew that alterations in language followed revolutions in morals and communicated the radically different psyches of successive ages. The emotive cry of primitive language was not dissociated from its object; in the miserable intermediary present state, the disjuncture between speech and object is total; in the future, language will again be related to its object. It is in talk about emotions that the current disarray is glaringly evident. No man of feeling can remotely comprehend what people in Paris salons, with their society jargon, are chattering about. The characters of *La Nouvelle Héloïse* speak the straightforward language of passion of another world, whatever the consequences. In their utopia of Clarens the five protagonists sometimes even return to the silence of the state of nature, when creatures communicated without speech.

In the *Discourse on the Origin of Inequality,* Rousseau exposes the folly and brutality of societal man. Since he has no spontaneous feeling of sympathy for a fellow creature in distress to drive him to his aid, he can reason himself into quiescence under the bed covers at night instead of responding to a cry for help. Preening himself with all manner of social graces, fripperies, arts, scientific pretensions, which are merely the means of accentuating his inequality with other men, he has developed complicated institutions, above all a property system, and has accumulated riches that are concentrations of his self-esteem and that perpetuate his sense of superiority. He needs the constant stimulation of strong drink and sumptuous food; at the same time his existence passes in continual fear of countless illnesses. In unending anxiety, he dies a thousand deaths. The distracted creature, man in present society, is wracked by frustrated passions that render him an enemy to himself. Though born free, he is straightway swaddled in rags, denied the natural desire for his mother's milk, enchained by the prohibitions of adults' rules, fettered by false social restrictions, and finally wrapped up again and shut into a coffin.

The lament on the human condition in anti-utopia is a foil for the euphoric ballad of the *moi* and the *moi commun*.

The beginning of awareness of the "I" goes back to the dawn of consciousness in mankind, and scholarly essays have attempted to render into modern languages what this "I" signified. But only since the seventeenth century has a vocabulary been created which, while its matrix is a religious idea of the soul and the weighing of its worth in a final judgment by God, assumes a secular form and grapples with the potentialities as well as the reality of the "I." Jean-Jacques Rousseau was one of the fashioners of the language of the ideal "I." In the *Emile* he offered the perplexed detailed guidance on how to mold the complete moi from birth through marriage in a series of stages. The vision on the road to Vincennes was an apparition of this moi abstracted from Rousseau's society, purified of its dross. In *Rousseau juge de Jean-Jacques,* he defined the moral character of the moi in a *monde idéal*—the phrase is his. In the *Confessions* he narrated the trials of a moi—Jean-Jacques himself—that, while far from perfect, had come through the ordeal of living as well as a man could in this vale of tears. He could pretend to himself that he was a free moi, he could in his fantasy live as a moi dependent upon no one and, for all his miseries and wrongdoings, present himself as a man of virtue in an evil world. He was at least a shadow of what a moi could be. The adoring letters written him by contemporaries testify that they were trying to absorb a bit of that ideal virtuous moi into their own souls by consulting him, reading his books, loving and worshiping him from afar. The imitation of Rousseau was a way of advancing toward the wholeness of the moi.

Instead of the cogito, a secret voice of conscience present within a man was emotional witness to the existence of his "I." To discover conscience, to ward off its corrupters, to nurture its spontaneous movements was the active way to create a good moi with a good and capable will. The seed of this moi was in everyman, but wicked, evil, enticing, vicious creatures were capable of destroying its goodness, robbing it of its natural virtue and humaneness. If these many-shaped bogeys were to be encapsulated into one terrifying monster, it would be the craving heads of desire that had far outstripped real, authentic human need and capacity. Contentment of the moi does not mean the death of desire or the enfeeblement of passion. But the passions had to be so trained that they would not exceed the needs and faculties of the particular unique moi of each stage in the life cycle of every individual. The infinitude of desire, competition in desires and their satisfaction, the desire that recognizes no limits, have to be curbed from early childhood on. The education of Emile is a contest between pupil and master in which the pupil's ultimate triumph consists in his desiring, both as a child and as a man, no more than he is capable of fulfilling by himself for himself. If the world of the child is circumscribed by the extent of his natural curiosity, the harmony of desire and need will be perfect. And the child is the prototype of the ideal man. The conquest of a child's immediate world of objects, the alleviation of real bodily pain—these are examples of authentic needs that have priority and are illustrative of what constitutes real need in the man. The growth of conscience, which in the end means natural empathy with a fellow creature's pain, is readily fostered by example. And only when the moral capacity is formed is the reasoning capacity to be developed—but never beyond necessity. By the time the boy reared under Rousseau's system reaches manhood, the accord between desire and need is perfect. We do not quite know what the limits of our faculties are, and Rousseau is not thinking in terms of some mathematical absolute. The moral, however, is reasonably sustained. If Emile or mankind or a nation or a world civilization lives in a fantasy of desire far outstripping its needs and its faculties it courts moral disaster.

The ideal moi has harmoniously educated manual and mental powers; it cannot conceive of *luxuria;* it is autonomous, entire, whole. It lives fully and totally within the bounds of time and space that happen to be its environment. Identity, the consciousness of self, grows like a plant. Once it is fashioned, man can preserve that self whatever the vicissitudes of fortune. The limitless development of the ideal moi in scientific knowledge and the quest for unending novelty only deprive the moi of the immediacy of joy in the present. Rousseau had a grave suspicion of the pleasures of dominion, either over persons or over nature. The intellectual pleasure of scientific curiosity was forthrightly rejected —Rousseau did not even bother to argue the point seriously. It was Auguste Comte in his second career as High Priest of Humanity who took a similar position a century later and gave "physiological" reasons for the superiority of an expansive, sentient moi over the rationalist moi dedicated to scientific inquiry.

In Western culture the quest for the moi had assumed a form that was probably closest to Rousseau's ideal in the paideia of the Moravian bishop Comenius, who had it from the Swabian Lutheran pastor Andreae. There was a spark of divinity in every man and to nurture it, to make it glow to the uttermost limits of each man's and woman's faculties, was a Christian mission. ("Development of capacities" was the phrase into which the process was translated in nineteenth-century Saint-Simonian and Marxist language.) Human beings living in the world had to be well equipped with a knowledge of things both for the sake of utility and for the glorification of God the Creator of things. In rebellion against rote learning and abstract formulas, the Pansophic utopians had hoped that men who would know real things rather than mere words would be universally united in language, thought, belief, even theology. They would be joined in knowledge and love, with emphasis upon knowledge that perfected moral behavior in a Christian society. There was to be no futile knowledge, no science whose immediate utility was not apparent. Differences in the character of children and men were recognized as reflecting the infinite creativity of the Divine and they were respected, within the fixed bounds of Protestant rules of conduct whose moral content was self-evident. Each stage in the ideal educational process, Comenius had taught, was to be in large measure sufficient unto itself. Rousseau wrote in the *Emile:* "Each age, each stage of life, has its appropriate perfection, the sort of maturity that is fitting for it."[9] The education of the ideal moi by Emile's tutor, which begins with the concrete objects of the natural environment and has a program appropriate for each successive stage, is a further elaboration of this Pansophist vision, though Jean-Jacques introduced a crucial new element. "Perfectibility" has been a tragic attribute of mankind when defined in terms of science, technology, and the amassing of unnecessary objects. But there is another way. Rousseau's kind of expansion of the moi allows for the raising of emotional, rather than rationalist, consciousness to a higher level.

In *Rousseau juge de Jean-Jacques* Rousseau presented the final version of a dream of the moi he had rehearsed time and again throughout his life. Here was unfolded the vision of the moral and emotional nature of the "I" in a *monde idéal* populated by men who had achieved complete identities, the wholeness of the moi. He offered a glimpse of this world in action. Rousseau the protagonist called upon *le français* to imagine an ideal world similar to the one he lived in, yet very different—a passing good definition of utopia. The physical nature of the earth remains fundamentally unchanged; but the emotions of all its inhabitants are mysteriously heightened, the arrangement of things is more perfect, forms are more elegant, colors brighter, odors more subtle. All objects excite admiration. Without benefit of psychedelic drugs Rousseau conjures up a world of nature so strikingly beautiful that it alters the human beings who dwell in it. Instead of the suspicious, cruel, plotting creatures familiar to us, men are suddenly aglow with love for one another. The source of the metamorphosis is nature itself. Men are inspired to place themselves in harmony with its glories and are fearful only lest their presence contaminate it.[10]

As among Rousseau's contemporaries, the passions are still the driving forces behind a man's action in the monde idéal; but passions have become simpler, purer, livelier, and more ardent. Even in the benighted creatures of present society, original impulses are good and are directed toward self-preservation and happiness. But in the world of today these spontaneous initial feelings bump up against a thousand obstacles as they seek fulfillment, and they are diverted from their straight path. The emotions become so tangled in their circuitous attempts to overcome the impediments in their way that they never reach their destination and men forget what the object of their desire was in the first place. A cumbersome accumulation of irrelevant social artificialities makes them lose sight of what track they are pursuing.

The soul of the moi, the seat of its will, has grown soft and weak so that it is only feebly responsive to the "impulse of nature." As a consequence, when it hits its first obstacle, the will is sharply deflected from its original purpose— Rousseau uses the image of a billiard ball striking a wall and moving off at an angle. But in the monde idéal men have strong, willful souls and are like balls shot out of a cannon: They fly straight and either overcome the obstacles they aim at or are shattered by them.[11] If the soul obeys natural passion it is either victorious or it perishes. In this our miserable world men sidestep objects so often that they may finally end up somewhere relatively safe, but it is somewhere else, far from the place they had set out for.

The inhabitants of the ideal world preserve their bonds with nature and their souls have therefore lost nothing of their original vigor. If the soul follows the dictates of the elemental passions, it is preoccupied only with objects that concern *amour de soi,* love of self, a desire for self-preservation, and such feelings are, paradoxically, naturally loving and gentle. But man in his present wretched estate, living in a world overcrowded with superfluous objects, becomes obsessed with the things that stand in the way of his desire to the point where the ultimate goal is lost sight of and the feelings themselves turn irascible and hating. Thus the primal emotion of love of self, which is good and absolute and self-moved, gets transformed into *amour-propre,* self-esteem, a feeling derived from comparison with others, a relative, reactive emotion. The man of self-esteem no longer desires a thing for itself, but covets what belongs to someone else in order to outdo and surpass him. He has only preferences, not genuine desires, and fundamentally he no longer wants an object for the direct, unalloyed pleasure the thing itself brings but seeks it only for the loathsome satisfaction of depriving and injuring someone else.

The monde idéal is a utopia of passionate desire of the ego, emancipated from spurious, adventitious needs and from desires not freely generated by the self in its wholeness but merely responsive to the rules of emulation. Rousseau's moral critique speaks to us today as directly and forcefully as it did to his contemporaries. The inhabitants of his ideal world, while primarily animated by love of self, have expansive souls and can embrace many persons. Unmoved by appearances, "they pass their lives in enjoyment, doing each day what seems good for themselves and right for their fellows, without regard to the judgment of men and the caprices of opinion."[12] As he contemplated the decadence of his own society Rousseau found the telltale symptom of its disease in the loss of any strength of passion. Strong feelings were not easily deflected from their course, feeble ones were. His contrast between two lovers, one ardent, the other cool, was a homely illustration of the point. Both would hate a rival, that was natural; but the quality of their hatred would be substantially different. The indifferent lover would become obsessed with his rival, and after his love had waned and vanished he would hate the competitor even more violently than before because his love was intimately bound up with self-esteem. On the other hand, the ardent lover hated his rival only because he loved, and when he had ceased to love his hatred would be dissipated. The inhabitants of Rousseau's ideal world were like the true lover; his contemporaries, the false one. Frenchmen, cool and artificial—he had in mind the fashionable type known as the *petit maître*—even when moved by passions, experienced only secondary and derivative, not primary, emotions. A century later Friedrich Nietzsche would still be fascinated by a similar moral dichotomy, which he translated into a contrast between the scheming slave-person, the man of *ressentiment,* and the spontaneous, open, noble extrovert. As late as the summer of 1936 both Rousseau and Nietzsche, excerpted in chapbooks, figured among the idols of the Spanish anarcho-syndicalists.

It may be, Rousseau concedes, that in the ideal world men in general would not be more virtuous than we are today, but they would love virtue more.

Given their headstrong passions, they might commit crimes out of desire and love of self; but since their souls were sound and unsullied, they would know what true virtue was. Men in the ideal world would be constantly forced to combat their potent evil passions and they might ultimately succumb to them, exhausted by the struggle. But such an occasional defeat would occur in despite of their strong wills. They were not capable of willing anyone harm, of feeling envenomed hatred and envy, of treachery or deception. Such men, even if guilty of *crimes passionnels,* were not wicked.

Far from being revolutionaries dedicated to the institution of an egalitarian social order, the men of Rousseau's ideal world were content with their station in life and did not seek to rise above it, since social appearances meant nothing to their happiness, and inner feeling everything. If the object of their desire was below them in station they went for it, caring naught about public opinion, but respecting only the authenticity of their desire. They were sensuous and voluptuous—their sensibilities were sharper than ours—but they did not hanker after riches because they knew that true pleasure was not dependent upon wealth and they loved their liberty too much to undergo the servitude necessary for the acquisition of a fortune or to endure the worry of preserving it. Rousseau's construct of the moral system of the monde idéal justified his own conduct after his break with the philosophes, when he fled their Paris society—a philosopher who abandoned his fellowmen. But he had no alternative in the present state of society, assailed and battered as he was by the passions of his own self-esteem (not love of self), for he too had been corrupted by the world in which he lived, and while he remained in society he was merely serving as an impediment for the passions of self-esteem of which others were possessed. He was losing his way in this emotional labyrinth, and if he took refuge in isolation he would at least do no harm. Rousseau the true philosopher pitied the blindness of men more than he was angered by their malice, and when he repulsed the assaults of his enemies it was only for self-preservation, not out of vengeance.

His vision of the two worlds explained why Rousseau's works had been misunderstood and why he had been considered an aberration of nature. Jean-Jacques, though living in this world amid corrupted men whose system of emotions revolved only around self-esteem, had some drives that were identical with those of the inhabitants of the other world, the monde idéal; he was therefore an alien. Initiates of the enchanted world—few in number—recognized one another by the exaltation of their souls. (Students of German Romantic literature will recognize in *die schöne Seele* the counterpart of Rousseau's sublime creatures.) A man motivated by the love of self of the monde idéal would invariably express himself differently from ordinary people. Either one was a part of that world and spoke its language or one was not. Rousseau's contemporaries could not comprehend his strange speech and therefore misread his writings.

The Primitive and His Social Counterfeit

The first book of the *Discours sur l'inégalité,* or *Second Discourse,* written a full quarter of a century earlier, presents a similar model of the monde idéal in the guise of a natural or original state of man. It portrays in detail the psychological and moral features of the noble primitive and sets him off against an anti-model, an anti-utopian man in modish Parisian society, the "social" man who had sunk to the depths of dissoluteness and depravity, who had removed himself almost as far as he could from the state of nature. Rousseau started out with the anti-utopia of present-day man, his distorted moral nature, his false values, his impaired physical and spiritual health; he then inverted the attributes, called them by opposite names, and emerged with an ideal image of man in the state of nature, natural man. Building utopia as antithesis to reality, a kind of counterpoint, is one of the oldest devices in the utopia-writer's repertory. In the *Discours,* Rousseau constantly flashes before our eyes intimate scenes of Parisian life to make us savor the bliss of natural men the more.

Man in the state of nature is robust, content with little food, unafraid of the future; he delights in the immediacy of existence. He wants no more than he has the capacity to grasp at the moment, and therefore he knows neither greed nor resentment. His needs are simple—sleep, acorns, copulation—and these desires are instantaneously fulfilled. Though there are natural inequalities of strength among men in the state of nature, the inequalities have not been exacerbated by inequities, accumulations of the products of the arts and sciences in the hands of some men but not others. Natural man kills his enemy or his rival, but he kills in self-preservation and not out of mere competitiveness. This was the vision that overwhelmed Rousseau in the forest of Compiègne and plunged him into an ecstatic trance.

Man (or the man-beast) in the state of nature as delineated in the first book of the *Second Discourse* may have been too rough-hewn even for Rousseau; in the second book he painted a more socialized state, and some would consider this halfway house Rousseau's preferred utopia. At an intermediate stage after the fatal instinct of perfectibility had already manifested itself but before the full development of the arts and sciences had ravaged mankind, men lived in simple huts in the bosom of nature and made merry together at communal celebrations. Rousseau's "intermediate" natural man is still fiercely independent: he does not have to play the hypocrite, to flatter and to fawn. We who live in an artificial society are constantly gnawed by the haunting memory of that earlier state.

The utopia of the independent, fulfilled moi is Rousseau's most popular message to the modern world. Its existence is so pervasive an assumption in Western society that any educator who challenged it as an ideal would be forthwith banished. The Rousseauan "I" is alive in the rhetoric of the present-day quest for identity, in a whole series of theses about total self-actualization from Marx through Maslow. "Actualization," of course, has a way of changing direction: For Marx its content was scientific and aesthetic creativity, while for Marcuse it has become primarily aesthetical and sexual. The essential content for Rousseau's moi was still moral conscience, religious wonderment, and emotional directness.

The Collective Moral Body

But what of the other Western utopian feeling, the yearning for a *moi commun* that Rousseau made the cornerstone of a "political theory" which promised to provide justification for the existence of the state? The fantasy of the moi, when it encounters the equally potent dream of a moi commun, a new state of social being, may be difficult of fulfillment. The demands made by the moi commun, even if hidden or camouflaged, are absolute and compelling. And if the grasping for the moi commun is superficially appeased in ways that Rousseau would have condemned as societal frauds and artifices, the moi is betrayed to its innermost depths.

The paradox of Rousseau's utopia is obvious. No one has preached more eloquently the absolute uniqueness and inviolability of the moi, the need for an arduous education to achieve its wholeness and integrity; and no one has demanded with more fervor that in the social state this moi become so identified with a moi commun that neither in *raison* nor in feeling shall the will of the moi be in conflict with that moi commun. The greatest moral suffering of mankind derives from the wild incoherence of individual and common wills. How bring them into a natural harmony?

The degree of potency with which to invest community feeling was perhaps the oldest of controversies in the rational Hellenic discourse on ideal states, fundamental to Aristotle's critique of the *Republic*. In the *Contrat social* Rousseau, in the Platonic rather than the Aristotelian chain, reserves nothing for the individual away from the Platonic integral whole. In the sixth chapter of Book I he dramatizes the revolution of the compact, when in a moment the individual loses his private being and the act of association creates a "collective moral body . . . which by this same act acquires its unity, its moi commun, its life, and its will."[13] He wrote out a formula in the *Emile* for eliminating any antagonism between the moi and the moi commun: "Natural man is all for himself. He is the numerical unity, the absolute whole, that has no relationship but with himself or his like. Civil man is only a fraction of a unit that depends upon the denominator; its value lies in the relationship with the whole, which is the social body. Good social institutions are those that are best able to change man's nature, to take away his absolute existence in order to give him a relative one and to translate the moi into a communal unity, with the result that each individual no longer thinks of himself as one, but as part of the unity, and has feelings only in the whole."[14]

Rousseau's arithmetical imagery is only partially successful, but his idea of the moi commun persisted and has been reiterated by a line of powerful thinkers who invented different phraseology for the conception. Dom Deschamps, the strange Benedictine author of the communist and primitivist *Le Vrai système,* with whom Rousseau conducted a mild intellectual flirtation in the 1760s, distinguished with scholastic subtlety between the whole that was still a composite of parts, and wholeness, whose existence he raised to a law of the social order of the same universality as gravity. Movement to wholeness was the destiny of man. Fourier invented a passion, though it was only one among many, that he called unityism, and it was to pervade the phalanstery. The Saint-Simonians wrote alternately of a new Christianity, interpreting the Gospel in Rousseau's spirit, and of *amour* as a unifying force that through time was constantly enlarging its orbit from family to tribe to nation until it would encompass all of humanity with the same intensity that was once restricted to the intimacy of the family. Young Marx wanted a fully developed, well-rounded sensate moi (a man of rich and deep sense)[15] completely aware of itself and its uniqueness, and at the same time a moi commun that was not a mere numerical majority but a will expressive of the essence of the human, an organism in which everyman participated without consciousness of his separateness. The collective unity of a certain type of communist theory is the fulfillment of a

Rousseauan fantasy, and so is the glorification of *Gemeinschaft* in late nine-teenth-century German sociology.

Where did Rousseau find a simulacre of a moi commun? In Sparta, Republi-can Rome, Geneva, Corsica, the little village at the foot of the Alps that he invented in the *Nouvelle Héloïse*. There, at Clarens during the harvesting of the grapes, he conjures up something of the spirit of ideal community. For a mo-ment the peasants and bourgeois and lords are united in labor and honest al-lowable pleasures—Jean-Jacques never had anything against good wine. Julie distributes functions and everyone naturally knows his place. (Any peasant who breaks the pastoral mood with excess or indecency is sacked.) Social classes do not matter in this community, when the sentiment of the communal moi has penetrated all bosoms.

Despite their affinities, Rousseau's solution to the predicament of man, who needs to find his entire self and at the same time to lose it in an authentic moi commun, could not satisfy completely either the Dom Deschamps or the Grac-chus Babeuf type of social theorist. In Jean-Jacques's evocation of the spirit of the collective moi, its religious emotion, its love, so perfectly merged the "I" in the moi commun that degrees of wealth and status were not felt. But in one tradition stemming from the theory of the moi commun the organismic whole required absolute equality. This was the direction in which Dom Deschamps was trying to pull Rousseau. Without absolute equality there would be envy and the wholeness of the whole could never be achieved. Dom Deschamps judged Rousseau's moi commun inadequate and told him so. It was not enough of a whole, since private property and the family prevented the crea-tion of real, total community. Babeuf moved along the same path, drawing the implications of Rousseau's two *Discourses* to their extreme conclusion, pre-pared to abolish altogether whatever was in short supply, to sacrifice all arts and sciences in order to create the ideal symphysis.

The harmony of the Rousseauan vision was irreparably disrupted by the spread of science and technology, when desire became dynamic and infinite and was virtually identified with need. Rousseau never seriously engaged with science and technology, despite the fulminations of the *First Discourse*. Keeping up with burgeoning desire became a critical utopian problem, entailing a con-stant theoretical reordering of economic and political systems. Saint-Simon, the Saint-Simonians, and Marx hailed the dynamism of desire for new sensate objects and for infinite knowledge. They were committed to a dynamic growth of needs and desires forever, generating what Rousseau would have considered constant imbalance and unhappiness. Rousseau knew that disequi-librium between escalating desire and real need would destroy fellow feeling among human beings. In this vital respect the ascetic anarchists of the nine-teenth century were aligned with Rousseau against Marx, and in their recent revival they use Rousseauan rhetoric, often without knowing it. As one wryly contemplates today's explosive and fragmented society, pullulating with new needs and inauthentic desires, one understands the force of Rousseau's argu-ment.

To the extent that Rousseau had an institutional utopia embodying his eu-psychia, it was outlined in the *Contrat social* and in his projected constitution for Corsica. The haven could be a small city-state much like his native Gen-eva, where, in his fancy, men had managed to preserve some of those moral and psychological qualities that once distinguished the primitive in the early stages of his emergence from the state of nature. (Our present knowledge of the bitter class conflicts that tore through eighteenth-century Geneva makes us appreciate the dimensions of Jean-Jacques's mythomania. Jean Starobinski, one of the subtlest commentators on Rousseau, believes that it was the oppressive Geneva of his childhood which turned him into the eternal outsider.) A small mountain people like the brave supporters of the Corsican insurgent Paoli, untainted by the evils of civilization, could keep out the corrosive forces of hypersophisticated arts and sciences, refuse to imitate the mammoth dynastic states. Where the society was already a colossus, not much could be done to rescue it except to realize its condition and try to slow down the process of decline. This was the time-honored nostrum of the doctor of the state in the face of inevitable death, a role in which Jean-Jacques occasionally cast himself.

Rousseau and the Revolution

There is no reason to take Rousseau's strictures against revolution as mere acts of prudence; for the author of the second book of the *Discours sur l'inégalité*, political revolutions undertaken by the slaves of an artificial morality in a modern state would only bring about the worst of all possible tyrannies. But this was not the way a younger generation in the 1780s read Rousseau's works.[16] They really believed that they could establish a society with a new consciousness in the middle of Paris. In the years following Rousseau's death, they took his ideal world seriously as a practical prospect, and though they embarked upon the course of the Revolution with a wide variety of political models, Rousseau was exalted as the prophet by all of them, the more so because he had not been too circumstantial in proposing plans and methods of action. The Jacobin utopia incorporated in the works of Saint-Just, the futurist visions of Mercier and Condorcet, the communist utopia of Babeuf's conspiracy, and the erotic utopias of Restif de la Bretonne and the Marquis de Sade without exception acknowledged Jean-Jacques as their ancestor. He emerged triumphant in the Revolutionary era because the novel sensibility he had generated could be bound up with widely varied political movements and moral doctrines that rationalist analysis might find conflicting. Rousseau idealized a new state of emotion in which local, fanatical, religious, and personal feudal loyalties would be replaced by the allegiance of one contented national family of Frenchmen who wanted few material things, loved one another, and miraculously thought and felt alike. They would no longer suffer from the discord of contradictory wills, but would achieve harmony in one general will.

With *La Nouvelle Héloïse* and the *Emile,* Rousseau fashioned models of a new sensibility. Men, and even more, ladies, were thenceforth prepared to be carried away by waves of tender feeling and torrents of virtue. If read in the light of his lifelong utopia of the monde idéal, *La Nouvelle Héloïse* was perhaps the most revolutionary and influential of all Rousseau's works: Seventy-two editions were recorded by the turn of the century. A society that would make all its members feel with the same passionate sincerity as Rousseau's characters— that was the ideal state of man. Rousseau summoned all Frenchmen to express their natural emotion. Hundreds of letters addressed to him bear witness that he had come to represent an emotional emancipation. It was now allowable for everyman to utter what he felt in his sentiments of love. Why not in his feelings of rage against the aristocratic evils of society?

Voltaire had made anticlericalism a la mode; he provided the new negative identities, priests instead of devils and Huguenots. Rousseau gave Frenchmen, and other Europeans, too, characters with whose virtue they could associate themselves. The anti-aristocratic element in Rousseau is less blatant than the anticlericalism of Voltaire, but it runs deeper. In attacking the conventions of society he was undermining a particular style of life, that of the nobility, the *petit maître,* the arrogant fops with all their posturings and insincere compliments. As the elaborate manners of French aristocrats were being aped by petty German princelets and the bourgeois of Europe, Rousseau exhorted the plebeians to be themselves. Goethe, for one, heard the call and repeated the message in *Werther,* in *Wilhelm Meister,* in *Die Wahlverwandschaften.* If society was corrupt, ordinary humans were less corrupt than the titled upper classes—they still had some uncontaminated instincts. While the cautious philosopher turned his head away, Rousseau reminded the people, ordinary fishwives spontaneously intervened to stop a murderous quarrel. The vicious aristocrats in Laclos's *Les Liaisons dangereuses* were the other side of Rousseau's coin. These monsters of depravity were forever lying, intriguing, plotting, deceiving one another, and in the end they were caught in their own web. The official condemnation of *Emile* and the *Contrat social* and their public burning by the hangman added the touch of martyrdom necessary for a religious leader and Rousseau was apotheosized by the Revolution. He was *le révolutionnaire malgré lui.*

Rousseau's dramatic phrases imprinted themselves deeply on the consciousness of men of the pre-Revolutionary period. He said with eloquence what they were thinking or feeling in some inchoate manner. Dissatisfaction with one's estate had become widespread and it was now more frequently allowable to vocalize one's grievances, a growing permissiveness that culminated in one of the great outpourings of universal discontent, the hundreds of *cahiers de doléances.* A Jansenist peasant's son escaping to the city (Restif), a rich artisan's son ending up in the bohemia of Paris (Diderot), an illegitimate son of a noble (d'Alembert), a disbelieving monk (Dom Deschamps), a clerk searching for titles to lands in feudal documents (Babeuf), a disinherited son spurned by his unnatural mother (Saint-Just), a restless scion of one of the great aristocratic families (Henri de Saint-Simon)—Rousseau spoke to all of them. And one should not forget those disgruntled lawyers, Robespierre and Danton, and that rejected doctor of talent, Marat. Rousseau splashed the whole of existing society with the epithets corrupt, hypocritical, lying, diseased, wretched, self-deceived, indifferent. He ruthlessly stripped off veil after veil to reveal the moral void of his world. He did not concentrate his attack on the monarchy or the *parlement* or the aristocracy or the bishops of the church, or any particular class or officer of the state, but sweepingly denounced the whole of civilization, calling it degenerate physically and morally. Your father was corrupt if you were a son, your patron if you were a bum, your superior officer if you lacked enough influence at court for advancement, your bishop if you were a wavering priest, your absentee lord if you were a steward, your aristocratic *lycée* classmate if you were a commoner.

When Rousseau's castigation of the society was seconded by aristocrats who no longer believed in themselves and in their right to privilege, they were signing their own death warrants, a rather frequent kind of scribbling among ruling classes. The promise of a monde idéal peopled with men who followed the dictates of their passions and were the more virtuous for it was soothing to those whose ambitions had been thwarted by a restrictive order that had lost its sacred aura. Men of the most diverse origins, whose feelings had been fashioned in Rousseau's school of psychology and rhetoric and who had glimpsed the moral beauty of his monde idéal, were prepared for a revolution. Few may have understood the intricacies of the theoretical argument in the *Contrat social,* but everyman could feel the force of the final apostrophe of the *Discours sur l'inégalité:* "It is manifestly against the law of nature, however one defines it, that a child should command an old man, that an imbecile should lead a wise man, and that a handful of people should be bursting with a superfluity of things while the hungry multitude is in want of the necessities of life."[17]

Since the French Revolution there has been a multiplication of little utopian communities to which men and women have flocked, for a few years at least, to create a moi commun. Nationalists of all colors, Marxist-Leninists, Maoists, even anarchists, have promised moi communs of various sizes, mostly on a larger scale. Even the prospect of one universal moi commun has been extended. In these movements, as in Rousseau, the moi commun was not merely a state or a polity; it was a pervasive emotion. In the nineteenth and twentieth centuries, those who joined together to bring about the new communal moi, either of a patriotic nationalist or communist internationalist character, experienced in the course of their struggles the creation of the communal will; at times it was akin to the "oceanic feeling" that has been used to define religious emotion. When men have known this feeling in the generosity or madness of youth they often cling covertly to the memory of its warmth after they have grown old and staid. Some are not emancipated from its tenacious hold even when their reason rebels against it.

In the past, at least according to the history books, there were religious societies that allowed for both a unique fulfillment of the moi in its particular relationship to God and a covenant of believers who created a brotherhood in God. In modern times synthetic religions or secular total systems of belief have aspired to reproduce similar conditions or have promised to make Rousseau's utopian fantasy a reality. They have usually ended up as caricatures. The devotees of a French cult of the 1830s, which had adepts throughout the world, proclaimed themselves "Children of Saint-Simon," their founding father, as there were brothers in Christ and sons of Abraham. To answer the criticism that their new religion would run the risk of a loss of the moi in its excessive stress upon the bonds of love and community, the Saint-Simonians had their names embroidered in large letters on their blue tunics. In variant forms Marx preached the "self-actualization of the individual" and in his rare utopian excursions raised the prospect of a communal moi in which creativity, participated in by all men, would lend wholeness to existence. But the communist countries that have enshrined his doctrines have manifested capability only for promulgating the dry formalism of a moi and a moi commun without their substance. When the heroic period of the seizure of power has passed, their new commonalties recall the last stages of societal degeneration in Jean-Jacques's *Second Discourse,* a world of men ranged in a hierarchy to kick and be kicked.

Western democracies in the tradition of Locke and Montesquieu have made attempts to demarcate with legal specificity and sometimes virtuosity the lines that protect the moi from any interference and to circumscribe the area in which society takes total possession. The intention at the core of this philosophy has been to leave the moi free to create its own content or to leave it as empty of coherent meaning as a creature can be and yet survive. The liberal constitutional state has in theory been divested of emotionality, and rational law and written tradition have pretended to be absolute, though always subject to simple rules of utility such as the self-preservation of the political body. This arrangement has provided a viable society that satisfies many elementary needs, opens wide the gates of curiosity, and allows for the expression of numberless desires. But its very neutrality ignores the powerful primitive yearning for a moi commun and reduces its binding emotions to weak links, while the individual moi as an integrated whole, an Emile perfect in his entirety, is a haphazard of fortune.

If one examines Rousseau's conceptions of the moi and the moi commun, not as component elements of a political theory that has to show a modicum of logical consistency, but as coexistent desires, the richness of his utopian vision and its power may be highlighted. The pathos of the human condition lies in wanting identity and community too, and both in full measure. Upon rereading, Jean-Jacques's rhetorical, rationalistic conciliation of the contradictions between the moi and the moi commun offers no great satisfaction. But though he spoke to another world, his diagnosis of the *mal moral* still bears credence, in part because it is not enchained with bonds of a parochial historical analysis. He carries conviction when he lays bare the inauthenticity of the conflicted moi that triumphantly announces its self-actualization and the fraudulence of the synthetic moi commun that is preached from political pulpits. To the self-tortured vagabond Jean-Jacques, who so deeply craved to be both his unique self in all its fullness and a citizen of the moi commun of a Heavenly Geneva, we owe a prophetic, sibylline, and maybe even true, discourse on the state of man.

18

Freedom from the Wheel

IF A LITERATE Christian European in the early eighteenth century had been asked what were the prospects for the future of mankind, he might have answered that there would be a second coming of Christ followed by a Last Judgment, or that there would be an indefinite continuation of the same pattern of political history with which he was familiar—some states would prosper and others decline. If he were a millenarian he would point out that men were living in the sixth millennium since Creation and that the earth was not scheduled to last more than six thousand years; thus the Sabbath would not be long delayed. Had he by chance been touched in the head by the Prophets of London, his prognostications would have been even more precise. The wars of Louis XIV would have been recognized as the fulfillment of the prophesied struggle between Gog and Magog or the temporary triumph of the Antichrist, further signs that the Messiah was at hand. Such interpretation of prophecy could not always be practiced with impunity. In England the foretellings of imminent destruction might be deemed too vivid, likely to create tumults among Her Majesty's subjects, and the prophet might well be exposed in pillory at Charing Cross to dampen his enthusiasm—a punishment meted out to Fatio de Duillier, a young Swiss mathematician who was a favorite of Isaac Newton's.[1] Another friend of Newton's, the theologian John Craig, worked out mathematical formulas to show that the Second Coming was due when the memory of the original witness to Christ had been entirely eroded, a historical process of attrition that was calculable with precision.[2]

One did not have to be a devout Christian to believe in the future destruction of the world. A Stoic secularist of the Enlightenment who took his Seneca seriously could learn from the *Natural Questions* that universal deluges and conflagrations were in the nature of things, that the good principle became exhausted with time and a cosmic renewal was periodically necessary. The subsoil was soaked with subterranean streams ready to burst the crust of the earth whenever the tenuous balance of the elements was upset. Eruptions of the waters might alternate with great fires and mankind was left in doubt as to the particular manner of the cosmic catastrophe.

The Prevalence of Cyclical Theory

The idea of the great conflagration or the periodic deluge had more than a passing revival in eighteenth-century thought. It was one of the oldest historical conceptions of Western man, and probably can be traced back to the early river valley civilizations of the Tigris-Euphrates. In Plato's *Critias* the myth of the submersion of Atlantis as told by Egyptian priests to Solon is narrated. The apocalyptic vision from late Judaism and early Christianity coalesced with the Greek version of the more ancient Babylonian myth that was probably their common origin.

In the eighteenth century a new secular translation of the apocalypse was driving out the traditional religious one. The new geology and paleontology found the conception of one great deluge or periodic world floods a useful way to explain the bizarre rock formations, lofty mountain ranges, canyons, straits, and isthmuses that marred the rotundity of the globe. Religious geologists like Burnet and Whiston had still adhered to the conception of one great flood in harmony with the text of Genesis; atheists who accepted the theories of the eccentric young engineer Nicolas Boulanger, a member of Baron d'Holbach's circle, were not content with the single geological revolution of the planet and hypothesized a long series of upheavals each one of which wiped out virtually every vestige of previous civilized existence. What survived the catastrophes were a few physical remnants of the many floods, seashells swept to the mountaintops by colossal waves, and the mythic traditions of all peoples, which in distorted form and with a religious envelopment preserved the memory of the terrible events mankind had once suffered.[3]

The Lisbon earthquake, the volcanic eruptions of Mount Aetna, and the mid-eighteenth-century excavations at Herculaneum were reminders that geological revolutions on the planet were real possibilities with which mankind might have to cope again. Count Buffon's history of the planet was perhaps the most widely known account of the transformations of the earth published in the latter part of the century; but though his descriptions of the early breaking apart of continental land masses were frightening, the moral of his geological tale had its consolations: The earth was simmering down, becoming more stable, almost "reasonable" in its behavior.

Boulanger's hypothesis, though mocked by German literary philosophers such as Herder, was not without its serious adherents and counterparts. Geological experience was cyclical—the term is Boulanger's in *Antiquity Unveiled* —and man, who is bound to nature, though he might in short terms achieve progressive, enlightened happiness, in the long run had to submit to the ineluctable rhythm of nature. The relationship between Boulanger's theory and that of his ancient Stoic predecessor Seneca was generally recognized, and those who took a Christian view of the end of the world were at pains to refute them both.

As long as the elements of nature were in equipoise all would go well, but a periodic imbalance was to be expected and a catastrophe inevitable. The eccentricities of the comets might not be divine portents to Pierre Bayle or most of his religious contemporaries, as they had still been to great astronomers like Riccioli and to run-of-the-mill believers in judicial astrology; but the possibility of a comet's coming too close to the earth for comfort was not discounted by Halley himself (and he was reputed to be a disbeliever). Newton occasionally talked of the universe as "running down" and requiring rectification. Once he even referred to the satellites as spare planets of sorts that God kept in reserve for the period after the destruction of the earth—a notion that, divested of its religious origins, reappears in twentieth-century science fiction. In short, some form of the Platonic tradition of the Great Year—a confluence of planets, an upheaval in the balance of the elements, an exhaustion of nature necessitating renewal through either divine intervention or some autonomous force in the universe—was a fixture of eighteenth-century thought. A large number of Europeans felt human destiny was earth-bound or nature-bound in a commonsensical way. Man in history was surely not "free," since the overall pattern of his physical existence was determined by planetary revolutions, geological catastrophes, the seesaw of exhaustion and replenishment, and a host of other natural phenomena.

In sheer bulk most of the theories of history that can be identified in eighteenth-century thought are either cyclical or committed to the metaphor of flux and reflux. Vico's *ricorsi* as a law of nations is a full-blown illustration of this type of thinking adapted to human affairs. Hume's flux and reflux between monotheistic and polytheistic religious attitudes in *The Natural History of Religion* was a forthright denial of the unilinear Christian theory of history, whether it led to heaven or to hell. Winckelmann's concept of progression and decline in the history of art in antiquity, Montesquieu's charting of grandeur and decadence in Rome, the exemplar empire, Herder's extension of the major characteristics of the Winckelmannian cycle to the history of *Völker* all militated against a world view of absolute progression, and were inimical in spirit to a utopian state of man in the end of the days. Neither Rousseau nor Montesquieu conceived of particular societies that would be everlasting. They were doctors of the polity who might advise on how it might manage to live longer, but there are no intimations of immortality for any political order. John Adams, one of the Americans of his day who had a passing acquaintance with European thought, was an avowed enemy of the prophets of progress.

The body of cyclical thought in the eighteenth century, though rich and varied, should, however, not be construed as a direct attack on the illusions of progress, because the illusions themselves had not yet possessed European thought to the point where they blotted out rival conceptions. The underlying ideas of Turgot's *Sorboniques* (1750) had to await Condorcet's *Vie de Turgot* in 1786 and the *Esquisse* of 1795 to receive wide currency in print; Herder's concept of *Fortschritt,* ambiguous as it is, does not take shape until the 1780s. Lessing's hundred aphorisms and Kant's essays that debate the problem of a cyclical theory are works of the eighties and nineties. When the idea of progress first occurred to Turgot it was in response to a prize essay contest on the causes of artistic decadence, a characteristic aesthetic concern in the 1740s and 1750s.

Despite literary disputations about the ancients and the moderns and the manifest triumphs of the arts and sciences recorded by academies and in the *Encyclopédie,* where moral issues were involved much eighteenth-century thinking on the subject of progression had not moved away dramatically from the Renaissance doctrine of the wheel. Francis Bacon could expound in the same work his convictions about the cumulative effect of learning and his cyclical conception of moral stages—and he felt that his society was in a low state. The philosophical historian Louis Le Roy could be a modernist, plead for the scientific emancipation of his fellowmen from the authority of the ancients, write hortatory addresses calling upon his contemporaries to fling themselves into scientific research with renewed energy, and yet hold to a fundamental theory of the circular vicissitudes that was phrased in classical language, replete with borrowings from Aristotle's *Politics.* Such earlier Renaissance ideas were constantly rehearsed by the *philosophes.*

It is only in the latter part of the eighteenth century that the debate on the idea of progress, on the utopia of the good future time, was joined in earnest—and it was difficult to find thoroughgoing progressists. Turgot tried to convince Hume of the idea and failed, Kant directed himself against Moses Mendelssohn, who had attacked the thesis propounded by Lessing in *The Education of the Human Race.*[4] Goethe, unmoved by Herder's enthusiasm, wrote letters from Italy reflecting deep skepticism about his friend's unfolding of a happy future for mankind. While the President de Brosses accepted the superiority of the state of civilization over fetishism, he was none too sure of the enduring quality of the contemporary triumphs of reason. Holbach's vision of a superstition-free society provoked a trenchant riposte in Frederick II's cynicism. Edward Gibbon is perhaps typical of the ambivalence that characterized the attitude of many major intellects toward the idea of progress in the last decades of the eighteenth century. He too had inherited the Renaissance belief in the vicissitudes and was reluctant to predict the heights to which the human species might aspire in its advance toward perfection. Nevertheless, he reflected at the conclusion of Chapter 38 of the *Decline and Fall of the Roman Empire,* "it may safely be presumed, that no people, unless the face of nature is changed, will relapse into their original barbarism." His proof was that not even the Romans in decline had fallen so far as to renew the "human feasts of the Laestrygons on the coast of Campania."[5] But to promise his fellow men freedom from anthropophagy was no resounding affirmation of the certain boundless progress of civilization, though it went further than many thinkers of the older generation of Anglo-French culture were prepared to venture.

The idea of inevitable political decadence coexisted in eighteenth-century thought with the idea of progress in certain fields of human endeavor. At a moment when the life sciences were finding a place in the roster of respectable forms of knowledge there was a common analogy with death in organic process. But there were also numerous studies of what was called declension or decline and fall that proceeded without any support from biological analogy and still relied on the mechanical metaphors of the popular Newtonian world machine. Winckelmann in his periodization of the history of Greek art claimed that his four epochs were derived from the five stages or degrees in any physical movement—inception, increase, perfection, deceleration, and end. When Hume in his *Natural History of Religion* referred to a flux and reflux of ideas or to a mounting up to the more abstract conception of monotheism followed by a descent to polytheism, he was adopting a terminology derived from celestial mechanics. In Vico the image of the wheel dominates the idea of the *ricorsi.*

Perhaps the terms historical optimism and historical pessimism are not an appropriate dichotomy for eighteenth-century thought because the second term introduces alien overtones of feeling that were not necessarily experienced by men who denied the theory of moral or religious progress. Pessimism is a nineteenth-century neologism. In emancipating themselves from Christian terrorism, which in its Calvinist form prognosticates a hell so crowded that there is no standing room and a heaven with wide-open spaces and a few fluttering angels here and there, philosophes looked at the historical world with what they thought were pagan, pre-Christian eyes. Societies, like men, were fated to die. But this did not mean that in the absence of a permanent utopia, or of a Christian heaven and hell, the modern Stoic should refuse to exert himself *pro bono publico.* Man's passion for fame could serve as a counterpoise to his niggardly egotistic tendencies. Neither Voltaire nor any of the other major *philosophes* ever spoke slightingly of the natural human craving for glory, even when they refused to recognize moral progress in history.

In the eighteenth century it was still possible for the philosophes to combine an underlying feeling of the inevitability of decay and death in all things—art, science, the prosperity of the state, virtue—with the position that life and the pursuit of happiness or the public good were worthwhile. In Boulanger's bizarre theory, the two notions were joined in a way that was at first totally incomprehensible to a later age, which made of the dogma of unlimited progress the very raison d'être of moral action. For Boulanger, while the civilized world was destined to be destroyed periodically and there was nothing to circumvent it, it was the duty of the philosopher here and now to rid mankind of the false myths of divinity and a punishing God, myths generated by the last deluge and conflagration, and to proceed with the work at hand, the attainment of such happiness as mankind might yet enjoy before the wheel again began its descent. Fourier's nineteenth-century theory rested on a similar combination of cosmic assumptions: There was a finite, preordained time span for the earth; therefore it was all the more urgent that mankind speed on its way to the age of harmony and spend its allotted time in instinctual gratification instead of self-denial. A circular historical theory could live with meliorism in action.

Montesquieu's history of Rome gave the classical analysis of the death of a great and glorious empire. At times it reads like a Greek tragedy. Rome had a fatal flaw inherent in its courageous military expansion. It suffered from overextension—the vice of its virtuous noble character. This conception of the fall of Rome runs through many eighteenth-century histories, narrative and philosophical. The moral of the tale was not to overextend. The wise legislator would analyze the character of his people and seek to discover a counterpoise to its fatal flaw. The character was determined by the complex of factors known as climate, but the lawgiver could within limits—though only within limits—fight the determinations of climate. There were always elements of decay in societies, tendencies running contrary to their nobler aspirations. If these corrupting elements were not rectified, the societies would be destroyed; if they were caught in time, the polity could be restored to health temporarily, until the next bout with its characterological malady. The mechanism had to be constantly repaired. In this narrow sense, some eighteenth-century philosophico-historical thinkers were committed to a limited futurist conception; but its conservative penchant hardly allows it a place in the grand conceptualizations of euchronia, in which Time itself becomes the bearer of a cornucopia of happiness for all mankind.

Edmund Burke seemed to approach close to Montesquieu's image of the constancy of the good society as long as it was led by wise and experienced doctors whose advice was followed whenever the body politic was assailed by illness. Burke rejected a cyclical as well as a progressionist pattern. The good society was neither young nor old, but was always being restored in one of its parts so that it was ever changing and yet ever the same. If it violated the rule of its own inner organic balance, it would be destroyed as France had been by revolutionaries, as the radical Englishmen would destroy England if their false French ideas were allowed to possess and poison hearty English breasts. Burke was thus neither optimist nor pessimist, neither progressive nor reactionary, but a believer in the art of "maintaining," an end that was probably Montesquieu's ideal. The good society had no history, and if a polity remained true to its pristine spirit it would suffer neither revolution nor quick death; it would endure for a long time in a state of sameness.

How often in the eighteenth-century moralists and moral historians does one read praise for the society without a history! History meant wars, devastations, religious persecutions. Machiavelli's sense of the extension of power as an end in itself outraged the philosophes, though probably all of them would have condoned wars against superstition or against corrupt governments like that of the Turkish Empire. To the extent that they idealized China, it was a consequence of their view that its society had reached a high level of excellence and preserved itself on that plane. Repetitiveness as a self-destructive, stultifying rut is a new conception that represents a sharp disjuncture in Western thought. The need for dynamism, aggrandizement, change, expansion in all branches of human activity was first given voice by Turgot; the reality of eternal change was first seen as a religious good, fulfillment of a divine plan, by Lessing. Limitless progress, a utopia inherent in the very nature of the historical process, is a novum of the closing decades of the eighteenth century that had to overcome a wide variety of contrary intellectual currents. The burden of proof, justification of a belief in the idea of progress, was on the philosophical innovators.

Seventeenth-century participants in the Battle of the Ancients and the Moderns, in a counterattack against the diehards who contended that the ancients were unsurpassable giants in all spheres of creativity, showed that the moderns had demonstrated capacities in literary invention and in a number of new technologies. For more than two centuries defenders of the moderns had reiterated as if by common design that they had brought into the world such useful techniques as printing, the compass, and gunpowder. But this kind of claim to superiority was a mere embryo of the full-grown utopia of future perfectibility. Early utterances about the advantages and utility and even aesthetic worth of one innovation or another hardly constituted a wide-ranging utopian vision. Only Turgot, Condorcet, and Kant succeeded in transforming the idea of progress into a utopia that embraced the whole of existence. Their secular euchronia was a flight of the imagination into a qualitatively different human condition. While it has become common to trace the remote origins of this utopia back to the late Renaissance and on occasion even to classical antiquity, its mature version belongs to the latter part of the eighteenth century, when the old static pictorial utopia of calm felicity gave way to a dynamic vision of a future ideal of man in this world. As the doctrine of indefinite or infinite progress came to prevail in Western thought, the point furthest removed in future time was by definition the era of the optimum republic. This represented a revolutionary moment in the discursive utopia of the West.

The Awakened Sleeper

Simultaneously the fictional utopia adopted an entirely new device for depicting an ideal society, one thrust into future time instead of faraway space. The protagonist of Mercier's novel *L'An 2440* had been conversing far into the night with an Englishman who was haranguing him about the wretched state of France, while he tried to argue that conditions were improving. When the discussion was over, he sank into a deep sleep, from which he awakened 672 years later (Mercier's work was begun in 1768, he informs his readers). As was his habitual regimen, he went out-of-doors for a stroll, unaware of the passage of time and expecting to encounter the usual sights and sounds. The shock was immediate and profound. Avenues were broad, people walked in an orderly manner, staying on the right or the left in accordance with their destination. Instead of a riot of carriages endangering passersby, vehicles were reserved for the aged and for officials, and there were no boisterous mobs of people bruising and crushing one another in the crowded space. The Louvre had been completed, the formidable Bastille leveled to the ground. In the center of Paris ample, comfortable hospitals, theatres, houses had been constructed. Streets, empty of prostitutes, were brilliantly illuminated. The very temper of Parisians had been altered. They went their way cheerfully and did not importune the 700-year-old stranger gawking at the new world, but treated him with unaffected politeness. The sneering, mocking inhabitants of the old Paris had been transfigured. Mercier had taken as the epigraph of his book a thought from Leibniz: "The present is pregnant with the future."[6] And Leibniz was the underlying inspiration of the entire work. The point of gravity in utopia was dramatically shifted from the present or near present to distant generations not yet born. "Would the world have been made only for such a small number of men as now cover the face of the earth?" Mercier asked rhetorically in his introduction, "What are all the creatures who have existed compared with all those whom God could create? Other generations will come to fill the space that we now occupy. They will appear upon the same stage, behold the same sun, and push us so far back into antiquity that there will remain of us neither trace, nor vestige, nor memory."[7]

The awakened sleeper achieved distance in time, as in the Morean utopia the adventurous navigator had achieved distance in space. Mercier's hero opened his eyes to a Paris that was the actual fulfillment of the wildest progressionist dream. Society in the course of something over five hundred years had fashioned itself into a terrestrial urban paradise where reason and utility reigned supreme. Science and learning and diligence were esteemed and everyone was happy. The book became a prototype for a long line of imitators who broke with the Morean model and tried to communicate the reality of an ongoing self-transforming utopia.

But of far greater moment in the history of Western thought than Mercier's 1771 fictional rendering of the futurist utopia were the writings of the philosophers, who drafted reasoned demonstrations that the utopia of progress was either inevitable or at least highly probable. The two Frenchmen, Turgot the older and Condorcet the younger, were intimately connected with each other. Condorcet was Turgot's biographer, he was called his chevalier, and his own work was a development and expansion of the unpublished sketches of his predecessor. Kant was a loner living in Königsberg, a German university city on the Baltic Sea, far from the Parisian center of the intellectual universe. The French and German doctrines of progress, as they emerged in historico-philosophical essays, were rather dissimilar in tone, character, and content, each in its own way setting up a frame for a utopia of progress that dominated the mind and sensibility of its respective national society for more than a century. With these philosophers we enter the world of the full-fledged utopian system-makers whose comprehensiveness and universalism have possessed the secular utopia ever since. Speaking-picture utopias still had their uses, but they paled beside the vigorous new theoretical structures that usurped the power and the glory, first of systematic philosophies and then of established religions.

19

Turgot on the
Future of Mind

IN 1750 a young bachelor of arts, scion of an illustrious Norman family, the Prior Anne Robert Jacques Turgot, Baron de l'Aulne, delivered two lectures in Latin before the Sorbonne at the opening and conclusion of the academic exercises called the *Sorboniques*. Together they framed a new conception of world history from remotest antiquity to the present and constituted the first important version in modern times of the ideology of progress.[1]

Abbé, Philosophe, King's Minister

Turgot's theses had been born amid great personal spiritual travail, as befitted so momentous a pronouncement. For three months before the delivery of the first oration he had been profoundly disturbed—in a letter to his brother, a Knight of Malta, he described himself as in a depressed state—and only after a most flattering triumph had been assured did he completely recover.[2] The Cardinal de la Rochefoucauld himself was in attendance at the 23-year-old scholar's initial performance on July 3, 1750, which to all appearances launched the idea of human perfectibility under solemn ecclesiastical auspices. The academic stronghold of the Catholic faith seems a strange podium for the propagation of a view of mankind which in its ultimate consequences was more potent than the wit of Voltaire and the mechanistic materialism of La Mettrie in deflecting Western consciousness from a religious to a utilitarian earthly morality. Now that the twentieth-century Catholic Church has become progressive and oriented toward organized social amelioration, the absurdity of the mid-eighteenth-century confrontation may seem less flagrant, but retrospective reflection on the scene is enough to make one believe in the dialectic. From the same building where the young Turgot was lodged there regularly resounded thunderous condemnations by the Faculty of Theology against heretical works of philosophy. In the very bosom of the old religion of sin, death, and salvation was born the new religion of earthly immortality.

Nominally Turgot's discourse was a eulogy of Christianity, but to extol the ancient faith he could find no more appropriate and lofty praise for the creed of his audience than an array of historical proofs positive that the Christian religion, far from being an agent of the forces of darkness—as clandestine atheists were bruiting it about—had been the moving spirit in the progress of mankind since the fall of the Roman Empire. The truth of Christianity vindicated by the idea of progress and a harangue on the "utility of religion" were dangerous apologias, but it would seem that the mid-eighteenth-century church was grateful for approval from any quarter.[3] Turgot's defense of Christianity had marked affinities with laudatory chapters on the moral truths of Catholicism in the *Esprit des lois*. Montesquieu had already anticipated a number of Turgot's arguments when he demonstrated that on balance, historically, the social vir-

461

tues of religion had outweighed its iniquities—but this was a rather weak bulwark for the church militant. The singular form of approbation voiced by these aristocratic defenders of the faith robbed Christianity of transcendence and ultimately left it so enfeebled that religion was constrained to conduct the great spiritual debate on the adversary's favorite field of combat, worldly usefulness.

In no single work published during his lifetime did Turgot ever amplify the theses of his orations of 1750; but a substantial number of fragments and outlines first collated by Dupont de Nemours under the Empire, the articles prepared for the *Encyclopédie*, scattered reflections in his essays on language and economics, verbal traditions incorporated by Condorcet in his biography of 1786, and letters to philosophical contemporaries, when assembled together, constitute a grand body of doctrine with a reasonable measure of consistency. Turgot, who shed the cloth and became one of the great administrators of France, was an innovator in the study of philosophical history, however sketchy and unfinished his brief texts may be. Had he ever written the projected universal history about which he talked at length to Condorcet instead of spending himself in abortive attempts at a rehabilitation of the French state, he would have ranked with Vico as a creator of the "new science." Even during his lifetime his ideas were far more widely diffused than the meager record of his publications would indicate.[4] Though he rejected their blasphemies, Turgot was one of the great heroes of the philosophes. As a man of action, albeit a failure, the promulgator of the six edicts of 1776 gave daring expression to Enlightenment theory. When the dying Voltaire, on his last triumphant journey to Paris in 1778, grasped the hands of the fallen minister, kissed them, and bathed them in tears, the skeptical king of the epoch symbolically embraced the idea of progress and the Leibnizian theodicy which *Candide* had so uproariously caricatured.

Turgot, of the middle generation of the philosophes, younger than Voltaire and Rousseau, older than Condorcet, despite his great talents was a blocked, frustrated man, unfulfilled. Houdon's statue has caught his melancholy air; one senses a touch of genius which was never quite realized, a sort of eighteenth-century French presage of John Stuart Mill.

In April and May 1776 the "good Turgot," whose whole being was devoted to the happiness of mankind, whose ministerial edicts were intended to alleviate the sufferings of his fellows and to save the kingdom of the young Louis XVI who had called him to his side, found himself beset by widespread hunger riots, the *guerre des farines*. These popular uprisings, now considered rehearsals for the great tumults which followed twenty years later, were largely spontaneous, though the intrigues of the courtiers and of the farmers-general whose interests where threatened by the six edicts played some role in rousing the populace.[5] Turgot approved severe measures of suppression, and a number of rioters were hanged from a high gibbet "as an example." The monarchy survived the incidents, but Turgot's enemies used the opportunity to perfect a cabal, and the minister was dismissed. Turgot foresaw the doom of the monarch he served—on one occasion he recalled to his sire the fate of Charles I— but to what avail? In a youthful *pensée* Turgot had already dwelt on the curse of the power of prescience. "If a man could foresee with certainty all the events which depend upon chance and if he directed his conduct in the light of this knowledge, he would pass for a lunatic because men would not understand his motives."[6]

The papers of this enigmatic man kept in the Château de Lantheuil in Normandy have not revealed his secret—if there was one. There are rare expressions of warm affection between the Abbé Turgot and the young abbés with whom he studied at school and who offered him friendly advice on the early drafts of his discourses and prize essays. Of the two chief aides during his tenure of office, Dupont de Nemours seems to have been the object of intense paternal feeling (there are three hundred letters covering a period of twenty years); with Condorcet the relationship was more philosophical. Both worshiped him as a heroic model. "If ever friendship deigned to inhabit a temple on earth it was the heart of M. Turgot," Dupont de Nemours wrote in the introductory volume to the first edition of Turgot's works. "He joined the sensitivity of a young man and the modesty of a respectable woman to the character of a legislator for whom the administration of an empire was not above his capabilities, a man worthy of influencing the destinies of the world."[7] In the salons of the great ladies of the ancien régime Turgot was a brilliant star, but not even a breath of scandal about him can be detected in the memoir writers. During the crisis of 1776 when attacks rained upon him, a false catalogue of imaginary books in the Abbé Baudeau's library was circulated: along with run-of-the-mill titles like *L'Homme au masque*, *Consultation de médecine sur les délires de M. Turgot*, and *Le Nouveau Machiavel*, there was listed an *Antigunaika, ouvrage composé par M. Turgot, avec une préface du frère orateur Diderot*, a crude attempt, in the manner of contemporary libels, to cast doubt upon his interest in women. There is a tradition that Turgot had once asked for the hand of Mlle. de Ligniville, who presumably rejected him in favor of Helvétius. This scion of the great Turgot family—named after the god Thor, according to one etymology—was a shy man with a tendency to obesity whose reticence was often mistaken for arrogance. His dedication to the life of reason sometimes made incomprehensible to him the ways of men who were differently motivated.

The Baron Turgot would no doubt have resented being included as the first prophet of progress. A man of orderly administration in the provinces and in the ministries, a frequenter of the great Paris drawing rooms where nothing was more alien than enthusiasm, he was worlds away from the spluttering Prophets of London of 1707, those refugees from the Cévennes who foretold the doom. But, for all that, he was the true initiator of the rationalist prophetic tradition. Dismayed as he would have been by the end of the catena, by the rigid dogmatism of an Auguste Comte or the more fanciful hallucinations of a Fourier, Turgot despite his personal diffidence must take his place at the head of the procession. First among moderns he foretold the future of reason.

Novelty or the Rut of Sameness

Turgot's philosophy of progress was firmly rooted in the current sensationalist theory of knowledge. The capacity of man to receive new impressions from the outside world, to combine them, and to reflect upon them was an ultimate assurance of the inevitable and indefinite advancement of the human mind. Sheer accumulation of experience in time was the underlying process of the education of mankind, as it was for the child. In the primordial stages of historical development the motives of human beings are nakedly passionate and they partake of almost no reflective elements. Men are goaded into action by their pains and their pleasures, their lusts and their necessities, their hunger, their thirst for power and conquest. Only in the latter days of Enlightenment have rational forces begun to assume direction of world history.

This recognition of the predominance of the passionate rather than the rational element in the history of mankind raised for Turgot a problem common to most exponents of temporal teleologies: how could a being who to the ordinary observer has acted primarily, if not solely, out of passion, whose conduits open to the external world are mere sensations, ever achieve a transcendent destiny called Reason? Turgot's man, though created by God, is bound by the laws of the Locke-Condillac epistemology, and within this framework he must accomplish his historic mission: become a civilized moral being living up to the standards of eighteenth-century Christian Stoicism; exert ever greater control over nature through technology; acquire and preserve beyond the possibilities of destruction an increasing body of knowledge about himself and about the physical world; achieve and sustain a measure of artistic creativity.

In most of their writings the philosophes, and Turgot among them, prided themselves on their emancipation from the *esprit de système* which they associated with scholasticism and the secular philosophical system-builders of the seventeenth century. They were confident of the purity of their empirical method; they looked only at the facts. But often enough the categorical denial of innate ideas or a priori axioms was only a preparatory device which preceded a dogmatic affirmation of innate sentiments or principles of behavior. Western thought has experienced its greatest difficulties in driving out the demon of the absolute; if he was exorcised from the mind he sought refuge in feelings. Thus Rousseau, for example, in his *Discourse on Inequality,* invented the tragic "instinct" of perfectibility to explain man's unfortunate emergence from the lowest stage of the state of nature. Turgot posited a similar principle, which, though he shunned the word rendered odious by Locke, was virtually "innate." There is for Turgot a basic drive in human nature to innovate, to create novelty, to bring into being new combinations of sensations. And once this novelty-making impulse has been assumed, rock bottom has been reached. One either accepts or rejects it.

Simultaneously Turgot identified in civilized society a hostile negating principle which, through the operation of institutions, had always sought to stall man in the rut of sameness, in a routine, in a state of treadmill repetitiveness. World history turned into a war eternal between these polar principles. In depicting the struggle, Turgot was of course no indifferent bystander, for the battle between the spirit of novelty and the spirit of routine, between the desire for movement and the tendency toward quiescence, was the underlying conflict of human destiny, a new philosophical version of the religious war between good and evil.

This idea of innovation remained the basic new concept in Turgot's view of the historical world. Traditional society had accepted a changeless state of being as the greatest good. In the most ancient documents of Near Eastern civilization the plea to the gods for an enduring order was the prayer behind the quest for peace. When messianism with its foretelling of a great transformation appeared in Judaic and Christian history its promise of a radical metamorphosis was invariably considered a dangerous disruptive agent by the rulers of society. With an acute sense of self-preservation institutionalized religions have always fought the millenarians. Change of the earthly order and a prediction of the change were equally disturbing. In the midst of wars and in conquest, traditionalist societies invariably aimed at establishing a stable, enduring, even immutable order. Turgot may have considered himself a devoted servant of the French monarchy, but no principle was more inimical to its preservation than his absolute commitment to eternal change and perfectibility.

By raising the spirit of novelty to the level of a major passion of human nature, Turgot established a fundamental distinction between the physical and the moral sciences, one that was increasingly emphasized as the eighteenth century passed its halfway mark. In that Socratic age, along with deep respect for the new physics there were real misgivings about man's complete immersion in the universe of the natural philosophers. The eighteenth-century moralist, though fascinated by the Newtonian world machine, a model he longed to imitate, was not without hidden doubts about its applicability to the social sciences. The facile analogy between the movement of the spheres obeying the law of gravity and a harmony in human relationships that would reflect the natural order, a frequent correspondence, was not always convincing. A number of major eighteenth-century thinkers, though committed to the principle of the existence of moral scientific laws, dwelt upon the differences as well as the similarities between the two orders of nature and of man. Vico's *Scienza Nuova* was a deliberate attack upon preoccupation with the laws of matter, the lesser element, to the neglect and abandonment of the laws of men and nations which had their own peculiar character. Vico had made a great show of contrasting the loftier, nobler truths of his new science of history and human experience with the more limited certainty of the mathematical world of the Cartesians—a paradox to the average intellectual of the age. Rousseau, following up his earlier attack on the arts and sciences, had shouted a challenge in his *Second Discourse:* "It is of Man that I shall speak"—and he meant that he was again dealing with human problems, not the laws of nature and the achievements of technology, even though in the next breath he rendered obeisance to the Newtonian image. By contrast, Montesquieu's great masterpiece of mid-century Enlightenment was still written in the shadow of the old subservience to Newtonian physics, and his model was basically mechanistic; the good polity was subject to technical breakdown because of a failure to operate in accordance with its true character, and the genius-legislator by fathoming the spirit of a nation's laws could effect a restoration, set the machine working once more so that it might continue its orderly revolutions. "Ed io anche son pittore," Montesquieu had affirmed without modesty before the unveiling of his fundamental law of climate, the equivalent of universal gravity in physics. Turgot drew upon Montesquieu for factual information, but he abjured the slavish patterning of the science of man after the science of physics. Though far from emancipated from mechanical imagery, he introduced another dimension: if the physical order expressed its innermost being in the principle of recurrence, the human order had a unique principle all its own, an antithetic principle—Progress. While Turgot rarely used organismic similes, he was already affirming the intrinsically different nature of the world of men, in which the repetitive movements were far outstripped by the novelties.

The order of men was an endless innovation. But the new was not a mere fortuitous alignment and realignment of elements in the Epicurean manner. In human events real, lasting, and enduring novelty was being created. The new configuration brought about by each successive age was not merely a replacement of one set of forms by another, nor was it only a rectification of an old structure. There was a process of eternal transmission, an ever-growing accumulation, an increasing inheritance, a sort of vast worldly repository of intellectual merit. The variations brought forth in history were additive, and the piling up of new experience was the law of mankind. Civilized man was distinguished from the savage and from the child precisely because he had recorded more diverse and complex combinations—the language of Locke's epistemology.

The constancy of the physical order had so ravished men's minds in the eighteenth century that the apparently accidental and chaotic human order had begun to appear inferior. Turgot's idea of progress, by sharply distinguishing the human order and discovering in it a relative superiority, reestablished its faltering status. In this discovery there was an admixture of Christian apology and humanism. Mankind was vindicated, was restored to a central position in a separate historical world, and was granted a quality which no other part of the natural order could pretend to possess. Man was also rescued from the Epicurean view of the world, which had many somber attractions for the eighteenth-century philosophical historian. While Turgot's historical universe could not boast the obvious constancy of physical nature where events repeated themselves, it was blessed with a more sublime rule of constancy, the extraordinary law of steady perfectibility. Sameness and repetition, the very attributes which men contemplated with admiration in nature, were evil if they long endured in the world of men. Constant inconstancy, eternal change and progress, were the true distinctions of mankind.

The opening periods of the second *Sorbonique,* the *Tableau philosophique des progrès successifs de l'esprit humain,* contrasted the rival virtues of the two orders:

The phenomena of nature, subject to constant laws, are enclosed in a circle of revolutions which are always the same. Everything is reborn, everything perishes, and through successive generations in which vegetation and animal life reproduce themselves time merely restores at each instant the image which it has caused to disappear.

The succession of men, however, presents a changing spectacle from century to century. Reason, the passions, liberty, produce new events without end. All ages are linked to each other by a series of causes and effects which binds the present state of the world with all those which have preceded it. The conventional signs of language and writing, affording men the means of assuring the possession of their ideas and of communicating them to others, have fashioned of all detailed forms of knowledge a common treasury, which one generation transmits to another like a legacy that is ever being augmented with the discoveries of each century, and thus the human race, considered from its beginnings, appears to the eyes of a philosopher to be one immense whole which, like every individual, has its infancy and its progress.[8]

Turgot's conception of the progressive accumulation of knowledge through time, particularly in the physical sciences, was hardly an unheralded novelty by the mid-eighteenth century. Roger Bacon had probably had at least an inkling of the idea. Francis Bacon's *Novum Organum* and Bernard Fontenelle's *Digression sur les anciens et les modernes,* written incident to the famous literary "quarrel," have been recognized as respectworthy antecedents. Passages in

Descartes and particularly Pascal's *Fragment de préface sur le traité du vide* were forerunners insofar as they conceived of the accretion of scientific truth through the mere performance and recording of new experiments over the centuries. Turgot's theory rested upon a far broader concept. In contrast to Pascal's severe restriction of the idea to the physical sciences, accompanied by tortured doubts about the meaning of this progress to man's moral and religious nature, Turgot extended progress to virtually the whole realm of being and implanted it as the central shaft of a system of worldly morality.

Turgot's theory mirrored a profound revolution in man's attitude toward change which in the eighteenth century imposed itself with ever greater force in western European society and was soon to conquer the world. He had a pervasive psychological horror of the static, his friends have reported, and in public office he was always impatient of any curbs on his zeal to reform and rearrange whatever ancient practices came within his jurisdiction. In a playful couplet Voltaire said that Turgot did not quite know what he wanted but he was sure it would be something different. In violent rebellion against traditionalist society, as chief minister of Louis XVI he spearheaded its disruption with new ways of thought and new methods of action. He seemed to revel in its breakup. Turgot had an almost twentieth-century sense of the rapid flux of events, a succession of changes so fast that it was almost impossible to grasp the meaning of a stable structure. In the "Plan d'un ouvrage sur la géographie politique" he expressed this feeling in a brilliant aperçu. "Before we have learned that things are in a given situation they have already been altered several times. Thus we always become aware of events when it is too late, and politics has to foresee the present, so to speak."[9]

In the plan of the second discourse at the Sorbonne, "movement" was described as the primordial force which dispelled chaos. Only through movement had men acquired ideas of distinctiveness and of unity. If an innate sense of movement were not an aspect of human nature, men would have contented themselves with mere sensation and they would never have established differences. If they did not synthesize new combinations of feelings to yield novel reflections, they would have gone on perceiving the same things without change forever throughout history. Fortunately movement had always thrust objects into fresh relationships. Wars, migrations, catastrophes had made discoveries possible by allowing for unprecedented confluences of events. If man were not submitted to such violent stimuli, he would lapse into a state of somnolence and barren decay followed by death. In Vico's doctrine the energizing drive had to be roused by necessity. Surely Turgot's early man—and perhaps man in all ages—had to be provoked and excited to produce new ideas, to assimilate new juxtapositions of phenomena. Any mutation—and he used the word—was desirable, even if it should temporarily lead men astray, because something was to be learned from any occurrence.[10] It was preferable to allow men to wander into dangerous pathways and break their legs rather than to limit experience and to promote the false belief that perfection had already been attained. Error was more salutary than imitation, he declared with an almost romantic defiance, anticipating Schiller's defense of a similar paradox. Turgot sanctioned the free exercise of caprice as long as it did not harm other persons. In a fragment on morals written when he was a young man, he attacked the "sheeplike conformity" which society called "good sense."[11] His belief in the right to error expressed itself in an absolute intellectual openness. "He tolerated equally," wrote Condorcet, "both Pyrrhonism and the staunchest belief in opinions opposed to his own."[12] Since mere repetition added nothing to the total acquisitions of mankind, "to progress," in one of its nuclear definitions, came to mean simply to innovate, to make the new, without an implied judgment of worth and excellence, and in this crude form the idea has often been adopted in Western society.

Turgot's disrespect for the dead weight of the past was dramatically set forth in his *Encyclopédie* article "Foundations." If all the graves that had ever been dug had been preserved, it would be necessary in order to cultivate the soil to overturn "these sterile monuments and to stir the ashes of the dead to nourish the living."[13] He was prepared to violate the wishes of ancestors if their endowments, their ancient wills, usurped the needs of their descendants and barred them from access to the tremendous hoards of wealth controlled by monasteries. If past generations impeded the free enjoyment of liberty, the wills of the ancestors should be annulled. The past had to be overcome, brushed aside, lest it gain a stranglehold on the unborn. Living meant an eternal breaking out of old forms, an emancipation, a liberation. When Turgot tried to refashion the traditionalist monarchy of France he was acting out his own philosophy of history. In the edict of 1776 suppressing the *jurandes* he proclaimed the "right to work" as the possession of every man, an "inalienable right" of humanity[14]—familiar language that year, but his words should not be interpreted with the socialist overtones of 1848. Work was eulogized as the creative act of man cleansed of the stigma of original sin; and even though rooted in necessity it was the key instrument of liberty. Since any activity was potentially productive of innovation, it contained the germ of progress. To shackle work with the restrictions of the feudal system, with prohibitions and tariffs, was to smother the possibilities of change. Limitations on the movement of grain among the provinces, on the free circulation of ideas, on the mobility of labor, on the accessibility of knowledge were kindred antiprogressive regulations. Whatever was fixed, set, hardened, a religious dogma or an economic restriction, literally anything that might block new combinations of ideas, was a source of evil, deadly.[15] Turgot's prognostication of the independence of the American colonies was the expression of a libertarian desire of the philosopher of progress, even though his analysis preserved the form of a cold diplomatic state paper.[16] Turgot favored all freedom from tutelage, any independence, because these political acts of liberty were conditions precedent to creative innovation. The very term liberty lost its medieval connotation of a privilege and became the right to bring into being what had not existed before. Turgot knew that the present and the future were locked in a sequence of relationships with the past, but there are few thinkers who have respected its survival less.

The archenemy of progress, the sickly tendency toward repetition and sameness, had historically sunk whole societies in a rut where they languished and died. "It is not error which is opposed to the progress of truth; it is not wars and revolutions which retard the progress of governments; it is softness, stubborness, routine, and everything which leads to inaction."[17] The spirit of routine tended to become the controlling force in any intellectual elite which managed to seize power before it was permeated with a full consciousness of the morality of progress. Turgot's favorite illustration was the mandarin class and his evidence the well-nourished eighteenth-century debate on the character of the despotism of China. Here was a classic example of a society in which rational scientific progress had so far outstripped the spirit of liberty and moral progress that the rulers created a monopoly for themselves, froze education, and insisted upon mere traditional reiteration. Though the scientific level the Chinese mandarins had attained was high, their whole intellectual world became desiccated because it was static. Sects of every kind, philosophical as well as religious, faced the debilitating influence of the spirit of routine when they enjoyed power for long. Turgot was so wary of this pernicious proclivity of sects to stereotype their ideas that he even abandoned the philosophes of the *Encyclopédie,* repelled by their dogmatism. Only with great reluctance did he concede to his friend Condorcet, the Permanent Secretary of the Academy of Sciences, that academies might conceivably serve a useful purpose during a brief transitional period. In the bright future of mankind he saw no more need for these learned assemblies than for other corporate bodies tainted with the stigmas of feudalism. The esprit de corps was in itself a stultifying evil. A few common projects of direct benefit to the participants he was willing to tolerate, though not without misgivings. His historical appreciation of the sects and ancient priesthoods of Babylon and Egypt was barbed with an antagonism which derived from his hostility toward the theologians who had trained him. The definition of a priesthood as a conspiracy to withhold religious truth in order to maintain uncontested sway over the people was common enough in eighteenth-century Europe. Turgot added the further reflection that in time these intellectual monopolists lost the capacity to understand their own traditional learning; and whatever scientific treasure they had amassed soon either evaporated or was destroyed by a superior force. The accumulation of scientific knowledge required absolute freedom of inquiry—a Turgot conception which became a cornerstone of liberalism in modern times, a highly controversial contention that has often proved itself to be an article of the new faith rather than a historical proposition that is universally applicable. Hume, Turgot's friend, doubted it when the idea was first propounded.

Turgot was openly dissatisfied with the great Montesquieu's typology of polities based on climate or geography. He posed a fundamental dichotomy between those societies which featured a maximum of mobility in all branches of human activity and those which were hostile to movement. Montesquieu had betrayed a strong preference for a political configuration in a state of balance, perhaps with tension in the atmosphere, but with equilibrium maintained. Turgot extolled every manifestation of expansiveness and condemned every form of self-containment as deadening. A precondition of progress was that a society be wide open to the spirit of change, that it welcome energy and action. Progress required a climate in which novelty was passionately sought after, not only tolerated. Turgot's philosophy of history anticipated the mood of the Revolution.

Genius the Dynamic Agent

In Turgot the idea of progress had not yet become completely dehumanized. There was a unique being, the genius, who played a crucial role as its dynamic

agent. There were continually new encounters, new contingencies, unprecedented relationships in the world, but most of them passed unperceived, leaving no lasting imprint on a human mind, and they were gone forever. A living
intermediary was necessary for the consummation of the progressive act; a
human being had to experience the sensations, make the proper combinations,
and after reflection create a new truth. The genius was that receptive mediator
who grasped novelty, who was unbound by previous modes of perception,
and who dared to articulate what he saw. History functioned through the genius—the new Logos—and if unfavorable circumstances prevented him from
exercising his superb talents on the novel play of events, progress was temporarily arrested. Turgot, unlike Montesquieu, was in search of a human moral
force, rather than a physical force such as the challenge of the environment, to
spark the movement of world history. In his theory of genius and its relation
to the dynamics of progress, Turgot discovered a uniform single principle operative everywhere that could account for diversity in the tempo and character
of progress in time and place without abandoning the whole mechanism to
Epicurean chance.

Though Turgot recognized only minor differences in the natural physical
equipment of men, he did establish a "real inequality" in the character of their
souls, and though he confessed to his inability to define the causes of genius, he
was convinced of its qualitative superiority. His appreciation of genius was in
the romantic spirit of one segment of eighteenth-century thought and has its
parallel in Diderot; Turgot, however, introduced none of the psychic complexities which were raised by *Le Neveu de Rameau*. Turgot's genius was a
more old-fashioned, respectable figure, one who could still be admitted into
Fontenelle's academic society. But Turgot created the type in the philosophy
of history, and he grew in stature until he ultimately became Hegel's demonic
world-historical hero-monster, the embodiment of Spirit at a crucial *Moment*.

Turgot still dealt with his genius as a mechanical principle, since the most
important thing about him was the mathematical frequency of his appearance
in the world. The problem of the relative number of geniuses emerging in various historical periods had been debated in the course of the late-seventeenth-
century quarrel between the ancients and the moderns. In their zeal to prove
that it was possible for contemporary literature to be as great as the creations of
the classical world, the moderns had steadfastly maintained that nature was
equally prolific of genius in all times and in all places. For evidence of this constancy in the fertility of nature they used homely analogies. Since trees were
obviously no thicker in antiquity than in modern times, why should genius
then have been more plentiful or more sublime? The eighteenth century
tended to regard an increase in the population of a society as an absolute good.
For Turgot, who believed in a fixed ratio of genius births to ordinary births at
any historic moment, the modern increase in the number of inhabitants was
especially felicitous, for it presaged a greater yield of geniuses. "Genius is
spread among mankind like gold in a mine. The more ore you take out the
more metal you will get." [18]

Turgot introduced a new twist into the old conception of genius. To be sure,
the extraordinary man was a natural phenomenon that appeared at more or
less equal intervals throughout history, the same natural potential being present in an identical amount, but the crux of the problem of genius lay else-

where. Circumstances in the world of political reality and in the accidental world of the natural genius either fostered his development or crushed him. Therefore the first task which Turgot posed for humanity was to actualize genius more frequently and to minimize the instances when a born genius was lost to mankind and to progress. If under favorable conditions in a given society many potential geniuses were trained to their full capacity, progress was assured. If only a few were suitably perfected, at best the age might become an epoch of conservation. And should genius be generally suffocated by external conditions, a temporary decline might set in. Thus the preservation of the genius and the maximization of his talents became the central function of the good society, for he held the power of the keys of progress. A whole moral system was involved in this rather simple idea. Those forces which stifled genius were evil and those which fostered it, allowed it to attain fruition, were good. During the long historic past the central role of genius had not been recognized, with the result that mankind had benefited from only a small proportion of the geniuses whom nature had proffered to civilization. This waste of genius in the world economy of knowledge had retarded progress.

All of the utopian projects for the subsidization of genius drafted by Condorcet and Saint-Simon at the turn of the century were direct outgrowths of Turgot's stress upon the critical role of genius in the historic process. The rather fanciful and complicated mechanical schemes they devised were specific responses to the problem of how to salvage more geniuses and how to increase their productivity, since both of these heirs to the Turgot conception were convinced that genius set the pace of development for progress. The rate of the fulfillment of genius established the overall rate of progress in an absolute sense.

Language the Vessel

One factor above all others determined whether the perceptions of genius were destined to become part of the main stream of universal progress or whether they were fated to be forgotten in the darkness of time: the ready accessibility of an appropriate vessel for the containment of ideas, an orderly language.[19] If for reasons related to the political life of nations—wars, conquests, turmoils— no proper language was fashioned, novelty would sprout in vain. Normally in the great civilizations the genius had available adequate symbols for the preservation of his thoughts and their transmission to posterity. In the future language was destined to become an even better instrument; it would be stripped of its rhetoric, cleansed of its ambiguities, so that the only means of communication for true knowledge would be the mathematical symbol, verifiable, unchanging, eternal. The ideal of Descartes's clear and distinct ideas, terminological economy, would become a reality.

In the past one of the unfortunate consequences of the conquest of a decadent higher civilization by vigorous barbarians had been the linguistic confusion which followed the disaster. A long period of time elapsed before the victors and the vanquished merged their different forms of speech and, during the interval, language, the only receptacle for the storing of scientific progress then available, was lacking. Geniuses continued to perceive new phenomena, but since they were deprived of a stable body of rational linguistic symbols their observations were stillborn. During the barbarian invasions of Western Europe the Latin language, which previously had diffused works of speculative science, was adulterated by admixture with primitive tongues. The babel of languages resulted in a protracted period of intellectual sterility during which it was impossible for a creative genius to express himself because there was no settled linguistic medium for scientific thought.[20] Turgot compared this historical situation to the pouring of two different liquids into a bottle; a passage of time was required before their fusion could be effected, before the murky color was dissipated and a new homogeneous fluid appeared. The Middle Ages were that long interval during which favorable linguistic conditions were created for the Renaissance emergence of genius. In the Byzantine Empire a stultification like that in the medieval West had occurred, but there at least the speculative science which the ancients had accumulated could be preserved intact, for in this isolated society continuity of language with the source of knowledge in Greece had never been severed.

Language was not only a means of communication for new ideas, it was also a repository for the history of progress. In an article on languages which Turgot had projected for the *Encyclopédie* but which, like so many of his plans, never came to fruition, he intended to show that throughout the ages language was an index of the stadial development of nations, since words were invented only when there were ideas demanding utterance. The mere existence of certain words was witness to a complex civilization.[21] Should two nations "unequally advanced in their progress" intermingle, the more highly civilized people, even if defeated, would predominantly color the new language-fusion because they alone possessed words corresponding to the more complicated ideas of a rich social fabric. Thus even when a decadent civilization succumbed before young barbarians its idea structure would survive. Language recorded the triumph of real progress in science even amid the ruins of once glorious empires. This conception of the history of language and literature as the embodiment of the successive stages of human development had of course been more copiously presented in the axioms of Vico's *Scienza Nuova*, but there is no evidence of any direct influence. In his *Réflexions sur les langues*, a youthful polemic against Maupertuis written about 1751, Turgot proposed historical semantic studies as the clue to mythology and to the illumination of prehistoric traditions. "The study of language, if well done, would perhaps be the best of logics. In analyzing, in comparing the words of which they are fashioned, in tracing from the beginning the different meanings which they acquired, in following the thread of ideas, we will see through which stages, through which metamorphoses men passed . . . This kind of experimental metaphysics would be at one and the same time the history of the human mind and the history of the progress of its thoughts, always fitted to the needs which gave birth to them. Languages are at once their expression and their measure."[22] Like many of Turgot's insights, the formula is so laconic, so apparently casual, that it would pass unnoticed were we not already sensitized to the ideas by parallel themes in other eighteenth-century thinkers.

The primitive language structure of each nation had developed independently but along similar lines, because the sensations from which speech derived were the same. While Turgot was not as militantly antidiffusionist as Vico, he had broken completely with the traditional theory of language. By mid-century there was already widespread disbelief in the orthodox notion that language was born a complete and perfect rational instrument, a fully developed means of communication which Adam already possessed in the Garden of Eden. Though still utilizing subterfuges necessitated by censorship, the weight of opinion tended to establish a hypothetical historical pattern for the growth of language, from the first emotive grunts of man in the state of nature, through a period of sentence structure, to the highest form of expression in a mathematical formula. This ideal history of the origins and development of language had roots in Locke, was repeated in Condillac, in Adam Smith, in Monboddo, in the *Encyclopédie,* in Rousseau, in Hume, and could count even respectable English bishops among its adherents. Language had become the record of the human intelligence as it passed from a stage in which man, like a child or a savage, could only record the concrete, to the highest levels of abstraction, those mathematical symbols in which neither human feelings nor concrete objects obtruded. Along the way men had resorted to images, similes, poetic metaphors, admixtures of ideas and sensations. There were transitional stages during which both language and thought lacked the precision and the conciseness of the French spoken in Mlle. de L'Espinasse's salon; but even the most philosophical language was vastly inferior to a theorem as a method of rational discourse.

In all of these stadial views of human development, whether the mirror of mankind was the history of language, of writing, of religion, of civilization, of perception itself, there was one recurrent theme: the record revealed a steady rationalization of man at the expense of his emotional and imaginative faculties, a constant movement toward greater abstraction. As in Vico, Turgot's fragments also recognized a stage of human consciousness which was so primitive that man could only give voice to his ideas in myth, in metaphor, in pictorial images. And for Turgot, as for Hume, there is a manifest superiority in the abstract attitude over the concrete. Turgot was ultimately led by his worship of reason to prefer the purest mathematical abstraction over all other forms of knowledge and to look upon the metaphors and images in which the ancients communicated their ideas as a sort of baby talk, expressive perhaps, but a form that had to be outgrown. Eighteenth-century French thinkers like Turgot were conscious of the death of the poetic spirit in their society, and they did not regret it.

In his theory of language Turgot was skirting the borders of one of the commonest and yet most controversial conceptions in modern philosophies of history, the idea that there has been an evolvement of human modes of perception, that the differences between the primitive and the civilized are qualitative, and that they can be defined as different mentalities. Thinkers from a wide variety of disciplines seemed to be groping in this general direction throughout the eighteenth and early nineteenth centuries until the idea culminated in Comte's law of the three states, a source from which it was diffused throughout modern psychology and anthropology—though by no means without challenge. It has often been pointed out that a number of passages in Turgot already contain this positivist law in embryo.[23] Knowledge had once been exclusively theological, then it turned metaphysical, and finally it was becoming positive. By the theological stage Turgot—writing in the tradition of Fontenelle and paralleling the works of his friends Hume and de Brosses on the natural history of primitive religion—meant the propensity of men to project intelligent divine power into all manner of objects and forces in nature. The metaphysical described a stage when knowledge was thought of and expressed in terms of essences. The final or third stage was one in which men recognized the real objective nature of things and were beginning to formulate their relationships in mathematical terms. Language had recorded this growth of human modes of perception, and in their normal development all peoples would have to pass from one stage to another. In a general historico-philosophical sense Turgot conceived of progress as the ascent of mankind from one state of perception to another, each step accompanied by the introduction of new signs and symbols.

This aspect of Turgot's theory of progress can be interpreted as an extension to the historical process of Condillac's epistemology as presented in the *Essai sur l'origine des connaissances humaines*. Those conditions which Condillac found necessary for the original acquisition of abstract thought in an individual were discovered to be the motive drives in the progress of the species throughout time. The stimulating effects of intricate and numerous social communications, the existence of a language whose symbols were clear and distinct rather than blurred, a sense of the fragility and susceptibility to error of even the greatest intellects, the importance of chance are all ideas he drew directly from Condillac. What Turgot did was to translate the investigation from an abstract inquiry into how human knowledge should be acquired by an ideal pupil under the direction of a philosophical tutor, to the vast canvas of the history of mankind, and thus to fill in with empirical detail that ancient analogy between phylogeny and ontogeny. Mankind did in fact amass its knowledge in precisely the same way as every newborn child. Its mistakes have been numerous but it has learned from experience, and in the future it may be able to minimize error by perfecting its geniuses, the men who have special talents for the manipulation of symbols and the combination of ideas. Condillac's "operations of the soul and the causes of its progressions"[24] were transmuted by Turgot into the operations of the human mind or mankind and its progressions.

Ethnology the Record

Universal progress has left a record of its movement from one stage to another that is far more complete and circumstantial than written historical documents and even language; this is the living record of ethnology, the actual existence of aboriginal tribes and nations dispersed over the face of the globe, each on a different level of culture.[25] The travel literature and the missionary reports on primitive, barbaric, semibarbaric, and heathen civilized societies had come to constitute an indisputable body of data for any scholar to examine and for any intrepid explorer to verify, proving without recourse to conjecture that there had in fact been a stadial development of mankind. Contemporary barbaric societies were vestiges of previous stages; primarily because of their isolation, they had become frozen at a given moment in time or they were developing more slowly. "In the overall progress of the human mind, all nations start from the same point, proceed to the same goal, follow more or less the same path, but at a very uneven pace," Turgot wrote in the article "Etymologie" in the sixth volume of the *Encyclopédie*.[26]

The idea that savage societies were exemplars of what the more advanced civilizations had once been was by the mid-eighteenth century no longer startling, but not until the writings of Turgot and de Brosses[27] in the 1750s did this momentous hypothesis become the springboard for grandiose conceptions of stadial progress. For Turgot the ethnographic record contained the whole history of the species, so that by moving throughout the world from one primitive society to another the philosopher could—if he wisely chose appropriate examples—establish the true historical series from the most barbaric through the most enlightened. Turgot defined the quintessential nature of the series as it advanced from one stage to another in terms of a history of changing capacities of perception, or at least different ways of confronting the external world, transformations in the human mind which were by no means accidental but were clearly ranged in an order of being from the less to the more perfect. The societies that exemplifed the stadial development formed a historical roster of excellences in which the primitive savage was the inferior and the civilized Frenchman the most recent expression of the superior.[28]

Political geography, as Turgot outlined the discipline in one of his unfinished sketches, became the description of world areas in the light of his one central theme: How proximate was each society, barbaric or civil, to the bellwether nation leading the movement of progress? Or was a people perhaps veering in the opposite direction, toward decadence, and eliminating itself from world history? When Turgot propounded his conception of progress he never implied that all nations were progressing regularly in a straight line and at an even tempo. He was neither so simple nor so obtuse as to envisage simultaneous unchecked development, though this has sometimes been inferred in crude distillations of his theory. On the contrary, in the spirit of Vico and Montesquieu and Gibbon, he was acutely conscious of the phenomenon of grandeur and decadence, of growth, maturity, fall, and decline.[29] What he intended to demonstrate from the record of world historical geography was that some society was always carrying the torch of progress forward; when it was about to be extinguished in one society the sacred fire was seized by another. As one haven of science crumbled there was always another polity which inherited the discoveries and, after an interval necessary for assimilation, advanced still further. "Thus it has happened that in alternating periods of agitation and calm, of good and evil, the total mass of the human species has moved ceaselessly toward its perfection."[30] Turgot was not precise in his definition of the societal unit in which progress was incorporated; most often he drew examples from large areas like the Greek world, the Roman Empire, Christendom, or China, though sometimes he used an individual dynastic state or even an American tribe. This vagueness in the establishment of the unit of discourse makes it difficult to relate the cyclical patterns of individual societies to the world development of progress which, mutatis mutandis, assumes a role analogous to Hegel's World Spirit triumphing amid the tragic death of cultures. The linking of individual instances of growth and decay with the central thread of world development has been the rock on which the most magnificent constructs of philosophical history have foundered, and Turgot was often hard put to document the transmissions, particularly from Rome to medieval Europe, though he managed to squeak through with a felicitous use of metaphor.

Political geography endowed with a time dimension became universal history. At most a few names had to be added, the key inventive geniuses and the towering political figures. History, almost entirely divested of its heroic qualities, became a record of the relations of societies to one another spatially and temporally. The images with which Turgot tried to communicate these relationships remained predominantly spatial.[31] There was distance in time as there was distance in space, and each people, nation, and tribe could be located in time on some rung of the ladder of progress with the same precision as it could be fixed in space on a world map.

The "Plan d'un ouvrage sur la géographie politique" was an outline of history demonstrating in schematic form how from a diversity of peoples on different levels of civilization one enlightened world with a uniform culture would inevitably result. The whole process was depicted in a set of geometric images. In the beginning there were numerous isolated units; with time, in any world area, the nation which had surpassed others in progress became the center of a group of political satellites. The same process was repeated in various parts of the globe which had no contact with one another. Ultimately the independent constellations extended their circles until they collided and established relations through war and commerce. In the end of the days the major political areas would coalesce, and one world whose boundaries were coterminous with the physical world would be created. Turgot extolled this ideal of one political world not only because it would unite men but because it would provide an opportunity for the maximum interpenetration of diverse perceptions among the greatest number of human beings, the necessary prerequisite for accelerated progress. The uniformity and insipidity of one world was an idea remote from his imagination.

Anatomy of the Four Progressions

Progress naturally divided itself into four subsidiary progressions, and Turgot anatomized them, established their mutual relationships, and derived from them a law of unequal development. These types of progress were identified with distinct areas of human creative activity: speculative science, technology, moral behavior, and artistic expression. The "inequality of the progressions" was a central thesis, for he had discovered in each progression a different pattern of growth, and when referring to them as a group he constantly used the term in the plural, *les progrès,* a form that Condorcet retained in the *Esquisse.* Thus there was uneven development of progressions within a society as there was among various geographic entities throughout the world, a law which accounted for the extraordinary diversity of human experience despite the identity of mankind's underlying historic destiny. What conditions, asked Turgot the philosophical historian, had in the past furthered one or more progressions, and what had been the negative elements destructive of progress or blocking its path? Since progress is the integrating concept which bestows meaning upon the history of man, since it is virtually the sole historical subject, this experience of the progressions in the past will enlighten mankind about its future prospect. The diagnosis of the progressions is preliminary to a prognosis.

Of all the progressions, the technological had been the hardiest growth of man's genius, the least evanescent, for mechanical capacities were common, shared by a vast number of human beings, and it would be impossible to destroy totally the productive techniques of artisans even during periods when the political framework of society was shattered. Because the body of men who practiced mechanical arts was large, the chance of novelty was greater than in other forms of progress, for the incidence of genius was the same in all fields. Since artisans dealt with elementary needs of life, were plentiful and yet indispensable, the mechanical arts were perfected by the "mere fact that time passed."[32] Once a new device had been invented and accepted by the artisans it was hard to envisage its abandonment, because the advantages of the innovation were manifest to utilitarian common sense. Since the preservation and transmission of technology were not dependent upon language, it could even survive a barbarian conquest. No tyrannical power had a special interest in interfering with the artisan's processes of cloth manufacture. As a consequence, technological discoveries had accumulated throughout history at a relatively even tempo; and during long epochs progress in the mechanical arts had continued without interruption even while science and artistic creativity had suffered a total eclipse. Turgot appreciated the technical progress achieved in medieval Europe, a rare insight for an eighteenth-century philosophe, and he was one of the first to suggest that the regeneration of speculative science in the Renaissance had been facilitated by an antecedent succession of mechanical inventions during the Middle Ages: the introduction of maritime instruments, the magnifying glass, and, most important of all, the art of printing, which diffused scientific knowledge over a wide area, made the discoveries of the ancient Greeks generally available, and stimulated potential geniuses by making them aware of the achievements of their predecessors. Up to the eighteenth century, science owed more to technology than technology to science, a relationship which Turgot was prepared to see reversed by the imminent revolutionary explosion of speculative science.[33] Whatever the past interdependence of science and technology, for the future the scientists were the unchallenged vanguard of the battalions of progress.

The fine arts was one area of creativity where Turgot modified his theory of limitless infinite progress. In the literary quarrel of the ancients and the moderns he still found for the giants of antiquity. Aesthetic achievement was the tenderest plant of human genius, sensitive to political contingencies. Good taste, which had to prevail in a society before genius in the fine arts could be honored, was fragile and delicate, and it could be easily corrupted by decree throughout a whole civilization if a capricious ruling prince were imbued with bizarre or fantastic notions of the beautiful. Of all forms of human expression, art was the most vulnerable to the influence of a hostile environment. Turgot clung to the neoclassic idea that the Augustan Age had reached the artistic zenith, a level that might perhaps be equaled again under proper guidance but could never be surpassed. Knowledge of the fine arts, unlike knowledge in the mechanical arts and in speculative science, was not cumulative; hence the very concept of progress was not, strictly speaking, applicable in this sphere. Atrociously bad taste could predominate in the same age in which mechanical arts were accomplishing marvels of engineering. The Gothic cathedral which Turgot, in conformity with the prevailing judgment of the eighteenth century, considered a monstrosity, was a superb expression of man's ingenuity in the mechanical arts. Men still had not learned how these structures had been raised by the medieval artisans, but there was no doubt about their hideousness.

Turgot had no conception of the high seriousness of art. While discovery in mechanical arts and speculative science was part of an infinite movement, the fine arts aimed only to please. Once the philosophical canon of the pleasurable had been established on the basis of a knowledge of human psychology—which was uniform—a specific art object either obeyed and conformed to the rules or violated them. While other branches of human endeavor were infinitely expansible, progress in the arts of poetry, painting, and music was bound by intrinsic natural limitations. Since our artistic sensibilities were restricted by the nature and sensitivity of our organs, once perfection had been attained in the Augustan Age later generations were reduced to mere imitation of these models. At most there might conceivably be an improvement in the technical media of artistic production, never progress in art itself. Turgot the poetaster and translator of Vergil and Horace was unable to extol the creations of eighteenth-century France above those of the Romans, and he expressed a measure of contempt for those who deluded themselves that they were perfecting the arts when they were only rendering the artistic object more complex. "The knowledge of nature and of truth is as infinite as they are," he wrote in the second *Sorbonique*. "The arts whose purpose it is to please are as limited as we are. Time continually brings forth new discoveries in science, but poetry, painting, music have a fixed limit which the genius of language, the imitation of nature, and the sensibilities of our organs determine . . ."[34]

By contrast moral behavior was clearly subject to improvement, though what he meant by the moral implied a set of fixed criteria, ideals common to the wise philosophers of his age, generally accepted by Hume and Montesquieu, Beccaria, Lessing, and Kant. The moral was a combination of Stoic virtues and rules of general conduct with a measure of utility, the whole suffused with Christian love and charity. Future moral progress signified the end of war, cruelty, and crime, and the extension of virtues throughout all strata of European society and among all the nations of the world. It entailed the general practice of tolerance and leniency and obedience to reason, acceptance of law out of rational conviction rather than any dread of worldly punishment or superstitious fear of torments in Hell. If men acted solely on grounds of utility and reason, if they extended free inquiry and assimilated its scientific findings into the practical sphere of everyday action, then they were progressing. To the degree that man became mild, gentle, loving, tranquil, his moral behavior was improving.

Turgot never fell in with the rabid anticlericalism of some of his Encyclopedist friends, even after he had left the Church. He retained a profound respect for the moral virtues of Christianity, which he considered a further purification and not a corruption of natural religion. Under the canopy of the medieval Church the bestial nature of the northern barbarians had been tamed and in time they had been transformed into polite, reasonable, well-behaved, compassionate members of society.[35] Christianity had abolished slavery, prohibited infanticide, established asylums for the sick and the weak, preached brotherhood and love. The church had been one of the great civilizing and moralizing forces in the history of mankind. His friend and loyal disciple Condorcet, alive to bloody religious persecutions, inquisitions, massacres, and crusades, was unable to stomach this summation of the historical evidence.

About the future moral progress of mankind, however, Condorcet and Turgot were in agreement. The reduction of morals to a science of observation would inevitably lead to the wider prevalence of those ways of conduct which every philosophe appreciated and whose essence was an extension of altruism, "contributing to the happiness of others."[36]

The Demonstration of Inevitability

Turgot's doctrine supported itself on two central arguments: an empirical proof that progress had in fact occurred in the past from the dark primitive stage of humanity's origins through the enlightened present; and a demonstration that since retrogression was no longer possible future progress was inevitable. The past history of progress had been proved by ethnology. The prediction of its future was based upon an evaluation of the increasing momentum of progress, its accelerating tempo; upon estimate of the global diffusion of enlightenment; and finally upon the observation that all knowledge was actually in the process of becoming encased in mathematical symbols which granted it certitude. Historical reflections in the grand manner of a Bossuet illustrated these bold and novel ideas in the Sorbonne discourses, refuting both pessimist Christian theologians and antihistorical philosophes who tended to regard the past as a meaningless parade of crimes and cruel accidents. Hitherto, Turgot conceded, progress had been consistently waylaid by two enemies: Either barbarian invasions overwhelmed societies that had attained a high level of civilization and temporarily stifled the progress of science; or advanced societies became corroded by an equally vicious internal disease in their own bodies politic, that spirit of routine, the rut, which was always for him the very incarnation of evil. In the future, however, these two dread enemies of progress would be powerless, since the eighteenth-century reality of a unified world civilization had rendered it impossible for mankind as a whole ever again to suffer stagnation or catastrophic relapse. Knowledge of science was now so widely diffused among societies throughout the world that even the irruption of a barbarian horde intent upon devastation, even suppression by an obscurantist tyrant, could not wholly extinguish the light of progress. In the past the isolation of political societies had rendered them peculiarly susceptible to internal putrescence, but henceforward if a nation tended to fall into a stagnant state, either it would be forcibly awakened, shaken out of its torpor by commercial stimuli from abroad, or it would be conquered by a more vigorous nation which would ultimately inherit its progress. To the extent that war had kept humanity alert and constantly aroused it had not been an unmitigated evil. In the future this terrible remedy might not be necessary, but it was always available to assure humanity's forward movement.

Turgot tended to evaluate progress in two dimensions. One was intensive, vertical so to speak, the accretion of units of scientific truth in time; the other was extensive, horizontal, and entailed the gradual sowing of these scientific truths throughout the world until ultimately no area would remain barren. During his retirement Turgot toyed with inventions of cheap processes for the reproduction of writing, in order to multiply communications and extend progress among those elements in society which were still beyond its pale. The extension of the communications network became a crucial practical measure for the acceleration of the progressive process and was in harmony with the other elements in his theory. Increase communications and an ever greater number and variety of new idea combinations would be transmitted to an ever larger number of human beings. Among those exposed to the new configurations would be a new quota of geniuses who would grasp the meaning of novel contingencies, formalize them, and make them a part of the accumulating body of world knowledge. To learn truth and to spread it was the essential social mission of man bequeathed by Turgot to his disciple Condorcet. "To know the truth in order to make the social order conform to it, that is the sole source of public happiness. It is therefore useful, even necessary, to extend the limits of knowledge . . ."[37]

To gather new peoples under the protection of science was from the beginning a vital element in the idea of progress. When no spot on earth was excluded from the illumination of science, then and only then was it safe from an attack by the forces of evil and ignorance, free of the threat of submersion by waves of darkness from beyond the pale of the civilized world. Only thereafter would intensive scientific progress be accelerated indefinitely, without setback or impediment. Europe's mission to civilize the world was for Turgot, as it was later for Condorcet and Saint-Simon, a necessary requirement for its own development. No region of the globe, however enlightened, could enjoy perfect tranquillity as long as savages lurked on the rim of civility. Since temporarily at least barbarians throttled a more advanced culture when they took possession, the mere existence of an uncivilized penumbra endangered civilization. The function of enlightenment was to draw the whole of the world into the orbit of civilization as an absolute insurance against retrogression. Turgot's rational belief in the inevitability of future progress was bolstered by his confidence that eighteenth-century Europeans were in manifest control of the savage world and had only to disseminate their teachings to eradicate the last remnants of the historic dread of barbarian invasions which hung over them. Intensive and extensive progress were thus interrelated; they fortified each other and were dependent upon each other.

Turgot's optimism derived from the realization that the growth of science had by now gathered so great a momentum that interruption of the process had been rendered impossible. *Vires acquirit eundo*. In the early stages of history the plant of civilization could be trampled down by outsiders, the horde, or it could be shriveled from within by sloth, luxury, an absence of challenge. But the strength and the speed of movement achieved in modern times made every progression easier and every backward lapse more improbable. An accelerating wheel became the image of progress.[38]

Finally, the richest source of confidence for the believer in the inevitability of progress lay in the special mathematical character of all forms of scientific knowledge in recent ages. Mathematics, of which Turgot had only an amateur's smattering, was for him the loftiest expression of human thought, at the summit of intellectuality. In mathematics and only in mathematics did Turgot feel an absolute sense of security about the survival of acquired knowledge. Throughout his life he had toyed with fantasies about devoting himself to science, and he was always wistfully contrasting the turbulent, ungrateful, political world in which, alas, he had expended his energies as an administrator with the peaceful, finite, enduring world of science from which the rhetoric and the prejudice that governed the politics of men had been expunged. On August 24,

1761, he had written to Voltaire: "I have the misfortune to be an Intendant. I say misfortune because in this century of quarrels there is no happiness but in living philosophically among one's studies and one's friends."[39] Science to Turgot connoted the mathematical world, the realm of the purest of the sciences, the ideal form of knowledge. Here was certainty for this uneasy intellectual.

The progress of speculative science was now solidly safeguarded by the new symbolic forms which knowledge had assumed since the Renaissance. Once mathematics had become the universal language of science, intellectual progress would be emancipated from the historical vicissitudes to which the ordinary spoken vernaculars were subject. Mathematical language would soon set up an impregnable barrier against retrogression. To reduce all knowledge to mathematical symbols would become the highest achievement of mankind. For the moment only the social sciences seemed to be standing apart; but their mathematization was the inevitable next stage of intellectual progress. In the formula no room was left for the vague, for the exaggeration of enthusiasts, for superstition—the great vices of mankind. The mathematization of the study of man would become a double security against antiprogressive forces, for moral knowledge would find itself protected by the armor of numbers and equations, and moral problems would be removed from the disputes of the marketplace where they always provoked destructive violence. In his last years Turgot, wracked with the pains of illness, drew consolation from the vision of humanity on the threshold of this wondrous transmutation of knowledge, a leap comparable in his mind to the passage of human speech from a myth-ridden, metaphoric, poetic language to the relatively rational style of the contemporary European world. As long as mankind relied upon language and rhetoric to express its truths, knowledge would inevitably become polluted with chimeras of the imagination, with personal prejudice. Even civilized languages, rational instruments of communication though they were, had never succeeded in freeing themselves from their primitive origins and remained encumbered with similes and images which obfuscated rational thought. There was always something suspect about an idea that was not mathematicized because it was subject to passion, to political influences, to the weaknesses of the imaginative faculty. In the past, scientific knowledge had been acquired rather haphazardly, and as a consequence of unpropitious external circumstances it had been stagnant for long periods at a time. Only since the regeneration of the sciences through mathematics had a long succession of geniuses been steadfastly adding to this body of knowledge and at the same time extending the dominion of science over new peoples who had once been victims of superstitious belief or obscure theological reasoning. In technical terms the new vista opening before Turgot was the imminent application of the calculus of probabilities to human behavior, thus the invasion of a whole moral world from which mathematics had previously been excluded.

Turgot is in a long tradition of French thinkers ranging from Descartes through Paul Valéry who have sought refuge in mathematics as an ultimate haven. When all other arguments in support of the inevitability of future progress were momentarily weakened by the spectacle of the real world with its oppressive stupidity and irrationality, the triumph of the mathematical spirit was a last resort. As long as the knowledge of abstract relationships in the mathematical world was growing there was progress. The final consolation lay in the existence of the equation. Princes might prove weak and false, but nothing could assail one's confidence in a theorem.

As a result of the manifold demonstrations of inevitability the burden of proof was shifted to the shoulders of the antiprogressists. Wherefrom was the antiscientific destructive storm to blow if enlightenment became universal? To impede the natural impetus of scientific progress a countervailing force equally potent was required. Since there was no such power on the historical horizon, progress would be "indefinite" or without limit, like an infinite progression in mathematics.[40]

Progress a Theodicy

The progressists have sometimes been read and interpreted as if they were continually mouthing optimist shibboleths. Turgot, whose half-smile sometimes disturbed contemporaries, was not immune to moments of disenchantment and even despair. Declarations of war by the philosophical monarchs of the Enlightenment evoked from him a cry of horror. "Poor humans!" he exclaimed in a letter of March 19, 1778, reporting to his friend Dupont de Nemours the imminent outbreak of hostilities in Germany and in Turkey.[41] He sighed when he contemplated the enduring stupidity of his race. Few of the eighteenth-century philosophes were naive or blissfully unconscious of contradictions in their own optimist posture. Turgot was gnawed by a deep sense of the persistence of tragedy in the human condition. In a letter to Condorcet in 1772, four years before the failure of his attempt to rescue the monarchy from collapse, Turgot revealed his feeling of futility about administrative reforms and confided a secret conviction that men would probably never overcome the evils they inflicted upon themselves, that physical ills and moral grief would always be with them. Progress would therefore have to limit itself to the eradication of "artifical evils" generated by ignorance.[42]

Turgot's optimism was rarely without qualms. His economic theory had led him to rather gloomy conclusions about any possible improvement of the lot of the ordinary worker, who was bound by a law which limited him to a subsistence level of wages—an antecedent of Marx's iron law.[43] Turgot's version of the utopian idea of progress did not involve any total elimination of evil, error, or misery from an empirical view of human experience. The Turgot who at the height of his powers was rejected by the King and ousted by a palace cabal was not the simplistic unquestioning believer in progress that some of the popularizers of his ideas have made him out to be; and neither was Condorcet, who after overthrowing the King found himself condemned to the guillotine in absentia; and neither was Saint-Simon, the perennial failure who cried out with anguish at the sight of the terrible harvest of death during the Napoleonic wars; and neither was Comte, who saw the Europe of 1848 bathed in a bloody fratricidal class war. None of these men were starry-eyed fools repeating stereotyped formulas about progress and the betterment of mankind. They all saw progress as an overcoming of contrary forces in organized society, in physical nature, in man himself. They were wrestling with the problem of evil which reappeared in a new mask in each generation, its most recent embodiment the forces of antiprogress. The war of good and evil, of Christ and Antichrist, became the war of progressive history and antihistory. Process, movement, social dynamics did not lose their Christian moral overtones. The doctrine of progress was born in the bosom of Christianity, and Saint-Simon and Comte even tried to retain the epithet "religious" as a key descriptive word for their new progressist systems. Turgot was aware of the overwhelming potency of the deadening forces of tradition and routine, Condorcet of the power of tyranny, sect, and lust for dominion, Saint-Simon and Comte of the divisive forces of anarchy which endangered the cohesion of the social fabric. The evil passions and even the dissolving demons of madness were not unknown to the philosophers of progress.

In the last analysis their systems were fervent attempts to solve the theodicy problem and to give meaning to historical experience once the sanctions of future rewards and punishments were removed. If Providence was a source of goodness, why the long chronicle of wars and devastations, the spectacle of crimes and barbarities perpetrated throughout the ages? The answer is common to most eighteenth-century philosophers of history—in this respect Turgot's concept is only one offshoot of a general theme. Without the impetus of the aggressive, evil passions, without the ambitions of individuals, the "leading strings" of nature, there would have been no progress in the early stages of history and man would have been doomed to peace and mediocrity.

The ambitious ones themselves in forming the great nations have contributed to the design of Providence, the progress of enlightenment, and consequently to the increase of the happiness of the human species, a thing which did not at all interest them. Their passions, their very rages, have led them without their knowing where they were going. I seem to see an immense army all of whose movements are directed by a great genius. At the sight of the military signals, at the tumultuous noise of the trumpets and the drums, the squadrons move forward, the horses themselves are driven by a fire which has no purpose. Each section makes its way over obstacles without knowing what may result. Only the chief sees the effect of so many related steps. Thus the passions multiplied ideas, extended knowledge, perfected minds, in default of the reason whose day had not yet dawned and which would have been less potent if it had reigned earlier.

Reason, which is justice itself, would never have carried away what belonged to another, would have forever banished war and usurpation, would have left men divided into a mob of nations, isolated from one another, speaking different languages.

Limited, as a result, in their ideas, incapable of progress in any branch of knowledge, of science, of art, of civility, which is born of the meeting of geniuses assembled from different provinces, the human species would have forever remained in a state of mediocrity. Reason and justice, had they been hearkened to, would have fixed everything—approximately the way it happened in China.[44]

The attainment of the providential (or nature's) purpose—progress—required the free play of the passions. This did not mean that individual acts of wickedness were willed by God, pleaded the former theologian Turgot. Since men committed these acts, they had to bear the moral responsibility. Progress merely utilized the opportunities created by the self-willed men who broke the moral law. And they thereby unwittingly achieved a divine purpose. The idea of progress thus comes to the rescue of the religious man who might otherwise have begun to question divine guidance of the world of men steeped in evil. Vice is enlisted in the service of progress, and progress in turn becomes a part of Christian apologetics.

An individual immoral deed, inspired by personal lust, can generate historical forces which lead to the perfection and humanization of the species. This theodicy, which explains the emergence of objective good for mankind from subjective evil intent, was one of the most persistent motifs in eighteenth- and early nineteenth-century philosophies of history. With variations it can be found in Vico, Herder, Kant, and Hegel as well as among the progressists of the French school. Inevitably the philosophical historians were forced into a divorcement of the will of individual morality from the unfolding of a rational purpose in history. Turgot was the first of the French group to resort to this justification of God's way in time, the equivalent of what Vico had called a civil theology. Even in its later development the secular idea of progress was never completely divested of the theological robes in which it had made its first appearance at the *Sorboniques*. Whatever the balance of good and evil in the world may be at any specific moment, the historic ledger always shows a credit in favor of the good. Ever since his youth Turgot, who had read Leibniz,[45] had been profoundly disturbed by the question of the origin and purpose of evil in a world that was created by a God who was perfect good. His article on Manichaeism for the *Encyclopédie* had wrestled with this, "the hardest and thorniest problem which presents itself to the mind."[46] The idea of progress provided the solution. "He saw in physical Evil, in moral Evil," Condorcet reported, "only a necessary consequence of the existence of sensitive beings capable of reason but limited. The perfectibility with which a few species, and in particular the human species, are endowed is a slow but infallible remedy to these evils."[47] And it was this insight into progress which, to the obvious annoyance of his anticlerical friend, sustained Turgot in the belief in a beneficent, providential design. "The universe viewed in its totality, in the whole range of the progressions, is a most glorious spectacle, witness to the wisdom which presides over it."[48]

Validation of the passions, however, was usually limited by Turgot to the past. Once enlightenment had spread over the world this stimulus to progress would no longer be necessary, since full-grown reason should be able to care for its own and humanity's future development. The evil passions that had been useful in the infancy of the species would be superfluous in man's mature rational age. Turgot recognized the complexity of the individual drives which had motivated the great discoveries of the past, and he refrained from emphasizing exclusively either love of knowledge or a quest for glory. A human desire for fame, he realized, had hitherto limited researches which required many generations to achieve fruition, but he was hopeful that in the future society, with the equalization of wealth and a diminution of the importance of political action, more men of talent would devote themselves to the pursuit of reason without the excitation of the passions.[49] With time, Turgot hoped, reason would occupy more and more space in the finite area of the spirit, casting out the disorderly passions and limiting severely the scope of the imagination. Emotion would thus be progressively blotted out until in the end of the days there would be only reason. The improverishment of the spirit under the hegemony of pure reason did not trouble the eighteenth-century philosophe, because as he saw the world about him—the prejudice, the superstition, the ignorance, the fanaticism—he felt that mankind had only begun to fight the battle of rationality. The prospect of an undernourishment of the passions and the imaginative faculties for the sake of reason did not yet appear real to men of

Turgot's generation. He was acutely aware of how young was the reign of reason—only the mathematical sciences had pursued appropriate analytic methods before the end of the seventeenth century—if measured against the background of historic time.[50] When Turgot contemplated the irrationality of the world, he derived consolation from the simple historical realization that the mathematical perception of the universe was so relatively recent an acquisition of the human spirit that its influence upon laws and morals had not as yet had an opportunity to make itself felt.[51]

At the close of the biography of his friend, Condorcet presented an Isaiah-like vision of the end of the days as it had been unfolded to him in Turgot's conversation. Most of the elements in this progressist heaven he later repeated in the last part of the tenth epoch of his own *Esquisse,* the form in which the ideas penetrated European thought.

He [Turgot] hoped that day would come when men, disabused of the fantastic project of opposing nation to nation, power to power, passion to passion, vice to vice, would occupy themselves with hearkening to what reason would dictate for the happiness of humanity. Why should politics, based like all the other sciences on observation and reason, not be perfected in the measure that one brings to observations more subtlety and exactitude, to reasoning more precision, profundity, and good judgment? Shall we dare to fix what point could be attained in this field by minds fortified by a better education, exercised at an early age in the combination of the most varied and extensive ideas, accustomed to manipulate more general and easier methods? Let us beware of despairing of the human kind. Let us dare to envisage, in the immensity of the centuries which will follow us, a happiness and an enlightenment about which we cannot today even form a vague and indefinite idea. Let us count on that perfectibility with which nature has endowed us, on the power of genius from which long experience has taught us to expect prodigies, and let us console ourselves for the fact that we shall not witness those happier times with the pleasure of foretelling them, of enjoying them in advance, and perhaps with the even sweeter satisfaction of having accelerated that all-too-distant epoch by a few moments.[52]

In the correspondence of his last years Turgot recorded the progress of the American Revolution, the Gordon riots, the outbreak of the war with Turkey, and the ravages of the mutual passion which consumed his friends Madame Helvétius and Benjamin Franklin (who was then seventy-three). He watched these events with tender sympathy for the victims of war and civil strife and emotional excess. These were moral ills of which men had not yet been cured, and perhaps the pains were destined to endure for some time, like the gout with which both Turgot and the sage from Philadelphia were afflicted. Turgot's disgrace provoked no misanthropic outburst. If he was outraged at his betrayal by the King, there is no report of his indignation. The slightly skeptical smile continued to hover about the lips; it is preserved in Ducreux's pastel in the Château de Lantheuil. Not so his faithful lieutenant Condorcet. In a letter to Voltaire he gave vent to his anger with a vehemence that Turgot would never have permitted himself:

I have not written to you, dear illustrious master, since the fatal event that has robbed all honest men of hope and courage. I waited for my wrath to cool down somewhat and for grief alone to remain. This event has changed all of nature for me. I no longer take the same pleasure in looking at the beautiful countryside where he would have spread happiness. The spectacle of the gaiety of the people makes my heart ache. They dance as if they had lost nothing. The wolves from which you delivered the countryside of Gex are going to invade the rest of France, and two years of abstinence have transformed their thirst for the blood of the people into a fury. Would you believe they dared demand that no writing against them be allowed and that this vile progeny of lackeys, bitches, and pimps of the past century be respected? They want to muzzle us out of fear lest the cries which our pain tears from us trouble their peace. This is where we have fallen, dear illustrious master, and from what a lofty pinnacle!

The day of the philosophes was drawing to a close, and the men of action were about to take over. If the conspiracy of the privileged ones ousted the last hope of France there were other means of bringing about the triumph of reason. Condorcet recovered from his dejection, girded himself for war, and flung himself into the revolutionary battle. In his turn he suffered the fate of the philosopher engaged—as had his master.[53]

20

Condorcet:
Progression to Elysium

SOON AFTER the Marquis Jean-Antoine-Nicolas Caritat de Condorcet, born in 1743, had turned four, his father, a dashing cavalry officer, died.[1] His fanatically devout mother, possessed with the idea of consecrating her son to the Virgin, kept him in skirts until he was eight. Finally rescued by his uncle, the Bishop of Lisieux, he was turned over to the Jesuits to be educated. "Hardly had young Condorcet opened his eyes," wrote Arago in a paper delivered before the Academy of Sciences in 1841, "than he found himself surrounded by the highest dignitaries of the church and the sword. His first guides, his first teachers, were Jesuits. What was the result of so extraordinary a confluence of circumstances? In politics a total rejection of any idea of hereditary prerogative; in matters of religion skepticism pushed to its extreme limits."[2]

A Snowcapped Volcano

Young Condorcet was quickly recognized as a mathematical genius and his geometry was much appreciated by his contemporaries, though his reputation in this branch of knowledge has not endured. After 1770 he joined the philosophical coteries, virtually abandoning his mathematical studies to become a *politique*. During Turgot's brief ministry, when the philosophes descended in a body upon the royal offices and were awarded sinecures, Condorcet received the mint, as Newton once had in England.

The official portrait of Condorcet depicts a man devoted to the life of reason, a mathematician, a permanent secretary of the Academy of Sciences, an exponent of the middle way in revolutionary politics, an adherent of the Girondins who broke with them in the end and died hated by all parties—in short, a philosophe. But Condorcet's intimate friends knew that an explosive, passionate nature was being held in check—a "snowcapped volcano" was d'Alembert's mot.[3] Beneath the surface Condorcet hardly resembled that image of the cool, unbiased scientist that he had set before himself as the perfect model of the man of the future. There was even a malicious streak in the official of the greatest scientific body in France. Some of the grand *éloges* of his dead colleagues, like the piece he delivered on the naturalist Buffon, were written with tongue in cheek; he was laying on the rhetoric, he confessed to a friend, to repay the eminent Count in kind for the bombastic rodomontades of his voluminous works.

Condorcet's sentimental correspondence with Mme. Suard, the wife of a literary man of the period (the letters, now in the Bibliothèque Nationale, have been published only in inadequate extracts), spanning a period of more than two decades, reveals a complex, emotional introvert. Mme. Suard's manuscript notes on their exchange, written years after Condorcet's death, show her extraordinary perspicacity about the man, even though her remarks are sometimes tinged with venom. In the letters Condorcet the High Priest of the Temple of Reason aptly described himself as a "romanesque" character. While in the public eye he was the learned aristocrat, orderly to the point of obsession, a diligent worker in the vineyard of science, above all a calm and quiet intellectual, beneath the rather phlegmatic exterior was a frightened man who for years lived in a dream of romantic love. "I shall continue out of habit to occupy myself, but not from a desire for glory, because that would be wasting my time, and after all, if I had as much as Newton, would I be more loved?"

As an eighteenth-century philosophe was likely to do in his private chamber, Condorcet submitted his feelings to probing psychological analysis, and was aware of his own overwhelming need for suffering in love. The philosophical historian of human progress was an anxious man, always expecting catastrophe. Commenting on his perennial uneasiness, he wrote to his confidante: "Perhaps this derives from an instinct fashioned by the habit of suffering which tells me that what is bound to hurt me will happen." Condorcet leads one to reflect on the strange paradox of a modern man whose inner emotional anguish is accompanied by a compensatory historical optimism which knows no limits. "My nerves only bother me from time to time, and what remains of my physical and moral ills is a sadness, a little imbecility, and much laziness. What you tell me of your reflections does not surprise me. Such is the misfortune of the human condition. The idea of the necessary flight of our happiness can suffice to poison it, while the idea of the flight of our miseries does not suffice to console us." The love-friendship with Mme. Suard, which remained Platonic—for seven years Condorcet lived in a chaste ménage à trois with the Suards—gave rise to transports in which a boyish sentimental love, almost puppy love, had banished philosophy. "If it were possible for me to believe in a god, I would be persuaded that a beneficent divinity has united itself with your body as an example to the world and for the happiness of the elect."[4]

Mme. Suard, who had a number of philosophes on her string, accepted his adoration for years, and she was no doubt flattered by his devotion, though at the same time she felt a measure of disdain for his softness and servility in intimate relationships. When on two occasions during the course of their long correspondence Condorcet was struck by a passion for another woman, Mme. Suard remarked in her notes upon his abjectness, the same utter submissiveness, the "weakness of a slave" (his childhood in female dress had left its mark). The first object of his affections, a Mme. de Meulan, the wife of a *receveur de finances,* led him on, watched him dance attendance on her, and then dropped him. The second, to whom he succumbed at the age of forty-two, was the beautiful Sophie de Grouchy, twenty-three-year-old daughter of a noble family which had fallen on evil days. During this courtship Condorcet was beside himself. To Mme. Suard he seemed to have lost all self-respect. Condorcet had always dreamed of a perfect love to which he and his partner would surrender themselves utterly. He would give his life for six months of such a love, "qu'il aimerait d'amour," he once confessed to Mme. Suard. When he offered his hand, Sophie de Grouchy was still possessed by a lover (either the Duke de la Rochefoucauld or Lafayette) who was himself married and therefore not free. It was Condorcet who had to beg Sophie's hand from her paramour. Sophie de Grouchy was infatuated to the point where the entreaties of her mother were unavailing, and she accepted Condorcet only after her lover had relinquished her and given his consent. The whole agitated affair is described by Mme. Suard, a participant observer and far from disinterested, for she was loath to lose the loyal admirer who could always be counted upon to turn up at ten in the evening. Mme. Suard has blamed Sophie de Grouchy for the total transformation of Condorcet's personality in succeeding years and for the revolutionary excesses to which he abandoned himself. She depicts Sophie de Grouchy as an intriguer who was impressed by Condorcet's income and an ambitious woman who used him as a tool.

This was pure cattiness. Sophie de Grouchy was one of the brilliant hostesses of the end of the ancien régime whose salon became an intellectual center for philosophes and politiques from both sides of the Atlantic. Her wit and charm are extolled by the memorialists. Michelet has written of her noble and virginal figure fit for a Raphael model of Metaphysics—for Mme. Condorcet was a lady philosopher who translated Adam Smith's works on moral sentiments and the origin of language and herself composed letters on sympathy.[5] There is some truth to the allegation that it was she who pushed her rather retiring husband into the revolutionary turmoil. She was if anything more rabid in her anticlericalism than he was. While Condorcet had a horror of tumults and a fear of the tribune and at one point wrote to Mme. Suard, "I am a royalist," at his wife's instigation he became an activist, a republican, a pamphleteer using all the tricks of the trade, a president of the Legislative Assembly. There is one opinion that Mme. Condorcet, presiding over her salon, was even more influential in directing Girondist policy than Mme. Roland. During the Great Days, Mme. Condorcet demonstrated with the people in the streets. Swept along by the revolutionary tide, Condorcet framed constitutions, drafted legislation, reorganized the educational system. But these ci-devant aristocrats could never be radical enough for the Revolution, and at the crucial moment of the great divide, the verdict on the King, Condorcet voted for a severe penalty short of death, which led to his proscription. (The specific reason in the act of accusation was his publication of an attack on the Jacobin constitution accusing its authors of an attempt to restore the monarchy—an extravagant demagogic appeal of which he was capable in the heat of controversy.)

In 1793 the Marquis de Condorcet, the last of the philosophes, the friend of Voltaire, Turgot, and Cabanis, was hiding from Robespierre's police in the house of Mme. Vernet near Saint-Sulpice in Paris. Condemned as an enemy of the Republic, he had been received by the widow of an artist in her modest establishment when it was too dangerous for him to secrete himself in the home of more prominent friends. For months elaborate security measures were in force to alert the self-immured scientist-politician-philosopher in the event of a Jacobin search for suspects. He had no illusions about his survival. "I shall perish like Socrates and Sidney, for I have served my country," reads a stray fragment.[6] In his clandestine chambers, to keep from despair and to ward off distraction, he composed an *Esquisse d'un tableau historique des progrès de l'esprit humain,* spinning out an epic from his own body of accumulated knowledge, with little recourse to books. Forewarned of an imminent raid, he escaped through the gates of Paris in disguise, only to be captured by sansculottes in an obscure tavern on the outskirts of the city. He died in their detention room in Bourg-Egalité, either from apoplexy, from an embolism, or in the Stoic manner by a self-administered poison with which Dr. Cabanis had provided him.[7] In 1795, when his last testament to humanity was posthumously published, three thousand copies were purchased for distribution by the National Assembly of the Directorate, symbolic recognition that his theory had become official revolutionary doctrine after the Terror.[8]

To his daughter, who Michelet claims (with a measure of poetic license) was conceived on the day the Bastille fell,[9] Condorcet bequeathed a testament of another character, an eighteenth-century man's warning against the ravages of the passions which is almost a confession.

I shall not give you useless advice to avoid the passions and to beware of excessive emotionality. But I shall tell you to be sincere with yourself and not to exaggerate your emotions, either out of vanity or to flatter your imagination or fire someone else's imagination. Fear the false enthusiasm of the passions. It never compensates either for their dangers or their misfortunes. It may be that one is not sufficiently master of one's heart to refuse to listen to it, but one is always capable of not exciting it, and that is the only useful and practical counsel which reason can give to emotion.[10]

In the hour of the hunted philosopher's need, Mme. Condorcet, the philosophical, aristocratic beauty, and the loyal friend, Mme. Suard, were both put to the test, and each comported herself in her own manner. Sophie de Condorcet, disguised as a peasant girl, mingled with the mob around the guillotine in order to make her way through Paris undetected when she paid her visits to the attic on the rue des Fossoyeurs (now rue Servandoni). To earn a living in the hard winter of '93–'94 she opened a store and sold underclothes. When the revolutionary patriots made their regular perquisitions in the hope of finding a clue to her husband's whereabouts she somehow preserved herself and her daughter by distracting them with quick sketches and pastel drawings. As conditions became even grimmer, she was forced to apply for a divorce—with Condorcet's secret consent—in order to evade the law against the wives of proscribed citizens and to protect the property of their child. What had once been a marriage of convenience had ripened into a profound affection. Her last letters to Condorcet show the full measure of the woman, passionate, realistic, true. "O that I could give my life for you. I am having a good vest made for you. Avoid the dampness and preserve yourself for this child . . . Your misfortunes devour my being. My soul is in the same torment as yours. I have the same horror as you for this camouflaged rupture, but between me and this lying shadow I see the interest of our child . . . "[11]

After Condorcet left Mme. Vernet's garret and succeeded in getting beyond the gates of Paris, he sought asylum in the house of the Suards in the country, where they were outwaiting the Terror. M. Suard refused the bearded and disheveled Condorcet for the same reasons that rational men have always found to abandon or betray their tracked friends. They had a "servante patriote." "I saw this man leave," Mme. Suard later wrote in a privately printed memoir on her husband, "but I only saw his back and his posture alone filled me with the greatest pity. Without turning he was looking for something in his pockets, something he did not find. He departed and M. Suard came to tell me that it was M. de C * * * who had been so dear to us. Ah, how fortunate that he had not presented himself to me first! Seeing him in this state I would have allowed a cry of anguish to escape from my heart: it would have betrayed him and I would have been disconsolate forever."[12] The false note in this sentimental outburst still jars.

In the shadow of the guillotine Condorcet had composed a dramatic paean, a passionate affirmation of rationalist faith, the climactic expression of the eighteenth-century quest for reason in history. The temper of the times had altered the calm, majestic assurance with which his predecessor Turgot had unfolded his ideas half a century before. Condorcet was writing amid hostile forces, in defiance of them, for the enemies of mankind were lurking all about him, and at the moment the tyrant seemed to be triumphant over virtue. In the decades since 1750 the conception of progress had broadened; it had been sparked by a sense of revolutionary urgency which Turgot's mid-century philosophical reflections often lacked. During the Revolution Condorcet had experienced life situations that Turgot the philosophical statesman had only comprehended abstractly. Condorcet had witnessed the declaration of war against the chosen nation by the aristocracies and clerisies of the world. The practicing savant, secretary of the Academy of Sciences, an exemplary agent of intellectual advancement, had soiled his hands in the blood and dirt of the Revolution, and he spoke to posterity like a prophet who had seen the people, one who knew their refractory ways but would bend them to the inevitable yoke which was their worldly destiny.

Condorcet was profuse in acknowledgements to his predecessors, Turgot and the two Englishmen who were the subversive bêtes noires of Edmund Burke's *Reflections on the French Revolution:* "We have witnessed the development of a new doctrine which is to deliver the final blow to the already tottering structure of prejudice. It is the idea of the limitless perfectibility of the human species, a doctrine whose first and most illustrious apostles were Turgot, Price, and Priestley."[13] But the writings of his antecedents were too sketchy and dispersed ever to become popular. The *Esquisse* was the form in which the eighteenth-century idea of progress was generally assimilated by Western thought. Condorcet wrote his manifesto with full awareness of its world revolutionary significance. Those who came after him had no choice but to affirm allegiance as did Godwin, Saint-Simon, and Comte, or to proclaim their hostility as Malthus did on the very title page of his pessimist *Essay on Population,* which appeared as a formal refutation of the French philosophe.[14] When the traditionalists of the de Maistre school declared war on eighteenth-century ideology they were engaged in controverting the arguments of the *Esquisse,* even when it was not mentioned by name. DeBonald anathematized it as the "Apocalypse of the new Gospel."[15]

Condorcet's conception of progress is by no means restricted to the *Esquisse;* it is the very lifeblood of all his intellectual labors, whether he is studying laws of probability in social phenomena, drafting constitutional norms for the revolutionary state, writing popular journalism, preparing *éloges* in the tradition of Fontenelle for deceased academic colleagues, collecting contemporary philosophical works for a world library of knowledge, or outlining projects for universal education. To be fully appreciated, the text of the *Esquisse* must be supplemented by a set of parallel chapters that amplify three of the epochs, documents published in the Arago edition of Condorcet's works in the 1840s.[16] Particularly revealing are the often-forgotten section which parallels the fourth epoch and a commentary on the *New Atlantis* of Francis Bacon, both of which were attached to the 1804 edition of the *Esquisse* and exerted a profound influence on Saint-Simon and Comte.

The Mechanics of Secular History

The *Esquisse* set forth the historical great chain of being: "We pass by imperceptible gradations from the brute to the savage and from the savage to Euler and Newton."[17] The term *progrès* and its derivations broke through all hitherto accepted bounds of meaning and became at one and the same time a capsulated description of empirical history, a charted goal for men's activities in the present and in the future, a definition of the good at any historic moment, and an identification of the moral man. Progress was a capacity inherent in the growth of rational intelligence. Less of a philosopher than Turgot, Condorcet merely accepted and incorporated his predecessor's psychology and epistemology. In the very first stage of his spiritual existence man's ability to make "new combinations" was already fully formed, and the secret of his progressist nature resided in his natural talent and desire to innovate. The tempo of progress was not uniform throughout history, either in Condorcet's version or in Turgot's. The early stages of barbarism had witnessed only a feeble development because man, weighed down by the repetitive labors of hunting, fishing, and agriculture, did not have sufficient leisure to effect the progress-bearing "new combinations." Higher civilizations resulted from the accident of a surplus that allowed some men to devote themselves completely to observation and to meditation—a formula that should be familiar to Marxist historians of the growth of consciousness, though no direct Condorcet influence need be traced since the idea had become commonplace by the 1840s. Unlike their more primitive necessitous forebears, reads the Condorcet account of the dawn of reason, the men of civilization had the time to study the new phenomena that chance had thrown in their path. Progress was still, as with Turgot, dependent primarily upon the individual act of a man of extraordinary talent, but a different emphasis altered the role of genius. For Condorcet each invention had to fulfill a social need at a given historic moment before it could be adopted by the people. Turgot was absorbed in the personal fate of the genius, whom inimical political conditions might crush. While Condorcet honored and extolled the genius, he shifted the focus to the state of society and its general readiness to assimilate an invention once it had seen the light. Throughout Condorcet's work the crucial instant of the progressive act was not the initial discovery, but its acceptance. In filial deference to Turgot the title of the *Equisse* retained an intellectualist and elitist bias, but in the working out of the historical process the concept was weighted heavily in the direction of the social.

Condorcet the secularist could no longer derive the idea of progress from God, making of it a new eighteenth-century attribute of divinity.[18] Vico, Turgot, and Herder had reassured themselves of the existence of historical laws in the world by fashioning arguments touched with theology and teleology. It has been rightly said that for German thought enlightenment usually meant the enlightenment of theology. Could a rational God have bestowed the reign of law upon the movement of the planets, upon organic and inorganic matter, and have abandoned human history to mere accident? Could a God who was infinite goodness have created the noblest of His creatures and then rendered his life on earth a meaningless, disorderly succession of events which would arouse disgust in a rational man? Herder's answer was a pious negative. Could Nature have endowed man with reason and afforded no opportunity for its unfolding in time? asked Immanuel Kant; for surely the half-bestial man of the present hardly represented the total fulfillment of rational and ethical capacities. Turgot's historical theodicy still reflected analogous quasi-religious reasoning. But for Condorcet the godless one, who wished to commit himself to the teleology of progress, none of these religious props was available to bolster his confidence.

From the outset Condorcet stripped the historical process bare of its ceremonial Christian elements. It was no longer a civil theology as with Vico, nor a theodicy as it had been with Turgot. Condorcet self-consciously secularized his master's world history and injected it with a virulent antireligious bias, though the dynamic forces on earth remained unchanged even after the guiding hand of God through time had been removed. History lost a transcendental sanction, but the substantive worldly goals of Turgot were preserved intact and the motive psychological drives of men were unaltered. Instead of Providence working through history, henceforward history would have to function only through itself. Progress became an autonomous human creation free from divine will or direction. Instead of pointing up a unique, divinely ordained quality in human history as distinguished from natural history, Condorcet resorted to the complete identification of history with the other sciences. Even if it were not a science of absolute prediction like physics, it could still preserve the fundamental character of science by calling its findings truths with a high degree of probability. Condorcet was willing to submit historical hypotheses to the same rigorous tests of necessity and constancy that prevailed in the other disciplines. Armed with the theory of probability, he could then integrate the historico-social sciences with the physical sciences and dispense completely with theology.

Through his disproof of the idea of "necessary connection" or simple causality, Hume as much as any other philosopher had brought about a rapprochement between the social and the physical sciences; for if absolute law was denied to the physical sciences then both forms of knowledge were reduced to the level of sciences of probability. When Condorcet wrote about "general and constant facts" he meant facts of a general enough character to permit of reasonably accurate prediction. In this respect all phenomena, both human and physical, could be viewed as on the same plane. "They are equally susceptible of being calculated," he wrote in a manuscript, "and all that is necessary, to reduce the whole of nature to laws similar to those which Newton discovered with the aid of the calculus, is to have a sufficient number of observations and a mathematics that is complex enough." [19]

After his traditional obeisance to scientific method in the tenth epoch of the *Esquisse,* which lacked only a formal acknowledgment to the philosophy of Chancellor Bacon for completeness, Condorcet launched into an excursus on "our hopes" for the future, by which he meant those hopes of the philosophes transcribed by himself which, according to the empirical evidence of history, had a reasonable probability of fulfillment. Gliding from a rationalist statement of scientific methodology to wishing is not so rare in the science of society as to warrant comment, but the ingenuousness of the transition in Condorcet is truly disarming.

In Condorcet's view the study of history could accomplish for mankind most of the functions that August Comte later arrogated to the science of sociology. It was "a science to foresee the progressions of the human species,"[20] a science of prediction, and the capacity to foretell was a source of vast power. It made it possible "to tame the future."[21] Through the separating out of obstacles and aids, which could then be recorded on the debit or the credit side of the ledger, past history could be made to yield the key to future development, because in an old-fashioned sense it was a storehouse of moral lessons teaching humanity what to elect and what to reject, how to minimize historic pain and regulate the temporal dimension of achievement. History could indicate, by what would now be called extrapolation, the general future tendency of the evolution of the human mind; delving into the record of past transformations was no mere idle amusement, for it instructed men in the art of directing progress. "These observations on what man has been and what he is today will later lead to the means of assuring and accelerating the new progressions which human nature still permits him to hope for."

History also served as a prophylaxis against prejudice. At moments this faithful devotee of reason called upon history to deflate the arrogance of self-complacent rationalists who imagined themselves totally emancipated from the parochial attitudes of their own age. "He who limits himself to knowing only the epoch in which he lives, even if it enjoys a marked superiority over its predecessors, exposes himself to the danger of partaking of all its superstitions; for each generation has its own, and it would be exceedingly dangerous to fancy oneself so close to the ultimate limits of reason that one no longer had to fear these prejudices."[22]

While there is a determined progressive development—absolute retrogression is impossible—whose grand sweep mankind can no longer defy, there remains a quasi-independent human force which sets the pace or the measure of progress and affects environmental conditions more or less favorably. Though the present state of knowledge guarantees a happy future for the overall movement of world history, a human variable can alter the methods whereby felicity may be attained. "And in order that the happiness which it promises us shall be less dearly bought, in order that it may spread with greater rapidity over a very extensive area, in order that it may be more complete in its results, do we not need to study in the history of the human mind what impediments we still have to fear, what means we possess for surmounting them?"[23] Condorcet adopted Turgot's arguments demonstrating the past reality and future inevitability of progress as foregone conclusions and then reshaped the whole problem: What was the most efficient, gentle, and easy method for the attainment of perfectibility?[24] In the *Fragment de justification* of July 1793, he described his own life's mission in precisely these terms. "Long since persuaded that the human species is infinitely perfectible, and that this perfection . . . cannot be arrested but by physical revolutions of the globe, I considered the task of hastening progress to be one of my sweetest occupations, one of the first duties of a man who has strengthened his reason by study and meditation."[25]

The narration of the first nine epochs of world history in the *Esquisse* reveals the natural motivation of mankind to have been a steady agelong pursuit of utility. There are passages in which progress is called an "instinct" or a "transcendent goal"; as epoch after epoch is analyzed, as the concrete discoveries, inventions, and moral leaps are described in detail, it becomes abundantly clear that there is one fundamental utilitarian drive in man; if left to his own devices he will invariably pursue the useful and the pleasurable, Hume's *utile et dulce,* in the ordinary economic sense of the eighteenth-century Encyclopedists.[26] From the primitives upward, whenever men realized that a practice, often discovered by chance, consumed less energy, was less costly, afforded more enjoyment, they adopted it. It was this identification of the *progressus* of mankind with the law of least action which was to arouse the towering rage of Nietzsche, guardian of the Will, against these passive optimists. For Condorcet every major progress was a conclusion reached by reasonable men thoroughly imbued with the spirit of rational utility. The momentous advancement in morals depicted in the second epoch, for example, when men stopped strangling their war captives, was the direct consequence of a tidy bit of commonsensical bookkeeping which convinced the conquerors that a healthy young slave was worth more in productive labor than the cost of his subsistence. Before such rational propositions mankind had to bow. Of course, at crucial moments the intervention of genius—a genius of utility—was often required to point out the new profit before the mass of ignorant, unthinking mankind could perceive it. This principle of utility was the driving force in all times and places and led to identical institutions under like circumstances. Common needs produced similar utilitarian solutions, ran the eighteenth-century ditty. Institutions such as feudalism were not peculiar to Western Europe, Condorcet argued, but a universal form "found almost everywhere in the world at all stages of civilization each time that one and the same territory was occupied by two peoples among whom victory had established an unequal heredity."[27] This type of world-historical thinking was most congenial to monistic philosophes of the eighteenth century. Court de Gébelin's Great Order of needs is the obvious parallel —and Condorcet knew his *Monde primitif.* If men were left to operate freely, "naturally," they would, he believed, produce a series of functional innovations which continuously increased their happiness. Condorcet was not a profound theoretician of human motives, and his historical world view should not be oversystematized. There are times when, in the spirit of d'Alembert's *Discours préliminaire,* he joined to utility an abstract concept like scientific curiosity as a progressive drive of mankind; but for the most part history was a succession of recognized needs and appeasements of needs in the course of which man was accumulating an ever-greater stockpile of scientific and moral truths.

That this smooth progression had not always been the past experience of mankind was due to the intrusion of nonfunctional, false, religious ideas that confused men, disrupted and distorted the normal, "natural" operations of their utilitarianism. The injection of alien motives had resulted in the war of progress against prejudice, which had become the substance and central theme of history. But the triumph of Locke's sensationalism, that incomparable tool for the analysis of ideas, would henceforward serve as "an eternal barrier between mankind and the old errors of his infancy, which should prevent him from ever being returned to his former ignorance by new prejudices . . . "[28]

In the past there had been grave setbacks. "Would anybody imagine that the whole system of human faculties in all individuals could have always made

such methodical progress that in no part of the system would either distur-
bances or disorders ever result, that all the faculties would perfect themselves
at one and the same time, in accordance with a felicitous sense of proportion,
steadfastly maintaining among the parts an equilibrium most favorable to the
happiness of the whole species?"[29] Such absolute balance would have been impossible; hence the variety of historical vicissitudes and the unevenness of development among peoples and individuals. History had been a worldly battleground between those forces advancing real utility and those suppressing it in
the name of a religion, a philosophic system, or a tyrannical lust for domination. This is a somewhat differently accented translation of the struggle between the promoters of novelty and the adherents to routine which Turgot
had described. More explicitly than in Turgot, religious bodies in all ages harbored evil antiprogressive elements and their opponents were the legions of
the good. The plots of organized castes and priesthoods to maintain themselves (the deceivers) in power, and their deliberate conspiracy to keep the
mass of the people, the duped, in ignorance through imposture were a hackneyed theme in eighteenth-century thought to which Condorcet gave final expression. Ultimately the enthroned sacerdotal tyranny was undermined because the sane spirit of men, of virtuous souls, of natural utilitarians broke
through the hard crust of lies imposed by the theological conspirators and resumed the quest for truth. Falsehood could not be maintained forever, for the
priests soon contradicted themselves and revealed their own inconsistencies.
Throughout the historical drama there is a conviction that virtue must triumph
in the end and that however oppressive may be the dominion of darkness and
evil, man's dogged inquiring energy in search of the useful will finally reassert
itself.

The first nine epochs of the *Esquisse* are largely a tirade against clerical enemies. Turgot had still found a respectworthy place for Christianity in the development of rational thought; unlike his predecessor, Condorcet was fighting
l'infâme. The arraignment of priests and religious impostors of all nations
grows into a tiresome harangue. In refutation of his friend's appreciation of the
benign role of the church in softening the barbarians of the north, Condorcet
cried out, "The blood of millions of men massacred in the name of God still
steams about us. Everywhere the earth which supports us covers the bones of a
barbaric intolerance."[30] The medieval Cathari are depicted as heroic figures,
the first who dared to reject the lies of the conspirators, and the brutal subjuga-
tion of the heretics by the fanatical armies whom the priests unleashed against
them is bewailed as the sad loss of brothers in progress and revolution. But
happily the defeats of the righteous are always temporary, the forces of light
suppressed in one area reemerge in another, and no power or violence is
mighty enough to choke off the diffusion of new ideas.

The historic, almost Zoroastrian combat between enlightenment and obscurantism had been marked by a series of great technological and scientific discoveries, which became the natural benchmarks of Condorcet's world tableau.
The early stages of civilization were relatively simultaneous developments in
different parts of the globe, for primitive human nature was everywhere the
same; only with the flowering of Greek genius was there a breakthrough of a
unique course of rational progress in Europe. But, alas, the Greek system-
makers, the sectarians of the schools, brought about their own downfall; Con-

dorcet abhorred the institutionalized knowledge of Greece and Rome and of the Chinese mandarins almost as much as he did that of the medieval School-men. Metaphysicians and system-makers in all ages, men with a tendency to raise questions for which mankind would perhaps never have answers and to construct "a philosophy of words" as a response, were as inimical to progress as priests and religious enthusiasts.[31] True knowledge was restricted to what he called the "sciences réelles,"[32] by which he meant precisely what Mme. de Staël and Saint-Simon did a few years later when they introduced the neologism "sciences positives": simple, straightforward empirical science, preferably with a mathematical base—that alone was authentic knowledge accumulating in time. Philosophies were disguised religions and they invariably led to the decline of true science. In its hour of triumph Christianity had merely picked up the debris of twenty rival Greco-Roman sects and systems which had battled one another into a state of exhaustion under the Empire, and this was "the signal for the total decadence of the sciences and of philosophy."[33] Medieval Christianity, a dismal period of retrogression after the bloom of Greek genius, was the target of his persistent, bitter eloquence. "Theological reveries, superstitious impostures are the only expressions of human genius, religious intolerance their only morality, and Europe, compressed between sacerdotal tyranny and military despotism, awaited in blood and tears the moment when new knowledge would allow it to be reborn to liberty, to humanity, and to virtue."[34] For Condorcet the world was still witnessing a death struggle between Christianity and progress, the great irreconcilable polar opposites both in scientific and in moral values.

The progressist angel of salvation appeared in the guise of the scientific Arabs, who transmitted back to Europe what the Greeks had discovered, the Romans preserved, and the Middle Ages destroyed. The anticlerical philosophe would naturally rather see the new illumination come from Islam than from Christendom. Condorcet was less impressed than Turgot by medieval developments in the mechanical arts as a prelude to Renaissance science. The medieval world was really a dark age. With the restoration of the arts and the sciences mankind had to resume progress where the ancients had left off, expunging a whole era of human existence as sterile.

In the great revival after the Middle Ages the art of printing occupied a crucial position, for in this instrument the conspirators of evil were confronted with an invention which could spread scientific truth over so vast an expanse of territory that suppression became virtually impossible. As in Turgot, the extension of progress, the massive quantitative promulgation of the new ideas, would henceforward fundamentally alter the balance in the conflict between light and darkness. During the initial stages of the antireligious struggle the enemies of the priestly conspiracy had been forced to be circumspect. Men but recently emancipated from superstition had not dared attack frontally; they had introduced their ideas stealthily into books read by the upper classes, had resorted to wit rather than overt invective, and had thus hoodwinked the persecutors of truth. To render the breakdown of the medieval sacerdotal system plausible, Condorcet dreamed up a counterconspiracy of truth, secret societies of philosophical adepts whose traces had been lost. He even hazarded the wild guess that the Knights Templar had been a clandestine organization of this character, sworn to the propagation of truth, and that this was the real reason for their suppression. When he asked himself what manner of men were they who risked combat with priestly authority, his rather insipid answer was that "those who had a sounder mind, a more open, elevated nature . . . fought for the cause of men against the priests."[35]

The history of the progress of the human mind became the chronicle of the princes of the intellect who at eight or nine critical moments set the spirit of man free. Each stage was a separate act in the drama, and the argument was a repetitive one: There was always a body of wily men, a heroic genius, a conflict of power, a moment of triumph followed by a regrouping of the agents of evil who, bloated with the new knowledge acquired through the discoveries of genius, again closed the gates of the temple of reason and practiced the wicked rites which they fashioned into a tradition. The drama was usually enacted with aristocratic characters as in classical tragedy. The people themselves played virtually no role in the historic process. Condorcet was fully conscious of the inclination toward decadence, particularly among the priestly or philosophical conspirators. In the early stages, after the infusion of a new potion of energy from the free genius, even the theological systematizers were inventive, but as time passed and they were subject to no new stimuli their works became stale and hackneyed; and in the end they could not even comprehend their own traditions. Wicked priests made use of the temporal arm of cruel tyrants, but the evil ones invariably fell out among themselves like a band of thieves. Each side summoned new forces, uncommitted men, and these aides in an internecine conflict among obscurantists grasped the opportunity to insinuate fresh ideas into the discussion. Both traditionalist rivals were constrained by their own abominable lust for power to employ the good geniuses, and in time, once they had been allowed into the city, the newcomers took possession of the ideology which had been sapped of its vital force.

Condorcet, like many modern philosophers of history prior to Hegel, made frequent use of a primitive sort of historical dialectic. Since history was a conflict of the forces of good and evil and since evil had been triumphant for many centuries, the progressionist had to demonstrate how contradictory forces could arise in the bosom of an old order. One example of the process was the growth of learning in the later Middle Ages, despite society's commitment to obscurantism and sheer power lust. The priests, in the very act of strengthening their offensive against the secret propagators of truth, had to study the liberal arguments that were being propounded against them. Similarly they were constrained to become learned in order to fabricate evidence bolstering their own position against secular rivals for power. Kings in their turn had to establish schools for jurisconsults in an effort to uphold their temporal regimes. Thus in the very ranks of the fanatics, despite the self-interest and ill will of priests and lords, learning and knowledge were diffused, and in the desperate attempt to consolidate the power of superstition a new light was kindled.

The crusades were another example of Condorcet's crude "dialectic" of history. Religious prejudice had impelled Christian Europeans to fight in the East, but from the wars there stemmed consequences disastrous to the feudal antiprogressist regimes. The crusades weakened the power of the seigneurs. Men were brought into close relations with the Arab peoples and their learning so that, ultimately, if the late medieval Christians did not surpass Arab science they at least came to equal it. "These wars undertaken for the cause of superstition served to destroy it."[36] Even scholasticism, for all its excessive subtleties and its false ideas, developed the human mind and became "the first origin of the philosophical analysis which has since been the fecund source of our progress . . . This scholasticism did not lead to the discovery of truth; it did not even serve for its discussion, for a good appreciation of its proofs; but it sharpened the minds . . . "[37]

Condorcet's treatment of the discovery of cannon and gunpowder was perhaps his most striking instance of progressist good emanating from tyrannical evil. The new weapons were retrogressive agents if evaluated in terms of eighteenth-century pacifist morality, for they increased the terrible potentialities of destruction. In its long-term effect, however, the cannon poured forth a host of salutary results. Warriors became less ferocious because gunpowder obliged them to fight at greater distances from one another. The heavy cost of military expeditions made even the most bellicose nations devote themselves to commerce and the arts of peace in order to be able to finance their wars. Finally, the discovery of gunpowder reduced the likelihood that a sudden invasion of barbarians, possessed by blind courage, would be able to crush less warlike, civilized peoples. "The great conquests and the revolutions which follow them have become almost impossible."[38] Gunpowder reduced the superiority of the mounted knight and in the long run diminished the prestige of the nobility. Thus an invention which had threatened to destroy the human species removed the last obstacles to the attainment of real liberty and equality among men. The "cunning of reason" is a perennial conception of philosophical history; virtually all the modern prophets resort to it. "The very passions of men, their interests falsely understood, lead them to spread enlightenment, liberty, happiness, to do good despite themselves"[39] was Condorcet's simplistic expression of the idea in one of his manuscripts.

In Condorcet's secular history those who denied liberty, particularly in the pursuit of science, were the wicked ones, and in this respect the rigid philosophical system-builders were thrown into the same category in progressist Hell as the theologians and priestly dogmatists. The early sections of the *Esquisse* continue the Turgot tradition with an indissoluble association of liberty and progress. Whenever there had been decadence, a temporary blotting out of progress—as under the latter-day caliphs, in China, or in medieval Christian Europe—Condorcet found explanations almost exclusively in the imposition of tyranny and the crushing of liberty. The absolutist institutions of Christianity had been antihuman not only because of the cruelties they perpetrated upon their enemies but because they denied mankind the full measure of progress under freedom it was naturally capable of achieving.

In the nineteenth century this narrative of events became the unimpeachable framework for any popular liberal anticlerical view of world history. But in his espousal of liberty as the dynamic of progress Condorcet soon encountered a dilemma, and a tension was introduced into the heart of his system, perhaps the pivotal development in the history of the concept—a still unresolved dilemma. There came to be an issue, even a contradiction, between liberty and the optimum tempo of progress. Essentially the problem was posed for the future of mankind; in the past it had not been pressing since the historic spiritual powers and their organizational embodiments had always degenerated into antiprogressive strongholds. Medieval Christianity never impressed Condorcet as the repository and preserver of the acquisitions of mankind, as it had the young Turgot, for he saw only its repressive sword cutting off genius in its prime, stifling truth. The proclamation of freedom of inquiry had hitherto been the natural rallying cry of progressists. But what of the future? Was the rule of liberty applied with Turgot's absolutism the best way for the attainment of maximal progress as fast as humanly possible? Or was there another road? The union between liberty and progress might be rent asunder, and liberty might yield before the prospect of accelerated development under organization with its necessary restrictions. This alternative had many ramifications in Condorcet's theory, which then became more than a mere rehearsal of his admired predecessor's reflections.

Progress in Equality

For Turgot the diffusion of progress still resembled a benevolent act of enlightened monarchy; in the hands of Condorcet progress in equality became an intrinsic constituent element in the idea. To render men more or less equal assumed moral value and was a goal virtually independent, to be pursued in and of itself. The extension of enlightenment among the nations and a diminution of inequalities was for Turgot primarily intended to moralize the people, but there was always another purpose too, one rooted in aristocratic suspicion—to safeguard the acquisitions of humanity from an uprising of the ignorant mob. In Condorcet there is an appreciation of the positive uses of democracy for progress which the prerevolutionary noble philosophe could not wholeheartedly entertain. Condorcet altered Turgot's theory of the incidence of genius, the idea that it was a fixed though infinitesimal proportion of the population in any epoch, by proposing a critically different ratio: The creative scientists were a proportion of all persons subject to the influence of rationalist education. If the state provided instruction for a vastly increased number of inhabitants, the total of productive scientists would multiply astronomically. The agent of progress was still the scientist, but in Condorcet he was less the unique genius of Turgot, less the rare colossus of the mind, and more a statistical probability of mass enlightenment.

Condorcet faced one of the central historic problems of the idea of progress —the relative worth of intensive scientific progress among the elite and of extensive progress of scientific knowledge among the masses. Which should be preferred? He was consistently opposed to the double-truth doctrines which had become current among deists and one wing of the philosophes, the idea that there was one truth for the masses and another for the elite, who alone could comprehend science and the mathematical world. This was for Condorcet dangerous thinking which had served as the basis for the domination of society by a hieratic priesthood. In the Orient the exclusive concentration of truth in the hands of an elite had resulted in the desiccation of scientific creativity. Condorcet democratized the idea of progress. He was so worried that progress might be crushed by an educated class with a monopoly of knowledge that he was even willing to sacrifice to a degree the intensification of scientific knowledge among the elite—this was the critical test—in favor of its propagation among the masses. It was salutary, for example, to abolish Latin as the exclusive language of scientific communication, even at the risk of placing additional burdens upon scholars who henceforth would have to spend time learning many languages. The use of the vernacular for their publications would prevent the scientists from becoming an exclusive clique, creating two distinct classes, the learned and the ignorant, and curtailing the progress of the "mass of the human species."[40] Condorcet himself was highly conscious of the distinction between the two measures of progress—one intrinsic and intensive, the other extensive—which in Turgot was only implicit. "We shall distinguish between the progress of science itself, which can be measured only in terms of the totality of the truths it has uncovered, and the progress accomplished by a nation in each science, a progress measured both by the number of people who are acquainted with the most common and the most important truths and by the number and the nature of the truths generally known."[41] In passages of the ninth epoch Condorcet clearly reduced the prestige of pure scientific discovery and made it the handmaiden of popular well-being. Meaningful history consisted in tracing the consequences of a new scientifc discovery, a new system of laws, or a political revolution, as they affected "the most numerous portion of each society . . . For this is the real object of philosophy, since all intermediary effects of these same causes can only be considered forces ultimately working on those who truly constitute the mass of humanity."[42]

Only in the progress of the mass of mankind could there be an ultimate value judgment. Did a man really deserve his titles to glory? The people would decide. Had human reason really progressed, had there been a real perfection of mankind? Only by examining the condition of the people could one judge. Progress usually starts with a scientific discovery, but the purpose of its development has to be popular utility. In the past the two basic forms of progress, the moral and the scientifc, had not always been compatible. A high level of scientific information had once been the monopoly of a sacerdotal class which used its knowledge for ends diametrically contrary to the moral progress of their society. The tragic fault lay in the very fact of exclusivity. As soon as modern science reached a "certain point" of advance among a number of nations and penetrated among the mass of people in any one nation whose language and relationships were universal (France seems the chosen one), an unbreakable bond between scientific and moral progress would be forged. The past had witnessed elite scientific progress which could be abused; the future popularization of science would make its freezing into a hieratic system—the death of progress—impossible.

The hopes for the future that Condorcet was able to find within himself could be reduced to three (even the sworn enemy of the Catholic Church, when driven to prophecy, was triadic), and they all dealt with the principle of equality. Before his mind's eye loomed a plateau of excellence in science and well-being which was occupied by the French and Anglo-American nations. (He was thus one of the first to conceive of an Atlantic community.) In time the other peoples of the globe would rise to a status more or less equal with this lofty plane. Similarly there was an eminence of scientific knowledge and well-being in the elite of each nation, and progress would signify the raising of all men in a polity close to this level. His third hope was a desire for the perfection of man in a biological sense. This too was a development which would affect all men more or less equally through the inheritance of acquired characteristics.

Condorcet proceeded to test the empirical validity of these desires for equality. Was there any evidence that they would be fulfilled? His response assumed the form of rhetorical questions which no son of the Revolution, whatever his party, could answer in the negative. Were there peoples on earth condemned to live forever without liberty and without reason? Was there any inherent necessity for the wide disparities in scientific knowledge and general well-being among nations—was the existence of barbarous peoples inevitable? Were gross inequalities in the enlightenment and prosperity of various classes in a nation necessary conditions of the civilized state? He could find no basis for replying affirmatively; therefore the converse was true.

The wide inequalities of contemporary society were due to a mechanical defect in administration, in social art. There was nothing irremediable in civilization which required the persistence of such flagrant differences. Condorcet was not free of the Rousseauan conception of a blissful state of nature, and he accepted the argument of the *Second Discourse* in a modified form: up until the Age of Enlightenment the growth of the arts and the sciences had been accompanied by an unfortunate maximization of the original natural, though slight, inequality among human beings. Before men had acquired talents and the vanities of amour-propre and comparative morality, the inequalities at birth, the natural inequalities, had been of no great significance. Only when an individual man accumulated great powers in the state of civilization did horrid and unnatural inequalities become the very basis of an oppressive social organization. Fortunately, in the immediate future a counter-tendency would make itself felt, a momentous turn in the history of human inequality on earth. While the arts and the sciences were preserved and their progress was furthered, a concomitant decrease in inequality among men would manifest itself. The strengthening of this development would become one of the main efforts of conscious future action, the practical goal of the "social art." Absolute equality would never be reached nor was it desirable, for there were benign inequalities, special excellences, unique attributes and capacities, which Condorcet's intimate friend Cabanis was to comment upon in his famous papers before the Institute in 1794–1795. These were to be fostered not for themselves but because paradoxically they accelerated general equality. The natural inequalities of Turgot's men of genius—and that is what Condorcet counted on—would, if afforded a favorable environment, spread a high measure of equality through their contribution to the general utilitarian progress of civilization. Natural inequalities would endure, but they would no longer entail dependence, impoverishment, or humiliation for the great mass of mankind.

Reaching a status of relative equality meant becoming citizens in a free society, and this presupposed minimal physical, intellectual, and moral attainments. Human beings all had a natural capacity for reason which had to be nourished with knowledge until they were capable of discerning truth from falsehood, thus emancipating themselves from traditional prejudices, foremost among them religious superstitions. Men had to be aware of their rights as citizens and to be in a position to exercise these rights freely and independently. The use of judgment demanded a certain physical ease. Natural faculties and the conveniences of living had to be sufficiently developed lest men be too wretched to fulfill their elementary citizenship obligations. A prelude to freedom and true equality was the existence of a general social climate in which stupidity and misery were accidents, the rare exceptions rather than the habitual fate and norm of mankind. Condorcet the intellectual was far from indifferent to ordinary material wants. Their gratification was a condition precedent, it was almost taken for granted, to any future evolution. He reaffirmed, like Bacon and Leibniz before him, the relationship between progress in science and technology and the raising of the general level of prosperity. At the end of the eighteenth century the utility of science, aside from its value as a search for truth, was just becoming a widespread popular notion. For Condorcet this was the point of contact between intellectual and moral progress.

Condorcet's estimate of the world political situation confirmed him in the hypothesis that the ideal of equality was in fact in the process of realization. All enlightened men on earth had already accepted the principles of the French Revolution. Their diffusion was so wide that no counterforce could prevent their eventual penetration everywhere. In the new dawn the universal values of the Declaration of the Rights of Man could not remain the monopoly of a spiritual clique. Once the truths of the French Revolution were taught in the huts of enslaved peoples, their rational capacities would be awakened and they would fight to secure for themselves the same rights enjoyed by Europeans. Condorcet drew a grim portrait of the colonial slave living in mute indignation; but he was nevertheless a man, and it required only a spark to arouse in him all his human qualities. Condorcet perhaps telescoped the periods of eighteenth-century colonialism, nineteenth-century imperialism, and twentieth-century independence, but sub specie aeternitatis he still deserves to retain an honorable place in the fraternity of utopian emancipators of all oppressed races and peoples.

The movement toward equality would not proceed at the same tempo and in the same manner throughout the whole world. There was uneven development, to borrow Marx's later phrase. The political action of individual governments would determine the manner in which the egalitarian revolution took place. Among some nations a recognition of the inevitability of the process would bring about a peaceful transition; among others stubborn, blind resistance on the part of the tyrants who held the reins of governance would provoke outbreaks of violence. The burden of choice between a peaceful and a chaotic transition was thrust upon those who now exercised power. Revolution would be the fate of those polities which refused to accept the verdict of history. But in either event the final consequence, a world converted to the French Revolutionary ideology, was preordained.

With time all nations and peoples of the earth would climb toward the high level of civilization and enlightenment achieved along the shores of the Atlantic, the area that was the pacesetter of universal egalitarian progress. This presupposed the abolition of slavery, of colonial domination, and of the exploitation of one political society by another. The methods by which this was achieved—peaceful or violent—were less significant than the fact that total world civilization among relative equals was a necessary aspect of total progress. In one curious passage Condorcet conceded the remote possibility of an irruption of barbarians from the plateau of Tartary to cut short European and hence world progress, but it was only a passing reflection. Europeans would soon increase so rapidly that they would overflow onto other continents, civilizing and assimilating backward peoples. The horrors of the enslavement of native populations which the Abbé Raynal had depicted with indignation in the *Histoire philosophique* would then give way before a universal education program directed by altruistic white Europeans bearing science. In Saint-Simon the idea later assumed the form of a white European's mission or crusade to uproot the primitive religions of Asia and Africa and impose scientificism. There was only one true form of knowledge allowable, and any other spiritual existence or culture represented a grave danger. The progressists had so absolute a faith in the objective validity of their scientific utilitarian civilization that its universal propagation as a perfect good was never questioned for a single moment. The Europocentrism of the liberal idea of progress exemplified by Condorcet became one of its more naive though deep-rooted preconceptions.

The Scientific Society

The important element introduced by Condorcet into the idea of progress was not the commonplace that the study of the past would help man in the future, a frequent variation on any moralizing history, but the sense of tempo, the belief that philosophical history, if deciphered, would teach man how to affect the historic timetable. That progress was inevitable after a certain stage of human development Turgot had already demonstrated. What then was a worthy human purpose in life and what should be a man's individual role? Condorcet's solution is a prototype for similar, nineteenth-century theories in Saint-Simon, Comte, and Marx. There was a peculiar merit in accelerating the rate of progress. Since it was defined in terms of utilitarian good, the sooner it dispensed its bounty the better. To hasten the end was a longing of medieval mystics. Worldly progress, infinite and inevitable, had no final historic moment like an apocalypse, but there was nevertheless an implied virtue in the acquisition of more felicity as fast as possible. A hypothetical maximum pace could be achieved if the total human effort were expended, and there was an inference that failure to fulfill one's progressist mission to the utmost was sinning against humanity. Once progress had become the absolute of human behavior there was an implied immorality in not bringing quickly to fruition the complete development of which humanity was capable at any moment. A delay in the discovery of abstract truth was not an innocent failing, because progress in science could overnight—this was uncontested—be transmuted into moral progress and happiness. To decelerate the pace for whatever reason was therefore a great iniquity, for it was a refusal to bestow happiness upon fellow men. Driven one step further it became an act of treachery against humanity.

The eighteenth-century ideology of progress has long since engulfed the politics of the world, East and West. Some of the real differences between them are mechanical and organizational: how fast shall the tempo be accelerated and what price in liberty shall be paid at any given stage of development? Condorcet was one of the first modern thinkers to explore the problems entailed by the painful alternatives.

Throughout the *Esquisse* and the fragments attached to it Condorcet communicated the feeling that mankind stood at one of the great divides in history, an emotion he shared with two other philosophical geniuses, one old, the other young, who were alive at the moment of the French Revolution—Kant and

Hegel. The conviction that the whole human race was on the verge of a great bound forward into another realm of social being made Condorcet a militant activist and persuaded him to venture, perhaps without full consciousness of what the decision might imply, upon a plan for the ordering of world progress. Turgot had conceived of liberty as the absolute prerequisite of progress, the very air in which it breathed most easily. Suddenly the problem of tempo intruded, raising the provocative query whether under liberty mankind was in fact achieving the maximum harvest extensively and intensively of which the species was capable. Once progress became the moral absolute, then even liberty could be called upon to bend, at least a little. Throughout his description of the mechanics for the realization of his utopia, Condorcet tended to soften the contradiction between liberty and progress, to show that men would be drawn to organization freely and of their own will, to demonstrate that at this advanced stage a rational order necessarily required complete organization. At times he expressed confidence that it would be feasible to enjoy the benefits of organization and of liberty too. By introducing libertarian safeguards he hoped to avoid the more flagrant impositions and dangers of institutional control, which he had studied, examined, and inveighed against so dramatically in his universal history. He was often markedly uncomfortable with the denial of absolute liberty, but ultimately in the name of progress he allowed himself to be enticed into the new order.

A side glance at the realities of scientific organization at the turn of the eighteenth century may highlight the novelty of Condorcet's break with existing practice. Despite a few instances of international cooperation, particularly in the gathering of astronomic data, seventeenth- and eighteenth-century scientific discovery had been the work of lone individuals, men of heroic genius. During the revolutionary era learned societies of Paris and the provinces offered prizes on a heterogeneous array of research topics, and a substantial number of scientists were salaried by the state in professional schools and institutes; but in these endeavors public attention and sponsorship were always concentrated upon isolated individual performance. A deep-rooted hostility to the *esprit de système* which the *idéologues* had inherited from Condillac rendered them inaccessible to the notion of collective experimentation; it savored too much of a School, which cramped initiative. Scientists were empiricists who published their discoveries as they made them, without subscribing to preconceived "metaphysical" ideas of any master, and somehow their total effort added up to human perfectibility. Free enterprise in business was paralleled by private research in the sciences, and benefits to humanity would accrue from both. In the universities, learned societies, and academies, general consciousness of a European intellectual community had been fostered over the centuries, but it had bred a zealous spirit of competition among scientists rather than any tendency toward combination or coordination. Bitter controversy over the priority of scientific discoveries was a symptom of this contentious rivalry. The republic of science was not necessarily a happy family. And not all its members considered themselves professional scientists rather than individuals who practiced science as an avocation out of sheer curiosity. After Condorcet's death, with the establishment of the Institute and the great schools, the adoption of a universal system of education, and the promulgation of Napoleon's decree demanding regular reports from the various classes of the Institute (before he

reorganized the Class of Political and Moral Sciences out of existence), communication among scientists and scholars became more intimate and regular—
there was a growing professional consciousness—and at formal sessions the
presidents of the several classes rendered verbal obeisance to the idea of the
unity of science. Despite the more frequent assemblages, however, there was
no interference with the individual scientist as he chose his subject and conducted his research in private. The announcement of prize competitions by the
various classes of the Institute focused attention upon specific problems in separate areas of knowledge, but there were no coordinated efforts at their solution. Nor was there any interdisciplinary body charged with the formulation
of problems in accordance with a preconceived scientific scheme. In this historical environment the plans of Condorcet, and the later ones of Saint-Simon,
for the universal administration of science were revolutionary proposals that
went against the grain of existing mores.[43]

Drawing his inspiration from Francis Bacon's description of the activities of
Salomon's House of science on New Atlantis, Condorcet proposed a voluntary
organization of world scientists acting under a common direction and in accordance with a "perpetual" plan of research. His commentary on the *New Atlantis* was one of the last things he wrote. Viewed historically the manuscript
was a key work of transition between eighteenth- and nineteenth-century
thought. The bulk of what Condorcet said in the *Esquisse* is readily assimilable
with conceptions of the late 1700s; the new emphasis on organization, however, was destined to become so overpowering in its intensity that it has by
now drowned out most other elements in the idea of progress. For Condorcet,
writing on the eve of his death, this was a realistic program of action which
would surely be put into effect within the next few generations and might even
be initiated in his own. The piece is what the editors of the 1840s called it, a
fragment, and its tone is discursive; he is answering arguments against the feasibility of the heterodox proposal, refuting an imaginary skeptical interlocutor
in the classical utopian manner.

The guiding brain of Condorcet's plan was a supreme body for the direction
of science, independent of all state institutions, even those operating under an
egalitarian political system. While making men more or less equal was an immediate social goal, Condorcet was well aware that the spirit of equality could
degenerate into low envy of excellence, that mediocrity hated dangerous rivals
and feared "a penetrating and severe judge in the most modest talent."[44] For all
his insistence upon equality in his social and political theory, he recognized the
intellectual gulf which separated those people who had managed to acquire
sufficient knowledge to carry on the ordinary functions of society from the
outstanding scientists of genius for whom the acquisition of truth was the all-
absorbing passion of their entire lives. What then could prevent the leveling
spirit, albeit on a high plane of excellence, from interfering with the progress
of new scientific investigations organized internationally, which genius alone
could appreciate?

It was a precondition of Condorcet's utopia of science that the bulk of mankind would be emancipated from the grosser errors of superstition and that
scientific achievement, in lieu of power, riches, and military glory, would become the channel into which men of talent naturally drove their energies. The
problem for the future was less the intrusion of a stupid tyrant or mass igno-

rance than how to assure the superiority of the real genius over the charlatan, how to safeguard mankind from embarking upon useless projects which might attract run-of-the-mill rational men but were not the most urgent needs of science. In effect, how would elitist science, having accepted organization for the sake of accelerated development, maintain its independence and deal with democratic controls in an egalitarian society?—a not unfamiliar query in the eighth decade of the twentieth century. Ordinary men could think only in terms of their immediate needs and desires, and if they had a dominant voice in the organization of science it would be almost impossible to agree upon the support of a grandiose plan which would break through the natural limitations of time imposed upon one scientist or national scientific group. Bacon had dreamed of a monarch who would undertake scientific projects beyond the capacity of any one genius, but there was no assurance for Condorcet that a great king, even if he could be interested in science rather than hunting, would further studies which served the total requirements of science and humanity rather than those which attracted his fancy or increased his power.

Since only scientists could appraise the needs of their discipline, Condorcet contrived a mechanism aimed at guaranteeing their independence from outside influences and at the same time preventing their passions from exerting deleterious effects upon the choice of projects, yet providing for a maximum coordination of all creative efforts. As a *politique* Condorcet was one of the great protectors of the absolute rights of the individual in the face of the state, but when it came to the organization of science new elements were abruptly introduced into his system of values. The individual scientists of the future, even the geniuses among them, would not be able to achieve great progress as long as they continued to operate in isolation, even if they maintained casual contacts with one another. Since the really important discoveries of the future necessitated observations in places dispersed over the whole face of the globe and over a period of many generations, an overall plan for the collection of data, guaranteeing constancy of observation and uniformity of method, was indispensable. The lone scientist could not undertake projects of this scope because of the limitations of his mortality and of his resources. The new areas of knowledge to be explored henceforth depended upon a massive quantification of scientific experiments and observations.

Like most of his contemporaries, Condorcet was smugly convinced that problems of scientific theory had all been solved or at least were on the verge of solution. His world organization took for granted a common self-evident methodology which was easy of access; modern questions in the philosophy of science did not perturb him, and the prospect of accumulating ever more data and of establishing appropriate correlations among them seemed endlessly fruitful. With scientists agreed upon method, there was a common standard for the evaluation of the separate parts of whatever grand plan was adopted. Scientists could not, without violating their own natures, their inner sense of what was right, espouse a project which was useless or irrelevant. There persisted, to be sure, that old canker of envy and competition, especially among men in the top grades of a scientific hierarchy, and this might lead to conflicts over who should direct the supreme body of science. To mitigate these antagonisms he suggested that final judgment of rank come not from the rivals themselves but from the lower echelons, lesser men, but persons informed, impartial, and free from the passion of rivalry because they were either younger or humbler scientific workers who recognized the limitations of their status. Even if the army of scientists should err somewhat in their selection, the consequences would not be disastrous for mankind, since rough justice was all that was necessary. Quacks and fakers had to be excluded, and for this purpose the judgment of the informed corps of scientists in each discipline was adequate. The opinion even of rational, educated laymen, on the other hand, would not suffice.

Before it could be instituted, the perpetual and universal society for the progress of the sciences had to face stubborn obstacles in human wills and passions. What would persuade the scientific great to abandon the splendid autocracy of their individual laboratories and to join in the common world enterprise? Condorcet's answer was threefold: First, there was a growing consciousness in every field that the problems of science had become far too vast for any one man to aspire to solve them alone. Second, the imminent tremendous increase in the total number of creative scientists would lead to cooperation. In the tenth epoch of the *Esquisse,* by the simple process of multiplying the existing ratio of scientists to educated persons by the prospective factor of increase in the number of men with adequate schooling, he had arrived at the conjecture of àn array of scientists that was staggering, at least to the imagination of an eighteenth-century man. In this multitude there would be esteem for everybody, but no single individual genius would tower above the body of science like a Newton. Therefore great scientists, more or less equal in capacity, would not hesitate to welcome one another in joint enterprises. Third, the scientists would rush to participate in the universal society out of curiosity and for the pleasure of learning new truths, passions that in the real scientist overcame and superseded the natural egotistic desire for individual fame.

In his politics Condorcet had provided for frequent revisions of the French constitution. Fearful (as his friend Turgot had taught him to be) of the dangers to intellectual progress of falling into a rut, into a set pattern, he allowed for the review of his scientific grand design by each new generation. The eighteenth-century philosophes, possessed by the spirit of innovation, were wary of the dead hand of the past, and Condorcet was loath to allow the originators of the scientific plan to force future generations into fixed grooves of research. But there was an equivalent hazard if there were no continuity from one epoch to another. In answer to the argument that a partisan contentious spirit in a succeeding age might jettison the whole plan, not only amend it, he recalled that in the history of science the conservative, traditionalist, repetitive spirit had been predominant and was far more to be feared than innovation. The risk of a subsequent overturning of the applecart was dismissed with a reiteration of his basic premise that a scientific methodology universally agreed upon would have established general standards which no scientists in the future would dare to violate. Thus there could be revisions of the overall plan without an interruption of the accumulative process of research from one generation to another.

Embryonic elements of the cooperative spirit destined to permeate the whole corps of world scientists were already present among contemporaries. Scientists reacted with great excitement to the announcement of every new discovery, even if it took place in the most distant land. Why would they be less moved by the annual revelation of the new harvest of truths yielded by

their common labors? Science, like all human institutions and social relationships, had to be purified of its "fanaticisms," the self-interest, ambitions, and
predilections of its practitioners. This was to be accomplished by a technique
similar to that which Condorcet had applied to other social problems, the elaboration of an appropriate administrative device, an institutional arrangement
under which it became difficult, almost impossible, for the individual passion for fame to find expression at the cost of excellence. In the end, world
science would be freed from the dross of personal prejudice; it would become
objective.

There lurked another menace to the realization of Condorcet's collegiate
body of progressive scientists, rivalry among the scientific disciplines. To off-
set this spirit of corps competitiveness Condorcet preached a sermon on the
unity of the scientific system and illustrated the interdependence of the social
and the mathematical and physical sciences. While each scientist's natural preference for his own discipline would not disappear, Condorcet's faith resided in
the diffusion of the general concepts of every branch of knowledge among all
scientists. With the propagation of the idea of the universality of science, the
rivalry among its branches, if not abolished, would at least abate. An exaggerated estimation of one's own science was a trait of mediocrities who were
incapable of rising to the top ranks of the profession and therefore consoled
themselves by trumpeting the preeminence of their special field.

A primary characteristic of Condorcet's scientific society was its independent voluntary nature; it was not state-directed, and scientists joined it freely
because they were convinced that it fulfilled their most expansive hopes. This
was his facile verbal conciliation of liberty and organization. There had been
momentous individual discoveries in the past, and even if the anarchic play of
scientific investigation continued, some new truths would emerge fortuitously
in the course of future centuries; but "the plan" would greatly increase the
quantity of discoveries, their realization would become more certain, the element of chance would be minimized, and, above all, the time factor would be
sharply reduced. A rhetorical question was addressed to those men of science
reluctant to join the society: By what right did they deprive whole generations
of mankind of the enjoyment of the fruits of their researches because of their
stubborn unwillingness to organize? It was immoral not to have given birth as
soon as possible to a discovery that was potentially feasible; it was an act of
perfidy against the ideal of scientific progress. To hasten the revelation of truth
with its humanitarian consequences was an article of the scientist's creed. To
delay it was antiscientific.

According to one version of the organizational mechanics of Condorcet's
scientific society, those who subscribed to a "Fund" could participate in the
election of a small number of scientists whose function it would be to draft the
overall plan of operations. On the eve of his death in 1794, after his dismal
experiences in the Legislative Assembly, Condorcet was none too sanguine
about the efficiency of great public bodies. He therefore advised that the election of the scientists be arranged in writing, without speeches. "One must in
general avoid any large meeting. This is the only means of obtaining true
equality, of avoiding the influence of intrigue, of charlatanism, and of verbiage;
of conserving for simple truth the whole of its empire, of being led by knowledge and not by passions."[45] Condorcet the scientific expert was becoming

uneasy about democratic parliamentary procedures. He died before his distrust
of revolutionary assemblies was given forthright public expression; his successors Saint-Simon and Comte would no longer be bound by a populist past.

In return for a contribution to the fund, each subscriber received scientific
papers and a decennial report on new discoveries (omitting those of too recent
date). While a contributor might designate the particular project on which he
wanted his money spent, a tenth of all collections automatically became part of
the budget for the maintenance of the long-term or perpetual projects. Condorcet was still on the alert lest any one generation exercise an excessive influence on the future progress of science by abandoning certain branches of
knowledge completely. In the decisions of the elected scientists, a very high
majority would be required for the alteration of a basic part of the plan, a simple plurality for modifications of detail. A periodic renewal of a third of the
directing body—perhaps a chance recollection of the American Constitution
—would assure continuity without allowing scientific school prejudices to become deeply entrenched. Though state aid would not be rejected, it would be
subject to the same conditions as the subscriptions of other members. The scientific society might avail itself of governmental facilities, but the character of
the free relationship between a public power and an autonomous association
had to be preserved. Since the "historical review" had taught him that whenever state power became the controller of science decadence invariably set in—
as with the Arabs—he was opposed to direct governmental participation in his
scientific society. "It is for the association alone to judge in an independent
manner what it believes should be undertaken for the progress of the sciences.
It is for the public power to judge, with the same independence, which of these
projects appears to merit either its concurrence or its munificence."[46] A self-
imposed neutrality on the part of the modern state in its relations to science
was one of Condorcet's more naive illusions. The organizer of science tried to
balance nicely elements of innovation and conservation, elements of freedom
and constraint.

Condorcet's commentary on the *New Atlantis* was only a fragment and he
never had an opportunity to iron out its inconsistencies. It is thus not quite
clear whether the basic unit of the society's organization is a state or the whole
world. He began by referring to the "general union of the scientists in a universal republic of the sciences," and then somehow switched to a national unit.
In the end he reverted to the prospect of a world scientific society and proposed among its labors the establishment of a universal language and the
somewhat cryptic (though at the moment highly relevant) "execution of a
monument which shelters the sciences even from a general revolution of the
globe."[47]

From the Institut de France manuscripts it appears that while Condorcet was
confident that the spread of knowledge virtually insured mankind against any
recrudescence of barbarism, it could not be safeguarded from "an upheaval of
the globe which, without entirely destroying the human species and without
swallowing up in an eternal abyss the monuments that had been raised, would
nevertheless cause the arts and sciences and their fragile repositories, including
all the languages spoken today, to disappear." This was an obvious echo of the
ingenious theories of Nicolas Boulanger. Condorcet grappled with the idea
of how progress might survive the apparently inevitable cataclysms of na-

ture, and he finally found an answer in the lesson of the Egyptian hieroglyphs. If contemporary mankind incorporated its knowledge in symbolic forms and engraved them on steles capable of surviving the most terrible castastrophes, a future philosopher, a Plato for example, would somehow be able to divine their meaning even though he understood none of the languages. In this way even after the deluge mankind would not have to start from scratch but could move forward from a high level of scientific knowledge.[48] The theme of total destruction will occur again among the utopians, especially in Saint-Simon's early writings and in Fourier. Condorcet's solution is a passionate expression of the will to render eternal the scientific treasure house of man.

Work Projects

Perhaps the most remarkable aspect of Condorcet's theory is his blueprint of practical works for the realistic utopia of the future. This guesswork of genius actually foretold the direction of scientific inquiry in many fields for the next hundred and fifty years. Such prognostication about the prospect of science by scientists is one of the great self-fulfilling prophecies of the modern era.

The second part of the fragment on the *New Atlantis* presented a catalogue of the areas of research most appropriate for a society which had burst the narrow limitations of time and space in planning for the future. Daily and perpetual observations in astronomy, meteorology, the natural history of man, and rural economy seemed the most fruitful activities. If organized on an international scale astronomical observatories could be located on optimum sites at appropriate intervals. Meteorological stations could be dispersed in the same way. (Condorcet raised the possibility of using mechanical instruments to make and record observations.) Most of all he concentrated on projects which assembled quantities of data relating to the science of man. Two methods were proposed, one involving the general observation of the total population of a country, another, the intensive investigation of a limited number of specimens. Vital statistics would use the former, medicine the latter technique. Together these studies would solve all medical and moral problems, would cure disease, end epidemics, increase longevity, and lead to the "limitless perfectibility of the human faculties and the social order."[49] The republic of science would undertake a study of all factors that affected the deterioration of the human mechanism: heredity, education, climate, the laws, occupations, pleasures, habits, exercises. Scientists would measure the influence of race. The relations among human physiology and intellectual powers and moral behavior presented perplexing problems to the eighteenth-century philosopher of progress, for which he expected solutions from the scientists of the future. "We know that absolute equality of aptitudes does not exist at the moment of birth, neither for any of our senses, nor for any of our faculties. But new observations alone may teach us whether there exist between the differences which one can notice in physical organization and the variations in the intellectual faculties determinable relationships or whether our knowledge must forever be limited merely to knowing that these relations exist. The same reflections apply to our moral faculties."[50]

Condorcet propounded a series of questions on the relations between physiology and psychology to which, after a century and a half of research, few answers are yet available. "Are human faculties perfectible only by the perfection of the organs which produce them? Can the faculties be perfected only by the progress of methods for the development of the organs, for directing them, strengthening them through exercise . . . ?"[51] He wondered whether a state of moral virtue might not be produced in man by a combination of institutional changes and improved heredity to the point "where every action contrary to the right of another man will be as impossible physically as an act of barbarism committed in cold blood is today for most men."[52] He looked to a quantification of data for confirmation of his intuitive belief that differences in the moral and intellectual aptitudes of the two sexes had been grossly exaggerated.

Other experimental proposals ranged from mineralogy, organic chemistry, geography, to human and animal anatomy. Since world prosperity might lead to an increase in population and tax the world food supply, Condorcet advised the organized scientists to study methods for the maximum utilization of foods and fuels, to investigate the nutritional elements in various products, the feasibility of manufacturing animal and vegetable substances artificially, the utilization of substances which were wasted, the possibilities of diminishing consumption without a concomitant loss of enjoyment. The institutional and technological problems of a society devoted to the pleasure principle were discussed, but the moral absolutes of hedonism were never called into question. These practical researches might not carry much glory, but for that very reason they should be undertaken by the universal society.

In the gamut of suggestions there is a marked de-emphasis of physics and mechanics, understandable in an age which imagined that the fundamental principles of these sciences had been established forever, that the possibilities of new findings were on the verge of exhaustion. The life sciences and the social sciences had now become the focus of scholarly attention, and it was precisely these areas of knowledge that depended upon quantification of data, requiring the cooperation of a vast number of researchers. Condorcet had not broken with the dominant mathematical spirit; by utilizing the calculus of probabilities in the social sciences he proposed to "mathematicize" social phenomena and finally to introduce predictability and law into the science of man. In his famous edition of Pascal in 1776 (the philosophes were always itching for a confrontation with the man in whom they recognized their profound enemy), Condorcet attacked him for sharply bifurcating the world into two separate kingdoms, the mathematical and the moral, allowing certitude to the former and abandoning the latter to despair and impotent confusion. There was now a bridge between the realms, Condorcet maintained, the calculus of probabilities, and once this discovery was applied moral problems would be resolved as scientifically as geometric ones. He rejected the famous Pascalian distinction between the *esprit géométrique* and the *esprit de finesse;* their methods were similar, not contradictory. In response to Pascalian jeremiads on the feebleness of human knowledge, Condorcet countered again and again with the new panacea, the science of probabilities.

In 1785 he had written a long technical treatise entitled *Essai sur l'application de l'analyse à la probabilité des décisions rendues à la pluralité des voix* to demonstrate in a specific sociopolitical case study the feasibility of reducing moral data to mathematical terms. This had been a favorite topic of conversation with the middle-aged Turgot; even in moments of doubt it had led Condorcet to hope that the "human species would of necessity make progress toward happiness and perfection."[53] While Condorcet was not confident that all aspects of human behavior could be presented in mathematical form, he drafted an impressive list of social phenomena which were amenable to statistical calculation by governments or learned societies.[54] His technique for forecasting majority decisions, the central proposition of his work, is of more than passing interest to the contemporary public opinion analyst. Condorcet the professional mathematician, even more than his friend the great bureaucrat, remained suspicious of truths which had to be clothed in eloquence and thus suffered from an "admixture of hyperbole." His own revolutionary experiences as a politician, a pamphleteer, a committee reporter on educational projects to the National Assembly, and a framer of constitutions only fortified his skepticism about the validity of knowledge which could not be mathematicized.

A brief article published posthumously in the *Journal d'instruction sociale* set forth the first principles of a mathematical social science (*mathématique sociale*) with even greater detail than his earlier, prerevolutionary work. Since all judgments and opinions were based upon an almost automatic presumption of probability, there would always be an advantage on the side of the man who acted by scientific calculation over the one who merely responded by instinct or routine. Those truths which were impervious to calculation were in effect so vague that they were useless because they could not be applied. Truths arrived at by abstract reasoning alone could become transformed into their very opposites, into mere prejudices, when they were raised to a level of generality not appropriate to them. The "new science" would be of particular significance during the aftermath of a revolution which called for political and moral decisions based upon data computed with precision in order to establish truths beyond the realm of passion and the sophisms of self-interest. A revolution confused values, and only by invoking mathematical clarity could the dangers of the stormy period during which the passions dominated action be passed in safety.

In the same article Condorcet spelled out the theoretical justification for the application of mathematics to political and moral sciences: it was a direct derivation from the fundamental idea of equality. Our essential sensate similarity made us calculable. "Since all men who inhabit the same country have more or less the same needs and since they also generally have the same tastes and the same ideas of utility, what has *value* for one of them generally has it for all."[55] By following out this postulate it would be possible for the state to estimate probabilities of desire and to legislate accordingly. In his last manuscripts there continually obtruded grave misgivings about the decisions of any public bodies which were not technically competent as experts. With the accumulation of sufficient data and the application of the calculus of probabilities the state could be run by social mathematics—without debates. With one stride the first sociologist of scientific creativity traversed the age of middle-class parliamentarism and arrived at the ideal of the all-knowing scientific technician as the ruler of society.

The Pleasures of Foretelling

Moral progress ended up as a conditioning process, functioning through education and the exercise of the laws, which made a man identify his own interest with the common interest, constrained him to harness his immediate, direct,

egotistic desires and passions and to act in harmony with the dictates of universal reason and justice—alternative ways of defining the "common interest."
That legitimate human rights never could be in contradiction one with another
was an axiom of the optimist moralism of the age. If they appeared to be at
odds, then error had crept in somewhere. Almost all social conflicts were the
result of inadequate institutional and juridic mechanics, amenable to easy remedy. The contests among men which seemed at first glance to defy any possible settlement, conflicting passions for the same person, for example, were
minor exceptions to the general principle, and even they were subject to institutional control; the intensity of passion in such rivalries could be reduced. "I
believe," Condorcet concluded in his *Fragment de l'histoire de la xe époque*, "that
I have proved the possibility and indicated the means of resolving what is perhaps the most important problem for the human species: perfectibility of the
broad masses, that is to say, the problem of rendering right judgment, an independent sound reason, an enlightened conscience, a habitual submission to the
rules of humanity and justice, almost universal qualities, so that as a consequence the normal state of man is guided by truth even though subject to
error, is subordinate in its conduct to the rules of morality even though sometimes drawn into crime, is nurtured on gentle and pure feelings that unite him
to his family, to his friends, to the unfortunate, to his country, to the whole of
humanity, even though he is still susceptible of being led astray by personal
passions—a state in which man is as happy as he is permitted by the pains, the
needs, and the losses that are the necessary consequence of the general laws of
the universe." [56]

When rational conduct finally became normative behavior for all mankind
(with only rare lapses into crime and injustice), then a state of society would be
reached where the whole emphasis of human activity could be shifted. In this
happy age the state would be administered by officials who exercised the
powers of office for brief periods of time, because the minimum aptitude requirement necessary for the posts was within the common capacity of all men
and offices were readily interchangeable among average citizens. There would
be no special bureaucratic class trained in the operations of the state, and public
office would not be sought after as a great honor, for it would merely be a
commonplace function. No corps would have a vested interest in government.
In this ideal state the laws would not allow for the concentration of great fortunes in a few hands. Though there would be no communism of property, the
gulf between the richest and the poorest would be narrowed by abolition of
the economic measures which in the past had fostered the accumulation of
wealth and by insurance schemes which protected all men from the miseries of
unemployment and of abject poverty. The passion for riches would be diminished because great fortune would no longer be an important source of distinction—no more than would be the governing power—and it would confer no
unusual privileges upon its holders.

Though glory in war had long since ceased to attract mankind after the dethronement of the tyrants who originally provoked international strife, men
were still zealous for esteem and they still had a drive to surpass other men; the
competitive spirit was inborn and could not be completely eradicated. As in
Turgot, there is a feeling that emulation is a necessary stimulus to action and a
safeguard against lethargy. What should these new men of the future, well

conditioned and well nourished, do with themselves? What activities would then attract men of energy and zeal, since they could not excel in war, government, or wealth? Condorcet's plan for the organization of a society for the advancement of scientific research was the only possible outlet. Man was thus turned by Condorcet into a scientific animal, the direct consequence of his being a rational animal. The whole of society would be deliberately organized for the production of scientists and science. His imagination was excited by the prospect of a vastly increased annual yield of science and technology as a direct result of the mere multiplication of science-producing, educated men. The world of nature would be opened up to exploitation. The food supply could be increased virtually indefinitely. If the population problem should ever become troublesome, then rational man would know how to curtail his breeding propensities. Before Malthus' attack, Condorcet clearly foresaw many of the difficulties which a rapid increase in population would entail. His answers may not satisfy neo-Malthusians, but they have a straightforward commonsense ring which belies the caricatures that have been made of the utopians. In the end of the days he may turn out to be more realistic than his matter-of-fact critics. "If from the perfection of hygiene there results a greater life span, a greater fertility, the survival of a greater number of children; if the perfection of medicine postpones the decline of life and the death of most individuals; if this increase of population exceeds the limit which the annual production of materials of consumption can attain, will not the human race find itself unable to escape destruction. . . ?"[57] Condorcet's panacea is simply contraception. Modern man can regulate his reproduction without curtailing his pleasure. In warrior societies the prevention of births was looked upon with horror because a large population was necessary for conquest. The church, which viewed all pleasure as a crime, had naturally condemned sexual gratification without intent to reproduce. When rational men of the future controlled parenthood, contraception would reduce infidelity and perversion. If the love of children is real, then an element of calculation must enter into their birth. There might come a time when a further population increase would be considered contrary to the general interest.

Condorcet was equally forthright in his manuscript discussion both of medical cures for venereal disease and of the nature of contraceptive substances. In publishing his work his executors were far more circumspect. He refuted the argument that these medicines would lead to venereal excesses. If there was a way of rendering all mushrooms less indigestible and of eliminating the poisonous ones, would anyone argue that such discoveries should be kept secret because they might lead to gluttony? He recognized that any scientists of his day who presumed to read papers on sexual diseases would be expelled from the academy. For the future he expected open treatment, without prudery, of medical questions which were of vital concern to the health and pleasure of mankind.

Condorcet also examined the complicated consequences of a hypothetical scientific discovery which might render it possible to predetermine the sex of offspring. Would males motivated by prejudice and passion tend to increase the number of women disproportionately in order to have younger girls available for their lusts? After going through an elaborate calculus of desires he reached the comforting conclusion that in the future the number of the two sexes would remain more or less equal despite the capacity to produce a given sex at will.[58] In his discussion of artificial insemination Condorcet hinted at the improvement of the species through eugenic measures. The absolute equality between the sexes which he foresaw led him to interesting psychological insights into the nature of the love relationships resulting from the new independence of women. "Everything which can contribute to rendering individuals more independent is also a good relative to the happiness which they can reciprocally bestow upon each other; their happiness will be greater when the individual action is more voluntary."[59]

But had he never foreseen the possibilities of fantastic new weapons of destruction in flying machines or balloons? "I shall not stop over the futile fear of dangers which might result from the art of traversing the air," he wrote with assurance in one manuscript, "because since it would be impossible to keep it secret, the capacity to harm cannot be increased without augmenting that of defense."[60] Nonetheless he was at times troubled by the idea that some unnamed discoveries, which could not be ruled out as possibilities, might impede the march of perfectibility. Such transient misgivings, however, remained buried in his manuscripts.[61]

Without fear of illness and starvation man would become gentle and the problem of criminality would be reduced to insignificance. Once the scientists discovered and promulgated the laws of happiness it was inconceivable that men should be so stupid as not to implement them. If chemistry found a new dye it was immediately utilized; why should sound social law not enjoy similar instantaneous application and spontaneous acquiescence? When retrogressive institutional sources, the external causes of evil, were removed, man would be left with his pristine virtue, free to further the advancement of science. Through technological improvements man's senses would receive a new extension into what Sébastien Mercier had called the two infinities, the telescopic and the microscopic worlds. This sensory progress could be achieved without altering human nature, but there was also a prospect of organic improvement in the human mechanism. That acquired characteristics were inherited was a widespread hypothesis among many eighteenth-century thinkers well before Lamarck's exposition of his evolutionist thesis in 1801. This doctrine, perhaps more than any other belief, was proof positive for Condorcet in the tenth epoch of the *Esquisse* that the intellectual and moral attainments of one generation could be passed on intact to its successor. Any possible remnant of doubt about the inevitable and infinite progress of the human spirit was dispelled once the human organism was shown to be subject to biological perfectibility. Progress was indefinite. This became its quintessential attribute. It vied with and replaced the infinity of God. Only after having reached one high level could man even conceive of the still loftier peaks which loomed ahead. The wildest visions could not foretell the ultimate capabilities of man, because it would require a far more developed mind even to imagine them. The favorite analogy in Condorcet's theory is the mathematical progression toward infinity.

The totality of nature may never be known, but that does not mean that any specific thing is unknowable. There is only the not yet known. This is another sense in which progress is infinite—the continuous acquisition of the not yet known at the same time that man recognizes his incapacity ever to possess the whole of knowledge. Man's constant struggle with refractory nature, utilizing the laws wrested from nature as the most powerful weapon leading to its sub-jugation—a conception later dramatized by the Saint-Simonians and Marx—was portrayed with eloquence in many of Condorcet's minor published works and in his manuscripts. In the *Mémoire sur l'instruction* he wrote of the "eternal conflict between nature and genius, between man and things." He described the assault in grand terms: "Interrogated everywhere, observed in all its as-pects, attacked simultaneously by a variety of methods and instruments capa-ble of tearing away its secrets, nature will at last be forced to let them es-cape." [62] In his acceptance speech before the Academy of Sciences he had announced, "Every discovery is a conquest over nature, and over chance." [63] While man is subject to the laws of nature, "he has the power of modifying these laws, of making them contribute to his well-being. This power may be feeble and insignificant in each individual, but if it is observed in the species and exercised over a great span of many generations, ever growing with the progress of the human mind, it can ultimately balance that of nature." [64] This is the most daring manifesto of eighteenth-century hubris—man and nature enter the arena of the distant future equal in strength.

The movement of future progress described by Condorcet can be likened to the advance of the whole of mankind on an open plain. In the front rank, ahead of their fellow men, the scientific elite are dashing forward at a speed that is continually being augmented; behind the main body portions of humanity lag because they have been duped by Machiavellian despots and their priestly min-ions. But the forward thrust of the great scientists is of such Herculean power that it pulls the whole of mankind along with it. And as they advance in time men are ever healthier, happier, more acute in their sense perceptions, more precise in their reasoning power, more equal in wealth and opportunity, more humane in their moral behavior.

The vision was so compelling that judgments of worth could henceforth be expressed only in terms of the conception of perfectibility. The good of all fu-ture generations—not the individual, not the nation, not even the age—was the proper criterion for human action. Moral judgment was the verdict of all future time.

How was it possible for a materialist, a sensationalist, a believer in the rather simplistic code of the harmony of self-interests, to achieve this intense passion for progress and work? The doctrine of benevolence, the outgoing compassion of man, had come to the rescue. Natural man had sympathy for his kind—that was an innate characteristic of his emotional being, Rousseau and a long line of Scottish moralists had taught. When in his fantasy Condorcet extended sym-pathy from contemporary mankind to all future generations of humanity a vast new horizon was opened. *Bienveillance* was now borne aloft on the wings of infinity. Once aware of this sympathy, man in the present could enjoy the delights of the future by working toward it or by mere contemplation of the ultimate bliss. The last page of the *Esquisse* is a noble period depicting the con-solations of the idea of progress even under the reign of a tyrant and an obscu-rantist. [65] To sustain the utilitarian martyr, Progress—the new god of the age—had arrogated to itself a tender solace of the old religion, the dream of future beatitude. "In the contemplation of this vision he receives the reward of his efforts for the progress of reason, for the defense of liberty. He then dares to join his exertions to the eternal chain of human destinies. There he finds the true recompense of virtue; it lies in the pleasure of having accomplished an enduring good, which fate will never again destroy by an unfortunate reversal restoring prejudice and slavery. This contemplation is for him an asylum where the memory of his persecutors cannot pursue him. Living in thought with man reestablished in his rights as well as in the dignity of his nature, he forgets the man whom avarice, fear, or envy torments and corrupts. Then he truly is with his equals in an Elysium which his reason has been able to create and which his love for humanity embellishes with the purest joys."[66] Here the eighteenth century left its final message to the ages.

21

Kant: Beyond Animality

IN AN ESSAY, "Idea for a World History from a Cosmopolitan Point of View," published in the *Berlinische Monatsschrift*, 1784, Kant set forth the underlying principles of the German school of the progressive utopia.[1] This is a strange piece from the author of the categorical imperative, one of the rare instances in his philosophical writings when he ventured to speculate about the historical world and the ideal condition that was its end. The argument has none of the rigor of his thinking in other fields of philosophy. It is not at all formidable, this polite essay on the purpose and meaning of history as an introduction to euchronia, and it has an emotional quality that the professorial bachelor of Königsberg hardly ever allowed to intrude into his writings. The spirit of Jean-Jacques the passionate critic of the societal order informs the piece, not that of Hume the dialectician. It represents Kant's utopia and his belief, sometimes a bit faltering, that mankind was getting there, a German version of the dream of reason and of the triumph of instinctual repression as the only ideal worthy of man.

There are three other essays in which Kant's utopia of the end of the days found expression: the extended reviews of Herder's *Reflections on the Philosophy of History of Mankind*; an essay *Eternal Peace* (perhaps the most widely known of his minor works); and his ambiguous testament, *The Battle of the Faculties*.[2] These writings supplement the central propositions of the "World History from a Cosmopolitan Point of View." Their conclusions are the same; but the tone of resolute belief in a utopia beyond animality sometimes gives way to ambivalence and paradox.

The Telos of History

At the very outset of his essay on world history Kant posed the central question of a telos in the historical world and answered it affirmatively in a succinct formula of the Second Thesis: The goal of history was the development of man's reason. Reason (*Vernunft*) in this context is defined as a creature's capacity (*Vermögen*) to extend the principles (*Regeln*) and purposes (*Absichten*) of the use of all his forces far beyond his *Naturinstinkt*. Moreover, reason knows no bounds to its projects. The development of man's reason implies the flowering of all human faculties beyond the instinctual, those desires that man has in common with the other animals. By reason Kant here means man's capacity to know the physical world, to dominate it, to know himself and his passions, above all to control them and to construct an ethical society in which moral imperatives are obeyed and evil instincts repressed.

It is immediately apparent that of all the multifarious faculties and capacities, the one that occupied the place of honor among the materialist and sensationalist theoreticians of progress on the west side of the Rhine, man's capacity for happiness, is conspicuously absent. The telos of the French philosophes is deliberately denied as a historical purpose of Nature: God created man not for instinctual happiness and fulfillment, but for the actualization of his unique rational capacities. Contrary to the doctrine of pleasure, in Kant's essay man was made solely for the development of that which is distinctively human, his capacity to build a moral social order. In the seventeenth and eighteenth centuries, as in all ages of rationalist thought, extended inquiries were undertaken into the qualities or faculties that distinguished man from beast. Today the answer would probably be man's symbol-making capacity; Rousseau wrote of his innate, tragic faculty of perfectibility; Kant, his reason.

There is something troublesome for Kant about the growth of reason in the species as the mark that distinguishes man from all other living beings. At first sight it seems to undermine one assumption of purposefulness in all other aspects of biological creation. Every animal except man totally fulfills himself in his own individual lifetime. Man too has a side of his being that is wholly actualized. The bestial capacity to desire does not need development; it is present in all its maturity here and now. But reason is clearly unfulfilled in man as we know him. It required no accumulation of empirical evidence to demonstrate that man's potentially ethical nature, an aspect of his reason, had not yet been actualized in the year 1784. Even to a casual observer of the world—and though Kant never traveled outside the port city of Königsberg he had a keen sense of reality—it was obvious that man was not behaving in the fullness of his rational capacities. One hears the resounding echo of Rousseau: The creature walking the streets of the cities in 1784 is not wholly man; he is the defective version belonging to the present corrupt state of society. Contemplate man's history and condition, and the spectacle fills one with revulsion. This being, by definition made for reason and for ethical behavior, is a monster in war, in lust, in torture, in madness. Can this be man?

Everything in the world has an essential nature that is adapted to an end. If man's nature is reason and he is not fulfilling it in his lifetime—and who among us leads the life of reason?—there must be an explanation. The fulfillment cannot be deferred to heaven because Kant has abolished it; it must therefore take place in the next remotest condition, the historical future. Nature has to fulfill itself in man as in all other creatures, else there would be disorder. In his *Reflections on the Philosophy of History of Mankind,* Herder defends the same proposition with an a fortiori argument that has a more theological tinge. Is it imaginable, he asks, that God in His wisdom and infinite goodness would bestow order and purpose on the physical universe and leave the world of man, the noblest part of His creation, without plan or purpose, a mere haphazard of kaleidoscopically changing events? God could not be so malevolent, thus there must be a historical plan. This is, of course, merely a transposition of one of the stereotyped traditional arguments for the existence of God. Kant reasons in much the same way. Nature has a purpose in all its manifestations. Man's purpose is not accomplished in his lifetime. Therefore it must be fulfilled historically in the life of the species. If this were not so, nature would be lawless in a vital area and this is not admissible. Today man may not be much better than a brute, but his destiny is human. Kant was profoundly affected by Rousseau's writings—once he missed his daily walk, so meticulously timed that the burghers of Königsberg fixed their watches by it, because he was reading *Emile.* In bringing future history to the rescue of man, Kant paralleled the Rousseau of the *Contrat social*.

If one studies the French believers in progress of the late eighteenth century, the idea is inescapable that man is already quite an accomplished fellow, that Anglo-French society has already gone far up the ladder of progress, and that its mission now is to spread enlightenment to the dark corners of the world so that benighted peoples may catch up with the forerunners of civilization along the Channel. Despite his dismal personal fate, Condorcet felt that the Revolution had opened wide the gates of utopian heaven. He took pride in man's achievements thus far and had boundless confidence in his future accomplishments. In Kant, on the other hand, there was doubt whether man had even reached the halfway mark in his development—witness the fact that his destructive passions had not even begun to be curbed. In this sense he conveys the same feeling that Herder does in passages of the *Reflections*. Man's humanity is still in the far distance. The Frenchmen of the Turgot-Condorcet school judged of the future primarily in terms of progress in the arts and sciences. While Kant does not go the whole way with Rousseau in proclaiming their iniquity, he considers them matters of relative moral indifference. Kant was close to the merchants of Königsberg—a famous painting depicts them dining together—but the commercial and technological achievements which their world represented were in his eyes mere baubles. His euchronia was not founded on sensate improvements.

But though distinguished from the dauntless optimists of the Condorcet persuasion, Kant is not to be identified with Pascalian or traditional religious pessimism. His view is quite as dark as Pascal's, if contemporary man is measured and judged by the moral criteria of the categorical imperative; but it is optimistic sub specie aeternitatis in repudiating the wretch depicted by Pascal as the real human being. For Pascal, the great mathematician, the crippled and torn creature is the ultimate possibility in this world, though man may accumulate vast stockpiles of scientific knowledge. For Kant, the man of his day is nothing but a moral embryo. Though he agrees with Pascal that all man's works are morally tainted, he foretells a future perfection, embodied in a euchronia.

Kant's assertion that man's reason would fulfill itself in time inevitably provoked a question: If it was ordained that man would ultimately be rational, then why had nature not formed him a rational creature at the outset? Why the historic suffering of the species? If the telos was reason, why create a passionate beast? To this problem Kant, like a number of other eighteenth-century thinkers, Turgot among them, offered a version of what became in Hegel the cunning of reason. In the early stages of mankind the passions were necessary because they stimulated man to action, to the exercise of his faculties, to the discovery of new capacities. In Vico the idea of God, the sublime religious conception, was born of terror. In Turgot war, the greatest of scourges, led to the development of the arts and sciences. Similarly, Kant argued that if man had remained in a peaceful Arcadia he would never have become anything but a shepherd. He might have been happier—Kant's Arcadia is the parallel to Rousseau's state of nature—but he would have been nothing but a peasant dolt.

Kant aimed his darts directly at the work of Herder, who had propounded the outlandish idea that every *Volk*, even the most primitive, contained within itself the principle of its own happiness. Kant's review of the early volumes of Herder's philosophy of history was devastating. The master knew the weak points in his student's armature and he cut into him without mercy. In Kant's confrontation with Herder the special character of the master's dream of reason is carved in bold relief. Herder's design of some more or less pleasurable, growing self-fulfillment that could be called happiness, radically different among individual peoples and races, was diametrically contradictory to Kant's conception of one universal, absolute, ethical destiny for the whole of mankind. This was the real issue beneath the snide thrusts and counterthrusts that followed one another in rapid succession in the first volume of Herder's *Reflections,* Kant's reviews and essays, and Herder's responses in later volumes. What could it mean to say, asked Herder in obvious allusion to Kant's relentlessly austere vision of the moral man of the distant future, that man as we know him here is made for the infinite growth of his mental powers? Are all generations of the race really made for the last generation, which would then be enthroned on the dilapidated framework of the happiness of all preceding ones?

Kant's morality was total and the partial benefits of civilization failed to impress him. If at one moment he wrote with a measure of respect about the halfway mark in the achievement of nature's telos for man, in the next he pointed at the fraud beneath the façade of civilization and gave voice to his revulsion at the sight of wicked man in language that would do justice to a hellfire preacher. In Kant's pronouncements not much is cumulative in the struggle for an ethical structuring of life; man arrives at it by trial and error, he hits upon it, but the method is not quite known. If the pietist mood in his writing is given weight, man appears to be either saved (permeated by the categorical imperative) or damned (acting in violation of it). In the "World History from a Cosmopolitan Point of View," Kant speaks of the next duty of man as the establishment of a just civil constitution, as if there were a set series of stages in the historical moralization process; but this constitution does not solve the moral problem because the steps are primarily logical and not chronological. Herder sensed that the realization of Kant's totalitarian moral ideal could come only in the end of the days and that intermediate historical life was of relatively little worth.

Kant pounced on the postulate in Herder that each individual contained within himself his own criterion of happiness. For Herder this meant that each Volk held within it a unique genius, a character that was the soul of its being, and that the geniuses of different peoples were not comparable. They were variant embodiments of the divine in the plenitude of creation, whether they were worm-eating Californians or ancient Greeks. In his review, Kant used Herder's first volume, where these ideas were elaborated, as a jumping-off place for a reiteration of his old disdain for sensate happiness as a moral category. "Does the author really mean that if the happy inhabitants of Tahiti, never visited by civilized nations, were ordained to live for thousands of years in their quiet indolence, a satisfactory answer could be given to the question as to why they existed at all, and whether it might not have been just as well if this island had been populated with happy sheep and cattle as with happy human beings living in mere sensual pleasure?"[3]

The concept of happiness or contentment was excluded from Kant's view of the historical universe. Such a conception might be applicable to timeless heaven, where there was a monotonous chanting of hallelujah, he mocked in an essay on "The End of All Things," but for this world it was unimaginable. "For the state in which man is at present always remains an evil, comparatively with the better into which he is ready to enter; and the representation of an infinite advancement to the [goal] is at the same time a prospect in an infinite series of evils which, though they are outweighed by the greater good, do not allow the contentment, that he cannot conceive but by the [goal's] being finally reached, to find place."[4] If happiness had been the end of man, nothing would have occurred in history and man would not have developed his rational faculties far beyond the instinctual. This theme reappears in later philosophies of history with a thousand faces; it is still recognizable in Arnold Toynbee's chapters on challenge and response in the birth of civilization. Mankind had to be sparked into action. The passionate conflicts among individuals were necessary in order to make them, like trees in a forest, grow tall, erect, well-formed, striving heavenward. The branches of a tree in isolation might grow in all directions and present a shapeless spectacle.

Was the leitmotif of world history a progression in reason, or was the history of mankind a pluralist spectacle in which many relatively autonomous groups known as *Völker* lived out their existences in fulfillment of their varying essences or substances through a period of time that was analogous to a life cycle? Like human characters, the "substances" of different peoples, in Herder's psychological language, would tend to have leading or dominant passions. Rationality might figure significantly in one Volk, a sense such as hearing or sight in another. The fuzziness of Herder's Volk spirits was intellectually distasteful to the master of the categories. And when Herder proceeded to amalgamate his pluralist history of nations with a rather mystical concept of human evolution into a higher stage in the great chain of being, Kant dismissed his former student as an incorrigible *Schwärmer*.

Kant analyzed the mechanism of nature's plan in fashioning man to rationality. Neither original human nature nor the process was such as to make the education of mankind a pleasurable experience. Suffering and hardship were its fate. Two powerful, contradictory drives were in tragic conflict with each other in a struggle akin to Rousseau's war of societal and natural man, or Diderot's inner battle between natural and artificial man (or Freud's tug-of-war between the superego and the id for whatever remains of the shrunken ego). In Kant's language man had a desire for total freedom, a freedom that no society had ever tolerated. The individual craved limitless freedom to express his individual desires and will, absolutely, without any restrictions. But man also had a need for sociability, for other human beings. There was, unavoidably, an eternal *antagonism* (Kant used the English word in his text) between the two desires.[5] But—strange cunning of nature—matters worked out in such a manner that man's most violent asocial desires brought about the ultimate ethical improvement of his being, his progress in reason.

In all of the rationalist teleologies of the German school, Hegel's included, rational behavior does not come about through rational intent. The history of mankind is not the history of the slow growth of reason through the accretion of knowledge or through the promulgation of laws by wise legislator-kings who make their subjects more moral and reasonable. That is not the course of nature and the historical process. Indirection is the divine way. In the beginning there was evil passion, irrational desire, the favorite example of which, after the emergence of Frederick the Great, was war. Kant lived all his life on the borderland between the Empress Catherine's expansive Russia and the new Prussia bent on aggrandizement, and Königsberg was overrun by Russian troops. Kant showed how the evil passion of aggressive monarchs could bring about the moral improvement of mankind. To finance their wars the monarchs had to collect more money in taxes, but since only the burghers could produce the needed specie, their peaceful, ethically superior labors had to be granted royal support. Modern war, moreover, required an effective legal organization of society. For this purpose education had to be fostered, and rational values, rather than superstition, instilled among the people. The monarchs who initiated wars were driven by sheer lust for power, for territorial expansion, but the consequences were the spread of education and lawful behavior and the end of internecine quarrels within the boundaries of the dynastic state. The knowledge and organization necessary for destruction would lead to the abolition of war—perhaps. There is always an implicit doubt.

As Kant spins out the argument, the next stages of human development involve the establishment of a just civil constitution within each state and eternal peace among the states. These, however, are not the final goals of mankind. The introduction of the rule of universal law is not the telos, but a condition precedent to the flowering of human rationality. The civil constitution is the sole political environment that can sustain an ethical being. Only from this platform can the ascent to the next stage be accomplished. Kant lived during the last period of the dynastic state, with its petty monarchs absorbed in senseless foreign wars while at the same time they were creating mechanisms for the maintenance of the king's peace within the realm. But he had long realized that ethical existence was indivisible. If there was no external peace there could not be a credible public morality within the state. As long as men killed one another for the state, the possibility of moral behavior anywhere was excluded. Plato had entertained the fantasy that the guardians of his Republic could act like benign, domesticated animals toward the citizenry and ferocious beasts toward strangers. Kant early made the reflection that as long as there was war there could be no rational ethical creature living above instinct, no matter how lawful the internal order of his society.

The French Revolution posed dilemmas for many of the German intellectuals at the end of the eighteenth century. At first they hailed it in great numbers. Young Hegel, perhaps prematurely, saw in it the enthronement of reason, ethical reason triumphant. Reason had been officially proclaimed as the guiding principle of a great state. As the Revolution brought in its wake international war and the Terror, most of the German thinkers, like the young English poets, defected. Goethe accompanied the Duke of Weimar to the front, Schiller and Herder joined the anti-French reaction. Kant alone in isolated Königsberg continued to defend the Revolution. His little essay on universal history helps to explain his later position, which was rooted in the dialectical sense that all great achievements had been born of violent clashes, that out of the lust for power and equality somehow a respect for individual man emerged. The Kant of the categorical imperative in personal behavior condoned terror, at least in a historical context. History achieved the highest moral ends by violating elementary individual moral principles. Hegel would proclaim this bitter dictum with great eloquence in his description of the world-historical figure who, in fulfilling the needs of Spirit, crushes many a tender flower. This notion of the higher morality of the historical process had earlier won an apology from Kant, the sternest German moralist of them all. Its consequences for German conduct and the morality of modern man are tragic.

Only in the final proposition of his essay on cosmopolitan history does Kant come around to the title, an idea for a universal history from a cosmopolitan (the German is *weltbürgerlichen,* which perhaps should be rendered world-civil) point of view. In this excursion into universal history he considered himself a Kepler, not a Newton; he was casting forth a number of ideas, not actually writing the history. If his propositions were accepted, a history could be written with a new focus, the chronological presentation of the growth of a just civil constitution from the Greeks and the Romans through the barbarians and down to modern times. This would be the only meaningful history, the history of man's becoming a moral creature by fulfilling his nature amid a display of passionate inclinations. History would then become rational; nature or nature's God would be vindicated in action. Events could be judged by a new standard: Did they contribute to the moralization of man, his civilization in the true sense? Any other history was but a tale of individual passions. Kant's cosmopolitan history recalls the proposal of his contemporary Lessing in the equally brief *Erziehung des Menschengeschlects* (1780), the education of mankind. Kant argued for a history of the species, not of states and empires. Political chronicles had meaning only insofar as they revealed changes in the history of the species. He found at last the *Leitfaden* that he had set out to discover at the opening of his piece, the plan of nature.

Schiller openly announced that his lectures on universal history would be based on Kant's schema. In the nineteenth century there would be a number of even more famous attempts to write this history of mankind encapsulated in a gnomic concept like *Vernunft*—not the least of them Hegel's history of *Geist,* or Spirit—and they would have more than passing resemblance to Kant's project, or at least to his work in combination with Herder's.

The Transformation of the Inner Man

In Kant's philosophy of history, man was born to suffering as the spur to the unfolding of his ethical being. Among the French progressists, even if there is an admission that in the past there have been evil days of dark fanaticism, henceforward, under the guidance of mathematical reason and with the help of physiological knowledge, progress will come rather facilely. In the German intellectual world there is no creation without pain and travail, from Kant's conception of man's asocial sociability, through the Nietzschean conceptualization of creativity as a consequence of brutal frustration. There must be a dialectic that involves chaos and destruction or an overcoming of contrary forces. The historical process is never a smooth-flowing increase, a growing abundance.

The German school is Protestant in a deep theological sense, whether the writers were true believers or not—and Kant in solemn university processions marched up to the portals of the Königsberg church without entering. There is no reliance on good works, on externals, on mechanics, on a quantitative accumulation of artifacts and their diffusion, on the development of the arts and sciences. Moral transformation is an inner illumination that takes place in crisis. Great truths have to be wrung from nature. The idea predominates that man has paid dearly and must continue to pay dearly for his moral triumphs. The French conceptions of progress feature the steady acquisitions of mankind in obedience to a rational recognition of the utility of new things. There may have been interruptions due to the short-lived triumph of the evil ones—priests and tyrants in various guises—but these have merely been temporary breaks. In the German world what comes easily is considered rather trivial. The Anglo-French-American idea of progress has remained essentially additive. The German ideal is the transformation of man's nature, a change that requires conflict, hardship, a clash of titanic forces, a dialectic, a conversion.

These very different ends have sometimes been expressed in later European thought by a contrast between the rival ideals of civilization and culture. In general the men west of the Rhine have seen the problem in terms of civilization, activity, goods, sensate realities; east of the Rhine there has been an idealization of *Kultur,* which relates to the nature of the inner man. Throughout the nineteenth and early twentieth centuries the Kantian notions of Kultur, however modified, permeated the Germanic world. No more than Hamann, his mystical, antirationalist neighbor in Königsberg, was Kant impressed with the external triumphs of civilization. He saw social graces, hypersensitivity to artificial concepts of honor, outward decency of conduct. But had man become more ethical? There was only a façade of containment of the beast. Often Kant was nauseated as he contemplated man. How believe that a truly moral being would come forth from the chaos? Logic rather than observation led Kant to affirm that there was ethical progress.

The Kantian image is that of humanity training itself, a long and arduous task. Reason is a capacity that grows slowly, it is not instinctive. Human capacities are fortified only through trials (*Versuche*), exercise (*Übung*), education (*Unterricht*); and no individual can himself live long enough to go through the entire course, to attain the full rational capacity to which the species is destined. Kant's fateful decree of nature, to which only German speech gives an appropriate Lutheran intonation, has willed that everything over and above the mechanical arrangement of man's animal nature, the part with which he was endowed, should be wrung from himself, and he is to have no reward but what he achieves beyond instinct through his own efforts. Man shall make himself, that was nature's awesome rule. Nature was parsimonious; she granted man no fine equipment like other animals, no claws, no fur. She intended that he make these things for himself in order that he might strengthen his capacities in the process. Nature wanted to fashion a man, not a sleepy beast. It cared more for his rational self-esteem (*vernünftige Selbstschätzung*) than for his happiness and well-being.[6] Nature denied him ease, gave him only potentialities. Man's way to salvation was not through good works set out before him in a church, but through his struggle with his own evil nature to reach faith. At another point in his essay on universal history Kant stopped to muse how strange it was that one generation was called upon to live for another, for a future generation. Such subordination of one generation to another made sense only if one believed in the rational development of the species. Otherwise the conscious serving as a stepping stone for the future was incomprehensible.

The principle of antagonism, which Kant elevated to the equivalent of a Newtonian law for the historical world of men, would recur again and again in various forms among thinkers of the first half of the nineteenth century, in Saint-Simon, the Saint-Simonians, Hegel, and Marx. There is ever present in man the dialectical drive to individuate himself, which is at odds with the need to socialize his existence. This absolute self-will, divorced and in defiance of any social considerations, man senses in himself and recognizes in others. Its existence makes of his life an eternal state of tension and rouses him to action. In defense of his individuality he is paradoxically moved to social action. For man by nature is lazy, Kant learned from Rousseau, and without the stimulus of conflict might do nothing. But when his passions are awakened, he has the three libidos of *Ehrsucht, Herrschsucht,* and *Habsucht,*[7] desires for fame, dominion, and possession, and though these desires are in themselves egotistic, they breed social talents and rationality and man thereby tames his own nature. Out of evil comes good, out of a pathological situation of antagonism and competitiveness the human faculties are perfected. Without this tension of asocial sociability all of man's abilities would remain dormant, but his destiny is growth. Man would like the ease of harmony, but nature knows better what is good for the species; it has decreed discord. The essentially tragic plight of man is revealed. What is good for man as an individual—peace and tranquillity—is not good for mankind. Kant has also resolved the problem of Job and of Leibniz' theodicy in one breath. Evil, clashes, wars, passions are requirements for the development of reason, which as it ripens will in turn emancipate man from these lusts and vanities. Whether the sum total of happiness or misery is greater is irrelevant, because happiness is not the end of man in the world order.

The first immediate manifestation of rationality after a period of strife is the establishment of a citizen society. The similarity of this idea to that of the citizen society of the *Contrat social* is unmistakable. Citizenship in Kant's liberal society is perhaps the best definition of one type of freedom. It becomes the underlying presupposition of liberal history, as Kant writes of freedom under external laws combined with irresistible force. Both elements are present in the just civil constitution. On the one hand there is individual freedom; on the other, absolute power vested in society. While a synthesis is achieved in an ideal constitution, tension remains between them. The realization, after many trials and bloody internecine wars, that men could not live in wild, self-willed freedom has forced them to submit to this constitution. It was necessity, not rational comprehension, that brought about the legal order. But does the civil constitution with its absolute power crush freedom? For Kant the seminal element of growth and creativity, man's will, remains strong; society merely tames it, channelizes it, directs it. Kultur is the process of taming freedom without stifling it, and the result is the optimal social order, the highest expression of man's nature. But Kultur involves mankind's overcoming its own asocial instinct, disciplining itself so that true freedom can grow. Progressive history is the acquisition of Kultur.

Kant's optimism was never naive. Man was an animal who needed a lord, a *Herr,* to break his anarchic individual will and force it to obey *einem allgemeingültigen Willen*—Rousseau's *volonté générale* in German dress.[8] Whether the

Herr is one man or a group of men, he is still a lord, and the perennial problem of who guards the guardians is central in Kant's ideal society—perhaps not wholly or adequately resolved. Granted that there must be a rule of law, a civil constitution, who but a man can enforce it? Montesquieu and Beccaria felt that they had achieved the purpose of justice when they depersonalized the law; Kant was not so easily satisfied. In quest of a way out he offered the possibilities of good will and experience. Such a solution, if it was ever embraced, could only come late in the history of mankind. Somehow an identification of human will with right recognized for its own sake ultimately had to transpire. The nature of man had to be prepared to receive the just civil constitution—the ideal of law had to be internalized, one would now say—yet at the same time man's nature could not really be perfected until a just civil constitution was in force. In the world of Immanuel Kant on the borderland of the Slavic wilderness, there were no comforting assurances of man's eventual triumph. At times Kant was overwhelmed by a Protestant sense of human frailty. Man was like warped wood, and nothing truly perfect could be carpentered from crooked, warped wood.

It is only in other works by Kant, *The Metaphysics of Ethics* and the *Groundwork of the Metaphysic of Morals,* that we gain an insight into the actual content of morality if man's reason should ever come to full fruition under a just civil constitution. Moral action would result from the reign of law internalized. The good and the pleasurable are quite distinct from each other. Pleasure, Kant contends, is the consequence of the influences of purely subjective causes upon the will of the subject. These can vary with the susceptibility of this or that individual, but a rational principle of morality is valid for all in all times and all places. Previous ideal systems of morality have been based on what Kant calls hypothetical imperatives. An action was deemed good because it was a means to something else. A truly rational morality requires that the action be good in itself; it is a categorical imperative. The categorical imperative from on high makes its demands on moral man: "Act only on that maxim through which you can at the same time will that it should become a universal law," and "Act as if the maxim of your action were to become through your will a Universal Law of Nature."[9]

There is only one being in the world, man, who is an end in himself, not merely a means to something else. Rational beings are by definition persons, not things, and moral action with respect to persons ought to be motivated by considerations of their being absolute ends in themselves. The practical moral imperative then becomes: Always act so as to treat humanity, the rational human being, whether in your own person or in the person of another, as an absolute end, never as merely a means. In an ideal moral world there would be no contradiction or conflict between these rational imperatives, the law of the state, and the inclination of men's wills and desires. The will would be free and autonomous because it would be ruled not by sensate desires, interests, contingencies, circumstances, external force, but by itself. It would be an absolute good will, the embodiment of the categorical imperative, and would be governed by one precept only, that the principle of every action had to be capable of being made a universal law. Granted man's natural instincts, the adoption of this universal criterion was not much in evidence in the world Kant saw about him, and at times he doubted that it was ever attainable. But without this practical enforcement through free will there could be no morality.

The Prospect of Eternal Peace

Such considerations underlay Kant's reflections on universal peace in his essay *Zum ewigen Frieden*. Morality could not be bound by the limits of an individual state, and if man remained within the confines of the just civil constitution, he would not be fulfilling the requirements of the categorical imperative. Kant moves to the international plane, to relations among states, where he finds the same asocial passion embodied in every sovereign nation. At present man does not behave like a rational human being on the state level, any more than on the individual level. Were men rational they could deduce the necessity for eternal universal peace rationally, or perhaps they might read the *Metaphysics of Ethics,* which with impeccable logic deduced the necessary universal moral principles. But though man has the capacity for reason, in the practice of everyday life he does not behave rationally. It is nevertheless his destiny to be forced into ethical behavior by nature. Here again, just as the results of his brutish, individual lust led him to the commonwealth, so the bloody experience of his warlike asociability is inevitably leading him to eternal peace and the idea of a world federation.

Kant's doctrine of the prospects for peace is rooted in the same teleological arguments with which he had begun his essay of 1784 on world history. How could nature be rational in some of its parts, the universally accepted Newtonian laws, and not in others? Was peace to depend merely on a chance concatenation of circumstances like the Epicurean configurations of atoms? Were universal disaster and universal order equally possible? Kant like Herder had moments of doubt about the meaningfulness of universal history, but he always returned to the thesis that if the species was ever to fulfill its rational nature, there had to be a cosmopolitical state. Though he paused to speculate about what would happen to man if the challenge of conflict, the tension of asocial sociability, were removed, he did not linger long over the problem of universal quiescence that from time to time troubled the peaceful philosophes. To Kant eternal peace was so remote, like the reign of mathematical reason to the French, that the inertia it might bring in its wake was not of major concern.

Kant asked himself an empirical, matter-of-fact, historical question, a rare inquiry on his part. What is the state of the categorical imperative in the world today? Has there been improvement in the moral nature of man that would support the teleological argument? Kant's response, in sharp contrast with the buoyant optimism of the French school in the latter part of the eighteenth century, is a halting, almost skeptical affirmation that the historic patient shows some small signs of betterment. He repeated this qualified verdict in a jesting manner in one of his very last writings, *Der Streit der Fakultäten* (The Battle of the Faculties). The societies he examined were in a state of violent, inhuman competitiveness. Translated into the terms of his metaphysics of morality, that meant they were actuated by external, not autonomous, factors, and were using one another as means, not ends. But the consequences of this competitiveness were not wholly negative for man's future development, since their ambitions forced monarchs to effect internal reforms and no European societies were in a state of somnolence. Increased commerce had brought greater individual freedom and greater enlightenment. War itself was demonstrating the realities of the interrelationships among states and was leading to European union.

Granted that Kant comes out on the side of the angels in *Eternal Peace,* the generally gloomy tone of numerous other works, not often quoted, must be hearkened to. The scatological origin of man on earth, a fancy to which Kant was hardly committed and which he quoted from a "Persian witling," is a rare departure from sobriety that nevertheless gives an insight into Kant's deep sentiments about the character and condition of man.

Paradise, the abode of the first human pair, was placed in heaven, in which are to be met with garden-trees enow, loaded with the most delicious fruits, whose superfluity, after being eaten, loses itself by insensible perspiration; a single tree in the middle of the garden excepted, which bears a charming fruit, it is true, but which cannot be perspired. As our first parents, notwithstanding the prohibition, desired to eat of it, there was, in order that they should not defile heaven, no other advise than that one of the angels showed them the earth at a great distance, and said, *that is the jakes of the universe,* conducted them thither to do the needful, left them there, and flew back to heaven. Thence sprang the human species upon earth.[10]

In the imagery of Kant's last essay in *The Battle of the Faculties,* mankind comes to perpetual peace only out of sheer exhaustion, after having been sorely injured time and again while thrashing around like a wild bull.[11] The philosopher who launched the Promethean slogan of the Enlightenment, *Sapere aude* (albeit as the movement was drawing to a close), had more than passing doubts about the historical perfectibility of man. But he simply could not entertain the two major alternatives to this idea: the religious terrorist view that the world represented universal retrogression, or the Abderite view that man was just aimlessly clowning about. Since it had not been demonstrated that perfectibility was impossible, he felt it a moral imperative to believe in the possibility and to act *as if* it were feasible, thus helping to bring about the desired end. The fact that in the past things had not grown better was neither a pragmatic nor even a theoretical argument against continuing to try; after all, men had not previously succeeded in riding in aerostatical balloons. The present age was superior in self-reformation despite the increasing prevalence of talk about moral degeneracy. Mankind had already risen to a higher ethical level that enabled it to see farther ahead, and this very improvement had sharpened man's moral criticism of himself.

Kant's argument was by far the most sophisticated among the progressists, as he was the greatest dialectician among them. And his version of the cunning of reason (or of nature, or of Providence) is the most complex, though similar ideas can be found in Turgot and Condorcet. The vast potential for destruction that he saw concentrated in the new nation-states would force them to enter into a "cosmopolitical constitution," just as the "violence on all sides" had forced men to subject themselves to public law within states. And if men feared the despotism of one universal state, they would out of interest have to opt for a confederation and a law of nations.

Kant's world confederation out of self-interest was based on economic considerations, which were determinative to an eighteenth-century rationalist: the rising cost of standing armies, general inflation, the mounting national debt. Impotence might finally achieve what good will ought to have done, but could not. If the nation rather than the prince had the deciding voice in a declaration of war, an inevitable development of the just civil constitution, then, argued Kant, out of interest the people would refuse to expose themselves to a holocaust. Thus each generation could advance out of self-love, not love of the good. This is so patently a translation of Smithian economics into morals and history that it is surprising how infrequently it has been noticed. The economic self-interests of individuals lead to a harmony of interests; the warlike desire for aggrandizement becomes so powerful that men, faced with annihilation, choose peace.

Kant was well aware that great statesmen had always derided projects such as those of the Abbé de Saint-Pierre and Rousseau; and he too felt that universal peace preserved only by the principle of the balance of power was precarious. But, paradoxically, eternal peace would ultimately come to the nations of the earth in despite of themselves, because of their very warlike instincts. That was mankind's destiny, and it was the part of morality and reason to act in accordance with it, not obstruct it. "Fata volentem ducunt, nolentem trahunt." Kant the conceptualizer of a utopia beyond animality was a most reluctant utopian, but he was in the great tradition. After all, the most humble storybook utopian reached his blessed isle only after a shipwreck or an arduous trek through dangerous territory. When utopia became removed in time rather than space, history was the punishing terrain man had to traverse.

PART V

A Revolutionary Diptych

Nic. Ed. RESTIF, Fils-EdME.
1785.

Restif de la Bretonne

engraving by Berthet after Binet
for *Le Drame de la vie*, 1793

22

New Faces of Love

THE EIGHTEENTH-CENTURY utopia culminates in two works of the years 1795–96 that are not ordinarily juxtaposed. Babeuf issued the *Manifesto of the Equals* and plotted to establish the communist agrarian utopia through a coup d'état; de Sade's *Philosophie dans le boudoir,* with its declaration of freedom from all repression and its demand for endless sexual excitement as the only goal worthy of a French republican, made its unnoticed appearance. But neither Babeuf nor de Sade stood alone: De Sade should be coupled with his rival Restif de la Bretonne; Babeuf, too, has a revolutionary utopian pendant in Saint-Just, who preceded him to the guillotine. There are two saints in each panel with the Goddess of Liberty hovering over all of them. Each pair bears a different attribute of its martyrdom: one, love; another, equality. They warrant separate consideration.

Sexuality in Enlightenment Thought

Aside from radical conceptions of the polity and of property relations, the eighteenth-century utopian novel introduced a striking innovation that achieved universality: the exploration of a variety of sexual patterns and rules for a new régime domestique that would hardly have been sanctioned by the monogamous, patriarchal, sacramental family order of Catholic France. As the seventeenth-century Christian character of utopia began to wear off, utopian fantasy allowed itself to encompass in print a broad gamut of sexual possibilities. Particularly after the discovery of the Blessed Isles of the South Seas and the publication of travelers' reports, many composed in Paris garrets, a flood of utopias depicting sundry exotic forms of marriage and sexual relations inundated Europe. Since many of the new utopias were situated in a climatic zone where the bounty of nature was overflowing and little or no labor was required, work regulations, no longer meaningful, gave way to plans for sexual gratification. Institutional arrangements were subordinated to the perfect fulfillment of erotic passion; in the South Seas of eighteenth-century exotic dreams there was nothing much else to do but make love.

Inspired by the discovery of Tahiti and the simultaneous de-Christianization of Europe, utopias looked toward greater sexual freedom as a primary ideal, or at least pleaded by implication for the mitigation of existing legal restrictions, with their cruel punishments for adultery and homosexuality. Christian monogamy, not rooted in nature, was exposed as both hypocritical and provocative of strife. A freer sexuality, it was argued, would not lead to the disruption of the social order and the exacerbation of hostile emotions among men, but on the contrary would contribute to peaceful, amicable relationships. The sexual practices described by Diderot in the *Supplément au voyage de Bougainville* are pleasurable yet innocent, not debauched, without deleterious consequences for moral character or order in Tahitian society. In a confrontation of native mores with European hypocrisy, embodied in the hapless chaplain of Bougainville's ship, the salutary humanist consequences of sexual freedom are overwhelmingly demonstrated: Women are treated as subjects, not objects, happiness is generally diffused, and no one wears a mask.

Community of women and children, though strictly supervised, had been proposed often before in utopias of the ancient and Renaissance worlds, for eugenic purposes and the good of the state; but the audacious and scandalous ideas voiced during the Enlightenment, even if not meant to be taken literally, reflected a fundamental change in attitude toward sexual fulfillment for the individual. These ideas, moreover, were not restricted to an aristocratic class, but had resonances in the rich gutter literature of the age. Some of the novels were doubtless mere divertissements: They bordered on erotica and were intended to shock or titillate. Others, though disguised as entertainments, raised basic questions about Western morality enforced by religious law. Two of the most notorious writers, Restif de la Bretonne and the Marquis de Sade, advanced highly original solutions to the problem of the need for love and sexual pleasure that have had a long and checkered subsequent history in utopian thought.

The corpus of utopian fiction teems with sexual alternatives that range from the slightly modified conventional to the extravagant. Louis Rustaing de Saint-Jory's *Les Femmes militaires: Relation historique d'une isle nouvellement découverte* (Amsterdam, 1736) calls for the total equality of rights and privileges between the sexes, in education, warfare, love, and governance, with equal access to all dignities and offices spelled out and differences in the behavior patterns of the sexes virtually eradicated. Males and females alternate on the throne. A noble pride shines on the faces of the girls, a charming modesty distinguishes the men. All move with extraordinary ease and grace because, the astonished visitor to their Kingdom of Manghalour soon discovers, they are ambidextrous— equality has even banished right-left dominance. The ideal of unisex had assumed a rather bizarre form in an earlier work, Gabriel de Foigny's *Les Avantures de Jacques Sadeur,* located in the *terra incognita australis* and first published late in the seventeenth century. Foigny there depicted an isle of hermaphrodites, who, in a variant of the Adamic manner, procreated from the thigh. But this physiological uniformity was too absolute for Saint-Jory, who was teaching equality between the sexes in capacities, skills, and rights as a moral doctrine, not abolishing the traditional modes of reproduction. Another group of utopias, in revulsion against the mincing ways of the *petit maître,* moved in a contrary direction, accentuating the differences rather than the similarities in the roles of male and female, while submitting both to a rigorous new order that broke with lifelong monogamy and substituted an annual ritualized reassignment of partners. In Restif's *Dédale français,* the Megapatagonians change wives each year, with interim periods of enforced chastity to stimulate desire afresh. Still other utopias, those of de Sade and Choderlos de Laclos's evocation of primitive woman in a state of nature, abolish all lasting sentimental and legal ties—love is the great lie—leaving sexual relations completely promiscuous, though with a bias in favor of the aggressive need of each individual. In Laclos's *L'Education des femmes* (1785), the natural woman is the counterpart or caricature of the natural man conjured up by Rousseau in the *Discourse on Inequality*. She seizes a male who captures her fancy, copulates, and abandons him. She nurses her children, but after lactation ceases she separates from them and forgets their existence. She is so strong that if she embraced a contemporary *petit maître* she would crush him. Sex without love is the perfect relationship, which complements the portrait of coldly manipulated love among the jaded aristocrats in his *Liaisons dangereuses.* There are many instances of regulated polygamy and, under certain conditions, polyandry. In Tompson's *Histoire d'un peuple nouveau dans l'isle de la raison* (1757), which pretends to be the translation of an English work by the captain of the vessel *Boston,* newly returned from China, eight men and four women living together without jealousy comprise the rational and natural marital unit, because, the author confides, "woman has received from nature a greater aptitude for and a stronger tendency toward plurality."[1] In scores of novels the moral of the tale is the injustice of woman's subordination to the caprices of men and the legal order they have imposed. The demand for equality is widespread, though most authors are not sanguine about the prospects for change.

The medical articles on marriage in the *Encyclopédie* had noted the deleterious consequences of severely repressed sexuality. "All practitioners," writes a contributor, "are agreed that the different symptoms of vapors or hysterical afflictions that attack girls and widows are a consequence of the deprivation of marriage. It is in fact observable that wives, especially those happily married, are ordinarily free of them, and that these maladies are very common in the vast establishments harboring a large number of girls who are obliged by duty and estate to keep their virginity." One article even approves of a doctor's masturbating a patient suffering from "uterine fury."[2] The relationship between female hysteria and sexual deprivation, recognized in the sixteenth century and dilated upon in a work so widely read as the *Encyclopédie,* had to be "rediscovered" by German clinicians toward the latter part of the nineteenth.

But in eighteenth-century utopias there is also a trend diametrically opposed to candid, forthright sexuality. Lovemaking is sentimentalized as an "Embarkation for Cythera" in a mist of quietly playful beatitude, a fantasy of eternal dalliance. An earthly paradise is the setting for *fêtes galantes.* Watteau, the wistful consumptive who died at the age of thirty-seven, is the painter of this utopia of ethereal love. Some pass the time gently pushing a beloved on a swing, their most strenuous exertion; others strum a guitar. Morelly's *Naufrage des îles flottantes, ou Basiliade du célébre Pilpai: Poëme héroïque, traduit de l'Indien* (1753) is the tale of a Zoroastrian-like assault by evil forces on an island of calm and perfect felicity, to which peace is restored after a bit of geological hocus-pocus. Sensual love is coated thickly with sentimentality, though at moments the pornography is scarcely hidden beneath a sprinkling of long-drawn-out "Ahs." The consummation of love among the young on Morelly's tropical isle is a festive communal occasion with appropriate adornments: garlands, dancing, singing, joyous laughter. All this is conceived as natural, the converse of contemporary aristocratic excess and debauch. Equality reigns on the island, by which Pilpai understands that everybody is accorded the sure and pleasant means of procuring all the delights of life, "chacun selon son goût."[3]

One can sometimes discover in secular utopias such as Mercier's *L'An 2440* radical counter-tendencies to the plea for women's liberation, a demand that the husband's authority over his wife be reenforced rather than weakened. Mercier would prohibit dowries by law, so that women should be chosen for their amiability, not their money; but to make up for the financial deprivation, he would grant the husband the right to divorce his wife without resort to religious agencies or drawn-out legal proceedings if she proved to be not to his liking. Roman marital law was Mercier's model. The obligation of pleasing a spouse would restrain a female's vices, assure domestic tranquillity, and accentuate the differences rather than the similarities between the sexes. This was very much in the spirit of Mercier's friend Restif—neither philosophe ever accepted by the intellectual elite. Restif and Mercier expressed the anxieties of little bourgeois on the rise having trouble with their women, who had begun to adopt the spendthrift ways of the upper classes and ape their licentiousness. Mercier's solution was inspired by the image of Roman republican virtue with its chaste and noble women, inferior to their husbands in law but achieving a partnership in virtue. The Church, of course, was aware of the problems of familial relations and what was believed to be the spread of promiscuity. To stem what they thought was a rising tide of venereal vice, the Church launched a counteroffensive in the form of the *culte de la rosière,* a celebration of virtue in the villages during which the young girl voted the most chaste was ceremoniously crowned in the presence of clergy, local lord, and assembled peasantry. In its way this was as utopian as the more fanciful literary proposals, given the indivisibility of virginity and what we are told about the reality of sexual conduct under the ancien régime.

While in many eighteenth-century utopias love has been pushed into the center of the stage, there is no exclusive face of love. The dominant tone is gentle; turbulence and tension are rare. But in the underground the two forbidden utopians, Restif and de Sade, created a new literary sensibility and posed a new diabolical ideal. Love as mastery and power found verbose expression in their writings, though until its closing decades the age was far too committed to the Apollonian to take much notice. Playing blind man's buff in a Watteau paradise, most utopians did not know, or pretended not to know, of the ideals being manufactured for the Revolutionary period in the imaginary torture chambers of de Sade. For all their prolixity the divine Marquis and the perverted peasant intruded into the calm felicity of the age-old utopian tradition with rude violence. Though hundreds of exotic utopias, enlightened-despotism utopias, robinsonades are now forgotten, de Sade and Restif, like Fourier, have been revived in the twentieth century. As utopian explorers of sexuality they tapped a new vein.

Rivals at Unveiling

De Sade and Restif were for a long time classified as pornographers, though each fancied himself the only authentic, unhypocritical moralist of the age. To our knowledge they never met in the flesh, but Restif loathed de Sade and directed an *Anti-Justine* against him; and de Sade wrote contemptuously of Restif. Both were polymorphously perverse, at least in their imaginings, though de Sade had a marked preference for flagellation and Restif was a passionate shoe-fetishist. In July 1789 the Marquis de Sade and Restif were probably as close to each other as they ever got. While the Marquis, one of the five remaining prisoners inside the Bastille, urged on the people of Paris by shouting encouragement through a pipe stuck out of his cell window, Restif the peasant's son was wandering about the city in terror of the canaille, yet too curious to stay in hiding. He shuddered as he saw the guts of de Launay, governor of the Bastille, dangling from the handle of an executioner's hatchet.

Following a period of apprenticeship to a printer in Auxerre, Restif had settled in Paris and virtually confined himself to that island in the middle of the Seine where the city was born. For years he made a nightly circumambulation of the island, scribbling on walls and parapets with an iron key hundreds of Latin abbreviations commemorative of sexual anniversaries. During the Revolution, though often theatened by gangs of young hoodlums as a "suspect," he persisted in his appointed rounds, watching, listening, gathering stories for his *Les Nuits de Paris, ou Le Spectateur nocturne,* perhaps the most graphic description of the Revolutionary capital—at least to our contemporary taste. No witness of the Revolution has captured the violence and cruelty of the people with more compelling effect than this peasant's son turned literary hack. By nature timid and cowardly, Restif, who dubbed himself the *hibou,* had to propel himself into his nocturnal adventures; he was constantly testing himself. Despite numerous accusations lodged against him, he managed to stay out of jail, pursuing young girls with ever more intense ardor, plagued by venereal diseases, overcome at last by impotence. Under the Empire he served as a police spy and minor functionary and earned a decent funeral. His most elaborate utopias, the five-volume *Idées singulières* and the *Dédale français,* were written before the Revolution, but even later he returned to reporting on occasional utopian ventures among French artisans.

Restif and de Sade were prolific, compulsive writers, and, judged by most literary canons, both were colossal failures. Many of the stories composed by Restif are dull, and the long-drawn-out regulatory procedures in his utopias are oppressive. De Sade's repetitive scenes of torture pall. Both are uneven writers, as might be expected of great neurotics. Despite their turgidity, however, de Sade's works contain succinct epigrammatic utterances about human nature, and Restif's descriptions of major events in the Revolution have long been used by historians casting about for local color in the accounts of perceptive eyewitnesses.

De Sade and Restif are utopians, perhaps less respectable than the rest, but legitimate members of the profession. Though Martin Buber did not include them in his book, they too have left us paths to utopia. On one level of consciousness Restif's bliss may have resided in a pretty shoe and de Sade's in a knout; but their utopian works transcended their own obsessions and set forth proposals for a future society that are in many ways an appropriate climax to the eighteenth-century sensationalist utopian tradition. When private fantasts of genius like Jean-Jacques Rousseau, Restif, de Sade, and Fourier generalize their none-too-secret personal longings, they become utopians despite themselves. A narcissistic shell could not contain them. Restif was more deeply committed to his utopia than was de Sade, who in *La Philosophie dans le boudoir* may have been pulling the self-righteous Jacobin leg of his contemporaries. The works of neither fit well into such categories as the Edenic or the Promethean utopia; at times they are, rather, caricatures of both. Restif constructed a super-rationalist society in which a piling-up of ordinances assured social tranquillity; de Sade invented libertine heroes who used their passionate stick whenever it could be set aflame. Under de Gaulle, France felt itself sufficiently imperiled morally by de Sade to prohibit his old-fashioned writings, which had little to do with the life or death of the First Republic, let alone the Fifth. The recent revival of interest in him is doubtless related to the massive diffusion of pornography through all media. But he has also fascinated intellectuals like Simone de Beauvoir and Albert Camus, who have stretched the philosophical implications of de Sade's ideas to their uttermost limits.

The Marquis de Sade has been portrayed as a symbol of the corrupt, dying aristocracy of the ancien régime; but the image falls apart when Restif the "perverted peasant," son of a stalwart, respected, Jansenist Burgundian farmer, appears by his side kneeling in adoration over the foot of a beloved. Restif is in many ways the more difficult figure to grasp. He published well over two hundred volumes, including *Le Coeur humain dévoilé,* setting the type for many of them himself; only a few of de Sade's works were printed during his lifetime and many of his writings, above all the scores of notebooks of *La Nature dévoilée,* were burned under the Restoration by his priggish son, who pursued his father after death with the same vindictiveness with which his wife had hounded him in life. Restif's style lacks the elegance and smoothness the philosophes achieved, but his narratives sometimes have the rough-hewn, stark simplicity, complete with imitations of popular speech, that has come to be associated with modern writing. His works sold well and he was called the *Rousseau des ruisseaux,* the "Rousseau of the gutters," or the "chambermaids' Rousseau"; but he also had avid readers in high places, among the French nobility and litterateurs outside the official circle of the philosophes. His friend Sébastien Mercier considered him the greatest innovator of the age, and among his admirers were Grimm, Julie de l'Espinasse, Benjamin Constant, Stendhal, Gérard de Nerval. Like so much that was powerful in eighteenth-century writing—one thinks of Rousseau and Diderot—his work was most appreciated by the Germans, and he won the praises of such knowers of men as von Humboldt, Schiller, and Goethe. But somehow he never quite reached the height of notoriety or the acclaim of the Marquis de Sade, and his jealousy was boundless. Restif's *Anti-Justine* by a perverse logic outdoes de Sade in parading varieties of sexual experience for the ostensible purpose of curing mankind of its addiction to vices—recalling that sanctimonious Gandhian who when admonished for his profligate tastes assured his critic that the wildly erotic temple carvings to which he was devoted were didactic portrayals of everything one must not do.

Restif was an authoritarian utopian sinner with the fixations and persecution mania of the authoritarian. He hid in dark corners. He was envious of de Sade, the disdainful aristocrat who rejected virtue and flaunted those perversities before which Restif sometimes hesitated, satisfying himself as best he could with his protective fetish, the dainty little shoe. Restif eulogized the orderly life of his austere father, adored the monarchy, the Republic, the Directory, Napoleon, every authority in turn as replacements of God. De Sade railed at God as the enemy of man with a fiery violence that no member of Holbach's circle had achieved. De Sade and Restif were rivals at unveiling, tearing the masks off themselves and those they saw about them. When a social order is dissolving some of its members will strip the body before it is cold. They perform autopsies on the carcass while it still has a breath of life in it. If de Sade and Restif are considered as brothers in the fraternity of utopians, it is more difficult to find an appropriate niche for the divine marquis than for the perverted peasant. The black humor that is interspersed with prophetic pronouncements blurs the image of de Sade as utopian. Restif conforms more closely to the type of world-reformer-with-a-system that will predominate in the first half of the nineteenth century.

The Divine Marquis

The Marquis Donatien-Alphonse-François de Sade was born in Paris on June 2, 1740, of an ancient Provençal family related on his mother's side to the younger branch of the House of Bourbon. His maternal uncle, the Abbé de Sade d'Embreuil, a solid *érudit,* directed his early education. At ten he was enrolled in the Jesuit college of d'Harcourt, and at fifteen he took part in the Seven Years' War as a cavalry officer. In 1763 he married Renée-Pélagie Cordier de Launay de Montreuil, who bore him two sons and a daughter. Within five months of the marriage began the half-century of his private battle with the religion of virtue personified by state power. The embodiments of authority changed from the absolute Bourbon monarchy to the Revolutionary government to the Napoleonic dictatorship; but whatever incarnation the religion of virtue assumed, de Sade remained in jeopardy. He fared best during the early years of the Revolution and under the Directorate, when four of his novels and a number of political pamphlets were published. During the ancien régime he was jailed for brief periods on charges of homosexuality, sodomy, and murder, but he always managed to escape, until he was struck down by a lettre de cachet. According to a catalogue he drafted after enduring ten years of continuous imprisonment, by October 1788 his most important works had already taken shape—the *Dialogue entre un prêtre et un moribond, Les 120 Journées de Sodome, Aline et Valcour,* the first *Justine,* and most of his short tales.

After de Sade's liberation from royal prisons in April 1790 (he had been transferred from the Bastille but remained incarcerated for nine months thereafter), he led an exemplary Revolutionary career as a secretary of the Section des Piques, and was active in reorganizing the hospitals of Paris. Rearrested in the summer of 1793, this time as a relative of aristocratic émigrés, he was moved from prison to prison until he was lost in the shuffle and evaded the guillotine because he could not be located. A rare interval of freedom, from October 13, 1794, through March 6, 1801, was succeeded by another arrest, not for acts committed but for words—his authorship of the scandalous, ten-volume *La Nouvelle Justine, ou Les Malheurs de la vertu, suivie de L'Histoire de Juliette sa soeur* (1797).[4] The peripatetic prisoner was again shunted from jail to jail, until he was finally locked up in a madhouse in Charenton through arrangements with his family, who agreed to pay his board. This former convent of the nuns of Picpus was run by one Belhomme and attended by the great alienist Pinel. De Sade's friend Mme. Quesnet accompanied him to the asylum, and until 1808 he was allowed to direct theatrical performances that attracted the notice of Parisian seekers after novelty. (The extent to which other patients rather than townspeople participated in the plays is problematic.) He died on December 2, 1814, at the age of seventy-four, having been sequestered for a total of thirty-four years.

De Sade's *Les 120 Journées de Sodome, ou L'Ecole de libertinage (The 120 Days of*

Sodom, or The School for Libertinism), written in 1785 and first published by Eugen Dühren in Berlin, 1904, is a meticulously regulated and mechanical utopia. It resumed the tradition of Thomas Artus' *Les Hermaphrodites* (1605). The heroes and victims of both sexes are locked into the Château of Stilling, from which there is no escape; any attempt to leave is punishable by death. In the secret society of the Château, a hundred and twenty days of debauch are orchestrated in the presence of an *historienne*. The victims and the lords alike are subjected to inflexible rules, aimed at maximizing the pleasures of the active protagonists. In the Renaissance, philosophical Platonists like Patrizi of Cherso had composed aristocratic utopias in which the whole order of a *città felice* was arranged for the primary purpose of allowing a noble elite to pursue a life of contemplation. De Sade created an aristocracy of libertines who, within the confines of their castle walls, ruled another type of perfect society, the incarnation of evil, through a mechanism that allowed them to reach the heights of carnal pleasure to which man's limited bodily nature could aspire. One type should not be admitted to the utopian canon while barring the other. Both are ideal forms whose attainment is impossible.

The rationalistic, mechanistic element in most utopias has been frequently remarked upon. De Sade's utopia of the 120 days of Sodom is regulated like clockwork. Its lack of feeling can bore or terrify; nothing accidental is permitted, nor is any individual idiosyncrasy tolerated, since split-second timing is required for carrying out the total sexual enterprise in its perfection. The director for the day, the appointed female historian, is in charge of the scenario. Our present-day word scenario, which has become a part of the vocabulary of planned projects involving war and peace, life and death for the planet, can be appropriated for a description of the Sadean utopia and draws the two performances closer together. Like de Sade's daily exercises, war-game rooms have their male and female historical recorders and participant observers.

De Sade conceives of all sexuality as domination. His societies, composed of numerous persons, are divided into two sectors—on the one side, companions in domination, on the other, helots who perform their will. These microsocieties of lords and slaves have in common with the Morean utopia their autarchic character. And since they are devoted primarily to the total fulfillment of sexual desires, they are not alien to that utopian genius Fourier, though he extends some of the Sadean liberties to all members of the phalanstery instead of limiting them to a few masters. Fourier is a democratized and sublimated Sadean. De Sade's utopia drove the demand for freedom from repression to its ultimate consequences. The orgies of his four heroes know no bounds; they sequester cohorts of human creatures to serve their every changing desire. The libertines are supermen with an enormous capacity for food, drink, and sexual excitement, three appetites that must be controlled and manipulated for maximum satisfaction, since the heroes of pleasure are subject to the same ills of surfeit that beset other men and must recuperate in order to resume. Like Plato's Republic, de Sade's utopia is exclusive and aristocratic, with the heroes of pleasure replacing the Platonic guardian-heroes of continence. The fatal flaw in de Sade's utopia is man's incapacity to exist autonomously on the sensate level and the frequent need for the introduction of moral elements into the surrounding environment in order that sacrilege, matricide, and other exquisite pleasures may be relished the more. The utopia enshrines a moral corruption that needs innocence to prey upon, and innocence is difficult to manufacture. Someone must believe in God in order to give significance to the celebration of a Black Mass.

De Sade's first utopias to appear in print were digressions in Letter XXXV of *Aline et Valcour, ou Le Roman philosophique,* published in eight volumes in 1793. In this novel one Sainville sets off in search of his wife Léonore, who has been kidnapped by a noble Venetian libertine. In recounting the tale of his travels through Europe and Africa to the Indian Ocean, he dwells with circumstantial detail upon the institutions, customs, and daily life of two societies he has encountered, one called Butua, ruled by an anthropophagous prince who is wholly evil, the other the magical island of Tamoé, the perfection of goodness. In these two excursions de Sade approximated the standard eighteenth-century formula of an imaginary utopian society described by a European. Egalitarian Tamoé is the stereotyped and less interesting utopia, the commonplace eighteenth-century blessed isle. Costumes are identical, fortunes the same, passions are stifled by the suppression of luxury, and laws are few because vices are rare. In Tamoé, no one controls the actions of others, and naked-breasted women diminish, rather than stimulate, desire. Butua is the obverse of Tamoé. As Sainville the European wanderer approaches Butua, he witnesses the slicing up of a prisoner tied to a tree. We have now entered the black world of de Sade. Ben Mâacoro, King of the cannibalistic Butuans who are neighbors of the warring Jagas, has a Portuguese counselor named Sarmiento, a former administrator who had fled his native land when he could no longer hide his malfeasance in office. The utopia of Butua is revealed in a dialogue between Sainville and Sarmiento, both philosophers but exponents of contradictory views on moral relativity and Sadean pleasures. As he munches away on his Jagas, the ex-European assures the virtuous Sainville that there is no taste that cannot be acquired through habit, that everything in the world serves and profits nature.[5] In the kingdom of Butua the rulers exercise open, absolute power over their ravaged subjects. Here the Sadean heroes are installed at the apex of the state, they are not a secret band within a state as in *The 120 Days of Sodom.*

De Sade's counter-utopia is the existing society of Europe, where virtue exacts its terrible punishments "against nature" through the agency of remorseless, self-righteous state power. Since the respectable European Sainville tells the story, the tone of the narrator is indignant against the Butuans, the most cruel and dissolute people on earth. But protected by this mask of virtue, de Sade unveils the evil society of Butua as unhypocritical and naturally good in its consequences. The dialectic is involuted: Sainville, a representative of the evil society of virtue, bears witness to the existence of a Sadean society of pure but just evil in contrast to the unnatural society of Europe, which commits cruelties in the name of virtue. The conversation between Sarmiento and Sainville covers the major moral questions of the Enlightenment. The confrontation is critical. If Sarmiento's amorality was victorious the whole structure of Enlightenment thought would collapse, a destruction that de Sade relished as he bestowed upon the disabused anti-philosophe one laurel wreath after another. Sainville can hardly hold his own. He is no more successful than the chaplain in the *Supplément au voyage de Bougainville* or the philosophe in *Le Neveu de Rameau.*

The people of Butua and their neighbors the Jagas wage eternal warfare against each other, occasions for conquest and the rituals of sensual destruction. The Butuans are free from feelings of pity and fear of death. Public butcher shops sell human flesh. There is a kind of commerce between these neighbors: The media of exchange are slaves, women, and children, to be used for work and pleasure. Butuans have a number of advantages over the anxiety-ridden Europeans, we learn in a passage that could have been lifted out of Rousseau. Without care for the morrow, they enjoy the present as best they can, and they never foresee the future. They have no recorded history and remember nothing of the past, not even their ages. Fear of a serpent-god, whose idol they regularly anoint with blood, is their only religion. Their chiefs practice capricious cruelty, burning or massacring whole villages solely out of commitment to the principle of amusement.

The Sadean utopian argument is ambiguous. Is this really the utopia of Sadean evil, or is it rather a depiction of European despotism in war and peace, beside which the Sadean pleasures appear innocent? Nietzsche would later maintain that meting out punishment was primarily an act of the strong imposing their will upon victims, the transgression of the criminal being a mere pretext for the enjoyment of this pleasure. De Sade's Butuans anticipated the Nietzschean principle pictorially. Punishment was simply an excuse for arranging hunting parties to track down the supposed miscreants and experience the delights of executing them.

In only one work did de Sade depart from the exclusively aristocratic pattern of his scatological and sadistic, anal and oral, and sometimes genital, erotic novels, and that was in *La Philosophie dans le boudoir,* published in the libertine Paris of 1795. The participants in an orgy, drawn from various social classes, are resting after one of their colossal, multifaceted sexual bouts requiring prodigious force and precise timing, since five persons, male and female, are involved in the structuring of simultaneous orgasms. The reputedly greatest debauchee of the age, who directs and coordinates the party, entertains his companions with a newspaper article setting forth a new constitutional law for the French Republic worthy of truly free citizens. In this document the normally elitist Sadean utopia is extended to all members of society equally. It is based on the principle that no one may deny a citizen the satisfaction of any of his erotic desires. Nothing so universal had been imagined since Aristophanes' *Parliament of Women,* though in the ancient dystopia the old crones were in the privileged position and young men had to comply with their wishes by a law of the Athenian Assembly, which had been packed by women in disguise. At times the long discussion of perfect social laws for the French Republic appears to be tongue-in-cheek. The extent of de Sade's earnestness in each of his constitutional proposals is impossible to measure. Scholarly attempts to pin down Thomas More in his whimsical moods have not been rewarding enough to justify putting the Marquis to the question.

De Sade donned the costume of the French egalitarian republic, Jacobin style, as he drove to their ultimate conclusion many of the preconceptions behind the revolutionary slogans. If all citizens were really to be "enfants de la patrie" in the fullness of meaning of the phrase in the "Marseillaise," then he drew the eminently Platonic deduction that the family with its rival loyalties must be abolished. Children, moreover, should in the manner of the ancients be allowed to live or die depending solely upon the need and interests of the *patrie*. Weaklings ought to be killed at birth without pity, a sniveling emotion that he despised.

Having banished God, de Sade based his order on nature and the purity of the pleasure principle. Occasionally he was willing to convince a novice in debauch that a certain amount of pain had to be endured, as in pedicatio, in order to reap a greater harvest of pleasure, for this was nature's way. But though pleasure was preceded by pain, the interval between them was never to be long. With the pleasure principle as his guide, he tackled directly the customs that ought to govern that sovereign pleasure in the optimum republic, sex. His rules are simple: The state should establish institutions where anyone, male or female, may order anyone else to an assignation, during which the summoned one must be totally submissive to all the desires, whims, and caprices of his fellow man or woman, however unpleasant they may be. This law is the logical consequence of the supreme dictate of the pleasure principle. It also simultaneously serves another purpose: The state becomes more secure because man's despotic nature, which seeks the untrammeled expression of its free and arbitrary will, is thus fully appeased in well-regulated houses and there are no aggressive drives left which, under other less fortunate constitutions, are directed against the state and its order. De Sade had at his disposal none of the statistical apparatus of modern scholars, who have so skillfully demonstrated to their own satisfaction the correlation between sexual frustration and the political revolutionary temperament, but he propounded the same thesis. In defense of his insistence that the laws provide for the practice of sodomy, he hazarded the estimate that such penchants were quite widespread and that their denial was a serious and dangerous curtailment of liberty.

In *La Philosophie dans le boudoir,* de Sade pleaded eloquently for female equality. He argued that women had been doubly disadvantaged by existing laws and customs because, though their rampant desires were even more tyrannical and pressing than men's—a stock French view of female sexuality since the Renaissance—men alone led relatively unrestricted sexual lives. If the cruelty of women could only be appeased in the course of sexual activity, they would no longer have to find an outlet in acidulous verbal aggression. The rights of half the human species were defended with the fervor of the later Saint-Simonians. The theory that frustrated passions sought alternative means of satisfaction found an echo in Charles Fourier, who cites de Sade's works— one of the rare acknowledgments of his indebtedness to a moralist predecessor.

Adopting the rhetoric of the radical egalitarians, de Sade denounced the existing sexual order as one based upon a monopolistic conception of property. The exclusive ownership of persons in the prevailing family structure was contrary to nature and to the spirit of the French Republic. He saw no contradiction between the liberty of the one who desired and the legal compulsion of the summoned sexual partner to obey, since the constraint did not entail permanency of property-holding. The rights of pleasure had precedence over the rights of ownership. While under the existing marital system women were owned in exclusivity, a fountain was enjoyed by all without being possessed by anyone. Enduring sexual possession is a great Sadean evil and love is its primary symptom. In a true republic, emotional ties are reserved only for the state; among individuals there are nothing but temporary contractual engagements for pleasure, without loyalty or moral involvement beyond the moment of enjoyment.

In the Sadean utopia the state is necessary chiefly for defense against enemies; outside of this function it may establish facilities of various sorts, but may not promulgate punitive laws. The typical eighteenth-century naturalistic utopia of calm felicity took care of the problem of crime by presupposing that in an economy of plenty, situated in the bosom of nature, with its inhabitants assured a sound moral education, breaches of the written or implicit code of laws would be rare. De Sade would not abandon his utopia to any such facile cult of virtue. Thievery, rape, and murder would continue to be frequent; but the French Republic should not make crimes of these natural acts. If the Republic is to survive against enemies its people must be alert, lively, in a state of aroused passion as befits warrior citizens; it cannot lapse into quiet and indolence. Why should theft be punished? Rather, the man who is robbed should incur the anger of the law because he was not vigilant enough to prevent the theft. Stealing, moreover, will help to equalize wealth, which is desirable in a free republic. Rape fazes de Sade no more than theft, while sentences of death for rape arouse his indignation. What has been lost in rape? The pain of the victim is trivial if measured against the pleasure of the rapist possessed by a tyrannical passion. De Sade argues in a similar manner about "unnatural" sexual relations, which were subject to gruesome punishments in the eighteenth century. Such erotic feelings are common, they cause no harm, and if the example of the ancients were followed homosexuality would be encouraged to make warriors the braver.

Murder is perhaps the most difficult act to strike from the roster of the penal laws, but in his reasoning de Sade demonstrates the same ingenuity as in his treatment of theft, rape, and sodomy. The murderer is forced to commit the act by nature, and how can nature in one of its manifestations be denied? Moreover, what has the murderer done but return a body to nature, where it will bring forth new life in the form of little insects? The punishment of murder is based upon the anthropocentric conception that there is something unique and sacred about human life and an implied denigration of the other creatures that would spontaneously arise out of a corpse. All ancient peoples permitted, even encouraged, infanticide. If the warrior Republic condones killing in battle, why does it follow a different principle within the state—a paradoxical turn of thought that Kant was using at about this time in behalf of eternal peace. The state had no right to execute a murderer who had acted out of passion and thus to perpetrate another murder—this time in cold blood and without even the defense that it was compelled by a natural criminal impulse. "The law, cold in itself, cannot be accessible to the passions that can legitimize in man the cruel act of murder."[6] Since it is dangerous for a state to let its citizens become too docile, the murderer's passion should be appreciated, and the state should not intervene to punish him, although his victim could be freely avenged by others.

If France is to be a free state there must be true liberty—the freedom of the passions, all the passions, de Sade insisted with an absolutism before which even Fourier, who was doubtless influenced by him, recoiled. True liberty means total self-fulfillment in all one's desires under any circumstances. The moral logic is so relentless that at times it seems to triumph even over its own paradoxes. De Sade outdoes the *enragés* among the sansculottes. If there is liberty of conscience and of the press, there must be liberty of action except in those matters that strike directly at the roots of government. De Sade had learned well the lessons of juridical and cultural relativism which so many of the philosophes, including the most respectable Président de Montesquieu, had been teaching. Were a society based on real liberty and equality, there would be no room for criminal laws. De Sade still talks of virtues and vices, in the language of his time. Nature needs them as complements of existence, and he fails to comprehend why their often nebulous distinction should become a basis for criminal prosecution.

Both Restif and de Sade rest on the same premise in their discursive utopias: A society can ensure happiness only if its laws honestly reflect the ways of nature. Present conditions are analyzed and demonstrated to be unnatural and productive of great unhappiness, while the ancients and contemporary savage societies as revealed by the travel literature are admired for respecting nature's laws. Once in a while Chinese customs are cited for support, and in rare instances even Thomas More, who was known and misquoted by both Restif and de Sade, is dragged in as a witness.

In defense of his scandalous ideas, de Sade mockingly used the same bombast Revolutionary orators did in proclaiming self-evident truths. One is, however, brought up short by the commonsensical plea that while murder ought to be allowed within the confines of the Republic, the Revolutionaries should be extremely cautious about extending war into foreign countries. Let France establish the Sadean Republic of true liberty within the borders of one country, and then all other nations would spontaneously emulate her without the need for a military crusade—Sadeanism in one country rather than world revolution. In these passages, at least, de Sade seems to be writing with genuine feeling and conviction.

The same holds for his works on religion. His attacks on the belief in God and fear of the afterworld have an authentic Lucretian quality, as he depicts with unmistakable sincerity the misery caused by religious chimeras. Let there be no religious crimes of any sort, he commands. And he goes further than a plea for mere toleration; he claims the right to ridicule, to treat religious rituals as if they were theatrical performances. *Plus de dieux, Français, plus de dieux,* if you want to safeguard yourselves against despotism. He was imbued with the spirit of the ancient Critias doctrine of the political origins of the gods in a tyrant's plot, revived in the eighteenth century, and he borrowed a page from Shaftesbury on religious enthusiasm: Do not overthrow the idols in anger, pulverize them in play, and the belief will fall by itself.

As for the golden rule of morality, de Sade attacked it with the same vehemence that Freud would muster some hundred and forty years later. An injunction to love one's neighbor as one loves oneself is absurd because it is impossible and against all the laws of nature. Perhaps we can exhibit the affection of brothers and friends who live together, but nothing more intense. We can work out reciprocal rules of humanity and benevolence; but let us not expect the same degree of energy in these relationships among all people—some are just naturally cold. De Sade pleads for the diversity of individual psychic needs. There can be no universal laws in this respect, any more than all soldiers can be outfitted with the same size clothes. The Fourierist utopia is in the making. "It is a frightful injustice to demand that men of unequal characters should bend themselves to equal laws; what suits one is not at all suitable for another."[7] De Sade is not being facetious; he knows that there cannot be separate laws for each individual; therefore he counsels only a few general rules to which men with different characters can adapt themselves readily. Above all, the laws must be lenient. If your reputed justice strikes down a man who is incapable of binding himself to your law, de Sade exclaims, is it not as guilty as if it punished a blind man for not differentiating among colors?

The Perverted Peasant

A peasant's son, a printer, a textbook case of shoe-fetishism, Nicolas Edme Restif de la Bretonne had a utopian plan for the general reformation of mankind in one fell swoop. The inventor of a science-fiction fantasy many of whose prophecies would become plain realities, he dreamed of air fleets, missiles, a world of microbes. He broke with Newtonian time and the reason of the Newtonian world machine. As his sexual debility became more pronounced with age, his fantasies grew wilder. In his imagination he would overturn this world with a new technology and new rules of love. But in many of his utopian projects the strict discipline of his Jansenist father took over. "Children are the prolongation of the life of fathers," Restif declared with simple factualness in *La Vie de mon père*.[8] In his utopian regulations he craved the authority against which his nature rebelled. One has to await Fourier, who learned a thing or two from him, to find a more compulsive and fixated creation or one as fertile in utopian details that fill up every crevice of existence and leave nothing to chance, that provide for every contingency. The elements of the total utopia of the next century are here—a cosmography, a microscopy, an analysis of man in all possible situations. Restif felt constantly persecuted by enemies, real and imaginary, coalescing into a hostile phantasmagoria. At the same time he desired to break out of his self-imposed imprisonment, to fly to the ends of the earth, to the spaces between the planets.

To want to possess the world and to be possessed by a little shoe, to dream of new orders of man and nature and to be trapped by an infantile memory that imprisoned his sexual being in an attempt to recover a past odor or sight once experienced by an infant crawling among the feet of the giants who surrounded him and whom he recreated in his fantasy of the Megapatagonians—this was Restif's destiny. He was a builder of imaginary kingdoms over which he lorded. Many utopians, including the saintly More, shared that fantasy. Restif recorded how as a child-shepherd in Burgundy he once took ceremonial possession of a hillock and conducted his young playmates about his domain. Sometimes he was a priest in a white shirt performing religious rites. One day the ten-year-old shepherd led his two sheep and goats to the hillock. Filled with memories of the Old Testament, which his father read to the assembled family and farm laborers every night, he saw himself a patriarch-founder of a new kingdom. He raised an altar to God in the form of a pyramid of stones and was about to burn some brush in sacrifice when a bird of prey plunged down upon a starling. With his stick he struck the ravisher, broke its wing, and then in an ecstasy sacrificed the evil one that had intruded upon his peaceable kingdom, for he was lord and priest of all he surveyed and he meted out punishments. Restif had a vocation to legislate for the world. When he was the "owl" surveying the whole of Paris as it slept, reporting on its sins and vices, he was giving expression to another aspect of the same omnipotence fantasy.

In the 1770s and 1780s Restif wrote out plans for a new world in the utopian style. He had led a tumultuous life in search of excitement and now that he was growing old he would issue laws for mankind, distributing rewards and punishments like a Moses. By that time the biblical dream of his boyhood had become crowded with images of the customs of a host of nations about which he had read in travel books. His regulations were severe and Deuteronomic in spirit—he was repeating the austere rule of his Jansenist father in a new language—but his domain was far broader than the ancestral fields of the Restifs; he had come to encompass all of Paris and from Paris the entire world. Though he lived on the Ile Saint-Louis, he felt deep aversion for the city he explored. It was Gomorrah, a conviction bolstered by his immersion in the passionate writings of that other wanderer, his master Jean-Jacques. The good life could only be established away from these vicious, filthy, cantankerous, thieving artisans and shopkeepers of Paris among whom he dwelt. In utopia he returned to his father's house, which, enlarged, became the egalitarian society. Unlike the authors of the classical isolated island utopias, Restif embraced the universalism of the philosophes. His system was to be worldwide and uniform, worthy of humanity everywhere, and he demanded its implementation by all sovereigns in one dramatic fiat.

Restif surpassed his father and his grandfather in the stringency of his ordinances. In his ideal kingdom new Restifs would not be allowed to behave as he had; they would be severely punished if they tried to violate the absolute rule of the social order. No peasant play in the haystack would be tolerated. Education, courtship, marriage, sexual intercourse, everything would be regulated. The elders would keep a book of merits and demerits and the award of pretty girls in marriage would depend upon obedient behavior. The supervisors of Plato's *Laws* were lenient compared with the watchful crones and graybeards of Restif's society.

Restif came from a formerly Protestant area whose inhabitants had not migrated despite persecutions, but had clung to their old ways even when with Henry IV they returned to the Catholic Church. Edme Restif, his father, was a *roturier*, a peasant landowner, but also a *lieutenant de bailliage* and a sort of justice of the peace who handed down verdicts in accordance with the customary law. His second marriage was the union of an irascible man of forty-five and a lively widow of twenty, and Restif believed himself destined to be of hot temper because he was conceived in passion. Born October 23, 1734, he was about twenty when Rousseau's *Discourses* came off the press. Physiologist Restif had been told that he was nursed not by his mother but by the most ardent woman in the canton. Restif's self-analysis awakened early sexual memories of the caresses and spankings of his sisters. It was while crawling at the feet of the priest, picking up bits of wafer, that by chance he lifted the petticoat of a little girl and encountered her slipper, the softest, silkiest thing he ever touched. The outcry of the child and the whipping that followed seemed to form the elements of an event that determined his sexual fixation. He was early introduced to sexual play by neighbors and sisters and to perversities by parents and

schoolmasters who whipped naked buttocks of girls and boys with equal abandon. He slept at the foot of his parents' bed and was awakened by grimacing
demons.

Most of Restif's books are shot through with philosophical and moral homilies. Sometimes they drown out the entertaining anecdotes and stories, brief
and pointed like the accounts of old-time columnists or windy and inflated like
a contemporary novel. Everything is uneven in Restif, the style, the level of
thought, the pace. His writing is without form; volumes are poured forth in
compulsive oral debauches. There are many new worlds to create. Anxiety is
all-pervasive and can only be allayed by endless activity, writing, watching,
seducing, suffering, rehearsing his suffering. Restif is no heedless Don Juan—
he does not make his conquests gaily, he is captured. And the pathetic fellow is
terrified of death at the hands of brigands and revolutionaries. He grows old
and he feels it, particularly in bed. The venereal diseases come and go, are
driven underground by quacks and doctors whom he alternately worships and
reviles. Somehow he never manages to get much money from his books—
they are all more or less clandestine, and pirated editions, easily and frequently
produced, sell more cheaply than the originals. Restif rants against the usurpation of the most sacred form of property, literary property.

As an apprentice printer Restif had fixed upon the person of the master's
wife, Mme. Fournier, as his *maman*. These young vagabonds in search of
mothers, Jean-Jacques and Nicolas, found them in older women, but their real
yearning was for fathers whose love had been denied them. They carried their
little perversions through life—Jean-Jacques his pleasure in being spanked by
women, Restif his passion for a pretty female shoe. Sexual fulfillment was a
fantasy; reality reduced them to impotence. In their social utopias, elements of
their private fantasies intrude in various disguises: To be free and to be in
chains, to worship the father and to defy him constantly. These are men of
acute sensibility; they seem to have delicate skins like women, and each touch
leaves an indelible mark. The caress of a sister, the scratching of a nurse, everything is remembered. They have extraordinary recollections of sentimental
and sensual experience. They celebrate a masculine ideal. The effeminacy of
the *petit maître* repels them, for it reminds them of their own sexual ambivalence. Restif's response to Rousseau's works was that of a younger brother. He
hated and adored him, recognized himself in him and rejected him even as he
continued to ape him. Both ended their lives in delusions of persecution and
megalomania. Comparing their flashes of genius, Paul Valéry, not a casual
judge, has raised Restif above Jean-Jacques.

By contrast with de Sade's rather broad-stroked constitution in *La Philosophie dans le boudoir,* whose intent remains problematic to the end, Restif de la
Bretonne's series of books, written in the decades before the Revolution, contain one of the most detailed and meticulously elaborated systems in the history of utopia. In five works that constitute a whole, all aspects of existence are
covered. The form is architecturally clumsy. The fictional envelopment of
each work is an exchange of letters in the manner of Richardson and Rousseau
among a group of characters who reappear in every volume. Some of the tales
they relate to one another illustrate the principles of the utopia proper, which is
always a set of rules and regulations that one of the correspondents drafts. Of
the five works, the *Andrographe* (1782) deals primarily with the education of

boys and is the pivotal utopia. *Les Gynographes* (1777) had performed an analogous function for girls. Together these are the heart of the system and there are cross-references between them. The *Thesmographe* (1789) is Restif's incorporation of the same rules into a code of laws; but it also represents a relaxation of the lofty ideals of the utopia. It is the equivalent of Plato's *Laws,* the second-best utopia, when the perfection of the *Republic* seems unattainable. The other two utopias deal with specific, rather narrow, social problems and were theoretically to have been integrated with the *Thesmographe*. One, *La Mimographe* (1770), treats of the regulation of the theater in an effort to suppress the license that has been associated with it. The other, the *Pornographe* (1769), is not really pornographic at all, though the title helped to fix the literary image of Restif; it is a proposal for the regulation of houses of prostitution primarily to prevent the venereal diseases that had caused Restif so much agony and had driven him to become the victim of some of the most eminent medical charlatans of the age.

Restif appended to the texts of these five volumes, to which he gave the overall title *Idées singulières,* long, discursive notes written by himself or collected from his friends in the literary bohemia in which he moved. These display much anthropological erudition, derived from the bulging storehouse of contemporary travel literature. The scholarly extravagance was meant to justify his proposals as conforming to the "law of nature," to show that they were in harmony with primitive custom, but also to prove that his system was superior to any other that had ever existed. In addition to the *Idées singulières,* Restif experimented with the more common eighteenth-century utopian form in a sort of *voyage imaginaire*—*La Découverte australe, ou Le Dédale français* (1781), where his ideas were far less rigidly formulated—and in various digressions in the vast body of disjointed stories that he published.

In the *Idées singulières* Restif imposed a Calvinist order upon his ideal society and punished violations with merciless severity. By his own account the seducer of hundreds of girls, from his first adventures in Auxerre through his last enfeebled years in Paris, he fancied himself the savior of others from moral depravity by the enforcement of stringent regulations—and what a grandiose sadomasochistic system he invented! There is one vice that he abhors more than any other: Homosexuality is the great social evil, or, what is the same to him, the tendency of both sexes to so alter their roles that they become almost indistinguishable. He runs counter to the utopian currents of the seventeenth and eighteenth centuries that, following the Platonic tradition, envisaged an erosion of differences between the sexes as a positive development. "The two sexes are not equal. To make them so is to denature them."[9] Restif, disciple of Rousseau, was at war with effeminacy. Of course, like Jean-Jacques, he may have been battling his own inclinations, for, despite his hundreds of "conquests" real or imaginary, he betrays a feminine sensibility, a softness traditionally associated with women, at least *in illo tempore.*

The male in Restif's utopia is dominant, authoritative, decisive; the female, obedient and receptive, formed to please the male and to be deferential to him. (One sees the shadow of Restif's wife, a hellion who flaunted her infidelities and defied his every wish.) Since a confusion of sexual roles is the major source of disorder in society, radically different educational systems are prescribed for the two sexes in order to accentuate distinctions rather than blur them. From swaddling for girls but not for boys, to writing for boys but not for girls (because there is no utility for them in the art and it might give them notions), the educational conditioning is aimed toward one end: to foster maleness and femaleness as unique attributes of the sexes and to eliminate ambiguity. Only in this polarization will there be complete happiness in the relations of male and female. It is Restif's underlying thesis that women are now discontented because there are no real men to govern them; despite their bluestocking pretensions, they suffer from the male's abdication of his role. In Restif's utopia, along with a patriarchal authority go terrible punishments for adultery; they may have been no harsher than existing French law in theory, but they were designed to be administered with utopian thoroughness.

Restif devised a complex system to keep alive the sexual desires of the newly married for each other. His method is the opposite of de Sade's. Instead of eternal satisfaction and renewed stimulation, Restif heightens sexual tension by denying easy fulfillment. Other restrictive utopias, those of Vairasse and the *Ajaoiens* of the pseudo-Fontenelle, reflected a popular conception that sexual overindulgence was unhealthful for the progeny. Restif is moved less by this consideration than by the aim of keeping sexual desire at its peak. Up to the age of thirty-five, the pair do not live together and the male must invent ruses to foil the vigilance of the parents, whose duty it is to try to prevent sexual congress. The play becomes intricate and the virtuosity of the lover in circumventing parental guards is much admired in the ideal society.

Though Restif was still too closely tied to the Jansenist tradition in which he had been reared to accept the extreme position of Helvétius that there could be no inherited bad character, he was convinced of the ease with which children could be formed into a new mold. Restif recommends for all classes a rigorous education from the age of three to twelve modeled on the hard regimen of a peasant's son: coarse and simple food, a straw bed, rough clothing, plenty of exercise until the age of nine, useful labor until twelve, then preparation for a future career by continual practice, with little leisure. The purpose of all this activity is clear-cut; it is the same idea that underlay English nineteenth-century public school education. Tire the boy out so that the "passions" will be silenced until he reaches twenty. Restif would institute this toughening-up process of the young man in the name of the pleasure principle: Pleasures are reserved for his maturity. Contemporary society, as Restif described it, was yielding to the caprices of its children and cultivating a race of sybarites. Those parents who thought that their permissiveness was merely a passing indulgence without consequences were ruining their offspring, since everything left a profound trace in this early period of habit formation. Restif echoes the psychology of Descartes's *Treatise on the Passions:* The earliest imprints are virtually ineradicable.

The theory of pleasure is based upon the idea that retention, holding back of immediate fulfillment, is vital to happiness, which consists less in actual enjoyment than in being in a position to hope for enjoyment. The key point of Restif's calculus of felicity is so to distribute the rewards of society that enjoyment can be relatively constant throughout the life cycle. Pleasures depend upon novelty, and they can be prematurely used up if indulged in too early. His whole utopia is built around the maintenance of a state of high tension and anticipation and the avoidance of surfeit. He goes to extraordinary lengths to devise laws and restrictions that erect barriers to easy appeasement, in order that his creatures may live in joyous expectation of satisfaction. This may be the model of pleasure he learned in the whorehouses of Paris. It was the only way to be spared the fate of the nobility, whose jaded scions he had encountered in their futile quest for pleasure. Instead of de Sade's vision of total immersion in sensations, with brief intervals of respite for renewal of capacity, Restif operated in terms of the multiplication of obstacles or the postponement of pleasure. His scheme is a careful attempt to balance the delight of ready gratification against the emptiness of satiety, an ever-present threat for him. But there must always be hope of ultimate reward in order to sustain the effort and the tension.

Before the Revolution, Restif was already beginning to point an accusing finger at Rousseau, though he derived from him. It was perhaps not his fault, Restif conceded, but Rousseau, egregiously misinterpreted, was filling the young with vain pride. They believed that reading him made them as wise as their elders. Instead, the way of the Egyptians should be imitated; knowledge should be doled out piecemeal throughout life, lest premature knowledge that one is incapable of understanding make one arrogant.

Restif ends up with a nightmare of Deuteronomic prohibitions. The goal is the establishment of a reign of virtue in which all, or almost all, will be saved through fear of the condign punishments that surround the regulatory procedures, and through competition for honors and dignities. In the utopia of the *Andrographe* there is equality of opportunity in the contest for the prizes of virtue. Once a classification of persons has been set by the supervising elders after the conclusion of the educational period, mobility downward is determined by the commission of felonies and upward by the performance of outstandingly meritorious acts.

The society is stratified in two fundamental ways. One is natural, the ordering by age-groups and years of matriculation in school in order to enforce the unqualified respect and obedience due all elders. Decisions are as firmly in the hands of the gerontocracy as in Plato's *Laws*. Functions in society are distributed primarily according to seniority, a system meant to assure a high degree of equality since certain privileges are reserved for each age-class and no callow youth will usurp the dignified offices of his seniors. The age stratifications give all citizens some respectworthy occupation to look forward to at every stage in the life cycle, as long as they remain virtuous. There are no refuse heaps for unwanted old men: The aged supervise, determine and mete out punishments, keep the books of merits and demerits. This is more than a structure based on traditionalist authority. There is an underlying hedonist argument that if the young or middle-aged taste all the varied rewards of life prematurely, they will have nothing to look forward to later. Here the lonely *hibou* who nightly roamed the Ile Saint-Louis speaks for himself after sexual potency has waned and the erstwhile adventurer has been reduced to a mere *voyeur*. He is echoing the biblical lament: Do not cast me off in my old age. The charming and wild M. Nicolas had already begun to feel the tedium of life in his forties. The second mode of classification is by virtue and capacity within each age-group, the different classes marked by distinctive colored insignia, as they had been among Vairasse's Sevarambians. A person, however, is not necessarily all of one color, because his degree of excellence in different fields of endeavor varies, and so he may have an orange vest and a blue coat. Though a man may rise a notch or drop a notch in later life, the significance of the classification is greatest at the conclusion of the educational process and on the eve of marriage. Then the young men of the highest virtue get first choice among the girls, who cannot refuse them except for a cause that must be proved and under pain of great punishment, such as being held over to another year or dropping back to the end of the line. An ascetic economic equality generally prevails, though the austerity of life is relieved by *fêtes champêtres,* orderly and chaste. Natural beauty and virtue are the two highest values in the utopia and the deformed are thrown into the same category as the villainous. There is competition, but it is strictly supervised and the prizes are honors rather than goods.

Restif knows that his project of reform can never be executed until there is a union of the wills of all men in a nation, which he concedes to be almost impossible. Yet he is driven to write this romance of virtue and happiness in order to perform a benevolent act for humanity by presenting it with a divine gift, his project. (Rousseau's rhetoric becomes wooden among his epigoni.) Restif is aware that the minutiae in his plan are burdensome, but his compulsive personality will not be denied: All the regulations, without exception, are essential, and any deviation from the set rules would be a grave danger to the system. What separates the realm of virtue from the realm of vice is the iron boundary of the regulation. Someone must punish and someone must be punished. Restif may distinguish among the violations for purposes of chastisement, but there is a Judeo-Protestant chasm between sin and non-sin. Restif mixes the severest Protestant ethic with the language of the philosophes. He attacks the Jansenists, but is himself a master of ascetic rule-giving. He places himself in the utopian tradition of Plato, Thomas More, the Abbé de Saint-Pierre, and, of all people, Raoul Spifame, a sixteenth-century eccentric who fancied himself the King of France, and whose code of laws for the realm was republished in part in 1775.

Restif is an upstart, a peasant's son taught to be an artisan, a printer who breaks into the literary world of Paris, albeit its less respectable circles, and at least sometimes, if only for a lark, is received and flattered by the more debauched among the wealthy bourgeois and even the nobility. He never gains entrée to the great salons, but he attends the parties of actresses and a few elegant ladies. Is he of "the people," whose manners he described in hundreds of volumes and among whom he engaged in the sexual adventures that absorbed his existence? He had no love of the *populace.* "I confess," he wrote in a "Postscript" to the seventh volume of *Les Nuits de Paris,* "that I trembled whenever I saw the common people in a state of agitation, and I trembled because I know them, because I know how deep was their hatred against anyone who is well off, an eternal, violent hatred . . . Once this ferocious beast believes that it may dare do so, it will overturn everything. I am so scared of them that I would be afraid to write or print this if they read. But this *populace* of whom I speak does not read. It will never read as long as it is the *populace.* I know the people better than the officials can, better than the bourgeois, better than the police, because they are masked before them while I live with them. They speak before me without constraint . . . Anarchy is the greatest of evils in every country in the world. Who would tolerate it in his family? . . . Everything the Government does is grand and noble. Its sacred authority, like unto the Paternal-Power, gives to the great family of the State the security and tranquillity necessary for the sciences and the arts."[10] Clearly the *populace* needed Restif's intricate and comprehensive system in order to hold its vices in check and guide it, even against its will, to a general reformation of its nature.

Restif readily calls down upon himself an accusation of hypocrisy: His eternal simpering about virtue in the midst of his own rather debauched existence, even if half the stories he tells about himself are untrue, is nauseating. By contrast, de Sade is a breath of aristocratic candor and defiance, though the air may be fetid with feces. De Sade is the outspoken enemy of virtue, the philosopher and defender of crime. Like Rousseau, Restif uses his works as a formal public confessional that is meant to absolve him of the sin of his vices. But the show of utter frankness, the piling up of detail are telltale signs that he has withheld what is most painful; his are ritual purifications. "It is because I have the courage to undress naked before you, to expose all my weaknesses, all my imperfections, all my baseness in order to make you compare your fellows to yourself, that I merit your thanks and friendship. The effort I make is so heroic that it should wipe out all the wrongs I have committed against society, purge me of them, and rank me among its benefactors."[11]

In his utopias his surrogate self, that is, the boys of the *Andrographe,* were let off less easily. In fantasy he had himself scourged, branded, and exiled for the sexual liberties that in real life he allowed himself to expiate with a mere verbal self-castigation, in itself not entirely unpleasurable. Of course his confessions are also lies—he has told of many vices only to hide the vice of which he is most fearful, the desire to be fornicated by his mother, or, faute de mieux, her shoe. His frequently expressed horror of homosexuality is suspect. The harshness and contempt with which cripples are treated is of the same order; and so is his obsession with incest, his fantasy that many of the girls he fornicates in middle age are really the natural daughters of the girls he seduced in his youth.

"When dissolution has blown its breath over a society, when the human mind has to be reborn, when old beliefs have to die, there comes a last man who summarizes and incarnates in himself this need for dissolution. This last man of the eighteenth century was Restif. It was not Diderot, it was not Voltaire, it was Restif. Yes, in the eyes of the philosopher who analyzes the spectacle of the world in depth, Restif, poor Restif, the Irus of this century, is the king of this century, for he is its extreme limit and its perfection, *finis et terminus ultimus.*"[12] This was the judgment of the Saint-Simonian Pierre Leroux.

23

Equality or Death

PLATO'S DISTINCTION between the principles underlying an ideal city that emerge from philosophical discussion and a portrayal of the ideal city in motion holds for the corpus of utopias in eighteenth-century France. On balance, Enlightenment works of utopian philosophical thought—and Rousseau fits into this general category—are far more original in their insights and in the long run may have exerted a more direct influence on significant men of action during the Revolutionary era than the flood of utopian novels, despite their surface appeal to larger numbers of people.

Communal Cures for Souls

Simon Nicolas Henri Linguet, Jacques Brissot de Warville, the Curé Meslier, Dom Deschamps, the Abbé Mably, Morelly, Restif de la Bretonne, and a host of minor theorists whose names were for a time lost in obscurity, but who are now a special preoccupation of the Werner Kraus school in East Germany, are writers who moved in a different orbit from the *patres majores* of the Enlightenment. A trenchant analysis of class conflict, demands for social and economic equality as well as political justice, even dialectical turns of thought alien to most philosophes have been discovered in their writings. In the official history developed by Friedrich Engels, Mably and Morelly took their rightful places as communist thinkers between the Levellers of the English Revolution and Babeuf of the French. Publicists like Linguet and Brissot de Warville were protean Paris types, fellows living by their wits, who did not know quite where to land politically or socially, and they spun off in all directions with radical proposals for the complete reorganization of society. Diderot felt that Linguet, whom Marx later admired, had the lie in the soul. Yet Restif de la Bretonne immortalized Linguet as the wise Teugnil of Megapatagonia in *La Découverte australe*. Restif himself, whose *Andrographe*—much admired by Benjamin Franklin— was subtitled *Idées d'un honnête-homme sur un projet de règlement, proposé à toutes les nations de l'Europe pour opérer une Réforme générale des moeurs, et par elle, le bonheur du Genre-humain,* and Morelly, who wrote the communist *Code de la Nature, ou le véritable esprit de ses lois,* belong among the philosophical utopians as well as among the utopian novelists who exploited the taste for erotica. Restif sententiously declared: "There can be no virtue without physical and moral equality."[1] And even Morelly's novel *Naufrage des îles flottantes* stretched the definition of equality to include easy access not only to the means of subsistence but to "all the pleasures of life."[2]

The social origins of the authors of the egalitarian discourses are varied: They tend to come from the poorer professional classes and include clerks, doctors, small-town priests, even a Benedictine monk. Restif, the prosperous peasant's son apprenticed to a printer, is an exception. As for Morelly, we do not even know his first name; he is a blank, though it has been conjectured that he was a school teacher. The egalitarian doctrines were concentrated in France, without significant echo in eighteenth-century England or elsewhere on the Continent, where outright attacks on the private ownership of property were virtually nonexistent before 1789. The English had had their experience with a world upside-down and were convalescing.

No one, to our knowledge, has yet drawn up a complete list of the French pre-Revolutionary treatises and projects for universal reformation. A good number of them, like those of Deschamps and Meslier, remained in manuscript during the lifetime of their authors and some are now lost. (The archives of local French academies are yielding a rich harvest of unpublished projects, the plans of defeated candidates in prize competitions.) Babeuf's youthful correspondence with the permanent secretary of the Arras Academy records the intense excitement with which the future leader of the Conspiracy of the Equals read one of these anonymous plans.[3] Which particular philosophical utopia ignited the spark in a young revolutionary and drove him to risk his life for the transformation of mankind is unknowable; the combustible quality of a work is not related to its excellence.

Egalitarian utopian themes of the eighteenth century were of a different order from both the communist tradition of antiquity and More's or Campanella's limited espousal of "community." The new concepts culminated in Babeuf's *Manifesto of the Equals,* a document that inaugurated the modern era of radical action utopias. While the late-eighteenth-century communist views attracted only a limited number of adherents at the time, in the nineteenth century these writings were recognized as a primary source for communist theory —Buonarroti, a survivor of the Conspiracy, was the intermediary in their resurrection in the 1830s—and Engels even thought of having some of them translated into German as part of a communist library. The continent, Spartan character of most of the egalitarian utopias is still in harmony with one strain of eighteenth-century thought; but the occasional emphasis upon "community of ownership" embracing the whole economic order, rather than equality in individual property holdings, is an innovation.

A psychological dimension that prefigures nineteenth-century theories distinguishes many communal utopias of the period before the Revolution. They may propose radical political and economic changes in order to bring about the new human condition. They may advocate the abolition of private property and sexual possession. But the diagnosis of the social ills takes place on the moral and psychological levels, and the demonstration of the cure is on the same plane. The state is not a primary agent of the transformation; often it is bypassed. Conversion to faith in the utopia occurs through the word or the dialectical movement of history. Without great interest in or any understanding of the realities of the economic process, this group of utopians focused upon the psychological consequences of the privatization of objects, both persons and things. Either mankind would be converted to sociability and the esprit behind the laws of private property in goods and bodies would be transformed, or regeneration could not take place. Montesquieu had had a great deal to say about the difficulties of altering an esprit overnight. But the utopians forgot his lessons when they were in a sanguine mood. Though they were for the most part ignorant of the keen analysts of the economic process in

France and England, their writings were usually made of sterner stuff than the flood of speaking-picture utopias that inundated the Continent.

The solitary Benedictine Dom Deschamps, who in 1761 tried in vain to convert Rousseau to *le vrai système,* was in the classical utopian mold. Under the protection of the Marquis Voyer d'Argenson, Léger Marie Deschamps was for many years a man of great prestige in his monastery outside Saumur, where he filled the office of *procureur.* This stubborn Breton who lost his faith through reading the Old Testament was nonetheless a zealous administrator and doughty defender of his priory in the law courts. Excerpts from his manuscripts were not published until the nineteenth century, and only in the twentieth has he come into his own. For him Rousseau was a prodromus. His own system was unique, radical, went to the roots of things, would found moral behavior on an indisputable metaphysical principle. His *vrai système* was constructive, not merely destructive. The *Encyclopédie* might bring about a revolution in religion, manners, and government, but it could do nothing more with its demi-enlightenment. This kind of revolution was as dangerous as it was useless. Moral evil, a consequence of man's ignorance of the metaphysical principle of wholeness in all being, was the cause of the present state of depravity, which would continue with more or less the same intensity even if external changes occurred.

Deschamps was in one sense a hangover from the seventeenth century. He was a great system-builder, a new Bacon or a new Comenius, who held the key to the enigma of all being. Deschamps's version of the civil war that raged in the breast of every man living in the present wretched state of civilization, the *état des lois,* is hardly to be compared with the analysis in Jean-Jacques's *Discourses;* often it is crude, even ungrammatical. But Deschamps's doctrine is an arresting example of the utopias inspired by the early Rousseau. Though not too well known, Deschamps's system has the attraction of being metaphysically complete and absolute.

Our laws rein in our natural drives and constantly oppose them; but the drives, seeking to go their own way, rise in revolt. The result is a state of violence. We are in perpetual contradiction with ourselves and with one another. We are always suspicious, masked, pained. We go about fearing our own kind, and we end up doing them harm either to avenge what they have done to us or to parry what they may do to us. Desire, frustration, pointless aggression against imaginary threats poison our lives. If this moral sickness is displayed by the side of psychic health, who would not prefer the new state of morality to the old? It does not matter whether a man is a prince or a peasant, the condition of the laws today holds him in its grip. Men are like galleyslaves under the rod of master-kings. But, adds Deschamps, anticipating the reflections of the aged Diderot and Hegel, in many respects the master-kings march under the rod of their own subjects, on whom they are dependent. Man could arrive at such analytic reflections and entertain the possibility of an optimal *état social* only after having experienced the most extreme tribulations. The savage on first coming into the state of society could no more have felt the social sickness than a newborn babe.

Deschamps addressed himself with fervor to the literate philosophes who were his fellow sufferers, exhorting them to heed his counsel and to accept a system of perfect unity over the whole face of the earth with men leading totally communal lives, mutually strengthened, and, he added as if in after-thought, "against all the other species." No one more or less happy than an-other was the only psychic state in which one could enjoy happiness without fear of another. No envy and no jealousy. No more of the vices that domesti-cated animals contract among men. "It is enough to replace moral inequality and property with moral equality and the community of goods to efface all the moral vices that reign over humanity."[4]

Men struggle to acquire knowledge of all things in heaven and on earth. With a felicitous admixture of Pascal and Rousseau, Deschamps condemns the frantic quest for more and more things as an evasion, a vain attempt to get outside of our suffering selves, while inside there is chaos, a mass of warring ideas and interests that never leave us at peace. That man had always sought tranquillity Deschamps proved from the myths of the golden age, paradise, the age of Astrea, pastoral literature, all of which he interpreted as psychologically authentic documents that illuminated human yearning under the present cor-rupt state of the laws. The future state of morality would be far simpler. It would be denuded of the flowery paraphernalia of paradisaical fantasies.

For Deschamps the difference between appearance and reality is nowhere more stark than in our (and by "our" he means the upper-class intellectuals for whom he is writing) view of the lower classes. We treat them roughly and think we are better off than they are; actually we suffer psychically far more than they do. And they have far less need of the *état de moeurs,* the ideal state, than we do. Deschamps is the self-conscious apostle to the tortured intellec-tual. Cast off your psychic woes in the only way possible, by establishing an order without property and moral inequality. When Deschamps finally got around to it, he unveiled the particularities of his utopia, one that would hardly have appeased the needs of the guests at the Baron d'Holbach's dinner table, despite Diderot's fleeting enthusiasm for Deschamps's world without *meum* and *tuum.* Deschamps envisaged a society divided into communal groups where all men and women would live together in one hut, work together at simple tasks, eat vegetarian food together, and sleep together in one big bed of straw. No books, no writing, no art—all that would be burned. The example of fathers would be sufficient teaching for children. There would be no *hommes cultivés* to live parasitically off the poor. The anti-intellectualism of Rousseau is driven to its ultimate conclusion by Deschamps, even as de Sade in his black utopia drew Rousseau's longing for heightened passionate sensibility to its ex-treme end.[5]

Deschamps's *état de moeurs* provides a happy physical existence. In a veritable prefiguration, or caricature, of Marx's *Gotha Program Critique,* he expressly condemns the separation of mental and physical labor, which he avoids by abolishing intellectuals, and he rules out the specialization of physical labor by having workers pass from one simple task to another. Beyond a few iron uten-sils no metals are necessary. Work is indistinguishable from pleasure or amuse-ment. There are no factitious entertainments, only satisfaction of *les vrais besoins de l'homme.* Groups freely joined in labor and love cooperate with one another, but, unlike Rousseau's *monde idéal,* Deschamps's is a low-keyed eu-psychia, without passions, without distinctions between men and women, without outbursts of laughter or crying. Sexual appetites are appeased with no more ado than eating, drinking, sleeping. One day is as happy as the next.

Children belong to society and they learn to perform with their hands all necessary tasks, including elementary surgery. Mothers give freely of their milk to the young and the very old. Language becomes purified, simple, and stable, since there is no changing substance, intellectual or emotional, to which it has to respond. The members of this society have no need to study logic because they are natually logical. Truth is naked and requires no embellishments.

The utopian state has *douce sérénité, candeur naïve, simplicité aimable,* and at the end a *mort douce.* In passing, Deschamps drops a psychological observation that some geriatricians have recently made with greater pomposity—men usually die as they have lived, and in his ideal society they pass their years tranquilly. There is no mourning because there has been no great psychic investment in any individual.

It was the metaphysical underpinning of Deschamps's system that intrigued the philosopher Jean Wahl. The attraction that moves human beings toward their "principle," which is the whole and is an entity that is different from the sum of its parts, is of the same order as that which moves inanimate things to their center. The contrary force is the spirit of independence, individuation. Private possession of land and women has introduced the moral evil disrupting the natural tendency toward union and wholeness. Universal union is humanity's true principle. In a dialectical movement man is destined to pass stadially from the state of savage nature, through the social state, to the true system of the *état de moeurs,* or the truth. The principal evil of the present state of mankind lies in the laws, and eupsychia demands a condition without, or virtually without, laws. For Deschamps the existence of property in objects and women is the main reason for the proliferation of legislation. Abolish both forms of property and no laws will be required.

Deschamps tried hard to peddle his *vrai système* among the philosophes. Rousseau conducted a correspondence with him in 1761 and 1762 but refused to read the full text, since Deschamps could not guarantee that it would make him happier. Diderot saw Deschamps three or four times in 1769, talked his way through a few parties with him, wrote with some enthusiasm about the manuscript, and never thoroughly read it. D'Alembert said metaphysics was not his specialty. And Helvétius warned Deschamps to be cautious about publishing the system. M. de Voyer, Deschamps's sponsor, passed the manuscript off as his own, and for his pains got from Voltaire in 1770–1771 a grapeshot volley of complete skepticism about human nature and morals. Deschamps proved to be good litmus paper for testing the measure of the philosophes's commitments.

The philosophes were more amenable to the intellectual legacy of the Curé Meslier, but only because they missed its utopian constructs. Being wafted up into a state of communal utopia was clearly a professional hazard of members of the clergy who had lost their traditional faith. The Curé Meslier's testament of 1733 was first published in an extract in 1762; the *Bons sens,* imputed to Meslier, appeared in 1772 under the Baron d'Holbach's supervision, and the *Catéchisme du Curé Meslier* under the atheist Sylvain Maréchal's in 1789. These constituted the anticlerical part of his doctrine, which the philosophes welcomed in concert. Only in the nineteenth and twentieth centuries were the rest of Meslier's writings published.[6] There the social doctrines appear as an integral part of the attack on Christianity and are used to demonstrate that the Christian religion could not be true since it tolerated private property, inequality of status, and despotism.

Meslier was more violent than the monk of Saumur would ever be. The powerful of the earth should be strangled with the guts of priests because they live in pleasure while the people suffer. Meslier's post-strangulation utopia is a world in which men behave with justice and natural equity. In present society, on one side of the social barrier there reigns pride, on the other, hate. A few croak from overeating and the rest starve. One group lives in a sort of paradise, the others languish in a hell. Yet nature had made all men equal, and all had an equal right to live and walk upon the earth. If all property were divided equally, everybody could be happy. If marriage were dissolvable, no conjugal unions would be wretched. In the good future condition there will be a reasonable hierarchy and a limited subordination; but men of the same parish will live in common, directed by the wisest and the best.

Meslier would reach utopia through violent revolution; Deschamps would proceed through conversion alone. Meslier calls for tyrannicide and union against the enemies of mankind. His posthumous advice to his parishioners, the peasants whom he had always defended against their lords, included the hatching of secret plots, the concealment of food, the hiding of sons to keep them out of the army, and finally an uprising.

By comparison with the ascetic communal utopias of Deschamps and Meslier, who meant what they said and were all too ready for action programs, the Abbé Mably's views were only those of an eighteenth-century salon communist. For him equality was a feeling, a sentiment, associated with self-respect. He was essentially a Christian moralist who preached against luxury in the name of a moderate asceticism and as a preventive against the sin of arrogance. "I believe that equality, the modesty of our needs, preserves in my soul a tranquillity that opposes the birth and growth of passions."[7] Mably associated private property with some sort of fall, either from Eden or the state of nature; and the acquisition of a sense of absolute property could be related to corruption and to an absence of Christian *caritas*. Private property was tainted and had to be redeemed in a new order of community. But for Mably such notions remained Platonic ideals; nothing would have horrified him more than to be classed with incendiary revolutionists. He was castigating the men of "large-scale" industry and commerce, who cared nothing for community and a great deal about the free expression of their individuality in the marketplace. Mably's equality was something out of Plutarch's "Lycurgus" or out of Plato; it applied to no class and really meant no harm to anybody except the great bankers and entrepreneurs, who fell into the category of the conscienceless rich and could be castigated with impunity by the moralists.

Morelly the unknown one grounded his communal utopia, the *Code de la nature* (1755), on feelings of fraternity and humanity that would lead to a natural ascetic egalitarianism. The first stage of his historical triad consisted of an original paternal government of one or more families characterized by sentiments of affection and tenderness among communal brethren in imitation of the fathers—remarkably unlike Freud's primitive horde. The corruption of pristine communal feelings of sociability in the second stage of mankind came as a consequence of the multiplication of families and migrations. To inaugurate the third stage Morelly prescribed a reconstitution of agricultural communes and the imposition of tough sumptuary laws that would allow communal feelings to be revived. There would be rational work rules, strictly regulated conjugal relations, severe punishments for crime, all to reanimate the first natural law of sociability. For Morelly, more than the necessary would endanger equality, lead to the vice of *luxuria,* and destroy fellow feeling, which was the heart of his utopia. Marx liked to quote Morelly on the barrenness of family life based on property arrangements, and on the atrophy of the affections under the system of private ownership. Abolish property and the family would flourish in natural affection again. Morelly's *Code de la nature* enjoyed a certain notoriety in the eighteenth century because it was in print and was attributed to Diderot, while much of Meslier and all of Deschamps languished in manuscript. Once Morelly was picked up by Babeuf he became a catalyst of revolutionary action.

Despite superficial resemblances to the ideas of Plato and More, the *Code de la nature* initiated a new utopian form, a detailed secular egalitarian constitution, ready-made for promulgation in an agrarian society. Harrington and most other seventeenth-century projectors had not espoused equality in economic terms, and the English radicals of the Civil War were still in the religious millenarian tradition. In the sixteenth and seventeenth centuries there had been egalitarian, direct-action utopians—Müntzer and the Anabaptists, Campanella, Winstanley—but their moment of fame or notoriety passed quickly. Morelly and other eighteenth-century utopians drafted concrete communist plans for future implementation that had offspring. Morelly really expected to see his code of laws adopted, and it is known to have exerted a powerful influence upon Babeuf's Conspiracy of the Equals. We are dealing here not with the egalitarian household economies of Thomas More's *Utopia,* which retain a certain individual autonomy, but with the blueprint of a full-fledged communist society and a demand for the immediate institution of equality in all things.

In the pre-Revolutionary period there were other pleas for equalizing possessions and restraining the acquisition of private property that can readily be misconstrued if pulled out of context. A philosophical position in favor of community and equality would not necessarily bring down a death blow from either ecclesiastical or royal censors. Such ideas had been espoused by the Fathers and Doctors of the Church, and the unbridled acquisition and use of private property still remained under a cloud even in the eighteenth century. Avarice and gluttony had been condemned for too many centuries and the communal obligations of Christians had been preached with too much vigor to make the abstract ideas of community and equality pejorative in themselves. There was also authoritative literary support for these conceptions among the lawgivers of antiquity—Pythagoras, Lycurgus, Plato—whom educated men revered. Those communist theorists who had not broken with the ecclesiastical establishment—such as the Abbé Mably—and had presented their views in the form of dialogues with an antique mise-en-scène, or those identified with the small-town artisan world like Jean-Jacques, could inveigh against the usurpations of the rich and bewail the sufferings of the poor without any revolutionary intent. They were merely opposed to unchecked private enterprise, as were state absolutists and mercantilists.

But a gulf separates the communism of Mably, Morelly, Dom Deschamps, or the utopians who depict communal holdings in lush tropical islands of the South Seas, where food is for the asking anyway, from the conspiracy of Babeuf, hatched during the French Revolution. This is not to say that the run-of-the-mill, pre-Revolutionary theoretical treatises were stillborn. The idealization of community and equality fed Babeuf, Blanqui, and even Marx with arguments rationalistic and emotional—though Marx was never as tolerant of these eighteenth-century fancies as Engels. The revolutionaries from Babeuf on meant it literally when they demanded absolute equality and community. This was not the first time that abstract concepts of one generation—academic discourses on the origin of inequality and the like—were seized upon in a completely different spirit by the next.

Despite a current vogue for the minor egalitarian utopians of the eighteenth century, who have come to play an exaggerated role among Eastern and Central European and, to a lesser degree, French, historians in antiquarian search of communist "origins," it is still Jean-Jacques Rousseau who looms as the towering utopian figure of the age. Only he conjured up a state of utopian consciousness that, thanks to the magnificence of the language in which it was clothed and the vital emotional resources it drew upon, became an intoxicating element in all modern mass movements calling for the annihilation of ego-wills and their merging into a powerful undifferentiated whole. In the creation of a revolutionary rhetoric that moves men's souls the quantity of curious pamphleteers is not transformed into quality. In this realm Jean-Jacques reigns in solitary splendor. And nowhere is his direct impact more forcefully illustrated than in the visions of his two fanatical disciples who lost their heads during the Revolution, Saint-Just and Babeuf.

These were men of sentiment who had become committed in their teens to Jean-Jacques's revolution of virtue. Under a new order men would be forced to be virtuous—by Saint-Just, through "republican institutions," by Babeuf, through egalitarian economic and social practice. One would limit property to thirty French acres per person, the other would establish absolute communism in all things. In both there is a goodly dose of suspicion against men of esprit. Saint-Just considers them tricky sophists who would oust innocent virtue; Babeuf fears their superiority as a threat to real equality. Saint-Just's exaltation of the inner voice of conscience over reason springs right out of the homily of the Vicar of Savoy in *La Nouvelle Héloïse:* "I do not like newfangled words; I recognize only what is 'juste' and 'injuste.' Such words are readily understood by the consciences of all men. Further definitions must be tried by conscience alone. 'Esprit' is a sophist that leads the virtues to the scaffold."[8]

Despite glaring differences in their conceptions of equality, Babeuf and Saint-Just have much in common. Both represent the revolutionary utopias of the little men before the industrial revolution. Their ideal images are Spartan and republican Roman. The Revolution, which suddenly accelerated the tempo of existence, brought young men into positions of prominence, where they had a chance to give voice to their utopias. When the Revolutionary leaders were still adolescents, Voltaire and Rousseau, Diderot and d'Alembert had already died. Saint-Just and Babeuf were among those who clamored for "utopia now"—they were no philosophes—and both were cut down at an early age.

Through Terror to Egalitarian Virtue: Saint-Just

Saint-Just, a member of the Convention at the age of twenty-four, was guillotined along with Robespierre two years later, in July 1794, after a brief moment of triumph during which he attempted to impose a Jacobin utopian model on France. A present-day historian of the Revolution, Albert Soboul, writes of him as one of the major political intelligences in history and dwells on his "serene vigor," a somewhat hyperbolic assessment, but he is an interesting type case. In 1952 the publication of Saint-Just's *Fragments sur les institutions républicaines,* a notebook, focused new light on the raw materials for his utopia. They are stream-of-consciousness reflections jotted down during odd moments between proclamations of terror. Liberties had been taken with the original manuscript in a prior edition of 1800, where references to men and events of the Revolution had been excised, and the whole had been tinted to resemble a remote, timeless utopia in the classical manner. By contrast, the fragments now have something of the appeal of a painter's sketches—they are spontaneous and immediate and capture the fugitive moment.

Both Saint-Just and Babeuf were the sons of fantasts, men given to inventing for themselves heroic and aristocratic pasts. Saint-Just, born in the Nivernais in 1767, came of a line of farmers and notaries; his aging father had concocted an aristocratic name, Louis-Jean de Saint-Just de Richebourg. A year after the son, Louis-Antoine-Léon, was born, his parents left him in charge of a nurse and an old parish priest. By the time the parents returned he was four, a child given to violent outbursts of temper. His father died, and the task of raising the boy was left to his mother, who utterly failed to cope with him. As an adolescent, the future ascetic revolutionary aped aristocrats in dress and extravagance whenever he could get hold of the money. He was handsome, and he passed himself off as the Chevalier Léonard-Florelle de Saint-Just de Richebourg. In the course of a protracted struggle with his mother he ran away with the family silver and jewels. He suffered from agonizing headaches, consulted doctors, wrote distracted letters to his mother in their name imploring her forgiveness and pleading for help.

His mother had him imprisoned in the Châtelet in order to persuade him to mend his evil ways. After his release he ended in Rheims, where he studied law and soaked up revolutionary doctrines; Rousseau was his master. Saint-Just's eloquence made him the center of an admiring circle of friends. In 1789 his two-volume epic, *Organt, poëme en vingt chants,* was published in Paris with the place-name "Au Vatican." In uninspired doggerel, it sang of the adventures of the bastard son of the Archbishop of Senlis. Its licentious episodes are a discordant note in the career of the future high-priest of virtue.

The little boy who had been abandoned by his wicked mother found refuge in *la patrie:* He became a tribune of the Revolution. Saint-Just's personality perplexed contemporaries: In private, he was courteous and sometimes merry; in public, he spoke laconically and with chilling disdain. He had learned to conceal his emotions beneath a rigid, impassive exterior. The arrogant and ruthless revolutionary proved to be an effective administrator when delegated to handle military affairs. Friends and enemies alike testify to his erect bearing and the extraordinary beauty—somewhat effeminate—of his face. This was the archangel of the Jacobin Terror and its utopian.

Saint-Just's ideal society as it evolves in the *Institutions républicaines* would be a polity composed of peasants, artisans, and a few shopkeepers—a mirror of eighteenth-century France—after the heads of banking, commerce, industry, the church, and the aristocracy had been lopped off. This was presumably what ordinary people wanted. Throw the great out of all government posts, freeze the prices of all products of primary necessity, set the wages of labor and the allowable profits forever, and men will be virtuous and contented. Small holdings of private property, the key to the lives of the people, have their justification in the satisfaction of simple physical needs; when prices rise to levels higher than those that seven-eighths of the population can pay, maxima must be established by law. The republic provides everyone with the means of subsistence in quantities sufficient for living, but not for superfluous luxuries.

This Jacobin utopia of the little people makes no dogmatic demand for a communal system. The Jacobin sansculottes of Paris, who had few "proletarians" among them—their ranks being filled with shopkeepers, artisans, and members of the poorer professions—were against what would later become "capitalism" and the great bourgeoisie, but they were not opposed to individual property because most of them had a bit of it. The Jacobins pleaded only that their modest possessions be preserved from the gluttony of the big fish that were threatening to devour them. They looked upward with resentment, not downward upon those who had nothing at all. Let everyone have a modicum of property, instill in the young ineradicable virtues, and a patriotic republic composed of men of the same temper and same communal will would be assured.

Toward the great ones who could manipulate wages and prices Saint-Just vowed implacable enmity, because they were identified with the international bankers and aristocrats who had no loyalty to the France of the little fellows with something to defend, citizens whose parcel of property was a part of their persons. The Jacobin conception of equality meant more or less equality achieved through radical political measures that killed off the engrossers and the aristocrats. The ideal was traditionalist. These Frenchmen of the Revolutionary period wanted what they thought was a return to a society of shopkeepers, master artisans, and their journeymen, living in harmony with small landholders who tilled their own soil—the good society that would remain forever after the powerful aristocrats, rapacious financiers, and greedy merchants had been destroyed. Saint-Just was in favor of dividing up the large holdings that his ancestors, as *régisseurs du château,* had administered for absentee nobles. An honest country *manoeuvrier* needed land, but no more than the thirty French acres that Saint-Just would allow each man in his ideal republic.

This disciple of Rousseau was no atheistic materialist; his elder brother in virtue, Robespierre, had delivered himself of an attack against the godless Encyclopedists, and both of them worshiped the Supreme Being. Saint-Just had no use for grand historical conceptions. Once the large estates of the aristocrats had been broken up, it would be possible, through political institutions, to settle this world of shopkeeper-artisans and small landowners into a fixed position for all time. Saint-Just could write of "immortal institutions" that would be impervious to the intrigues of factions. His tactic was the most simplistic and traditional of utopian devices, "to enchain crime with institutions."[9]

The rationalist Encyclopedists, when they concerned themselves with economic problems, favored greater production and expansive industry, a very different social ideal, along with science and advanced technology—attributes of a dynamic society. Saint-Just and Robespierre were among the last of the great static utopians of calm felicity, perhaps their caricature. Fénelon's agrarian utopia differs from Saint-Just's in placing a benign hierarchy on top of the small landowner; but the prevailing temper is similar, and the ideal remains a classic agrarian idyll of individual small producers. Saint-Just and Robespierre departed from many of their predecessors principally in believing that this idyll could be achieved speedily and through violent means. In this respect they resemble in spirit the ancient Judeo-Christian writers who foretold the apocalypse—widespread destruction followed by an eternal Sabbath.

The militancy inherent in Saint-Just's *Republican Institutions* is that of a class beleaguered on all sides by hostile forces while it is attempting to freeze history. Opposed both to egalitarian communists and to the great bourgeois and aristocrats, it has to fight against the old and the new men of power in order to achieve a stable, everlasting society of virtuous artisans, shopkeepers, and small landowners. The Rousseauan formula has become stereotyped in Saint-Just's notes: "You know well enough that man is not born wicked; it is oppression that is wicked."[10] The philosophes, who saw themselves as members of an international republic of virtue, were in their own minds free of the bonds of authority, though they were occasionally victims of tyrannical oppression. Saint-Just and Babeuf aimed to make their utopias a universal reality, for they were of the next generation. They had taken Rousseau at his word, but they would add a new ingredient: Constrain men to be virtuous by wielding instruments of terror through a committee of public safety or a revolutionary committee with dictatorial powers, and the triumphant reign of virtue would be inevitable. Both young men were destroyed; one had tasted blood, the other never got beyond threats to purge society of its enemies.

Cold, objective, impersonal justice was what Saint-Just demanded. Laws and morals ingrained into mankind would rule, not men. Saint-Just combined his Montesquieu with his Rousseau: The *moeurs* determine the laws, therefore internalize the laws so that they become *moeurs,* by force if necessary. Laws that do not correspond to *moeurs* are meaningless. First establish republican institutions, then engrave virtuous laws and customs in the consciences of men and the constitution will be immune to the normal vicissitudes of empires. Montesquieu and Rousseau still wrote with a world-historical assumption that decline was unavoidable and the wise legislator, like the skillful doctor, at most could only stave off decay. After the death of the philosophes, Saint-Just and Babeuf lived in the illusion of a state impervious to time and corruption, under an ideal of unchanging or virtually unchanging laws.

The republic of virtue could not be achieved by the mere proclamation of what was right; this was the awesome lesson of Saint-Just's revolutionary experience. There had to be an energizing force to make a revolution, yet order had to be maintained and goals established for all time. Unperturbed by these seemingly contradictory psychological requirements for the realization of utopia, Saint-Just resorted to analogy. "One can impose order on a fiery, vibrant city, even as nature does on a racehorse (*coursier*) and on a volcano."[11] The desired "spirit" of his ideal society was an admixture of contrary tempers: He would give the French people "manners" that were at once "gentle, energetic, sensitive, and implacable against tyranny and injustice."[12] The day he was convinced that this was impossible he would stab himself.

Saint-Just is one of the first theoreticians of terror as the necessary path to utopia if any obstacles should stand in the way of a republic that has virtue as its guiding principle. The concept has been traced back to Marat as early as 1770, but the dubious honor of introducing it into the general political vocabulary of modern times belongs to Saint-Just and Robespierre working in tandem. "What do they want," Saint-Just asks with his brutal platitudinous rhetoric, "those who want neither virtue nor terror? Force does not make a thing either reasonable or right. But it is perhaps impossible to do without it, in order to make right and reason respected."[13] But at other times in the *fatras* of contrarieties that fill his notebooks there is an apparent awareness of the futility of terror, even an outburst of despair. "The Revolution is congealed. All principles have been weakened. All you have left are red caps borne by intrigue. The exercise of terror has jaded crime as strong drink jades the palate."[14] The secular inquisitor, without the sustenance of an immanent God, has his moments of doubt.

The *Institutions républicaines* outlines the educational plan for a Jacobin utopia with circumstantial detail, most of it old and hackneyed, worn-out bits from the seventeenth and eighteenth centuries. If anything, it preaches a harder primitivism than most of its predecessors. Young blades like Saint-Just and Restif, who, after sowing their wild oats, glimpsed abstract virtue, are characteristically prodigal with stringent measures for implanting morality in future generations. Saint-Just decrees that from the ages of five to sixteen boys should live in community away from their parents, their diet limited to fruit, roots, milk products, bread, and water, while girls are raised at home. Boys have thus had only five years with their parents before they are surrendered to *la patrie*. Free from cruel wicked mothers like his own, the boys of future generations will be nurtured by the motherland itself. From fifteen to twenty-one they receive apprentice training on the job, but not from their fathers. Their education is intended to create Spartan mentalities that will activate their robust bodies. They are taught brevity and simplicity of speech. Odes and epics are used to inspire them, but there are no school prizes for rhetoric and no declamations. As children they form battalions that are prototypes of Fourier's *petites hordes* and armies of adolescents, utopian mechanisms with a long future history in writers as varied as Wilhelm Weitling and Edward Bellamy. Everyone dresses alike during the educational process; from sixteen to twenty-one all wear the worker's costume, from twenty-one to twenty-five, the soldier's uniform. Thereafter they labor at honest artisan and agricultural occupations.

Saint-Just's eulogy of the moral virtues of hard labor is all the more affecting because he never engaged in any. In the persistent Morean tradition, he is antagonistic to a commercial economy and to money as generating all the evils of society—the former spendthrift has forsaken his old ways, at least in print. Historically and politically one tends to make much of the differences between the Jacobin private-holding utopia of Saint-Just and the communism of Babeuf, but both are ascetic and static. "Everyone must work and they must respect one another," Saint-Just laid down in his commandments. "If everyone works, abundance will flow again. We will need less money. Vice will disappear . . . When Rome lost its taste for work and lived on the tribute of the world it lost its liberty."[15] The economic principle is simple. "We ought to have neither rich nor poor."[16]

The political structure is permeated by a Rousseauan imperative of the need for absolute centralized power; the federalism of the Girondins is the great destructive bogey. "There is federalism in fact, even though a government may be united in theory, if each city, each commune can isolate itself out of self-interest. What happens is that each commune then keeps its products on its own territory and all goods are consumed on the spot. The goal of a government opposed to federalism is not unity for the sake of the government, but for the sake of the people. We must therefore keep people from isolating themselves in fact."[17] Jacobin authoritarian centralism, however, is combined with an idealization of the nuclear family as the source of national strength, despite the fact that boys are outside the family jurisdiction from five to twenty-five. "The liberty of the people resides in its private life. Do not disturb it," he admonishes.[18]

Saint-Just's republican utopia ends up as a collection of formulas abstracted from Jean-Jacques, with the elimination of any intermediary loyalties between the family at one end and *la patrie* at the other. Since this young lawgiver had nothing of Jean-Jacques's passionate style, he was feeble in cementing relations among producing families through the agency of "affections" and the natural need for mutual exchange. These were the benign catchwords on which the idea and the reality of terror, "but of necessity," were grafted.

The Manifesto of the Equals

Gracchus Babeuf's father, Claude, was a retired officer of the Austrian army, in which he had served for many years as a soldier of fortune. In 1742 he managed to get a pardon for his earlier desertion from the army of the French King, and thereafter he eked out a miserable existence as an employee in an office for collecting the salt tax. A man touched with mythomania, he wove tales around his service abroad and the birth of a son, François Noël, in 1760. In his turn the son, Gracchus Babeuf—the name he bestowed upon himself when he was reborn a revolutionary—embroidered equally extravagant fantasies in telling about his origins to his own beloved son Robert, later renamed Emile in honor of Rousseau. After Gracchus' execution Emile continued to embellish the Babeuf legend, so that in the end an epic hero was created. Was Gracchus Babeuf originally named Noël to commemorate his birth on Christmas Day, or was he really born on November 23, as the baptismal record states? Had his father been a major in the Austrian army and tutor to the future Emperor Leopold, who in gratitude for his ministrations later offered Gracchus a high post, which the young republican, already an enemy of kings under the ancien régime, contemptuously rejected? Was the father a kindly educator who himself taught his son the rudiments of Latin, German, and mathematics, or did he beat the lad with some regularity to instill knowledge and virtue into him as a rough soldier might? Was Gracchus' mother a respectable female companion to a country noblewoman or was she a mere servant girl? Of Gracchus Babeuf's tenderness to his own wife and many children there is a record in family letters and in correspondence with the famous Dubois de Fosseux, secretary of the Arras Academy, who guided young Babeuf before the Revolution. Later, Babeuf favored the execution of the King and was a friend of Marat; but there is no evidence that he was one of the more bloodthirsty creatures whom the Revolution allowed to fulfill their dreams of violence and destruction.

As a child, François Noël had been something of a prodigy and had basked in the praises of those about him. The crisis of adolescence had brought an outburst against the authority of a father over seventy: The young Babeuf threw away his books and refused to touch a pen. Using the revolutionary language that was already in the making, in retrospect he saw himself living in a "state of anarchy." Apparently one still could not trifle with the rule of a truculent soldier grown old, and François Noël was kicked out of the house.

Left on his own, he became a ditchdigger for the construction of the Picardy canal, a job that quickly drove him to find a less onerous way of earning a living. Since he was proficient at reading and writing, clerking was a possibility, and he secured a place with one Hullin de Flixécourt, near Abbeville, who taught him to be a *feudiste,* a title searcher for local aristocrats who sought to rediscover and reinstitute feudal dues that over the years had fallen into desuetude. By twenty-eight he had already internalized the vocabulary and imagery of Jean-Jacques's writings: In an autobiographical fragment he could look back at his expanding "little self-love," not a pejorative phrase in Rousseau's lexicon, when men admired his skill in arranging the papers of the Ferme de Saint-Quentin even though he was an autodidact. Freed from a domineering father, he fell under the rule of new masters who exercised their power more subtly by aiming darts at his tender soul. He was treated as an underling. Babeuf recorded humiliating incidents, when he, a professional, a feudiste, a clerk, a correspondent of the secretary of the Arras Academy, had to take his meals with the servants in the houses of the petty nobles who engaged him. The Conspirator of the Equals was born during one of these traumatic occasions. The final wound was perhaps inflicted by the tone of his employer's voice or the disdain in a grimace. The humiliated one was proud. He knew that he was worth more than the aristocratic dotards whose false titles he examined and the lazy monks whose ecclesiastical rights he was paid to defend.

Babeuf's rebellion was not a continuous attack on the regime; during one period in the 1780s there was a bare possibility that the feudiste could be assimilated into the existing order. As learned provincial academies proliferated in eighteenth-century France, it became allowable to entertain all manner of projects for the good of mankind, for Frenchmen were living in the reign of Louis the Just. Babeuf's experience was not unique. The respectable academies were the incubators of revolutionaries. Who could tell whether a young man would grow into a monster or a victim of the Revolution after being fed books and verse and scientific projects by a hard-working rich farmer and local notable serving voluntarily as secretary of a provincial academy that was building up a network of correspondents? Who could identify the future leaders in this seemingly innocent intellectual pastime? Robespierre presented a few innocuous papers to the Academy of Arras when he was a lawyer practicing there; and Babeuf corresponded assiduously with its permanent secretary. The ties of the minor notable of Arras, Dubois de Fosseux, and Babeuf, the impoverished feudiste of Roye who never saw him, were developed in more than a hundred letters that cover the whole range of concerns among men of the Enlightenment, before its feeble light was blotted out by the blazing red sun of the Revolution. Despite age differences, the pen-friends corrected each other's grammar, haggled about proper usage, discussed agricultural projects, debated abstract moral questions as equals. Should the Academy of Arras permit the public reading of certain poems at the risk of causing sensitive ladies invited to attend the sessions to swoon? Should the apathetic man who escaped the ravages of the passions be preferred to the man of sensibility who was battered by the assaults of violent emotions?

In the mid-1780s utopian projects were springing up on all sides, and no subject was prohibited as long as its terms were abstract enough. Megalomaniacs mingled with practical projectors and the proposals of both were considered without discrimination. The language of the times had begun to fall into set formulas that could be sprinkled over any piece of writing: prejudices, feelings of humanity, the philosophical century, reason, happiness, sensibility, betterment. There were plans for agricultural reform and limitation of the size of landholdings; "systems" sprouted overnight, foolproof methods for determining the worth of all things and reducing them to values mathematically calculated. Babeuf added his mite to the flood. He boldly suggested a discussion of the abstract possibilities of an egalitarian system, couching his ideas in long-winded philosophical periods that in seven years would be totally transformed, chopped up into the staccato phrases and slogans of the *Tribun du Peuple.*

Dubois de Fosseux was Babeuf's philosophical father; the rough old soldier who was his biological father was replaced by the gentle, loving secretary who nourished him with books, deferred to his opinions, asked for his judgments. Though Babeuf married and sired children, he retained something of the adolescent about him. He wished to read everything, to know everything, to encompass the whole world. In March 1787 Dubois and Babeuf exchanged notes on grand plans of reformation, and on the nineteenth, Dubois sent him the outline of a work whose prospectus bore the promising title "L'Avant-coureur du changement du monde entier par l'aisance, la bonne éducation et la prospérité générale de tous les hommes, ou prospectus d'un mémoire patriotique sur les causes de la grande misère qui existe partout et sur les moyens de l'extirper radicalement." It appears to have been written by one Claude-Boniface Collignon of Orleans and ultimately appeared with the name of Louis-Pierre Couret de Villeneuve of Orleans as editor. Was this the spark that set Babeuf aflame, or was it Morelly's *Code de la nature,* the more accepted, traditional inspiration of Babeuf's conspiracy?

Babeuf continued his duties as a feudiste with growing repugnance until the day when he joined in the burning of the iniquitous records in the castle that had been the source of his livelihood. From an obsequious servant of local aristocrats he became one of the more vocal Picard proponents of a popular movement against the payment of taxes—first on liquor, then on anything—a spokesman for popular causes who drafted petitions of protest and hawked incendiary pamphlets. During the early years of the Revolution, he oscillated between Paris and the provinces, in search of a livelihood and justice for the persecuted revolutionaries. A few days after the Bastille was stormed he was in Paris, but his family back home could not live on the feeble prospect that he would collect some arrears on the debts the vanishing nobles owed him for establishing their rights to augmented feudal dues, services rendered that had now lost their meaning. Forced back into the provinces, away from the grand stage of the Revolution, Babeuf grasped every opportunity to become the local revolutionary hero. The inner man was not a glib egalitarian, whatever his public utterances might be. His view of the world recognized two types of people, the Roman heroes and the "multitude." From the outset of his political career he felt a pathos of distance between himself and the masses who had "prejudices," who had to be won over, conquered, led. The idea of the dictatorship of a revolutionary elite was born early in his career, long before the Conspiracy; it was already implicit in the address of the patriots of Roye that he drafted in March of 1790. A firebrand who terrified the more respectable revolutionary notables and even defied emissaries from Paris, he ultimately became their Mirabeau, the locals said.

In Roye, where the march of the Revolution was slower-paced than in Paris, Babeuf earned the hatred of those who had managed to acclimate themselves to the Revolution, and they had him imprisoned as an incendiary. After he was freed, as the more ardent patriots became appreciated the friends of liberty appointed him a minor official to help direct the sale of confiscated national properties, until a charge of collusion with purchasers was leveled against him. He pleaded an inadvertent mistake, but the penalty meted out this time by the judge was severe—twenty years in prison and a loss of civil rights. The social changes in the provinces during the early years of the Revolution were less dramatic than in Paris sections, and sometimes the old local notables simply moved into new Revolutionary offices, or a few new faces appeared, manipulated by the same powerful figures in the background. Babeuf's enemies were legion, a multitude of "perverse ones"; they poisoned his existence, kept him in a continual state of agitation. He managed to evade the arm of the law and was swallowed up in the turmoil of Paris, getting a job in a bureau that supervised the provisioning of the city through the intercession of the atheist Sylvain Maréchal, who would later be the actual author of *The Manifesto of the Equals*. But the provincial administrators tracked him down and had him jailed once again. He won his liberty at last in July 1794, through the good offices of Maréchal and a prosecutor by the name of Polycarpe Pottofeux, an ardent Jacobin who refused to abet the reactionaries' persecution of a patriot.

There are enraged ones eternally possessed who never have moments of self-revelation. Babeuf is not among them. He was always introspecting and telling about himself, sometimes too much, obfuscating with the sheer profusion of the disclosures. The Rousseau who dominated his thought was not the Rousseau of the abstract political theory, the Rousseau who could reason and argue with virtuosity in classical terms, but the Rousseau of the *Discourses*, who was ferocious in his sense of independence, who had discovered the self and dared talk about it without shame. Like Rousseau, Babeuf wrote his *Confessions*, though they were rather pallid and thin by comparison. He composed long letters about his father, wrote autobiographical sketches, narrated his life before the High Court of Vendôme that tried him. This great "conspirator" was incredibly outspoken. In his newspaper, the *Tribun du Peuple*, he described the frenzy with which he composed his articles and the intricate ritual he had evolved to galvanize himself into a proper state of excitement. He was quite

capable of unburdening himself to total strangers and analyzing his most intimate feelings to a man he had never seen face to face. There was a certain
naiveté, an ingenuousness, about him. And after all, it was not much of a conspiracy, that plot hatched in the Café des Bains-Chinois (not far from the Directory's intelligence bureau and the police station) with a police agent in constant attendance.

Babeuf hated the existing social order, whose humiliations he had endured
as a clerk, and it was now permissible to hate vehemently, to give utterance to
feelings that had been choked up. The Revolution encouraged men who had
been silenced by fathers and masters and superiors to shout at the tops of their
lungs. Babeuf, who had once sorted the papers of the aristocrats, had gone
back to the documents and found the real origins of their possessions, those
feudal "rights" that they were bent on restoring. He could reveal the truth
about their usurpations, print pamphlets and penny newspapers that exposed
and denounced them, turn the world topsy-turvy, as he wrote in his autobiography,[19] raise the lowly to the clouds, and care nothing about the great ones.

With the outbreak of the Revolution, Babeuf found himself. He made his
debut as a publicist with a brochure proposing fiscal reform to the government
(1790). By August 20, 1791, he knew that he was good for nothing else but
revolutionary action. The philosophical ideas with which he had played as a
young man were no longer adequate. He was still uncertain of his way, but he
understood the process that was seething within him. He was surprised to find
that he had become unfit for anything but journalism (*publicisme*) and matters
related to legislation—meditation on the true principles of what the laws
should be and their implementation. Before the Revolution Babeuf had dabbled in pure theory; as the Revolution progressed, he became ever more deeply
involved in action. Not long before the Conspiracy of the Equals was crushed,
his journal *Le Tribun du Peuple* called for a new apocalypse: "All evils have
reached their peak. Things cannot get worse. A cure can come about only
through a total upheaval!!! Let confusion reign! Let all the elements be confounded and entangled, let them clash with one another! May everything return to a primitive chaos, and out of the chaos may a new, regenerated world
be born."[20]

When Babeuf had become head of the Directory of the District of Montdi-
dier he laid before his compatriots a formal statement of his conception of the
office. This was not mere verbiage. He had found his "idea" where Rousseau
would have directed him, in the depths of his soul. He would be incorruptible,
just, impartial; he would not behave toward his fellow citizens with the arrogance of a ci-devant magistrate. No doffing of caps before *him!* Citizens were
expected to wear the *bonnet rouge* when they visited the administration building, and not to remove it in the presence of officials.[21] No one, not even a
conqueror of the Bastille, could outdo him in patriotic fervor from the very
first day of the Revolution. Viewed in the light of his self-image as the incorruptible one, the charge of venality in office must have been psychically
devastating.

The idea of equality as one of the central concepts of the Western utopia was
a long time aborning. In the utopias of the Stoics and the early Christians, satisfaction of the need for equality in and of itself had begun to assume an ever
more prominent position. The Platonic struggle with evil in the soul was in-

corporated, but that very contest made all men relatively equal, and the Christians held forth the promise of paradise for the victors at the end of the days. The longing for calm felicity was recognized, but its attainment often had to be postponed until the saved were gathered into the heavenly city. There are many periods in Roman and Christian history, however, when the utopian passion for *worldly* equality among all men erupted in violent outbursts: the uprising of the slaves under Spartacus, medieval peasant revolts, the egalitarian millenarianism of the later Middle Ages and of the Reformation in the Rhineland and Central Europe. The teaching of the brotherhood of man in primitive Christianity was literally interpreted and became a utopian text expressive of this need for equality. The promise of equal access to salvation for all mankind imparted an emotional intensity to Stoic philosophical reflections on universal brotherhood that firmly established equality as a utopian need in the Christian world, probably an ineradicable one in Western society.

After Thermidor, while hailing the end of the Terror, Babeuf violently attacked the government for its failure to deal with inflation and the widespread misery it entrained. A favorite song by his collaborator Sylvain Maréchal, "Dying of hunger, dying of cold," was chanted in the cafés of Paris, while Babeuf's journal demanded the abolition of private property and the institution of egalitarian communism. In 1796, together with his confederates Darthé and Buonarroti, he formed the Conspiracy of the Equals to overthrow the Directorate. When the plot was discovered and he was arrested, *The Manifesto of the Equals* was found among his papers. The *Manifesto* gave a revolutionary cast to Morelly's plan for agrarian communism in the *Code de la nature*. It stressed the equal need for food, which should be as free as sunshine and water. There was also a deliberate and momentous decision among the members of Babeuf's Conspiracy to reject equal, private, individual holdings, an institution of More's *Utopia,* in favor of communally held property as the only feasible way to enforce equality. For the Babouvists the social problem was simple: Inequality in the distribution of goods (production problems tended to be sidestepped) was the source of all evils in society. The utopia of the insurrectionary leaders revolved around one principle: The new order of things could never permit sumptuary inequality to secure a foothold. Since inequality was the prime evil, they reasoned, two alternative paths were open to them. The first led to the establishment of equal individual ownership, some variation of the agrarian law of the Gracchi or what they knew of Spartan equality from Plutarch, the formula of many agrarian utopias that posited equal division of the land. But the conspirators, though it is unlikely that they had read Hume's classical arguments against the feasibility of keeping individual holdings equal, opted for the other alternative, the establishment of the community of goods and works. Finding a precedent in ancient history, they believed that a system of this sort had once actually prevailed in France prior to the Roman conquest. They were aware of individualist proclivities, but, heedless of Montesquieu, were stubbornly determined to give Frenchmen new "customs" by changing the laws.

Though individual rights were recognized, the individual right to property was replaced by the right to an existence as fortunate as that of all other members of the body social. This was the zenith of egalitarian utopian thought. All men would not only have an equal right to life, liberty, and the *pursuit* of happiness; in the new rhetorical promise they would actually be guaranteed an existence as "fortunate" as that of their neighbors. The idea of responsibility insinuates itself: There is an equal obligation to be associated in communal works. The Babouvist utopia is still essentially agrarian, and its organizational problem is reduced to the administration of agricultural production on a cantonal basis, though the specialized work of artisans is appreciated as contributing to the good of the community—not unlike Thomas More's Utopia in this respect. The aim of work is to provide *surabondance,* great abundance, of those things that are necessary, in order to prevent shortages, as well as to produce those—and only those—amenities that are not prohibited by public custom. While Babeuf's optimum society guaranteed the full provision of necessities and countenanced a few superfluities, it frowned upon exotic and enervating luxuries.

Under no circumstances would the iron law of equality be broken. If anything was not divisible among all, it would be wholly denied to all. Equality required a continent, almost ascetic, community, in which shirkers would be severely punished. Absolute, really absolute, equality, immediately established, was the paramount human need, not in its vague French Revolutionary sense, which could be twisted linguistically in almost any economic or social direction, but in plain terms—one man should not have more of anything than another. If there is not enough to go round, abolish the thing itself, Babeuf insisted. This egalitarian communism was founded upon the idea of the virtual replication of needs, desires, and abilities among all citizens. Its intolerance of any distinctions was fierce. To be equal, not to suffer the pain of a superior's slights or power or authority—that was to set the tone of life, and all else was to be sacrificed to it. "We are equal, is it not so?" the *Manifesto* asked rhetorically. "Well, we henceforth intend to live and to die equal, just as we were born; we want real equality or death, that is what we need. And we shall have it, this *égalité réelle,* no matter what the price . . . Woe to anyone who shall offer resistance to so keen a desire . . . May all the arts be destroyed, as long as we have *égalité réelle.*"[22] The Babouvist dogma of immediate equality lived on in the popular French communist tradition that Buonarroti revived in the late 1820s and 1830s.

Thomas More in the *Utopia* had established a category of men specially endowed for the exclusive pursuit of intellectual activities; *The Manifesto of the Equals* announced that it would let all the arts and sciences perish if they endangered equality. The snobbishness and restrictiveness of the pre-Revolutionary academies, Rousseau's condemnation of the arts and sciences as the particular adornments of those who would exacerbate men's natural inequalities, confirmed an anti-intellectualist streak in egalitarians *à outrance* that harks back to the sixteenth century. Müntzer's populist egalitarianism had been bitter in its mockery of the engrossers of learning. And Winstanley in the seventeenth century had exhibited the same bias in his agrarian equality: The monopolizers of learning in the universities were on a plane with the usurpers of property. There was a deep-rooted mistrust of specialists trained in the art of government—a Platonic ideal—because they would have an inevitable penchant for exaggerating their services to society and thus would break the law of equality.

The Babouvist order expected to render labor as painless as possible. Though Babeuf had not yet arrived at Fourier's full-blown conception of "attractive labor," in some measure the attraction of pleasure was already associated with work and Babeuf dragged in a whole bag of motives, an admixture of egotist and communal passions, that would stimulate men to work in the future society of equals—love of country, the encouragement of habit, public approbation, the "attrait du plaisir." Work was no longer its own justification; it had a rationale outside the realm of Christian theology and original sin. The amount of work was not gauged by any mechanical standard such as fixed hours of labor. Duties were proportioned to a man's strength and the hardship of the task performed. As an incentive to the more robust to accept inequality in work obligations, which would benefit the weak, he introduced the reward of public gratitude.

Technology and science were prized less for themselves than as aids to the maintenance of equality. Buonarroti, writing in 1828 at a moment when Luddite machine-breaking had erupted in the textile centers of France, was aware that mechanization could create suffering and unemployment. As he recollected Babeuf's thought more than three decades later, in the system of community technology would be used to minimize the difference between the weak and the strong. Thus the Buonarroti of 1828, at least, was not a romantic revolutionary dogmatically opposed to science and technology as threats to equality. The problem of equal work clearly preoccupied him at that time. The system of egalitarian community would itself lead to better utilization of resources and to lightening the burdens of individual labor. It might be useful to divide work into two categories, light and heavy, and call upon every man for some of both. He also wished to consider in the assignment of jobs the diminution of strength with age. At one point Buonarroti set up as a criterion the "capacité du travaillant," about the same time that the Saint-Simonian slogan "De chacun selon ses capacités" was being formulated. His ascribing to Babeuf, who thought primarily in agrarian terms, conceptions related to embryonic French industrialization in the 1820s is probably anachronistic.

After Babeuf's Conspiracy had been successful, the whole of France was to become one administrative unit, because no village by itself could provide amply for the needs of its inhabitants. In the 1790s the memory of famine in one province and plenty in another was still vivid. Under the aegis of the Babouvist utopia, those who lived in less fertile areas would no longer be condemned to misery. The extension of the idea of community to the entire country would insure its impregnability and spread a feeling of happiness and fraternity among all the citizens. Buonarroti saw further advantages to community in breaking down localism by requiring all capable citizens to participate in the distribution network. There is an almost Saint-Simonian emphasis on the utility of multiplying the arteries of communication within the realm. Foreign commerce would remain a national enterprise in what was to be essentially a system of state communism.

According to Buonarroti's account, the conspirators realized that all Frenchmen had to be animated by great patriotic ardor if the system of equality in community was to operate successfully. What they had to offer was another version of the Jacobin "love of country" inculcated into the young through state education. The nation became the primal object of sentimental attachment, to which family affections and relationships were subordinated. The Babouvists dreamed of a "true fraternal union of all Frenchmen," an emotion-laden phrase that would come alive again in the nineteenth-century oratory of political leaders who abominated egalitarian communism. In the 1790s the plotters already lived in a fantasy of this national brotherly love: "This thought ravished our conspirators with its delights and was the soul of all their plans," Buonarroti recollected.[23]

The agrarian idyll of Babeuf drew its imagery from a variety of sources. Rousseau was omnipresent and so was Morelly; but Babeuf also remembered his Plutarch. According to Buonarroti, Lycurgus was seen as nearly reaching the goal of society fixed by nature.[24] And though the *Manifesto of the Equals* was drafted by the militant atheist Sylvain Maréchal, the moderate tone of life was set by the Archbishop of Cambrai's *Telemachus*. Tranquillity permeated men's souls, married couples were more loving, old age was unmarred by anxieties, children were always cared for. The antiurbanism of Jean-Jacques triumphed: "There will be no more capital city, no more large cities . . . those vast agglomerations destructive of morals and of people."[25] Simplicity prevailed in private life and architectural magnificence was restricted to a few public buildings. There was cleanliness without godliness. Everyone wore loose-flowing, healthful clothing and no one was ruled by frivolous fashion. There was a decent French national costume for everybody, and the only deviation from uniformity was color denoting age groups and occupations—a utopian stereotype inherited from Vairasse and Restif.

The conspirators were aware that the joys the egalitarian society could offer were not riotous; but the satisfactions of serenity and true happiness far outbalanced the depraved pleasures of a handful of corrupt usurpers. These wicked ones had to be brought around to more "reasonable opinions" either willingly or if need be by force.[26] Above all, softness and boredom had to be kept from gaining the upper hand. Only on rare occasions had the possibility of boredom in utopia reared its ugly head and gaping yawn, and it is surprising to find it even mentioned in the Babouvist temple of egalitarian virtue—though boredom does not linger long. There are approved ways of spending leisure hours—physical exercise, cultivation of the mind, educating the young, learning to use arms (France was still an embattled utopia), conducting military maneuvers, worship of an abstract Divinity, apotheosizing great men, participating in public games, arranging holiday decorations, perfecting the useful arts (there is no particular interest in abstract academic science), study of the laws, witnessing public deliberations. With all these laudable activities from which to choose, why should anyone be bored?

Like all traditional utopians, the Babouvists were conscious of the paramountcy of the educational process in ensuring the success of their system. The new values had to be so profoundly internalized that they would never be questioned. In his evocation of the spirit of Babeuf, Buonarroti eulogized the new paideia. "The masterpiece of the art of politics is to alter the human heart through education, example, persuasion, public opinion, and the attraction of pleasure in such a way that it will never be able to give birth to any other desires than those that tend to make society freer, happier, and more lasting."[27] In *Le Tribun du Peuple* (issue of 9 frimaire, an IV), Babeuf in a virtual paraphrase of passages from the *Discourse on Inequality* had warned the people of the perils of monopolized education, the real instrumentality of power in a ruling class. "Education is a monstrosity when it is unequal, when it is the exclusive patrimony of only a portion of the association. Then it becomes, in the hands of this portion, a hoard of weapons, a stock of arms of every type, with the aid of which the superior portion combats the other, which is totally disarmed, and as a consequence easily succeeds in strangling it, deceiving it, despoiling it, shackling it with the most humiliating chains."[28]

Buonarroti's reconstruction of what the conspirators planned for the period immediately after the triumph of their coup d'état became a manual for revolutionaries of the mid-nineteenth century. The concept of the revolutionary dictatorship of the proletariat, which Marx first made explicit in the *Gotha Program Critique* of 1875, owes much to these formulations. The Babouvist tactical advice, however, when read in an age of sophisticated guerrilla warfare, exudes a certain quaintness. "If things went badly, arrangements were made to obstruct the streets and to pour on the troops torrents of boiling water mixed with vitriol and a hail of rocks, tiles, slate, and bricks."[29] If the conspirators were victorious, there were preparations for the exercise of revolutionary justice in an orderly manner, not untouched by a spirit of forgiveness. As revolutionary vengeance goes, Babouvism was among the less bloody cults of mankind, at least in its prospectus. "The crime was evident; the punishment was death; a great example was necessary. Nevertheless we wanted this example to bear the mark of rigorous justice and of a profound feeling for the public good. It was decided that the people who had led the insurrection would hear a detailed and circumstantial report of the treachery of which they had been the victims and they would be invited to exempt from proscription those among the accused who had strayed in a pardonable manner from the simple morals of the people or those who had rendered to equality some signal service during the course of the insurrection, and who could therefore be forgiven their political faults."[30] The members of the insurrectionary committee were so convinced of victory that they constantly meditated upon the steps leading to the new order of things, which would of necessity have to be centralized in their hands before the "definitive legislation of equality" could be promulgated.[31]

Babeuf's conduct at his Vendôme trial set a precedent for the use of the establishment's judicial procedure to broadcast revolutionary doctrine. He constantly interrupted the prosecutor, refusing to play the compliant victim and throwing the judges into confusion. Classical rhetoric flowed from the mouth of an antique Roman in modern dress. Two days after his imprisonment Babeuf addressed a letter to the Directorate: "Death or exile would be for me the road to immortality and I shall march in that direction with heroic and religious zeal."[32] At one dramatic moment, by prearrangement, Babeuf and his fellow conspirator Darthé tried to rob the oppressors of their victims by stabbing each other. But the noble Romans were out of phase, and, as Buonarroti reports, "the fragility of their daggers, which broke in their hands, did not allow the condemned to deprive each other of life."[33] On the guillotine Babeuf joined the ecumenical roster of utopian martyrs.

PART VI

The Union of Labor and Love

Charles Fourier

lithograph by Dedupart
Bibliothèque Nationale, Paris

24

The Battle of the Systems

GREAT INTELLECTUAL discoveries have generally sprung forth uniquely from the brain of one creator, though on occasion they have appeared in duplicate, engendering bitter controversies over priority of invention. Only rarely have major innovations assumed as many as three different shapes at about the same time. The emergence of utopian socialism, with its revolutionary views of work and love, was a novum of this character. With an uncanny simultaneity, the secular European spirit received three alternative embodiments in Henri Saint-Simon, Charles Fourier, and Robert Owen. Their class origins, personalities, occupations, and educations were diverse, their prose styles equally turbid, their destinies not dissimilar. All three were the progenitors of "movements," schools of thought and action that proposed to reorganize society radically by implementing the ideas of the founders. They were united in a single common goal, the resolution of the crisis of the age, recognized as a crisis in man's capacity to find satisfaction in his work and emotional relationships; but, understandably, the movements were hostile to one another, rivals as they were for the allegiance of mankind as it faced a momentous decision in the newborn nineteenth century. Humanity stood bewildered at the crossroads or so the social philosophers thought, dredging up a Herculean metaphor; it was a matter of life or death that men choose the correct path and not prolong present suffering by following false prophets who pointed in the wrong direction. The three great utopians repeatedly rehearsed the annals of mankind from the beginning of time to demonstrate that their epiphany was the instant of the great divide. There may have been other crucial happenings in the past, other troublous times, but somehow the gravity of the hour was qualitatively different from everything that had gone before both in its intensity and in its pivotal significance for world history. A momentous event was about to transpire. After the travail of rebirth had passed, mankind would emerge—or would be catapulted—into a new world. The tonal effects of these crisis-crying prophets have been assimilated so thoroughly by modern man that they are today the hackneyed accompaniment of even the most casual social or political utterance. A century and a half ago the warning calls still sounded anguished.

The Utopian Triplex

Saint-Simon, Fourier, and Owen unveiled the future and in the same anxious breath tried to control it by persuading their contemporaries to adopt willingly and without bloodshed the course they were ultimately destined to take anyway. They were intoxicated with the future: They looked into what was about to be and found it good. The past was a mere prologue and the present a spiritual and moral, even a physical, burden that at times was well-nigh unendurable. To convince their contemporaries of the virtues of their systems, the founders and their principal disciples wrote books that became canonical texts and availed themselves of what were then relatively new instruments for proselytizing and winning publicity. Journals and newspapers were started to further the cause, pamphlets were issued in which the replacement of minuscules by majuscules connoted urgency. Lectures and meetings were organized at which the spoken word fortified the printed one with the emotive power of oral persuasion. Today we have only the dead pulp of printed messages and cannot recover the affective tones of heated discussions in great public assemblies and small clandestine gatherings, as the movements spread from an Anglo-French nucleus far east into Russia and overseas to the United States.

Collectively, the utopians invented a new vocabulary of social thought: They either took familiar terms and invested them with fresh emotional intensity, changing their meaning in the process, or they coined neologisms. Crisis, moral, social, socialism, progress, harmony, movement, school, happiness, system, revolution, attraction, antagonism, repulsion, love, passion, instinct, mutual, association, ability, need, education were combined in phrases that illuminated a newly discovered firmament. The three major (and many minor) contemporary utopian movements shared a similar, if not identical, set of metaphoric concepts.

For the Saint-Simonians the primary evil attribute of society was antagonism (a derivation from Kant's essay on cosmopolitan history); for Owen it was repulsion. For the Saint-Simonians the good attribute was love or attraction; for Owen it was charity or attraction; for Fourier it was passional attraction. The same Newtonian scientific image had penetrated, and diffusion and influences need not be proved, though specific interrelationships can readily be documented. In 1828, for example, a twelve-page pamphlet entitled *Political Economy Made Easy: A Sketch by M. Charles Fourier, Exhibiting the Various Errors of Our Present Political Arrangements* was presented to the Owenite London Co-operative Society by its translator. While the bulk of the text was incomprehensible to anyone not already conversant with Fourier's private language, it was distributed by the society and Robert Owen could well have read there that the ultimate solution to social problems lay in the "analysis and synthesis of passional attraction." His eclectic mind might have picked up the Fourierist term *attraction* (if not the substance of the idea), for it crops up in his later writings; or he may have derived it from a score of similar sources.

The parallel chronology of the utopian movements confirms the power of the historical moment to use different types of mentality for the same general end. The utopian founders were born within a decade or so of one another (Saint-Simon in 1760, Fourier and Owen in 1772), experienced their first revelations between 1799 and 1803, surfaced in public print between 1808 and 1812, achieved a final doctrine by the 1820s, and then repeated themselves for the rest of their lives—with a goodly number of variations and contradictions. Death came at more widely spaced intervals: Saint-Simon's in 1825, Fourier's in 1837, and Owen's in 1858, a longevity that perhaps explains the numerous deviations in his thought from one period to another.

Saint-Simon was a warm, vivacious, and seductive person who entranced young men with his energy. After his death they became the oratorical transmitters of Saint-Simonian ideas; Saint-Simon himself had not harangued public assemblies. Fourier was thin, short, tight-lipped, never known to laugh, bitingly sarcastic, solemn. He prevailed by the sheer cogency of massive detail in his system. When the Fourierist "societal school" came into the hands of speech-ifying lawyers, the doctrine fared better, though the new leaders felt called upon to bowdlerize Fourier's writings on sex in order to propagate them. Owen was his own organizer, expounder, and lecturer, exuding a confidence that captivated listeners of all classes. His capacity to utter the most outrageous ideas as if they were self-evident matters of fact astounded enemies and sup-porters alike. The Saint-Simonian and Fourierist movements assumed new life after their founders' deaths. The Owenites lost their independent existence when Owen finally joined the spirits with whom he had been in touch; his surviving followers tended to merge with other social activists, preserving only a vague identity.

Saint-Simon was present in the flesh only in the inchoate stage of the move-ment, which reached its zenith in the early 1830s. Though Owen himself was a man of both theory and practice and his activities stretched over many decades, his international reputation was at its height in the twenties. He survived to organize a world congress for universal reform in 1855, having participated in launching both the English cooperative and the trade-union movements in ear-lier decades. Fourier's fame was greatest in the early forties.

The intellectual and emotive influence exerted by these three men and the movements inspired by their scriptural writings was not restricted to true dis-ciples. Their ideas were alive in the intellectual underground of the nineteenth century long after the surface ripples of their direct action had vanished. Fourier and Saint-Simon have even enjoyed revivals of sorts in the twentieth century, Saint-Simon after World War I and Fourier in the 1960s. All three were swallowed up by Marxism, but they were not always well assimilated, and from time to time certain prickly elements have disturbed the internal processes of the victorious movement that transcended them.

The three founders had had personal experience as practical agents, with varying success, in either commercial or industrial enterprises, and could boast that their knowledge was not derived from study alone. They were not mere bookish outsiders diagnosing the economic and social system. Their reading was sporadic, and as autodidacts they made a virtue of their academic deficien-cies, heaping contempt upon the official schools of learning. Pointing to the pedants, they declared themselves fortunate to have escaped the stultification of social science in the universities.

The New Messiahs

With utter faith in their election, they stepped into the age-old roles of saviors and messiahs. They sometimes imagined that in their persons the Messiah himself had already arrived. Saint-Simon thought he was the reincarnation of Socrates and Charlemagne; the disciples evoked the analogy with Jesus; Fourier, though not given to historical learning, demonstrated from Scripture that his appearance had been foretold; Owen identified himself with both Jesus and Columbus. Like all prophets, they suffered moments of doubt and defeat, but these were usually well concealed, sometimes even from themselves. Mag-nificent obsessives, their entire beings were one with their systems, and ene-mies of the grand designs they had constructed became threatening violators of their bodies. A quantum of persecution mania has often been infused into the blood of system-builders. While they were aware of their own weaknesses and appealed to all men of good will to aid them with money, advice, specialized knowledge, such assistance was acceptable only on their own terms. They were the leaders, others could only be loyal and obedient disciples. Though they were hostile to Jacobin revolution and Napoleonic dictatorship, the stamp of the Age of Napoleon was upon them. The first embryonic projects of Saint-Simon and Fourier were actually addressed to the First Consul, who already loomed as an omnipotent colossus. If he would only adopt their plans, success was assured; they were prepared to act as powers behind the throne. After Napoleon's death the utopians frantically searched for other patrons, and they appealed to a motley crew—bankers, czars, kings, American congressmen, English nobles.

They fancied themselves extraordinarily acute observers who had culled their systems directly from the book of life, from intimate experience with all classes of society. Newton was their favorite hero and they imagined themselves achieving for the social universe what he had for the physical. Out of a multiplicity of personal observations, equivalent to social experiments, they had arrived at the final synthesis, a few simple laws. Their findings were scientific because they were based on "demonstrable facts" (Owen), "positive facts" (Saint-Simon), "actual observations" (Fourier). Historical facts were admissible on the same level as contemporary facts because there was one human nature, modifiable only by conditions and circumstances. Grand historical patterns were more persuasive to Saint-Simon and the Saint-Simonians than to Owen or Fourier and their schools, but even among the Saint-Simonians, philosophico-historical knowledge did not detract from the paramountcy of their probing analysis of their own society. They were the omniscient social doctors in the immediate crisis, and they proffered mankind a universal panacea, an elixir that was bound to be efficacious because it was the fruit of the inviolable social laws they had discovered.

Though there is no evidence that the three ever met, they were in the same place at the same time. From 1825 to 1832 Fourier lived in a rented room on 45 rue de Richelieu, in Paris; Saint-Simon had died nearby on the same street in 1825. Owen visited Paris in 1818, though at that point he tended to consort with prominent educators, not with freakish utopians.

On his way to Aix-la-Chapelle where he presented his projects before the Congress of the Holy Alliance, Owen was led about the city by Marc Auguste Pictet of Geneva, who introduced him to Cuvier, the autocrat of French science, and he was invited to present a formal report on the New View of Society to the Académie des Sciences. The serious spread of Owenite ideas in France was due to Laffon de Ladébat's 1821 translation of Henry Grey Macnab's *Impartial Examination of the New Views of Mr. Robert Owen*. Fourier, who was no great reader of books, got his impressions of the rival system through periodical notices and at one time he hoped to be invited to an Owenite colony to expound his ideas, a utopian fantasy of forbearance.

In different degrees the utopian movements were conscious of one another's existence, but like some plants drawing sustenance from the same soil, they were violently inimical to one another. While Saint-Simon himself made no reference to Fourier and Owen, his disciples were acutely sensitive to the competition when they went on propaganda missions. When Fourier in 1824 heard of Owen's experiments at New Lanark, he looked upon them as merely demonstrating the truth of his own phalanx system. Fourier knew that he had preceded Owen in publishing the plan of an industrial-agricultural community— the idea of the phalanx dated back to 1808—and when his British counterpart won public acclaim he openly charged him with plagiarism. But Owen also knew that he had anticipated Fourier in the implementation of the "idea" in his own factories while Fourier was still advertising for a benefactor to finance a practical trial. The argument over priority of invention was more emotional than rational, since there were only formal similarities between the simple projects of Owen and the intricate system of passional series which Fourier devised in 1808 and to which he gave definitive form in 1823. Owen practiced before he theorized; his system was finally perfected only in 1849, when his projects had failed and he had alienated virtually every class of English society in its turn, including the workingmen, whose aggressive political activities bordering on violence in behalf of the Charter he had rejected as diversionary. The rival utopians of the first half of the nineteenth century were not avid readers of one another's works—which did not prevent them from denouncing one another and making charges of burglary when they detected remote similarities among the systems.

Fourier had lumped together Saint-Simon and the Saint-Simonians, Owen and the Owenites, and blasted away at them with a barrage of denigrating and scornful invective in a pamphlet of 1831. As a rule he appeared less informed about Owen than about the Saint-Simonians, whose sacerdotal nonsense was the principal target of his attack. Owen had defeated himself, Fourier gloated; the collapse of the Owenite experiment at New Harmony, Indiana, was proof positive that the doctrine was false. The Saint-Simonians were too pusillanimous even to try out their system. Instead of teaching mankind how to quadruple production through labor in attractive association, both groups lost themselves in side issues, the Owenites attacking all religion, the Saint-Simonians inventing a new one.

They [the Saint-Simonians] preferred the ignoble role of ascetic charlatans worthy of the nineteenth century, suspect and dangerous schismatics . . . dogmatic plagiarists without any idea of their own, speculative chameleons, changing their system ten times over, and scientific cossacks pillaging and appropriating the ideas of others. They only have one praiseworthy principle, which is not theirs, *to reward each one according to his capacities and his works*. This is the wish that respectworthy authors have always expressed, ever since the abolition of slavery. But it was necessary to find a way of implementing this equitable division in accordance with each man's work and talent. I discovered this method in 1822.[1]

Fourier's key to the system lay in short and frequently changing work sessions, in the gaiety of free work groups, supplanting the tightness and boredom of the traditional family, in a multiplicity of options, in abundance of food and drink instead of uniformly bad feeding. Owenites and Saint-Simonians were the blind leading the blind.

When in the 1830s missionaries of the Saint-Simonian religion, dressed in full regalia—blue tunics and shiny black belts of leather—tried to establish propaganda centers in England, one Edward Hancock, a lapsed Owenite, took it upon himself to warn his compatriots against both heresies, Robert Owen's

Community System as well as the "Horrid Doings of the Saint-Simonians."
The "New Moral World" was nothing but a "New Moral Mistress" and both
systems of socialism were mere disguises for instructing females in the art of
prostitution.

The contest between the Fourierists and the Saint-Simonians for the alienated souls of Europe and America is one of the unwritten secret histories of the
nineteenth century. The passionate debates occasioned by these competitive
systems have been forgotten, like the battles of the mystery cults in the Roman
Empire; they were later dwarfed by the appearance of the triumphant Marxist
ideology. In their day, however, "the possessed" of Russia were torn by these
alternative moral ways and so were the more respectable idealists of New
England.

It sometimes happened, as one moved away from the utopian centers in
France and England, that the distinctions between the doctrines which seemed
so crucial to rival disciples became blurred, especially when knowledge of the
theories was derived from hearsay or secondary and tertiary sources. During
the early 1830s, Alexander Herzen and his friends turned to both Saint-Simon
and Fourier for sustenance. The poet Ogarev, who was a member of the
group, has recreated the religious atmosphere of the vague romantic Russian
socialism of 1833:

> I remember a small room five *arshin* long
> The bed and the chair and the table with the tallow candle
> And here three of us, children of the Decembrists
> Alumni of the new world
> Disciples of Fourier and Saint-Simon
> We swore to dedicate our whole lives
> To the people and their liberation.[2]

But for the most part such syncretism was frowned upon, and acerb discussions among the standard-bearers of rival cults lasted far into the night.

Yet the coteries of the great utopians were rather fluid in their composition.
Once committed to the quest for an absolute system, young men moved from
one to another; it was not rare for the truth-seekers to run through two or
three systems in the course of a lifetime. There were the usual cries of treachery, the same bitter gnashing of teeth that had been heard fifteen hundred years
before among the early Christian sectaries and would be heard again among
the communists and socialists of the third and fourth decades of the twentieth
century.

The projects of Robert Owen and Charles Fourier, the two major
early-nineteenth-century apostles of the small community movement, were
markedly different in character from previous European establishments of self-
sufficient communes, which had always been sustained by a religious law.
Though neither Owen nor Fourier was a militant atheist and they used the
name of God to identify a life-giving principle, He was not a personal God and
was never called upon to intervene in the life of the newly founded secular
communes.

Owen and Fourier had in common a total negation of the existing industrial
system, whose miseries they knew from experience with running factories or
selling factory products; complete confidence in the gradual contagion of the

communal movement, leading to a belief that a single successful experiment based upon their principles of organization would provide an example so compelling that, better than any arguments, it would persuade the rest of mankind to adopt their system; a faith in a psychological doctrine of motivation whose laws they had discovered; a rejection of violent revolutionary action as a means of changing the social system; and an appreciation of the vital significance of childhood education. They parted ways on the principle of equality, on the relative significance of reason and passion in the human constitution, on the role of manufacturing in the communal settlement, and, most important of all, on the nature and quantity of allowable instinctual pleasure. In the mature version of his system, Owen would inaugurate his experiment with instant equality in work and rewards, as he did in the village of New Harmony, Indiana. Fourier allowed for different levels of capital investment by phalansterians and graduated rewards, though his promise of returns on investment, expressed in terms of real sensate enjoyment, made the lot of the poorest man in a phalanstery superior to that of a Rothschild. Owen would educate through the cultivation of reason and by teaching children through habit to imitate only rational behavior; that meant temperance, gentleness, absolute truth-telling, contentment with limited sensate pleasure, joy in conversation, reading, dancing, singing. Fourier would have his phalansterians fulfill all their desires to the utmost, no matter how esoteric they might be, and cultivate the need for complex sounds, smells, sights, tastes, and touches as a virtue, not an excess. Thomas More's sixteenth-century "honest allowable pleasures" could well have been the model for Robert Owen's conceptions, while Fourier thought of himself as the discoverer of vast new amorous worlds for all mankind.

Owen and Fourier hoped to see their new forms of organization grow within the body of the old system, but independent of it, and they expected to be granted tolerance because no present government would be threatened by them. They had a common commitment to peace, gradualism, and nonrevolution. Since they were not subversive they saw no reason for governmental interference, and Owen did in fact lecture on his communal system before the most improbable audiences, including the President and Congress of the United States. Fourier's disciples in the Icarian movement were not quite so fortunate: They were hounded by the French police, who were in terror of public tumults and revolution, and suspicious that the movement, despite its protestations of nonviolence, was merely a cover for dangerous clandestine political action.

Though for a time in the early 1830s the Saint-Simonians maintained a settlement in Ménilmontant, where on a Sunday the bourgeois of Paris came to watch the educated sons of respectable citizens dirtying their hands by digging the soil, the main thrust of the movement was not directed toward establishing small communities. The Saint-Simonians aimed at persuading the bankers, industrialists, and proletarians to institute their system by a total reorganization of the whole scientific-technological society, without resorting to its fragmentation into small units of the Fourierist or Owenite type.

All three utopian sects were inevitably torn over the issue of compromise with the ruling establishment. In the beginning they professed doctrines that could not be changed one iota in theory or practice lest the perfect edifice collapse. But as time went on they were willing to sacrifice some parts that offended prospective converts. They wrote somewhat different versions of the gospel, with an eye to honoring group prejudices. Like Saint Paul, they were prepared to speak to each man in his own language as long as they might win his concurrence on fundamentals of belief. Their preachments to all classes, each in terms of its interests, were often disingenuous, but by their own lights not false. It was for men's own good that different features of the same doctrine were highlighted, because it was in fact beneficial to all mankind and the method of proselytizing had to be flexible.

Saint-Simonism, Fourierism, and Owenism were all eudaemonistic systems based on the self-actualization of individuals in a state of community, though they differed sharply about what should be actualized. Owen's concentration on the fulfillment of what he held to be an ordinary man's natural reason sounded like old-fashioned, restrictive, Enlightenment philosophy by comparison with the expansive French worshipers of the emancipated passions of men and women. But they all bear witness to the stirring recognition that came to many Europeans after the turmoil of the Napoleonic wars that the old order could not be restored and that men had been set adrift morally, economically, socially, intellectually. Along with the Romantic poets, the utopians lamented the isolation and fragmentation of society, each in his own rhetoric. The English and French phrases are so similar that they sometimes give the impression of being translations of each other. Owen's strictures against British society in the second decade of the nineteenth century parallel in spirit the Fourierist and the Saint-Simonian critiques of French society of the same period. The social order had fallen to pieces, turned against itself, and harmony could be instituted only in some communal system. George Mudie, editor of *The Economist: A Periodical Paper Explanatory of the New System of Society Projected by Robert Owen . . . and of a Plan of Association for Improving the Condition of the Working Classes* (1821–1822), wrote in his journal: "It appears to be indisputable that all men pursue happiness; and that happiness can only be attained by the possession of abundance, and by the cultivation of the physical, moral and intellectual powers . . . and that the proposed societies offer the only means of giving abundance and intellectual and moral excellence, to all mankind."[3] Physical, moral, and intellectual capacities and needs were Saint-Simon's trinity too at this period, though he was far more enmeshed in the question of primacy among the three than were the English.

On the sociological level one is arrested by the utopians' deflection of primary concern from the state and from the definition of power to social relationships and religion. Amid the complex diplomatic intrigues and wars of the dynastic states of the West and a succession of bloody political revolutions in which men fought and died for liberty and dominion, these philosophical utopians essentially turned their backs on the state. It is a comprehensible repudiation in a society that witnessed the promulgation and annulment of political constitutions at regular intervals. No basic metamorphosis seemed to take place during the frequent transfers of power from one regime to another. Authentic human relationships as envisaged for the ideal societies were not dependent upon evanescent political forms. The history of politics described nothing more than the changing of the guard. The utopians were determined to discover the core of human nature and to build a new social structure with the hard blocks of reality—man's reason, instincts, desires, needs, capacities. Each utopian might draw his plan and manipulate his materials differently in setting up the model of a good society, but the problem of the state apparatus and the overriding role it had assumed in fostering and inhibiting satisfactions escaped all of them. The state was a scaffolding, a tool, a superstructure, a covering—distant from the heart of the human condition. The political order was looked down upon as a residue of the past which had to be circumvented—they did not say destroyed because they were peace-loving utopians—so that men might come face to face with their authentic problems, which were moral, social, and religious. They would gladly avail themselves of the services of political leaders to inaugurate the new order, but such aid was considered merely an auxiliary mechanism.

The utopians foresaw the calm dissolution of the crisis of the age. Resembling the comforter of the Second Isaiah rather than the grim punisher of the First, they were bearers of good cheer. "The golden age of the human species . . . is before us," said Saint-Simon.[4] "Breathe freely and forget your ancient evils," Fourier encouraged the inhabitants of Europe in the midst of the Napoleonic slaughter, "Abandon yourselves to joy, for a fortunate invention finally brings you the social compass." Père Enfantin addressed the unbelievers in 1832, "O you whose somber sadness and stubborn regrets remain obstinately bound to the debris of the past, O you who doubt of your victory and vainly seek joy and repose in the society which you have fashioned, dry your tears and rejoice, for I have come in the name of God, of Saint-Simon, and of my Fathers to make you see the brilliant colors that will soon burst forth before your eyes."[5] Owen announced the imminent dawn of the new order in the first number of the *New Moral World* on November 1, 1834: "This . . . is the Great Advent of the World, the second coming of Christ, for Truth and Christ are one and the same. The first coming of Christ was a partial development of Truth to the few . . . The second coming of Christ will make Truth known to the many . . . The time is therefore arrived when the foretold millennium is about to commence." On the outside of Owenite buildings the letters C.M. were prominently carved, signifying the Commencement of the Millennium.

25

Saint-Simon: The Pear Is Ripe

OF ALL THE MODERN utopians the Count Claude Henri de Rouvroy de Saint-Simon was the most picaresque; he resembled a character out of *Gil Blas* more than a traditional seer.[1] But when the spirit of foretelling hovers about, it may possess the most unlikely subjects. Born in Paris on October 17, 1760, he belonged to a collateral branch of the same family as the famous Duke, author of the voluminous *Memoirs of Saint-Simon* on the court of Louis XIV and the Regency. Traditions about his youth gathered by disciples depict him as stubborn and self-willed, in such continual and bitter conflict with his father that the elder Saint-Simon once imprisoned him for his contumely. At the age of seventeen, the young Saint-Simon received his first military commission, and in 1779 he set sail from Brittany with the Touraine Regiment to fight in the War for American Independence, not as a dashing volunteer, but as a line officer obeying royal orders. After participating in a number of engagements in the Antilles, his contingent joined Washington at Yorktown. During the battle he acquitted himself creditably in command of a section of artillery and was later elected a member of the Society of Cincinnatus in recognition of his services. The French continued the war in the West Indies after Cornwallis' capitulation, and Saint-Simon saw action again at St. Kitts. In the great naval engagement—disastrous for the French—between the forces of Admirals Rodney and de Grasse in April 1782, Saint-Simon was on the flagship. Stunned by a cannon ball, he was taken prisoner in the general surrender, and was interned in Jamaica. After his liberation, he presented to the Viceroy of Mexico his first grand project, a plan for an interoceanic canal running through Lake Nicaragua—and he was rebuffed.

Back in France, Saint-Simon was promoted at regular intervals, but the life of an officer in barracks was dull, and he took leave from the army. In Holland in 1786 he involved himself in an abortive plan to join the Dutch and the French in an attempt to drive the English out of India. Then he turned up in Spain, where in cooperation with Count Cabarrus, father of the future chief mistress of Barras, he sponsored another unsuccessful canal project, to link Madrid with the sea. While in Spain he met a Saxon, Count Redern, the Prussian Ambassador, who lent him a sum of money presumably for investment in French securities—the beginning of a strange relationship.

The Grand Seigneur Sansculottes

Upon his return to France during the early months of the Revolution, Saint-Simon commenced to play a complicated role, commuting between Paris and the provinces. In Falvy, Marchélepot, Cambrai, Péronne, towns near his ancestral estates, he acted the enthusiastic partisan of the Revolution, helping to draft local cahiers, presiding at popular assemblies, delivering revolutionary speeches, and commanding the national guard at moments of crisis. Simultaneously he bought extensive church lands with small down payments, profiting from the steady drop in the value of the assignats. On September 20, 1793, when the Jacobin wave was high, Saint-Simon formally abdicated his noble name and titles and assumed an earthy peasant surname, Bonhomme. Numerous acts of republican virtue, the adoption of aged citizens and the purchase of animals for needy peasants, brought him favorable repute among the local people of his ancestral communes. In Paris, by laying out small deposits, he came into the possession of mansions of nobles who had emigrated or been guillotined. Since he had made his first investments with money given him by Count Redern, he was under the impression that they had established an informal partnership in which he was the active member. To play safe, the deals were negotiated under a host of false names. The enterprises were vast and rumor embroidered them; there was even a tale that he had made a bid for Notre Dame de Paris. Saint-Simon habitually resided near the Palais Royal and frequented the society of other speculators, a motley group in which international bankers, foreign spies, Dantonists of the right, and Hébertists of the extreme left were intermingled. They led licentious lives, in sharp contrast with the Incorruptible One who dominated the Committee of Public Safety. When Robespierre finally moved against the whole crew, he was able to throw their heads into a common basket by using the police agent's technique of guilt by association.

Saint-Simon was arrested, though probably in error, on November 19, 1793, during one of the roundups of international bankers and foreign agents. The government seems to have been looking for the Simon brothers, who were Belgian bankers. In prison Saint-Simon protested his innocence in a long, carefully drafted memoir to the Committee of Public Safety, and the local patriots of Picardy, among whom the ex-noble had shown his revolutionary zeal on more than one occasion, wrote numerous testimonials of civic virtue for him. He behaved most circumspectly in the antechamber of death and cautiously avoided participation in any of the plots against Robespierre which General Ronsin was hatching among the desperate men in the prisons.

Saint-Simon never was tried before the revolutionary tribunal and he survived the Terror. The original down payments on his vast holdings in Paris and the provinces had preserved his title to these properties even while he was in prison, and once he was liberated he came to own them outright by paying the balance of the price in almost worthless assignats. He led a wild life as a member of the Barras circle, toying with Directory politics, new constitutional schemes, and all manner of novel industrial and commercial projects. In his salon he entertained lavishly, and invited as his guests bankers, politicians, intellectuals, and artists. He played the Maecenas and subsidized bright young scientists. Learning intrigued him as much as finance, and he dabbled in all the mathematical and physical sciences, in the psychology and social doctrines of the idéologues. He was a brilliant conversationalist, witty, obscene in the fashion of the Directory, cynical, and yet moved by a strange passion for projects to revolutionize science and society. During this period his plans never went beyond the animated talk of the dinner table.

Count Redern appeared in Paris in 1797 and for a while gorged himself on the *punch aux oeufs* and truffles that Saint-Simon served. But he was growing uneasy both about the extravagance of his partner's expenditures and the wild financial and industrial projects which he was promoting. Saint-Simon thought that Redern was a philosophical soulmate, and when the German asked for a dissolution of their partnership he nonchalantly left the details to his discretion. Redern drew up the documents which broke their financial union and Saint-Simon took his share, withdrew from business, and determined henceforth to study and to work solely on projects for the betterment of mankind.

Saint-Simon was married on August 7, 1801, to Alexandrine-Sophie Goury de Champgrand, the daughter of a former comrade in arms and fellow speculator of the Palais Royal. It appears to have been a marriage of convenience. She was penniless and he wanted an elegant hostess for his salon. Sophie was a literary lady and she brought a contingent of artists, composers, and musicians to their parties. In later life she described her embarrassment when Saint-Simon tried to go back on the chaste arrangement he had made with her. She was amused but also somewhat frightened by his philosophical projects, and on June 24, 1802, they were divorced.

That same year Saint-Simon traveled to Switzerland, where, according to Saint-Simonian tradition, he proposed at Coppet to Madame de Staël, recently bereaved of her husband. What was probably the first edition of the *Lettres d'un habitant de Genève* was printed in Geneva during this trip. It was addressed "*à l'humanité.*" The edition which became more generally known was entitled *Lettres d'un habitant de Genève à ses contemporains* and was distributed if not actually published by a Paris bookseller in 1803. Both editions were anonymous and neither bore a place or date of publication. A copy was addressed to the First Consul from Geneva, accompanied by a curious letter, full of adulation, soliciting his opinion of the work. The *Lettres d'un habitant de Genève* was ignored by contemporaries, and Saint-Simon never made reference to it in later life. His disciple, the eminent mathematician Olinde Rodrigues, discovered the work in 1826 and reprinted it in 1832. A strange first book for a middle-aged adventurer to produce, it is the only serious writing of his prosperous period. Almost all the ideas he later developed in his streams of reiterative pamphlets are here in embryo. During the two or three years after the appearance of the *Lettres d'un habitant de Genève,* Saint-Simon spent the rest of the fortune allotted to him by the dissolution of the Redern partnership, and by 1805 he was penniless.

Saint-Simon's passion for knowledge grew stronger in his poverty. He spent long nights spinning out his philosophical projects, until he fell ill and spit blood. When he had reached the depths of misery, a savior appeared in the person of his former servant Diard, who took him under his care and provided for him. Curious scientific intuitions poured forth in an outburst of disorganized tracts: *Introduction aux travaux scientifiques du XIXe siècle* (1807); *Nouvelle encyclopédie* (1810); *Histoire de l'homme* (1810); *Mémoire sur la science de l'homme* (1813); *Travail sur la gravitation universelle* (1813). When he could not afford to print he copied in manuscript. As soon as a mere sketch of an idea was completed, he sent it around to members of the Institute, to scientific establishments, and to the Emperor. Accompanying letters asked financial aid to help him complete his projects; but he needed more than money; he wanted advice and criticism, most of all sanction and praise. Most scientists did not even deign to cut the pages of the brochures addressed to them, and copies were discovered untouched in their libraries after their death. At best, they sent formal notice of receipt. The crueler men among them mockingly expressed their lack of interest in his plans. Cut to the quick, Saint-Simon rejoined with bitterness, challenging the scientific geniuses of the age to spiritual combat. His letters became a series of wild ravings about genius, his mission, and the persecutions he endured from his enemies. Interspersed among the psychopathic tirades there are moving passages about his passion for glory, written in the grand romantic manner. A family genealogy traced the Saint-Simons back to Charlemagne, and on more than one occasion his great ancestor appeared to him in a vision. They both had the same mission, separated though they were by a thousand years—the spiritual and temporal reorganization of European society.

During this period Saint-Simon turned to a more practical solution of his financial troubles by reopening in public his final property settlement with Redern, who had in the meantime become a respectable French property owner engaged in useful agricultural and manufacturing projects. Saint-Simon moved to Alençon to harass Redern in the province where he was gaining prestige, but he failed to make any headway, and during one of the journeys he fell seriously ill. Descriptions of his state sound like madness. He was put into a private hospital for the insane in Charenton and was treated by the famous Dr. Pinel.

But the man rebounds. Sometime before 1814 he recovered. To get rid of his pretensions to a portion of his ancestral estate, his own family settled a small annuity upon him. When he returned to Paris during the Hundred Days he even got a post in the library of the Arsenal. The darkness seems to have left his brain, and at fifty-four he embarked upon a new career. The scientific projects were forgotten, he never mentioned the strange brochures of the Empire, and he became an active political polemicist during the Restoration period.

Apparently Saint-Simon had enough money to hire a secretary, and he soon attracted respectable friends and collaborators. From then on he never worked alone; there were always young men by his side who edited his copy, joined with him in publication, and accepted his guidance. He had an eye for brilliance. The first of a series of secretaries was Augustin Thierry, the future historian, with whom he published a scheme entitled *De la réorganisation de la société européenne* during the Congress of Vienna. It was more than an adaptation of the Abbé de Saint-Pierre's plan for universal peace, which it resembled superficially; Saint-Simon placed his emphasis on an integral federation of Europe, the cornerstone of which was to be an Anglo-French alliance. Another thesis put forth in the pamphlet concerned the superiority of the modern commercial over the military nation, an idea which Benjamin Constant was developing with greater subtlety.

The political brochures that Saint-Simon wrote during the First Restoration and the Hundred Days won him admittance into the circle of liberal economists and publicists identified with Jean-Baptiste Say and Charles Dunoyer. He ceased to be treated as a mere crackpot, though he was still considered "an original" by his more sedate friends. His baptism of respectability was so efficacious that he was even received in the salons of the Parisian bankers Laffitte and Ardouin. The new relationships included enterprising industrialists such as Ternaux, the great textile manufacturer. Saint-Simon became a member of a party. The bourgeoisie, which had grown fully conscious of its power under Napoleon even when dominated by him, was now confronted with a serious attempt on the part of the émigrés thirsting for vengeance to reconstitute intact the ancien régime with its noble prerogatives and disparagement of industry and commerce. There was developing a full-blown struggle of a new ruling class against the restoration hopes of the old, and it was being fought out in a parliamentary regime. Saint-Simon became a more or less official propagandist for the bourgeois. He organized a series of periodical publications: *L'Industrie* (1816–1818); *Le Politique* (1819); *L'Organisateur* (1819–1820); *Du système industriel* (1821–1822); *Catéchisme des industriels* (1823–1824); *Opinions littéraires, philosophiques et industrielles* (1825). The issues appeared intermittently, in part to evade rules of censorship on regular serial publications, but chiefly because there were always money troubles. On more than one occasion he went beyond the polemical line that his proper banker and industrialist friends were ready to support. While they were willing to have him extol the virtues of the industrial class and its historic right to assume control of the state, they were not yet prepared to attack frontally the power of the revived Catholic Church. When Saint-Simon used such dangerous phrases as "terrestrial morality," which would not have troubled in the least an eighteenth-century bourgeois, many of the Restoration bankers dropped him cold.

In February 1820 he had an even more unfortunate experience. *L'Organisateur* had included in its very first issue a literary artifice—the famous Parable—in which Saint-Simon contrasted the possible consequences to France of the death of her foremost scientists, artists, artisans, industrialists, and bankers with the death of all the leading nobles and officials of the bureaucracy. On February 13, Louvel assassinated the Duke of Berry, and Saint-Simon was tried as one of the moral instigators of the crime. It was a profound affront to a man who abhorred revolutionary violence with a consistency which was remarkable in a figure so mercurial. He managed to escape punishment after a complicated judicial proceeding.

Augustin Thierry, a collaborator of 1814, soon left him, and in his place came a young graduate of the Ecole Polytechnique, Auguste Comte. The new secretary had a well-organized mind and a forceful, logical method of presentation. At first he allowed himself to be known as a pupil of Saint-Simon's, but he soon chafed at the subordinate position. After Comte's defection, Saint-Simon made the acquaintance of several medical men, a Dr. Bailly among them, who were fascinated by his ideas on the physiology of society. But his worldly success was far from brilliant. The infelicitous reference to "terrestrial morality" and his trial of 1820 made most respectable bourgeois shy away from him. They had more discreet plans for seizing power. He was again forced to beg for alms to support his little household, which had acquired a mistress and a dog. One day in 1823, after recommending his Julie to the industrialist Ternaux, in a fit of despair he shot himself. But he was found in time, doctors were called, and the only injury discovered was that one of the shots had penetrated an eye.

He lived for two years longer. A new group of friends appeared, among them two young Jews whose academic careers had been brusquely interrupted by the restrictions against them reimposed by the Restoration. They were Léon Halévy, father of the future playwright of the Second Empire, and Olinde Rodrigues, one of the real innovators of nineteenth-century mathematics. The young men were thirsting for a new morality to fill the emptiness of their souls, and Saint-Simon provided the gospel in the *Nouveau Christianisme* (1825). He conversed with Olinde Rodrigues for many hours during his last years, and in this manner the oral tradition of the master's ideas was transmitted to the disciples. Many of his keenest reflections never appeared in print; they either evaporated in conversation or were received and passed on by Rodrigues. During the last months before his death in 1825 the group began planning a new journal to be called *Le Producteur*.

Science Dethroned

Though he knew virtually no science, in all his writings Saint-Simon had a great deal to say about scientists and their unique role in modern society. In one of his autobiographical fragments he confessed that an understanding of the character of men of science had always been his paramount interest in listening to their conversation. During the quarter-century of his creative intellectual life he adopted a wide variety of changing attitudes toward them, many of which were doubtless colored by the reactions of individual scientists and of the dominant scientific schools to his person and his doctrine. Nonetheless his conception of the role of the scientist is a fruitful vantage point from which to examine the whole body of his writings. It is one of the most persistent motifs, recurring time and again with different variations. His early works, completely in the Condorcet spirit, had raised the scientists to the apex of society; by Saint-Simon's death science had been dethroned—a revolution in the spiritual conception of nineteenth-century prophets of progress that distinguishes them from their eighteenth-century predecessors. Saint-Simon still honored the scientists, though he made them share their social hegemony with others; in Auguste Comte's final phase, technical science as it had been practiced since the Renaissance would be banished.

In the *Lettres d'un habitant de Genève à ses contemporains* Saint-Simon discussed the problem of the role of the scientist as the crux of the contemporary social disarray in France. His class analysis of the French Revolution and its aftermath, in an essay whose originality Friedrich Engels admired and perhaps exaggerated, defined the underlying development of the whole epoch as a conflict between the propertied and the propertyless. A third element in the struggle, the scientists were a floating elite with no natural class alignment; they were mobile and could be recruited to one or the other side of the dichotomic conflict. Though numerically weak, the scientists held the balance of power and could therefore throw victory in the class war to the contestant they favored. In the French Revolution, Saint-Simon reminded his respectable readers, the scientists had sided with the men without property, and the consequence was upheaval, bloodshed, and chaos. It was to the interest of both hostile social classes to put an end to the crisis of the times, and this could only be achieved by neutralizing the political power of the scientists. Blandly Saint-Simon advised the rival temporal classes that the best way to reach this reasonable solution was to elevate the scientists to the summit of the social structure

and to subordinate themselves to their rational commands. If scientists organized the spiritual world, social conflicts would cease and men would attain
terrestrial happiness.

The intellectual origins of this conception are not hard to identify. They derive from Condorcet, from Cabanis, and from the idéologues who, prior to
their fatal political miscalculation in sponsoring Napoleon, dreamed of such a
hegemony of science under the benign tutelage of a modern Marcus Aurelius.
Saint-Simon went a step further than Condorcet and the idéologues when he
explicitly summoned all classes in world society to establish a new universal
spiritual power in the form of the scientific priesthood of the Religion of Newton. Aside from the synthetic character of the ceremonials he proposed—
rather creaky contrivances after the manner of the Directorate theophilan-
thropic cults—his founding of the sacerdocy of science was based upon a number of rationalist and historical considerations which were current at the time.
There was a widespread consensus that a people had to have some religious
beliefs and institutions in order to preserve order and that even if atheism was
an ideal for the elite there had to be an exoteric religious doctrine for the mass
of the people. The theory of Charles Dupuis, propounded in his *Origine de tous
les cultes,* that all ancient religions were really codifications of scientific knowledge was adapted by Saint-Simon for practical religious purposes. The new
religion which he at one point dubbed Physicism was thus merely a modern
application of respectworthy time-honored usages among mankind.

The rule of the priest-scientists would end the moral crisis of the age and
would give impetus to a vast expansion of scientific knowledge. New sciences
would become "positive" in an appropriate hierarchical succession from the
less to the more complex, culminating in the science of man. As a consequence
of the creation of this elite the men with the greatest energies and capacities
would no longer pour their efforts into wars of destruction, but would become
productive scientists—the same idea which Condorcet had already suggested
in one of his manuscript elaborations of the tenth epoch of the *Esquisse.* "No
more honors for the Alexanders! Long live the Archimedes!"[2] was Saint-
Simon's hortatory way of predicting this inevitable ideological metamorphosis. In the *Lettres* he expressed confidence that both antagonistic social classes
would not fail to subscribe to the religious fund rendering scientists absolutely
independent of the temporal powers: the men of property in order to be reassured about what they were most interested in, possession of their property
and freedom from revolution; the propertyless in order to be saved from becoming cannon fodder in war.

Once Saint-Simon fell into penury under the Empire, his bitter personal experiences with the official scientists of the Napoleonic hierarchy roused him to
a frenzy of violence against them. In his paranoid state he fixed on Laplace and
Bouvard of the Bureau of Longitudes as his archenemies, the men who were
preventing the sublime truths of his *Introduction aux travaux scientifiques du XIXe
siècle* from being recognized. His conception of the scientist's role became
more complicated. On the one hand he still held firm to the idea that the individual scientist was the seminal historical force, a thesis he demonstrated in
numerous truncated aperçus on the history of world science; in fact historical
epochs were definable primarily in terms of their scientific geniuses. But
simultaneously in his scattered unfinished works of the Empire he adumbrated

a kind of scientific historical determinism in which the person of the scientist was eclipsed by the absolute and anonymous rhythm of scientific evolution. According to his formula the historical process of science, like all fundamental movements both physical and spiritual, required an alternativity of analysis and synthesis. Thus in the development of modern science, the age of Descartes had synthesized, Newton and Locke had analyzed, and now a new synthesis was to follow, a synthetic genius of science had to arise.

This scheme for the history of modern science was the rational kernel in his otherwise pathological attacks against the contemporary Napoleonic scientists. Instead of proceeding with the new synthesis which was their historically ordained mission in accordance with the law of alternativity which he had propounded, the school scientists were continuing to act like epigoni of eighteenth-century science and were becoming mere particularizers, detailists. "You gentlemen are anarchist scientists. You deny the existence, the supremacy of the general theory,"[3] he charged in a series of violent letters. The great Napoleon had summoned them for a report on the needs and mission of science, and they continued to conduct their individual experiments oblivious of historic duty, in open defiance of the true destiny of nineteenth-century science. They were thus at once traitors to science, to history, and to Napoleon. The science of the nineteenth century had to develop a unified plan, to construct a new view of the world, to oust old-fashioned religion and purge education of residual elements of superstition. Scientists had to cooperate and associate among themselves in the production of a new encyclopedia based upon a principle of synthesis that would replace Diderot's merely destructive encyclopedia; they had to fit their individual studies into an organic whole and then to crown their labors with social physiology, the newest of the sciences, in which was hidden the secret of man's salvation. Instead scientists were piddling away their time egotistically on their own petty disordered experiments. "The philosophy of the eighteenth century was critical and revolutionary, that of the nineteenth will be inventive and organizational," was the motto of his new encyclopedia.[4] Saint-Simon knew that the synthesis of the coming century would have a single principle, and he divined a priori that the principle would be Newton's law of gravitation, an idea which was by no means limited to physics but could be extended to chemistry, physiology, and the science of man. What he desperately needed was the aid, the collaboration, of technicians and other scientists—the very men who spurned him.

During the period of Saint-Simon's gravest psychic crisis, in 1812–13, when the slaughter in Europe was at its height, his rage against the indifference of the scientists mounted to a frenetic violence. At first he distinguished between the mathematical and the life scientists. He had quickly become disillusioned with the *brutiers,* for unlike Condorcet he saw no prospect for the solution of the social problems of mankind through the application of the calculus of probabilities. Many fragments directed against the mathematical and physical scientists hiding behind their "ramparts of X and Y," coldly indifferent to the fate of man, serving in the destructive corps of all the armies of the Continent, have a contemporary poignancy. With sarcastic contempt Saint-Simon ordered the inhuman *brutiers* from the height of the scientific eminence. He demoted them in esteem. For a while the only hope lay in the biologists, physiologists, and social scientists. Dr. Burdin, a surgeon in the armies of the Revolution, had once told him that the new science would be born when someone synthesized the writings of Vicq-d'Azyr, Cabanis, Bichat, and Condorcet, and Saint-Simon long clung to this expectation as the salvation of Europe. But there were times when even the life scientists seemed to have been engulfed in the general chaos. In his madness he cried out for the creation of a scientific papacy, for the summoning of great international councils of science to save mankind.

Saint-Simon's recuperation from his breakdown coincided with the end of the Napoleonic wars and the respite of Europe. As he emerged into the light his attitude toward the scientists underwent a drastic change. In the early years of the Restoration, when he gave ever greater prominence to the organizing role of the *industriels* in society, the scientist lost status by comparison. There are a number of different versions of his shifting sociological theory, but they all have in common a uniform devaluation of the role of the scientist in society. At times he thought of an ideal duumvirate with more or less equivalent status for scientists and industrialists, the one representing the spiritual, the other the temporal power, and he refashioned his whole philosophy of modern history along the lines of a novel pattern: the replacement over the centuries of the medieval priestly and military ruling classes by the scientists and the bourgeois. This historical conceptualization, which has since become a platitude of Marxist universal history, had many dialectical turns of thought: The new scientific elite did not succeed the old priesthood in a mechanical manner; in the very bosom of the medieval sacerdotal class the modern scientists occupied positions from which they were able to carry on their destructive warfare against religion. But despite this rather traditional dualism—the two swords—in which the scientists seem to represent a growing independent spiritual force, in the early Restoration writings Saint-Simon tended more and more to subordinate them to the industrialists. Sometimes he tried to use old projects, like his encyclopedia, as a device for the forging of a common militant consciousness between the scientists and the industrialists, but on many occasions he forthrightly proclaimed that it would be best for society as a whole if the industrialists became in the last analysis the final judges of the value of what the scientists accomplished. When he was most deeply under the influence of the French liberal economists Dunoyer and Jean-Baptiste Say he found no objection to considering the achievements of the scientists as mere commodities whose worth was to be estimated by the industrialists in terms of their practical needs and desires. His disenchantment with the official scientists was so profound that he could no longer conceive of them as playing a role of primacy in society. They were not heroic leaders but mere followers. Most of them lived on sinecures and emoluments from the state, and any overt opposition to the retrograde Bourbon aristocracy was too much to expect of them. They were timid and pusillanimous. Their intellectual productions were worthwhile —and they were not to be classed with useless bureaucrats, generals, and priests—but as often as not Saint-Simon came to see them as underlings. In some writings he merely grouped the scientists along with other useful persons such as entrepreneurs and workers under the general rubric *industriels,* which grew to be an overall category of productive people in every conceivable occupation who were contrasted with the *fainéants,* the do-nothings.

Unfortunately for his material well-being, try as he might Saint-Simon could not long rest content with his limited role as a moderately successful propagandist for the bourgeois. As soon as he broke loose and propounded in *L'Industrie* the crucial need for a terrestrial morality, he was thrown back into the problem of the competitive roles of the scientists and the priests. One of his solutions, during the period when he was still eager to retain the financial support of the nonrevolutionary Restoration businessmen, was to propose a transitional stage for society during which the priests of the old religion would be taught more and more science in the seminaries, so that those who in fact controlled education would promote the ideology of science while still wearing clerical garb. To avoid the horror of revolution and the evils of precipitous change Saint-Simon would advise the priests to become scientists—or he would have the Papacy order them to do so. Existing conditions in the spiritual world of the Restoration were morally intolerable because the great learned organizations were in the hands of scientists, while the educational system was still under the control of priests who knew no science, a fatal division which resulted in chaos. Perhaps if the priesthood could be converted to science no class revolution in the spiritual realm would even be necessary, as a mere transition would suffice. Of one thing Saint-Simon was certain: The scientific ideas of the elite of savants were penetrating all elements of the population, even the lowest classes, and the ultimate expulsion of existing orthodox religious ideas was inevitable.

In the final stages of Saint-Simon's doctrinal development, roughly after 1822, the scientists had to share their elite position not only with the administrative directors of society but with a third ruling group, the moralist leaders of the New Christianity. Religious and scientific functions were conceived of as distinct, requiring different capacities. In this period Saint-Simon came to realize the full social implications of an idea which he had first discovered in the writings of the physiologist Bichat. There he found a separation of all men into three natural classes, psycho-physiological types so to speak, in each of which one quality predominated, the motor, the rational, or the emotive. During his last years Saint-Simon adopted this triadic division as the ideal structuring of the good society of the future as contrasted with the existing unnatural roles into which men were cast by the status of their birth and by haphazard. In the new world of Saint-Simon, men would engage in motor activity either as administrators or workers, in pure rational research as scientists, or, as moralizers and inspirers of mankind, in appealing to human emotions through preaching and the arts. Since under this "industrial system" each man would be fulfilling his natural capacity to the utmost, there would be no misfits and no class conflicts. Each "capacity" would labor in its respective branch and would evince no desire to encroach upon the province of another. Perfect harmony would prevail, the power state would disappear, and men would be directed to the exploitation of nature instead of exercising dominion over one another. While Saint-Simon tended to conceive of the three capacities of acting, thinking, and feeling as mutually exclusive, he did make exceptions; in one of his works he even had a prophetic insight into the future central role of the engineer in the industrial system. In Saint-Simon's classificatory order the engineer combined the characteristics of both the administrator and the scientist, and he could therefore serve as an ideal intermediary in the implementation of the grandiose projects of the new society.

A substantial portion of Saint-Simon's writing in his final years was devoted to the drafting of blueprints for the administrative organization of the future world. Their detail is often tedious, but they have one constant element: All organs of administration—he eschewed the term government—were so arranged that each of the three fundamental natural classes was always represented in what he called the "high administration of society" in the fulfillment of its special capacities. As a rule, under the new division of labor the emotive or moralist branch tended to initiate projects, the scientific to criticize and evaluate them, and the administrators to execute them. In these ideal constitutions the scientist was thus cast in a rather uncreative rationalistic role; he was more often the emendator than the original inventor. The scientist seemed to represent the analytic spirit more and more, and Saint-Simon had come to appreciate the originality of the poet and the moralist above the talent of the scientist. In principle the three capacities were equal in worth, but if the spirit rather than the letter of Saint-Simon's last writings is considered, the scientist has somehow become the least preferred of the three brothers, and the religious leader who teaches men to love one another is awarded ever greater prestige. The cynic of the Directorate was on the way to becoming a Saint-Simonian.

The final article in a collection of essays Saint-Simon published in Paris in 1825, the *Opinions littéraires, philosophiques et industrielles,* was a discussion among representatives of the triumvirate who were destined to direct the future society. It was entitled "L'Artiste, le savant et l'industriel." The mission of his profession set forth by the scientist was precise: It was another plea for a general theory to encompass all the sciences rather than allow each of them separately and in isolation to achieve a high degree of abstraction; but there was also a new emphasis in this work upon the relations of theoretical science to "practice." As a consequence of the new social philanthropic tendency of his lifework, Saint-Simon insisted upon a reorganization of both science and education for practical purposes, which meant a speedy increase in the production of goods. The scientist's utilitarian and even "proletarian" goals were set forth with simple frankness. "What are the general applications of mechanics and of all the other sciences by means of which the most numerous class of producers will be able to increase its comforts and diminish its physical exertions, with the result that the price of human muscular labor will rise in direct relationship with the perfection of scientific processes? In a word scientists will undertake a series of works directly intended to perfect industrial arts."[5] While the scientists as a corps retain their dignity, they are forced out of their isolation—pure theory in any particular science is thrust aside—and all their works are specifically applied to the needs of technology, which alone is able to bestow a new worth upon the manual laborer. Human activities are set in a new hierarchy of values: Science is subordinated to technology and technology is made to serve not profit making but the appreciation of that element in production which is not mechanical—the human component.

From Equality to Organicism

Saint-Simon has one underlying preconception which is identical with the outlook of the old philosophical egalitarians, the conviction that the ideal forms of the good society must be congruent with what is natural in man. From a cursory reading of the physiologists, however, Saint-Simon came away with a different version of the natural: the natural was inequality. He inveighed against *philosophisme* for its ignorance of the simple physiological facts, positive scientific facts, which had since been set forth by Cabanis and Bichat. Confirmed in the belief that physiology was the only sound foundation upon which to construct a social theory, he experimented with variant schemes of social classification, and the plan he devised in the final phase of his thinking was a direct adaptation of the Bichat typology. His three social functions and three mutually exclusive social classes corresponded to the physiologist's three human types.[6] First society needed scientists to discover positive laws which in turn could be translated into guides for social action. This scientific capacity—the brain type, which he sometimes called the Aristotelian capacity—if given free play would fulfill the mission which Condorcet had proposed for the leading scientific intellects. Bichat's motor capacity was transformed by Saint-Simon into the industrial class. Most of mankind, whose primary aptitude was the motor capacity, were destined to remain manual laborers, though a small elite of this class with essentially the same kind of talent would become the administrators of the temporal affairs of society—the men who organized states and directed public works and engineered vast projects for the exploitation of nature. Saint-Simon's third class, which corresponded to Bichat's sensory man, were the artists, poets, religious leaders, ethical teachers, whom he sometimes identified with the Platonic capacity. In the last years of his life, when he emphasized the religious character of his doctrine, he endowed the sensory aptitude with special worth since he considered it capable of overcoming the atomist, egoist, egalitarian propensities of the contemporary world in crisis. The men of sentiment would give the new industrial society its quality and cohesive humanitarian spirit.

The good society thus represented a harmonious association or cooperation of men fundamentally dissimilar in their most essential natures, organized in three natural classes. Together they embodied the total needs of mankind—rational-scientific, manual-administrative, sensory-religious. The eighteenth-century philosophes, even when they admitted human inequalities, had still insisted upon organizing the state and society around those elements which men had in common, their natural equalities and relatively equal capacity for governance and the holding of public office. Saint-Simon and all later organicist doctrines which derived from him may have taken for granted some of the equal juridical rights of the philosophes, but they then proceeded to fashion society out of the different clays which were the raw materials of human nature. All men were not equally capable of participating in the administration of society. The new philosopher of society approached the whole problem with the initial preconception that the physiological and psychological differences of men were the very brick and mortar of the perfect social edifice.

The presumption is overwhelming that each man seeks to express his own and not an alien nature, that he desires to live and work in the classification where he has natural endowments, be they scientific, administrative, or poetic capacities. Saint-Simon here adapted one of the major contentions of the de Maistre and de Bonald theocrats, who steadfastly maintained that men were not driven by a passion for equality with other men of higher status or greater wealth, but really had a profound desire to remain in their own traditional occupations and to continue to express themselves in the traditional roles into which they had been cast at birth. They wanted not equality but the expression of their true social natures. Saint-Simon merely translated this conception into "scientific" terms: Men by nature desired not equality with others but the expression of their intrinsic and immutable physiological aptitudes. The Aristotelian idea that every being seeks a fulfillment of its essential character or nature has found an echo both in the theocratic and in the Saint-Simonian theories. It is a dogma that no man would be so monstrous as to desire to exercise administrative functions if he were born with a scientific capacity; at least, no good social order would allow such an anarchic misplacement of human talent. In the Saint-Simonian world outlook, organic inequality among men, inequality in the social hierarchy, and difference of social function were natural and beneficent, wholly superior to the *égalité turque* of the Jacobin revolutionaries, which was an equality of slavery beneath an omnipotent state authority.[7] Born unequal in their faculties, men required a society in which each was allotted a function. If a man operated in a social class to which he did not naturally belong, performing functions for which he was not naturally equipped, he would be wasting his own talents and reducing the total creative potential of humanity. Among Saint-Simon's last words to his favorite disciple was a definition of the quintessential goal of his doctrine and his life's work: "to afford all members of society the greatest possible opportunity for the development of their faculties."[8]

Talleyrand's image of the national workshop propounded in his report on the reorganization of public education survives in Saint-Simon's writings, where the goal of the new society is maximum production through maximum utilization of individual capacities. In Saint-Simon's vision of the golden age of plenty, the emphasis is placed upon ever more production and creation, rather than upon consumption and distribution. The banquet spread before mankind is so sumptuous that dwelling upon material rewards, so characteristic of a world of scarcity, seems to be beside the point. Saint-Simon's humanitarian doctrine thus incorporated the Condorcet principle that society could be organized so that misery and ignorance became accidents rather than the norm of human experience.[9]

Perhaps the difference between Saint-Simon's and the eighteenth-century conception has its crux in a new view of humanity. Instead of the man of reason as the most perfect expression of humanity toward which all men are striving, Saint-Simon thinks of man now and in the future as at once rational, activist, and religious, at once mind, will, and feeling. His ends are moral, intellectual, and physical, three major areas of human effort corresponding to the aptitudes of the artist, the scientist, and the industrialist. This is the whole man, whose being is paralleled in the organization of the healthy body social. If man is primarily a rational animal and the highest form of reason is mathematics, the Turgot-Condorcet egalitarian ideal of rational units behaving in accordance with mathematicized social rules is comprehensible. But if humanity is a composite whose various manifestations include the predominantly activist or religious as well as the rationalist, social structure, reflecting and embracing the variety and diversity of men, will be organismic, a harmony of complex, different, and essential parts.

The organismic society, unlike the atomist egalitarian society, which functions like mechanical clockwork, requires a "vitalist" element—some pervasive emotion, feeling, or belief to give life to the body. Though the eighteenth century had developed the concepts of benevolence and humanity as characteristics of natural men of virtue, Saint-Simon in the romantic temper infused the idea of the love of humanity with an emotional drive which it had lacked in the minds of the philosophes. Love was the fluid which coursed through the body social, gave it movement and energy. In Saint-Simon's judgment the equal atoms of the eighteenth-century world view were always on the verge of strife; his ideal of love created an organic harmonious whole out of society's vital parts. Men hungered for this comfort on the morrow of a quarter-century of world revolution which had loosened the very bonds of society. The need for the emotionalization of relationships if society was not to fall apart and disintegrate into its discrete elements had been dramatized by Burke and de Bonald and de Maistre. Saint-Simon by his own testimony was communicating the same urgent longing of men for a society in which they could feel themselves integral parts, an organic society, as contrasted with a state in which isolated units competed and fought with one another. Egalitarianism had come to represent the eternal struggle of equals in a world of cold and brutal competition.

In the good society a natural elite corps (he was directly influenced by the contemporary analogy of Napoleon's *troupes d'élite*), one with authentic, proved capacities, directed the various classes. Leadership was not, as the doctrine of popular sovereignty held, a generalized capacity in which all men were more or less equal and which made it feasible and natural for offices to be elective. In the organic society, workers instinctively rendered obedience to their natural superiors, their "chiefs," in their own class.[10] The idealized image of the Napoleonic army, in which ordinary soldiers had risen to be marshals, in which rank was at least in theory the reward of talent and merit, was a prototype for Saint-Simon's utopian civilian society.

Since it was in the very order of the universe that men should be unequal, instead of attempting to level these differences Saint-Simon, in the spirit of Bichat's physiological doctrines, held that it would be beneficial to the whole of society to emphasize them, to nurture and develop the uncommon and extraordinary capacities in individual men. Saint-Simon denied that Negroes were equal to Europeans.[11] Among Europeans themselves there were professional and class distinctions which he called "anomalies." The corps of the nobility and the clergy in European society had originally been founded upon just such organic anomalies in the human species. Though these anomalies had become attenuated through the centuries, the egalitarian philosophes had made a fatal error when they proclaimed the abolition of all specialized corps simply because the existing elites in name had ceased to be elites in fact. True scientists of society would not try to minimize unique excellences, but would devote themselves to the regeneration of specialized corps, confining their membership to the men who were patently superior, those who had the most marked "anomalies."

Saint-Simon's doctrine of what he called the "great trinity" of capacities was further developed by the Saint-Simonians, but this is one area in which they remained mere emendators, adding little that was new. At most they emotionalized a problem which Saint-Simon had set forth in rationalist terms.

The Twilight of Power

In the *Introduction aux travaux scientifiques du XIXe siècle,* Saint-Simon had shown his awareness of the universality of the power drive. "Every man, every grouping of men, whatever its character, tends toward the increase of power. The warrior with the saber, the diplomat with his wiles, the geometer with his compass, the chemist with his retorts, the physiologist with his scalpel, the hero by his deeds, the philosopher by his combinations, all struggle to achieve command. From different sides they scale the plateau on whose height stands the fantastic being who rules all of nature and whom every man who has a strong constitution tries to replace."[12]

Saint-Simon's Restoration works established a sharp distinction between the exercise of power by ruling classes in the past and the direction of the future industrial society which would become the function of entrepreneurial and scientific chiefs. The prospect of the survival of power, with its dread military and psychological consequences, into the golden age seemed to poison the benign placidity of free labor in association in the ideal state of mankind. Struck by the ubiquity of the power lust, Saint-Simon in his later works squarely met the challenge which it represented to his entire system. In a significant passage in the ninth letter of *L'Organisateur* he dismissed as irrelevant to the discussion furious madmen like Napoleon who reveled in the exercise of arbitrary power for its own sake, for such men were monstrosities. This was a typical eighteenth-century way of dealing with the abnormal; it was eliminated from consideration. As for the rest of mankind, there was a happy way out of the contradictions with which persistent and omnipresent human aggressiveness confronted the good society: The civilizing process tended to transfer the object of the power lust from men to nature.

By power Saint-Simon meant the exercise of any force by one human being upon another, an act of dominion essentially vicious. Power would not be necessary in the future industrial society composed of men freely utilizing their capacities. The energy which had previously been wasted upon the exercise of power over men would be channeled in another direction, toward the ever more intensive exploitation of nature. "The only useful action that man can perform is the action of man on things. The action of man on man is always in itself harmful to the species because of the twofold waste of energy which it entails. It can only be useful if it is subsidiary and if it supplements the performance of a greater action on nature."[13] This succinct expression of a new moral ideal for the industrial society captured the imagination of later socialist theorists and found an echo in their writings.

The historic substitution of nature for man as the object of aggression, so provocatively suggestive of both Marx and Freud, nurtured Saint-Simon's optimistic belief that with time not only intellectual but moral progress was feasible. Despite the fact that the most recent embodiment of the great demon of power lust was still alive on the rock of Saint Helena, Saint-Simon forecast the ultimate quiescence of the evil.

Along with his teachings that man's body influenced his mind, Cabanis had dwelt upon the reciprocal influence of the *moral* and the *physique,* an idea Saint-Simon had always found congenial. This doctrine allowed for the possibility that, with a great development of man's scientific knowledge, his passions

might be bridled. Society had already given promise of the eventual pacification of the power lust. Saint-Simon proved by homely example that the seductions of industrial civilization were becoming so potent that most men would
sacrifice even the exercise of absolute power to enjoy their pleasures in the
peace of the new society—vide the English nabob who after years of service in
India preferred the simple comforts of rural England to arbitrary dominion in
Bengal.

Since the natural elite of the industrial scientific society was based upon
sheer capacity, talents which presumably all men could instantaneously recognize, there was no room in the society of the future for class and power conflict. Men found their way into the elite because their natural aptitudes drew
them there. The prospect of jealousies and internal struggles within scientific
elites did not disturb Saint-Simon. The act of appreciation of superior genius
appeared to be miraculously free from the baser passions. As for conflicts
among coequal bodies of the elite, such as the scientists and the industrial entrepreneurs, they were beyond the realm of possibility. The innermost desire
of each member of an elite was the exercise of those aptitudes and functions in
which he excelled. It would therefore be contrary to nature for a scientist, for
example—a theoretician—to covet administrative powers, or for an industrialist to presume to seek membership in a scientific corps. Such capacities,
Bichat had taught, were mutually exclusive, and in the good society each man
would find his proper place. In the new moral order, "know thyself" would be
read "know thy capacity."

In past epochs of civilization there had been internecine strife among the ruling classes because these classes were constituted as agencies for the exercise of
superior power over all men. The medieval nobles were inflamed by a desire to
control the inhabitants of ever more extensive territories, the clergy to enjoy
absolute mastery over the minds of their parishioners. Such corps ambitions
had to clash because they vied for exclusive power. In the industrial scientific
society, basic drives would be turned outward toward the world of objects.
The scientist was discovering the deepest truths of nature and the industrialist
was harnessing the refractory forces of nature, two different, noncompetitive
functions. The direction of men in the new society was only an ancillary phenomenon to the exploitation of nature, both in the spiritual realm and in the
temporal. Dominion over men was indivisible, whereas the management
of nature could be separated into specialized functions, eliminating power
conflicts.

In the industrial scientific society all capacities were given free play. Saint-
Simon himself did not overstress the hierarchic nature of this society. He was,
of course, not completely emancipated from a classical denigration of manual
labor; the scientists and the industrial chiefs were endowed with special excellence. But, for all that, no working function in society was disdained in and of
itself. "All men shall work" was still the commandment of the new order.
Men's labors varied with their capacities. As for their rewards, Saint-Simon
was not an egalitarian. He dismissed the problem with the assurance that each
member of the body politic would be recompensed in accordance with his investment, a vague formula which left room for differentials in material emoluments. "Each person enjoys a measure of importance and benefits proportionate to his capacity and to his investment. This constitutes the highest degree of

equality possible and desirable."[14] Saint-Simon always focused on production, impediments to production, methods for increasing productivity; the rules governing the distribution of rewards were reduced to issues of a secondary nature, for amid the great superfluities of the society of producers there would surely be enough for the needs of all men. The social organism was guided by an ideological absolute that discouraged too wide a disparity between the rewards of one man and those of another. The primary goal was to raise the physical and moral well-being of the poorest and most numerous classes. While Saint-Simon rejected Condorcet's equality as an ideal, he never raised the incentive of class divergences as the motive drive animating the social body.

The only sound system was a functioning class society in which the roles of the men who administered were mere extensions of their social occupations. The "high administration of society," that clumsy phrase which he preferred to both "state" and "government," required no special aptitudes or talents and no specialized personnel beyond those occupied in directing normal social functions. There was no need for a government expert or a man trained in administration. Before the triumph of the industrial society men had been governed, in the order of the future they would be administered. The old and the new leadership were different because they reflected this underlying transformation in the nature of human relationships. Saint-Simon was emphasizing the distinction between the exercise of power based on physical force and of direction founded on a recognition of superior capacity in the elite, between the command function and the organization of an association for the common welfare. At first sight it might seem utopian to turn society over to a group of administrators after men for centuries had accustomed themselves to the absolutes of governance, power, and dominion. Saint-Simon pointed out, however, that in his day many pivotal economic institutions already in operation had dispensed with the command function and were voluntary associations—the banks, insurance companies, savings societies, and canal construction companies. These administered societies were models for the total society of the future, and he anticipated no special difficulties incident to the enlargement of the unit of administration. Society itself was one large national workshop with more varied activities, though none essentially different from those of a canal construction company.

The transfer of political power from the noble class to the chiefs of the industrial class—"professors in administration"—who in their factories and banks and companies had already been virtually exercising civil administration, would not be perplexing to the mass of the workers, since they had long since grown accustomed on the job to an appreciation of these entrepreneurs as their natural leaders. In the new order, entrepreneurial leadership would simply be extended from individual factories to the requirements of the "high administration of society." For the proletariat such a scheme of things would involve a return to a more normal relation in which they would no longer have to deal with two leaderships, one political and one civil; the chiefs of daily work would be at the same time the chiefs of the total society. Thus there would eventually be created an organic integrated society in which men would cease to be pulled in two opposite directions by rival forces. Similarly, the unification of the spiritual power in society, ending the present division between the clergy and the scientists, would not be a disturbing novelty for the mass of the people but would represent a desirable amalgamation replacing the confusion which had hitherto bedeviled them.

Class conflicts would be banished from the new society. Since the capacities of real classes could not overlap, what could they fight about? Since men of a class would seek to excel in their natural aptitudes, there could be only rivalry in good works, not a struggle for power.[15] When class chiefs owed their prestige to their control of men, they could fight over one another's "governed," but since there would be no governors and no subjects, from what source would class antagonism be derived? Within a class, men of the same capacity would be striving to surpass one another with creations whose merits members of the class would be able to evaluate. Between classes there could only be mutual aid. There was no basis for hostility, no occasion for invading one another's territory.

In a few key paragraphs of his tract *Suite à la brochure des Bourbons et des Stuarts,* published on January 24, 1822, Saint-Simon expressed in capsule form his whole concept of the natural elite in a society without power. "All privileges will be abolished and never reappear since the most complete system of equality which can possibly exist will be constituted. The men who show the greatest capacity in positive sciences, in the fine arts, and in industry will be called by the new system to enter the top echelon of social prestige and will be placed in charge of public affairs—a fundamental disposition which destines all men possessing a transcendent talent to rise to the first rank, no matter in what position the chance of birth may have placed them."[16] The whole social structure thus constituted would have as its goal the implementation of a *révolution régénératrice* throughout the European continent.

The more Saint-Simon analyzed the governmental functions of the state, the less use he found for its existence. His industrial society could operate with administrative and scientific capacities alone, without men adept at wielding force. The existing governmental system, which he hoped to replace in the near future, had raised men to office not because they demonstrated special talents, but because they had cunning and knew how to acquire and to manipulate power.[17] Their evil genius would be thwarted in the productive society of the future.

In the modern world the only useful work was scientific, artistic, technological, industrial (in the broad sense of the term); everything else was parasitic. Hitherto despite the fact that society had had to squander a large proportion of its energies on struggles for power, it had nevertheless managed to achieve a high level of prosperity. A fortiori, what great accomplishments was humanity capable of if men ceased to spend themselves in power conflicts and devoted themselves solely to cooperative labor!

After Saint-Simon had surveyed the various branches of the Bourbon government, he came to the conclusion that only the police power had some justification for existence. Though he made this grudging admission, he assigned the police a subordinate position in the industrial society, severely reducing the exalted status it enjoyed under the Bourbons. At times he even eliminated the maintenance of order as a formal attribute of the state. "This function," he wrote, ". . . can easily become almost in its entirety a duty common to all citizens . . ."[18] His state virtually "withered away," though he did not use the phrase.

In the good society, governmental action—by which Saint-Simon understood the command function—would be "reduced to nothing, or almost nothing." Since the goal of society was general happiness and happiness was defined as the development of the arts and sciences and the diffusion of their benefits through technology and industry, only managerial action would be required. Inevitably the progress of industry would reduce poverty, idleness, and ignorance, the chief sources of public disorder, and thus the need for most governmental functions, even the police, would dissolve. The industrial society, by eradicating the causes of disorder, made it possible virtually to eliminate the state. Granted a thoroughgoing economic liberalism—free trade, no domestic governmental regulation of industry and commerce, an inevitable reduction in crime, a foreign policy committed to peace—it seemed difficult to discover any broad areas in which the state could operate. Ultimately decisions affecting the body social would be impersonal and would be reached like other positivist scientific conclusions. "Decisions can only be the result of scientific demonstrations, absolutely independent of any human will . . ."[19]

However much Marx differed from Saint-Simon in analyzing the historical process, there was agreement between them that the new society emerging from the last conflict of systems or classes would witness the twilight of power and the cessation of power conflicts among men. Both saw power and aggressiveness not as ineradicable characteristics of man but as transient historical manifestations generated by previous, imperfect social systems and destined to perish with them. Their optimism was a corollary to their analysis of the classes designated as the agents of the last revolution. The "industrials" were by definition productive entrepreneurs to whom the spirit of war and conflict was alien; it would be contrary to their nature to become intoxicated with power. The proletarians were in their nature men who worked, not men who exploited, hence they could not engineer a proletarian revolution and thereafter exploit others. The simplicity with which socialist theory turned its head away from the realities of power was the great blind spot of its outlook.

The New Christianity

Saint-Simon's various religious posturings froze in a final attitude in the *Nouveau Christianisme,* published shortly before his death. The work was originally intended as an essay in the second volume of the *Opinions littéraires, philosophiques et industrielles,* but the urgency of the political and moral crisis moved him to issue it separately, and it appeared early in 1825, preceded by an unsigned introduction from the pen of Olinde Rodrigues which was an effort to smooth the transition between Saint-Simon's earlier philosophical works and the religious proclamation. The favorite disciple was only partially successful, for there is a chasm between the two careers which cannot readily be bridged in a few pages.[20]

As a manifesto of the New Christians, this last publication of Saint-Simon's is not a very pungent piece of writing. In many respects it is his dullest work. The tract has no clear plan; it is verbose and repetitive, and its occasional flights of fancy invariably fall flat. Nevertheless it was revered by his disciples as the final testament of Saint-Simon, and they strove to discover in it a hidden sense. Unfortunately for his reputation as a theorist, his name has been identified with this work above all others.[21]

Even in this tract the break with past doctrine is not absolute. Saint-Simon is still the philosopher of an industrial-scientific-artistic society organized as an "aristocracy of talent." He still is the enemy of the warrior nobility and the do-nothings. He still indulges in dialectical turns of thought, contrasts of epochs, of moral systems, of emotional drives. The heart of his whole system, however, has changed, for it is first and foremost a religion.

The *Nouveau Christianisme* is cast as a dialogue between an innovator (a New Christian) and a conservative, during the course of which the conservative is converted rather effortlessly. The opening lines announce the innovator's credo, his belief in the existence of God, in straightforward catechismic affir- mations. The dialogue ends with a proof that Christianity is a religion which must have been inspired by divine revelation. Forgotten are the Physicism of the Empire and the sacrilegious Dupuis theory. In the New Christianity, reli- gion was no longer the mere expression of general science, even though scien- tific knowledge was a major prerequisite for the priesthood. The essence of Christianity was its moral content. Dogma and ritual in great religions were only utilitarian addenda, handmaidens of the moral principles, which were timeless and not subject to change; the philosopher who once used the phrase "nineteenth-century morality" had recanted his heretical, relativist doctrine. Only the physical sciences have had a history and there has been progress in the accumulation of their data. Since the revelation of Christ, morality has had one principle and only one. The absolute perfection of this abstract moral truth could not be altered in time, even though the appropriate application of Chris- tian morality would still be subject to the law of change and progress. In brief, the Christian moral principle was eternal; only its historical embodiment was relative.[22]

The Christian religion, said Saint-Simon, was summed up in one sublime commandment, the golden rule: Men should behave toward one another like brothers.[23] When the conservative expressed incredulity at this succinct reduc- tion of Christianity, he was silenced with Saint-Simon's monist dogma: "It would be blasphemy to presume that the All-Powerful One founded his reli- gion on several principles."[24] The Christian apostles had taught this principle of brotherly love in its original simple form in the primitive catechism.[25] Preached to a society that was still divided into two classes, the Roman masters and their slaves, it was a lofty, revolutionary principle. The early Christians were thus daring moral reformers whose principles were to dominate the medieval system. In the heyday of its power, Christian papal society went a long way toward the practical application of the Christian catechism in the abolition of slavery. But the injunction of the catechism—to love one another as brothers—was not in its primitive form the ultimate embodiment of the Christian principle.

By the fifteenth century the primitive sense of the Christian principle had already become outmoded and urgently needed rejuvenation, but unfortu- nately the Catholic clergy, secure in their institutional powers, opposed any changes in the original expression of the moral principle. What was worse, they became inveterate enemies of its practical implementation, unlike their medieval predecessors, and they had remained so ever since. In the *Nouveau Christianisme* Saint-Simon threw caution to the winds. He arraigned the Papacy and the Catholic hierarchy before the bar of primitive Christianity and accused them of heresy. His language and tone were no longer circumspect; he labeled them Antichrists. They were heretics because for four hundred years the Christian principle had needed new raiment, and they refused to recognize its plight. It was no longer sufficient to preach brotherly love, for with the progress of science and the discovery of new worlds it was incumbent upon the Church to recast Christianity into a morality which taught that to labor for the amelioration of the lot of the poorest and most numerous classes in society was man's goal on earth. The services of the New Christianity would not be concerned with disputations about dogma but would concentrate on extolling those who upheld the new principle and condemning those who opposed it.

Saint-Simon repeated his earlier strictures against violence and his absolute belief in the powers of persuasion. Propagation of the Christian doctrine by force was contrary to Christianity itself. With this principle he hoped to reassure the rich, who might otherwise be terrified lest the poor, having most to gain from the New Christianity, resort to revolution to inaugurate it speedily. As he explained, he had long delayed the promulgation of the religious cult of his system because he wanted the rich first to become familiar with his scientific and industrial doctrine so as to be convinced that he was not an egalitarian subversive preaching against them. His earlier works had demonstrated the real character of the industrial society. The rich had nothing to fear from the New Christianity because the grand projects he planned, the universal exploitation of world resources, affording full employment, could be undertaken only under their direction and to their incidental enrichment. The industrial society with the New Christianity as its moral principle was a capitalist society working under a profit system. Saint-Simon saw no inconsistency between entrepreneurial activity and the moral ideal of the New Christianity. In this sense he was one of the great ideologists of modern philanthropic capitalism.

The treatment of the spiritual power of the old order of society always posed a troublesome problem for Saint-Simon. The old Christian clergy of Europe had failed in their function as an intellectual elite, and they had to disappear. But the fate of this class was more disturbing than was the destiny of the military rulers of society. There was no conceivable continuity between the functions of a warrior noble class and a new industrial class, so that the framework of the former could not be preserved to house the latter. The spiritual power seemed to have greater continuity from the Middle Ages to modern times, since in medieval Europe the Christian clergy were the repositories of whatever scientific knowledge was available and they were also the protagonists of the only moral principle in society. It would perhaps have been desirable, in the name of an orderly transition, for the Christian clergy to have assimilated the new science and the new version of the humanitarian principle of early Christianity rather than for the class of scientists to develop outside the Church. Saint-Simon was not intent on destroying the clergy, but on transforming their nature. Unfortunately the European clergy, having failed to keep abreast of scientific knowledge, had forfeited their right to function as society's intellectual elite. They had become a corps stronghold of superstition and false ideas, which they were defending against the new scientists merely out of a desire to maintain themselves in power.

The failure of the clergy to preach the moral law of Christian brotherly love was fatal to their continuance as a spiritual force. Whereas the medieval clergy as the spiritual power had pretended to supremacy over the feudal classes or at least to a status of equality with the feudal-temporal force, the modern religious leaders had resigned themselves to complete dependence upon Caesar and his heirs in all the European political societies. The need for moralists, scientists, teachers of the newly discovered truths, even theologians as formulators of the truth into religious principles, still existed, but the clergies of the formal European religious faiths were no longer capable of filling this spiritual office and therefore had to vanish as classes in their existing role. Perhaps a few of them would be assimilated among the leaders of the new Academy of Reasoning or the Academy of Sentiment, but the old religious organizational structures, mere shells of their former selves, would have to be divested of their spiritual power. If the Christian churches persisted in trying to hold the minds and the passions of men in their grip, they would have to be destroyed after a few individuals had been integrated into the new spiritual bodies. Saint-Simon did not expect this process to be a very profound shock to the European spirit since for hundreds of years the scientists had been slowly absorbing the prestige which was being lost by the clergy. Most people, even those in the lowest ranks of the industrials, no longer gave credence to the clergy's superstition-laden explanations of natural phenomena, so that the abolition of the clergy as a class would involve nothing more than the continuation of a process which was already far advanced. The acceptance of the New Christianity as the religion of the scientific industrial society would be the climax of this development. The old clergy having betrayed their trust as professors of morals and guides of sentiment and teachers of progressive scientific truth, their duties would be assumed by new classes composed of artists, poets, moralists, scientists, new theologians.

In his last work Saint-Simon wrote about the "church" of the New Christianity, his "mission," and the "voice of God" speaking "through his mouth." He referred to the "revelation of Christianity" and to its "superhuman character."[26] By this time the religious phrases had probably ceased to be mere literary artifices with him, as he had truly come to believe that Christianity was a unique historical experience and that he was the messiah of the new creed. In an early passage of the *Nouveau Christianisme* he made explicit reference to the messianic belief of the Jews and implied that he was its fulfillment. But despite the grandiloquent phrases, nowhere in the whole work is there an iota of what has traditionally been described as religious sentiment or expression. The word "mystical" has a negative connotation whenever he uses it, for his New Christianity is founded upon the truths of positive science and the one absolute moral principle of all time—brotherly love. It is even difficult to identify this religion with romantic pantheism and the romantic religious posturing which was in vogue in Europe during this period. Saint-Simon took occasion to condemn in passing the tendencies toward the "vague" in contemporary German literature, where romantic religiosity had struck deepest roots. His use of the arts in the propagation of the faith is a far cry from Chateaubriand's revelation of the beauties of Christianity. Chateaubriand tried to illustrate the genius of

Christianity by pointing to the sublime creations its spirit had inspired; Saint-Simon would employ the artists as mere agents, to rouse men to action in harmony with the New Christianity's philanthropic moral principles. The final rewards of his new religion were not dissimilar from the promise which Diderot extended to the moral man who by his services to science and by his philanthropy had deserved well of humanity—the preservation of his memory among posterity. The gulf between Saint-Simon and traditional faiths is so unbridgeable that it would be presumptuous to embrace his humanitarian creed and the Judeo-Christian revelations under the same rubric of religion, were it not for the fact that the actual practice of many Jewish and Christian modernists is far closer to Saint-Simon's morality religion than to orthodox belief.

At the outbreak of the French Revolution Saint Simon was almost twenty-nine years old, and the basic emotional pattern of his own personal life had been set in the sensuous, irreligious climate of the later eighteenth century.[27] But with the Restoration he revealed a remarkable sensitivity to the temper of the new generation born at the turn of the century and to its peculiar emotional needs. The religious and moral vacuum of post-Napoleonic France, so poignantly described by de Musset in *La Confession d'un enfant du siècle*[28] and by Stendhal in *Le Rouge et le noir,* was unbearable for many young men—the legion of Julien Sorels who had inwardly broken with traditional revealed religions, yet had found nothing to fill the emptiness. Olinde Rodrigues, the tense, emotional mathematician who became the constant companion of Saint-Simon's last days, no doubt strengthened his early intuition that a new morality and a new organic age had to assume a religious form. The Catholic revival in the romantic manner ushered in by the works of men like Chateaubriand was one of the officially approved religious solutions proffered to these young men. The *Génie du Christianisme* was an attempt to make the old religion palatable by embellishing it with the aesthetics of romanticism. But this religion of "sentiment" which passed for the revived Catholicism was rejected by many young intellectuals. Saint-Simon's New Christianity was more eclectic: In many ways it provided an ideal moral and religious syncretism. He praised the rationalist creations of the scientists and the speculations of the entrepreneurs; he dipped their ethics into a bath of moral sentiment, the love for humanity, and called it religion. Saint-Simon himself could not quite improvise the requisite romantic style and imagery for this new religion, which in his hands remained simple, amystical, at times crudely rationalist. Within a few years after his death, the young men who formed a cult in his name unabashedly drank in the metaphors and poetic conceptions of contemporary Catholic thinkers and emerged with a special cult jargon and ritual. It was a feat of exegesis to use the trite doctrinaire text of the *Nouveau Christianisme* in a public evangelism. There is none of the Saint-Simonian mysticism in the master's own written works, though he might conceivably have been swept along with his young men had he lived. Saint-Simon actually had in preparation a third dialogue which was to cover the morality, the worship, and the dogma of the new religion as well as a credo for New Christians. But he died before it was completed.

In Saint-Simon's Empire writings the history of scientific development had been established as an alternativity of epochs of synthesis and generalization and epochs of analysis and particularization. The *Nouveau Christianisme* revived this terminology, extending it far beyond the limits of a scientific method, adapting it to describe the whole social and moral order. First, there was an age of generalization:

From the establishment of Christianity until the fifteenth century the human species has principally been occupied with the coordination of its general feelings and the estab- lishment of a universal and unique principle and with the foundation of a general insti- tution having as its goal the superimposition of an aristocracy of talents over an aristoc- racy of birth, and thus with submitting all particular interests to the general interest. During this whole period direct observations on private interests, on particular facts, and on secondary principles were neglected. They were denigrated in the minds of most people and a preponderance of opinion was agreed on this point, that secondary princi- ples should be deduced from general facts and from one universal principle. This opin- ion was a truth of a purely speculative character, given that the human intelligence has not the means of establishing generalities of so precise a nature that it would be possible to derive from them as direct consequences all the particulars.[29]

This was the medieval outlook with its monist absolute, one is tempted to say the "thesis." Then followed the second stage, the contrary movement of this trinity—the history of Christianity from the Reformation to the present. During this second era, a new spirit of particularization, specialization, indi- viduation replaced generalization. This next epoch was clearly the antithesis, the contradiction of the first.

Though Saint-Simon does not use any of the Hegelian dialectical language he does express the concept: "Thus the human spirit has followed, since the fifteenth century, a direction opposed to what it had followed up to this period. And surely the important and positive progress which resulted in all our fields of knowledge proves irrevocably how much our ancestors in the Middle Ages were deceived in judging the study of particular facts, of second- ary principles, and the analysis of private interests to be of little utility."[30]

This second, antithetic movement of Christian history bore with it spiritual faults of its own, particular to its specializing, individualizing nature. Saint- Simon described again the malady of the modern age of self-centered, egotis- tic, isolated units, the moral parallel to the dominant trend of scientific particu- larization.

Moral deficiencies of the second movement of Christian history necessitated another reversal of the trend, away from particularization, individuation, ego- tism, but in this, Saint-Simon's last formula for the alternativity principle, he did not call for a complete turning back to the general. He ended with an ap- peal for the coexistence of individuation and generalization, not quite a new synthesis, but a civilization in which both antithetical elements were present. "It is therefore very desirable that the works which have as their object the perfection of our knowledge relative to general facts, general principles, and general interests should promptly be activated and should henceforth be pro- tected by society on a basis of equality with those works which have as their object the study of particular facts, of secondary principles, and of private in- terests."[31] A simultaneous advance on both fronts, the synthetic and the par- ticularistic, was the ideal course for the new religious society.

With less warrant Enfantin and Eugène Rodrigues later read into Saint- Simon's works other trinitarian formulas such as God, Man, and World, or the Infinite, the Ego, and the Non-Ego. Their doctrine moved further and further away from his positivism and shot off into a world of sensual mysticism alien to Saint-Simon's thought. On the other hand, it would be difficult to reduce Saint-Simon to a matter-of-fact philosophe of the simple, idéologue persuasion.

As he lay dying, Saint-Simon gathered his disciples about him.

The pear is ripe, you must pluck it. The last part of our work will perhaps be misunderstood. By attacking the religious system of the Middle Ages only one thing has been proved: that it is no longer in harmony with the progress of positive science. But it was wrong to conclude that religion itself has tended to disappear. Religion must bring itself into harmony with the progress of the sciences. I repeat to you, the pear is ripe, you must pluck it.[32]

26

Children of Saint-Simon:
The Triumph of Love

WHEN THE SAINT-SIMONIAN movement was founded by Olinde Rodrigues on the morrow of the master's death, it attracted a heterogeneous group of brilliant, disturbed young men—Buchez, Holstein, Arlès, Bazard, Fournel, Enfantin, d'Eichthal, the Pereires, Michel Chevalier, Duveyrier, Barrault.[1] They proselytized throughout Europe—though they usually preferred to convert in Paris—organized missions to the working classes, lectured in hired halls, contributed to newspapers and journals (*Le Producteur* and *Le Globe* became their official organs), were worshiped and denied. Soon they betrayed a characteristic common to young sects, religious and secular, Christian, Marxist, and Freudian—they fought bitterly among themselves. Violent personal rivalries for power and profound doctrinal differences developed in the church, and in the heat of the controversy the two antagonisms became inextricably confounded with each other.

Rehabilitation of the Flesh

Enfantin, a strikingly handsome man touching thirty, an engineer graduated from the Ecole Polytechnique, the son of a bankrupt businessman, quickly rose to be head of the Saint-Simonian hierarchy in the sacred college, though he had seen Saint-Simon in the flesh only once and there is no record of the master's judgment—his dog Presto is reported to have barked his disapproval. Père Enfantin presided over a succession of heartrending schisms, melodramatic temporary reconciliations, and final excommunications, accounts of which found their way into print immediately after their occurrence. The lives of the fathers were stenographically reported. When Buchez, Bazard, and Rodrigues himself were ultimately separated from the Saint-Simonian family and church, the surviving faithful redoubled their devotion to the new pope. They had all been committed to the rehabilitation of the flesh and to the commandment "Sanctify yourselves in work and pleasure." They were united in their resolve to establish a new organic order in which the senses would be gratified through the flowering of art, science, and material prosperity; but Enfantin's theological postulates, his androgynous image of God, and his apparent sanction of promiscuous love relationships passed beyond the point of tolerance for some of the adepts. When Rodrigues counterattacked he charged Père Enfantin with the very vices which their religion had come to remedy in contemporary society—destructiveness and revolutionary negation.

Saint-Simonian meetings were often disrupted by hoodlums hired by prominent citizens who feared that the cult would seduce their young. Stendhal's Lucien Leuwen, it will be remembered, threatened his banker father that he would run off and become a Saint-Simonian if his wishes were not acceded to.

The noisy debates among the apostles transpired in an atmosphere of general hysteria which induced seizures and fainting spells. Men saw visions of Christ and Enfantin. Edouard Charton, a Saint-Simonian preacher, has left a description of his initial terror, followed by a flood of free associations and by a passionate evocation of his experience when, in the presence of the Father, the gift of tongues was upon him. "Soon I could hear myself speak. I slowly became master of myself. I felt carried away by a torrent of thoughts and I took courage. I let my memories roam slowly from one event to another . . . If I aroused pity for the miseries of the people, I really was cold, I was hungry. If I bemoaned the grief of the isolated, betrayed man, I suddenly felt myself enveloped by the loneliness of my student room or the disdainful looks of men rejecting my entreaties. I was happy because I lived in body and soul with a greater intensity than I ever had before in my life! My whole being expanded and filled the hall . . . Borne aloft by my emotions as if they were powerful wings, I floated beneath a mysterious sky."[2] At meetings of the Saint-Simonian family "members of the proletariat" who were one moment burning with hatred against the privileged orders found themselves overcome by love as they embraced young nobles before the whole assembly, all joined as children in Saint-Simon.[3]

The strange fascination that Enfantin exercised upon the disciples was a troublesome memory years later when most of them had resumed respectable careers and had become successful bankers, engineers, entrepreneurs, and artists of the Second Empire. The search for the Female Messiah, the emancipator of her sex, for whom Enfantin was only a precursor, the expeditions to North Africa and the Middle East, degenerated into opéra bouffe and the movement petered out. The sentimental doctrines of the cult soon melted into the general romantic temper of the period. Triumphant international Victorianism put a determined stop to the easy talk of free love, but even in death Saint-Simonism remained one of the most potent emotional and intellectual influences in nineteenth-century society, inchoate, diffuse, but always there, penetrating the most improbable places. Paradoxically enough, the Saint-Simonians exerted an enduring influence in the business world, where they provided an ideology for expansive nineteenth-century capitalism in the Catholic countries of Europe. The Saint-Simonians left their mark on the projects of the Crédit Mobilier, the railway networks of the Continent, and de Lesseps' Suez Canal; their economic teachings have been traced to even more remote areas, the works of Visconde Mauá, the Brazilian entrepreneur, and of Lamanski, a pioneer of Russian industrialization. In the period between the First and Second World Wars there was talk of a neo-Saint-Simonian revival among French and German captains of industry.

Today one is more drawn to the psychological theories of the Saint-Simonians and the vivid portrayal of spiritual anguish in their public confessionals. Piercing insights into the nature of love and sexuality, which outraged the good bourgeois of the 1830s and brought down the police upon the Saint-Simonians, now have a greater appeal than economic doctrines which have become rather commonplace. Enfantin dared to discuss sexual repression with frankness in an age grown unaccustomed to such ideas since the Restoration had reimposed a restrictive system of public moral behavior from which at least the upper classes of eighteenth-century society had felt themselves emancipated. Saint-Simonian schisms were usually provoked by quarrels over the degree of sexual emancipation allowable in the new world. The more sedate among them would countenance divorce, but insisted on monogamy. For a brief period at least Enfantin preached free love with the same unrelenting absolutism with which Turgot had once espoused freedom of thought and economic action.

In the first public exposition of their doctrine in a hall on rue Taranne in 1828–1829, the Saint-Simonians were still demonstrating the positive scientific character of their teachings in language reminiscent of both Condorcet and Saint-Simon. This was their last obeisance to reason. When they proclaimed themselves a religion, as distinguished from a movement, their orators repudiated the groveling adjustment to contemporary taste which had characterized the scientific and historical proofs of their lecture series, published as the *Doctrine de Saint-Simon*. At a ceremony on November 27, 1831, Enfantin solemnly announced, "Up to now Saint-Simonism has been a doctrine and we have been doctors. Now we are going to realize our teachings. We are going to found the religion . . . We are now apostles."[4] As religious teachers they spoke directly to the hearts of men, to the downtrodden workers, to the enslaved women of the world, to moral men in conflict with themselves in all ranks of society. They were resolved to awaken the dormant feelings of love in mankind not by historical disquisitions and not by denunciations of the evils of the existing order, but by the beautiful example of their love for one another. Those Saint-Simonians who survived the great schisms voluntarily submitted to the discipline of the hierarchy, adored the Father, and ennobled the commonest labor by performing it with devotion in their retreat in Ménilmontant on the outskirts of Paris. Their sermons depicted the happiness of a future world where the passions were free, where both jealousy and indifference had been extirpated, where each man loved and worked according to his capacity, where the flesh was not mortified, where monogamy was not imposed but was practiced spontaneously—though only by the monogamous. In the religion of Saint-Simon dullards and sluggards in love would be aroused by the inspiration, the exhortations, and if need be the personal ministrations of the high priests and priestesses. For the nonce, alas, the seat of the Mother beside Père Enfantin was left vacant. In this second phase—when the preachments of the Saint-Simonians became dogmatic and they abandoned demonstrations from philosophical history—ritual, drama, costume, and music were introduced to fire the imagination of prospective converts. More and more they sought to pattern their actions after those of the early Christians. Enfantin's vest, a relic which has been preserved in the Bibliothèque de l'Arsenal, was a symbolic garment: Since it could only be laced in back, to don it required the assistance of another human being—a witness to the unity and brotherhood of man.

The religion turned its light on man's sexual nature and its relation to his intellect, on the psychic debasement of women, on the nature of love and God. On November 19, 1831, in a lesson to the Saint-Simonian assembly, Enfantin developed a complex theory of love and proposed a new sexual order based on the realities of human affections to replace the monogamous marriage which recognized no divorce. First he distinguished between two types of love, expressive of fundamentally different psychic natures, the constant and the fickle.

"There are beings with profound durable affections which time only knits more closely. There are other affections which are lively, quick, passing but nonetheless strong, for which time is a painful, sometimes an insupportable, trial."[5] To subject both characters to the legal arrangements which conformed only to the passionate desires of the monogamous entailed emotional misery and inevitably resulted in social chaos. Enfantin identified three forms of love relationship instead of one, and he sanctioned them all without praise or blame: the intimate, the convenient, and the religious. Intimate affections could be equally profound whether they were enduring or fleeting, as long as they were consummated among characters of the same type. When on occasion two contradictory personalities established relationships, the love was to be labeled convenient or casual. A third love, which he called religious, was the unique attribute of the Saint-Simonian sacerdocy—the priest's love for the two natures, which he understood equally well. "Thus with respect to morality the temple is divided into three parts, which correspond to the three faces of love —casual affection, profound affection, and calm or sacerdotal affection which knows how to combine them one with another."[6] What Enfantin meant by free love was the freedom to love in accordance with one's psychic nature, not universal promiscuity or universal evasion of the moral order through fornication and adultery.

How can one give both psychological types satisfaction and a rule at the same time? How can one safeguard exclusive love from the abnormal exaltation which renders it vicious and also protect it from the disruptive influence which the character of the other series, the Don Juan, exercises on the person of its choice? How preserve (no less important, despite what Christian prejudice has been able to do and still does to favor exclusive love) the individual who has this progressive love, who does not stop at one because he has loved one, but can, after having loved one, move toward another if the second is greater than the first—how preserve such a person from the anathema, condemnation, and contempt which Christianity hurls against him and from the impositions of persons endowed with exclusive affections sanctified by Christian law?

The solutions lay in the Saint-Simonian doctrines of the rehabilitation of the flesh, the emancipation of women, and the hierarchic priesthood of love, whose guidance was essential to avoid emotional abuses.[7]

The Saint-Simonian rebuttal of the bourgeois defenders of the family was full of scorn for the moralists whose hypocritical code was preserved only by the acceptance of prostitution and by the social toleration of adultery—the bourgeois safeguarded the chastity of their own daughters by "levying a tribute upon the daughters of the poor who walked the streets." Abel Transon's sermon on the *Affranchissement des femmes* on January 1, 1832, was a tender defense of the prostitutes of Paris, the modern Magdalens.[8] The later Marxist derision of bourgeois morality and Victorian spirituality drew heavily from Saint-Simonian and Fourierist sources. If progress came to signify the liberation and full expression of the whole man, his total personality, then sexual actualization had to be recognized as good, sexual repression as an illness which affected man's rational capacities adversely. Progress should not be restricted to the advancement of reason at the cost of a drying up of the fonts of love. As long as one vital drive in man's nature was curbed there could be no true happiness. For a brief period the Saint-Simonians, at Enfantin's command, attempted what would now be called sublimation in their retreat in Ménilmontant, in denial of the popular interpretation of their religion as gross sensuality. They were preaching the triumph of love, not mere carnal passion, but the distinction was difficult to communicate in nineteenth-century Christian bourgeois society, and when the rehabilitation of the flesh became a central dogma of the new religion, a rich vein of crude humor was discovered by contemporary journalists, who exploited it to the utmost. Enfantin's truth was not understood at the time by his revilers; the Saint-Simonians were expressing profound psychological realities which could not be assimilated by even the most perceptive idéologue observers of the human drama—men like Stendhal, for example, who wrote a witty though superficial pasquinade against them, joining the pack whose inner corrosion he knew so well. Sometimes it is difficult to believe in the authenticity of the Saint-Simonian love experience, and there is much that seems artificial in their aping of Christian models. Enfantin's withdrawal with a party of forty disciples to a house in the district where he had spent his childhood, the resurrection of the image of the Father and the bestowal of the august title upon a young man with a "childish" name, the quest for the Mother in distant lands, the reliance upon adolescent forms like an "initiation," all bear witness to the perturbed affective natures of the cultists. On June 6, 1832, before assuming the Saint-Simonian dress, Retouret ceremoniously turned to Enfantin: "Father, once I told you that I saw in you the majesty of an emperor . . . the goodness of a Messiah. You appeared formidable to me. Today I have felt how profoundly tender and gentle you are. Father, I am ready."[9] For all the tinsel trappings, the Saint-Simonians voiced subconscious longings whose very existence the bourgeois of Paris dared not admit.

The Saint-Simonians came to realize that women, one half of humanity, with their unique capacity for feeling, tenderness, and passion, had been suppressed for centuries because the Judeo-Christian tradition had identified them with evil, with the flesh, and with the grosser parts of human nature. The Saint-Simonian proclamation of the emancipation of women, Fourier's masterful depictions of their real needs and wants, and Comte's idealization of his beloved angel broke not only with Catholicism but with the eighteenth-century tradition of many philosophes, who even in their most expansive moods had regarded women as either frivolous or lesser human beings. This superior attitude had still been Père Simon's. For the Saint-Simonians and for Fourier the emancipation of women became the symbol of the liberation of bodily desires. If capacities were to be expressed in all their wholeness, the sexual desires of men, and women too, would have to be fully appeased, not as inferior but as noble, integral functions of the body. Once the Saint-Simonians denied the Christian dichotomy of the body and the soul a pronouncement of instinctual emancipation had to follow.

The Malady of the Age

The Saint-Simonians startled the intellectuals of Europe with a cry of despair, "Progress is in danger!" Civilization itself was threatened with total dissolution. The crisis of the times which Saint-Simon had diagnosed earlier in the century had been prolonged for decades; continually aggravated, it was undermining the whole social structure. The elementary bonds of human relations were being loosened. Faith in the eventual restoration of sanity and in the progress of humanity was unshaken among the Saint-Simonians, but what a terrible moral toll was being exacted from their generation, living in a twilight world when that-which-had-been no longer held men's allegiance and that-which-would-be was not yet believed. "Gentlemen," began the lecturer at the opening session of the exposition of the *Doctrine de Saint-Simon* on December 17, 1828,

Viewed as a whole, society today presents the spectacle of two warring camps. In one are entrenched the few remaining defenders of the religious and political organization of the Middle Ages; in the other, drawn up under the rather inappropriate name of *partisans of the new ideas*, are all those who either cooperated in or applauded the overthrow of the ancient edifice. We come to bring peace to these two armies by proclaiming a doctrine which preaches not only its horror of blood but its horror of strife under whatever name it may disguise itself. *Antagonism* between a spiritual and a temporal power, *opposition* in honor of liberty, *competition* for the greatest good of all—we do not believe in the ever-lasting need for any of these war machines. We do not allow to civilized humanity any *natural right* which obliges it to tear its own entrails.[10]

The degradation of the age was described by the Saint-Simonians in images less powerful than Balzac's but with the same moralist intent. Love relations were false; young girls were decked out by their parents to increase their value like slaves on the auction block. Since egotism colored all human relationships, in order to get people to perform an act of charity one had to invite them to a ball. The Greeks were being oppressed by the Turks, but no European nation rose to their defense and Christians traded with the persecutors. Fashionable atheism was proof that there were no ties, either to God or among men. An act of devotion or love was met with a sneer. Indignation at the persistence of social conflict was dismissed with the cynical reflection that such had always been the nature of man. "We have spared you the grief one experiences in penetrating into the intimacy of those families without faith and without belief which, turned in upon themselves, are linked to society only by the bond of taxation."[11] The malady of the age was an atrophy of love and association. "If one takes away the sympathies which unite men to their fellows, which cause them to suffer of their sufferings, take pleasure in their joys, in a word live their lives, it is impossible to see anything else in society but an aggregate of individuals without ties or relationships, having nothing to motivate their conduct but the impulse of egotism."[12]

A passionate indictment of their selfish generation was the leitmotif of everything the Saint-Simonians wrote and taught. It struck a responsive note in the audience of the Salle Taitbout and among correspondents throughout the world who recognized that the disease was their own. "Yes, my friend," wrote a gentleman from New York to *Le Globe*, "for twenty years I have been a Saint-Simonian in my inner being."[13] The Saint-Simonians brought to a reconsideration of the problem of progress their own anxieties, their thirst for faith, their fear in the face of a moral vacuum, their self-disgust with indifference and verbal atheism, above all, horror of their incapacity to love. Though they were not acquainted with the Hegelian idea of alienation, they described many of the symptoms of the spiritual malaise which Marx dwelt upon a decade later.

The Saint-Simonian inquiry into the state and destiny of economic production, science, and art in a world of disorder and confusion, of political and moral anarchy, drew a bleak picture. Industry was in a state of chaos. The cutthroat competition among entrepreneurs had brought about a haphazard distribution of productive forces accompanied by periodic crises during which competent managers lost their fortunes in bankruptcies and masses of workers starved. The common people refused to be comforted by the assurance of the economists that free enterprise and the introduction of machinery would ultimately lead to increased employment. The disorder, secrecy, and monopoly which interfered with technological improvement, the incompetent direction of industry by men who had nothing to recommend them but inherited wealth, the sufferings of the proletariat, the indifference of the economists who devoted their studies to a description of competitive antagonisms rather than to devising means for their alleviation, the absence of a central direction to industrial life which would allocate instruments of production in accordance with need and capacity—these were both the symptoms and the causes of the prevailing industrial anarchy. The possessors of capital were idlers, merit went unrewarded, gains were distributed in a chance manner. Laissez-faire had resulted in a colossal waste of human energy: technological potentialities were not fulfilled and material production was only a fraction of capacity. The physical misery of fellow humans left most men cold. Economic antagonism was the rule of industrial relations between workers and employers, when the true nature of man was pacific, cooperative, loving, and associative. "What is unbridled competition but murderous war, which perpetuates itself in a new form, of individual against individual, nation against nation? All the theories which this dogma tends to foster are based only on hostility."[14]

Science was in the same sorry state. Here the disciples repeated Saint-Simon's strictures against the piddling practitioners who were content with their anarchic laboratory observations and kept amassing insignificant details without a general theory, without a unified direction, smug in their little niches, callous to the woes of the rest of the world and the fate of humanity, cold *brutiers*. The competition which raged among the industrialists was paralleled among the scientists; they were absorbed in precedence of discovery, and in the absence of a general allocation of scientific resources they repeated one another's experiments, squandering their own and humanity's genius. In academies they convened in the same room, but that was the extent of their association. There was no overall scientific plan. Teaching and research were two separate compartments and what one branch knew was hardly ever communicated to the other. There were hundreds of analytic scientists, no synthesis. There were isolated discoveries, but no concerted attempt to apply them for the good of mankind through technology. Again, laissez-faire in science was dissipating energies upon useless projects.

Most pitiable was the state of the fine arts, a form of expression which in every age faithfully mirrored the moral nature of man. Unlike the creative geniuses of Greece and medieval Europe, contemporary artists had been reduced to the role of satirists who mocked their society or elegists who bewailed the state of mankind. They represented no great affirmations. Unless men believed in something, whether it was war or religion or humanity, there could be no grandeur in the arts. In the absence of a common ideal, the fine arts were mere evocations and reflections of the prevailing anarchy.

When the Saint-Simonians reached maturity a new generation of poets and dramatists had begun issuing manifestoes against the classical spirit and proclaiming the rebirth of poetry. The outburst of romanticism bestowed new worth upon aesthetic genius and gave the lie to those pessimists of the previous generation who had maintained that science could achieve victories only at the expense of the poetic spirit. The regeneration of the fine arts—though devoid of the wished-for vital spirit—convinced the Saint-Simonians that man could develop a more fertile imagination along with a more productive intellect and a vast material expansion of civilization. The fine arts, instead of being doomed—a common eighteenth-century attitude—might even become the most magnificent embodiment of human creative capacity. By comparison with masterpieces of beauty, the sciences appeared cold and lifeless; the passion for science which Condorcet had extolled so eloquently in his fragment on the *New Atlantis* was surpassed by a new enthusiasm for literature, painting, and music. Within a decade Saint-Simonian doctrines were absorbed by poets and artists throughout Europe who established no formal ties with the church, but who gave voice to its ideology. In this sense writers as widely dispersed as Alfred de Vigny, Ogarev, Carlyle, Heine, and the poets of young Germany were Saint-Simonians; even Victor Hugo paid his debt to Enfantin in a famous letter. Progressive humanity, the idealization of love, of association, of brotherly feeling, of outgoing emotion, appeared as new subjects capable of inspiring an artist to accomplishments superior to the work of the *Grand Siècle* with its exaltation of military glory. The notion of socially conscious art and literature, which has in the last hundred and fifty years spawned so many worthless documents and a few works of genius, was born among the Saint-Simonians. To sing of productive humanity and not of warriors would be the artistic ideal of the new order. To warm men's hearts grown frigid in the contemplation of neoclassic forms was the poetic mission. Poetry was no longer condemned to a repetition of the ancient myths; it had acquired a vast corpus of novel situations drawn from human history in all times and places, the whole gamut of human emotions, not the few permissible ones presented on the traditional stage. There were new feelings to be experienced and new priests of sentiment to be ordained.

While the Saint-Simonians' ideology of love and humanity as a cure for the *mal du siècle* evoked a widespread emotional response, the purely religious doctrine of the cult was a dismal failure: It was a manufactured religion whose raw materials were easily recognizable. When they called religion "the synthesis of all conceptions of humanity, of all ways of being," and preached that "not only will religion dominate the political order but the political order will be in its ensemble a religious institution, for nothing can be conceived outside of God or developed outside of His law," [15] it sounded as artificial and rusty as the writings of Saint-Simon himself concocting rituals for the Religion of Newton, expounding Physicism, or teaching the New Christianity. One group of Saint-Simonians had been exposed to German intellectual influences, particularly Gustave d'Eichthal and Eugène Rodrigues, and through them the amorphous pantheism of eighteenth-century German religious thought infiltrated France. The young Rodrigues had translated Lessing's aphorisms on the *Erziehung des Menschengeschlechts,* which are redolent with a romantic Spinozism that has little or nothing to do with the hard geometric propositions of which Spinoza's ethical system was originally constructed. The Germanic *Schwärmerei* invariably fell flat when it was presented in Cartesian French; it lacked authenticity. The Saint-Simonians' talk of a unitary law and of a providential plan, of the inevitable religious revival—for by definition all organic periods had to be religious—is deficient in feeling-tone. After Enfantin made the image of God androgynous a few loyal Saint-Simonians died with the "Father-Mother" on their lips, but though the Saint-Simonian religion may have for a fleeting moment inspired the adepts at Ménilmontant to ecstasy, its sermons sound imitative, mechanical, and stereotyped. No doubt some of them had religious experiences in William James's sense of the term, felt newborn upon conversion, and at least for a time were in a state of love which they indentifed with God; but a mere handful, perhaps only Holstein, Enfantin's oldest friend, were sustained in this emotion to the very end. Their historic proof that a new religion must be born after the incredulity of their own generation was nothing more than the threadbare analogy—worn even thinner since—between the contemporary world and the latter days of the Roman Empire. If the taste of their cynical age was bitter on their parched lips, there is little evidence that their thirst for a new religion was ever quenched by the ceremonies which Enfantin and Chevalier contrived—perhaps to stimulate themselves as much as their disciples.

The Social Trinity

Aside from the religious beliefs and paraphernalia of the cult, which rendered them notorious, the Saint-Simonians bequeathed to Western civilization a solid, relatively systematic body of social thought. Many of their ideas penetrated European socialist party programs in the form of slogans; others were more widely if more thinly disseminated. Since the original writings of Saint-Simon were almost impossible to come by, his ideas were generally fused with those of the school in the commentaries of the thirties and the forties. As propagators of a "progressive" theory, the Saint-Simonians had no inhibitions against putting into Saint-Simon's mouth words he had never uttered, if these were considered necessary developments of his thought. In general the rationalist and historical doctrines, which antedated the religious phase, found readier acceptance than Enfantin's mystical lucubrations in the *Physiologie religieuse,* but the two periods are to be distinguished more by the views that were accented and the style of preaching than by any fundamental cleavage in ideas.

The very definition of man had been changed by the Saint-Simonians; hence the nature of his evolution—the term became common—had to be reinterpreted. In one of his aspects man was still a rationalist, scientific, calculating utilitarian, who through time was fulfilling his needs; but what a feeble, one-sided identification of his glorious self this Turgot-Condorcet man had become in the eyes of the romantic Saint-Simonians of the thirties! They never outrightly denounced their spiritual ancestors, the eighteenth-century French forerunners. They paid them due homage, but they also adopted additional fathers in progress from across the Rhine, Kant and Herder and Lessing, and introduced that lone Neapolitan, Vico. The foreign thinkers endowed the Saint-

Simonian image of man with moral and emotional depth. The eighteenth-century progressists knew well enough that man in their age was not yet a rational utilitarian, but they firmly believed that he would become one, for that was his destiny. The Saint-Simonians invoked Saint-Simon and Vico and ultimately Plato to reveal a different man, a tripartite man, a being who was at once a rational scientist, a practical industrial activist, and a man of feeling and moral drives, a creature of emotion. Since this was the real total man, any theory which limited him to one aspect of his triadic nature was a false representation of his sacred personality. In Turgot and Condorcet and the early Saint-Simon the conclusion is inescapable that the history of mankind since primitive times had demonstrated the flowering of rational capacities at the expense of imaginative and passionate nature and that they deemed this one-sided evolution good in an absolute sense. For the Saint-Simonians progress was never encased within the relatively finite compartment that a rationalist view pre-established, a world in which one withdrew from the passions what one bestowed upon reason, a closed economy with a fixed quantum of energy. Saint-Simonian man had infinite capacities in all directions; he could at one and the same time progress in power over nature, in expansive feeling, and in the endless accumulation of knowledge.

The redefinition of the nature of man by the Saint-Simonians had moved far away from the rather mechanical Bichat typology. The three cardinal capacities were present in all men, and in the good society they would all be nurtured and developed. The Saint-Simonians recognized that men were not equal and tended to excel in one or another talent, that each man had a specialized capacity which would require separate training; but while Bichat seemed to posit a finite store of energy that was concentrated among different people in uneven proportions, the Saint-Simonians regarded all capacities as endlessly expansive. What they rejected were the exclusivity and limitations of all previous definitions of man. Man was at once utilitarian and religious and activist: morality had a sanction in use, in God, and in nature all at the same time. The Christian duality of the spiritual and the corporeal, the contempt for the body and its desires, the eighteenth century's hypertrophy of reason and its implied denigration of the creative imagination, and the Stoic repression of feeling were all banished. Man appeared with both his body and his soul, loving, with an insatiable thirst for learning, boundlessly dynamic in his conquests of nature. In the hundred years of prophecy Turgot's "progress of the human mind" became the Saint-Simonian "progress of the general emancipation of humanity."

As in all triadic systems ancient and modern, the role, relative potency, and position of excellence of the three elements composing the unity was a harassing problem. It invariably led to disputations. Saint-Simon himself had wrestled with the three capacities and had offered his alternative, often contradictory solutions; and the great heresiarch Comte struggled with the new trinity, producing complex, subtle responses worthy of a latter-day Greek Father of the Church. The relations among the capacity to reason, to act, and to feel became central to Saint-Simonian theology. The ideal of equivalence among the three has always been difficult to maintain—Christianity with its trinitarian definition of God had a similarly irksome intellectual problem which found expression in thousands of volumes and cost hundreds of thousands of lives. What was man, after all: Was he *primarily* a rational, a sentient, or an activist being? Which psychological type should rule the world? Which should lead in the march of progress and which should docilely accept subordination? The eighteenth-century rationalists faced none of these prickly questions because the reign of reason as an ideal was virtually unchallenged. Saint-Simon and his disciples, the true and the dissident, had to make a configuration out of the different natures which comprised the human soul, and however much they pleaded for the parallel worth of knowing, feeling, and acting, discoursed on their common interdependence, praised their mutual indispensability, the very idea of hierarchy raised questions of precedence, and the worm of rivalry among the three equally noble parts crept into the bosom of the doctrine. Though Plato's triad was always in the background of the Saint-Simonian system, the outright subordination of the nonrational capacities in the ancient myth made direct references to him uncongenial.

The Saint-Simonians accentuated the final phase of the tradition of their master and elevated to preeminence the "artists"—their generic name for what he had called the Platonic capacity—a category that extends far beyond painters, poets, and musicians, and embraces all moral teachers, whatever may be their instruments of instruction. If man was tripartite his emotional being was the most developed side of his nature in the good, healthy, organic periods of human existence. The crisis of modern times was primarily an emotional one and the malady of the age a morbidity of the sentient capacity. Mankind's talent for love had shriveled. The scientific capacity, if left to itself, would become glacial, merely critical; science was always useful, but it would be dangerous if allowed to dominate society. Since the sentient capacity was the clue to man's religious future—the major problem of human existence—clearly the man of feeling was the ideal personality type, before whom his brothers in humanity had to incline slightly, even if they did not quite genuflect. The man of moral capacity set goals and inspired his brethren with the desire to achieve them. By his side the scientist who merely accumulated observations was a frigid analytic agent, indispensable for progress, but surely not to be ensconced on the throne. The Saint-Simonians were among the first to voice their horror of the neutrality of science.

The appeal of this idealized artist-poet-priest type to the romantics who listened to the exposition of the *Doctrine de Saint-Simon* was overwhelming. A fusion of religious and aesthetic enthusiasm had been achieved by eighteenth-century German writers; it was an underlying tenet of Chateaubriand's religiosity in France; Saint-Simonism was thus sowing in well-ploughed fields. Even before the Saint-Simonian preachers mounted the rostrum, the young poets of Europe had already arrogated to themselves the emotional direction of mankind which the clergies of all nations were allowing to slip from their grasp. Since feeling was all, the artist-poet-musician with the most acute sensitivities could best express man's moral nature and reawaken dormant moral sentiments. The romantic genius was *Obermann*, Vigny's *Chatterton*, Hölderlin, Beethoven—all Christlike martyrs—not the rationalist scientist-geniuses of Turgot and Condorcet. It was most flattering to the poets of Western romanticism to find themselves raised to the pinnacle of society—albeit the society of the future—at a time when they were disdained by the successful, activist, philistine bourgeois and treated with cold indifference by the rationalist men of letters and science in the academies.

From Antagonism to Association

Unlike their autodidact master, the Saint-Simonians incorporated philosophical history from beyond the boundaries of France. In addition to members of the school the principal agents of transmission were Victor Cousin, who had popularized Kant and Hegel in his lectures, and Michelet, who had translated Vico a year after Saint-Simon's death. When Edgar Quinet adapted Herder, the chain was complete. Kant's theory of history, developed in his brilliant little essay of 1784, provided the Saint-Simonians with a key formula that explained the historical process.

The word and the concept of Antagonism introduced into the cult from Kant's essay were endowed by the Saint-Simonians with an easy optimism that the philosopher of Königsberg never expressed. The history of mankind became the record of the evolution of this primary immoral passion and of the variegated forms that it had assumed through time. The Saint-Simonians were rectilinear progressists, for whom the feeling of antagonism was subject to modal changes in a continuous series—to adopt their language for a moment; in the large they contemplated history as a temporal process in which the quantity of overt antagonism in the world underwent a steady diminution as the result of a salutary transformation of human institutions. In the beginning, ran the Saint-Simonian account of Genesis, there had been only isolated families, each of them held together by enmity toward all other families on the globe—the maximum possible extension of the hostile feeling. Only within the confined orbit of this primeval human association did even a glimmer of harmony and love prevail. With time, as the organizational forms of society encompassed ever greater numbers of persons, advancing in a series from the family to the tribe to the city to the nation to the multinational religion, the sum total of possible antagonisms among persons decreased arithmetically and the love relationships within the broader social unit increased in a like proportion.

World history thus became the study of the general diffusion of love and the contraction of antagonism, a new adaptation of the geographic analogies which Turgot and Condorcet had once used to describe the spread of scientific enlightenment and the gradual blotting out of obscurantism. A history of the progressions of love replaced the successive advances of mind.

In its detail Saint-Simonian history is not quite as simple as this image at first implies. While antagonism assumed new shapes—city wars, national wars, religious wars—the old conflicts were not completely eradicated within the inflated structures of association, so that even after international religious societies were organized the spirit of hostility within the family based upon age and sex differences, within the city based upon families, and within the nation based upon cities tenaciously persisted. Love had never taken complete possession of even the most intimate associations of the older "in-groups"—to employ a contemporary barbarism. A Saint-Simonian view of the world as it stood on the threshold of association and love gave rise to the paradoxical reflection that there was still pervasive antagonism throughout human society both on an international and on an intimate personal level; on the verge of universal love, the world was riddled with hates. The conflicts might be said to have diminished within the limits of the smaller associations only in the sense that they had become attenuated and milder in their overt expressions. Men were no longer commonly anthropophagous.

Another facet of antagonism which had undergone a series of quantitative, measurable changes was manifested in the economic exploitation of one man by another, in the treatment of men as objects rather than persons. (Here the Saint-Simonians clearly drew on Beccaria and Kant.) In the earliest times men devoured their captives, then with progress they merely killed them, and finally they enslaved them. The first modes of the series were lost in prehistory, but the later forms of exploitation were known and recorded in the successive institutions of slavery, serfdom, and free labor. Legally, at every one of the stages, there had been some further limitation upon the absolute power of the exploitation of man by man. The progress of love was thus demonstrable, though complete freedom had not yet been achieved and in the condition of the modern proletariat—the indignity of the term, connoting the status of workers as a mere child-bearing mass, made it repugnant to Saint-Simonians —remnants of the ancient forms of exploitation had survived. There were vital respects in which modern workers were still slaves and serfs—a common theme in the contemporary literature depicting the wretchedness of the laboring classes in Western society. But though exploitation was an abominable reality of the organization of work, a review of its history proved that in long terms it was a waning form and that association and sociability were steadily gaining the upper hand. "National hatreds are diminishing every day and the peoples of the earth who are ready for a total and definitive alliance present us with the beautiful spectacle of humanity gravitating toward *universal association.*" [16]

The Saint-Simonians had still another way of interpreting the past, one derived directly from Saint-Simon, which involved the introduction of an alternating rhythm into world history, a heartbeat of the historical process. Among the Saint-Simonians it took shape as a succession of organic and critical epochs; they fixed the terminology, though Saint-Simon had already described the phenomenon. The organic was a period in which individuals were tied together by some common bond—be it war or religious faith—in which there was at least a harmony between spiritual and secular powers, education trained men to a set of common values, the moral and material forces in the society were not in flagrant contradiction with each other, there was organization and order. The order may have been rooted in false scientific assumptions, as it was in the Middle Ages, and the moral level of an organic epoch may have been relatively low, as it was in the Greek world; but these ages were sound, healthy, human, harmonious, social, integrated—they merited the positive adjectives in the Saint-Simonian vocabulary. It was unfortunately the nature of the historic process for these organic epochs to become disturbed and ultimately to disintegrate. The causes of the disruption could be found in the inadequate level of moral, scientific, and activist achievement of previous societies, in the internecine rivalry among the leading capacities, and in the persistence of superannuated organizational forms. The organic epochs were invariably fol-

lowed by critical epochs which had a deplorable, even a tragic, historic function to perform, for it was their mission to criticize and to destroy the old organic institutions that had once held a society together, to mock and to attack
its values, to annihilate its ruling groups, an ugly thankless task which had
usually brought to the fore analytic character types, men who could dissect and
anatomize but not create. At this point the Saint-Simonians modified somewhat their master's conception. He had depicted the alternativity of the organic and the critical almost exclusively in class terms, the version in which the
doctrine penetrated Marxist thought. His new classes, both spiritual and temporal, had grown in the very bosom of the old order and had secretly waxed
powerful beneath the surface of the overt political institutions until they were
mighty enough to overthrow the dominant forces and assume control themselves. The initial period of class revolt was drawn by Saint-Simon in heroic
terms: His most elaborately developed illustration, the combat of the modern
industrial-scientific powers against the medieval military-theological ones,
was marked by a strong Condorcet-like jubilation at the triumph of rational
good over superstitious evil. The Saint-Simonians were consistently pejorative
toward critical epochs. Destruction was a necessary clinical operation, and they
occasionally recognized the force and the vitality of those engaged in wiping
out antiquated scientific and moral ideas and decrepit temporal rulers whose
day had passed, but once the ancient beliefs had lost their sway over men's
hearts and minds, there followed a most terrible period of human history, an
age of nothingness, of the void, of indifference, of isolation, of egotism, of
loneliness, of psychic suffering, of longing. The Saint-Simonians were describing the Roman Empire before the triumph of Christianity and their own miserable century. The portrayal of the darkness before the dawn in the Saint-
Simonian sermons made them documents of spiritual self-revelation, mutatis
mutandis like the writings of the early Church Fathers.

From de Maistre, Bonald, and Ballanche they drew an idealized image of
medieval Europe, the last great organic epoch of history, an age of love, devotion, and duty, when men had faith, when they belonged, when society had
unity and order. Their romantic medievalism was transparent. In destroying
the abstract values of Condorcet's progressist school—the ideals of equality,
rational science, and liberty—they also turned his philosophical history topsy-
turvy. The good ages were those in which spiritual and religious authority
were spontaneously respected, in which there was no conflict, no opposition,
no contradiction, no dissension.

Saint-Simonians had one rational method for the propagation of the new
doctrine, the demonstration through an array of empirical evidence that the
attainment of a society of universal love was historically inevitable. Their
theme was not novel; the idea of a historical series, prevalent enough in eighteenth-century thought, was continued on into the nineteenth, strengthened
by the addition of analogies from biological growth. The mathematical series
never lost its fascination even after organic concepts describing evolution had
been introduced, since the organic metaphors could not render the idea of infinity so convincingly as an arithmetic progression without end. In the organic
image the fear of death or the notion of mere cyclical recurrence always lurked
in the background, and at moments the most ardent of the progressists, like
Saint-Simon and Fourier, succumbed to the prospect of inevitable degenera-

tion. Infinite organic growth was hard to conceive, while a long series moving in one direction and begging for extrapolation was irresistible. Why should the course be reversed? If in the past there had been temporary stoppages and even brief setbacks, the Saint-Simonians' theory of progress improvised specific ad hoc excuses to explain away the insignificant deviations from the main current of history.

Each According to His Capacity

The only solution to the crisis of the times was the moral transformation of mankind through the religion of Saint-Simon. To join the Saint-Simonian movement was an act of commitment to the future progress of man, an act of faith in his potential development. It involved a spiritual conversion from egotism, the dominant morality of the age, to humanity, the moral law of the future. The dawn of a new religious epoch was inevitable because the law of progress foretold another synthesis after the atheism and emotional barrenness of the second stage of the critical epoch. But the process could be delayed or hastened, and it was the mission of the Saint-Simonians to put an end to an age of disbelief and anarchy and to inaugurate the new world, to regenerate mankind. The leaders of the cult knew their historic role well—they were the Fathers of the Church, come after Saint-Simon to spread the new doctrine. The renovation of man would now be total; this was the last stage of provisional history and mankind was about to make the leap into definitive history, a world of order, limitless progress in the flowering of all capacities, a world without antagonism, virtually without pain, a world of love, unity, and cohesiveness. The members of the movement practiced those virtues which would become normal among all mankind in the future. The movement, the religion, was the new world in miniature.

The prevailing chaos resulted from the repression of true capacity and excellence among industrialists, artists, and scientists and the haphazard disposition of human energies in accordance with hereditary privileges and antiquated legislation. The principle of the new order would be antithetical: "Each according to his capacity! Each capacity according to its works!" became the Saint-Simonian motto. In the social organism there was an optimum spot for every individual, and its discovery was the end of the social art. It was an unquestioned presupposition of Saint-Simonism that each man's capacity was clearly definable by a hierarchy of experts whose authority culminated in the priests and priestesses of the new religion, and that each man would willingly crawl into his appointed cubbyhole in the perfect system. This did not involve a destruction of personality or liberty—the Saint-Simonian preachers thus quieted the qualms of their audience of romantic individualists—but a genuine fulfillment. "Our religion does not stifle liberty," Père Barrault assured his listeners on November 27, 1831, "it does not absorb sacred personality. It holds each individual to be saintly and sacred. Since it promises classification according to capacity, does this not guarantee each man the preservation and development of his own native physiognomy, his own particular attitude, under a name which belongs only to him?"[17]

In order to achieve the proper distribution of capacities two profound changes had to be effectuated in the order of Western society. First the property system had to be reorganized, and then a new educational system introduced. The transmission of property through inheritance had to be abolished, even though private property was preserved as an institutional instrument to reward merit. Inheritance had become the vicious mechanism for the induction of incompetents into the administration of society, where they created anarchy and stifled progress. Their posts rightfully belonged to men of capacity. Order required the reward of each according to his works, and the intrusion of inherited wealth rendered any such allotment for merit impossible. The Saint-Simonians, who always thought of themselves as men of moderation, sharply distinguishable from the revolutionaries, drew the attention of their listeners to the numerous transformations which property had undergone in historic times in order to present the abolition of inheritance as a mere step in a long series—the final metamorphosis.

Absolute equality in property would entail equal awards for unequal merit, and such communism was contrary to human nature. "We must foresee that some people will confound this system with what is known under the name of *community of goods*. There is nevertheless no relationship between them. In the social organization of the future each one, we have said, will find himself *classified* in accordance with his capacity, rewarded in accordance with his works; this should sufficiently indicate the inequality of the division."[18] But while capacities and works and rewards were all unequal in the new society, the dimensions of differences were not conceived of in our contemporary terms, and the pursuit of inequality, the desire to outstrip one's fellows, was never envisaged as an energizing drive of society. Inequality resulting from rewards according to works was a consequence, not a goal. Like Condorcet, the Saint-Simonians knew that in the new distribution of functions in accordance with technical capacity partiality would sully the purity of the moral world, but that was not the issue, they maintained, anticipating the arguments of their opponents; in their day there was chaos and misery in a society of misfits, in the future "errors, accidents, and injustices will only be exceptions."[19]

In the economic realm Saint-Simonism became a utopia of finance capital. The whole industrial mechanism was envisioned as one vast enterprise presided over by a unitary directing bank which dominated the rest and was able to weigh accurately the various credit needs of all branches of industry. "Let us transport ourselves to a new world. There proprietors and isolated capitalists whose habits are alien to industrial labors no longer control the choice of enterprises and the destiny of the workers. A social institution is invested with these functions which are so badly filled today. It presides over all exploitation of materials. Thus it has a general view of the process which allows it to comprehend all parts of the industrial workshop at the same time . . ."[20] There would be a central budget which on the credit side consisted of the "totality of the annual products of industry,"[21] the gross national product of present-day parlance. On the debit side were the requirements of the various subsidiary credit institutions and the banks of the specialized industrial branches. In this bankers' dreamworld the demands of centralized supervision and of local special institutions were delicately balanced—in a way, the contemporary practice, though not the theory, of all highly organized economies of the "capitalist" or "communist" variety. The Saint-Simonians recognized that there would be competitive claims from various branches of industry, a thorny problem verbally resolved with the slogan that allocations would be made "in the interests of all."[22] In the last analysis decisions on individual demands were evaluated by the experts, or "competent chiefs," prototypes of our contemporary planning commissioners.

There has been some attempt to fit the Saint-Simonians into a history of totalitarianism. Their contempt for liberalism and the franchise gives a semblance of verisimilitude to the charge that they were precursors of fascism, though a hierarchical conception of order is not necessarily totalitarian. In many respects they proposed to run the capitalist economic and social order the way it actually has been run in the welfare state since World War II. Heavy death duties are virtually the equivalent of a Saint-Simonian abolition of inheritance, and the central financial institutions of most governments exert no less power over the distribution of credit to industry than the central banks projected by the Saint-Simonians. Business, the army, and the university are hierarchical structures in which directives are issued from the top and diffused through various echelons, despite the continued existence of residual democratic forms and the occasional influence of a ground swell of opinion from below. In the most advanced societies the course is open to scientific and artistic and industrial talent, and sheer incompetence even when buttressed by hereditary wealth is no longer generally tolerated. Women are moving toward real as contrasted with theoretical equality, and the greatest good of the greatest number is universally accepted by all nations in solemn assembly.

Perhaps the only tenet of Saint-Simonian doctrine that has not fared well in the twentieth century is the proclamation of the triumph of love. While the necessity for its existence has been preached often enough in the church and in the university, love seems to have encountered almost insurmountable obstacles. Ours is an orderly, hierarchical society, open to capacity that is rewarded according to its works, but it is hardly a loving society. The "lonely crowd" of David Riesman would fit into any Saint-Simonian course of lectures diagnosing the ills of that world.

Education for Love

Since a whole aspect of man's instinctual nature, his capacity to love, had atrophied, leaving him only a part-man, a totally reshaped educational system was urgently required to rectify the basic failings of the old order. The progress of science and industry had so far outstripped man's emotional development that there was a grave imbalance in the human condition. Mankind had to be taught to feel again. Nourishment of the moral sentiment became the paramount objective of the Saint-Simonian educational system. Teaching the love of humanity would warm all relationships grown tepid in the critical epoch and rescue a society which had lapsed into emotional sterility. If the capacity to love were developed among all men a state would ultimately be reached where each individual would spontaneously subordinate his particular interest to the good of mankind. Men would be conditioned to love as they were now trained to self-seeking, self-interest, and antisocial behavior.

The Saint-Simonians were adroit in refashioning the educational techniques of Catholicism to fit the new religion. "This does not mean," the Saint-Simonian lecturer explained to his audience of unbelievers, "that the same practices and the same forms would be perpetuated, that the catechism and the rituals, the stories which once inspired the faithful had to be preserved intact . . . Analogous though improved methods would be utilized to prolong the education of man throughout the whole course of his life."[23] The confessional, far from being scorned as an instrument of clerical domination, was praised as an ideal way of instilling moral values. The Saint-Simonians revamped it into a "consultation"—shades of the psychoanalytic couch—and extolled it as a health-giving agency that during moments of acute personal crisis could be used to bind men's souls to the service of humanity. In the confessional-consultation "less moral and less enlightened men seek the knowledge and the strength they lack from their superiors in intelligence and in order."[24] Preaching would have the same function as in the Catholic Church, and prayers would be directed to a humanitarian God and Father-Mother. In their public utterances the Saint-Simonians invariably treated Catholicism with the respect due a worthy departed ancestor—an attitude which the official ecclesiastical hierarchy failed to appreciate. Enfantin went so far in adapting Catholic theological terminology that the Pope was constrained to place the *Physiologie religieuse* on the Index lest confusion be sown among the faithful.

Since all moral truths were not rationally demonstrable, the bulk of mankind would have to accept religious teachings on authority, as they had in the old Church. While the philosophes had always relied on the logical proof of their ideas in a popular, easily presentable form that rendered them self-evident, and had looked forward to the time when all men were amenable to reason, Saint-Simonian doctrine was heavily dosed with elitist snobbery. The attitude toward the proletariat was loving but paternalistic; hence the frank recourse to preaching ex cathedra: "The results of social science can be presented to most men only in a dogmatic form."[25]

In practice Saint-Simonian education would take place on two levels, the general and the special. The physiologist Bichat had stressed the specialized inborn character of human capacities, a view which favored a highly professionalized system of education. Since the Saint-Simonians agreed with his theory in its broad technical outlines, they were committed to the training of specialists in three separate departments. "There will be three kinds of education, or rather education will be divided into three branches which will have as their object the development of, one, sympathy, the source of the fine arts, two, the rational faculty, the instrument of science, and finally material activity, the instrument of industry." But the Saint-Simonians recognized grave dangers of disunity if this specialized education were allowed to dominate society exclusively. "Since each individual, whatever his aptitude may be, is nonetheless also loving, endowed with intelligence and with physical activity, it follows that all men will be subject to the same triplex education from their childhood until their classification into one of the three great divisions of the social order."[26] Under the Saint-Simonians education would thus be at once particular and common. The simultaneous capacity for both the specific and the general was a unique characteristic of the new age and distinguished it from all past organic periods; in the future men would be able to live as specialists and yet would not be cut off and isolated from the totality of their fellows. The curriculum fabricators of the American university in the seventh and eighth decades of the twentieth century, with their "general education" and "core curricula" neologisms, may be surprised to learn that they have been unconscious disciples of the Saint-Simonians. Like Molière's *bourgeois gentilhomme,* they have been speaking prose without knowing it.

The Saint-Simonians would have been antagonistic to the easy liberalism and skepticism which underlies some American general education programs. There is, however, a substantial body of American educators who would be quite at home among the Saint-Simonian preachers determined in the face of engulfing moral chaos to hold back the flood and stop up the dike with their didactic index fingers. "To inculcate in each one the sentiment, the love of all, to unite all wills into a single will, all efforts toward the same goal, the social goal, that is what one can call *general education* or morality." Out of fear of anomie and moral rootlessness they may yet end up subscribing to the Saint-Simonian unitary law. "Every system of moral ideas presupposes a goal that is loved, known, and clearly defined . . ."[27]

Despite the Saint-Simonians' roseate and comforting portrayal of the future, the passage from the egotist to the altruist society presented almost insurmountable hurdles to the educators of mankind in Balzac's France. As long as the contemporary world was steeped in blind self-love and carping negation, how could the organic society with its cohesive morality ever come into being? Marxism later introduced the idea of a total, destructive revolution to clear away the debris of the old society and permit a fresh start in the industrial, scientific, and moral spheres. But since the Saint-Simonians steadfastly denied the creativity of violence and of the revolutionary act, how could mankind ever escape from its impasse? "The word upheaval is always associated with a blind and brutal force having as its goal destruction. Now these characteristics are alien to those of the doctrine of Saint-Simon. This doctrine does not itself possess or recognize for the direction of men any other power but that of persuasion and conviction; its end is to construct and not to destroy; it has always placed itself in the ranks of order, harmony, edification . . ."[28] In imitation of Christ they ended by identifying the means with the end. Only the preaching of love was capable of arousing feelings of love and of leading to the establishment of a society in which love would blossom. They rejected social revolution because love could not be born out of the hatred of class conflict. Their apostles to the proletariat taught them to love their superiors in the social hierarchy and promised that a paternal love would embrace them in return. To add yet another form of antagonism—class conflict—to a society riddled with hatreds would only delay the dawn of the age of love. In the Saint-Simonian world the concept of hierarchic order assumed a transcendent value and became associated with love. Turgot's grand affirmations of absolute liberty and the quest for novelty as the guarantees of progress were reversed. Anarchy, unguided action, revolutionary movements were now the hidden forces of antiprogress. The Saint-Simonians went far in the denunciation of liberty of conscience, and their mockery of the weakness of individual reason had a de Maistrian flavor. Free will suddenly emerged as a cover for caprice, threatening society with dissolution. The liberals' conception of order as an equilibrium of contrary forces, a derivative from Montesquieu's division of powers, was censured as merely negative. Order preserved by naked power, by the hangman, was equally unpalatable. Instead the Saint-Simonians tried to envisage order as a creative force, the spontaneous expression of love enlisted under the banner

of progress. The general will turned loving—named without benefit of Rousseau—was eulogized as the highest good, preservative of order.

But what about the inhibition and punishment of malefactors? How was the
illegal defined in a society educated to love? Like Fourier and Comte the Saint-
Simonians, who had many lawyers among them, never managed to arrive at a
satisfactory solution to the penal problem. They either hedged or dismissed the
issue as unimportant. There was an underlying presumption that if all men
were allowed to follow the inclinations of their natural capacities in love, reason, and action there would be no great need for legal restraints, since everybody would be satisfied. At worst a few isolated abnormalities might have to
be repressed. Often they repeated the view of the eighteenth-century rationalists who considered crime in the good society of the future a rare monstrosity
or an illness that could be treated as a concern of social hygiene. The Saint-Simonians categorically affirmed that the existence of repressive penal laws was
proof of serious defects in the educational system—a fault they would quickly
remedy. Montesquieu had already said that condemning a man to death was a
symptom of a sick society. Saint-Simonism provided for no elaborate state apparatus; there were merely a religion and an administrative mechanism under
which it was easy for the elite in each section of society to evaluate human
action in terms of its contribution to social welfare and to remunerate individuals in accordance with their works. The "liberties" of the philosophes, the
English liberties, were not considered as abstract inalienable rights; they were
judged only in terms of their social consequences. In the organic society of the
future there was no liberty to support the forces of retrogression, of social illness, of indifference, of destruction and conflict, of aggressiveness, and of
human exploitation. There was the positive liberty to express one's creative
love, to exercise scientific reason, and to exploit nature in association with
other men. Legislation, insofar as it was necessary, rewarded the altruistic social virtues and penalized the egotistic vices, though, they were quick to add,
punishments would not be severe. They meant never to employ the death penalty, long prison terms, or police bayonets in the streets. In the new world the
mere announcement of the moral law would exert a potency hitherto unknown. Judges would not be moved by vengeance and the purpose of punishment would be the rehabilitation and the regeneration of the felon. "The penalties inflicted on the propagators of antisocial doctrines will above all serve to
protect them from public wrath,"[29] an insidious argument that has become all
too familiar in the modern communist state to justify severe punishments,
though the Saint-Simonians did not echo Rousseau's summary and brutal condemnation of the violators of the general will in the *Second Discourse*. The
ideals of leniency and clemency advanced by the great eighteenth-century lawgivers Montesquieu and Beccaria were incorporated into Saint-Simonian doctrine, a saving grace.

At this point one is confronted with difficulties in conveying the general
tenor of the Saint-Simonians' future society. In theory at least they extended
the area in which crime would be punishable far beyond the carefully fixed
boundaries of liberal constitutional jurisprudence. They departed from the traditions most nobly represented by Montesquieu and Mill, who staunchly rejected vague and sentimental criteria in constructing a system of law. For the
Saint-Simonians there would be crimes against science as well as industrial

crimes, and, to round out the trinity, moral crimes which impeded the progress of sympathy and love. They failed to provide their listeners with specific examples of these new types of wrongdoing, whose amorphous nature itself renders them suspect. The apparent readiness to punish unbelievers inevitably evokes the memory of wholesale accusations of disloyalty to the state and crimes against society for which twentieth-century men have been tried and condemned. The specter of emotional and moral as well as scientific and industrial control hovers over the Saint-Simonian system, and Rousseau's censor rears his ugly head. Nevertheless it seems farfetched to relate the Saint-Simonians on these grounds to the monster states of Hitler and Stalin. True, the Saint-Simonian political formulas emphasized emotion rather than reason, hierarchy, elitism, and organicism; in these respects their theories bear superficial resemblance to some of the lucubrations of twentieth-century fascism. The ecclesiastical nonsense of the cult, however, should not obscure the fact that their image of society was founded first and foremost upon the expectation that there would be an upsurge of Eros in the world, that men would become more loving—a rather dubious assumption, though one that is not to be laughed out of court by the true skeptic. The totalitarians, and sometimes nominally libertarian democracies, have operated against their opponents with an apparatus of terror—this has been the heart of their power system. The Saint-Simonian society was founded upon relations of love among members of a hierarchy. This may be ridiculous, unfeasible, nonrational humbug, but it is totalitarian only in the sense that love may be. The Saint-Simonians were committed to the winning of converts solely through preaching and persuasion. To relate all the images of "authoritarianism" and "totalitarianism" to these tender failures of the 1830s entails driving their ideas to conclusions they never entertained. Saint-Simonians talked and quarreled far more about love, all sorts of love, then they did about authority. They never spilled a drop of blood in their lives and in middle age they became respectable bourgeois. There was something unique about the German experience under the Third Reich. Remembrance of it should not be diluted by the discovery of antecedents that are of a qualitatively different character. The Saint-Simonians may be cast into liberal hell, but there they will probably encounter as many lovers and passionately fixated men as Dante did in Christian hell.

The Trial

At Ménilmontant the Saint-Simonians had labored and got calluses on their hands. Their master had commanded, "All men must work." Daily life was regulated by a monastic rule: At set hours there were parades, recitations, songs, symbolic acts celebrating the virtues of work. In later years the poet Maxime du Camp gathered recollections of their magnificent costumes from former members of the cult. "The trouser was white, the vest red, and the tunic blue-violet. White is the color of love, red that of labor, and blue that of faith. The costume signified that Saint-Simonism was founded on love, that it fortified its heart with labor, and that it was enveloped in faith. The headdress and the sash were left to individual choice. Since all men both in this world and in the hereafter are responsible for their own lives, the name of every Saint-Simonian had to be inscribed in large letters on his breast."[30] Watching the

Saint-Simonian spectacle became the object of Parisian outings to the country; on holidays there were as many as ten thousand persons in attendance, separated off from the performing priests, priestesses, and their acolytes by a colored ribbon. The outrageous lectures of the Salle Taitbout and the goings-on in the outskirts of Paris had turned Saint-Simonism into a public scandal, but it was difficult for the government to decide upon the grounds for prosecution. Were they a subversive political movement or were they a religion, whose assemblies were protected by the laws, or were they common embezzlers who had hoodwinked the simpleminded into placing their patrimony in the hands of the church? After protracted investigation the Saint-Simonians were indicted for various felonies—some for embezzlement, others for outrages against public morals. The embezzlement charge was never proved in court.

When they were brought to trial on August 27 and 28, 1832, the faithful ranged themselves in a hierarchical order and paraded from their retreat all the way through Paris to the Palais de Justice. The heroic moment of Saint-Simonism had arrived.[31] From the instant the colorfully bedecked adepts entered the courtroom until their final condemnation the trial was repeatedly disrupted by dramatic incidents. The advocate-general, M. Delapalme, used the case as an opportunity to rally opinion in defense of the state and its moral system, both of which had been rather shaken by the uprising of the Lyons proletariat. "We have a society, we have a social order, good or bad we must preserve it."[32] He terrified the members of the jury by raising the specter of a revolution at their very doorstep. Evidence that the Saint-Simonians had divided up their Paris propaganda organization by faubourgs was conclusive proof that an insurrection was being plotted. For the moral and sexual doctrines of the Saint-Simonians he expressed revulsion and contempt. The accused had rejected legal aid, insisting on the conduct of their own defense or the appointment of female Saint-Simonians as counsel. When Charles Duveyrier became obstreperous, the presiding officer threatened to appoint a spokesman for them against their will; whereupon Duveyrier had a fit of temper and pointed to an array of legal talent that was sitting in the visitors' section watching the show. "A lawyer! I told them when I came in that I am being charged with saying that everyone was living in a state of prostitution and adultery, but you are in fact all living in that state. Well, have the courage to say so out loud. That is the only way you can defend us."[33]

The first day, in his defense against the accusation that the Saint-Simonian doctrine preached an orgiastic indulgence which would sap the moral foundations of society, Enfantin distinguished between the "rehabilitation of the flesh" which he espoused and the "disorder of the flesh" prevalent in existing society. He turned the tables on the proper bourgeois who had found an ideal mouthpiece in the advocate-general. The Saint-Simonians recognized different kinds of love, he explained, and provided for their regulation through the sacerdotal office. Failure to concede the existence of variations in love had resulted in the deceptions and evasions of contemporary marriage, the great moral lie. As he developed his argument, it became apparent that the reorganization of the love life of mankind was the major concern of the age, to which the organization of property and industry were subordinate. The evils of inheritance and the miseries of the working classes had further confused sexual relations by forcing girls into prostitution. By refusing to admit the legitimate demands of the body and the sacred rights of beauty, which should not be subject to the economic power of property, Christian society had deformed and crucified love. When free and natural relations were suppressed, love itself was rendered ugly. In the name of amorous compacts entered into only by free mutual consent, the Saint-Simonians condemned prostitution and adultery. The bourgeois, they charged, were preserving these vicious human institutions in behalf of the property system, the monogamous family which was its adjunct, and Christian asceticism. It was the Saint-Simonians who upheld purity in love, who espoused an ideal love based upon equality of the sexes and free expression of true desire, while the defenders of the existing moral order were furthering promiscuity, the purchased and enslaved love of prostitutes, and the uneducated, unregulated loves of men and women who, for want of a priesthood to guide them, were wallowing in degraded affections that were bought or clandestine.

Enfantin adverted once again to the intimate connection between the disorders of love and the anarchy of private property relations in existing society. His graphic, sometimes crude, imagery depicting the alienation of both human force and human beauty did not spare the sensitivities of his audience.

I have devoted myself to a religion unfurling the banner of universal association. How could I not be moved by the spectacle of a struggle which divides all classes? Look at the people. They sell their bodies to labor; they sell their daughters' flesh to pleasure and to shame.

The young and old, the beautiful and distorted, the elegant and boorish, all take part in the orgy. They squeeze and they tread upon the flesh of these women as if they were grapes of the vine—women glowing with freshness or already stained with mud, women plucked before their time or savory and mature—they bring them all to their lips only in order to cast them away with contempt . . . All in this great Babylon drink the wine of a frenzied prostitution.[34]

The president, who had showed signs of ill-contained impatience during the long speech, postponed the session to the following morning with the remark: "The defense is degenerating into a scandal."

The next day Enfantin took a quite different tack. In a self-conscious manner, whose motives he openly explained to the court, he taught the audience a lesson in the superiority of emotions and of tactile values over reason. While the advocate-general ranted about the violation of articles in the penal code, Enfantin with majestic calm extolled the power of beauty. He slowly surveyed the judge, the jury, and the prosecutor with his magnetic eye, forcing them into uncontrollable outbursts of rage as he lingered over every one of them, caressing them, thus demonstrating by example the greater strength of his moral being expressed in the eye over their rationalistic juridical arguments. He was the Father preaching, not defending himself. At a signal, the slightest movement of his brow, members of the cult spoke or were silent. The protracted pauses charged the atmosphere in the courtroom. When the judge tried to break the tension by asking, "Do you want to compose yourself?" Enfantin replied, "I need to see all that surrounds me . . . I want to teach the advocate-general the potent influence of form, of the flesh, of the senses, and for that reason I want him to feel the eye." "You have nothing to teach me, neither about looking nor anything else," was Delapalme's exasperated retort. Enfantin was unperturbed. "I believe that I can reveal the whole of my thoughts on my face alone . . . I want to make everyone feel and understand how great is the moral force of beauty, in order to cleanse it of the stains with which your contempt has caused it to be sullied."[35] Despairing of ever getting this romantic hero, who used the techniques of Mesmer popularized in the feuilleton novels everyone was devouring, to return to the well-trodden paths of legal procedure, the president closed the session and the good bourgeois on the jury proceeded to find the Saint-Simonians guilty.

Thirty Years After

The sentence of the court, a year in jail, was generally condemned as harsh by the press—but it served the purpose of the July Monarchy. The Saint-Simonian world of illusion was dissipated in Sainte-Pélagie—the same prison where Saint-Simon had once been incarcerated during the Revolution—not through cruel treatment but by leisure, good feeding, and the constant mutual proximity of the elect. Michel Chevalier, who had been the great activist of the movement, controlling the funds, editing the publications, administering the affairs of the church, answering a voluminous correspondence, finally became alienated from the Father.

The July Monarchy liberated them both after they had served seven and one-half months of their term, but the movement and the religion never recovered. Chevalier was accepted back into society almost immediately, and he effected his rehabilitation by conducting an official mission of inquiry into the administration of public works in the United States and Mexico. He ended up as one of the more prominent senators of the Second Empire, an official economist, though he never quite divested himself of the social ideology of the cult. There was a Saint-Simonian flavor to everything the worthy Senator Chevalier accomplished for the Napoleonic economy; even the trade treaty with Cobden was swaddled in slogans about universal brotherhood among nations. In a letter of February 20, 1832, he had called himself one of those "hierarchical men"—we would now say organization men.[36] The switch of allegiance from Enfantin to Napoleon III was profitable. Père Enfantin's "return to the world" was not quite so easy. After he dropped his sacerdotal manner he eked out an existence in various jobs, a long series of fiascoes. He finally was named an administrator of the Paris-Lyons-Marseilles railroad, a merger of smaller companies that he had been instrumental in effecting. This was in his eyes no mere mundane economic transaction but a presage of the great communications networks of the future which would unite all mankind. He lived on for thirty-two years after his release from prison, and even after his formal abdication he remained the Father for some of the followers.

The cloud of make-believe was not suddenly dispelled for the Saint-Simonians at a single moment: Their fantasies lingered on even after they had become respectable bourgeois seemingly undifferentiated from other successful businessmen of the July Monarchy and the Empire. Not that the dissolution of the sect went smoothly; there were ugly contests about the disposition of the funds of the new religion, and Enfantin found himself denied more than thrice by the closest of his sons, Chevalier. Though most of the Saint-Simonians who reentered the world carried something of their old views with them, the doctrine was diluted. They completely abandoned the sexual theories of the cult. The more acceptable ideas about banking, credit, and the financing of grand projects for science and economic development cropped up in the chancelleries of Napoleon III.

The fates were not equally kind to all of the rehabilitated Saint-Simonians. Many died of the fever in Egypt, where Enfantin had pursued the Suez canal project with his customary tenacity. The Pereires were the most successful: Their titanic struggle with the Rothschilds for domination of the French banking system became the most important single episode in the financial history of the nineteenth century. In their multifarious activities the Pereires clung to the illusion that their temple of Mammon had been sanctified by the commandment to improve the lot of the most numerous and poorest classes. To his dying day Enfantin, the ambiguous seer who could write treatises on railroads one day and mystic outpourings on the true nature of love the next, freely expressed the two sides of his nature. His flirtation with Napoleon III did not sit too well with some of the faithful, but since it was not successful his incorrigible activism was forgiven. His last project of the 1860s, the opening of a vast "intellectual credit" for brilliant young university graduates with only their brains as security, was rejected by his former sons, who began to find his name embarrassing in any association. A plan for a new encyclopedia, which Chevalier and the Pereires supported, was the occasion for an act of public repudiation from which Enfantin never recovered.

Some members of the cult remained loyal to the end, as did Arlès and Lambert. Most of them forgot their sectarian quarrels, and as aged men with flowing white beards they confessed to one another that the period of the rue de Monsigny and Ménilmontant had been the peak experience of their lives. The fascination Enfantin exerted upon men and women alike remains something of a mystery, hard to explain solely in terms of his beauty and his charm. He surely was not a towering intellect. There was a craving for a new translation of the concept of love, and he seems to have provided it for the disciples both in the gentleness of his person and in the mystic outpourings of his works. The *Physiologie religieuse* (1858) sounds today like sheer balderdash because he really was a mediocre writer, but he did manage to arouse enthusiasm when he preached of man's all-consuming need to love. He was a mystic manqué. His interpretation of the symbols of the Eucharist in human terms, describing the universal community of flesh and blood, outraged Catholics. The extended eulogies of the senses and of the various parts of the human body have a Whitmanesque flavor. To an extraordinary degree he felt communion with all living men even when the verbiage in which he clothed his sentiment was trite and wooden. Like Feuerbach's parallel system, Enfantin's theology transformed the worship of a God who allowed His son to become a man into an adoration of man who was God. Perhaps most appealing was Enfantin's conception of existence as an eternal giving of the self to others in the myriad relationships of everyday life until in the end of the days a man had transferred his whole being to mankind. No man dies because with the exhaustion of age there is nothing left to die, and all that was once part of a man lives on transmuted in others, in humanity. "I affirm," he wrote in his last testament, *La Vie éternelle,* "that I live outside of myself as certainly as I live in myself. I feel this as much in what I am as in what I hate; I feel myself live wherever I love, absent and dead in whatever I condemn; whatever I love increases my life, whatever I hate deprives me of life, robs me of it, defiles it."[37] As the medieval mystics invented a vocabulary to communicate the sentiment of merging with the Godhead, Enfantin tried to render into words his sense of fusion with all persons living and dead. It was a manifesto against the sensationalist philosophes who had introduced into the world the image of the individual as a hard-knit little body, preferably made of marble, standing in splendid isolation ready to receive specific stimuli from the outside. "Man does not give himself life, he receives it; one does not lose it, one gives it. This is what I call being born and dying . . . This absolute individualization of a being whose destiny is essentially collective establishes among beings a disunion, a dissociation, a disaffection, and hence a radical absolute egotism against which all the faculties of my soul are in revolt . . . I wish to feel my life penetrate into the life of those I love, whom I teach, as well as into this work which I am writing at this moment and for which I desire an eternal life. But this is only one side of the question. I believe myself loved. I have been and I am always being taught. I am myself the creation of another, worked upon, cultivated, nourished, fashioned by the friendly hands of my brothers and of the whole of nature."[38]

The Saint-Simonians help us to comprehend that total merging of identities that men of the nineteenth and twentieth century experienced when they successfully lost self-awareness in the ardent periods of nationalist, socialist, and communist movements. They were swimming in the infinite, in universal brotherhood. Both Mazzini and the socialists could read the Saint-Simonians and feel that their emotions were being faithfully reported. But humanist mysticism of this character can only be practiced by a select group; it is no more a popular manifestation than was Christian mysticism in the Church. The more effective organizers of the international communist movement and the militant nationalisms of every stripe have usually been endowed with claws as well as arms outstretched in brotherly love. The vision of the Saint-Simonians implied the possibility that a great mass of mankind could actually live for long periods in a state of loving so intense that the boundaries between the ego and the outside world would become blurred. Perhaps the Saint-Simonians at Ménilmontant did in fact experience this state for a brief moment—but then followed the cool awakening, as on that terrible day when Delaporte the true disciple realized that the Father was "neither Moses nor Christ, neither Charlemagne nor Napoleon—that he was only Enfantin, only Enfantin."[39]

27

Fourier: The Bourgeoning of Instinct

FRANÇOIS MARIE CHARLES FOURIER was born in Besançon in 1772, the son of a prosperous cloth merchant.[1] Traditions about his childhood preserved among disciples document the history of the great neurotic in the making. At five he took the oath of Hannibal against commerce. There followed a period of religious terror—dread of the cauldrons of Hell for having committed all the sins in the catechism. At the age of seven he confessed to fornication and simony. During the Revolution he participated in the Lyons uprising against the Convention and conceived a horror of social turmoil. His patrimony, which at one time had been considerable, was confiscated in the siege; imprisoned, he barely escaped being included in a convoy of counterrevolutionary victims who were executed en masse. For a brief period he was drafted into the cavalry, and the image of Fourier on horseback rekindles one's admiration for the French Revolutionary organizers of victory.

Life of a Salesman

In 1779 Fourier became a traveling salesman. On one of his business trips to Paris that year the young provincial from the Franche-Comté saw an apple in Février's Restaurant. Its price on the bill of fare was fourteen sous; in his home town a hundred pieces of superior fruit could be bought for the same cost. Clearly something was wrong with a state of society that tolerated such differentials. When in later years he recollected the dining room scene he placed the event in its true historical perspective. There had been four apples in the world: two were destined to sow discord and two to create concord. While Adam and Paris had brought misery to mankind, Newton's apple had inspired the discovery of the basic law of attraction which governs physical motion, and its complement, Fourier's apple, had moved him to formulate the law of passionate attraction which would inaugurate universal happiness. Such contemplative episodes made up the drama of his life. There were no heroic actions, no grand love affairs, perhaps no amorous relationships at all. Once he perceived that civilization was corroded with vice, Fourier retired into his private world and to remain pure held himself aloof from society. Only the few disciples whom he acquired in the last decades of his life believed that he would ultimately be recognized as the greatest man in history.

Fourier the bachelor lived alone in a garret and ate table d'hôte in the poorer Lyons restaurants, disliked children and spiders, loved flowers and cats, had a mania for measuring things with a yardstick cane, had a sweet tooth, could not digest bread, adored spectacles and parades, loathed the philosophes and their Revolution as much as he did rigid Catholicism. From all accounts he was a queer duck. Men called him mad, but no evidence has been adduced to sustain this clinical diagnosis; his autopsy revealed no signs of brain damage. Of course he talked to himself, worked in fits of excitement, could go without sleep for a week, was incapable of concentrating on any one job for long (the butterfly temperament of his own description), was quarrelsome, especially with members of his family. His writings emanated from the madhouses of Charenton, was the verdict of contemporary journalists, though this was a far less derogatory judgment than they imagined. Under Napoleon these institutions were inhabited by no mean knowers of man—the Marquis de Sade, Henri de Saint-Simon, Choderlos de Laclos.

Fourier's habits were meticulous, his manner frigid. One sometimes wonders whether this inventor of the system of passionate attraction ever experienced one. He could be a great hater, violently suspicious, and he showed mild symptoms of paranoia, but he also felt infinite pity for mankind, was acutely sensitive to the sufferings of the hungry and to the monotony of their lives. Acquaintances have described Fourier's fixed and abstracted gaze as if he were in a continual state of ecstasy; but he had an excellent memory, which he nourished with an endless supply of facts seemingly gathered at random. Once the idea of the phalanstery had taken shape, every chance bit of information was assimilated into the infinitely detailed and complicated system of living and working arrangements which he projected. Fourier was constantly collecting, counting, cataloguing, and analyzing. If he took a walk in Paris and a small hotel appealed to him, its proportions became the basis for the architectural framework of a phalanstery building. He seemed indifferent to the seasons and the temperature. His disciples realized that he was incapable of adapting himself to his environment and for the sake of the system tried to protect him from the sharper blows of fortune, but was he for that reason to be labeled daft? Quite on the contrary, the world and civilization were mad and he could prove it. "Only in attraction," he wrote in "La Nouvelle Isabelle," a manuscript published by his followers in Volume 9 of *La Phalange,* "should men have sought the interpretation of the social laws of God and of our common destiny. Despite this our planet is twenty-five centuries late in studying attraction. After such flightiness, after such insanity, is it not reasonable to maintain that there are crazy planets as there are individuals, and that if there were insane asylums for crazy planets one should send ours there for having wasted twenty-five hundred years . . . ?"[2]

The initial major formulation of Fourier's doctrine, the *Théorie des quatre mouvements et des destinées générales,* appeared in 1808, about the same date as Saint-Simon's first signed publication and Hegel's *Phenomenology.* Pierre-Joseph Proudhon, a young printer in Lyons, remembered setting it up in type; the utopians had a way of rubbing elbows with one another. For three decades Fourier kept repeating what was essentially the first draft of his theory, issuing amplifications, abridgments, and summaries. *Le Nouveau Monde industriel* of 1827, the only version which excluded the annoying cosmogony, was probably the most successful. (Fourier wrote in his own hand on many copies that anyone who understood Chapters 5 and 6 of this work had grasped his true meaning.) The previous year he had moved to Paris, where he was employed as a correspondence clerk in the wholesale house of Messrs. Curtis and Lamb of New York on the rue du Mail.

During the last period of his life Fourier spent a great deal of time alleviating the specific pains of civilization among individuals: he would intervene to get overworked servant girls better jobs and he would wait on petty bureaucrats for hours to arrange for the pensions of war veterans. In his decline he seems to have found especial pleasure in the company of Madame Louise Courvoisier, *veuve* Lacombe, a sister of the Keeper of the Seals under Charles X. Just Muiron, his first and most loyal disciple, was deaf, and since they communicated in writing even when they were together many direct solutions to the problems of phalanstery have been preserved. On October 9, 1837, Fourier died in his flat on rue Saint-Pierre Montmartre. Victor Considérant, who took over control of the school, was a man of different stripe. Under his direction Fourierism became a political and social movement involved in the subversion of the July Monarchy, and there was far greater emphasis on the structure of capitalism than on the anatomy of love, which for Fourier had always been the central problem of man in civilization.[3]

For the half-million volumes on morals and philosophy which had accumulated through the ages Fourier had nothing but contempt. Since he consulted few books after the rather stereotyped classical education of his youth, whatever he knew about the world was drawn from three primary sources: from introspection into his own desires and fantasies, from the newspapers which he read avidly, and from talk. As a traveling salesman he had observed men in all ranks of society, had noted their conversation; as a resident of pensions he had listened attentively to the local scandalmongers. These people showed him what men and women really longed for and what they loathed. Of the scabrous side of family life he learned in the coaches of the commercial travelers and from his openly promiscuous nieces. Of the cheats of commercial civilization he was amply informed in the business houses where he worked long hours. His understanding of industrial relations came from inside the shops of Lyons, not from treatises on political economy. "I am a child of the marketplace, born and brought up in mercantile establishments," he wrote in *Le Nouveau monde industriel,* "I have witnessed the infamies of commerce with my own eyes, and I shall not describe them from hearsay as our moralists do."[4] Long before the uprisings of 1831 and 1834, when for the first time threatening banners of the proletariat, "To live working or to die fighting," were borne aloft, he had known of the perennial war between the great merchant-manufacturers and the silk workers who depended upon them for their livelihood. In Lyons he had seen cutthroat competition, social hypocrisy, prostitution. What did he need books for? The moralists had written dissertations about what men ought to desire, how they ought to behave; he knew directly what passions men yearned to gratify. To afford them total fulfillment was the simple, obvious solution to the problem of man's happiness—the creation of a society without repression. It was Fourier's mission to convince mankind that the system which he had laboriously spun out was preferable to the tawdry world of civilization depicted in the daily press. To his dying day he failed to understand how anyone could refuse the happiness of his post in phalanstery and continue to endure the wretchedness, the chaos, and the frustrations of the life every man knew.

The works in which Fourier phrased and rephrased the system he had invented are full of neologisms, repetitions ad nauseam, and plain nonsense. There is an eccentric pagination, numerous digressions and interpolations break the argument, and references to minor events of early nineteenth-century history can have meaning only to a scholar of the period. The neologisms are particularly irritating because they require interpretation, a guess at his meaning, and are virtually untranslatable. Silberling's *Dictionnaire de sociologie phalanstérienne* is useful only to those who have already been initiated into the secret world.[5] Fourier was conscious of the fact that he was pouring forth a torrent of newfangled words, and in his manuscripts he occasionally indulged in light self-mockery on this account. "Hola, another neologism! Haro on the guilty one! but is this any worse than *doctrinaire?*"[6] Readers of the works published during his lifetime and of the extracts from his manuscripts gleaned by members of the *Ecole sociétaire* after his death generally put him down as turgid, incomprehensible, confused, and boring. Examination of the thirty-odd dossiers of his papers in the Archives Nationales leaves a surprisingly different impression. Fourier could write succinctly, with straightforward logic; he had a mordant wit and his style flowed freely. One approaches these documents expecting a cramped minuscule hand as in the columns of an obsessive accountant. Instead one finds that his handwriting has a gay swing to it and is remarkably clear. Fourier's insights came out best in brief aphorisms, in a few pungent formulas. Throughout his life he kept jotting down catch phrases in notebooks and on stray sheets, all too many of which have been preserved. "We must have something new. Fruitless attempts for 3000 years. Ergo absolute denial. Integral exploration. New sciences. Doubt everything."[7] This was the system in shorthand set down in moments of illumination, lest he forget. But the system-maker in him had to put these flashes together, and then the trouble began. He strung his individual pieces on a chain and forced them into a mechanical order. A single page or a paragraph, when the original inspiration was let alone, stands out like a life-giving spring in the desert. When he mulled over the texts preparatory to publication he usually smothered them with an avalanche of detail. Recourse to the manuscripts, even when the same ideas lie buried in his printed works, restores to his conceptions a vitality which the published writings have often lost.

Fourier's frequent and often successful play on words can hardly ever be rendered into another language, and his peculiar brand of humor is not readily comprehensible. The closest friends of this lonely man never heard him laugh; his analyses of existing social institutions betray an awareness of the ironic beneath the ponderous didactic mask, but the irony is always searing and the jokes are chastisements.

The detail of Fourier's descriptions, the endless minutiae of arrangements covering every aspect of life in the state of harmony, mark the obsessive. The style is often jerky. Each point is a hammer blow, delivered with violence. Fourier was voicing the common pain of an age confronted by the breakdown of traditional forms, an anguish which he perhaps felt with greater sharpness than did others. The longing for order which he depicted with such poignancy was a cry from the soul of early industrial society. His fantasy world of unfulfilled desires, unlike the imaginings of countless other isolated men, was somehow transmuted into an ideal system of social organization which came to exert a strange fascination upon small groups of people throughout the civilized world, from the depths of czarist Russia to the wilds of transcendentalist New England. If the higher mental systems are sublimations of ungratified desire, Fourier's obsessional structure is a typecase, for virtually every pattern of labor and of love proposed for the phalanstery can be traced back to the unappeased needs of this sequestered man. Whatever the satisfaction that Fourier derived from this subtle delusional system, it has meaning to us across the decades because the everyday horrors he painted are still ours, and his infantile fantasies are shared by those of us who are not yet resigned to the reality principle. The system has many virtues, above all its humanity. Since Fourier read himself into the whole keyboard of psychological types and endeavored to find solutions to all their problems, he was embracing the totality of mankind with its manifold woes, its secret desires, and its obstinate fixations. No one, not even the child Fourier, was rejected.

And who can say whether his system is not the true balsam for our pains? Who knows whether the phalansterian formula does not hold within it the secret of future happiness? Has it ever been tried precisely as Fourier prescribed? The abortive nineteenth-century experiments, the Brook Farms and the New Harmonies, were not conclusive, for in none of them was Fourier's requirement that each phalanstery include every one of the 810 possible combinations of psychological character punctiliously observed. Fourier's phalanstery has no more been disproved than Plato's Republic.

From the very beginning Fourier, like Saint-Simon, was convinced of the imminent acceptance of his projects for the transformation of mankind. If France could waste blood and treasure on the false systems of the Revolution and the Empire, why should it not invest the paltry funds necessary for the implementation of the true one? This born enemy of rationalism could not understand unreason in others, a not infrequent failing. Throughout his life, the salesman of Lyons was on the lookout for a powerful client who would buy his system. If only a potentate or a millionaire would try out the plan on one square league of territory, mankind would be overwhelmed by the sight of real human happiness under harmony, the whole world would have to accept an irrefutable scientific demonstration, and everybody would flock to phalansteries to taste of their delights. Every day on the stroke of twelve he made a point of returning to his lodgings to wait for the appearance of the Maecenas who would somehow, of his own accord, arrive to consult with him on the practical details for the establishment of a model. Fourier never stopped writing letters to prospective patrons and scheming to receive some notice, however paltry. He sent his work to John Barnet, the American consul in Paris, assuring him that his system was a better way of winning the savage Creeks and Cherokees to the United States than waging war against them, an assertion that cannot be readily disproved. In Aberdeen, Scotland, a prize competition was announced for the best work demonstrating the goodness of God— precisely what Fourier's doctrine of the passions had done. Confident that the reward was his he was eager to despatch his proofs to the committee, but a little paranoid imp prevented him, insisting that the august Scottish judges should formally request a copy of his essay so that his authorship might be publicly established in advance, a reasonable precaution in case he should die in the interim and his work fall into the hands of plagiarists. In 1817 Fourier turned to the Russian Czar, offering him the tetrarchate of the world if he instituted the new system and promising him that under the influence of phalansterian labors the climate of his empire would become as pleasant as Italy's. On another occasion he tried to bribe the Rothschilds with the Kingdom of Jerusalem if they would finance his projects. If only the King of France would order the founding of an experimental phalanstery! Once admitted to a three-minute interview, he was certain to convince him. The archives of the July Monarchy are laden with Fourier's repeated efforts to reduce his system to a brief memorandum fit for hasty ministerial consumption.

Even though their conversion would immensely facilitate the transition to the new society, Fourier's appeals were not limited to the great and the powerful. In the second and third decades of the nineteenth century, the popular journal with its glaring advertisements began beating upon the consciousness of Europe with a drumlike persistence hitherto unknown, and he adopted its techniques in his writings. Since results alone counted, his style often lapsed into turns of phrase that sounded like newspaper copy. He wanted to shock, to startle, to cajole, and any mechanism that drew attention served. The printing of key words in block letters, the frequent capitalization, the repetition of stock phrases, are symptoms of Fourier's neurosis, but they also mirrored a new social aspect of modern existence. He was a forerunner of the great advertising heroes. The Saint-Simonians, who were sharply attuned to the psychic tendencies of their society, were equally confirmed believers in publicity—the word was becoming common—and they employed the same oratorical rhythms which the French Revolution had insinuated into European speech. To bring happiness to mankind Fourier had to break through the barrier of public silence and ignorance, to acquaint men with the reality of the phalanstery, so patently superior to civilization. And paradoxically the tools he was constrained to use were the very newspapers which reflected the falsehoods of contemporary civilization. Fourier dreamed of performing some dramatic act which would be reported and would attract attention to himself. Though he had been imprisoned under the Terror, in later years the state did not favor him with a public prosecution as it had Saint-Simon, and he never achieved notoriety. The press usually passed over his books in silence and they remained piled up in the back rooms of his printer and bookseller.

In practice the grand neurotics cannot abide by their absolutist resolves, and while proclaiming the indivisibility of truth in the system of phalanstery as contrasted with contemporary deceptions, Fourier used methods to hoodwink people into the new order as one would entice children with candy. But his lies were not comparable to the lies of civilization, because once within the gates of Eden men would see with their own eyes that happiness was prepared for them. Fourier frequently tried to pass off his total revaluation of morals and society as a mere "industrial reform." It was as if he hoped to introduce phalansteries and drag mankind to harmony while it was unaware of what was happening. His purpose was clear, to arouse little or no political and religious controversy while he turned the world topsy-turvy. "What is Fourierism?" he asked in a disingenuous letter to the *Gazette de France.*

I do not know. My theory is the continuation of Newton's on attraction. In this new mine he exploited only the material vein, I exploit the industrial. I am a continuator and I have never countenanced the name *Fouriériste.* My theory of society is not concerned with any religious, political, or administrative reform, but solely with industrial reform applied to the functions of agronomy, manufacturing, housekeeping, commerce, and general studies. If any of my disciples touches on prohibited subjects it is outside of my doctrine and concerns me no more than the divergent opinions of royalists and republicans. My discovery serves everybody without distinction of opinion—king or shepherd, the prodigal and the miserly. I have disciples from among various religions, Catholics, Protestants, Greeks, Jews, and so on. I ask of them no account of their religious beliefs because the societal mechanism of which I am the inventor is applicable to all religions, with the exception of the bloody ones which immolate human victims and the coercive ones which persecute for differences of opinion or which accept the slavery of workers and the sale and confinement of women.[8]

To reassure the religious, Fourier loudly proclaimed his belief in God; his most bombastic charge against critics was that they were atheists because they condemned the passions which God had created. Fourier's theology was not the most sophisticated part of his system. His God did not intervene in the details of this planet's operations, because He had millions of other worlds to look after; He had provided men with the instrumentalities for happiness and it was for them to divine the secret of their use. There were no individual rewards and punishments, only global ones. Because of the backwardness of the planet in discovering the key to the true system, deceased humans were now in a sort of limbo waiting expectantly for the triumph of attraction on earth so that they might be free to join universal materiality and thus have a chance to reappear on some more fortunate globe.

Toward the end of his life Fourier experienced a grave disappointment as he saw the rival sects of Owen and Saint-Simon winning adherents, or at least notoriety. The spectacle was doubly painful: on the one hand they were disseminating false doctrines and misleading humanity; on the other hand they were stealing his ideas and distorting them. The public interest which the rival sects aroused was a sign that mankind was ripe for a new system; the errors they propagated were therefore all the more vicious. The Owenites were usually fought with ad hominem arguments against Robert Owen and his dictatorial ways, but since the American experiments had already discredited him the Saint-Simonians became Fourier's chief target. He was acute enough to put his finger on a fundamental divergence between his system and theirs. The Saint-Simonians were principally preoccupied with a moral revolution, presuming to inaugurate the new era by preaching against idleness and hereditary wealth, by instructing the workers in the ways of obedience to their hierarchical superiors, by sermonizing about universal love. They were trying to change human nature. Fourier on the contrary took man as he was, a creature of passions and desires, and by combining the passions rendered him happy. "I am the only reformer who has rallied round human nature by accepting it as it is and devising the means of utilizing it with all the defects which are inseparable from man," he wrote to his disciple Victor Considérant on October 3, 1831. "All the sophists who pretend to change it are working *in denial of man,* and what is more, in denial of God since they want to change or stifle the passions which God has bestowed on us as our fundamental drives . . ." The Saint-Simonians were always talking about a hierarchy of functions in the good society—precisely what he had been preaching since 1800 in his doctrine of the ordered passional series. "You see that in this question of hierarchy, as in everything else, the Saint-Simonians take the skeleton or the shadow of my method and denature it by changing the name . . . They want no hierarchy except in the ranks and degrees of their priests who rule arbitrarily over the whole social system, especially in the evaluation of capacities."[9] The Saint-Simonians pretended to make everybody love all mankind; this was an impossibility since amorous sympathies were selective. Their tripartite division of capacities into physical, moral, and intellectual merely vulgarized his more complex series. "These scientific pirates" stole his concepts of talent and labor and transformed them into "capacities" and "works." When a M. de Corcelle took Fourier to one of the sessions of the Saint-Simonians, he was demonstrably jealous of the vogue they enjoyed, and after the meeting he exploded, "What a pitiful thing it is! Their dogmas are like hatchet blows and yet they have an audience and subscribers." [10] Fourier sent Enfantin a copy of his *Nouveau monde industriel* and vainly implored the Saint-Simonians to make an experiment of his system.

There is an extraordinary chronological parallel between the fortunes of Saint-Simon and Fourier in the dates of their first conceptions, their first printed works, and their first acquisition of disciples in the year 1825. Despite Fourier's angry denunciations, the Saint-Simonians obviously did not plagiarize from him, any more than did the ancient prophets from one another. They were tuned in on the same celestial stations and listened to the sighs of the same wretched humanity. Saint-Simon had had the good fortune to die in time and to become immortalized among disciples who fought over the true interpretation of his message. Fourier with bad grace survived for about twelve years after a school and a movement had been founded, and the Fourierist journals and public lecturers were constrained to propound the doctrine under the hawk-eye of the master. It was an embarrassment for his followers when the old man lived on, criticizing their every move, snarling at them, monopolizing their periodicals with his writings, carping at every proposal that did not emanate from him. They wished that he were dead, if only for the sake of Fourierism. After their original message has been delivered, messiahs must die.

The first phalanstery was finally organized in—of all places—Rumania, where a journalist who had returned from Paris persuaded a noble landowner to experiment with the system among his serfs in Scâeni (then in Bulgaria). [11] Unfortunately the phalanstery aroused the enmity of surrounding landowners who feared the contagion of such dangerous practices, and they invaded, crushing the society of labor and love with firearms. The phalansterians are said to have been valiant in defense of their system and there remains a wall, honored as a historic monument by the present Rumanian Soviet state, where the Fourierist peasants took their last stand. The commune of Scâeni is today the seat of a cooperative dominated by an intrinsically un-Fourierist emotional atmosphere. When Mikhail Vasilevich Petrashevsky, the Russian revolutionary of 1848, tried to practice Fourierism among the peasants of his own poverty-stricken estate in the region of Saint Petersburg, he inspired less enthusiasm among the occupants of the communal house. One night he found it burned to the ground, probably the act of the peasants themselves. [12] In 1865, in a hilarious short story, Dostoevsky poked fun at the petty bureaucrat Ivan Matveitch, who, having been accidentally swallowed by a crocodile at an exposition in Saint Petersburg, had resolved in the depths of the beast's bowels to "refute everything and be a new Fourier"; but some sixteen years earlier Dostoevsky had stood before a firing squad, sentenced to death for adherence to the Petrashevsky Fourierists. In 1841 Elizabeth P. Peabody enthusiastically announced glad tidings to the readers of the Boston *Dial,* "We understand that Brook Farm has become a Fourierist establishment. We rejoice in this, because such persons as form that association will give it fair experiment. We wish it God-speed. May it become a University where the young American shall learn his duties and become worthy of this broad land of his inheritance." For more than a year the *New York Tribune* was used by Albert Brisbane to advance the cause of Fourierism in his regular column—he had been initiated into the system in Paris by its inventor, at five francs a lesson. An authentic and complete history of Fourierism and its influence would have to cover much territory, settlements ranging from the prairies of mid-nineteenth-century America to the kibbutzim of modern Israel. One thing is certain, the Master would have rejected each and every one of them as vicious falsifications of the doctrine.

Death to Philosophy and Its Civilization

Fourier's basic method involved a deliberate total denial of all past philosophical and moralist schools. *Ecart absolu,* he called it. Its definition came early in the *Théorie des quatre mouvements,* a methodological addendum to the Cartesian doubt. "I assumed that the most certain means of arriving at useful discoveries was to remove oneself in every sense from the methods followed by the dubious sciences which never contributed an invention that was of the remotest utility to society and which, despite the immense progress of industry, had not even succeeded in preventing poverty; I therefore undertook to stand in constant opposition to these sciences."[13] The accumulation of hundreds of thousands of volumes had taught mankind nothing. Libraries of tomes by pompous and sententious thinkers had not brought man one inch closer to happiness. Fourier's own theory of the passions occupied a position of unique importance in the history of scientific discoveries. It had not really mattered that men were ignorant of the movements of the planets before Copernicus, of the sexual system of plants before Linnaeus, of the circulation of the blood before Harvey, of the existence of America before Columbus; but every delay in the proof and inauguration of the system of passionate attraction was felt in the flesh of mankind. Each year wars destroyed a million lives and poverty at least twenty million more—procrastination took a heavy toll. Since most great revolutionary geniuses had been forced to pursue mean occupations, Fourier's own humble condition was no test of the merit of his system. Metastasio had been a porter, Rousseau a menial worker, Newton a clerk in the markets (*sic*).[14] He now joined this august company by adopting the same underlying dialectical principle of écart absolu which had guided them—a complete reversal of the philosophical ideas which had held mankind enchained for three thousand years. "He isolated himself from all known pathways."[15] Ecart absolu was developed independently later in the century by Nietzsche in quest of a new moral system, and the same formula reappeared again in Rimbaud. André Breton correctly recognized in Fourier an important predecessor of his own surrealist school and filially composed an *Ode à Fourier.*

The two abstract concepts of philosophy and morality could vie for supremacy as the blackest of Fourier's many bêtes noires. When the *Revue encyclopédique* finally deigned to publish an article on his works they were classified under the hated rubric "philosophy," much to the dismay of the loyal disciple Just Muiron, who on May 12, 1832, wrote to Clarisse Vigoureux: "Philosophy!! Oh! did the Master hit the ceiling? I am terribly afraid."[16] And now in the second century after his death Fourier is again ill used by the fates—called a utopian and joined with his mortal enemies in a single volume. The respectworthy general ideas of eighteenth- and early nineteenth-century thought—virtue, enlightenment, emancipation, rationalism, positivism, industrialism—were for Fourier empty shibboleths, words instead of things. Progress, the grandest concept of them all, the crowning glory of Turgot and Condorcet, Saint-Simon and Comte, was an iniquitous deception because it pretended to improve civilization and this was patently impossible. Civilization had to be destroyed, it could not be amended. For Fourier civilized society was a prison: the philosophes were trying to ameliorate conditions in the prison, he to break its bars and escape.

In Fourier's imagery the historical world was at once stadial and cyclical. It was mankind's destiny to climb upward through a series of sixteen or so fixed epochs from the depths of savagery until the zenith was reached in harmony. Never at a loss when nomenclature had to be invented, Fourier's brain, jungle-like in the fertility of its private language, devised a terminology for each of the stages in the series up the ladder and back again. The progression is not infinite, for after the passing of harmony man is ordained to trudge laboriously down sixteen steps to a societal form even more primitive than savagery, at which point he fortunately will disappear in a general dissolution of the earth. In the Fourierist dream a striving for progress in happiness is intimately associated with a vision of final destruction. Mankind was summoned to the worldly pleasures of the phalanstery but was offered no promise of eternity. The earth's delights were real but necessarily transitory: therefore carpe diem. With meticulous care Fourier estimated the approximate time periods originally allotted each of the sixteen successive upward stages in the historic calendar, but since the schedule was not inflexible it was possible to abbreviate intermediate periods and to accelerate the process from savagery to harmony. A heightened tempo of change was even more urgent in the Fourierist order than in Condorcet's, because man's total destiny on earth was so pathetically finite. Hastening to the felicity of harmony would lengthen the duration of the period of perfect happiness mankind might enjoy. To the degree that man was left to languish in a state of "civilization" or in preharmony interludes such as "guarantism" or "sociantism," whole generations were being robbed of their portion. The quantum of history was fixed; it could be passed either in misery or in supreme happiness. This was a human choice. Fundamentally the successful speeding up of the pace of evolution depended upon the propagation of the correct theory, as it had with Condorcet and as it would with the major ideologists of the nineteenth century.

Fourier singled out the Jacobins as the historic archenemies of the human race, the misleaders of humanity into the blind alleys of false doctrine. They were the reactionaries who stood for the perfection of the purported moral values of civilization when its complete abolition was required. They preached the Stoic ethic of self-denial and the merits of competitive commerce when mankind craved pleasure and order; their cult of virtue was the essence of anti-harmonious evil. Futile political revolution shed blood without even the redeeming feature of Napoleonic carnage—the prospect of the unification of mankind. In its pretense of discovering happiness in liberty, equality, frater-nity, and the moderation of desire the Jacobin philosophy was the embodiment of anti-Fourierism.

A counterpoint between the emotional and physical sufferings of man in the state of civilization and the perfect happiness attainable in the phalanstery runs through all of Fourier's works. As Burke well knew when he attempted to combat the French Reign of Virtue, there is no way to refute a utopia. Try as you may to demonstrate that the ideal structure is impossible of realization, that evils will inevitably crop up to poison the harmony, that the proposed system is contrary to powerful interests, that it violates our knowledge of human nature and contradicts the wisdom of the ages, utopians like Fourier insistently direct you to take another look at the cheats of contemporary civili-zation, at the falsehoods which contaminate all human relationships in society as it is now constituted, until you recoil with horror, shouting as you join the movement, "Take me to the phalanstery!" The spirit of Jean-Jacques, the enemy of the philosophes, hovers over every line that Fourier wrote. The play of contrast between natural man and artificial man of the *Discourse on Inequality* is reflected in the antithesis of the happy man in the phalanstery and the wretched man of civilization.

Man's desire to fulfill the totality of his passionate nature was the will of God. Since nature and nature's God had bestowed passions upon man, they must be afforded absolute free expression. Even Rousseau had usually avoided an extreme naturalist position by stopping at the bar of Stoic moderation. In Fourier's vocabulary moderation, along with liberty and equality, was a gross, pejorative word: to curb, to restrain, to repress a desire was contrary to nature, hence the source of corruption. Nature never decreed moderation for every-body; surely nature never ordained moderation in all things for everybody. Fourier derided the philosophical moralists for their betrayal of the much-vaunted empirical method when they argued about what men *should* be like, what they *ought* to do, what sentiments they *ought* to have. Their discussions were chimerical nonsense, their morality high-flown dicta whose hypocritical authors never practiced their own preachments. Fourier began not with the ra-tional principles of natural law but with an inquiry into what men actually wanted, their basic drives and passions. Despite the destined historical move-ment of mankind through a total of thirty-two stages up and down the ladder of progress, basic human passions had remained and would remain the same in all times and places and could be identified and described. Only the opportuni-ties for the expression of the passions had differed from epoch to epoch. Since the passions were constant, human history was a study in varying degrees of repression.

Ever since the dawn of civilization three thousand years before, the external physical forces of nature had been sufficiently harnessed by man to allow for the total fulfillment of all the desires of all human beings on the planet; it had been theoretically possible during all those centuries for miserable mankind to leap out of civilization into harmony. The crisis of passionate man was thus not a novelty of the recent transition epoch between feudal and industrial so-ciety. Gratuitous evil had been the lot of mankind ever since an equilibrium between desires and satisfactions had become abstractly possible. In the recent period, following the development of science and the wide extension of commercial relations, the gap between society's potential capacity to appease desires and the restrictive self-denials imposed by civilization had become ever wider, not narrower. The progress of the arts and sciences had not been paralleled by an increase in gratification. The state of civilization had been protracted far beyond its allotted span of time—the period when it was extending human capacities; it had multiplied artificial restrictions, curtailed pleasure, extended repressions. Under civilization neither rich nor poor had realized their full measure of potential enjoyment.

Fourier had been advised by his more cautious disciples to withdraw his reflections on love in order to make his ideas on the organization of labor more palatable to philosophers, less outrageous to rational civilized society. But this was the very heart of the system of harmony. "Love in phalanstery is no longer, as it is with us, a recreation which detracts from work; on the contrary it is the soul and the vehicle, the mainspring, of all works and of the whole of universal attraction." Imagine asking Praxiteles to disfigure his Venus. "I'd rather break the arms of all the philosophes than those of my Venus; if they do not know how to appreciate her, I'll bury her rather than mutilate her."[17] Let philosophy go to the depths of the Hell from which it came. Fourier would prefer to commit his theory to oblivion rather "than alter a single syllable" to please this nefarious clique. In his absolutism and his obsessions he was a worthy successor of Jean-Jacques. The philosophers must either accept the whole theory down to its minutest detail, the arrangement of the last mechanism of the passionate series—or nothing. There would be no compromise with philosophy and civilization. The system was a total truth which had to be preserved entire; modify its slightest aspect and it would be destroyed.

The philosophes were the infamous ones to be crushed; Fourier was the anti-Voltaire. Contemporary followers of the pretentious eighteenth-century moralists who believed in the perfectibility of reason had formed a cabal—he sounds Burkean in his imagining of the plot—to suppress invention in general and the one inventor in particular who could assure the happiness of mankind. The new philosophical superstition, the exaltation of reason at the expense of the passions, had to be obliterated to make way for the Fourierist truth. The morality preached by the philosophers of all ages had always been a hypocritical mask. Paris and London were the principal "volcanoes of morality" which each year poured forth on the civilized world veritable torrents of moral systems, and yet these two cities were the bastions of depravity. Athens and Sparta, the ancient centers of philosophy, had espoused pederasty as the path of virtue.

In the divine designation of insignificant Fourier as the bearer of the new doctrine of salvation there was a symbol, a correspondence with the ancient choice of a poor carpenter to defeat the scribes. "Finally to complete the humiliation of these modern titans," he wrote in the *Théorie des quatre mouvements,* "God decreed that they should be beaten by an inventor who is a stranger to the sciences and that the theory of universal movement should fall to the lot of an almost illiterate man; it is a store clerk who is going to confound these libraries of politics and morals, the shameful fruit of ancient and modern charlatanism. Well! It is not the first time that God has used a lowly man to humble the great and has chosen an obscure man to bring to the world the most important message."[18]

The works of Fourier leveled the most circumstantial attack on the uses of civilization since Rousseau. What Fourier lacked in style he made up in profusion of detail. The cheats of ordinary commercial arrangements, the boredom of family life, the deceits of marriage, the hardships of the one-family farm and the miseries of pauperism in the great cities, the evils of naked competition, the neglect of genius, the sufferings of children and old people, the wastefulness of economic crises and wars added up to a total rejection of civilization as a human epoch. Proof positive that it was quintessentially unnatural lay in the fact that children and savages, who were closest to nature, would have none of the ways of civilization until they were violently forced into its toils. The coercive mechanisms of society disguised as reason, duty, moderation, morality, necessity, or resignation did not work. In order to maintain its dominion the apparatus of mercantile trickery and morality called civilization had been constrained to rely upon more terrible contrivances: the executioner and his accessories, the prisons and the bastilles. "Try to suppress these instruments of torture and the next day you will see the whole people in revolt abandoning work and returning to the savage state. Civilization is therefore a society that is contrary to nature, a reign of violence and cunning, and political science and morality, which have taken three thousand years to create this monstrosity, are sciences that are contrary to nature and worthy of profound contempt."[19] The natural goal of man was an affluence of pleasures and riches, not penury, chastity, and self-sufficiency; order and free choice, not individualistic anarchy; instead of the negative philosophy of repression, the positive one of attraction. Civilized doctrines of "the wealth of nations" had merely succeeded in covering the immense majority of laborers with rags. The lot of ordinary people under civilization was worse than that of animals.

Fourier arraigned the supposed achievements of the industrial revolution, charging that men had been more wretched since the introduction of the steam engine and the railroad than they had been before. The steam carriage and the steam boat, which rivaled the grasshoppers and the salmon in their velocity, were beyond doubt fine trophies for man, but these prodigies were premature. Under existing conditions of civilized society they did not lead to the goal of augmenting in steady proportions the well-being of all social classes—rich, comfortable, middle, and poor. There was a gulf between progress in material industry and backwardness in industrial politics, or the art of increasing the happiness of nations in proportion to the progress of their labors. Men were retrogressing in the very branch of knowledge most useful to them. Among the hardest-working nations—England, Ireland, and Belgium—the poverty-stricken class included as many as thirty out of a hundred; in areas that were not industrialized—Russia, Portugal—the number of indigents was three out of a hundred, ten times less than in industrialized countries. In terms of genuine progress the social system was therefore a contradiction, an essentially absurd mechanism whose elements of potential good only resulted in evil. This was the art of transforming gold into copper, the fate of any business in which philosophical science had become involved. Philosophy had tried to direct monarchs and peoples. Where had it led them? Sovereigns were falling into debt, running to usurers, and vying with one another in ruining their states while the peoples who had been promised happiness were experiencing a hard time getting work and bread and were never sure of having it on the morrow.

Such were the fruits of the science of deception called political and business economics. Let false progress be recognized for what it was, mere nonsensical social change that, like a horse, moved round and round without getting anywhere.

Fourier's writings became the locus classicus for descriptions of the evils of capitalism, the thievery of the stock market, the "corruption of commerce," the miseries of economic crises, the hoarding, the speculation. The civilized order was like a dinner table at which the guests fought with one another over every morsel, while if they lived amid the abundance of the phalanstery each man would graciously serve his neighbor. How could moralists pretend to be shocked by the intricate love relations in the state of harmony when they tolerated with equanimity the crowding of men and women into the attics of Lyons as if they were herrings in a barrel? Of all the consequences of industrial and commercial anarchy Fourier was most profoundly angered by the squandering of natural resources and the products of the earth, because this represented an absolute diminution of potential pleasure for mankind. His witness of the dumping of boatloads of rice during a famine in order to sustain high prices assumed the same symbolic significance as his vision of the costly apple. The intermediaries in the contemporary social mechanism who were not directly related to production—housekeepers, soldiers, bureaucrats, merchants, lawyers, prisoners, philosophers, Jews, and the unemployed—were useless and parasitic; they lived at the expense of producers, savages, barbarians, and children.

Fourier's critique of civilization concentrated on the portrayal of its pervasive poverty. Virtually all men—not only the proletariat—are poor, because their passions are unfilfilled, their senses are not appeased, their amorous emotions are curbed, and their naturally complex social sensibilities can find outlets only in pitifully limited channels. As a consequence all men are bored. In civilization the distinction between the rich and the poor remains an important one because among the rich a small minority may even today enjoy a measure of satisfaction, while the poor are almost totally deprived. If the gastronomy of the rich is mediocre, the poor suffer hunger in an absolute sense. If the rich can at least partially alleviate their ennui by changing women and occupations and by satisfying their senses with music and beautiful sights, the poor man bound to his small agricultural plot is condemned to long hours of repetitive labor and is almost completely bereft of pleasures. A holding based on the organization of the family is far too circumscribed a unit for the contentment of man. While the most obvious distinction between the rich and poor is economic, the concepts of richness and luxe (and its opposite, poverty) acquired far broader connotations in Fourier. The idea of luxury has no pejorative overtones; richness is one of the basic desires of all men; it identifies a way of life in which there is a continual experience of a wide variety of sensations and in which the opportunities for gratification are ample. Real passionate richness is what Fourier is extolling, not mere richness of wish or fantasy; being rich implies active indulgence in sensuous delights. Fourier cleansed luxury of its Christian theological stigma and demoted poverty from its ideal position as a crowning virtue. "Poverty is worse than vice," he quoted from his Franche-Comtois peasant compatriots. In the state of civilization class conflict has become endemic because the poor who are ungratified hate the rich who seem to be fulfilled (though in reality they are not) and the rich are fearful of the poor who might deprive them of their pleasures. The view of the class system of domination as a form of instinctual repression—which Freud hinted at in his last works—was developed extensively by Fourier.

Family life, the key social institution of the civilized state, was Fourier's most compelling example of an unnatural institution holding men in its iron grip, bringing misery to all its members. While upon casual inspection the patriarchal monogamous family of the French appeared to establish a system under which the males were free to satisfy their sexual passions outside of the marital bond without suffering derogation and only the females were enslaved, the realities of contemporary marriage were oppressive to men and women alike. The legal fettering of women's desires had resulted in the invention of countless subterfuges to evade the law and in the diffusion of a general hypocritical spirit throughout society. Cuckoldry was rampant. Fourier's anatomy of modern adultery with its intricate categories and typologies—he identified some sixty-odd ideal situations, varying subtly with the temperaments of the threesome involved and their social status—is a triumph of psychological analysis which earned the plaudits of no less an observer of the human comedy than Honoré de Balzac. The husband is by no means the only sufferer and ridiculous figure in the drama, for the adulterers never appease their real passions and have to pay dearly for the mere semblance of contentment.

From his conversation with men boasting about their conquests, Fourier, not yet equipped with the delicate statistical techniques of contemporary sexologists from Indiana, arrived at the gross estimate that on the average each member of the female sex contracted six liaisons of fornication before marriage and six of adultery after marriage. But what about the exceptions, he asked rhetorically in a section of the Traité de l'association domestique-agricole piquantly entitled "Equilibre subversif." There goes a man who claims that he has taken a virgin to wife. He has, he says, good proofs. Maybe, if he married her young enough. But if she has not, before marriage, provided her quota of illicit loves to maintain the "subversive equilibrium," she will have to compensate by twelve liaisons of adulterous commerce after marriage. "No, says the husband, she will be chaste. I shall see to it. In that case it is necessary that her neighbor compensate by twenty-four infractions, twelve in fornication and twelve in adultery, since the general equilibrium requires twelve times as many illicit liaisons as there are men."[20] Granted the relative accuracy of his informants, Fourier's computations were impeccable.

Fourier's mordant descriptions of supposedly monogamous marital relations in a state of civilization were designed to silence those critics of free love in the state of harmony who had denounced its bestial materialism. Marriage in contemporary society, he wrote in the Théorie de l'unité universelle, is "pure brutality, a casual pairing off provoked by the domestic bond without any illusion of mind or heart. This is the normal way of life among the mass of the people. Dulled, morose couples who quarrel all day long are reconciled to each other on the bolster because they cannot afford two beds, and contact, the sudden pinprick of the senses, triumphs for a moment over conjugal satiety. If this is love it is the most material and the most trivial sort."[21]

The desires of most people are polygamous, witness the secret bacchanalia which take place in small villages and the virtual community of women which prevails among the rich. The great "passionate" lie of love in the state of civilization is rooted in the philosophical dogma that all men and women are the same in their wants. This is simply not true. Men and women have different love needs at various periods in their life cycle. Even persons of the same age group have widely divergent amorous tendencies ranging from the extreme of inconstancy—the Don Juan type among men—to the rare extreme of monogamy. To subject them equally to the same rigid law must inevitably yield a harvest of unhappiness for all.

The gospel of Fourier was the ultimate triumph of the expansive romantic ideal. True happiness consisted of plenitude and the enjoyment of an ever-increasing abundance of pleasure. Man's goal was not the attainment of illusory juridical rights but the flowering of the passions. Though civilization was originally an advance over savagery, patriarchy, and barbarism, in its present decadent state its superiority was not marked enough to attract either savages or barbarians. In the civilized world anarchic competition, monopoly, commercial feudalism, business speculation were despoiling the earth, spreading misery, fostering thievery in the guise of commerce. Men with diverse passionate natures were constricted within the bonds of monogamous marriage, which forced them to seek other sexual pleasures clandestinely. Man had a progressive need for ever more multifarious luxuries of the table; such gastronomic pleasures were now denied to the vast bulk of the population and the destiny of a substantial portion was hunger. Men were bored by a dull family life under civilization, and at their parties and in their clubs there was a frantic though vain attempt to escape tedium, the corrosive enemy of the species.

The Twelve Passions

"Passionate attraction" was defined by Fourier at the opening of *Le Nouveau monde industriel* as "the drive given us by nature prior to any reflection, persistent despite the opposition of reason, of duty, and of prejudice . . ."[22] At the core of his system was the identification of the passions of man—his fundamental instinctual drives—which like the signs of the zodiac, the gods of Olympus, and the apostles were twelve in number. Unfortunately he changed his nomenclature from time to time, introducing neologisms in "-ism" and "-ique," competing with the coiners of stylish philosophical slogans. Nevertheless the passions can be described and rendered into English. The whole system is an organic one, conceived as analogous to a tree—Saint-Simon's favorite simile too. From the trunk, which is labeled *unityism,* stem the three main branches of the passions, the luxurious, the group, and the serial. When unityism is treated as a distinct passion it is the one that links a man's happiness with all that surrounds him, with the rest of mankind. Sometimes it is another name for that general outgoing feeling which contemporaries translated as philanthropy and which Saint-Pierre had called *bienveillance;* it is not alien to the benevolence of the Scottish moralists. When Fourier was at a loss for positive ways to communicate his meaning he defined unityism as the polar opposite of egotism, the all-pervasive emotion of the state of civilization. Unityism set the dominant tone of the state of harmony; it integrated all other passions, and therefore was appropriately the trunk of the tree.

The first branch of the passions was the luxurious one, a category designating the desires of the five senses. Every passion in this branch had an internal and an external manifestation. The internal signified the mere healthy physical capacity to give the senses great development, a respect in which human beings by nature varied. In the state of civilization the external luxurious fulfillment of the passions of the senses was dependent upon wealth; hence the anomaly, characteristic of this vicious human condition, that persons with fine appetites and vigorous stomachs capable of grand gastronomic feats were starving, that men with the subtlest musical sensibilities could never hear an opera, while those who were tone-deaf attended concerts for mere show. By virtually abolishing the barrier of penury, harmony would allow for the flowering of any inner sense. Fourier would enrich sight with the elegant structures of careful city planning, hearing with fine music; he would open up unexplored opportunities for the development of the sense of taste—on one journey this poor clerk, the inmate of provincial boardinghouses, had met Brillat-Savarin himself.

The four group passions, another branch, were called also the affective passions and comprised the desires for respect (our translation of the passion for honor), for friendship, for love, and for parenthood. Like the passions of the senses, they not only differed in intensity among individuals but their actualization assumed divergent forms in each of the thirty-two basic epochs of social movement through time, from Edenism up the scale to harmony and down again to dissolution. While the familial passion, for example, might linger on during the transition period from civilization to harmony, it would finally disappear in the perfect order of free love. In civilization parenthood was one of the most frustrated forms of affection because the intensity of feeling that flowed from the superior to the inferior was never balanced by an equal reciprocal emotion on the part of the inferior. A father loved his child at least three times more than his love was returned; in harmony no father would be repressive—the educational system allowed for. pampering—and therefore no child could resist loving his father. (Though the love relationship might never be equal, the discrepancy would be narrowed to at least a ratio of three to two.)[23] Everything in civilization was upside down; since the familial passion had been elevated to primacy at the expense of the other affections, the whole emotional system had become gangrenous with falsehood.

The three passions of the last branch, called the serial or distributive, were the most difficult to describe because in the state of civilization they were either unknown or frustrated. These were the passion to make arrangements (the concordant or the composite), the passion for intrigue (the discordant or the cabalist), and the passion for variety (the changeling or the butterfly). The existence of these passions had once been recognized by the primitives, but only in harmony would they be satisfied. "Here lies the secret of the lost happiness which has to be rediscovered," Fourier wrote in the *Quatre mouvements*.[24] The serial passions were the drives of the socializing mechanism; their intervention, which led to the creation of multifarious forms of association, made it possible for the sensory and the affective passions to achieve realization. Since these crucial instrumental—perhaps catalytic—passions were suppressed in civilization, this state could never allow for the harmonious expression of any passion.

While the philosophes and the Saint-Simonians, as well as Comte, were prophesying an eternal Sabbath, a peace in which the elements of conflict were eliminated from human relationships, Fourier was analyzing the benign effects of the passion for discord, a notion which Georg Simmel elaborated later in the century in his sociology of conflict. The cabalistic spirit was an excellent mechanism with which to electrify the mass of workers and cause them to perform miracles. The passion for intrigue, which stimulated men to a great variety of combinations, kept them alert, interested, informed about the affairs of others in old age (in the passive cabalistic sense), had to spend itself in civilization in card playing and gambling, substitute "intrigues" to which bored people resorted because there were no opportunities for real ones. Fourier knew that some men, the cabalistic types, loved complex relationships, and he provided conditions in phalanstery under which they would be able to exercise their imaginative capacity for effecting novel combinations. The passion to emulate would not be stifled but heightened; there would be all manner of contests in phalanstery among age-groups and work crews on the same project, but since these parties were not fixed organizations the competition would never continue between the same groups, and it would have none of the destructive qualities of rivalry in a state of civilization. It was of the English playing-field type, without acrimony or excessive hostility. For the performance of various functions during the course of a day in phalanstery the same individuals would be opponents and loving associates. Those who in the morning might belong to rival cabbage-growing teams would by evening be cooperating with each other in an orchestral performance and vying with another group. The plurality of associations took the sting out of competition; the emphasis was always on the relations of love and friendship within the work unit, not on the hostility to a rival group; but the stimulus of emulation was recognized as an indispensable ingredient.

The order of the phalanstery took cognizance of the reality that many men, like butterflies, would, if they could, flit from one occupation to another, from one woman to another. These "papillon" desires would be appeased by allowing for frequent changes of occupation and of loves. At present men were almost universally condemned to labor inhumanly long hours fettered to the hoe or to the industrial machine. The most remarkable aspect of the organization of labor in harmony was the regularity of the shift of work from one job to another; sessions of labor or of entertainment rarely lasted longer than an hour even among the poorer members of the phalanstery. This helped to combat boredom, which for Fourier was always one of the most painful consequences of civilization.

A major vice of civilization, the desire for domination, was transformed in phalanstery. Men changed their occupations frequently during a day, work groups were composed of rich and poor alike, all age-groups and both sexes were represented, the members had different talents and pursued their tasks with varying degrees of assiduity, and no one man was always the leader—he might be a captain one hour, a lieutenant the next, and a mere private the third. Thus no classes of superiors and inferiors that endured for a whole day could ever be established, and the problem of power was resolved. There were numerous honorific offices in the world of phalanstery, and men, women, and children were always being awarded posts of honor and respect (the two were virtually identical), graduated up to the world throne of omniarchy. Everybody received some honor and respect. Ambition permeated the social order; the need for respect was wholesome; it was destructive only if it was exclusive and manifested itself as an all-consuming lust for power. Since affections were always allowed free play in phalanstery there was no shame attached to being subordinate or passive in love, friendship, or organized activity.

All passions created by God were naturally good and harmonious if they were afforded maximal expression. The order of harmony was ever vigilant that every one of the twelve basic passions be well nourished. Man was by nature cooperative, loving, philanthropic, a creature with expansive capacities for enjoyment—he only needed an appropriate order based on a recognition of the mechanism of the passions. This order had to await the inventive genius of Fourier, the Columbus of the social world, as he liked to call himself. The object of the phalanstery was not regimentation for its own sake; the order had to be complex because it was the only true way to provide for the intricacy of human emotions.

Fourier's determination of the size of the phalansterian unit which in harmony was to replace the family was made by an analysis of the passions. He arrived at a minimal figure of twice 810 persons. There were in reality an infinite number of human character combinations, since any man was a composite of twelve passions each of which had a wide range, not counting the manias which were rare distortions of the passions but were present in every man to some degree. Nevertheless, for purposes of the economy of the phalanstery, he was willing to reduce men to 810 fundamental passionate combinations. For a rich life in the phalanstery all of the types in both sexes would have to be represented; usually he felt that a random sample of about 1,700 to 1,800 persons would yield the required full quota. The phalanstery would thus be a meeting place of diverse types who because of their very diversity could fashion by their own will a multiplicity of relationships of love and labor.

While most choices in phalanstery would be spontaneous, on occasion gifted psychological directors might intervene with advice. There would be a sort of card catalogue where each of the basic 810 types was identified, and if a weary traveler arrived in a phalanstery he could approach the proper bureau, be interviewed, have his character determined, and within a few hours find himself in the presence of a partner with whom he would be able to establish immediate amorous relations. (This is the fantasy of the traveling salesman who spent restless lonely nights in grubby provincial hotels.) Typologizing was to be an intrinsic part of the system, and the wise men who intuitively recognized psychological types would be highly paid in phalanstery because they could suggest perfect work-love combinations.

Passions would be enjoyed vicariously as well as actively, and older people in particular were not deprived of detailed information about the newest amorous intrigues in the haylofts of phalanstery, because each age-group had a right to all possible pleasures. The mood of the phalanstery was peaceful, nondestructive, and nonviolent, and yet it was lively, rich, and joyous, an uninterrupted Saturday-night party, one grand weekend of horticulture and arboriculture, operas, parades, banquets, and lovemaking. Only the destroyers of life, insipidity and dullness, were banished.

A revolutionary educational policy was the heart of the phalansterian system. Whereas civilized education repressed and denatured the faculties of the child, the new education was aimed at what would now be called "self-actualization," the development of *all* the physical and intellectual faculties, especially the capacities for love and pleasure.[25] While the deathbed message of Saint-Simon to his disciples also committed them to this ideal, different spirits permeate the two systems. The Saint-Simonians tended to categorize men into fixed professional types and to build their society out of gigantic corporate blocks; Fourier composed his harmonious phalansterian worlds out of psychological elements which happened to have individual embodiments. If in both systems the end was the creation of a new social being, Fourier's individuals were allowed to fulfill themselves passionately to a degree that the Saint-Simonians would not have conceived of. Their doctrine was fundamentally sociological and his psychological. Both systems were expansive in contrast with Owen's rather barrackslike monastic communism which created equality by decreasing consumption, and both valued physical as well as moral passions, at least in theory; but the Saint-Simonians often opted for the sublimation of desires as a high level of existence, while Fourier accepted gross oral and genital gratifications, if they were not harmful to others, as legitimate, desirable expressions of the real man.

Once modern moralists had become acutely conscious of the cultural relativity of customs and manners, they set out in quest of some new Petrine rock on which to raise their edifice. The eighteenth-century utopians chose reason as the only sure haven, even though aware that it was subject to the violent buffetings of emotion and to massive tidal waves of passion. Fourier's relativism forced him to seek out the passions as the only secure foundations because in common experience they alone counted: their potency was in a ratio of twelve to one if compared with reason, and nothing could be done to alter the relationship. "Since customs and morality are conventions which vary in accordance with each century, each country, and each legislator, there is only one way to arrive at moral stability: rallying customs around the desires of the passions, for these are invariable. In what century, in what place, have they bent before our systems? They march triumphant and unperturbed along the road which the Author of their movement has laid out for them. They overturn all obstacles, and reason will not prevail against them. What is the use of beating against this rock?"[26] For Christianity and for its eighteenth-century opponents the passions were shifting sands, their essential definition was changeability and transience. Fourier's paradoxical transvaluation made them the only authentic stable force throughout time.

Love in the state of harmony recognized the simple truth that in any coupling a great number of different amorous modes would prevail: Love might be purely physical or purely spiritual, a combination of physical and spiritual elements on the part of both persons, or physical alone on one side and spiritual alone on the other. A delicate yet frank examination of the characteristics involved in a love relationship would bring about optimum fulfillment in the state of harmony—a condition which was rarely possible in civilization. Fourier was aware of a dialectical quality in most passionate relations. In some, as in ambition, there was a natural submission of the weaker to the stronger; in others, as in love and the family, a contrapuntal submission of the stronger to the weaker.

Of the various "ways" toward the pursuit of happiness that Freud outlined in a famous passage of *Civilization and Its Discontents,* Fourier would have chosen the path leading to substantial and immediate gratifications. To Freud's argument that in the nature of things pleasure can only follow upon the tension of deprivation Fourier would have replied that there was room enough in most people's lives for a great increase in direct and varied pleasures because men were in fact in a grave state of deprivation. Fourier would not on principle have been opposed to what Freud called sublimation, but he would have left this effort to those who desired it. As for the uses of tension in creating the possibility of pleasure, this involved the very heart of the mechanism of attraction for Fourier. He made use of an arsenal of "distributive" and "affective" passions in order to maximize pleasure and to prevent the intrusion of that state of boredom which kills passion. The Fourierist system has been likened to a bordello where various stimulants are administered to provoke the capacity for pleasure. Fourier would have contended that in a state of harmony there was nothing intrinsically wrong about desires aroused in this manner. They were vicious in civilization only because the labors were not free and voluntary.

The attempt to reduce the laws governing the passions of man to a handful, the adaptation of Newtonian terminology, and the frequent use of mathematical-physical analogies were characteristic of the quest for certainty in the science of man during this period. Saint-Simon's early writings had seized on the monist principle of gravity as the key to the universal system. Fourier's four "movements" of the passions were similar imitations of science. "For passionate attraction is as fixed as physical. If there are seven colors in the rainbow there are seven primitive passions in the soul. If there are four curves in the cone there are four groups of passionate attraction whose properties are the same as those of conic sections. Nothing can vary in my theory," he had written in the first fragmentary exposition of the doctrine.[27] The analogy between the psychological world and the Newtonian physical universe, this new version of the ancient comparison of the microcosm with the macrocosm, could not be driven further. Perhaps the manifesto of the whole system had already been issued in the *Lettre au grand juge,* a strange communication that Fourier had addressed to the attorney general under Napoleon back in 1799. "What does happiness consist of but in experiencing and satisfying an immense quantity of passions which are not harmful? That will be the fortune of men when they are delivered from the civilized, barbarous, and savage states. Their passions will be so numerous, so fiery, so varied, that the rich man will spend his life in a sort of permanent frenzy and the days which are today twenty-four hours long will pass as if they were one."[28] Fourier's works on the future happiness of mankind were an attempt to communicate a state of permanent orgasm. If the passions were good, then eternal convulsion was bliss itself.

The aims of the phalanstery were the attainment of riches and pleasures; or both could be combined to describe the common goal as the expansive enjoyment of rich pleasures. This would be achieved by uniting pleasure with work, making work attractive, establishing an accord in the distribution of rewards to three "faculties" (capital, labor, and talent), and spontaneously amalgamating unequal classes. Work in phalanstery is attractive because it is never mere labor out of necessity but is always related to one or more of the fundamental passions with which all men are endowed. Primarily men proceed to satisfy their passions; in the course of this delightful pastime they labor. The biblical curse has been lifted.

The ideal society was not a grouping together of people who were more or less similar and hence compatible with one another. In phalanstery there would be an assembly of dissimilar character types and ages. Instead of conformities and identities Fourier maximized differences and created as many novel combinations as possible while still keeping his basic societal unit within manageable limits. He inquired into the unique characteristics of each age-group, and instead of subjecting all human beings to the uniformity of family life he made them happy by allowing for the particular social arrangements which were most passionately attractive at each stage in life. Children love to move about in hordes, to parade and display emblems; with appropriate organization and incentive he could even make the dirty work of the phalanstery attractive to this age-group. Work on the manure piles, which had disturbed Nathaniel Hawthorne during his stay at Brook Farm,[29] had been amply provided for by Fourier. "The natural penchant of children for filth becomes the charm and the bond of the series. God gave children these strange tastes to provide for the execution of various repulsive tasks. If manure has to be spread over a field, youths will find it a repugnant job but groups of children will devote themselves to it with greater zeal than to clean work."[30] Among the young and the middle-aged he recognized love as the dominant passion, and the major labors of society would be organized around their manifold love relationships. Work performed by groups bound together by amorous ties would be far more productive than the labors of competitive civilization. Only the aged tended to be naturally familial, and there was room for the appeasement of this desire too. None of the age-group relations of love and labor were stereotyped. Allowance was made for the mutual passions of older men and young girls, older women and young boys. All human beings could be fitted into some symbiotic love relation; there were no absolute misfits in the fantasy world of lonely Charles Fourier. In and of itself work was neither a blessing nor a curse, but men drawn to labor in common by the attraction of sexual passion would find even work pleasurable.

In rebellion against scholastic theology and the intricacies of the royal administration of France, the philosophes and their Revolutionary followers had eulogized sacred simplicity and a mechanical order in which all the parts were virtually interchangeable. Fourier rejected the simple as false and evil, and insisted on complexity, variety, contrast, multiplicity. His denunciations of the metaphysical order of the philosophers are reminiscent of Burke, though he never read him. Since man was a psychologically complex creature he needed an intricate social order to fulfill the design of his nature.

Repressions and Manias

"Nature driven out through the door comes back through the window," Fourier wrote to the *Gazette de France*.[31] The whole system of repression is, according to Fourier, based on the assumption that man is free to choose between succumbing to the so-called destructive impulses or resisting them. The premise is false. Nothing can be done to curb the natural passions under civilization short of the use of inhuman instruments of oppression. Man's only alternative is a choice between a vicious civilized state and a virtuous phalansterian one. Once they are thrust into civilization most men cannot resist the forces which lead them to what is known as evil. "Perhaps a few individuals with weak passions seem to be less driven and they give the appearance of having the faculty to repress their passions"—shades of Nietzsche—"but the mass will never repress theirs." What happens in civilization is that the repressed passions assume a different external form. "Hence the development which, after Horace and La Fontaine, I have called the countermovement (*contremarche*) and re-currence of the passions deprived of expression. These produce a double evil instead of the double good which might have been born of their direct development."[32] The pivotal social science was the analysis of the twelve "recurrent" passions or counterpassions, the malignant transformations of the benign. If, for example, the normal desires for fame and for love do not have natural outlets, they are turned into perversions of the passions: the ambitious ones become philosophes and the amorous ones prostitutes. "It is then that one realizes the stupidity of the philosophes who want to repress, compress, and suppress nature and the passions."[33] The same theme was repeated in *Le Nouveau monde industriel*: "It is easy to compress the passions with violence. Philosophy supresses them with a stroke of the pen. Prison bolts and the saber come to the aid of gentle morality. But nature appeals from these judgments. It recaptures its rights in secret. Passion stifled at one point reappears in another, like nature contained by a dike; it is driven in like the humor of an ulcer closed too soon."[34]

In the state of harmony the patently destructive passions are not sublimated, they are merely channelized and used in a salutary manner by being appropriately combined with others. Fourier's employment of the little hordes of boys that love to wallow in dirt is a classic example of the technique; as disposers of filth, they contribute to the mechanism of harmony. Moreover, Fourier the eternal bookkeeper added, they are economical agents since they are paid only in *fumées de gloire* (clearly a pun on *fumier*).[35] His treatment of a potential Nero is equally well known, a device often adopted by Eugène Sue in effectuating a sudden reformation of the characters in his novels. The rehabilitation of Slasher in *Les Mystères de Paris* is completely in the Fourier spirit. If a Nero is harassed and repressed up to the age of sixteen, at twenty he becomes like a powerful torrent that breaks the dike and ravages the countryside. "This is the effect of morality which while trying to repress and to change the passions merely irritates them and treats them as infamous in order to excuse its ignorance of the proper method of employing them." The remedy for Nero is simple: "From an early age he will be attracted to work in the butcheries."[36]

The distortion of salutary passions into vices as a direct consequence of repression is one of the more original psychological reflections of Fourier. To describe the dynamics of the phenomenon he invented a special vocabulary which is perhaps neither better nor worse than the one that has come to dominate our common modes of expression, and he garnered a few case histories to support his abstract system. In Volume 9 of *La Phalange* the disciples rescued the following strange passage from the debris of his manuscripts:

Every passion that is suffocated produces its counterpassion, which is as malignant as the natural passion would have been benign. The same holds true for manias. Let us give an example of their suffocation.

Lady Strogonoff, a Moscow princess, seeing herself grow old, became jealous of the beauty of one of her young slaves. She had her tortured; she herself pricked her with pins. What was the real motive behind these cruelties? Was it really jealousy? No. With-out knowing it the woman was in love with the beautiful slave in whose torture she participated. If someone had presented this idea to Madame Strogonoff and arranged a conciliation between her and her victim, they would have become very passionate friends. But instead of thinking of it, the princess fell into a counterpassion of a subver-sive character. She persecuted the person whom she should have cherished, and her fury was all the greater since the suffocation derived from a prejudice which, in hiding the veritable object of her passion from this lady, did not even leave her the possibility of an ideal development. A violent suffocation, which is the nature of all forced privations, leads to such furies. Others have exercised in a collective sense the atrocities which Ma-dame Strogonoff practiced individually. Nero loved collective cruelties or their general application. Odin had made of them a religious system and de Sade a moral system. This taste for atrocities is nothing but a counterpassion, the effect of a suffocation of the passions.[37]

Fourier's appreciation of the nature of primitive religious ritual and of the character of de Sade's writings is rare in this period. It is an axiom of the sys-tem that virtually all sadistic passions could be turned into wholesome express-ions. In Fourier this is accomplished without sublimation into the higher men-tal systems; and the newly directed passions lose nothing of their vivacity and intensity—a proposition that Freud generally denied.

With a sense of compassion hitherto unknown in psychological literature Fourier confronted the problem of hidden manias, and when they were not harmful to others he defended their right to existence as a part of man's nature. "After the many insults which have been heaped upon the self-love of civilized men, I am finally going to rehabilitate them in their own eyes and become the champion of every one of their manias. I am going to teach them to be proud of all the ludicrous secret feelings which bewilder them and which everyone conceals, even the amorous extravagances which readily lend themselves to jokes . . ."[38] Though his definition is somewhat cryptic, the notion of a mania as a secondary passion should attract the interest of sexologists. "Manias are diminutive passions, the result of man's need to create stimulants for him-self. This can give rise to superstition and is, so to speak, the root of spiritual manias. In love, especially when one seeks an ideal happiness in a habit that is in itself often indifferent, manias develop very actively."[39] Normally the twelve passions in their various combinations grouped themselves into 810 types; but the manias were outside the keyboard of the passions. If they were as frequent as 1 in 810, they were still intramanias; if as rare as 1 in 100,000, clearly extramanias. "The passionate manias, both *intra* and *extra* keyboard, are innu-merable, for each person can have many in relation to each passion, many in love, many in friendship, in ambition, and even in the passions of the senses." Fourier's formal definition of a mania in his manuscripts was not very satisfac-tory. "I call deviation or mania in passion every fantasy which is considered unreasonable and outside of the circle of the passion, outside of its admissible development."[40] The rare manias arrested Fourier's particular attention; if they were infinitesimal in number in the world, they would be especially significant in the study of psychological prognoses called horoscopes, for the very infre-quency of a mania made its effect the more readily calculable. All manias were to be investigated with respect: men were without prudery in harmony. Fourier was conscious of the prejudices he would have to overcome in reha-bilitating manias that were seemingly useless and extremely bizarre, especially since the amorous passion itself was not yet recognized in its own full rights.

The ultimate purpose of conducting psychological studies was the prediction of human character by the establishment of physical and psychic correspondences. Calculations based on his 810 basic types would be extended through many generations with the purpose of foretelling the appearance of manias in an active, passive (we would now say latent), or mixed state—social hygiene. If at an early age a child showed the identifiable manias of a future monster, men would know soon enough to keep him away from the throne. In this respect Fourier differentiated his system not only from the rival sects of Owen and Saint-Simon but from the phrenologists with whose character typologies he had certain marked affinities. The phrenologists were only willing, on physiological grounds, to indicate the psychological propensities of an individual; they would never hazard a guess about what circumstances might do to alter them. Fourier's system, on the contrary, not only analyzed character but so fashioned the external circumstances of society that a sound development of natural tendencies was predetermined.

In proclaiming absolute freedom from repression Fourier had to face the problem of sexual perversions. He certainly would protect the young from them. In the case of older people, he seems to have hedged. In public he solved the problem by asserting dogmatically that virtually all perversions and vices were the direct consequence of repression. If the banquet of nature were free, he maintained in a passage reminiscent of Montesquieu's *Spirit of the Laws,* pederasty and Sapphism would disappear. Alcoholism too was a consequence of deprivation, and if liquors were available in abundance there would be few addicts. Moralists preached their doctrines of repression in order to preserve society—at least that was the pretense—but Fourier doubted profoundly whether moral sermons had ever repressed anything. The real agencies of repression were other, he repeatedly affirmed in crisp language that is a strange echo of de Maistre's defense of the executioner. "It is not morality but the bayonet which represses the weak; and supposing it were a good to repress the passions, is the whole thing not illusory as long as this repression cannot be extended to the powerful, to Nero and Tiberius, to Genghis and Attila, who still have the capacity to persecute a hundred million men? As for the common people whom one pretends to repress, in all countries they abandon themselves to every vice which force cannot reach, such as embezzlement and adultery . . . Morality is impotent in repression without the gibbet and bayonets, the pivots around which all human legislation revolves."[41]

But what about murder and robbery: Were these not malevolent passions which had to be repressed? Here again Fourier stuck by his contention that in and of themselves there were no evil passions; there were only corrupted developments of originally salutary passions, for in the perfect harmony of God's creation there were no qualities which did not serve a purpose. Fourier's system merely drove to their absolute conclusion the arguments that seventeenth- and eighteenth-century Christian virtuosi had used to demonstrate God's perfection from a contemplation of rational purposiveness in the most minute physical and biological phenomena in the world.

God had to create bloodthirsty characters. Without them there would be neither hunters nor butchers in harmony. It is therefore necessary that there be among the 810 character types a certain number of naturally ferocious ones, who are actually very wicked in the present order where everything suffocates and irritates the passions; but in harmony where the passions find an easy expression the bloodthirsty man, having no cause to hate his fellows, will be drawn to exercise himself on animals . . . Thus ferocity, the spirit of conquest, robbery, concupiscence, and many other unsavory passions are not vicious in the seed; only in growth are they rendered vicious by the civilization that poisons the mainsprings of the passions, which were all considered useful by God, who created none of them without assigning to it a place and a purpose in the vast harmonious mechanism. As soon as we wish to repress a single passion we are engaged in an act of insurrection against God. By that very act we accuse Him of stupidity in having created it.[42]

Little did Leibniz reckon where his philosophy of universal harmony could lead.

The Delights of Phalanstery

Fourier's treatment of the education of the young in phalanstery has attracted special attention because he dissolved traditional family relationships. Any coercion in the process of upbringing would be prohibited. Methods would be found for giving free expression to the unruly as well as to the docile child, and teachers chosen whose characters harmonized with the various types of children. They would be enticed by ruses to perform unpleasant yet necessary tasks such as reading and writing. Instead of the nightmare of howling children in a state of civilization, Fourier opened up the prospect of cooperative young ones engaged in contests, marching in parades, working, and learning what every good phalansterian should know through actual practice, taught by professors who were well paid and had achieved a new dignity in society. If children broke the rules, they would be subject to the reproof of their comrades, a sort of gentle mockery rather than punishment, and when the child returned to the bosom of his parents at night they could overwhelm him with love and affection without endangering the educational process or spoiling him.

Amorous adolescents and young people would be allowed to contract a wide variety of relationships, some constant, others promiscuous, depending upon their innate character structures, the reality of their passions. This would end hypocrisy in love. One partner would not be condemned to monogamy while the other was free to love at will—the common practice of the rich man in civilization. Contracts of work and love would somehow be supervised, but the punishments for their breach are not always clearly defined. Group opinion, it seems, would exercise its pressure by making the delinquents feel ashamed. With Fourier, as with the Saint-Simonians, penal problems do not loom large, because there is an underlying assumption that once opportunities were open for passionate expression, no one would feel that the contract freely entered into was onerous. Since the dissolution of relationships would be easy, men would tend to abide by those they accepted without the imposition of external force—a highly dubious assumption.

Fourier preserved private property in his system; he rewarded purchasers of shares in phalanstery according to their investment. He railed against the Saint-Simonian abolition of inheritance and against any preachments of communistic economic egalitarianism as unnatural. This was no follower of Babeuf; a passion for equality is somehow not recognized in the keyboard. There would be disparities of income in the phalanstery and therefore distinctions in the degree of pleasure attainable by those who had greater or fewer economic resources. When he described a typical day's program of work and pleasure for a rich man and for a poor man there turned out to be substantial differences in the refinement of the pleasures available to them. Members of the Fourierist movement later tended to minimize these distinctions and to emphasize economic communism, but they were probably not so far wrong in interpreting the master's ultimate goal as a superficial reading might indicate. In phalanstery every one was so gloriously rich in a psychic and an emotional sense that the variations in degrees of enjoyment measured in accordance with wealth became insignificant. Wines, for example—and his receipted bills in the Archives Nationales indicate that Fourier was quite interested in the subject as a major source of gastronomic pleasure—that were served at the poorest table in phalanstery would be of a quality superior to the finest Romanée-Conti reserved in civilization for only a few of the richest men in France. With the prevalence of such real luxury everywhere there could be no class alignments on the basis of wealth. While the differences existed, they did not matter. Moreover, there was great social mobility, and men and women would shift easily from one economic category to another because passions, not money, would dictate amorous alliances. Fourier's preservation of a rudimentary economic hierarchy at times seems a mere stratagem to win rich adherents in a blinded world of civilization where men do not recognize true values—their own desires.

Fourier took a similar position with respect to the family. He did not abolish it outright; but in phalanstery there were so many other ways of achieving passionate fulfillment that with time this antiquated institutional form would just drop by the wayside—vanish without anyone's noticing its disappearance.

Superior creative talents in any branch of activity would be rewarded with astronomic royalties which made the contemporary compensation of a writer or a composer appear puny by contrast. The expansion of creative talents among phalansterians would assume gigantic proportions; under instinctual freedom geniuses would proliferate like rabbits. Fourier's obscurantism was directed against moralists and philosophers, not against mathematical scientists and artists. "When the globe shall have been organized and brought to a total of three billion inhabitants, there will normally be on earth thirty-seven million poets the equal of Homer, thirty-seven million mathematicians the equal of Newton, thirty-seven million authors of comedies the equal of Molière, and the same number in all other conceivable talents (these are estimates). It is a great error to believe that nature is miserly in talents; it is far more prodigal than our desires and our needs. But one must know how to discover and develop the seed. About this you are as ignorant as a savage is about the discovery and the exploitation of mines."[43]

In the choice of his ideal unit of about seventeen hundred persons he was in the ancient Platonic tradition which could only conceive of good societies as small. In making the basic work form agricultural he was giving voice to the small townsman's horror of the vast agglomerations of Lyons and Paris. But Fourier did not abandon his phalansteries to peasant idiocy and isolation. There would be traveling groups of artists who knitted phalansteries together not only in one nation but in different parts of the world; extraordinary excellence in any field was universally shared, not monopolized. There was even a vague hierarchical set of international political powers, culminating in an omniarch—a position which he offered Napoleon in his first work. Through its combined efforts the world union of phalansteries would change the physical face of the earth so drastically that the weather would everywhere be affected and the very polar regions of the earth made habitable—no longer so absurd a notion as it appeared to the shortsighted journalists of Fourier's France.

Fourier knew that he had aroused great enmity among the respectable middle-aged defenders of the family; after one year in phalanstery the rigorous moralists would become the most ardent admirers of the system of free love. The corps spirit of the vestal virgins would defend the chastity of young girls —those who chose this way of life—far more effectively than the watchful eyes of bourgeois parents. Aging men and women would find young lovers without losing their self-respect, because the organized groups of *bayadères*, female fakirs, bacchants, and magicians would appease all desires and be paid by society, not the individual. Fourier was one of the first to dwell on the psychic isolation of the aged, condemned to the company of babies for conversation. The twentieth-century medical science of geriatrics would have much to learn from his reflections.

Fourier always maintained that his theories of love had been completely misunderstood by his critics, who applied them to the present debased state of civilization, whereas they were intended for a purified humanity. "People keep judging the innovations I have proclaimed in accordance with the results they would bring forth if amalgamated with civilization, a condition in which they would only produce material and spiritual infamies."[44] How could the existence of corporations of voluptuaries be reconciled with a civilized order which is infected with venereal diseases? How could such corporations be organized before mankind had been cleansed by a universal quarantine—somewhat difficult to implement, to be sure—one of the first public measures of the unitary order? The same incompatibility existed in the moral sphere. Would not the *bayadères* willing to devote themselves to the service of the contemporary vulgar rabble be even more crapulous than they? "All the arrangements of free love are reserved for a period when the physical and moral being of people shall have been transformed, and it is ridiculous to think that I ever had the notion of fully applying this new system to the present-day mob. But our great minds do not want to wait until an inventor has explained his plan to them; they anticipate his reasoning and know better than he does what he has not yet communicated . . . To condemn without listening, that is the rule of the modern philosophers who brag that they have perfected the perfection of perfectibility."[45]

In the stage called *Sériosophie,* which precedes harmony, when men are still in the process of developing the passionate series, great sensitivity would have to be exercised during the ritual of choosing among partners to make certain that no pain was inflicted on rejected suitors. At a ball no individual invitations would be extended from a man to a woman; instead there would be multiple requests signalized by the deposition of symbolic torches before each woman, and when she finally made her selection the refusal would be "composite"; it would never be given directly and verbally and thus would not wound any one individual. Should there be only two requests, the woman must accept them both lest a singular refusal result. Fourier's psychology was founded upon the premise that in plurality and complexity there lay salvation and happiness; in multiplicity there was freedom. The dangerous relationships were the limited ones, because in exclusivity there lurked disasters—an idea Freud recognized on more than one occasion.

Ordinary services would be performed by special corps who were paid as a unit, and their choice of a person to serve was dependent on mutual friendship and inclination, a relationship in which pleasure on both sides would grace every minor act of attention. Division of the emoluments of the service corps was directed by a group council that were easily informed of the relative devotion of the various members. Their judgments would never be unfair, for though passion might blind an individual to prefer his favorite, it could not mislead ten to twelve persons, pronouncing a collective judgment on the assiduity and the dexterity of one. "In short, the complex is always just and true, the simple always false . . ."[46]

Without a passionate mechanism there was emotional chaos. Civilized institutions created universal frustration, the false mechanism. The social art consisted of skill in manipulation—this was the Fourier doctrine with which, much to his dismay, the philosophe Condorcet might have been in abstract agreement. But there was also a profound difference between them. Condorcet saw the passions as disruptions of an ideal Stoic calm; while one could not do without them, they had to be moderated. They were the winds that gave movement to the sailboat, but they also dashed it against the rocks. Fourier's passions all served a noble purpose; they were numerous and good. Man could do nothing about their God-given nature; what he could do was to provide for their burgeoning and to establish appropriate social institutions for their guidance.

No projects combined the expansive potentialities of the union of labor and love more felicitously than the "harmonious armies" which Fourier described in his books and manuscripts (the long unpublished gray notebook series).[47] These vast enterprises would come into being only after harmony was well established and therefore prepared to undertake the colossal public works necessary to reforest the mountain chains of the world, to force rivers back into their proper channels, and to repair the ravages of nature caused by the negligence of the civilized stage of mankind. Industrial armies might comprise as much as 2 or 3 percent of the total population; an empire the size of Britain could recruit 600,000 a year and disperse them over various parts of the globe. "Harmonious armies" would not be condemned to arduous labors alone. Women would be attached to them, and besides cooking and performing fine arts in the evening, each one of them would provide for the sexual needs of three to four men. "Most women of twenty-five have a temperament suited to this role, which will then become a noble one." The honored ladies who had contempt for that "egotist love called fidelity"[48] would be consecrated to the service of the fatherland in order to charm young men into working in the armies without pay. This counting-clerk utopian was always intent upon running his grand projects as economically as possible.

The bacchantes would in no way resemble modern courtesans or camp followers. They would have ranks bestowed upon them in accordance with their capacities, and a lady marshal would command cohorts of fifty to a hundred thousand women whose feats would be reported in phalansterian newspapers throughout the world. There would be wars in harmony, but what delightful wars! Armies composed of men and women in equal numbers would do combat with each other, but no one would be killed. Positional warfare, as in a game of chess, would dominate the field and neutral judges award the palms of victory. Prisoners would belong to the conquerors for a period of one to three days. A battalion of men divided up among a battalion of women would have to follow their orders, and the young women warriors might, out of sympathy, occasionally lend their young captives to older women. If the fellows did not behave gallantly with the aged and satisfy them, their imprisonment would be prolonged. Similar fates awaited young female captives, who would be awarded to venerable old men. Since the only real vices recognized in harmony were lying and deception, couples contractually committed to fidelity would by agreement be allowed to grant each other periods of sexual liberty, especially when the "harmonious armies" came marching through their territory. Time and again Fourier reiterated that all this would become feasible only when the last generation of civilization—the generation of the wilderness—had disappeared and reason dominated love relations.

The term reason at first sounds incongruous in a Fourier manuscript. Was this not the shameful hallmark of the philosophical enemies of mankind? But Fourier endowed reason with new attributes. "What is reason in the state of harmony? It is the employment of any method which multiplies relationships and satisfies a great number of individuals without injuring anybody. A beautiful woman operates in contradiction of this rule if she wants to remain faithful and to belong exclusively to one man all her life. She might have contributed to the happiness of ten thousand men in thirty years of philanthropic service, leaving fond memories behind among these ten thousand."

In the state of harmony punishments for secret infidelity were inflicted by courts of love. A young woman culprit, for example, might be ordered to keep herself at the disposition of a worthy member of the phalanstery for a day or two. In general Fourier was not too disturbed by such infidelities, because no real evil had been committed. After all, amorous relationships had been multiplied, and that was a good in and of itself. The young man who was condemned must perform his corvée for an old crone with courtesy "because the old lady is free to grant or to refuse the certificate of good conduct upon which his absolution depends." Failure to obey a *cour d'amour* led to exclusion from pleasures and employment; hence the young persons would obey with alacrity. The system is so arranged that "no age capable of love is frustrated in its desire."[49]

Many of the facile objections which have since been raised against the system were already answered by Fourier somewhere in his voluminous manuscripts. What happens in phalanstery when two men are in love with one woman? How is the rejected suitor treated? Fourier was not at all fazed by this unfortunate circumstance. In the state of civilization the fellow would probably become a misanthropist, but nothing of the sort occurs in the state of harmony, because a special corps of fairies (*fées*) take hold of him, women skilled in playing on a man's accidental sympathies. Using techniques based upon passionate identities and contrasts they divert him from his fixed attraction. This type of magnetism is a recognized positive science in the phalanstery, a branch of medicine.[50]

When it came to elaborating the details of the system of harmony, Fourier the structure-builder was never at a loss. The printed word has not caught up with his manuscript plans for the architecture of buildings in phalanstery, for the regulation of the complex, free labor exchange with its myriad contractual forms, for the celebration of banquets and fêtes, for the pyramidal grouping of phalansteries on various levels from the individual unit through the caliphate, the empire, the caesarate, to the omniarchy of the world. His relentless vengeance against Paris expressed itself in reducing the capital to a mere caliphate while Nevers—perverse choice—became the center of the French empire.

In final defense of Fourier it should be remembered that some of the wildest reveries imputed to him, such as the prognostication that men of the future would grow tails with an eye in them, were the inventions of his detractors. Since our recent experiments with interplanetary instruments and our manipulation of the weather, cosmological fantasies have become somewhat less ridiculous. The idea that under certain conditions the ocean would change from its present saline state into a not unpleasant lemonade may not bear immediate conviction, but a reasonable skeptic would hardly be willing to assert the stable character of the sea for all future geological time. When Fourier described the copulation of the planets he was difficult to follow, though many of his more respectable philosophical predecessors had heard the music of the spheres. The cautious may suspend judgment on his prospect of an aromatic revolution generated by the harmonious labors organized in the new industrial society. But we have no right to dismiss him for these conceits. His reflections on the relationship between love and work, the ideal of total self-fulfillment, ought not to be treated lightly by an age which has swallowed the values of the new psychology. If Freud transformed into a permissive father becomes the savior, Fourier will have to be revered as a worthy forerunner.

The Mask of Harlequin

Of all the nineteenth-century system-makers Fourier has left behind the most complete documentation for a study of his character structure. The published works, the manuscripts which members of the Fourierist movement issued posthumously, and the unpublished dossiers in the Archives Nationales respond to any sounding with a rush of evidence. But the meaning of this profusion of evidence is difficult to unravel.

In a manuscript entitled "Le Sphinx sans Oedipe ou l'énigme des quatre mouvements," published in 1849, Fourier wove a fantasy describing how he had deceived the philosophes. Like Saint-Simon he conceived of his system as an act of aggression against the philosophical authorities; and in his war with "them," the all-powerful fathers, only stratagems and guile could prevail. Because he knew his theory would clash with accepted opinion, would be ridiculed by the "philosophical cabal," and would be covertly plagiarized, he had to devise a way of presenting his ideas so that nobody should doubt his title to them even though they long remained hidden and came to light only generations later. Since men were incapable of reasoning when their prejudices were shocked too profoundly, he had schemed to catch them off their guard. Introspective Fourier was well aware that bizarre forms came naturally to him, but on this occasion he had deliberately assumed a peculiar habit. It was a ruse to sound out the age, to see how contemporaries would react to his ideas. Or it was a trap set for the pretentious, cunning Parisians. Surely his first book and its title were strange, but they were less strange than its judges were obtuse when they failed to detect the masquerade which had been dictated by prudence.[51] The cosmogonic theories were the sections of his work which attracted the eye and called forth the sneers of reviewers in the 1820s, while virtually nothing was said about his social system. Precisely what he had wanted. The artifice had been successful—he had purposely included these sensational fancies to distract attention from his two revolutionary attacks, one directed against the family, the other against the economic system. His cosmogony had convinced men that he was a visionary, and nobody prosecuted visionaries; in the meantime his ideas on the family and the economy, on love and on labor, had been allowed to insinuate themselves slowly into the consciousness of his contemporaries. He had intentionally assumed the mask of Harlequin;[52] playing the court fool, he had been allowed to say things that would otherwise have been prohibited.[53] Another way of putting it was even more involuted. Knowing that all philosophers were intolerant of new ideas, he had adopted a trick from the confessional: Just as the canny penitent slips a major sin among a host of venial ones, in the *Quatre mouvements* Fourier had concealed his reflections on free love among a mass of notions on planetary changes which he touched up with obscenity—"the pearl in the mud."[54]

Fourier had triumphed in his contest with the philosophers; he had successfully outfoxed the potential plagiarists; they had been repelled by his undemonstrated cosmogonies and had turned away. Despite the jeering reception in the newspapers, it was not he who had been rejected and mocked; grand strategist of society, he had outwitted all his enemies. Nobody, none of the smart Frenchmen, had guessed the riddle. The laugh was on them, the wiseacres of Paris who wrote witty feuilletons about him, *le fou du Palais Royal*. It was they who were mad, they who were fools. He had planned it all that way in 1806, when he first surveyed the soil in which he would have to sow his doctrine. His book was a scout sent out beyond the front lines to observe the enemy. The newspapers said the work lacked method: It had the method of an enigma.

One of his manuscripts described an imaginary dialogue between the inventor of the compass and the philosophers of Athens, who treated him as a madman and sent him to an asylum to be cured. In the course of the conversation, in order to humor him, they publicly conceded the one point that he was intent upon—they admitted that he had discovered the needle and that any benefits which derived from it were henceforth traceable to him alone. Fourier did not care that they considered him daft as long as his authorship of the system was recognized for all eternity. If Fourier's explanation of the secret of the *Quatre mouvements* were accepted, many of his extravagances would have to be interpreted in a different spirit. Actually, much of this is a later rationalization constructed to steel himself against ridicule; this divided man may have believed in his cosmogonies at some moments and at others have been so ashamed of them that he chose to deny them and to pass them off as mere window dressing. Like other neurotic geniuses, Fourier was shrewd when he played the fool, and at times he really was the credulous fool. The ambiguity remains.

There was a sadistic element in this builder of a utopia of love. He feasted on dreams of glorious vengeance against his generation, against the philosophers, against Frenchmen, especially Parisians—against all those who had mocked him. The punishments he meted out to his detractors were terrible. Paranoid elements are almost always latent in the great structure-builders; in Fourier they rise to the surface—nothing is hidden. Fourier proclaimed his resolve "to punish his century."[55] Ultimately he might relent and publish his latest findings, but only in bits and pieces, tantalizing his contemporaries, making them suffer for their doubts about his truth. In later writings he demonstrated that the decision to vent his wrath upon his compatriots had been fully realized in the final stages of the Napoleonic wars. Suppose the inventor of the physical compass had kept his discovery secret, what shipwrecks, what destruction would have been visited upon mankind—"he would have punished the whole world."[56] Frenchmen had suffered a similar chastisement for their refusal of the social compass. "More than any other people, they have been victims of the protraction of the state of civilization from which I could show them a release. The fates have pursued them and their chief since 1808. They have been punished." Frenchmen had missed a historic opportunity by making fun of him in 1808. If they had accepted the system straightaway they would have been able to grasp the initiative in the diffusion of uniform communications, signs, and measures. Eventually a new international language would be invented, but for an interim transitional period French would have been used and Frenchmen would have been in great demand throughout the phalansteries of the world. They lost their chance. Fourier recounted the punishment of France for the neglect of his first work in terms that evoke de Maistre's divine scourge, the Revolution visited on the land for its abandonment of the true religion. The chronological coincidence is perfect: in 1808 the *Quatre mouvements* was published and in 1808 the war in Spain broke out, the beginning of the defeats of France. "Opprobrium, ruin, public servitude, finally all the calamities which have assailed and devoured her, date from the period when she disdained the discovery of the calculus of attraction. The capital where this discovery was derided has been invaded twice, sullied by the outrages of its enemies. France thought she would rule the world; she has become its plaything. I repeat: if I had any power over destiny, would I have been able to demand of it a more remarkable vengeance?"[57] Fourier's megalomaniac fantasies were vivid and bloody. It was he who condemned France to a horrible retribution, he who had secretly resolved to wait until France had lost another million heads in combat before he published further details on the operation of the system. "Finally the year 1813 amply paid this tribute of a million heads which I had imposed on France. There is today even a surplus of three to four hundred thousand heads in the massacre."[58]

Paris was Fourier's immediate adversary because there the false, lying monopoly of philosophical journalists reigned supreme. In Paris opinion had to be bought and he was no Croesus. What did they expect, that he who had discovered the secret of human happiness should come to them—who by right should be his suppliants—on bended knee? Fourier hated Paris with the passion of a provincial unrecognized, disdained by the coteries among whom he could make no headway. In the end of the days he would be avenged: the capital of the world would be set up in Constantinople, and Paris would be humbled even as Paris had humiliated him.

To throw his contemporaries into utter turmoil, Fourier slyly raised the prospect of his own death—what if he died before the printing of his system, and his invention were lost forever? Then indeed they would have cause to wail. Fourier shot out sibylline utterances, refusing to tell his ungrateful generation on what evidence they had been based. Let them be tormented with curiosity while he kept his secret; he wanted them to be sorry, to grieve over having missed the opportunity to learn the truths of the new science. He acted out childish fantasies; how they, the civilization of the nineteenth century, would regret him when he was gone, how they would miss his theories, mourn the loss of the clue to mankind's happiness.

But what really was there beneath this mask of Harlequin which Fourier was so anxious to display? Like many of the great neurotics, there was some measure of everything in him. Many of his descriptions of life in phalanstery are the obvious daydreams of the deprived; the gastronomical bouts and jolly companies are the wish fulfillments of a poverty-stricken man condemned to lonely 25-sous meals, and the amorous feats he depicted with such obvious relish the longings of one who was probably impotent.

When one moves from this realm of simple frustration to look deeper, the waters become troubled. There are passages in Fourier's writings which more than hint at masochist and perhaps homosexual elements that are not infrequent accompaniments of sadism. After denouncing the overlordship imposed by males in civilization and hailing Catherine the Great for having "crushed the masculine sex underfoot," Fourier let a fantasy escape in the *Théorie des quatre mouvements:* "To confound the tyranny of men there should exist for a century a third sex, male and female, one stronger than man. This new sex would prove with a beating of rods that men as well as women are made for its pleasure; then one would hear men protest against the tyranny of the hermaphroditic sex and admit that force should not be the sole rule of right."[59]

If Fourier's descriptions of the destructiveness of children mirror his own suppressed desires—his wrecking of an orchard at the age of three was a persistent childhood memory[60]—if his threats to France are reflections of his massive sadism, then the transformation of the daydream of total annihilation into a utopia of love follows the rule of his own system. The extremes touched, and what he called a counterpassion became operative. Similarly, a Freudian might interpret Fourier's overflowing love for all humanity as a transmuted fear of punishment for its opposite, the hidden wish for universal destruction. That a vision of total love was born of fantasies of hate would surely not have astonished Nietzsche, the analyst of *ressentiment.*

The New World of Love

With the publication of the unexpurgated manuscript of *Le Nouveau monde amoureux* in 1967, many new details of Fourier's intimate life were revealed, as he probed into his own sexual nature to illustrate his theory of love. In this work, the most extensive summary of his system, he openly avowed his manias in the hope that his candor would encourage others to become less reticent about theirs and through analyzing themselves discover their authentic being. Fourier never quite plumbed his innermost parts with the power of a Freud, but in his vivid perception of the social atmosphere in the "state of civilization" in which the *manies,* or fixations, masked themselves he displayed a touch of genius. Not until he was thirty-five, he reflects, did he discover his special predilection for lesbians. At that point he suddenly became aware that he had always loved and favored them. Upon self-analysis he realized that this mania was in perfect accord with his essential personality type, the *omnigyne* or *omnitone,* a human with seven dominant spiritual passions, one of the rarest of all characters in the taxonomy of sex. "In the whole world there are roughly 26,400 people like me (if one calculates at the rate of 33 per million) because every male omnigyne is necessarily a Sapphianist or a protector of lesbians, just as every female omnigyne is necessarily a pederastite or a protectress of pederasts. If this were not the case, these personalities would lack their pivotal quality in love, which is an impulse of philanthropic dedication to the opposite sex and to everything that might please it in both the ambiguous and direct modes . . ."[61] Fourier knew that like all "civilized" people he had once condemned and ridiculed homosexuals, even while concealing a strong affection for homosexual females. But he was hardly to be blamed for not recognizing a penchant so rare in the Occidental world, though one much esteemed in China, where the Emperor had been depicted on a circular couch surrounded by active lesbians.

In the *Nouveau monde amoureux* Fourier prophesied uneven development in the radical restructuring of labor and love. The domestic and industrial economies would be quickly transformed in the new "state of harmony" without offending anybody, because their advantages would be patent. Men would have to be more cautious, however, about religious and moral innovations that might outrage consciences. Even though it was a rule in harmony to authorize any practice that multipled amorous relationships and gave pleasure without doing injury, in the initial stages Harmonians would be rather cautious about incest. Thus the "industrial mechanism" would be revamped first, while "passionate refinement" would have to wait for a higher stage of harmony—a delightful prefiguration of the Marxist timetable. Fourier saw himself as the drafter of the general theory of harmony in all its complexity; its implementation in detail would respond to particular contingencies.[62] And though all amorous forms met with his approval, he too accepted a hierarchy of values. The highest good was clearly the multiplication of amorous relations; that was taken for granted. But in the end the more spiritual and intricate loves would be preferred to the simpler and grosser ones. There were even proper manners in amorous behavior: It was bad form not to leave a legacy to a love partner of some months' duration; thousands of transient affairs and participants in orgies need not be remembered.

In the 1960s and 1970s the rediscoverers of Fourier were right to see in him a predecessor of Freud, though on occasion they were carried away in their exaltation of the French prophet of a new world of love. Fourier, who acknowledged de Sade as an intellectual ancestor, remains a vital link between the scandalous late-eighteenth-century philosophe and the respectable late-nineteenth-century philosophe who was the founder of psychoanalysis.

28

Owen's New Moral World

On July 30, 1817, Robert Owen crossed the Rubicon with an announcement in the London press that he was resolved to engage in battle with the errors and evils of all contemporary systems, civil and political. No quarter would be asked and none given until their final abolition was expressly desired by all parties, including those who now felt a strong interest in preserving them. The principles and practices he espoused in their stead would be able to stand on their own rational foundation, irrespective of any individual personality. But at forty-six Owen was prepared to present himself naked to his enemies and defend every act of his past behavior.

The Illuminated Mill Owner

In his letter to the newspapers, Owen offered the public the detailed curriculum vitae of a self-made man who had climbed up the ladder of industrial achievement step by step, one job after another, until he reached the top as owner of the mills and ancillary establishments at New Lanark in Scotland. These accomplishments proved that he was no impractical dreamer and guaranteed the merit of his new system of society. "I was born in Newton, Montgomeryshire," he wrote, "left it, and came to London, when about ten years of age; soon after went to Mr. James M' Guffog, of Stamford in Lincolnshire; where I remained upward of three years; returned to town, and was a short time with Messrs. Flint and Palmer, London Bridge. I went afterwards to Manchester, and was some time with Mr. John Sattersfield, whom I left, while yet a boy, to commence business on a limited scale in making machinery and spinning cotton, part of the time in partnership with Mr. Jones, and part on my own account. Afterwards I undertook to manage the spinning establishments of the Late Dr. Drinkwater of Manchester at the latter place and at Northwich in Cheshire, in which occupation I remained three or four years. I then formed a partnership to carry on a cotton-spinning business with Messrs. Moulson and Scarth of Manchester; built the Chorlton Mills, and commenced a new firm, under the designation of the Chorlton Twist Company, along with Messrs. Borrodale and Atkinson, of London, and Messrs. H. and J. Barton and Co., of Manchester. Some time afterwards we purchased the mills and establishments at New Lanark, where I have been before the public for eighteen years past."[1]

Forty years later, at the promptings of friends and faithful disciples, the dying old man of eighty-six composed an autobiography (which did not get far beyond the early 1820s) that was somewhat more revealing about the crucial psychic events of his life than this drab business chronicle. The writer of tract after tract on the abstract principles of the formation of human character allowed his readers a look into what he believed had fashioned his own. The analysis, in conformity with his axiomatic precepts, demonstrated conclusively the paramount significance of external circumstances. When he was about five, in a hurry to dash back to school, he took a spoonful of hot flummery, scalded his stomach, and fainted. The accident had a tremendous influence upon him, he assured his readers. It made him incapable of digesting anything but simple food and in small quantities at a time, which in turn led him to give heed to the effects of different qualities of food on his changed constitution and thereby bred in him the habit of close observation and continual reflection. Only once was he chastised by his parents, when his father whipped him at his mother's behest. Hearing indistinctly one of her commands, he had responded "No," and, having uttered the word, he obstinately refused to retract it. "You may kill me but I will not do it," was the stubborn response as the whipping continued. The contest of wills was decided in his favor, and ever after he was convinced that correction was pernicious and injurious to both punisher and punished. At ten he underwent a religious crisis occasioned by the reading of Methodist books borrowed from three maiden ladies. The deadly hatred among Jews, Christians, Mohammedans, Hindus, and Chinese led him to conclude that there was something fundamentally wrong with all religions. Once he stuck his finger into a keyhole and had to cry for help to extricate it. Another event he recalled was nearly drowning and being saved by a spotted horse. Explaining the meaning of fingers shoved into keyholes was not part of his psychological system. But the spotted horse stayed with him and henceforward he favored the type, an early impression on the mind that fitted neatly with his doctrine of association.

Owen's natural intellectual gifts as a child had been noticed, and the libraries of the learned men of the town of Newton—the clergyman, physician, and lawyer—were open to him. Before the age of ten he had read *Robinson Crusoe, Pilgrim's Progress, Paradise Lost,* Harvey's *Meditations among the Tombs,* Young's *Night Thoughts,* Richardson's novels, the voyages of Captain Cook and other explorers, the history of the world, lives of philosophers and of great men. The literature he devoured mostly celebrated man's daring and capacity for achievement in this world, but dark romantic contemplations of death were there in the background. One has the feeling that there was a saturnine, melancholy side to Owen's nature, ordinarily covered by a gloss of official optimism. If the child Robert Owen needed further stimulus to deeds of greatness, it was provided by his ordinal position in the family, the last but one out of seven.

During his first thirty years, this son of an artisan apprenticed to a draper was unusually enterprising. While living in Manchester, he not only effectively managed a cotton-spinning mill but he was active in the Literary and Philosophical Society—this was no countinghouse boor. And though he was so shy with women that he lost his first love for lack of courage to declare his sentiments, he succeeded in winning in marriage the daughter of the onetime owner of the New Lanark Mills. The former Miss Dale bore him many children, but apparently the union was not otherwise blessed.

From 1800 to 1812 Owen enjoyed outstanding success as a businessman; the most important cotton-spinning factory in Britain was under his direction, and at the height of the Napoleonic wars he was earning enormous profits. The good fortune of this industrious father of a large family testified to the substantial rewards awaiting those who expended their energies in hard work. He was a model and an inspiration. But about 1812 the signs of a transformation became visible. Instead of sticking to his grindstone and deriving satisfaction from his prosperity, Owen began to absorb himself more and more in the moral and economic condition of his workers and in plans for their education. His autobiography would have us believe that the vast project he was to undertake in transforming New Lanark into an exemplary settlement of contented workers had occurred to him in a flash as soon as he saw the factory on the Clyde in 1799. Before long, Owen extended his concerns to all of mankind.

What made this go-getting textile manager and owner stray from the traditional path of his calling and become enmeshed in schemes of universal rehabilitation? Philanthropy was one of the spiritual inheritances of the Enlightenment and it could possess an entrepreneur of lowly origins as well as a declassed scion of the nobility like Saint-Simon or the son of a bankrupt French cloth merchant like Fourier—the morbus striketh where it listeth. As long as Owen's projects had the appearance of charity that uplifted the drunken, shiftless workers, his ideas were listened to sympathetically by the respectable classes of England and Scotland, especially since his business continued to make a profit. *A New View of Society: or, Essays on the Principle of the Formation of the Human Character* (1813), with its stress on rationalist training and individual reform, could hardly be regarded as a revolutionary document. But in 1817, like Saint-Simon and at about the same time, Owen began to deliver himself of slashing criticisms of the whole economic and social order; what was even more outrageous, he attacked the institution of the family in forthright terms and denounced organized religion. The philanthropist whose establishment had become a showpiece for inquisitive English and foreign visitors was turning into a scandal.

In 1824 the middle-aged mill owner with disturbing notions about a "new moral world" went even further: He decided to quit the scene of his economic triumph in New Lanark and to implement his peculiar doctrines on virgin soil in America. Within a period of three years he broke with business, invested almost the whole of his fortune in a village at New Harmony, Indiana, moved his children (but not his wife) there, and conducted a utopian experiment that ended in disaster.

Upon his return to England, a poorer though not less ardent proselytizer, Owen found that he had made converts, especially among the literate working classes. He was catapulted into the leadership of a workingmen's federation. And after its disintegration, he still remained the head of a devoted sect of Owenites, whose journals, among them the *New Moral World,* were of European repute. Friedrich Engels was counted among the contributors; some of the best early reports of the vicissitudes of Continental utopian sects and movements came from his pen and were carried by this periodical. The aging Owen continued to travel and lecture, propagating his ideas among all who would listen. Like Fourier, he outlived himself, and toward the end he became a spiritualist, establishing contact with a motley crew of incarnations that included Lord Byron, Thomas Jefferson, the Duke of Wellington, Robert Burns, Mehemet Ali—personages he had once admired. Even the dead had a stirring role to play in the transformation of society. Reluctant, perhaps, to see his own career terminate with the approaching close of his life, Owen published in 1853 *The Future of the Human Race,* in which he predicted the coming of a peaceful revolution through the agency of "departed spirits of good and superior men and women."[2] Marx never alluded to Owen's designation of these cohorts of spirits as agents of the new society.

When Owen had taken over the management of the cotton mills at New Lanark, he found a working community already in existence. It had been recruited by his future father-in-law, David Dale, who provided houses for families of good moral character and shelter for a sizable number of abandoned children over nine fit to work, sent up by the parishes. Widows were encouraged to take jobs in the mills. Discipline was maintained throughout a thirteen-hour day, with breaks for breakfast and dinner, and there was rudimentary schooling after work. Owen was nevertheless faced with drunkenness and slothful habits, despite the harsh regimen of the factory system. It is one of the bizarre manifestations of the historical dialectic that English socialism, long identified with Owenism, was born out of these working-class barracks dominated by a Calvinist ethic. Owen's initial experiments at New Lanark strengthened discipline, increased productivity, and welded communities out of mere agglomerations. To the economic ingredients of an orderly factory system he added the voice of Reason, which, it is said, acted as a persuasive guide to community in New Lanark under his watchful eye, but lost its effectiveness whenever the philanthropist turned his back.

Owen stood at the pinnacle of a regimented paternalism and dealt with his workers through a system of subalterns. It did not occur to him that men would ever balk at unquestioning submission to his wise commands. He reasoned his workers out of drunkenness and irregular habits and into perfect communal order, using a mechanical monitor and relying on the reprimand as his only punitive instrument. The monitor, a creature of wood and wire, standing beside each machine, showed different colors that rated the worker's assiduity or delinquency. A worker could appeal from the judgment of the overseer who manipulated the dummy directly to Robert Owen. Somehow none ever did. Owen instituted an educational system for the children of New Lanark that molded them through the power of habit, the psychological weapon he worshiped as a new god. He shaped good moral characters fit to live in a new moral world. His militant attacks on priestly religion, which got him into trouble with the upper-class philanthropists, did not blind him to the virtues of the strict discipline of the religious communities established by the Rappites and Shakers; he merely substituted his own secular millenarianism for their religious one.

Owen's first full-fledged utopian plan, as distinguished from his earlier endeavors to suppress alcoholism among his workers and provide schooling for their young, was embodied in a *Report to the Committee of the Association for the Relief of the Manufacturing and Labouring Poor,* presented in March 1817, in which he analyzed the severity of the post-Napoleonic economic crisis and proposed the formation of self-sustaining communities of unemployed workers, victims of technological advances and prey to vice and misery. Their living quarters were to be arranged in rectangular units complete in themselves that would meet all the educational and social needs of the 1,200 or so inhabitants. Immediately beyond these enclosures would be structures for mechanical and manufacturing purposes, and, farther away, agricultural establishments.[3] The original proposal, modest in its scope and restricted to the indigent, was soon expanded to become the organizational formula for a wide network of communities. At first the villages were to be voluntary associations varying with the income level of the members—Fourier's phalansteries allowed for similar gradations—and they would coexist with other manufacturing enterprises based on current practices. The small-unit example would attract adherents on its own merits. Its gradual adoption and spread would then usher in a new millennium whose virtues Owen could sing in the old biblical language: "Even now the time is near at hand . . . when swords shall be turned into ploughshares, and spears into pruning hooks—when every man shall sit under his own vine and his own fig-tree, and none shall make him afraid."[4]

In Owen's report to the County of Lanark in May 1820, the founding of "villages of unity and mutual cooperation," with capital supplied by private subscribers, was turned into a system of cooperative socialism that would encompass the earth. Agricultural and manufacturing elements were to be intermingled in the villages. But the work system was not the main focus of Owen's reformation. He saw in these ingatherings an opportunity for transforming the character of the indigent by altering their environment. The villages, set in remote places uncorrupted by the prevalent evils of working-class society, would afford the philanthropic projector an opportunity to remold the poor as if they were children. A new generation of rational beings would arise on British soil.[5] Owen had a way of soaring from the particular to the timeless universal. Initially his was just another one of scores of attempts to shape a poor law in the spirit of Christian charity; but like parochial English utopian projects of the seventeenth century, it burgeoned into a panacea for the organization of work among men everywhere. In one of its aspects Owen's plan was a reversion to the idea of communal moral responsibility to provide employment for the meritorious poor, which had been widely replaced by the Speenhamland system of granting relief to the destitute through meager allowances charged to the parishes. Other Scottish philanthropists had notions similar to Owen's, if more limited, but unlike him they did not link indigence and immorality with the need for rationalist education and training; nor did they alarm their fellows by proclaiming adherence to the principle of absolute equality.

Owen was of the normative, rationalist Enlightenment school that believed moral conduct could be inculcated by systematic training leading to habit formation, since all men were equally capable of listening to the voice of reason and could be persuaded by argument. Rational behavior was ordinarily conceived in terms that would be acceptable to any frugal, upright man. Owen saw the social environment as corrupting the poor workers and making them unproductive. The new society would convince them that it was better to be rid of their vices, would instill in them habits of orderliness and cleanliness, and would educate their children so that they could imagine no other way of life. Rule II adopted by one of the many organizations Owen put together, the British and Foreign Philanthropic Society of 1822, defined its purpose as "the permanent relief of the labouring classes, by forming communities of mutual interest and cooperation, in which by means of education, example, and employment, they will be gradually withdrawn from the evils induced by ignorance, bad habits, poverty and want of employment."[6] For such ideas to gain even minimal acceptance, the pessimistic Calvinism of the Kirk had to be modified by Enlightenment rationalism and there had to be some belief in the possibility of reform. This development had in fact occurred among some segments of Scottish society in the late eighteenth century, perhaps more visibly than in England. And one part of Owen remained in this respectable tradition.

As Saint-Simon had terrified his industrialist and banker supporters with his proclamation of the need for a "nineteenth-century morality," as distinguished from the eternal Christian gospel, so Owen handicapped himself with his virulent anticlericalism, his refusal to countenance religious education in any form in his plan, and his essays on the formation of character that abolished original sin and denied moral accountability. But it was just this uncompromising antireligious strain in Owen that endeared him to Marx and Engels and was a factor in winning for him benign treatment at their hands, while they were put off by the religious balderdash of the Saint-Simonians. However naive his utopianism, an anticlerical could not be all bad. Christians attracted to Owen were dismayed by his apostasy, but usually solaced themselves with the reflection that true practical Christianity and Owenism would ultimately converge.

Though his name was joined with Saint-Simon and Fourier, Owen had nothing of Saint-Simon's vision of the industrial-scientific dynamism of society, or of Fourier's conception of the intricacy of the human passions. Of all the major utopian socialisms, the Owenite and in general the English type represent the purest longing for the old agrarian way of life as the indispensable path to utopia—and this despite the fact that the communitarian idea sprang up in the cotton mills of New Lanark. Theoretically, Owenite doctrine presented itself as favoring a combination of manufacturing and agriculture in self-sustaining villages to create a balance of activities; in practice, the Owenite community turned out to be agricultural and crafts were treated as necessary but subsidiary elements. (Owen had once favored spade husbandry because it would engage a greater number of the unemployed.) While divorce was allowable, the family nevertheless remained the unit of social life. Owenites never accepted the realities of mammoth industrialization as did the Saint-Simonians, nor the radical reorganization of sexual life demanded by Fourier. Instead they wanted to revive the virtues of the rural English village, enhanced by rationalist character formation through schooling. Saint-Simon himself in his last works had looked forward to the grand progress of scientific technology to lighten the physical burdens of manual labor. Owen still clung to the illusion of the moral worth of hard work, and Owenite sympathizers from among the upper classes had the same predilection—toil in a morally prophylactic village setting was ennobling for the workers of the world. In the end Thomas Spence, the Chartist Bronterre O'Brien, and the Owenites shared the same kind of agricultural utopian dream.

In May 1842 the *New Moral World* reported that Owen was turning his back on industrialism: "[He would be] very sorry ever to have a cotton factory again, for the substantial wealth of the world is only obtained from land."[7] This physiocratic declaration reveals the essential quaintness of Owenism, always on the point of regression. In nineteenth-century utopianism there is a divide between those who undertook to grapple with the scientific-technological civilization and those who, without actively joining the Luddites, were reliving the old agrarian utopia in an emended form. Owen's attitude toward industrialization was ambiguous at best. His early writings described the ravages of the factory system in graphic language. Cotton mills were "receptacles, in too many instances, for living human skeletons."[8] Such denunciations were accompanied by demonstrations to factory owners that their profits would increase if they paid more heed to their living machines. In later writings Owen advanced antitechnological arguments that were in harmony with the Romantic poets' attack on science and technology and their longing for a return to the agrarian past.

The Great Error

Were mankind aligned on opposite sides of the nature-nurture controversy, the utopians among them would be found in the camp of the nurturists. Since the fifteenth century, secular utopians have believed, almost without needing to make their views explicit, that the environment in which children are reared and mature persons go about their business is the major determinant in fashioning their character and subsequent pattern of conduct. They may have differed about which aspects of the environment exerted the most potent influence—was it the architecture of the city, the educational system, social and political arrangements, the organization of work relations, the form of religious worship?—but they would join in agreement on the power of human institutions to create both good and evil. Among the modern utopians, Robert Owen is probably the most self-conscious behaviorist and it is difficult to find in more recent utopians of that school anything more than glosses on his principles. "Any general character, from the best to the worst, from the most ignorant to the most enlightened, may be given to any community, even to the world at large, by the application of the proper means."[9] An individual could not fashion the appropriate immediate environment for the formation of rational character leading to the greatest happiness of the greatest number, but society could and should.

An epistemology of sorts and an implicit philosophy of history backed up Owen's behaviorist utopia. World history past, present, and future was divisible into two segments, one in which irrationality, even insanity, characterized virtually all human relationships, and one, whose moment was just come, in which rationality would predominate. The whole of past and most present behavior were blind to reason in action because men were steeped in error and were bound by a false association of ideas. Minor errors of perception and superstitious beliefs were malignant, but one Great Error held mankind in thrall, and this was the religious falsehood that an individual of his own free will could choose to perform acts that were either good or evil. In fact, a man had no such liberty. He was born into a specific environment in which evil influences were compelling, he was reared to accept lies, and he lived out his life subject to erroneous ideas. As a consequence, the creature was blindly selfish, cruel, lying, hypocritical, addicted to vices, criminal, generating his own unhappiness. Societies and religions fixed blame upon the individual for his acts, whereas in truth he was blameless, merely a product of circumstances and iniquitous arrangements. Owen presents the unusual spectacle of a mill owner who, instead of inveighing against the shiftlessness, drunkenness, sexual immorality of workers, finds them innocent victims of circumstance.

Owen's critique of his society, while it never quite achieved the pungency of

Fourier's, was as all-embracing, and at moments a trenchant phrase breaks through the monotonous portrayal. Owen knew the horrors of the factory system in its formative period and dwelt with passion upon the physical and moral degradation of men, women, and children entrapped by it. Though committed to the omnipotence of the environment, he could fall into a eugenic mood in which he saw the physical species of British workers as definitively corrupted by disease, or at least in danger of such a fate if conditions were not improved. The injuries inflicted by the factory system were of a different order of magnitude from those suffered by farm laborers. Were the present system to continue, the whole of mankind would degenerate.

How had the present evil world come about? What is Owen's etiology of the Great Error? Sometimes it is the priesthood that is responsible, at least for marital evils. There are the accumulated errors of irrational ancestors. Secondary causes easily account for some aberrant behavior: For example, fear made moral cowards of those who had discovered the true facts but dared not proclaim them. But an explicit *fons et origo* of error is conspicuously absent from Owen's writing. Once original sin was thrown out, there was nothing to replace it.

Owen's simple environmentalist conception, what others mocked as his "one idea," was the cornerstone of his whole system, and detractors did not discourage him. If mankind would only accept this one idea with the same fervor with which they had hitherto denied it, a host of salutary consequences would naturally flow from it. "It is a law of nature, obvious to our senses, that the internal and external character of all that have life upon the earth, is formed *for* them and not *by* them; that, in accordance with this law, the internal and external character of man is formed *for* him; and *not by* him, as hitherto most erroneously imagined; and, therefore, he cannot have merit or demerit, or deserve praise or blame, reward or punishment, in this life, or in any future state of existence."[10] This one idea, encapsulated in the motto "The character of man is formed *for* him, not *by* him," was emblazoned on the masthead of the *Crisis,* the journal Owen edited in the early thirties. His portrait, a sketch of an ideal square agricultural-industrial village, and the slogan about character formation became the three fundamental elements symbolizing the movement.

The leaps from one assumption to another in the numbered arguments of Robert Owen take place as if they were links in an iron chain of logic. If men were convinced that no individual was responsible for his moral condition and it was created only by environmental circumstances, they would have to behave toward one another in a "new, sublime, and pure spirit of charity, for the convictions, feelings, and conduct of the human race."[11] All punitive measures were irrational, as proved by the beneficial effects that resulted when barbaric methods were abolished in reformed asylums and schools. The time was approaching when innumerable maladies physical, mental, and moral would disappear. The rule would be to govern or treat all society as the most advanced physicians cared for their patients in the best arranged "lunatic hospitals," which were distinguished by forbearance and kindness and full allowance for every paroxysm of the peculiar disease of each patient.

Owen's proclamation of the end of individual responsibility was repeated over and over again in different contexts; a section of his universal code of laws was provocatively entitled: "On the irresponsibility of man." It made him anathema to the clergy of all religions and undermined the moral basis of any existing government or punitive law. By the same token, it won him the admiration of Karl Marx. While Marx assented to Vico's historico-philosophical dictum that man makes his own history, his reference was to man the species. Individual men, or at least social classes, were the products of their moment in time and the particular role they performed in the productive relations of their society. Marx would always insist that, though an extraordinary individual like himself or Owen was capable of transcending the circumstances of his birth, in general men were products of their environment, as Owen put it.

The emphasis upon external circumstances as the key to character formation was read by Marx in a sympathetic spirit because there was something anti-idealistic, matter-of-fact, practical about Owen's unphilosophical formulations that made them preferable to the pomposities of the German philosophers who had invaded the radical world. The Owenite utopia offered a naive, behavioristic solution to all problems that was not alien to theoretical or practical Marxian utopistics.

Man can never attain to a state of superior and permanent happiness, until he shall be surrounded by those external circumstances which will train him, from birth, to feel pure charity and sincere affection towards the whole of his species—to speak the truth only on all occasions, and to regard with a merciful disposition all that have life . . . such superior knowledge and feelings can never be given to man under those institutions of society which have been founded on the mistaken supposition that each man forms his own *feelings* and *convictions* by his *will,* and therefore has merit or demerit, or deserves praise or blame, or reward or punishment, for them.

. . . Under institutions formed in accordance with the principles of the rational system of society, this superior knowledge, and these superior dispositions, may be given to the whole of the human race, without chance of failure, except in cases of organic disease.[12]

By nature man was not only rational but benign and loving, if he was led to make the correct association of ideas. Men's desires would be temperate if they were shown the reason for temperance. Their capacities could be developed in many directions, including the ability to govern themselves.

Character formation had to begin as soon as a child could walk; hence the early establishment of play areas in New Lanark. Engraving the crucial first impressions upon a child's brain could not be entrusted to parents who had been imbued with false ideas. Most of Owen's writings were devoted to demonstrating that character formation depended upon the principles of those who managed it, not on the individual, for a man could not make himself and therefore he was not free or accountable. The single exception was Owen, discoverer of the Great Error, himself partly a product of circumstances, albeit favorable ones for the inauguration of the new system. There were times when Owen saw the character of man as a compound of his qualities at birth and the circumstances in which he was afterward placed, with the constant action and reaction of the one upon the other; but in his last important work, *The Revolution in the Mind and Practice of the Human Race* (1849), circumstances, nurture, arrangements far outweighed the significance of congenital qualities, which, though fostered in the utopian townships, were useful primarily to lend diversity to society. Owen's mechanisms for inducing a rational state of mind in his workers were precisely those used by benign animal experimenters, with emphasis on positive reinforcement rather than punishments. The New Lanark factory where Owen was Father and Master was the first industrial social laboratory in the modern world. As early as 1813 he had written in his *New View of Society:* "Withdraw those circumstances which tend to create crime in the human character, and crime will not be created. Replace them with such as are calculated to form habits of order, regularity, temperance, industry; and these qualities will be formed."[13]

The Marquis de Sade had used the argument that *all* actions were natural, hence their perpetrators were devoid of responsibility and should be free from any punishment for the rape, torture, murder of their fellows. Robert Owen never voiced approval of abhorrent actions. He was opposed to punishment because men were victims of circumstance and not to be held accountable for their wicked deeds: "The laws of man create crime, and then punish it in the individual, whose character they have previously formed to commit the crime."[14] But when Owen assured the rulers of the earth that under a system of independent home colonies of 500 to 3,000 persons all human needs would be satisfied, he meant only rational needs. None other came to his enlightened lips. A rational education would make impossible the passionate propensities and extraordinary appetites that de Sade and Fourier had extolled.

The Gradual Transition

Owen protested tirelessly in lectures and public addresses on both sides of the Atlantic that his project was to be instituted with the least possible disturbance of existing economic relations. As in the thought of Saint-Simon and Fourier, the French Revolution still loomed ominously in the background, and Owen had no wish to foment disruption and rebellion. The psychological principles underlying a peaceful transition to the new moral world are a simple extension of the eighteenth-century doctrine of association. Under the old system of error, somehow or other ideas became associated in wrong combinations; these now had to be "unassociated" and the true associations knitted together, a process that might last a few generations. "There must be no attempt to change governments or society by violence. Anger, in its various stages towards extreme violence and deadly conflict, indicates similar degrees of insanity and madness."[15] The transition could be effected by all governments simultaneously through the newspapers within the course of a single year, if only they turned to the advocacy of rational principles. Owen's fundamental tenet was reiterated so often it became like a religious litany. The new technology for creating wealth with little manual labor would eliminate poverty once the true principles of society were instilled in all human beings. Hence the ease of the changeover from one system to another. Marx in his estimate of Owen passed over his militant antirevolutionism.

When the turgid rhetoric was put aside, it became clear that the transition would be effected by an unusual concatenation of circumstances that required an act of illumination. There arose a man, none other than Robert Owen, who, through a study of the past and present social and psychological facts of world history, which by his own testimony to the American Congress he had absorbed five hours a day for twenty years, had discovered the one idea that was the fundamental law of human nature. He communicated his knowledge first to a few men capable of enlightenment and then to the governments of the whole world, who would proceed to institute a new system of education first among a few workers' colonies and then throughout the globe. The crucial assumptions were that Owen was capable of communicating his system and that from the very beginning a select body of men were capable of receiving it. Nothing accounted for his extraordinary appearance on earth and the exercise of his power of persuasion, elements that Owen's major utopian competitors had also presumed, each in his own case. The Reverend J. H. Roebuck in public debate in 1837 made the impertinent reflection: "Mr. Owen cannot explain to us consistently with his scheme, how out of the rubbish of the old irrational world, he sprang up so beautifully rational."[16] Marx eschewed a theory of individual behavior and dealt with classes and systems; Owen was locked into his individualist behavioral psychology, which had no exits.

The problems of transition to the new society were left vague. Owen had nothing "rational" to say about the relations of the existing agricultural and manufacturing system and the new cooperative villages until he came forward with his "new" theory of value, which made labor the basis of all valuation in the new society. This "discovery" became a moral imperative: Since the principle was true, it had to be accepted. Perhaps the accumulation of scientific data in recent ages and the extraordinary technological advancement that had increased productivity many times over provided firm enough arguments to overcome the prevailing "irrationality"; but it is difficult to understand how, even granted Owen's unique enlightenment about the law of nature, his findings could impress others. There was of course his thirty-year experience in the spinning mills of New Lanark with the systematic transformation of his "operatives" from drunken, shiftless creatures into the best workers in the world, a metamorphosis witnessed by aristocrats, their expert advisers, and numerous foreign visitors, empirical demonstration of the truth of the system and its dominant idea. Even if men would not listen to abstract reason, they could not fly in the face of an experiment of such long duration. Owen's ceaseless lecturing, book writing, propaganda were directed to one end: to convince the powerful, preferably heads of state, that the movement from irrationality to rationality could be achieved peacefully and gradually, bringing happiness to all, rich and poor, aristocrats, red republicans, socialists, and communists.

When in *The Revolution in the Mind and Practice of the Human Race* Owen asked "What was to be done?"—that favorite nineteenth-century refrain of practicing utopians—he established his authority to speak as a universal reformer by citing once again the three decades of his administration of the mills of New Lanark. They had taught him that mankind was infinitely malleable, "ductile," he said, but that an appropriate physical and moral environment had to be installed before the new man could be turned out. Owen was prone to resorting to metaphors from industry and commerce, and he thought of social renovation the way he would the introduction of a new manufacturing process. He conceived of himself as "chosen" long before he indulged in spiritualist séances and held converse with great heroes of the past. He was uniquely fitted to effect the transformation in the work system because he had served in every rank, from his post as usher in a school at the age of seven, through apprenticeship to a draper, and finally to his elevation as manager and owner of mills. And he had seen the world—at least France, Jamaica, Mexico, and the

United States. Everywhere he had met men of all classes and had had the opportunity to study precisely how their particular systems of ideas had been molded by their environments.

Current political demands of the working classes for universal suffrage were irrelevant distractions that would only lead to further upheavals. Marx's conception of the auto-emancipation of the working classes through economic and political action was totally alien to Owen, despite his paternalist flirtation with the labor movements. Chartists such as Henry Hetherington perfectly understood this, and while their *Poor Man's Guardian* could praise Owen's philanthropy, it rejected his constant assertion of the futility of political action and the winning of constitutional rights. Though Marx would join Owen in the prospect of the ultimate withering away of the political state, he would differ from him on tactics. For the transition period to communism, Marx valued political agitation as a mechanism that would help create communist consciousness, while Owen saw politics only as another force contributing to the current state of anarchy. Philosophical freedom and dignity were as meaningless to Owen as they are to a contemporary behaviorist like Skinner.

Owen consistently condemned sharp revolutionary disjunctures. It was not to the interest of contemporaries that their social institutions remain forever unchanged, but on the other hand it would be deplorable if any one of them should be prematurely or suddenly destroyed. It was evident that the peace and safety of all demanded that these institutions and social practices be gradually superseded by others. Owen likened the peaceful transition to utopia alongside the old system to the building of railways while the old roads remained undisturbed. Governments would merely have to appoint a committee of seven intelligent, practical men who would be in charge of enlisting all the unemployed into a civil army to be reeducated so that they could introduce the institutions of the new scientific and rational society "gradually, peaceably, and wisely," without interfering with any existing government or public or private interests.[17]

Fourier had imagined a huge army of adolescents who would be driven by an exploratory passion to reconquer the wastelands of the world and who in passing would seek the fulfillment of their sexual needs in grand mock battles of the sexes. The German artisan Weitling saw industrial armies in quasi-military dress as appropriate for production and he called for strict discipline among them. Bellamy would later continue the tradition of the work army for his ideal society of the future. For Owen the civil army of the unemployed was the perfect instrument to effect the gradual changeover from private interests to socialism, though he did not intend the army to be a permanent institution of the new society. The authoritarian way had found early acceptance in the communist utopia of Babeuf, and under a variety of names, with differing degrees of the Spartan rule, a long line of utopians from Owen through Marx resorted to it, especially for that irksome interim when the old man was not yet dead and the new one had not yet been fully formed. Moses' "arrangements" for the Jews in the wilderness, which required a forty-year hiatus before the triumphal entry into the promised land, was a deep Judeo-Christian cultural memory and the death of the old generation an archetypal solution. An authoritarian dictatorship of the proletariat was the mechanism Marx introduced into the *Gotha Program Critique* to protect communism in its fledgling stage, but some of his utopian predecessors, especially those who eschewed violence, had earlier concocted milder schemes. Owen's was among the more disarming because of its built-in time limitation. The wretched state of human existence would slowly give way to a scientific and rationally constructed society.

The Rectangular Townships

The townships delineated in *The Revolution in the Mind and Practice of the Human Race* are the final embodiment of his utopian thought, far more concrete than his earlier, long-winded discussions on the formation of character. He had learned something, but not much, from the fiasco at New Harmony a quarter of a century before. Marx was right in refusing to reduce Owen to a promoter of cooperative "boutiques," even though the spread of small-scale cooperative enterprises was the movement through which Owen probably exerted the greatest direct influence upon English society. In the circumstantial detail of the ideal township Owen's utopia comes to life.

Both the Saint-Simonians and Fourier had preserved many elements of the capitalist private property system. Only the later Owen was decisive in demanding communal exploitation of township fields, which surrounded a quadrangle of living quarters; as a practical businessman he had concluded—and he supplied comparative illustrations of income and expenditure—that cultivation in common would be more economical. At one time Marx thought this a cogent proof of the superiority of a communist system. For Owen, the ultimate justification for cultivating the land in common was its beneficent effect on character formation. "The land will be cultivated as one farm property divided, under one general management, and will thus yield all the advantages of large and small farms, without the many disadvantages of the one or the other.

"By this arrangement for cultivating the land, in connexion with those for manufacturing, and both being united with the domestic arrangements and education, it will be easy in execution to have only superior circumstances in every department, to the entire exclusion of all vicious, injurious, or inferior circumstances." [18]

The township would be governed directly by all trained and educated members who had reached the age of thirty; there would be no tumultuous elections. All three of the great utopians shared a profound antagonism to political life as separated from the actual administration of production. In the townships, men and women in full vigor from thirty to forty would join the Home Department. The main body engaged in domestic management would thus be remarkably stable, since only about a tenth would be renewable each year. At forty, citizens would enter the Foreign Department, and at sixty they were entirely free of governmental obligations. With this fixed order of responsibility there could be no political contests. Life really would begin at sixty, when each as he saw fit could devote himself to public betterment; and the freedom and ease would make for longevity. (Bellamy adopted a similar scheme in *Looking Backward*.) The Foreign Department created road links among townships, arranged for the establishment of new townships when population increased to the allowable limit, and exchanged scientific, technological, and cultural information.

Owen's townships of 500 to 3,000, the parallel to Fourier's phalansteries of

1,800, had "no useless private property,"[19] no rewards and punishments. They were joined in circles of tens, hundreds, thousands, and still larger units until the whole world was encompassed, again a pattern not unlike Fourier's. Individual townships would exchange surpluses, but they were essentially self-sufficient. There was no expectation of irrational behavior in these small local societies, though provision was made for its treatment should it chance to break out. Present-day readers can hardly study the passages about the care of "moral invalids" without sensing a presage of things to come. No matter how radically an English utopia strives to oust the punitive through the door of its ideal society, it manages to creep in through the window. "All individuals, trained, educated, and placed, in conformity with the laws of their nature, must, of necessity, at all times, think and act rationally, unless they shall become physically, intellectually or morally diseased; in which case the council [of the township] shall remove them into the hospital for bodily, mental, or moral invalids, where they shall remain until they shall have been recovered by the mildest treatment that can effect their cure."[20]

Where authority was involved, Owen was full of contradictions. On one page full liberty for the individual to express all his thoughts "upon all subjects" was reckoned a requisite for human happiness; eight pages later the reader encounters regulations "to prevent injurious expressions of opinion or feelings arising among the adult members of the Township."[21] The behavioral system Owen as mill owner had instituted at New Lanark somehow fell apart in the freedom and equality of New Harmony, Indiana; but the theory rolled along in periodical after periodical, public meeting after public meeting, book after book, as if nothing adverse had occurred. Defeats might whip Owen, but they never forced him to change a word once uttered. Marx admired Owen's tenacity, his refusal to bend in order to court popularity.

By 1849, the township of about 2,000 had usurped the role of what we now call the nuclear family as Owen's basic unit of existence. The township as "parent" served as an agent of the creative power of God in maintaining universal harmony. Harmony could not be achieved without equality as a unifying principle, and equality meant fulfillment for a variety of characters, not the imposition of uniformity. At times *The Revolution in the Mind and Practice of the Human Race* reads like an anglicized version of Fourier, the extravagances toned down, reason and science substituted for the passions as the key words. However naive Owen's home colonies may have appeared to Marx, he praised him for respecting equality in self-expression and for providing that the fulfillment of needs be directly organized by society, without the burdensome Fourierist holdover of disproportionate return on investment in each phalanstery. The limitation in size of the township was determined by Owen's contention that about 2,000 persons of all ages and sexes were the optimal number that could be housed in buildings forming a rectangle. The complex was superior to a royal palace, in that it offered the utmost in private and social accommodation and comfort as well as education and amusement. Public buildings would include colleges; private quarters would be assigned in terms of marital status and individual disposition. Apartments and accommodations of varied types were planned, though here a certain uniformity had to prevail lest a person suffer the slight of having another of the same age better housed than himself or herself.[22]

The townships were to be surrounded with gardens, pleasure grounds, and intensively cultivated estates on both sides of the railways that would traverse every country. Thus food would no longer have to be transported to over-crowded cities where it would arrive in deteriorated condition; instead, the inhabitants of ideal townships would live in the midst of their food supply. A thousand to two thousand acres of farmland girding the residential buildings would more than amply nourish the inhabitants.

Marx preferred the Owen of the post-1820 period and ignored the earlier works. He found congenial Owen's exposition of the general socialist idea of labor as the sole basis of value and the affirmation of plain equality as a goal in speeches and lectures of the twenties and thirties. Robert Owen of New Harmony, Indiana, on July 4, 1826, had called for liberation from privilege or individual ownership, absurd and irrational systems of religion, and marriage based on individual property. The 1830 *Lectures on an Entire New State of Society* described private property as an emanation of ignorant selfishness. And in *Lectures on the Marriages of the Priesthood* (1835), marriage was denounced as a satanic device that changed "sincerity, kindness, affection, sympathy and pure love into deception, envy, jealousy, hatred and revenge."[23]

Owen's attacks on marriage, property, and religion, the unholy trinity, which appeared in his lectures of the 1830s and in *The Book of the New Moral World,* resulted in his ostracism from respectable society. There were English booksellers who refused to stock any of his writings. The bitter denunciation of a marriage system that made divorce painfully difficult would seem to stem from personal experience—though a veil is drawn over the intimate details of the personal relations between Robert Owen the artisan's son and the daughter of Dale the manufacturer. In his polemical works Owen mixed eugenic arguments with descriptions of the psychic depredations of this priestly institution. Everything in the existing system of marriage was leading to the degeneration of the race; it put barriers in the way of eugenic improvement. Females in particular suffered under the present regimen, which brought them to insanity and suicide. Traditional marriage enslaved women who could not endure their husbands and caused them to bear untold miseries in silence. These "priestly" marriages from which there was no escape were a source of wretchedness among all classes. They encouraged men to make choices contrary to sound and natural eugenic principles because they were enticed by the rich dowries feeble women offered to prospective husbands.

For the townships Owen advocated sexual equality pure and simple in education, rights, privileges, and personal liberty. In this pure democracy there would be no motive for sexual crime, and sexual disease would soon be eradicated. Virtually all marital difficulties would dissolve, since partners would be chosen for the general sympathies of their natures. Owen could conceive of no other legitimate basis of coupling. Existing priestly marital laws had created and forced upon the human race more frustration of natural innocent feelings, more loathsome afflicting diseases, more monstrous crimes, more murders, more disordered fancies and more insanity than the human mind was capable of imagining, especially since these terrible evils had been concealed. If the doctors, police authorities, and keepers of madhouses would speak out, mankind would learn of the terrible injustices and anguish generated by the present system; it revealed men as less rational than all other animals, which, lacking a meddlesome priesthood, instinctively pursued what they wanted.

Childhood was the crucial formative period—Owen always stressed the significance of the early months of life—yet this was the age most neglected. The abuse of children was not physical alone; it formed in them evil habits and they were as if lost for life. Owen's descriptions of incompetent, punitive masters join those of seventeenth-century utopian emancipators of children like Comenius, who had written of schools as slaughterhouses. When in 1816 Owen opened an Institution for the Formation of Character in New Lanark, he gave explicit instructions to its teachers: They were never to beat children, and were to address them with pleasant countenance and in a kindly tone of voice. If parents attended the lectures he hoped that even they would profit from them. They could learn to apportion their earnings rationally, creating a fund to relieve anxieties for the future instead of wasting money on drink.

Children had to be made rational through knowing themselves, a knowledge attained by investigating facts. The consequence would be the drying up of anger, ill will, envy, jealousy, and other repugnant emotions. Only when all children passed through the same general routine of education, domestic teaching, and employment, as they would in the townships, would happiness become possible for them. Parents were too partial to their offspring to educate them, even if they had the pedagogic machinery at their disposal—an old communitarian utopian saw. Only the townships were large enough to maintain the necessary and suitable instrumentalities for fashioning a superior, useful character. At every age there would be particular educational techniques to fit the growing physical and mental capacities of the students and their altered propensities.

Owen assured his readers that the affections of the biological family would not be weakened by communal education. Now limited to the family, the affections would be extended so that the disposition to take undue advantage of others would be curbed. Freud later claimed, as Aristotle had before him, that the communal diffusion of affections diluted them. Owen adamantly held to the evidence of his thirty-year experience in New Lanark that the natural affection between parents and children was not diminished under a communal system. His thesis was simple: If an egalitarian democratic character was to be shaped, it could not be achieved within the egotistic confines of the small family unit.

Perfect equality throughout life was "the only foundation for a certain bond of union among men, and for an elevated state of society."[24] Answering an unseen interlocutor, Owen refuted the argument that such equality in his ideal townships would entrain monotonous uniformity. The bogey had been raised against the Saint-Simonians, and it has never been laid to rest. Owen denied that there was any necessary connection between drab sameness and complete equality. "In every case, the Township will form those general arrangements that will supply all equally, according to age, with the best of everything for human nature, at each divisional period of life; and apply the faculties and powers of each, without exception, for the benefit of the individuals of the Township, and of the extended circle of the federative unions."[25] Owen allowed that each person was born with a different compound of qualities, and in practice it would be discovered that this diversity was necessary and useful in the order of nature; but this did not mean that a superior quality should provide a pretext for breaking the rule of equality, since the merit was given by God, not earned.

Owen granted that in the past an occasional lawgiver like Lycurgus of

Sparta had succeeded in developing a uniform, one-sided, "sectional" character that excelled in military prowess; but the progress of human knowledge now demanded rational men and women, fully formed mentally, morally, and physically. Though Owen did not get far away from the language of the spinning-mill owner, in essence he was in the same philosophical tradition as that governing the other romantic utopians, Marx included—the self-actualization of the individual in all his capacities. The complete flowering of a man's natural gifts under a social arrangement of equality was likened to the production of a fine textile. "The machinery is now required to manufacture from human nature this superior fabric, for the benefit of all who live, and for future generations." The establishment of the township system would increase happiness in a ratio of 2,000 to 1 compared with the present individualistic system. Owen's "laws of the universal rational constitution, for the government of the human race collectively,"[26] guaranteed total self-fulfillment.

The mid-nineteenth-century revolutionary excitement in France and England, the two most energetic and advanced nations of the globe, heralded what was to come—full and complete equality. "It is the pure principle of democracy, carried out to its full extent in practice, that can alone carry the human race onward toward the highest degrees of perfection."[27] Utopian happiness could not be restricted to a particular class or geographic section. All of the human race shall be happy, or none.

The Onward Spirit

The scientific laws of human nature, discovered by Owen, would transform the world into a terrestrial paradise, in which the "onward spirit" of each inhabitant would operate against the existence of any cause of evil.[28] Concern for the well-being and well-doing of every individual in society would generate in every man "the highest rational enjoyments" to the greatest practicable extent. The Benthamite adaptation is patent, the belief in the malleability of every human being is unquestioned, the identity of individual and collective happiness has never been more dogmatically asserted. The rub lies hidden in the "rational" of the highest rational enjoyments, a nineteenth-century version of the "honest allowable pleasures" of Thomas More, whose *Utopia* the Owenites freely excerpted and published in their journals.[29] These anticlerical dissenters, of course, could not have anticipated that in the twentieth century More would be formally declared a full-fledged saint.

Though Owen's militant anticlericalism caused him the greatest difficulties in the propagation of his system, he was neither an unrelenting atheist nor a materialist. His nine laws on the principles and practices of rational religion set him somewhere between a deist and an agnostic, but he still posited a single creating force for all existence. His murky theology was not acceptable to any religious establishment or sect in England. He maintained that "all facts yet known to man indicate that there is an external or internal Cause of all existences, by the fact of their existence; that this all-pervading cause of motion and change in the universe, is that Incomprehensible Power which the nations of the world have called God, Jehovah, Lord, etc., etc.; but the facts are yet unknown to man which define what that Power is."[30]

In his old age Owen reverted to the language of Christian millenarianism, which he mixed with a hodgepodge of pseudo-scientific cosmological notions.[31] When a bit of Lucretian atomism seeped into his view of the universe, he saw its elements in a constantly changing pattern of repulsion and attraction, continually forming new compounds. This perception of the physical world in no way hindered his belief in material and spiritual progression. Owen regularly quoted the Scriptures, albeit with commentaries that were far-out even for independent Dissenters, many of whom nevertheless joined his movement. When he lectured to his workers on Saint Paul's First Epistle to the Corinthians, he linked the Christian idea of charity with the greatest happiness of the greatest number deriving from the practice of enlightened self-interest, a stew that only a Bible-ridden Benthamite could readily digest.

Owen did not contemn the spiritual leaders of Western society, neither Plato nor Jesus, who was for him a "genuine socialist." Unfortunately their doctrines had been perverted by the practices of unknowing and misguided disciples, who had honored the principle of repulsion instead of attraction. It was the ecclesiastical establishments of all religions and the formal worship of God that drew Owen's fire; the ritual mummery was meaningless. For man, an insect upon a planet, a grain of sand in the universe, to imagine that he could glorify the Origin of all things with his trivial, fatuous, ceremonial acts was the most irrational of conceptions. In short, God was indifferent to the laudations of puny man. Behind Owen's conviction of the possibility of a rational society and the fashioning of mankind to goodness lay the ultimate belief that all being was an expression of the divine creative force. When Marx and Engels enrolled him under their materialist banner, they were turning a deaf ear to his spiritualism, which allowed for the existence of recognizable beings after death and for man's ability to communicate with them. Neither for Robert Owen nor for his son Robert Dale Owen, who became a naturalized American citizen and when Minister of the United States in Naples frequently participated in spiritualist séances, was there a conflict between such beliefs and the universal truth of the Owenite system as the only way to a new moral world.

Over the centuries the English utopian tradition has largely gone its own parochial way, and though in broad lines it is related to Continental developments it often spawns figures who have a special character: the Catholic martyr who invented Utopia, the Diggers and Ranters of the Civil War, the eighteenth-century dissenting clergyman who expounded anarchism in two volumes, and the authoritarian cotton manufacturer who founded the socialist community of New Harmony, not to speak of that indescribable assortment of intellectuals in the Fabian Society who debated with one another about utopian values. The English utopians displayed neither the philosophical vigor of the Germans nor the political and psychological acumen of the French. More than other utopian creators they prided themselves on their moral principles, and the most irreligious English socialist community seems to incarnate a Dissenter sermon. At some point, common sense and self-evident propositions are left behind, and plain psychological data about man's nature and history are blithely ignored.

PART VII

Marx and Counter-Marx

Karl Marx in his last years
painter unknown

29

Marx and Engels in the Landscape of Utopia

AMONG THE HUNDREDS of disparate pronouncements on human need in modern times, two are curiously linked. The first is from *King Lear*. After the King had been mercilessly nagged by his daughter to dismiss his retainers as serving no *need* for a retired monarch, he roared with rage:

> O! reason not the need; our basest beggars
> Are in the poorest thing superfluous:
> Allow not nature more than nature needs,
> Man's life is cheap as beast's. Thou art a lady;
> If only to go warm were gorgeous,
> Why, nature needs not what thou gorgeous wear'st,
> Which scarcely keeps thee warm. But, for true need,—

The other declaration was made by a great admirer of Shakespeare who knew large parts of his plays by heart, the middle-aged Karl Marx, in a letter written to his follower Wilhelm Bracke on May 5, 1875. It was published posthumously in 1891 by Friedrich Engels, who captioned it *Critique of the Gotha Program of the Social Democratic Party*. In our time the aristocratic *Almanach* with which the city of Gotha was long associated has yielded to the *Critique*. The political circumstances that called forth the letter—Marx's attempt to supervise from his exile in London, to control from afar, the compromise draft prepared at Gotha by two hostile branches of the German party, the Eisenachians (who followed Marx) and the renegade Lassalleans—are by now generally forgotten, and so is Engels' motive in dispatching the letter to Karl Kautsky's journal *Die Neue Zeit*, where it was unceremoniously followed by Max Schippel's article "Zuckersteuer und Zuckerindustrie." Fundamentally, Marx in 1875 felt that a new party program was supererogatory; the *Manifesto*, cogent and lucid, had been around for popular consumption since 1848, and the publication of another statement of principles was likely to be obfuscatory. Moreover, neither Marx nor Engels had been consulted about the new articles of unification, which had come as a bolt from the blue, and the leaders of the world communist movement were angry. But since the German and international tactical situation demanded Marx's immediate intervention (he was under simultaneous attack from anarchist Bakuninists as well as reformist Lassalleans), the ailing patriarch of the revolution, in despite of his doctor's orders, laboriously wrote out line-by-line glosses on the draft, and then concluded them with a mock-religious "Dixi et salvavi animam meam."[1]

The Banderole

For a time the glosses on the Gotha Program had great prestige in the communist thought of the West because they were quoted as authoritative by Lenin in *State and Revolution* and by other theoreticians whenever party conflicts raised issues of doctrinal purity in the face of "opportunism." Among other things, the *Critique of the Gotha Program* contained a clear-cut passage on the "revolutionary dictatorship of the proletariat" as the appropriate transitional stage between capitalism and communism.[2] By now, perhaps, the tactical measures and programmatic criticisms painfully spelled out are considered too old for service even by the most devout European followers of Marx, though the East German official history of the German working-class movement still calls the hallowed text the most important theoretical document of Marxism after the *Communist Manifesto* and *Das Kapital*. It is reported that peasant communes in China discuss the *Critique* in their educational assemblies, and faint echoes of its phraseology can be detected in the constitution of the People's Republic of China. In that portion of the globe at least, time and space have not diminished the reverence for Marx's utterances, though whether the Chinese analyses of his words bear any kinship to their original meaning is another matter. In the West, the centenary of the *Critique* was not marked with anything like the festive reconsiderations that accompanied the anniversary of *Das Kapital*'s appearance in 1867; but the utopian principles enunciated in Marx's letter to Bracke continue to resound throughout the world. The banderole inscribed "From each according to his abilities, to each according to his needs" may be getting a bit frayed with age, but it is still fluttering in the winds of doctrine, belief, and hope. In the *Critique* Marx distinguished for the first time between Phase I of communist society, during which real equality could not yet be instituted because economic and cultural resources were too limited, and Phase II, the higher plane of communism. These paragraphs embodied a full version of Marx's utopia, one of his very rare descriptions of the future communist world.

Both Marx and Engels on occasion had a word of approval for old utopian socialists and communists as antecedents[3]—Thomas More, Thomas Müntzer, and the Levellers faithfully reflected the conditions of their times—but what had been innocent daydreaming up to about the end of the eighteenth century could not be considered so thereafter, for the later utopians, without any sense of the objective conditions of their society and its historical development, were spinning purely subjective fantasies that distracted the proletariat from its destined political mission. Once Marx and Engels had come onto the world stage, any utopian survivors had to be repudiated in principle, since they had been transcended by scientific socialism. The idea of utopia acquired heavily pejorative overtones in communist thought. As the appointed guardian of true revolutionary consciousness, Marx was formally obligated to combat every utopian system that raised its empty head—Owenite, Saint-Simonian, Fourierist, Blancian, Proudhonian, Stirnerian, Weitlingian, Bakuninist, Lassallean, Dühringian, in fact any deviation from the realistic and correct doctrinal position set forth in the writings of Marx and Engels. "Utopian" was usually an epithet of denigration to be splashed onto any theoretical opponent. If a roundabout story is credible, as he advanced in years Marx continued to reject the very idea of a utopia. Georges Sorel in the *Réflexions sur la violence* (1908) reported that, according to the economist Professor Lujo Brentano, Marx wrote the English Positivist Edward Spencer Beesly in 1869: "The man who draws up a programme for the future is a reactionary."[4]

In daily practice the position Marx and Engels assumed with respect to their utopian forerunners was far more complex and on occasion even they might lapse into utopian glossolalia. Despite the persistence with which they belabored some contemporary utopians, essential parts of the *Critique of the Gotha Program* were in fact the answer to a utopian inquiry that Marx himself had initiated: "What transformation will the nature of the state undergo in a communist society? In other words, what social functions will then remain that are analogous to present-day state functions?" This question could only be answered "scientifically" (*wissenschaftlich*), he declared in the *Critique;*[5] but some pages back, a grand apostrophe had already escaped him and he was caught in the utopian web.

In a higher phase of communist society, when the enslaving subordination of the individual to the division of labor, and with it the antithesis between mental and physical labor, has vanished; when labor is no longer merely a means of life but has become life's principal need; when the productive forces too have increased with the all-round development of the individual, and all the springs of shared wealth flow more abundantly —only then will it be possible completely to transcend the narrow horizon of bourgeois right and only then will society be able to inscribe on its banners: From each according to his abilities, to each according to his needs [*Jeder nach seinen Fähigkeiten, jedem nach seinen Bedürfnissen*]![6]

Implicit in this passage is the quintessential problem of what are and what are not human needs that has always been at the core of utopian thought in the West. The question of need has been analyzed in abstract philosophical terms, as in Plato's *Philebus,* or in concrete physiological terms. Distinctions have been established between need and desire, between authentic and inauthentic needs. The relationship of needs and abilities in Marx's utopian thought can perhaps best be established, not in an isolated or autonomous commentary on the brief, laconic phrases of the *Critique,* but in juxtaposition with the views of the French and English utopian communists and socialists who antedated him and whose followers survived to bedevil him, and in relation to his own views on other occasions. The French and English utopian tradition about the future of society was the most serious body of utopian thought with which he was confronted. Except for the memory of Thomas Müntzer there was no German social utopia that earned the respect of Marx and Engels, and Müntzer was too remote to be used as anything but a fetish. Marx had a way of defining himself by negation, but he did not live by refutation alone, and the encyclopedic and synthesizing mind of this man deeply immersed in the culture of his age managed to assimilate the ideas of his enemies even while he was berating them. A hundred years after it was written, the *Critique of the Gotha Program* can be most effectively illuminated if it is restored to the utopian landscape in which it was originally planted.

Crude Leveling

Marx was aware from his reading of *The Conspiracy of the Equals,* by Philippe Buonarroti, a survivor of the plot, that there had been a deliberate and momentous decision among the members of Babeuf's inner circle to reject the equal, private, individual holdings of More's *Utopia* in favor of communally held property as the only feasible way to enforce absolute equality after the Revolution. The Babouvist dogma of *immediate* equality had also lived on in the popular French communist tradition that Buonarroti had resurrected in the 1830s. When the young Marx was exposed to Babouvism, he rejected it totally and unequivocally. His loathing for instant egalitarianism was a constant of his thought from his first appearance in the political arena. While he could treat more tenderly the egalitarian communistic utopians of the eighteenth century that he knew, Mably and Morelly, their identification with the consequences of their thought in the mad Babouvist uprising caused even these guileless ones to be smeared.

In the *Communist Manifesto* of 1848 the Babeuf type of communism was labeled *reaktionär*. "It teaches a general asceticism and a crude leveling."[7] From the 1840s onward, Marx, who saw himself as coming to mankind in order to establish a communist system for a dynamic, world technological-industrial mechanism inherited from bourgeois capitalism, heaped scorn upon the eighteenth-century French founders of "optimum little republics" based on egalitarian principles and their nineteenth-century German imitators with their "Federal republics with social institutions" and vapid egalitarian slogans.[8] The German scribblers of the Gotha Program of 1875 had fallen into the same oratorical trap, and he would have none of them. The notes that preceded Engels' *Anti-Dühring* (whose express purpose was to distinguish authoritatively between utopian and scientific socialism) are spotted with similar sneers, witness that the two men were on the same track. "To want to establish Equality = Justice as the highest principle and the ultimate truth is absurd." Ahistorical manifestoes like the Gotha Program were drivel for both of them. "So the concept of equality itself is a historical *Produkt* to whose working out the whole of prehistory is necessary," wrote Engels, "it has not existed as truth from all eternity." When Engels heard talk of a sudden communist revolution against the "existing military bureaucratic state," he could only liken such political insanity to Babeuf's attempt "to jump immediately from the Directory into communism."[9] As late as 1885, recollecting the Babouvist influence in the secret organizations of the League of the Just and the League of Communists of the 1840s, Engels continued to denounce them for their derivation of community of property from the *principle* of equality rather than seeing communism as an outgrowth of the historical process.[10] Inequalities were inevitable in the first phase of communism as it would emerge, after long birth pangs, from capitalist society, Marx insisted in his *Critique,* and for Social Democrats promiscuously to advertise promises of equality was a base deception. Justice (he meant distributive justice), the law of a society, could not be more effective than its economic structure and the cultural level dependent upon it would permit. True equality had to await the higher stage of communism.

Once the idea of absolute equality, in the Babouvist sense, as a human need had become deeply entrenched in certain branches of French communist thought of the 1830s and 1840s, usually among the violent direct actionists such as Auguste Blanqui, it had to be recokoned with. But immediate equality as a goal clashed sharply with other utopian needs as they had been set forth by those seminal utopian thinkers and their followers who had moved in a very different direction from Babeuf's: Saint-Simon, Fourier, and Owen. These were men toward whom both Marx and Engels had adopted a negative attitude in the *Communist Manifesto,* which was a utopian's due. But despite their criticism, ambivalent feelings colored their treatment.[11] All utopian thought was inimical to scientific socialism, but some conceptions were less inimical than others. In the collected works of Marx and Engels there are scores of citations dealing with Saint-Simon, Fourier, Owen, and their followers, and they range from contempt to generous praise. The writings of these utopian socialists left an indelible stamp on the banderole of the *Critique of the Gotha Program*.

Utopian Socialists

The minds of Saint-Simon, Owen, and Fourier, all autodidacts, had been fashioned by the Anglo-French Enlightenment thought of pre-Revolutionary Europe. Marx and Engels represented a very different world—Rhineland society half a century later—and they were illustrious products of the organized German university system of the early forties. But from the beginning of their self-awareness as revolutionaries, they had to cope with the curious, often absurd, writings of these three men, whom they somehow recognized as respectworthy predecessors. Utopian socialist thought had first taken shape during the Napoleonic period, contemporaneous with the Hegelian philosophy, and the young men had a love-hate relationship with both. They knew their fathers and had to transcend them.

The identification of the mutually unsympathetic persons of Saint-Simon, Fourier, and Owen as a utopian trinity was becoming general in the 1830s. Fourier himself had singled out Saint-Simon and Owen as his two major rivals in the hostile pamphlet of 1831, *Pièges et charlatanisme des deux sectes: Saint-Simon et Owen, qui promettent l'association et le progrès* (Snares and Charlatanism of the Two Sects: Saint-Simon and Owen, Who Promise Association and Progress), and in a series of articles in the Fourierist journal *La Réforme industrielle ou Le Phalanstère* of July 1832 that covered the whole utopian spectrum under the title "Revue des utopies du xixᵉ siècle." Jérôme-Adolphe Blanqui (respectable brother of Auguste), *Cours d'économie industrielle*, 1837–1838, listed Saint-Simon, Fourier, and Owen as *socialistes modernes*. Nonsectarian Europeans probably were first alerted to the triple threat of the new utopians when Louis Reybaud's *Etudes sur les réformateurs contemporains ou socialistes modernes* was published in 1840 and crowned by the Académie des Sciences Morales et Politiques. After critically dissecting Saint-Simon, Fourier, and Owen, Reybaud had added an appendix on Thomas Müntzer, associating the utopians with memories of the bloody uprisings of the Reformation.

Marx and Engels fell naturally into the current mode of grouping Saint-Simon, Fourier, and Owen as the principal socialist or communist sectarians of Europe. They might turn for casual reference to any of the numerous other systems, but these three were preoccupations throughout their lives. When Marx and Engels formed their enduring emotive and intellectual alliance in the 1840s they mounted a stage literally swarming with utopian systems, but they quickly distinguished antagonists of parts from the small fry. Though they once hailed the *Garantien der Harmonie und Freiheit* (Guarantees of Harmony and Freedom, 1842) by the German tailor Wilhelm Weitling as an example of what German proletarian genius could achieve, they soon judged his thought for what it was, a loose amalgam of Saint-Simonian and Fourierist notions. For the historian, Weitling's *Gerechtigkeit* (Justice) remains a moving autobiographical witness of the mind and feelings of a nineteenth-century, self-taught artisan; Marx and Engels came to treat him with the same contempt they visited upon Proudhon and Bakunin.[12]

Over the decades Marx's and Engels' appreciation of the utopian triumvirate of Saint-Simon, Fourier, and Owen swayed with the subject under discussion and the political exigencies of the times, whether they lumped the three together or carefully separated the triplex into its component parts. Engels was always more tolerant of "originals" than his partner and he had a deeper and more enduring affection for the dead *prodromoi;* but these are differences of degree, not fundamentally opposed attitudes. Marx and Engels often used the great utopians as foils in the course of attacks on Proudhon and the Germans— the True Socialists, Bruno Bauer, Weitling, Dühring. And, with the rarest of exceptions, they treated the three as men of consequence, even when they had to mow them down. Perhaps the high point of their esteem was reached late in their lives, in Engels' introductions to the 1870 and 1875 editions of *Der deutsche Bauernkrieg (The Peasant War in Germany)*. "German theoretical Socialism will never forget that it stands on the shoulders of Saint-Simon, Fourier, and Owen, three men who despite their fantasies and utopianism are to be reckoned among the most significant minds of all times, for they anticipated with genius countless matters whose accuracy we now demonstrate scientifically."[13] The image of dwarfs standing on the shoulders of giants seeing further than the giants themselves, which the passage evokes, has had a long history in Western culture. It was not habitual for Marx and Engels to dwarf their own historic roles, but there the unusual tribute stands.

Marx and Engels had read deeply in modern utopian literature before 1848 and at one point planned to have the foreign works excerpted and translated into German as educational materials for German workingmen. During the later years of exile in England they returned to the utopians, coming upon insights that had escaped their notice before, and reporting on them to each other with excitement. In the hiatus of the middle years, when it was vital to differentiate themselves from the host of rival system-makers dead and alive, they may have been more severe in their negation. As the former Saint-Simonians, turned bankers and senators, became a mainstay of Napoleon III's dictatorship, antagonism toward the disciples spilled back onto their ancestor; but Marx and Engels were generally careful to differentiate between the philosophico-historical sweep of Saint-Simon and the behavior of the ex-Saint-Simonian capitalists who ran the Crédit Mobilier.

As far back as 1845–46, Marx and Engels had already reached a reasonably consolidated position on the communist and socialist utopian "systems" that had mushroomed all over Europe. Instead of rejecting them outright as "dogmatic-dictatorial" as the German True Socialists did, they began to see the utopian systems as products of their time and the character of their authors. Fourier, they wrote in *Die deutsche Ideologie (The German Ideology)* had developed his views in an authentic poetical spirit; Owen and Cabet, lacking his imagination, had invented their utopias with businesslike calculation or juridical slyness. As the working-class parties of Europe evolved, these "systems" would become source books of popular slogans. Nobody could accept literally all of Owen's plans, which he continually modified in accordance with the class he was propagandizing—an observation not meant to be pejorative. Only the German True Socialists, who pretended to speak for eternity, were ridiculous.[14] Utopians like Owen who acted for their time served a salutary purpose. In praising him, Marx and Engels may even have provided posterity with a clue as to how they expected their own works to be read, hoping men would take into account the time and place of their utterances and the particular audience they were addressing. If their works were read in this spirit today much Marxological quibbling about consistency would evaporate into thin air.

In the *Communist Manifesto* of 1848, Owen's home colonies and Fourier's phalansteries were derided as castles in Spain, but they were explained historically rather than merely dismissed: Saint-Simon, Fourier, and Owen had sprung up in the undeveloped, early period of the war between the proletariat and the bourgeoisie.[15] Their definitive judgment on utopianism as an intellectual phenomenon was formulated by Engels in 1878, in *Herrn Eugen Dühring's Umwälzung der Wissenschaft (Herr Eugen Dühring's Revolution in Science)* where he drew careful distinctions between the early nineteenth-century utopians, who were justified because they "had to construct the outlines of a new society out of their own heads, since within the old society the elements of the new were not yet generally apparent," and the utopian social order constructed by the likes of Dühring "out of his sovereign brain" eighty years later. This purported "authoritative system" was winning converts in the Social Democratic party of Germany and was a real threat to the Marxist doctrine of scientific socialism. Things had come to a pretty pass when Dühring's confused rhetoric had to be considered seriously. In the text of Engels' classical work, the deflation of the pompous German professorial man-of-all-knowledge was accompanied by the elevation of each of the major utopians of the first decades of the nineteenth century.[16]

Doughty Robert Owen

But for all Marx's and Engels' appreciation of the utopian threesome, it was Owen whom they singled out for special praise—all the more perplexing in the light of what is known of his life and works. The rose-tinted Owen is an anomalous portrait in the Marxist gallery, where rough caricature tends to predominate. In the years that followed the Revolution of 1848, when the Owenites and Fourierists were shrunken into sects and the Saint-Simonians defected to the capitalists, Marx preserved a soft spot for the Robert Owen who had cast his lot with the working classes. Owen had a conception of a new world, Marx wrote to Ludwig Kugelmann.[17] Owen was in favor of the direct socialization of work. His establishment of connections between productive labor and the education of children and cooperatives had once been mocked, but many of his ideas had since been incorporated into laws. In fact they had become so widely accepted that they were beginning to serve as covers for new ways of swindling the working classes. *Das Kapital* quoted as authoritative the observations of Owen the manufacturer on the deleterious effects of the existing factory system upon the body and spirit of the average worker.[18] From Owen, Marx took testimony that the machine had deprived human nature of its resilience and reduced to a minimum its capacity to offer resistance to oppression. As late as 1877, when Marx was gathering up what he owned of Owen's works for Engels, who was reviewing the whole experience of utopian socialism, he came upon *The Revolution in the Mind and Practice of the*

Human Race; or, the Coming Change from Irrationality to Rationality (1849) and promptly bestowed upon it his accolade—"a very important work."[19] The dictatorial Owen of the experiments in harmony and Owen the aged spiritualist were forgotten.

When the Owenites gave Marx trouble in the International by refusing to recognize the importance of strike movements in consolidating the consciousness of the working classes, he turned to the memory of Robert Owen with a measure of nostalgia. He, unlike his followers, Marx believed, had never had any illusions about the widespread benign consequences of cooperative factories and stores. The factory system was for Owen the point of departure of the social revolution and he was regarded as a brother-in-arms. According to Marx, Owen had accepted industrialization, was an atheist, did not hesitate to rebel against the bourgeois law of marriage. Above all, Owen, along with Engels and the great parliamentary inquiries into the factory system, had laid bare for Marx the grim realities of the capitalist mode of production and its recent history. Owen's experiences in New Lanark proved to Marx and Engels that communist man could not emerge full-grown from primitive communal society, as some Russian theorists were beginning to argue. In Scotland Owen had wrestled with workers who had just outgrown a broken-down, Celtic, communistic clan system; they were no more amenable to his social ideas than other English proletarians. "It is a historical impossibility for more primitive forms to resolve conflicts with which the higher are unable to cope," Engels wrote.[20] Marx's utopia could not violate the rhythm of history and its iron laws.

Owen had enjoyed the unwavering admiration of Friedrich Engels from the time of his youth. Writing for the *Schweizerischer Republikaner* (Swiss Republican) of June 9, 1843, he voiced a preference for the English over the French socialists because men like Owen were practical and could deal with concrete realities; in particular, they were not afraid to attack openly all churches. Owen dared to proclaim that marriage, religion, and property had been the major sources of human misfortune since the beginning of the world. Engels was preserving the sequence of a broadsheet of 1839, *Robert Owen on Marriage, Religion, and Private Property, and on the Necessity of Immediately Carrying into Practice the "Rational System of Society," to Prevent the Evils of a Physical Revolution.* In the *Anti-Dühring*, written thirty-five years after his Swiss article, Engels still used virtually the same formula, albeit reversing the order of Owen's targets, in a lavish eulogy. "There were three great obstacles which above all seemed to block the path of social reform: private property, religion, and marriage in its present form."[21] The last phrase in the title of the 1839 broadside, "to Prevent the Evils of a Physical Revolution," was not dwelt upon; neither was the main thrust of the *Outline of the Rational System of Society* (1840?), which offered itself as the only effective remedy for the evils in the world and promised that its immediate adoption would tranquilize society. For all time Robert Owen, the former manufacturer, was enshrined among the heroic figures of the class struggle. "Banished from official society, banned by the press, impoverished by the failure of communist experiments in America in which he sacrificed his whole fortune, he turned directly to the working class and worked among them for another thirty years. All social movements, all real advances made in

England in the interest of the working class were associated with Owen's name."[22]

Writing for the Owenite *New Moral World,* Engels had contrasted the no-nonsense approach of the English with Cabet's Icarians, who in their propaganda tried to identify communism with true Christianity.[23] To the extent that Marx and Engels were capable of close relations with workers and their leaders, the English were their favorites. They might be naive, but they were not lost in philosophical vapors like the Germans. Since the English inhabited the most advanced industrial country and were free of religious hangovers, they were ideal agents of the communist revolution. In the sixth chapter of *The Holy Family* Marx and Engels used the visions of Fourier and Owen as bludgeons with which to beat down the "critical" philosophy of Bruno Bauer, who had failed to realize that the so-called "spiritual" advances of mankind, which were the core of his concern, had been achieved in contradiction to the interests of mankind. By contrast, Owen's expectation of a collapse of civilization as he knew it was a genuine, radical critique of society. Owen was sound because he based his thought on a radical materialism that derived from Bentham and harked back to the French materialists of the eighteenth century, an "authentic humanism" that was a "logical" foundation for communism. Owen was a communist of the masses because he recognized in contemporary punishments and rewards the sanction of social class divisions and the absolute expression of base slavishness.[24] Owen had achieved real victories in his fight to protect the health of child workers and to curtail the hours of labor. He embodied both theory and practice—even as Marx and Engels did. In the early 1840s, Engels had recognized as worthwhile enterprises Owen's proposals for home colonies, in which two to three thousand persons would be engaged in both agriculture and industry under rules that allowed for complete freedom of thought and less stringent marital and criminal laws. In 1844, reporting to the *New Moral World* on the rapid progress of German communism, he assured the Owenites that the German leaders had no intention of remaining mere theoreticians. One of their number was engaged in a review of all communal plans, including the experiment in Harmony. Engels expressed confidence that the experience of the communes would give the lie to those who asserted that workers could not live and work together without constraint.[25]

The Saint-Simonians had never outrightly rejected private property, only inheritance, and Fourier's elaborate scheme of remuneration made Marx bristle when it was labeled communist. Owen alone seemed to recognize the worth of the direct social organization of labor. Saint-Simon's play with a New Christianity and Fourier's preservation of God as the ultimate sanction for his system put Marx and Engels off. There was something straightforward about Owen's anticlericalism. They never commented on the Owenites as a millenarian sect, and they overlooked the imitation of forms of religious organization, with *The Book of the New Moral World* (1836) replacing the Bible, a book of Social Hymns that incorporated creed, catechism, and articles, and *The Social Bible* (ca. 1840), an outline of the "rational system of society." Owen remained the philanthropist who had transcended his class status as a manufacturer and had turned to the working classes. In 1866—no glorious period of his own life—Marx described Owen in terms that raised him to the level of a model hero: He was one of those "really doughty natures who, once having struck out on a revolutionary path, always draw fresh strength from their defeats and become more decisive the longer they swim in the flood tide of history."[26]

In 1878 Engels found in Owen's *Book of the New Moral World* "not only the most clear-cut communism possible, with equal obligation to labor and equal right in the product—equal according to age, as Owen always adds—but also the most comprehensive project of the future communist community, with its groundplan, elevation, and bird's-eye view."[27] Praise for such utopian baubles is completely alien to the normal intellectual style of Marx and Engels, and the superlatives with which they both showered Owen remain puzzling. They had identified themselves with this man of many projects who refused to recognize defeat and was intent upon saving humanity and the working classes in despite of themselves. Owen the blind authoritarian in utopia escaped them.

Marx and the Saint-Simonians

On his deathbed, Saint-Simon had reflected that if he had done anything for mankind, it was to proclaim the need for the free development of distinctive natural talents. "Talents" was his word and the Napoleonic overtones are patent; the Saint-Simonians later called them "capacities." Among them, fulfillment of capacities became the new formulation of the primary need in utopia. *Une capacité,* around the time of the Restoration, acquired the meaning of a man expert in some branch of activity as well as the expertise itself. (It had a scientistic significance.) "C'est une capacité" was said of a person—of Flaubert's father, a noted doctor, for example. The final utopian goal was no longer equal access to a sufficiency of food and drink and knowledge, which, though it was hardly a reality in early nineteenth-century France, could be hypothetically assumed in any futurist vision of the development of great productive resources. What was now at issue was the realization of man's creative potential, his professional capacity, his innate talent, but with modern scientific, not Platonic, connotations. Marx in his early period highlighted free creativity as the primary attribute of man under communism; his conception of creativity was tinged with the values of both French and German Romanticism and involved the expression of the unique inner self of each man. A new typology of human personality formulated by the Saint-Simonians for utopian man, though it bears some intellectual resemblance to the Platonic division of golden, silver, and brass men, has very different roots. Men needed to actualize their psychic beings in at leat two major areas: creative work and ideal sexual relationships. And these, it was newly appreciated, were complex and varied, not easily subsumed under egalitarian rubrics, except perhaps such coveralls as equal access to self-actualization.

On the morrow of the July Revolution, the Saint-Simonian Fathers had issued a proclamation abolishing inheritance and setting forth the new hierarchical principle: "Each will be placed according to his capacity and rewarded according to his works." "Each according to his capacity, to each capacity according to its works," was emblazoned on the masthead of their newly acquired newspaper, *Le Globe.* In their sermons and formal expositions of the doctrine, they testified to their recognition of varied sexual needs with "rehabilitation of the flesh" and "emancipation of woman." They introduced novelty into the political vocabulary: "The end of the exploitation of man by man; its replacement with the exploitation of nature by man," and "Performance of the function to which a man's natural calling destines him." Other battle cries were "Each one pursuing his own capacity in order that its products may be distributed to each one according to his works," or "To each, labor according to his calling and rewards according to his works," or "An education and function that conform to one's natural calling and a reward that conforms to one's works."[28] The Saint-Simonians were clearly adapting religious terminology—*oeuvres, vocation*—for their program. And in his turn Marx utilized the Saint-Simonian language. Though he could never stomach Saint-Simonian religious verbiage, the *Critique of the Gotha Program* phrase "From each according to his abilities" has an unmistakable Saint-Simonian resonance. This is not to say that Marx consciously plagiarized it; but the Saint-Simonian proclamation "Each will be placed according to his capacity and rewarded according to his works" is a pretty fair statement of Marx's expectations for the first phase of communist society.

When the Saint-Simonians became involved with the Female Messiah and made the banking system the administrative heart of their economy, Marx ridiculed them, and he derided as hypocrites the former adepts who had turned into supporters of Napoleon III and had become prosperous international financiers. Nevertheless, he and Engels continued to study the writings of Saint-Simon as they had done since their twenties. In *Die deutsche Ideologie (The German Ideology)* of 1845–46, Marx, who occasionally flaunted his pedantic scholarship, had torn to shreds *The Social Movement in France and Belgium* (Darmstadt, 1845) by Karl Grün, a leader of the True Socialists, for its misquotations of Saint-Simonian and Fourierist writings.[29] After Marx's death, Engels, and later Lenin, applied words like "genius" to Saint-Simon for some of his insights into the conflict of classes.[30] Abhorrent though the Saint-Simonian principle of hierarchy was to Marx and Engels, they could not fail to recognize the affinity between their own and the Saint-Simonian outlook for the future world—an endlessly dynamic prospect founded upon the boundless expansion of science and technology, exploitation of the inexhaustible natural resources of the globe, and the flowering of human capacities.

Sexuality, Fourier, and Marxist Need

Fourier had posed the problem of the other half of Marx's banderole, "To each according to his needs," with startling originality. The older utopian ideal of Western man was shifted dramatically away from calm felicity, achieved through more or less equality, to the excitement of novelty and of rich sensation as the supreme need. As men were different, so did their needs vary. Individual fulfillment called for a communal society of great variety, an idea that would later reappear in its Marxist incarnation as the need of every individual to enjoy a communal existence as the precondition for personal self-realization. Through reflection in the "other" and in social action each man's being was realized. In *The German Ideology*, Marx wrote: "Only in a state of community with others has each individual the means to develop his predispositions in all directions; only in a state of community will personal freedom thus become possible."[31] The reaffirmation of man's social nature in utopian thought may now sound trite; but in its day it had a psychological dimension that went far beyond the old saw about man being a political animal and served as a negation of a presumed bourgeois doctrine of absolute individualism. Though in his published works Fourier avoided discussion of homosexual needs, his manuscripts, especially the *Nouveau monde amoureux* (The New Loving World),[32] ranked them along with any others.

But Fourier's utopia of maximal dynamism in action and in sensation was too far-out to be acceptable in the nineteenth century, even in radical circles. His own disciples censored his writings. Socialist thinkers of the Victorian world, like Marx, could not endure this utopia in all its nakedness; it reeked of the brothel. Many of Fourier's manuscripts were not published until the 1960s, when there was a recrudescence of interest in his utopia of the free satisfaction of all psychophysical needs because it had found contemporary parallels in such men as Wilhelm Reich, Norman Brown, and Herbert Marcuse in one of his moods. Marx was clearly exposed to Fourier's conception of needs and read his critical anatomy of the cheats of industrial civilization and the hypocrisy of bourgeois social values with an appreciative eye. But he was not ready to follow Fourier in his labyrinthine analysis of psychosexual needs, and was resentful whenever the name "communist" was attached to him. Marx's own language remained properly vague and philosophical when he depicted man's relations to the sensate world of objects, human and natural.

If in rationalist and argumentative propositions with respect to the philosophical character of communism and historical materalism Marx and Engels had no significant disagreements (*pace* those who have tried to drive a wedge between them), differences in the modes of life of the communist Dioscuri may suggest differences in their attitudes toward sex and the family. Nonetheless, when they paint the transfigured family of the future, their palette is the same. Marx was brought up and remained enclosed for all ostensible purposes within the boundaries of the Western Judeo-Christian family as it had evolved into its bourgeois form by the nineteenth century. His youthful correspondence with his father affords an inkling into the traditional love-hate relationship with which he was grappling. The early love for Jenny von Westphalen of the petty Rhenish nobility, an alien both to the religion of his two rabbinic grandfathers and to the world outlook of the apostate Enlightenment lawyer who was his father, is a romantic idyll that, with heavily clouded periods, endured the dangers of revolutionary outlawry and the gnawing dread of proletarianization in dismal London flats. The sick Marx, alone in a hotel in Algiers and seeking alleviation of the respiratory diseases that plagued him, conjured up in a letter to his friend Engels touching images of the Jenny who had sustained him.[33]

Whether or not Marx dallied with the maid, Helene Demuth, or had an illegitimate son—since the publication of his daughter Eleanor's papers it seems hard to reject the evidence that Freddy Demuth was the son of Marx and not of Engels—Marx's notion of family life was normative-Victorian. He reigned over his household with the dignity of a benevolent lord, and heroic Helene held the establishment together. Jenny often had vapors. When marriage proposals for his daughters were in the offing, his inquiries about a prospective son-in-law resembled those of any other loving, tender, yet wary, middle-class father of the period. Wherever his personal impulses may have led him, the destruction of the institution of the nuclear family was not an integral part of his utopia, and those twentieth-century societies that have accepted his philosophical guidance have not tampered with the family structure beyond the assertion of a measure of female equality in relationships. In the 1870s, Marx and Engels occasionally exchanged notes on the sexual customs of the medieval Welsh and passed on to each other somewhat salacious jokes about them; but in general the traditional monogamous family structure was not attacked in public. In fact, wiping out the evils of capitalism would render familial ties less constrained by economic considerations, more open, and more loving—that was a recurrent Marxist promise over the decades. In the 1840s, Marx was already quoting Morelly on the deleterious psychic effects of private ownership on marital relationships. "Interest denatures the human heart and spreads bitterness over the most tender relations. These are transformed into heavy shackles that our married couples hate, and they end up hating themselves." [34] One might point in contradiction to a footnote in *The German Ideology,* "That the supersession of an individualist economy cannot be divorced from the supersession of the family is self-evident"; [35] but this was a solitary manuscript observation of the forties, part of a polemic with German ideologists who denied that the family had its origin in production relations and talked of the "concept of the family" as a timeless absolute. In the manuscripts of 1844, while Marx continued to treat of sexuality in the same abstract terminology as need, alienation, and work, there is the prospect that in the communal state sexual relations will become uniquely human, transcending animality. Nothing resembling the concreteness of Fourier's understanding of sex is in evidence. The brilliantly mocking excursion on the abolition of the family in the *Communist Manifesto* patently refers to the bourgeois family.

Friedrich Engels, of a prosperous Barmen family of manufacturers who had a branch of their cotton mills in Manchester and whose surplus value supported Marx for decades through the agency of their aberrant son, by repute was sexually more adventuresome than his colleague. Though Engels' relationships with an Irish working-class girl and, after her death, with her sister—the latter union was consummated in marriage—were constant enough by the Victorian canon, the impression is inescapable that he lived less conventionally and comprehended the Fourierist sexual fantasies more readily than did "Old Nick." In his brief sketch of the history of changing forms of love and sexuality Engels could write of Anacreon, with no more than a flicker of the Victorian eyebrow, that "sexual love [*Geschlechtsliebe*] in our sense was of so little concern to him, even the sex of the loved person was all one to him." [36] But when Engels inherited Marx's notes on the anthropologist Lewis H. Morgan's *Ancient Society* and expanded them into a full-blown work, *Der Ursprung der Familie (The Origin of the Family),* 1884, in which he spelled out the derivation of the family from production relations, he probably stated the definitive views common to both of them on the historical transformations of the family and its possible future, views that were not always acceptable to the German Social Democrats and English "socialists" among whom he lived and died. As he examined Morgan's historical hypothesis, the outrageous Fourier's stadial theory of the growth of civilization took on new meaning, and he wrote to Kautsky on April 26, 1884: "I must show how brilliantly Fourier anticipated

Morgan in so many things. Through Morgan, Fourier's critique of civilization appears in all its genius."[37] But this did not imply acceptance of the bewildering multiplicity of sexual patterns prescribed by Fourier for "harmonian society." Engels' prognostication of the future of the family after the abolition of property was not at all Fourierist. He argued that, with female equality, optional divorce when love vanished, the end of prostitution and of covert polygamy, the marital bond would become tighter than ever, since it would be the product of free choice. En passant, Engels delivered himself of sententious sexological opinions in the temper of the age: "The duration of a seizure of sexual love for an individual is very different for different individuals, particularly among men," or "Sexual love is by its very nature exclusive."[38] His descriptions of the contemporary bourgeois family were in the acerb Saint-Simonian and Fourierist spirit, but the communist future would nurture a loving, monogamous, and lasting relationship.

Neither Marx nor Engels, gentlemen from the Rhineland who spent most of their adult lives in England, was preoccupied in his writings with the complexities of sexual needs that concerned the Saint-Simonians and even more Fourier. The all-round (allseitig) development of man in Marx's utopia is approached rather gingerly when it comes to sex. Herbert Marcuse's emphasis on aesthetic-sexual needs as the authentic, vital needs of a new free society, which so titillated the generation of 1968, is a shift that the Victorian Marx never made. Reading into him the validation of such needs had to await twentieth-century Freudo-Marxists. Fourier's chief innovation, the expansion of sensations and sexual capacities in all directions as superior to rational capacities, escaped Marx or repelled him. He was much more restricted in his outlook and recognized as legitimate only reasonable, refined, and decent needs— which stopped far short of Fourier's equation of desires and needs. Marx was still too deeply imbued with the rationalist tradition of Plato and More to allow free play to all psychosexual desires as authentic needs. By no means was appeasement of desire necessarily salutary: English workers could be enslaved the more readily by catering to their taste for carousing in taverns. Marx's diagnosis of the function of drink among the English working classes is paralleled by Marcuse's depiction of the capitalist use of sex to dull the mass of the workers and rob them of true consciousness.

The Realms of Freedom and Necessity

Marx refused to identify work with pleasure in Fourier's terms, and the attractiveness of labor was not bound up with erotic stimulus. Though in most of his writings Marx did not envisage the abolition of work, he expected that it could ultimately be reduced to a minimum number of hours. Total freedom from necessity was unlikely, though it might be possible to surmount the antithesis between free time and work time. The most famous passage on the subject appears toward the end of the third volume of Kapital, which Engels edited:

Just as the savage must grapple with nature in order to satisfy his needs, sustain his life, and procreate, so must civilized man, under all forms of society and all possible modes of production. With man's development, this realm of natural necessity is broadened because his needs become more extensive; but simultaneously the forces of production that satisfy these needs are increased. Freedom in this realm can be achieved only when communized man, the associated producers, regulate their material exchange with nature in a rational manner, when they bring it under their communal control, instead of being dominated by this exchange as if by a blind force, when they accomplish this with the least possible expenditure of their strength and under conditions that are the most worthy and most fitting for their human nature. But this always remains a realm of necessity. Beyond this realm begins a development of human powers that are ends in themselves, the true realm of freedom. This realm of freedom, however, can only flower on the foundation of the realm of necessity. The shortening of the working day is its fundamental prerequisite.[39]

These phrases have led to all manner of verbal leaps from the realm of necessity to the realm of freedom. The then United States Secretary of State in a Labor Day 1975 address (read by Ambassador Moynihan) before the United Nations General Assembly, a number of whose member nations were on the brink of starvation, seized Marx's rhetoric and transcended it: "Throughout history, man's imagination has been limited by his circumstances—which have now fundamentally changed. We are no longer confined to what Marx called the 'realm of necessity.'"[40]

In Phase I of Marx's communist world, work would no longer be dehumanizing because man would not be pouring his being into a fetish of his own making, a machine belonging to others, and he would be rewarded for the whole of the labor he invested without sacrificing a surplus to the capitalist. The same amount of labor that he gave to society in one form he would get back in another. This considers individuals only as workers. In Phase II, however, though performing equal labor, one individual might in fact receive more than another because as unequal individuals their needs differed. The division of physical and mental work would tend to be obliterated, the distortion of personality in highly specialized tasks would be eliminated, and the realm of freedom would be approached. There is a passage of *The German Ideology* in which the young Marx, despite his distaste for Fourier on sex, seems to cut a page out of Fourier's work plan—the liberated man will go hunting, fishing, shepherding, or engage in intellectual pursuits at will—though the digression in which Marx describes this free movement from one occupation to another in the course of a day, ending with after-dinner indulgence in criticism of the critical philosophy, is partly satirical, despite the fact that it has sometimes been read straightfaced by the more earnest Marxologists.[41] At points in his manuscripts, Marx is full of praise for Fourier's conception of childhood without repression and his permissive system of education. But the *Critique*, seen in its historical context of the 1870s, ignored Fourierist psychosexual needs and concentrated primarily on bread and butter and shelter, health insurance, and a guarantee of leisure. Marx did not have to alarm the proper Social Democrats to whom he addressed himself with the intrusion of Fourierist thoughts on free love. What Marx implied in the *Critique* was that in the higher stages of communism the elementary needs of a man and his family for food and housing and care during illness would be met by society, irrespective of the quantity of social labor he was able to contribute. Marx recognized that there were differences in skills, hence his dictum: "From each according to his abilities"—that phrase with a Saint-Simonian ring; but the returns would be determined not by labor performance or labor value produced, but by sumptuary needs, measured by the size of a man's family and its requirements. Beyond the work economy, he unfolds a vision of abundance and self-actualization. The banderole is quite devoid, however, of more complicated Fourierist or Saint-Simonian notions on sexuality, even though the language is historically related to these conceptions.

The actual phraseology of Marx's slogan is approximated even more closely on the title page of Papa Etienne Cabet's Fourierist *Voyage en Icarie* (1840), where the formula is writ large: "To each according to his needs, from each according to his strength"; and by Louis Blanc, whose woolly doctrines are a potpourri of socialist and communist thought of the 1840s. Blanc, that Lilliputian anti-hero of 1848, whom Marx despised as much as he did any revolutionary leader—and that is no thimbleful of contempt—prefigured the Marxist formula in later editions of his *Organisation du travail*. This turgid work had a significance in both France and England in the mid-nineteenth century that is difficult to appreciate. Blanc pontificated that in the ultimate stages of socialism there would be true equality only when "each man . . . will produce according to his faculties and will consume according to his needs." Quoting himself on an earlier occasion, he continued:

There are two things in man—needs and faculties [though Blanc fought the Saint-Simonians, he adopted their terminology]. Through his needs man is passive, through his faculties he is active. Through his needs he calls his fellows to his aid; through his faculties he puts himself at the service of his fellows . . . According to the divine law written into the constitution of every man, great intelligence presumes more useful activity but not more considerable compensation. And the inequality of aptitudes could not legitimately result in anything but the inequality of duties. A hierarchy of capacities is necessary and fruitful; recompense in accordance with capacities is more than just disastrous—it is impious.[43]

Of course, by "needs" Blanc, too, meant material needs dependent upon each man's strength and state of health, not Fourier's esoteric needs.

The anarchist Pierre-Joseph Proudhon took a special delight in exercising his mordant wit on the "socialist" Blanc and his followers, tearing apart the slogan on capacities and needs in a perfect state of association that Marx later adapted in the *Critique of the Gotha Program*. "You say that my capacity is 100; I maintain that it is 90. You add that my need is 90; I insist that it is 100. There is a difference of 20 between us on need and capacity."[43] (Proudhon, who had a strangely prophetic insight into some of the inherent tendencies of Marxist thought, in 1851 was already making sport with the elements that were later combined in the banderole.) Louis Blanc's formula struck roots in the French working classes, and thirty years later, on October 7, 1882, it reappeared in *Le Prolétaire,* an organ of the French Socialist Revolutionary Workers' Party, as "Chacun donnant selon ses forces recevra selon ses besoins." Marx's son-in-law Paul Lafargue was disturbed by this revival of Blanc's slogan, which carried with it a promise of instant implementation, and wrote Engels to complain. Marx, on the Isle of Wight and ailing, was silent; by this time he was approaching the end.[44]

Marx's banderole, with its sibylline proclamation "To each according to his needs," could mean all things to all men. In the mouth of a direct-actionist it could become demagoguery, deluding the workers with false promises. To ordinary socialists it could mean eventual satisfaction of their plain wants and desires. And for intellectuals it was pregnant with philosophical connotations that evoked an ideal state. The phrase harked back to Rousseau and Kant, who had given voice to the true need of a self-aware man—the need for a society in which the moral worth of personal action did not derive from external constraint but was the expression of the inner self and had absolute value in and of itself. Even today the banderole raises an image of universal psychic harmony in which the antagonisms between the individual and society are resolved under conditions that allow for the preservation of personal identity and complete self-actualization.

Isaac Newton framed no hypotheses and Karl Marx wrote no utopias; that was the official stance. But in neither case was the position in fact maintained. If one does not restrict oneself narrowly to the phraseology of the *Critique*'s banderole and assimilates to it Marx's related pronouncements, the full dimensions of his utopian dream come into view. Though he never wrote dull utopian stories, he encapsulated his utopia in a series of succinct, memorable phrases that in our time have exerted an especial fascination over vast numbers of intellectuals. Their mere recitation over and over again is hypnotic, like certain rhythms of popular music; one begins to feel as if one were already living in that paradisaical state.

Marx came early to utopia, and the longing never abated, though the language of the utopia changed at various stages of his life. In a letter of 1837 to his father, the adolescent student first raised the curtain on his secret search for a total moral system to replace the "old gods," a pursuit that drove him to nights of relentless study and perhaps a temporary breakdown of sorts. By 1844, the manuscripts show, he had found his way out of the maze with his own economico-philosophical creed for a communist society composed of unalienated men—couched in the jargon of German Romantic philosophy. These manuscripts, prepared when Marx was twenty-six, were perhaps the most seductive of his texts for the mid-twentieth century. The utopia achieved its clearest universal voice in the *Communist Manifesto* of 1848. What could be more in the Romantic utopian spirit of the times than the prophecy: "The old bourgeois society with its classes and its conflicts of classes gives way to an association where the free development of each individual is the condition of the free development of all"?[45] In his late fifties, the sick man, writing glosses on himself and on his enemies in the *Critique of the Gotha Program,* epitomized his vision in apothegms that are still accepted as final ends for man in many parts of the world. Marx combined the underthought of German philosophy in its Hegelian version with the rhetoric of the French utopians, which, unlike German philosophy, was easily adaptable to the styles of popular expression in any country, and with the rational argumentation of English economists amended and presented as science to give solidity to the whole structure. Marxists of later generations could stress one or another of these elements, transforming the whole in accordance with the passing needs of time and place. The amalgam became as flexible and plastic as the original Christian utopia of the ancient world, and it has enjoyed a signal success for much the same reason that Christianity and barbarism once triumphed over the Romans.

Marx's utopian formulas can be garnered from a period of more than three decades in his now published manuscripts and in printed books. They always have reference to the higher stage of communism, called Phase II in the *Critique,* after the inadequate Phase I has been left behind. It has been the function of modern Marxology to bind these phrases together into a system, but perhaps something of their original quality can best be communicated by presenting them in their pristine, free-floating state: "Free development of the individual . . . Development of personality . . . Self-actualization of the individual . . . To set in manifold motion the many-sided developed predispositions [*Anlagen*] of men . . . Only in community will personal freedom be possible . . . Men become masters of their own socialization."[46] Add to these the texts on freedom from necessity, the need for community as a precondition of individual self-realization, and the morality plays about the end of alienation that embarrass Adam Schaff and more sophisticated Marxologists. There are elements in this litany that are markedly Saint-Simonian and Fourierist in tone, expressive of the same Romantic temper. Other elements have counterparts and parallels in contemporary German philosophy. But whatever their source, they are now part of one composite confession of faith. A time may come when the sonorous bits of rhetoric strewn throughout the works of Marx will be fused into a unified liturgical chant whose origins are lost in obscurity.

The Saint-Simonians and even Owenite popularizers thought in terms of the progressive self-actualization of the species man, with the complete actualization of his three major capacities—scientific, emotive-moral-artistic, and manual-administrative. They avoided boxing themselves into a single capacity for each man, and provided for general education in which all three types of capacity would be nurtured until the special capacity manifested itself. Marx's *uomo universale,* too, allows for outstanding predispositions in one direction, along with the general development of all talents. And his idea of a capacity, which may be inferred from specific images and analogies in his writings, was not far removed from that of the Saint-Simonians and most other utopians of the time: Left free to himself, a man would demonstrate either artistic or scientific-rationalist excellence. The Saint-Simonians had a hierarchy of values: In the end, the moral-religious-artistic inspirational capacities were awarded primacy. Marx did not share their predilections, and surely would have excluded the religious capacities. The Saint-Simonians would also have had an organizational hierarchy of excellence within each capacity, while Marx contented himself with perfect spontaneity of expression and bypassed hierarchy or avoided it. In this respect he has been "improved" by Marcuse, for whom hierarchy holds no terrors. But the basic conception of self-actualization of innate predispositions is about the same in Marx as in the Saint-Simonians. Though Marx normally rejected the hierarchy of values, he clearly had a preference, which left traces in chance conversations and obiter dicta, for the human rationalizing capacity. Paul Lafargue, who first met him in 1865, describes him as constantly citing a provocative Hegelian reflection: "Even the criminal thought of a scoundrel is grander and loftier than the marvel of the heavens."[47] Marx himself was committed to the unrelenting exercise of organized thinking, and Lafargue's later exposition of the utopian "right to idleness" would hardly have enjoyed his approval. Under communism the intensity of *activity,* a later version of creativity, would increase rather than diminish.

The Saint-Simonians were strong on the potentialities of technological development, and would manipulate productive capacities so as to minimize manual labor insofar as possible. Among them there was not quite the bold fantasizing in which Marx indulged in a passage where he foresaw technological progress reaching so high a level—virtual automation—that man's relation to the machine would become purely intellectual-scientific guidance. Total technology is the ineradicable signature of the Marxist utopia.

Despite obvious differences, the Marxist slogans can be set into the Fourier–Saint-Simonian chain of filiation without violating their spirit. They are all inhabitants of the same expansive Romantic utopia of self-actualization in varied directions, a boundless drive of the individual and of mankind. There was one branch of utopian thought, however, to which Marx had a profound, abiding, and unmitigated antipathy—the ascetic tradition that runs from Babeuf to Buonarroti to Proudhon and on to Bakunin (the Bakunin of theory, not of real life). They represented the false route. Their thought, based upon a severe limitation of human needs, was essentially static, opposed to the expansion associated with the machine, to great productivity, to the multiplication of goods, and to the grand advancement of science and the arts. In a word, it was reactionary, petty bourgeois. One of Marx's principal objects in writing his *Critique of the Gotha Program* was to have excised from the draft every word of egalitarian rhetoric, associated in his mind with the French egalitarian communist and anarchist tradition. Equality now, immediate and absolute, had failed to recognize the historical need for vast technological development as a prerequisite to realizing "from each according to his abilities, to each according to his needs." (Looked at a century later, the compromise Marx's supporters achieved in the German Social Democratic Party of 1875 after the reception of his *Critique* is ludicrous—*Jedem nach seinen vernunftgemässen Bedürfnissen* ["To each according to his reasonable needs"].)

Equality was Marx's eventual goal in Phase II of communism, but equality in the rich satisfaction of material and intellectual needs in a dynamic economy —not returns, equal in their paltriness, for labor expended in a primitive, artisan-like system à la Proudhon, not a holding back of technology, not the anti-intellectualist asperities of Babeuf and Bakunin. Irrespective of the other bases of Marx's conflict with Proudhon, there was deep antagonism to his cramped, moralistic individualism, bounded by an artisan's horizon, whereas Marx in the *Critique of the Gotha Program,* as elsewhere in his work, opted for the free-flowing expansion of wealth in association. When the communist artisan Wilhelm Weitling tried to offer an example of capitulation to a wild, egotistic desire by a worker of the future with extra chits to spend in his utopia, the most self-indulgent act he could imagine was the purchase of a watch with a second hand. Marx's was a wide-ranging vision in the spirit of the Romantic utopians, and this helps to account for its rehabilitation among the children of 1968. But then they betrayed the angelic Moor by demanding utopia now and flirting with Ludditism.

Remote from us as the alternatives of an ascetic Babouvist egalitarian or a rich Saint-Simonian–Fourierist orientation may be, they are far from irrelevant in the present-day world. They still represent different utopian choices in the contemporary revolutionary arena: absolute equality here and now at all costs, or dedication first to the expansion of productive capacities, with the hope of ultimately realizing the banderole of the *Critique of the Gotha Program* in its fullness of meaning in the distant, distant future.

A hundred years after the composition of the *Critique of the Gotha Program,* Marx's words are enjoying a great triumph. Close on to a half of the world's population is hovering between Phase I and Phase II of communism. And there is not a political leader East or West, North or South, so steeped in reaction he would not on appropriate occasions affirm his allegiance to the principle that all men should have their needs fulfilled and natural potentialities developed to the utmost. The Constantines of the world preside at councils where Marx's banderole is duly unfurled; and though slaughter is threatened over its interpretation, history teaches that the correct reading will eventually prevail. If a Diogenes redivivus should point out that such casual phrases of the *Critique* as "dictatorship of the proletariat" have sometimes been translated into massacres of millions of human beings, the true believer will remind him that the historical process has always been profligate of lives. There is every reason to expect that the preaching of Marx in this classic of communist thought will bear the same relationship to communist societies of the future that the Sermon on the Mount does to Christianity.

30

Comte, High Priest of the Positivist Church

MARX TOOK virtually no cognizance of Auguste Comte until the 1860s, when the name cropped up in a letter to Engels announcing that he was studying Comte "on the side" because the English and the French were making such a fuss about the fellow. What they found attractive about him, Marx judged, was his pretension to encyclopedism and *la synthèse*. As for himself, his preference for Hegel was unchanged. The Comtean system was pitiful if compared to Hegel's: Since Comte was a mathematician and physicist by profession he may have surpassed him in details, but Hegel's generalizations, even in science, were far more important. "And this Positivist muck appeared in 1832!"[1] When Marx was preparing the *Civil War in France,* his original draft included a piece called "The Workers and Comte." There he summarily dismissed him as of no account. "Comte was known to the Paris workers as the prophet of personal dictatorship in politics, capitalist rule in political economy, hierarchy in all spheres of human activity, even in science, the creator of a new catechism, a new Pope, and new saints to replace the old ones."[2] By the 1880s Engels was outrightly accusing Comte of plagiarizing Saint-Simon's encyclopedic ordering of the sciences.[3] When it came to rival systems, Marx and Engels wielded a sledgehammer.

Auguste Comte is a loner in the history of utopian thought. His derivation from the tradition of Condorcet and Saint-Simon is patent, but in the end he stood apart, creator of a structure of mammoth proportions. If Marx paid Comte scant attention, by the 1850s Comte was no longer reading anything but his own works and did not notice Marx. Anarchism was the prime enemy of Comte's system. He saw the political and social consequences of its triumph after 1789 so clearly that he had no need to assimilate the works of "anarchist" writers. Comte was at the same time the denial of the French age of prophecy and its most pathetic climax. His vision was at once abstract and intimate.

The Master Denied

In no other modern philosopher has the rationalist fantasy been so inextricably bound up with private life.[4] In 1817 the former Polytechnician Auguste Comte, then only nineteen, was wandering about Paris at loose ends with no particular occupation, when a friend introduced him to the aging Saint-Simon. The impecunious petty bourgeois from the south was at first dazzled by the philosopher who had preserved the buoyancy of a young man and the elegant manners of an aristocrat. When Comte became his secretary and "adopted son," Saint-Simon presented him to the circle of liberal economists, paid him whenever the rich industrialists and bankers sent money, and in long conversations expounded his scientific and social system. At the beginning it seemed that their talents complemented each other and that the relationship would yield a rich intellectual harvest. Unfortunately there were obstacles in the way of any lasting collaboration. In his very first independent pamphlets, *Séparation générale entre les opinions et les désirs* (July 1819), *Sommaire Appréciation de l'ensemble du passé moderne* (April 1820), and *Prospectus des travaux scientifiques nécessaires pour réorganiser la société* (May 1822), Comte revealed his fundamental disagreement with Saint-Simon's plans; he was again bringing to the fore the philosophy of the sciences which had troubled Saint-Simon in the brochures of the Empire, but had since been abandoned for practical considerations. Believing it vain to attempt the solution of the social problem before mankind had, for guidance in the wilderness, the steady light of a settled comprehensive philosophy, Comte continued his mathematical studies and engaged in researches in the other sciences, with the aim of actually creating that synthesis of all knowledge which Saint-Simon had merely sketched in a page of the *Mémoire sur la science de l'homme*. Only after the synthesis was achieved would the temporal world end its internecine struggles, because it would then have before its eyes, in detail, the elaborated system of positive science and positive politics. Before the grandiose revelation of the true laws of the polity, the forces of anarchy would give way. Formulated in a simple manner, the theoretical controversy with Saint-Simon was concentrated in one problem. Could scientific truth alone force men to act in accordance with its precepts, as Comte then thought, or should practical men of action forge ahead, allowing scientists to trail after them with advice, as Saint-Simon had come to feel after his disillusioning experiences with the savants of the Empire? In the spring of 1824 the quarrel that had long been smoldering flared up. The final rupture ended an uneasy communion between two of the most extraordinary thinkers in modern times. Their friendship degenerated into a fishwives' squabble which, as might be expected among philosophers, had a universal resonance.

After Saint-Simon's death, though Comte at first disdained any part of the Saint-Simonian *Le Producteur,* his need for money induced him to become a collaborator—*à contre-coeur* because he anticipated the irksome censorship of "Rodrigues et compagnie." In the end Comte's association with the disciples was short-lived. He could not stomach their deification of the master, and by 1828 he was already poking fun at their plan to found a new religion, a "sort of incarnation of the divinity in Saint-Simon." [5] Bitter was his disillusionment when he found that Gustave d'Eichthal, his one disciple, to whom he had freely unburdened himself of his grievances against Saint-Simon, to whom he had confided his most intimate philosophical and psychological reflections, had been swept along by the religious wave of the Saint-Simonian school. On December 7, 1829, he sent d'Eichthal a biting, sarcastic letter, enclosing an entrance card to the reopening of his private course on positive philosophy: "Since the change of direction which your mind has just taken, I must admit to you that I no longer count on you for anything. You are on so sublime a summit that you must, even against your will, pity our wretched positive studies, which you no longer need and which on the contrary would trouble your theological labors." [6] When the Saint-Simonians transformed themselves into a religious cult and their meetings became a public scandal which ultimately brought them before the King's Bench, Auguste Comte took himself off.

Wicked Wife and Good Angel

In 1822 Auguste Comte walked into a bookstore and recognized behind the counter a girl whom he had once picked up in the Palais Royal. Comte renewed the acquaintance, and within a year they merged their living quarters, later formalizing the common-law marriage.

The opening lectures of Comte's course on positive philosophy, which he conducted privately in his apartment in 1826, had a small but illustrious audience; but before the thirteenth session he suffered his first psychic breakdown. For the next fifteen years Mme. Comte wrangled with this mad genius; while no succeeding outburst was as wild as the first one, he never completely recovered. At the height of an attack scenes of violence were frequent. Between crises, his smoldering fury spent itself on his wife and on academic colleagues. In 1842 Mme. Comte left his bed and board for the last time—there had been intermittent separations—but this strange, tenacious woman kept turning up again, and in 1850 it was her intervention with the Ministry of Education which made it possible for Comte to continue the popular lectures to which he clung so desperately—rare moments of public recognition. The vengeance with which Comte pursued his wife in later years was monstrous.

The history of Comte's academic life was a record of defeats whenever he was proposed for a full chair either at the Polytechnique or in the university. Public denunciations of his perfidious colleagues were accompanied by vain appeals to the ministries, outbursts of wild paranoia against detractors, calls to the world to avenge the wrongs perpetrated against him. The accusations he leveled against the academic intriguers were true enough; and the more he reviled his adversaries the more convinced they became that they did not want him in their company. For most of his adult career he eked out an existence as an entrance examiner at the Polytechnique, and in his last years even this was denied him.

In 1844, after the definitive estrangement from his wife, Auguste Comte fell in love with Mme. Clothilde de Vaux, a woman of about thirty abandoned by her husband. While their affections began on a lofty spiritual plane, Comte importuned her with his physical needs, and when entreaties failed he was not beyond using the threat that her denials were endangering his health and upsetting his cerebral hygiene. Their emotional tug-of-war ended in tragedy— Comte was again on the verge of madness and his beloved became afflicted with a disease, probably tubercular, which brought on her death. The last months of her life were tormented with the contradictory advice of rival physicians, Comte's maniacal pretension to supervise personally the direction of the cure, violent quarrels between Comte and the dying young woman's family, which at one point led to his expulsion from the sickroom. When he was called back toward the very end, he bolted the door of the death chamber, excluding her parents so that Clothilde died in his presence alone.

The Two Careers

The first series of private lectures on the positive philosophy had been attended by Blainville the physiologist, Dunoyer the economist, and the naturalist

Alexander von Humboldt. When the course was resumed in 1829 after the attack of insanity and the attempts at suicide, Broussais the phrenologist, Dr. Esquirol, and Fourier the mathematician were in the audience. But during that long and troubled period from 1830 to 1842—years of tremendous intellectual concentration, plagued by marital difficulties, mental aberrations, poverty, and a vain search for some academic position which would be worthy of him—the brilliant reputation of Comte's youth gave way to ridicule in official learned circles. A contemporary bibliography listed him as already dead.[7]

The six volumes of the *Cours de philosophie positive* (1830–1842), composed in isolation during years of wretchedness, were an attempt to synthesize the particular studies of individual scientists by sharply marking the bounds of every form of knowledge and drawing from each the essence of its philosophic generality. It involved writing a history of science—which is still worth reading for its extraordinary flashes of insight—as well as arranging the sciences in a hierarchy of complexity which would prove that each had in turn progressed first from a theological into a metaphysical and then into a positive state. The drama of the work was the struggle of positivist, nonmetaphysical, and nontheological truth with the remnants of antiquated intellectual forms which still sought to corrupt it. Religion and sentiment were banished as the handmaidens of theologians and metaphysicians; the *Cours* was at once a new *Organon,* a new *Methodus,* and a new philosophy of history. Comte sharpened spiritual distinctions: The scientists could no longer continue the cant of their old procedure, tinkering with the particular tools of their special discipline and at the same time worshiping at the shrine of final causes. He demanded that they be thoroughly consistent, that they abide by the philosophical implications of their scientific endeavors, and that they recognize in every particular experiment some additional element to the great structure of positive science. The *Cours* had a style that was dull, dry, and lumbering. While the positive philosophy did not help many scientists in their labors, it was adopted by a few litterateurs who needed an overall pattern for their popular scientific notions.

Inevitably, the appearance of the *Système de politique positive* from 1851 through 1854, which proclaimed love as the motive force of mankind, was a violent shock to the select group of Comte's rationalist admirers. As he laboriously evolved a special calendar for his church and multiplied ritual observances for the Religion of Humanity, he seemed to be denying the very spirit of his previous works. Many considered his change of front a treacherous defection to those forces of darkness which he had driven forth from the positive system. Between the *Cours* and the *Système de politique positive* he had risen from the depths of misery to a mystical love so overpowering that true disciples looked on in dismay and outsiders scoffed. The publication of the correspondence of Clothilde de Vaux and Comte, his annual written confessions after her death, and his prayers to her memory have not added to his philosophical stature, though they reveal a complex emotional being.

After Clothilde's death Comte's whole life became devoted to a religious worship of her image. Those disciples who had admired his powerful mind watched with troubled spirits as he embarked upon a system which was deeply colored by elements of religious mania. Yet to Auguste Comte the positive church seemed the natural fruition of an original plan which he had developed in his earliest pamphlets in the 1820s. The scientific synthesis of the *Cours* had only been a foundation. His friends knew nothing of the youthful writings in which he had expatiated on the power of the sentiments and of the imagination in moving mankind to action and had praised spontaneous religious faith as the force which would again bring intellectual and moral unity to humanity. They had never read those passages in which he had extolled the organic unity of medieval Catholicism in the language of de Maistre. Even before Comte met Clothilde de Vaux he wrote to Mme. Austin on April 4, 1844, complaining that she was unjust in interpreting positivism as anti-emotional: "Believe me, I know how to cry, not only in admiration but also out of sorrow, above all sympathetic sorrow. As for prayer, it is really only a particular form in the old order of ecstatic emotions, or general emotions, whose indestructible core will always be a part of human nature, whatever its mental habits may become."[8] Comte himself recognized that there was a difference of emphasis in what came to be called his two careers. In the first period he had considered himself primarily an Aristotle, and in the second he had become a Saint Paul, but the elements of the second period had already existed in embryo in the first. The social opuscules of his youth support his contention. As conclusive proof of the unity of his work Comte reprinted six of these brochures as a general appendix to the fourth volume of the *Système de politique positive* (1854).

When the committed rationalists in his circle realized the new turn in his thought, they slowly withdrew. The head of the French group was Littré, and the leaders of the English were Mill and Lewes, three men who had been among the first to call the world's attention to the positive philosophy. Littré was profoundly upset by his inability to accept the positive polity with the same passion with which he had espoused Comte's philosophy, and fell upon the notion that only a serious mental strain, the consequence of some organic illness, could have produced the positivist church and its ritual.[9] Littré's manipulations did not end with Comte's death; while proclaiming their love for Comte, Littré and Mme. Comte tried to have his final testament legally annulled and sought to eradicate the memory of the second period of Comte's writing, embalming the founder of the positive philosophy as a figure dissociated from the worshiper of Clothilde de Vaux. They joined in a formal declaration that Comte had been mad, but in a final trial in 1870, after many years of litigation, the true disciples won their case, and Comte's Religion of Humanity was not mutilated.[10] "Positivism consists essentially of a philosophy and a polity. These can never be dissevered," maintained the English disciple Dr. Bridges, and most scholars of Auguste Comte have acquiesced in this view.

The High Priest of Humanity

When Comte apotheosized Clothilde de Vaux as the spiritual symbol of the Virgin Mother, superior even to himself, who was only the High Priest of Humanity, and established her grave as a place of sacred pilgrimage, his cult suffered the ridicule of all fabricated ceremonials that fail of acceptance by a sufficient body of believers to become sanctioned vehicles for the expression of religion emotion. For Comte it was now science and excessive absorption in rationalist analysis that became suspect, dangerous for the spiritual well-being of mankind. The philosopher of positivism ended up rejecting a large proportion of the works of science as futile. As his view of the good life became ever more restrictive and cramped, less expansive and sensate, modern science and technology which provided great abundance and riches became distracting superfluities. Comte accepted a social system based upon a division between the rich and the poor, but neither grouping was of fundamental importance since the end of man was the training of his emotional being to sublimated love. A mania for regulation possessed him and he set up rules of conduct to govern each epoch in a man's life; the transitions from one to another stage of being were marked by rigid sacramental performances. Order became more vital than progress. The multiplication of new artifacts of any nature—scientific or industrial—became an anarchic impediment to good disposition and arrangement. The positivist law of family life demanded a vow of eternal widowhood, and divorce was refused. The world would be made continent and puritanical. The commandments preached "Love your neighbor. Live for others"—but a cold chill came to pervade the chambers of the Comtean mission.

From the chair of the High Priest of Humanity in his apartment on the rue Monsieur-le-Prince, Auguste Comte contemplated the Revolution of 1848, the bloody June Days, and the rise of the dictator Napoleon III. These misfortunes had been visited upon the Occident because it was ignorant of its true historic destiny. The epoch of the positive polity had arrived, but instead of reading its laws as they had been expounded in Comte's writings, humanity was wasting its divine forces in material conflicts and civil strife. There was warfare of diverse doctrines at a time when the essence of humanity should be unity; there was revolutionary antagonism to the religious principle when the very being of mankind was religious—in the positivist sense. All past history had been a battleground for partisan spirits. Revolutionaries of the gospel of 1789 (the first year of anarchy) and their philosophers were besmirching the noble morality of the Middle Ages, when all men should have realized that medieval civilization was one of the most progressive forms of social synthesis. Men of religion were in their turn denouncing the great cultural productions of classical antiquity and decrying the achievements of science, when these were necessary prolegomena to the new state of postivism. If the warring factions accepted the world-historical outlook that Comte had revealed to them, they would understand that all history had borne good fruits, and that whoever would act with wisdom in the future had to preserve for mankind the creations of past civilizations and incorporate them into his being, without rancor and without hatred for any age. There was but one power in the world capable of judging history with justice, a power embodied in the High Priest of Humanity who, while synthesizing the past, would impart to the annals of mankind a unity of movement and purpose which it would be difficult to violate in petty quarrels of the moment.

In the Revolution of 1848 Comte saw the Occidental world at a point of final crisis, and only he could save it from the chaos and anarchy in which it was seething. The Positivist Society, which had formed itself about Comte, formulated a pretentious plan of action for the Provisional Government, and Comte was willing to establish contact with the most violent of the revolutionaries, even Barbès and Blanqui, if only their movement could be diverted into a positivist channel.[11] But Paris was a city of barricades, strewn with the corpses of the proletariat. Comte called the spirits of social peace, but alas they would not answer. The coup d'etat of December 2 caused disruption in the Positivist Society.

But the belief of the High Priest of Humanity in the power of the idea, of the true philosophic and religious system, was so all-absorbing that the nature of the political regime became a matter of indifference. The state was but a subject ready to take on the coloration of the positive religion once the executive power was enlightened. A disorganized revolutionary government that presented the spectacle of warring factions would be less amenable to the propaganda of the idea than a dictatorship that was concentrated in one man. Convert this man and the cause of positivism would be won. Saint-Simon and Fourier had addressed their early memoirs to Napoleon I; Comte was willing to accept Napoleon III if only he would become a positivist.

Though secretly tormented by the indifference of scholars and scientists Comte continued to mount giant block upon giant block in the construction of his great pyramid. After the *Cours de philosophie positive* and the *Système de politique positive,* there appeared in 1856 the first volume of the *Synthèse subjective,* also called the *Système de logique positive.* Works for the next few years were planned and announced in advance: for 1859 the *Système de morale positive* or the *Traité de l'éducation universelle,* and for 1861 the *Système d'industrie positive* or the *Traité de l'action totale de l'humanité sur sa planète.* Comte was writing for the future, for the men of 1927 perhaps, when, as he analyzed the course of events, the positivist regeneration of the Occident would be accomplished, at least among the souls of the elite. Few men have had a more poignant sense of their historical mission. "Living in an anticipated tomb, I must henceforth speak a posthumous language to the living, a form of speech which is as free from all manner of prejudices, above all the theoretical ones, as our descendants will be. Up to now I have always had to speak in the name of the past, though I was continually aspiring toward the future. Now I must interest the public of the West in the future state—which irrevocably follows from the totality of the various anterior modes—in order to discipline them at the same time that I consecrate them." [12] Toward the end of his life, Comte was deeply involved in spreading the doctrine among the noblest members of all classes of society. He was aware that neither of his two major works could reach broad masses of people. Therefore he undertook positivist propaganda (the word is Comte's) by composing in 1852 a *Catéchisme positiviste* for the use of women and workers, and in 1855 an *Appel aux conservateurs* for the education of contemporary political leaders. And there was some response: In the fifties a heterogeneous group of disciples from all over the world came to pay homage to the founder of positivism.

As Comte regulated his own diet and arranged hours for prayer and work with obsessive punctuality, so he multiplied ritualistic details for the Religion of Humanity. The positive sacraments became the manifest symbols of the new educational process: the presentation of the infant, initiation at fourteen, admission at twenty-one, destination at twenty-eight, marriage before thirty-five, maturity at forty-two, retirement at sixty-two, and finally the sacrament of transformation. [13] In the end the evil ones, the suicides and the executed, or those who had failed in their duty to humanity, were relegated to the field of the forgotten, while those upon whom the final judgment of Incorporation was favorable were transferred to the Holy Wood which surrounded the Temple of Humanity.

In France, Comte was not read during his lifetime. Ridicule was heaped upon him as just one of the numerous religious messiahs who had come forth with panaceas for universal peace and happiness. His aloofness from the class struggle made his writings meaningless to the revolutionaries who were organizing the workers with the slogans of communism and socialism. To sectors of the middle class who were seeking parliamentary reform in the Revolution of 1848 his philosophy was of no importance. His teachings were quite superfluous for those trying to defend the existing property system, because they had no need of his theocracy to ensure their domination. Many of the leaders of the Second Empire were Saint-Simonians, some of whom were still giving lip service to the humanitarian ideals of their master. The hierarchy of Auguste Comte and his spiritual tyranny were not consonant with their expansive activism.

Ultimately Positivism, like many of the other great dogmatic structures of modern times, exerted its greatest influence in those countries which were comparatively backward in their cultural and economic development. It had its attractions for the intelligentsia of Russia in the sixties and seventies.[14] In South America it became the ideal formula among those members of the upper classes who had abandoned the Catholic Church and yet did not wish to grope in the darkness of skepticism. Positivism was acceptable to them as an organic philosophy of life which provided for the status quo of class relationships and demanded only that order and progress become the general ideological principles of political and social action. Brazil inscribed the motto of Comte's church, *Ordem e Progresso,* on its national flag and accepted Comte as its official philosopher.[15]

Positivism in England was a movement of some strength, especially after Mill briefly espoused its cause; but in the long run the English felt no need for it, for Herbert Spencer had provided them with essentially the same doctrine in a native mixture that rivaled the original in pomposity and long-windedness.[16] There were stray groups of Positivists in Holland, Italy, Sweden, and the United States. When on January 1, 1881, Edward Spencer Beesly celebrated the Festival of Humanity in London, he could speak of a union of all Positivists, comprised of members in Havre, Rouen, Mons, Rio de Janeiro, Dublin, New York, and Stockholm, who were at that moment turning toward Paris, where Pierre Laffitte, the successor of Comte as the head of the Positivist Society, was conducting the ceremonials in the very abode of the Master.[17]

The Law of the Three States

Progress became the definition of social dynamics—we have been propelled into the jargon-world of sociology by its founder—as Order was the key to social statics. Progress is the development of Order, or Progress is the dynamic form of the static concept of Order. The social series, another way of identifying the philosophy of history, was an extension of the animal hierarchy and was governed throughout by the same fundamental principle: a simultaneous evolution toward the complex, the harmonious, and the unified. Passing from the lowest inorganic state to Humanity, Comte's hypostatization of the highest state of social being, forms became ever more complicated and more tightly integrated. Historical progress dealt with the evolution of the higher forms of social dynamics, but it was rooted in a psychology of human nature that was enduring and unchangeable.

The most comprehensive way of formulating the totality of the historical process was the law of the three states, even though in the narrow sense it referred primarily to the evolution of human intelligence. Comte was heir to Turgot's idea that a higher stage of mind was achieved at the expense of a diminution of subjective imaginative fancy, and to Hume's definition of man's primitive religious feeling in *The Natural History of Religion* as a total immersion in primary passions of fear and hope accompanied by little or no capacity for abstraction. Following Vico, Saint-Simon, and the Saint-Simonians, Comte focused on the nature of the psyche in every epoch, and the history of human intelligence became for him, as it had been for his predecessors, a history of religion.

To define the first and most primitive state of man, Comte employed a variety of terms which require translation; he called it spontaneous and fictitious — we might say today that it was freely creative and subjective, that it had relatively little to do with the outside world of objects. Fetishism, a term he borrowed from de Brosses's little essay *Du culte des dieux fétiches,* was the first, totally subjective explanation of man's relationship with external reality. Theologism, with its subsidiaries polytheism and monotheism, though it had a separate name, was still a part of the primary state, the provisional pattern of human intelligence which was inevitably destined to be superseded not only for historical reasons but because man's perception bore within itself the inherent necessity of evolution into a new form. The logic of history had psychological foundations. Comte's descriptions of the passing from one phase of development to another within theologism were circumstantial and ingenious, replete with illustrative materials his predecessors had been ignorant of, since his prodigious memory had assimilated and stored the contents of new works of erudition. The second or transitional state he labeled metaphysicism; its essential character was abstraction. The medieval theologians were the major intellects of the metaphysical and their monotheism was typical of the tail end of theologism merging into metaphysicism. Using metaphysicism to define medieval philosophy was bewildering, but it served to fill a pressing psychic need on Comte's part, to differentiate his categories from those of Saint-Simon, who had stuck to commonsensical nomenclature, with theology as the spiritual expression of the medieval mind and metaphysics as the intermediary form between theology and positive science. Needless to say, Comte's verbal switch did not profoundly alter the nature of the evolution both of them described. Positivism, whose characteristic was demonstration, was the third and definite state or stage of human evolution. It was only a few centuries old, it had not yet eradicated the remnants of metaphysicism, and many ages lay before it. A high degree of subordination of subjectivity to the objective world was its most noteworthy attribute. Mankind had thus moved in a direction that was the polar opposite to primitive fetishism, it had passed from subjectivity to objectivity. But here Comte raised an ominous warning: There was grave danger in the total elimination of creative subjectivity; merely objective perception could lead to idiocy.

Pursuing another parallel which Saint-Simon had already explored, Comte correlated the three stages of progressive intelligence with three forms of social activity. (Saint-Simon had still referred to spiritual and temporal powers.) The ancients had been military and aggressive conquerors who organized labor as slavery; the medievals had also been committed to warfare, but unlike the peoples of antiquity their military tactics tended to be primarily defensive—they locked themselves behind the ramparts of their castles—and this slackening of the offensive warrior spirit gave birth to a transitional form of activity which allowed for the growth of industrial labor. In the positivist epoch a free proletariat became the dominant pattern for the organization of labor. With variations in vocabulary—modern sociology has come by its terminology legitimately, from the father—this theme had been constant in French philosophical history since Turgot. Comte explained the conflict between the activists and the intellectuals in the first two stages of social dynamics on the ground that these elements were competitive with each other—as Saint-Simon had—and he forecast the elimination of the conflict in the third and final stage because scientific positivism in intelligence and industrialism as a method of work organization would be compatible, not rival.

Usually there was a third law (sometimes it was expressed not as a separate law but merely as a derivation of the two preceding ones) which illustrated moral or emotional progress. The third series fitted perfectly with the other two—all the gears of social dynamics mesh. The progress of sentiment, which the Saint-Simonians had described as the growth of love in an almost identical form, could be traced in the extension of the area of consciousness over which affects of sympathy had power. The higher stages of this development were the direct moral consequence of progress in intelligence and activity: Growth in love was thus a derivative form. The ancients had recognized only civic sentiments, the medievals a wider sphere designated as collective European consciousness, and the moderns under positivism were destined to render sympathy universal, the loftiest moral ideal, at once the most complicated and the most unified. The same moral progression of sentiment could also be expressed conversely as a decreasing egotism, a condition marked by a steady weakening of nutritive and sexual instincts and an increase of altruism. Comte too had undergone the influence of Kant's concept of antagonism and had set up a world history of progress around the idea of decreasing rivalries and increasing love relationships among humans. As a characteristic index of this development he pointed to the growing social and moral role of women, who symbolized the affectionate element. As a final, fourth law of social dynamics Comte included the philosophical key to the history of scientific development which had already been expounded in the *Cours*, the idea that the sciences progressed in chronological order from the simplest to the most complex, culminating in sociology—an idea that is directly traceable to Saint-Simon's earliest works and that he in turn owed, on his own testimony, to Dr. Burdin, surgeon in the armies of the Republic.

Order and Progress

Comte faced the problem of the boundlessness of future progress and of the geographic areas in which his laws of social dynamics operated with more forthrightness than some of his predecessors. Like Fourier in this respect, he entertained the possibility of ultimate decline and death, carrying out the onto-genetic analogy, though he was quick to reassure his contemporaries that it was far too early to determine the shape of the downward stadial course of mankind. While Saint-Simon's theory was Europocentric and its universaliza-tion depended upon the conquest of other continents by the industrial-scien-tific ideology, and the Saint-Simonians felt that scholarship was not yet suffi-ciently advanced to document their thesis with Asian analogies, Comte made his law of the three states equally applicable throughout the world. Ultimately every region would have to pass through the same stages, but—and here was the escape clause—the evolution could be accelerated by a more intense rate of progress in non-European areas. Like children, the savages might be able to jump over the metaphysical stage and emerge as full-fledged positivists; only fetishism was a necessary condition. He even allowed for slight variations—he called them "oscillations"—apparent minor movements of retrogression, though in universal terms the overall development was inevitable and abso-lute.

Comte's vision diverges fundamentally from Saint-Simon's less in the no-menclature of the historical periods than in the complete abandonment of indi-vidual self-realization for a new emphasis on the total absorption in social statics and social dynamics. Saint-Simon in his last words to his disciple Olinde Rodri-gues had still insisted on the development of individual capacities. Men were to be joined in association and love, but the individual would not be lost—this was a Saint-Simonian pledge to prospective converts. With Auguste Comte the Great Being became the time-bearing ocean in which all men were en-gulfed. The individual found his true fulfillment only by subordinating his subjectivity. The impression is inescapable that in the positivist religion there is a total loss of personality as man is merged in the perfect transcendent unity of Humanity. The late Teilhard de Chardin, the eminent paleontologist and theoretician of human evolution who prognosticated a similar development for the species, was fully aware of the affinities between his own philosophy and Comte's.

The other unique element in the Comtean doctrine is the richness of the psy-chological characterization of the three stages of consciousness. In a most re-vealing excursus in the third volume of the *Système de politique positive* Comte reported that during the course of his madness in 1826 he had acquired a per-sonal conviction of the truth of the law of the three states. Under the impact of mental strain he had felt himself regress backward through various stages of metaphysics, monotheism, and polytheism to fetishism, and then, in the pro-cess of recuperation, he had watched himself mount again through the progressive changes of human consciousness, at once historical and individual, to positivism and health.[18] This was a far more profound conception than the rather commonplace analogy between phylogeny and ontogeny to which Saint-Simon had regularly adverted. Comte experienced these stages as dis-tinct states of consciousness fundamentally different from one another. When a man went mad and there was a derangement of psychic processes he naturally fell back along the same historic path of development. This embryonic Com-tean version of the idea of a collective consciousness, its origins and growth, and the view of regression as at once a return to the infantile and to the primitive had many eighteenth-century roots, but never before in the literature of psychology or sociology had these conceptions been developed with comparable vigor. Comte raised the theory of progress to a new level when in addition to technological, scientific, intellectual, and moral progress he envisaged a progressive growth of consciousness and proceeded to define its constituent historical elements. At the same time he had the extraordinary insight that as mankind advanced, the earlier stages of consciousness would not be completely sloughed off and forgotten forever, but on the contrary every child born in the new humanity would reexperience the history of the race and pass through the successive orders of intelligence in the course of its education. In previous stadial theories there is an impression of completeness in each stage: Once man has achieved a higher level the old forms are abandoned. For Comte, who had known madness, the fetishist world was an ever-present reality, and in his religious philosophy he wrestled with the problem of preserving the direct and immediate emotional responses which characterized primitive religion even in the positive polity of the future.

Auguste Comte's predilection for the institution-bound priest was reflected everywhere in his philosophical review of history. Whenever a sacerdotal body appeared upon the scene mankind was at least temporarily in secure hands. From the lying trickster priest of Condorcet to Comte's benign ecclesiastical authorities who at every crucial moment in history ordered human intelligence and feeling, there had been a complete volte-face. Even the fetishist priests, about whom de Brosses had written in 1760 with mixed horror and contempt as the heart of primitive darkness, in Comte's analysis became wise leaders who turned the subjective cause-seeking of savages to a moral purpose, the creation of communal sentiment among primitive mankind. The later metaphysicians who directed the transitional stage from theologism to positivism were the spiritual leaders who deserved the least praise in the whole history of mankind; they had in fact given no general institutional direction to human endeavors. The anarchic potentialities of metaphysicism were always so powerful that it colored their works, and whatever was sound and progressive in their epoch was to be credited to the secret undercover operations of the positivist spirit at work in their midst and not to the abstractions of philosophy. The positivist priesthood that Comte was initiating was destined to resume the direct creative tradition of mankind, which ran from the priests of fetishism, through the Catholic Church, to the high sacerdotal authority of the new religion.

Historical crises occurred when there was a grave imbalance among the progressions and in the arrangement of the various human creative capacities, when the industrial-political or the ideological maturation of a new epoch was either too sluggish or too precipitous. In the third volume of the *Politique positive,* Comte's interpretation of the outbreak of the French Revolution is characteristic of his thinking and expression. He descends from a dogmatic statement of the grand laws of social dynamics in the opening chapter to illustrate their workings in the "facts" of history.

This fatal inversion was above all the result of the inadequate harmony between the two evolutions, negative and positive, one of which then required a renewal which the other could not direct. All beliefs had been dissolved, and the regressive dictatorship, which held together the wreckage of the ancien régime, found itself irrevocably discredited. At the same time, feelings, which alone support that kind of society, already had undergone an intimate transformation as a result of the anarchy of thoughts, as shown by the steady diminution of feminine influence and the growing insurrection of the mind against the heart. On the other hand, science remained limited to inert nature and even tended toward academic degeneration. Philosophy, for lack of an objective base, spent itself in thin aspirations toward a subjective synthesis. Since organic evolution was incapable of satisfying the needs manifested by the critical movement, a social upheaval then became inevitable . . .[19]

The providence of the Great Being could not be demonstrated more conclusively.

While the broad lines of the development of the Great Being were fixed by the laws of social dynamics, there was a sense in which human "modificability" played a role, albeit a restricted one. There was sometimes choice between serving a positive or a negative force, even though the overall course itself was objectively determined. Much as Comte dwelt upon the "spontaneous emergence" of new aspects of the Great Being in the historical process, he was, perhaps more than any other thinker before the triumph of depth psychology, aware of the tremendous weight of the generations of the past in delimiting the scope of any novel action. The new, if it was to be more than a mere expression of caprice and anarchy doomed at the very moment of birth, had to take its properly ordained place in the historic queue. No disorderly breakthroughs could be countenanced; if they occurred they had no real, that is, lasting, existence. The past determined the future so overwhelmingly that every action, every sprout of intellectual and moral growth, was relative to what had gone before.

Since harmonious unity—the Saint-Simonians would have said an organic synthesis—is the only good society, Comte's historical enemies were those intellectual, activist, or emotional forces which failed to contribute to social integration on an ever-higher plane of existence—the destructive critics, the revolutionaries, in a word, the anarchists. Saint-Simon's attack against the "liberals" became Comtean tirades against the "revolutionary anarchists" who had initiated the "great crisis," the men of 1789. Traditionalists like de Maistre were less dangerous to progress than the revolutionaries because they at least understood the need for the creation of a collective consciousness. The theocratic school's utopia of the organic society was the great divide in this respect between the two eighteenth-century progressists Turgot and Condorcet and their nineteenth-century followers Saint-Simon and Auguste Comte. Whereas Turgot had been almost pathologically afraid of sameness and its deadening effect on man, Saint-Simon and Comte saw in those who desired novelty and innovation for their own sake an even greater danger. Both of them raised the specter of formlessness as the dread antiprogressist force, a French sociological tradition which culminated in Durkheim's conception of anomie. A change in politics or science which was not organically integrated was for Comte destructive of the good order—it was like an act of historical regression either in an individual or in humanity. Throughout his historical presentation Comte was ever vigilant to apprehend the violators of the preordained historical timetable and to censure them retroactively. Condorcet's flogging of science and technology into ever-faster accomplishments was not the part of the *Esquisse*

Comte admired. The progressions of intelligence, activity, and emotion ideally should march in step, three abreast.

Moral Love and Gay Science

Nineteenth-century European thought had a penchant for total systems at once grand in scope and minute in their detail, full of generalities and particularities. The future was the whole purpose of Comte's colossal labors—*savoir pour prévoir*. The detail with which he prophesied about calendars, holidays, and sacraments has repelled the skeptical, though it should not have because in his capacity as High Priest of Humanity he was actually instituting the future which he depicted, perfect model of a self-fulfilling prophet. After long travail, having become successfully identified with the Great Being, he had only to interrogate himself about his own spontaneous desires to know what the future would be—a procedure which has been followed unconsciously by many dissenters from the positivist religion.

In the temporal order the rulers of the future Comtean society would remain the capitalists, and he was not afraid to flaunt the name in the face of the revolutionary radicals of 1848. These men would remain responsible for the material arrangements of the world because they controlled its wealth and were by nature gifted in the activist art of manipulation. In effect they would be more like economic administrators than domineering potentates. Comte had in mind men such as the philanthropic textile manufacturer of the Restoration, Baron Ternaux, who had befriended him during the lean period when he lived in Saint-Simon's shadow. He saw no reason to alter the satisfactory existing order under which the capitalists controlled the instruments of production. Though there would be no legal or institutional checks upon the free utilization of their talents, there were other restraints of far greater potency than mere state legislation. Rational scientists, no longer supreme but influential in their own sphere, were a complementary force engaged in ordering society through their control of the educational system. Once the moral goal was set and made explicit, capitalists and scientists would operate harmoniously without conflict. Since Comte's utopia was not an expansive sensuous society, the production of novelties which appealed to the senses and the conduct of researches such as astronomic investigations of distant planets would be frowned upon as futile. In his popular works when he was proselytizing "conservatives" and "proletarians" Comte never outrightly condemned the luxuries of capitalists; they were allowed their excesses without censure; theirs were peccadilloes which he tolerated, not ways of life establishing the moral tone of the society. His description of the really distant future leads one to surmise, however, that the forbearance of the Great Being in this respect would not be of long duration. Comte's extreme personal asceticism during the second phase of his philosophical career was projected onto the whole of society. The preservation of a stable temporal order was far more important than the intrusion into the system of new artifacts, which would disrupt the fixed spiritual arrangements that he planned for mankind.

Though the Saint-Simonian goal which dedicated the whole of society to the improvement of the moral and physical lot of the poorest and most numerous classes was not accepted, Comte did take for granted that capitalists who had adopted the device of the positive religion, *To live for others,* would provide for the fulfillment of the indispensable material needs of all human beings. In addition he relied upon the new dignity which would be achieved by the two most oppressed classes of existing society to infuse a totally different spirit into the contemporary egotistic industrial-scientific order. Women and proletarians were the classes whose elevation Comte, along with most other reformers of the thirties and forties, predicted. Both had similar natures: They represented the simple, tender, loving element in mankind whose true force consisted not in ruling but in modifying the selfish character of the rulers in the very process of being ruled. The proletarians who had the power of numbers would not use their brute strength to achieve a false equality contrary to human nature, Comte preached on the morrow of the June Days. Instead, the moral influence they exerted on the capitalists would put an end to class conflicts and persuade the economic directors of society to behave toward their proletarians as loving parents would to children. In the family—the central unit of existence, absorbing many emotions now dissipated on public bodies— women would exercise a similar paramount influence. They would be universally recognized as morally superior to men—as Clothilde de Vaux was to Comte—and though they were dominated and enjoyed no independent existence, either in life or in death (for even their positivist immortality was bound up with the fate of their husbands), they suffused the whole of society with a gentle warmth.

After the provisional period of theologism and the transitional period of metaphysicism the positivist priesthood would inaugurate definitive history. The new religion from which God was banished would consciously reorient social relationships by locating the focus of existence in the Great Being, the source of moral judgment in the future as it had been the end of moral and psychic development in the past. "Happiness as well as duty consists in uniting oneself more closely with the Great Being which epitomizes the universal order."[20] With the triumph of the positive religion, sociology, a political science, would be transcended in the hierarchy of knowledge by morality.

Relations among the sciences in the encyclopedic hierarchy were not conceived of simply as a mechanical succession in which the lower forms served as a mere base for the higher ones. As in the Marxist relationship of substructure and superstructure there was a reciprocal interplay of forms among the various echelons in the ladder. The final transformation of man's moral being was dependent upon the perfection of the biological sciences, primarily through the development and extension of the ideas of Gall and Broussais, whose phrenological discoveries Comte considered pivotal in the science of man since they established specific connections between physical brain areas and intellectual, emotional, and activist expressions. Toward the end of the first volume of the *Système de politique positive,* he defined the moral problem in an adaptation of their physiopsychological jargon: "how to make the three social instincts, assisted by the five intellectual organs, surmount as a matter of habit the impulses resulting from the seven personal tendencies, by reducing these to the minimum of indispensable satisfactions in order to consecrate the three active organs in the service of sociability."[21] Moral education metamorphosed the nature of biological functions by developing some and atrophying others. Man the agent could be perfected through a complex educational mechanism which supervised every age-group in the life cycle through the successive ministrations of mothers, teachers, and priests, leading to a total improvement in spontaneous biological action-responses which could be measured in terms of the growth of love, altruism, living for others. Personality, an odious word in the Comtean vocabulary reminiscent of the anarchy of late metaphysicism, was not meant to flower but to merge in the totality of existence, past, present, and future.

All sciences on the lower levels of the encyclopedic scale would be affected by the moralization of man because the loving sentiment would pervade the scientific experiment and enrich it. Comte had a full awareness of the gap that separated a mere intellectual comprehension of a phenomenon from an emotional experience of the same event—an idea which has often been touted as a discovery of late-nineteenth-century German sociology. Comte repeatedly protested to those of his disciples who maximized the distinction between his two careers that in the essays of the 1820s he had already announced a revolution of sentiment and the institution of a new moral authority as the inevitable development of the present epoch, but at that time his understanding of the necessity had been chiefly intellectual. Not until his first profound experience of love, when he had felt in his own soul (the word was allowable to connote a combination of mind and feeling) the moral effects of a sublime selfless passion for another person, was he able to institute a new religion which would operate through love and metamorphose those who lived in the Great Being from self-loving into other-loving.

The temporal order of the future did not occupy a central place in Comte's considerations because in the end this was the lesser order. If capitalists were allowed their profits and the direction of the economy were entrusted to their hands they would not be encouraged to produce material objects that man could really do without. The sensuous desires to which modern industry caters were destined to become ever-weaker manifestations of human existence; with the enfeeblement of the nutritive and sexual passions there really was no wide field open for the expression of capitalist productivity. The boundless exploitation of nature in which the Saint-Simonians reveled was not a part of the Comtean dream. In bowdlerized language which spared the sensitivities of his Victorian readers Auguste Comte foretold the end of sex in the fourth volume of the *Politique positive*. It was "presaged by the growing development of chastity, which, proper to the human race, at least among males, shows the physical, intellectual, and moral efficacy of a sound employment of the vivifying fluid . . . Thus one conceives that civilization not only disposes man to appreciate woman more but continually increases the participation of the female sex in human reproduction, ultimately reaching a point where birth would emanate from woman alone."[22]

Indispensable sustenance of the body—but no more—was the restriction imposed upon the appetites. From the time of his first mental crisis through the climax of his love for Clothilde de Vaux, Comte established a relationship in his own life between the curtailment of a sumptuary superfluity or extravagance and the unveiling of new philosophical vistas—he had in turn denied himself tobacco, coffee, and wine at each point in the progression. And since Comte conceived of himself as a symbolic embodiment of the man of the future, what was good for Comte was good for mankind. Time and again there are hints in his writings that sensual gratification denied was transmutable into vast resources of spiritual power of an intellectual or an emotional character. The direct connection between his sublimated love for Clothilde de Vaux and the massive outpourings of his last years was the most conclusive evidence of his theory. The period of the *Système de politique positive* and the *Synthèse subjective* can hardly be looked upon as a creative decline, however little one may be attracted by the prospects which the High Priest held out for humanity.

Natural science had been a necessary introduction to the final science of morality; but knowing physical relationships was not an end in itself. Comte's parsimonious system allowed for the expansion of technical science only insofar as it was related to the ordering of human relationships and the stimulation of progress in love. Beyond that point professional virtuosity was wasteful, and Comte was prepared to decree a breaking of the chemists' retorts and the biologists' test tubes as well as a burning of the books if sheer curiosity multiplied information beyond the point where it was assimilable by the study of man. Comte and Fourier would have lighted the firebrand together and both would be preaching eternal love—and yet what different faces of love—as they destroyed the intellectual accumulation of the ages in its name.

Comte's vision of the future moral life on earth, for there is no other, at times seems unbearably dull, but there is another aspect to the man and his doctrine which is often obscured by the dark austerity of his mien. The second volume of the *Système de politique positive* extrapolated lines of human development which, though they may not suit the taste of contemporary sybarites or the men of action engaged in a struggle for power, cannot be lightly dismissed as baseless conjecture. In the hypothetical distant future state man is virtually liberated from work and the subsidiary intellectual occupations which have been dependent upon labor as a necessity. Not every type of work enjoyed Comte's moral sanction. "Activity dictated by our physical needs exerts an influence that is doubly corrupting, directly on the heart, indirectly on the mind." Freedom from work whose only real justification is the biological need to keep the body alive would be easily achieved. "It will only be necessary that the preparation of solid food habitually require as little trouble as our liquid or gaseous nutrition does today."[23] After the ages of slavery and labor there would follow an epoch in which man's intellectual and emotional nature—as Comte defined it—would enjoy free play. During the course of his historical review of human activity Comte referred to the "destructive instinct," which he sometimes called more energetic than the constructive one,[24] but all this was forgotten when he turned to the future. The destructive instinct had been stimulated by necessity, but once man is emancipated from physical needs and abandons his meat diet he will become spontaneously loving and his altruist nature will express itself in all its fullness. The parallel to Marx's utopia in *The German Ideology* is provocative. For the first time in the history of man, freedom from necessity will allow for the development of pure consciousness, the essential human nature. But with Marx the image is far more intellectualist (though he had his Fourierist moments too) while with Comte the emotive capacity tends to prevail. In the end of the days the inhabitants of the Comtean and the Marxist worlds would never recognize one another and become reconciled.

"We must now evaluate what our intellectual existence will be like," Comte begins blandly in the second chapter on social statics in the *Système de politique positive,* when he allows himself to be catapulted into a fantasy world that is one of the most charming of the unscientific utopias. For once the dry, obsessively precise mathematics teacher seems to have thrown his textbooks out of the celestial windows and abandoned himself to the Italian operas whose delights he relished but could not often afford. There will be virtually no development in technological thought because such practical speculations have always been sparked by physical needs, and these, as he has shown, will be appeased with the expenditure of little or no work. Perhaps the free intellect will still occasionally erect scientific models which derive from simple analogies. But science will not be the main channel into which human intelligence flows. Aesthetic works will attract the energies formerly spent upon scientific and technical labors, since this is a natural predilection of the human desire for expression and is not born out of mere necessity. Instead of devoting himself to the elaboration of scientific constructs that are remote and complicated, man will seek the most direct means of self-expression and he will find them both in art and in the expansion of his emotive vocabulary. Intelligence will thus become bound up with love and sympathy to a degree that has never been feasible under the reign of technical science. Man's need for activity will not disappear even though he is freed from the burdens of labor, but the nature of action will be profoundly changed. Domestic animals, all of whose needs are provided for, do not cease to express themselves; instead of being scavengers they become playful. "In a word, acts would essentially be transformed into games, which instead of being preparations for active existence would constitute pure means of exercise and expansiveness." No longer absorbed by work enterprises of an external character, action will involve itself in the organization of fetes that develop the mutual affections—chaste ones of course—of the participants. The aesthetic will prevail because it has a more direct physiological relationship to the emotions than have either science or industry. "We shall then exercise no other activity, but the perfection of our special means for expressing affection, as we shall cultivate no other science but the *gaie science* naively preferred by our chivalrous ancestors."[25] Nietzsche's *Gaya Scienza!*

31

Anarchy and the Heroic
Proletariat

ANARCHISM APPEARED in the mid-nineteenth century as the most serious radical utopian alternative to Marxism. Though "anarchism" is derived from an ancient Greek root, the order of anarchy as a utopian condition for mankind dates from the end of the eighteenth century. It was not yet used as a substantive in a positive sense, however, even by William Godwin, the ex-Dissenter clergyman who in 1793 first presented its fundamental principles in an extensive two-volume treatise on a society without property or governing authority.

The Five Pillars of Anarchy

Godwin's *Political Justice,* a verbose work composed in long Latinate periods, had none of the epigrammatic pungency of the seventeenth-century Civil War literature of the Levellers, Diggers, and Ranters from which its idea system was partially derived. It was a reasoned academic discourse that laboriously refuted the contract theories of Locke and Rousseau on the ground that one generation did not have the right to commit its successors to a bond or an agreement upon which they had not entered and called for the restoration of the natural right of every man to remain unfettered by laws and rules in whose framing he himself had not directly participated. The traditional arguments safeguarding accumulated property as an inalienable right were dismissed in the name of a natural law that recognized only equals. The Dissenter "independancy of private conscience" was transformed into the individual's right of free action untrammeled by any sovereign or property-holding power. The natural goodness of man, set forth in Rousseauan terms, was called justice and bore with it assurance that once the wicked institutions of society were made to disappear each individual in his conduct toward another would be illuminated and moved by the same power of reason. Men would then live in peace and tranquillity without the intervention of any external force. The dictates of Dissenter conscience became the rational foundation of a state without government, a condition of absolute freedom that would allow the human spirit to soar to heights of achievement hitherto unattained.

Since humans were sociable animals, they would spontaneously group themselves into neighborly communes, where they would work and eat in a society of complete equality. No distinctions of sex would break the natural law of equality. Marriage would not bind a person to his mate for any longer than he willed, for mutuality would prevail in all relationships. Godwin delivered himself of grand excursions on the dynamic potentialities of total freedom. He pleaded for a wholesome state of mind, unloosed from shackles, in which every fiber would be expanded according to the independent and individual impressions of truth upon it. But before his little anarchic parishes could function there had to be a psychic revolution. The conviction had to become deeply engraved on the minds of all men that their genuine wants were their only just claim to the acquisition of goods. Unnecessarily consuming objects that might benefit another, or appropriating property to gain ascendancy over others, would in the future state become as abhorrent as committing murder. The conversion had to precede the implementation of the utopia.

Godwin's communal parishes could have recalcitrant members, and he relied on psychic sanctions to bring them into line, the primitive technique of shaming so often resorted to by puritanical and savage societies. Not having heard of the tyranny of the big beast of public opinion in Stendhal's small town, he proposed the little general will of parish neighbors as a preventive of crime in the future society. "No individual would be hardy enough in the cause of vice, to defy the general consent of sober judgment that would surround him. It would carry despair to his mind, or which is better, it would carry conviction. He would be obliged, by a force not less irresistible than whips and chains, to reform his conduct."[1] Something of the punitive spirit of Rousseau's *Social Contract* had seeped into the anarchic eupsychia of Godwin. But his anarchic commonalty was far less anti-intellectual than Dom Deschamps's, and ultimately it was the cultivation of the spark of reason in all men that would guarantee the benign nature of the utopia without governmental authority.

The popularity of *Political Justice* among a generation of young English poets, especially Southey and Coleridge, owes much to the completeness of the argument, which under successive headings destroyed the underpinnings of church and state. A plan of Southey and Coleridge in 1794 to found a "Pantisocracy" on the banks of the Susquehanna River in Pennsylvania, where property would be held in common, was based on the idea of making men virtuous "by removing all Motives to Evil—all possible temptations."[2] In the sixth of Coleridge's youthful "Lectures on Revealed Religion," his paean to Universal Equality and his description of the dread disease of Inequality owe equal debts to Rousseau and Godwin, though the idea of common ownership to which he subscribed at this period seems closest perhaps to the views of Robert Wallace, author of *Various Prospects of Mankind, Nature, and Providence* (1761), a rare English proponent of equal division of produce among the producers.[3] The Pantisocratic project was aborted, and the world outlook of Southey and Coleridge changed in a conservative direction. It was Shelley who became the poet of libertarian anarchy (and Godwin's son-in-law). For a time, contemporary events in revolutionary France had encouraged adolescent dreamers to embrace the system of *Political Justice*.

The weightiness and turgid style of Godwin's volumes, which cost three guineas, saved the author from prosecution—such expensive books were not considered dangerous. But this most comprehensive attack upon the institutions of England survived, and the ideas in a crude form were picked up by organizations of English artisans, who discovered in *Political Justice* a worthy substitute for the Bible. In the end the work remains a sport, the strawlike sustenance of Robert Owen, founder of the first English socialist colonies, that most authoritarian of ideological masters in utopia—no mean distinction among the willful leaders of utopian socialism—the master of the regulation of simple people with a Sinai of prohibitions, all promulgated in the name of sovereign reason. In the second half of the nineteenth century Godwin was also occasionally read on the Continent and he was assimilated into the anarchist canon, though the impetus behind most European anarchist thought came from less parochial sources than the mental exercises of a former English clergyman. The main body of modern anarchist theory was composed by a quadrumvirate beginning in the 1840s—Proudhon, Max Stirner, Bakunin, Kropotkin. They do not form a chain so tightly linked as the utopian socialist prophets of Paris, but they are interrelated, and in the leaflets of the political anarchist movement one or another is constantly quoted with reverence.

There is no significant utopian novel or full-bodied description of a future utopian society whose author would identify himself as an anarchist. Virtually all versions of the doctrine—and the varieties are as numerous as the militant individualists who subscribe to it—condemn detailed depictions of the anarchist society of the future as a heresy, since the world of anarchy following upon the imminent revolution, the abolition of government, the destruction of capitalism, and the outlawing of property in the bourgeois sense of private monopolistic ownership would be a spontaneous creation of the free, untrammeled spirit of the men of that fortunate time, not fettered to any previously formulated plans or dogmas. A utopian blueprint of anarchy would be self-contradictory, internally inconsistent, and anathema to anarchists, who are ardent believers in reason and the scientific method. An outsider might hazard the opinion that William Morris' "Nowhere" comes pretty close to the condition for which many anarchists have expressed longings; but unfortunately Morris after his ideological conversion considered himself a Marxist, and Marx has been the bête noire of every self-respecting anarchist since his first encounter with Proudhon in the 1840s. Yet anarchist writers or theoreticians have inevitably been seduced, as Marx himself was, into utterances about what an ideal world should be like after the great outburst of destruction that would bring the new man into being, and anarchist journals have been as contentious and hairsplitting as their Marxist counterparts in distinguishing true from false principles.

If seen from within, anarchy is a doctrine of individualism à outrance, and one man's anarchy can hardly be another's. No-government, anarchy, was a wished-for state in Western man's fantasy long before it became a full-blown ideology. It would be possible to link one version of Zeno the Stoic, surely Diogenes the Cynic, popular cokaygne utopians of all times, late medieval and early Reformation millenarians, perhaps a few English Ranters of the seventeenth century, and the Marquis de Sade in a hypothetical genealogy of Anarchy. But most modern anarchists have been fervent atheists who have equated divine and state coercion—which would exclude religious anarchists of the past—and the profoundly ascetic or puritanical streak in modern Anarchy would blackball the divine Marquis. Tolstoy has been considered a religious anarchist and there has been a small anarchist movement within the American Catholic Church. The church-burning anarchists of the Spanish Civil War of 1936–1938, however, would not have considered them normative anarchists. The search for common denominators in the anarchist utopia is of necessity the act of a nonparticipant inquirer; to an observer, even though emancipated from the nineteenth-century stereotype of the bearded incendiary with bomb in hand, the anarchist is nevertheless a definable species in utopia.

If William Godwin is regarded more as a precursor than an integral member of the modern order, the anarchist utopia is essentially a nineteenth-century creation, its major formal theorists an improbable group. The father of the movement, Pierre-Joseph Proudhon, a French autodidact-printer who invented the famous slogan "Property is theft!" was a prolific author whose complicated paradoxes have been more appealing to intellectuals than to workers, though his ideas have seeped down to the masses. Two Russian nobles, Mikhail Bakunin of the hereditary nobility (equivalent to English country gentlemen), an erratic giant, voracious and violent, and Prince Peter Kropotkin of the titled nobility, a former page at the Czarist court and geological explorer of Siberia, who in his English exile came to represent the respectable side of the movement, were activist theoreticians with a large popular following. Finally, a meek German teacher in a Berlin school for girls, Johann Caspar Schmidt, who hid his identity under a tough nom de plume, Max Stirner, provided a philosophical statement of anarchy in Hegelian jargon, *Der Einzige und sein Eigenthum* (*The Ego and Its Own*), 1845. Stirner was a loner and his influence was marginal, though Marx took the trouble to ridicule him as Sankt Max in a famous section in *Die Heilige Familie* (The Holy Family). On occasion popular anarchist movements have incorporated strange gods into their pantheon—Rousseau and Nietzsche, for example—but on the whole, anarchists have not been hero-worshipers. Enrico Malatesta returning to Italy from exile after World War I sternly reproved his adulators for the excessive ardor of their welcome.

In practice, the utopia of anarchy found adherents in diverse groups in Europe and America that have little in common—among the artisans of the Swiss Jura, French syndicalists, isolated groups of Italian and Andalusian peasants, immigrants in the slums of large American cities. Direct-action anarchist leaders, charged with preparing the climate of revolution by perpetrating symbolic acts of terror against individuals who incarnated the evils of the existing state system, committed assassinations that had tragic consequences both for their victims and for the followers who were swept away by their rhetoric. Whole villages of peasants in Andalusia, Italy, Russia were for a brief moment possessed by a secular millenarianism that lasted until the police authorities brutally suppressed them. As the assassinations multiplied, the security forces of all states resorted to the recruitment of agents provocateurs whose contingents sometimes exceeded in number the authentic members of the secret cells under surveillance. Anarchist leaders often perished in their assassination attempts, but occasionally they escaped from one fiasco to replay their tragicomic roles in another part of the Continent. These incidents recall the local delusions of the Reformation period.

With improved means of communication and the vulnerability of modern technologized societies to flash attacks, intermittent outbursts such as those of the American Weathermen, the Japanese bands of terrorists, and the Red Brigades of Italy can have massive consequences that bookish anarchists never dreamed of, and the cruelties of Sergei Nechaev, the Russian monster who dominated university cells in St. Petersburg in the 1860s, are surpassed by his present-day descendants in Tokyo and Berlin. The destructive needs of a Bakunin or a Malatesta, or the mad fantasies of a Nestor Makhno, or the barbarities of American Weathermen and Japanese and Italian terrorists seem totally divorced from the doctrines of anarchist utopians like Godwin, Proudhon, and Kropotkin, who eschewed violence or conceived of it strictly as a defensive weapon to be used only in extremis. The rhetoric of the anarchist philosophers, however, is far from dead, and continues to reverberate in the proclamations of both violent and philosophical anarchists whatever new names they adopt. The gory anarchist utopia lives alongside the Tolstoyan vision of Christian love.

Perhaps the unifying element in modern anarchy has been its negation of the Marxist utopia. From the beginning, men like Proudhon and Bakunin and the Russian anarchists of the twentieth century defined themselves in opposition to the revolutionary tactics that Marx early introduced into the anticapitalist movement and that they found abhorrent. There is a famous letter of Proudhon to Marx after their meeting of 1846 in Paris, in which the French printer cautioned Marx against falling into the error of his "compatriot Luther." Proudhon warned against turning the "revolution" into a new dogmatic religion and the "movement" into a new authority, and strongly advocated keeping it alive through perpetual dialogue. "I applaud with all my heart," he wrote to Marx on May 17, "your idea of bringing into the open all opinions. Let us conduct a good, honest polemic. Let us give the world the example of a wise and prescient tolerance. But because we are at the head of a movement let us not turn ourselves into the leaders of a new intolerance or pretend to be the apostles of a new religion, even if this is the religion of logic, the religion of reason. Let us gather up, let us encourage, all differing points of view. Let us condemn all exclusions, all mystifications. Let us never consider that a problem has been exhausted. And when we have used up our last argument, let us begin again, if need be, with eloquence and irony. On this condition, I shall be delighted to join your association. If not, no!"[4]

Proudhon rejected centralized leadership for the revolutionary struggle and the dictatorship of the proletariat under a chosen directorate for either the initial or the subsequent stages of the path to utopia. Bakunin, a domineering authoritarian personality with more than his share of human frailties, including an excessive capacity for alcoholic consumption and a weakness for young revolutionary fantasts like Sergei Nechaev ("the boy," as he affectionately called him in English), combated Marx's influence in the Workingmen's International to the point where at one moment he effectively controlled the voices of a majority, forcing Marx to transfer the executive body to New York, far from the scene of action. The public oratorical passion of this colossus (in private, a man ridden with anxieties over his impotence) triumphed over the learning of the doctor of philosophy from Jena. While Marx laboriously defined his concepts and elaborated his theory of the stages of revolution, making each development depend upon the level of technology achieved and the degree of worker organization in process, Bakunin demanded immediate action, spurned tight control of the movement (at least in theory), extolled the spontaneity of the masses. His philosophy of history was a patchwork; in his ultimate vision there was more than a little suspicion of science and technology on the grand scale, as there was in Proudhon's world view. Only the geologist Kropotkin developed a scientific foundation for anarchism, in which anthropology, biology, and history all pointed to inevitable victory for the doctrine. His *Mutual Aid: A Factor of Evolution* (1902), the product of observation and reflection, was first published as a series of articles in the *Nineteenth Century* to counter the antiprogressionist and anti-utopian preconceptions of some forms of Social Darwinism. Kropotkin's work was designed in particular to refute the position taken by Thomas Huxley in his article "The Struggle for Existence in Human Society" that life was inevitably a continual and remorseless battle of man against man.[5]

Anarchists generally turned their backs on the existing political institutions that the bourgeoisie were creating; they wanted not to seize the state and its controls in the Marxist manner but to pulverize it. Participation in political processes entailed some form of recognition of the state, and the purists among the anarchists were on guard against contamination by such activity. The idea of a long political struggle, of availing themselves of recognized electoral and parliamentary instrumentalities, was odious to them. The true anarchist stands aside in his pristine virtue until the moment of apocalyptic revolution, or at most, in the prerevolutionary period he may form voluntary groups among his fellows for mutual aid, but only on condition that they are totally separated from the state. Anarchist worker unions grew out of this conception.

At every stage in modern revolutionary history, conflict with Marxists divided the working-class movements of Europe into hostile camps. Anarchists were willing to join in loose federations of believers and even hold international meetings for mutual consultation; but never would they allow a majority vote to dominate a minority or control its action. The corrupting consequences of engaging in bourgeois politics were delineated by Proudhon with prophetic fervor. In all its forms the state was an object of execration. In 1914, while the political socialists of the world united in going to war for their respective capitalist countries, anarchists looked upon such involvement with revulsion, except for Kropotkin, who opted for the Allies and drew down upon himself the condemnation of his fellow believers. Only in the early years of the Russian Revolution did some anarchist groups consent to cooperate with the Bolsheviks against their common enemy, for which they were rewarded with the signal honor of being the first dissidents to be liquidated.

Viewed historically, the fundamental cleavage in anarchist thought is between the anarchist individualists and those who since Kropotkin have come to be known as anarchist communists, though there are many subgroups in each category. In *The Conquest of Bread* Kropotkin prophesied: "Every society, on abolishing private property will be forced, we maintain, to organize itself on the lines of Communistic Anarchy. Anarchy leads to Communism, and Communism to Anarchy, both alike being expressions of the predominant tendencies in modern societies, the pursuit of equality."[6] By contrast, so rigid in his individualism was Proudhon that he was suspicious of too tight an organization of production even in a cooperative form. His ideal for the future remained the free individual producer or artisan creator, and associations were to be kept to a minimum. Mutually beneficial contracts were freely entered into and terminated at will in his society of small farmers and artisans, and men got what they worked for. Since a medium of exchange was necessary for the independent producers, Proudhon invented labor checks that cleared through a Bank of the People. In time there were variations on these techniques and many of them became the basis of cooperative societies that functioned within the capitalist system. In the utopia, however, there was to be no state, no coercion, no large-scale enterprise. This mutualist anarchy of Proudhon's in the hands of others could assume rather more organized forms than he would have sanctioned. Syndicalists, for example, conceived of the occupational *syndicat* as the most appropriate unit for establishing anarchy, without returning to the regressive economic forms for which Proudhon had a nostalgia. In France, Italy, and Spain, syndicalism, using the general strike as the final revolutionary weapon, came to regard itself as the instrument for the institution of anarchy. The unions of the future would by definition avoid all the evils of a state bureaucracy, and their few agents were to be paid no more than their ordinary members. Society would become a loose federation of unions.

Kropotkin conceived of his "commune," in his fancy an adaptation of the Russian peasant mir, as the unit of both production and consumption, and in place of the elaborate Proudhonian system of exchanges he in effect embraced a standard similar to Marx's in the *Critique of the Gotha Program*. Though there was a fundamental difference. What for Marx was the postponed "higher stage" of communism was in Kropotkin's plan to be instituted immediately on the morrow of the revolution and not deferred to some unspecified future period of technological maturity. Each citizen would take from the common stock what he needed, irrespective of what he produced, and it was assumed that under the new condition of communist anarchy every man would contribute the fullness of his powers. In many respects Kropotkin moved to the other end of the spectrum, away from William Godwin's individualistic anarchism where each independent farmer and artisan both produced and exchanged necessities. *La Conquête du pain* (*The Conquest of Bread*), 1892, Kropotkin's most popular work, laid down the organizational principle of communistic anarchism: "All things are for all men, since all men have need of them, since all men have worked in the measure of their strength to produce them, and since it is not possible to evaluate everyone's part in the production of the world's wealth."[7] But this anarchist communism envisaged no coercion by a state authority—at most, social persuasion of recalcitrants. For Kropotkin the formula of each man's taking goods in accordance with the precise amount of labor he had contributed was impossible to calculate. How could one assess the appropriate portion of an inventor in his invention, or the part due the schoolteacher who had taught him to read and write? Since complex mutualist divisions were impracticable, there had to be a rule of community under the anarchist order. It is hard to see how Kropotkin's anarchy can live under the same roof with Proudhon's. But at the same time, in his popular exposition of the doctrine in *Paroles d'un révolté* (The Words of a Rebel), 1885, a collection of pieces first published in the journal *La Révolte* (1880–1882), Kropotkin was careful to differentiate his plan from the tradition-bound Russian peasant collectivity that had been Bakunin's model. Since Kropotkin was intent on preserving the fluidity of all economic and social relationships, the utopian structure he outlined was lost in a cloudy haze. "For us, Commune is no longer a territorial agglomeration," he wrote, "it is rather a generic name, a synonym for the grouping of equals knowing neither frontiers nor walls. The social commune will soon cease to be a clearly defined whole. Each group of the commune will necessarily be drawn toward similar groups in other communes; it will be grouped and federated with them by links as solid as those which attach it to its fellow citizens, and will constitute a commune of interests whose members are scattered in a thousand towns and villages."[8]

After a period among the workers in the Jura, during which he may have preached violence as the path to the world of anarchy, Kropotkin turned milder and in his London exile was known as a saintly philosopher. He was the theoretical anarchist whose studies of animal behavior, essentially based on recollections of his youthful explorations in Siberia, proved that wolves did not behave in accordance with the prejudicial Hobbesian metaphor, but roamed in cooperative packs and never killed one another, thus providing a "scientific" basis for the anarchist expectation that when men had been removed from the capitalist environment they would freely work together without strife. This was the other face of anarchy, delineated by the benign lover of mankind who was eminently acceptable to literary circles in Edwardian England. It was a far cry from the strident pronouncement with which modern anarchy had first broken upon radical Europe in 1842, when the expatriate Bakunin, under the influence of young Hegelians, delivered himself of an apocalyptic vision of the future in two parts in a pseudonymous pamphlet entitled *Die Reaktion in Deutschland: Ein Fragment von einem Franzosen* (The Reaction in Germany: A Fragment by a Frenchman). The angel of death appears glorifying the creative power of destruction. "Let us put our trust in the eternal spirit which destroys and annihilates only because it is the unfathomable and eternally creative source of all life. The passion for destruction is also a creative passion." The comforter speaks in a bastard tongue, part residue from Bakunin's early Greek Orthodox training and religious crisis that culminated in atheism, part ill-digested Hegelian verbiage. "There will be a qualitative transformation, a new, living, life-giving revelation, a new heaven and a new earth, a young and mighty world in which all our present dissonances will be resolved into a harmonious whole."[9]

Of all the anarchists Proudhon was by far the most powerful writer.[10] He was a moralist with a touch of genius, a prophet immune to high-flown rhetoric, who looked for precise answers to sharp questions on human conduct and had the capability of cutting a loosely woven argument to shreds. Proudhon's writings bristle with paradoxes, the most noteworthy of which is his definition of property in existing society. You bourgeois are afraid of the workers, the dangerous classes, because you fear that they will rob you and plunder and destroy; but it is you who are the real thieves. The very foundation of your existence, property, is theft.[11] This outrageous wordplay had an enduring resonance in anarchist thought. Embattled on two fronts, Proudhon lashed out against the plutocrats and their capitalist society in its state of economic and moral disintegration, and then turned to the left to demolish the systems that pretended to replace the old order—the socialist, communist, and sundry other doctrines of association in vogue in the 1840s. "What is Association? It is a dogma . . . Thus the Saint-Simonian school, going beyond what it received from its founder, produced a system; Fourier, a system; Owen, a system; Cabet, a system; Pierre Leroux, a system; Louis Blanc, a system; like Babeuf, Morelly, Thomas Morus, Campanella, Plato, and others, their predecessors, each one starting with a single principle, gave birth to systems. And all these systems, excluding each other, are equally progressive. Let humanity perish rather than the system, this is the motto of the utopians, like that of fanatics of all ages."[12]

A Hesiod redivivus, Proudhon was no facile optimist, but a preacher who would lead the nineteenth century back to the values of true liberty and justice, mocking the false shibboleth of equality. Genuine relationships were self-interested and contractual. The good society would be an intricate fabric of agreements among individual men without the intervention of any alien power or third party. Perhaps "associations" might be necessary in order to make use of complex machines, he grudgingly conceded, but in this combine no other principle would be involved than in any ordinary mutualist arrangement. Over and over again Proudhon insisted on a few pat solutions. Interest rates should be reduced to a fraction of a percent—there should be virtually free credit—and funds should be granted to men on the basis of their competence. Human skill was a far more secure warranty than anything a capitalist could offer. Once credit was allocated, the society would function without need of further intervention.[13]

For Proudhon, appreciation of the dignity and essential respectworthiness of each human being, whoever he might be, was the cardinal principle of anarchy. Upon this rock the mutualist society was to be built. This single idea, reiterated throughout his works, letters, and private notebooks, impressed itself on French dissenting opinion beyond the anarchist ranks. For some intellectuals it became the foundation of a new morality. Men, treated as equal in dignity, would thereby have equal access to the sources of credit, allowing them either individually or in groups to produce whatever objects of consumption they were capable of making. Simply by virtue of his being, a man was entitled to free credit; his word was his bond. A contract was the sacred obligation of free individuals as they exchanged the fruits of their labor. All ties were loose, and the superior workman would be rewarded according to his "works." Absolute equality of returns was not a goal; but since credit was free there would be no monopolies and any virtuous man could enter the productive market and earn his family's keep. A network of mutual exchanges, though assuming different forms in Proudhon's schemes and in later adaptations, always excluded accumulation of property, which in its contemporary form was theft. Somehow the free workers would eschew luxuries; mutual services would take care of all reasonable necessities; and no man would try to pierce the armor of individual dignity with which his fellow was clothed. Respect rather than happiness was the touchstone of existence. The worth of men's work would vary, but the intricate fabric of mutual consent would imperceptibly generate a feeling for community. Since there would be no state authority and no coercion, the hard problem remained how to achieve the consent of the refractory ones. The anarchist solution, following Godwin, was usually social pressure of a psychological character. Individualism was also slightly amended to provide for those incapable of producing and exchanging. Neither of these exceptions, however, was considered a grave departure from principle.

Unlike the contemporary Saint-Simonians and Fourierists, Proudhon apotheosized the nuclear family, dominated by the working male, as the atom of social existence, and females were kept under a misogynous cloud. In *La Pornocratie, ou Les Femmes dans les temps modernes* (Pornocracy, or Women in the

Modern Era), receding from the position taken by Godwin more than half a century before, Proudhon was scornful of the Saint-Simonian Prosper Enfantin and his "emancipation of woman"; for Proudhon, the family was an indissoluble androgynous unit in which there could not be total equality, the male being superior to the female in the ratio of three to two. Instead of opening the doors to the outside world, Proudhon closed the family in upon itself.[14] The family was excluded from the rule of Anarchy.

In *Idée générale de la révolution au xix* *siècle: Choix d'études sur la pratique révolutionnaire et industrielle* (*The General Idea of the Revolution in the Nineteenth Century: Selected Essays on Revolutionary and Industrial Practice*), 1851, Proudhon wielded the bludgeon of a courtroom lawyer. He demanded a yes or no answer from his adversaries, the believers in the new gospel of communist association. "It is one of two things: either association is compulsory, and in that case it is slavery; or it is voluntary, and then we ask what guaranty the society will have that the member will work according to his capacity and what guaranty the member will have that the association will reward him according to his needs. Is it not evident that such a discussion can have but one solution—that the product and the need be regarded as correlated expressions, which leads us to the rule of liberty, pure and simple?"[15]

Since 1840 Proudhon had provocatively identified himself in public as an anarchist. For him the word anarchy signified the abolition of coercive authority in the state, on the land, and in money, and the end of the aristocratic landowner, the big capitalist, the monopolist. Though he abhorred the utopians, in the *Idée générale de la révolution au xix* *siècle* he spelled out the principles of a revolutionary utopia with oratorical simplicity:

Society has to be turned inside out, all relationships inverted. Yesterday we walked with our heads down; today we keep our heads up, and all this without any interruption in our lives. Without losing our personality we change our way of existence. This is the Revolution of the nineteenth century.

Is not the major decisive idea of this Revolution: "No more Authority," neither in Church nor State, neither in land nor in money? . . .

No more authority! This means a free contract instead of an absolutist law, voluntary transactions instead of the intervention of the State, equitable and reciprocal justice instead of sovereign and distributive justice, rational morality instead of revealed morality, a balance of forces substituted for a balance of powers, economic unity in place of political centralization. Once more, is this not what I have the right to call a complete reversal, an about-face, a Revolution?[16]

Proudhon's nostrums were simple: education, free credit, free association. Once credit was free, the true economic forces of society would reach a state of equilibrium under which social life would organize itself spontaneously, without profiteering and with everyone selling at a just price set by universal consent. Proudhon dreamed of a peasant and artisan utopia, restoring the virtues of justice and liberty that had supposedly prevailed among the ancient Gauls, Celts, and Druids—a belated French version of the Norman-yoke thesis of English radicals of the Civil War. Though Proudhon is unlikely to have known Godwin's *Political Justice*, he proposed a similar agricultural utopia of individual holdings, whose worker-owners would have no need of the state or organized society. "Anarchy," he wrote in an article addressed to Pierre Leroux on December 3, 1849, "is the condition of existence of adult society, as hierarchy is of primitive society, and there is ceaseless progress from the one to the other."[17]

While middle-class intellectuals like Marx dreamed of a world in which the realm of necessity was rationalized and controlled and manual labor virtually abolished, workers like Proudhon exalted the creative values of work. By implication, Proudhon was also throwing darts at the notions of Fourier and the later Comte that work should be like play. In his notebooks, Proudhon composed quasi-religious eulogies of labor. "To work is to produce from nothing . . . By virtue of this reality, man is made as great as God. Like God, he draws everything out of the world. Cast naked on the earth, among the brambles and thorns, in the company of tigers and serpents, hardly finding enough to live on . . . without tools, models, provisions, or acquired experience, he cleared the land, laid out plots, and cultivated his domain. He actually embellished nature. He surrounded himself with marvels unknown to the ancient author of things, and he brought forth luxuriousness where the Creator had granted merely profusion. At the beginning of society there was only matter; there was no capital. It is the worker who is the true capitalist; for to work is to produce from nothing; and to consume without working is not to exploit capital but to waste it . . ."

In Proudhon's mystique of work, labor is neither punishment nor necessity. Labor is not so essentially unpleasant that it has to be rendered "attractive" in Fourier's sense or superseded, for it is itself "immaterial, imperishable, unconsumable, immortal, always living, always creating, always spontaneously tending, by virtue of itself and without any external help, to actualize itself."[18] Work for work's sake is a denigration, for then it would only be play, like the Olympic games and medieval jousts, which soon degenerated because they were not tied to utility.

The debate on the nature and organization of work in an ideal human condition lay at the heart of Proudhon's anarchist, as well as nineteenth-century socialist and communist, utopias. Industrialization and a new sense of social malleability required utopian reconsideration of the meaning of work. Labor as a human value had not been problematic as long as man's capacity to produce was limited to the bare necessities at most. But industrialization brought surplus and with it choice. Should the quantity of labor invested by each man be kept relatively constant as the new technology was allowed to satisfy ever more luxurious desires, or should consumption be stabilized and the hours of labor be reduced? The alternatives had already presented themselves in petto to Thomas More's Utopians, but with the prospect of infinitely expanding productive capacity the nature and worth of labor beyond a minimum became fateful for the utopian thinker. For a German artisan utopian like Wilhelm Weitling, freedom and justice meant in part maintaining a harmony between desires and the capacity of production. While not a Spartan, Weitling could see no point in burdening the individual and society with excessive desires for objects that went far beyond need. Though under Fourier's influence in other respects, a poor Christian worker like Weitling could not countenance without some shame the notion of an infinity of expansive sensate pleasures. Proudhon started out with a different premise. It was the original *moral* value of work that fulfilled a real need; work was creative, but it also had to be truly useful. Real work, work that produced goods and knowledge, would always entail too much sacrifice and perseverance ever to become identifiable with mere play or with Fourier's passions, fugitive things in themselves. Such an association would rob labor of its quintessential dignity.

Marx could not endure either Weitling's religious preaching or Proudhon's moralizing of work. And yet in one respect, their descriptions of the dehumanizing quality of the contemporary division of labor, Marx and Proudhon have much in common. Work, Proudhon maintained, should be the emanation of a complex intelligence which in stages performs a total, creative act. Instead of operating as that intelligence, man had been reduced to the status of a hammer or a wheel. Originally, the division of labor was to have freed man from serfdom, from bondage to the soil. Instead he had been tied to one part of a job in a factory. This impoverishment would end in the utopian future when each man had access to free credit and could start producing as an independent being. Proudhon's attack on alienation is always expressed less in economic than in psychological terms. "Man has been constricted into routine labor which, far from initiating him into the general principles and secrets of human industry, closes the door on every other occupation. His intelligence was first crippled, then stereotyped and petrified. Apart from what is related to his job, which he flatters himself that he knows but to which he brings only a feeble conception and a rote-like habit, his soul has been paralyzed with his arm . . . Soon the monotony of the work with all its disgust begins to be felt. The supposed worker becomes aware of his degradation. He tells himself that he is only a cog in the bosom of society. Slowly despair possesses him; his reason, since he lacks positive knowledge, loses its equilibrium, his heart becomes depraved . . . They aimed to mechanize the worker; they did worse, they made him one-armed and wicked."[19] But none of the socialist utopias with which Proudhon was acquainted offered anything to restore individual dignity to the worker and to make him whole again, master of his own creation, rewarded in accordance with his own total efforts. All other reforming schemes always ended up either as a hierarchical corporation, a state monopoly, or a despotism of the community.

Unlike the aging Kropotkin of a later period with his soupy optimism, Proudhon infused the anarchist tradition with a tragic sense of life. There are moments when the eternal struggle of man with his needs, with nature, with his fellows, with himself appears to be his inevitable lot. But under anarchy there would at least be justice. Each man would have his due, according to his works. No one, however, would be coerced into philanthropy, and if the strong helped the weak, they would do so out of generosity and with good grace. "Man is very willing to obey the law of duty, serve his country, and oblige his friends, but he wishes to labor when he pleases, where he pleases, and as much as he pleases. He wishes to dispose of his own time, to be governed only by necessity, to choose his friendships, his recreation, and his discipline; to act from judgment, not by command."[20] Bakunin and Kropotkin talked the language of historical determinism, adapting Hegel to demonstrate the inevitability of anarchy. Proudhon, though flaunting the dialectic in his autodidactic way and publicly subscribing to the doctrine of progress, in private correspondence aired his doubts without restraint. Societies, generations, whole races, could go astray and fall into a "definitive and irremediable aberration," he wrote to Jérôme-Amédée Langlois on May 18, 1850. Mankind was at the crossroads and had to will its own salvation, choosing between virtue and vice, equality and exploitation, Jesus and Malthus. On other occasions, Proudhon could swing into a mood of wild optimism and predict the demolition of the state in six weeks.[21]

The harsh realism of Proudhon, like the fierce egotism of Max Stirner's philosophical tirades, created a tough-minded, anarchist utopian strain that eschewed sentimentality. Proudhon, of course, would have disavowed the mindless violence with which anarchy has been associated in reality as well as in popular mythology. The theoreticians of anarchy have always maintained that their vision represented true order and that the existing society of economic anarchy was a dehumanizing disorder. But anarchy could lead in all directions and in the course of the decades Proudhon, for one, spawned diverse progeny, from the most practical initiators of small production cooperatives to fabricators of heroic utopian mythologies. One of them was Georges Sorel.

The Coming Age of Heroes

In the well-stocked tool kit of Georges Sorel, the retired engineer turned philosophe, there were few epithets more deadly than "utopian." When he wanted to belabor a writer or politician as a vain, rationalistic drafter of inane plans of social reform to which he tried to bend reality, falsifying here and there with deliberate cheats, Sorel called him a utopian. What he saw in utopias was nothing but the touched-up photograph of ugly contemporary society, like his master Proudhon, who thought of utopians as "more or less retrograde, mirrors of reactionary types."[22] The basic elements of utopias were derived from the present; the utopian merely juggled them into a new configuration and added a few so-called improvements. Utopias were schemes of compromise, palliatives, blueprints for the future that obfuscated the palpable, insoluble, social conflicts of an epoch by pretending to show the hostile contending forces or classes a way out of their dilemmas, a roseate prospect of social peace. All this was illusory; utopia dulled man into a state of somnolence.

Despite his antipathy to the term, it is obvious even after a brief immersion in his writings that the anti-intellectual Sorel protests too much. He had a utopia of his own, whose characters were drawn not from a distant island but from the historical experience of Western man. He may have fancied himself a herald of man the master of his destiny, but he was a descendant of Don Quixote rather than Prometheus. Sorel's is a utopia of heroic conduct, though he differs from Cervantes in one vital respect: There are not two ideal human natures, there is no Sancho Panza to sustain the heroic knight. Sorel's utopia was made up of all knights and no squires.

He came to this utopia as most utopians have, out of a radical negation of the present. And once his central theme took shape, he nourished it with a motley array of impressive writers from the past. Karl Marx was at the head, but he was in need of revision, and there was Marx's enemy Proudhon, too; Henri Bergson's élan vital rubbed shoulders with the pragmatism of Charles Peirce and William James; and finally there was Nietzsche. Giambattista Vico was incorporated, though not as he had been romanticized in Michelet's translation; the Vico who came into the works of Sorel had, without his knowledge, been baptized by Nietzsche. These intellectual progenitors of Sorel's were joined by a changing group of friends, collaborators, and idols, from Fernand Pelloutier through Charles Péguy, from syndicalism to the Action française; and, toward the end of Sorel's life, Lenin appeared drawing up the rear. The conversations with a young friend, Jean Variot, held over the years, bear testimony to the fascination that Lenin and Mussolini came to exert on this former devotee of revolutionary syndicalism.[23] The migration from Anarchism to Fascism and authoritarian Communism has not been infrequent in Western thought. Sorel remained an abstract theorist and never bloodied his hands as he moved in and out of various French intellectual cliques. What ties him most firmly to the Western anarchist tradition is his absolutism, his admiration for asceticism, and his quest for the heroic.

In the eighteenth century, one freakish utopian constructed an ideal primitivist society literally by cutting out and stringing together passages from exotic travel literature. Georges Sorel's is a utopia of many colors whose eclectic character might long since have condemned it to oblivion, were it not for the scandal of a good bourgeois composing a work provocatively entitled *Réflexions sur la violence*. All revolutionary creeds are nurtured by the fantasy of a cult of heroes. Sorel raised the heroic to the level of an ideal psychic state, the only one worthy of man. The cause for which one sacrificed one's life was less significant than the personality created in the course of the battle. The exponents of the existential philosophy of European intellectuals in the period after the Second World War would blush to be identified with so turgid and inelegant a writer as Sorel—Albert Camus, in accepting his Nobel Prize, called upon the shades of Nietzsche, not Sorel, as his hero—but the Sorelian creed fits well into the anarchist critique of Marx, and in the Paris uprising of 1968 the staid Sorel, who had been forgotten by all political parties when he died in 1924, was briefly resurrected. In 1968 members of a generation far removed from the corrupt politics of the Third French Republic somehow turned to this middle-class dreamer of heroic violence for sustenance—a symbol of the growing impoverishment of the utopian imagination among middle-class radicals. If there had been something incongruous in the shocking declarations of the good bourgeois of Cherbourg in the first decade of the century, the spectacle of students sixty years later feeding on reheated Sorelian fantasies of glory was pathetic.

Sorel's work was rooted in the political and social events of France during his lifetime, especially the dissolution of the French radical left, which had been the party of the Commune and had held the French army at bay for months, into an assortment of political parties known officially as Socialists, Radical Socialists, and other variations on the generic name. The Socialist party in France in the latter part of the nineteenth century nominally belonged to the Second International founded by Karl Marx; in theory at least its leaders subscribed to the idea that class conflict unto the death was the only authentic social reality and that under capitalism a dichotomous class conflict was becoming progressively accentuated. The science of economics provided objective reasons for believing that capitalism, as a consequence of a law of inner development, was headed for a *Zusammenbruch*, a total collapse and breakdown. The function of a politically conscious socialist or a communist was to take his place in the vanguard of the working classes and to train and organize them for the day when they would be called upon to seize power in the state in order to establish the dictatorship of the proletariat. This remained doctrine for the record, the party congress, and Fourteenth of July speeches.

When on the morrow of the defeat in the Franco-Prussian War and total collapse of the Commune the French parliamentary system of the Third Republic slowly took shape, the members of the French Socialist party were, like their counterparts the German Social Democrats, faced with a dilemma: to vote or not to vote in parliamentary elections. And at a later date the even more crucial question arose as to whether or not to become *ministres*. Those socialists who opted for voting in the parliamentary elections of a capitalist republic and ultimately for accepting portfolios as socialist ministers of state in a republican regime were not starved for arguments. The vote would give them representatives in government who would be able to mount the tribune in the Chamber of Deputies and deliver sermons on the true nature of socialism to Paris and to the universe. As members of parliamentary committees they would be able to influence social legislation, shorten the working day, perhaps obtain pensions for the aged, see to it that rules of hygiene were enforced in factories and that security measures were adopted in mines. When the socialists became ministers they might even be able to exert pressure and influence on the capitalists who owned the mines and factories to increase wages. They could protect workers' organizations from the arbitrary power of the reactionary law code and thus give them added leverage in pressing for higher wages. In international affairs they would always align themselves on the side of peace against imperialist adventures, and they could unmask the hypocrisy of the army as it revealed itself in the Dreyfus case. They could broaden the educational system, even curb the brutality of the hated flics. This was the political fantasy of the French Marxist revolutionary socialist with a none-too-secret passion for the ballot.

But there were working-class parties in France under anarchist and syndicalist influence that closed their ears to these siren songs and obstinately refused to participate in the government, despite its promises. The anarchists who depended upon Bakunin rather than Marx, along with one wing of the trade-union movement, denounced the contamination of proletarian virtue that would inevitably result from commingling with the oppressive bourgeois state and its minions. In his *Reflections on Violence* Georges Sorel, as pungently as any writer, gave sharp expression to this fear of assimilation with the bourgeois, and much of what he saw in day-to-day political and social practice bolstered his arguments. The working-class representatives in parliament, and, even more so, their ministers, quickly became little bourgeois—this was the indictment. Their dress changed, their tastes in wine and women became more luxurious, and soon their ideas were bourgeoisified. The hard core of proletarian morality, which both Marx and Proudhon posited, each in his fashion, disintegrated. The parliamentarians took graft, got involved in public scandals, made vast sums out of running newspapers, helped settle strikes for a consideration. Of their preparliamentary socialism they retained a socialist vocabulary lurid with bloody slogans about the final battle; but in their daily lives they were bourgeois with the rest of them, polishing their tarnished ideological brass whenever they had to take to the hustings. In practice they represented reasonable compromise, social peace, an end to the disastrous strikes. In principle they were opposed to adventures in imperialist exploitation, but a well-placed overseas investment was not beyond them, especially if it helped increase the revenues of their socialist newspapers.

Against these subverters of the proletarian ideal Georges Sorel arose in indignant protest like an ancient prophet or a modern Calvinist. These men were betrayers, falsifiers, crooks no better than the bourgeois. "These politicians want to reassure the bourgeoisie and promise it that they will not allow the people to abandon themselves to their anarchic instincts. They explain to the bourgeoisie that they have no thought of crushing the great machine of the State. It follows that the sensible socialists," wrote Sorel with irony "want two things: to get control of this machine to perfect its wheels and make them function for the best interests of their friends and to render the government stable, which will be most advantageous for all business men."[24] But if this had been Sorel's total achievement, he would have left no deeper imprint than scores of other debunkers of socialist duplicity, or for that matter the mockers of every man with high principles of morality, a lust for fast women, and large bank accounts. Instead, Sorel raised the immediate political situation in France to the level of a universal conception of man which, though it sometimes appears parochial because of its absorption with passing issues of public malfeasance in the late nineteenth and early twentieth centuries, does occasionally escape from its circumstantial limitations and rise to a certain grandeur.

Searching for a counterforce to the soft bourgeois and the socialist petty bourgeois, he ransacked world history for heroic movements of religious, social, and political action. It was not the individual heroes upon whom he focused or the ideological content of the movements, but their abstract heroic idealism or beliefs or constellations of moral principles. Participation in a heroic movement—any heroic movement—with its self-abnegation, its rejection of sensate indulgence, its emotional commitment, its self-sacrifice unto death is singled out from among all other activities as the ideal human condition. Epochs in which such movements had appeared and struggled for victory were expressions of a higher species of man.

From Vico, Sorel took the idea of the *ricorsi,* defined in more social and human terms than Nietzsche's eternal recurrence with its pseudoscientific physicists' paraphernalia. Vico had described three ages that followed inevitably upon one another throughout history over and over again, the age of the gods, the age of heroes, and the age of men. The age of men in the *Scienza nuova* represented for Vico, as Sorel read him, a measure of rational superiority over the age of heroes, but a decline in emotive and passionate power, in poetry, symbol-creating, and grandeur. The age of men developed a system of law and reason that eventually degenerated into a hypersophistication, what Vico called the barbarism of the intellect. It was then that a Divine Providence in His beneficence initiated the cycle of social life once again with a return to savagery, and there followed a repetition of the sequence of the age of gods, the age of heroes, and the age of men.

What Sorel derived from Vico—and his interpretation differs radically from that of many modern commentators—was a sense of the emotive breakthrough of a new belief embodied in a heroic society that might be cruel, but that created a way of life which stamped its character on a culture. Sorel was convinced that the latter-day Age of Reason, which rationalized, theologized, organized, made neat and pat the powerful spontaneous early credo of a heroic culture, was a falling off from the pinnacle of human capacity. Throughout, Sorel adored the primitive imagination, all robust even though crude, and scorned the degeneration of the ideal, whatever it might be, at the hands of its meticulous, orderly expositors. Clearly he had in mind the contemporary socialist intellectuals of France and political misleaders of the potentially heroic proletariat. "So-called municipal socialism which transforms workers into functionaries in a bureaucracy has created a category of privileged individuals in the midst of the proletarian mass. The existence of this caste is dependent upon the success of a party and develops none of the feelings that socialism needs to foster."[25] His conception was enriched with other examples drawn from world history. As in Nietzsche, his philosophy of history ended with a dualistic moral typology, the reign of the heroes whom he worshiped alternating rhythmically with the domination of the unheroic rationalists whom he despised and treated as corrupters of the truth.

In *Le Procès de Socrate: Examen critique des thèses socratiques* (The Trial of Socrates: Critical inquiry into the Socratic propositions), 1889, Sorel's first major work, the traditional image of the heroic Socrates confronting death was rejected. He became the traducer of the values of heroic Greek culture, one of the quibblers and deceivers and wordmongers of the rising urban civilization of Hellas who ultimately brought about its doom. After the heroic Greek warriors, Sorel exalted the monks of the communities of primitive Christianity. He glorified the ascetic ideal along with Proudhon, whose moral outlook colored all Sorel's writings, and in historical Christianity he found striking examples of self-denying anti-utilitarian movements that he would have had the working classes of France 1890 emulate, converting the trade unionists into martyrs prepared to sacrifice themselves on the altar of a proletarian revolution. Utopians in other ages had been given to archaistic daydreaming. Sorel's desire to clothe the working classes of Paris in monkish habits is one of the more extravagant acts of utopian transvestism. He painted a dramatic contrast between the monks of the desert, those small, isolated communities, seemingly powerless, who ultimately sapped the strength of the Roman Empire, and ecclesiastical, theological, decadent Christianity. There was a modern parallel: Noble working-class *syndicats* would effectively undermine the mighty structures of the slothful, pleasure-ridden capitalists. The accolade of virtue was bestowed upon the primitive Christian saints, the medieval monastic orders in their initial stages, and finally upon the brave Calvinist communities of believers who had risked their lives in a sea of Catholics. Small bands of heroic men of the faith had wrought the triumph of the Christian myth; Sorel now exhorted to victory a heroic proletariat, imbued with a new myth.

Sorel's heroic man had always thirsted after the mythic, and he was fully man only when completely possessed by it. But the authentic myth was not the travesty of image-making to which business—capitalistic, political, and academic—has sometimes reduced the idea. Sorel's myths were autonomous creations, while the others were characteristically manufactured by hyper-rationalist manipulators. The authentic myth could only come into being of its own momentum. Sorel denounced the despoilers of a great myth in the making, the swamping of the heroic action of the contemporary proletariat by parliamentary intriguers. Only history, not man, could make a myth. "The true vocation of intellectuals is the exploitation of politics. The role of the politician is analogous to that of the prostitute and requires no industrial aptitude," wrote the staid bourgeois engineer living at Boulogne-sur-Seine, using a comparison with which he was obviously ill at ease.[26]

Sorel conceived of world history as a succession of creative myths that originally possessed small, tightly knit elites; through their heroic devotion, the mythic ideal came to dominate the whole of a culture for a time. The previously enthroned myth which the new creative myth replaced had by then grown flat and stale, a coin worn thin. It had been rationalized to extinction and the ruling classes themselves no longer believed in it; they merely gave it lip service. The two typecases of this sort were the ruling classes at the end of the ancient world, whose more recent historiography Sorel had analyzed in the focused light of his thesis, and the contemporary flabby bourgeoisie of the nineteenth century.[27] They could not resist for long a new militant elite inspired by a fresh-born myth. The ancient myth was Christianity; the new myth was the class conflict followed by the establishment of a society of producers à la Proudhon, based upon *syndicats* as the key units of organization, communities without a special authority, without a state, without benefit of false-hearted intellectuals and socialist phrasemakers—agglomerations of simple noble workers, producing and exchanging their goods, laboring enough to have a continent existence removed from extravagant sensate desires. In Fernand Pelloutier, the doctrinal teacher of French syndicalism, he found a theoretician, in Kropotkin's denial that factories required military discipline to function well, a supporter. In a note headed "The Socialist Future of the *Syndicats*" Sorel attacked the prevalent conception of the technological imperative of industrial regimentation. "Modern production requires the mutual cooperation of the workers, a voluntary coordination, systematic relations which transform the accidental aggregate into a body where man reveals himself as a species . . . One cannot expect shopkeepers to understand these things."[28]

There is one element in his grand fantasy that Sorel exploded into an apocalyptic event: the general strike of the proletarians. The idea itself was not a new one; it was probably first set forth in print by a London tavern keeper whose establishment was frequented by workers in the 1820s. On one Great Day the workers of a nation or of the whole world, already neatly organized in *syndicats,* would proclaim the general strike. All the facilities of bourgeois life would be abruptly halted, and in the face of this unanimity among the workers the middle classes would throw in the sponge and turn the society over to them. The goal of the heroic proletariat would be achieved. A historic myth like the general strike was not a truth in any positivistic, scientific sense—it would become a reality and a truth only when men passionately believed it.

This essentially mythic prospect of the general strike was supposed to exert upon workers the same powerful fascination as the Apocalypse, Resurrection, and Last Judgment had upon early Christians. It did not matter whether the takeover following the general strike would actually transpire in the direct manner Sorel outlined or whether there would be a series of combats. The keystone was the myth itself, the faith in the myth true or false, the unreasoning confidence that would give cohesion to working-class groups and bind them in a creative, communal will. For Marx's insistence upon the forging of a revolutionary communist consciousness—a rationalist conception if ever there was one—Sorel would substitute a blind belief in the general strike as the myth that would triumph because of its overwhelming emotional appeal. From an inchoate mass the proletariat, under the spell of the myth, would be shaped into a unified force. Sorel was indifferent to the technical accuracy of the prognoses of Marxist economics; the myth would make the general system true. The pragmatism gone mad of some student confrontations in the late 1960s was imbued with the same spirit: Action and will first, thought to follow in the rear.

This mysticism of action and denigration of thought are easily perceived to be the intellectual's self-loathing. There is a quest for activity that will make the thinking egotist oblivious of himself through submergence in a movement. That movement must be expansive, capable of endless dilation until it swallows up the whole universe of man. It must promise justice, recreate a moral atmosphere, shed blood if necessary, demand devotion to the point of self-sacrifice, pose issues in such a manner that they cannot be compromised, loathe haggling, disdain reasoning in propositions because those who have followed reasoners through long and tortuous alleyways have ended up in a cul-de-sac.

Sorel identified as dangerous enemies of the proletarian utopia the French imitators of the German Social Democratic revisionist Eduard Bernstein. Bernstein's name had become widely associated with a watery revision of the Marxist doctrine to allow for a nonrevolutionary gliding from a state of capitalism into socialism without a total breakdown of the system, without violence, without any interruption in the cultural continuity of society. For Sorel this revisionism was the greatest peril to the myth of class conflict, general strike, proletarian identity, monastic isolation, and cohesion. It could be likened in its absurdity to an appeal directed to a militant Church Father of the late Roman Empire that a compromise be effectuated between Christianity and paganism. The potency of the proletarian myth resided in its revolutionary fervor. Any talk of peace implied the destruction of its very essence. How the new society of producers would come into being, the process itself, was the core of the revolution, not a peripheral matter of techniques or mere mechanics.

To Sorel there was no such thing as abstract truth. The myth proved itself in action; it could not be demonstrated by rational argumentation. Inevitably he latched on to some versions of the pragmatist philosophy of William James to bolster his theory. (James's will to believe, with its brilliant complement, the analysis of the varieties of religious experience, was brother to the Sorelian conception.)[29] Ideas were real insofar as they served life, and some of the most bizarre and irrational ones fulfilled life-giving purposes. Religious illumination in the end created a new man. Sorel, a Marxist, would shake himself free of the rationalist Hegelian framework of Marxism and salvage the emotional appeal of the proletarian revolution. His Marxism was a peculiar syncretism. The materialist theory of history was fundamentally correct: New technological and economic conditions dictated the emergence of new myths. But once they were born they achieved a life and potency of their own. Marx had underestimated the compelling power of emotion and of irrational drives; these alone were creative. In *The Illusions of Progress,* Sorel disassociated Marx's determinism from his general theory and repudiated its Hegelian roots in order to preserve the creativity of the myth of the proletariat. "The march toward socialism will not come about in a manner as simple, as necessary, and consequently as easy to describe in advance as Marx had supposed. Marx's Hegelian leanings led him to admit, without being generally aware of it, that history advances (at least with regard to peoples considered to be blessed with a superior civilization) under the influence of the force of the mysterious *Weltgeist*. This ideal agent imposes on matter the obligation of realizing ends whose logical order is finally discovered by men of genius. Like all romantics, Marx supposed that the *Weltgeist* operated in the heads of his friends."[30]

On the subject of violence, the most notorious element in Sorel's proletarian myth, he was often paradoxical. The bourgeois engineer who lived a retiring life with his wife was deliberately trying to *épater le bourgeois*. His apology for violence assumed many forms. He assured the bourgeois that violence had always been an expression of man's relationship to man. Contemporary Frenchmen should not pride themselves on the taming of man in their society; he had remained as intractable as ever, only becoming more cunning—a recognizable Nietzschean theme and one upon which Freud would dwell. All great movements—Christianity, the French Revolution—had had their violent moments; why suppose that violence would abruptly disappear from human nature? But having indulged in this forensic play, Sorel repeatedly affirmed that he was not an apostle of violence exulting in rivers of blood. If the myth was to live, conflict and open clashes were inevitable. Real, not factitious, confrontations of the two hostile moralities of the bourgeoisie and the proletariat would take place. If the workers were well organized, however, the final showdown need not be too destructive of human life. The eventual settlement did not have to take the shape of a barbaric obliteration of culture, as some bourgeois fearful of the "dangerous classes" had prophesied. In arguments that find parallels in Lenin's writings, Sorel often observed that in any conflict it was the bourgeois who usually took the brutal offensive. As an amateur historian, he comforted his contemporaries, as he incited them to battle, with the reflection that the number of early Christian martyrs was probably exaggerated by the hagiographers.

Georges Sorel would have his Proudhon and his Marx too. From Proudhon he learned a fierce hatred of the state and its institutions, an emotion heightened by his experience of the parliamentary regimes of Europe before World War I, a trust in the spontaneity and heroic qualities of small groups working for themselves, expressing their will in labor rather than political chatter, and above all his admiration for self-sufficient, ascetic men. The free *syndicat* or voluntary union of workers on a small scale was the ideal form of proletarian life which he hoped would triumph over the financiers and corrupt politicians, especially the socialists like Jaurès, who rose to fame through the strength of their saliva. From Marx Sorel derived the myth of the victorious proletariat and its history. It was not scientific socialism that made him adhere to Marxism, nor the Hegelian determinism that was attached to the doctrine, but the force of the proletarian myth, embodied in a class that would be made to believe in its own power and virtue. The historical position of the proletariat rendered them capable of believing in the will of their class. On the other hand, they could be hoodwinked by socialist politicians who put the workers to sleep with fantasies of the inevitable coming of a Marxist society and became as addicted to soft living as the decadent bourgeoisie. Bureaucratized Marxism robbed the proletariat of will and spontaneity, of vital energy. In the anarchist

Proudhon, Sorel recognized the spirit of the future, in Marx stripped of his positivistic scientism the grand formulator of the proletarian myth.

Though at one time he played with monarchism as a possibility, Sorel never believed deeply in its prospects because its leaders were too literary and had no popular base. In the end, either Mussolini or Lenin would do; they had the genius to rouse their countrymen from the torpor of finance capitalism and the corruption of talking politicians. They could achieve what Proudhon hoped for—release energies, make men creative, rescue them from sloth. This amalgam of the spirit of anarchy destroying an old order gone soft and the Marxist myth of an order rooted in the might of the proletariat is composed of elements from antagonistic sources; but this is not anomalous in the history of Western utopian thought.

"Le Violent," as the courteous, gentlemanly Sorel was called, was committed to a utopia of absolute principles internalized by a heroic proletariat reaching the height of human capacity in the course of the struggle against the existing bourgeois order and its state. There was, of course, no final conquest because the utopia lay in the conflict itself. Progress as an abstract philosophy of history was illusory, but in this respect Sorel was not alone among utopians. A cyclical conception of history, even a tone of pessimism and irony, has been combined with an activist utopia. Here he was closer to Proudhon than to the Marx of the Eternal Sabbath after the revolutionary apocalypse. Sorel had no fantasy of a new man everlasting. He wanted to make a heroic noble warrior in life and work of the man whom he saw before him, but he never imagined that man would remain in so exalted a condition.

As a popular theorist—and he is surely not a major thinker—Sorel has been adapted for diverse ends. Mussolini was reputed to have been inspired by him, though recent literature on the formative period of Italian Fascist thought indicates that Sorel was picked up by Il Duce after he was already in power and was preening himself with an intellectual ancestry. In his last years Sorel himself would praise anyone who stood up to fight for his "myth," and when the French proletarian movement became bureaucratized he turned both to the rightist nationalists of the Action française and to Lenin, with equal aplomb, as agents of the heroic utopia. The heroic utopia is an essential ingredient of contemporary movements of violent protest against social injustice and is the energizing drive behind that potent, unpredictable international force, terrorism. One group's hero is another's treacherous villain.

It is difficult to maintain vast numbers of people in a constant state of heroic fantasizing, but the annals of modern rebellion are not lacking in protagonists of an ascetic, heroic character. Many possessed by the abstraction of a heroic utopia can slide from one ideal to another, relatively indifferent to the content of the utopia. Nationalism, anarchism, communism, even bourgeois democracies have produced their heroic corps. Whoever they are, their major figures are touched by a rhetoric that is not very different from Sorel's—its attractions are fateful. The heroes come from all classes and nations. Because of the highly technical organizational requirements of heroic action, leaders in modern times are often recruited from the middle classes.

Sorel's continued appeal probably rests on his powerful invective against social hypocrisy, against bombastic oratorical principles. The Sorelian myth should be distinguished from the Hitlerian great lie, because the myth is not a mere instrumentality, not a deception, but a morality, a way of life that becomes a higher truth as it is embraced by heroic adepts. Sorel was not an image maker or a mythmaker. He found the myth in the heart or emotions of a new proletarian elite, a potential body of heroes, and he aimed to protect the myth from destruction in its early fragile, vulnerable stages. In sum, his utopia is a rather baroque version of a death–and–resurrection fantasy for mankind. There is a certain apprehensiveness in Sorel's thought. Without any countervailing force, the evil in nature would triumph; hence the urgent necessity for heroic moral action to stave off decay. In the absence of a myth, of moral enthusiasm, societies tend to crumble. At heart this doctrine is not alien from that of either Spengler or Toynbee. The bourgeois have no morality, Saint-Simon had said earlier in the century; no justice, Proudhon charged; no myth, Sorel accused.

PART VIII

The Twilight of Utopia

William Morris

frontispiece to E. L. Cary,
William Morris, 1902

32

Utopia Victoriana

THE FIRST SEVEN decades of the nineteenth century had produced a vast body of polemical, critical thought about the nature of contemporary society, accompanied by grand discursive systems that laid down the principles for a future ideal world. During this period there were few novels of intrinsic worth dealing with a utopian society. Cabet's *Voyage en Icarie,* Hawthorne's disenchanted tale about Brook Farm, *The Blithedale Romance,* and Chernyshevskii's *Chto delat'? (What Is to Be Done?),* written in the Peter-and-Paul Fortress in 1862 and published in 1863, all reflect earlier utopian thought, but they are weak renderings of the power and complexity of the great systems. In the European political arena utopian thought tended to become indistinguishable from solemn revolutionary pronouncements or nonrevolutionary radical party programs. The utopian polemist was often engaged in the formation of a social movement or a political alliance, and painting pretty pictures of the future, though occasionally resorted to, was not a favored method of winning converts. The major demonstrations of the inevitability of utopia were historical and scientific or Christian and moralist. The declaration of immediate revolutionary objectives—the English Charter, the French right to work—or the promulgation of a set of utopian principles was enough to attract true believers. As the slogans were orated, the mere sound of the words induced a utopian state of feeling. Humanity, the end of exploitation, brotherhood, universal suffrage, liberty, equality—each new adept read into the phrases the satisfaction of his most expansive desires.

By the 1870s, after the defeat of the Paris Commune, it was becoming evident even to the more militant that there would be no world revolution, at least for a while, that a new social structure would not be installed overnight. The wars of the utopian systems that had developed in the first half of the century continued, but they were fought in secret revolutionary conclaves or within the councils of recognized political parties, whose radical reform programs were now conceived as long-term enterprises. With their chicanery and compromises and internal struggles, the radical organizations began to resemble markedly the older political parties.

The Rebirth of the Utopian Novel

Since the revolution itself was indefinitely postponed and men were deflected from direct action, the time was propitious for a rebirth of the utopian novel. Its tone would befit a nonrevolutionary age. It was not strident or violent; a rose-colored portrayal of the future replaced the call to arms. The enthusiasm generated among the readers of these novels, who formed societies, clubs, even international associations to discuss the good life depicted by the authors, intrigues the analyst of a century later. That Edward Bellamy's *Looking Back-*

759

ward, 2000–1887 (1888), Theodor Hertzka's *Freiland: Ein sociales Zukunftsbild* (*Freeland: A Social Anticipation*), 1890, William Morris' *News from Nowhere; or, An Epoch of Rest, Being Some Chapters from a Utopian Romance* (1890) inspired thousands of people with what they believed to be a new and unprecedented vision is difficult to credit as one struggles through their didactic, wooden prose. While a utopian innovation makes its appearance from time to time, particularly in William Morris, for the most part these novels and the scores of contemporary imitations that shall be nameless are derivative, syncretistic, and infinitely boring. They are patchwork utopias, and anyone addicted to nineteenth-century utopian literature can detect in them bits and pieces of the thought of Fourier, Saint-Simon, Weitling, Proudhon, Marx, Auguste Comte. Marx was rarely named, but he cast a long shadow. Though largely unread, his ideas, like musk, had begun to suffuse the intellectual atmosphere. Even in novelistic utopias written to forestall a bloody Marxist revolution, categories of his thought penetrated as the new visionaries proposed to do what he had always rejected—portray in detail a future social order. Paradoxically, utopian novels such as Bellamy's *Looking Backward* were assimilated into communist propaganda, and if Marxist leaders like Lenin refrained from violating Marx's prohibition against painting images of the future, street-corner orators were far less hesitant about lifting large sections from the novels in order to capture their audiences.

In the Marxist world Chernyshevskii alone among the utopian novelists of the nineteenth century enjoyed a special dispensation. The aging Marx kept Chernyshevskii's portrait in his study and often expressed admiration for the revolutionary who languished in czarist prisons; Lenin admired him as a great Russian socialist.[1] The novel *What Is to Be Done?*, which portrayed the new human being in the person of the austere, heroic, rationalist, unsentimental Véra Pávlovna, founder of cooperatives of seamstresses, was hardly Marxist in spirit, for it believed in conversion by persuasion, but it appears to have exerted a profound emotional effect on Lenin. It is known that the book was a favorite of his elder brother, the revolutionary executed by the czarist regime, and that Lenin treasured his brother's copy. The novel left its trace at least in the title of one of Lenin's most trenchant revolutionary pronouncements on communist tactics. But the other Victorian utopian novels were of a different character, and had Marx lived to read them they would doubtless have called down upon themselves the same sneers that he bestowed upon Cabet's *Voyage en Icarie*. His taste in literature ran to the tragic—Shakespeare and the Greek dramatists.

The thornier problems of man's affective and psychic relationships, expressly his sexuality, which had absorbed Saint-Simonians and Fourierists, and the apocalyptic prologue that was bound up with the Marxist utopia were bypassed in the Victorian utopia, as the novelists set about fashioning pleasant state socialist or free socialist or state capitalist utopias. No blood was shed in the storybook transition from anarchic industrialism to the agreeable planned society. The Victorian family was preserved intact, with all its saccharine-sweet male-female relationships and its prudery. Labor, production, and consumption were rationally organized in a variety of ways: by making credit freely available in the manner of Proudhon, or by allowing for associations of workers who would have access to free capital without interest, or by the formation of industrial armies under state control. Marx's labor theory of value in a vulgarized form was often at the bottom of these pictures of working societies. Each man had a right to the full fruits of his labor—that was the overriding principle. How to measure the value of different types of labor allowed for the introduction of numerous variations on a theme, and most of the utopias became a bookkeeper's dream of glory. Idleness was prohibited and the leisure classes abolished, as the utopias offered equal opportunity to the industrious and basic equality among all men. Hunger, want, unemployment, and disease were quickly eliminated. Security was provided for the sick, the aged, and the very young. Elements of incentive were incorporated in the society but there were no gross inequalities; elements of economic freedom were preserved but there was no abject poverty. Monopoly capital was universally recognized as the prime evil. Regulated state capitalism or state socialism, in which merit was rewarded and people lived more or less equally, avoided the horrors of revolution and permitted an easy changeover to the new order.

One way to bring about the new society under a constitutional democracy was to vote for the establishment of state enterprises that would attract labor, pay the workers in scrip honored in government-owned, non-profit-making stores, while private enterprise would see its labor force slowly dwindle away and its gold become worthless. The former exploiters would be left to wither on the vine or to seek equal treatment in government industries. The whole "revolution" was envisaged as peaceful and gradual, though it required no more than a generation to be effected. The Marxist threat of the slaughter of the bourgeoisie was dispelled, the class war would not materialize, and the dictatorship of the proletariat would never be installed. Small wonder that the easy birth of the new society as recounted by Edward Bellamy allayed the apprehensions of middle-class intellectuals and literate artisans on the morrow of the Haymarket riots in the United States.

Though many of the novelistic utopian societies of the latter part of the nineteenth century were socialist in character, their socialism was less total and uncompromising than that of Marxist doctrine. Like the "revisionism" of the turn of the century among Social Democrats, it could take on different colorations in the countries of the Western world. It might eschew the very name socialism because of its dangerous associations and call itself nationalism, as in Bellamy's work. Oscar Wilde and George Bernard Shaw and the English Fabians were utopian socialists of this vintage. In the same spirit Theodore Herzl wrote a Zionist utopia of state socialism, *Old Newland*. The social utopia could even start out as an imperialist venture—without conflict, of course: Hertzka's *Freeland* began with a peaceful invasion of Kenya.

Looking Backward

Edward Bellamy from Chicopee Falls, a small textile town in western Massachusetts, editor of a newspaper in Springfield for many years, Theodor Hertzka, a Viennese economist who was suddenly overwhelmed with the vision of his *Freeland* as a solution to the class struggles in Europe, and William Morris, the Oxonian pre-Raphaelite who always considered himself a disciple of Karl Marx, make strange bedfellows. And yet their novels, which were surely read by more people in the nineteenth century than the combined writings of Saint-Simon, Fourier, Comte, and Marx, exude a common spirit and belong together. Victorian socialism is perhaps the best label for their teachings. Whether they were writing under the reign of the great Queen herself, under the Emperor Franz Josef, or under President Grover Cleveland, their utopias reproduce the same genteel atmosphere, in which lady and gentleman converts to solidarity and the communal ideal carry on their anemic, passionless activities and pallid relationships. The literary devices that introduce the utopias differ. Bellamy's hero, a proper Bostonian suffering from insomnia, is mesmerized in an underground bedchamber where he has sought refuge from noise and awakens in the year 2000. Hertzka reports on the colonization of a piece of Masai territory. And Morris' hero has a vision as he lies in bed in a dingy Hammersmith house in London. But if there were a population exchange among them, all the inhabitants would readily adjust to their new utopian environments. Nor would the citizens of other utopias composed during the period—and even a gifted writer like Anatole France tried his hand at the genre in *Sur la pierre blanche* (*The White Stone*), 1903—be aliens in this imaginary world. The futuristic gadgetry of Jules Verne's imaginary societies is only more abundant and prophetic than Bellamy's stage props, which make life in late-nineteenth-century utopia so stagnantly comfortable, notwithstanding Bellamy's formal commitment to a doctrine of spiritual advancement. Despite their socialist trappings, these are essentially nostalgic utopias that have either facilely tamed or bypassed the dynamism of industrial-scientific civilization.

With all the triteness of invention in *Looking Backward,* the explicit psychological ideal that Bellamy posed for his society has a measure of interest: Perfection is defined as the negative of present reality, the reverse of what he saw in the lonely crowd of Boston in the 1880s, "faces unmarred by arrogance or servility, by envy or greed, by anxious care or feverish ambition, and stately forms of men and women who had never known fear of a fellow man or depended on his favor."[2] The utopia had returned to calm felicity as embodied in Victorian gentility. Grandeur was not entirely eradicated, but restricted to "gorgeous public palaces"; dwellings, while simple, were full of conveniences.[3] Through the utopia runs an American modification of the Rousseauan concept of independence. The frontiersman's or colonist's freedom from fear of his fellow man—perhaps always something of a fiction—was here recaptured. *Looking Backward* thus has two themes. The obvious one is an emphasis on the joys of the year 2000 by contrast with the woes of 1887, the other is a longing for an early America, utopianized, that had vanished. In a postscript that took the form of a letter to the editor of the *Boston Transcript,* Bellamy unequivocally claimed his place in the ranks of progressionists, with sentiments that echo, perhaps unconsciously, those of the early Saint-Simon: "*Looking Backward* was written in the belief that the Golden Age lies before us and not behind us, and is not far away."[4]

A Victorian ambivalence toward sexuality that pervades Bellamy's novels is evident in one of his notebooks (now at Harvard), where the rhetoric sounds like a travesty of classical figures of speech: "So shall passions, the strongest in man's nature, which have hitherto been chiefly directed to his preservation by their diversions into sexuality and the family relations, be directed to the general advancement and elevation of the human type; just as a steamship when driven by tempests has to put all her steam to work to keep from drifting to leeward, but when the storm ceases, by aid of the said steam power, is able to rush like a railroad train on her course."[5] The idea of sublimation has never received a more technological, if unpoetic, expression.

Bellamy is far more absorbed with the problem of incentives in a socialist economy than any of the other major Victorian utopians, and his recipe is an admixture of kindergarten prizes and quiet threats of harsh deprivation. Prizes are given to virtually everybody; and only the most incompetent and inveterate idlers fail to rise at least a notch in the course of their working careers. Gradations and minor promotions within each class are numerous, since it is intended that no form of merit should go wholly unrecognized. But the stick is there, in the background. Bellamy does not share William Morris' or even Hertzka's confidence in human nature; his Calvinist undergarments show. Though their description may not occupy much space, cruel sanctions are invoked against malingerers in the industrial army: "A man able to duty, and persistently refusing, is sentenced to solitary imprisonment on bread and water till he consents."[6]

Salaries are equal, and men vie for status and honor instead of wealth. When Bellamy wishes to mark differences in position, he has recourse to an element from the oldest utopian tradition of Western society, sanctified in Plato and Hesiod, a variant on the myth of the three metallic races: "Every industry has its emblematic device," explains Doctor Leete to the awakened dreamer, "and this, in the shape of a metallic badge so small that you might not see it unless you knew where to look, is all the insigns which the men of the [industrial] army wear, except where public convenience demands a distinctive uniform. This badge is the same in form for all grades of industry, but while the badge of the third grade is iron, that of the second grade is silver, and that of the first is gilt."[7]

Men strive without monetary recompense because the high places in the nation are reserved for the highest class of persons. Rank in the industrial army is the only avenue to honor and prestige, except in art and the professions. Distinctions based upon merit, not wealth, are good in and of themselves, and position and respect are recognized as having intrinsic worth. There are also a few perquisites, minor privileges, and immunities enjoyed by men who attain to the superior class. Effort is rewarded; but though the stronger are selected as leaders for the "interest of the common weal,"[8] the principle of equality is not grossly violated. At the highest levels, men exert themselves from an inner need for achievement. The aristocracy of merit is not trumpeted, paraded, or advertised. It is intended to arouse as little envy as possible among the less successful; yet there is constantly before every man's eye the desirability of reaching the grade next above his own. Bellamy's is a subtly scaled meritocracy, in a setting that combines American competitiveness with a welfare society of relative equality in goods and services.

In the national organization of labor with its numerous offices of employment exchange, every man naturally and spontaneously selects "the harness which sets most lightly on himself . . . that in which he can pull best."[9] Natural aptitudes and equal education are the keys to the system; neither mercenary considerations nor social prejudices hamper men in the choice of their life's work. But the harness remains the symbol of the new society. All must pull, fit themselves into the right harness or it would chafe. Work is not idealized; it is a disagreeable obligation to be discharged with the greatest dispatch. Hours are short, there are regular vacations, and men pant for the moment of liberation from the industrial army at forty-five, when real enjoyment begins. Longevity makes this final period the important part of life. There is a reversal of the contemporary values of stages in the epigenetic cycle.

Women also belong to the industrial army, but as an auxiliary force under their own general-in-chief, who, by the way, occupies a post in the presidential cabinet. Marriage does not exempt women from labor service. As Dr. Leete explains, they "have no house-keeping responsibilities now, you know, and a husband is not a baby that he should be cared for."[10] The good doctor contrasts the lot of women in his society with the constricted, unhappy lives of nineteenth-century women, rich or poor, who had no interests beyond the family and "no refuge in the breezy outdoor world of human affairs" from the great sorrows and petty frets that beset mankind. The symbol of female equality in the new Boston is the credit card, issued for a sum as large as that allowed the men. But equal status does not imply unisex; the differences between the sexes are accentuated rather than obliterated, with the result that "the piquancy which each has for the other" is enhanced. Since both share alike rights, privileges, and obligations, girls no longer want to be boys, parents no longer prefer male children, and with no anxieties about earning a living, much more thought is devoted to the tender passion. Moreover, the power of women to bestow happiness on men has increased proportionately with their own contentment.[11]

When Dr. Leete tries to explain what cements the society, he falls back upon the early-nineteenth-century principle, or feeling, of solidarity or humanity or brotherhood of man. "The title of every man, woman, and child to the means of existence rests on no basis less plain, broad, and simple than the fact that they are fellows of one race—members of one human family."[12] Through education these fine phrases become "as real and as vital as physical fraternity."[13] Hertzka gets by, or almost, without this emotion; he tries to build his society on old-fashioned, utilitarian self-interest. In Morris the system itself generates fraternity as a flame does heat. Bellamy, in answer to the question as to why everybody has a right to equal sustenance, again moves into an economic argument based on a diluted Marxist value theory: All of us in this generation have inherited the accumulated technological achievements of previous generations of mankind, and every man alive today has a right to an equal share in this treasury.[14] All past humanity is one value-creating, laboring body to whose products we are heir.

But in the end the justification for the system is its rational efficiency and lack of waste. And Bellamy introduces an ominous analogy: "The effectiveness of the working force of a nation, under the myriad-headed leadership of private capital, even if the leaders were not mutual enemies, as compared with that which it attains under a single head, may be likened to the military efficiency of a mob, or a horde of barbarians with a thousand petty chiefs, as compared with that of a disciplined army under one general—such a fighting machine, for example, as the German army in the time of Von Moltke."[15]

Hertzka's Freeland

Dr. Theodor Hertzka belonged to the Manchester school of Austrian economists; in 1872 he became economics editor of *Die Neue Freie Presse,* Vienna's most important newspaper; and in 1886 he wrote a ponderous work entitled *Die Gesetze der sozialen Entwicklung* (The Laws of Social Development). Then this respectable mentor of the Austrian bourgeoisie had a sudden illumination, and produced a utopian novel called *Freeland,* a vision of the future society. The economist turned fiction writer achieved an instantaneous success: The German edition of 1890 was promptly translated into English, and in cities and towns throughout Germany and Austria, Freeland societies mushroomed, very much like the spontaneous multiplication of Bellamy societies about the same time. At a meeting of the International Freeland Society in Vienna, it was announced that a tract of land in British East Africa had been put at the society's disposal.

In the introduction to his novel, Hertzka avowed himself a disciple of Mill, Marx, and Darwin, and declared his society to be a combination of their ideas stripped of their erroneous and odious notions. The new order would be as liberal and free as Mill would have desired, but it would forever emancipate mankind from the periodic crises of overproduction and the catastrophic class conflicts that were becoming endemic in the European world. The technological society was here to stay, but it was not indissolubly linked with a system of protective duties, cartels, trusts, guild agitations, and strikes. All of these evils were manifestations of the desperate resistance of the classes engaged in production to the deleterious consequences of the anarchy engendered by monopoly. It was absurd that advanced technology and increasing facility in the production of wealth should bring only misery and ruin in their train.

Darwin provided Hertzka with metaphors about the necessity of man's adjusting to his new technological environment: He must either adapt or perish. Darwin's law of evolution in nature taught Hertzka that when social arrangements ceased to be optimal and were no longer consonant with the contemporary conditions of human existence, they had to be replaced by new ones. "For in the struggle for existence, that which is out of date not only *may* but *must* give place to that which is more in harmony with the actual conditions." [16] The languages of Darwin and Marx were wedded to each other. Marx had been mistaken in arguing that capitalism stopped the growth of wealth by crises of overproduction for the market; the present system was flawed because it prevented the consumption of the surplus produce. If a mechanism could be invented for providing capital without infringing on individual liberty or violating justice, if the levying of interest could be abolished without resorting to communistic controls, a free social order of capitalists operating in association would arise. Easy credit and the end of monopoly would allow for the best of both worlds. Individual freedom would be secure and the evils of capitalism that now inhibited consumption would be banished. The staid economist waxed dithyrambic: "My intense delight at making this discovery robbed me of the calm necessary to the prosecution of the abstract investigations upon which I was engaged. Before my mind's eye arose scenes which the reader will find in the following pages—tangible, living pictures of a commonwealth based upon the most perfect freedom and equity, and which needs nothing to convert it into a reality but the will of a number of resolute men."[17]

Hertzka compared himself to Bacon: As his seventeenth-century forerunner had abandoned his scientific studies for a time in order to compose the *New Atlantis,* so Hertzka had interrupted his academic pursuits to write a "political romance" based on sober reality.[18] The initial founders of Freeland would not be philanthropists but hardheaded men acting out of individual, commonplace self-interest. The structural unit would be the voluntary organization of workers in a specific occupation who had banded together in order to get the full produce of their labor and to whom credit was generously available without charge. This type of organization had to be cleansed of every remnant of the old, servile relationship to an employer, thereby solving successfully the problem of social emancipation.[19] The desiderata of a free, cooperative industrial enterprise were set forth in an example: To establish an iron works in Freeland it was not imperative that the workers themselves be versed in every aspect of iron manufacture. All they had to know was what sort of persons they should place at the head of the enterprise and how to delegate to them sufficient authority to manage the work properly, while never letting the reins of control slip from their own hands. At the outset of Hertzka's rational, liberal system, a committee to rule on applications for funds is chosen among the workers' associations petitioning for capital. Later, as the initial outlays are repaid by profitable ventures, surplus capital is so great that credit is virtually for the asking. The ultimate principle of *Freeland* is that every citizen has a right to the fruits of existing productive capital, which itself is ownerless. The sharp light of universal publicity puts an end to the secrets and conspiracies of monopoly. The incentive remains self-interest, for every member has a claim on the net profits proportionate to the amount of work he has contributed. Some allowance is made for older workers, and the pay of directors is determined by giving their participation a value in ordinary work hours.

The body of the novel is devoted to the story of the settlement of the first Freeland by colonists who accepted the principles of the association, along with reports from starry-eyed visitors who saw it operating in high gear. The members of the society meeting at The Hague under the direction of the economist Karl Strahl adopted all decisions unanimously and voted to establish their utopia in Kenya among the nomadic Masai. Africa was chosen to avoid colliding with existing societies, as early utopians had once sought refuge in the American Midwest. The site of the colony was a mountainous district to the east of the Victoria Nyanza, between latitudes 1° north and 1° south and between longitudes 34° and 38° east. In planning for the settlement, the colonists ordered four light steel mortars from Krupp in Essen. The object was not to use the murderous weapons against any foe, but, if occasion arose, to preserve peace the more easily through the terror the mortars would inspire.[20] When an advance party of Freelanders met up with the Masai, the Africans were assured that they would not be forced to give up any land, even though the Europeans could compel them to do so. If, however, free passage through Masai territory were not peaceably granted, the Freelanders would know how to impose their will.[21] While ancient voyagers to utopia had had to contend with terrible storms and shipwrecks, the obstacles of the optimistic Freeland settlers were easy to surmount. The expedition to their chosen homeland ran like a well-organized safari—a few cannonballs shot into the air and the most ferocious savages were transformed into blood brothers.

Rhapsodic visitors a few decades later found a society with all the physical comforts of capitalism, the freedom of liberalism, the security of socialism, and the merriment of a Wienerwald carnival. At the National Palace of Freeland sat twelve supreme boards of administration and twelve representative bodies. For the rest, it was a land of workers' associations open to all newcomers who wished to join in a particular enterprise. There were large departments of statistics, warehouses, and banks, but the Freelanders economized on other state expenditures since they required neither judges, nor police, nor soldiers. Criminals were considered morally diseased and were treated medically. Women teachers who had flocked to the settlement were quickly snatched up in marriage and they ran ideal ménages. An Italian diplomat who sojourned among the Freelanders was much taken with the graceful, princesslike ladies colorfully dressed in raiment that recalled ancient Greece. Everyone was "cultured," even tillers of the soil, usually Negroes with a higher level of civilization than rural Europeans. The whole land was an Eden, illuminated by electric arc lamps. "Imagine a fairy garden covering a space of nearly forty square miles, filled with tens of thousands of charming tastily designed small houses and hundreds of fabulously splendid palaces; add the intoxicating odours of all kinds of flowers and the singing of innumerable nightingales—and set all this in the framework of a landscape as grand and as picturesque as any part of the world can show; and then, if your fancy is vigorous enough, you may form some mild conception of the delight with which this marvellous city filled me . . . In many of the houses which we passed could be heard sounds of mirth and gaiety . . . the shores of the lake were full of life every evening until midnight . . . On broad airy terraces and in the gardens around them sat or sauntered the inhabitants in larger or smaller groups. The clinking of glasses, music, silvery laughter, fell upon the ear; in short everything indicated that here the evenings were devoted to the most cheerful society."[22] A new era had been inaugurated in architecture, whose nobility of form rivaled the Grecian and whose grandeur outdid the most massive Egyptian monuments.[23] Bathing establishments were luxurious, and so were theatres, opera houses, and concert halls. Private houses were unique in aspect, half-Moorish, half-Grecian. Hertzka was answering the charge of dull uniformity that utopias like Cabet's had provoked.

The Cokaygne utopia of Attic comedy with its abundance of sensate pleasures was reborn with appropriate Victorian restraints. Technology and a rational organization of labor took the place of ancient magic and gave the imaginary society verisimilitude and, alas, a deadly earnestness. *Freeland* is gadgety, full of push-button telephones and labor-saving machinery, like Bellamy's *Looking Backward*. Air is artificially cooled, mildly "ozonized." The Italian diplomat gets better service from "iron slaves" than he ever received in the Hotel Bristol in Paris. The servant problem has been eliminated: In response to a bell, a worker from an Association for Rendering Personal Service appears. While the household sleeps, the Association worker cleans, moving about with such celerity that 181 man-hours of labor a year suffice to maintain a tidy home. Competition among the Personal Service Associations keeps domestic help on their toes and transforms them into zealous artisans. There are no attendants at dinner to inhibit the company. A cupboard in the dining room wall yields an "inexhaustible series of eatables."[24] The Food Association stocks hot and cold dishes in separate compartments and does the washing up. The Freelanders ride around on velocipedes whose motive power resides in the elasticity of a spiral spring wound up tightly in workshops of the Association for Transport. The vehicle can move at eleven miles an hour for twelve miles, when its springs have to be changed at a service station. Lake streamers do not belch smoke nor do their whistles shriek. But attention to material comfort implies no slight to the life of the mind. "The academies, museums, laboratories, institutions for experiment and research seemed endless."[25] Libraries have lost their forbidding aspect and the hush of sacred precincts; in addition to storing books, they serve as cafés and conversation salons, amenities in the care of the Association for Providing Refreshments, and people frequent them to study, entertain themselves with books, or chat with acquaintances.[26]

Beneficent social institutions have decreased the incidence of disease, and for those who fall ill sanatoria are widely available, so that there are no poor sick lacking treatment. Physicians are publicly paid officials who have passed their examinations, and aspirants are trained by accompanying their elders on house visits. Even in this area freedom is not infringed upon, and anyone can practice medicine, though the possibility that a doctor without credentials will attract patients is remote.

The Freelanders look younger than their years, and goodness and nobility of mind are impressed upon their features. The tone of society is so cheerful, pleasant, and benign it is difficult to remember that at the precise moment when Hertzka was fabricating his African utopia in Vienna, his neighbor Sigmund Freud was making discoveries which put the quietus on such fantasies, at least for a generation.

Morris from Nowhere

In William Morris' *News from Nowhere,* an old antiquarian succinctly defined the fundamental principle of the new society as "freedom for every man to do what he can do best."[27] This ideal was predicated on a number of prior conceptions—that there was such a thing as a unique capacity in every man, that if men were free they would choose to express that unique capacity, and that it was best to organize society on the basis of unique capacities. Beyond the innate need for self-actualization, men sought a great variety of things; but there were some they really wanted in contrast with others they only appeared to want. The discernment of this distinction was the psychological key to Morris' utopia.

Simplistic utopian psychology usually assumed that if a group of people voiced their collective demands and published a manifesto, they meant what they said. They knew what they wanted, so to speak. Ever since Thomas More, utopians had distinguished between desires they allowed and desires they would repress. In Morris, the answer is on the face of it more subtle. Men truly wanted only *some* of the products of labor; desires for other products were factitious or false. Morris analyzed the old economic system as loaded with fake, artificial "necessaries" created by the capitalist market in a never-ending series. In his mind, these were clearly distinguishable from the genuine necessaries, but the evil capitalistic system had rendered men incapable of perceiving the difference. And by involving themselves in the breeding of sham needs, men became burdened with excessive labor. Work in itself was not an evil—quite the contrary—but a prodigious amount of labor that was repugnant to them and gave them no artistic satisfaction was a major source of unhappiness. The market economy had constrained men to work for superfluous products for which they had no proper use. Artificially stimulated consumption had tied them to the system. Once its chains were broken by the revolution and, in a state of calm self-analysis, they sought to know their authentic needs, the inhabitants of Nowhere would find that they had to do only a modicum of work to supply their wants. Morris' utopia is anti-Fourierist and anti-expansive, since the multiplication of desires and their amplification and orchestration are not good in and of themselves. Left to act without coercion, in perfect freedom, men would not crave excess in anything. Fourier had dangled the ancient Cokaygne fantasy before prospective converts—a plethora of gastronomic delights at each of the five to seven meals a day served up in the phalanstery. Morris' public restaurants served meals that were dainty. His citizens did not seek gross oral or genital gratification—any more than Morris himself did in his personal life.

Morris sometimes starts at the other end of the sumptuary problem and poses the question as to what work is intrinsically good and what work is evil. One answer is that work leading to the production of fraudulent, sham necessaries is evil. Another is set forth in a discussion of machinery: Only work that is pleasurable is good. Here we have returned to the Fourierist world, though with a difference. The conception of attractive work has been taken over from Fourier, but the basic principle of attraction has changed. While for Fourier labor was palatable only in combination with libidinal relationships, for Morris attraction rests on the satisfaction of an artistic need within man. Not since the architectural ideal-city plans of the Renaissance had the aesthetic propensity of mankind occupied so pivotal a position in Western utopian thought. There was no blind Luddite antagonism toward machinery, but Morris was less impressed with the benefits of technology than either Hertzka or Bellamy. Though his utopians did not discard the machines inherited from the past that were useful in the light of the new standards, they were not intoxicated with innovative mechanization and were quite willing to be regressive in this area of human endeavor; when the machines failed to produce works of art, they were quietly scrapped one after another. The formula is simple: If the labor is irksome, relegate it to the machines; if it is pleasurable—and it is assumed that a great many people will discover a natural pleasure in performing manually a variety of tasks—then let it be done by hand. Morris' young people revel in gathering the harvest without mechanical aids. If for some people *all* labor were irksome, there would be trouble in utopia; but Morris did not entertain this possibility because of his presumption of an inborn desire to express oneself in work. He did not conceive of the diabolical manipulation of the libido so that work would appear essential and even agreeable when in fact it was not.

Since the economic crises of the nineteenth century were attributed to overproduction and an incapacity to dispose of surplus products, Morris' *Nowhere* offered a pat solution. Hours of labor could be reduced to a necessary minimum and whatever energies were left could be expended upon ornate architecture. Ornamentation would recognize no surplus in this aesthetic. "And indeed I do think that the energies of mankind are chiefly of use to them for such work, for in that direction I can see no end of work, while in many others a limit does seem possible."[28] In the history of the revolution as recounted by the men of Nowhere, pleasure in work as art developed spontaneously when the burdens of overwork for the world market were removed. A yearning for beauty was naturally awakened in men's minds once they had stopped producing for production's sake and had the opportunity to make each thing an excellent specimen of its kind. Here was the idealized medieval artisan of the pre-Raphaelites, a character who on occasion had even popped his head out of the pages of *Das Kapital*. At one stage in the evolution of Morris' utopian society there was anxiety lest there be a scarcity of pleasurable work to do, "a kind of fear growing up among us that we shall one day be short of work. It is a pleasure which we are afraid of losing, not a pain . . ."[29] But on reflection this eventuality was excluded, for it was realized that when the necessaries had been provided, men could turn to grand architecture, like the medieval cathedral, where all manner of creative instincts would find ample fulfillment in labor. Morris, who had an incorrigible predilection for the decorative, which he associated with the exuberance of life, had his utopians combine the best qualities of the northern Gothic with those of the Saracen and the Byzantine, a potpourri not unknown in the skyscrapers of the twentieth century before the "functional" revolution.

There are no snakes in Ireland and no government in Nowhere. Units of management called communes, wards, or parishes operate by majority rule; but the minority are excused from participating in an action of which they disapprove. While mid-century utopians like Proudhon and Weitling had devised various types of chits and special workbooks and personal credit schemes as part of a system of incentives and control and these persisted in Hertzka and Bellamy, William Morris spurned such mechanics. Since man's need for work was an expression of his innermost being—he called to witness his romantic medieval artisans and cathedral builders, who toiled not for grub but to fulfill themselves—there were for him no chits, no credit cards, no central bank, nothing but artisan-artists joyously at work. In Chapter 15, entitled "On the Lack of Incentive to Labor in a Communist Society," the standard anti-utopian argument is summarily dismissed. The reward of labor is life. The reward for especially good work is the reward of creation, God's reward. "Would you send in a bill for begetting children?"[30] Morris apostrophizes in a rare allusion to sexual pleasure.

Marx had still looked upon most work as part of the realm of necessity. Morris stressed the positive aspect of work and transformed it into an aesthetic experience. "*All* work is now pleasurable; either because of the hope of gain in honor and wealth with which the work is done,—which causes pleasurable excitement, even when the actual work is not pleasant—or else because it has grown into a pleasurable *habit*, as in the case with what you may call mechanical work; and lastly (and most of our work is of this kind) because there is conscious sensuous pleasure in the work itself; it is done, that is, by artists."[31]

Morris joined Proudhon in insisting that free work was a human expression of high seriousness. The biblical curse had been lifted and the Aristotelian repugnance to labor as slavery had been overcome. Work was neither a Benedictine prayer nor a Puritan duty. It was, in the tradition of the Saint-Simonians, the ultimate manifestation of the human. Labor was not alienated, not "objectified." Men worked in order to live happily, and instead of having the product of their labor taken from them, they freely gave it away. Aristotle's fear that equality meant the end of liberality has been dispelled: There is the greatest possible opportunity for liberality as all things are handed out unstintingly for the asking by fellow artisans. The artistic imperative salvages all labor from drudgery.

Proudhon had considered labor an act of personal affirmation, but his writings convey the impression that he was a crypto-Jansenist. The task had to be arduous, even painful, to be regarded as work. There was a dread of softness, anxiety that if labor became too easy then the working class, which should be noble and heroic, would become as degenerate and effete as the aristocrats and monopoly capitalists. Proudhon aimed to preserve the work ethic and its virtues without the bourgeoisie. Morris did not shrink from ease, even laziness, though total idleness would have been considered a malady in Nowhere.

The physical and moral consequences of this regimen are among the most fortunate aspects of Nowhere. As in Freeland, the inhabitants look younger than in "unsocial" countries because one ages less quickly if one lives among happy people. Morris, like Bellamy and Hertzka, celebrates the frank openness and joyous countenances of his people. Everyone has a kindly air. The women, rather pre-Raphaelite in appearance, dress in un-Victorian, colorful costumes, and sartorial individualism is encouraged. The argument that socialism entrains uniformity is quickly refuted. Even esoteric antiquarian interests and the higher mathematics are tolerated, though they are looked upon as foibles rather than the noblest expressions of man, which remain handicrafts on the simplest level and great monuments of architecture on the most complex. Bellamy's characters even in their emancipation are still buttoned-up Bostonians, who spend much of their time passively listening to telephonic music in a specially constructed chamber. For all its benign aspect, their utopia is regimented, especially in education and the industrial army. Hertzka's Freeland is an amusement park, where neither aggression nor frustrated sexual desire ruffles the calm of life. There is a premium on good manners and girls with a taste for refined ways train as ladies-in-waiting to virtuous women of genteel, rather aristocratic demeanor. The people of Nowhere are less prim. They go barefoot when they choose and enjoy the outdoor life. Their world is easygoing, untrammeled by the outworn conventions and traditions of another age. Elements of that eerie, elegiac tale of a natural agricultural matriarchy in a new Britain—W. H. Hudson's *A Crystal Age* (1887)—may have crept into Nowhere.[32] Even children have freedom to learn or not to learn, and are not submitted to bookish knowledge without purpose.

There was a new religion in Morris' world, the "religion of humanity," which borrowed its name from Comte but was very different in character from anything he had taught his disciples, for it was without hierarchy or ritual. Morris believed that all men would love one another if they were lovable, hence his circular prescription: Make men commonly beautiful of body, free, happy, and energetic, and they will be naturally loving. The exploitation of nature that he dreamed of was not aggressive; he was not committed to Saint-Simonian gigantism. Nature was to be bettered, not worsened, by contact

with man; that is, nature was to be glorified. The sublimity of nature surrounding human beings would in turn make them more beautiful and more
lovable, and they would then enthusiastically embrace the religion of humanity. Morris was anticipating—and refuting in advance—the acidulous observation of the aged Freud that it was impossible to obey the injunction to love
one's neighbor when often he was not lovable.

Despite the ethereal, pre-Raphaelite atmosphere of his utopian society, Morris took cognizance of the uncontrollable passion, the overwhelming desire,
that could occasionally disrupt the relaxed, loose-jointed order of Nowhere by
robbery or murder. To show his awareness of the demonic, he describes a wild
outburst provoked by unrequited love. The guilty aggressor is killed in the
fray, but having taken a human life—though accidentally—the lover isolates
himself to cure his psychic wounds. Crime, even aggressive crime, is not punished; sometimes it is considered insanity and treated medically as in Hertzka's
Freeland.

There is perhaps a soupçon of Darwinism in *News from Nowhere*, though it is
hardly a Darwinian utopia. "How to take the sting out of heredity has been
one of the most constant cares of the thoughtful men among us."[33] The inhabitants of Nowhere are not eugenicists in any coercive sense, but it is assumed
that if healthy women reach maturity in a favorable environment, their maternal instincts will flourish, and that children born of natural and healthy love
will be more beautiful. Improvement in good looks is demonstrated scientifically by a comparison with photographs of previous generations, a smug pro-
vincialism that blissfully ignores the relativity of aesthetic criteria. Love remains almost statically Victorian, in contrast with the complete transformation
of the ideal of work. True, there is equality among the sexes, easy separation
when marital difficulties arise, good maternal care. But the tone of amorous
relations is touchingly old-fashioned. A beautiful young woman enters the
room, stops short on seeing Dick, and flushes red as a rose; but she faces him
nevertheless. His whole visage quivers with emotion.

Yet the Victorianism in *News from Nowhere* is liberated in some respects.
Morris does not pretend that all the troubles besetting the sexes have been resolved. Sometimes he conveys an almost Humean sense of the mingled pain and
pleasure that go to make up the life of mankind. But at no point is there any
doubt that happiness far outbalances unhappiness in the new society.

33

Darwinism, the Ambiguous Intruder

WHILE EIGHTEENTH- and early-nineteenth-century utopian thinking still fitted in neatly with physical science in the shape of the smooth-flowing Newtonian world machine—it had served as a model for both Saint-Simon and Fourier, who fancied themselves Newtons of the social universe—in the latter part of the nineteenth century two scientific hypotheses about the nature of man appeared at first to raise insurmountable barriers to the prolongation of the utopian dream: the discoveries of Darwin and of Freud. Both were shattering to those men of the nineteenth and early twentieth centuries who had visions of a peaceful, orderly, progressive world from which antagonism and aggression had been virtually banished and where man's creativity would flower, culminating in a utopian world order, either with or without revolution. The biological destabilization of species man, conceived in vague terms by literary philosophers in the eighteenth century, became a serious prospect with the spread of Darwin's thought. The utopian propensity suffered what appeared to be a mortal blow as the fundamental biological nature of the creature who was being utopianized became problematic. The Freudian threat came somewhat later, but its impact was equally staggering.

The New Cosmic Pessimism

Darwinism was rapidly assimilated into the major intellectual currents of the age—no one could remain indifferent to its implications. For Marx it strengthened the conviction that a bloody revolutionary struggle, as contrasted with gradual reform, was inherent in nature; for the captains of industry and European imperialist adventurers it was proof positive that nature enjoined the powerful to dominate and the fittest to survive; for some utopian fantasts it offered the possibility, for good or for evil, of a new man with entirely different physical and psychic equipment. Among utopians of the past there had been hints that the species man might undergo fundamental biological changes through the transmission of acquired characteristics or as a consequence of the atrophy of organs and appendages from disuse; Auguste Comte had forecast female self-fertilization without the intervention of male sperm. But for more than four centuries most utopians had operated on the premise of a stable biological nature that included unchanging sensory and cerebral systems. Suddenly vulgarized Darwinism opened up a new prospect. If the anthropoid had been modified in the past, why should it not continue to evolve in the future? And who knew what direction the evolution of the various species might take? In Darwin's friend Thomas Huxley the theory induced cosmic pessimism rather than an optimistic vision of a benign development of gentle human qualities as they were appreciated by a well-bred Victorian. That Social Darwinism in many of its forms was a gross distortion of Darwin's thought is irrelevant. Phrases such as the "struggle for existence" came to imply that raw tooth-and-nail conflict was embedded in man's nature. Bloody images intruded into the dreams of the utopians. Darwin himself was anything but a jolly utopian, and in the end the black mood generated by his theory was consonant with his own miseries, whether their origin was a specific physical disease acquired during an expedition, or a psychic malady, or a combinaton of both.

The initial impact of Darwinism on literature produced a spate of worlds peopled by creatures who once were men, in successive, later stages of their biological evolution or degeneration. Such writings, often in novelistic form, presented largely negative, or at best ambivalent, utopias. The loathsome species whose chilling aspect and newly acquired physical and mental powers terrified such residual humans as they encountered could have no place in a humanist utopia and prefigured the death of utopia as an ideal city in the Greek tradition. In general the transformed beings had moved toward omnipotence and a diminution of human affect. Beast-machines, emotionally impoverished, existing only to exercise power, became stereotypes whose origins in social reality were all too evident.

What another race alternative to men would be like was a query that did not have to await the formulation of a scientific theory of evolution. A well-worked theme in Hellenistic novels had treated of the voyages of Europeans to Ultima Thule and to the land of the Hyperboreans, where they discovered many weird species. The tradition persisted, from medieval travel accounts like those of Mandeville through eighteenth-century extraordinary voyages, cabalistic tales, and fantastic stories. The accounts of real travelers of the sixteenth and seventeenth centuries made wild reports credible, and eighteenth-century utopias and dystopias introduced societies of men with extra heads or with wings, or creatures with a combination of animal and human characteristics, to illustrate their moral lessons. Swift's Yahoos are perhaps the most famous animals spawned by the utopian-dystopian imagination. In the early part of the nineteenth century the biological prodigies were slighted in favor of man-made monsters like the one Mary Shelley's Frankenstein created. But with the spread of Darwinism an abrupt change in tone occurred. The prospect of a strange new species was no longer a mere literary conceit invented for didactic purposes or for entertainment; it became a reasonable possibility in the portrayal of future animal destiny. The Western imagination began to play a dangerous game. As in past fantasies, new creatures were being dredged up from some primitive unconscious, but this time the sport had a scientific foundation. In Sumerian creation myths all kinds of monsters had been put together by gods in their experimentation with *membra disiecta*. Now the utopian novelist, having imbibed a draught of popular Darwinism, could be like unto the gods in his reckless creativity.

In the concerns of writers of Darwinian futurist novels, the political or religious reborn man was replaced by a biologically transformed being. Not only a new order, but a new specimen who was gifted with "unnatural powers" was brought forth. This offshoot of the utopian tree was radically different from the men who inhabited the social utopias of the early nineteenth century, from the rational, unalienated men of Marx's future world, and from the proper Victorians who moved stiffly through the romances of state socialism that poured from the printing presses in the latter part of the century simultaneously with the Darwinian novels. To be twice born had become a worn-out eupsychian enterprise, well established in religious traditions; to be born two-headed was a far graver matter. When the argumentative social utopias of the first decades had been succeeded by the pleasant speaking pictures of the Utopia Victoriana, predicting happiness under an ideal social system, men were still kept biologically intact and had preserved their essential humanity; any alterations were of a purely moral or religious character. Perhaps there was a reshuffling of the passionate and intellectual drives, with one strengthened at the expense of another. Or there were changes in the quality of love, a movement away from self-love toward solidarity, a shifting balance in egoist-altruist feelings. But the Darwinian theory of biological mutations expanded futurist potentialities to an infinite degree. The literature that grew out of Darwinism, beginning with Edward Bulwer-Lytton's *The Coming Race* (1871), proliferated like jungle vegetation, and half a century later merged into a genre known as science fiction, which ended up saturating the imaginative life of a large portion of mankind.

In the novels, futurism of a Darwinian cast was often wedded to extrapolations of contemporary scientific and technological changes already in process. In order to survive in a radically altered physical environment consequent on accelerated advances in science and technology, the human animal had to adapt itself, to undergo fundamental modifications. Sometimes the results of technological gigantism and new scientific powers are depicted before physical transformation has set in, and sometimes a series of stages is outlined in which the end product is totally unrecognizable as a human. Evil forces maximized in the future are often envisaged in combination: an uncontrolled technology that destroys nature; a Darwinian evolutionary deviation that makes the humans unadapting, or so adapted to specialized functions that they become only part human; the multiplication of devices of control, first technological and more recently pharmaceutical. Many stories make plots of sorts out of a rebellion, in the name of love or freedom or both, of those who represent the old values against the controlled, technological, eugenicized society. The uprising is usually suppressed.

Bulwer-Lytton in *The Coming Race* was perhaps the first to explore the possibilities of magical technological energies in a Darwinian context. His story centers around all-purpose "vril-power" (an obvious portmanteau of will-power and virile-power), which could be terribly destructive, annihilating instantaneously like a death ray, or marvelously curative and rehabilitating when used to charge a bath. With this tremendous capacity to enforce their wishes and guarantee their position, the coming race settles into inactivity after the age of childhood and finishes up in indolence. They rank repose among their chief blessings, and abandon all activity to the young, who still engage in killing primitive monsters as if in sport, or in colonizing new territories. But grown-up Vril-ya rest quietly since they are without cupidity or ambition to spur them to action. Even their luxuries are innocent.[1]

H. G. Wells, the pivotal figure in the development of this type of literature, was a student of Thomas Huxley and was early affected by his gloomy outlook. Wells's first and perhaps only great work, *The Time Machine: An Invention* (1895), was a composite of Darwinian and Marxist elements. The utopian

vehicle was a machine that propelled an inventor-scientist into a series of future ages, each more terrifying than its predecessor. The major plot revolves
around the decent, respectable Victorian's experience in one epoch, the world
of the "Eloi" and the "Merlocks." Social change resulting from scientific and
technological innovation induces biological modifications, as each of the two
major classes in society, defined in Marxist language as workers and exploiters,
grow apart and adapt physically to their sharply different conditions of existence. In the biological-social novel of fantasy that Wells raised to the level of
literature, the changes are nightmarish breeders of unprecedented evils. The
Eloi, those who dwell in the sun, as contrasted with the Merlocks, or proletarians, who live underground and cannot tolerate light, have gone a step farther than Bulwer-Lytton's Vril-ya. The rulers of past societies have developed
so complex a technology and so clear-cut a division of labor that their descendants can spend all their time in play and banqueting after the manner of the
inhabitants of Lucian's Blessed Isles. They occupy themselves with dancing,
drinking a kind of ambrosia, and sleeping. The science and technology of
which their forebears were masters no longer interest them; their buildings are
allowed to fall into decay; the scientific and technological artifacts have been
relegated to museums, which arouse nobody's curiosity; and every night a few
Eloi are devoured by the hungry Merlocks.

For a time technological developments appeared to exert force in two opposing directions. They found expression in both utopias and dystopias, sometimes written by the same author at different points in his life. In Wells's *When
the Sleeper Wakes* (1899), the gigantism of technology has led to mass enslavement; in *The Time Machine,* to a ruling class become so effete that they are
good for nothing but food for the distorted underground workers who prey
upon them. In his *Modern Utopia* (1905), however, Wells has become converted
to hope. A dynamic technological society of joy and endless movement run by
an ascetic elite of Samurai is the ideal, a banality subsequently repeated for decades in scores of his novels and essays. There is not a single fresh idea in the
whole lot. A later novel in the early Wellsian spirit, William Olaf Stapledon's
Last and First Men: A Story of the Near and Far Future (1930), carries its society
through eighteen stages of evolution. In one of them a Chinese scientist who
discovers what is called "subatomic power" creates a force that is capable of
great good and great destruction, but is at first used for annihilation.[2] In the
fabrication of futurist nightmares Wells has remained the dominant influence;
his doggedly utopian novels have had fewer progeny.

There is a temptation to become overly impressed by the technological and
scientific predictions of the futurist novels of the nineteenth and twentieth centuries. One marvels that their authors foresaw flying machines, washing machines, radio, television, tape recordings, subatomic energy, moving road systems, rapid transit on the ground and in the air, medical advances—though
they were incapable of imagining a new emotion. Jules Verne was so meticulous about the scientific validity of his works that they hardly kept ahead of the
next phase of actual development and are thus quite outdated as fantasies.
Wells in his early period did not impose such narrow scientific limitations
upon himself, and ventured to conjure up societies with powers that are not
yet even in the drawing-board stage. What he lost in scientific plausibility he
gained in imagination—until he began to read old utopias and persuaded him-

self that he was the originator of a unique, dynamic technological utopia that would save the world, when in reality he was merely piecing together stray bits from Plato, More, and Saint-Simon. As he jumped from bed to bed in his personal life, he preached of a new order that would end war and distribute commodities equitably, a world society whose austere, ascetic ruling elite, with high intellectual entrance requirements and no vices, would nobly shoulder the burdens of Plato's guardians.

The novels inspired by popular Darwinism and the new technology, though barely utopian, use the standard literary device of a stranger coming upon an alien society and reporting on what he has seen of its institutions and manners, and what he has felt about its tone of life. These novels are Darwinian in the sense that the new society always represents a much later stage of biological development. Before the prospect of physical transformations was accepted as scientifically feasible, the outsider merely had to travel to another part of the globe to discover the utopian society; now new techniques for bridging a gap of hundreds of thousands of years had to be invented. Falling into a hole in the earth and landing upon a society underground had been tried in the eighteenth and nineteenth centuries in fantastic tales such as the Danish professor Baron Ludvig Holberg's *Nicolai Klimii Iter Subterraneum, Novam Telluris Theoriam, ac Historiam Quintae Monarchiae . . . Exhibens* (*Nicholas Klim's Underground Journey, Setting Forth a New Theory of the Earth and the History of the Fifth Monarchy*), 1741. In this tale of adventure, with its mock millenarian echoes, the hero happens upon a civilization of sensate mobile trees. In Holberg's fable a bizarre species that has many reasonable customs superior to the irrationalities of the European world is used primarily to satirize human frailties by contrast. The same mechanism was adopted by Bulwer-Lytton, whose stranger descends into the nether regions to find a society in a more advanced state of evolution endowed with powers his contemporaries dream of but do not yet possess. Wells, more innovative than Bulwer-Lytton, relied on technology to transport the hero through the ages into a future more than 800,000 years hence. But in neither case are the visitors overwhelmed with admiration for what they see. Bulwer-Lytton recognizes the advantages of the new society and he even eulogizes the social state of Vril-ya because it contrives to harmonize into one system "nearly all the objects which the various philosophers of the upper world have placed before human hopes as the ideals of a Utopian future."[3] But his hero finally has to confess his boredom with the life of the new world in the lower depths, despite the fact that a Vril lady has fallen in love with him. Wells's Victorian scientist is horrified at the consequences of a class-bifurcated society that through adaptation has become physically differentiated to the point where two distinct species emerge, one of which feeds on the flesh of the other. The ascent of man becomes the descent of man—though not in Darwin's sense; it leads into monstrous byways where evolution cannot be identified with perfectibility.

Such biological-futurist portraits have since reached the proportions of an avalanche, with seemingly endless variations; but as with many of the primitivist utopias of the eighteenth century, the repetitiveness is oppressive. The world of horrors in which the evolutionary process has gone madly awry can be differentiated from the society of still recognizable men endowed by technology with absolute control over the environment, over other men, and over immeasurably destructive instruments. Yet the emotional tone of both kinds of fiction is meant to inspire dread in the reader. And the visions may be reasonably accurate prognostications—that is the lingering suspicion.

Utopian ardor, inhibited by the powerful scientific influences generated by Darwin—though they did not stop the flow of incredibly dull novelistic utopias in all European languages that merely rehashed old social utopian themes —was further dampened by the experience of two world wars, a mass slaughter of innocents, and the murderous aberrations of new social systems in the making which unfurled the Marxist banderole in many different colors. The dystopia had its brilliant moments in the works of Yevgeny Zamiatin, Aldous Huxley, and George Orwell in successive decades. It derived further impetus from the revolutions of the twentieth century, communist and fascist, though the original fount remained the early Wells, as any old-fashioned tracer of literary themes can detect at a glance.

Teilhard de Chardin to the Rescue

But despite the flood of bitter mockery unloosed by the dystopians, the utopian energy of man was not irretrievably dissipated. The creature, it seems, could not stop dreaming even as he stood beneath the gallows of the atomic launching pads. Certain of the hopes of Morean and Saint-Simonian utopias had in the meantime become partial political realities, through social legislation, in restricted areas of the world; or they had at least been incorporated as programmatic statements of intent by major institutions. The social encyclicals of Pope John XXIII, the speeches of Nikita Khrushchev at Soviet party congresses, and the preambles to Democratic party platforms are a fairly wide-ranging sample of the deep penetration of early-nineteenth-century utopian motifs into the contemporary political rhetoric. Henceforth mankind only had to face the nettlesome problems incident to the implementation of these lofty purposes; a vague consensus about their merit had seemingly been achieved. Traditional utopian oratory saturated the atmosphere of party debate until the whole world became transformed into a deafening chorus of utopian crickets and one had to be a subtle cricket oneself to differentiate one from another. As new theological utopians appeared they evolved a theology of hope both in and out of the churches.

Simultaneously with the realization of some reforms that once would have been deemed wildly utopian, in the realm of pure thought Western writers undertook to do battle with both the Darwinian and the Freudian pessimistic denial of the utopian promise, and in the course of their counterattack developed the new utopian styles that are peculiar to the first half of the twentieth century. The confrontation of utopia with biological transformism had started in the nineteenth century, and the battle is still in its early stages as the passive biological fatalism of early Darwinism gives way to the activist prospect of biological engineering.

A group of imaginative life scientists first modified the emotional temper of Darwinism. They asserted that a benign spirituality was about to possess the whole of mankind and become a permanent acquisition of the species, that we were on the point of ascending to a higher stage in the autonomous and irreversible evolutionary process. Physical-biological evolution had virtually reached the utmost limits, they said—the size of the brain had hit a plateau since Neanderthal—and the development of man, who now had the power to control his own destiny, must henceforward take place in the realm of mind or spirit. Instead of being associated with tooth-and-nail capitalism, rampant nationalism, and aggressive imperialism, the theory of evolution, in a Kropotkin-like mood, had moved away from dramatization of the individual struggle for survival to envisage a future world peopled by humane, cooperative, totally conscious beings. The German romantic idea of a leap into a higher state of consciousness, a rather metaphysical concept, was replaced by an assertion of psychosocial evolution that purported to have roots in the sciences of anthropology, paleontology, and biology, broadly interpreted. Pierre Teilhard de Chardin wrote of a noösphere, a universal belt of psychosocial forces; Julian Huxley, somewhat less Platonic, preferred the term "noösystem." Both of them conceived this new world of consciousness to be Stage Three in the evolution of matter, which had already passed through a historical metamorphosis from the inorganic into the organic. But for all the scientific learning that buttresses their predictions, within the context of this book their views can only be looked upon as a dream of reason.

The future expanding order of psychosocial inheritance, they foretold, would result in earlier internalization in the child and in ever more complex psychic awareness in the adult. Through the progressive intimacy and density of the network of human communications throughout the world, a peaceful and universal morality would be achieved. In the course of time the process of natural selection would fortify the new ethical order by showing biological preference for those with superior fitness in adapting to it. The old warfare between nature and culture would be abolished since both would be dominated by rational man.

The Jesuit paleontologist Teilhard de Chardin emerged as the central prophetic figure of this twentieth-century cosmic historical utopia, with his arms outstretched to embrace humanist English biologists as well as French Marxists, among whom he was for a time assimilated. "Mankind," he wrote in *Le Phénomène humain* (*The Phenomenon of Man*), first composed in 1947 though it remained unpublished for nearly a decade, "the spirit of the earth, the synthesis of individuals and peoples, the paradoxical conciliation of the element with the whole, and of unity with multitude—all these are called Utopian and yet they are biologically necessary. And for them to be incarnated in the world all we may well need is to imagine our power of loving developing until it embraces the total of men and of the earth."[4]

Though throughout his life he was an obedient son of his Order and insisted upon the Christological aspects of his doctrine, Teilhard's writings were subject to a monitum from the Vatican. He would perhaps have objected to the tearing of his ideas out of their "Divine Milieu" (the title of one of his works), but he nevertheless belongs among the scientists rather than the theologians. His underlying thesis was simplicity itself. If since Cro-Magnon man there has been no perceptible physical evolution of the species, wherein lies our superiority? Only in the existence of a transmitted social and psychic order that begins to be absorbed at an early age. The knowledge that sustains this order has accumulated through centuries of time, and future evolutionary progress may be defined as the continuing growth of this vast treasury.

The vision first came to Teilhard in the mud and slime of the trenches on the Western front where he served as a chaplain during World War I; it persisted through years of exile in China, where his Order had sent him because of the heterodoxy of his opinions. His posthumous works have the compelling force of a voice from the grave calling man to a new life. Teilhard de Chardin's is a strange historical mysticism in a new language—new, that is, to those who never heard of Giordano Bruno. Teilhard is not bound to the dualism of spirit and matter; materialist is an epithet that no longer frightens him. He sings religious hymns of praise to primeval matter as ultimately creative of the highest values of spiritual love. At a given moment, matter gives birth to consciousness, and consciousness, now spread over the peoples of the whole planet, by dint of the sheer physical concentration of a growing population must give rise to a universal human consciousness—he names the process hominization—that will transcend the old individualism.

What Teilhard intoned in a sibylline style, the English and American biological theorists have been expressing in plainer prose, without commitment to Christ and within a purely humanist frame. As Teilhard de Chardin devoted his life to a redefinition of Christology in the light of the new evolutionary vision, so the brilliant English and American biologists have conciliated their new world view with traditional Darwinism by revising its implications. Biology has moved away from dramatization of the individual struggle for survival to the idea of evolution by rational choice or direction toward a goal defined in terms, not of the virile he-man caricatures of the English eugenicists and the German race theorists of the late nineteenth century, but of humane, cooperative, loving, totally conscious beings. These scientists have put a new Darwin by the side of Teilhard de Chardin's new Christ. J. B. S. Haldane's man of the future will be "more rational and less instinctive than we are, less subject to sexual and parental emotions, to rage on the one hand and the so-called herd instinct on the other."[5] Julian Huxley has a vision of "psycho-social selection" that is unique to man and "decides between alternative courses of cultural evolution." This mechanism, he says, "must be primarily psychological and mental, involving human awareness instead of human genes."[6] At one of the darkest moments of the present century, in the midst of World War II, Huxley reaffirmed his optimism, countermanding the dark vision of his ancestor: "Man represents the culmination of that process of organic evolution which has been proceeding on this planet for over a thousand million years . . . The appearance of the human type of mind, the latest step in evolutionary progress, has introduced both new methods and new standards. By means of his conscious reason and its chief offspring, science, man has the power of substituting less dilatory, less wasteful, and less cruel methods of effective progressive change than those of natural selection, which alone are available to lower organisms."[7] Hermann J. Muller is perhaps more hortatory than prophetic, but the biological utopia of universal love eugenically controlled is for him at least a prospect. "The rapid upgrading of our intelligence must be accompanied as closely as possible with a corresponding effort to infuse into the genetic basis of our moral natures the springs of stronger, more genuine fellow-feeling."[8]

These scientists belittle the prophets of doom and those so engrossed in the pettiness of living that they fail to appreciate the grand design of the future happiness of mankind, which, to be sure, is more cerebral than sensate, more spiritual and artistic than physical—in the desexualized Comtean, rather than Fourierist, tradition. From the viewpoint of the scientists, ours is an age of crisis not because two economic systems are at war, or because subject races throughout the world are demanding their share of goods and their right to participate in universal self-awareness, or populations and armaments are increasing in unprecedented numbers: These are conceived merely as the birth pangs of the new man. It is an age of crisis in the sense that a new humanity with a sharpened awareness and a deeper consciousness is being forged. Ordinarily this process would be thought of as requiring millennia in the evolutionary timetable; but some scientists are more sanguine. Undaunted by the horrors of the twentieth-century world they are confident that we are actually witnessing the initial breakthrough into the new age. They speak in Nietzschean terms—one hears echoes of *ein Bruch, ein Zwang*. To these scientists the contemporary revolution is a leap, not a slow acceleration, and they cite examples from the early history of evolution to justify their conception of discontinuity. In a letter written shortly before his death, when the nations of the world, East and West, agreed to cooperate in the scientific investigations of the geophysical year, Teilhard de Chardin playfully yet enthusiastically proclaimed it the first year of the noösphere.

The life scientists were joined by a number of eminent philosophers of history, who seemed agreed that the next stage of human life either must or is likely to entail a spiritualization of mankind and a movement away from absorption with aggressive power and instinctual existence. Arnold Toynbee used the term "etherialisation" for what Teilhard de Chardin in his private language called "hominization," and Karl Jaspers, a second "axial period" of spirituality similar to the age of the prophets. For what is the fable of the sleeper on the ledge of a mountainside, which Toynbee has preserved from the first volume to the last, but a historian's utopian dream? One ledge separates the primitive world from the age of civilizations. But this age is drawing to a close, and the rule of circularity that governed Toynbee's twenty-one known specimens of civilized society in the past is not applicable to the future. Civilization with its inner cyclical dialectic of growth and destruction is about to be transcended. When mankind reaches the next ledge above, new rules will prevail in what Toynbee, a somewhat reluctant utopian, tentatively defined as a spiritual world of brotherhood and communion.

Once we are committed to this ideology of cosmic evolution, the narrow five millennia of recorded history with their minor progressions, regressions, cycles, and sinusoidal curves appear terrifyingly diminished. And yet the neo-evolutionists would insist that their teachings are raising man to a higher rather than a lower place in the scheme of things. Far from being dethroned as the king of nature, he is restored to a grander position than he occupied before the Copernican revolution. The earth may now be a mere planet moving around the sun, but man is no longer confined to it. His spiritual energy, his reason, his brain power, his psyche, his consciousness have become the center and the purpose of the whole universe, of the cosmic process. The old Adam was ruler of the beasts but subservient to his Creator and on a lower rung than the angels. The new Adam, as a result of his own will and struggle, towers in the forefront of all being, the end of billions of years of history—an intoxicating conception, frightening in its hubris, if there are gods to envy him.

The complex interplay between Darwinian evolutionary theory and euchronia is far from over. If under the first impact of Darwinism utopian expectations began to fade because in a fundamental sense it was impossible to build a vision of a future society on the soft foundations of primitive slime that might propagate new creatures with unknown capacities and needs, the neo-Darwinians succeeded in restoring the shapeless blob that was future man to his accustomed settled form. At most he will become endowed with a largish egg-shaped head. Unfortunately the breaking of the genetic code has restored the conditions that obtained before Teilhard and Julian Huxley wrote their cosmic utopias, and has again brought utopia into a state of perfect disequilibrium. The newly acquired potential capacity to manipulate the genetic bank of future ages has bestowed upon man the powers of good and evil as these words have been understood since the birth of the Christian utopia. As usual, science fiction anticipated the event by sketching out the activities of scientific geniuses or mad-geniuses who could make life and fashion it into a variety of shapes. The prospect of the naked, unchecked power of biological creation again darkens the horizon and once more casts ugly doubts upon the reign of euchronia. The future is misty. What do all the consoling apothegms of the French utopians and of Marx amount to if somehow the evil ones—whoever they may be—have acquired the instruments not only of technological production but of human reproduction? Despite admonitions that the prophecies of genetic omnipotence are premature, evolution has reappeared in a Janus-like mask. Condorcet once predicted that man would some day be able to determine the sex of the unborn and he discussed abuses to which this might lead. The new biology extends with the same hand the promise of eradicating diseases and preventing deformities and the threat of new tyrannies in the mode of pessimistic science fiction, the dominant tone of sophisticated Western writing in this genre. The hazards of experimentation with recombinant DNA leave most of us in a state of bewilderment. The scientific utopia of Bacon and Condorcet has lost its innocence. And though Soviet science fiction was for decades boisterously optimistic, even there new tonalities can be heard that render problematic any future triumphs in the manipulation of biological processes—witness the Soviet film *Solaris* (based on the Polish novel by Stanislaw Lem) with its evocation of the terrors of a collectivity of official academic Fausts, who can no longer distinguish between their own imaginings and the scientific reality they once worshiped.

The Bimorphic Vision of Bernal

Ultimately, the future of utopia is bound up with the destiny of science and scientists in modern society. If the Spenglerian analysis of the decline of civilization proves accurate and the wishes of the Luddite, antiscientific exponents of the counterculture and its utopia come true, or if controls over the instruments of atomic destruction lapse, the problem of a future utopia solves itself. There may some day be a renewal in another state of man, but the prospect of such a beginning recalls the fate of those refugees from disaster, as Plato described them, after one of the periodic cataclysms to which nature was subject. Under those circumstances, connections with the utopian past of Western man are likely to be tenuous at most. But what if none of these developments takes place? In that event the utopia of the scientists, which has been popularized in the speaking pictures of science fiction, becomes the most provocative of potentialities, especially since the visions of the scientists transcend the limits of political and religious structures.

The hegemony of scientists over society is a utopia that had its origins in the seventeenth century, and has gathered strength from Bacon's *New Atlantis* through Condorcet's *Commentary on the New Atlantis,* Saint-Simon's Religion of Newton, Renan's *Dreams,* and the present-day popularizations of science fiction. Whether the scientists themselves run the world as secular administrators, don priestly robes, or act as advisors imitative of Aristotle in his fabled relationship with Alexander, they are depicted as an elite in effective control of the world. The brief works of two important twentieth-century scientists, the crystallographer J. D. Bernal and the physicist Freeman Dyson, may serve as examples of the contemporary version of the scientific utopia. These men have used the instrumentalities of predictive science to arrive at patterns that fit into the utopian sequence as we have known it in the past.

A few years before the aging Freud delivered his analysis of man's discontent with contemporary civilization, young Bernal presented his tripartite division of man's concerns in a remarkable essay, *The World, the Flesh and the Devil* (1929). Before the proliferation of scientistic works on the near future, often called futurology (since Ossip Flechtheim invented the term), Bernal made a distinction between short-term prognoses, in which desires seriously distort perceptions, and those relating to the distant future, with which we are less emotionally involved. For Bernal there were patent disadvantages in the predictions of the distant future, but in the end they were less alarming than corruption of short-term prophecies by the immediacy of our desires. Long-range predictions suffered from our incapacity to separate "the axiomatic bases of the universe" from the historic accidents of our society. As a consequence, Bernal saw most of mankind bound by static conceptions despite overwhelming evidence of accelerating change. But a paradox lies behind this dynamism. While desire is the major agent of change, actual change is rarely what we desire.

Man's grappling with the massive, unintelligent forces of nature was set in the place of primacy, a position that Freud would hardly have awarded it. Bernal, with the gift of scientific prophecy, envisaged an artificial world in which man's imposition on nature would not be limited to mere modification of stones, metals, wood, and fibers. The massive, clumsy age of metals having been surpassed, man would be a free molecular architect creating a world of fabric materials, strong, light, and elastic, that would imitate the balanced perfection of the living human body. Energy would be transmitted by low-frequency wireless waves, and the high-frequency light waves of the sun would be captured. Food production would be a mere chemical problem. The freedom from necessity of the nineteenth-century romantic utopians would become a reality. At this point the earth-centered, traditional, human Marxist utopia and Bernal came to a parting of the ways, though in his time he would hardly have recognized the profundity of the cleavage. This bearer of the scientific culture's dynamism could not endure the idea of his being a Prometheus bound to the surface of the earth, subject to the caprices of geology. The conquest of space was the next assignment. Bernal's man on earth might be freed from needs as Marx had conceived them, but the exploration of the universe became a new necessity from which the rationality of man would never be emancipated.

Bernal's projections of permanent spatial colonies built by attaching a space vessel to an asteroid, hollowing it out, and using the material to build a protective shell have found many applications in science fiction; his description of space rockets and the manner of landing from them had elements of plain scientific prediction, since fulfilled. He was eloquent in his eulogy of the optimum living, the openness, and freedom of existence within the confines of a protective shell in outer space. One is reminded of the womblike security of traditional utopian societies combined with the freedom of movement of paradisaical fantasies, those of the young Newton, for example. Bernal renewed the hope: "We should be released from the way we are dragged down on the surface of the earth all our lives: the slightest push against a relatively rigid object would send us yards away; a good jump and we should be spinning across from one side of the globe to the other."[9] By the time the transition to shell-asteroid existence had taken place, men would have become so absorbed in science as a way of life that large numbers of people would no longer be necessary for cultural pursuits. The further affirmation of the current movement toward the abstract in art would reach a point where communion with untouched nature was no longer required. Variety would be produced not by individuals in an earthly community but by the diversity of tendencies on different asteroid colonies in the solar system. When these got crowded, adventurers—the embodiment of the necessity for exploration—would set out beyond the bounds of the system on voyages that could last for hundreds of thousands of years. Ultimately man would invade the stars, organizing them for human purposes, and most of the sidereal universe would be inhabited.

But man, Bernal remarks in one place, has had far less experience with understanding and changing himself than with altering his environment. Compared to the radical transformations of the physical environment through space science that he believed to be inevitable, what eugenicists were proposing seemed trivial modifications, merely rendering the species beautiful, healthy, and long-lived. Man's exploratory curiosity would eventually go farther, Bernal believed, than the most daring eugenicists in refashioning the species. With the development of surgery and physiological chemistry, the radical alteration of the body would become scientifically feasible. Mankind would no longer allow evolution to work the transformations, but would deliberately copy and short-circuit its methods. Bernal's vision was rooted in the Hellenic assumption that the development of man's mental capacity was unique and inescapable. The limbs of a contemporary civilized worker were mere parasites, devouring nine-tenths of his energy. There was "blackmail" in the exercise limbs needed to prevent disease, and the body organs wore themselves out supplying the physiological requirements of these essentially useless appendages.[10] As an alternative to this grossly inefficient creature, whose destiny was ever more complex thought, Bernal dreamed up what he called a "fable," a remarkable, interventionist fable. He imagined a physiologist who, after an accident, had to decide whether to abandon his body and keep his brain suffused with fresh and correctly prescribed blood, or to die. If he chose to live as brain, he did not have to suffer isolation since it was a mere matter of delicate surgery to attach nerves permanently to an apparatus that would send out messages and receive them. In a few years, Freud would be writing about man's unease with his technological achievement and its artificial limbs, without knowing of the 29-year-old British scientist's fantasy. Freud and his patients would be left behind on earth by Bernal, in pursuit of their balanced eudaemonistic utopia of achievement and pleasure, while he resorted to mechanical sublimation through the willed severing of heads from bodies among the more rationalist adventurers. He conjectured that during a transitional stage on the way to decapitation they might utilize the many superfluous nerves with which the body is endowed for various auxiliary and motor services.

Bernal's ideal life cycle starts in an ectogenetic factory. Man is then allowed 60 to 120 years of unspecialized existence during which he can occupy himself with traditional pleasures; thereafter he will be prepared to leave the body which he has sufficiently exploited and become a transformed, physically plastic man. "Should he need a new sense organ or have a new mechanism to operate, he will have undifferentiated nerve connections to attach to them, and will be able to extend indefinitely his possible sensations and actions by using successively different end-organs."[11] This will require the surgical intervention of a medical profession that will be chiefly in the mechanized hands of such transformed men. In Bernal's final state of man, there is a brain inside a cylinder with nerve connections immersed in a liquid of the nature of cerebrospinal fluid. The historian of utopian imagery cannot help recalling that Simon Magus conceived of paradise with its rivers as a symbol of the womb and its conduits of nourishment and that one of the favorite locations for utopia has been an island surrounded by waters. The ultimate twentieth-century scientific fantasy of the living brain preserves its original womblike encasement.

The Pansophic utopia of the seventeenth century was a vision of what Europe and the world could become if the new system of scientific knowledge were instituted. Condorcet's euchronia, wholly oriented toward the future, was an ideal portrait of a society virtually ruled by scientists, totally devoted to scientific advances that would alleviate pain and to the raising of all mankind to more or less equality. In the twentieth century the scientific utopia is set off both in space and time from mother earth. Bernal and his astronauts would abandon the earth because not all men are capable of pursuing the destiny of scientific inquiry. The earth would be left to those who continue to pursue an old-fashioned utopia, while the more advanced species of man moves off into a hollow asteroid to achieve decorporealization and inevitable transformation into a cerebral mechanism of hitherto unimagined power and sensitivity. The man who chooses the way of exploration, adventure, and mental triumph ends up as part of a multiple unit of consciousness capable of existing even after an individual brain in the collective has died and been replaced. The new unit of existence is immortal, while old parts are discarded and new ones produced. Condorcet had been mocked by the religious leaders of early-nineteenth-century France as pretending to everlasting life through science. Bernal in a fantasy reminiscent of Auguste Comte's merging of all men into one Great Being, laid out the scientific particulars for the attainment of immortal consciousness.

More than forty-three years later, in the "Third J. D. Bernal Lecture," delivered at Birkbeck College, London, in 1972, Freeman J. Dyson used the title of Bernal's work as a text and then took off on his own speculations about the future of mankind. Dyson's utopian fantasies are to be sharply differentiated from a futurology that simply projects present tendencies. They are utopian in the same sense that Leibniz' projects were. Among the numerous possibilities open to mankind, it was the duty of man to discern that path of collective activity which promised most to the achievement of *bonté générale*—in Leibniz' terms, activity consonant with the will of God and obedience to his commandment to practice Christian charity. Dyson, in a secular spirit, also identified many possibilities in the world: nuclear warfare, the total pollution of the atmosphere, universal starvation. What he proposed was a lateral solution to man's problems, a lateral movement propelled by an examination of two major new scientific developments: the potentialities of discoveries in molecular biology and the habitability of comets and utilization of their energies.

The needs that sparked this magnificent fantasy were perhaps not evident in earlier ages, though they may have underlain other manifestations of the utopian propensity in the past. In Dyson's thought the exploratory need becomes acute with the realization that there are no more places left on earth to discover. The exploratory need is related to a desire for privacy or for living in small independent units that are free from the omnipresent manipulatory powers of a central government of a vast state or empire. There is a presumption, based on the historical experience of Athens and Florence, that limited size will allow for greater creativity and perhaps an elevation of the genetic drift. Dyson's ideal appears to have some kinship with the anarchistic utopia of Proudhon and the "grand designs" of seventeenth-century New England colonial settlements (Dyson himself recognized the latter analogy). Anxiety over human aggressiveness in his comet settlements, easily reached by space ships, is mitigated because triumphing over the environment becomes a major cohesive force. And even if not eliminated, aggression in the small group remains on the limited scale of either Athenian or Florentine city-state warfare.

Commitment to the total exploitation of whatever technological possibilities proceed from the mastery of the new principles of biology underlies Dyson's utopia. The direction could conceivably be what has been called "genetic surgery." "The idea is that we shall be able to read the base-sequence of the DNA in a human sperm or egg-cell, run the sequence through a computer which will identify deleterious genes or mutations, and then by micromanipulation patch harmless genes into the sequence to replace the bad ones."[12] Dyson refuses Jacques Monod's scornful rejection of the illusion that remedies are to be expected from current advances in molecular genetics. While agreeing that the complexity of interactions among the thousands of genes in a human cell probably makes it advisable to declare a moratorium on genetic surgery until we have learned vastly more, Dyson is confident that it will yet play a role in man's future. The small colonies inhabiting space ships might allow themselves the freedom of experimentation with genetic surgery still prohibited on earth.

Dyson also has a series of alternative utopian solutions on a more modest level. Even if the manipulation of human genes is excluded there still remain other ways that might be pursued in relation to the scientific triumphs in biology and physics, biological engineering and self-reproducing machinery. "Biological engineering means the artificial synthesis of living organisms designed to fulfill human purposes. Self-reproducing machinery means the imitation of the function and reproduction of a living organism with non-living materials, a computer-program imitating the function of DNA and a minia-ture factory imitating the funtions of protein molecules."[13] Dyson has in mind the extension of the art of industrial fermentation to produce microorganisms equipped with enzyme systems tailored to our own design. Biological engi-neering could even venture from an enclosed biological factory to the more hazardous step of letting organisms loose into the atmosphere to scavenge and mine, to clean up the natural environment (disturbed by human technology), and to produce almost all the raw materials necessary for our industry and our existence.

Historically, extraterrestrial utopias have been located on other planets, ex-cept for a few rare underdeveloped seventeenth-century platforms floating in space. For colonization Dyson turns away from the planets and Bernal's aster-oids to the space around the solar system populated by huge numbers of comets, small worlds a few miles in diameter, rich in water and other life-sus-taining chemicals. He estimates that the total population of comets loosely at-tached to the sun must be numbered in the thousands of millions. The whole universe is crowded with comets of the order of a light-day or less away from one another. Since the comets have the basic constituents of living cells—water, carbon, and nitrogen—they lack only two essentials for human settle-ment, warmth and air. Through biological engineering men could design trees with leaves having a special skin that permits growth in "airless space by the light of a distant Sun," say as distant as the orbits of Jupiter and Saturn.[14] Everything is provided for: The oxygen the leaves manufacture is transported down to the roots of the trees (which have gradually melted the interior of the comet) and is then released into the areas where men live among the tree trunks and other flora and fauna. Since the comet is only a few miles in diame-ter the force of gravity is so weak that a tree can grow wondrously tall. From a comet ten miles in diameter trees can rise out into space for hundreds of miles, collecting the energy of sunlight from an area thousands of times as large as the area of the comet itself. "Seen from far away, the comet will look like a small potato sprouting an immense growth of stems and foliage."[15]

Unlike his predecessor Bernal, Dyson does not long for the absolute of an artificial environment, but seeks to preserve in outer space reminders of earthly existence. Nor does he totally disembody the creature man. In the period be-tween the two scientists, the emphasis seems to have shifted in descriptions of the drive behind the utopian flight to outer space. Bernal conceives of the human creature as pursuing the final destiny of his rationality when he cuts the umbilical cord that has tied him to earth and his own body; Dyson's adven-turers leave an earth whose existence has become intolerable, self-destructive, and invent rational solutions that preserve the species in a recognizable shape—the eugenicist's dream realized through new biological discovery.

Writers and readers of scientific fiction, that somewhat perverse modern utopia, have borne witness to the seminal character of Bernal's essay; Dyson will doubtless exercise a similar function in future stages of this non-art. In fundamental political outlook Bernal and Dyson, who did not know each other, would appear to be men of different worlds. Bernal came to identify himself with Soviet Marxism, while Dyson recalls the vestigial rugged indi-vidualist, no admirer of centralized authority under any rubric. Their conver-gence may demonstrate the degree to which utopian constellations of far-out predictive scientists transcend the bounds of political inclination.

34

Freudo–Marxism, a Hybrid for the Times

THE READAPTATION of Darwinism to serve the utopian ideal of a peaceful, rational, cooperative man was paralleled by the efforts of a group of psychologists, anthropologists, and philosophers to grapple with Freud and free him from the rather somber portrait of the future of mankind that he left behind, particularly in his last works. Freud had consistently aimed his sharpest darts against the promise that aggressiveness would be eliminated as a consequence of establishing a new order of property relationships, or of the abolition of property—the underlying assumption of most nineteenth-century utopians. Freud's death instinct may have been a relatively late introduction into his system, but the whole of his life work had already established a deep-rooted contradiction between civilization and worldly happiness. Deadly hostility against fathers and brothers was represented as virtually innate and only partially transmutable. In many ways Freud's was the most trenchant and devastating attack on utopian illusions—what he called the lullabies of heaven—that had ever been delivered.

Freud: Dark Cloud over Utopia

A doctor engaged in the cure of individual souls in distress and the teacher of a technical method to quiet anxiety and sometimes eliminate physical symptoms related to psychic anguish, Freud was also a philosophe with a generally unified concept of human nature, subject of course to the normal inconsistencies that crop up in the writing of any man who has labored for more than half a century and experienced the vicissitudes of changing time, place, and fortune. As a proper Viennese physician in the Hippocratic tradition, he sought to relieve pain without deeply questioning the ultimate purposes of his patients. Doubtless he was oversanguine at times about his psychic remedies, as he had been about cocaine as a panacea until it proved to be addictive. (For many years he continued to cherish the hope that ultimately some mental illnesses, like other diseases, would be amenable to chemical and biological cures. From this perspective, long-drawn-out analytic techniques would have to be conceived as temporary palliatives pending the discovery of effective drugs.) But he had a broad historical world view that can be separated from his role as a physician, a new version of the ancient dualism.

Freud posits two given drives or instincts in all human beings: the erotic, which joins the creature in love relationships with many persons and things, and the aggressive, which seeks to divide, destroy, and bring death. These instincts can be directed toward oneself as well as toward others, which often complicates their description and the diagnosis of their ravages. In the fragments of the pre-Socratic Agrigentine poet Empedocles, the alternativity of love and strife in the world was presented with moving simplicity, and Freud

—whether he knew it or not—remains bound to a traditional chain of thought derived from ancient Greece. Nothing in all time will alter the contrariety of forces operating in man. The loving and the aggressive cohabit in the same body and no social institutions or systems will totally exterminate one or the other. Since both derive their energy from a life-force, which in each individual is a finite quantity of potential energy, the triumph of one will, at one time or another, diminish its rival; but the eternal enemy, its opposite, is always lurking somewhere in the shadows of inner man. Most often these two drives are so inextricably intertwined that love toward one set of persons may be strengthened and nurtured, made more intense, only by aggression toward others. Freud has a way of generalizing these drives so that they become attributes of whole civilizations, some exhibiting a predominance of love, others the overbearing power of destruction.

Civilization and culture, in their loving and nonaggressive aspects joining millions together, have derived their energy by withdrawing it from that seemingly indestructible unit of social existence, the family. As a consequence, there is a latent antagonism between the demands of genital love, particularly in the female, and the uses of civilization. Woman for Freud has never really been reconciled to the purposes of civilization, which create competitive, though mild, loving relationships among men. If love and aggression, the only sources of pleasure, are given free rein, they become enemies of civilization and of their own host. Love uninhibited exhausts itself, spreads over a great number of objects with a devouring possessiveness—mother, father, brothers, and sisters. Nothing is left for culture to draw upon. The history of culture-building has therefore meant a constant curtailment of love objects and a limitation of the exercise of the love instinct to specific genital forms.

The aggressive feelings that have often surrounded the love object so that love becomes exclusive have given rise to multitudinous fears and anxieties, above all the fear of the powerful father who sees a rival in his son. There is a myth in Freud that at one time the brothers banded together and killed that father who tried to deny them any gratification and keep all women to himself. But the fear of the father and his reprisals lived on after his death. A modern man does not have to kill his father in order to become stricken with anxious terror; it is quite sufficient to wish the act. Moreover, the aggressive feeling of rivalry toward the father is never isolated, but is commingled with love and fear of losing that love. The rivalry of siblings merely presages the hostility toward all who come within a man's orbit in later life. Brothers and sisters may love one another, but must also hate one another. And despite the mythic pact of the brothers not to kill, to repress some quantum of their instinctual drive, they have to practice eternal vigilance against violation of the treaty.

The sexual development of each creature ideally moves through stages of oral, then anal, absorption before it finally settles into genitality. The earlier forms of gratification are not wholly abandoned and survive in the forepleasure of love play. But the ideal evolution—a sort of genital utopia—rarely takes place without disturbance, for all manner of events, premature disclosures, and premature experiences can give rise to definitive fixations which cripple genital sexuality and cause great unhappiness and displeasure. There is both a desire to move along the sexual escalator to genitality and a reluctance to abandon the earlier forms of libido, especially that of the first period of blissful, undifferentiated existence in the womb or at the breast. The successful achievement of the sexual pilgrim's progress is dependent upon two factors that are not always favorable: The biological endowment of the individual may unfit him for the climb; or circumstances, the world of reality, may wound him traumatically in these secret parts. In either event he is subject to pain and unhappiness.

Throughout history man has sought ways of mitigating his unhappiness and Freud lists many of them, along with a variety of techniques devised to overcome the pain temporarily. In an excursion of *Das Unbehagen in der Kultur* (*Civilization and Its Discontents*), 1930, he analyzed major sources of the unhappiness of man as he moves through life by dividing them into three categories: pain from one's body, from external physical nature, and from other human beings. In particular, the pain and unhappiness caused by other human beings appear ineradicable, the greatest disappointment of culture and civilization. Whatever reform in human relations is proposed bears a worm within it—an absolutist verdict that made Freud the dark prince of the modern anti-utopians. In order to avoid the pain inflicted by others, some have fled to the desert or to monasteries, where they have sacrificed the pleasures of love to protect themselves from the aggressions of their fellows. Others have built ideal worlds, imaginary utopias into which they have escaped. Still others have dedicated themselves to political programs of total radical reformation, perhaps next to religion the most illusory remedy.

Here Freud directs his attack at the Marxist utopia with which his system stood in open conflict. Aggression is an instinctual need and to trace back the major source of aggression of man against man to property ownership is nonsensical. Private property may be an instrument for the expression of violence, but if it were abolished the instinct would seek other outlets. Aggression antedates property ownership and can already be discovered in the nursery.[1] Why lull men to sleep with these fairy tales? The spirit of equality that communism purports to foster may be gratifying to some men but disastrously crushing to others. The excellent and the superior who find themselves leveled by the communist system suffer from this equality and the result may be a general depression of culture. In America—the land of his negative identity—Freud thought he detected the universal sign of the times, a distrust of worth. The history of group formations taught Freud that all loving, nonaggressive, ingroup relationships—nations, states, cultures—were formed at the expense of violent hostility to others, the out-groups. The chronicle of ethnic group formation ancient and modern provided him with a plethora of examples to support his thesis.

For Freud all cultures and civilizations were by definition repressive. They differed in the severity of their repression of manifestations of the aggressive instinct or of the erotic. Since individuals have a great variety of needs of differing intensities, some epochs and cultures are better for some individuals than others; that is, to some persons they offer greater opportunity for pleasure. If a man is demonstratively aggressive, he might be happier in a hunting society than in a tea-party society. Some societies are so punitive in their restriction of certain types of sexual relationship that they totally destroy creatures who would prosper in other states. Thus the inevitable inequality is twofold. All men are born unequal in their instinctual equipment and societies gratify these unequal men unequally. Freud, who died in 1939 and thus did not witness the recent sexual revolution, believed that the Western world had reached a high point of restriction on sexual gratification. Though the restrictions did not fall equally on all—the strong simply ignored them—a vast quantum of suffering was thus brought into the world. If Freud allowed himself a reformist aside it was at this point: Society, culture, civilization had gone far beyond their basic needs in imposing sexual prohibitions.

Most of the palliatives for pain that Freud described—distraction in work, sublimation in art, being in love, taking alcohol (he wrote before the emergence of the contemporary popular drug culture)—could be effective in various degrees under ordinary circumstances. But there were persons who could not manage to work out an appropriate diet of even partial alleviation. They were unable either to severely curb or to cut off the overt manifestations of the drives through some higher mental system. For these unfortunates there was only one way out. Those defeated in the battle for existence sought refuge in madness, with its total withdrawal from the world of men the aggressors. Having been subjected to the shocks of World War I and the presence of the Gestapo in his house on the eve of World War II, Freud was none too sanguine about the future of man. One consolation that he refused was the religious balsam. This was a return to the infantile, to the feelings of the child at its mother's breast, or to the naked fear of the omnipotent father. Unlike art, science, and technology, religion was vehemently rejected as unworthy of man, as pretending to powers it did not possess. It did not tell the truth, and confused a palliative with a cure.

In the end the paltry measure of happiness an individual might attain was dependent upon far more than an ideal social order: It was rather the result of a complex interplay between a man's psychophysiological nature and the particular forms of repression adopted at a given historical time in a specific culture. Some natures were doomed from the outset to suffer under certain cultural regimens, others to flourish; some sought refuge in insanity, while others could be restored through therapy to endure or tolerate what was essentially inimical to them. There are many ways to unhappiness in the Freudian philosophy. Civilization might create higher mental systems which contained the beast, but aggressiveness would inevitably erupt in a thousand guises. If primitive aggressiveness merely assumed different shapes throughout history, if the most that could be done in the name of civlization was to repress and sublimate, then the eudaemonist utopia was a flagrant absurdity. To the extent that Freud has a utopian ideal it remains a Kantian one: the development of all human capacities beyond the instinctual. The preferred historical state of man is the reign of de-emotionalized reason; but this is hardly in prospect.

For the mass of mankind Freud sees no final hope: They will continue to be brutish beasts vacillating between Death and Eros. Perhaps a few like himself or Einstein can achieve wisdom, can sublimate their aggressions successfully. These unhappy few are really believers in all the dictates of the Kantian moral imperative. Their solution is not happiness, a hedonist happiness, which in any ultimate sense is as impossible for Freud as it was for Kant or Epictetus or Epicurus. The universal moral values of Kant were taken for granted by Freud's small society. His psychoanalysis suffered no value crisis, because it was enveloped or swathed in a Kantian morality that the Germano-Judaic educational system under which he grew up took for granted. Trouble came to Freudianism after its sea voyage to the United States, when it found itself the official psychological remedy in a society that had no Kantian morality as a lodestar, nothing but a hypocritical Puritanism. In desperation an "ego psychology" was invented to preach a sort of attenuated moralism and serve as an ersatz for Kant.

The Eudaemonist Response

Many epigoni who were influenced by Freud's writings nevertheless tried to repulse his corrosive anti-utopian assault, to oppose his militant rejection of the socialist utopia, along with religious belief, as illusions unworthy of rational man. Some denied the existence of the death instinct and the inevitability of aggressiveness. Others gave lip service to Freud as a great destroyer of Victorian hypocrisy, as a critic, but would not grant that he had the genius to create a new vision of the world that might sustain mankind in the twentieth century. They wanted lullabies with fresh tunes. Still others quoted isolated texts that contradicted his generally pessimistic position, especially with regard to the creativity of earlier stages of the sexual cycle. They refused to accept his argument that for all time civilization could only be held together through the painful repression of libidinal energy. If they had a Hegelian bent, they conceded that at one time this libidinal energy may have been needed for civilization-building, but once a civilization of freedom from economic necessity had been achieved through technology, the repression and conversion were no longer necessary. They switched from Freud's negativistic emphasis upon the neuroses with the inevitable chronicle of widespread psychic malaise to optimistic affirmations of creative energy, and proclaimed actualization of the unique self as an absolute value that was not incompatible with communal love and cohesion. In their utopian rededication they moved in different directions. Some brought up in the Marxist tradition concentrated upon the end of a system of alienated labor—their psychological definition for competitive, exploitative capitalism—as a prerequisite for the establishment of that system of mental health which they identified with the abolition of instinctual repression. Others for a time reversed the priorities and appealed to politically revolutionary parties to place, in the forefront of their program and practice, freedom from sexual repression as a necessary prolegomenon to the achievement of political renovation. In either case the form and content of work—was it alienated or not—were intimately related to sexual emancipation.

Another orientation, related to Carl Jung, aimed to revitalize religion and fill the vacuum created by Freud's contempt. The archetypes and forms of mythic and religious experiences deeply embedded in the unconscious of everyman were not illusions but the stuff and nutriment of man's psychic salvation, without which he was destined to become spiritually impoverished, dry—a far graver danger than the material deprivation the social utopians hoped to eliminate. There came into being a whole spectrum of specialized psychological religions that promised eupsychias. A shift had taken place from the "best commonweale," which More located in a place, through the euchronia, which was set in a future time, to the eupsychia, the good state of mind that could be induced virtually in any place and at any time by an adept who exercised regularly. The eupsychians introduced shreds and tatters of assorted Oriental religions, which in their new milieu faddishly succeeded one another at a rapid pace, as the experimenters, in the manner of the late Romans, abandoned one panacea for another.

One is tempted to posit half seriously, half ironically, a law of the uneven development of utopian thought. Psychological utopias and their problems are most relevant in those areas where the economic utopia, at least on its elementary level, seems to have been realized and the social utopia of self-fulfillment in work is at least partially in effect. It is only then, perhaps, that the ultimate problems of happiness posed in sexual and religious terms become pervasive. They have always been present in some form, but the psychic pangs can be driven away by hunger and by thirst for creative knowledge. Once there are sufficiencies of food and jobs, the problem of human happiness becomes linked to psychic needs. We have reached a higher level of utopian needs, and who knows whether they are more or less painful when they remain unappeased?

The first important disciple of Freud's to attempt an adaptation of his discoveries to a more optimistic view of the future of man that would be consonant with the Marxist utopia was Wilhelm Reich. The Marxist and the psychoanalytic movements had once appeared on the European intellectual horizon as profoundly antagonistic. In the twenties, on the eve of the Nazi seizure of power, Reich broke ranks and summoned the German proletariat to abandon their exclusive fixation upon the Marxist sociological interpretation of man's historical destiny and to incorporate much of Freud's psychological theory of genitality into their world view—"Dialektischer Materialismus und Psychoanalyse" appeared in *Unter dem Banner des Marxismus* in 1929.[2] But Reich drew revolutionary consequences from the doctrine: Instead of a future civilization resting on heightened instinctual repression, he preached an apotheosis of the body in all its parts and a worship of the orgasm. Immediate radical sexual emancipation was for him a prerequisite to the achievement of a victorious social revolution; otherwise the potentially militant masses, enthralled by the repressive psychological forces of the Oedipal family structure, would be inhibited from active political rebellion. The two most important nineteenth-century, pre-Marxist utopian schools, the Saint-Simonian and the Fourierist, had intimately coupled free sexuality with work needs, but this bond had been neglected by the Victorian-Kaiser Wilhelm Marxists. Reich's original *Sexualpolitik,* which did more violence to Freud than to Marx, was an authentic return to the older tradition.

Those who followed Reich's path in the 1940s and 1950s, Erich Fromm, Norman O. Brown, and Herbert Marcuse, represent a characteristic resurgence of the Adamite utopia in a mechanized society where relationships are endangered by an atrophy of love. They negate the Freudian negation of the eudaemonist utopia. They reject the underlying dualism of his system and admit no intrinsic reason why the libido cannot enjoy free expression, once mankind has been emancipated from the economic and sexual repressions that may have been necessary for culture-building in lower states of civilization.

The posthumously published manuscripts of the young Marx were the proof text for Fromm's great conciliation. Like Hercules at the crossroads, modern man could have embarked upon a new order of free labor in companionship and love—Fromm's euphemistic restatement of the Fourierist utopia

—or he could have again allowed himself to submit to a pathological sado-masochistic order of society. Man seems to have chosen the second alternative, a competitive, power-dominated society in which "alienation as a sickness of the self" is well-nigh universal.[3] He will never be happy until he finds love and security in true democratic socialism. "Man today is confronted with the most fundamental choice; not that between Capitalism and Communism, but that between *robotism* (of both the capitalist and the communist variety), or Humanistic Communitarian Socialism."[4]

Norman Brown's utopia also derives from Freud. But he sees no reason for suffering through the later repressive stages of genitality when it would be more human, natural, and indeed pleasurable to stop at the period of greatest self-fulfillment, childhood sexuality. Wilhelm Reich's assumption that the sexuality which culture represses is normal adult genital sexuality is rejected as "simplified and distorted."[5] With a wealth of literary evidence from poets and mystics, Brown demonstrates that Freud's stage of childhood is what mankind has longed for through the ages, that the redemption of the body, the abolition of dualism, the dawn of Schiller's age of play or Fourier's "attractive work" is the final solution to the problem of happiness. Brown contends that Freud himself had sensed this in one of his moods but censored it in another. Brown, too, calls to witness the young Marx, though his utopia is in general less politically oriented than either Fromm's or Marcuse's. While his argument is not so skillful a dialectical exercise as Marcuse's, he pursues much the same course in turning Freud upside down. "The abolition of repression would abolish the unnatural concentrations of libido in certain particular bodily organs—concentrations engineered by the negativity of the morbid death instinct, and constituting the bodily base of the neurotic character disorders in the human ego . . . The human body would become polymorphously perverse, delighting in that full life of all the body which it now fears."[6]

Marcuse's Last Paradox

Marcuse's was by far the most popular and intellectually the most sophisticated attempt to amalgamate elements from Freud and Marx in a new utopian synthesis. Like many of the other Freudo-Marxists he was at once dogmatic, apocalyptic, and changeable. While *Eros and Civilization: A Philosophical Inquiry into Freud* (1955) is a critique of Freud in the name of an absconded Marx —who, by the way, is not mentioned in the text—*One-Dimensional Man: Studies in the Ideology of Advanced Industrial Society* (1964) represents a departure from Marx on a crucial point of doctrine, the historical role of the proletariat as the agent that would bring into being the new society. Marcuse quoted Freud against himself, often by removing passages from their context or treating tongue-in-cheek excursions as if they were earnest affirmations of principle. Marx of *Das Kapital* was neglected in favor of the sibylline phrases of the young Marx, that high-water mark of romantic utopian thought.

Marcuse accepted the idea that civilization-building in its early stages required the energy provided by libidinal repression. But once a high technology had been reached, when freedom from want and from the necessity of anything but nominal labor was an imminent reality, not a remote fancy, there was no longer any need for libidinal repression, the primary source of energy for civilization-building in Freud's closed system. Syncretic language coupled Marxist with Freudian terms, as in the portmanteau phrase "surplus repression," in the expectation that the verbal union would eventuate in a conceptual one.[7] The mix was appealing, particularly to those who felt the need for a psychology, more sophisticated than Marx's underlying utilitarianism, to supplement his philosophy and his theory of social development. The Freudian dispensation was retained as the psychology of prehistory, but the inevitability of repression, the social need for a heavy psychic toll once a society of plenty had been achieved, was flatly denied.

For the purposes of his argument, at least, Marcuse incorporated the basics of the Freudian system in its pure form, unadulterated by the neo-Freudians, but to his Hegelian-Marxist faith in the stadially developing consciousness of man, the idea that civilization must forever be nurtured and sustained by repressed libidinal energies was clearly abhorrent. In his utopia an era of general nonrepressive sublimation would be inaugurated by reactivating early stages of the libido. "The sexual impulses, without losing their erotic energy, transcend their immediate object and eroticize normally non- and anti-erotic relationships between the individuals, and between them and their environment . . . The pleasure principle extends to consciousness. Eros redefines reason in his own terms. Reasonable is what sustains the order of gratification."[8] Fourier never said more. But as in Fromm, the abolition of "surplus repression" would require political action as a prelude to the establishment of a new world. In *Eros and Civilization* Freudian pessimism was dissipated by the prophecy that once the repressive order of capitalism had been destroyed by the working class and the higher stages of communism achieved not only would men be free from necessity in an economic sense, but they would have the opportunity to fulfill the multiplicity and complexity of their psychosexual desires. Men would be twice liberated—from the fetters of capitalism and from the instinctual repressions of civilization.

A decade later, however, Marcuse sensed that the manipulatory capacities of capitalist society made this wished-for historical development problematic. In *One-Dimensional Man* optimism yielded to disenchantment. Marcuse had gone into the marketplace, having left the study where he could let a Freudian phrase cosset a Marxian one without looking at the world, or where he could indulge in what may have been an intellectual's jeu d'esprit. The reality he discovered was dark. The large-scale technological organization of power states had made it possible to enslave the libido to the machine of propaganda by awarding the masses spurious, addictive pleasures to assure their acquiescence in the maintenance of the existing political structure. Gratifications were immediate and tawdry, blotting out true human needs. The ordinary man had been seduced by a cheap and ubiquitous sexualization as a narcotic. Instead of the workers' seizing the instruments of production, the capitalists had seized control of the collective libido of their workers and manipulated it at will. Technology, while it built benign labor-saving devices and productivity-creating machines, had also made dramatic advances in the means of mass communication and had concentrated them in the hands of capitalists. They were able to enmesh the workers in their web, to forge psychic iron chains that held them captive. Technology had become an end in itself, its expansion an independent, autonomous, self-perpetuating phenomenon. The spirit of the new, rational, higher technology had invaded every nook and cranny of the society —the university, art, and the psyche of the workers.

The consequences were rampant false consciousness (Marcuse was still a book-carrying Hegelian) and failure on the part of Marx's chosen people, the proletariat, to realize the technological potentialities for the total emancipation of all mankind and to engage in revolutionary action. The masses now lived in a state of dull consent, of the somnolence of true consciousness, of preoccupation with vulgar, stupefying pleasures. Marcuse still appreciated the worth of historical civilization, but in the contemporary cultural world he saw only pitiable degeneracy in the miscegenation of capitalism and the libido. The language of intellectual communication had become concrete and self-sufficient to the point of eliminating all ambiguity, history, and potentiality. Industrial consumer societies constantly augmented false needs, absorbed the people in the acquisition of objects, and indefinitely prolonged the period of inauthentic necessity while the ruling classes continued to play their power games. A rational technology could appease many consumer demands, but the whole system was in the service of irrationality. A moon flight or a sophisticated military weapon was a superb example of the mighty collaboration of science, technology, and work for ends of questionable rationality. In their innermost beings men were alienated from the relentless pursuit of objects, but they were as if drugged with things that could not really satisfy them and with sexuality that was not a free expression of love. There is much to be said for this dismal portrayal and its critical philosophy, though Marcuse ignored the extent to which in the West pleasures and even a degree of self-realization have become possible for millions who in earlier societies knew only drudgery.

Marcuse's initial commitment in the 1920s and 1930s was to Marx; his interest in Freud came later. The cornerstone of Marx's social theory, however the texts may be contorted, has always been the labor theory of value. Under capitalism, massive technological structures and vast wealth rest on a forced levy upon the labor of a proletarian, conceived of primarily as a manual worker in an industrial society tied to the machine. As a consequence, the resolution of the contradictions of capitalism would come about only with the willed *self-emancipation* of the workers, who would seize the instruments of production and no longer give up, or alienate, a large part of their labor, their being, or an extension of their being, to an idle, nonproductive capitalist. By the second half of the twentieth century this analysis, with its central emphasis upon the maturing proletariat, was no longer so convincing to Marcuse as it might have been in pre-Hitler Germany, when Marcuse's thought was formed. Automation had made the worker a mere adjunct to the machine, almost supernumerary. Hence it became increasingly shortsighted to rely on the vanishing manual worker, or the cog-in-the-wheel industrial worker, to be the prime mover in a transition from capitalism to nonrepressive communism. In fact, Marcuse began to doubt whether the worker was a revolutionary agent at all. Marx had been aware that classes, which he treated anthropomorphically, could be hoodwinked, corrupted, deceived. But the utter degradation of the proletariat in the late stages of the industrial-technological epoch had not been foreseen and required a revamping of Marxist thought.

In *One-Dimensional Man* the inherited, deeply ingrained values of the aesthete and philosopher came into play. In our civilization there was ugliness, stupefaction, surfeit, no chance for the burgeoning of a true higher consciousness. In this mood Marcuse could sound like a moralist preacher extolling the loftiest spiritual values. He diagnosed acutely what had happened to philosophical knowledge, which had become technologized. When the technological spirit dominated a society everything in it partook of the same ruthless concreteness, immediacy, unambiguity, exactitude, precision. Because of its concentration on presentness, its pursuit of novelty, and its orientation toward practical achievement, this spirit neglected or wiped out the past, or, what is the same, technologized it. Ever the Hegelian, Marcuse discerned in this concretization that seemed to brook no otherness an intellectual weapon that stifled any revolt or opposition. Men became so saturated with the moment and its fullness that there was not a brain cell left to conjure up totally different possibilities, to imagine dialectically the opposite of what is.

Marcuse joined the large company of those who saw in the triumph of the technological spirit a desiccation of life and a shrinking of its dimensions. This has been one of the oldest critiques of industrial-scientific civilization. From its very beginning technology has been regarded with a certain uneasiness. In eighteenth-century Germany Herder, who probably saw few new machines in his lifetime, looked with wonderment at the immense potential power of technological achievement and then asked, "Power for what?" William Blake and Goethe both attacked Newton, the symbol of science, because he seemed to reduce life to mathematics, to the measurable. To Spengler, mammoth technology, like all gigantism, was a symptom of the decline of civilization. Marcuse was in a formative period when Spengler struck Germany in the 1920s and many overtones of his work can be rediscovered in a different setting. But what happened to the Marxist in Marcuse, faced with his own spirited, often incisive, attack on technological-industrial civilization? As early as his book *Soviet Marxism: A Critical Analysis* (1958), he had begun to perceive the convergence of the Russian Soviet and the Western technological spirit. The triumph of Soviet communism would have the same results as the spread of American technology.

The Hegelian philosopher of history had to find agencies of change, new embodiments of world spirit that grew out of existing conditions, but he could not hold fast to any instrumentality of liberation for long. Every so often he grasped at a new straw. If students rebelled against university authorities, for a moment he hailed them as the great predestined force of change; but when confronted by some of the consequences, he recoiled like any bookish professor. He then hoped the oppressed minorities of capitalist states who had been refused a place at the banquet table of the industrial-technological civilization would lead the way. But Marcuse knew that the minorities, like the workers before them, were all too ready to be ensnared by the mechanized fleshpots of the civilization. He toyed with the fantasy that the creative break in world civilization would come from the have-not nations, who would be warned by our spiritual distress and avoid its pitfalls. But he could hardly avert his eyes from the evidence pointing the other way, the bloody military coups launched in the new nations for the possession of the instruments of power. Marcuse was left with a patent revolutionary utopian need unfulfilled. Somehow history had to capture technology for the expansion of the human spirit in all its manifestations, for true freedom from necessity. But his own analysis and his fickle sin-

gling out of a succession of fateful heroes to effect the necessary change ended in
an impasse.

In July 1967 Herbert Marcuse delivered himself of a colloquy at the Free
University of Berlin, "Das Ende der Utopie." Its title was characteristic of his
normal dialectical play. What he meant was that utopia had stopped serving as
an object of derision and a contradiction of socio-historical potentialities, since
human capacity had now reached a level of achievement that made any transformation of the natural or technical environment feasible. Utopianism as a
special category of thought had lost its raison d'être, for everything, man's wildest dreams of plenitude, could become actual. The end of utopia was merely
the end of the old-fashioned limited utopia. Though the blasphemy did not
come to his lips, even Marxism itself had offered only finite possibilities; but
now that the forces of production generated by twentieth-century science and
technology had lifted off the lid, anything was conceivable and utopia could fly
to the highest vaults of heaven. And so Marcuse had turned a paradox: His
utopia was realistic. It was firmly grounded in the actual productive capacities
of advanced technology which, given the correct rational-organizational system, could do anything imaginable.

Since the material and psychic factors were now ready for the revolution
with its leap into freedom, why had it not occurred? In response to his self-
posed question, Marcuse explained that all the forces of existing society were
mobilized against its happening, one of the most profound bits of social analysis since Calvin Coolidge's conclusion that when many people were out of
work, unemployment resulted. There was a sort of conspiratorial organization
of "society as a whole"—Marcuse could no longer think in Marxist terms of
capitalists and proletarians—that opposed and resisted the transformation. If
Marcuse had been intermittently troubled by the difficulties of identifying a
revolutionary class in the most technologically developed capitalist societies, in
this lecture he took refuge in an old utopian bromide, common to infantile anarchists and vulgar Marxists, that the bearers of social revolution would fashion themselves into a vanguard in the course of the revolution itself and were
not "ready-made"; this reading of the Marxist gospel gingerly sidestepped the
whole issue.

Marcuse's end of utopia also spelled the end of history in the sense that the
future no longer needed to be the development or continuation of the past; the
creation of Marx's new man would be a sharp discontinuity, with no recognizable relationship to the previous history of mankind. Marx had still hesitated
on the brink of that leap from the realm of necessity (which even in its late
stages entailed some rationally organized work) into the realm of absolute freedom. Marcuse sportively reversed the traditional formula of the *Anti-Dühring:*
Instead of finding a way from old-fashioned utopianism to science or scientific
socialism, men could now open an untrodden path leading from scientific socialism to a new age of absolute freedom from necessity. Marcuse benevo-
lently applauded Marx for his negative appraisal of the old utopias, because the
objective and subjective conditions, those two pillars that support the world,
had not been ripe for the realization of their fantasies. Henceforward, however,
everything was possible; nothing was utopian in the traditional sense—or almost nothing. Marcuse was still prepared to apply the term pejoratively to
projects that violated physical or biological laws, though such categories were
also historical and subject to change.

This kind of thinking was marked by gross neglect of man's utopian past. Most rationalist utopias of the West have in fact been realizable within the framework of their existing intellectual and economic systems. It was not men's limited productive capacities that inhibited the founding of More's Utopian cities with their agricultural hinterland, Vairasse's *osmasies,* Campanella's City of the Sun, Lesconvel's physiocratic communities, Fourier's phalansteries, Owen's New Harmonies. In his writings Fourier had repeatedly denounced the West for having wasted three thousand years of opportunities for human happiness, since the agricultural and intellectual capacities of the ancients had been quite sufficient for the introduction of fully equipped phalansteries. The contradictions inherent in utopia—the refractory, destructive, power-lusting forces of Kant's *Heerschsucht, Habsucht,* and *Ehrsucht* (drives for dominion, possession, and prestige)—seem no more amenable to resolution in a technological-scientific world than in the agricultural society in which the modern Christian utopia was born. But Marcuse was not disturbed by such elementary psychological perceptions.

Marcuse made a belated discovery of what to a historian of utopian thought would be a banality: "Human needs have a historical character. Beyond animality all human needs, including sexuality, are historically determined and historically transformable. And the break with the continuity of needs, which carry their repression with them, the leap in a qualitative difference is not something made up but something which is inherent in the development of the forces of production. This has reached a level, where it needs new vital needs, in order to live up to its own possibilities."[9] Still clothed in Marxist robes, Marcuse naturally saw the new needs as negating the old ones inherent in the system of capitalist domination. The catalogue was long: the need to struggle for existence, to earn a living, to follow the achievement principle, to compete, to continue the wasteful, disruptive, endless productivity that is bound up with destruction, the need for repression of instinctual drives. In their place he set the need for rest; the need for privacy, either alone or with chosen others; the need for beauty, for unearned happiness. And the last utopian called for the recognition of a new anthropological need, emerging not ex nihilo, but out of prevailing conditions in the capitalist world. This need, hitherto unfelt by the majority of men, was the need for true freedom. In his youth he had prepared a bibliographical study of Schiller—and who knows but that he might have remembered the old poet's libertarian rhetoric. The new freedom would no longer be related to the satisfaction of mere material wants or to emancipation from alienated labor or even to immunity from "surplus repression." The novel, vital freedom would entail the birth of a "new morality" that would completely repudiate Judeo-Christianity. Marxism had to risk defining freedom in terms totally different from anything called freedom in today's political language. Fourier was signaled as an antecedent who had come closest to Marcuse's own conception of the distinction between the free and the unfree society.

Marcuse went beyond Marx, who had bound the new society too tightly to an increase in the forces of production, or so it seemed in the *Critique of the Gotha Program,* and urged a free discussion of the qualitative differences between the old and the new society. What was to be the earmark of utopia after the end of utopia? How did Marcuse distinguish himself from the predecessors and contemporaries who continued to wave the Marxist banderole: "From each according to his abilities, to each according to his needs?" His revised tablet of the law featured the aesthetic-erotic dimension. He was aware that Marx had still been reluctant to see work as play; the new utopia was destined to transcend him and to revive the Fourierist ideal that Marx had contemned. The needs Marcuse recognized as real could be fulfilled all at once under a transformed technological system in the advanced countries. What was involved was nothing less than a total revamping of existing industrialism, a reconstruction of cities, the elimination of the brutalities of capitalist industrialization. Marcuse was careful to disavow the romantic attack on technology itself. He called for a technology restored to its pristine virtue, cleansed of the evils of capitalism.

The Marcuse who will be remembered in the history of utopian thought was swept along on the high tide of prophecy. By one of those quirks of world spirit, in 1967 and 1968 he became the philosopher of a widespread student rebellion and the seer whose foretellings were read as the imminent future. When Marx himself, identified with the bureaucratized official communist parties of the world, was in large measure rejected by the student revolutionaries, Marcuse filled the vacuum with his Freudo-Marxist utopia. That students often read into him their own adolescent longings was helped, not hindered, by the opacity of his style. In that part of the world still under orthodox Marxist influence, most of it largely agricultural, there were no student rebellions and the new technology was both officially and popularly regarded as an absolute good because of an unsatisfied hunger for its products. But in what have been called the postindustrial societies, there was a growing unease over the technological colossus and its depredations. Young persons were repelled by the prospect of their enrollment in a capitalist technological society, and many of them discovered in the aging Marcuse a grandfatherly theorist who vocalized their apprehensions.

EPILOGUE

The Utopian Prospect

IF AN INQUIRY into the utopian thought of Western man has pretensions to being more than an academic or antiquarian exercise, it has to be aware of nagging questions in the background. Have we been discussing a propensity that had a beginning more than three thousand years ago, experienced glorious moments, and is now virtually exhausted or, what amounts to the same thing, is leading a treadmill existence, living on past performances repeated with only trivial variations? Are we witnessing a running down of the utopia-making machine of the West? Or is it only a temporary debility? Does the utopia of the counterculture herald an authentic rebirth? Must utopias henceforth be nothing but childish fairytales? Do the daring scientific fables of Bernal and Dyson, obedient to their rules of predictive science, represent the new utopia? Utopian thought, if it fulfills its function, is unpredictable, but the queries persist.

Somehow the utopian way of thinking and feeling, with its origins in the great historical visions of the golden age, of paradise, and of the fire-bringer Prometheus, sustained by both Judaic and Christian eschatology and embodied in hundreds of works in all European societies since the mid-fifteenth century, clings to life. The metaphor of the twilight of utopia suggests an impoverishment of the utopian imagination, not a prophecy of the end. There is no way of prognosticating whether the night will be long or short or whether the utopian propensity, which has enjoyed so long an existence in this culture, is drying up, any more than the death of the religious propensity could be prophesied. The jungle growth of new religious cults may be spelling either an end or a new beginning; the proliferation of present-day utopias of the antiscientific counterculture, of biological transformism, and of the humanization of outer space leaves us in the same state of doubt.

Over the centuries, a need once appeased may vanish from a culture's utopian scene, to be replaced by another. In some societies the satisfying of elementary hunger is no longer a need and cannot be made to reappear in utopia with conviction. What are now the deep-rooted social and psychic diseases that torment us most cruelly? An incapacity to love? A confusion of identity? A bewildering metaphysical anguish? An inchoate religious yearning? An unrequited passion for equality? An unappeased drive for exploration and challenge? Just as there are throughout the world different levels of economic growth and of acceptance of the ways of the scientific-technological civilization, so utopias responding to different wants coexist in a new babel.

For a great number of human beings on earth today the static Western utopias of the period before 1800, with their plans for an orderly society and adequate subsistence, are still pie in the sky; while for those who have abolished the scourges of hunger and plague but live amid atomic launching silos Kant's eternal peace remains a utopian fantasy. Among millions, the nineteenth-century ideal of self-fulfillment epitomized as freedom to work at tasks of one's own choosing is a far-off goal. Men of action in the political arena appear to be responding to the social demands of once silent classes and peoples that a century ago would have been dismissed as utopian. The most advanced and wealthy segments of Western civilization, where the division of labor is highly sophisticated, have become so absorbed with their intense and perhaps growing psychic malaise that they depute special writers to dream for them of a higher mental system totally possessing mankind, or of a childlike society without instinctual repression, offering complete self-actualization, overflowing with love and engaged with play, or of space colonies where men quench their thirst for exploration, continue to diversify the species, and populate the universe. Affluence even supports commentators on these utopias.

Utopians of the past have dealt with war and peace, the many faces of love, the antinomy of need and desire, the opposition of calm felicity and dynamic change, the alternatives of hierarchy or equality, the search for a powerful unifying bond to hold mankind together, whether universal love or a common identification with a transcendent being. They have either made aesthetic and individual creativity the key to existence or all but passed it by. They have concentrated on physical or mental pain as prime evils. At other times they have analogized the conduct of civilized men with animal or "primitive" behavior, with machines or cosmic forces. They have measured the changing needs of different stages in the epigenetic cycle and have conceived of better ways of being born and dying. The optimum unit of living has been weighed—the isolated self-sufficient individual, the family, the city, the nation, the world. Material and psychic preconditions of freedom have been explored, and the imperative of survival of the species has been proclaimed as beyond freedom and dignity. The historical record has been ransacked to demonstrate with evidence from the past not only what a re-created good society would be like, but when it would have to come into being.

One sometimes wonders whether the utopians have not pondered all the possibilities, identified all the ideal states and the worms that might corrode them. Is the West, which has had elements of utopian fantasy embedded in its culture for millennia, still capable of generating new shapes? A clean solar technology, an unaggressive yet creative man, a being cerebral though not dead to the exaltation of the passions, a lord of nature who lives in harmony with its rhythms, a deepening of inner life without falling into solipsism. The historian of utopian thought is at his best in understanding things post-festum. Having studied the fate of many prophets, he may have no ambition to be one, and when he falls among them he steps gingerly, leery of the contagion of the *morbus utopiensis.*

While the critic may not today discern any compelling new vision among the utopian ideals recently paraded in the marketplace, whether Teilhard de Chardin's noösphere or Marcuse's sexual-aesthetic self-actualization after the "end of utopia," he cannot conclude dogmatically that utopian thought is dead. By its very nature the utopian breakthrough is unannounced; that is what distinguishes it from the mechanical extrapolations of futurology. Though dystopian novels of the years immediately after World War II sold more copies than any utopia in human memory, with the possible exception of Edward Bellamy's *Looking Backward,* there followed a period during which the utopian propensity showed signs of stirring again. Aldous Huxley, author of the ironic dystopian *Brave New World* (1932), lived to write the utopian *Island* (1962), with its admixture of Oriental religious teachings and pharmacological conditioning. Youth movements and communal experiments throughout the world called forth a spate of discursive utopias and fantasies about new states of consciousness. There are those who believe that we have been witnessing an exuberant burgeoning of utopian thought. Others are more skeptical. Numerically, utopia may be thriving. The quality of present-day utopian creation is, however, as David Hume would say, "exposed to some more difficulty."

A Taxonomy of Contemporary Utopia

Though not nearly so complex a problem as that posed by seventeenth-century sectarian heresies, establishing appropriate categories for the varieties of present-day utopian experience bedevils the commentator. Like everything else in our society, utopias are becoming highly specialized. There are political utopias, religious utopias, environmental utopias, sexual utopias, architectural utopias, along with dystopias that portray the future as a living hell. Out of apocalyptic visions of human beings overpopulating the earth and clawing one another for survival, of nuclear disaster, of escaped pathogenic bodies heedlessly created by experimental scientists, are born new crisis utopias—grandiose fantasies of flight in which earth is abandoned to its fate and a new beginning made elsewhere. But for the most part the utopian bazaar is cluttered with old-fashioned wares that are all too familiar.

Of the utopias which accept the premise that innovative science and technology will progress forever, the most extensive are Marxist in inspiration, subject to historical and geographic variations. There are leaders in the Marxist world who stress egalitarian elements and look forward, in theory at least, to the abolition of distinctions between manual and mental labor, as predicated in Marx's *Gotha Program Critique*. Others have established systems that keep putting off the higher stage of communism, while the state apparatus grows octopus-like and a political hierarchy flourishes on sharp class distinctions. If revolutionary Marxism is still the dominant verbal utopia on the planet, in practice it is either spiked with fierce egocentric nationalism or diluted with socialist reformism. Marxist theoreticians pompously debate among themselves the question of whether "alienation" will persist in future phases of communism. After a time the conclusions of their hypersophisticated discussions fail to evoke the temporary suspension of disbelief that narrators returning from utopian islands once achieved.

The Marxist utopia exists today in a number of standardized versions: a Western socialist one—its utopian character is borderline—that is becoming ever more pragmatic and is merging with the ideal of the capitalist welfare state; Soviet Marxism, which on principle would cut itself off from its utopian origins but allows for a recrudescence of futuristic utopian speech on ceremonial occasions; Maoism, which at least at one time stressed egalitarian elements in the Marxist utopian heritage that Soviet Marxism deliberately neglected; and a dissident Marxism, which had a meteoric success in 1968, that would integrate Marx with the whole Western utopian tradition, emphasizing moral values rather than scientific socialism and at times denying the worth of theory altogether.

The phrases that define just where Soviet society stands on the path to utopia have changed subtly with each successive leader: Under Stalin it was "consolidation of socialism"; under Khrushchev, the initiation of "the full-scale construction of communism"; under Brezhnev, "the stage of developed socialist activity." On the fiftieth anniversary of the USSR in 1972 Brezhnev solemnly proclaimed: "The Soviet Union is moving toward communism," building a new, just, free society and an "indestructible fraternal union of many peoples."[1] Vacuous rhetoric is the vehicle for wornout conceptions in this official portrait of a Soviet utopia.

The Maoist utopia has followed a different verbal tradition. The timetable for the realization of the utopia has been revised as frequently as the precise prognostications of the coming of the Christian millennium; but the failure of a prediction has had little effect on the faith of true believers. On July 29, 1958, *Jenmin Jih Pao* (People's Daily) of Peking announced the imminent inauguration of communism. The quick realization of the dream of the young Marx and of the utopia of the *Gotha Program Critique* was assumed. "What will become of our future? A few years from now China will become a communist society. In that society, each and every person will be able to take up his position in the general division of labor—he will be able to farm, to work, to carry out several specialized fields of work, to participate in scientific research, and to write. In other words, each and every one of us will be an 'all round hand.'"[2] The abolition of any distinction between mental and physical labor and the development of the many-sided individual were promised in a Maoist translation of the original Marxian utopia. The Chinese foresaw instant achievement of goals in a great leap, while the Russians singled out those passages of the *Gotha Program Critique* that insisted on free-flowing abundance before the creation of full communist consciousness. Mocking the pants-less Chinese, on October 19, 1961, Khrushchev put his own gloss on the old banderole: "If we stated that we were introducing communism at a time when the cup was not yet full, it would not be possible to drink from it according to need."[3]

In one of Chairman Mao's last poems, *Reascending Chingkangshan,* the heroic spirit of his brand of utopian communism was dramatically contrasted with the matter-of-fact fleshly communism of his Russian enemies.

> We can clasp the moon in the ninth heaven
> And seize turtles deep down in the five seas.
> We'll return amid triumphant song and laughter.
> Nothing is hard in this world
> If you dare to scale the heights.

The Russians were satirized in a dialogue of two birds that echoes a theme from the universal Cokaygne utopia. The Russian bird promises:

> There'll be plenty to eat
> Potatoes piping hot,
> Beef-filled goulash.

To which the Chinese bird replies with contempt:

> Stop your windy nonsense!
> Look you, the world is being turned upside down.[4]

But the Chinese bird is now free of Mao . . .

In recent decades the stadial Marxist utopia has once again had to confront the Babouvist utopia of absolute egalitarianism. The utopian language that flashed through the Paris uprising of 1968 abounded in fantasies about free instinct and spontaneity, and turned its back on scientific-industrial dynamism as it vainly tried to emancipate itself from the shackles of Marxist political language grown sclerotic. Voices were raised committing the rebels to a utopian ideal without binding them to a particular political, doctrinal, or social apparatus. The new utopian ethic would not break with the past, but would be heir to the socialist ideas of all times and places as they had found expression in the wisdom of Greco-Roman and Oriental sages, the Christian heretics of the Middle Ages, and the nineteenth-century utopians. The new dissidents were prepared to include Marx, too, but turning the tables, they selected the utopian Marx and denied his pretensions to a scientific socialism. Return to utopia became the *mot d'ordre*. A pamphlet that was published by the Centre d'études socialistes reads: "The universal crisis of which we are today the witnesses and the victims makes the return to utopia the only rational solution that remains for a humanity threatened with annihilation. The new utopia will be made of theory and imagination, of calculation and invention, of the old and the new. It will attach itself to no authority, to no name, to no genius other than that of the anonymous masses, who in inspiring the thinkers of the revolution allowed them to report and to paint their dreams."[5] The walls of the Paris student quarter were covered with graffiti: "Utopia now. It's the dream that's real. You'll all end up croaking of comfort. Make love, not war. God, I suspect you of being a leftist intellectual. Long live Babeuf! Anarchy, that's I. We want music that is wild and ephemeral. A revolution that demands self-sacrifice for its sake is a revolution *à la papa*. The passion for destruction is a creative joy. Invent new sexual perversions. The prospect of pleasure tomorrow will never console me for the boredom of today."[6]

But '68 came and went and despite the sloganeering no new dreams were painted. In retrospect 1968 has taken shape as a *fête révolutionnaire,* a utopian upheaval of short duration that for a while destroyed existing relations in one Western institution, the university, and doused all other institutions with utopian rhetoric. The celebration over, things settled back into place, but only more or less. During the revolutionary moment there had been much oratory and some direct action, sexual and terroristic. Surrealism had been revived, Fourier and Bakunin awarded university chairs. Certain instruments of scientific and literary production had been smashed; enmities lasting longer than loves struck deep root; dignities were debased. When the trash after the trashing was cleaned up, the professors returned to their podia. Within a decade the student body began to change and the status quo ante bellum was restored, except that it seems a little more fragile. There is every reason to believe that such destructive outbursts of utopian energy will recur. Nineteenth-century anarchism is surfacing again in a benign political form—heresy of heresies—among Spanish anarcho-syndicalists, while Red Brigades of Italy and Germany grip whole societies with terror through an international network that defies the feeble countermeasures of men of order.

On August 4, 1977, German societies lost their outstanding exponent of the uses of utopia in the Marxist world, when Ernst Bloch died in Tübingen in his ninetieth year. Bloch had thought of himself as the activator of the transition from the possible to the actual or, viewed subjectively, from hope to fulfill-ment, the architect who in the wake of Marx would concretize utopia, a uni-versal concept that embraced all other higher mental systems. In the oratorical atmosphere of West Germany he had freely identified himself with Thomas Müntzer, quoting his sermons on *Aufruhr* (Uproar) and declaiming, "Right on, I want to be uproarious."[7] Though deeply rooted in traditional Marxist philosophy, Bloch praised utopia as an incomparable instrument of thought because it allowed a systematic exploration of a variety of specific possibilities. It was for him a critical weapon that made men aware of the imperfections of the present and spurred them to transform it in the light of the utopian revela-tions. Unlike Marcuse, Bloch never abandoned the Marxist hope of awakening the dormant consciousness of the proletariat. Bloch's German disciples con-tinue to work on his utopia of the concrete in an attempt to construct a bridge over the abyss of fascism and establish a living relationship between the uto-pian past of Western culture and the future of a new hope.[8]

   The political activity that goes on in Marx's name has only incidental rela-tionship to the jottings of 1844—so often invoked in contemporary Marxol-ogy—that constituted a 26-year-old's attempt to spell out his own hopes and those with which he would inspire mankind. In a way, official Marxist and proto-Marxist and pseudo-Marxist lands with theologized utopias that go along different paths have no need of new utopias, since by proclamation they *are* utopia or a mere stage or so away from it. Their self-criticism and doctrines of eternal revolution become a façade for Roman smugness. If a sufficient num-ber of human beings call themselves Marxists and live in Marxist societies, mankind may have entered an age when utopia-makers will be persecuted on the manifest ground that one cannot want what one already has. In its treat-ment of millenarian heretics, orthodox unutopian Christianity left behind a model of how to cope with such insurgency.

   An American utopia has been competing with the Marxist one in the con-coction of slogans. We have moved from New Deal to Fair Deal to New Fron-tier to Great Society to President Carter's inaugural excursion on "the Dream," *tout court.* Patently, the rulers of both communist and capitalist socie-ties have seized the rusty instruments of utopia for their ideological arsenal. Capitalist societies are not wanting in hortatory, bookish treatises that espouse ideal forms to be established within the existing scientific-technological frame-work, their obvious intent being the maximization of capacities for the con-sumption of goods and services. These low-keyed meliorist utopias address themselves for the most part to the creation of high technology, economic work organization, the structure of the family, and sexual relations, all tradi-tional topics. They propose ideal plans for eliminating psychosexual unhappi-ness, pollution, work-boredom, energy hunger. Their favorable prognoses are related to an ideal of abundance in the consumption of food and clothes and shelter. The run-of-the-mill consumer utopias that peddle a professional opti-mism concentrate on mechanical inventions and have little or nothing to say about changed social institutions for mankind. Walter Orr Roberts' *View of Century 21,* to cite an example of this pedestrian literature, foresees a pollution-free all-electric car, commuting on magnet control tracks, high-rise buildings that house hundreds of thousands of people, children who learn in private computer carrels, automated medical diagnoses, and two-week weather fore-casting. There is still a money economy run by private business, universal credit and computerized central file accounts, and bond issues to finance public improvements. In all respects, the visionary future is a mere intensification or accentuation of present reality and implies that a stamp of approval has been placed upon it—at least by the utopographer. Century 21 is only more of Century 20. In sum, both late-twentieth-century communism and capitalism in their dreamworlds present the exciting prospect of societies eating their way to the kingdom of heaven on earth without surfeit.

But utopias that incorporate into their systems a growing science and technology have been repudiated by those who reject constant innovation in favor of a posttechnological or antitechnological idyll, to follow upon a hypothesized nuclear catastrophe, a technology that self-destructs, or one that is deliberately restrained or allowed to fall into desuetude. Thomas More, when confronted with the eviction of agricultural laborers during the enclosure movement, wrote in an unforgettable line of his *Utopia* that the sheep were devouring the men. A sizable body of thinkers now see in technology a threat to our humanity: Machines are devouring the men. Even some scientists wish, at least secretly, that the tempo of growth were not quite so fast, in order that we might have an opportunity to reckon with its social consequences before they overwhelm us. As we reel under the impact of uncontrolled scientific-technological expansion, they wonder whether, in the light of the psychic consequences of gigantism, a utopian, rejecting Ludditism and the pastoral fantasy, could not explore other ways of harnessing the new technology. Could a technological development be imagined that would free man from the burdens of painful labor without uglifying and polluting nature and reducing human relationships to cold evasiveness?

In Germany a new type of utopia has begun to emerge from the homilies of men like Georg Picht that calls itself an *aufgeklärte*—enlightened—utopia. While Picht refuses to define its positive content, but rather establishes perimeters of reason that delimit what a utopia might seek, he pleads that science, the key to present-day utopia, should become totally self-conscious and aware of itself. Just as a true scientist would not falsify an experiment or intentionally draw erroneous conclusions from his data, so scientists should incorporate into their very beings the idea that the social consequences of their discoveries are an intrinsic part of the "scientific" considerations governing their experiments.[9]

When the ravages of industrialism first became evident in a few isolated manufacturing centers in England and France—and how puny these origins now appear—a prescient few, like Fourier, rang the alarm and called for a restructuring of society upon the basis of agricultural and horticultural communes, without sacrificing the pleasurable literary and artistic culture that had always been associated with urban agglomerations. Labor would be made attractive through love. Throughout the nineteenth century, communes were established in many parts of the world; virtually all were dismal failures and they often brought great suffering to their members, many of whom—like the French Icarians—died in fever-ridden swamps. In a dream of a nonindustrial England after a peaceful revolution, William Morris expounded the principle of a countertechnological movement that was perhaps more spontaneous, less obsessive, and less psychologically and sexually intricate than Fourier's, more concerned with the fulfillment of simple creative, aesthetic needs. After Morris, isolated communes continued to be founded, especially during the American Great Depression. And in the last decades, communal experiments of groups living on the land, with the object of minimal reliance on the corrupt city, have again multiplied in many parts of the Western world.

Abandonment of the city to barbarism may become an irreversible movement, while pastoral utopias spread over the countryside. One element of the ancient underthought of utopia, rationalist discourse about the ideal city, is being submerged by apocalyptic and millenarian visions. While paradisaical fantasies maintain a tenacious hold on our subconscious, it is today hard to conceive of an urban utopia—the Hellenic element has all but evaporated. The secular grouping of a large number of persons in an ideal urban society on the planet earth taxes our credulity, as controls over the physical environment become weakened beyond recovery. The utopias that are being carved out in distant places or in semi-isolated communities apart, but not too remote, from a teeming megalopolis and drawing on its resources, are brief excursions in applied utopistics that have sucked the last bit of marrow out of old utopian theories. Many of the rural communes that spring up in contemporary America, Great Britain, or New Zealand tend to eschew theory altogether and have no identifiable character. Their array of teachers and gurus have introduced no elements that were previously unknown, beyond perhaps the use of drugs as chemical agents heightening fraternal feelings among the members. Without a religious base these widespread experiments have a short life expectancy, about three years, the span of a serious love affair. They repeat the dismal experiences of nineteenth-century American utopian communities.

Idyllic, pastoral, anarchistic, universalist, syncretistic utopias may regularly possess young persons coming out into the world of science and technology, who weigh its worth and find it wanting. Their latest creation, the utopia of the counterculture, is a potpourri of outworn conceptions—a bit of transcendence, body mysticism, sexual freedom, the abolition of work, the end of alienation. A traveler among American utopian communes, Herbert A. Otto, has classified them in Utopia USA (1972): agricultural subsistence, nature, craft, spiritual-mystical, denominational, church-sponsored, political, political-action, service, art, teaching, group-marriage, homosexual, growth-centered, mobile or gypsy, street or neighborhood. A foreword to the book set forth the utopian credo of a man in flight to a rural commune.

People in communes are people who have decided that they will no longer take this immense social and economic creation on faith, that their environment will no longer be out of reach or understanding . . . We shall start with the land and only the land, a metacultural fact if ever there was one. And beginning here, naked animals on naked soil, at this biological irreducible, our construction will insist on a denial of as much of the mother culture as possible . . . If we were born in the suburbs, we shall be agrarians who live from land to mouth. If we were raised on a shallow and bastardized morality, we shall know each other in the profoundest senses, we shall love each other.[10]

The utopia of the counterculture may be associated with an emotional reinterpretation of Christianity; or it may seek spiritual sustenance from any number of ancient Oriental religions such as Zen Buddhism or Hinduism; or it may invent new psychological religions and ally itself with a quest for a highly privatized eupsychia. Theodore Roszak, who at one time made himself the spokesman of the utopia of the counterculture, in his reflections on the technocratic society and its opponents spoke with the voice of the shaman in an American idiom, calling upon the youth to "open themselves . . . and allow what is Out-There to enter them and shake them to their very foundations."[11] The antiscientific, antirationalist utopia of the counterculture dreams of a new consciousness to control existence. It is oriented toward present living, the immediacy of existence rather than an idealized future, and looks to the miniature rather than the large-scale model for fulfillment.

Of an entirely different order is the behavioristic utopia, with ties to the pre-World-War-I laboratories of Father Watson, who in a popular magazine called *Liberty* once published a crude utopian prospectus of what he could achieve for the good of the race if he were given free rein to use his techniques on society. The current behavioristic utopia has assumed a far more sophisticated envelopment in B. F. Skinner's proposed controls for the sake of cultural survival. Frazier, the founder of the community in *Walden Two*, exclaimed to his visitors with a gesture of impatience, "No one can seriously doubt that a well-managed community will get along successfully as an economic unit. A child could prove it. The real problems are psychological."[12] After accepting Skinner's perceptive formulation of a contemporary utopian question, we find his solutions rather old hat, a fusion of Morean and Owenite elements refurbished with experimental techniques. For what he considers the threadbare shibboleths of freedom and human dignity, Skinner substitutes the burning bush of survival, in whose name men should submit to the reinforcements of behavior that preserve the species: "What is needed is more 'intentional' control, not less, and this is an important engineering problem."[13] Science fiction has coopted the behavioral techniques and supplemented them with surgical and pharmacological devices. The profuse literature on imaginary societies dominated through psychological reinforcements resembles the classical dystopias of Wells, Zamiatin, and Orwell. In the 1970s the type has already mounted to about a tenth of all fiction that comes off the presses in the United States.

There are other more traditional utopian outlets in the revival of religion. A transcendental utopia can always be counted upon as a last resort when the hollowness of existence amid an accumulation of luxuries becomes burdensome. Children of the rich, overstuffed with the objects that Cokaygne utopias have always proffered, may show signs of satiety with the material goods of this world, as they opt for an apocalypse. And if the apocalypse comes, the Kinggom of Heaven cannot be far behind. Anticlericals may consider the attempt to rehabilitate the Christian utopia rather feeble, but in a society grasping at utopian straws it cannot be disdained. Though the seventeenth-century utopia of one global Christian republic has long been forgotten, ecumenical endeavors among the churches are making moderate headway. The religious unification of world society under a single head appears to have no great prospect, but religious and other transcendental beliefs are reemerging with new strength as elements in a psychic utopia. The vision of a theocratic utopia—Christian, Judaic, or Islamic—has assumed a variety of nostalgic, sometimes freakish, even sinister, forms. The rebirth of Christian faith in a heaven on earth, complete with millenarian paraphernalia, should not be eliminated from any twentieth-century overview. A Russian exile, Solzhenitsyn, has emerged as a combative protagonist of this type of utopia in the Greek Orthodox world, a witness to the enduring potency of the chiliastic vision. Solzhenitsyn has risen to smite the hosts of what Berdyaev called Caesaropapism and his medieval revivalism is applauded in the mightiest bastions of Western scientific culture. The Catholic Church had moments in the twentieth century when the utopian idea of "progressus" in a secular sense found its way into papal encyclicals and when radical transformations were achieved in ritual and church government. But there is also a countermovement. Recently the papacy has begun to issue explicit admonitions against worldly "utopian" expectations—along with critiques of existing society that are couched in the language of Marxist anthropology more often than in the rhetoric of the Church Fathers.

Back in 1951 the Protestant theologian Paul Tillich gave voice to his unease with obscurantist anti-utopianism and in some of his writings deliberately assimilated utopia into his theology. In the essay "Critique and Justification of Utopia," Tillich established a necessary bond between immanent and transcendental utopias. "A Kingdom of God that is not involved in historical events, in utopian actualization in time, is not the Kingdom of God at all but at best only a mystical annihilation of everything that can be 'kingdom'—namely, richness, fullness, manifoldness, individuality. And similarly, a Kingdom of God that is nothing but the historical process produces a utopia of endless progress or convulsive revolution whose catastrophic collapse eventuates in metaphysical disillusionment."[14] Recent German Protestant theologians have achieved marvels of syncretism, as theoretical strands of utopia and theology are woven together. In *Utopia as the Inner Historical Aspect of Eschatology* by Hans-Joachim Gerhard (1973), the "concrete utopia" of the atheistic Ernst Bloch is skillfully joined in unholy wedlock with Paul Tillich's theology.[15] Outside the established churches, universalist religious cults—newly manufactured—have rushed to fill a vacuum left by the ossification of both traditional religious and secular utopias. There are moments when, confronted by their profusion, we cannot escape the feeling that we are living among the mystery cults of the late Roman Empire. But the analogy is 150 years old, dating back to Henri Saint-Simon, and may therefore be suspect.

The utopia of science that transcends political boundaries may be the only one that shows some signs of real vitality. Explorations of inner space leading to esoteric religious or philosophical utopias are instrumentalities of privatization. They have been avenues of individual escape from ugly reality, and have often been symptoms of the breakdown of high civilizations. The scientific utopia, in discursive presentations by scientists, in science-fiction books, and in the literal "speaking picture" of the movies, may be the only form in which the utopian mode, born in a preindustrial age, is able to survive. Even here it is difficult to find a text that conveys the potential power of this relatively new utopia, except for Bernal's little book of 1929.

In our own time there has been an extraordinary increase of human capacity in two realms: Matter has been "vexed" to yield the secret of physical energy, and unlocking the secrets of heredity in organic existence has endowed mankind with the awesome power of self-alteration. When Francis Bacon, one of the most adventurous utopians of the past, proposed to investigate all things possible, the paths to his scientific utopia were finite and could still be enumerated. Genetic engineering now opens up countless avenues. As a consequence, in utopias of biological transformism there is a complete fracture with past traditions that had a semblance of continuity. The question of change in man's physical environment is equally open-ended. Previously, utopias were usually restricted in their selection of an ideal location: paradise could be on a mountain, in a fertile valley, on an open plain, in the bowels of the earth, in a two-layered city. Once possibilities are extended to millions of comets, each capable of a different kind of exploration, the physical landscape of utopia assumes a bewildering multiplicity of forms. Of course, despite his putative freedom man may still be limited in his choices on the subconscious level by his own utopian past and his sociobiological inheritance.

Utopian discourse can lose coherence when its frame is no longer recognizably human. At the same time, utopias that are merely variations on a Marxist theme, or small commune utopias, or anarchist fantasies, whose rhetoric cannot hold a blowtorch to an ancient apocalypse, become banal because by definition their assumptions of a relatively static biological creature and a familiar physical landscape ignore the universe that science and technology are unveiling before us. A Marxist discussion about the strategic alternative paths to utopia has all the excitement of an academic debate on procedures. For a long time, the utopian imagination may still be shackled by the formulas invented by earthlings with a recent anthropoid past, but a truly new utopia will hardly accept such confinement.

Just when magnificent new scientific powers have become available to us, we are faced with a paucity of invention in utopian modalities. There is a discordance between the expansion of revolutionary techniques in manipulating nature and the persistence of old-fashioned utopian wishes, holdovers from earlier agrarian or primitive nineteenth-century industrial societies. What distresses a critical historian today is the discrepancy between the piling up of technological and scientific instrumentalities for making all things possible, and the pitiable poverty of goals. We witness the multiplication of ways to get to space colonies, to manipulate the genetic bank of species man, and simultaneously the weakness of thought, fantasy, wish, utopia. Scientists tell us that they can now outline with a fair degree of accuracy the procedures necessary to establish a space colony in a hollowed comet or an asteroid. But when it comes to describing what people will do there, the men most active in this field merely reconstruct suburbia—garden clubs and all—in a new weightless environment. In the twentieth century the fantasies of science fiction have been largely derived from hard scientific knowledge supplemented by a few imaginative concepts. The social and psychological content of these fantasies, however, is generally threadbare. In the midst of a catalogue of the most breathtaking inventions there is emotional sameness and an adaptation to outer space of technocratic forms or fascist and communist mechanics of repression. Intricate technical procedures are outlined for the colonization or humanization of the universe, but the utopian institutions proposed for the society are hackneyed.

It is too early to pass serious judgment on the substance of the utopias of outer space, though a few eminent scientists embarked upon this path have hinted at their ideas of the possible character of new developments. Perhaps the details of their projections should not be taken too literally. Bernal's fable of the eternal human brain whose mechanical appendages are constantly being re-newed readily lends itself to caricature. In his hilarious *Futurological Congress* the Polish novelist Stanislaw Lem has enlarged upon Bernal's vision of biolog-ical engineering:

The third proposal was long-range and far more drastic. It advocated ectogenesis, prostheticism and universal transception. Of man only the brain would remain, beauti-fully encased in duraplast; a globe equipped with sockets, plugs and clasps. And powered by atomic battery—so the ingestion of nutriments, now physically super-fluous, would take place only through illusion, programmed accordingly. The brain case could be connected to any number of appendages, apparatuses, machines, vehicles, etc. This prostheticization process would be spread out over two decades, with partial replacements mandatory for the first ten years, leaving all unnecessary organs at home; for example, when going to the theater one would detach one's fornication and defeca-tion modules and hang them in the closet . . . Mass production would keep the mar-ket supplied with custom-made internal components and accessories, including brain-tracks for home railways, that would enable the heads themselves to roll from room to room, an innocent diversion.[16]

What strikes the eye in all of the contemporary scientific utopias is their re-jection of the ideal political order as the principal subject of inquiry, even as once the divine order was eliminated from utopia. Gerard O'Neill, one of the most enterprising exponents of the humanization of outer space, has tried to differentiate his projects from what he calls classical utopian concepts, at the same time that he deliberately separates himself from the Hellenic quest for the ideal city. "I have said nothing about the government of space communi-ties . . . I have no desire to influence or direct in any way, even if I could, the social organization and the details of life in the communities. I have no pre-scription for social organization or governance, and would find it abhorrent to presume to define one."[17] Where the scientists fear to tread, the science-fiction writers have rushed in with an avalanche of repetitive pulp in which despots dominate whole civilizations with an arsenal of gadgets.

There is only one contemporary field in which the utopian commitment arouses an immediate response of appreciation and delight. Twentieth-century visionary architecture is emancipated from the old set forms and appears to be a departure radical enough to harmonize in spirit with the potentialities of the scientific explorations of outer space. Architecture readily lends itself to uto-pian constructs. Paper is relatively cheap and an insight can be instantaneously captured without the verbosity of speaking-picture utopias or philosophical dialogues about perfect commonwealths. There is a sense in which space pro-grams may be conceived as airborne visionary architecture.

The question remains whether architectural environments can pretend to change human nature. The great composers of visionary architectural treatises in the past—Alberti, Boullée, Ledoux, Lloyd Wright—maintained that the creation of new physical environments would transform human beings. Some Italian planners who seek social renovation have turned to their antecedents for inspiration. Other architects have broken with the past so sharply that their designs, not intended as building plans, end up as subjective fantasies with no conceivable social content. Visionary architecture in this century has far out-stripped the other great moments of the genre—fifteenth-century Italy and late eighteenth-century France—in richness of invention, in the wildly revolutionary application of technology, and in the exploitation of new materials. The drawings of Paolo Soleri and Eric Mendelsohn and Arata Isozaki are among the most imaginative and authentically utopian creations of the age.[18] Perhaps the whole tradition of the written utopia may become extinct while the silent architectural drawing and the speaking film become the favored media of utopian expression.

Optare non Sperare

After we have passed in review a variety of Marxisms, orthodox and heterodox, anarchist revivals benign and terroristic, expansive and no-growth producer and consumer utopias, counterculture movements in many shapes and colors, updated behaviorist utopias of psychologically and pharmacologically controlled societies, transcendental utopias of established churches and new-fangled cults, scientific utopias of space colonies and biological engineering, and the grandiose visions of architectural planners, the contemporary world gives the appearance of pullulating with enough utopias to satisfy all tastes and desires. Yet simple observation has led us to the conclusion that, in the midst of societies seething with utopian experiments, there is unfortunately no significant utopian thought. It may be that somewhere an unnoticed Saint-Simon or a forlorn Fourier is building a new system in solitude, but their voices are drowned by the roar of self-proclaimed ideal societies in operation and the clatter of special effects produced by movie presentations of new worlds in outer space. If most states and empires profess what are in many respects the same stereotyped utopian goals, the words of the true utopian visionary can hardly be distinguished from the bombast diffused by those who control the instruments of emission.

Ever since Edmund Burke, intellectuals have been denounced for fomenting revolutionary terror with their dreams. In the world utopia runs amuck often enough. When the rationalist Hellenic element in the Western utopian synthesis is far outweighed by frenetic millenarian enthusiasm, the fanatics of utopia to whom the vision has been revealed can lead both their foes and their followers to the holocaust. The mass suicide of members of the Reverend James Jones's cult at Jonestown in Guyana on November 18, 1978, will long remain a symbol of utopian madness in action: Fragments of agrarian utopianism, fundamentalist Christianity, and Marxism possessed castoffs of twentieth-century civilization who had been manipulated by crude psychological-reinforcement techniques. In the past there have been utopian tragedies and utopian comedies. Now the bloody theatricalities of the Grand Guignol have been added to the annals of utopia.

In the latter part of the twentieth century the creative utopian spirit, as distinguished from utopias in action, has been further dampened by statistics-laden futurologists. The present-day world is teeming with prognosticators. We are drunk with the future, as nineteenth-century Romantics were drunk with the past. But as it complacently extrapolates its way into the future with tunnel vision, historical prediction has only limited access to lateral possibilities. The prognosticators, divine or human, inspired or insipid, have a way of leaving out the crucial unknowables, the vital unpredictables, while they befuddle us with inconsequential knowables. It could be argued that the historical process is pregnant, "interesting" in Nietzsche's sense, only at moments of disjuncture that by definition are not subject to projection. Trivialities are often foreseeable; eruptions that upset the cart as it laboriously grinds its way uphill, downhill, or in a circle are not. Futurological extrapolations of existing societal developments will doubtless continue, even though they are costly exercises that depend upon an adequate supply of graph paper; but in the end their mechanical anticipations of the next stage are not likely to destroy the utopian propensity, which makes a mockery of the planners. Man the innovator comes up with the unthought-of, leaving the model-builders and the futurological predictors holding their bag of forecasts and facile analogies in embarrassed irrelevance.

A critical overview of the continuities and ruptures in the utopian thought of the Western world has convinced us that utopian fantasies have yielded both good and evil in ample measure. The utopias have not always exerted the destructive influence imputed to them by their implacable enemies. A utopian's release of imaginative energies is often innocent, his reflection of the emotional reality of his times genuine. Experimenters tell us that as we sleep the eyeballs persist in going through their rapid movements four or five times a night, bearing witness to dreamwork. Western civilization may not be able to survive long without utopian fantasies any more than individuals can exist without dreaming. Historians of thought, while reporting that most utopian theory in their day is stale, flat, and derivative, may still wish for a fresh utopian vision to order the conflicting needs and desires of civilization. To cultivate wisely the ancient art of wishing as an antidote to the present saturation with the pseudoscience of prediction and the busyness of the masters of applied utopistics may be a paramount moral need of the age. But this is more a utopian wish than a great expectation.

NOTES

SELECTED BIBLIOGRAPHY

INDEX

Notes

Introduction. The Utopian Propensity

1. Sir Philip Sidney, *Defence of Poesie* (1595), in *The Complete Works*, III (Cambridge, Cambridge University Press, 1923), 15.

2. Ibid., p. 9.

3. John Donne, *The Satires, Epigrams and Verse Letters*, ed. W. Milgate (Oxford, Clarendon Press, 1967), p. 72. The poem has been dated 1597 or early 1598.

4. Sigmund Freud, "Psycho-Analytic Notes on an Autobiographical Account of a Case of Paranoia" (1911), in *The Standard Edition of the Complete Psychological Works*, ed. James Strachey, XII (London, 1958), 1–82.

5. *The Reign of George VI* (London, 1763).

6. Aristotle, *Politics*, trans. and ed. Ernest Barker (Oxford, Clarendon Press, 1946), p. 39 (2.1.1).

7. Henricus ab Ahlefeld, *Disputatio Philosophica de Fictis Rebus Publicis* (Cologne, 1704).

8. Robert von Mohl, "Die Staatsromane: Ein Beitrag zur Literaturgeschichte der Staatswissenschaften," *Zeitschrift für die gesamte Staatswissenschaft*, 2 (1845), 24–74.

9. Translated along with other Mannheim writings and published under the title *Ideology and Utopia: An Introduction to the Sociology of Knowledge*, trans. Louis Wirth and Edward Shils (New York, 1952).

10. Raymond Ruyer, *L'Utopie et les utopies* (Paris, Presses Universitaires de France, 1950), p. 9.

11. Georges Duveau, *Sociologie de l'utopie et autres "essais"* (Paris, 1961).

12. Frederik Lodewijk Polak, *De Toekomst is verleden tijd: Cultuur-futuristische Verkenningen* (Utrecht, W. de Haan, 1955), trans. as *The Image of the Future* (Leyden and New York, Oceana Publications, 1961).

13. Roger Mucchielli, *Le Mythe de la cité idéale* (Paris, Presses Universitaires de France, 1961), p. 170.

14. Jean Servier, *Histoire de l'utopie* (Paris, 1967).

15. Lewis Mumford, *The Story of Utopias* (New York, 1922).

16. Victor Dupont, *L'Utopie et le roman utopique dans la littérature anglaise* (Toulouse and Paris, 1941).

17. Miguel Avilés Fernández, ed., *Sinapia* (Madrid, 1976).

18. Aristotle, *Politics*, p. 39 (2.1.1).

19. Herbert Marcuse, *Das Ende der Utopie* (Berlin, 1967), trans. and pub. in *Five Lectures: Psychoanalysis, Politics, and Utopia* (Boston, 1970), pp. 62–82.

20. Sir John Mandeville, *Travels*, ed. and trans. Malcolm Letts from the Douai (1624) edition (London, Hakluyt Society, 1953), I, 205.

21. Giovanni Battista Ramusio, *Navigationi et viaggi*, 2d ed., I (Venice, 1554), 190r–191r.

22. *Plato*, trans. R. G. Bury, Loeb Classical Library, VII (Cambridge, Mass., Harvard University Press, 1952), 483 (Epistle VII).

1. Paradise and the Millennium

1. Samuel Noah Kramer, *Sumerian Mythology*, rev. ed. (New York, Harper & Row, 1961), p. 107.

2. "Enki and Ninhursag: A Paradise Myth," trans. S. N. Kramer, in James B. Prit-

chard, ed., *Ancient Near Eastern Texts Relating to the Old Testament,* 2d ed. (Princeton, Princeton University Press, 1955), p. 38.

3. "The Epic of Gilgamesh," trans. E. A. Speiser, ibid., pp. 95, 89.

4. Leroy A. Campbell, *Mithraic Iconography and Ideology* (Leyden, 1968), pp. 129–130.

5. Ernst Herzfeld, *Zoroaster and His World* (Princeton, Princeton University Press, 1947), I, 297, 299.

6. See Siegmund Hurwitz, *Die Gestalt des sterbenden Messias: religions-psychologischen Aspecte der jüdischen Apokalyptik* (Zurich, 1958).

7. *Sanhedrin,* trans. H. Freedman (London, Soncino Press, 1935), II, 601, 602.

8. Ibid., p. 659.

9. Ibid., p. 657.

10. Ibid., p. 663.

11. Ibid., p. 607.

12. *Baba Bathra,* II, trans. Israel W. Slotki (London, Soncino Press, 1935), p. 503.

13. *Kethuboth,* II, trans. Israel W. Slotki (London, Soncino Press, 1936), pp. 721–722.

14. *Pesikta Rabbati: Discourses for Feasts, Fasts, and Special Sabbaths,* trans. W. G. Braude (New Haven, 1968), I, 415.

15. *Kethuboth,* II, 721.

16. *Sanhedrin,* II, 613.

17. Ibid., p. 670.

18. *Seder Gan Eden,* in Adolf Jellinek, ed., *Bet ha-Midrasch,* II (Jerusalem, Wahrmann, 1967), 52.

19. Wolf Leslau, *Falasha Anthology* (New Haven, Yale University Press, 1951), pp. 84–85.

20. Hayyim Jacob Slucki, ed., *Midrash Konen* (Vilna, 1836).

21. Philo, *Questions and Answers on Genesis,* trans. Ralph Marcus, Loeb Classical Library (Cambridge, Mass., Harvard University Press, 1953), Philo Supplement I, 4.

22. Ibid., p. 8.

23. *Philo,* trans. F. H. Colson and G. H. Whitaker, Loeb Classical Library (Cambridge, Mass., Harvard University Press, 1929), I, 175, 189.

24. Hippolytus, *Philosophumena ou Réfutation de toutes les hérésies,* trans. A. Siouville (Paris, Rieder, 1928), II, 22–23. See also *Refutationis omnium haeresium,* ed. and trans. L. Duncker and F. G. Schneidewin (Göttingen, 1859), p. 245; and *The Ante-Nicene Fathers,* ed. Alexander Roberts and James Donaldson, V (Grand Rapids, 1951), 77.

25. Carl Jung, *The Archetypes and the Collective Unconscious,* in *Collected Works,* vol. IX, part I (London and New York, 1959), p. 81.

26. Adriaan Beverland, *Peccatum originale* (Leyden, 1679), pp. 33, 35, 37, 38. See also Martin Metzger, *Die Paradieseserzählung: die Geschichte ihrer Auslegung von J. Clericus bis W. M. L. De Wette* (Bonn, 1959).

27. A. Dupont-Sommer, *The Essene Writings from Qumran,* trans. G. Vermès (Oxford, Basil Blackwell, 1961), p. 327.

28. *Sanhedrin,* II, 665.

29. II Baruch 74: 1, in R. H. Charles, ed., *The Apocrypha and Pseudepigrapha of the Old Testament in English* (Oxford, 1913), II, 518.

30. II Baruch 73: 2, 4, ibid.

31. *Origen against Celsus,* book VII, chap. 9, in *Ante-Nicene Fathers,* IV (Grand Rapids, W. B. Eerdmans, 1951), 614.

32. *Irenaeus against Heresies,* book III, chap. 33, ibid., I (1950), 563.

33. *The Divine Institutes,* book VII, chap. 24, ibid., VII (Buffalo, 1886), 219.

34. St. Augustine, *De civitate Dei,* ed. J. E. C. Welldon (London, Society for Promoting Christian Knowledge, 1924), II, 642.

35. *City of God,* book XXII, chap. 30, trans. J. W. C. Wand (London, Oxford University Press, 1963), p. 416.

36. Emilien Lamirande, *L'Eglise céleste selon Saint Augustin* (Paris, 1963), p. 245.

37. *Enarrationes in Psalmos,* 84, 10, in *Corpus Christianorum: Series Latina,* XXXIX (Turnhout, Brepols, 1956), 1170.

38. Tertullian, *A Treatise on the Soul,* in *Ante-Nicene Fathers,* III (Buffalo, 1885), 231.

39. Tertullian, *Apology. De spectaculis,* trans. T. R. Glover, Loeb Classical Library (London, Wm. Heinemann, 1931), pp. 297-301.

40. St. Thomas Aquinas, *Summa contra Gentiles,* trans. English Dominican Fathers, IV (London, 1929), 300-303.

41. Moses Maimonides, *Hilkhot Teshuvah,* chap. 9:2, in *Mishneh Torah.* A Latin translation of this section was published under the title *Canones poenitentiae* (Cambridge, 1631).

42. Moses Maimonides, *Hilkhot Melakhim,* chap. 12:1-4, in *Mishneh Torah* (Vienna, 1842), part VIII, 166.

43. *The Zohar,* trans. Harry Sperling and Maurice Simon (London, Soncino Press, 1931), I, 101. The "Rav Mithivtha" covers folios 116b through 174a of vol. III of the Mantua edition of 1559.

44. Joachim of Fiore, *Liber cōcordie: Novi ac Veteris Testamenti, nunc primo impressus & in luce editus* (Venice, 1519), p. 21, col. c.

45. Joachim of Fiore, *Psalterium decem cordarum abbatis Joachim* (Venice, 1527), p. 260, col. a.

46. Marjorie Reeves, *The Influence of Prophecy in the Later Middle Ages* (Oxford, 1969).

47. Pierre Daniel Huet, *Tractatus de situ paradisi terrestris* (Amsterdam, 1698).

48. Lars-Ivar Ringbom, *Graltempel und Paradies: Beziehungen zwischen Iran und Europa im Mittelalter* (Stockholm, 1951). See also Howard Rollin Patch, *The Other World, According to Descriptions in Medieval Literature* (Cambridge, Mass., 1950); Elisabeth Peters, *Quellen und Charakter der Paradiesesvorstellungen in der deutschen Dichtung vom 9. bis 12. Jahrhundert* (Breslau, 1915).

49. See Peter Martyr, *De Orbe Novo* (Alcala, 1516).

50. Pierre d'Ailly, *Imago Mundi,* with annotations by Christopher Columbus (Boston: Massachusetts Historical Society, 1927), a photostat of the manuscript in the Biblioteca Capitular Colombina in Seville.

51. William G. Niederland, "River Symbolism," *Psychoanalytic Quarterly,* 26 (1957), 71-72.

2. The Golden Age of Kronos

1. William Woodthorpe Tarn, *Alexander the Great,* vol. II, *Sources and Studies* (Cambridge, 1948), 430-433; John Ferguson, *Utopias of the Classical World* (Ithaca, N.Y., 1975), pp. 108-110.

2. See, for example, Ferguson, *Utopias,* pp. 126, 142-145. T. W. Africa is skeptical of Iambulus' influence; see his "Aristonicus, Blossius, and the City of the Sun," *International Review of Social History,* 6 (1961), 110, 120ff.

3. *Hesiod,* trans. Richmond Lattimore (Ann Arbor, University of Michigan Press, 1959), p. 39.

4. Ibid., pp. 31-33. See Rudolf von Roth, *Abhandlung über den Mythus von den fünf Menschengeschlechtern bei Hesiod und die Indische Lehre von den vier Weltaltern* (Tübingen, 1860).

5. H. Diels, *Die Fragmente der Vorsokratiker,* 6th ed. (Berlin, Weidmann, 1951), I, 362-363, Empedocles, fragment 128. See G. S. Kirk and J. E. Raven, *The Presocratic Phi-*

losophers: A Critical History with a Selection of Texts (Cambridge, Cambridge University Press, 1957), p. 349, no. 466, for quotation.

6. Plato, *Republic,* trans. Paul Shorey, Loeb Classical Library (Cambridge, Mass., Harvard University Press, 1958), I, 305.

7. Plato, *Laws,* trans. R. G. Bury, Loeb Classical Library (Cambridge, Mass., Harvard University Press, 1961), I, 175.

8. Karl Müller, ed., *Fragmenta historicorum graecorum,* II (Paris, 1848), 233ff; Jean-Jacques Rousseau, *Discours sur l'origine . . . de l'inégalité,* in *Oeuvres complètes,* Pléiade ed., III (Paris, 1964), 199.

9. Aratus of Soli, *Phaenomena,* trans. G. R. Mair, Loeb Classical Library (Cambridge, Mass., Harvard University Press, 1960), p. 215.

10. Lucretius, *The Nature of the Universe,* trans. R. E. Latham, Penguin Classics (Harmondsworth, Penguin Books, 1951), p. 202, book V.

11. *Virgil,* trans. H. Rushton Fairclough, Loeb Classical Library, I (Cambridge, Mass., Harvard University Press, 1920), 28–33, Eclogue IV.

12. Ovid, *Metamorphoses,* trans. Frank Justus Miller, Loeb Classical Library (Cambridge, Mass., Harvard University Press, 1960), I, 9, 11.

13. Henri Saint-Simon, *De la réorganisation de la société européenne,* in *Oeuvres choisies* (Brussels, 1859), II, 328.

14. Homer, *Odyssey,* trans. A. T. Murray, Loeb Classical Library, I (Cambridge, Mass., Harvard University Press, 1974), 149, book IV, lines 561–569.

15. *Hesiod,* trans. Lattimore, pp. 37–39.

16. Homer, *Odyssey,* I, 241, book VII, lines 113–119.

17. Pindar, *Works,* trans. Lewis Richard Farnell, I (London, Macmillan, 1930), 333, fragment 129.

18. Plato, *Republic,* I, 131.

19. Joannes Stobaeus, *Eclogai,* in *Anthologium* (Berlin, Weidmann, 1958), I, 421ff, 448.

20. *The Fragments of Attic Comedy,* ed. and trans. John Maxwell Edmonds, I (Leyden, E. J. Brill, 1957), 247, 249. See also Athenaeus, *Deipnosophists,* trans. Charles B. Gulick, Loeb Classical Library, 7 vols. (Cambridge, Mass., Harvard University Press, 1927–41); and Campbell Bonner, "Dionysiac Magic and the Greek Land of Cockaigne," *Transactions and Proceedings of the American Philological Association,* 41 (1910), 175ff.

21. *Fragments of Attic Comedy,* I, 159.

22. Ibid., pp. 75, 81, 183.

23. Quoted in A. L. Morton, *The English Utopia* (London, Lawrence & Wishart, 1952), pp. 12–13, 15, 29.

24. *The Qur'ān,* trans. Richard Bell, II (Edinburgh, T. and T. Clark, 1939), 444, Surah XXXVII.

25. Pliny, *Natural History,* trans. H. Rackham, Loeb Classical Library, II (Cambridge, Mass., Harvard University Press, 1942), 379, book VI, 55; John Muir, ed., *Original Sanskrit Texts,* 2d ed., I (London, 1868), 491–494.

26. For an account of two utopias written by Dionysius Scytobrachion (second or first century B.C.) but lacking the philosophico-moral overtones of the others, see Ferguson, *Utopias,* pp. 123–124.

27. Theopompus of Chios, *Philippika,* book VIII, in Felix Jacoby, ed., *Die Fragmente der griechischen Historiker,* IIB (Berlin, 1929), 550–552, and in Karl Müller, ed., *Fragmenta Historicorum Graecorum,* I (Paris, 1885; 1st ed., 1841), 289–291, fragments 74–77; Claudius Aelianus (b. 170 A.D.), *Varia Historia,* ed. M. R. Dilts (Leipzig, 1974), pp. 48–50, book III, 18. For a general appraisal of Theopompus, see Kurt von Fritz, "The Historian Theopompos: His Political Convictions and His Conception of Historiography," *American Historical Review,* 46 (July 1941), 765–787; A. Momigliano, "Studi sulla Storiografia Greca del iv secolo a.C.: Teopompo," *Rivista di filologia,* n.s., 9 (1931), 230–242, 335–353 (*Terzo contributo alla storia degli studi classici,* Rome, 1966, 367ff); and Gil-

bert Murray, "Theopompus, or the Cynic as Historian," in *Greek Studies* (Oxford, 1946), pp. 149–170.

28. Tertullian, *Opera*, ed. Nicolas Rigault (Paris, 1634), pp. 132, 278.

29. Diodorus of Sicily, *Library of History*, trans. C. H. Oldfather, Loeb Classical Library, II (Cambridge, Mass., Harvard University Press, 1935), 31. Poggio Bracciolini's Latin translations of books I–V of Diodorus appeared first in Bologna, 1472, and many times thereafter in Paris, Venice, and Lyons.

30. See Diodorus of Sicily, *Library of History*, II, 36–37, n. 2.

31. Ibid., p. 41, book II.

32. Aelian, *De natura animalium*, trans. A. F. Scholfield, Loeb Classical Library, II (Cambridge, Mass., Harvard University Press, 1959), 357, 359, book XI.

33. Pomponius Mela, *De chorographia libri III*, ed. C. Frick (facsimile reprint of 1880 ed., Stuttgart, 1968), pp. 63–64, book III, 36–38, quoted from Arthur Oncken Lovejoy and George Boas, *Primitivism and Related Ideas in Antiquity* (Baltimore, Johns Hopkins University Press, 1935), p. 311.

34. Pliny, *Natural History*, II, 189, book IV.

35. Lucian, *A True Story*, book I, in *Works*, trans. A. M. Harmon, Loeb Classical Library, I (London, 1921), 251, 255; Diodorus of Sicily, *Library of History*, II, 65–83, book II; Giovanni Battista Ramusio, *Navigationi et viaggi*, 2d ed., I (Venice, 1554), 190r–191r, "Discorso sopra la navigatione di Iambolo Mercatante antichissimo"; Leo Africanus, *Description de l'Afrique, Tierce Partie du Monde* (Lyons, 1556), II, 113–125. See Elizabeth Visser, *Iambolus en de eilanden van de Zon* (Groningen, 1947); and David Winston, "Iambulus: A Literary Study of Greek Utopianism," Ph.D. diss., Columbia University, 1956.

36. Diodorus of Sicily, *Library of History*, II, 78–79, book II.

37. Callimachus, *Aetia, Iambi . . .*, trans. C. A. Trypanis, Loeb Classical Library (Cambridge, Mass., 1975), pp. 105, 107.

38. Diodorus of Sicily, *Library of History*, III (1939), 210–211 (n. 1), 215–227, book V, and 331–337, book VI; Lactantius, *Divine Institutes*, trans. Sister Mary Francis McDonald (Washington, D.C., 1964), pp. 49–52, 54, 57, 58, 59, 69, 91–92, book I. See Herman Franke van der Meer, *Euhemerus von Messene* (Amsterdam, 1949); Giovanna Vallauri, *Evemero di Messene: Testimonianze e frammenti, con introduzione e commento* (Turin, 1956); H. Braunert, "Die Heilige Insel des Euhemeros der Diodor Ueberlieferung," *Rheinisches Museum*, 108 (1965), 255–268.

39. The description of the Indian castes by Megasthenes is summarized in Strabo, *Geography*, trans. Horace Leonard Jones, Loeb Classical Library, VII (London, 1930), 67, 69, 81, 83, book XV; see also K. Müller, ed., *Fragmenta Historicorum Graecorum*, II (Berlin, 1848), 405ff. Herodotus' description of the seven-class division of Egypt appears in his *Persian Wars*, book II, chap. 164–168, in *The Greek Historians*, ed. F. R. B. Godolphin (New York, 1942), I, 158–159.

40. Athenaeus, *Deipnosophists*, VII (1941), 33, book XIV.

41. Antonius Diogenes, "Ta hyper Thoulen apista," is summarized in Photius, *Bibliotheca* (Paris, 1959–62), vol. II, sect. 166.

42. See Henry Reynolds, "Mythomystes" (1632), in J. E. Spingarn, ed., *Critical Essays of the Seventeenth Century* (Oxford, Clarendon Press, 1908), I, 176: "[W]hat can *Adonis horti* among the Poets meane other then *Moses* his *Eden*, or terrestiall Paradise . . . ?"

3. The Great Transmission

1. Kurt von Fritz, *Pythagorean Politics in Southern Italy: An Analysis of the Sources* (New York, 1940); John Earle Raven, *Pythagoreans and Eleatics* (Cambridge, 1948).

2. Plutarch, "Solon," in *Lives*, trans. Bernadotte Perrin, Loeb Classical Library, I (London, Wm. Heinemann, 1914), 453.

3. Ibid., p. 483.

4. Plutarch, "Lycurgus," ibid., p. 279.

5. Victor Ehrenberg, *The People of Aristophanes: A Sociology of Old Attic Comedy*, 2d ed. (Cambridge, Mass., Harvard University Press, 1951), pp. 360ff, 373.

6. Lucian, *A True Story*, book I, in *Works*, trans. A. M. Harmon, Loeb Classical Library, I (London, 1921), 285. See J. Bompaire, *Lucien écrivain: Imitation et création* (Paris, 1958).

7. Thomas More, *Utopia*, in *The Complete Works of St. Thomas More*, IV, ed. Edward Surtz and J. H. Hexter (New Haven, Yale University Press, 1965), 183.

8. Lucian, *A True Story*, book II, in *Works*, I, 317.

9. Ibid., p. 323.

10. Leonardo Bruni, *Epistolarum Libri VIII* (Florence, 1741), vol. II, book IX, no. 4, p. 148, Leonardo Bruni to Nicolaus Ceba.

4. The Passion of Thomas More

1. Desiderius Erasmus, *Opus Epistolarum*, IV, ed. P. S. and H. M. Allen (Oxford, Clarendon Press, 1922), 16, Erasmus to Ulrich von Hutten, July 23, 1519.

2. Ibid., p. 18.

3. Thomas More, *The Correspondence*, ed. Elizabeth Frances Rogers (Princeton, Princeton University Press, 1947), p. 6, no. 3, More to John Colet, London, Oct. 23, 1504.

4. More, *St. Thomas More: Selected Letters*, in the Yale Edition of Selected Works of St. Thomas More (modernized series), I, ed. Elizabeth Frances Rogers (New Haven, Yale University Press, 1961), pp. 4–5, no. 2, More to John Colet, London, Oct. 23, 1504; More, *Correspondence*, pp. 6–7, no. 3.

5. More, *Latin Epigrams*, ed. Leicester Bradner and Charles A. Lynch (Chicago, University of Chicago Press, 1953), p. 105, no. 242.

6. There was a life of Agis IV in Plutarch. See Plutarch's *Lives: Agis and Cleomenes*, ed. and trans. Bernadotte Perrin, Loeb Classical Library, X (London, 1921), 3–43. Professor T. W. Africa has kindly allowed us to read his paper, "Thomas More and the Spartan Mirage."

7. More, *Utopia*, in *The Complete Works of St. Thomas More*, IV, ed. Edward Surtz and J. H. Hexter (New Haven, Yale University Press, 1965), 19.

8. Ibid., p. 21.

9. Ibid.

10. Plato, *Timaeus*, trans. R. G. Bury, Loeb Classical Library (Cambridge, Mass., Harvard University Press, 1961), p. 23.

11. Ibid., pp. 45, 47.

12. More, *A fruteful, and pleasaunt worke of the beste state of a publyque weale, and of the newe yle called Utopia*, trans. Raphe Robynson (London, 1551), [m 8 recto].

13. More, *The History of King Richard III*, in *Complete Works of St. Thomas More*, II, ed. Richard S. Sylvester (New Haven, 1963), 3–4.

14. More, *The Answer to the first part of the poysoned booke . . . the Supper of the Lord* (1533), in *The Workes of Thomas More Knight . . . wrytten by him in the Englysh tonge*, ed. William Rastell (London, 1557), p. 1041, D, E.

15. Elizabeth B. Blackburn, "The Legacy of 'Prester John' by Damião á Goes and John More," *Moreana*, vol. 4, no. 14 (May 1967), pp. 37–98.

16. Later More cautioned against the "inordinate appetite of knowledge" as a "meane to drive an man out of paradise." *A Dialogue concernynge heresyes and Matters of Religion* (1528), in *Workes*, ed. Rastell, p. 242, AB.

17. More, *Utopia*, pp. 65, 67.

18. Ibid., p. 241.

19. More, *Lucianus Samosatensis*, in *Complete Works of St. Thomas More*, vol. III, part 1, trans. and ed. Craig R. Thompson (New Haven, 1974), pp. 25–43, 169–179.

20. More, *Utopia*, p. 221.

21. Ro: Ba:, *The Lyfe of Syr Thomas More*, ed. E. V. Hitchcock and P. E. Hallett (London, Oxford University Press, 1950), p. 86.

22. More, *Utopia*, p. 167.

23. Ibid., p. 175.

24. Ibid., p. 161.

25. See Lorenzo Valla, *De Voluptate* (written ca. 1431); and Don Cameron Allen, "The Rehabilitation of Epicurus and His Theory of Pleasure," *Studies in Philology*, 41 (1944), 1–15.

26. Amerigo Vespucci's *Quatuor Navigationes*, first printed in Italian in a rare Florentine edition of 1505/6, was appended to Martin Waldseemüller's *Cosmographiae Introductio* (St. Dié, 1507); for Vespucci's description, see a facsimile edition of the *Cosmographia*, ed. C. G. Herbermann (New York, 1907), p. 98.

27. More, *Utopia*, p. 117.

28. More, *Selected Letters*, p. 73, no. 6, More to Erasmus, London, Sept. 3, 1516.

29. Ibid., p. 90, no. 15, More to Antonio Buonvisi, London, January 1517(?).

30. More, *Correspondence*, p. 87, no. 31, More to William Warham, Archbishop of Canterbury, London, January 1517.

31. More, *Selected Letters*, p. 85, no. 11, More to Erasmus, London, ca. Dec. 4, 1516.

32. Ibid., p. 82, no. 10, More to Tunstal, London, ca. November 1516.

33. Ibid., p. 81, no. 9, More to Erasmus, London, Oct. 31, 1516.

34. Erasmus, *Opus Epistolarum*, IV, 21, Erasmus to Ulrich von Hutten, July 23, 1519.

35. More, *Utopia*, p. 37, Busleyden to More, Mechlin, 1516.

36. Ibid., pp. 14, 15, Guillaume Budé to Thomas Lupset, Paris, July 31, 1517.

37. More, *Selected Letters*, p. 85, no. 11, More to Erasmus, ca. Dec. 4, 1516.

38. More, *Utopia*, pp. 245, 247.

39. Edward Surtz, *The Praise of Pleasure: Philosophy, Education, and Communism in More's Utopia* (Cambridge, Mass., Harvard University Press, 1957), p. 1.

40. More, *Utopia*, p. 165.

41. More, *Eruditissimi Viri Guilielmi Rossei Opus Elegans, Doctum, Festium, Pium, Quo Pulcherrime Retegit, ac Refellit Insanas Lutheri Calumnias . . .* (London, 1523).

42. More, *The Apology* (1533), in *Workes*, ed. Rastell, pp. 863H–864A.

43. More, *Confutacyon of Tyndales answere* (1532), in *Complete Works*, vol. VIII, part 1, ed. L. A. Schuster, et al. (New Haven, 1973), p. 3.

44. Ibid., p. 179.

45. More, *Selected Letters*, p. 181, Epitaph (1533), sent to Erasmus.

46. More, *Confutacyon of Tyndales answere*, p. 3.

47. More, *Selected Letters*, p. 180, no. 46, More to Erasmus, Chelsea, June (?) 1533.

48. More, *Responsio ad Lutherum*, in *Complete Works*, vol. V, part 2, trans. Sister Scholastica Mandeville, ed. John M. Headley (New Haven, 1969), p. 870.

49. More, *Confutacyon of Tyndales answere*, pp. 307, 308.

50. John Foxe, *The Booke of Martyrs* (London, 1621), II, 353.

51. More, *A dialoge of comfort agaynst trybulacion made by an Hungaryen in laten, & translatyd out of Laten into French, & out of French into Englysh* (1534), in *Complete Works*, XII, ed. L. L. Martz and Frank Manley (New Haven, 1976), 83.

52. More, *A godly meditacion* (1534), in *Complete Works*, XIII, ed. Garry E. Haupt (New Haven, 1976), 227.

53. Petition of German Merchants to the Mayor of Cologne, March 3, 1526, J. Pierpont Morgan Library, New York, E-2, 45B.

54. More, *Confutacyon of Tyndales answere*, p. 5. More's bite was far worse than his bark, if he is to be compared to Foxe and his *Booke of Martyrs*. While Foxe wished to send no man to the stake, we are reminded by one of his apologists, "the same cannot be said of More nor even of Cranmer, both of whom have gained a reputation for gentleness and width of sympathy." J. F. Mozley, *John Foxe and His Book* (London, 1940), p. 158.

55. More, *Early Poems*, in *The English Works of Sir Thomas More* (1557), fascimile edition (London, Eyre and Spottiswoode, 1931), I, 341.

56. William Roper, *The lyfe of Sir Thomas Moore Knighte*, ed. E. V. Hitchcock (London, Oxford University Press, 1935), p. 21.

57. Ro: Ba:, *Lyfe of More*, p. 86.

58. More, *Workes*, ed. Rastell, pp. 81H, 9A, 1168G, 1244H, 81C, 1248H, 1298H.

59. More, *History of King Richard III and Selections from the English and Latin Poems*, in Yale Edition of Selected Works (modernized series), III, ed. Richard S. Sylvester (New Haven, 1976), 162.

60. Ibid., p. 116.

61. More, *Latin Epigrams*, nos. 22, 27, 28, 52, 57, 38, 56, 101, 243.

62. More, *A Treatise on Ecclesiastes 7*, in *English Works*, I, 474, 475, 479.

63. More, *De Tristitia Christi*, in *Complete Works*, vol. XIV, part 1, trans. and ed. Clarence H. Miller (New Haven, 1976), pp. 241–243.

64. Ibid., pp. 413–415.

65. Ibid., p. 457.

66. Thomas Stapleton, *The Life and illustrious martyrdom of Sir Thomas More*, part III of *Tres Thomae*, printed at Douai, 1588, trans. Philip E. Hallett (London, Burns, Oates, & Washbourne, 1928), p. 75.

67. More, *A dialoge of comfort agaynst trybulacion*, p. 98.

68. *Thomas More's prayer book*, a facsimile of the annotated pages, trans. with intro. by Louis L. Martz and Richard S. Sylvester (New Haven, 1969), pp. 27, 31, 32, 33, 34, 35, 37, 39, 45, 50, 52, 57, 60, 66, 68, 79, 88, 96, 98, 99, 100, 109, 111, 165.

69. Sigmund Freud, *Jokes and their Relation to the Unconscious*, in *The Standard Edition of the Complete Psychological Works of Sigmund Freud*, trans. and ed. James Strachey, vol. VIII (London, Hogarth Press, 1953); "Humour" (1927), ibid., XXI (1961), 161–166. Freud's dynamic explanation of the humorous attitude involves his whole system of displacement of large quantities of cathexis from the ego to the superego. "Look here! This is all that this seemingly dangerous world amounts to. Child's play—the very thing to jest about." This is the intention that humor fulfills, Freud maintains. When More's *Utopia* is closest to humor, it is the Utopian children who take over and deny the world of More's England: They transvalue the worth of gold and jewels and turn them into playthings.

In *Wit and its Relation to the Unconscious*, trans. A. A. Brill (New York, Dodd, Mead, 1916), Freud hazarded the "impression" that "the subjective determination of wit production is oftentimes not unrelated to persons suffering from neurotic diseases, when, for example, one learns that Lichtenberg was a confirmed hypochondriac burdened with all kinds of eccentricities . . . Persons having a powerful sadistic component in their sexuality, which is more or less inhibited in life, are most successful with the tendency-wit of aggression" (pp. 218, 219).

70. Freud, *Collected Papers*, V, ed. John Strachey (London, Hogarth Press, 1950), 217.

71. More, *Confutacyon of Tyndales answere*, p. 232.

72. Ro: Ba:, *Life of More*, pp. 89–90.

73. In another story (recorded in Foxe's *Booke of Martyrs*, II, 353) the beard figures in an incident that takes place on the scaffold: "Also even when he should lay downe his necke on the blocke, he having a great gray beard, striked out his beard, and said to the

hangman, I pray you let me lay my beard over the blocke, lest you should cut it; thus with a mocke he ended his life."

74. Ro: Ba:, *Lyfe of More,* pp. 123–124.

75. Foxe, *Booke of Martyrs,* II, 353.

76. Robert Southey, *Sir Thomas More or Colloquies on Progress and Prospects of Society* (London, 1829), I, 60ff.

77. Russell A. Ames, *Citizen Thomas More and his Utopia* (Princeton, Princeton University Press, 1949), p. 6.

78. More, *Utopia,* p. 241.

79. Ibid., p. 105.

80. Ibid., p. 243.

81. Ibid., p. 245.

82. [Jacobus Sobius], *Philalethis Civis Utopiensis Dialogus de Facultatibus Romanensium nuper Publicatis* (Basel, 1520).

83. Silvio Zavala, "Sir Thomas More in New Spain," *Recuerdos de Vasco de Quiroga* (Mexico City, 1965), pp. 99–116; Robert Ricard, *The Spiritual Conquest of Mexico* (Berkeley, 1966).

84. Quoted in N. Z. Davis, "René Choppin on More's *Utopia,*" *Moreana,* vol. 5, nos. 19–20 (1968), pp. 91–96.

85. More, *Tableau du meilleur gouvernement possible, ou l'Utopie de Thomas Morus . . . ,* trans. M. T. Rousseau (Paris, 1780), dedication to Vergennes.

5. *A Città Felice for Architects and Philosophers*

1. Ortensio Landi, *Commentario delle piu notabili, et mostruose cose d'Italia, & altri luoghi, di lingua Aramea in Italiana tradotto* (Venice, 1548).

2. Antonio Francesco Doni, *I Mondi* (Venice, 1552); *I Marmi del Doni, academico peregrino* (Venice, 1552–1553). See Cecilia Ricottini Marsili-Libelli, *Anton Francesco Doni, scrittore e stampatore* (Florence, 1960); Paul F. Grendler, *Critics of the Italian World, 1530–1560: Anton Francesco Doni, Nicolò Franco and Ortensio Lando* (Madison, 1969).

3. Ellis Heywood, *Il Moro: Ellis Heywood's Dialogue in Memory of Thomas More,* ed. and trans. Roger Lee Deakins (Cambridge, Mass., 1972).

4. R. O. Jones, "Some Notes on More's 'Utopia' in Spain," *Modern Language Review,* vol. 45, no. 4 (October 1950), pp. 478–482.

5. Lodovico Zuccolo, *Dialoghi . . . nei quali con varietà di eruditione si scoprono nuovi, e vaghi pensieri filosofici, morali, e politici . . .* (Venice, 1625), and *La Repubblica d'Evandria, e altri dialoghi politici,* ed. Rodolfo de Mattei (Rome, 1944), intro., pp. 7–30. Zuccolo had also attacked More in an earlier work, *Considerationi politiche et morali sopra cento oracoli d'illustri personaggi antichi* (Venice, 1621).

6. Francesco Patrizi da Cherso, *La Città felice* (Venice, 1553), excerpts from Carlo Curcio, ed., *Utopisti e riformatori sociali del cinquecento* (Bologna, Zanichelli, 1941), pp. 121–142. See Paola Maria Arcari, *Il pensiero politico di Francesco Patrizi da Cherso* (Rome, 1935); and Benjamin Brinckman, *An Introduction to Francesco Patrizi's Nova de Universis Philosophia* (New York, 1941).

7. Girolamo Cardano, *Encomium Neronis,* in *Opera Omnia* (Lyons, 1663), I, 179–220. See Jean Lucas-Dubreton, *Le Monde enchanté de la renaissance: Jérôme Cardan l'halluciné* (Paris, 1954); and A. Bellini, *Cardano e il suo tempo* (Milan, 1947).

8. Ludovico Agostini, *La Repubblica Immaginaria,* ed. Luigi Firpo (Turin, 1957), and *Esclamazioni a Dio,* ed. Luigi Firpo (Bologna, 1958). See Luigi Firpo, *Lo Stato ideale della Controriforma: Ludovico Agostini* (Bari, 1957).

9. More, *Utopia,* in *The Complete Works of St. Thomas More,* IV, ed. Edward Surtz and J. H. Hexter (New Haven, Yale University Press, 1965), 121.

10. Heinrich Brauer and Rudolf Wittkower, *Die Zeichnungen des Gianlorenzo Bernini* (Berlin, 1931), I, 85.

11. Carroll William Westfall, *In This Most Perfect Paradise: Alberti, Nicholas V, and the Invention of Conscious Urban Planning in Rome, 1447–55* (University Park, Pennsylvania State University Press, 1974).

12. Leone Battista Alberti, *Opere volgari*, ed. Cecil Grayson, 3 vols. (Bari, 1960–73); *Opuscoli morali*, trans. Cosimo Bartoli (Venice, 1568); *Momus o del principe*, ed. and trans. Giuseppe Martini (Bologna, 1942); *De Re Aedificatoria*, ed. Paolo Portoghesi (Milan, 1966); for an English translation, *Ten books on Architecture*, trans. into Italian by Cosimo Bartoli and into English by James Leoni, ed. Joseph Rykwert (London, A. Tiranti, 1955), a reprint of the 1755 edition, with the life from the 1739 edition. See Joan Gadol, *Leon Battista Alberti: Universal Man of the Early Renaissance* (Chicago, 1969); Girolamo Mancini, *Vita di Leon Battista Alberti* (Florence, 1882); Paul-Henri Michel, *Un idéal humain au xve siècle: La Pensée de L. B. Alberti (1404–1472)* (Paris, 1930); Rudolf Wittkower, *Architectural Principles in the Age of Humanism* (London, 1941); Giovanni Santinello, *Leon Battista Alberti: Una visione estetica del mondo e della vita* (Florence, 1962).

13. Filarete (Antonio di Piero Averlino), *Treatise on Architecture* (commonly referred to as *Sforzinda*), trans. and ed. John R. Spencer, 2 vols. (New Haven and London, Yale University Press, 1965). See Luigi Firpo, "La Città ideale del Filarete," in *Studi in memoria di Gioele Solari* (Turin, 1954), pp. 11–59; John R. Spencer, "Filarete and Central Plan Architecture," *Journal of the Society of Architectural Historians*, vol. 17, no. 3 (1958), pp. 10–18; H. Saalman, "Early Renaissance Architectural Theory and Practice in Antonio Filarete's Trattato di Architettura," *Art Bulletin*, 16 (1959), 89–106; Robert Klein, "L'Urbanisme utopique de Filarete à Valentin Andreae," in *Les Utopies à la Renaissance* (Brussels and Paris, 1963), pp. 209–230; Peter Tigler, *Die Architekturtheorie des Filarete* (Berlin, 1963).

14. Francesco di Giorgio Martini, *Trattati di Architettura, Ingegneria e Arte Militare*, ed. Corrado Maltese, transcription by Livia Maltese Degrassi, 2 vols. (Milan, 1967). See Allen Stuart Weller, *Francesco di Giorgio, 1439–1501* (Chicago, 1943); Roberto Papini, *Francesco di Giorgio architetto*, 2 vols. (Florence, 1946); Selwyn J. C. Brinton, *Francesco di Giorgio Martini of Siena, Painter, Sculptor, Engineer, Civil and Military Architect (1439–1502)*, 2 vols. (London, 1934–1935).

15. Weller, *Francesco di Giorgio*, app., p. 349, doc. 35, Federigo da Montefeltro to the Signoria of Siena, July 26, 1480.

16. Ibid., app., pp. 373–374, doc. 85, Duke Gian Galeazzo to the Sienese Balìa, July 8, 1490.

17. Francesco di Giorgio Martini, *Trattato di architettura civile e militare*, ed. Carlo Promis (Turin, 1841), p. 53, book II, 8, and p. 62, book II, 10.

18. Ibid., p. 71; see also Maltese ed., II, 360.

19. Quoted in Pierre Lavedan, *Histoire de l'urbanisme: Renaissance et Temps modernes*, 2nd ed. (Paris H. Laurens, 1959), p. 11.

20. Alberti, *De Iciarchia*, in *Opere volgari*, ed. Anicio Bonucci, III (Florence, 1845), 116.

21. Filarete, *Sforzinda*, I, 106, book VIII, fol. 61v.

22. Ibid., p. 41, book IV, fols. 23 r and v, and p. 47, book IV, fol. 27r.

23. Ibid., p. 16, book II, fol. 8r.

24. Ibid., p. 45, book IV, fol. 25v.

25. Ibid., p. 111, book IX, fol. 65r.

26. Aristotle, *Politics*, trans. and ed. Ernest Barker (Oxford, 1946), p. 68, book II, chap. 8.

27. Vitruvius, *On Architecture*, trans. Frank Granger, Loeb Classical Library, I (London and New York, Wm. Heinemann, 1931), 5, book I, preface.

28. Ibid., pp. 53, 55, 57, book I, chap. 6, and plate A.

29. Ibid., p. 121, book II, chap. 8.

30. Ibid., p. 27, book I, chap. 2.

31. Filarete, *Sforzinda*, I, 6, book I, fol. 2v.

32. Ibid.

33. Francesco di Giorgio, *Trattati*, ed. Maltese, I, plate 1, reproduction of MS Saluzz. 148, fol. 3, in the Biblioteca Reale, Turin.

34. MS Ashburnham 361, fols. 1 and 5r, in the Biblioteca Medicea Laurenziana, Florence. See G. Eimer, *Die Stadtplanung im schwedischen Ostseereich, 1600–1715. Mit Beiträgen zur Geschichte der Idealstadt* (Stockholm, 1961), p. 62.

35. Filarete, *Sforzinda*, I, 175, book XIII, fol. 100r.

36. Ibid., p. 222, book XVI, fol. 128v.

37. Vitruvius, *On Architecture*, I, 73–75, book II, preface.

38. Alberti, *Ten Books on Architecture*, pp. 67–68, book IV, chap. 2.

39. Ibid., p. 64, book IV, chap. 1.

40. Ibid., p. 66, book IV, chap. 1.

41. Ibid.

42. Ibid., p. 85, book V, chap. 2.

43. Filarete, *Sforzinda*, I, 146–150, book XI, fols. 84r–86r; Francesco di Giorgio, *Trattato*, ed. Promis, p. 53, book II, 8.

44. Filarete, *Sforzinda*, I, 45–46, book IV, fol. 26r.

45. Ibid., p. 49, book IV, fol. 28r, and p. 180, book XIV, fol. 103r.

46. Ibid., p. 6, book I, fol. 2v.

47. Ibid., pp. 282–283, book XX, fols. 165r and v.

48. Leonardo da Vinci, *I Manoscritti e i Disegni*, pub. by Reale Commissione Vinciana, V (Rome, Danesi, 1941), 29, fol. 16r, and 69, fol. 36r.

49. Ibid., pp. 28–29, fols. 15v and 16r. Summary follows translation by I. A. Richter, ed., *Selections from the Notebooks of Leonardo da Vinci* (London, Oxford University Press, 1952), pp. 213–214.

50. Patrizi, *La Città felice*, in Curcio, *Utopisti del cinquecento*, p. 136.

51. Ibid., p. 129.

52. Agostini, "L'Infinito," book I, part II, sect. 130, quoted in Firpo, *Lo Stato ideale della Controriforma*, p. 275.

53. Agostini, *La Repubblica Immaginaria* (book II, part II, of "L'Infinito"), ed. Firpo, p. 47.

54. Ibid., p. 74.

55. Filarete, *Sforzinda*, I, 248, book XVIII, fol. 144r.

56. Ibid., p. 254, book XVIII, fol. 148r, and p. 257, book XVIII, fol. 150r.

57. Doni, "Mondo Savio" (dialogue from his *I Mondi*), reprinted by Luigi Firpo in *Il Pensiero della Rinascenza e della Riforma*, vol. X of *Grande Antologia Filosofica*, ed. M. F. Sciacca et al. (Milan, 1964), p. 577.

58. Quoted in Hermann Bauer, *Kunst und Utopie* (Berlin, Walter De Gruyter, 1965), p. 1.

59. Agostini, *La Repubblica Immaginaria*, p. 63.

6. Heaven on Earth for the Common Man

1. Thomas Müntzer, "Protestation odder empietung Tome Müntzers vō Stolberg am Hartzs seelwarters zu Alstedt seine leere betreffende unnd tzum anfang von dem rechten Christen glawben unnd der tawffe (1524)," in *Schriften und Briefe*, ed. Günther Franz (Gütersloh, G. Mohn, 1968), p. 234. Hereafter referred to as Franz.

2. Jürgen Bücking, "Der Oberrheinische Revolutionär heisst Conrad Stürtzel," *Archiv für Kulturgeschichte*, 56 (1974), 177–197; A. Franke and G. Zchäbitz, *Das Buch der 100 Kapitel und 20 Statuten des sog. O R* (Berlin, 1967).

3. Adapted from translation by Gordon Leff, *Heresy in the Later Middle Ages* (Manchester, Manchester University Press, 1967), I, 373.

4. Theodora Büttner and Ernst Werner, *Circumcellionen und Adamiten* (Berlin, Akademie-Verlag, 1959), pp. 81–82; quotation adapted from Howard Kaminsky, *A History of the Hussite Revolution* (Berkeley, University of California Press, 1967), p. 405.

5. Walter Elliger, *Thomas Müntzer: Leben und Werk* (Göttingen, 1975), p. 17.

6. Martin Luther, "Eine schreckliche Geschichte und ein Gericht Gottes über Thomas Münzer, darin Gott öffentlich desselben Geists Lügen straft und verdammt," *Schriften,* XVIII, in *Werke: Kritische Gesammtausgabe* (Weimar, H. Böhlau, 1883–1957), 367.

7. Franz, p. 394, Müntzer to Count Ernst von Mansfeld, Allstedt, Sept. 22, 1523.

8. Luther, "Brief an die Fürsten zu Sachsen von dem aufrührerischen Geist," *Schriften,* XV, 213–215.

9. Erwin Mülhaupt, *Luther über Müntzer* (Witten, 1973), pp. 109–110.

10. Franz, p. 471, Müntzer to the people of Erfurt, Frankenhausen, May 13, 1525. Luther's Bible translation for Daniel 7:27 read, "Aber das Reich Gewalt und Macht unter dem ganzen Himmel wird dem heiligen Volk des Höchsten gegeben werden."

11. Numbers 19 refers to the purification required by the seventh day after touching a dead body. This is characteristic of Müntzer's free handling of the biblical text. Müntzer, "Auslegung des andern unterschyds Danielis dess propheten gepredigt auffm schloss zu Alstet vor den tetigen thewren Herzcogen und vorstehern zu Sachssen durch Thomā Müntzer diener des wordt gottes" (1524), in Franz, p. 251.

12. Ibid., p. 256.

13. Müntzer, "Hoch verursachte Schutzrede und antwwort wider das Gaistlosse Sanft lebende fleysch zu Wittenberg" (1524), in Franz, p. 329.

14. Franz, p. 434, Müntzer to the people of Allstedt, Mühlhausen, Aug. 15, 1524.

15. Ibid., pp. 454–455, Müntzer to the people of Allstedt, Mühlhausen, about April 26 or 27, 1525.

16. Ibid., p. 398, Müntzer to Hans Zeiss, Allstedt, Dec. 2, 1523.

17. Ibid., p. 256.

18. Ibid., p. 281.

19. Ibid., pp. 21–22.

20. Ibid., p. 403, Müntzer to Christoph Meinhard, "Auslegung des 18 Psalms," Allstedt, May 30, 1524.

21. Luther, *Briefwechsel,* III, in *Werke* (1933), 472, Luther to Nikolaus von Amsdorf, Wittenberg, April 11, 1525.

22. Luther, *Tischreden,* I, in *Werke,* 598.

23. "Bekenntnis Thomas Müntzers" (May 16, 1525), in Franz, p. 548.

24. Luther, *Briefwechsel,* III, 515, Luther to Johann Rühel, May 30, 1520.

25. Franz, pp. 473–474.

26. Ibid., pp. 543, 548.

27. Philipp Melanchthon, *Opera quae supersunt omnia (Corpus reformatorum),* ed. C. G. Bretschneider, vol. I (Halle, 1834), col. 744.

28. Georg Theodor Strobel, *Leben, Schriften und Lehren Thomae Muentzers des Urhebers des Bauernaufruhrs in Thueringen* (Nuremberg, 1795).

29. Elliger, *Thomas Müntzer.* The best Müntzer bibliography is on pp. 824–835.

30. Philipp Melanchthon, *Die Histori Thome Muntzers des anfengers der Döringischen uffrur* (Hagenau, 1525), quoted in Otto H. Brandt, ed., *Thomas Müntzer, sein Leben und seine Schriften* (Jena, E. Diederichs, 1933), p. 42.

31. Wilhelm Zimmermann, *Allgemeine geschichte des grossen Bauernkrieges,* 3 parts (Stuttgart, 1841–1843), III, 606ff, 766ff.

32. Friedrich Engels, *Der deutsche Bauernkrieg* (1850), trans. in *The German Revolutions,* ed. Leonard Krieger (Chicago, 1967), pp. 3–119; for Engels' appraisal of Müntzer, see esp. pp. 29, 30, 46ff.

33. Karl Kautsky, *Die Vorläufer des neueren Sozialismus,* 2nd ed. (Stuttgart, 1909), II, 42ff.

7. Pansophia: A Dream of Science

1. Pansophia, an ancient Greek word, was used by Philo, reappeared in the Renaissance, and gained wide currency in the seventeenth century.

2. Francis Bacon, *A Refutation of Philosophies (Redargutio Philosophiarum),* 1608, in *The Philosophy of Francis Bacon: An Essay on Its Development from 1603 to 1609, with New Translations of Fundamental Texts,* ed. and trans. Benjamin Farrington (Liverpool, Liverpool University Press, 1964), p. 109.

3. John Milton, *An Apology against a Pamphlet Call'd a Modest Confutation of the Animadversions upon the Remonstrant against Smectymnuus* (London, 1642), p. 10.

4. Descartes cast Bruno and Campanella into the same basket with Telesius, Basso, Vaninus as *novatores* from whom nothing was to be learned. Descartes, *Oeuvres,* ed. C. E. Adam and Paul Tannery, new ed., I (Paris, 1969), 158, Descartes to Isaac Beeckman, Amsterdam, Oct. 17, 1630.

8. Bruno, the Magus of Nola

1. Giordano Bruno, *De Immenso et Innumerabilibus,* bk. III, chap. 1, in *Opera Latine Conscripta,* ed. Francesco Fiorentino et al. (Florence and Naples, 1879–1891), vol. I, part i, p. 313.

2. Father Mersenne in *L'Impiété des Déistes* (Paris, 1624) attacked Bruno's idea of science in the name of the new science with a mathematical foundation. See Hélène Védrine, *La Conception de la nature chez Bruno* (Paris, 1967). Florio, *The Essayes* (1603), p. vii, reported Bruno's views on the importance of translation in the accumulative transmission of knowledge: "my old fellow Nolano taught publikely, that from translation all Science had it's of-spring. Likely, since even Philosophie, Grammar, Rhethoricke, Logike, Arithmetike, Geometrie, Astronomy, Musike, and all the Mathematikes yet holde their name of the Greekes: and the Greekes drew their baptizing water from the conduit-pipes of the Egiptians, and they from the well-springs of the Hebrews or Chaldees." Despite Bruno's expression of the idea of accumulation in astronomic knowledge in one passage of the *Cena de le Ceneri,* he held to the common doctrine of vicissitudes in all material things, which meant a movement from one state to its opposite: "Cossí tutte cose nel suo geno hanno tutte vicissitudine di dominio et servitú, felicità et infelicità, de quel stato che si chiama vita, et quello che si chiama morte; di luce, et tenebre; di bene e male." Giordano Bruno, *La Cena de le Ceneri,* ed. Giovanni Aquilecchia ([Turin], Einaudi, 1955), Fifth Dialogue, p. 217. See F. Saxl, "Veritas Filia Temporis," in *Philosophy and History: Essays Presented to E. Cassirer* (London, 1936), pp. 197–222.

3. Quoted in Dorothea (Waley) Singer, *Giordano Bruno, His Life and Thought, with Annotated Translation of "On the Infinite Universe and Worlds"* (New York, Schuman, 1950), p. 25.

4. Francis Bacon, *Historia naturalis et experimentalis* (1622), in *Works,* ed. James Spedding et al., II (London, 1857), 13.

5. Bruno, *Cena delle ceneri* (1584), in *Opere italiane,* ed. Giovanni Gentile (Bari, Laterza, 1907), I, 28.

6. Bruno, *De l'infinito universo et mondi* (Venice [London], 1584), trans. in Singer, *Bruno,* p. 20.

7. Domenico Berti, *Documenti intorno a Giordano Bruno da Nola* (Rome, 1880), pp. 32, 55.

8. On Bruno's sexual exploits, see the preface to his *De gl'heroici furori* (1585); Angelo Mercati, *Il Sommario del processo di Giordano Bruno* (Vatican City, 1942), p. 102; and Berti, *Documenti,* p. 9.

9. Berti, *Documenti,* pp. 7, 37.

10. See John C. Nelson, *Renaissance Theory of Love: The Context of Giordano Bruno's Eroici furori* (New York, 1958).

11. Berti, *Documenti,* p. 66; Vincenzo Spampanato, *Documenti della vita di Giordano Bruno* (Florence, 1933), pp. 108–109. The translation is by Frances Yates, *Giordano Bruno and the Hermetic Tradition* (Chicago, University of Chicago Press, 1964), p. 231.

12. Quoted and trans. in Yates, *Bruno,* pp. 211–212.

13. Bruno, *The Expulsion of the Triumphant Beast,* trans. and ed. Arthur D. Imerti (New Brunswick, N.J., Rutgers University Press, 1964), p. 268, emended.

14. Quoted from Yates, *Bruno,* p. 226.

15. Bruno, *Expulsion,* ed. Imerti, p. 246.

16. Luigi Firpo, "Il processo di Giordano Bruno," *Rivista storica italiana,* 60 (1948), 542–597; Vincenzo Spampanato, *Vita di Giordano Bruno con documenti editi e inediti* (Messina, G. Principato, 1921), II, 656.

17. *De l'infinito universo e mondi,* trans. in Singer, *Bruno,* p. 58.

18. *Expulsion of the Triumphant Beast,* quoted and trans. in Yates, *Bruno,* pp. 212–213.

19. On Bruno's trials, see Luigi Firpo, *Il processo di Giordano Bruno* (Naples, 1949).

20. Angelo Mercati, *Il Sommario del processo di Giordano Bruno* (Vatican City, 1942).

21. Giordano Bruno, *The Heroic Frenzies,* trans. and ed. Paul Eugene Memmo, Jr. (Chapel Hill, University of North Carolina Press, 1965), pp. 114–115, 117, 118.

22. Ibid., p. 122.

23. During the Venetian trial Bruno charged that Mocenigo had struck him in his *onore.* Spampanato, *Vita di Bruno,* II, 739.

24. Ibid., pp. 588–589.

9. Bacon, Trumpeter of New Atlantis

1. Adolf von Harnack, *Geschichte der Königlich preussischen Akademie der Wissenschaften zu Berlin* (Berlin, 1900), vol. I, part I, p. 174.

2. Francesco Grillo, *Tommaso Campanella in America: A Critical Bibliography and a Profile* (New York, 1954), pp. 97–98.

3. In 1631 the *New Atlantis* was translated into French, in 1633 into Latin; it was published eleven times from 1627 to 1676, and there have since been more than a hundred editions.

4. The inscription, a rewriting of the Vulgate, Daniel 12: 4, "Plurimi pertransibunt et multiplex erit scientia," appears on the frontispiece engraving of ships sailing forth in the *Instauratio Magna.* The engraving is reproduced in Francis Bacon, *Works,* ed. James Spedding et al., I (London, 1857), 119. In the *Redargutio Philosophiarum,* 1608 (*The Refutation of Philosophies*), he had already written: "Distant voyages and travels have brought to light many things in nature, which may throw fresh light on human philosophy and science and correct by experience the opinions and conjectures of the ancients. Not only reason but prophecy connects the two. What else can the prophet mean who, in speaking about the last times, says: Many will pass through and knowledge will be multiplied? Does he not imply that the passing through or perambulation of the round earth and the increase or multiplication of science were destined to the same age and century?" Benjamin Farrington, *The Philosophy of Francis Bacon: An Essay on Its Development from 1603 to 1609, with New Translations of Fundamental Texts* (Liverpool, Liverpool University Press, 1964), pp. 131–132.

5. Bacon, *Sylva Sylvarum: or a Natural History, in Ten Centuries* (1626 [1627]) in *Works,* II (1857), 666–667. See also Paul H. Kocher, "Francis Bacon and His Father," *Huntington Library Quarterly,* 21 (1957–58), 133–166.

6. Bacon, *Novum Organum,* in *Works,* IV (1858), 82.

7. Bacon, *The Wisdome of the Ancients,* trans. Arthur Gorges Knight (London, 1619), p. 131: "Let men therefore be admonished, that by acknowledging the imperfections of Nature and Arte, they are gratefull to the Gods, and shall thereby obtaine new benefits and greater favours at their bountifull hands, and the accusation of *Prometheus* their Authour and Master, (though bitter and vehement) will conduce more to their profit, then to be effuse in the congratulation of his invention: for in a word, the opinion of having inough, is to be accounted one of the greatest causes of having too little." (See also *Works,* VI [1858], 749.)

8. *The Wisdome of the Ancients,* trans. Knight, pp. 143–144. (See also *Works,* VI, 753.)

9. Bacon, *Natural and Experimental History for the Foundation of Philosophy: or Phenomena of the Universe,* in *Works,* V (1858), 131.

10. Bacon, *Temporis Partus Masculus (The Masculine Birth of Time),* in Farrington, *Philosophy of Francis Bacon,* p. 63: "Come, then let Aristotle be summoned to the bar, that worst of sophists stupefied by his own unprofitable subtlety, the cheap dupe of words . . . He composed an art or manual of madness and made us slaves of words."

11. Bacon, *Sylva Sylvarum,* in *Works,* II, 336, William Rawley, "To the Reader."

12. James Spedding, preface to the *New Atlantis,* in *Works,* III (1857), 122.

13. Bacon, *The Advancement of Learning and New Atlantis* (London, Oxford University Press, 1951), p. 277.

14. See, for example, *Works,* VI, 475.

15. Bacon, *Advancement of Learning and New Atlantis* (1951), p. 136.

16. James Spedding, *The Letters and the Life of Francis Bacon,* I (London, 1861), 109, Bacon to Lord Treasurer Burghley, ca. 1592.

17. Bacon, *Advancement of Learning and New Atlantis* (1951), p. 256, William Rawley, "To the Reader."

18. Ibid., pp. 285–286.

19. Ibid., p. 288.

20. See R. L. Colie, "Cornelis Drebbel and Salomon de Caus: Two Jacobean Models for Salomon's House," *Huntington Library Quarterly,* 18 (1954–1955), 245–260, for some of the ideas behind Bacon's proposed inventions.

21. Bacon, *The History of Life and Death, or The Second Title in Natural and Experimental History for the Foundation of Philosophy,* in *Works,* V, 215.

22. Bacon, *Advancement of Learning and New Atlantis* (1951), p. 291.

23. Ibid., p. 295.

24. Ibid.

25. Ibid., p. 297.

26. Ibid., p. 9.

27. Ibid., p. 10.

28. Bacon, *Temporis Partus Masculus (The Masculine Birth of Time),* in Farrington, *Philosophy of Francis Bacon,* p. 72.

10. Campanella's City of the Sun

1. Tommaso Campanella, "Quaestiones Physiologicae," in *Disputationum in Quatuor Partes Suae Philosophiae Realis Libri Quatuor* (Paris, 1637), p. 513.

2. Tommaso Campanella, *Lettere,* ed. Vincenzo Spampanato (Bari, Laterza, 1927), p. 133, Campanella to Monsignor Antonio Querengo, Naples, July 8, 1607, "dal profondo Caucaso."

3. Campanella, *Philosophia, Sensibus Demonstrata,* in *Octo Disputationes Distincta* (Naples, 1591), p. 320.

4. Luigi Amabile, *Fra Tommaso Campanella: La sua congiura, i suoi processi, e la sua pazzia* (Naples, 1882), III, 12, Giulio Battaglino to Usimbardi, Naples, Sept. 4, 1592.

5. Campanella, *Lettere*, p. 107, Campanella to Gaspar Scoppius, Naples, Kalends of June, 1607: "'Quomodo literas scit, cum non didicerit? ergone demonium habes?' At ego respondi me plus olei quam ipsi vini consumsise . . .'"

6. There is a reference to Bruno as "a certain Nolan" in Campanella, *Apologia pro Galileo, Mathematico Fiorentino. Ubi Disquiritur, Utrum Ratio Philosophandi, Quam Galileus Celebrat, Faveat Sacris Scripturis an Adversetur* (Frankfort, 1622), p. 9; trans. Grant McColley (Northampton, Mass., 1937).

7. Campanella, *Lettere*, pp. 165, 169, Campanella to Galileo, Naples, Ides of January 1611. He reminded Galileo of their meeting, and extolled him as the reviver of Pythagorean doctrines and the restorer of glory to Italy.

8. Campanella, *Lettere*, pp. 95, 98, Campanella to Gaspar Scoppius, Naples, May 6, 1607, and April 26–May 17, 1607.

9. In his letter to Cardinal Odoardo Farnese he admitted prophesying the "end of the world" in 1598. *Lettere*, p. 23, Naples, Aug. 30, 1606.

10. Amabile, *Campanella*, III, 195–196, doc. 269, "Atti institutivi del processo co' capi d'accusa," Sept. 1, 1599.

11. The official record read: "finxit non intelligere, et extra mentem esse." Amabile, *Campanella*, III, 263, doc. 312, "Esame del Campanella, che si mostra pazzo," May 17, 1600.

12. See Nicolaus Eymericus, *Le Manuel des inquisiteurs*, trans. and ed. Louis Sala-Molins (Paris, 1973), a translation of the Roman editions of 1585 and 1587.

13. This obviously did not appear in the printed edition of Rome, 1631: *Ad Divum Petrum, Apostolorum Principem, Triumphantem. Atheismus Triumphatus, Seu Reductio ad Religionem per Scientiarum Veritates, F. Thomae Campanellae . . . Contra Antichristianismum Achitophellisticum. Sexti Tomi Pars Prima . . .* (Rome, 1631). In the preface to the English translation of *De Monarchia Hispanica Discursus*, entitled *A Discourse Touching the Spanish Monarchy* (London, 1654), the Frenchman Jacques Gaffarel is quoted as describing Campanella "with the Calves of his Legs beaten black and blue all over, and with scarcely any flesh at all upon his buttocks; it having been torn from him peice-meal, to force him to the confession of such crimes as they had accused him of." See also Campanella, *Lettere*, pp. 21–22, Campanella to Cardinal Odoardo Farnese, Naples, Aug. 30, 1606.

14. For a portrait of Campanella around 1630 painted in Rome by Francesco Cozza (now in the Palazzo Caetani di Sermoneta in Rome) see opposite p. 16 in Tommaso Campanella, *Monarchia Messiae, con due Discorsi della libertà e della felice suggezione allo Stato ecclesiastico,"* a facsimile of the 1633 edition with a critical text of the *Discorsi*, ed. Luigi Firpo (Turin, 1960).

15. Descartes had dipped into the works of Campanella, which Tobias Adami had introduced in the 1620s. Writing to Constantin Huygens in March 1638 he referred to them with contempt, saying they had left nothing in his memory. And he bluntly refused Mersenne's offer to send him the 1638 edition of the *Philosophiae Rationalis et Realis Partes V*. Descartes, *Oeuvres*, ed. C. E. Adam and Paul Tannery, new ed., II (Paris, 1969), 48, 436.

16. See Gisela Bock, "Bemerkungen zur neueren Campanella-Forschung," *Quellen und Forschungen aus italienischen Archiven und Bibliotheken*, 51 (1971), 390–421.

17. Giovanni Di Napoli, *Tommaso Campanella, filosofo della restaurazione cattolica* (Padua, 1947), p. vii. Romano Amerio is the best representative of the position that Campanella developed from a youthful naturalistic to a traditional religious position. "Il problema esegetico fondamentale del pensiero campanelliano," *Rivista di filosofia neo-scolastica*, 31 (1939), 368–387.

18. Amabile records Campanella's confession of his simulation of madness and its cause in an "Appendix ad Amicum pro Apologia" (*Campanella*, III, 188, 189, doc. 268): "Falsitates et doli praevaluerunt ob Martialem Cometam in domo Mercurii carceres, aut

ob *quadratum* aspectum *Martis* et *Saturni* post terremotus. et nos dolis collusimus, et mendaciis ad vitam servandam."

19. For a review of scholarly controversy on the interpretation of Campanella's religious position, see Nicola Badaloni, *Tommaso Campanella* (Milan, 1965), pp. 7–35.

20. See "Canzone a Berillo (Basilio Berillari) di pentimento desideroso di confessione . . . ," in *Scritti Scelti di Giordano Bruno e di Tommaso Campanella,* ed. Luigi Firpo (Turin, Unione tip-editrice torinese, 1949), p. 377: "Io mi credevo Dio tener in mano, non seguitando Dio, ma l'argute ragion del senno mio . . ."

21. Campanella, *Lettere,* p. 76, Campanella to Philip III of Spain, Naples, April (?) 1607.

22. Ibid., p. 77.

23. Campanella, *Lettere,* p. 389, Campanella to Ferdinand de' Medici, Paris, July 6, 1638.

24. The first edition was Frankfort, 1623. There is a recent French translation, *La Cité du soleil* by Arnaud Tripet, with notes by Luigi Firpo, Geneva, 1972. Modern editions tend to be based on the Biblioteca Governativa of Lucca, MS 2618. For Italian editions of *The City of the Sun,* see Norberto Bobbio (Turin, 1942); and *Opere di Giordano Bruno e di Tommaso Campanella,* ed. Augusto Guzzo and Romano Amerio (Milan, 1956), pp. 1074–1116, *La Città del sole, dialogo poetico*.

25. See *Prodromus Philosophiae Instaurandae, Id Est, Dissertationis de Natura Rerum Compendium Secundum Vera Principia, ex Scriptis Thomae Campanellae Praemissum. Cum Praefatione ad Philosophos Germaniae,* ed. Tobias Adami (Frankfort, 1617). A sonnet by Campanella to Adami appears on p. 25.

26. See Campanella's *Apologia pro Galileo, Mathematico Fiorentino*.

27. In the unpaginated preface to his edition of Campanella's *Realis Philosophiae Epilogisticae Partes Quatuor, Hoc Est, De Rerum Natura, Hominum Moribus, Politica, (Cui Civitas Solis Iuncta Est) et Oeconomica, cum Adnotationibus Physiologicis* (Frankfort, 1623), Tobias Adami raised *The City of the Sun* above the ideal states of Plato and More.

28. In the *De Dictis Christi. Inediti. Theologicorum Liber XXIII,* ed. and trans. into Italian by Romano Amerio (Rome, 1969), p. 213, Campanella later proposed the institution of a religious order devoted to the practice of medicine.

29. Campanella, *La Città del sole e Scelta d'alcune poesie filosofiche,* ed. Adriano Seroni (Milan, Feltrinelli, 1962), p. 21.

30. Campanella republished in 1637 as *Disputationum in Quatuor Partes Suae Philosophiae Realis Libri Quatuor* the work Adami had printed in 1623 (*Realis Philosophiae Epilogisticae*), adding to each book a series of objections which he then refuted, after the manner of an academic or theological debate. The work was dedicated to Pierre Séguier, Grand Chancellor of France. In the refutation of the objections to his thought in the "Quaestiones super Tertia Parte Suae Philosophiae Realis, Quae Est de Politicis," he summarized the arguments that had been made against his political writings; pp. 100–112, quaestio IV, are an apologia for *The City of the Sun.* The "Quaestiones" appeared in an Italian translation in *Opere di Tommaso Campanella,* ed. Alessandro d'Ancona (Turin, 1854), II, 287–310, "Questioni sull'ottima republica."

31. Campanella, *Disputationum in Quatuor Partes,* p. 71, "Quaestiones super Tertia Parte." See also Campanella, *Syntagma de Libris Propriis,* ed. Vincenzo Spampanato (Florence, 1927); and Luigi Firpo, *Bibliografia degli scritti di Tommaso Campanella* (New York, 1940).

32. For an extreme statement of this position see Frances Yates, *Giordano Bruno and the Hermetic Tradition* (Chicago, 1964), pp. 376, 450.

33. Campanella, *Atheismus Triumphatus, seu Reductio ad Religionem per Scientiarum Veritates,* "Superiorum permissu." See "Risposte alle Censure dell' 'Ateismo Triunfato,'" in Campanella, *Opusculi inediti,* ed. Luigi Firpo (Florence, 1951), pp. 9–54.

34. Campanella, *Discourse Touching the Spanish Monarchy,* p. 47.

35. Campanella, *Lettere,* pp. 45–46, 48, 49, Campanella to Paul V, Naples, September 1606.

36. Campanella, *De Homine. Inediti. Theologicorum Liber IV,* ed. and trans. into Italian by Romano Amerio (Rome, Centro Internazionale di Studi Umanistici, Edizioni Rinascimento, 1961), p. 191.

37. Campanella, *Lettere,* p. 26, Campanella to Cardinal Odoardo Farnese, Naples, Aug. 30, 1606. See also ibid., p. 191, Campanella to Pope Paul V, Dec. 22, 1618.

38. See *Per la conversione degli ebrei (Quod Reminiscentur, Libro III),* ed. Romano Amerio (Florence, 1955). The full title of the complete work, *Quod Reminiscentur et Convertentur ad Dominum Universi Fines Terrae,* is derived from Psalm 21:28.

39. *Thomas Campanella, von der spanischen Monarchy, oder Auszfuehrliches Bedencken, welcher massen, von dem Koenig in Hispanien, zu nunmehr lang gesuchter Weltbeherrschung, sowol insgemein, als auff jedes Koenigreich und Land besonders, allerhand Anstalt zu machen sein moechte . . . Num . . . ausz dem Italianischen . . . in unser teutsche Sprach versetzt, und erstmals durch den offenen Truck in Tag gegeben* (Tübingen? 1620), trans. Christoph Besold. The *De Monarchia Hispanica Discursus* was, after *The City of the Sun,* his most frequently published work: two Latin editions, Amsterdam 1640, followed by others in 1641, 1653, 1709; two German editions, 1620 and 1650; two English editions, 1654 and 1660.

40. Campanella, *Quod Reminiscentur,* ed. Amerio, I, p. 81.

41. Campanella, *Discourse Touching the Spanish Monarchy,* chap. X, "What Sciences are required in a Monarch, to render him admired by all," pp. 45–49.

42. The *Discourse* was reprinted in 1660 as *Thomas Campanella, an Italian friar and second Machiavel. His advice to the King of Spain for attaining the universal monarchy of the world. Particularly concerning England, Scotland and Ireland, how to raise division between king and Parliament, to alter the government from a kingdom to a commonwealth. Thereby embroiling England in civil war to divert the English from disturbing the Spaniard in bringing the Indian treasure into Spain. Also for reducing Holland by procuring war betwixt England, Holland, and other sea-faring countries, affirming as most certain, that if the King of Spain became master of England and the Low Countries, he will quickly be sole monarch of all Europe, and the greatest part of the new world, translated into English by Ed. Chilmead, and published for awakening the English to prevent the approaching ruine of their nation. With an admonitorie preface by William Prynne of Lincolnes-Inne esquire* (London, 1660). Prynne's preface was dated Dec. 16, 1659.

43. Henry Stubbs, *Campanella revived, or an enquiry into the history of the Royal society, whether the virtuosi there do not pursue the projects of Campanella for the reducing England unto popery. Being the extract of a letter to a person of honour from H[enry]. S[tubbs]. with another letter to Sir N. N. relating the cause of the quarrel betwixt H. S. and the R. s. and an apology against some of their cavils. With a postscript concerning the quarrel depending betwixt H. S. and Dr. Merrett revived . . .* (London, 1670).

44. Campanella, *Discorsi della libertà, e della felice suggettione allo Stato Ecclesiastico,* (Iesi, 1633), pp. 5–14.

45. Campanella, *Monarchia Messiae* (Iesi, 1633), p. 8; *Discorsi della libertà,* p. 14.

46. Campanella, *Discourse Touching the Spanish Monarchy,* author's preface and pp. 2, 11.

47. Ibid., p. 230. The normal cyclical theory of world history was set forth in *Realis Philosophiae Epilogisticae,* ed. Adami, pp. 369–370, 393. The general section on Campanella's political thought is in *Pars Tertia Quae Est de Politica, in Aphorismos Digesta,* pp. 367–414. In the *Politica* each stage has its own symbolic figure (as in Joachim) and its own principle of corruption. The first stage was incarnate in Nimrod, the second in Moses, the third in Peter (p. 370). Joachim's triadic formula is used, its content transformed.

48. Campanella, *Discourse Touching the Spanish Monarchy,* p. 232.

49. See also *Lettere*, p. 374, Campanella to the Cardinal Duke de Richelieu, Paris, 1637: "et Civitas solis, per me delineata ac per te aedificanda." In the dedication to the Paris, 1637, edition of the *De Sensu Rerum et Magia* there is an appeal to Richelieu to build the City of the Sun.

50. *Ecloga Christianissimo Regi et Reginae in Portentosam Delphini . . . Nativitatem* (Paris, 1639). See modern edition by L. Firpo, *Tutte le opere* (Milan, 1954), I, 308, 310. Translation quoted from Frances Yates, *Bruno*, p. 391, n. 1.

51. Campanella, *De Dictis Christi. Inediti. Theologicorum Liber XXIII*, chap. 2, art. 1, pp. 37–53.

52. The *Metaphysica* was published in France in 1638. Its complete title was *Universalis Philosophiae seu Metaphysicarum Rerum iuxta Propria Dogmata Tres, Libri 18;* it was a long time in the making. This was the ultimate synthesis of Campanella's views on the principles and ends of the whole of reality. A first attempt at approaching the subject can be found in a *Metaphysica Nova Exordium* of 1590–1591; a new *Metafisica*, in Italian, is dated 1602, about the time of the composition of *The City of the Sun*. From then on successive versions were smuggled out to protectors and friends, stolen, destroyed, rewritten in Latin, lost, as he was moved from one dungeon to another. Time and again he recomposed the text de novo. Upon his liberation in Rome he sent the manuscript to a Lyons printer; the book was not published, and he had to pay thirty scudi to get it back. Only in 1638 did it finally appear, after further revisions and emendations. Other manuscripts had piled up in the interim, only a few of which were published in his lifetime.

11. Andreae, Pastor of Christianopolis

1. The Jesuits alerted Catholics to the dangers of this fraternity, which they considered a "rejetton du Luthérianisme, meslangé par Satan d'empirisme et de magie, pour mieux decevoir les esprits volages et curieux." Jacques Gaultier (Gualterius), S.J., *Table chronographique de l'estat du Christianisme* (Lyons, 1633), p. 889.

2. Descartes's dreams were recorded in Adrien Baillet, *Vie de Monsieur Descartes* (Paris, 1691). On the *Olympica* from which Baillet derived his account of the dreams, see *Oeuvres de Descartes*, ed. C. E. Adam and Paul Tannery, new. ed., X (Paris, 1966), 179–188. In the "Cogitationes privatae" Descartes recalls the dreams and the question from Ausonius, "Quod vitae sectabor iter?" (ibid., pp. 157, 216). On Descartes's curiosity about the Frères de la Rose-Croix, see Baillet and references to the unfinished "Studium bonae mentis" (*Oeuvres*, X, 191–203). See also Stephen Schönberger, "A Dream of Descartes: Reflections on the Unconscious Determinants of the Sciences," *International Journal of Psychoanalysis*, 20 (1938), 43–57; Henri Gouhier, *La pensée religieuse de Descartes*, 2nd ed. (Paris, 1972); Isaac Beeckman, *Journal tenu par Isaac Beeckman de 1604 à 1644*, ed Corneille de Waard, 4 vols. (The Hague, 1939–1953).

3. The most recent work on Andreae is the scholarly and thoroughgoing study by John Warwick Montgomery, *Cross and Crucible: Johann Valentin Andreae (1586–1654), Phoenix of the Theologians*, 2 vols. (The Hague, Nijhoff, 1973). In addition to the published writings Montgomery examined a dozen manuscripts, including a preaching diary, and seven hundred pieces of correspondence. While we have relied significantly on Montgomery's documentation, our point of view and interpretation differ from his. See also J. B. Neveux, *Vie spirituelle et vie sociale entre Rhin et Baltique au XVIIe siècle* (Paris, 1967); Will-Erich Peuckert, *Die Rosenkreuzer* (Jena, 1928), and *Pansophie*, 2nd ed. (Berlin, 1956); Paul Arnold, *Histoire des Rose-Croix et les origines de la Franc-Maçonnerie* (Paris, 1955); Gabriel Naudé, *Instruction à la France sur la vérité de l'histoire des frères de la Roze-Croix* (Paris, 1623); Andreas Libavius, *Analysis Confessionis Fraternitatis de Rosea Cruce* (Frankfort, 1615); Alfons Rosenberg's introduction (based on an unpublished work on Andreae by Ursula von Mangoldt) to a modernized edition of the *Chymische*

Hochzeit (Munich, 1957); Richard Kienast, *Johann Valentin Andreae und die vier echten Rosenkreutzer-Schriften* (Leipzig, 1926); Ferdinand Maack, ed., *Die Johann Valentin Andreä zugeschriebenen vier Hauptschriften der alten Rosenkreuzer* (Berlin, 1913); Harald Scholtz, *Evangelischer Utopismus bei Johann Valentin Andreä: Ein geistiges Vorspiel zum Pietismus* (Stuttgart, 1957); Hans Schick, *Das ältere Rosenkreuzertum: Ein Beitrag zur Entstehungsgeschichte der Freimaurerei* (Berlin, 1942).

4. Andreae, *Vita, ab Ipso Conscripta,* ed. F. H. Rheinwald (Berlin, 1849), p. 10, quoted in Montgomery, *Andreae,* I, 37, n. 66: "[The Chemical Wedding was] productive of a brood of monstrosities: a fantasy, which you may wonder was evaluated and interpreted with subtle ingenuity by some people, foolishly enough, in demonstration of the inanity of the curious." The *Vita* appeared first in a German translation, in the collection of D. C. Seybold, *Selbstbiographien berühmter Männer* (Winterthur, 1799). A diary, the "Breviarium vitae Andreanae potiora carptim libans," portions of which were published by Kienast from a Berlin manuscript (now lost), exists in another manuscript in the Herzog August Bibliothek, Wolfenbüttel. It is not to be confused with the published *Vita.* The *Chymische Hochzeit* was republished in Regensburg, 1781, in Munich, 1957, and in Stuttgart, 1957 (eds. Walter Weber and Rudolf Steiner). The *Fama Fraternitatis, oder Entdeckung der Brüderschaft des löblichen Ordensz RosenCreutzes . . . an alle Gelehrte und Häupter Europae geschrieben* was first published in Cassel, 1614, and bound with the *Allgemeine und general Reformation, der gantzen weiten Welt;* there followed editions in Frankfort, 1614, and Danzig, 1617. The *Confessio* was first published along with a second edition of the *Fama* in Cassel, 1615.

5. Johann Valentin Andreae, *Menippus sive Dialogorum Satyricorum Centuria Inanitatum Nostratium Speculum,* 2nd ed. (Cosmopoli, 1618; 1st ed., 1617), chap. 12, "Fraternitas," pp. 24–25; the section on "Utopia" is on pp. 122–123. There was also a Berlin, 1673, edition of this work.

6. The first part, *Invitatio Fraternitatis Christi,* also expressly opposed to Rosicrucianism, was published in Strasbourg, 1617.

7. Andreae, *Turbo, sive Moleste et Frustra par Cuncta Divagans Ingenium* (Helicone, iuxta Parnassum [Strasbourg], 1616). The German translation of 1907 by Wilhelm Süss is entitled *Turbo oder der Irrender Ritter vom Geist.* In the *Theophilus* (Stuttgart, 1649), pp. 89–90, Andreae loudly proclaimed his Christocentrism and rejected all other lawgivers: "Christianus homo non ad Romuli, aut Lycurgi, vel Draconis leges, sed Christi archetypum, corde, studio, opere . . . conformandus." The subtitle of *Theophilus* was *sive de Christiana Religione Sanctius Colenda, Vita Temperantius Instituenda, et Literatura Rationabilius Docenda Consilium.*

8. Andreae, *Turbo,* p. 164.

9. Andreae, *Mythologiae Christianae sive Virtutum et Vitiorum Vitae Humanae Imaginum Libri Tres* (Strasbourg, 1619), pp. 22–23, quoted in Montgomery, *Andreae,* I, 208.

10. See Ludwig Timotheus von Spittler, "Ueber Christoph Besolds Religions-Veränderung," in *Patriotisches Archiv,* ed. F. K. von Moser, VIII (Mannheim and Leipzig, 1788), 429–472.

11. "Once the capital of the world, now the capital of crime." Andreae, *Vita,* ed. Rheinwald, p. 36.

12. Andreae, *Seleniana Augustalia* (Ulm, 1649), p. 146. A second volume of correspondence with the Dukes of Brunswick-Lüneburg and others was published in 1654 under the title: *Sereniss. Domus Augustae Selenianae.*

13. See Montgomery, *Andreae,* I, 139. The painting is now in the Staatsgalerie in Stuttgart.

14. A translation by Andreae's descendant Hermann Viktor Andreae appeared as *Die Kämpfe des christlichen Herkules* (Frankfort, 1845).

15. Andreae to Comenius, Sept. 16, 1629, quoted in Montgomery, *Andreae,* I, 104, n. 317.

16. Andreae, *Amicorum Singularium Clarissimorum Funera, Condecorata* (Lüneburg,

1642), pp. 7–9, quoted in Montgomery, *Andreae*, I, 214–215. The two pamphlets, written in 1620, apparently were not printed and were lost until the mid-twentieth century.

17. Montgomery, *Andreae*, I, 82. In a letter of March 1, 1654, to Duke Augustus of Brunswick-Lüneburg (ibid., p. 52), Andreae wittily summarized his pastoral career: "Anno 1614. conduxit ad Laboratorium Vaihingam.

1620. produxit ad Directorium Calvam.

1639. pellexit ad Oratorium Studtgardiam.

1650. depressit ad Purgatorium Bebenhusam.

1654. eduxit ad Refrigerium Adelbergam. Dominus porro provideat."

18. *Vita*, quoted in Montgomery, *Andreae*, I, 114.

19. The German translation by D. S. G.[eorgi] was *Reise nach der Insel Caphar Salama* (Esslingen, 1741). Other works of Andreae were adapted into English by the mid-seventeenth century. John Hall, *Of the advantageous reading of history* (London, 1657), included *A modell of a Christian society*, which was a loose translation of Andreae's "Christianae Societatis Imago," and *The right hand of Christian love offered*, a translation of "Christiani Amoris Dextera Porrecta."

20. Andreae, *Christianopolis*, trans. Felix Emil Held (New York, Oxford University Press, 1916), p. 177. All quotations are from the Held translation unless otherwise noted.

21. Ibid., p. 176.

22. Ibid., p. 155.

23. Ibid., p. 198.

24. Ibid., p. 156.

25. Ibid., p. 217.

26. Ibid., p. 216.

27. Ibid., pp. 221–222.

28. Ibid., p. 222.

29. Ibid., p. 197.

30. Ibid., p. 198.

31. Andreae, *Christianopolis*, ed. Richard van Dülmen (Stuttgart, Calwer, 1972), p. 112 (authors' translation); *Christianopolis*, trans. Held, pp. 196–197.

32. *Christianopolis*, trans. Held, pp. 157–158.

33. Ibid., p. 169.

34. Ibid., p. 152.

35. Ibid., p. 187.

36. Ibid., p. 203.

37. Ibid., p. 205.

38. Ibid., p. 204.

39. Ibid., p. 151.

40. Ibid., p. 206.

41. Ibid., p. 159.

42. Quoted in Montgomery, *Andreae*, I, 140.

43. Andreae, *Vita*, ed. Rheinwald, p. 24, quoted by Montgomery, *Andreae*, I, 43–44, in translation.

44. Andreae, *Vita*, ed. Rheinwald, p. 277.

45. See R. E. W. Maddison, *The Life of the Honourable Boyle* (London, 1969), p. 71, for references to Andreae in letters of Hartlib to Boyle (1647).

12. Comenius and His Disciples

1. Samuel Sorbière, who saw Comenius in Holland in 1642, was shown his Pansophic manuscripts, which drew forth a series of ejaculations in print: "Johannes Amos Comenius, *Januae Linguarum* author, *Pansophiae* futurus, ostendit mihi codicem suum manuscriptum ad Pansophiam cudendam annotatorum. Quae farrago! Quae liturae!

Quae transpositiones! Jehu, vevohu, inscribi meritò potuissent." Quoted by C. E. Adam and Paul Tannery, the editors of Descartes's *Oeuvres*, new ed., III (Paris, J. Vrin, 1971), 722–723, note, from Samuel Sorbière, *Sorberiana* (Toulouse, 1691), pp. 74–75.

2. Comenius, *De Rerum Humanarum Emendatione Consultatio Catholica*, ed. Academia Scientiarum Bohemoslovaca, 2 vols. (Prague, 1966).

3. Ibid., I, 39.

4. See R. F. Young, *Comenius and the Indians of New England* (London, 1929), and *Comenius in England* (London, Oxford University Press, 1932), pp. 89–95.

5. Translated from the *Pansophici Libri Delineatio* in David Masson, *The Life of John Milton*, III (London, 1873; reprinted, Gloucester, Mass., P. Smith, 1965), 213–214.

6. Comenius, *A Generall Table of Europe* . . . (London, 1670), pp. 41, 43.

7. Cotton Mather, *Magnalia Christi Americana*, 1st American ed. from the London 1702 ed. (Hartford, 1820), II, 10. See also Matthew Spinka, *John Amos Comenius, That Incomparable Moravian* (Chicago, 1943); Pasquale Cammarota, *Introduzione allo studio di J. A. Comenius* (Salerno, 1968); Wilhelmus Rood, *Comenius and the Low Countries: Some Aspects of the Life and Work of a Czech Exile in the Seventeenth Century* (Amsterdam, 1970).

8. Masson, *Life of Milton*, III, 226.

9. According to Comenius, Descartes in the course of their conversation paid him a cryptic compliment: "Beyond the things that appertain to philosophy I go not; mine therefore is that only in part, whereof yours is the whole." See doc. I, "Komenský's description of the development of his plan for an encyclopaedia and a great college for scientific research, and of his visit to England in 1641–2, translated from Chapter 39 and following of the biographical fragment entitled *Continuatio admonitionis fraternae de temperando charitate zelo ad S. Maresium*, published at Amsterdam in 1669," in Young, *Comenius in England*, p. 50. Descartes nevertheless was highly critical of Comenius' *Pansophiae Prodromus*, which pretended to unify acquired and revealed truths. Descartes's *Judicium de Opere Pansophico*, addressed to Mersenne in 1639, was transmitted to Theodore Haak of the Hartlib group. See Descartes, *Oeuvres*, II (1969), 651–652.

10. Comenius, *Panegersia*, chap. 12, nos. 32, 36, in *Consultatio*, I, 95.

11. *De Novis Didactica Studia Continuandi Occasionibus*, in *Opera Didactica Omnia*, ed. Academia Scientiarum Bohemoslovenica (Prague, 1957; 1st ed., Amsterdam, 1657), vol. I, part II, p. 3.

12. See John Lewis Paton, "The Tercentenary of Comenius' Visit to England, 1592–1671," *Bulletin of the John Rylands Library*, 26 (1941–1942), 154.

13. Spinka, *Comenius*, 2nd ed. (New York, 1967), p. 31.

14. Comenius, *Pampaedia*, chap. 1, sect. 6, in *Consultatio*, II, 15.

15. *Pampaedia*, chap. 1, sect. 14, ibid., p. 16.

16. *Pampaedia*, chap. 2, sect. 8, ibid., p. 18.

17. Comenius, *The Great Didactic*, trans. M. W. Keatinge (London, 1896), p. 327, chap. 19, sect. 40.

18. Ibid., p. 333, chap. 19, sect. 53.

19. Ibid., pp. 336, 338, chap. 20, sects. 6, 10.

20. Ibid., p. 341, chap. 20, sect. 16.

21. Ibid., p. 325, chap. 19, sect. 36.

22. Ibid., p. 317, chap. 19, sect. 16.

23. *Pampaedia*, chap. 5, sect. 19, in *Consultatio*, II, 43–44.

24. *Pampaedia*, chap. 2, sect. 27, ibid., p. 22.

25. *Panegersia*, chap. 19, no. 31, ibid., I, 83.

26. *Pampaedia*, chap. 2, sect. 10, ibid., II, 18.

27. Milada Blekastad, *Comenius: Versuch eines Umrisses von Leben, Werk und Schicksal des Jan Amos Komenský* (Oslo, Universitetsforlaget, 1969), p. 630.

28. *Pampaedia*, chap. 5, sect. 1, in *Consultatio*, II, 40.

29. *Pampaedia*, chap. 5, sect. 28, ibid., p. 45.

30. *Pampaedia*, chap. 2, sect. 17, 25, ibid., pp. 20, 22.

31. Comenius, *Pansophia*, Fourth Stage, ibid., I, 287.

32. *Great Didactic*, p. 345, chap. 20, sect. 24.

33. Comenius, *Panorthosia*, chap. 15, sect. 16, in *Consultatio*, II, 299.

34. Comenius, *Didactica Magna*, in *Opera Didactica Omnia*, vol. I, part I, pp. 8, 15, and *Novissima Linguarum Methodus*, ibid., part II, pp. 283–284.

35. Quoted in John Warwick Montgomery, *Cross and Crucible: Johann Valentin Andreae (1586–1654), Phoenix of the Theologians* (The Hague, Nijhoff, 1973), I, 151.

36. Jvan Kvačala, *Die Pädagogische Reform des Comenius in Deutschland bis zum Ausgange des XVII Jahrhunderts*, I (Berlin, 1903), 200–203, Comenius to Andreae, Lüneburg, Aug. 22, 1647.

37. Comenius, *Pansophiae Praeludium*, in *Opera Didactica Omnia*, vol. I, part I, p. 442.

38. *A Reformation of Schooles, Designed in Two Excellent Treatises*, trans. Samuel Hartlib (London, 1642), p. 36.

39. Ibid.

40. Ibid., p. 37.

41. Ibid.

42. The title of the first edition is *Orbis Sensualium Pictus; Hoc Est, Omnium Fundamentalium in Mundo Rerum et in Vita Actionum Pictura et Nomenclatura* (Nuremberg, 1658).

43. *A Generall Table of Europe*, p. 257.

44. See J. E. Sadler, *J. A. Comenius and the Concept of Universal Education* (New York, 1966); *John Amos Comenius on Education*, intro. by Jean Piaget (New York, 1967; 1st ed., 1957).

45. Friedrich Althaus, "Samuel Hartlib: Ein deutsch-englisches Charakterbild," in *Historisches Taschenbuch*, ed. Wilhelm Maurenbrecher, 6th ser., 3rd year (1883), pp. 239ff.

46. Hartlib was, he says himself, "familiarly acquainted with the best of Archbishops, Bishops, Earls, Viscounts, Barons, Knights, Esquires, Gentlemen, Ministers, Professors of both Universities, Merchants, and all sorts of learned, or in any kind useful men." Henry Dircks, *A Biographical Memoir of Samuel Hartlib, Milton's Familiar Friend* (London, 1865), p. 4, Hartlib to Dr. John Worthington, Aug. 3, 1660.

47. John Dury, *A Memoriall concerning Peace Ecclesiasticall amongst Protestants* (London, 1641), preface.

48. John Winthrop, Jr., once described Hartlib as the "great intelligence of Europe." Albert Matthews, "Comenius and Harvard College," in Colonial Society of Massachusetts, *Publications*, 21 (1919), 171.

49. See Cressy Dymock (identified as author by Henry Dircks), *An Invention of Engines of Motion lately brought to perfection* . . . (London, 1651). Hartlib later grew disenchanted with Dymock's scheme. See Dircks, *Biographical Memoir of Hartlib*, pp. 91–93, and his *Perpetuum Mobile* (London, 1870), p. 35.

50. Masson, *Life of Milton*, III, 664.

51. *The Diary of John Evelyn*, ed. E. S. de Beer, III (Oxford, Clarendon, 1955), 162–163.

52. G. H. Turnbull, "Some Correspondence of John Winthrop, Jr., and Samuel Hartlib," in Massachusetts Historical Society, *Proceedings*, 72 (1957–1960), 39–40.

53. Comenius, *Korrespondence: Listy Komenského a vrestevníkú jeho* [Papers of Comenius and His Contemporaries], ed. Jvan Kvačala, II (Prague, Nákl. České Akademie, 1902), 11, Dury to Hartlib, Stockholm, Aug. 20, 1636.

54. Ibid.

55. Ibid.

56. Ibid., p. 16, Dury to Hartlib, Feb. 22, 1639. Even Hobbes has been discovered among the millenarians; see J. G. A. Pocock, "Time, History and Eschatology in the

Thought of Thomas Hobbes," in J. H. Elliott and H. G. Koenigsberger, eds., *The Diversity of History: Essays in Honour of Sir Herbert Butterfield* (London, 1970), pp. 179–181.

57. Comenius, *Korrespondence*, II, 80–81, Francouzský přítel [French friend] to Hartlib, Paris, May 15, 1643.

58. Ibid., pp. 81–82, Nejmenovaný [S. n.] to Hartlib, Amsterdam, June 25, 1643.

59. See, for example, his *Considerations Tending to the Happy Accomplishment of Englands Reformation in Church and State, Humbly Presented to the Piety and Wisdome of the High and Honourable Court of Parliament* (London, 1647), in which a parliamentary committee, seconded by learned divines, would promulgate practical reforms in a four-class society.

60. See Charles Webster, *The Great Instauration* (London, 1975).

61. Originally published as *Conatuum Comenianorum Praeludia* (Oxford, 1637).

62. Charles Webster, "The Authorship and Significance of *Macaria*," *Past and Present*, no. 56 (1972), pp. 34–48. Webster has identified Gabriel Plattes, inventor and author of treatises on agriculture and mining, as the author of *Macaria*. Plattes made separate proposals to Parliament that it equip a laboratory for him. In Kaspar Stiblin's *Commentariolus de Eudaemonensium Republica* (Basel, 1555), an appendix to *Coropaedia, sive de Moribus et Vita Virginum Sacrarum*, the island is named Macaria, its capital Eudaemon. Knowledge of Andreae's *Christianopolis* came to Hartlib through his relations with Comenius.

63. *Description of the Famous Kingdome of Macaria* (London, 1641), p. 13.

64. Ibid., p. 14.

65. *Reformation of Schooles*, pp. 3–4.

66. John Pell, *An Idea of Mathematics* (London, 1650), p. 41.

67. Cressy Dymock, *An Essay for Advancement of Husbandry-Learning* (London, 1651), p. 13.

68. G. H. Turnbull found among Hartlib's papers one entitled: "A motion for the Public good of Religion and Learning," which proposed an Office of Addresse and Correspondencie to be established by Parliament for the advancement of "religion, learning and ingenuities." *Hartlib, Dury, and Comenius: Gleanings from Hartlib's Papers* (Liverpool, University Press, 1947), p. 78. See also Turnbull's *Samuel Hartlib: A Sketch of His Life and His Relations to John Amos Comenius* (London, 1920).

69. Turnbull, *Hartlib, Dury, and Comenius*, p. 81. Turnbull believes Dury was probably the author of *A Further Discoverie* (p. 79, n. 1).

70. For a negative appraisal of the relations of utopia and science, see A. R. Hall, "Science, Technology and Utopia in the Seventeenth Century," in P. Matthias, ed., *Science and Society 1600–1900* (Cambridge, 1972), pp. 33–53.

71. Théophraste Renaudot, *Recueil général des questions traitées dans les conférences du Bureau d'adresse, sur toutes sortes de matières, par les plus beaux esprits de ce temps*, 5 vols. (Paris, 1666).

72. William Petty, *The Advice of W. P. to Mr. Samuel Hartlib. For the Advancement of some Particular Parts of Learning* (London, 1648).

73. Hartlib, *Considerations Tending to the Happy Accomplishment of Englands Reformation*, pp. 50–51.

74. Ibid., p. 47.

75. John Dury, *The Reformed Librairie-Keeper* (London, 1650), p. 20.

76. Ibid., p. 30.

77. Pell, *An Idea of Mathematics*, p. 44.

78. Dury, *The Reformed-School: and the Reformed Librairie-Keeper. Whereunto is added I. An Idea of Mathematicks II. The description of one of the chiefest Libraries which is in Germanie* (London, 1651), pp. 40–41.

79. Comenius, *A Generall Table of Europe*, p. 10.

80. Dury, *The Reformed-School*, p. 33.

81. Dymock, *An Essay for Advancement of Husbandry-Learning*, p. 3.

13. Topsy-Turvy in the English Civil War

1. British Museum, London, *Catalogue of the Pamphlets, Books, Newspapers, and Manuscripts Relating to the Civil War, the Commonwealth, and Restoration, Collected by George Thomason, 1640–1661*, 2 vols. (London, 1908).

2. Thomas Edwards, *Gangraena*, 3rd ed. (London, 1646), part I, p. 3.

3. Ibid., p. 4.

4. Ephraim Pagitt, *Heresiography* (London, 1645), pp. 30–34.

5. John Milton, *Areopagitica*, in *The Works*, ed. F. A. Patterson, IV (New York, Columbia University Press, 1931), 340–341.

6. Quoted in Christopher Hill, *The World Turned Upside Down* (London, Temple Smith, 1972), p. 28.

7. Gerrard Winstanley, *The Law of Freedom in a Platform . . .* (1652), in *The Works*, ed. George H. Sabine (Ithaca, Cornell University Press, 1941; reissued New York, 1965), p. 502.

8. Winstanley, *Fire in the Bush* (1650), ibid., p. 468.

9. Thomas Hobbes, *Behemoth*, ed. William Molesworth (1840; reprint ed., New York, B. Franklin, 1963), pp. 51, 53.

10. John Lilburne, Richard Overton, and Thomas Prince, *Picture of the Councel of State*, in William Haller and Godfrey Davies, *The Leveller Tracts, 1647–1653* (New York, Columbia University Press, 1944), pp. 194–195.

11. Ibid., p. 209.

12. A. S. P. Woodhouse, ed., *Puritanism and Liberty, Being the Army Debates (1647–1649) from the Clarke Manuscripts with Supplementary Documents, Selected and Edited with an Introduction* (London, J. M. Dent, 1938), p. 158.

13. J. Philolaus, *A Serious Aviso to the Good People of this Nation, Concerning that Sort of Men, called Levellers* (London, 1649), p. 3.

14. Ibid., p. 5.

15. Lilburne, Overton, and Prince, *Picture of the Councel of State*, in Haller, *Leveller Tracts*, p. 212.

16. John Lilburne and William Walwyn, *The Mournful Cryes of many thousand poor Tradesmen* (January 1648), quoted in D. M. Wolfe, ed., *Leveller Manifestoes of the Puritan Revolution* (New York, T. Nelson, 1944), p. 276.

17. Lilburne, Overton, and Prince, *Picture of the Councel of State*, in Haller, *Leveller Tracts*, p. 204.

18. William Walwyn, *A Still and Soft Voice from the Scriptures* (London, 1647), p. 15, reprinted as App. II (pp. 363–374) in D. M. Wolfe, *Milton in the Puritan Revolution* (New York, T. Nelson, 1941), p. 374.

19. Walwyn, *Walwyn's Just Defence against the Aspersions cast upon him* (1649), in Haller, *Leveller Tracts*, p. 353. See also W. Schenk, *The Concern for Social Justice in the Puritan Revolution* (New York, 1948), p. 41.

20. Lilburne et al., *An Agreement of the Free People of England. Tendered as a Peace-offering to this distressed Nation*, in Wolfe, *Leveller Manifestoes*, pp. 409, 407.

21. Ibid., p. 407.

22. [John Price], *Walwyn's Wiles* (1649), in Haller, *Leveller Tracts*, p. 303.

23. Lilburne et al., *Agreement of the Free People of England*, in Wolfe, *Leveller Manifestoes*, p. 402.

24. Lilburne et al., *A Manifestation . . . Intended for their full Vindication* (1649), ibid., p. 388.

25. Ibid.

26. C. B. Macpherson upholds the theory that the Levellers were not egalitarian democrats. See his *Political Theory of Possessive Individualism: Hobbes to Locke* (London, Oxford University Press, 1962), chap. 3, "The Levellers: Franchise and Freedom."

27. Lilburne et al., *A Manifestation*, in Wolfe, *Leveller Manifestoes*, p. 390.

28. Lilburne, *The Just Defence of John Lilburne* (1649), in Haller, *Leveller Tracts*, p. 452. See also Lilburne, *A Worke of the Beast, or A Relation of a Most unchristian Censure, executed upon John Lilburne* (1638), in William Haller, ed., *Tracts on Liberty in the Puritan Revolution* (New York, 1934), II, 3–34.

29. Lilburne, Overton, and Prince, *Picture of the Councel of State,* in Haller, *Leveller Tracts*, p. 228.

30. Marchamont Nedham, *The Case of the Commonwealth of England, Stated* (1649), ed. Philip A. Knachel (Charlottesville, University of Virginia Press, 1969), p. 96.

31. Ibid.

32. Ibid., pp. 109–110.

33. Henry Denne, *The Levellers Designe Discovered* (London, 1649), p. 8.

34. Edwards, *Gangraena,* part I, p. 36.

35. Overton, *An Arrow against All Tyrants* . . . (October 1646), pp. 3–4, quoted in Macpherson, *Political Theory of Possessive Individualism,* p. 140.

36. Lilburne, *In the Charters of London,* app. to *London's Liberty in Chains* (Dec. 18, 1646), quoted in Henry Noel Brailsford, *The Levellers and the English Revolution,* ed. Christopher Hill (London, Cresset Press, 1961), p. 117.

37. M. A. Gibb, *John Lilburne the Leveller: A Christian Democrat* (London, 1947), p. 345.

38. Winstanley, *The True Levellers Standard Advanced* (1649), in *Works,* p. 261. On Winstanley, see George Juretic, "Digger No Millenarian: The Revolutionizing of Gerrard Winstanley," *Journal of the History of Ideas,* vol. 36, no. 2 (1975), pp. 263–280.

39. Winstanley, *The True Levellers Standard Advanced* (London, 1649), title page.

40. Ibid., p. 6.

41. Winstanley, *The Saints Paradise* . . . (London, 1648), sig. A2, r and v.

42. Ibid., A3.

43. Ibid., p. 8.

44. Ibid., [A4].

45. Ibid.

46. Ibid.

47. Ibid., p. 3.

48. Ibid., p. 4.

49. Ibid.

50. Winstanley, *The Law of Freedom in a Platform,* in *Works,* p. 503.

51. Ibid., p. 507.

52. Ibid., p. 593.

53. Winstanley, *A Declaration from the Poore oppressed people of England,* in *Works,* p. 271.

54. Winstanley, *Fire in the Bush,* ibid., p. 457.

55. Laurence Clarkson, *The Lost sheep found: or, The Prodigal returned to his Fathers house, after many a sad and weary Journey through many Religious Countryes* (1660), quoted in Norman Cohn, *The Pursuit of the Millennium,* 2d ed. (New York, Harper and Row, 1961), pp. 351–352.

56. Edwards, *Gangraena,* part II, p. 126.

57. See ibid., *passim.*

58. Abiezer Coppe, *Second Fiery Flying Roll* (1649), quoted in Cohn, *Pursuit of the Millennium,* pp. 371, 378.

59. Ibid., pp. 372–374.

60. Coppe, *Some Sweet Sips, of some Spirituall Wine* . . . (London, 1649), p. 7.

61. *The Routing of the Ranters* (London, 1650), p. 4.

62. Coppe, *A Fiery Flying Roll,* quoted in Hill, *World Turned Upside Down,* p. 162.

63. This section draws on Bernard S. Capp, *The Fifth Monarchists: A Study of Seventeenth Century Millenarianism* (London, Faber, 1972), and Hill, *World Turned Upside Down,* though our interpretation of the materials differs.

64. Henry Archer, *The Personall Reign of Christ Upon earth* (London, 1642), title page.

65. Capp, *Fifth Monarchists*, p. 131.

66. John Tillinghast, *Generation-Worke, or, An Exposition of the Prophecies of the Two Witnesses*, 3d part (London, 1654), p. 221.

67. *A Witnes to the Saints* (London, 1657), p. 6, quoted in Capp, *Fifth Monarchists*, p. 133.

68. John Tillinghast, *Mr. Tillinghast's Eight Last Sermons* (1655), posthumously published with a preface by Christopher Feake (London, 1656), p. 59.

69. Quoted in Capp, *Fifth Monarchists*, p. 142.

70. Ibid., p. 144.

71. John Spittlehouse, *An Answer to one part of the Lord Protector's Speech: or, A Vindication of the Fifth Monarchy-men* (London, 1654), p. 13.

72. Capp, *Fifth Monarchists*, p. 144.

73. Ibid., pp. 145–146.

74. Ibid., p. 143.

75. See Peter Chamberlen, *The Poore Mans Advocate, or Englands Samaritan* (London, 1649), p. 49.

76. Capp, *Fifth Monarchists*, p. 149.

77. Quoted by Charles Blitzer, *An Immortal Commonwealth: The Political Thought of James Harrington* (New Haven, Yale University Press, 1960), pp. 3–4.

78. John Toland, "The Life of James Harrington," in Harrington, *The Oceana and Other Works*, 3d ed. (London, 1747), p. xv.

79. Cardinal Gasparo Contarini, *The Commonwealth and Government of Venice*, trans. Lewes Lewkenor (London, 1599), sig. A2v.

80. Robert Filmer, *Observations upon Aristotles Politiques, Touching Forms of Government* (London, 1652), p. 34.

81. Toland, "Life of Harrington," p. xxxiv.

82. Harrington, *Oceana*, p. 91.

83. Quoted in Blitzer, *Immortal Commonwealth*, p. 37.

84. Harrington, *Oceana*, p. 40.

85. Toland, "Life of Harrington," pp. xix–xx.

86. Harrington, *Oceana*, p. 212.

87. R. H. Tawney, "Harrington's Interpretation of His Age," Raleigh Lecture on History, 1941, *Proceedings of the British Academy*, 27 (1941), 209.

88. David Hume, "Idea of a Perfect Commonwealth," in *Essays and Treatises on Several Subjects in Two Volumes* (London, 1768), I, 565.

14. The Sun King and His Enemies

1. *Istoriia sevarambov* (Moscow, 1956).

2. Denis Vairasse, *Histoire des Sevarambes* (Amsterdam, 1702), I, 277. There was also an Amsterdam, 167–, edition.

3. *History of the Sevarambians* (London, 1738), p. 204.

4. Ibid., p. 202.

5. Ibid., p. 198.

6. Ibid., p. 200.

7. Ibid., p. 203.

8. Ibid., p. 202.

9. Ibid., p. 203.

10. *Histoire des Sevarambes*, I, 322–323.

11. François de Salignac de la Mothe Fénelon, *Correspondance* (Paris, 1827), VI, 411, May 8, 1703.

12. Ibid., I, 4, Fénelon to Marquis de Seignelai, Feb. 7, 1686.

13. Lionel Rothkrug, *Opposition to Louis XIV* (Princeton, Princeton University Press, 1965), pp. 239, 251, 255.

14. Ibid., p. 245.

15. Fleury, *Oeuvres*, ed. M. Aimée-Martin (Paris, 1837), p. 565.

16. Rothkrug, *Opposition to Louis XIV*, pp. 267–268.

17. Fénelon, *Correspondance*, VI, 275.

18. Fénelon, *Les Aventures de Télémaque* (Paris, 1822), p. 197.

19. See, for example, *Les Aventures de Télémaque* (Philadelphia, 1821).

20. Jeremy Bentham, *Works*, ed. John Bowring (Edinburgh and London, 1843), X, 10.

15. Leibniz: The Swan Song of the Christian Republic

1. In a sketch for a "Bibliotheca Universalis Selecta" prepared in 1689 for Theodor Althet Heinrich von Strattmann, Leibniz included under the heading "Narrationes rei-publicae fictitiae continent interdum monitum in veris regendis profutura": "*Utopia Mori*, Campanellae *Civitas Solis*, Verulamii *Nova Altantis* [sic], Nicii Erythraei [pseud. of G. V. Rossi], *Eudemia, Les oeuvres* de Cyrano de Bergerac; *Mundus alter et idem, La Reine de l'isle invisible*, Roman François. *Les Severabambes* [sic], et *la Terre Australe* [by Foigny]." *Sämtliche Schriften und Briefe*, ser. 1, *Allgemeiner Politischer und Historischer Brief-wechsel*, ed. Deutsche Akademie der Wissenschaften zu Berlin, V (Berlin, O. Reichl, 1954), 441. Most of Leibniz' utopian projects were first published from manuscript in vols. I and II (the ecumenical correspondence) and vols. V and VII (the academy plans) of Alexandre Foucher de Careil, ed., *Oeuvres de Leibniz*, 7 vols. (Paris, 1859–1875).

2. Gottfried Wilhelm Leibniz, *Die Werke gemäss seinem handschriftlichen Nachlasse in der Königlichen Bibliothek zu Hannover*, ed. Onno Klopp, ser. 1, *Historisch-politische und staatswissenschaftliche Schriften*, IX (Hanover, 1873), 58.

3. *In Comenii obitum*, in *Sämtliche Schriften und Briefe*, ser. 2, *Philosophischer Brief-wechsel*, ed. Preussische Akademie der Wissenschaften, I (Darmstadt, 1926), 201. See also ibid., ser. 1, I, 132; 2, I, 199–200; and on Andreae, ser. 1, VIII, 245, 302, 336, 363; Campanella, ser. 1, I, 92, 104, ser. 2, I, 14, 22, 176, 200, ser. 6, I, 265; Bruno, ser. 1, VI, 265, ser. 2, I, 176, ser. 6, I, 194; Bacon, ser. 2, I, 10, 14, 15, 80, 163, 171, 235, 247, 252, 253, 400, 466, 519, 554.

4. Herbert Wildon Carr, *The Monadology of Leibniz, with an Introduction, Commentary, and Supplementary Essays* (Los Angeles, 1930), pp. 3–4.

5. Vladimir Ivanovitch Guerrier, *Leibniz in seinen Beziehungen zu Russland und Peter dem Grossen* (St. Petersburg, 1873), p. 203, Leibniz to Golofkin, Jan. 16, 1712.

6. Leibniz, *Werke*, ed. Klopp, ser. 1, V (Hanover, 1866), 67–68, Leibniz to Duke Ernst August, 1680–1681 (undated letter).

7. See Paolo Rossi, *Clavis universalis: Arti mnemoniche e logica combinatoria da Lullo a Leibniz* (Milan, 1960).

8. Leibniz, *Werke*, ed. Klopp, ser. 1, V, 69.

9. Leibniz, *Grundriss eines Bedenkens von Aufrichtung einer Societät in Teütschland zu auffnehmen der Künste und Wissenschafften* (1671?), in *Sämtliche Schriften und Briefe*, ser. 4, *Politische Schriften*, ed. Preussische Akademie der Wissenschaften, I (Darmstadt, 1931), 530.

10. Leibniz, *Discours touchant la méthode de la certitude et l'art d'inventer pour finir les disputes et pour faire en peu de temps des grands progrès*, in *Die philosophischen Schriften*, ed. C. I. Gerhardt, VII (Berlin, 1890; reprint ed., Hildesheim, Olms, 1961), 178.

11. Leibniz, *Préceptes pour avancer les sciences*, ibid., p. 160.

12. Leibniz, *Discours touchant la méthode de la certitude*, ibid., p. 180.

13. Rudolf W. Meyer, *Leibnitz and the Seventeenth-Century Revolution*, trans. J. P. Stern from German ed., 1948 (Cambridge and Chicago, 1952), p. 96. See also *Ursachen warum Canstatt*, in *Sämtliche Schriften und Briefe*, ser. 4, I, 107–110.

14. Leibniz, *Discours touchant la méthode de la certitude*, in *Die philosophischen Schriften*, ed. Gerhardt, VII, 181.

15. Ibid., pp. 175–176.

16. Ibid., pp. 176–177; *Relation de l'état présent de la république des lettres*, in *Sämtliche Schriften und Briefe*, ser. 4, vol. I, p. 569; *Oeuvres*, ed. Foucher de Careil, III (1861), 1–41.

17. Leibniz, *Die philosophischen Schriften*, ed. Gerhardt, II (1960), 136, Leibniz to Antoine Arnauld, Venice, March 23, 1690.

18. See Leibniz, *Grundriss eines Bedenkens von Aufrichtung einer Societät;* Joseph, Ritter von Bergmann, "Leibnitz in Wien, nebst fünf ungedruckten Briefen über die Gründung einer kaiserlichen Akademie der Wissenschaften an Karl Gustav Heräus in Wien," and "Leibnitzens Memoriale an den Kurfürsten Johann Wilhelm von der Pfalz wegen Errichtung einer Akademie der Wissenschaften in Wien vom 2 Oktober 1704," in Kaiserliche Akademie der Wissenschaften, Vienna, Philosophisch-historische Classe, *Sitzungsberichte*, 13 (1854), 40–61, and 16 (1855), 3–22; and R. F. Young, *Comenius in England* (London, 1932), doc. IV, p. 62.

19. Young, *Comenius in England*, p. 62.

20. See Jean Baruzi, *Leibniz et l'organisation religieuse de la terre, d'après des documents inédits* (Paris, 1907), p. 100.

21. Leibniz, *Die philosophischen Schriften*, ed. Gerhardt, III (1960), 261, 262, draft of letter to Thomas Burnett, 1699.

22. Leibniz, *Confessio philosophi: Ein Dialog*, ed. Otto Saame (Frankfort, Klostermann, 1967), p. 110.

23. Baruzi, *Leibniz et l'organisation religieuse de la terre*, p. 95.

24. See his letter to Nicolas Rémond, from Vienna, Aug. 26, 1714, in *Die philosophischen Schriften*, ed. Gerhardt, III, 624–625.

25. See K. Bittner, "J. A. Comenius and G. W. Leibniz," *Zeitschrift für slavische Philologie*, 6 (1929), 115–145; 7 (1930), 53–93.

26. Leibniz, *Elementa Juris Naturalis*, in *Sämtliche Schriften und Briefe*, ser. 6, *Philosophische Schriften*, I, ed. Preussische Akademie der Wissenschaften (Darmstadt, 1930), 445.

27. Leibniz, *Modus Instituendi Militiam Novam Invictam Qua Subjugari Possit Orbis Terrarum: Facilis Executio Tenenti Aegyptum, vel Habenti Coloniam Americanam*, in *Sämtliche Schriften und Briefe*, ser. 4, I, 408.

28. Leibniz, *The Preface to Leibniz' Novissima Sinica: Commentary, Translation, Text*, ed. Donald F. Lach (Honolulu, University of Hawaii Press, 1957), p. 75.

29. Guerrier, *Leibniz in seinen Beziehungen zu Russland und Peter dem Grossen*, p. 178.

30. Leibniz, *Preface to Novissima Sinica*, p. 77.

31. See Leibniz, *Nouveaux essais sur l'entendement humain* (1703–1705), in *Sämtliche Schriften und Briefe*, ser. 6, VI, ed. Leibniz-Forschungsstelle der Universität Münster (Berlin, 1962), 56.

32. See Gottschalk Eduard Guhrauer, *Gottfried Wilhelm, Freiherr von Leibniz: Eine Biographie* (Breslau, 1846; reprint ed., Hildesheim, Olms, 1966), II, "Vita Leibnitii a se ipso breviter delineata," 52.

33. Baruzi, *Leibniz et l'organisation religieuse de la terre*, pp. 123–124.

34. Leibniz, *Oeuvres*, ed. Foucher de Careil, VII (1875), 512, draft of a letter to Peter the Great, Jan. 16, 1716.

35. Leibniz, *Werke*, ed. Klopp, ser. 1, IX, 373–374.

16. The Philosophes's Dilemma

1. *Encyclopédie, ou Dictionnaire raisonné des sciences, des arts et des métiers*, ed. Denis Diderot and Jean le Rond d'Alembert, 35 vols. (Paris, 1751–1780), "County of Rutland," XIV, 448.

2. *Encyclopédie,* "Encyclopédie," XII, 361.

3. Voltaire, *Correspondance,* ed. Theodore Besterman, X (Geneva, Institut et Musée Voltaire, 1954), 10, Voltaire to Pierre Robert Le Cornier de Cideville, Brussels, Jan. 9, 1740; see also ibid., LXII (1961), 141, Voltaire to Claude Germain Le Clerc de Montmerci, Aug. 25, 1766.

4. Ibid., LXIII (1961), 13, 19, Voltaire to Etienne Noël Damilaville, Oct. 10 and 15, 1766.

5. Ibid., LXII (1961), 185, Frederick II to Voltaire, San-Souci, Sept. 13, 1766.

6. Diderot, *Salons,* ed. Jean Seznec and Jean Adhémar, III (Oxford, Clarendon, 1963), 121.

7. Ibid., p. 122.

8. Ibid., p. 125.

9. Ibid., pp. 125–126.

10. Ibid., p. 126.

11. Diderot, *Correspondance,* IX, ed. Georges Roth (Paris, Editions de Minuit, 1963), 245–246, Diderot to Mme. de Maux (?), Paris, 1769 (?).

12. Ibid., pp. 127–129, Diderot to Sophie Volland, Paris, Aug. 31, 1769.

13. Ibid., V (1959), 245–254, Allan Ramsay to Diderot, January 1766.

14. Ibid., p. 244.

15. Diderot, *Apologie de l'Abbé Galiani,* in *Oeuvres politiques,* ed. Paul Vernière (Paris, Garnier Frères, 1963), p. 85.

16. Maurice Tourneux, *Diderot et Cathérine II* (Paris, 1899), p. 160.

17. Diderot, *Entretiens sur le fils naturel, Second entretien,* in *Oeuvres complètes,* ed. J. Assézat and M. Tourneux, VII (Paris, 1875), 108–109.

18. Diderot, *Observations sur Garrick,* in *Oeuvres,* VIII (1875), 350–351.

19. Diderot, *Le Temple du bonheur,* fragment, in *Oeuvres,* VI (1875), 438–439.

20. Diderot, *Correspondance,* XIII, ed. Georges Roth and Jean Varloot (1966), 71, Diderot to Madame Diderot, St. Petersburg, before Oct. 15, 1773.

21. *Encyclopédie,* XXV, 201.

22. Voltaire, *Essai sur les moeurs et l'esprit des nations,* in *Oeuvres,* ed. M. Palissot (Paris, 1792), XVI, 40.

23. Louis Antoine de Bougainville, *Voyage autour du monde* (Paris, 1771), pp. 98–102.

24. Ibid., p. 190.

25. Abbé Guillaume Thomas François Raynal, *Histoire philosophique des deux Indes* (Paris, 1780), II, 103.

26. Ibid., IV, 13.

27. Ibid., p. 39.

28. Ibid., p. 694.

17. The Monde Idéal of Jean-Jacques

1. *Boswell with Rousseau and Voltaire,* ed. Geoffrey Scott (Mt. Vernon, N.Y., 1928), pp. 56, 61–64; James Boswell, *Boswell on the Grand Tour: Germany and Switzerland, 1764,* in *The Yale Edition of the Private Papers of James Boswell,* ed. F. A. Pottle, IV (New York, 1953), 221, 223–224. The translation, which is republished in the Yale edition, is Scott's.

2. An autographed and annotated copy of Rousseau's Plato in Marsilio Ficino's Latin translation is in the British Museum. See M. J. Silverthorne, "Rousseau's Plato," *Studies on Voltaire and the Eighteenth Century,* 116 (1973), 235–249.

3. The books and papers of Saint-Pierre were handed over by his nephew to Rousseau in 1756. See C. E. Vaughan, ed., *The Political Writings of Jean Jacques Rousseau* (New York, 1962; 1st ed., 1915), I, 360.

4. Rousseau, *Lettres écrites de la Montagne,* in *Oeuvres complètes,* ed. Bernard Gagnebin and Marcel Raymond, Bibliothèque de la Pléiade, III (Paris, Gallimard, 1964), 697.

5. Rousseau, *Discours sur l'origine et les fondemens de l'inégalité parmi les hommes,* ibid., p. 123.

6. Rousseau, *Emile,* ibid., IV (1969), 351n.

7. Ibid., p. 277.

8. Rousseau, *Discours sur l'inégalité,* ibid., III, 122.

9. Rousseau, *Emile* (Favre manuscript), ibid., V, 157.

10. Rousseau, *Rousseau juge de Jean Jacques,* ibid., I (1959), 668.

11. Ibid., p. 669.

12. Ibid., p. 672.

13. Rousseau, *Du contrat social,* ibid., III, 361.

14. Rousseau, *Emile,* ibid., IV, 249.

15. Karl Marx, "Ökonomisch-philosophische Manuscripte" (1844), in *Marx-Engels Gesamtausgabe,* sect. I, vol. III, p. 121 (Berlin, 1932).

16. A pamphlet of 1789 entitled *Jean-Jacques Rousseau des Champs-Elisées à la Nation Françoise* carries a footnote that it is extracted from Rousseau's works on the rights of peoples and may be "useful to those who do not know the principles of this famous man, to whom France owes the present revolution."

17. Rousseau, *Discours sur l'inégalité,* in *Oeuvres complètes,* III, 194.

18. Freedom from the Wheel

1. See Manuel, *Portrait of Isaac Newton* (Cambridge, Mass., 1968), pp. 206–211.

2. John Craig, *Theologiae Christianae Principia Mathematica* (London, 1699).

3. Manuel, *The Eighteenth Century Confronts the Gods* (Cambridge, Mass., 1959), pp. 210–227.

4. Moses Mendelssohn, *Jerusalem: A Treatise on Ecclesiastical Authority and Judaism* (1783), trans. M. Samuels (London, 1838), II, 100–101; Gotthold Ephraim Lessing, *Die Erziehung des Menschengeschlechts* (1780), in *Sämmtliche Schriften,* 3rd ed. rev., ed. Karl Lachmann, rev. Franz Muncker, XIII (Leipzig, 1897).

5. Edward Gibbon, *The History of the Decline and Fall of the Roman Empire,* III (London, 1781), "General Observations," 639–640.

6. Leibniz, *Nouveaux essais sur l'entendement humain,* in *Sämtliche Schriften und Briefe,* ser. 6, *Philosophische Schriften,* VI (Berlin, 1962), 55.

7. Louis Sébastien Mercier, *L'An 2440,* new ed. (Paris, An X; 1st ed., 1771), I, xxxviii, note.

19. Turgot on the Future of Mind

1. There are three editions of the works of Turgot: the first, by Dupont de Nemours, 9 vols. (Paris, 1808–1811), secularized the religious tone of the Sorbonne discourses; the second was by Eugène Daire and Hippolyte Dussard, 2 vols. (Paris, 1844); the third and probably definitive edition was by Gustave Schelle, 5 vols. (Paris, F. Alcan, 1913–1923). Fragments of Turgot's work were translated into English in W. Walker Stephens, *The Life and Writings of Turgot, Comptroller General of France, 1774–1776* (London and New York, 1895); and there is a translation titled *On the Progress of the Human Mind,* with notes and an appendix by McQuilkin de Grange (Hanover, N.H., 1928). The *Textes choisis* by Pierre Vigreux (Paris, 1947) emphasizes economic thought. A collection of texts on Turgot's theory of progress has appeared in Spanish: *El progresso en la historia universal: Traducción del francés por María Vergara* (Madrid, 1941). Of the major works on Turgot, two appeared in the eighteenth century, written by devoted admirers and disciples: Dupont de Nemours, *Mémoires sur la vie et les ouvrages de M. Turgot* (Phila-

delphia [Paris], 1782); and Condorcet, *Vie de Turgot* (London, 1786). These really constitute the oral tradition and cannot be separated from the writings themselves. For a bibliography on Turgot see Frank E. Manuel, *The Prophets of Paris* (Cambridge, Mass.,
1962), pp. 319–320. The Schelle edition had a reimpression in Glashüten im Taunus,
1972, and there have been two recent compilations: *Ecrits économiques,* ed. Bernard Cazes
(Paris, 1970); and *Turgot on Progress, Sociology and Economics,* trans. and ed. R. L. Meek
(Cambridge, University Press, 1973).

2. Turgot to the Chevalier Turgot at Malta, July 31, 1750, in Schelle ed., I, 184.

3. Turgot, the man of taste, was sometimes self-conscious about the apologetics.
On one draft of the discourse he wrote, "All this has a didactic air." MS in Turgot archives, Château de Lantheuil, Normandy.

4. Condorcet, a jealous disciple, would not have agreed. "His real opinions were
not known. There existed in Europe only a very few men in a position to comprehend
them in their totality and to judge them." Condorcet, *Vie de Turgot,* p. 287.

5. See Edgar Faure, *La Disgrâce de Turgot* (Paris, 1961).

6. MS in Turgot archives, Château de Lantheuil.

7. Dupont de Nemours ed., I, 417–418.

8. Schelle ed., I, 214–215.

9. "Pensées diverses," ibid., p. 321.

10. "No mutation has taken place without producing experience, and without
spreading or ameliorating or preparing education." "Plan de deux discours sur l'histoire
universelle" (ca. 1751), Schelle ed., I, 285.

11. MS note in Turgot archives, Château de Lantheuil.

12. Condorcet, *Vie de Turgot,* p. 220.

13. Schelle ed., I, 593.

14. Ibid., V, 242–243.

15. *Tableau philosophique des progrès successifs de l'esprit humain* (1750), ibid., I, 222.

16. *Réflexions rédigées à l'occasion d'un Mémoire remis de Vergennes au Roi sur la manière
dont la France et l'Espagne doivent envisager les suites de la querelle entre la Grande-Bretagne et
ses colonies,* ibid., V, 416.

17. *Recherches sur les causes des progrès et de la décadence des sciences et des arts ou réflexions sur l'histoire des progrès de l'esprit humain,* ibid., I, 133.

18. "Plan du second discours sur les progrès de l'esprit humain," ibid., I, 302–303.

19. Abbé Etienne Bonnot de Condillac had already treated of the dependence of
genius on the availability of appropriate language forms. "Circumstances favorable to
the development of geniuses are found in a nation at the time when its language begins
to have fixed principles and set character. This is the epoch of the great men." *Essai sur
l'origine des connaissances humaines,* in *Oeuvres* (Paris, 1798), I, 437.

20. Turgot's whole discussion of language is clearly derivative from Condillac.
"Besides, it would show little understanding of the genius of language to imagine that
one could cause to be transmuted all of a sudden the most perfect forms from the most
crude. This can only be the work of time." Ibid., p. 440. "The success of the best organized geniuses depends completely on the progress of language in the century when
they live." Ibid., p. 439. This held equally true for literary and scientific genius: "The
success of Newton was prepared by the choice of symbols which had been made before
him." Ibid., pp. 438–439.

21. Similar ideas are expressed in the *Tableau philosophique,* Schelle ed., I, 223. Condillac in chap. XV, "Du génie des langues," of the *Essai sur l'origine des connaissances humaines* had already used language as the embodiment of the character of nations; Turgot
transferred the idea directly to historical stages. In this instance, as in many others, he
historicized Condillac.

22. Schelle ed., I, 347.

23. The following passage from Turgot is usually quoted (for example, by Robert

Flint, *The Philosophy of History in France and Germany* [London, 1875], p. 113) to illustrate the origins of the Comtean law: "Before knowing the connection of physical facts with one another, nothing was more natural than to suppose that they were produced by beings intelligent, invisible, and like to ourselves. Everything which happened without man's own intervention had its god, to which fear or hope caused a worship to be paid conforming to the respect accorded to powerful men—the gods being only men more or less powerful in proportion as the age which originated them was more or less enlightened as to what constitutes the true perfections of humanity. But when philosophers perceived the absurdity of these fables, without having attained to a real acquaintance with the history of nature, they fancifully accounted for phenomena by abstract expressions, by essences and faculties, which indeed explained nothing, but were reasoned from as if they were real existences. It was only very late that, from observing the mechanical action of bodies on one another, other hypotheses were inferred, which mathematics could develop and experience verify." Dupont de Nemours ed., II, 294–295. P. J. B. Buchez, *Introduction à la science de l'histoire* (Paris, 1842), I, 121, had already noted this similarity of ideas; it has been accepted by Jules Delvaille, *Essai sur l'histoire de l'idée de progrès jusqu'à la fin du dix-huitième siècle* (Paris, 1910), pp. 398–399. Auguste Comte acknowledged "the wise Turgot" as a predecessor, in the *Cours de philosophie positive,* IV, 201. Wilhelm Dilthey, in *Sitzungsberichte der Berliner Akademie,* 1890, p. 979, classified Turgot as a precursor of Positivism.

24. Condillac, *Essai sur l'origine des connaissances humaines,* in *Oeuvres,* I, 457.

25. "By observing the present one can see all the forms that barbarism has assumed spread over the face of the earth and thus, so to speak, the historical monuments of every age." MS notes, Turgot archives, Château de Lantheuil.

26. Schelle ed., I, 495.

27. Charles de Brosses, *Du culte des dieux fétiches* (Geneva, 1760).

28. In a very early work, the *Lettre à Madame de Graffigny sur les Lettres d'une Péruvienne* (1751), Turgot already expressed sharp divergence from the primitivists; there is no appreciation of man in the state of nature, and the primitive world is dark, ignorant, and cruel. Schelle ed., I, 243.

29. "Plan du premier discours sur la formation des gouvernements et le mélange des nations," ibid., p. 289.

30. "Plan de deux discours sur l'histoire universelle," ibid., p. 285.

31. "Plan d'un ouvrage sur la géographie politique" (1751), ibid., p. 257.

32. *Tableau philosophique des progrès successifs de l'esprit humain,* ibid., p. 231.

33. In a letter to Abbé Cicé (only a part of which is reproduced in Schelle, I, 108–109) Turgot emphasized the dependence of seventeenth-century speculative science upon a prior development of the mechanical arts. "At all times men have studied for their needs, and there have in all ages been workers who have known the physics of their jobs better than the physicists of their time." MS in Turgot archives, Château de Lantheuil.

34. *Tableau philosophique des progrès successifs de l'esprit humain,* Schelle ed., I, 227.

35. Ibid., pp. 199–200.

36. Condorcet, *Vie de Turgot,* p. 240.

37. Ibid., p. 251.

38. On the other side of the channel Richard Price was expressing a cognate idea in somewhat different similes at about the same time: "Such are the nature of things that this progress must continue. During particular intervals it may be interrupted, but it cannot be destroyed. Every present advance prepares the way for farther advances; and a single experiment or discovery may sometimes give rise to so many more as suddenly to raise the species higher, and to resemble the effects of opening a new sense, or of the fall of a spark on a train that springs a mine." *Observations on the Importance of the American Revolution and the Means of Making It a Benefit to the World* (London, 1785), pp. 3–4.

39. Dupont de Nemours ed., III, 448.

40. This definition is attributed to Turgot by Condorcet, *Vie de Turgot,* in *Oeuvres de Condorcet,* ed. A. Condorcet O'Connor and D. F. Arago, 12 vols. (Paris, 1847–1849), V, 14.

41. Schelle ed., V, 547. By no means did Turgot always sustain the youthful ecstasy of his 1750 *Tableau philosophique des progrès successifs de l'esprit humain* on the age of enlightenment: "Finally, all the shadows have been dissipated. What light shines in all directions! What a perfection of human reason!" Ibid., I, 234.

42. Turgot to Condorcet, Ussel, June 20, 1772, *Correspondance inédite de Condorcet et de Turgot, 1770–1779,* ed. with notes and intro. by Charles Henry (Paris, 1883), p. 88.

43. *Réflexions sur la formation et la distribution des richesses* (1776), Schelle ed., II, 537.

44. "Plan du premier discours sur la formation des gouvernements et le mélange des nations," ibid., I, 283. Kant, without referring to Turgot, developed a similar conception in his *Ideen.* This theme had been the heart of Vico's civil theology.

45. "The *Théodicée* of Leibniz should serve as a model for anyone who would put a vast erudition to use . . ." *Pensées,* ibid., p. 340. The Leibnizian influence is obvious throughout in Turgot. "I have also shown," wrote Leibniz, "that it is this Harmony that establishes the ties of the future with the past as well as of the present and what is absent." *Essais de Théodicée,* in *Opera Philosophica* (Berlin, 1840), p. 477.

46. *Encyclopédie,* X, 22.

47. Condorcet, *Vie de Turgot* (London, 1786), p. 212.

48. "Plan de deux discours sur l'histoire universelle," Schelle ed., I, 285.

49. Condorcet, *Vie de Turgot,* p. 279.

50. Ibid., p. 249.

51. Ibid.

52. Ibid., pp. 276–277. See the last passage of Condorcet's *Esquisse* (Genoa, 1798), p. 359, written as a consolation of philosophy.

53. *Oeuvres de Condorcet,* I (1847), 113–114.

20. Condorcet: Progression to Elysium

1. The original edition of Condorcet's *Esquisse* was published by P. C.-F. Daunou and Mme. M.-L.-S. de Condorcet in 1795. The edition cited here was published in Genoa, 1798. An English translation of the *Esquisse* by Thomas Churchill was published in London, 1795 (also in Philadelphia, 1796, and Baltimore, 1802); the modern rendering by J. Barraclough (London, 1955) corrects many obvious mistakes but sometimes loses the flavor of the original. An *Oeuvres complètes* in 21 volumes appeared in Brunswick and Paris, 1804, edited by Mme. Condorcet with the assistance of A. A. Barbier, Dr. Pierre Cabanis, and D. J. Garat. The standard edition of the *Oeuvres de Condorcet,* published by A. Condorcet O'Connor and D. F. Arago, appeared in 12 volumes in Paris, 1847–1849. (This edition is cited here.) A "Table alphabétique des oeuvres de Condorcet" and a "Table chronologique des oeuvres de Condorcet" are included in the standard edition, I, 641–646 and 647–652. Keith Michael Baker, *Condorcet: From Natural Philosophy to Social Mathematics* (Chicago, 1975), supersedes previous studies, and has a helpful bibliography, pp. 485–523.

2. Condorcet, *Oeuvres,* I, viii.

3. The classical portrait by Mlle. de l'Espinasse is in *Oeuvres,* I, 626–635.

4. Bibliothèque Nationale, Paris, N.a.fr. 23639, correspondence of Condorcet with Mme. Amélie Suard.

5. Marie-Louise-Sophie de Grouchy, *Théorie des sentimens moraux ou Essai analytique sur les principes des jugemens que portent naturellement les hommes . . . suivi d'une dissertation sur l'origine des langues. Huit lettres sur la sympathie,* 2 vols. (Paris, 1798). The most recent work on Mme. Condorcet is Henri Valentino, *Madame de Condorcet* (Paris, Perrin, 1950). For Jules Michelet's description see *Les Femmes de la révolution* (Paris, 1883), pp. 92–93.

6. Condorcet, *Oeuvres*, I, 608.

7. In *Les Indiscrétions de l'histoire*, 5th ser. (Paris, 1903–1909), pp. 339ff, Dr. Augustin Cabanès, on the basis of documents published by Marius Barroux in *La Révolution française*, 9 (1889), 173–185, concluded that Condorcet had died of a cerebral hemorrhage. For a rectification of details in Michelet's account of Condorcet's death, which most historians have followed, see Gérard Walter's notes to his edition of Jules Michelet, *Histoire de la révolution française* (Paris, 1952), II, 1304–1306.

8. Condorcet, *Oeuvres*, VI, 5.

9. Michelet, *Les Femmes de la révolution*, p. 94.

10. Condorcet, "Conseil de Condorcet à sa fille," in *Oeuvres*, I, 617–618.

11. Henri Valentino, *Madame de Condorcet*, p. 63.

12. Mme. Amélie Suard, *Essais de mémoire sur M. Suard* (Paris, 1820), p. 197.

13. Condorcet, *Esquisse* (Genoa, 1798), p. 250.

14. Thomas Robert Malthus, *An Essay on the Principles of Population, as it affects the future improvement of society. With remarks on the speculations of Mr. Godwin, M. Condorcet, and other writers* (London, 1798).

15. La Harpe and Chateaubriand spread the canard that Condorcet believed progress in science could render man immortal. François Picavet, *Les Idéologues* (Paris, 1891), p. 116n.

16. Epochs I, V, and X.

17. Condorcet, *Oeuvres*, VI, 346.

18. Condorcet's atheism was outspoken. The contention of O. H. Prior in his edition of the *Esquisse* (Paris, Boivin, 1933), pp. xi–xii, "He was certainly not an atheist," cannot be supported.

19. Quoted in Alberto Cento, *Condorcet e l'idea di progresso* (Florence, Parenti, 1956), p. 84, from Institut de France, MS 885, fasc. B, fol. 109.

20. Condorcet, *Esquisse* (1798), p. 24.

21. Quoted in Cento, *Condorcet*, p. 164.

22. Condorcet, *Mémoire sur l'instruction publique*, in *Oeuvres*, VII, 355.

23. Condorcet, *Esquisse* (1798), p. 26.

24. In his discourse of reception at the Académie Française, February 21, 1782, he had already made his commitment: "Each century will add new knowledge to the century which has preceded it, and these progressions, which nothing henceforth can either arrest or suspend, will have no other limits but those of the duration of the universe." *Oeuvres*, I, 390–391.

25. Ibid., p. 594.

26. Condorcet, *Fragment de l'histoire de la xe époque*, ibid., VI, 516.

27. Condorcet, *Esquisse* (1798), p. 58.

28. Ibid., pp. 236–237.

29. Condorcet, *Fragment de l'histoire de la première époque*, in *Oeuvres*, VI, 378–379.

30. Condorcet, *Vie de Turgot* (London, 1786), p. 10.

31. Condorcet, *Esquisse* (1798), p. 128.

32. Ibid., p. 88.

33. Ibid., p. 129.

34. Ibid.

35. Ibid., p. 162.

36. Ibid., p. 164.

37. Ibid., p. 168.

38. Ibid., p. 171.

39. Bibliothèque Nationale, N.a.fr. 4586, fol. 214.

40. Condorcet, *Esquisse* (1798), p. 210. A good deal of Condorcet's concern with the mass of the people was still quite abstract and remote. His articles on workers' education were rather patronizing: Since they would still have to labor six days a week he would limit himself to the inculcation of a few simple moral precepts and the teaching

of elementary laws of science. He seems to have been particularly annoyed by the religious ditties they sang while they worked; for these he would substitute moralizing rhymes, of which he left a few unfortunate examples:

Le travail est souvent le père du plaisir
Plaignons l'homme accablé du poids de son loisir

or

Les mortels sont égaux. Ce n'est pas la naissance
C'est la seule vertu qui fait leur différence.

Bibliothèque Nationale, N.a.fr. 23639.

41. *Esquisse* (1798), pp. 213–214.

42. Ibid., p. 302.

43. The idea of cooperative scientific ventures had already been mentioned a number of times by Condorcet in the course of his *éloges* of deceased colleagues. *Eloge de Haller*, in *Oeuvres*, II, 307: "The successive progressions of these sciences can be the result of the combined works of a great number of men." *Eloge de Linnaeus*, in *Oeuvres*, II, 342, described the worldwide cooperation between Linnaeus and his admirers in reporting new specimens.

44. Condorcet, *Fragment sur l'Atlantide*, in *Oeuvres*, VI, 600.

45. Ibid., p. 652.

46. Ibid., p. 657.

47. Ibid., p. 603.

48. Institut de France, MS. 885, fasc. C, fols. 9–10.

49. Condorcet, *Fragment sur l'Atlantide*, in *Oeuvres*, VI, 618.

50. Ibid., p. 600.

51. Ibid., p. 626.

52. Ibid., p. 628.

53. Condorcet, *Essai sur l'application de l'analyse à la probabilité des décisions rendues à la pluralité des voix* (Paris, 1785), p. i.

54. Ibid., p. clxxxvi–clxxxix.

55. Condorcet, "Tableau général de la Science, qui a pour objet l'application du calcul aux sciences politiques et morales," *Journal d'instruction sociale*, June 22 and July 6, 1795, in *Oeuvres*, I, 558.

56. Condorcet, *Fragment de l'histoire de la xe époque*, ibid., VI, 595.

57. Bibliothèque Nationale, N.a.fr. 4586, fol. 190.

58. Léon Cahen, in "Condorcet inédit: Notes pour le tableau des progrès de l'esprit humain," *La Révolution française*, 75 (1922), 199–212, published fragments from N.a.fr. 4586 entitled "Effet, dans l'état moral et politique de l'espèce humaine, de quelques découvertes physiques comme du moyen de produire avec une certaine probabilité des enfants mâles ou femelles à son choix."

59. Bibliothèque Nationale, N.a.fr. 4586, fol. 207.

60. Léon Cahen, "Condorcet inédit," p. 210.

61. Bibliothèque Nationale, N.a.fr. 4586, fol. 189.

62. Condorcet, *Oeuvres*, VII, 433.

63. Condorcet, "Discours lu à l'Académie des Sciences," ibid., I, 470.

64. Institut de France, MS 885, fasc. A, fol. 4.4°.

65. The *idéologues* of the *Décade philosophique* considered these last paragraphs as sublime as anything the philosophers of antiquity had written. Picavet, *Les Idéologues*, pp. 92–93.

66. Condorcet, *Esquisse* (1798), p. 339. After the sacking of Priestley's laboratory by a mob, Condorcet had written him in a similar vein from Paris, July 30, 1791: "The beautiful day of universal liberty will shine for our descendants; but we at least shall have witnessed the dawn, we shall have enjoyed the hope, and you, sir, you have accelerated the moment by your works, by the example of your virtues . . ." *Oeuvres*, I, 333–334.

21. Kant: Beyond Animality

1. Immanuel Kant, *Ideen zu einer allgemeinen Geschichte in weltbürgerlichen Absicht* (1784), in *Gesammelte Schriften*, ed. Königlich Preussische Akademie (Berlin, 1912), VIII, 15-32. See Emil L. Fackenheim, "Kant's Concept of History," *Kant-Studien*, 48 (1956-1957), 381-398; Frank E. Manuel, *Shapes of Philosophical History* (Stanford, 1965), chap. 4; Immanuel Kant, *On History: A Compilation*, ed. Lewis White Beck (Indianapolis, Bobbs-Merrill, 1963). Beck's translations have been adapted for this chapter.

2. Kant, *Rezensionen von J. G. Herders Philosophie der Geschichte der Menschheit* (1785), Ernst Cassirer edition, in *Werke*, IV (Berlin, B. Cassirer, 1913). *Zum ewigen Frieden: Ein philosophischer Entwurf* first appeared in Königsberg, 1795; the following year it was translated into French as *Projet de paix perpetuelle: Essai philosophique . . . avec un nouveau supplément de l'auteur* (Königsberg). *Der Streit der Fakultäten in drei Abschnitten* (1798), Cassirer ed., in *Werke*, VII (Berlin, 1922), 311-431; the second *Abschnitt* posed the question, p. 391, "Is the human species in constant progression toward the better?"

3. Kant, *Rezensionen*, p. 199.

4. Kant, "The End of All Things," in *Essays and Treatises on Moral, Political and Various Philosophical Subjects*, trans. William Richardson (London, 1798-1799), II, 436-437.

5. Kant, *On History*, p. 15, Fourth Thesis.

6. Ibid., p. 16, Fourth Thesis.

7. Ibid., p. 15, Fourth Thesis.

8. Ibid., p. 16, Fifth Thesis.

9. Kant, *The Moral Law; or, Kant's Groundwork of the Metaphysic of Morals*, ed. and trans. H. J. Paton (London, Hutchinson's University Library, 1948), pp. 88, 89.

10. Kant, "The End of All Things," p. 431.

11. Kant, *Streit der Fakultäten*, in *Werke*, VII, 407.

22. New Faces of Love

1. David Tompson, *Histoire d'un peuple nouveau* (London, 1757), part 2, p. 134.

2. *Encyclopédie*, XXI, 97.

3. Morelly, *Naufrage des îles flottantes* (Messina [Paris], 1753), II, 296n.

4. The first *Justine* had been published in 1791, in two volumes.

5. Marquis Donatien-Alphonse-François de Sade, *Aline et Valcour, ou Le Roman philosophique* (1793; Paris, 1956), II, 73, 80-81. On the Marquis de Sade see *Oeuvres complètes*, 15 vols. (Paris, 1962-1964); *Cahiers personnels, 1803-1804*, ed. Gilbert Lély (Paris, 1953); *Journal inédit (1807, 1808, 1814)* (Paris, 1970); Gilbert Lély, *Vie du marquis de Sade*, new ed. (Paris, 1965), and *Sade: Etudes sur sa vie et sur son oeuvre* (Paris, 1967); Simone de Beauvoir, *Must We Burn de Sade?* trans. A. Michelson (London, 1953); Pierre Favre, *Sade, utopiste: Sexualité, pouvoir et état dans le roman Aline et Valcour* (Paris, 1967); Roberta J. Hackel, *De Sade's Quantitative Moral Universe: Of Irony, Rhetoric, and Boredom* (The Hague, 1976).

6. Marquis de Sade, *La Philosophie dans le boudoir* (1795; Paris, Pauvert, 1954), p. 214.

7. Ibid, p. 213.

8. Nicolas Edme Restif de la Bretonne, *La Vie de mon père* (1779), ed. Marius Boisson (Paris, Bossard, 1924), p. 270. On Restif de la Bretonne, see *L'Oeuvre*, ed. Henri Bachelin, 9 vols. (Paris, 1930-1932); James Rives Childs, *Restif de la Bretonne: Témoignages et jugements; bibliographie* (Paris, 1949); Marc Chadourne, *Restif de la Bretonne: Le siècle prophétique* (Paris, 1958); Mark Poster, *The Utopian Thought of Restif de la Bretonne* (New York, 1971), bibliography, pp. 141-150.

9. Restif de la Bretonne, *Les Gynographes, ou Idées de deux honnêtes-femmes sur un projet de règlement proposé à toute l'Europe, pour mettre les Femmes à leur place, et opérer le bonheur des deux sexes* (Paris, 1777), p. 41.

10. Restif de la Bretonne, *Les Nuits de Paris, ou Le Spectateur nocturne,* vol. VII, part 14 (Paris, 1789), pp. 3356–3359.

11. Restif de la Bretonne, *Monsieur Nicolas, ou Le Coeur-humain dévoilé,* 16 vols. (Paris, 1794–1797), VII, 3906.

12. Pierre Leroux, "Lettres sur le Fouriérisme: Rétif de la Bretonne," *Revue sociale,* vol. 3, no. 7 (March 1850), p. 103.

23. Equality or Death

1. Restif de la Bretonne, *L'Andrographe* (Paris, 1782), p. 28.

2. Morelly, *Naufrage des îles flottantes* (Messina [Paris], 1753), II, 296n.

3. See François Noël (Gracchus) Babeuf, *Correspondance avec l'Académie d'Arras* (1785–1788), ed. Marcel Reinhard (Paris, 1961).

4. Dom Deschamps, *Le Vrai système,* ed. Jean Thomas and Franco Venturi (Geneva, Droz, 1963), p. 106.

5. Morelly shared this suspicion of excessive learning. In a ruined Temple of Reason the hero of the *Naufrage des îles flottantes,* Prince Zeinzemin, learns a vast accumulation of books is but "a deep abyss of uncertainty and of doubt in which the human mind floats not knowing where to land . . . a confused and disorderly pile of false opinions, repeated over and again, myths, tales, laws which everyone interprets according to his fancy" (II, 207).

6. Jean Meslier, *Oeuvres complètes,* ed. Jean Deprun et al., 3 vols. (Paris, 1970–1972). See also Maurice Dommanget, *Le Curé Meslier, athée, communiste, et révolutionnaire sous Louis XIV* (Paris, 1965).

7. Gabriel Bonnot de Mably, *De la législation, ou principes des lois,* in *Collection complète des Oeuvres* (Paris, 1794–1795), IX, 45.

8. Louis-Antoine de Saint-Just, *Fragments sur les institutions républicaines,* ed. Albert Soboul (Turin, Einaudi, 1952), p. 35. (This edition has French and Italian texts.)

9. Ibid., p. 33.

10. Ibid.

11. Ibid., p. 48.

12. Ibid., p. 47.

13. Ibid., p. 49.

14. Ibid., p. 52.

15. Ibid., pp. 54–55.

16. Ibid., p. 55.

17. Ibid., p. 46.

18. Ibid., p. 33.

19. Gabriel Deville, "Notes inédites de Babeuf sur lui-même," *La Révolution française,* 49 (1905), 37–44. See also Victor Moiseevich Dalin, *Babeuf-Studien* (Berlin, 1961); Maurice Dommanget et al., *Babeuf et les problèmes du babouvisme* (Paris, 1963); and R. B. Rose, *Gracchus Babeuf: The First Revolutionary Communist* (Stanford, Calif., 1978).

20. *Tribun du Peuple* (Paris, Editions d'Histoire Sociale, 1966), no. 35 (9 frimaire, an IV), p. 107.

21. Rose, *Babeuf,* p. 123.

22. Filippo Michele Buonarroti, *Conspiration pour l'égalité dite de Babeuf* (1828), new ed. (Paris, Editions sociales, 1957), II, 94–95.

23. Ibid., I, 164.

24. Ibid.

25. Ibid., p. 165.

26. Ibid., p. 169.

27. Ibid., p. 170.

28. Babeuf, "Manifeste des Plébéiens," in *Tribun du Peuple,* no. 35 (9 frimaire, an IV), pp. 104–105.

29. Buonarroti, *Conspiration pour l'égalité*, I, 148.
30. Ibid., p. 150.
31. Ibid., p. 85.
32. Ibid., II, 12.
33. Ibid., p. 44.

24. The Battle of the Systems

1. Charles Fourier, *Pièges et charlatanisme des deux Sectes Saint-Simon et Owen, qui promettent l'association et le progrès* (Paris, 1831), p. 47.
2. Cited in Franco Venturi, *Il Populismo russo* (Turin, Einaudi, 1952), I, 18.
3. George Mudie, in *The Economist*, 1 (1821), 338–339.
4. Henri Saint-Simon, *De la réorganisation de la société européenne*, in *Oeuvres choisies*, ed. C. Lemonnier (Brussels, 1859), II, 328.
5. Cited in Frank E. Manuel, *The Prophets of Paris* (Cambridge, Mass., Harvard University Press, 1962), p. 10.

25. Saint-Simon: The Pear Is Ripe

1. The pioneer scholarly work on Saint-Simon was Georges Weill, *Un Précurseur du socialisme: Saint-Simon et son oeuvre* (Paris, 1896); the first to use archival materials was Maxime Leroy, *La Vie véritable du Comte Henri de Saint-Simon* (Paris, 1925); the second volume of Henri Gouhier, *La Jeunesse d'Auguste Comte* (Paris, 1933–1941) is largely devoted to Saint-Simon. In Frank E. Manuel, *The New World of Henri Saint-Simon* (Cambridge, Mass., 1956), bibliographical references are included in the section of notes, pp. 371–423. See also, in Russian, Viacheslav Petrovich Volgin, *Sen-Simon i sen-simonism* (Moscow, 1961); and A. Levandovskii, *Sen-Simon* (Moscow, 1973).
   Olinde Rodrigues first attempted to collect Saint-Simon's works in *Oeuvres complètes de Saint-Simon* (Paris, 1832). The *Oeuvres choisies de C. H. Saint-Simon, précédées d'un essai sur sa doctrine*, ed. C. Lemonnier, 3 vols. (Brussels, 1859), and the *Oeuvres de Saint-Simon et d'Enfantin*, 47 vols. (Paris, 1865–1878), cited as *Oeuvres*, are two collections that complement each other. In 1966 six volumes from the *Oeuvres* were reproduced, and in 1973 the *Oeuvres choisies* was reprinted in Hildesheim. *Selected Writings* have been edited and translated into English by F. M. H. Markham (Oxford, 1952); other compilations have been published by Keith Taylor, *Henri Saint-Simon: Selected Writings on Science, Industry and Social Organization* (New York, 1975), and by Ghita Ionescu, *The Political Thought of Saint-Simon* (London and New York, 1976). Jean Dautry's *Saint-Simon: Textes choisis* (Paris, 1951) includes excerpts from manuscripts in the Bibliothèque Nationale and in the La Sicotière Collection which had not previously been published.
2. *Lettres d'un habitant de Genève*, in *Oeuvres*, XV, 22.
3. *Lettres de C.-H. Saint-Simon: 1re correspondance* (Paris, 1808), p. 74.
4. *Esquisse d'une nouvelle encyclopédie* (Paris, n.d.), p. 5.
5. *Opinions littéraires, philosophiques et industrielles* (Paris, 1825), pp. 374–375.
6. The "immortal physiologist" Bichat was by Saint-Simon's own testimony the source of his conception of mutually exclusive capacities, a theory which in *Du système industriel* he called a law of human organization. *Oeuvres*, XXII, 56. Xavier Bichat, *Physiological Researches upon Life and Death*, trans. Tobias Watkins (Philadelphia, 1809), pp. 112–113. The work was originally published in France in the Year VIII (1799–1800).
7. *Oeuvres*, XXII, 17n.
8. *Notice historique*, ibid., I, 122.
9. Condorcet, *Esquisse d'un tableau historique*, in his *Oeuvres*, ed. A. Condorcet O'Connor and D. F. Arago, VI (Paris, 1849), 238.
10. The idea of the natural elite was developed by Saint-Simon in *L'Industrie*, in

Oeuvres, XVIII, 142–145. The same conception had been adumbrated earlier in the fragment entitled "Sur la capacité de l'Empereur," in the *Introduction aux travaux scientifiques du XIXᵉ siècle*, in *Oeuvres choisies*.

11. *Oeuvres choisies*, I, 173.

12. *Introduction aux travaux scientifiques du XIXᵉ siècle*, ibid., p. 143.

13. *L'Organisateur*, in *Oeuvres*, XX, 192.

14. Ibid., p. 151.

15. Saint-Simon's solution of the problem of internecine conflict within the elite is reminiscent of Condorcet's treatment of jealousy among the scientists called upon to collaborate on grand international projects. "Once the true methods for studying the sciences, for making progress in them, are known, there cannot fail to exist among those who cultivate some one science with success a common opinion, accepted principles which they would not be able to transgress without violating an inner feeling, without giving themselves a reputation either for ignorance or for bad faith.

"These men are doubtless not exempt from the pettiness of self-love. They are not alien to jealousy. But they will not sacrifice to the impulses of these wretched passions the very object which inspires them." Condorcet, *Fragment sur l'Atlantide*, in *Oeuvres*, VI, 604.

16. *Suite à la brochure des Bourbons et des Stuarts*, in *Oeuvres choisies*, II, 444–445.

17. *L'Organisateur*, in *Oeuvres*, XX, 200.

18. Ibid., p. 202.

19. Ibid., p. 199.

20. The belief that Olinde Rodrigues wrote the introduction is based upon a manuscript note in a copy of the *Nouveau Christianisme* in the Bibliothèque de L'Arsenal, Fonds Enfantin, 7802 (132) 8. Hoëné Wroński once told Frédéric de Rougemont that the *Nouveau Christianisme* was not written by Saint-Simon. Frédéric de Rougemont, *Les Deux cités: La Philosophie de l'histoire aux différents âges de l'humanité* (Paris, 1874), II, 439. This evidence by a rival Messiah is naturally suspect.

21. In a letter to John Stuart Mill on December 1, 1829, Gustave d'Eichthal, who was a close friend of Olinde Rodrigues, described the new religious orientation of Saint-Simon's last period: "Saint-Simon, after having in his early writings tried to reorganize society in the name of Science, after having later renewed the same attempt in the name of Industry, realized that he had mistaken the *means* for the *end;* that it is in the name of their *sympathies* that one must speak to men, and above all, in the name of their *religious sympathies,* which should summarize all others." J. S. Mill, *Correspondance inédite avec Gustave d'Eichthal* (Paris, 1898), pp. 75–76. D'Eichthal had written in his letter of November 23, 1829, that for two years none of the disciples was able to grasp the full meaning of the *Nouveau Christianisme. Correspondance*, p. 57n. By December 1, 1829, the key had been discovered and the religion of Saint-Simon had been clothed in the language of romanticized Spinozism: "The religious doctrine of Saint-Simon has this *unitary* character which should gather about it all the men of the future. It puts neither *spirit* above *matter*, nor *matter* above *spirit*. It considers them as intimately united one with another, as being the condition one of the other, as being the two modes in which *being* is manifest, *living* being, *sympathetic* being." *Correspondance*, p. 74.

22. "But there is a science that is more important for society than physical and mathematical knowledge. It is the science that constitutes society, that serves as its base. It is morals. Now morals have followed a path absolutely contrary to that of the physical and mathematical sciences. More than eighteen hundred years have elapsed since its fundamental principle was produced, and since that time all the researches of men of the greatest genius have not been able to discover a principle superior in its generality or in its precision to the one formulated at that epoch by the founder of Christianity." *Nouveau Christianisme*, in *Oeuvres choisies*, III, 378–379.

23. "Les hommes doivent se conduire en frères à l'égard les uns des autres." Ibid.,

p. 322. It is not absolutely clear to which New Testament text he refers. It could be the King James version equivalent in Romans 13: "In love of the brethren be tenderly affectioned one to another." The epigraph of the *Nouveau Christianisme* was derived from passages in the French version of Romans 13: "for he that loveth his neighbor hath fulfilled the law . . . and if there be any other commandment, it is summed up in this word, namely, Thou shalt love thy neighbor as thyself."

24. *Nouveau Christianisme,* in *Oeuvres choisies,* III, 322.

25. The primitive catechism to which Saint-Simon referred expressed the golden rule in a negative rather than a positive form.

26. *Oeuvres choisies,* III, 379.

27. C. Lemonnier, in the *Revue des cours littéraires,* 21 (1876), 383, was of the opinion that a total view of Saint-Simon's works could, despite the contradictions, only lead to the conclusion that "he died as he lived, that he remained to the end in the ranks of the freethinkers." Professor Henri Gouhier's judgment is categoric: "The Saint-Simonism of Saint-Simon is not a religion, but a social philosophy disguised as a religion." *La Jeunesse d'Auguste Comte* (Paris, 1933–1941), III, 231.

28. See Alfred de Musset's description of the plight of his generation in *La Confession d'un enfant du siècle* (Paris, 1937), pp. 19, 24: "Alas! Alas! Religion is vanishing . . . We no longer have either hope or expectation, not even two little pieces of black wood in a cross before which to wring our hands . . . Everything that was is no more. All that will be is not yet."

29. *Nouveau Christianisme,* in *Oeuvres,* XXIII, 182–183.

30. Ibid., p. 184.

31. Ibid., p. 185.

32. *Notice historique,* ibid., I, 121–122.

26. Children of Saint-Simon: The Triumph of Love

1. The classical scholarly work on the Saint-Simonians remains Sébastien Camille Gustave Charléty, *Histoire du Saint-Simonisme* (Paris, Paul Hartmann, 1931), which superseded the pioneer study by Georges Weill, *L'Ecole saint-simonienne: Son histoire, son influence jusqu'à nos jours* (Paris, 1896). Henry-René d'Allemagne, *Les Saint-Simoniens* (Paris, 1930), is noteworthy primarily for its illustrations. Georg G. Iggers, *The Cult of Authority: The Political Philosophy of the Saint-Simonians, a Chapter in the History of Totalitarianism* (The Hague, 1958), identifies its orientation in the title. Both Charléty, pp. 365–379, and Iggers, pp. 195–203, have bibliographies. Charléty expanded Henry Fournel's meticulous *Bibliographie saint-simonienne* (Paris, 1833) to include the secondary literature up to 1931. For a study of the ideas of the Saint-Simonians, the *Doctrine de Saint-Simon: Exposition, Première année, 1829,* edited by C. Bouglé and Elie Halévy (Paris, Rivière, 1924), is the key work, profusely and brilliantly annotated. The *Doctrine* has been translated into English by Iggers (Boston, 1958). For bibliography, see Manuel, *The Prophets of Paris* (Cambridge, Mass., 1962), pp. 331–333. See also François Perroux, *Industrie et création collective,* 2 vols. (Paris, 1964–1970); Francesco Pitocco, *Utopia e riforma religiosa nel Risorgimento* (Bari, 1972); Claire Démar (d. 1833), *Textes sur l'affranchissement des femmes: 1832–1833,* bound with Valentin Pelosse, *Symbolique groupale et idéologie féministe saint-simoniennes* (Paris, 1976).

Enfantin's works were published in the eccentrically edited *Oeuvres de Saint-Simon et d'Enfantin,* 47 vols. (Paris, 1865–1878); his writings appear as vols. XIV, XVI, XVII, XXIV–XXXVI, XLVI. The two principal Saint-Simonian journals were *Le Producteur: Journal philosophique de l'industrie, des sciences et des beaux-arts,* 5 vols. (Paris, 1825–1826); and *Le Globe,* vols. IX–XII (Paris, 1830–1832).

2. Edouard Charton, *Mémoires d'un prédicateur saint-simonien* (Paris, 1831), pp. 22–23.

3. *Enseignement des ouvriers, séance du 25 déc. 1831* (Paris, 1832), pp. 16–17.

4. *Religion saint-simonienne: Cérémonie du 27 novembre* (Paris, 1831), p. 4.

5. *Procès en la cour d'assises de la Seine, les 27 et 28 août 1832* (Paris, 1832), p. 75, extract from an *Enseignement* of Nov. 19, 1831.

6. Ibid., p. 76.

7. Ibid., p. 78.

8. Abel Transon, *Affranchissement des femmes: Prédication du 1er janvier* (Paris, 1832).

9. *Retraite de Ménilmontant* (Paris, 1832), p. 15.

10. *Doctrine de Saint-Simon,* ed. Bouglé and Halévy, pp. 121–122.

11. Ibid., pp. 157–158.

12. Ibid., p. 340.

13. *Correspondance: Articles extraits du Globe* (Paris, 1831), p. 53.

14. *Doctrine de Saint-Simon,* p. 267.

15. Ibid., pp. 404–405.

16. Ibid., p. 164.

17. *Religion saint-simonienne: Cérémonie du 27 novembre,* p. 17.

18. *Doctrine de Saint-Simon,* p. 248.

19. Ibid., p. 353.

20. Ibid., p. 261.

21. Ibid., p. 274.

22. Ibid., p. 276.

23. Ibid., p. 347.

24. Ibid., p. 346.

25. Ibid., p. 343.

26. Ibid., p. 320.

27. Ibid., p. 323.

28. Ibid., pp. 278–279.

29. Ibid., pp. 382–383.

30. Maxime du Camp, *Souvenirs littéraires* (Paris, 1883), II, 124.

31. For descriptions of the trial see Charléty, *Histoire du Saint-Simonisme,* pp. 175–185; *Oeuvres de Saint-Simon et d'Enfantin,* VII, 197–256; d'Allemagne, *Les Saint-Simoniens,* pp. 294–302.

32. *Procès en la cour d'assises,* p. 63.

33. Ibid., p. 194.

34. Ibid., p. 212.

35. Ibid., p. 218.

36. F. B. Duroselle, "Michel Chevalier, Saint-Simonien," *Revue historique,* 82 (1956), p. 240.

37. Prosper Enfantin, *La Vie éternelle, passée, présente, future* (Paris, 1861), p. 49.

38. Ibid., p. 79.

39. Quoted in Charléty, *Histoire du Saint-Simonisme,* p. 324.

27. Fourier: The Burgeoning of Instinct

1. A summary of Fourierist studies may be found in Henri Desroche's introduction to Emile Poulat, *Les Cahiers manuscrits de Fourier: Etude historique et inventaire raisonné* (Paris, 1957), pp. 6–36, "Fouriérisme écrit et Fouriérisme pratiqué: Notes sur les études fouriéristes contemporaines." The bibliographical emphasis in this introduction is on the Fourierist school and the diffusion of Fourierism throughout the world rather than on the works of Fourier himself. Hubert Bourgin, *Fourier* (Paris, 1905), still remains the most comprehensive scholarly study of the man and his works; its bibliography is on pp. 17–45. M. Lansac, *Les conceptions méthodologiques et sociales de Charles Fourier* (Paris, 1926), has not superseded Bourgin's work. Charles Gide, *Fourier précurseur de la coopéra-*

tion (Paris, 1922–1923); C. Bouglé, *Socialismes français* (Paris, 1932); H. Louvancour, *De Henri Saint-Simon à Fourier: Etude sur le socialisme romantique français de 1830* (Chartres, 1913); and N. V. Riasanovsky, *The Teaching of Charles Fourier* (Berkeley, 1969), are significant studies of Fourier himself. See also Emile Lehouck, *Fourier aujourd'hui* (Paris, 1966); Fourier, *Histoire du cocuage,* ed. René Maublanc (Paris, 1974); Roland Barthes, *Sade, Fourier, Loyola* (Paris, 1971); Henri Desroche, *La Société festive: Du fouriérisme écrit aux fouriérismes pratiqués* (Paris, 1975); David Zeldin, *The Educational Ideas of Charles Fourier* (London, 1969); Jean Goret, *La Pensée de Fourier* (Paris, 1974); Pascal Bruckner, *Fourier* (Paris, 1975); Henri Lefebvre et al., *Actualité de Fourier: Colloque d'Arc-et-Senans* (Paris, 1975). The most significant bibliography of Fourierist literature, including separate sections on the works of Fourier, those of the school, periodicals, and books on Fourierism, is the inventory of the Fourierist collection in the Biblioteca Feltrinelli, Milan, first published by Giuseppe del Bo in the *Movimento Operaio,* n.s., 1 (1953), 73–130, 299–321, and expanded in 1957 as *Il Socialismo Utopistico: Charles Fourier e la Scuola Societaria (1801–1922), Saggio bibliografico* (Milan, 1957), pp. 1–111. An *Oeuvres complètes,* 6 vols., that appeared in Paris, 1841–1845, omitting Fourier's manuscripts published in *La Phalange,* has in some respects been superseded by the 10-volume *Oeuvres complètes* (cited here only in the case of *Le Nouveau Monde amoureux*) published in Paris by Editions Anthropos, 1966–1968.

2. "La Nouvelle Isabelle," *La Phalange,* 9 (1849), 237–238.

3. See Victor Considérant, *Exposition abrégée du système phalanstérien de Fourier* (Paris, 1846), the 3d edition of his lectures of 1841, a vulgarization and simplification of Fourier in which the whole system is reduced to the organization of labor.

4. *Oeuvres complètes,* VI, 398–399.

5. E. Silberling, *Dictionnaire de sociologie phalanstérienne: Guide des oeuvres complètes de Charles Fourier* (Paris, 1911).

6. Archives Nationales, Paris, 10 AS 20.

7. Ibid., 10 AS 20: notebooks.

8. Ibid., 10 AS 20.

9. Ibid., 10 AS 21 (13), Fourier to Victor Considérant, Paris, Oct. 3, 1831.

10. Charles Pellarin, *Fourier, sa vie et sa théorie* (Paris, 1849), p. 104.

11. Poulat, *Les Cahiers manuscrits de Fourier,* pp. 14–15.

12. See Franco Venturi, *Roots of Revolution: A History of the Populist and Socialist Movements in Nineteenth Century Russia* (New York, 1960), p. 83.

13. *Théorie des quatre mouvements et des destinées générales: Prospectus et annonce de la découverte* (1808), in *Oeuvres complètes,* I, 7–8.

14. Archives Nationales, 10 AS 20.

15. Ibid.

16. Ibid., 10 AS 40, Just Muiron to Mme. Clarisse Vigoureux, May 12, 1832.

17. *La Phalange,* 9 (1849), 200.

18. *Théorie des quatre mouvements,* in *Oeuvres complètes,* I, 143–144.

19. Archives Nationales, 10 AS 20 (3).

20. *Traité de l'association domestique-agricole* (1822), in *Oeuvres complètes,* II, 413.

21. *Théorie de l'unité universelle,* ibid., IV, 462.

22. Ibid., VI, 47.

23. *Du garantisme,* in *La Phalange,* 9 (1849), 328.

24. *Théorie des quatre mouvements,* in *Oeuvres complètes,* I, 115.

25. Archives Nationales, 10 AS 8.

26. Ibid., 10 AS 8 (4).

27. Charles Pellarin, *Lettre de Fourier au grand juge, 4 nivôse an XII* (Paris, 1874), pp. 24–25.

28. Ibid., p. 22.

29. Nathaniel Hawthorne was initially enthusiastic about his labors with the dung

pile of Brook Farm. He wrote to his wife on May 4, 1841: "There is nothing so unseemly and disagreeable in this sort of toil as thou wouldst think. It defiles the hands, indeed, but not the soul. This gold ore is a pure and wholesome substance; else our Mother Nature would not devour it so readily, and derive so much nourishment from it, and return such a rich abundance of good grain and roots in requital of it." *The Heart of Hawthorne's Journal,* ed. Newton Arvin (Boston, Houghton Mifflin, 1929), p. 73. By the beginning of June the tune had changed: "It is my opinion, dearest, that a man's soul may be buried and perish under a dung-heap or in a furrow of the field, just as well as under a pile of money." Ibid., p. 74.

30. "Notions préliminaires sur les Séries et l'éducation naturelle," *La Phalange,* 7 (1848), 138.

31. MS letter to the *Gazette de France,* Archives Nationales, 10 AS 20 (7).

32. Ibid.

33. *La Fausse industrie morcelée, répugnante, mensongère et l'antidote, l'industrie naturelle, combinée, attrayante, véridique, donnant quadruple produit* (Paris, 1835), pp. 360–361.

34. *Oeuvres complètes,* VI, 403.

35. MS letter to the *Gazette de France,* Archives Nationales, 10 AS 20 (7).

36. Ibid.

37. "Fragments," *La Phalange,* 9 (1849), 456–457.

38. Ibid., pp. 453–454.

39. Ibid., p. 454.

40. Ibid., p. 455.

41. Archives Nationales, 10 AS 8 (4).

42. Ibid.

43. *Théorie des quatre mouvements,* in *Oeuvres complètes,* I, 117.

44. *La Phalange,* 9 (1849), 204.

45. Archives Nationales, 10 AS 8.

46. "De la sériosophie," *La Phalange,* 9 (1849), 48.

47. Archives Nationales, 10 AS 8.

48. Ibid.

49. Ibid.

50. Ibid.

51. *La Phalange,* 9 (1849), 195.

52. Ibid., p. 194.

53. Ibid., p. 197.

54. Ibid., p. 202.

55. "Le Sphinx sans Oedipe ou l'énigme des quatre mouvements," *La Phalange,* 9 (1849), 204.

56. Ibid., p. 214.

57. Ibid., p. 223.

58. Ibid., p. 224.

59. *Oeuvres complètes,* I, 219.

60. After the incident he was called a "petit massacre, enragé d'enfant." *Théorie de l'unité universelle,* ibid., V, 41–42.

61. *Le Nouveau monde amoureux,* trans. and quoted in Jonathan Beecher and Richard Bienvenu, eds., *The Utopian Vision of Charles Fourier* (Boston, Beacon Press, 1971), p. 350.

62. *Le Nouveau monde amoureux,* in *Oeuvres complètes,* VII (Paris, 1967), 257.

28. Owen's New Moral World

1. Robert Owen, *A Supplementary Appendix to the First Volume of the Life of Robert Owen Written by Himself* (London, 1858), vol. I.A, app. I, p. 82.

2. Owen, *The Future of the Human Race; or a Great, Glorious, and Peaceful Revolution,*

Near at Hand, to Be Effected through the Agency of Departed Spirits of Good and Superior Men and Women (London, 1853).

3. Owen, *Supplementary Appendix*, vol. I.A, app. I, pp. 53–64.

4. Ibid., app. I, letter published in London newspapers of Sept. 10, 1817, pp. 132–133.

5. Ibid., app. S, "Report to the County of Lanark of a plan for relieving public distress and removing discontent, by giving permanent productive employment to the poor and working classes, etc." (May 1, 1820), pp. 261–310.

6. J. F. C. Harrison, *Quest for the New Moral World: Robert Owen and the Owenites in Britain and America* (New York, 1969), p. 29. On Owen see also John Butt, *Robert Owen, Prince of Cotton Spinners: A Symposium* (Newton Abbot, 1971); Ronald George Garnett, *Cooperation and the Owenite Socialist Communities in Britain, 1825–1845* (Manchester, 1972); V. G. Podmarkov, *Robert Ouén—gumanist i myslitel'* (Moscow, 1976); Owen Bicentennial Conference, New Harmony, Ind., 1971, *Proceedings: Robert Owen's American Legacy,* ed. Donald E. Pitzer (Indianapolis, 1972).

7. *New Moral World,* May 28, 1842.

8. Owen, *Supplementary Appendix,* vol. I.A, app. F, "Observations on the Cotton Trade" (January 1815), p. 17.

9. Owen, *A New View of Society,* First Essay, reprinted in *Life of Robert Owen Written by Himself* (London, 1857), I, 266.

10. Owen, *The Revolution in the Mind and Practice of the Human Race; or, the Coming Change from Irrationality to Rationality* (London, 1849), pp. 62–63. See also Owen, *An Address Delivered to the Inhabitants of New Lanark . . . at the Opening of the New Institution Established for the Formation of Character,* 2d ed. (London, 1816); *Essays on the Formation of the Human Character* (Manchester, 1837), p. 36 (a later edition of *A New View of Society: or, Essays on the Principle of the Formation of the Human Character* [London, 1813]).

11. Owen, *Revolution in the Mind and Practice of the Human Race,* p. 63.

12. Ibid., pp. 63–64.

13. Owen, *A New View of Society,* 3d ed. (London, 1817), Second Essay, p. 59.

14. Owen, *Revolution in the Mind and Practice of the Human Race,* p. 81.

15. Ibid., p. 141.

16. Quoted in Frank Podmore, *Robert Owen: A Biography* (New York, 1907), II, 500. See *Public Discussion between R. Owen . . . and the Rev. J. H. Roebuck . . . ,* 2d ed. (Manchester and London, 1837).

17. Owen, *Revolution in the Mind and Practice of the Human Race,* p. 71.

18. Ibid., p. 123.

19. Ibid., p. 65.

20. Ibid., p. 67.

21. Ibid., pp. 60, 68.

22. Ibid., p. 124.

23. Owen, *Lectures on the Marriages of the Priesthood of the Old Immoral World, Delivered in the Year 1835, before the Passing of the New Marriage Act,* 4th ed. (Leeds, 1840), p. 7. See also *The Book of the New Moral World, Containing the Rational System of Society, Founded on Demonstrable Facts, Developing the Constitution and Laws of Human Nature and of Society* (London, 1836), part 1.

24. Owen, *Revolution in the Mind and Practice of the Human Race,* p. 124.

25. Ibid., p. 73.

26. Ibid., pp. 75, 72.

27. Ibid., p. 76.

28. Ibid.

29. The *Cooperative Magazine and Monthly Herald* (London), no. 11 (November 1820), published excerpts from the "beautiful moral landscape" of *Utopia.*

30. Owen, *Revolution in the Mind and Practice of the Human Race,* p. 62.

31. See Owen, *The Signs of the Times: or, the Approach of the Millennium,* 2d ed. (London, 1841); and *The Inauguration of the Millennium, May 14, 1855, Being a Report of Two Public Meetings* (London, 1855).

29. Marx and Engels in the Landscape of Utopia

1. The original title in *Die Neue Zeit,* 9th year, no. 18 (1890–1891, part 1), pp. 561–575, was "Zur Kritik des Sozialdemokratischen Parteiprogramms." The version in the Marx-Engels *Werke* (Berlin, Dietz, 1956–1965), XIX, 13–32, returned to the original Marx manuscript and introduced a subtitle: "Randglossen zum Programm der deutschen Arbeiterpartei."

2. *Werke,* XIX, 28.

3. See, for example, Friedrich Engels, *Die Entwicklung des Sozialismus von der Utopie zur Wissenschaft,* ibid., p. 191. The work is alternatively known as *Anti-Dühring* and *Herrn Eugen Dührings Umwälzung der Wissenschaft.*

4. Georges Sorel, *Reflections on Violence,* trans. T. E. Hulme (New York, Peter Smith, 1941), p. 150.

5. *Werke,* XIX, 28.

6. Ibid., p. 21.

7. Ibid., IV, 489.

8. *Die moralisierende Kritik und die kritisierende Moral: Beitrag zur Deutschen Kulturgeschichte. Gegen Karl Heinzen von Karl Marx,* in *Marx-Engels Gesamtausgabe,* sect. 1, vol. VI (Berlin, Marx-Engels Verlag, 1932), p. 321.

9. Engels, *Materialen zum "Anti-Dühring" (Aus Engels' Vorarbeiten zum "Anti-Dühring"),* in *Werke,* XX, 580, 581, 587.

10. *Zur Geschichte des Bundes der Kommunisten,* ibid., VIII, 578.

11. Engels tended to be more consistently appreciative of their originality than Marx. In 1845 he even thought of having Fourier translated into German (minus the cosmology). He planned a library of socialist thought that would include excerpts from Morelly, Robert Owen, and the Saint-Simonians. See Engels to Marx, March 17, 1845, in *Werke,* XXVII, 24.

12. On Weitling, see Wolfgang Joho, *Wilhelm Weitling: Der Ideengehalt seiner Schriften, entwickelt aus den geschichtlichen Zusammenhängen* (Heidelberg, 1932), and *Traum von der Gerechtigkeit: Die Lebensgeschichten des Handwerksgesellen, Rebellen und Propheten Wilhelm Weitling* (Berlin, 1956); Carl F. Wittke, *The Utopian Communist: a Biography of Wilhelm Weitling, Nineteenth-Century Reformer* (Baton Rouge, 1950); and Waltrand Seidel Höppner, *Wilhelm Weitling, der erste deutsche Theoretiker und Agitator des Kommunismus* (Berlin, 1961).

13. *Werke,* VII, 541.

14. Ibid. III, 448.

15. Ibid., IV, 489.

16. Ibid., XIX, 190.

17. Marx to Ludwig Kugelmann, Oct. 9, 1866, ibid., XXXI, 530.

18. Ibid., XXIII, 317.

19. Ibid., XXXIV, 68.

20. Ibid., XXII, 428.

21. Ibid., I, 475.

22. Ibid., II, 139.

23. *New Moral World,* no. 25 (Dec. 13, 1844).

24. *Die Heilige Familie,* in *Werke,* II, 199.

25. *New Moral World,* no. 25 (Dec. 13, 1844).

26. Marx to Ludwig Kugelmann, Oct. 9, 1866, in *Werke,* XXXI, 530.

27. Ibid., XIX, 289.

28. See, for example, *Le Globe*, Nov. 5, 1831, and a brochure by Enfantin, *A tous: Religion Saint-Simonienne* (Paris, 1832), p. 2.

29. *Werke*, III, 473–518. *Die Deutsche Ideologie* is considered by the editors of the *Werke* to be the joint work of Marx and Engels, and the attribution to Marx is used here as shorthand for the collaboration.

30. See Frank E. Manuel, *The New World of Henri Saint-Simon* (Cambridge, Mass., 1956), p. 371, n. 1; and Lenin, *Imperialism, the Highest Stage of Capitalism*, in *Collected Works* (New York, International Publishers, 1927–1945), XIX, 196.

31. *Werke*, III, 74.

32. Published in Paris, 1967.

33. Marx to Engels, Hotel Pension Victoria, Algiers, March 1, 1882, in *Werke*, XXXV, 46.

34. *Die Deutsche Ideologie*, ibid., III, 517.

35. Ibid., p. 29.

36. *Der Ursprung der Familie des Privateigenthums und des Staats. Im Anschluss an Lewis H. Morgan's Forschungen* (1884), ibid., XXI, 78.

37. Engels to Kautsky, London, April 26, 1884, ibid., XXXVI, 143.

38. *Der Ursprung der Familie*, ibid., XXI, 83, 82.

39. *Das Kapital*, III, ibid., XXV, 828.

40. United Nations General Assembly, Seventh Special Session, *Provisional Verbatim Record of the Two Thousand Three Hundred and Twenty-Seventh Meeting, September 1, 1975*, p. 62.

41. *Werke*, III, 33.

42. Louis Blanc, *Organisation du travail*, 9th ed. (Paris, 1850), pp. 72–74; Blanc says he is quoting his own remarks in the *Histoire de dix ans*.

43. Pierre-Joseph Proudhon, *Idée générale de la révolution au XIXᵉ siècle* (1851), in *Oeuvres complètes*, ed. C. Bouglé and H. Moysset, III (Paris, Marcel Rivière, 1923), 174.

44. Friedrich Engels, Paul and Laura Lafargue, *Correspondance*, ed. Emile Bottigelli (Paris, 1956), I, 92, Lafargue to Engels, Nov. 13, 1882.

45. *Werke*, IV, 490.

46. See, for example, *Ökonomisch-philosophische Manuskripte aus dem Jahre 1844*, ibid., vol. XL, part 1, pp. 510–562 *passim*.

47. Paul Lafargue, "Karl Marx, Persönliche Erinnerungen," *Die Neue Zeit*, 9th year, no. 1 (1890–1891, part 1), p. 14.

30. Comte, High Priest of the Positivist Church

1. *Briefwechsel*, in *Marx-Engels Gesamtausgabe*, sect. 3, vol. III (Berlin, Marx-Engels Verlag, 1930), p. 345, Marx to Engels, July 7, 1866.

2. Marx, draft of April–May 1871 for "Bürgerkrieg in Frankreich," in *Werke* (Berlin, Dietz, 1956–1965), XVII, 555.

3. Engels, Manuscripts for "Dialektik der Natur" (1878–1882), in *Marx-Engels Gesamtausgabe*, sect. 1, vol. VIII (Moscow, 1935), p. 680.

4. For a bibliography on Comte through 1962 see Manuel, *The Prophets of Paris* (Cambridge, Mass., 1962), pp. 337–339. More recent works include *Correspondance générale et confessions*, ed. Paulo E. de Berrêdo Carneiro and Pierre Arnaud, 2 vols. (Paris, 1973); Pierre Arnaud, *La Pensée d'Auguste Comte* (Paris, 1969); Antimo Negri, *Augusto Comte e l'umanesimo positivistico* (Rome, 1971).

5. Comte, *Lettres à divers* (Paris, 1905), II, 104, Comte to Gustave d'Eichthal, Dec. 9, 1828.

6. Ibid., p. 107, Comte to Gustave d'Eichthal, Dec. 7, 1829.

7. His disciple H.-P. Deroisin offered striking proof of the obscurity which began to envelop Comte after his attack of insanity: "In 1828 the bibliographer Quérard gave

him as having already died in the beginning of 1827." *Notes sur Auguste Comte* (Paris, 1909), p. 27.

8. *Lettres à divers,* II, 276, Auguste Comte to Mme. Austin, April 4, 1844.

9. E. Caro, *M. Littré et le positivisme* (Paris, 1883), p. 120.

10. André Poëy, *M. Littré et Auguste Comte* (Paris, 1880), pp. 8, 9.

11. *Rapport de la Société positiviste par la Commission chargée d'examiner la nature et le plan du nouveau Gouvernement révolutionnaire de la République Française* (Paris, 1848).

12. Quoted by Henri Gouhier, *La vie d'Auguste Comte* (Paris, 1931), p. 277.

13. See Charles de Rouvre, *Auguste Comte et le Catholicisme* (Paris, 1928).

14. James H. Billington, "The Intelligentsia and the Religion of Humanity," *American Historical Review,* 65 (1960), 807–821.

15. On Positivism in Brazil see Antonio Gomes d'Azevedo Sampaïo, *Essai sur l'histoire du positivisme au Brésil* (Paris, 1899); Clovis Bevilaqua, *A philosophia positiva no Brasil* (Recife, 1883); Hermann Dohms, *Der Positivismus in Brazilien* (São Leopoldo, 1931); Sylvio Roméro, *O evolucionismo e o positivismo no Brasil* (Rio de Janeiro, 1895).

16. On Positivism in England see John Edwin McGee, *A Crusade for Humanity: The History of Organized Positivism in England* (London, 1931).

17. See Hermann Gruber, *Der Positivismus vom Tode Auguste Comte's bis auf unsere Tage* (Freiburg, 1891).

18. Comte, *Système de politique positive* (Paris, 1851–1854), III, 75.

19. Ibid., pp. 595–596.

20. Ibid., II, 466.

21. Ibid., I, 733.

22. Ibid., IV, 276–277.

23. Ibid., II, 141.

24. Ibid., p. 57.

25. Ibid., p. 145.

31. Anarchy and the Heroic Proletariat

1. William Godwin, *Political Justice* (London, 1793), II, 116. On Godwin, see John P. Clark, *The Philosophical Anarchism of William Godwin* (Princeton, 1977).

2. Samuel Taylor Coleridge, *Collected Letters,* ed. Earl Leslie Griggs, I (Oxford, Clarendon, 1956), 114, Coleridge to Robert Southey, Oct. 21, 1794.

3. Coleridge, *Lectures, 1795, on Politics and Religion,* in *The Collected Works of Samuel Taylor Coleridge,* ed. Lewis Patton and Peter Mann (Princeton, 1971), I, 218–219.

4. P.-J. Proudhon, *Correspondance,* ed. J.-A. Langlois (Paris, 1875), II, 199, Proudhon to Marx, Lyons, May 17, 1846.

5. Thomas Huxley, "The Struggle for Existence in Human Society," *Nineteenth Century,* February 1888; reprinted in *Evolution and Ethics* (New York, 1894).

6. Peter Kropotkin, *The Conquest of Bread,* ed. Paul Avrich (New York, New York University Press, 1972), p. 61. The work first appeared as a series of articles in *Le Révolté* and *La Révolte;* the original edition of the book, in French, was published in Paris, 1892.

7. Kropotkin, *Conquest of Bread,* p. 49.

8. Kropotkin, *Paroles d'un révolté,* quoted in George Woodcock and Ivan Avakumovic, *The Anarchist Prince: A Biographical Study of Peter Kropotkin* (New York, Schocken Books, 1970), p. 312.

9. Mikhail Bakunin, *Die Reaktion in Deutschland* (1842), quoted in E. H. Carr, *Michael Bakunin* (London, Macmillan, 1937), p. 110; the piece was first published in the *Deutsche Jahrbücher für Wissenschaft und Kunst* (Leipzig), Oct. 17–21, 1842. The scholarly edition of Bakunin's works (edited for the Internationaal Instituut voor Sociale Geschiednis of Amsterdam) was prepared by Arthur Lehning et al., *Archives Bakunine,* 6 vols. (Leyden, 1961–). See also Henri Arvon, comp., *Michel Bakounine ou la vie contre la*

science (Paris, 1966); Jacques Duclos, *Bakounine et Marx, ombre et lumière* (Paris, 1974); and Arthur Lehning, *Michel Bakounine et ses relations avec Sergei Nečaev, 1870–1872* (Leyden, 1971).

10. On Proudhon, see Edouard Dolléans, *Proudhon* (Paris, 1948); H. Lubac, *The Un-Marxian Socialist: A Study of Proudhon*, trans. Canon R. E. Scantlebury (London, 1948); George Woodcock, *Pierre-Joseph Proudhon: A Biography* (London, 1956); Alan Ritter, *The Political Thought of Pierre-Joseph Proudhon* (Princeton, 1969); Robert L. Hoffman, *Revolutionary Justice* (Urbana, 1972).

11. See his *Qu'est-ce que la propriété?* (Paris, 1840).

12. Proudhon, *Idée générale de la révolution au XIXe siècle* (Paris, 1851), p. 84.

13. See his *Organisation du crédit et de la circulation*, 2d ed. (Paris, 1848).

14. Proudhon, *La Pornocratie, ou Les Femmes dans les temps modernes* (Paris, 1875), pp. 9, 10, 11, 19.

15. Proudhon, *General Idea of the Revolution in the Nineteenth Century*, trans. J. B. Robinson (London, Freedom Press, 1923), p. 97.

16. Proudhon, *Idée générale de la révolution au XIXe siècle*, pp. 338–339.

17. Proudhon, "Polémique contre Louis Blanc et Pierre Leroux," in *Oeuvres complètes*, ed. C. Bouglé and H. Moysset, III (Paris, Rivière, 1923), 365.

18. Proudhon, *Carnets*, I (Paris, 1860), 77–78.

19. Proudhon, *De la justice dans la révolution et dans l'Eglise* (1848), part 3 (Paris, 1932), 84.

20. Proudhon, *What is Property?* trans. B. R. Tucker (New York, n.d.), p. 261.

21. Proudhon, *Correspondance*, III, 260, Proudhon to Jérôme-Amédée Langlois, May 18, 1850; Dolléans, *Proudhon*, p. 207.

22. Proudhon, *Idée générale de la révolution au XIXe siècle*, p. 191.

23. Jean Variot, *Propos de Georges Sorel recueillis par Jean Variot*, 4th ed. (Paris, 1935), pp. 81–86.

24. Georges Sorel, *Réflexions sur la violence*, 3d ed. (Paris, 1912), p. 238. The work was first published in 1906 as a series of articles.

25. Sorel, *Matériaux d'une théorie du prolétariat*, 3d ed. (Paris, 1929), p. 170.

26. Ibid., p. 98.

27. See Sorel, *La Ruine du monde antique*, 3d ed. (Paris, 1933).

28. Sorel, *Matériaux d'une théorie du prolétariat*, p. 162.

29. See Sorel, *De l'utilité du pragmatisme*, 2d ed. (Paris, 1928).

30. Sorel, *The Illusions of Progress*, trans. John and Charlotte Stanley (Berkeley, 1969; 1st ed., 1908), p. 207.

32. Utopia Victoriana

1. V. I. Lenin, *Collected Works*, XXXVIII (Moscow, 1961), 503–559.

2. Edward Bellamy, *Looking Backward, 2000–1887* (Boston, 1888), p. 438. Other relevant works by Bellamy are *The Duke of Stockbridge: A Romance of Shays' Rebellion* (New York, 1900); *Equality* (New York, 1897), a sequel to *Looking Backward; Plutocracy or Nationalism—Which?*, address at Tremont Temple, May 31, 1889 (Boston, 1889); *The Programme of the Nationalists* (New York, 1894). On Bellamy see Sylvia Edmonia Bowman et al., *Edward Bellamy Abroad: An American Prophet's Influence* (New York, 1962); Sylvia Edmonia Bowman, *The Year 2000: A Critical Biography of Edward Bellamy* (New York, 1958).

3. Bellamy, *Looking Backward* (1888), p. 438.

4. Bellamy, *Looking Backward* (New York, New American Library, 1960), p. 222. Subsequent quotations are from the 1960 edition.

5. Notebooks of Edward Bellamy, Houghton Library, Harvard University, Cambridge, Mass.

6. Bellamy, *Looking Backward,* p. 95.

7. Ibid., p. 94.

8. Ibid., p. 97.

9. Ibid., p. 101n.

10. Ibid., p. 172.

11. Ibid., pp. 174–175.

12. Ibid., p. 100.

13. Ibid., p. 99.

14. Ibid., p. 100.

15. Ibid., p. 165.

16. Theodor Hertzka, *Freeland: A Social Anticipation,* trans. Arthur Ransom (London, 1891), pref., p. vii; a translation of *Freiland: Ein sociales Zukunftsbild* (1890). Also by Hertzka are *Die Gesetze der sozialen Entwickelung* (Leipzig, 1886); and *Eine Reise nach Freiland* (Leipzig, 1893), a sequel to *Freiland.*

17. Hertzka, *Freeland,* pref., p. xxi.

18. Ibid.

19. Ibid., p. 95.

20. Ibid., p. 11.

21. Ibid., p. 30.

22. Ibid., p. 190.

23. Ibid., p. 202.

24. Ibid., p. 190.

25. Ibid., p. 202.

26. Ibid., p. 203.

27. William Morris, *News from Nowhere; or An Epoch of Rest, Being Some Chapters from a Utopian Romance* (London, 1891), p. 128. The work was first serialized in the *Commonweal* in 1890. For other works by Morris see *The Collected Works,* with intro. by his daughter May Morris, 24 vols. (London, 1910–1915); *Atalanta's Race, and Other Tales from The Earthly Paradise,* ed. O. F. Adams (Boston, 1888); *Chants for Socialists* (London, 1885); *Communism: A Lecture by William Morris,* Fabian Tract no. 113 (London, 1903); *The Earthly Paradise: A Poem,* 4 vols. (Boston, 1869–1871); *Gothic Architecture: A Lecture for the Arts and Crafts Exhibition Society* (Hammersmith, 1893); *Political Writing,* ed. with intro. by L. Morton (London, 1973); Peter Faulkner, comp., *William Morris: The Critical Heritage* (London, 1973). On William Morris see R. Page Arnot, *William Morris: The man and the Myth, Including Letters of William Morris to J. L. Mahon and Dr. John Glasse* (London, 1964); Philip Henderson, *William Morris: His Life, Work and Friends* (London, 1967); James W. Hulse, *Revolutions in London: A Study of Five Unorthodox Socialists* (Oxford, 1970); P. Meier, *La Pensée utopique de William Morris* (Paris, 1972).

28. Morris, *News from Nowhere,* p. 49.

29. Ibid., p. 127.

30. Ibid., p. 79.

31. Ibid., p. 127.

32. On Hudson, see John Towner Frederick, *William Henry Hudson* (New York, 1972).

33. Morris, *News from Nowhere,* p. 79.

33. Darwinism, the Ambiguous Intruder

1. Edward Bulwer-Lytton (Edward George Earle Lytton, First Baron Lytton), *The Coming Race* (New York, 1873), pp. 62–63.

2. William Olaf Stapledon, *Last and First Men: A Story of the Near and Far Future* (London, 1930), p. 36.

3. Bulwer-Lytton, *The Coming Race,* p. 141.

4. Pierre Teilhard de Chardin, *The Phenomenon of Man,* trans. from the French, *Le Phénomène humain,* by Bernard Wall (New York, Harper and Row, 1959), p. 265.

5. J. B. S. Haldane, *Everything Has a History* (London, Allen and Unwin, 1951), p. 288.

6. Julian S. Huxley, "The Emergence of Darwinism," in Sol Tax, ed., *The Evolution of Man: Mind, Culture and Society* (Chicago, University of Chicago Press, 1960), I, 20.

7. Huxley, *The Uniqueness of Man* (London, Chatto and Windus, 1941), p. 32.

8. Hermann J. Muller, "The Guidance of Human Evolution," in Sol Tax, ed., *The Evolution of Man,* II, 456.

9. J. D. Bernal, *The World, the Flesh and the Devil: An Enquiry into the Future of the Three Enemies of the Rational Soul* (London, K. Paul, Trench, Trubner, 1929), p. 22.

10. Ibid., p. 33.

11. Ibid., p. 37.

12. Freeman J. Dyson, *Third J. D. Bernal Lecture* (London, Birkbeck College, 1972), p. 6.

13. Ibid.

14. Ibid., p. 9.

15. Ibid., p. 11.

34. Freudo-Marxism, a Hybrid for the Times

1. Sigmund Freud, *Civilization and Its Discontents,* trans. from the German by James Strachey (New York, 1962), pp. 60–61.

2. Wilhelm Reich, "Dialektischer Materialismus und Psychoanalyse," in *Unter dem Banner des Marxismus* (Berlin, 1929), p. 144. Reich insisted that the society was sick as well as unjust, and his utopian mechanisms included proposals for the foundation of an international sexual-political organization. The purpose of his *Sexualpolitik* was not therapeutic in the sense of individual analysis. See his *Massenpsychologie des Faschismus: Zur Sexualökonomie der politischen Reaktion und zur proletarischen Sexualpolitik* (Berlin, 1933), p. 251.

3. Erich Fromm, *Beyond the Chains of Illusion* (New York, Simon and Schuster, 1962), p. 53.

4. Fromm, *Man for Himself: An Inquiry into the Psychology of Ethics* (New York, Rinehart, 1947), p. 363.

5. Norman O. Brown, *Life against Death* (New York, Vintage Books, 1959), p. 140.

6. Ibid., p. 308.

7. Herbert Marcuse, *Eros and Civilization: A Philosophical Inquiry into Freud* (New York, Vintage Books, 1961), p. 40.

8. Ibid., pp. ix, 204–205.

9. Marcuse, *Das Ende der Utopie* (Berlin, 1967), trans. and pub. in *Five Lectures: Psychoanalysis, Politics, and Utopia* (Boston, Beacon Press, 1970), p. 73.

Epilogue. The Utopian Prospect

1. Jerome M. Gilison, *The Soviet Image of Utopia* (Balitmore, The Johns Hopkins University Press, 1975), pp. 1–2, 61.

2. Ibid., p. 4.

3. Ibid., p. 7.

4. Mao Tsetung, *Poems* (Peking, Foreign Languages Press, 1976), pp. 50, 52.

5. Centre d'études socialistes, Paris, *Cahiers 91–93: Conseils ouvriers et utopie socialiste* (Paris, 1969), p. 14.

6. Julien Besançon, ed., *Les Murs ont la parole: Journal mural, mai 68* (Paris, 1968), pp. 14, 15, 25, 33, 34, 54, 174. See also Daniel and Gabriel Cohn-Bendit, *Obsolete Communism: The Left-Wing Alternative,* trans. A. Pomerans (New York, 1968).

7. Ernst Bloch, *Widerstand und Friede: Aufsätze zur Politik* (Frankfort, 1968), p. 100.

8. Arno Münster, ed., *Tagträume vom aufrechten Gang: 6 Interviews mit Ernst Bloch* (Frankfort, 1977), p. 118.

9. Georg Picht, *Mut zur Utopie: Die grossen Zukunftsaufgaben* (Munich, 1969).

10. Richard Fairfield, comp., *Utopia USA* (San Francisco, Alternatives Foundation, 1972), p. 3.

11. Theodore Roszak, *The Making of a Counter Culture* (Garden City, N.Y., Doubleday, 1969, p. 235.

12. B. F. Skinner, *Walden Two* (New York, Macmillan, 1962; 1st ed., 1948), p. 80.

13. B. F. Skinner, *Beyond Freedom and Dignity* (New York, Bantam Books, 1972; 1st ed., 1971), p. 169.

14. Paul Tillich, "Critique and Justification of Utopia," in *Utopia and Utopian Thought,* ed. Frank E. Manuel (Boston, Houghton Mifflin, 1966), p. 308.

15. Hans-Joachim Gerhard, *Utopie als innergeschichtlicher Aspekt der Eschatologie* (Gütersloh, 1973).

16. Stanislaw Lem, *The Futurological Congress,* trans. Michael Kandel (New York, Seabury Press, 1974; 1st ed., 1971), p. 130.

17. Gerard K. O'Neill, *The High Frontier: Human Colonies in Space* (New York, Morrow, 1977), pp. 198–199.

18. George R. Collins, *Visionary Drawings of Architecture and Planning: Twentieth Century through the 1960s* (Cambridge, Mass., MIT Press, 1979).

Selected Bibliography

This bibliography is intended to cover general studies on utopias and utopian thought, works treating significant historical segments of the subject, bibliographies of utopias and related subjects, and important anthologies.

Ackermann, Elfriede N. *Das Schlaraffenland in German Literature and Folksong*. Chicago, 1944.

Ahlefeld, Henricus ab. *Disputatio Philosophica de Fictis Rebus Publicis*. Cologne, 1704.

Armytage, Walter Harry Green. *Heavens Below: Utopian Experiments in England, 1560– 1960*. London, 1961.

Atkinson, Geoffroy. *The Extraordinary Voyage in French Literature before 1700*. New York, 1920.

—— *The Extraordinary Voyage in French Literature from 1700 to 1720*. New York, 1922.

—— *La Littérature géographique française de la renaissance: Répertoire bibliographique*. Paris, 1927.

—— *Les Relations de voyages du XVIIe siècle et l'évolution des idées*. Paris, 1924.

Baczko, Bronislaw. "Lumières et utopie." *Annales, Economies, Sociétés, Civilisations*, 26 (1971), 355–386.

Bailey, James Osler. *Pilgrims through Space and Time: Trends and Patterns in Scientific and Utopian Fiction*. New York, 1947.

Baldissera, A. "Il concetto di utopia: problemi e contraddizioni." In *Concezione e previsione del futuro*, ed. Gianni Giannotti. Bologna, 1971.

Baldry, H. C. *Ancient Utopias: An Inaugural Lecture Delivered at the University on 28 November, 1955*. Southampton, 1956.

Balmas, Enea Henri. "Cité idéale; utopie et progrès dans la pensée française de la Renaissance." *Travaux de linguistique et de littérature*, 12 (1975), 47–57.

Baudet, Henri. *Paradise on Earth: Some Thoughts on European Images of Non-European Man*. Trans. Elizabeth Wentholt. New Haven, 1965.

Bauer, Hermann. *Kunst und Utopie*. Berlin, 1965.

Bauer, Wolfgang. *China and the Search for Happiness*. Trans. Michael Shaw. New York, 1976.

Bergmann, Uwe, Rudi Dutschke, Wolfgang Lefevre, and Berndt Rabehl. *Rebellion der Studenten, oder, die neue Opposition*. Reinbek bei Hamburg, 1968.

Berneri, Marie Louise. *Journey through Utopia*. London, 1950.

Bestor, Arthur Eugene. *Backwoods Utopias: The Sectarian and Owenite Phases of Communitarian Socialism in America, 1663–1829*. Philadelphia, 1950.

Bettini, Leonardo. *Bibliografia dell'anarchismo*. 2 vols. Florence, 1976.

Biesterfeld, Wolfgang. *Die literarische Utopie*. Stuttgart, 1974.

Bingenheimer, Heinz. *Katalog der deutschsprachigen utopisch-phantastischen Literatur, 1460– 1960*. Friedrichsdorf, 1959–1960.

Bleiler, Everett F. *The Checklist of Fantastic Literature: A Bibliography of Fantasy, Weird, and Science-Fiction Books Published in the English Language*. Chicago, 1948.

Bleymehl, Jakob. *Beiträge zur Geschichte und Bibliographie der utopischen und phantastischen Literatur*. Fürth, 1965.

Bloch, Ernst. "Dargestellte Wunschlandschaft in Malerei, Oper, Dichtung." *Sinn und Form*, 5 (1949).

———— *Freiheit und Ordnung: Abriss der Sozial-Utopien*. New York, 1946.

———— *Geist der Utopie*. Munich and Leipzig, 1918.

———— *Philosophische Grundfragen zur Ontologie des Noch-Nicht-Seins: Ein Vortrag und zwei Abhandlungen*. Frankfort, 1961.

———— *A Philosophy of the Future*. Trans. John Cumming. New York, 1970.

———— *Das Prinzip Hoffnung*. 3 vols. Frankfort, 1959.

Bloomfield, Paul. *Imaginary Worlds, or, The Evolution of Utopia*. London, 1932.

Bouglé, Célestin Charles Alfred. *Les Idées égalitaires: Etude sociologique*. Paris, 1899.

Bowman, Frank-Paul. "Religion, Révolution, Utopie: Etude des éléments religieux dans les projets d'utopie d'avant et après 1789." In *Le Préromantisme: Hypothèque ou hypothèse?* pp. 424–442. Colloque organisé à Clermont-Ferrand les 29 et 30 juin 1972 par le Centre de Recherches Révolutionnaires et Romantiques de l'Université. Paris, 1975.

Buber, Martin. *Paths in Utopia*. Trans. R. F. C. Hull. London, 1949.

Cattarinussi, Bernardo. *Utopia e Società*. Milan, 1976.

Cesarini, Gianfranco. "Pensiero utopico e conflitto sociale." In *Studi e ricerche di sociologia*, ed. Alberto L'Abate. Pistoia, 1973.

Chesneaux, Jean. "Egalitarian and Utopian Traditions in the East." *Diogenes*, 62 (1968), 76–102.

Chinard, Gilbert. *L'Amérique et le rêve exotique dans la littérature française au XVIIe et au XVIIIe siècle*. Paris, 1913.

———— *L'Exotisme américain dans la littérature française au 16e siècle*. Paris, 1911.

Choay, Françoise, ed. *L'Urbanisme: Utopies et réalités; une anthologie*. Paris, 1965.

Cioranescu, Alexandre. "Utopia: Land of Cocaigne and Golden Age." *Diogenes*, 75 (1971), 85–121.

Clarke, Ignatius Frederick. *The Tale of the Future, from the Beginning to the Present Day: A Check-list of Those Satires, Ideal States, Imaginary Wars and Invasions . . . All Located in an Imaginary Future Period, That Have Been Published in the United Kingdom between 1644 and 1960*. London, 1961.

Cohn, Norman. *The Pursuit of the Millennium*. 2d ed. New York, 1961.

Corrodi, Heinrich. *Kritische Geschichte des Chiliasmus, oder, Der Meynungen über das tausendjährige Reich Christi*. 3 vols. Zurich, 1781–1783.

Croce, Benedetto. "L'utopia della forma sociale perfetta." *Quaderni della Critica*, vol. 6, no. 16 (1950), pp. 21–26.

Curcio, Carlo. *Utopisti italiani del cinquecento*. Rome, 1944.

Davenport, Basil, Robert A. Heinlein, C. M. Kornbluth, Alfred Bester, and Robert Bloch. *The Science Fiction Novel: Imagination and Social Criticism*. Chicago, 1959.

De Mattei, R. "Contenuto ed origini dell'utopia cittadina nel seicento." *Rivista internazionale di filosofia del diritto*, 9 (1929), 414–425.

Dermenghem, Emile. *Thomas Morus et les utopistes de la renaissance*. Paris, 1927.

Devine, Francis E. "Stoicism on the Best Regime." *Journal of the History of Ideas*, 31 (1970), 323–336.

Donner, Henry Wolfgang. *Introduction to Utopia*. London, 1945.

Doren, Alfred Jakob. *Wunschräume und Wunschzeiten*. Leipzig, 1927.

Dubois, Claude Gilbert. "De la première 'Utopie' à la première utopie française: Bibliographie et réflexions sur la création utopique au XVIe siècle." *Répertoire analytique de littérature française*, vol. 1, no. 1 (January–February 1970), pp. 11–32, no. 2 (March–April 1970), pp. 7–25.

Dubos, René Jules. *The Dreams of Reason: Science and Utopias*. New York, 1961.

Dupont, Victor. *L'Utopie et le roman utopique dans la littérature anglaise*. Paris, 1941.

Duric, Mihailo. "Die Doppelsinnigkeit der Utopie." *Praxis* (Zagreb), 8th year, nos. 1–2 (1972), pp. 27–38.

Duveau, Georges. *Sociologie de l'utopie et autres "essais": Ouvrage posthume*. Paris, 1961.

Eimer, Gerhard. *Die Stadtplanung im schwedischen Ostseereich, 1660–1715: Mit Beiträgen zur Geschichte der Idealstadt.* Stockholm, 1961.

Elliott, Robert C. *The Shape of Utopia: Studies in a Literary Genre.* Chicago, 1970.

Engelhardt, Werner Wilhelm. "Utopien also Problem der Sozial- und wirtschaftswissenschaften." *Zeitschrift für die gesamte Staatswissenschaft,* 4 (1969), 661–676.

Engels, Friedrich. *Die Entwicklung des Sozialismus von der Utopie zur Wissenschaft.* Hottingen-Zürich, 1882; 6th ed., Berlin, 1955.

Erasmus, Charles J. *In Search of the Common Good: Utopian Experiments Past and Future.* New York, 1977.

Eurich, Nell. *Science in Utopia.* Cambridge, Mass., 1967.

Falke, Rita. "Utopie und chimère." *Germanisch-Romanische Monatsschrift,* n.s., 6 (1956), 76–81.

———— "Versuch einer Bibliographie der Utopien." *Romanistisches Jahrbuch,* 6 (1953–1954), 92–109.

Ferguson, John. *Utopias of the Classical World.* Ithaca, 1975.

Finley, M. I. "Utopianism Ancient and Modern." In *Critical Spirit: Essays in Honor of Herbert Marcuse,* ed. Kurt H. Wolff and Barrington Moore. Boston, 1967.

Firpo, Luigi. "Il pensiero politico del Renascimento e della Controriforma." In *Questioni di storia moderna,* ed. Ettore Rota, pp. 345–403. Milan, 1948.

———— "L'utopia politica nella Controriforma," In *Contributi alla storia del Concilio di Trento e della Controriforma* (Quaderni di Belfagor, I). Florence, 1948.

————, ed. *Studi sull' utopia.* Florence, 1977.

Freyer, Hans. *Die politische Insel: Eine Geschichte der Utopien von Platon bis zur Gegenwart.* Leipzig, 1936.

Fuz, Jerzy Konstanty. *Welfare Economics in English Utopias from Francis Bacon to Adam Smith.* The Hague, 1952.

Garnier, Charles Georges Thomas, ed. *Voyages imaginaires, songes, visions, et romans cabalistiques.* 36 vols. Amsterdam and Paris, 1787–1789.

Gerber, Richard. *Utopian Fantasy: A Study of English Utopian Fiction since the End of the Nineteenth Century.* London, 1955.

Giamatti, A. Bartlett. *The Earthly Paradise and the Renaissance Epic.* Princeton, 1966.

Gibson, R. W., and J. Max Patrick. *St. Thomas More: A Preliminary Bibliography of his Works and of Moreana to the Year 1750.* New Haven, 1961.

Giordani, Pierluigi. *Il futuro dell'utopia.* Bologna, 1969.

Girsberger, Hans. *Der utopische Sozialismus des 18. Jahrhunderts in Frankreich.* 2d ed. Wiesbaden, 1973.

Gove, Philip Babcock. *The Imaginary Voyage in Prose Fiction . . . with an Annotated Check List of 215 Imaginary Voyages from 1700 to 1800.* New York, 1941.

Grimm, Reinhold, and Jost Hermand. *Deutsches utopistisches Denken im 20. Jahrhundert.* Stuttgart, 1974.

Guggenberger, Alois. *Die Utopie vom Paradies.* Stuttgart, 1957.

Hahn, Arnold. *Grenzenloser Optimismus, oder, Utopiologie, das ist, die Lehre von den Entwicklungsmöglichkeiten der Menschheit.* Winterthur, 1947.

Haken, Johann Christian Ludwig. *Bibliothek der Robinsone: In zweckmässigen Auszügen.* 5 vols. Berlin, 1805–1808.

Hartig, Irmgart, and Albert Soboul. "Notes pour une histoire de l'utopie en France au XVIIIe siècle." *Annales historiques de la Révolution Française,* 48 (1976), 161–179.

Hertzler, Joyce Oramel. *The History of Utopian Thought.* New York, 1923.

Hessen, Sergeĭ Iosifovich. "Der Zusammenbruch des Utopismus." In *Festschrift Th. G. Masaryk zum 80 Geburtstage,* ed. B. V. Iakovenko. Bonn, 1930.

Hevesi, Ludwig, collector. *Katalog einer merkwürdigen Sammlung von Werken utopistischen Inhalts (16.–20. Jahrhundert).* Intro. by Friedrich von Kleinwächter. Vienna, 1912.

Holloway, Mark. *Heavens on Earth: Utopian Communities in America, 1680–1880.* London, 1951.

Hommel, Fritz. *Die Insel der Seligen in Mythus und Sage der Vorzeit.* Munich, 1901.

Kampers, Franz. *Kaiserprophetieen und Kaisersagen im Mittelalter.* Munich, 1895.

Kateb, George. *Utopia.* New York, 1971.

——— *Utopia and Its Enemies.* New York, 1963.

Kaufmann, Moritz. *Utopias, or Schemes of Social Improvement, from Sir Thomas More to Karl Marx.* London, 1879.

Kautsky, Karl. *Die Vorläufer des neueren Sozialismus.* 2 vols. Stuttgart, 1895.

Kirchenheim, Arthur von. *Schlaraffia politica: Geschichte der Dichtungen vom besten Staate.* Leipzig, 1892.

Klausner, Joseph. *The Messianic Idea in Israel, from its Beginning to the Completion of the Mishnah.* Trans. W. F. Stinespring. New York, 1955.

Kleinwächter, Friedrich von. *Die Staatsromane: Ein Beitrag zur Lehre vom Communismus und Socialismus.* Vienna, 1891.

Klibanov, Aleksandr Il'ich. *Narodnaia sotsialnaia utopiia v Rossii.* Moscow, 1977.

Kolnai, Aurel. "La mentalité utopienne." *La Table ronde,* 153 (1960), 62–84.

Krauss, Werner. "Geist und Widergeist der Utopien." In *Perspektiven und Probleme zur französischen und deutschen Aufklärung und andere Aufsätze,* pp. 331–366. Neuwied, 1965.

——— "Quelques remarques sur le roman utopique au XVIIIᵉ siècle." In *Roman et Lumières au XVIIIᵉ siècle,* pp. 391–399. Colloque sous la présidence de Werner Krauss. Paris, 1970.

Krysmanski, Hans-Jürgen. *Die utopische Methode: Eine Literatur- und wissenssoziologische Untersuchung deutscher utopischer Romane des 20. Jahrhunderts.* Cologne, 1963.

Lachèvre, Frédéric. *Les Successeurs de Cyrano de Bergerac.* Paris, 1922.

Lang, S. "Ideal City from Plato to Howard." *Architectural Review,* 112 (1952), 90–101.

Lanternari, Vittorio. *The Religions of the Oppressed: A Study of Modern Messianic Cults.* Trans. Lisa Sergio. New York, 1963.

Lasky, Melvin J. *Utopia and Revolution.* Chicago, 1976.

Lavedan, Pierre. *Histoire de l'urbanisme.* 3 vols. Paris, 1926–1952.

Leff, Gordon. *Heresy in the Later Middle Ages: The Relation of Heterodoxy to Dissent, c. 1250–1450.* Manchester, 1967.

Levin, Harry. *The Myth of the Golden Age in the Renaissance.* Bloomington, Ind., 1969.

Lewis, A. O., Jr. "The Anti-Utopian Novel: Preliminary Notes and Checklist." *Extrapolation,* 2 (1961), 27–32.

Lichtenberger, André. *Le Socialisme au XVIIIᵉ siècle: Etude sur les idées socialistes dans les écrivains français du XVIIIᵉ siècle avant la Révolution.* Paris, 1895.

——— *Le Socialisme et la Révolution française: Etude sur les idées socialistes en France de 1789 à 1796.* Paris, 1899.

——— *Le Socialisme utopique: Etudes sur quelques précurseurs inconnus du socialisme.* Paris, 1898.

Liljegren, Sten Bodvar. *Studies on the Origin and Early Tradition of English Utopian Fiction.* Uppsala, 1961.

List, Günther. *Chiliastische Utopie und radikale Reformation: Die Erneuerung der Idee vom 1000-jährigen Reich im 16. Jahrhundert.* Munich, 1973.

Lovejoy, Arthur Oncken, Gilbert Chinard, George Boas, and Ronald S. Crane. *A Documentary History of Primitivism and Related Ideas.* Baltimore, 1935.

Macpherson, Crawford B. *The Political Theory of Possessive Individualism: Hobbes to Locke.* Oxford, 1967.

Mannheim, Karl. *Ideology and Utopia: An Introduction to the Sociology of Knowledge.* Trans. Louis Wirth and Edward Shils. London and New York, 1952.

Manuel, Frank Edward. *The Prophets of Paris.* Cambridge, Mass., 1962.

———— ed. *Utopias and Utopian Thought*. Boston, 1966.

———— and Fritzie P. Manuel, eds. and trans. *French Utopias: An Anthology of Ideal Societies*. New York, 1966.

Marconi, Paolo, ed. *La Città come forma simbolica: Studi sulla teoria dell'architettura nel rinascimento*. Rome, 1973.

Massó, Gildo. *Education in Utopias*. New York, 1927.

Mauzi, Robert. *L'Idée du bonheur dans la littérature et la pensée françaises au XVIIIᵉ siècle*. Paris, 1960.

Melchiorre, Virgilio. *La coscienza utopica*. Milan, 1970.

Messac, Régis, and Pierre Versins. *Esquisse d'une chrono-bibliographie des utopies*. Lausanne, 1962.

Metzger, Martin. *Die Paradieseserzählung: Die Geschichte ihrer Auslegung von J. Clericus bis W. M. L. de Wette*. Bonn, 1959.

Mitscherlich, Alexander. *Thesen zur Stadt der Zukunft*. Frankfort, 1971.

Molnar, Thomas Steven. *Utopia, the Perennial Heresy*. New York, 1967.

Morton, Arthur Leslie. *The English Utopia*. London, 1952.

Mowinckel, Sigmund Olaf Pyatt. *He That Cometh*. Trans. G. W. Anderson. New York, 1954.

Mucchielli, Roger. *Le Mythe de la cité idéale*. Paris, 1960.

Müller, Hans-Peter. *Ursprünge und Strukturen alttestamentlicher Eschatologie*. Berlin, 1969.

Müller, Wolf-Dietrich. *Geschichte der Utopia-romane der Weltliteratur*. Bochum-Langendreer, 1938.

Mumford, Lewis. *The Story of Utopias, Ideal Commonwealths and Social Myths*. New York, 1922.

Münter, Georg. *Idealstädte: Ihre Geschichte vom 15.–17. Jahrhundert*. Berlin, 1957.

Negley, Glenn Robert. *Utopian Literature: A Bibliography with a Supplementary Listing of Works Influential in Utopian Thought*. Lawrence, Kans., 1977.

———— and J. Max Patrick. *The Quest for Utopia: An Anthology of Imaginary Societies*. New York, 1952.

Neusüss, Arnhelm, ed. *Utopie: Begriff und Phänomen des Utopischen*. Neuwied, 1968.

Nipperdey, Thomas. *Reformation, Revolution, Utopie*. Göttingen, 1975.

Oyer, John Stanley. *Lutheran Reformers against Anabaptists: Luther, Melanchthon and Menius, and the Anabaptists of Central Germany*. The Hague, 1964.

Palóczi-Horváth, György. *Youth up in Arms: A Political and Social World Survey, 1955–1970*. London, 1971.

Parrington, Vernon Louis. *American Dreams: A Study of American Utopias*. 2d ed. New York, 1964.

Patch, Howard Rollin. *The Other World, according to Descriptions in Medieval Literature*. Cambridge, Mass., 1950.

Piechotta, Hans Joachim, ed. *Reise und Utopie: Zur Literatur der Spätaufklärung*. Frankfort, 1976.

Plattel, Martin. *Utopie en kritisch Denken*. Bilthoven, 1970.

Poehlmann, Robert von. *Geschichte der sozialen Frage und des Sozialismus in der antiken Welt*. 2 vols. 3d ed. Munich, 1925.

Polak, Frederik Lodewijk. *The Image of the Future*. 2 vols. Leyden and New York, 1961.

Ponten, Josef, Heinz Rosemann, and Hedwig Schmelz. *Architektur die nicht gebaut wurde*. 2 vols. Stuttgart, 1925.

Pritchard, James B., ed. *Ancient Near Eastern Texts Relating to the Old Testament*. 3d ed. Princeton, 1969.

Prys, Joseph. *Der Staatsroman des 16. und 17. Jahrhunderts und sein Erziehungsideal*. Würzburg, 1913.

Quabbe, Georg. *Das letzte Reich: Wandel und Wesen der Utopie*. Leipzig, 1933.

Quack, H. P. G. *De Socialisten: Personen en Stelsels*. 6 vols. Amsterdam, 1911–1912.

Reeves, Marjorie. *The Influence of Prophecy in the Later Middle Ages: A Study in Joachimism.* Oxford, 1969.

Renouvier, Charles Bernard. *Uchronie (l'Utopie dans l'histoire): Esquisse historique apocryphe du développement de la civilisation européenne tel qu'il n'a pas été, tel qu'il aurait pu être.* 2d ed. Paris, 1901.

Reybaud, Louis. *Etudes sur les réformateurs contemporains ou socialistes modernes.* 2 vols. Paris, 1840.

Richter, Peyton E., ed. *Utopias: Social Ideals and Communal Experiments.* Boston, 1971.

Rihs, Charles. *Les Philosophes utopistes: Le Mythe de la cité communautaire en France au XVIIIe siècle.* Paris, 1970.

Ringbom, L.-I. *Graltempel und Paradies: Beziehungen zwischen Iran und Europa im Mittelalter.* Stockholm, 1951.

Rixner, Thaddeus Anselm, and T. Siber, eds. *Leben und Lehrmeinungen berühmter Physiker am Ende des XVI und am Anfange des XVII Jahrhunderts.* Sulzbach, 1819–1826.

Rohde, Erwin. *Der griechische Roman und seine Vorläufer.* 4th ed. Hildesheim, 1960.

Rosenau, Helen. *The Ideal City: Its Architectural Evolution.* Rev. ed. New York, 1974.

Rossi, Paolo. *Clavis universalis: Arti mnemoniche e logica combinatoria da Lullo a Leibniz.* Milan, 1960.

Rössler, Dietrich. *Gesetz und Geschichte: Untersuchungen zur Theologie der jüdischen Apokalyptik und der pharasäischen Orthodoxie.* Neukirchen, 1960.

Rowley, Harold Henry. *Jewish Apocalyptic and the Dead Sea Scrolls.* London, 1957.

Ruyer, Raymond. *L'Utopie et les utopies.* Paris, 1950.

Salin, Edgar. *Platon und die griechische Utopie.* Munich and Leipzig, 1921.

Sanford, Charles L. *The Quest for Paradise.* Urbana, Ill., 1961.

Saxl, Fritz. "Veritas Filia Temporis." In *Philosophy and History: Essays Presented to E. Cassirer,* ed. Raymond Klibansky and H. J. Paton. London, 1936.

Schreiner, Joseph. *Alttestamentlich-jüdische Apokalyptik: Eine Einführung.* Munich, 1969.

Schulte Herbrüggen, Hubertus. *Utopie und Anti-Utopie: Von der Strukturanalyse zur Strukturtypologie.* Bochum-Langendreer, 1960.

Schwonke, Martin. *Vom Staatsroman zur Science Fiction.* Stuttgart, 1957.

Seibt, Ferdinand. *Utopica: Modelle totaler Sozialplanung.* Düsseldorf, 1972.

——— "Utopie im Mittelalter." *Historische Zeitschrift,* vol. 208, no. 3 (1969), pp. 555–594.

Servier, Jean. *Histoire de l'utopie.* Paris, 1967.

Soboul, Albert, ed. *Utopies au siècle des lumières.* Paris, 1972.

Soeffner, Hans Ullrich. *Der geplante Mythos: Untersuchungen zur Struktur und Wirkungsbedingung der Utopie.* Hamburg, 1974.

Stammhammer, Josef. *Bibliographie des Socialismus und Communismus.* 3 vols. Jena, 1893–1909.

Swoboda, Helmut. *Die Qualität des Lebens: Vom Wohlstand zum Wohlbefinden.* Stuttgart, 1973.

——— *Der Traum vom besten Staat: Texte aus Utopien von Platon bis Morris.* Munich, 1972.

——— *Utopia: Geschichte der Sehnsucht nach einer besseren Welt.* Vienna, 1972.

Thrupp, Sylvia L., ed. *Millennial Dreams in Action: Studies in Revolutionary Religious Movements.* New York, 1970.

Thyssen, Ole. *Utopisk Dialektik.* Copenhagen, 1976.

Tod, Ian, and Michael Wheeler. *Utopia: An Illustrated History.* New York, 1978.

Trousson, Raymond. *Voyages aux pays de nulle part: Histoire littéraire de la pensée utopique.* Brussels, 1975.

Tuveson, Ernest Lee. *Millennium and Utopia: A Study in the Background of the Idea of Progress.* Berkeley, 1949.

———— *Redeemer Nation: The Idea of America's Millennial Role.* Chicago and London, 1968.

Ullrich, Hermann. *Robinson und Robinsonaden: Bibliographie, Geschichte, Kritik.* Weimar, 1898.

Uscatescu, George. *Utopia y plenitud historica.* Madrid, 1963.

Les utopies à la Renaissance. Colloque international (avril 1961) sous les auspices de la Fédération Internationale des Instituts et Sociétés pour l'étude de la Renaissance et du Ministère de l'Education nationale et de la Culture de Belgique. Brussels and Paris, 1963.

Uxkull-Gyllenband, Woldemar, Graf von. *Griechische Kulturentstehungslehren.* Berlin, 1924.

Vennerström, Ivar. *Svenska Utopister.* Stockholm, 1913.

Versins, Pierre. *Encyclopédie de l'utopie, des voyages extraordinaires et de la science fiction.* Lausanne, 1972.

———— *Outrepart: Anthologie d'utopies, de voyages extraordinaires, et de science fiction, autrement dit, de conjectures romanesques rationnelles.* Paris, 1971.

Villgradter, R. F., and Friedrich Krey, eds. *Der utopische Roman.* Darmstadt, 1973.

Voigt, Andreas H. *Die sozialen Utopien: Fünf Vorträge.* Leipzig, 1906.

Walsh, Chad. *From Utopia to Nightmare.* New York, 1962.

Wandlungen des Paradiesischen und Utopischen: Studien zum Bild eines Ideals, ed. Hermann Bauer. Berlin, 1966.

Wijngaarden, Nicolaas van. *Les Odyssées philosophiques en France entre 1616 et 1789.* Haarlem, 1932.

Williams, George Huntston. *The Radical Reformation.* Philadelphia, 1962.

———— *Wilderness and Paradise in Christian Thought.* New York, 1962.

Winter, Michael. *Compendium utopiarum: Typologie und Bibliographie literarischer Utopien.* Vol. 1: *Von der Antike bis zur deutschen Frühaufklärung.* Stuttgart, 1978.

Index